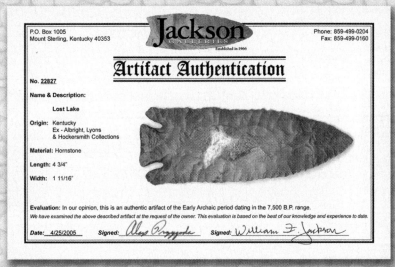

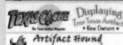

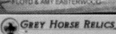

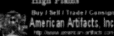

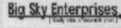

THE OFFICIAL OVERSTREET INDIAN ARROWHEADS IDENTIFICATION AND PRICE GUIDE

9th Edition

by Robert M. Overstreet

SPECIAL CONTRIBUTORS TO THIS EDITION:
Richard Michael Gramly, PhD • Duncan Caldwell

SPECIAL ADVISORS TO THIS EDITION:

David Abbott • Mark Berreth • Tommy Beutell • John Byrd
Joel Castanza • Dave Church • Jerry Chubbuck
Gary Davis • Tom Davis • Gary Fogelman • Jacky Fuller
Richard Michael Gramly, PhD
Ron L. Harris • Jim Hogue • Bill Jackson
Glenn Leesman • Randy McNeice • Bob McWilliams
Donald Meador • Roy Motley • Lyle Nickel
John T. Pafford • Rodney Peck
Alan L. Phelps • Floyd Ritter
Dwain Rogers • Dick Savidge • Mike Speer
Ben E. Stermer • Art Tatum • Carlos Tatum
Jim Tatum, PhD • Jeb Taylor • Larry Troman • Greg Truesdell
Eric C. Wagner • Sam Williams • Warner Williams
Jack Willhoit • Brian Wrage

HOUSE OF COLLECTIBLES  **NEW YORK**
GEMSTONE PUBLISHING, INC.

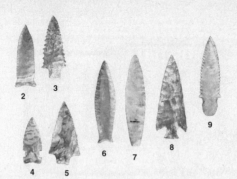

ABOUT THE FRONT COVER: The cover features a selection of points dating from 3,000 to 12,000 years old. **Back Cover-** from top to bottom: **1**-Adena from TN made from Sonora flint. **Front Cover: 2**-Greenbrier from TN made from Horse Creek chert; **3**-Kirk from TN made from Dover chert; **4**-Big Sandy from TN made from Buffalo River chert; **5**-Pickwick from AL made from red jasper; **6**-Cumberland from TN made from Fort Payne chert; **7**-Agate Basin from IA; **8**-Motley from LA made from Dover chert; **9**-Boggy Branch from GA. made from Coastal Plain chert. **Note:** Lightning and thunder were feared by man and beast alike in prehistoric times. Lightning strikes would topple trees, start forest fires and stampede bison herds. A testament to Paleo man's enchantment with lightning is illustrated by the discovery of a single bison skull found at a Folsom kill site out west that has a lightning bolt painted in red on its forehead. The cover lightning picture was photographed by the author almost 50 years ago.

THE OFFICIAL OVERSTREET INDIAN ARROWHEADS IDENTIFICATION AND PRICE GUIDE is an original publication of Gemstone Publishing Inc. and House of Collectibles. Distributed by The Random House Information Group, a division of Random House, Inc., New York, and simultaneously in Canada by Random House of Canada Limited, Toronto. This edition has never before appeared in book form.

HOUSE OF COLLECTIBLES
Random House Information Group
1745 Broadway
New York, NY 10019

www.houseofcollectibles.com

Overstreet is a registered trademark of Gemstone Publishing, Inc.

House of Collectibles is a registered trademark and the colophon is a trademark of Random House, Inc.

Published by arrangement with Gemstone Publishing, Inc.

Printed in the United States of America

ISSN: 1073-8622

ISBN: 0-375-72109-6

10 9 8 7 6 5 4 3 2 1

Ninth Edition-July 2005

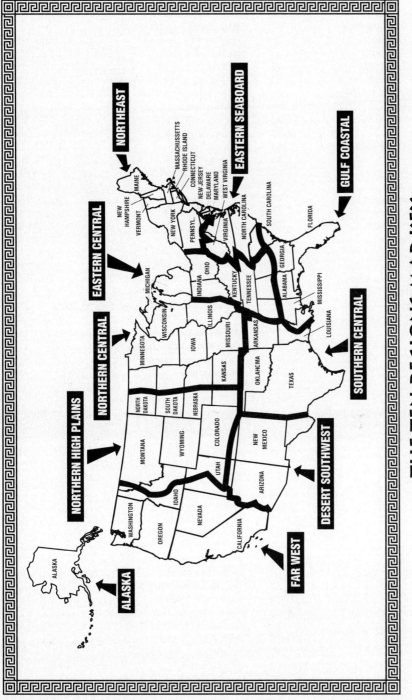

THE TEN REGIONS MAP KEY

This book is divided into ten regions and is set up starting with the Northeast and ending with the Alaska (east to west, right to left on this map). The Great Basin Westward region from the previous editions has been renamed the Far West region. This is your key to the contents of this book, and versions of the map highlighting each individual section appear at the beginning of each regional section.

Table of Contents

Advertisers

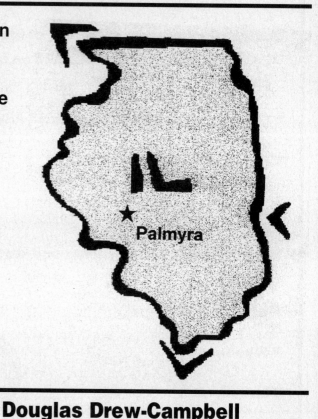

Acknowledgements

A very special thanks to Richard Michael Gramly, PhD for his well researched article specifically for this edition and for his contribution of photographs. Tremendous thanks is also given to my good friend Duncan Caldwell for his excellent article and price guide on "Collecting Old World Prehistoric Artifacts" and his contribution of many photographs as well.

Many thanks to Joel Castanza who has photographed and researched Alaska point types for the new section published in this edition for the first time.

My gratitude is also due the following people that so generously provided important data and or photographs used in this reference work: Don Adcox, Bill Breckinridge, Tom Byron (Byron Photography), Kevin Calvin, Richard Casson, Joseph Coody, Al Dows, Carol L. Fox, Steven Fox, William Garrett, Joe Girtner, Tony Hardie, Robert Hester, Wynn Isom, Nick Kassales, Steven Kirk, John Lake, Skip Lane, Michael Leggett, Jason Letts, Mike Manis, Steve McDonald, Randy McNeice, Norm McQuarrie, Pam McWhite, Rodney Michel, Phil Mize, Patrick W. Mueller, Stan Pflaum, Merlin Ray, David Richerson, Win Rider, George Roberts, Billy Roten, Bob Roth, William Roustin, Kenneth Rummel, George Scott, Don Seamans, William Jason Sockwell, William Taylor, Gary Todd, Allen Treichler, John Wanchic, Harmer Weichel, Jan Weisenfels, Jack Willhoit and Sam Williams.

I am also in debt to Pete Bostrom and Dr. Michael Gramly for their valuable advice in keeping me up to date with changes in the archaeological arena.

This book also contains photos from the collections of Ray Acra, Tom Addis, Dick Agin, Ralph Allen, Chuck Andrew, Robert Beasley, Jerry Beaver, Jim Bergstrom, Tommy Beutell, Ken Bovat (photographer, N.Y.), John Byrd, Roland Callicutt, Phillip H. Cain, Jerry Chubbuck, John Cockrell (deceased), Jim & Janice Cunningham, Leo Paul Davis, Kevin L. Dowdy, Tom Evans, Ted Filli, Gary Fogelman, Tom Fouts, Steven Fox, Jeff Galgoci, William German, Kenneth Hamilton, Scott Hanning, Jim Hill, Frank & Kathy Hindes, Bill Jackson, Mark L. Jewell, Glen Kizzia, Glenn Leesman, Mike Long, Skip Mabe, Edward Mason, Charles D. Meyer (deceased), Ron Miller, Sherri A. Monfee, Buzzy Parker, Floyd Ritter, George Roberts, Bob Roth, Arlene & Lori Rye, Richard Savidge, Charles Shewey (deceased), Mike Speer, Larry Allan Stanley, Scott Tickner, Brian K. Tilley, Kirk Trivalpiece, P.K. Veazey, R.S. Walker, Blake Warren, Warner Williams, Lyons D. Woody and John W. Young. We want to sincerely thank these people for making their collections available to us.

Gratitude is also due Tom Davis, Gary Fogelman, Jacky Fuller, Don Meador, Roy Motley, Dwain Rogers, George E. Rodieck, Jr. and Jack willhoit who spent so much of their valuable time taking photographs for this edition; to Art Tatum and Alan Phelps for their many hours of expert help, photographs and points sent in for photographing.

Thanks is also given to Jim Hogue who spent countless hours photographing collections in his area and writing descriptions of new types for this edition as well as for his excellent research into previously published reports on types.

Very special credit is due my wife Caroline, who not only advises cover and layout designs, but is of tremendous help to me at the artifact shows visiting and talking with collectors and dealers.

Thanks also to the staff of Gemstone Publishing--J. C. Vaughn (Executive Editor), Arnold T. Blumberg (Editor), Brenda Busick (Creative Director), Mark Huesman (Production Coordinator), Tom Gordon III (Managing Editor), Jamie David (Director of Marketing), Sara Ortt (Marketing Assistant), Stacia Brown (Editorial Coordinator), and Heather Winter (Office Manager)--for their invaluable assistance in the production of this edition.

Our gratitude is given to all of our special advisors for their dedicated advice and input as well as help in typing, grading, and pricing; and to those who wish their names not to be listed and to all of our advertisers in this edition.

PALAEO-AMERICAN RECYCLED ARTIFACTS: FLUTED POINTS AND DRILLS FROM THE VAIL CLOVIS SITE

By Richard Michael Gramly, PhD

American Society for Amateur Archaeology
North Andover, Massachusetts 01845
In collaboration with Valerie and D.C. Waldorf

The problem that we wish to explore with readers of this guide is how some Palaeo-American flaked stone artifacts were transformed by resharpening and recycling. Our focus will be projectile points, drills and kindred forms of the North American Fluted Point Tradition. Within any Stone Age industrial tradition there may be transformations not obvious to analysts; also, the pristine form of some flaked stone tools may be difficult to determine. However, well-documented artifact assemblages from briefly occupied archaeological sites of a single culture may aid in recognizing resharpened and recycled tools. The small artifact assemblages from such sites often reveal behaviors of individual ancient flint-knappers. Ancient knappers' level of skill varied, and the work of novices is often observed within the archaeological record. By "factoring out" (that is, eliminating from our consideration) whimsies and idiosyncracies, we can focus upon what was normal or "typical" behavior when recycling and refurbishing tools.

Fig. 1. Francis Vail at the Vail site – the first of Magalloway Valley Clovis sites to be discovered along the shore of man-made Aziscohos lake, northern Maine. 1979. R.M.Gramly photograph.

Such behavior, because it is patterned and recurrent, commands our attention. By understanding it, we can achieve a cherished goal of prehistorians everywhere – an ability to discriminate among ancient archaeological cultures.

The archaeological sites serving as the foundation for our arguments belong to the Magalloway Valley Palaeo-American Complex of northwestern highland Maine (Gramly 1988). The

Fig. 2. Aerial view of the Vail site (on right-hand bank of ancient channel of the Magalloway River) and Vail kill site #I (on opposite river bank along small stream draining pond) at a time of low lake level, 1980. R.M.Gramly photograph.

best known of ten sites constituting this 11,000 year-old archaeological complex is **VAIL** and its associated **VAIL KILL SITE** (Gramly 1982,1998). Information about the highly productive Vail Clovis encampment and kill site has appeared in American, Canadian (both in English and French), and European publications (see, for example, Schulze-Thulin 1995) Also, Vail and its sister sites are featured in a permanent exhibit about Maine prehistory at the Maine State Museum in Augusta, entitled "Twelve Thousand Years in Maine" (Bourque 2000). Even though much is known about the Magalloway Valley Palaeo-American Complex, more stands to be learned. The data presented here about fluted drills from the Vail site (where more examples of this peculiar toolform have been unearthed than anywhere else in northeastern North America) are products of fresh research by the authors. Studies of Vail site artifacts, archaeological features, diet of the site's occupants, and the ancient environment that existed within the Magalloway River valley during Clovis times are planned for the future.

The Clovis Toolkit of Northwestern Highland Maine

In various publications one of us (RMG) has argued that makers of fluted projectile points with deeply concave bases entered mountainous, northwestern Maine in pursuit of a favorite quarry – caribou. The crooked Magalloway valley, in places bound by sheer rocky ledge, offered several places to intercept caribou herds as they followed the Magalloway River to and from summer calving grounds. In most years the valley herd appears to have been hunted at the end of summer before the onset of winter and the rut. Then caribou were in their prime – their antlers hardened, their flesh well-larded, and with hides suitably thick for making clothing. This was the season when the Vail and the neighboring Adkins site were occupied, likewise the Upper and Lower Wheeler Dam encampments at the northern end of the valley (Gramly in press, a). The Morss site, on the other hand, was inhabited during the spring when caribou hides were thin and totally unfit for any purpose. The absence of endscrapers at Morss indicates that the hunters who camped there were interested only in meat (Gramly 2001 and reprint), intending to waylay pregnant caribou on their way to calving grounds and summer pastures in the mountains,

Fig. 3. Rock-rimmed pit or cache discovered at the Adkins Clovis site. A single tent structure that was inhabited by a reconnoitering party of Clovis hunters is being excavated (in background). 1984. R.M.Gramly photograph.

The absolute age of the Magalloway Valley Palaeo-American Complex is known through a series of radiocarbon dates on charcoal from the Vail site. The senior writer prefers the determination 11,120+/-180 years BP, which was furnished by a hearth feature (Feature 1) at Vail (Gramly 1982); however, others have argued that an averaged mean date of approximately 10,600 years BP is a better approximation of the Complex'es antiquity (Haynes et al. 1984). Whatever the true age, there can be no doubt that the environment of the Magalloway River valley then was quite unlike that of today. An open parkland tundra with groves of spruce likely existed, and caribou would have pastured on mountainous slopes covered with tundra vegetation surrounded by snow and bare rock.

Fig. 4. Flaked stone tools typical of the Magalloway Valley Palaeo-American Complex – all specimens shown here from the Vail site. *Top row from left,* knife/celt; two fluted projectile points; fluted drill, limace, awl; *middle row,* sidescraper, two endscrapers with graver spurs; *bottom row pièce esquillée* (wedge/chisel) and coronet graver. R.M.Gramly photograph.

Sites dating to the 11th and early 12th millennia BP in northeastern North America yield abundant fluted points that are variants of Clovis points from the type site at Blackwater Draw, New Mexico. One variety, which is well represented at Vail and another well-known eastern Clovis encampment – Debert in central Nova Scotia (MacDonald 1968) -- has a deeply indented basal concavity. This deep concavity resulted ftom successive, overriding channel flakes on each face – each requiring a striking platform to be set up for its removal. This Debert/Vail form of Clovis point, also known as a "Gainey point" to some writers, has been observed wherever caribou may have been the intended quarry. In my opinion Debert/Vail fluted points were tailored for lances or thrusting spears. Their deep basal concavities and thin lower margins made lances bearing them sleek penetrating devices – ones that could be used repeatedly upon caribou herds with deadly efficiency. This lance was equivalent to the iron-tipped "deer spear" wielded by caribou-hunting Indians and

Inuit during historic times in northern, interior Labrador (Turner 1894).

The senior writer is able to argue, on the basis of seven (!) conjoined, broken fluted points from the Vail Clovis site and its associated kill site, upwind and 150-200 m to the west, that annually a thousand or more caribou were bagged by the six groups of hunters encamped there (Gramly in press, b). In the course of ten hunting seasons, the Vail Palaeo-Americans may have killed and butchered 10-15,000 caribou, leading to destruction of the Magalloway Valley herd.

The need to process thousands of animals by six groups of Clovis hunters at Vail was demanding of equipment. Many flaked tools and tool-bits were resharpened and (ultimately) discarded at habitations, which to judge by the lack of structural traces, were tents. Well over 5,500 tools and tool fragments have been recorded from the site (Gramly 1995: Table 2), and I estimate that the full count is closer to 6,000. For a count of this size, there is surprisingly little debitage or flaked stone waste, amounting to only 8,000-9,000 items. Most of them are small flakes struck off during resharpening and maintenance of bifaces and unifaces.

The ancient knappers residing at Vail and other stations of the Magalloway Valley Palaeo-American Complex were frugal with toolstone. Sources of chert, quartz crystal, aphanitic felsites, and other quality raw materials lay scores and even hundreds of

Fig. 5. The four Clovis points from Vail kill site #I that survived with tips intact. R.M.Gramly photograph.

kilometers away and could not be accessed while hunters lay in ambush for passing groups of caribou. We unearthed no evidence in the valley of tools being made afresh from large masses of raw material; yet, the full complement of flaked tools that we have come to expect at sites of this antiquity and culture were present, namely:

In order of decreasing numerical abundance –

A. **Cutters** (includes utilized flakes, gravers, denticulates) 890
B. **Trianguloid endscrapers** 796
C. *Pièces esquillées* 619
D. **Sidescrapers** 182
E. *Limaces* (aka slug-shaped unifaces, groovers) 102
F. **Fluted points** 95
G. **Fluted drills** 77
H. **Other bifaces** 52
I. **Tool fragments** (mostly cutters and unifaces) 1919
J. **Choppers** 1
K. **Catalogued, unanalyzed** 16

TOTAL   4749

Sister sites of Vail elsewhere within this section of the Upper Magalloway River valley yielded the following totals of flaked stone tools: **Adkins** (151); **Morss** (62); **Big Brook**(6); **Lower Wheeler Dam** (177); **Upper Wheeler Dam** (90); **Cox** (2); **Wight** (4).

In sum, flaked tool analysts have a grand total of more than 5,200 catalogued Clovis tools and tool fragments from the Magalloway River valley with which to work. By all accounts it is a large sample, and provides a solid foundation for the statements we shall make about flaked tool refurbishing and recycling below.

Lithic Parsimony or How Did Fluted Point Users Treat Their Tools?

For parts of North America once covered by the Wisconsin glacier and some more southerly regions, as well, the oldest cultural manifestations of which archaeologists are aware belong to the Fluted Point Tradition. Included within this expansive, long-lived tradition are Clovis, Cumberland, Folsom, Crowfield, and Holcombe. The jury is still out as to which of these phases or archaeological cultures is oldest; however, the senior writer now believes that Cumberland may have been first on the scene. Further, it seems likely, in my opinion, that Cumberland was derived from a very ancient Early Lanceolate Tradition – representative artifacts of which are best known from discoveries in northern South America.

Whatever the ultimate derivation of the Fluted Point Tradition, it is evident that its bearers pioneered landscapes having challenging climates and seasonally fluctuating animal populations. Hunters armed with spears and javelins tipped with fluted points contended with seasonally transhumant animals and themselves became mobile like their quarry. All worldly possessions had to be carried on their backs, by sled (perhaps pulled by dogs), and in boats **OR** they were cached for reclaiming at times when it was more convenient. Likewise, excess food (meat, fish, fat), hides for clothing, and raw materials critical for their survival had to be deposited securely against animal scavengers and human thieves. Life must have been demanding, and ingenious solutions to the problems of transporting heavy loads and storing goods must have been required.

Fig. 6. A **multi-purpose** Clovis tool – a combination celt and knife from the Sugarloaf site, Connecticut River valley, MA. Length = 15.5 cm (over six inches). This implement could easily have been converted to a fluted projectile point, when needed. R.M. Gramly photograph.

One way of reducing weight was to design **multi-purpose tools**, that is, tools that with just slight modification of their haffing could be used for entirely different purposes. For example, a narrow end of a large flaked stone biface might be employed as a celt or adze; however, with its handle changed to a different position – parallel to the long axis of the biface -- it might be used with a slicing motion as a knife. A **composite tool** was another answer to the need to keep the weight of loads for transport to a minimum. In this case working edges of specific function were combined on a single tool. It is not uncommon to encounter a tool with 3-5 different working edges in tandem. A common combination is a denticulate (saw) + cutter + scraper + borer. Many composite tools appear to have been hand-held, making it easier perhaps to bring to bear a selected working edge.

Fig. 7. A **composite** Clovis tool — a snapped serial graver (saw) that has been combined with a sidescraper from the Vail site, ME. This specimen, which is in the center of the middle row, was retouched as a scraper after breakage. R.M. Gramly photograph.

A toolform that the senior writer has often observed within tool-kits cached by Palaeo-Americans of the Fluted Point Tradition is the **multi-dimensional tool**. Such a tool, be it a knife, adze/celt , scraper, or chopper, is usually impressively large – much larger and heavier than objects of "ordinary" size that were abandoned at Palaeo-American encampments. The maker of a multi-dimensional tool expected to convert it to a tool of another function and/or shape when it had become dulled or exhausted or as it was needed for service at a critical moment. A multi-dimensional tool might have endured several transformations before ultimate discard. Since flakes struck off during any episode of conversion might have served as cutters or other delicate instruments, it is possible to regard multi-dimensional tools as cores – although it is doubtful that their maker conceived of them in this way.

There are many examples of multi-dimensional tools within the Palaeo-American archaeological record, and here we illustrate a

Fig. 8. A **multi-dimensional** Clovis tool – a platter-like biface from the Anzick burial site, MT. At 14 inches long (!) this fragmentary biface is the largest flaked tool in the assemblage. Photo courtesy of Donald Simon.

Fig. 9. A **multi-dimensional** Clovis tool from the Anzick site, MT. Here a platter-like biface, once eight inches long, has been snapped in two creating two new bifaces. One has been retouched as a knife or scraper; while, the smaller one is well-suited for conversion into a fluted projectile point. Photo courtesy of Lithic Casting Lab.

few from unquestioned contexts that are associated with makers of fluted points. The best known and studied discovery of multi-dimensional tools is the Anzick site, southern Montana (Lahren and Bonnichsen 1974). Among the more than 100 Clovis flaked stone artifacts there were several, platter-like, thick bifaces of impressive dimensions. They belong to a class of objects well-known for Clovis culture east of the Mississippi River (see Gramly 2000: Figure 13 for an example from Massachusetts) and west of it (see Frison and Bradley 1999: Plates 54-56 for specimens belonging to the Fenn Cache, Utah?). Wilke and others (1991) have argued that platter-like bifaces were used as knives or butchering tools but were destined to be snapped into large segments – each segment available for reduction into another bifacial knife or an early-stage fluted

point perform and so forth. Flakes removed during such transformations might, of course, have been used for many purposes.

While 1) multi-purpose, 2) composite, and 3) multi-dimensional tools from fluted-point Palaeo-American sites are themselves fascinating topics for analysts, the focus of our paper is yet another class of objects -- tools recycled from broken or damaged tools. In our opinion tools converted from otherwise worthless items are the most elegant testimony to Palaeo-Americans' ability of coping with challenges. No better example of lithic parsimony during the Fluted Point Tradition can be offered than the broken fluted points that were recycled as drills at the Vail Clovis site, northwestern Maine.

Fig. 10. A **multi-dimensional** Clovis tool – another platter-like biface. This wide, well-crafted biface over eight inches long was found at the Simon site (Simon Clovis Cache), Big Camas Prairie, ID. Photo courtesy of Lithic Casting Lab.

Activities of the Magalloway River Clovis Band

The senior author has argued (Gramly 1988) that the first Clovis folk to enter the Magalloway Valley were a party of hunters who were accomodated within a single tent, approximately 5m in diameter, at the Adkins site. They had come from the southwest carrying flaked tools made of raw materials outcropping in southwestern Maine (quartz crystal), central New Hampshire (various felsites), and Vermont (cherts). This reconnoitring party of hunters chose to dwell at a narrow S-bend of the valley, which is here bounded by steep rocky hills and sheer ledge. We have termed their encampment the Adkins site for a Maine game warden, Charles Adkins, who abetted its discovery. Caribou moving past Adkins would have been forced to the flat valley floor by difficult terrain, giving expectant Clovis hunters opportunities for ambush. Hunting must have been good

Fig. 11. Caribou – the presumed principal quarry of the Magalloway Valley Clovis band. It is likely that the Magalloway Valley herd, estimated at 10,000-15,000 animals, was destroyed after 10 seasons of heavy hunting and may never have regenerated during the Clovis era. R.M. Gramly photograph taken in 1976 at Ramah Bay, Labrador.

for this pioneering party, as they constructed a substantial cache for storing surplus. When excavated by us, this neatly made, rock-rimmed cache-pit was found to be empty; when full, it may have contained the butchered remains of at least a dozen caribou – a handy larder for returning hunters in the following year

The potential of the valley having been tried and proven, additional parties of Clovis hunters subsequently converged upon it. With the risk of poor hunting seen to be low, as many as six families left erstwhile haunts in southeastern Vermont and New York's Hudson valley, assembled at Vail, and erected tents -- one for each hunting family. Vail lies only a kilometer north of Adkins and is downwind and convenient to a strategic interception point for caribou herds moving downvalley. In essence, here caribou had to negotiate the shallow outlet stream of a deep spring-hole or pond, and as they emerged from the water and shook themselves (as caribou are fond of doing), they were lanced. The pond (on the right) and an ancient channel of the Magalloway River (on the left) confined the caribou herds and made them better targets for waiting hunters. Judging by the quantities of flaked tools left behind and other lines of evidence, Vail hunters may have returned to the valley at least 10 times – perhaps during successive years. Eventually the valley herd was annihilated and the band moved on towards better prospects in virgin lands northward and eastward

Fig. 12. A just-discovered, intact Clovis point, Morss site, Magalloway Valley, ME. The Morss site was occupied by an under-strength Clovis band during the spring when caribou were moving towards their summer pastures and calving grounds. R.M. Gramly photograph.

In later years the same or another(?) Clovis band returned to the Magalloway valley to try its luck with a fall hunt. Earlier that year, perhaps, elements of the group invested the valley -- certainly well remembered for the plenty it had afford-

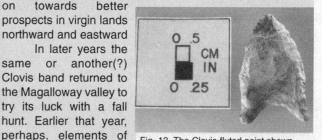

Fig. 13. The Clovis fluted point shown being excavated at the Morss site (preceding photograph). It is heavily resharpened and may have been abandoned intentionally. R.M.Gramly photograph.

ed! -- on the occasion of a spring hunt when caribou headed towards their mountain pastures and calving ground. This spring encampment we have identified as the Morss site, which lies a kilometer north of Vail (Gramly 2001). The fall encampment, when the full band likely was present, is termed "Wheeler Dam" and consists of a site with five tent-places (Lower Wheeler Dam) and a nearby -- just

Fig. 14. 1986 excavations at the Upper/Lower Wheeler Dam Clovis sites. These encampments represent resettlement of the Magalloway Valley – likely during a fall hunt of caribou by a full-strength Clovis band of six families. R.M. Gramly photograph.

Fig. 15. Rare Clovis point of quartz crystal, Lower Wheeler Dam site. Pete Bostrom photograph, used by permission.

a short walk away -- smaller site with a single tent-place (Upper Wheeler Dam). Insofar as we may judge by the raw materials used for flaked tools discarded at both these locations, the band re-entered the Magalloway Valley from the northeast. Rather than directly re-inhabit the Vail site, which ages-old beliefs (superstitions) may have cautioned them against doing, the reconstituted Magalloway Valley band of six families decided to test the potential of another ambushing spot 10-12 km north of Vail, Adkins and

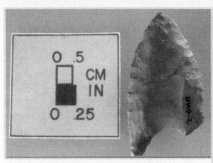

Fig. 16. Exhausted and damaged Clovis point abandoned at Upper Wheeler dam tent-site. R.M. Gramly photograph.

Morss. The six Wheeler Dam loci are immediately east (and thus downwind) of a remarkable rocky ridge that cuts across this part of the upper Magalloway Valley. Caribou moving downvalley would have been directed by the ridge and may have offered good targets to concealed Clovis lancers. Despite the advantageous situation, the luck of Clovis hunters appears to have been poor and was hunted for one season only.

In sum, it is possible to argue that the upper Magalloway Valley was pioneered by a single family or hunting party from the southwest, inhabited intensively by a large Clovis band for a decade, and finally abandoned when prey became scarce. The valley was re-inhabited sometime afterward during spring and fall hunting seasons – perhaps in the same year. The valley caribou herd, however, had not regenerated sufficiently for sustained hunting, and the Magalloway was abandoned once again – this time forever by users of Clovis points. As many as 10,000-15,000 animals may have been killed during the memorable hunts at Vail. Processing each year's kill of 1000-1500 animals required a large space; and a paramount problem would have been how to transport tons of surplus meat, fat, hides, sinew, and antler (for implements) to winter encampments in the south. Of course, some surplus may have been cached; indeed, our excavations at Vail to date have revealed two oval cache pits to the rear of habitation loci (see Gramly in press, b), and others are sure to exist in association with the four remaining, repeatedly occupied, tent loci. Still, such small chambers dug into the frozen earth could have accommodated but a fraction (perhaps only 10%) of the bounty accumulated each season by the practiced, lance-wielding Clovis hunters of Vail.

It is the senior author's belief that -- apart from implements needed to kill, to butcher and to prepare caribou hides for clothing and tent covers – flaked stone stone tools were used by Vail site occupants primarily to ready loads for transportation to distant winter camps. The Vail folk's acute need for bulk transport is likely to have been met by constructing sleds, sledges or toboggans. Although a small, deep river once flowed right by Vail and might have been navigable, boat transport of surplus alone would have been difficult. First, there would have been the problem of early icing, and second, an impressive waterfall with a drop of nearly 100 m over a kilometer had to be negotiated just 1-2 days travel downstream by boat. In choosing a water route, laborious portages would have been unavoidable. Hauling loads on sleds, sledges or toboggans with the aid of dogs (if available), on the other hand, would have presented fewer problems and provided greater freedom of travel. There is, of course, the possibility that a combination of a boat and sledge was used for long-distance transport (the sledge to haul boats at portages) -- in which case a water route down the Magalloway may have been used.

Building a boat, sled, sledge or toboggan ftom raw materials available within a park tundra is no mean feat. Many lashings, whether of spruce root or caribou sinew, would have been needed in constructing any of these conveyances -- were they at all similar to those used by historic Eskimo or Inuit of Alaska (see Murdoch 1892 for a discussion). Many holes would have had to be bored in wood, bone and ivory -- the common construction materials employed by Eskimo. For boring, historic people used bow-drills (pump-drills) and augers. Both devices were once widely distributed across North America and likely saw service for millenia -- beginning perhaps as early as the fluted point, Palaeo-American era.

Clovis Hunters at the Vail Site: Efficiency of the "Deer Lance"

The remarkable discoveries of four (4) intact and eight (8) tip and mid-section fragments of fluted projectile points at the Vail kill site in the course of our 24 years of involvement in the Magalloway River valley are proof of what Clovis lancers were using to kill caribou. We have been able to conjoin basal fragments of fluted points excavated from the Vail habitations to seven (7) of the eight (8) lance-tips at the kill site on the opposite shore of the ancient Magalloway River. Because matching basal fragments are derived from all six of the repeatedly occupied tent-locations, it is evident that Clovis hunters from all tents were equally involved in the destruction of the Magalloway valley herd.

Refitting of so many projectile point fragments, separated for at least 11,120 years, is unprecedented in the annals of North American archaeology. Only the Murray Springs Clovis site, Arizona, has furnished stone tool analysts with matching fragments of widely separated projectile Palaeo-American points (Haynes 1982:387).

At Vail the length of "working" fluted points ranged from five inches (125 mm) to as little as two inches (50 mm). The shortest complete Clovis point from the Vail kill site (two inches long) is clearly heavily resharpened. Nonetheless, this particular lance-tip retains its original basal width and configuration. Another short, heavily reworked point, however, has lost some of its basal width due to a new, angled cutting edge. Such an odd, substandard point with its greatest width at the base is termed a "Redstone type" by some collectors and analysts. I see little merit in this designation, as this particular shape was merely an expedient and made a poor cutting instrument, at best, It was derived from a damaged, standard Clovis point (of the Debert/Vail form) that at the time of initial manufacture had a greatest width forward of its ground hafting area.

Three of the four unbroken Clovis points at the Vail kill site had lengths of only 2-2 1/4 inches), They may have been abandoned intentionally after the spears, to which they were affixed, broke. These points were hardly worth the trouble of rehafting -- although it strikes us if raw material were scarce, they could have been recycled as drills. Perhaps at the times of abandonment, their owners were well supplied with toolstone and did not need these worn-out tips for conversion to drills?

One magnificent Clovis point, perfect in every detail and perhaps never before resharpened, was lost at the Vail kill site. It measures just short of four inches (98 mm) in length. It shows us how sleek and well-made Clovis points from the Valley could be. Of the 95 Clovis projectile points at the Vail site, it is arguably the only pristine example and is mute tes-

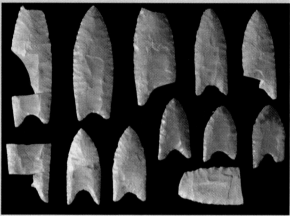

Fig. 17. The twelve fluted projectile points from Vail kill site #1. Seven of the eight Clovis point tips and mid-sections from the kill site have been conjoined to basal fragments discovered at habitations on the opposite bank of an ancient channel of the Magalloway River. R.M.Gramly photograph.

timony to the real rarity of Clovis points of fine form and flnish. Oddly, this Clovis point is fluted only once on each face and has a relatively shallow basal concavity – unlike the vast majority of Magalloway Valley points. It conforms in most respects to fluted points from the Clovis type site at Blackwater Draw, New Mexico (see, for example, Boldurian and Cotter 1999: 59). It is evidence that the often-heard argument for the separateness of Eastern and Western Clovis points, persistent within some intellectual circles, may be overdrawn

The seven (7) Vail Clovis points that are fully or partially restored from fragments recovered from the kill and habitation loci constitute an interesting lot. Three of the tips or mid-sections from the kill site have been conjoined to full-width basal fragments with both ears intact, which we unearthed at tent-sites. The lengths of these bases (as measured upward from the ears) are: 37 mm.; 25 mm; and 23 mm – making all three rather short for recycling into fluted drills or anything else. The other four (4) restored Clovis tips or midsections from the kill site are matched to equally short bases (25 m or less); worse, these particular bases are snapped in half – their ears separated. One wonders whether the ears were snapped apart during actual hunts or during re-arming, when Clovis craftsmen had to laboriously strip away old sinew bindings in order to fit their lances with new stone tips? The broken ears belonging to bases of deeply indented fluted points could not be put to use and were discarded.

In addition to the four complete fluted points and seven fragmentary point tips and mid-sections that conjoin with basal fragments from the habitations, there is a single tip from the kill site that has yet to be matched with its base. Perhaps one day it will be discovered within eroded sands of the Vail encampment? There is the possibility, however, that this base was transformed into a fluted drill and will never be identified.

One imagines that a caribou hunt at the Vail site was a wild affair. Perhaps a dozen or more spearmen, stabbing and yelling, intermingled with "family" groups of 30-50 caribou trying to elude their killers. In the heat of the moment some lances would have missed their intended mark and would have hit bone at glancing angles, snapping their stone points. Because they were securely bound, most broken Clovis points (with all their fragments still together) would have been returned to camp for re-tipping or recycling as drills. Some Clovis point tips, including the eight (8) specimens discovered at the kill site, may have split their bindings and have fallen underfoot – only to be lost among thick tundra growth

Fig. 18. 1980 excavations of Locus C, Vail site, Maine. This tent-site among six repeatedly occupied habitation spots at Vail yielded the greatest number of fluted drills, suggesting that a craftsman owning a drill apparatus once dwelled here. R.M. Gramly photograph.

Sixty of the 62 fluted drills presented in this study are derived from fragmentary fluted projectile points and all of them appear have been recycled from bases of broken fluted points – points that perhaps were returned still hafted on their owners' lances. Many tips of these same snapped lance-points may have been re-based and re-used in the hunt. Fluted point basal fragments converted to drills must have been longer than 25-26 mm, which is the average length of 16 intact, fluted point bases abandoned by Clovis tool-makers at Vail (as described in Gramly 1984, Table 2, p. 115). If we take into account discarded fluted drills and all isolated basal fragments of fluted points scattered around the Vail habitations, lances were refurbished upwards of 100 times. It follows that in the course of 10 successive hunting seasons, each of the six hunting parties (families) at Vail had to repair one or two of its "deer spears". To us, this amount of damage seems to be normal or expectable "wear and tear" given the hard service asked of lances. A spear tipped with a fluted point was obviously a deadly efficient tool, and in the right hands it might dispatch 100-200 caribou before breakage.

Fig. 19. Fragmentary fluted drill (V. 1920/2541) as it was unearthed from shallow forest soils at Locus C, Vail site, 1980. R.M. Gramly photograph.

Fluted Drills – Their Distribution and Character

The typical fluted drill is a small triangular biface with its greatest width from ear to ear across the base and a squared, spatulate or rounded tip showing considerable edge wear. In most cases fluted drills bear remnants of channel flake scars belonging to the fluted projectile points from which they were transformed. Also, in the usual case, one of the ears of a fluted drill is derived from a fluted point; while, the other ear was shaped afresh by a Clovis knapper.

Fluted drills are a widespread, but rare, toolform (Gramly 2000: 25-6). They are on record for the Folsom Phase of the Fluted Point Tradition in the American West, and they have been observed at sites in Indiana, Ohio, Pennsylvania (Bob Young, personal communication), Maine, and Nova Scotia (the Debert site - McDonald 1968). The Vail site has yielded more fluted drills (N=77) than any other Palaeo-American encampment in northern North America. The only fluted point site that appears to have more drills than Vail is the monumental Bull Brook camp, eastern

Fig. 20. A base of a fluted drill (V. 13040) fresh from the sands at Locus E, Vail site, 2002. The Vail site has yielded more drills of any sort than any other Palaeo-American, North American site. Photo courtesy of Kirk Spurr.

Massachusetts. Strictly speaking, the Bull Brook drills are different from those at Vail, being unfluted with rounded bases. Analysts and Bull Brook excavators have termed them "twist drills" (Grimes 1979).

Hampering our understanding of the distribution of fluted drills is the possibility that many have been mis-identified as "Redstone points" or some other Palaeo-American tool type. A case in point is the fluted drill pictured in a 1977 issue of the *Central States Archaeological Journal* (24-3: 138). This specimen, which is nicely fluted on one of its faces, is clearly a reworked fluted projectile point, and is now only two inches long. Although it has a squared tip making it typical of many drills discovered at the Vail site (but unlike any known fluted projectile point), nevertheless an erroneous attribution was made. This drill was discovered within the city limits of Indianapolis, Indiana, and to our knowledge is the only specimen on record for that state. Yet we may wonder how many other mid-Western fluted drills have gone unrecognized?

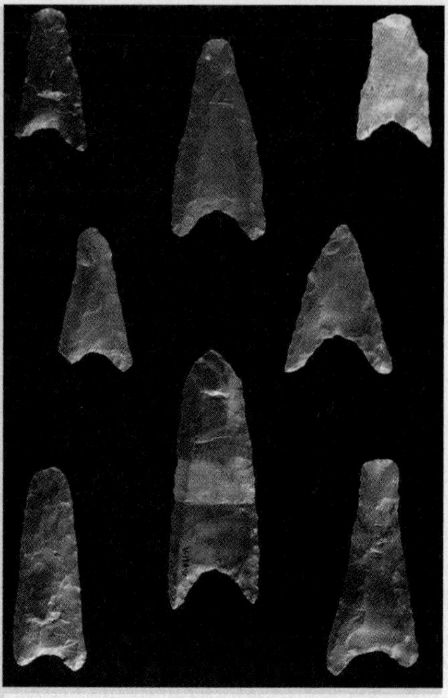

At Vail fluted drills have been unearthed or were collected from the eroded surface of all six repeatedly occupied habitation loci (tent spots). Two loci (C and E) yielded the highest number of drills, although Locus C seems to have had a denser concentration. Matching pieces of two fluted drills were collected at widely separated tent locations (Locus C and Locus E; Locus A and Locus D), suggesting that a single drill apparatus may have been carried about by its owner or shared among families. When a fluted drill tip snapped off during use, the apparatus with the drill base was carried away (by its owner?) for refurbishing.

Fig. 21. Series of drills (most are fluted) from the Vail site showing a range of size, form, and raw material. Length of longest = 56 mm. (just over two inches). Photo courtesy of Lithic Casting Lab.

Our intention here is to summarize the senior author's observations about Vail site drills, in particular, data about their dimensions, weight, nature of fluting, wear resulting from use, and other attributes. Hopefully this information will help guide collectors who stand to encounter this curious tool. Both photographs and exact, measured drawings by V. Waldorf will be used to illustrate the range of drill forms discovered at Vail.

Fig. 22. Fluted drill of reddish-brown chert (V. 3708/13047) recovered in two fragments from Locus E. One fragment was discovered in 1980 and the matching piece 24 years later. Note heavy polish resulting from use at tip. Photo courtesy of Lithic Casting Lab.

Having defined the range of attributes of fluted drills and what constitutes a "typical" specimen (with mean values for all dimensions, etc.), we will next explore how drills may have been hafted. Here experimental replication and the use of fluted drills will be discussed by experienced flintknapper, D.C. Waldorf. Archaeological evidence at the Vail site shows quite clearly that a drill apparatus may have been shared by members of the Vail band. Not all families may have owned the device and relied upon the generosity of their fellows.

It is our belief that, however fluted drills were hafted, may have been used, and shared, their abundance at Vail reflects the unique character of this site and its associated killing ground. Since it was a seasonal camp and hunting was good, hauling away surplus caribou meat, fat, and other parts would have been a recurrent, vexing problem -calling for Clovis ingenuity to solve. Fluted drills may have been indispensable in the construction of sleds, sledges, toboggans and/or boats at Vail and wherever else in northern North America this implement has been found.

Fluted Drills – The Measured Series from Vail

First, we should restate that as of January, 2005, a total of 77 whole or fragmentary specimens, completed or unfinished, representing 62 individual drills is on record for the Vail site. They appear to be distributed unevenly across the Clovis encampment; our understanding, however, is complicated by the fact that 37 drills were collected from displaced erosional sands and cannot be attributed to specific tent-loci. Loci with drills are: **A** (1); **B** (2); **C** (16); **D** (5); **E** (12); **F** (3); **H** (1).

Of the 62 drills we note that 15 have been restored from two or more fragments, found separately by various investigators since 1972. As already noted, two of these restored 15 link widely separated tent-loci (C-E, A-D), and constitute proof of equipment sharing among the Vail band.

Thirty-five (35) of the 62 Vail drills have tip-sections in a sufficiently good state of preservation for use-wear to be observed. This wear, which evinces how drills were hafted and employed, consists of step-fracturing and polish. The locations of step-fractures are most revealing. One drill was reversed in its haft, giving it, in effect, two tips for drilling.

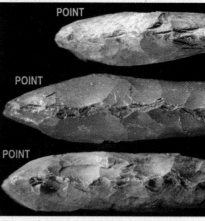

Fig. 23. Step-fractures resulting from use, fluted drills from the Vail site. Photo courtesy of Lithic Casting Lab.

Catalogue Number	SIDE A		SIDE B	
	LEFT EDGE	RIGHT EDGE	LEFT EDGE	RIGHT EDGE
1. 1979/3 + 13040	--	X	X	X
2. 3708 + 13047	X	X	X	X
3. 5375	X	X	X	X
4. 1979/342	--	X	--	X
5. 1979/345	--	--	X	X
6. 4650	X	X	X	X
7. 4224 +13063	X	X	X	X
8. 1979/97 + 1979/332	X	X	--	X
9. 2211	X	X	X	X
10. 5092 + 5379	--	--	X	X
11. 2545	X	--	X	X
12. 1979/324	X	X	X	X
13. 2134	X	X	X	X
14. 2324	X	X	X	X
15. 1979/21	X	X	--	X
16. 1979/329	X	X	X	X
17. 1979/719 + 6860	X	--	X	X
18. 1980/1813	X	X	X	X
19. 4674	X	X	X	X
20. 6696				
A. end #1	X	X	X	X
B. end #2, reversed haft	X	X	--	X
21. 5374	X	X	X	X
22. 1979/22 + 1979/331 + 6277	X	X	X	X
23. 1979/35	X	X	X	X
24. 1979/20	X	X	X	X
25. 1979/348	X	X	X	X
26. 1979/315	--	X	X	X
27. 5377	X	X	X	X
28. 1979/330	X	X	X	X

29. 1979/341	--	X	X	X
30. 2537	X	X	X	X
31. 8259	X	X	X	X
32. 2538 + 2544	X	X	X	X
33. 1979/343	X	X	X	X
34. 10798 + 2068	--	X	X	X
35. 13043	X	X	X	X

Drills with wear on both edges on both sides 24
Drills with wear on one side only 2
Drills with wear on both sides, one edge no wear 9
Drills with wear on both sides, two edges no wear 1

Had Vail drills been rotated in a preferred direction, then one would expect to find a high number of fluted drills with wear on the same edge on both sides. Such is not the case – only one drill showing such evidence (1979/342). Our semi-qualitative method of observation, of course, is hardly perfect, and undoubtedly the senior author failed to note step-fracturing in a few instances. Even so, a preponderance of drills with wear on both edges and on both sides can only mean that drills were rotated to the right **AND** left. Immediately it comes to mind that a bow or pump drill may have been used – like those employed by Inuit (Eskimo) in recent times. Yet, a T-handled auger or gimlet with a stone tip would have suffered wear of the same sort if its user had not favored one direction or another when twisting it into the work. Replicative studies by D.C. Waldorf, to be described below, however, have proved decisive and favor of only one of these possible implements -- the auger.

While findspots of drills tell us **who used them**, and use-wear on drill-tips informs us **how they were hafted**, only dimensional attributes and shape reveal **what size holes** drills made. Of importance in determining hole size are 1) distance from the tip to the "wear-point" forward of the haft – giving the depth of the hole; 2) width of a drill at the wear-point – giving oral diameter of hole; and 3) width of drill tip – giving the "effective" diameter of the hole. If drilling were pursued from both sides of the work, of course, the depth of a hole could be (at most) doubled.

Based upon measurements of 42 specimens, the mean distance between tip and wear-point was found to be 18.8 mm +/- 3.8 mm, or approximately 3/4 of an inch. Doubling this figure, gives I 1/2 inches as the maximum thickness of raw material that could be perforated by the Clovis tool-users at Vail. A hole of this depth would penetrate all but the thickest caribou antler, and if starting grooves were scraped out before drilling, any caribou antler could be fully penetrated.

The mean width at the wear-point of 50 fluted drills that were intact enough for measurement was found to be 11. 8 mm. +/- 1. 7 mm. or just under a half-inch. The more critical attribute, mean width of the tip, for a group of 42 drills with their tips intact was 7.6 mm, +/- 1.1 mm or slightly more than a quarter-inch. A cord or lashing of this diameter, whether made of spruce root, sinew, or *babiche* (green hide strip), would be very strong. Traditional snowshoe web lacing employed by American Indian and French Canadian woodsmen is hardly 1/8 inch in diameter; while web lacing for the seats of furniture (and the floors of cargo-sleds) is seldom wider than a quarter-inch. In our opinion the fluted drills of Vail were capable of making large enough holes for constructing a substantial conveyance assembled from animal bones and antler. Were wood used in a conveyance's framework, however, obviously it would have first been spilt into slabs or boards 1 1/2-2 inches thick or less. For splitting the many wedges or *pièces esquillées* unearthed by us at the Vail site would have served admirably.

As for the gross shape and character of the Vail fluted drills -- aspects most interesting to collectors of Palaeo-American artifacts – we note the following:

I. 89% of drills at Vail are fluted on at least one face; 80% are fluted on both faces.

II. Channel flakes range in length from 4.4 mm. to 39.5 mm, with means of 18.0 mm, +/- 6.0 mm (obverse side) and 14.4 mm. +/- 5.3 mm (reverse side).

III. The mean greatest thickness is 5.8 mm +/- .8 mm (somewhat thinner than fluted projectile points).

IV. The mean basal width, also the greatest width, of Vail fluted drills 17.5 mm, +/- 2.9 mm with a range of 11.6 mm. to 30.0 mm. This width is hardly 3/4 of the average basal width of fluted projectile points. In nearly all instances the lower edges (area of the haft) show grinding – just like fluted projectile points.

V. As a relic of their transformation from fluted projectile points, drills have relatively deep basal concavities (on a sample of 43 drills mean depth is 4.4 mm +/- 1.5 mm). In most cases the basal concavity has been ground for secure hafting.

Since nearly all drills were converted from fluted projectile points, not surprisingly the range of raw materials employed in their manufacture is identical to that of the spearpoints. Most common is a chert that is gray-green in color (when fresh) but has weathered to various shades of gray, tan, brown, and buff in the chemically active forest soils of the Magalloway River valley. This chert is likely a Cambro-Ordovician stone with abundant radiolaria from New York State's Hudson Lowland, otherwise known as Normanskill chert.. Also used for drills were: 1) a lustrous gray chert of high silica content derived from outcrops near Lake Champlain and 2) a yellow-brown chert or jasper of unknown origin. Only one drill was made of this jasper – likely foreign to northern New England: likewise, in the Vail projectile point assemblage there were only three fluted points fashioned of it.

In sum, the ancient Clovis knappers of Vail used basal fragments of projectile points longer than 25-26 mm. (an inch) for the manufacture of drills. Since most projectile points at Vail are fluted on both faces (a few, however, are fluted on just one face or rarer – on neither face!), it follows that most of the drills recycled from points bear channel flake scars on both faces. In order to maximize the length of drills, ancient knappers made one long edge run diagonally across a broken base and maintained a rough symmetry by flaking a new ear. Too, the basal concavity of the original fluted point was preserved during recycling; however, its depth was reduced slightly upon conversion to a drill. As a final measure, the edges of fluted rills in the area of the haft received a thorough grinding. Clearly, they were expected

Fig. 24. Bow drill apparatus used by the Central Eskimo (see Boas 1888: Figure 475).

to endure hard service just as the "deer spears" did. On the average, a Clovis household broke one drill during every season's residence at the Vail site.

The fluted drills of Vail are easily recognized artifacts and help characterize a "northern facies" of Clovis culture. While, drills are known for other phases and expressions of the Fluted Point Tradition, their shapes differ from those of the Magalloway Valley Palaeo-American Complex and may not have been recycled from pre-existing toolforms.

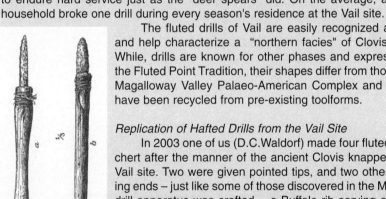

Fig. 25. Spindle and rotater-cup (socket held by mouth of user) of a bow drill apparatus used by point Barrow Eskimo (see Murdoch 1892: Figure 150).

Replication of Hafted Drills from the Vail Site

In 2003 one of us (D.C.Waldorf) made four fluted drills of chert after the manner of the ancient Clovis knappers at the Vail site. Two were given pointed tips, and two others had bulbous, expanding ends – just like some of those discovered in the Magalloway Valley. A bow-drill apparatus was crafted -- a Buffalo rib serving as a bow and a chunk of moose antler becoming the rotater-cup or socket. Hardwood spindles were employed for hafting the fluted drill-points. The rig was a workmanlike copy of bow-drills like those once used by Inuit (Eskimo) craftsmen of Point Barrow and elsewhere across the Arctic.

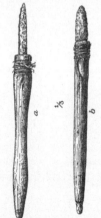

Fig. 26. Spindles tipped with flaked stone drill-points, Point Barrow Eskimo (see Murdoch 1892: Figure 159).

The first item selected for perforating was a red cedar stick. The pointed drill worked best; however, at a depth of 1/2 inch it began to bind, putting the drill-tip in peril of snapping. Also, it took considerable finesse in applying proper downward pressure upon the bow-drill to keep it cutting and not flying free of the socket. The bulbous-ended fluted drills performed poorly and tended to bind in the hole. All in all, the experiment was very unsatisfactory and drove us to use a simpler, T-shaped auger or gimlet.

Substituting softer Scotch pine for the cedar, a 1/2-inch deep hole was augured within two minutes! For this initial penetration a pointed fluted drill was used. Replacing it with a bulbous-ended example, the hole was broadened and increased to a depth of 3/4 inch within 10 minutes. According to Waldorf (2004: 20), the "trick" was "..to rotate the drill... 180 degrees, back and forth two or three times, after which the shaft was rotated 1/4 turn. Then this drilling motion was repeated." Once a rhythm was established, drilling the relatively soft pine (similar in hardness to the spruce and fir that existed at the Vail site during the Clovis era) was easy. Boring harder wood, like hickory, with an auger was much more difficult and time-consuming. Also, with hickory the chert drill-tips began to suffer damage when they became stuck in the hole.

Fig. 27. Awl or gimlet used by the caribou-hunting Neneot (Naskapi) Indians of interior Labrador to bore holes in wood (see Turner 1894: Figure 142).

For drilling antler Waldorf experimented only with a bow-drill armed with a pointed, chert tip. This combination worked relatively well on this tough raw material. In five minutes of vigorous drilling a hole 3/16 inch deep was produced. Although the stone drill-tip sustained considerable wear during this phase of the experiment, it was still sharp enough for additional work – had it been necessary.

In conclusion, both bow-drill and auger (gimlet) are effective, but much depends upon the raw material being drilled. A combination of drill-points (pointed- + bulbous-ended) advanced the job and gave the speediest outcome. Of course, we can never be certain that speed or "'workplace efficiency" was an important consideration to Clovis tool-users. However, given the rigors of a neo-Arctic climate that likely held sway in northern, interior North America during that ancient era, it is possible they, like most cultures of the modem era, set a premium upon tools that performed smoothly and quickly. There is one thing of which we can be sure, namely, the Vail site inhabitants' innate ingenuity to get jobs done on schedule and "under budget". We observe how they employed multi-purpose, composite, and multi-dimensional flaked stone tools as well as how they were able to transform worthless junk (fragmentary fluted points) into valuable implements (fluted drills). Across a gulf of hundreds of generations we are compelled to admire such artful behavior by Clovis folk, wondering only what were their other masterworks of perishable materials, which (alas!) we shall never witness.

References Cited

Boas, Franz
    1888 The Central Eskimo. *Sixth Annual Report, Bureau of Ethnology, Smithsonian Institution.* Washington, D.C.

Boldurian, Anthony T. and John L. Cotter
    1999 Clovis Revisited. *University of Pennsylvania, University Museum Monograph* 103. Philadelphia.

Bourque, Bruce
    2000 *Twelve Thousand Years: American Indians in Maine.* University of Nebraska Press. Lincoln.

Gramly, Richard Michael
    1982 The Vail Site: A Palaeo-Indian Encampment in Maine. *Bulletin of the Buffalo Society of Natural Sciences* 33. Buffalo, New York.
    1984 Kill sites, killing ground and fluted points at the Vail site. *Archaeology of Eastern North America* 12: 110-121.
    1988 *The Adkins Site: A Palaeo-Indian Habitation and Associated Stone Structure.* Persimmon Press. Buffalo, New York.

1995 The Vail Palaeo-Indian site, Maine: Fifteen years after the excavation. *The Amateur Archaeologist* 1(2): 46-64. Ameican Society for Amateur Archaeology. North Andover, Massachusetts.

1998 Vail site. Pp. 863-864 in Guy Gibbon (ed.) *Archaeology of Prehistoric Native America: An Encyclopedia*. Garland Publishing, Inc. New York.

2000 *Guide to the Palaeo-American Artifacts of North America*. 3rd edition. Persimmon Press. Buffalo, New York.

2001 (also available as a reprint, Persimmon Press)
The Morss fluted point site, northwestern Maine. *The Amateur Archaeologist* 7(2): 77-96. American Society for Amateur Archaeology. North Andover, Massachusetts.

In press, a
The Upper/Lower Wheeler Dam sites: Clovis in the Upper Magalloway River valley. *The Amateur Archaeologist* 11 (1). American Society for Amateur Archaeology. North Andover.

In press, b
Recent archaeological fieldwork at the Vail Clovis habitation and kill site, NW Maine. *The Amateur Archaeologist* 11 (1). American Society for Amateur Archaeology. North Andover.

Grimes, John R.
1979 A new look at Bull Brook. *Anthropology* 3(1 & 2): 109-130, State University of New York at Stony Brook.

Haynes, C. Vance
1982 Were Clovis progenitors in Beringia? Pp. 383-398 in *Paleoecology of Beringia*. Academic Press. New York.

Haynes, C. Vance, D.J. Donahue, A.J.T. Jull, and T.H.Zabel
2004 Application of accelerator dating to Fluted Point Paleoindian sites. *Archaeology of Eastern North America* 12: 184-191.

Lahren, Larry and Robson Bonnichsen
1974 Bone foreshafts from a Clovis burial in southwestem Montana. *Science* 186:147-50.

MacDonald, George F.
1968 Debert: A Paleo-Indian Site in Central Nova Scotia. *National Museum of Canada Anthropology Papers* 16. Ottawa.

Murdoch, John
1892 Ethnological Results of the Point Barrow Expedition. *Ninth Annual Report, Bureau of Ethnology, Smithsonian Institution*. Washington, D.C.

Schulze-Thulin, Axel
1995 *Indianer der Urzeit*. Eugen Diedrichs Verlag. Munich.

Turner, Lucien M.
1894 Ethnology of the Ungava District, Hudson Bay Territory. *Eleventh Annual Report, Bureau of Ethnology, Smithsonian Institution*. Washington, D.C.

Wilke, Philip J., J. Jeffrey Flenniken, and Terry L. Ozbun
1991 Clovis technology at the Anzick site, Montana. *Journal of California and Great Basin Anthropology* 13(2): 242-272.

Waldorf, D.C.
2004 Fluted drills and reamers from the Vail site. *Chips* 16(1): 15-21. Flintknapper's Comer, Greasy Creek Holler, Washburn, MO 65772.

IS YOUR COLLECTION WORTHY?

Should your collection be recorded for posterity and shared with your fellow enthusiasts? If you'd like to submit photos or be an advisor, please contact Bob Overstreet on our toll free line at (888) 375-9800 ext. 401 or by email at obob@gemstonepub.com.

When photographing your collection for submission, photos should be 300 dpi in full color with a ruler showing in the picture for reference size.

We want your help!

LAKE MOHAVE
13,200 B.P., CO

LAKE MOHAVE
13,200 B.P., OR,
ground stem

CLOVIS
11,500 B.P., TN.
hornstone

LAKE MOHAVE
13,200 B.P., CO

GRAVER
11,500 B.P., OR,
agate

HASKETT
12,000 B.P.,
OR, basalt

REDSTONE
11,500 B.P., AL,
Fort Payne chert

CLOVIS
11,500 B.P., FL

CLOVIS
11,500 B.P., FL,
red agate

CLOVIS
11,500 B.P., IL
Burlington chert

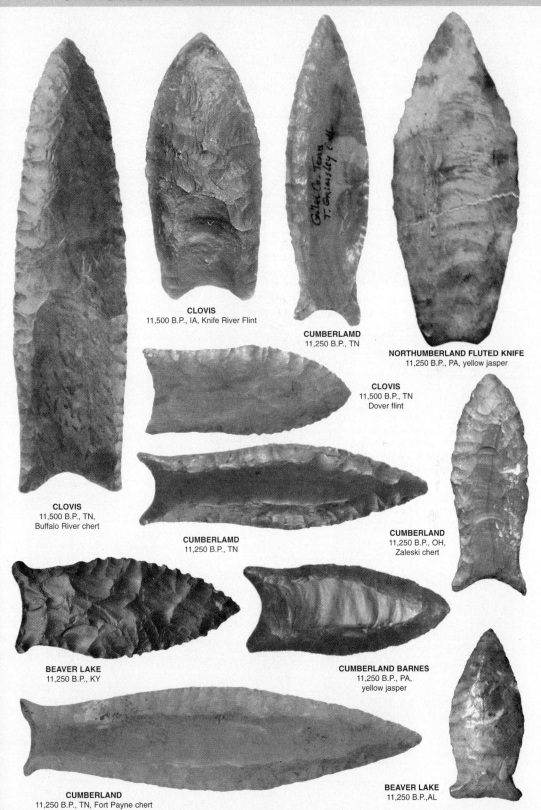

CLOVIS
11,500 B.P., IA, Knife River Flint

CUMBERLAMD
11,250 B.P., TN

NORTHUMBERLAND FLUTED KNIFE
11,250 B.P., PA, yellow jasper

CLOVIS
11,500 B.P., TN
Dover flint

CLOVIS
11,500 B.P., TN,
Buffalo River chert

CUMBERLAMD
11,250 B.P., TN

CUMBERLAND
11,250 B.P., OH,
Zaleski chert

BEAVER LAKE
11,250 B.P., KY

CUMBERLAND BARNES
11,250 B.P., PA,
yellow jasper

CUMBERLAND
11,250 B.P., TN, Fort Payne chert

BEAVER LAKE
11,250 B.P.,AL

PLAINVIEW
11,250 B.P., IL,
Burlington chert

PLAINVIEW
11,250 B.P., OK

GOSHEN
11,250 B.P., OK

PLAINVIEW
11,250 B.P., NM

PLAINVIEW
11,250 B.P., CO,
Alibates dolomite

BLACK ROCK CONCAVE
11,000 B.P., OR, agate

PLAINVIEW
11,250 B.P., MO

PLAINVIEW
11,250 B.P., KS

CROWFIELD
11,000 B.P., OH,
Delaware chert

COUGAR MOUNTAIN
11,000 B.P., OR,
oolitic jasper, ground stem

CRESCENT
11,000 B.P., OR

FOLSOM
11,000 B.P., OK,
Alibates dolomite

FOLSOM
11,000 B.P., IA,
Knife River flint

FOLSOM
11,000 B.P., WI,
silicified sandstone

CRESCENT
11,000 B.P., OR, obsidian

CRESCENT
11,000 B.P., OR, basalt

FOLSOM
11,000 B.P., NM

MILNESAND
11,000 B.P., NM

MIDLAND
11,000 B.P., TX

FOLSOM
11,000 B.P., CO,
Alibates dolomite

SILVER LAKE
11,000 B.P., NV, chisel tip

KENNEWICK
11,000 B.P., OR, obsidi-
an

LIND COULEE
11,000 B.P., OR

BOLEN BEVELED
10,500 B.P., FL

MILNESAND
11,000 B.P., TX

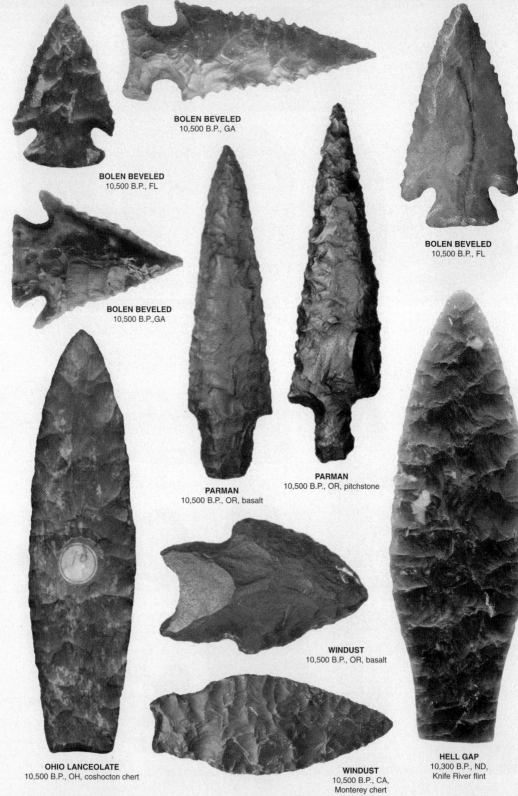

BOLEN BEVELED
10,500 B.P., GA

BOLEN BEVELED
10,500 B.P., FL

BOLEN BEVELED
10,500 B.P., FL

BOLEN BEVELED
10,500 B.P.,GA

BOLEN BEVELED
10,500 B.P., FL

PARMAN
10,500 B.P., OR, basalt

PARMAN
10,500 B.P., OR, pitchstone

WINDUST
10,500 B.P., OR, basalt

OHIO LANCEOLATE
10,500 B.P., OH, coshocton chert

WINDUST
10,500 B.P., CA,
Monterey chert

HELL GAP
10,300 B.P., ND,
Knife River flint

AGATE BASIN
10,200 B.P., OK

AGATE BASIN
10,200 B.P., ND, Knife
River flint

AGATE BASIN
10,200 B.P., OR
obsidian

AGATE BASIN
10,200 B.P., MO

AGATE BASIN
10,200 B.P., IA

ALBERTA
10,000 B.P., OR,
obsidian

BIG SANDY
10,000 B.P., KY,
red jasper

BIG SANDY
10,000 B.P., AL

BIG SANDY
10,000 B.P., TN

ALBERTA
10,000 B.P., OR, dacite

CACHE RIVER
10,000 B.P., LA

CACHE RIVER
10,000 B.P., AR, agate

CODY KNIFE
10,000 B.P. OR, obsidian

COLDWATER
10,000 B.P., TX,
petrified wood

COWHOUSE SLOUGH
10,000 B.P., S. GA

DALTON
10,000 B.P., S. GA

DALTON
10,000 B.P., IL, fluted

EDEN
10,000 B.P., CO
Alibates dolomite

DALTON
10,000 B.P., MO

DALTON
10,000 B.P., OK

HOLLAND
10,000 B.P., TX

EDEN
10,000 B.P., OK

EDEN
10,000 B.P., TX
jasper

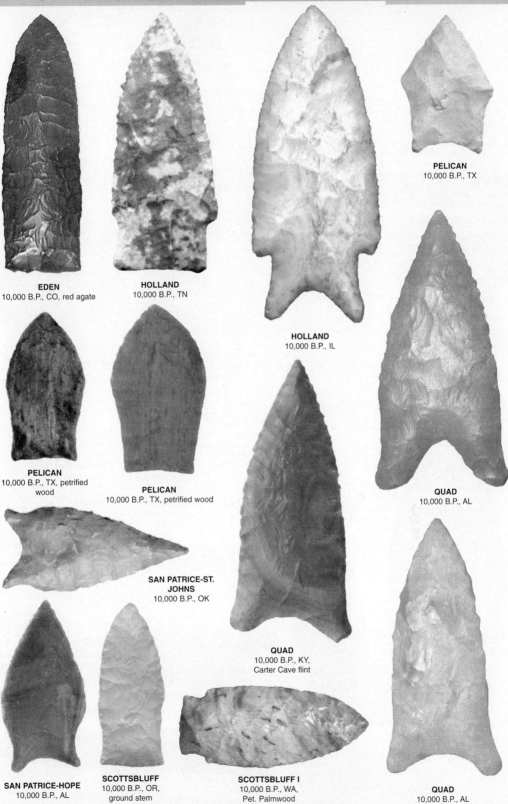

EDEN
10,000 B.P., CO, red agate

HOLLAND
10,000 B.P., TN

PELICAN
10,000 B.P., TX

HOLLAND
10,000 B.P., IL

PELICAN
10,000 B.P., TX, petrified wood

PELICAN
10,000 B.P., TX, petrified wood

QUAD
10,000 B.P., AL

SAN PATRICE-ST. JOHNS
10,000 B.P., OK

QUAD
10,000 B.P., KY, Carter Cave flint

SAN PATRICE-HOPE
10,000 B.P., AL

SCOTTSBLUFF
10,000 B.P., OR, ground stem

SCOTTSBLUFF I
10,000 B.P., WA, Pet. Palmwood

QUAD
10,000 B.P., AL

SCOTTSBLUFF II
10,000 B.P., TX, ground stem

SCOTTSBLUFF I
10,000 B.P., OR

SCOTTSBLUFF I
10,000 B.P., OK

SCOTTSBLUFF II
10,000 B.P., MO, Mozarkite
chert, glued

SIMPSON-MUSTACHE
10,000 B.P., FL

VICTORIA
10,000 B.P., NM

WHEELER
10,000 B.P., AL

SPEDIS I
10,000 B.P., OR, chalcedony

SIMPSON
10,000 B.P., FL

SPEDIS I
10,000 B.P., WA,
tan agate

WHEELER
10,000 B.P., WV, black Zaleski chert

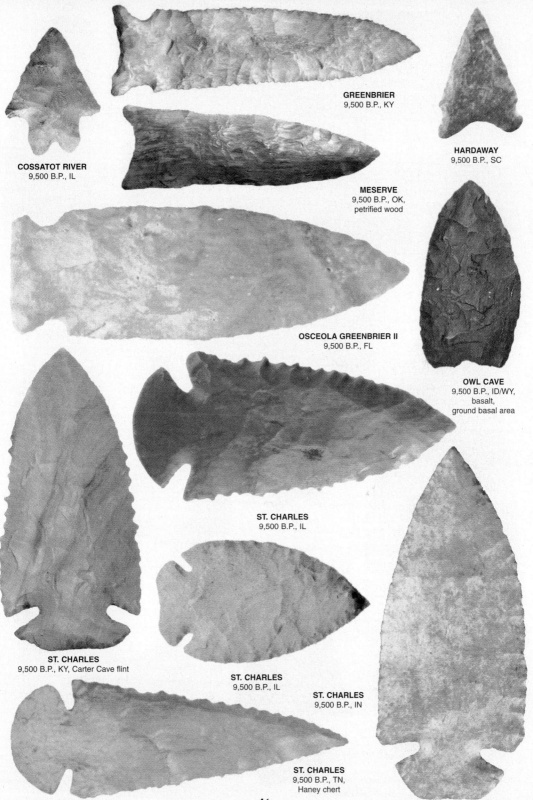

GREENBRIER
9,500 B.P., KY

HARDAWAY
9,500 B.P., SC

COSSATOT RIVER
9,500 B.P., IL

MESERVE
9,500 B.P., OK,
petrified wood

OSCEOLA GREENBRIER II
9,500 B.P., FL

OWL CAVE
9,500 B.P., ID/WY,
basalt,
ground basal area

ST. CHARLES
9,500 B.P., IL

ST. CHARLES
9,500 B.P., KY, Carter Cave flint

ST. CHARLES
9,500 B.P., IL

ST. CHARLES
9,500 B.P., IN

ST. CHARLES
9,500 B.P., TN,
Haney chert

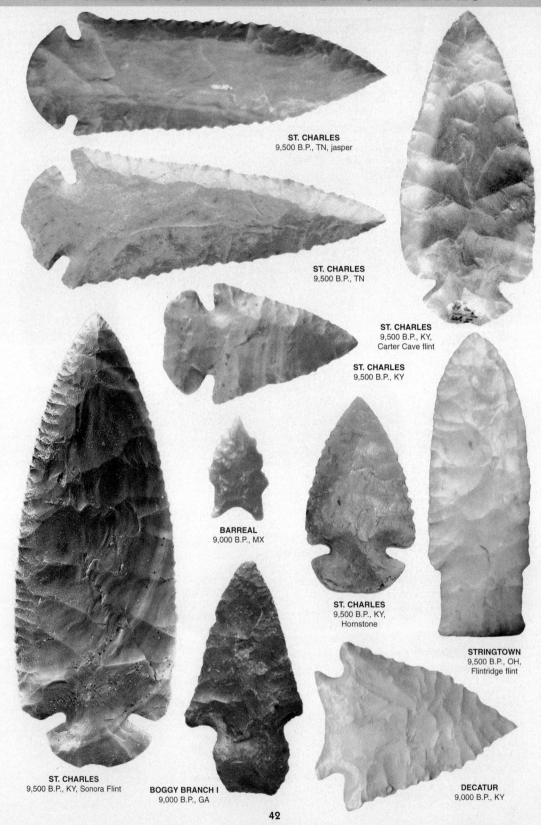

ST. CHARLES
9,500 B.P., TN, jasper

ST. CHARLES
9,500 B.P., TN

ST. CHARLES
9,500 B.P., KY,
Carter Cave flint

ST. CHARLES
9,500 B.P., KY

BARREAL
9,000 B.P., MX

ST. CHARLES
9,500 B.P., KY,
Hornstone

STRINGTOWN
9,500 B.P., OH,
Flintridge flint

ST. CHARLES
9,500 B.P., KY, Sonora Flint

BOGGY BRANCH I
9,000 B.P., GA

DECATUR
9,000 B.P., KY

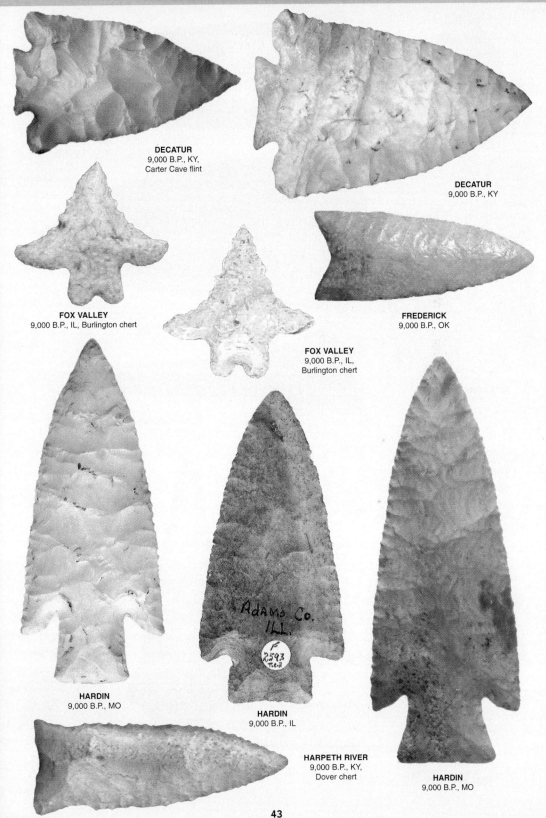

DECATUR
9,000 B.P., KY,
Carter Cave flint

DECATUR
9,000 B.P., KY

FOX VALLEY
9,000 B.P., IL, Burlington chert

FREDERICK
9,000 B.P., OK

FOX VALLEY
9,000 B.P., IL,
Burlington chert

HARDIN
9,000 B.P., MO

HARDIN
9,000 B.P., IL

HARPETH RIVER
9,000 B.P., KY,
Dover chert

HARDIN
9,000 B.P., MO

KIRK STEMMED
9,000 B.P., GA

KIRK CORNER NOTCHED
9,000 B.P., IL, Pitkin chert

KIRK CORNER NOTCHED
9,000 B.P., IL

KIRK STEMMED Drill
9,000 B.P., KY, drill

KIRK STEMMED
9,000 B.P., KY

KIRK STEMMED
9,000 B.P., KY

LECROY
9,000 B.P., KY

KIRK STEMMED
9,000 B.P., GA

KIRK STEMMED
9,000 B.P., KY

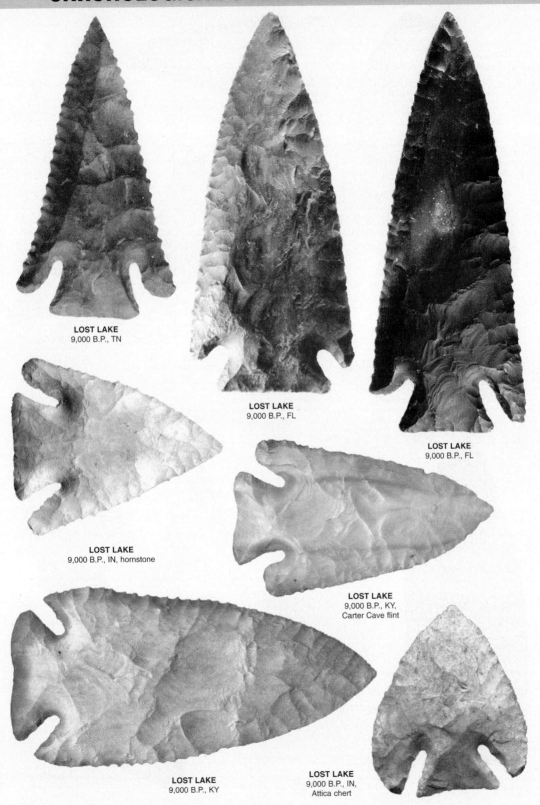

LOST LAKE
9,000 B.P., TN

LOST LAKE
9,000 B.P., FL

LOST LAKE
9,000 B.P., FL

LOST LAKE
9,000 B.P., IN, hornstone

LOST LAKE
9,000 B.P., KY,
Carter Cave flint

LOST LAKE
9,000 B.P., KY

LOST LAKE
9,000 B.P., IN,
Attica chert

RICE LOBBED
9,000 B.P., OK

NEUBERGER
9,000 B.P., MO

SAN JOSE
9,000 B.P., NM

SAN JOSE
9,000 B.P., CO
jasper

STILWELL
9,000 B.P., MO,
Burlington chert

SAN JOSE
9,000 B.P., NM

SAN JOSE
9,000 B.P., CO
jasper

VAN LOTT
9,000 B.P., SC

WACISSA
9,000 B.P., FL

STILWELL
9,000 B.P., OH, Coshocton

STILWELL
9,000 B.P., MO

WACISSA
9,000 B.P., SC

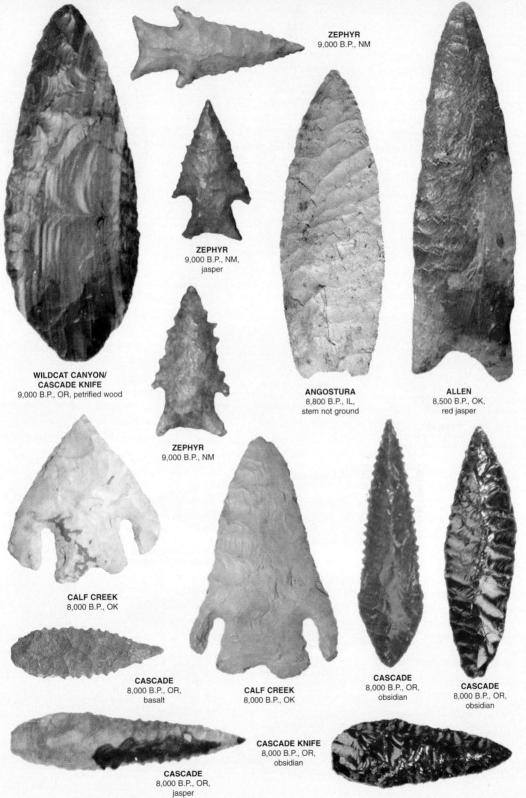

ZEPHYR
9,000 B.P., NM

ZEPHYR
9,000 B.P., NM,
jasper

**WILDCAT CANYON/
CASCADE KNIFE**
9,000 B.P., OR, petrified wood

ANGOSTURA
8,800 B.P., IL,
stem not ground

ALLEN
8,500 B.P., OK,
red jasper

ZEPHYR
9,000 B.P., NM

CALF CREEK
8,000 B.P., OK

CASCADE
8,000 B.P., OR,
basalt

CALF CREEK
8,000 B.P., OK

CASCADE
8,000 B.P., OR,
obsidian

CASCADE
8,000 B.P., OR,
obsidian

CASCADE KNIFE
8,000 B.P., OR,
obsidian

CASCADE
8,000 B.P., OR,
jasper

47

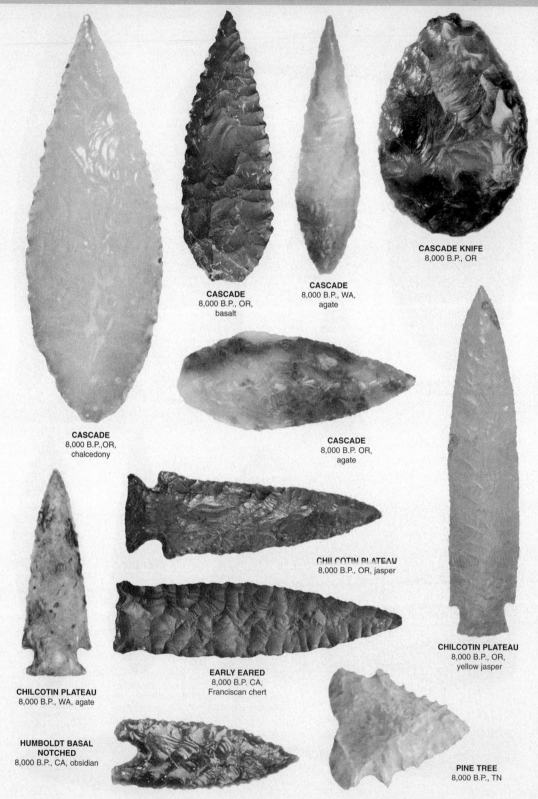

CASCADE KNIFE
8,000 B.P., OR

CASCADE
8,000 B.P., WA,
agate

CASCADE
8,000 B.P., OR,
basalt

CASCADE
8,000 B.P.,OR,
chalcedony

CASCADE
8,000 B.P. OR,
agate

CHILCOTIN PLATEAU
8,000 B.P., OR, jasper

CHILCOTIN PLATEAU
8,000 B.P., OR,
yellow jasper

CHILCOTIN PLATEAU
8,000 B.P., WA, agate

EARLY EARED
8,000 B.P. CA,
Franciscan chert

HUMBOLDT BASAL
NOTCHED
8,000 B.P., CA, obsidian

PINE TREE
8,000 B.P., TN

PINE TREE
8,000 B.P., KY

PINE TREE
8,000 B.P., KY, hornstone

PINE TREE
8,000 B.P., TN, Dover chert

PINTO BASIN
8,000 B.P., OR, obsidian

PINTO BASIN
8,000 B.P., OR, obsidian

PINTO BASIN
8,000 B.P., OR, obsidian

PINTO BASIN
8,000 B.P., CA, obsidian

PINTO BASIN
8,000 B.P., OR,
obsidian,
ground stem

PINTO BASIN
8,000 B.P., CA,
obsidian

PINTO BASIN
8,000 B.P., NV

ST. TAMMANY
8.000 B.P., MS

BITTERROOT
7,500 B.P., OR,
banded obsidian

WELLS
8,000 B.P., TX

CONERLY
7,500 B.P., KY

HOWARD COUNTY
7,500 B.P., MO

NEBO HILL
7,500 B.P., MO,
Burlington chert

RIO GRANDE
7,500 B.P., TX, rootbeer flint

RIO GRANDE
7,500 B.P., CO,
Petrified palmwood

HOWARD COUNTY
7,500 B.P., IL

ABASOLO
7,000 B.P., TX

ATLATL VALLEY
TRIANGULAR
7,000 B.P., ID, chalcedony

ATLATL VALLEY
TRIANGULAR
7,000 B.P. WA,
beveled base

BELL
7,000 B.P., AR

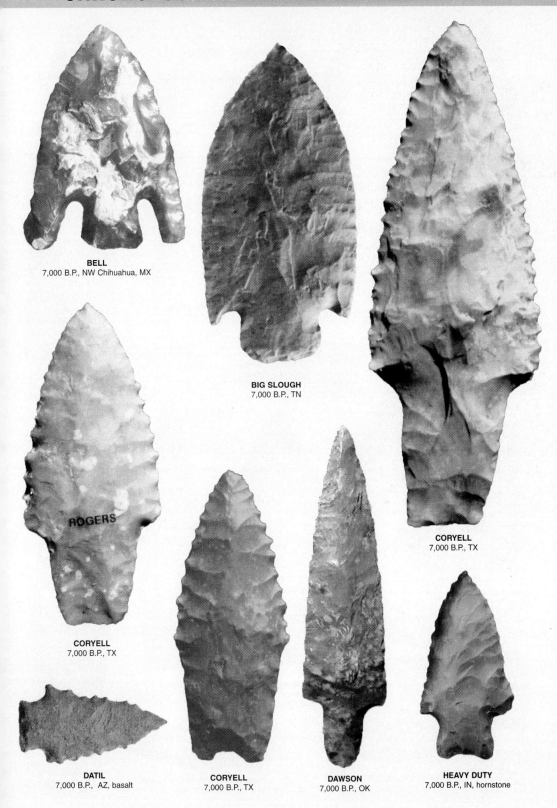

BELL
7,000 B.P., NW Chihuahua, MX

BIG SLOUGH
7,000 B.P., TN

CORYELL
7,000 B.P., TX

CORYELL
7,000 B.P., TX

DATIL
7,000 B.P., AZ, basalt

CORYELL
7,000 B.P., TX

DAWSON
7,000 B.P., OK

HEAVY DUTY
7,000 B.P., IN, hornstone

HEAVY DUTY
7,000 B.P., IN, hornstone

HEAVY DUTY
7,000 B.P., OH, Flint Ridge flint

HICKORY RIDGE
7,000 B.P., IL

**HUMBOLDT CON-
STRICTED BASE**
7,000 B.P., OR, ground
base

HICKORY RIDGE
7,000 B.P., OK

**HUMBOLDT CON-
STRICTED BASE**
7,000 B.P., CA

**HUMBOLDT CON-
STRICTED BASE**
7,000 B.P., CA

**HUMBOLDT
TRIANGULAR**
7,000 B.P., OR, obsidian

**HUMBOLDT
CONSTRICTED BASE**
7,000 B.P., OR, ground base

**HUMBOLDT
CONSTRICTED
BASE**
7,000 B.P., OR

HUMBOLDT CONSTRICTED BASE
7,000 B.P., OR

HUMBOLDT CONSTRICTED BASE
7,000 B.P., NV

**HUMBOLDT
TRIANGULAR**
7,000 B.P., OR

MARION
7,000 B.P., FL

NEWNAN
7,000 B.P., FL

NIGHTFIRE
7,000 B.P., OR, obsidian,
broken & glued

NIGHTFIRE
7,000 B.P., OR, obsidian

NIGHTFIRE
7,000 B.P., OR,
basalt

NEWTON FALLS
7,000 B.P., TN, Horse Creek chert

NEWTON FALLS
7,000 B.P., OH/KY

NIGHTFIRE
7,000 B.P., OR, ignimbrite

NORTHERN SIDE NOTCHED
7,000 B.P., OR, obsidian

**NORTHERN SIDE
NOTCHED**
7,000 B.P., OR, basalt

NORTHERN
7,000 B.P., OR, obsidian

NORTHERN
7,000 B.P., OR, obsidian

NORTHERN
7,000 B.P., OR, obsidian

NORTHERN
7,000 B.P., OR, obsidian

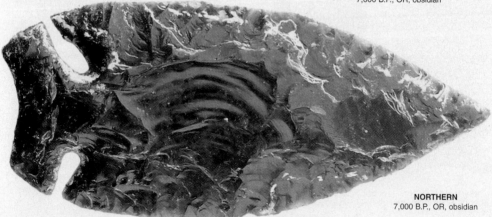

NORTHERN
7,000 B.P., OR, obsidian

NORTHERN
7,000 B.P., OR, obsidian

OSCEOLA
7,000 B.P., MO

OSCEOLA
7,000 B.P., IL

SEARCY
7,000 B.P., AR, type site

WENDOVER
7,000 B.P., OR,
obsidian

ESCOBAS
6,500 B.P., CO

ESCOBAS
6,500 B.P., AZ

ESCOBAS
6,500 B.P., CO,
jasper

PENTAGONAL KNIFE
6,500 B.P., OH, Flintridge flint

SUDDEN
6,300 B.P., CO

PENTAGONAL KNIFE
6,500 B.P., OH

PENTAGONAL KNIFE
6,500 B.P., OH, Flintridge
flint

SUDDEN
6,300 B.P., CO

SUDDEN
6,300 B.P., CO

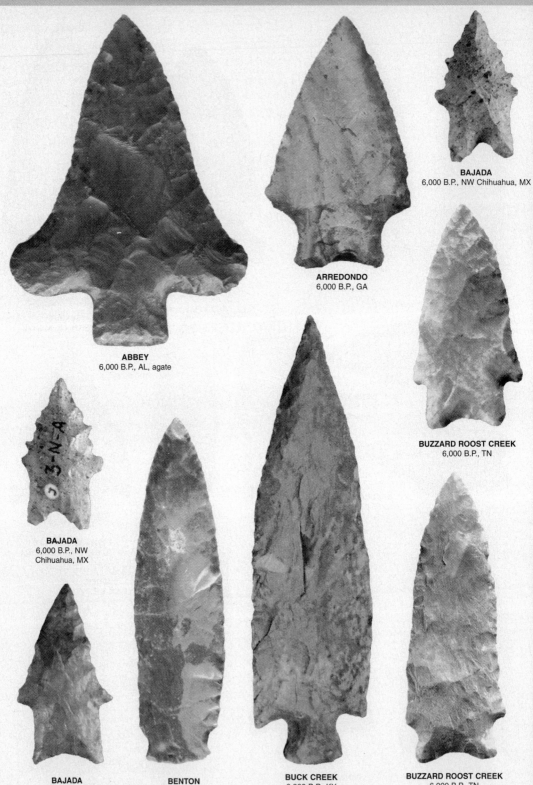

ABBEY
6,000 B.P., AL, agate

ARREDONDO
6,000 B.P., GA

BAJADA
6,000 B.P., NW Chihuahua, MX

BAJADA
6,000 B.P., NW
Chihuahua, MX

BUZZARD ROOST CREEK
6,000 B.P., TN

BAJADA
6,000 B.P., NM

BENTON
6,000 B.P., TN

BUCK CREEK
6,000 B.P., KY

BUZZARD ROOST CREEK
6,000 B.P., TN

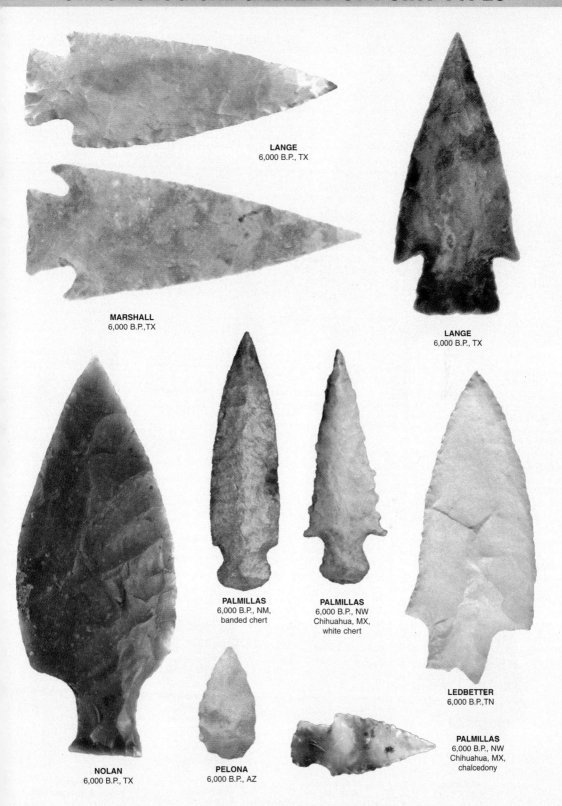

LANGE
6,000 B.P., TX

MARSHALL
6,000 B.P.,TX

LANGE
6,000 B.P., TX

PALMILLAS
6,000 B.P., NM,
banded chert

PALMILLAS
6,000 B.P., NW
Chihuahua, MX,
white chert

LEDBETTER
6,000 B.P.,TN

PALMILLAS
6,000 B.P., NW
Chihuahua, MX,
chalcedony

NOLAN
6,000 B.P., TX

PELONA
6,000 B.P., AZ

PEDERNALES
6,000 B.P., TX

PANDALE
6,000 B.P., TX

PEDERNALES
6,000 B.P., TX

PEDERNALES
6,000 B.P., TX

PICKWICK
6,000 B.P., TN

PICKWICK
6,000 B.P., KY

PEDERNALES
6,000 B.P., TX

PICKWICK
6,000 B.P., TN, Dover chert

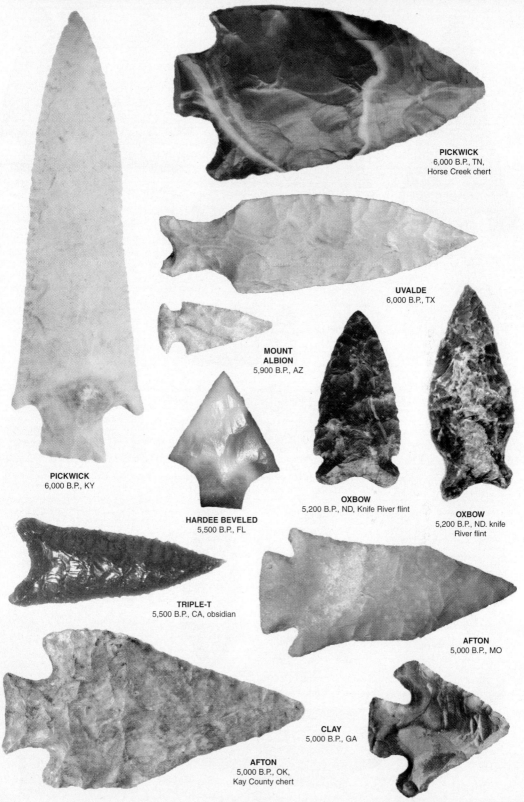

PICKWICK
6,000 B.P., TN,
Horse Creek chert

UVALDE
6,000 B.P., TX

MOUNT ALBION
5,900 B.P., AZ

PICKWICK
6,000 B.P., KY

OXBOW
5,200 B.P., ND, Knife River flint

OXBOW
5,200 B.P., ND. knife River flint

HARDEE BEVELED
5,500 B.P., FL

TRIPLE-T
5,500 B.P., CA, obsidian

AFTON
5,000 B.P., MO

CLAY
5,000 B.P., GA

AFTON
5,000 B.P., OK,
Kay County chert

CLAY
5,000 B.P., GA

CLAY
5,000 B.P., GA

COLD SPRINGS
5,000 B.P., OR

COLD SPRINGS
5,000 B.P., OR, agate

CRESCENT
5,000 B.P., MX, chalcedony

COLD SPRINGS
5,000 B.P., OR,
red jasper

COLD SPRINGS
5,000 B.P., OR, basalt

CULBREATH
5,000 B.P., FL

EXOTIC
5,000 B.P., OR

GATECLIFF
5,000 B.P., OR

EXOTIC
5,000 B.P., OR

GATECLIFF
5,000 B.P., OR

GENESEE
5,000 B.P., NY

MANZANO
5,000 B.P., NM

PUTNAM
5,000 B.P., FL

MONTELL
5,000 B.P., TX

SAVANNAH RIVER
5,000 B.P.,GA, petrified peat bog, ground stem

SAVANNAHA RIVER
5,000 B.P., TN, quartzite

MULBERRY CREEK
5,000 B.P., TN

OTTER CREEK
5,000 B.P., VT, quartzite

Introduction

Hunting arrowheads has been a popular pastime for many Americans over the past one hundred years. Even the Indians themselves cherished and collected rock crystals, gem stones, and points. In the past, large collections were put together with very little effort, since few people hunted and the supply of good artifacts was plentiful. Plowed fields along creeks and rivers, as well as river banks and dry lake beds, are the most popular places for hunting relics, as the early Indians built their villages and hunted game in such locations. The Indians' food supply, such as fish, game, mussels, etc. lived in or along rivers, creeks, springs, ponds, swamps and lakes. Early man preyed on this abundant food supply, migrating along these water routes, moving from place to place in search of better hunting grounds, as the game became depleted.

Fields are plowed in the Fall or Spring of each year. The most likely sites for hunting, of course, would be the large flat areas close to the original river or creek banks. Hunting in areas that may be large enough to support a small village and are on high ground, protected from a flooding river, are especially productive places. Village sites were usually built where a creek converged with a large river. Field hunting should be attempted after a hard rain. Heavy rains will create deep gullies and washed-out areas exposing the relics.

Here is where you can get lucky, especially if you are the first person in the field. All a collector has to do is walk along and pick up pieces of history. Be sure to ask permission before entering private property. Most farmers will give permission to enter their land if approached in a friendly manner.

Plowed fields next to springs and cave openings have also produced relics. Such a place is Castillian Springs, just above Nashville, Tennessee. Here, next to the spring, there are salt licks for animals. The Indians occupied and lived in this area for thousands of years from the Paleo to Woodland periods and later. The herd animals would always migrate here for salt and watering, providing the Indians with plentiful meat and nourishment right in their own backyard. Erosion around the spring has in the past produced many excellent artifacts. From fluted points to Doves, to Lost Lakes, to stemmed types, this area has been rich with many types of points.

Another similar site is Nickajack Cave and its surrounding fields, just below Chattanooga, Tennessee. Overhangs and rock shelters along rivers and creeks where early man lived, as well as river lands, have produced fine artifacts as well.

In the 1930s, the blow-outs, or dust storms, in the plains states produced many fine projectile points. The top layer of soil blew away, exposing relics left centuries ago by the Indians.

Sand bar hunting along the Tennessee River became possible after the Tennessee Valley Authority built their dams and began controlling the river level in the 1930's. During the development of the TVA system, hunting was excellent. Lake levels were dropped during the winter months, exposing the sand bars which were originally high areas in the now inundated fields along the river channel, where the early Indians built their villages and camp sites. As winter storms raged through the Tennessee Valley, the lake levels would rise and fall and the racing river would cut into the sand bars, exposing relics for anyone to merely come along and pick up.

Today most of the sand bars and plowed fields in many states have been "hunted out." But the energetic hunter can still find new relic-producing sites if he gathers his facts, follows all leads, studies maps of likely areas and hunts whenever he can. Sooner or later he will get lucky.

However, most collectors are neither energetic nor imaginative, and build their collections by systematically purchasing specimens one at a time. **Genuine** points can be found for sale at relic shows, and sometimes in local collections that come up for sale. **Warning:** fake relics (all recently made and aged) are being offered to the public everywhere as genuine prehistoric artifacts. Knowing the history or pedigree of a point is very important in the process of determining whether or not it is a genuine pre-Columbian piece. Before purchasing a relic from anyone, be sure the dealer will guarantee it to be a genuine, pre-Columbian artifact, and will give you your money back should you later discover otherwise. Many reputable dealers will give you a money back guarantee. Whenever possible, you should have an expert examine any and every piece for its authenticity before you buy.

> Most points illustrated in this book are shown actual size and are believed to be genuine prehistoric artifacts. We have gone to great lengths to insure that only authentic points are included. Any errors discovered will be deleted in future editions. This is not a "For Sale" list of points. The illustrated examples are for identification and value purposes only.

HOW TO USE THIS BOOK

This book is set up by regions of the country to make it easy for you to classify your collection. All points in each region are arranged in alphabetical order. First turn to the region that applies to you. The book is set up beginning with the Northeast section, continuing westward to the Alaska section. The ten regions are: Northeastern, Eastern Seaboard, Gulf Coastal, Eastern Central, Southern Central, Northern Central, Desert Southwest,

Northern High Plains, Far West and Alaska.

CLASSIFICATION: Projectile points come in many shapes, colors and sizes. Their quality varies from thick, crude forms to very thin, beautifully flaked, symmetrical specimens. Over the past fifty years, hundreds of points have been classified and given names. The names of people, rivers, creeks, lakes, mountains, towns, etc. have been used in naming point types. Many of the types come from sites that were excavated from undisturbed stratigraphic layers where carbon dating was made. These forms of data are important in placing each type in time and showing the relationship of one type to another. You will soon see that most of the early types evolved into the later forms.

This book includes as many point types as possible with the idea of expanding to more types in future updated editions as the information becomes available to us. The point types are arranged in alphabetical order by section of the country. The archeological period and approximate dates of popular use are given for each point type. A general distribution area is given, along with a brief description of each type. There are several factors that determine a given type: 1-Shape or form. 2-Size. 3-Style or flaking. 4-Thickness or thinness. 5-Kind of material.

NEW ARROWHEADS LISTED

The field of Archaeology is an on-going science where sites are constantly being found and excavated. Occassionally, new types are discovered, named and reported in their published literature. As a result, the interrelationship of types, their age, as well as geographical dispersion is always changing. Due to this, the region boundaries may change in future editions. We are constantly on the outlook for photographs as well as the documentation of these types so they can be added to future volumes of this book. The author would appreciate receiving any photos and reports of this nature.

ARROWHEAD VALUES LISTED

Values listed in this book are for your information only. None of the points shown are for sale. Under each type, we have attempted to show a photographic spread of size, quality and variation of form (where available), from low to high grade, with corresponding prices. All values listed in this book are in U.S. currency and are wholesale/retail prices based on (but not limited to) reports from our extensive network of experienced advisors which include convention sales, mail order, auctions and unpublished personal sales. Overstreet, with several decades of market experience, has developed a unique and comprehensive system for gathering, documenting, averaging and pricing data on arrowheads. The end result is a true fair market value for your use. We have earned the reputation for our cautious, conservative approach to pricing arrowheads. You, the collector, can be assured that the prices listed in this volume are the most accurate and useful in print.

The low price is the wholesale price (the price dealers may pay for that point). **The high price** is the retail price (the price a collector may pay for that point). Each illustration also gives a brief description pointing out special features when applicable. The prices listed have been averaged from the highest and lowest prices we have seen, just prior to publication. We feel that this will give you a fair, realistic price value for each piece illustrated. If your point matches the illustrated example in both size, color, and quality, the listed value would then apply. **Warning:** The slightest dings or nicks can dramatically drop the grade and value of a point. Please see Grade vs. Value following this section.

HIGH PRICE- RETAIL PRICE, LOW PRICE - WHOLESALE PRICE

IMPORTANT NOTE: This book is not a dealer's price list, although some dealers may base their prices on the values listed. The true value of any arrowhead is what you are willing to pay. The top price listed is an indication of what collectors would pay while the lower price is what dealers would possibly pay. For one reason or another, these collectors might want a certain piece badly and will pay over the list price for comparable quality. This commonly occurs on many high grade, rare points.

DEALER'S POSITION

Dealers are not in a position to pay the full prices listed, but work on a percentage depending largely on the amount of investment required and the quality of material offered. What a dealer will pay depends on how long it will take him to sell the individual piece or collection after making the investment; the higher the demand and better the grade, the more the percentage. Most dealers are faced with expenses such as advertising, travel, telephone and mailing, rent, employee salaries, plus convention costs. These costs all go in before the relics are sold.

The high demand relics usually sell right away but the lower grades are difficult to sell due to their commonality and low demand. Sometimes a dealer will have cost tied up for several years before finally selling everything. Remember, his position is that of handling, demand, and overhead. Most dealers are victims of these economics.

How to Grade Points

Before a point's true value can be assessed, its condition or state of preservation as well as quality must be determined. The better the quality and condition, and the larger the size, the more valuable the point. Perfect points that are classic for the type, thin, made of high quality materials with perfect symmetry and flaking are worth several times the price of common, but complete, low grade field points.

FACTORS THAT INFLUENCE THE GRADE AND VALUE OF POINTS:

Condition: Perfection is the rule. Nicks, chips, and breakage reduce value.

Size: Everything else being equal, a larger point will grade higher than a smaller point and larger points are worth more.

Form: The closer a point comes to being a classic for the type, the higher the grade and value.

Symmetry: Points with good balance and design are higher grade and worth more.

Flaking: Points with precision percussion and secondary flaking, a minimum of hinge fractures and problem areas are higher and worth more. Points with unusual flaking patterns, such as collateral or oblique transverse, enhance grade and value.

Thinness: The thinner the better.

After all the above steps have been considered, then the reader can begin to assign a grade to his point. Points are graded on a scale of 1 to 10+, where a 10+ is the best and a 1 is the lowest grade for a complete point.

GRADING DEFINITIONS

Grade 10+: The exceptional perfect point. One of the few half dozen best known to exist. Perfect in every way, including thinness, flaking, material, symmetry and form. The best example you would ever expect to see of any given type. This grade is extremely rare, and applies to medium to large size points that normally occur in a given type.

Grade 10: A perfect point, including thinness, flaking, symmetry and form. This grade is extremely rare, and applies to <u>all</u> <u>sizes</u> of points that normally occur in a given type. A point does not have to be the largest known to qualify for this grade.

Grade 8 or 9: Near perfect but lacking just a little in size or material or thinness. It may have a small defect to keep it out of a 10 category. Still very rare, most high grade points would fall into this category.

Grade 6 or 7: Better than the average grade but not quite nice enough to get a high ranking. Flaking, size, and symmetry are just a little above the average. Points in this grade are still very hard to find in most states. A very collectible grade.

Grade 4 or 5: The average quality that is found. The flaking, thickness, and symmetry is average. 2 or 3 very minute nicks may be seen but none that would be considered serious.

Grade 1-3: Field grade points that have below average overall quality. Better points with more serious faults or dings would fall into this grade. The most common grade found and correspondingly, the least valuable.

Broken points: Usually little to no value. However, good high grade broken backs of popular type points have fetched good prices. Examples would be Paleo points and many of the rare Archaic beveled and notched types.

PRICING POINTS

After a point has been graded and assigned a grade number, it should be compared with similar points in the alphabetical listings. The prices listed will give the reader a guide as to the probable value of his point, but be careful, compare grade with grade. If your point has a little ear or tip broken, the value is affected drastically. Of course, state of perfection, thinness, rarity of type, quality of material and flaking, and size all enter into determining a value. Usually with everything being equal, the larger the size the higher the price.

Many factors affect value and should be considered when determining a price for your point. Besides those listed under Grading Points, the following should be considered:

FACTORS THAT INFLUENCE VALUE:

Provenance: When a point has been properly documented as to where and when it was found and by whom, the value increases. Points from key sites such as the Clovis site in New Mexico, the Quad site in Alabama, the Nuckolls site in Tennessee, the Hardaway site in North Carolina, etc. increases value. Well documented points from famous collections show increased value. Points that have been published show an increase in demand and makes them easier to sell (the wise investor should have all points checked before purchase, whether published or not, because many fakes have been published as genuine). Local points usually bring higher prices than imports from other states.

Material & Color: Most points are made of common local gray to brown cherts, but the type of material can enhance value.

Points made from colorful or high quality material such as agate, petrified wood, agatized coral, quartz, crystal, flint, jasper, Horse Creek chert, Buffalo River chert, Flint Ridge chert, Carter Cave chert, Dover chert, etc. will increase value. Some materials became glassier and more colorful when heat treated by the Indians and would enhance the appearance. Certain local materials are more collectible in various states, such as rhyolite in North and South Carolina, Dover in Tennessee, Carter Cave chert or Kentucky hornstone in Kentucky, Flint Ridge chert in Ohio, Knife River flint in North and South Dakota, jasper in Pennsylvania, agatized coral in Florida or petrified wood in Arizona and New Mexico. Usually, points that are transparent or have pretty colors alone will sell for higher prices.

Symmetry: The left and right sides of points must be balanced to receive the highest grades. Value decreases as symmetry is lost.

Rarity: Obviously, some point types are scarcer and much harder to find than others. For instance, Clovis, which is found in most of North America, is more common than Folsom, which is rarely found in just a few western states. Paleo points are much more rare out west than in the east.

Popularity of Type: Market demand for certain point types can greatly influence the supply and value. The value of these points can vary with changing market demands and available supplies. Points with slight damage, such as a nick off the tip or wing, suffer a cut in value of about 60 percent. Medium damage, such as a missing wing, will cut the value about 90 percent. Field grade pieces and halves are usually sold at five dollars per gallon. The very best points have no top retail price and are always in very high demand. Local points are usually worth more in the area where they are found.

Grade and Its Effect on Value

Presented below are examples of the same point type in grades 10 through 3 and the effect on value. All are equal size and quality, except for the defects. These examples illustrate how value drops with grade. True number 10s are rare and the slightest dings or nicks can easily cause the value to drop dramatically.

When the novice grades points to determine value, it is a common mistake to grade his #5s and #6s as #9s and 10s. True 9s and 10s must be superb. They have to be perfect for 10s and near perfect for 9s, thin, symmetrical, and of high quality to reach this grade. Color, translucency and high quality material enhance value.

When dealers look at a collection to buy, they are faced with the economics of having to buy the whole collection to get the few points that they really want. For example, a virgin collection of 1000 complete points, all found by the owner, that is still intact and not picked over, would break down as follows: 92% (920 points) would be low grade, worth below $20 each with the remaining 8% worth $20 or more each. As you can see, most collections are loaded with low grade points making it very difficult for anyone to pay a large price just to get the few choice pieces.

Material increases value

"Bullseye" in hornstone

Perfect corners

Dovetail, grade 10
Value $1500

Dovetail, grade 10
Value $1000

Slight edge nick

Small tang nick

Dovetail, grade 9
Value $600

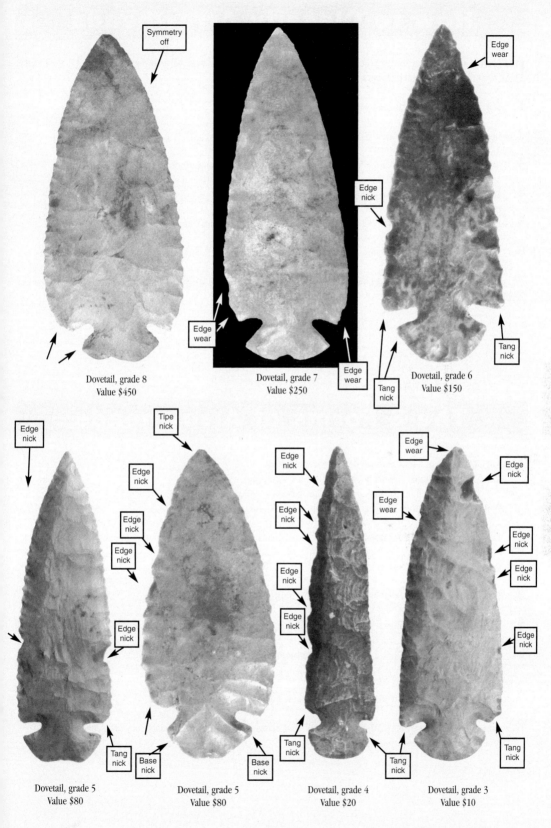

Symmetry off

Dovetail, grade 8
Value $450

Edge wear

Dovetail, grade 7
Value $250

Edge wear

Edge wear

Edge wear

Edge nick

Tang nick

Edge wear

Edge nick

Tang nick

Dovetail, grade 6
Value $150

Edge nick

Dovetail, grade 5
Value $80

Tipe nick

Edge nick

Edge nick

Edge nick

Edge nick

Tang nick

Base nick

Dovetail, grade 5
Value $80

Base nick

Edge nick

Edge nick

Edge nick

Edge nick

Tang nick

Dovetail, grade 4
Value $20

Edge wear

Edge nick

Edge wear

Edge nick

Edge nick

Edge nick

Tang nick

Tang nick

Dovetail, grade 3
Value $10

How to Classify Arrowheads

It's as easy as **one, two, three** (well, seven actually) if you take the following steps. All arrowheads, according to their shape, have been divided into eight different forms listed below.

1. The country is divided into ten sections.

2. Decide which of the categories #1-8 listed below that your point belongs.

3. Go to the Thumbnail Guide at the beginning of the section that applies to your locale.

4. Match your arrowhead to one of the photos in that section.

5. Look up the name under the photo that matches your point in the alphabetical section.

6. Look at the numerous examples, actual size, and make a more detailed comparison.

7. If your point still does not match exactly, go back to the **Thumbnail Guide Section** and look for another match and start over with step four.

The 8 Forms of Arrowheads

1. **Auriculate.** These points have <u>ears</u> and a concave base.
   A. Auriculate Fluted. A fluted point is one that has a <u>channel flake</u> struck off one or both faces from the base.
   B. Auriculate Unfluted. All other eared forms are shown here.

2. **Lanceolate.** Points without **notches** or **shoulders** fall into this group. Bases are round, straight, concave or convex.

3. **Corner Notched.** The base-end has corner notches for **hafting**.

4. **Side Notched.** The base-end has side notches for **hafting**.

5. **Stemmed.** These points have a **stem** that is short or long, expanding or contracting. All stemmed points have **shoulders**.

6. **Stemmed-Bifurcated.** Since a number of stemmed points occur that have the base split into two **lobes**, they have been grouped together.

7. **Basal Notched.** This form has notches applied at the **base**.

8. **Arrow Points.** These points are generally small, thin triangle and other forms grouped for easy identification.
   *See glossary for underlined words.

The following drawings illustrate point nomenclature used by collectors and professionals everywhere for point shapes and features.

Auriculate Forms

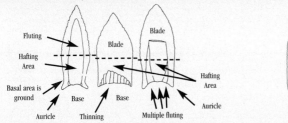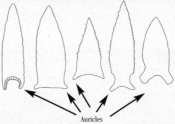

- Fluting
- Hafting Area
- Basal area is ground
- Auricle
- Blade
- Base
- Thinning
- Blade
- Base
- Multiple fluting
- Hafting Area
- Auricle
- Blade

Auricles

This is the basic form of the Paleo Period. Flaking tends to be parallel and the entire hafting area is usually ground.

Lanceolate Forms

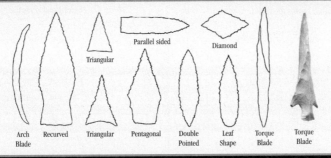

- Parallel sided
- Diamond
- Triangular
- Arch Blade
- Recurved
- Triangular
- Pentagonal
- Double Pointed
- Leaf Shape
- Torque Blade
- Torque Blade

Basal, Corner & Side Notched Forms

BASAL NOTCHED

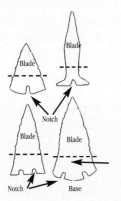

- Blade
- Blade
- Notch
- Blade
- Blade
- Notch
- Base

CORNER NOTCHED

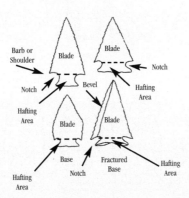

- Barb or Shoulder
- Blade
- Blade
- Notch
- Notch
- Bevel
- Hafting Area
- Blade
- Blade
- Base
- Notch
- Fractured Base
- Hafting Area
- Hafting Area

SIDE NOTCHED

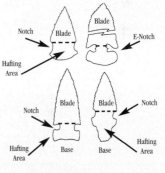

- Notch
- Blade
- Blade
- E-Notch
- Hafting Area
- Notch
- Blade
- Blade
- Notch
- Hafting Area
- Base
- Base
- Hafting Area

Basal notched forms appeared in the early Archaic Period and reappeared in the Woodland Period. Not a popular form of hafting since only a few types are known.

Corner notched forms appeared in the early Archaic Period and reappeared again in the Woodland Period and lasted to Historic times.

Side notched forms began in Transitional Paleo times and persisted through the Archaic Period, reappearing in Woodland times lasting into the Historic Period.

Stemmed Forms
(These drawings apply to points of all sizes)
Basal edge types   Shoulder types

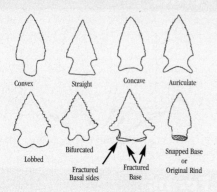

Convex · Straight · Concave · Auriculate · Lobbed · Bifurcated · Fractured Basal sides · Fractured Base · Snapped Base or Original Rind

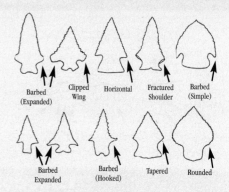

Barbed (Expanded) · Clipped Wing · Horizontal · Fractured Shoulder · Barbed (Simple) · Barbed Expanded · Barbed (Hooked) · Tapered · Rounded

Note: The **Basal Edge** begins the hafting area of a point.

Note: The **shoulder** divides the blade from the hafting area.

Stemmed Forms
(Hafting Area Types)
(These drawings apply to points of all sizes)

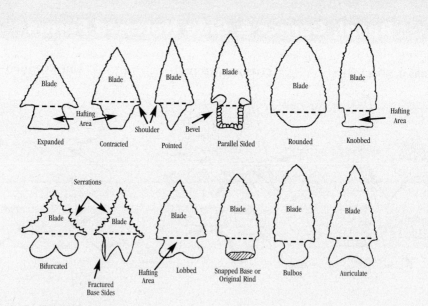

Expanded · Contracted · Pointed · Parallel Sided · Rounded · Knobbed · Blade · Hafting Area · Shoulder · Bevel

Bifurcated · Fractured Base Sides · Hafting Area · Lobbed · Snapped Base or Original Rind · Bulbos · Auriculate · Serrations · Blade

Note: Stemmed types began as early as the Paleo Period, but didn't really become popular until the Woodland Period. Consequently, this form has the most types and is the most difficult to classify.

Blade Beveling Types   Blade Edge

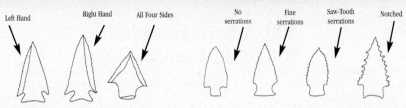

Note: Alternate blade beveling began in the early Archaic Period and continued into the Woodland Period. Beveled points are very popular among collectors.

Distal Ends

Note: The distal end of a point is located at the very tip and describes the shape of the penetrating part of the knife or projectile point.

Point Cross-Sections
(These drawings apply to points of all sizes)

Elliptical   Round   Uniface or Plano-convex   Median Ridged   Rhomboid   Flattened   Fluted

Note: The cross-section of a point represents its form if broken at mid-section.

Flaking Types
(These drawings apply to points of all sizes)

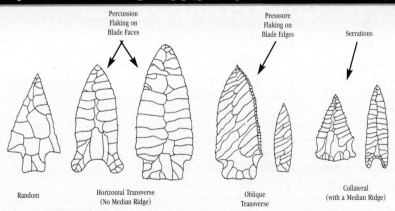

Percussion Flaking on Blade Faces   Presssure Flaking on Blade Edges   Serrations

Random   Horizontal Transverse (No Median Ridge)   Oblique Transverse   Collateral (with a Median Ridge)

Note: Points are rough shaped with an elk antler billet or hammer stone. Then fine pressure flaking is applied to the blade and stem edges with a sharp pointed antler. Billet and deer antler are alternated until the point is finally finished. During the flaking process, edges are lightly ground to prevent hinge fracturing on the blade edges.

Cultural Periods

The American Indian
Middle to Eastern U.S.

(Includes sections: Northeast, Eastern Seaboard, Gulf Coastal, Eastern Central, Southern Central and Northern Central) (Only carbon dates are used) (Calculated dates would be older)

Paleo ....c. 11,500 - 10,000 B.P.
Late Paleo ....c. 11,000 - 10,000 B.P.
Transitional Paleo ....c. 10,500 - 9,000 B.P.
Early Archaic ....c. 10,000 - 7,000 B.P.
Middle Archaic ....c. 7,500 - 4,000 B.P.
Late Archaic ....c. 5,000 - 3,000 B.P.
Woodland ....c. 3,000 - 1,300 B.P.
Mississippian ....c. 1,300 - 400 B.P.
Historic ....c. 450 - 170 B.P.

Note: The dates given above are only approximations and should be used in a general context only. This data is constantly being revised as new information becomes available. **B.P. means "before present."** In 1998 new data was released to correct previously published dates acquired through carbon dating. All points are now older than first realized.

The American Indian West

(Includes sections: Desert Southwest, Northern High Plains and Great Basin-Westward)

Paleo ....c. 13,200 - 8,000 B.P.
Early Archaic ....c. 8,000 - 5,000 B.P.
Middle Archaic ....c. 5,100 - 3,300 B.P.
Late Archaic ....c. 3,400 - 2,300 B.P.

Desert Traditions:

Transitional ....c. 2,300 - 1,600 B.P.
Developmental ....c. 1,600 - 700 B.P.
Classic ....700 - 400 B.P.
Historic ....c. 400 - 170 B.P.

Note: The dates given above are only approximations and should be used in a general context only. This data is constantly being revised as new information becomes available. **B.P. means "before present."**

Collecting Points

WHY COLLECT PROJECTILE POINTS?

Whether you collect ancient Chinese cloisonné, Egyptian tomb pieces, or projectile points, there is a particular satisfaction in possessing a piece of history from the distant past--to hold in your hand an object that was made by someone thousands of years ago.

Projectile points may very well be the earliest evidence of man's ability to create, style, and manufacture objects of symmetry and beauty. If you ever have the privilege of seeing an exceptional piece, made of the finest material, and flaked to perfection, take a close look. You will soon realize that these early tools of man were made for two reasons: function and beauty. They represent a unique art form crafted by the world's earliest artists. Unique, because, like snowflakes, each specimen is an original and no two are exactly alike.

Many different materials were utilized in crafting these points. From crude slate, conglomerate or quartzite, to high quality flint, agate, jasper, chalcedony, petrified wood or volcanic obsidian, the list is endless. The Indians went to great lengths to obtain high quality material from the popular flint and chert quarries known to them, such as Dover in Northwest Tennessee, Flint Ridge in Ohio, and the many obsidian sources of the west. It is believed that extensive trade networks for flint and other objects were established in the earliest times and extended over vast areas from coast to coast.

The variations in shape and flaking style are clues to dating and identifying point types. The novice should study points from the different periods illustrated in this book and become familiar with the various styles produced. Generally speaking, the older Paleo and Archaic types are better made, exhibiting the finest flaking, thinness, edge work, and symmetry ever produced by man. The earliest points are mostly auriculate or eared. Some are grooved in the center or fluted. Later, these forms basically became side-notched, corner-notched, basal-notched or stemmed. With the introduction of the bow, most points became smaller and lighter with stemmed bases. However, during the Woodland period, Paleo auriculate and Archaic notched forms reappeared for a short period of time.

Some collectors specialize in a particular type, while others try to assemble a collection of many shapes and types. Most collectors are only interested in points from their immediate locale, and only if found by them. However, this author has learned after many years of hunting, that the only way to put together a quality collection is through intelligent buying. It's a rare occurrence today to find an outstanding piece for your collection by hunting in the field.

FIRE DAMAGED POINTS

Points made of flint, chert, chalcedony, and other materials are susceptible to damage when in close contact with fire and heat. This can occur when points shot at an animal are left in the butchered meat that is cooked over a fire. Fire damaged flint reflects a rather unique appearance, usually a circular pitted, or pock-marked look not unlike miniature moon craters.

There have been theories that the intense heat of fire actually brings about a molecular change or rearrangement of molecules. This undue stress or tension causes a change in the material which induces the pock-marks to form. This has been questioned and criticized by some geologists who flatly state that no such action takes place.

(Examples of fire damaged points) Note typical pitting damage to the surfaces.

The acceptable and more logical explanation is that the change is purely physical. That is, the heat from the fire is applied and transferred in such a random and uneven manner that the coefficients of contraction and expansion cause the damage or pitting.

The resultant conflict of expansion and non-expansion coefficients flake off the flint material due to tensions within itself. The resultant flake is quite different from a pressure or percussion flake in that it is circular and, of course, non-controllable. The examples illustrated show points with the typical pitting associated with fire damage.

Example of a repaired impact fracture. The point was retipped.

Impact fracture located at the tip

Left: Example of a long impact fracture that runs almost to the base.

IMPACT FRACTURES

When spear and arrow points are thrown or shot, they sometimes collide with hard objects such as bone in animals or rock or wood when the target is missed. If the angle at the point of impact is just right, the resulting blow will fracture the point, forming a flute or channel that runs from the tip toward the base. In other examples the fracturing will run up the side, or the tip of the point will simply snap off. Occasionally, these broken points with impact fluting are remade into new points with the flute channel still visible (see illustration). These should not be confused with real fluted Paleo points that were found by later Indians and rechipped into a more recent point, also with the fluting still present.

Points with well defined impact fractures are interesting additions to any collection and should not be overlooked when going through the junk boxes.

HAFTING

All finished arrow points and most knives were made to be inserted or tied onto a shaft or handle. To prevent movement, sinew, gut, and rawhide were used to tie the stone blades onto the shafts or handles. Fibers from hair and plants (grasses, tree bark, yucca, vines, etc.) were also employed for lashing.

Pitch, asphalt and resin were used as adhesives (when available) to glue the lashings to the stone and shaft. In some of the western states where climates are very dry, complete specimens of arrows and knives have been found preserved in caves. On

Above: A very rare example of an 9,000 year old Kirk Corner Notched point with original hafting petrified to the base. Reverse side shows a brown stain where hafting was.

Above: A complete knife with bone handle and flint blade recovered in eastern Colorado. Note drilled hole in handle

Above: Rare examples of hafted arrow-points on wooden shafts. All were found in New Mexico or Nevada. The binding is fashioned of fibres from a local plant.

Above: A complete knife with bone handle and flint blade recovered 4 feet below the floor of a dry cave in Fort Rock desert in south central Oregon. Note the tally marks at the rear of the handle and the gut hafting and gum or asphaltum adhesive cementing the blade to the handle.

rare occasions complete arrows and knives have been found with hafting completely intact. Of course, during the Indian wars out west in the 1800s, perfect hafted specimens were collected and saved from the battlefields as well. Cane and many types of wood were employed for arrow shaft usage while bone, ivory and wooden handles were crafted for holding the knives.

DATING AND NAMING POINT TYPES

For decades, professional archaeologists and collectors have been interested in the age and classification of projectile points. Of course the best information has come from archaeologically controlled scientific excavations where exact locations, cultural association, and carbon dating of associated matter with point types was made.

The carbon deposits from animal and vegetable remains are taken from these stratigraphic layers and dated through the carbon-14 process and other techniques. This gives an age for each layer and its associated artifacts. In 1997, it was reported that all previously published carbon-14 dates are now slightly older than realized. Adjustments should be made on a logarithmic scale with age. **Clovis** is now believed to be about 2,000 years earlier.

Many of these sites were occupied for thousands of years by various peoples who left projectile points around their campfires, buried for future discovery with thousands more lost through usage and breakage. The face of the land next to rivers where many of these sites are, is always changing due to flooding. Indian villages and campsites were either being eroded away or buried under silt deposited by the flooding river. Later, the sites that were destroyed would become occupied again, waiting for the next inundation. Over a period of thousands of years, these sites accumulated many stratified layers of silt, some of which contain evidence of human occupation. The most recent culture would be near the top with the oldest at the deepest levels.

Some of these excavated areas produce important point types which were named after the site from which they were found. Sometimes popular "type styles" such as **Clovis** are found all across the country while others are very localized and found only in a few counties. Some of the more famous type sites are **Cahokia** at St. Clair and Madison counties in Illinois, **Eva** and **Nuckolls** in northwest Tennessee, **Quad** and **Pine Tree** in northwest Alabama, **Black Rock Concave** in Black Rock Desert, Nevada, **Clovis** near Clovis, New Mexico, **Folsom** near Folsom, New Mexico, **Golondrina** in Val Verde Co., Texas, **Graham Cave** in Montgomery Co., Missouri, **Hardaway** in Stanly Co., North Carolina, **Hell Gap** from Hell Gap Valley in Wyoming, **LeCroy** in Hamilton Co., Tennessee, **Midland** near Midland, Texas, **Milnesand** in Milnesand, New Mexico, **Motley** in northeast Louisiana, **Plainview** near Plainview, Texas, **San Patrice** in DeSoto Co., Louisiana and **Sandia** from the Sandia Cave near Albuquerque, New Mexico. There are many more sites too numerous to list here.

These excavations have provided valuable information about point types and their cultural relationships. Papers published (by the archaeologists who worked the sites) about these excavations were the first attempt at typing or classifying projectile points. These papers and books are still important reference sources today and belong in every reference library.

How Points Were Made

Decades ago this author was spending his weekends hunting rivers, fields and streams for the elusive #9s and 10s but usually coming home with the average 3s and 4s. His hunting territory covered several states including dozens of private farms, rivers, creeks and lakes. The usual procedure when hunting on private land was always to ask permission. This required a short visit with the owner who would be sizing you up before allowing access to his land. Some of the farmers were very suspicious of strangers because of their hidden whiskey stills.

During these interesting visits, I would hear stories of how the farmers thought the Indians made arrowheads. A common tale was that the Indians would heat up a container of water. After getting it as hot as they could, they would take an eagle feather, dipping it in the scoulding water, then carefully releasing drops onto the flint causing an immediate fracturing to occur. Eventually they would end up with a finished arrowhead. Although this story was pretty common, I don't think any of the farmers ever tried it to see if it would really work.

Actually flint tools are made by the art of knapping flint. Hundreds of thousands of years ago, far away from this country, early homo erectines learned how to knap flint. The earliest forms from Africa have been dated to 2.2 million years ago. Secrets of the knappers art came with the first peoples to inhabit the Americas. Beginning with Paleo Man the best sources for quarrying flint and chert were soon found. The technique of exposing flint to heat to change its molecular structure making it more "glassy" and easier to flake was learned prior to Paleo times. Heat treating changes the color as well, sometimes making it difficult to match the altered stone with local sources.

Examples of a group of spent cores made from spalls.

Although small points were crafted from local materials such as small nodules that can be found along rivers and streams, the larger points were made from a large nodule. The flintknapper takes the nodule and knocks off a chunk forming a spall. He then strikes off long slivers that can be crafted into points. As the slivers are struck off, a circular core is formed. Eventually the core is discarded and the process starts over. Flint flakes can be removed easily in the direction of the force applied. Indians used hammer stones, elk billits, and other tools in rough shaping the stone through percussion blows. After a suitable form was achieved with the proper thickness, the final shaping was accomplished using tools such as the fine tips of antlers. This procedure is called "pressure flaking" and was carefully applied to all edges and was used to create the notches on side and corner notched points.

Buying Points

FINDING VERSUS BUYING POINTS

Why would a collector want to buy points instead of just finding his own? The answer to this question is very simple. Many people who collect just don't have the time to spend hunting in the field. In most cases, you can buy points cheaper than you can find them, when you consider travel, lodging, food, and the money you could be earning if you were at home. But the best reason for buying is to acquire quality pieces that are not available or found in your immediate area of hunting. Not all collectors are fortunate enough to live in an area that produces high quality material. Many collectors hunt in plowed fields that do sometimes produce high quality points, but unfortunately most are broken or chipped by the plow and cutting harrow.

One collector lived and hunted in central Alabama and Mississippi for ten years, keeping every piece that was found. Later, when he took a realistic look at his collection, it was only worth about $1,000.00 and the points in the collection looked very common. He began selling everything but the most perfect pieces. He used the money to finance hunting trips to other areas that were strong with quality points, and also began to buy nice pieces as they became available. His previous collection was basically all the same color. He soon found that points from other areas were more colorful, and within three years he had built a large collection that anyone would be proud to own. He kept up this style of collecting for several years and has owned many super quality pieces worth a substantial amount of money. If he had not ventured out into other hunting areas his collection today would still be worth little and of low quality. Try acquiring a quality item, whether it be stone, bone, pottery, or flint. After all, isn't this what collecting is all about?

HOW TO BUY AUTHENTIC RELICS

The best way to recognize an old point is by knowing how both river and field patination affect the type of flint from which the point is made. Each point type also has its own style of chipping that you should study and understand. A Paleo point never has random flaking, while Archaic and Woodland points do. You should understand that changes in patination along the edges or near the tip of an arrowhead are signs of rechipping. Hinge fractures are good indicators to the authenticity of a point. An old point will patinate underneath the hinge fractures while recently applied patina will only be on the surface. Hold the point up to a light source and look along the edges for restoration. You can also lightly tap the surface of a point with a steel knife blade to find a restored area. The restored spot will have a dull sound. Restored areas will also look different under a black light.

If you go to a show, flea market, or someone's house to buy relics, you should first size up the collection or inventory that is for sale. Look for any questionable pieces. If the relics past the test, then you must assess the seller. If he looks untrustworthy, you should probably not take the risk.

But if you are convinced the person is of good character and the piece you want really looks good and authentic, you could use the following guidelines to protect yourself. First, ask for a money back guarantee in writing. Some dealers will comply but may put a time limit on it. Also ask if the point has been restored or rechipped. Second, you could ask for a <u>satisfaction guarantee.</u> This means that if you do get a piece that becomes questionable later, you would be able to trade it for another item of equal value that you feel is a good authentic piece. This arrangement would help you feel more secure about what you are buying. Third, especially if a lot of money is at risk, you should tell the person that you want to send the relic to someone for authentication before the sale is final. If a lot of money is at risk, you may want to get more than one opinion. Ask around to find out who the best authenticators are for your area.

There is a lot of competition in the Indian relic market. Some people will condemn a competitor's piece to persuade you to buy from them. They will also try to buy a good item from you at a cheap price. Others may say a relic is bad just to convince you that they are experts. To be truly knowledgeable in Indian relics, this book will help, but you need to learn as much as you can. Study the flint types of your collecting area and how they look with natural patination. Learn to match flaking styles with types. Simply look at as many good authentic points as you can. Remember, the people who think they know more than everyone else are usually the ones who get burned.

Market Reports

Photographs of needed types have been pouring in from collectors over the past two years. It has been impressive how many individuals now have scanners and/or digital cameras and have been able to email pictures to me for inclusion in future editions of this book. If you have points worthy of inclusion, shoot or scan at 300 pixels/ inch with a ruler along side and email to: (obob@gemstonepub.com). Be sure to send location, type, material, etc. with each picture.

The arrowhead market has continued to show growth in many areas with points from the Paleo period leading the way. Fluted points of all types continue to sell for record prices everywhere. Early Archaic beveled types have shown increased demand as have the smaller, true arrowpoints. Points made of exotic or colorful materials are in the most demand as are all higher grade examples of most types. Low, field grade points continue to languish with slow sales.

Certification has become more and more widely used. It is important before spending a large sum of money for a point that you have the benefit of an expert opinion, and it should be someone of your choice. There are quite a number of people papering points across the country. Be sure to check their reputation before choosing the right certifier to certify your points. On expensive points, it might be wise to have at least a couple of experts see the point before spending your money.

The following market reports were prepared by some of our advisors from around the country and are included here for your information.

Mark Berreth - (Relics From the Past)
Far West Section

The market for Western relics continues to explode due to high demand. This trend should continue because most artifact-rich land is Federal land and off limits to collecting. The result is that very few new relics are available to satisfy demand of new and existing collectors. New supplies only become available when an old time collection that was found before 1979 is sought out and broken up to be sold. The result is higher and higher prices for Western relics.

Field grade relic values have seen a modest increase in price while mid-grade artifacts have done better than the general stocks & bonds market. G-9 and G-10 grade relics continues to soar ever higher and should continue to do so because the people who seek out the old large collections and break them up to the public keep most of the G-9 and G-10 material for themselves. The result is that high grade material does not become available very often and when it does, the phrase "You can forget about trying to buy it for high book value" definitely applies.

Columbia Plateaus, Cascades, Early leaf, Paleo, Hells Canyon, Quillomene, Humboldts, and all agate points and blades are in very high demand. Pentagonal knives, Mule Ears, Rabbit Island and Elkos continue to lag the market and are real sleepers in my opinions.

The Internet has exploded with dealers in the last two years and will probably continue to grow modestly in the next two years. Most dealers have good return policies and guarantee that what they sell is authentic and legally collected.

Do not buy from any dealer who does not guarantee what they sell was legally collected and give at least a 30-day inspection and return period. You cannot genuinely decide if you like a rock until you have it in your hand.

Buying relics through Internet auctions can be perilous but also very fruitful. The thing you must do is buy from someone with a high seller rating and one who gives a 30-day or better inspection period. If you do not do this, you will get burned – it's just a matter of how many times. There are lots of reputable sellers on eBay and other auction sites and they will give you these guarantees and inspection periods. Rocks are like any other antique or collectible; if it seems too good to be true, it probably is!

Enjoy your hobby and buy what you like in whatever condition you can afford. This hobby is very interesting and can also be profitable.

John Byrd - Piedmont, SC
High Plains Section

In recent years there have been an increasing number of new collectors who are looking at Indian artifacts purely as an investment. Because the artifact market is continually evolving, it is important to understand the changes taking place in order to achieve the most from your investments. For this reason, I would encourage readers to study each of the market reports and pay attention to those growth trends that are being reported by the majority of these reports.

Over the past several decades, the extremely high grade artifacts – G-9 and G-10 – have increased in value far faster than the more moderate grades. Partially because of this, professional grading is becoming almost as important as authentication. Quality is very subjective and the interpretation of what constitutes a high grade specimen varies according to who is providing the description and what their interest is in the particular item. Over the past several years, I have been asked to provide almost as much grading and valuation services as authentications. The day of collectors being willing to just take a seller's word as to an item's grade has passed. We all have a tendency to esteem those particular artifacts we personally own too highly. When considering grading, I use a point system that takes a number of factors into consideration; I believe this approach will become the standard over the next few years.

Obviously, the very high grade artifacts have seen the greatest increase in value. But over the past few years, a number of very well known old time collections have come on the market and been broken up among the collecting community. Among these have been many items with incredible provenance and most of these have appeared in numerous publications over the years. These items have brought premium prices even though they may only have been of moderate grades. I think these well known and highly published old time artifacts will continue to escalate in value and help shape the market over the next several years.

For years, Paleo Indian points were the hottest thing on the market, but this trend has really cooled. It appears that the trend was perpetuated by a handful of big time collectors with deep pockets, and as those individuals have become less interested, the feeding frenzy for Paleo has subsided. Paleo points are still very collectible and highly sought after, but it is much more difficult to get the same high dollar amounts one could get a few years ago. This market niche is still alive and well but not seeing tremendous growth.

Nothing has more radically changed the artifact market than the Internet and online auctions, especially eBay. This allows every imaginable person to instantly become an international dealer, which can be good or bad. No place is filled with more fake artifacts and unscrupulous dealers than these auction sites, and it has become a nightmare for many innocent, unknowing collectors. As never before, I cannot stress enough: Know who you are dealing with. When considering bidding on an item, don't just look at the hype and the description, but check that person's feedback and find out what kind of guarantee they offer. If they will not allow you to return any item you are not satisfied with, then you should consider not bidding. One of the most positive things to occur because of Internet sales of artifacts is the formation of AACA (Authentic Artifact Collectors Association). Members of this organization agree to follow high standards of integrity that are designed to protect you, the collector. So when participating in an online auction or an Internet sale, don't be shy about asking if a person is a member of the AACA, and look for the AACA logo that many dealers will display on their listings.

Everybody wants to know what is going to be hot over the next few years and what is not. None of us have a crystal ball, but there are currently some noticeable trends that I expect to see continuing. For years, many collectors were afraid of obsidian because they had a hard time telling if it was old. Consequently, western artifacts from that lithic were selling at low prices. This is no longer the case today, and obsidian along with all of the Northwestern lithics has become extremely popular. In the last guide, I introduced you to the phenomenon of the incredibly high quality arrowheads from the Sahara desert in northwestern Africa. My prediction for this market has not decreased in the least because the quality is so high and the prices so low. In the past two years, I have sold several hundred thousand of these African gem points, something not even possible with North American artifacts. Look for the high quality African material to become scarcer and increase in value.

Unfortunately, not everything continues to escalate in value as fast as the overall market. Indian jewelry and rugs are prime examples. You will see a few spikes where exceptional examples bring good prices but overall this end of the market has gone down. Just go to the shows and you will see there are fewer and fewer dealers of these items all the time. I sell artifacts from across the entire country and there are two areas where I see prices for stone really slowing down: Florida and Texas. I do not attribute this so much to a lack of collector interest as I do the fact that I think artifacts from those regions were over-priced for years and now the market is simply leveling off.

We all need to remember that this is supposed to be a hobby. Find an area of collecting that you consider fun and satisfying and go in that direction. There is nothing I would rather see happen than our children becoming interested in collecting, not for the monetary gain but for the many other rewards we enjoy. No matter where you live, it is still possible to go out and find arrowheads – what an opportunity to get permission from the landowners and spend some time with your family. There is something about picking up even the most insignificant arrowhead off the ground with which buying and owning the most valuable of specimens cannot compare.

The market has strengthened considerably over the last couple of years. It seems the uncertainty about the economy has eased and spending has increased. This has increased the sale of authentic artifacts. Attendance at shows is up and the resulting sales have been strong. Auction sales, however, seem to have grown more than shows. Sales and attendance have to be stronger than they have been in years. Internet sales seem to have leveled off. The influx of new collectors coming from the web has slowed down. A few years ago, there were plenty of new collectors that only stayed in the hobby for a few years and then quit. This was most likely caused by the vast number of reproductions available on the Internet and all of the negativity on the online bulletin boards and chat rooms. It seems that most everyone has now found their niche and new collectors are being educated rather than scared away. One excellent online association can be found at www.theaaca.com.

As far as certain types of relics, bannerstones had a great run but have slowed down a little. High end flint, as always, continues to increase in value and makes a great investment. Lower end pieces also have seen good sales. Mid-range relics are a little stagnant but should come back around.

As always, buy from reputable dealers who back their relics with good guarantees. Don't be afraid to ask questions from the seasoned collectors and learn all you can. Read as much as you can and get all the hands on experience you are able to. This is a wonderful hobby that can bring years of enjoyment.

Not a lot has changed in the marketplace for Indian artifacts in the Northeast for the past several years. The market remains alive and well and prospering. Through the course of any given year, a number of older collections, or artifacts from older collections, surface in the marketplace. Some of these come up at auction. These auctions are usually well attended, but attendance and participation is relative to the caliber of the artifacts available.

A curious thing I've noted over the years is that it isn't the collectors that always pay out-of-line values. For example, in early spring 2005, I attended an auction in southeastern Pennsylvania. It was an old estate and there were many collectibles on hand such as guns, chairs, bottles, traps, etc. And there were artifacts. This presented a diverse assemblage and thus a diverse group of people was on hand. There were some nice items involved, but it was apparent that the cream of the crop was probably kept by the family or sold out of the collection. Several large frames were offered, and each had from 40 to 100 points, some in arrangements. Some frames had scenes or designs for the backgrounds. A frame that had a real value of $250-300 sold for $2,000. I witnessed eight or nine of these frames sell for at least 2-3 times what they were actually worth. The coup de grace was a frame of black chert points, 80-100, nice but not killer. The actual value was $500-750 perhaps, but the bidding finally stopped at just over $6,000 and there was a buyer's premium to boot. None of the artifact people I knew were doing the buying.

There are several possible explanations. Perhaps family members were insuring that they got some of the collection. Perhaps other local collectors were making sure that some things stayed local. It could be that some people who knew little about artifacts saw the high prices and decided they had to have some of those valuable things.

At an auction just featuring artifacts, prices are generally more sane, and depending on just what is on sale and how many other sales there may be at the same time or in the near future or recent past, some good buys can be had. Actually, it doesn't seem to matter how many auctions there are. I haven't been to one recently where they gave things away. Have you?

The market in the Northeast is fueled by such auctions, and also by the hundreds of collectors that attend flea markets, antique malls, household garage sales, and auctions on a weekly basis. These all add significant numbers of items to the marketplace. There are all sorts of stashes and hordes of cigar boxes filled with artifacts. Most, not all, are localized. Some contain artifacts from travels while others have artifacts from old dealers. Others are personal, local finds.

This is the way of things, and it will continue. Collectors will constantly be on the alert for fake or fraudulent points, reworked points, points labeled incorrectly as to type or area, and of course gray ghosts and eccentrics. There's another odd thing that can be noted with some old time collectors. They got hooked up with some of the early dealers, and whether they just kept ordering or the dealer kept pushing, some of these collectors ended up with literally hundreds of eccentrics, buffalo, horned toads, birds, snakes and fishhooks. Goodness sakes, the fishhooks! And there's usually an assortment of sawn blade gray ghosts from 6-10 inches or larger.

The point is that some of these early collectors operated in a vacuum, didn't associate with other collectors, and didn't learn much. So they became reservoirs, which I'm sure some early dealers exploited. Depending on where the collector was from and what he could find locally, some of those things had to be attractive. If all a person found was 1-3" black chert or rhyolite points, then a 6" gray ghost was heaven.

Much of the material coming to market in the Northeast originates in Pennsylvania, New York, or New Jersey. The far Northeastern states historically haven't offered a lot, and this continues to be so. This is unfortunate, as the occasional collection or item that does come along can be unique to those areas. Some nice bannerstones, slate items, slate daggers and points, gouges, Atlantic Phase Blades and so on, all come from the far Northeastern states.

At auctions and privately, the caliber of artifacts seldom fail to realize good value, often top dollar, and sometimes perform above expectations. At a recent auction, one of the top sellers was a Beaver Lake point of 4"+, an exquisite and fine specimen. It sold for $2,500 and will surely bring more in the future. Another flint piece sold well. It was a 6" Robbins Adena made of Flint Ridge flint and brought $1,400. An effigy bone comb sold for $1,000, a 3.25" Clovis type fluted point from New York State brought $1,500, a 3.5" Holcomb type fluted point from Canada brought $1,400, and a stone maskette fetched $950; all were top sellers.

Fluted points maintain their values. Good ones with good documentation, as just noted, sell right well. Those of 2" or so sell in the $500-1,000 range depending on the material, quality and history. I see similar points on Central and Midwestern price lists for twice or thrice the price. Must be the Certificates of Authenticity (COAs) offered with them, for surely our points are often the equal or better.

Beaded items are and have been the real top dollar items at auction. There are lots of reproductions, but get a good pipe bag or leggings or moccasins or painted rob and there will be absentee bids and phone bidders along with those present. The items bring thousands of dollars.

Pottery from the Northeast still isn't getting quite the respect it deserves, fortunately for those few who actively pursue this line. Complete vessels, perhaps with a little restoration, used to sell for $200-400. They're at least doubled now and $800-1,000 might be paid for a good specimen such as a plain Owasco or Clemson's Island punctate of 8" in height. Make it an Iroquois or Susquehannock pot with effigies and add at least half as much. Pipes are always a collector favorite. Clay or stone pipes that are plain, complete, nearly so, or with a little restoration, sell for $150-400. A nice effigy clay pipe of similar status would be $750 and up. Finer specimens and types that are rarer bring thousands.

Bone and antler items are always hit and miss. They don't seem to be high on many collectors' want lists. This is interesting since not many of them are coming out of the ground and onto the market anymore. Perhaps the interest isn't there because most collectors will never find some of these things.

Bone awls sell for $15-35 and more if they are exceptional or incised. Bone fishhooks sell for $100-300. Antler harpoons, depending on length, sell for $75-200. An effigy bone comb has been previously noted at $1,000, while another partial sample sold for $75.

Good flint of any type will not wait long for a buyer. Nice Adena points of size sell well as noted as do many of the more recognizable types such as Dovetails, Hardin Barbed, and the more localized Pennsylvania types like Perkiomen Broadpoints, Orient Fishtail, Piedmont points and a host of others. A 3.5" Perkiomen point made of jasper sold for $700, while another of Onondaga sold for $550. A Lehigh Broadpoint of a couple inches sold for $150 while a 4" Genesee sold for $225. Anything of jasper does well in Southeastern Pennsylvania. These are of course top of the line and better quality items. Flint of all descriptions and price ranges is available, especially at shows like the 3-4 sponsored by IACANE (Indian Artifact Collectors Association of the Northeast). Dealers and collectors come from many states to put up displays and buy, sell, or trade artifacts. No other states in the Northeast sponsor any shows at all, while auctions may occur in several states throughout the year. Most of the shows, by the way, also have demonstrations of flintknapping and atlatl throwing, all of which have proven popular over the years.

Stone tools are numerous in the Northeast – celts, adzes and axes. As always, the majority are field grade, discarded by the Native Americans and often bounced around in the fields by farm equipment. Such things sell for $5-25. Better items begin to bring money in the $50-75 dollar range, and an exceptional one will see prices from $300-1,000. Gouges sell well, even so-so specimens, as they're not all that common. A few collectors are specializing in these and ulus. Good specimens will sell for $15-250, an exceptional one for $750-1,000.

There are also those who specialize in ground slate points and copper items. Few of these hit the market in any given year. A slate point of 2-3" will bring $75-250. Make that point 4-5" and $500-750 is likely. Any copper points, celt or tool is worth a couple hundred at least, the price going up with size and condition. A tanged copper spear, 6" but cleaned, is still worth $300-350.

A fair supply of bannerstones exists in the Northeast and there's great interest in them, from salvaged or unfinished, to the mediocre, to the fine. Salvaged, broken or unfinished stones can sell for $25-250, especially some of those abandoned just before completion. Complete but not great examples sell for $250-600. Exceptional examples sell for several thousand dollars. Basically, the same could be said for slate gorgets and pendants, though such items worth thousands of dollars are very rare.

At most auctions, particularly of older collections, which become more and more scarce with the passing years, there is an array of points from the Central states, pottery from the Southwest, and maybe even some Eskimo bone and antler items and some Danish celts or daggers or holed axes. These sell commensurate with their quality, and if extra nice will draw phone and absentee bids from far and wide.

The interest in ancient relics has not abated nor been stymied by any real or perceived economic boom or bust. It continues on, steady if not getting better price-wise for solid artifacts. I predict 2005 will witness the continuation of this trend. This material is just too interesting and fascinating for it to be otherwise.

Tony Hardie
Far West Section

The artifact market conditions in the Northwest are showing moderate to high demand with interest continuing to grow in the East where a lot of material seems to be headed. In the past couple years, there seems to have been a large collection or two for retail sale available every six months or so, with small 1,000 piece sets being the average. Recent collections have originated mostly from Washington and Oregon as well as some from Nevada, BC and Alaska. The old time collectors of the 1940s and '50s are now in their 80s and 90s and most are getting ready to part with their lifelong accumulation of collected items that they have amassed. This seemed to have dried up in 2004 and prices did go on the rise.

Most artifacts from the Northwest remain affordable, especially field to mid-grade quality points and blades, thus allowing newer collectors and even more experienced ones to build frames and displays of artifacts with a very modest investment. The market trend indicates a continued supply of the field to mid-grades priced under $50 at auction and on websites such as ours. The higher end G-8 to G-10s are continuing to disappear as well as the rare types and larger sizes over 3"+. The savvy well-educated collector can still find some good deals. The top G-9 and G-10s are selling much higher than the listed book prices and will probably remain that way with this new edition. If you can get any items in these grades for the prices they list for, they are a great investment as I foresee a steady increase in their value over time. Top grade items are not being found anymore in these areas, so most have already found their way to museums and private collections.

2005 seems to have brought a few larger collections to light and this material is now being distributed through the market. Good quality mid- and top grade Great Basin obsidian artifacts continue to rise in value and remain very liquid on eBay and through website sales.

The top grade larger blades and gem quality points of spectacular flaking, minimal defects and best materials are always and will remain in very high demand; they don't seem to last long when listed on our website. Klickitat, Columbia Plateau, Humboldt, Cougar Mountain, Parman, Elko and Northern Fox Ear variants are just a few of the hot selling types in the Northwest right now. Most collectors as a whole appear to be willing to acquire investment grade artifacts at prices in the $100-500 range a lot more often over the past two years as well.

Over the long term, it looks like the ever-shrinking availability of larger well-documented legally obtained artifact collections that are rumored to be waiting for market conditions to improve are being slowly bought up. There will not be a better time than now to acquire quality top grade Western-Great Basin artifacts as well as the better grade Columbia River and BC material.

Ron L. Harris - Hickory, NC
North Carolina Piedmont Section

Interest and activity in the hobby of Indian arrowhead collecting in the Carolina Piedmont has notably increased in the region since publication of the last Overstreet guide two years ago. Months ago, the economy was in a bad slump. As a result, the buying and selling of arrowheads was in a decline despite the continued intense interest in the hobby. Currently, the economy appears to be on the upswing with more expendable income available. Collectors, dealers and hobbyists have become more aggressive and active in their buying, selling, trading and investment endeavors.

New collectors and their collections have frequently popped up, but most of their acquisitions are as a result of purchases at artifact shows and/or from existing private collections that become available from time to time. It has become extremely difficult, if not impossible, to begin a decent arrowhead collection based entirely on personal finds. This is mainly due to the lack of availability of hunting grounds or sites that have been destroyed or covered by commercial construction, road building, housing developments, decline of farming, etc.

The Piedmont Archaeological Society of North Carolina & South Carolina has played an important part in contributing to the continued interest and growth of the hobby. Often, artifact shows such as those sponsored by the Society are now the only source for enthusiasts to select and acquire quality genuine artifacts for their collection. Items offered at the shows range from field grade to high quality specimens, and of course, the price varies accordingly.

Annually, the Society sponsors several Indian artifact shows at various venues in the region. The shows consistently attract numerous collectors, dealers, enthusiasts and members of the general public not only from the two Carolinas, but from Virginia, Kentucky, Tennessee, Georgia and Alabama as well.

The Piedmont Archaeological Society website features interesting topics, show dates and collection photographs that can be accessed and viewed via the Internet at www.pasnsc.org.

The Genuine Indian Relic Society recently sponsored its first artifact show at Fletcher, N.C. (near Asheville) in western North Carolina. The attendance and artifact displays were a huge success, and the GIRS indicates the show will become an annual event. More information on the GIRS can be obtained at www.thegirs.com.

Along with the increased interest in the hobby of arrowhead collecting, the value and prices of the artifacts has increased proportionately. For example, ten years ago, common field grade points sold for about $2-3 each. Today these same points sell for around $8-12 each depending on the size, quality and sometimes quantity purchased. Upper end high grade artifacts in the G-8, G-9 and G-10 range command significantly higher prices as has been observed at recent shows and in private sales in the region. Certain high quality Woodland triangle points, the Yadkin for example, sold for as much as $400.

Top grade Archaic points, especially the corner-notch variety, have brought prices anywhere from a low of $100 to a high of $2,500. The most popular early points include the Hardaway-Dalton, Hardaway Corner-notch, Palmer and Kirk. Later Archaic points that are popular and compete for high prices for quality specimens include the Stanly, Morrow Mountain, Guilford and Savannah River varieties.

Paleo points are and have always been the top attention getter in all regions, and fine specimens continue to bring premium prices, especially those exhibiting fine Paleo flaking along with good fluting, color and symmetry. Included in this category are Eastern style Clovis, Simpson, and Redstone. Sales in the region for some of these high quality points have ranged generally from $300-3,000.

When it comes down to actually evaluating a particular type point in a given region, either for the purpose of buying or selling, Overstreet continues to be the foremost guide for both the beginning hobbyist and the advanced and experienced collector or dealer.

A common sense approach to consider when buying or selling artifacts is this: The actual value of an arrowhead or collectible is governed or influenced by size, quality, scarcity, and regional availability as well as the interest or motivation of the buyer and the willingness of the seller. The actual value on certain high quality or rare artifacts is difficult to place. It all boils down to the fact that it takes a willing buyer and a willing seller coming to terms at the right time on an agreeable price and/or trade. Many collectors specialize in certain artifact types while others simply collect artifacts from their immediate county, state or region. Some even elect to accumulate a general collection from many regions of the country. Typically, a collector will pay more for an artifact from his immediate locale more so than one from a distant state or region.

Most everyone has an inborn sense of curiosity and discovery and that is why it is so enjoyable (if you still have the means and opportunity) to discover an arrowhead in a freshly plowed field, following a good hard rainfall. Like for most people, you are hooked after finding your very first arrowhead, and this frequently leads to the very enjoyable lifetime hobby of collecting Indian arrowheads. There is something very special in being the first to discover a discarded or lost arrowhead that once was a very essential tool made and used by ancient Man for survival and existence hundreds and even thousands of years ago. One can only stand in awe while admiring a new find or acquisition and wondering about its origin and purpose through the ages. If only rocks could talk! Happy hunting and collecting.

Bill Jackson & Alex Przygoda- Mt. Sterling, KY
Great Basin & Northern Central Sections

The artifact market continues to offer tremendous collecting pleasure as well as potentially lucrative financial rewards so long as one is knowledgeable on the subject and deals with honorable trustworthy individuals whose good reputations precede them.

The key to navigating in today's artifact market is learning to know with certainty whether or not an artifact has true antiquity. In just the past few years, many individuals have appointed themselves artifact authenticators. That is good...if, in fact, they issue certificates of authenticity with the benefit of the experience one needs to accurately judge whether a piece is old or was made last week by a clever faker who has utilized modern techniques to age his pieces. Not all authenticators use the same standards to arrive at their decisions, and as such, there are occasions where authenticators will disagree. This can be very confusing for new collectors. We urge those who have made, or plan to make, a considerable investment in artifacts to do your "due diligence," and learn for yourselves the features that distinguish ancient from modern.

In this regard, the best advice we can offer is for you to invest in a microscope with built-in illumination and use it! Learn what makes a piece unquestionably old, how to tell if the patination is ancient or if it was chemically induced last week, and beware of "dealers" who offer no money-back guarantees of authenticity with their artifacts. Believe us, it is not rocket science. You can learn to determine the difference; it simply requires your effort. For those interested, we continue to offer classes teaching the methods we at Jackson Galleries employ to evaluate artifacts.

That said, we have observed that the artifact market itself has changed dramatically over the last two years and these changes need to be seriously considered. More and more folks are using the Internet to buy and sell their artifacts. As such, the amount of fraud perpetrated through this medium has gone up tremendously. We only recommend buying from dealers who offer a reasonable return period on their items (14 days or more) to allow for timely inspection. We see that prices online are far more volatile right now than in recent years, which we now believe is a direct result of the amalgam of reproductions and real pieces marketed through the same venues. In this period we have seen artifacts that in our opinion should command high prices sell very inexpensively while pieces that we know to be reproduction have brought some extreme prices. To gain the best understanding of pricing trends, the major dealers will publish catalogs and the prices they ask will likely represent fair market at that time. Subscribe to the catalogs, study, and begin to track your observations.

One constant we can point out with certainty is that 'perfect' artifacts continue to command higher and higher prices. Lesser grades will always have less appeal and will tend not to appreciate nearly as rapidly or steeply as the higher grade material. While we are no longer actively dealing in North American Artifacts, preferring to offer our authentication services instead, the market trends are the same across almost all realms of collectable antiquities whether it be ancient Roman, Greek, Egyptian, North American, Pre-Columbian, or Oriental items. No matter what you choose to collect in the ancient antiquities realm, to build your collection in today's market you can spend your time continuously searching for bargains on the Internet or elsewhere, and/or you can decide to collect from major dealers (the majority of whom advertise within the pages of this publication) and build a solid collection that is bound to appreciate. Either way, it can be tremendous fun. All else aside, remember to always make your collecting fun! The joy is in the chase, the history, and the electrifying connection with the past. Study, learn, hunt, and enjoy. Good luck and good collecting.

Donald E. Meador - Dallas, TX
South Central Section

Texas has enjoyed a very good market for the past 15 to 20 years. The market has drawn more outside collectors with increased prices on higher quality pieces. A lot of outside money is coming into the relic market now.

We still enjoy a lot of good artifact shows here in Texas and the surrounding states. The crowds are becoming larger at all shows. Most buyers require an authentication paper from a reliable source. A lot of collectors still have hunting sites, which are the setting for good prices, and some prefer to go on organized digs.

Many old collections have come into the marketplace by either consignment or sold intact as a unit. I see a lot of new type collections now, which is a nice way to start, and then upgraded or added to with available pieces.

Paleo points have led the way as far as prices go, but top quality Archaic pieces are in good demand.

Recent sales in the area of Grade 8 to 10 pieces of 4-5 inches are: Allen 5" $3,000-10,000; Barber 4-5" $3,000-15,000; Clovis 4-5&1/2" $5,000-25,000; Eden 4-6" $4,000-25,000; First View 4"+ $5,000-20,000; Folsom 2" $5,000-20,000;

Midland 3-4&1/2" $2,000-10,000; Milnesand 3-5" $2,000-15,000; Pelican 2-4" $1,000-5,000; Plainview 4-6" $3,000-15,000; Scottsbluff 4-6" $3,000-10,000; Alberta 4-6" $2,500-10,000; Base Tang Knives 4-6" $2,000-5,000; Castroville 4-6" $1,000-5,000; Corner Tang Knives 4-7" $2,500-10,000; Covington 4-6" $1,000-2,000; Golondrina 3-5" $2,000-5,000; Marcos 5"+ $2,000-4,000; Nolan 5"+ $1,000-2,000; Victoria 4" $2,000-5,000; San Saba 5"+ $3,000-5,000; Midbank Tang Knives 3-5" $2,000-5,000; Marshall 5"+ $1,000-2,000; Kinney 5"+ $500-1,000; Gahagan 5"+ $1,000-2,000. Top quality Bird points of two inches or more are bringing $200-1,500. The most sought after material is rootbeer, agate, alibates, petrified word, Georgetown, and Edwards Plateau.

Collecting is one of the most healthy activities that one can get involved in. It gives a person the opportunity to travel and meet a lot of very nice people. I recommend buying all the reading materials you can. Study them closely when you start collecting. Get a mentor to talk with and don't buy from him or anyone that authenticates artifacts that you are buying. Always ask for a history on pieces and buy with a return guarantee for two weeks to 30 days to look at a piece to see if you like it.

Good luck in your future with artifacts. I hope you find it as rewarding as I have.

Rod Michel
Far West Section

The demand for NW Coast, Columbia River, and Great Basin Indian artifacts has been increasing every year since 2000. Most collectors are seeking arrowheads, projectile points, knives and tools that grade in the G-7 to G-10 range. For many years, the valuations of Western material has lagged that of the Plains, Midwest and South, but in the past 18 months this has changed dramatically. Obsidian artifacts made of triple flow, Burns Green, mahogany, rainbow, zebra stripe and translucents are very hot, especially anything of good size over 3" long. The notched and lanceolates are in high demand owing to their sophisticated style and exceptional fine pressure flaking as a rule rather than as an exception. Simply put, obsidian was plentiful and easy for the early peoples to work into whatever form they chose due to its predictable fracturing patterns. Agate, petrified wood, and jasper are far scarcer, especially in the larger points, due to scarcity of suitable material. Granted, abundant smaller arrowpoints exist of "color," but this is because these are made of an abundance of small river cobbles, in particular the Mid- and Lower Columbia River region. Basalts are lagging way behind in price, but this represents an opportunity for the type point buyer for whom material is secondary to considerations of obtaining the finest examples.

We have been seeing more clients who are priced out of their Eastern markets coming to us searching for fine artifacts that they can afford. It seems that each dealer in the West is carving out niche markets; in my case, I have been working hard to win clients who are looking for Paleos, Archaics, and specialized tool forms. Many people desire to own Blackrock Concaves, Hasketts, Cougar Mountains, Cody Complex, Lind Coulee, Intermontane Stemmed, Crescents, Clovis, Lake Mohaves, Cascades, Parmans, and Owl Caves. Generally a

trickle of these desirable points are becoming available through the online auctions houses and some are on various dealers' websites, but the vast majority are being bought and sold in private transactions among collectors. Probably the best way for someone to get the better points is to develop a dialogue with other collectors, with a bit of mutual courtesy and respect going a long way to opening doors of opportunity. Also, patience and a willingness to take a legitimate offer when presented is a successful approach to building fine frames and a good collection. I cannot over-emphasize the importance of making friends with other people who collect the types and grades of artifacts that you wish to obtain. Also, it is important to insist that the sellers give you a written guarantee of ancient authenticity on all artifacts that you buy, not to mention protecting yourself by demanding a written statement of provenance as well. Further, using the services of a credible authenticator who specialized in Western artifacts is an additional layer of protection for your investment.

Excellent arrowpoints of all types such as Columbia Plateau, Eastgate, Wallula, Gunthers, Alkali, Rose Springs, and Deserts are available often. In particular, the Deserts represent some of the best bang for your buck this year. It is possible to buy G-8 to G-10s for less than $150 on a consistent basis. The higher end Columbia Plateaus, Eastgates, and Klickitats can command price tags in the $300-1,500+ range for the elite sweeping barb gems. The more colorful the agate and the finer the tips and barbs or variations in the material, the stronger the demand. If you are seeking type points or solid frames, there are many good quality mid-grades that can be bought in the $20-50 range.

Elkos, Snake River, Hells Canyon, Gatecliff, and Northerns are also very desirable types. The larger and the more exaggerated the tips and barbs the better, also increasing the demand. The best of this bunch will set you back anywhere from $50 for a good mid-grade specimen all the way up to $1,000+ for the cream. Some of the most elite examples illustrated in museums or journals are nearly unobtainable to any of us. That being said, sometimes one will pop up, and they never last for sale very long. The moss agates are probably the scarcest, followed by the petrified wood and colorful jaspers. Any obsidian with extra embellishment such as zebra banding, mottling, ghost points within as sometimes happens with rainbow, and sheen add artistic dimension and should be regarded in a higher light and usually are in the bottom line pricing. Some notable sales include Wolf Ears selling for $1,500-2,000; Elkos for $850-1,200; and Gatecliffs sold over $750.

Large knives with respectable thinness and fine flaking are another artifact group that people are seeking. The translucent gem materials rule this group in valuation with the higher grades seeing values at around $100-300+ per inch. The opaque ones made of gray sucrosic obsidians and basalts tend to lag in the $50-100 per inch range. Very few unbroken specimens of chalcedony or agate are known. There seems to be an abundance of knives that are broken and glued, and these generally sell at an 80-90% discount to comparable complete examples. The additions of basal tangs add value and are far scarcer than the average leaf shaped form. In addition, uniface knives are doing extremely well among collectors building fine frames or Archaic and Paleo-Archaics. Also, specialty knives having graver spurs, burins and spokeshaves are sophisticated relics that the market valued so highly, and to me add even more to curating the piece. We have seen several large knives sell this past year in excess of $1,000 each with the occasional specimen fetching over $1,500.

Lanceolates, darts, and defensive daggers or thrusting spears are another group that people associate with Western North America. Many darts that measure 2" or less can be obtained for around $35-75 each, while the longer lances over 4" are becoming much tougher to find and generally range from $100-500+ per inch depending on the type, caliber, material, and provenance. The defensive daggers can be made of the most beautiful material because this was a personal piece for the owner that protected him against hostile tribes and animals. The flaking on these relics tends to be extremely controlled pressure, often with ribbon flaking or horizontal transverse and fine edge pressure workmanship. They are also thin and lenticular and sometimes rhomboid in the case of Kennewicks. The broken and glued examples will command $100-150 per inch, while the Mint complete specimens get $250-500+ per inch.

Points made of slate or bone are characteristic of the NW Coast. Many of these were ground in ancient times using abraders and polished with shark or fish skin. The range of use can be for harpoon toggle heads for sealing all the way up to heavy duty whaling spears made of nephrite jades. The rare bone point can turn up on the market too, and we have seen examples made of mussel shells as well. Harpoons with serrations or carving are artistic pieces unto themselves and have been selling for around $50 for the mid-grades and up to $1,000+ for composite harpoons having both the bond or antler shaft plus a stone point. In purchasing these items, sometimes the specimens have been preserved using white glue and water to prevent stress fractures and expansion of the material as it dries out, causing damage. Provenance and reputation of the dealer is very important when considering these objects. The distribution ranges from California all along the West Coast along British Columbia into Alaska. This is a niche market with an upside to it for the investment-minded collector.

In conclusion, the market for Western artifacts has grown every year since the new Millennium and it looks like it is going to continue to do so long into the future. A good word of advice is to network with reputable people who collect relics you wish to obtain and insist upon written guarantees of ancient authenticity (30 days minimum) along with a conditional money back guarantee that the relic can be returned in the same condition as sent. Further, you cannot go wrong by collecting what you personally like first and foremost, because the worst that can happen is you decide to resell your arrowhead is that you get to keep the piece a while longer. Lastly, the better the flaking, material and quality, the higher the valuation of the piece. Never let a few bucks get in the way of owning a fine caliber specimen that you really want. Most of us who have been collecting a long time have been down that road. Pick up the phone and call the seller and do your due diligence. This can go a long way in negotiating a better deal or avoiding a potentially bad one. I wish everyone the best!

Roy Motley
Northern Central Section

In the last two years, we have seen the stock market and economy go up and down on a regular basis. Despite this uncertainty, I've observed mostly positive signals in the Indian artifact world. Interest is very high. More and more people are looking for artifacts and notable successes have been seen. Several large old time collections have been placed on the market. Many new collectors have entered the hobby, bringing new enthusiasm. More and more folks see this hobby as a fun way to invest some of their hard-earned dollars. Price tags remain varied with something for everyone. High quality pieces have seen their values soar. There has also been an increased desire shown by both collectors and dealers to have their artifacts authenticated by qualified individuals.

John T. Pafford - Eva, Tennessee
Eastern Central Section

Over the past two years, the artifact collecting market has experienced numerous challenges in the face of continuing growth and interest. Although artifact prices have remained relatively unchanged to slightly increased, the dynamics of the market have changed considerably. As reported in the last edition, an influx of artifacts from well-known collections has created unprecedented availability of high quality items in every category from flint to stone and pottery. Although this has caused increased interest in the collecting community, the market has been faced with trying to absorb not only the surge of available artifacts but also the record setting prices associated with these pieces. This phenomenon has caused a domino effect where additional collectors have decided to place their collections up for sale. The reasons for this have resulted from both an unwillingness to continue collecting in the face of ever-increasing prices and a desire to take advantage of a prime selling opportunity. In the midst of the confusion, modern reproductions with fraudulent provenances have made a startling appearance on the market both in quality and quantity. The combination of high priced authentic pieced and numerous high quality reproductions has caused an overall decrease of collector confidence. In response, almost every dealer has offered some type of authentication service to promote confidence in the marketplace. Many collectors have now started seeking out numerous authentication certificates on a single piece to ensure their confidence in an artifact's authenticity.

Although many collectors have left the hobby, numerous new collectors have taken their place. This new breed of collectors has primarily focused their interest on high quality pieces with excellent documentation. As a result, the market has experienced an increase of interest that has taken place with the increased availability of artifacts. This has limited the otherwise detrimental market impact of reproductions and over abundance of high quality authentic pieces. Therefore, prices for high quality well-documented flint artifacts have continued to escalate, especially those from the Paleo and early Archaic time periods. Although demand for Paleo pieces such as Clovis and Cumberland has remained in demand, highly documented quality early Archaic examples such as Dovetail, Lostlake, and Hardin have dramatically increased in value. Values for Woodland pieces such as Adena and Copena have at best held constant over the last two years while prices for high quality Woodland and Mississippian triangular points have increased.

Artifact sales that I am aware of: 4" Clovis $3,500; 4-3/8" Clovis $6,500; 4" super Cumberland $15,000; 4" broken Cumberland $1,500; 6-1/4" damaged Cumberland $10,000; 5-1/2" Dovetail $6,500; 4" Dovetail $6,000; 4" Lostlake $6,500; 4-3/8" Hardin, one of the best, $15,000; 5" Motley $3,500; 4" serrated Kirk $1,500; 6" Adena $1,000; Mississippian triangles from $75-250 each.

Dick Savidge
Northeast Section

I see a trend of more and more young collectors, especially women, coming into the collecting field.

Auction prices are holding high, especially the quality pieces. Axes – really nice ones – are finally bringing the prices that I feel they are worth. It has been a long time coming in this area.

Be aware that there are a lot of fellows getting into the flint knapping area and they are getting very good at it. We have come across quite a few Clovis points that are being reproduced and they are showing up in the market as if they are old. This is a scary situation, so please be aware of it.

IACANE Association sponsors approximately four shows a year in Pennsylvania. I'd like to advise anyone that has any artifacts in question to attend one of the shows to get quality advice from any one of these dealers.

Arlie (Art) D. Tatum
Southwest Section

The future looks great. Some fine Paleo points are still being found, some from surface collecting. Also, some grade 9 and 10 Archaic points have seen their values increase. The lower grade points remain about the same in value. As the economy decreases, fine artifacts are a good investment. Artifacts are not renewable, but the dollar is.

Restoration of slightly damaged points is becoming more acceptable. I remember when incomplete fossils were shunned by collectors. Now they are completely accepted and even duplicated parts are traded by museums. Restored pottery is now accepted. It is only a matter of time until restored points are also more accepted by collectors. I want to emphasize that there is an important point to remember: Restoration, for me, refers to perhaps 15% or less of the point that needs to be restored. More than this leans toward duplication or reproduction. As the number of G10 points found decreases, restoration on beautiful but slightly damaged points needs to be increased. Photos taken before restoration are a necessity. The quality of the restorer's work is also important. The bulk of the available points may need restoration, so this facet of the hobby needs to be increased. I enjoy looking at a complete relic as much as I do a beautiful pot or dinosaur skeleton.

Some new point types are being found in the Southwest. I have seen many that are not typed. Those collectors wanting one of each type will raise the prices on these new ones since there are not enough to fill the market demand.

Watch out for the new insurgence of fakes on the market. Three main reasons: the rising demand, new ways of chemically treating points to age them, and the eBay opportunity. Get reliable sellers and the best authenticators as your guide to buying.

A few years ago at the Tucson Gem & Mineral Show, some Neolithic points from the Sahara Desert or Northwest Africa were offered for sale for $1-2 each. This year, prices ranged from $15-25 and up. How quickly they learned the American market!

Most of the area in New Mexico is BLM land and military, and of course Texas has private land, so it is quite restricted for the arrowhead hunters. However, Mother Nature with her wind and water exposes more artifacts for the diligent seeker. Some exciting relics have recently been found. Surface hunters have recently found two Folsom points, three Clovis points, some Frios, Bells, Zephyrs, serrated Lermas, side notches, and points not typed. Three things you get from relic hunting: exercise, relics and camaraderie. And you know two out of three isn't bad as we say out here.

Greg Truesdell
Northern Plains and Far West Sections

What an interesting hobby we have gotten ourselves into. It isn't like flying radio-controlled airplanes or driving those radio-controlled four-wheel drive trucks. And no, it isn't as easy as coin or stamp collecting, where authentication services are all on the up and up. No, we decided to collect something in a field where there are over 25,000 or more well made fake artifacts surfacing every year. In a field where anyone and everyone can say that they are an authenticator – after all, it doesn't take a college degree – there are only a few good ones. Now we all know who the good ones are and who the bad ones are – at least I hope we do – as some of the prices seen for top notch artifacts are astronomical.

Here in the Northern Plains and in the Great Basin, prices for top grade artifacts have continued escalating at an incredible pace. We have seen Nightfires sell for $3,000 and Cougar Mountains for $7,000. Some Columbia Plateaus made of agate are going for $1,500 each no matter what this or any other guide book says. I have seen Wallulas command as much as $750, and that's for an artifact that is only an inch long. And if you want to talk high dollars – as if those numbers aren't high enough – some Folsoms, Edens, Scottsbluffs and Clovis have sole in the $20,000 range.

Demand for lower grade artifacts is also on the rise, with obsidian finally starting to bring what it is worth. While there have been a couple of very large collections entering the market with artifacts in all grades, it doesn't seem to have slowed demand for arrowheads.

A good collection can be started for a small investment, but I would rather recommend that new collectors buy the best that they can afford, as these will be easier to trade in for better material at a later time. Also, collectors should use authenticators familiar with their area of collecting; a local person has most likely seen more of that material than an authenticator a thousand miles away. That said, there are a couple authenticators who have seen so much material from all over the United States that they can tell you if a rock is good whether it is from the Great Basin or Florida.

The top authenticators for the Great Basin and the Northern Plains are people like Jackson Galleries, Jeb Taylor, Steve Wallman and Ben Stermer.

In closing, we believe that the artifact collecting community is stronger than ever and will continue to grow as long as a child can reach down and pick up something that Man made thousands of years ago. The more fakes the artifakers make, the more real collectors need to learn, and that is what's happening. Good luck and good collecting.

Eric C. Wagner - AACA Vice President
Eastern Central Section

In the mid-Ohio valley, relic prices have been steady for the past two years with slight increases. Buying G-7 and above relics is like having money in the bank as the prices always increase.

Paleo points, as always, are the leaders in price and demand. In the Archaic points, I see Lostlakes as a distant third to Dovetails and Thebes points. Dovetails are always a collector's dream and Thebes have increased in value and popularity. If you can get your hands on a nice Thebes E-notch, then do so. They are very rare in higher grades. Decaturs are another Archaic type that is rarer than most people think in all grades. As far as Woodland period points go, Hopewell points have a large following. But it's the Adena type that is on the rise in value. I feel that currently Adenas are one of the most undervalued point types. Drills are also undervalued in my opinion. If you look at large field found collections, you will notice that 90% of the drills are broken. Three inch plus drills in undamaged condition can be bought for $90-150 and are quite a deal. I see perfect large drills going nowhere but up.

The hardstone market has really risen in the past couple of years. Axes have always had good value and they are going up. The celt and pestle market used to be awfully weak but in the past couple of years I've seen prices and demand dramatically increase.

Slate artifacts are very rare and carry value accordingly. Quality Gorgets, Pendants and Bannerstones increase in value yearly and should continue to do so.

Recent observed selling prices: 3-1/4" Carter Cave Dovetail G-8 $400; 3-3/4" Ft. Payne Adena G-7 $195; 4-3/4" highly polished hematite axe G-9 $995; 4" highly polished celt G-10 $295; 2" serrated Palmer G-8 $125; 5-1/2" 3/4 raised groove axe G-9 $695; 3-1/8" Ft. Payne Clovis G-9 $2,800; 3-3/8" Hornstone Hopewell G-8 $265; 4" banded slate pendant G-8 $295; 1-1/2" Ball Bannerstone G-7 $325.

I've seen a lot of reproductions floating around in all relic types. Please insist on a return period in writing. Use an authenticator or a knowledgeable collector to help you sort out the fakes. Also remember that if a relic seems like a steal, it's probably the seller trying to steal from you! Best wishes in your collecting endeavors.

Jack Wilhoit
Gulf Coastal Section

Paleo and Archaic Points have increased in value greatly during the past two years. Large points in grades 9 and 10 made of translucent materials such as coral and high grade Coastal Plain Chert are bringing the highest prices.

Recently, a Mustache Simpson Point brought $10,000, a Newman Point totaled $10,000, and a River Clovis was purchased for $8,500.

Mid-grade points have decreased in price and low grade points have decreased even further.

Points and blades made from Tallahatta Quartzite have increased in price, especially examples made of Snow Flake Variety. Tallahatta Quartzite has a very limited distribution area. Most of the points made of this material are found in Choctaw County, Alabama and surrounding counties, including a few in southeastern Mississippi. A few points made of this stone have been found as far away as Florida, Georgia and Louisiana. Examples of artifacts made of Tallahatta Quartzite were found at the Poverty Point Site in northeast Louisiana.

Artifact shows in the Gulf Coast Region have been well attended with a high degree of interest by collectors and the general public. I believe that artifacts from the Gulf Coast Region will be in demand for many years to come.

Warner B. Williams
Eastern Seaboard Section

The market in our region continues to increase for the top quality points. Points in the 9 and 10 category usually bring what a collector is willing to pay while the lower grade points in the 1 to 5 category have become less desirable. The 6 through 8 category points have had a nominal increase since the publication of the eight edition of the Overstreet Guide.

Collectors are more cautious than ever due to the impact of modern day points. The risk of acquiring a modern made point unaware is high when the collector is purchasing an arrowhead made of stone for which they are unfamiliar. Knowing the patina, type, flaking, appearance and feel of the stone is very important.

I have collected Indian arrowheads for 58 years and 95% of the collection is from the Central North Carolina Region. The 1200 points in the 9 and 10 grade classification are made of rhyolite. I know rhyolite well but I am unfamiliar with the majority of stone from other regions.

There are several reputable dealers across the country who sell artifacts which are authentic and guaranteed. Collectors and dealers must know the stone inside and out. If there is any doubt, walk away.

One big influence in our market today and in the future will be the youth. There are different levels of collecting from the astute collector to the very young. A number 3 grade to a child is a number 10. It is imperative that we keep the market growing among young collectors by encouraging them at every opportunity.

During the first weekend in March for nine consecutive years, I have shown my entire collections at our local library. The public interest in our area has greatly increased. I feel it is beneficial to the hobby to share it with the public, which I have found brings me great joy as well.

What would happen if...

Thousands of fine people lost their lifetime hobbies in the recent hurricane season. Collectibles ranging from important Native American artifacts, to basement model railroad layouts and glass figurines were sadly destroyed. Did insurance help many of these victims? In too many cases, the answer was, "NO."

I've been a collector all of my life—even before I became the owner of a firm that specializes in providing insurance for thousands of collectibles. I know what it's like to lose the treasures of a lifetime hobby. Here's a lesson I learned that I'd like to pass along to you: Homeowners insurance is rarely, if ever, adequate for your hunting and fishing collectibles. Take a minute now and call, write or e-mail us for brochures that can help your peace of mind.

Dan Walker

We INSURE Hunting & Fishing Collectibles at Attractive Rates.

- **Sample collector rates:** $3,000 for $12, $10,000 for $40, $25,000 for $106, $50,000 for $216, $100,000 for $316, $200,000 for $476. Above $200,000, rate is $1.60 per $1,000.

- **Our insurance carrier** is AM Best's rated A+ (Superior).

- **We insure scores of major collectibles from Native American artifacts to toys**. "One-stop" service for practically everything you collect.

- **Replacement value.** We use expert help valuing collectible losses. Consumer friendly service: Our office handles your loss—you won't deal with a big insurer who doesn't know collectibles.

- **Detailed inventory** and/or professional appraisal not required. Collectors list items over $5,000, dealers no listing required.

- **See our website** (or call, fax, e-mail us) for full information, including standard exclusions.

VISA MasterCard DISCOVER

Get A Rate Quote!
Call Toll Free:
1-888-837-9537
Fax: (410) 876-9233

CIA Collectibles Insurance Agency

P.O. Box 1200-IA • Westminster MD 21158
E-Mail: info@insurecollectibles.com

www.collectinsure.com

COLORADO

Bob's Flint Shop
P.O. Box 4889
Grand Junction, CO 81502
Ph: (877) 244-8998
Email: bobsflintshop
@bresnan.net
Web:
www.arrowheads.com/bobs

Dream Spears
108 Country Club Park Rd.
Grand Junction, CO 81503-1610
Ph: (970) 241-3050
Email: sales
@dreamspears.com
Web:
www.dreamspears.com

FLORIDA

Paleo Enterprises
P.O Box 82098
Tampa, FL 33682
Ph: (813)632-8579
Web:
www.paleoenterprises.com

ILLINOIS

Drew-Campbell Indian Artifact Authentication
271 E. King St.
Palmyra, IL 62674
Ph: (217)436-2624
Email: grahamcave1
@msn.com

INDIANA

First Mesa
P.O. Box 1256
South Bend, IN 46624
Ph: (574) 243-2296
Web: www.firstmesa.com

KENTUCKY

Bluegrass Case Company
P.O. Box 982
272 Airport Rd.
Stanton, KY 40380
Ph: (888) 668-9871
Fax: (606) 663-6369
Email: support
@bluegrasscase.com
Web:
www.bluegrasscase.com

Davis Artifacts Inc.
P.O. Box 676
449 Oak Ridge Drive
Stanton, KY 40380-0676
Fax: (606) 663-4370
PH: (606) 663-2741
Email: tomdavis@mis.net
Web:
www.tomdavisartifacts.com

Jackson Galleries
P.O. Box 1005
Mt. Sterling, KY 40353
Ph: (800) 466-3836
Web:
www.jacksongalleries.com

Goodflint.com
P.O. Box 30304
Bowling Green, KY 42101
PH: (270) 782-7494
FAX: (270) 783-0624
E-Mail: goodflint
@goodflint.com
Web: www.goodflint.com

Prehistoric Artifacts
P.O. Box 30304
Bowling Green, KY 42102
Ph: (270) 782-7494
Fax: (270) 783-0624
Email:
goodflint@goodflint.com
Web: www.goodlfint.com

The Indian Shop
W.V. Hilliard
P.O. Box 246
Independence, KY 32403

MARYLAND

Collectibles Insurance Agency
P.O. Box 1200-IA
Westminster, MD 21158
Ph: (888)-837-9537
Fax: (410) 876-9233
Email: info
@insurecollectibles.com
Web: www.collectinsure.com

MISSOURI

KRM Consultants
29802 SE Moreland Sch. Rd.
Blue Springs, MO 64014
Ph: (816) 229-6025
Email: krmconsultants
@aol.com

NORTH CAROLINA

Warner B. Williams - Indian Artifact Collector
607 Back Creek Road
Asheboro, NC 27205
PH: (336) 625-6042
Email: warnerarrows
@triad.rr.com

OHIO

Back to Earth
17 North LaSalle Drive
South Zanesville, OH 43701

RHODE ISLAND

Arrowheads.com Karl Kilguss & Associates
535 Centerville Rd.
Warwick, RI 02886
Ph: (401) 737-0500
Email: kkilguss@aol.com
Web: www.arrowheads.com

WASHINGTON

Intermountain Art
P.O. Box 14758
Spokane, WA 99214
PH: (509) 924-0280
FAX: (509) 924-0294
E-Mail: randallm1
@mindspring.com
Web: www.bestartifacts.com

WYOMING

Jeb Taylor Artifact Evaluation
P.O. Box 882
Buffalo, WY 82834
Ph: (307) 737-2347
Email: jeb@rangeweb.net

CANADA

BC Artifacts
P.O. Box 71088
7921 120 Street
Delta, BC V4C 8E7
Ph: (604) 501-1768
Cell: (778) 386-3110
Web: www.bcartifacts.com

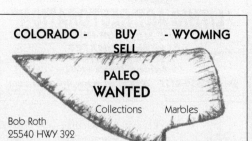

NORTHEASTERN SECTION:

This section includes point types from the following states: Connecticut, Delaware, Maine, Maryland, Massachusetts, New Hampshire, New Jersey, New York, Pennsylvania, Vermont.

The points in this section are arranged in alphabetical order and are shown **actual size**. All types are listed that were available for photographing. Any missing types will be added to future editions as photographs become available. We are always interested in receiving sharp, black and white or color glossy photos, color slides or high resolution (300 pixels/inch) digital pictures of your collection. Be sure and include a ruler in the photograph so that proper scale can be determined.

Lithics: Materials employed in the manufacture of projectile points from this region are: argillite, Coshocton chert, Coxsackie chert, crystal quartz, dolomite, felsite, Helderberg cherts, jasper, Ledge Ridge chert, milky quartz, Onondaga chert, quartzite, rhyolite, shale, siltstone, slate, vein quartz.

Important sites: Bull Brook (Paleo, Ipswich, Mass.), Burwell-Karako (Conn.), John's Bridge (Early Archaic, Conn.), Neville (Early Archaic, Manchester, NH), Plenge (Paleo, NJ), Shoop (Paleo, Dauphin Co., PA), Vail (Paleo, Maine), Titicut (Early Archaic, Bridgewater, MA), Wapanucket (Middleboro, MA).

Regional Consultant:
Gary Fogelman

Special Advisors:
Dr. Richard Michael Gramly
Richard Savidge

NORTHEASTERN POINT TYPES
(Archaeological Periods)

PALEO (11,500 B.P - 8,000 B.P.)

Agate Basin
Amos
Beaver Lake
Barnes(Cumberland)

Clovis
Crowfield
Debert
Graver

Haw River
Holcomb
Northumberland Fluted
 Knife

Ohio Lanceolate
Redstone
Scraper

EARLY ARCHAIC (10,000 B.P - 6,500 B.P.)

Angostura
Arden
Brodhead Side-Notched
Charleston Pine Tree
Dalton Classic
Dalton Nuckolls
Decatur
Hardaway
Kanawha

Kessel
Kirk Corner Notched
Kirk Stemmed
Kline
Lake Erie
LeCroy
Lost Lake
MacCorkle
Muncy Bifurcate

Neville
Palmer
Penn's Creek Series
Penn's Creek Bifurcate
St. Albans
St. Anne
St. Charles
Stanly
Stark

Strike-A-Lite I
Stringtown
Susquehanna Bifurcate
Taunton Riv. Bif.
Thebes

MID-LATE ARCHAIC (6,000 B.P - 4,000 B.P.)

Atlantic Phase Blade
Bare Island
Beekman Triangular
Boats Blade
Bone/Antler
Brewerton Corner Notched
Brewerton Eared Triangular
Brewerton Side Notched
Burwell
Chillesquaque
Crooked Creek
Dewart Stemmed

Drill
Duncan's Island
Eshback
Exotic
Genesee
Ground Slate
Guilford
Hoover's Island
Jim Thorpe
Kittatiny
Lacawaxan
Lamoka

Lycoming County
Merrimack Stemmed
Morrow Mountain
Newmanstown
Otter Creek
Patuxent
Pentagonal Knife
Piedmont, Northern
Piney Island
Poplar Island
Savannah River
Snook Kill

Squibnocket Stemmed
Squibnocket Triangular
Swatara-Long
Taconic Stemmed
Vestal Notched
Virginsville
Vosburg
Wading River
Wapanucket

TERMINAL ARCHAIC (3,800 B.P - 3,000 B.P.)

Ashtabula
Conodoquinet/Canfield
Cresap
Drill
Drybrook Fishtail

Frost Island
Koens Crispin
Lehigh Broadpoint
Mansion Inn Blade
Meadowood

Normanskill
Orient Fishtail
Perkiomen
Schuylkill
Susquehanna Broad Point

Wayland Notched

EARLY-MIDDLE WOODLAND (2,800 B.P - 1,500 B.P.)

Adena
Adena Blade
Adena (Robbins)
Erb Basal Notched
Forest Notched
Fox Creek

Garver's Ferry
Greene
Hellgramite
Hopewell
Kiski Notched
Oley

Ovates
Piscataway
Port Maitland
Randolph
Sandhill Stemmed
Shark's Tooth

Snyders
Strike-A-Lite II
Tocks Island
Vernon
Waratan

LATE WOODLAND (1,500 B.P - 500 B.P.)

Erie Triangle
Goddard
Jacks Reef Corner
 Notched

Jacks Reef Pentagonal
Levanna
Madison
Raccoon Notched

Rossville
Susquehannock Triangle
Web Blade

HISTORIC (350 B.P - 200 B.P.)

Trade Points

NORTHEASTERN UNITED STATES
THUMBNAIL GUIDE SECTION

The following references are provided to aid the collector in easier and quicker identification of point types. All photos are exactly 30% of actual size and are proportional to each other. Each point pictured in this section represents a classic form for the type. When a match is found, go to the alphabetical location of that type for more examples in true actual size.

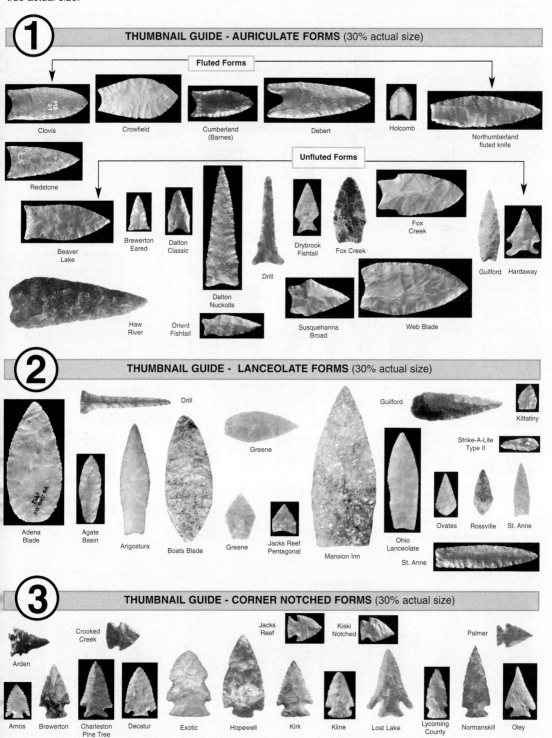

1 THUMBNAIL GUIDE - AURICULATE FORMS (30% actual size)

Fluted Forms

Clovis · Crowfield · Cumberland (Barnes) · Debert · Holcomb · Northumberland fluted knife

Redstone

Unfluted Forms

Beaver Lake · Brewerton Eared · Dalton Classic · Drybrook Fishtail · Fox Creek · Fox Creek · Guilford · Hardaway

Drill

Dalton Nuckolls

Haw River · Orient Fishtail · Susquehanna Broad · Web Blade

2 THUMBNAIL GUIDE - LANCEOLATE FORMS (30% actual size)

Drill · Guilford · Kittatiny

Greene · Strike-A-Lite Type II

Adena Blade · Agate Basin · Angostura · Boats Blade · Greene · Jacks Reef Pentagonal · Mansion Inn · Ohio Lanceolate · St. Anne · Ovates · Rossville · St. Anne

3 THUMBNAIL GUIDE - CORNER NOTCHED FORMS (30% actual size)

Crooked Creek · Jacks Reef · Kiski Notched · Palmer

Arden

Amos · Brewerton · Charleston Pine Tree · Decatur · Exotic · Hopewell · Kirk · Kline · Lost Lake · Lycoming County · Normanskill · Oley

95

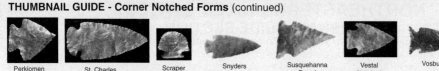

Perkiomen · St. Charles · Scraper · Snyders · Susquehanna Broad · Vestal Notched · Vosburg · Wayland Notched

④ THUMBNAIL GUIDE - SIDE NOTCHED FORMS (30% actual size)

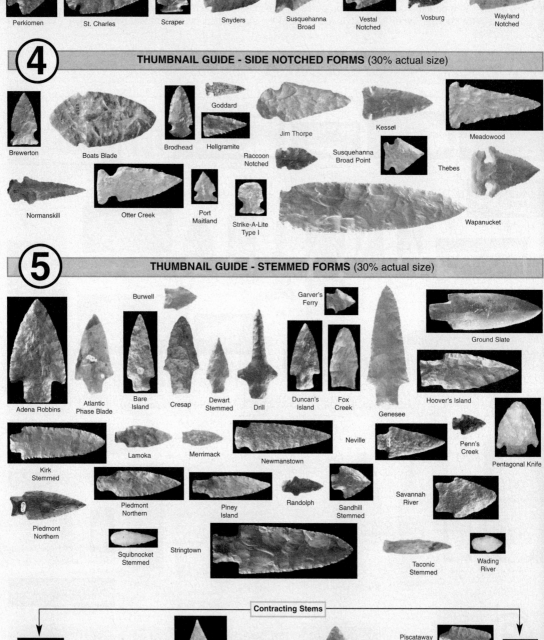

Brewerton · Boats Blade · Brodhead · Goddard · Hellgramite · Jim Thorpe · Raccoon Notched · Susquehanna Broad Point · Kessel · Meadowood · Thebes · Normanskill · Otter Creek · Port Maitland · Strike-A-Lite Type I · Wapanucket

⑤ THUMBNAIL GUIDE - STEMMED FORMS (30% actual size)

Burwell · Garver's Ferry · Ground Slate · Adena Robbins · Atlantic Phase Blade · Bare Island · Cresap · Dewart Stemmed · Drill · Duncan's Island · Fox Creek · Genesee · Hoover's Island · Kirk Stemmed · Lamoka · Merrimack · Newmanstown · Neville · Penn's Creek · Pentagonal Knife · Piedmont Northern · Piedmont Northern · Piney Island · Randolph · Sandhill Stemmed · Savannah River · Squibnocket Stemmed · Stringtown · Taconic Stemmed · Wading River

Contracting Stems

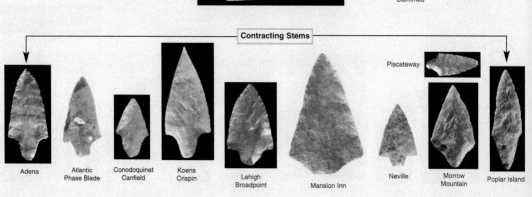

Adena · Atlantic Phase Blade · Conodoquinet Canfield · Koens Crispin · Lehigh Broadpoint · Mansion Inn · Piscataway · Neville · Morrow Mountain · Poplar Island

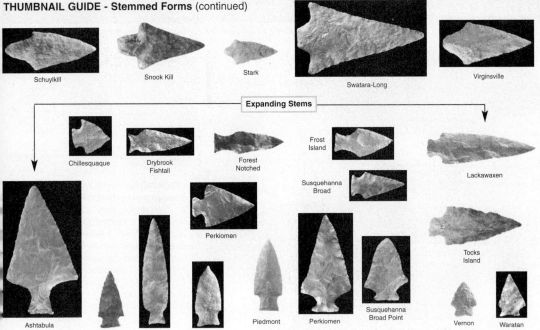

Schuylkill

Snook Kill

Stark

Swatara-Long

Virginsville

Expanding Stems

Chillesquaque

Drybrook Fishtail

Forest Notched

Frost Island

Lackawaxen

Susquehanna Broad

Perkiomen

Tocks Island

Ashtabula

Normanskill

Orient

Patuxent

Piedmont

Perkiomen

Susquehanna Broad Point

Vernon

Waratan

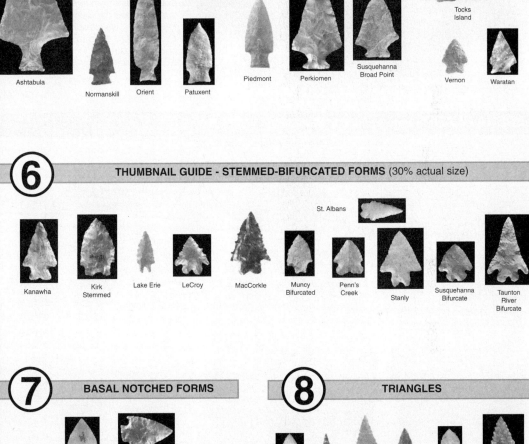

(6) THUMBNAIL GUIDE - STEMMED-BIFURCATED FORMS (30% actual size)

St. Albans

Kanawha

Kirk Stemmed

Lake Erie

LeCroy

MacCorkle

Muncy Bifurcated

Penn's Creek

Stanly

Susquehanna Bifurcate

Taunton River Bifurcate

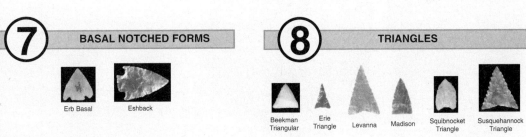

(7) BASAL NOTCHED FORMS

Erb Basal

Eshback

(8) TRIANGLES

Beekman Triangular

Erie Triangle

Levanna

Madison

Squibnocket Triangle

Susquehannock Triangle

ADENA - Late Archaic to late Woodland, 3000 - 1200 B.P.

(Also see Adena Blade, Koens Crispin, Lehigh, Neville, Piney Island, Turkeytail)

G4, $8-$15
NY

G7, $35-$50
W. PA

Quartzite

G7, $35-$65
Middlewsboro, Ma

LOCATION: Northeastern to Southeastern states. **DESCRIPTION:** A medium to large, thin, narrow, triangular blade with a medium to long, narrow to broad rounded "beaver tail" stem. Most examples are from average to excellent quality. Bases can be ground. Has been found with *Nolichucky, Camp Creek, Candy Creek, Ebenezer* and *Greenville* points (Rankin site, Cocke Co., TN). **I.D. KEY:** Rounded base, woodland flaking.

ADENA BLADE - Late Archaic to Woodland, 3000 - 1200 B.P.

(Also see Adena, Turkeytail)

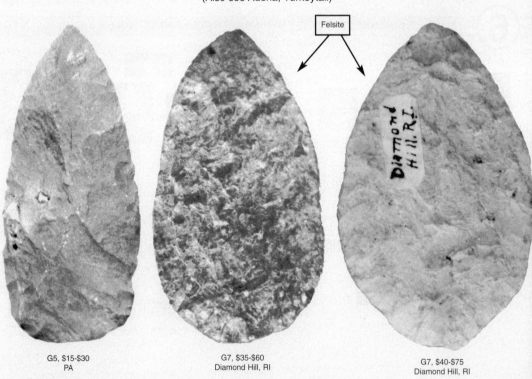

Felsite

G5, $15-$30
PA

G7, $35-$60
Diamond Hill, RI

G7, $40-$75
Diamond Hill, RI

LOCATION: Southeastern to Northeastern states. **DESCRIPTION:** A large size, thin, broad, ovate blade with a rounded base and is usually found in caches. **I.D. KEY:** Woodland flaking, large direct strikes.

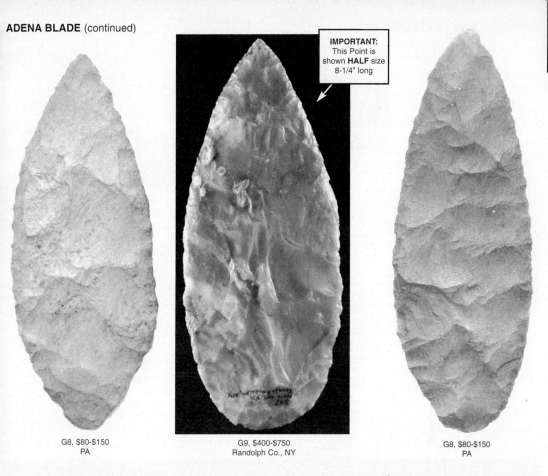

IMPORTANT: This Point is shown **HALF** size 8-1/4" long

G8, $80-$150
PA

G9, $400-$750
Randolph Co., NY

G8, $80-$150
PA

ADENA - ROBBINS - Late Archaic to Woodland, 3000 - 1800 B.P.

(Also see Duncan's Island, Genesee, Neville and Piedmont)

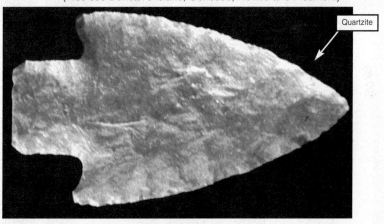

Quartzite

G8, $150-$250
Montgomery Co., PA

LOCATION: Eastern to Southeastern states. **DESCRIPTION:** A large, broad, triangular point that is thin and well made with a long, wide, rounded to square stem that is parallel sided. The blade has convex sides and square to slightly barbed shoulders. Many examples show excellent secondary flaking on blade edges. **I.D. KEY:** Square base, heavy secondary flaking.

99

ADENA-ROBBINS (continued)

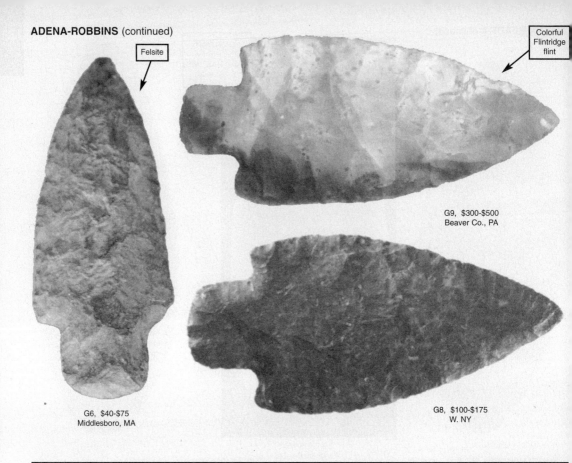

Felsite

Colorful Flintridge flint

G9, $300-$500
Beaver Co., PA

G6, $40-$75
Middlesboro, MA

G8, $100-$175
W. NY

AGATE BASIN - Transitional Paleo to early Archaic, 10,500 - 8000 B.P.

(Also see Angostura, Eden and Greene)

Chert

Quartzite

G4, $40-$75
Lycoming Co., PA

G6, $80-$150
Northampton Co., PA

G5, $60-$100
Berks Co., PA

G4, $80-$150
Lehigh Co., PA

G6, $80-$150
Lancaster Co., PA

LOCATION: Midwestern to Northeastern states. **DESCRIPTION:** A medium to large size lanceolate blade, usually of high quality. Bases are either convex, concave or straight, and are usually ground. Some examples are median ridged and have random to parallel flaking. **I.D. KEY:** Basal form and flaking style.

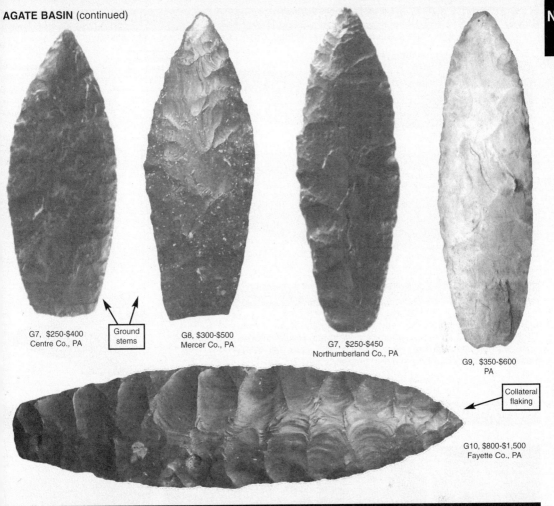

G7, $250-$400
Centre Co., PA

Ground stems

G8, $300-$500
Mercer Co., PA

G7, $250-$450
Northumberland Co., PA

G9, $350-$600
PA

Collateral flaking

G10, $800-$1,500
Fayette Co., PA

AMOS - Early Archaic, 10,000 - 9000 B.P.

(Also see Charleston Pine Tree, Kirk Corner Notched, Palmer)

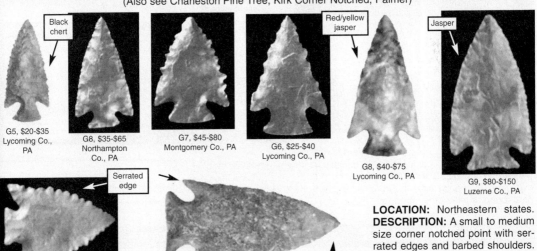

Black chert

G5, $20-$35
Lycoming Co.,
PA

G8, $35-$65
Northampton
Co., PA

G7, $45-$80
Montgomery Co., PA

G6, $25-$40
Lycoming Co., PA

Red/yellow jasper

G8, $40-$75
Lycoming Co., PA

Jasper

G9, $80-$150
Luzerne Co., PA

Serrated edge

G9, $90-$175
MD

G2, $8-$15
Lycoming Co., PA

Restored tip & tangs

LOCATION: Northeastern states.
DESCRIPTION: A small to medium size corner notched point with serrated edges and barbed shoulders. The base is straight to convex. **I.D. KEY:** Edgework.

ANGOSTURA - Early Archaic, 10,000 - 8000 B.P.

(Also see Agate Basin, Clovis-unfluted, Eden, Greene, Guilford and Plainview)

Black/brown chert

G9, $250-$400
Barre, MA

Yellow jasper

G9, $25-$500
Lehigh Co., PA

LOCATION: Eastern states. **DESCRIPTION:** A medium to large size lanceolate blade with a contracting, concave base. Both broad and narrow forms occur. Flaking can be parallel oblique to random. Bases are not usually ground but are thinned. **I.D. KEY:** Basal form, early flaking on blade. Very rare for the NE.

ARDEN - Early Archaic, 9000 - 8000 B.P.

(Also see Charleston Pine Tree)

LOCATION: Northeastern states, especially New York. **DESCRIPTION:** A small to medium size, serrated, corner notched point with barbed shoulders and an expanded stem. **I.D. KEY:** Basal form, one barb round and the other stronger.

G2, $2-$4
NY

ASHTABULA - Late Archaic to Woodland, 4000 - 2500 B.P.

(Also see Koens Crispin, Lehigh, Perkiomen and Susquehanna Broad)

Banded shale

G3, $12-$20
Lycoming Co., PA

G3, $12-$20
Lycoming Co., PA

G10, $800-$1400
Broome Co., NY

G3, $15-$25
Columbia Co., PA

G8, $400-$750
Union Co., PA

LOCATION: Northeastern states, especially Northeastern Ohio and Western Penn. **DESCRIPTION:** A medium to large size, broad, thick, expanded stem point with tapered shoulders. **I.D. KEY:** Basal form, one barb round and the other stronger.

IMPORTANT:
These Ashtabulas are shown half size

ATLANTIC PHASE BLADE - Late-Terminal Archaic, 4300 - 3700 B.P.

(Also see Boats Blade, Koens Crispin, Savannah River, Schuylkill and Snook Kill)

LOCATION: Massachusetts and surrounding states. **DESCRIPTION:** A medium to large size point with squared to tapered shoulders and a short, parallel sided to tapered stem. The base is generally straight. **I.D. KEY:** Base form.

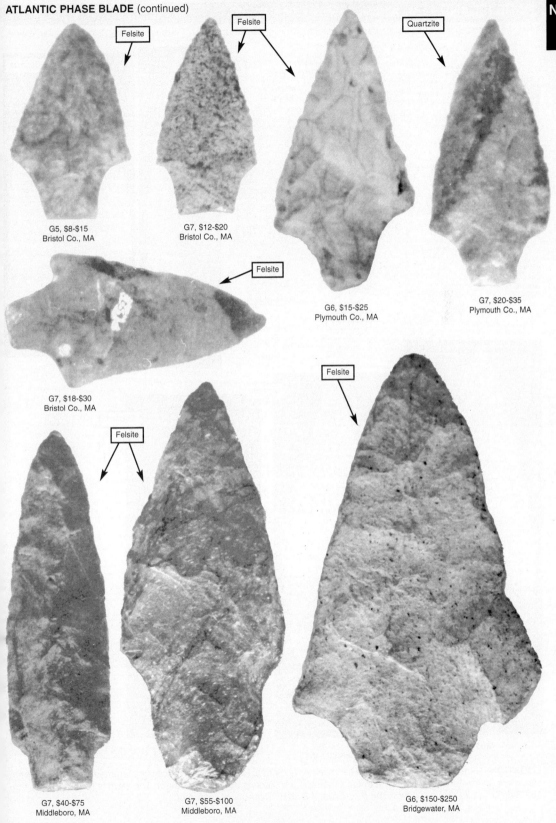

Felsite

Felsite

Quartzite

G5, $8-$15
Bristol Co., MA

G7, $12-$20
Bristol Co., MA

Felsite

G6, $15-$25
Plymouth Co., MA

G7, $20-$35
Plymouth Co., MA

G7, $18-$30
Bristol Co., MA

Felsite

Felsite

G7, $40-$75
Middleboro, MA

G7, $55-$100
Middleboro, MA

G6, $150-$250
Bridgewater, MA

BARE ISLAND - Late Archaic, 4500 - 1500 B.P.

(Also see Duncan's Island, Lackawaxen, Lamoka, Neville, Newmanstown, Piedmont, Piney Island, Poplar Island, Snook Kill)

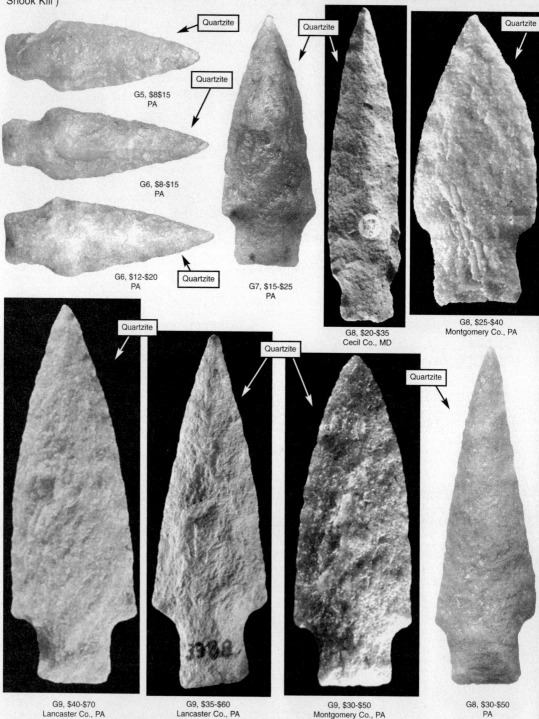

Quartzite

G5, $8$15
PA

Quartzite

G6, $8-$15
PA

G6, $12-$20
PA

Quartzite

Quartzite

G7, $15-$25
PA

Quartzite

G8, $20-$35
Cecil Co., MD

Quartzite

G8, $25-$40
Montgomery Co., PA

Quartzite

Quartzite

Quartzite

G9, $40-$70
Lancaster Co., PA

G9, $35-$60
Lancaster Co., PA

G9, $30-$50
Montgomery Co., PA

G8, $30-$50
PA

LOCATION: Northeastern states. **DESCRIPTION:** A medium to large size, narrow, thick stemmed point with tapered shoulders. One shoulder is higher than the other and the blade is convex to straight. The stem is parallel to expanding. Similar to *Little Bear Creek* in the Southeast. **I.D. KEY:** Narrow stemmed point.

BEAVER LAKE - Paleo, 11,250 - 8000 B.P.

(Also see Clovis Unfluted, Cumberland and Orient)

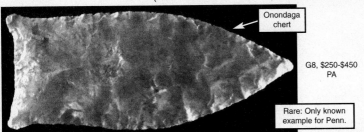

Onondaga chert

G8, $250-$450
PA

Rare: Only known example for Penn.

LOCATION: Southeastern to Northeastern states. **DESCRIPTION:** A medium to large size lanceolate blade with flaring ears. Associated with *Cumberland*, but thinner than unfluted *Cumberlands*. Bases are ground and blade edges are recurved. **I.D. KEY:** Paleo flaking, shoulder area.

BEEKMAN TRIANGULAR - Mid-late Archaic, 4800 - 4500 B.P.

(Also see Madison, Squibnocket Triangle and Susquehannock Triangle)

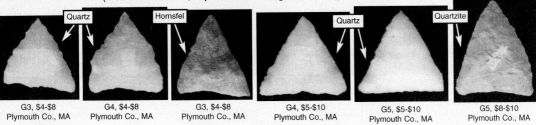

| Quartz | Hornsfel | | Quartz | Quartzite |

G3, $4-$8
Plymouth Co., MA

G4, $4-$8
Plymouth Co., MA

G3, $4-$8
Plymouth Co., MA

G4, $5-$10
Plymouth Co., MA

G5, $5-$10
Plymouth Co., MA

G5, $8-$10
Plymouth Co., MA

LOCATION: Northern Pennsylvania into New York, New Jersey and Massachusetts. **DESCRIPTION:** A small size, short, triangular point with a broad, straight to concave base. Bases are ground. **I.D. KEY:** Equilateral triangle with ground base.

BOATS BLADE - Late to Terminal Archaic, 4300 - 3700 B.P.

(Also see Adena Blade, Atlantic Phase Blade, Mansion Inn, Web Blade)

Glued

G3, $30-$50
Bridgewater, MA

Rare notched form

Half restored

G6, $25-$40
Middleboro, MA

$12-$20
Bridgewater, MA

LOCATION: Southern New England states. Type site is in Dighton, MA. **DESCRIPTION:** A large size, broad, bi-pointed blade of good quality. Rarely, examples exist with side notches.

BONE/ANTLER - Mid-Archaic to Historic, 4500 - 100 B.P.

(Also see Trade Points)

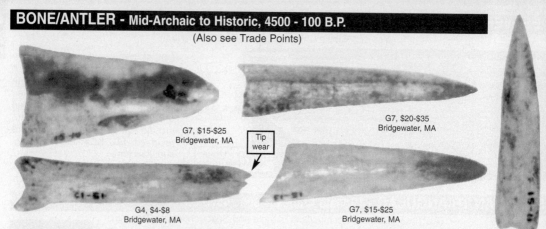

G7, $15-$25
Bridgewater, MA

Tip wear

G7, $20-$35
Bridgewater, MA

G4, $4-$8
Bridgewater, MA

G7, $15-$25
Bridgewater, MA

G6, $12-$20
Bridgewater, MA

LOCATION: Northeastern states. **DESCRIPTION:** A medium to large size lanceolate point carved from deer or Elk antler or from bone.

BREWERTON CORNER NOTCHED - Middle to late Archaic, 6000 - 4000 B.P.

(Also see Crooked Creek, Jacks Reef, Kirk, Kiski, Lycoming County, Normanskill, Palmer & Snyders)

Black flint

Base nick

G5, $6-$12
Monroe Co., PA

G6, $6-$12
Lycoming Co., PA

G5, $5-$10
Lycoming Co., PA

G5, $8-$15
Lycoming Co., PA

G6, $8-$15
Lycoming Co., PA

G6, $8-$15
Northampton Co., PA

G6, $8-$15
Carbon Co., PA

Black chert

Minor basal corner dings

G10, $25-$40
Columbia Co., NY

G6, $15-$25
Columbia Co., NY

G7, $15-$30
Columbia Co., NY

G5, $15-$25
Columbia Co., NY

G6, $18-$30
Columbia Co., NY

LOCATION: Eastern to midwestern states. **DESCRIPTION:** A small to medium size, thick, triangular point with faint corner notches and a concave, straight or convex base. Called *Freeheley* in Michigan. **I.D. KEY:** Width, thickness.

BREWERTON EARED-TRIANGULAR - Middle to late Archaic, 6000 - 4000 B.P.

(Also see Fox Creek, Steubenville & Yadkin)

Tip wear

Felsite

Felsite

Jasper

Felsite

Felsite

G4, $3-$5
Plymouth Co., MA

G6, $3-$6
Plymouth Co., MA

G8, $3-$6
Plymouth Co., MA

G7, $4-$8
Plymouth Co., MA

G7, $4-$8
Northampton Co., PA

G7, $5-$10
Plymouth Co., MA

G8, $8-$15
Plymouth Co., MA

G10, $25-$40
Norfolk Co., MA

G7, $4-$8
Chester Co., PA

LOCATION: Eastern to midwestern states. **DESCRIPTION:** A small size, triangular, eared point with a concave base. **I.D. KEY:** Small basal ears.

BREWERTON SIDE-NOTCHED - Late Archaic, 6000 - 4000 B.P.

(Also see Meadowood, Otter Creek, Perkiomen, Susquehanna Broad)

Vein quartz

Felsite

G5, $4-$8
Lycoming Co., PA

G4, $3-$6
Lycoming Co., PA

G4, $4-$8
Bres, CT

G5, $4-$8
Lycoming Co., PA

G8, $15-$25
Luzerne Co., PA

G7, $12-$20
Lycoming Co., PA

G4, $4-$8
3 Mile Isle, PA

G8, $15-$25
Lycoming Co., PA

G8, $8-$15
Luzerne Co., PA

G7, $8-$15
Lycoming Co., PA

LOCATION: Eastern to midwestern states. **DESCRIPTION:** A small size, thick, triangular point with shallow side notches and a concave to straight base. **I.D. KEY.** Small side notched point.

BRODHEAD SIDE-NOTCHED - Early Archaic , 9000 - 7000 B.P.

(Also see Bennington Quail Tail, Brewerton, Crooked Creek, Kiski, Lycoming Co. & St. Charles)

G5, $5-$10
Lycoming Co., PA

G7, $12-$20
Lancaster Co., PA

LOCATION: Northeastern states. **DESCRIPTION:** A medium size, side to corner notched point with an expanded, convex base. The notching occurs near the base and are wide. **I.D. KEY:** Wide notches, convex base.

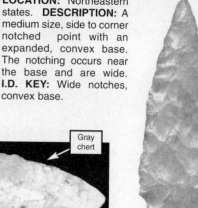

G7, $15-$25
PA

G7, $12-$20
Lycoming Co., PA

G6, $8-$15
Lycoming Co., PA

Gray chert

G7, $15-$25
Lycoming Co., PA

BURWELL - Late Archaic, 5000 - 4000 B.P.

LOCATION: Northeastern states. **DESCRIPTION:** A small size, parallel stemmed point with weak, tapered shoulders and a short blade. The base is concave. **I.D. KEY:** Broad, parallel stem, tapered shoulders.

G6, $4-$8
Washingtonboro, PA

CHARLESTON PINE TREE - Early Archaic, 8000 - 7000 B.P.

(Also see Arden, Kirk Corner Notched, Lycoming Co., Oley, Palmer, Vestal Notched, Vosburg)

G3, $5-$10
Lycoming Co., PA

G6, $25-$40
Lycoming Co., PA

Oblique flaking & median ridge

Gray chert

G6, $35-$65
Mifflin Co., PA

G9, $35-$65
NY

Restored ear

G5, $25-$50
Lycoming Co., PA

LOCATION: Eastern to Southeastern states. The St. Albans site is in West Virginia. Points here were dated to 9,900 B.P. **DESCRIPTION:** A medium to large size, corner notched, usually serrated point with parallel flaking to the center of the blade forming a median ridge. The bases are ground and can be concave, convex, straight, bifurcated or auriculate. Called *Pine Tree* in the Southeast. **I.D. KEY:** Archaic flaking with long flakes to the center of the blade.

CHILLESQUAQUE SERIES - Mid Archaic, 6,000 - 5,000 B.P.

(Also see Lycoming County Series and Penn's Creek Series)

LOCATION: Northeastern states. **DESCRIPTION:** A small size, corner to side notched, basal notched, triangular to expanded stem point. Shoulders can be strong to tapered. **I.D. KEY.** Wide side to corner notches.

G5, $5-$10
Lancaster Co., PA

CLOVIS - Early Paleo, 11,500 - 10,600 B.P.

(Also see Crowfield, Cumberland, Debert, Holcomb & Redstone)

Onandaga flint

Onandaga flint

Flint

Flint

G3, $80-$150
Lancaster Co., PA

G5, $250-$400
Lycoming Co., PA

G5, $275-$500
Lycoming Co., PA

G5, $275-$500
York Co., PA

G5, $275-$500
Lycoming Co., PA

G5, $350-$600
Lycoming Co., PA

Serrations added by a later culture

Jasper

Crystal

G6, $450-$800
Columbia Co., PA

G6, $450-$800
Ontario, Canada

G6, $400-$700
S.E. PA

G6, $450-$800
Northampton Co., PA

G3, $250-$400
Franklin Co., PA

Onondaga flint

Gray flint

Fire damage

G7, $600-$1000
Lycoming Co., PA

G7, $800-$1500
Berk Co., PA

LOCATION: All of North America. **DESCRIPTION:** A medium to large size, auriculate, fluted, lanceolate point with convex sides and a concave base that is ground. Most examples are fluted on both sides about 1/3 the way up from the base. The flaking can be random to parallel. The oldest point type in the hemisphere. Materials used in this area are: Argillite, black flint, chalcedony, conglomerate, coshocton, coxsackie, jasper, Onondaga, quartz crystal, quartzite, rhyolite, shale & upper Mercer black chert. **I.D. KEY:** Auricles and fluting.

CLOVIS (continued)

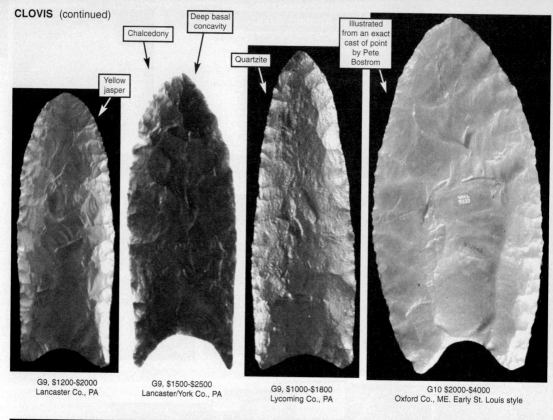

Yellow jasper

Chalcedony

Deep basal concavity

Quartzite

Illustrated from an exact cast of point by Pete Bostrom

G9, $1200-$2000
Lancaster Co., PA

G9, $1500-$2500
Lancaster/York Co., PA

G9, $1000-$1800
Lycoming Co., PA

G10 $2000-$4000
Oxford Co., ME. Early St. Louis style

CONODOQUINET/CANFIELD - Late Archaic, 4000 - 3500 B.P.

(Also see Dewart Stemmed, Duncan's Island, Lehigh, Lamoka, Morrow Mountain, Neville, Piscataway, Sandhill Stemmed)

Onandaga flint

Siltstone

Siltstone

G5, $4-$8
Lycoming Co., PA

Rhyolite

LOCATION: Northeastern states.
DESCRIPTION: A medium size, narrow, contracted stem point with sloping shoulders. Base is rounded to pointed.
I.D. KEY: Base form.

G5, $4-$8
Lycoming Co., PA

G5, $4-$8
Lycoming Co., PA

G6, $5-$10
Union Co., PA

Tip wear

G3, $4-$8
Lycoming Co., PA

G4, $4-$8
Lycoming Co., PA

Rhyolite

Rhyolite

110

CRESAP - Late Archaic to Woodland, 3000 - 2500 B.P.

(Also see Adena, Adena Robbins)

Felsite

G6, $35-$60
Bridgewater, MA

LOCATION: West Virginia, Kentucky, into Massachusetts. **DESCRIPTION:** A medium to large size point that has a medium-long contracting stem and slight shoulders. The base is usually straight. Stems can be ground. Associated with the early Adena culture. **I.D. KEY:** Long "squarish" tapered stem.

CROOKED CREEK SERIES - Archaic, 6000 - 4000 B.P.

(Also see Brewerton, Decatur, Dovetail, Kiski, Lycoming County and Palmer)

LOCATION: Northeastern states. **DESCRIPTION:** A small to medium size, short, corner to side notched point with a broad base that has rounded to squared corners. Shoulders are barbed to rounded. **I.D. KEY:** Short, notched point with a large base.

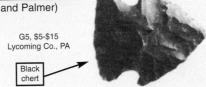

G5, $5-$15
Lycoming Co., PA

Black chert

CROWFIELD - Late Paleo, 11,000 - 10,000 B.P.

(Also see Clovis, Cumberland, Debert, Holcomb, Parallel Lanceolate, Plainview)

G6, $150-$250
Tioga Co., PA

All have ground stems and bases

Hand held to show quality and size

Restored tip

Flute channel

G8, $600-$1000
Chilhowie, VA

G8, $400-$750
NY

$400-$750
Chautauqua Co., NY

Extremely thin

Side wear

G8, $1000-$1750
Chautauqua Co., NY

G10, $1000-$1800
NY

Not fluted

CROWFIELD (continued)

Possible Hi-Lo type?

Multiple fluting

Flute channel

Black chert

Hand held to show quality and size

Multiple fluting

Broken & glued

Tip wear

G10, $1400-$2250
PA

G10+, $2500-$4500
Chautauqua Co., NY

G6 $2500-$3500
SW Ontario, Canada

G2, $2000-$3000
SW Ontario, Canada

LOCATION: Northeastern states. **DESCRIPTION:** A medium size,very thin, auriculate, fluted point with a concave base. Commonly multiple fluted and the basal area is ground. This point is widest near the tip. Believed to be later than *Clovis*. Cross section is as thin as *Folsoms*. **I.D. KEY:** Multiple flutes, blade form.

CUMBERLAND (Barnes) - Paleo, 11,250 - 10,000 B.P.

(Also see Beaver Lake, Clovis, Crowfield, Debert, Holcomb, Plainview, Redstone)

Black chert

Jasper

G7, $300-$500
PA

G7, $600-$1000
PA

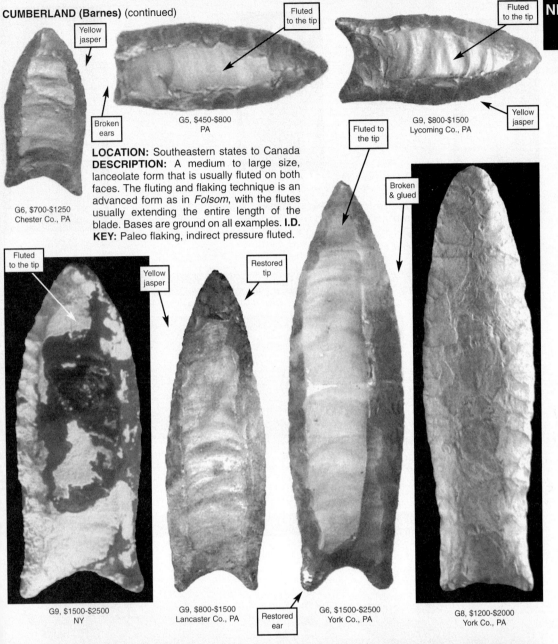

CUMBERLAND (Barnes) (continued)

Fluted to the tip

Yellow jasper

G5, $450-$800
PA

Fluted to the tip

Yellow jasper

G9, $800-$1500
Lycoming Co., PA

Broken ears

LOCATION: Southeastern states to Canada
DESCRIPTION: A medium to large size, lanceolate form that is usually fluted on both faces. The fluting and flaking technique is an advanced form as in *Folsom*, with the flutes usually extending the entire length of the blade. Bases are ground on all examples. **I.D. KEY:** Paleo flaking, indirect pressure fluted.

Fluted to the tip

Broken & glued

G6, $700-$1250
Chester Co., PA

Fluted to the tip

Yellow jasper

Restored tip

G9, $1500-$2500
NY

G9, $800-$1500
Lancaster Co., PA

Restored ear

G6, $1500-$2500
York Co., PA

G8, $1200-$2000
York Co., PA

DALTON CLASSIC - Early Archaic, 10,000 - 9200 B.P.

(Also see Clovis, Crowfield, Debert, Hardaway, Holcomb, Plainview)

Quartzite

Tip wear

G3, $25-$40
Lycoming Co., PA

Red jasper

G4, $40-$75
Jefferson Co., PA

Miilky quartz

G7, $30-$50
Plymouth Co., MA

DALTON CLASSIC (cont'd)

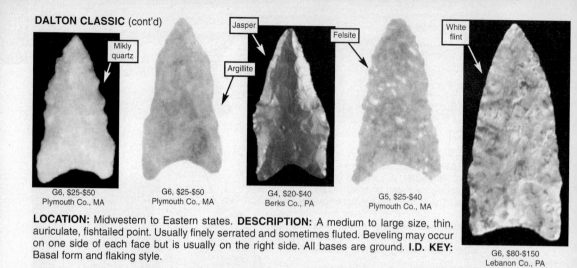

Mikly quartz

Jasper

Argillite

Felsite

White flint

G6, $25-$50
Plymouth Co., MA

G6, $25-$50
Plymouth Co., MA

G4, $20-$40
Berks Co., PA

G5, $25-$40
Plymouth Co., MA

G6, $80-$150
Lebanon Co., PA

LOCATION: Midwestern to Eastern states. **DESCRIPTION:** A medium to large size, thin, auriculate, fishtailed point. Usually finely serrated and sometimes fluted. Beveling may occur on one side of each face but is usually on the right side. All bases are ground. **I.D. KEY:** Basal form and flaking style.

DALTON-NUCKOLLS - Early Archaic, 10,000 - 9200 B.P.

(Also see Angostura, Dalton Classic, Plainview)

G10, $1200-$2000
Chester Co., PA, Yellow Jasper.

LOCATION: Midwestern to Northeastern states. Type site is in Humphreys Co., TN. **DESCRIPTION:** A medium to large size variant form, probably occuring from resharpening the *Greenbrier Dalton*. Bases are squared to lobbed to eared, and have a shallow concavity. Bases are ground and some examples are fluted. **I.D. KEY:** Broad base and shoulders, flaking on blade.

DEBERT - Paleo, 11,000 - 9500 B. P.

(Also see Clovis, Crowfield, Cumberland, Dalton, Holcomb)

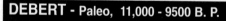

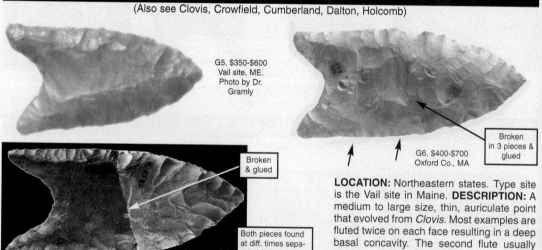

G5, $350-$600
Vail site, ME.
Photo by Dr.
Gramly

Broken
& glued

Broken
in 3 pieces &
glued

G6, $400-$700
Oxford Co., MA

Both pieces found
at diff. times sepa-
rated from kill and
camp site. Note
patination variation.

G6, $600-$1000
Vail Debert site, ME, Photo courtesy Dr. R.M. Gramly.

LOCATION: Northeastern states. Type site is the Vail site in Maine. **DESCRIPTION:** A medium to large size, thin, auriculate point that evolved from *Clovis*. Most examples are fluted twice on each face resulting in a deep basal concavity. The second flute usually removed traces of the first fluting. A very rare form of late *Clovis*. **I.D. KEY:** Deep basal notch.

G2, $125-$200
Vail site, ME. Photo by Dr. Gramly

$40-$75
Vail site, ME. Photo by Dr. Gramly

G10, $2800-$4500
Oxford Co., ME (St. Louis style)

G9, $2500-$4000
Snyder Co., PA. Yellow Jasper.

Fluting channel

Note deeply indented bases

Classic form

Broken with two pieces

Broken with two pieces

DECATUR - Early Archaic, 9000 - 3000 B.P.

(Also see Charleston Pine Tree, Dovetail, Kirk, Kiski, Lost Lake, Palmer)

Gray flint *Tip damage* *Gray flint* *Restored tip* *Fractured base*

Fractured base

G2, $3-$5
Lancaster Co., PA

G5, $25-$40
Northumberland Co., PA

G2, $5-10
Lycoming Co., PA

G7, $125-$200
Union Co., PA

Gray flint *Fractured base*

G6, $25-$45
Northumberland Co., PA

LOCATION: Eastern states. **DESCRIPTION:** A small to medium size, thin, serrated, corner notched point that is usually beveled on one side of each face. The base is usually broken off (fractured) by a blow inward from each corner of the stem. Sometimes the sides of the stem and backs of the tangs are also fractured, and rarely the tip may be fractured by a blow on each side directed towards the base. Bases are usually ground and flaking is of high quality. **I.D. KEY:** Squared base, one barb shoulder.

115

DEWART STEMMED - Late Archaic, 5000 - 2500 B.P.

(Also see Bare Island, Duncan's Island, Garver's Ferry, Lamoka, Merrimack, Neville, Piney Island)

G4, $3-$5
Divers Isle, PA

G4, $4-$8
Peach Bottom, PA

G4, $4-$8
Northumberland Co., PA

G6, $5-$10
Northumberland Co., PA

G6, $5-$10
Lycoming Co., PA

LOCATION: Northeastern states. **DESCRIPTION:** A medium size, narrow, stemmed point with strong shoulders. Tips are sharp and the stem is parallel to contracting. The base is normally unfinished. **I.D. KEY:** Unfinished base.

DOVETAIL (See St. Charles)

DRILL - Paleo to Historic, 11,500 - 200 B.P.

(Also see Graver, Randolph and Scraper)

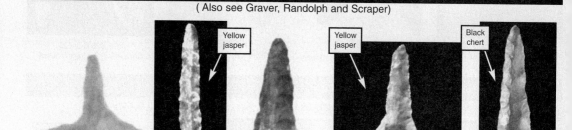

G3, $8-$15
Plymouth Co., MA

G4, $20-$35
Lycoming Co., PA

G3, $12-$20
Columbia Co., NY

G3, $20-$35
Monmouth Co., NJ

G5, $20-$35
Lycoming Co., PA

G3, $5-$10
Plymouth Co., MA

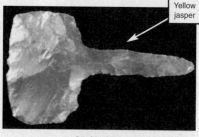

G5, $25-$40
Carbon Co., PA

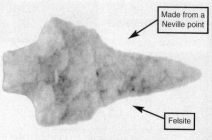

G5, $20-$35
Plymouth Co., MA

LOCATION: Everywhere. **DESCRIPTION:** Although many drills were made from scratch, all point types ended up in the drill form. Usually, heavily resharpened and broken points were salvaged and rechipped into drills. These objects were certainly used as drills (evidence of extreme edge wear), but there is speculation that some of these forms may have been used as pins for clothing, ornaments, ear plugs and other uses. **I.D. KEY:** Very narrow blade form.

116

DRILL (continued)

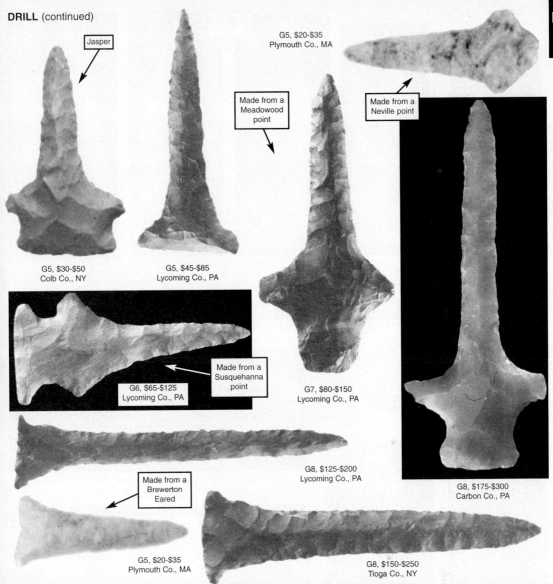

Jasper

G5, $30-$50
Colb Co., NY

G5, $45-$85
Lycoming Co., PA

Made from a
Meadowood
point

G5, $20-$35
Plymouth Co., MA

Made from a
Neville point

Made from a
Susquehanna
point

G6, $65-$125
Lycoming Co., PA

G7, $80-$150
Lycoming Co., PA

G8, $175-$300
Carbon Co., PA

Made from a
Brewerton
Eared

G8, $125-$200
Lycoming Co., PA

G5, $20-$35
Plymouth Co., MA

G8, $150-$250
Tioga Co., NY

DRYBROOK FISHTAIL - Late Archaic to Woodland, 3500 - 2500 B.P.

(Also see Forest Notched, Frost Island, Orient, Patuxent, Perkiomen, Susquehanna Broad)

G5, $12-$20
Centre Co., PA

Onondaga
flint

LOCATION: Northeastern states. **DESCRIPTION:** A medium size, narrow, triangular point that expands towards the base. Shoulders are rounded and taper into an expanded base. The base is straight to concave. Some examples have basal ears that are rounded to pointed. **I.D. KEY:** Basal form, rounded shoulders.

G3, $5-$10
Forge Isle, PA

G4, $8-$15
Luzurne Co., PA

G7, $20-$35
Lycoming Co., PA

DRYBROOK FISHTAIL
(continued)

Onondaga flint

G6, $25-$40
Union Co., PA

G7, $30-$50
Centre Co., PA

G7, $35-$60
Lycoming Co., PA

G6, $35-$60
Lancaster Co., PA

G8, $40-$70
Columbia Co., PA

DUNCAN'S ISLAND - Mid to late Archaic, 6000 - 4000 B. P.

(Also see Bare Island, Dewart Stemmed, Neville, Newmanstown, Piedmont, Piney Island)

G4, $5-$10
NY

Quartzite

Quartzite

G8, $30-$50
PA

Quartzite

Quartzite

G8, $30-$55
PA

G5, $18-$30
Lancaster Co., PA

G7, $20-$35
Montgomery Co., PA

Argillite

G6, $40-$75
PA

LOCATION: Northeastern states. **DESCRIPTION:** A medium to large size stemmed point with convex sides and a medium length square stem. The base is usually straight to slightly convex. Shoulders are straight to tapered. **I.D. KEY:** Square stem.

ERB BASAL NOTCHED - Mid-Woodland, 2000 - 1200 B.P.

(Also see Eshback, Oley)

G5, $8-$15
NJ/PA

Quartz

Quartzite

Quartz

G8, $15-$30
Montgomery Co., PA

G6, $12-$20
Union Co., PA

G6, $12-$20
NJ/PA

G8, $30-$50
Luzurne Co., PA

G7, $25-$40
Centre Co., PA

G7, $25-$40
Union Co., PA

LOCATION: Northeastern states. **DESCRIPTION:** A small to medium size, broad, basal notched point. Tangs can drop even with or below the base. **I.D. KEY:** Basal form.

ERIE TRIANGLE - Late Woodland, 1500 - 200 B.P.

(Also see Levanna, Madison, Susquehannock Triangle, Yadkin)

LOCATION: Northeastern states. **DESCRIPTION:** A small size, thin, triangular point with sharp basal corners and a straight to concave base. **I.D. KEY:** Triangular form.

G5, $3-$8
Lycoming Co., PA

ESHBACK - Late Archaic, 5500 - 3500 B.P.

(Also see Erb Basal Notched, Oley)

G4, $8-$15
Monroe Co., PA

G6, $15-$25
Northampton Co., PA

G7, $30-$50
Northampton Co., PA

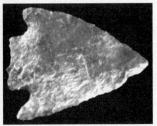

G8, $35-$60
Lycoming Co., PA

G6, $12-$20
Lycoming Co., PA

119

ESHBACK(continued)

LOCATION: Northeastern states. **DESCRIPTION:** A small to medium size, broad, basal notched point. Tangs can extend beyond the base. Bases are straight, concave or convex. Similar to *Eva* points found in the Southeast. **I.D. KEY:** Basal form.

G7, $20-$35
Lycoming Co., PA

Vein quartz

G9, $40-$70
Montgomery Co., PA

EXOTIC - Mid-Archaic to Mississippian, 5000 - 1000 B.P.

Double notching

LOCATION: Throughout North America. **DESCRIPTION:** Many of these forms are altered, known point types. Others resemble animal effigy forms while others may be no more than unfinished and unintentional doodles.

G9, $40-$70
PA

FOREST NOTCHED - Early Woodland, 3000 - 2000 B.P.

(Also see Drybrook, Frost Island, Orient, Patuxent, Perkiomen and Susquehanna Broad, Table Rock)

LOCATION: Northeastern. **DESCRIPTION:** A medium size, narrow point with very wide side notches. The basal area is relatively long and expands. The base is straight. Shoulders are rounded. **I.D. KEY:** Base form and rounded shoulders.

G6, $5-$15
Clinton Co., PA

FOX CREEK - Woodland, 2500 - 1200 B.P.

(Also see Dalton and Savannah River)

Rhyolite

Purple argilite

Base nick

Shale

G3, $6-$12
Union Co., PA

G4, $6-$12
Lycoming Co., PA

G3, $5-$10
Northumberland Co., PA

G3, $6-$12
Lycoming Co., PA

LOCATION: Northeastern states. **DESCRIPTION:** A medium size blade with a squared to tapered hafting area and a straight to concave base. Shoulders, when present are very weak and tapered. **I.D. KEY:** Basal form.

120

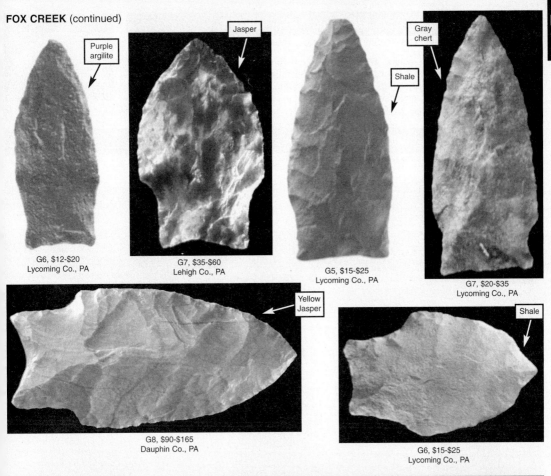

G6, $12-$20
Lycoming Co., PA

G7, $35-$60
Lehigh Co., PA

G5, $15-$25
Lycoming Co., PA

G7, $20-$35
Lycoming Co., PA

G8, $90-$165
Dauphin Co., PA

G6, $15-$25
Lycoming Co., PA

FROST ISLAND - Late Archaic - Early Woodland, 3200 - 2500 B.P.

(Also see Drybrook, Forest Notched, Orient, Patuxent, Perkiomen, Susquehanna Broad)

G6, $15-$25
Lycoming Co., PA

G6, $15-$25
Lycoming Co., PA

G6, $15-$25
Centre Co., PA

G6, $15-$30
Lycoming Co., PA

G7, $30-$50
Clinton Co., PA

LOCATION: Northeastern states. **DESCRIPTION:** A medium to large size expanded stem point with rounded shoulders. Side notches are broader than the *Forest Notched* type. **I.D. KEY:** Long expanded base, rounded shoulders.

121

GARVER'S FERRY - Late Woodland, 1800 - 1300 B.P.

(Also see Crooked Creek, Dewart Stemmed, Lamoka, Merrimack, Neville, Wading River)

LOCATION: Northeastern states. **DESCRIPTION:** A small size dart point with a short stem that is slightly expanding. The base is straight. Some examples are corner notched. **I.D. KEY:** Basal form, early flaking. **I.D. KEY:** Expanded stem, small size.

G6, $5-$10
Lycoming Co., PA.
Red Jasper.

GENESEE - Late Archaic,   5000 - 4000 B.P.

(Also see Bare Island, Neville, Newmanstown, and Piedmont)

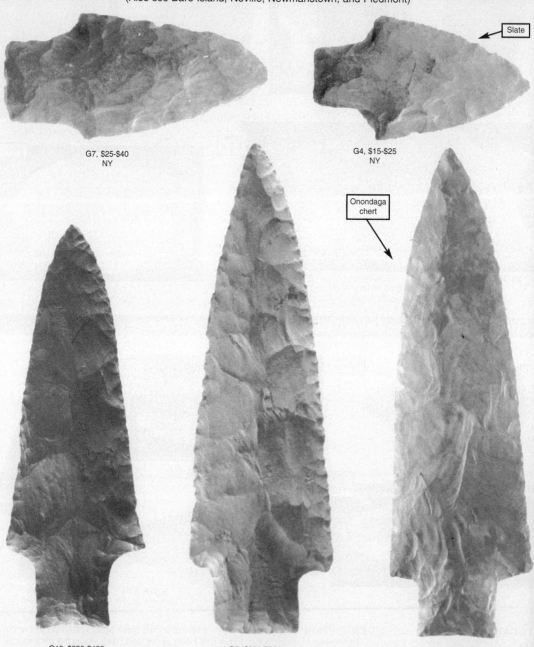

Slate

G7, $25-$40
NY

G4, $15-$25
NY

Onondaga chert

G10, $250-$400
NY

G9, $200-$350
NY

G10, $250-$450
Lancaster Co., PA

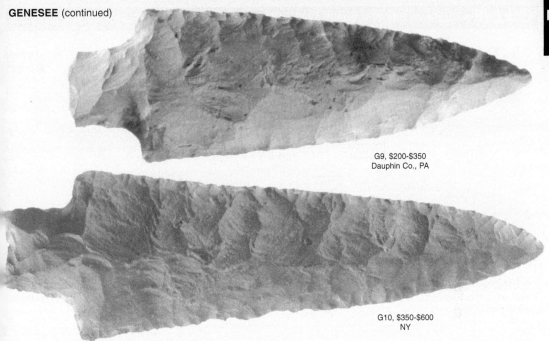

G9, $200-$350
Dauphin Co., PA

G10, $350-$600
NY

LOCATION: Northeastern states. Named for the Genesee Valley located in New York state. **DESCRIPTION:** A medium to large size point with prominent shoulders, a thick cross section and a squarish base. Shoulders can be straight to tapered to slightly barbed. Basal area can be ground. **I.D. KEY:** Squarish stem, strong shoulders.

GODDARD - Mississippian, 1000 - 800 B.P.

(Also see Jacks Reef & Raccoon Notched)

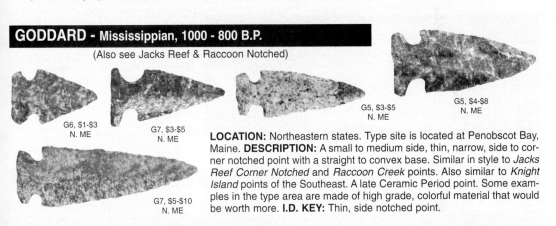

G6, $1-$3
N. ME

G7, $3-$5
N. ME

G5, $3-$5
N. ME

G5, $4-$8
N. ME

G7, $5-$10
N. ME

LOCATION: Northeastern states. Type site is located at Penobscot Bay, Maine. **DESCRIPTION:** A small to medium side, thin, narrow, side to corner notched point with a straight to convex base. Similar in style to *Jacks Reef Corner Notched* and *Raccoon Creek* points. Also similar to *Knight Island* points of the Southeast. A late Ceramic Period point. Some examples in the type area are made of high grade, colorful material that would be worth more. **I.D. KEY:** Thin, side notched point.

GRAVER - Paleo to Archaic, 11,500 - 4000 B.P.

(Also see Drill & Scraper)

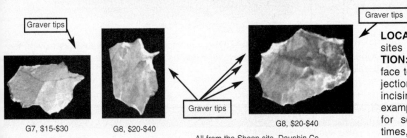

Graver tips

Graver tips

Graver tips

Graver tips

G7, $15-$30

G8, $20-$40

G8, $20-$40

All from the Shoop site, Dauphin Co., PA. Onondaga chert.

LOCATION: Paleo and Archaic sites everywhere **DESCRIPTION:** An irregular shaped uniface tool with sharp, pointed projections used for puncturing, incising, tattooing, etc. Some examples served a dual purpose for scraping as well. In later times, *Perforators* took the place of *Gravers*.

GREENE - Middle to late Woodland, 1700 - 1200 B.P.

(Also see Agate Basin, Angostura, Eden & Mansion Inn)

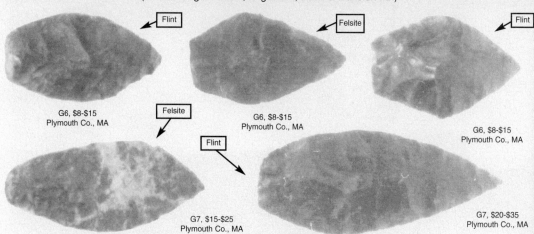

Flint

Felsite

Flint

G6, $8-$15
Plymouth Co., MA

Felsite

G6, $8-$15
Plymouth Co., MA

Flint

G6, $8-$15
Plymouth Co., MA

G7, $15-$25
Plymouth Co., MA

G7, $20-$35
Plymouth Co., MA

LOCATION: New York into Massachusetts and Connecticut. **DESCRIPTION:** A medium size, fairly broad lanceolate point with a tapering basal area and a straight base. Some examples form a pentagonal shape. **I.D. KEY:** Ovate to pentagonal form.

GROUND SLATE - Archaic, 6000 - 4500 B.P.

(Also see Bare Island)

LOCATION: Northeastern states. **DESCRIPTION:** A large size stemmed point completely ground from slate. Bases vary from expanding to contracting. Often found with notches in the stem. Examples of facial grinding of flaked Paleo and Archaic points have been found in the Eastern U.S.

G6, $125-$200
New England

GUILFORD - Middle Archaic, 6500 - 5000 B.P.

(Also see Agate Basin)

Round base form

Guilford Yuma form

G6, $15-$25
MD

G7, $8-$15
NY

LOCATION: Eastern seaboard to Northeastern states. **DESCRIPTION:** A medium to large size, thick, narrow lanceolate point. The base varies from round to straight to eared. Another variation has weak shoulders defining a stemmed area. **I.D. KEY:** Thickness, early parallel flaking.

HARDAWAY - Early Archaic 9500 - 8000 B.P.

(Also see Dalton-Greenbrier and Palmer)

HARDAWAY (continued)

G7, $55-$100
Taunton, MA

Felsite

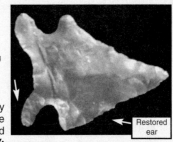

G3, $10-$20
Lycoming Co., PA.
Yellow Jasper.

Restored ear

LOCATION: Eastern states. Type site is in Stanly Co., NC, Yadkin River. Very rare in Northeast. **DESCRIPTION:** A small to medium size point with shallow side notches and expanded auricles forming a wide, deeply concave base. Ears and base are usually ground. This type evolved from the *Dalton* point. **I.D. KEY:** Eared form, heavy grinding in shoulders, paleo parallel flaking.

HAW RIVER - Transitional Paleo, 11,000 - 8000 B.P.

LOCATION: Eastern seaboard to Northeastern states. **DESCRIPTION:** A medium to large size, broad, elliptical blade with a basal notch and usually rounded barbs that turn inward. **I.D. KEY:** Notched base.

G8, $40-$75
NY

HELLGRAMITE - Early Woodland, 3000 - 2500 B.P.

(Also see Brewerton, Kessel, Kirk, Meadowood)

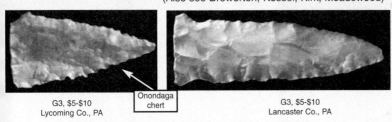

G3, $5-$10
Lycoming Co., PA

Onondaga chert

G3, $5-$10
Lancaster Co., PA

LOCATION: Northeastern states. **DESCRIPTION:** A small to medium size triangular point with very weak side notches. The blade edges are finely serrated and the base is straight to convex. **I.D. KEY:** Weak notches, serrated edges.

HOLCOMB - Paleo, 11,000 - 10,000 B.P.

(Also see Clovis, Crowfield, Cumberland, Dalton, Debert, Plainview)

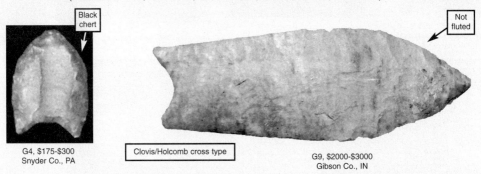

Black chert

G4, $175-$300
Snyder Co., PA

Clovis/Holcomb cross type

Not fluted

G9, $2000-$3000
Gibson Co., IN

LOCATION: Northeastern states. **DESCRIPTION:** A small to medium size, thin, fluted point with a concave base. Basal area is ground. More than one fluting strike is common. **I.D. KEY:** Small fluted point.

HOLCOMB (continued)

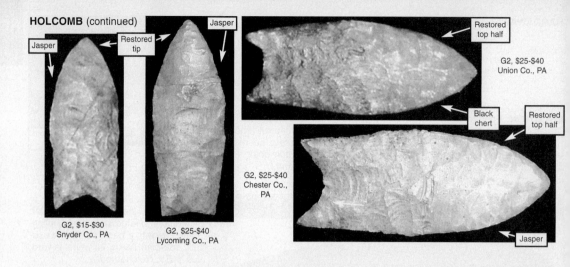

Jasper

Restored tip

Jasper

Restored top half

G2, $25-$40
Union Co., PA

Black chert

Restored top half

Jasper

G2, $15-$30
Snyder Co., PA

G2, $25-$40
Lycoming Co., PA

G2, $25-$40
Chester Co., PA

HOOVER'S ISLAND - Archaic, 6000 - 4000 B.P.

(Also see Bare Island, Duncan's Island, Genesee, Lackawaxen, Newmanstown, Patuxent, Piedmont, Piney Island)

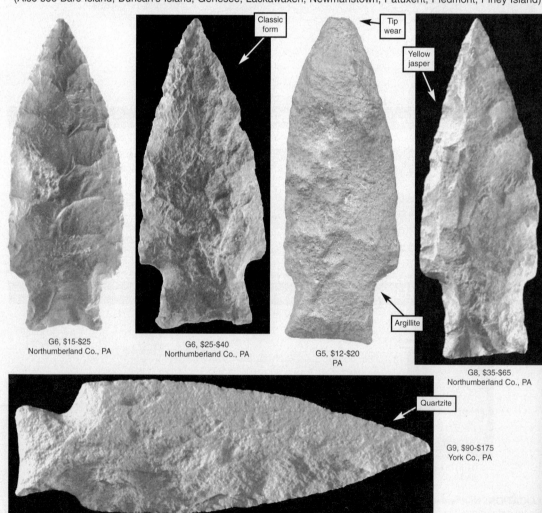

Classic form

Tip wear

Yellow jasper

Argillite

G6, $15-$25
Northumberland Co., PA

G6, $25-$40
Northumberland Co., PA

G5, $12-$20
PA

G8, $35-$65
Northumberland Co., PA

Quartzite

G9, $90-$175
York Co., PA

HOOVER'S ISLAND (continued)

LOCATION: Pennsylvania to northern Maryland. **DESCRIPTION:** A medium to large size, broad, expanded to parallel stemmed point. Bases are straight to concave. Basal corners are sharp. Shoulders are tapered to rounded. **I.D. KEY:** Sharp basal corners, tapered shoulders. Belongs to the Piedmont series and is also known as *Southern Piedmont*.

HOPEWELL - Woodland, 2500 - 1500 B.P.

(Also see Brewerton, Normanskill)

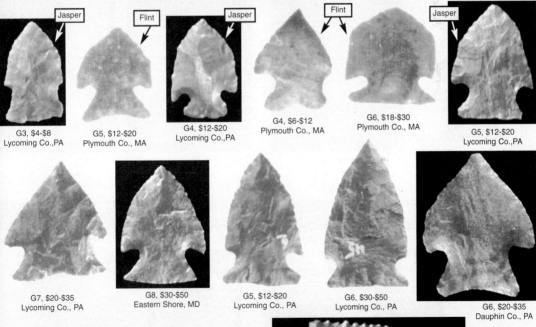

Preform

G6, $15-$30
Lycoming Co., PA

G5, $25-$40
PA

LOCATION: Midwestern to eastern states. **DESCRIPTION:** A large size, broad, corner notched point that is similar to *Snyders*. Made by the Hopewell culture.

JACKS REEF CORNER NOTCHED - Late Woodland to Mississippian, 1500 - 1000 B.P.

(Also see Kiski, Lycoming Co., Oley, Palmer, Raccoon Notched, Vosburg)

Jasper

Flint

Jasper

Flint

Jasper

G3, $4-$8
Lycoming Co.,PA

G5, $12-$20
Plymouth Co., MA

G4, $12-$20
Lycoming Co.,PA

G4, $6-$12
Plymouth Co., MA

G6, $18-$30
Plymouth Co., MA

G5, $12-$20
Lycoming Co.,PA

G7, $20-$35
Lycoming Co., PA

G8, $30-$50
Eastern Shore, MD

G5, $12-$20
Lycoming Co., PA

G6, $30-$50
Lycoming Co., PA

G6, $20-$35
Dauphin Co., PA

LOCATION: Southeastern to Northeastern states. **DESCRIPTION:** A small to medium size, very thin, corner notched point that is well made. The blade is convex to pentagonal. Some examples are widely corner notched and appear to be expanded stem points with barbed shoulders. **I.D. KEY:** Thinness, sharp corners.

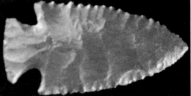

G7, $30-$50
Northumberton
Co., PA

JACKS REEF CORNER NOTCHED (continued)

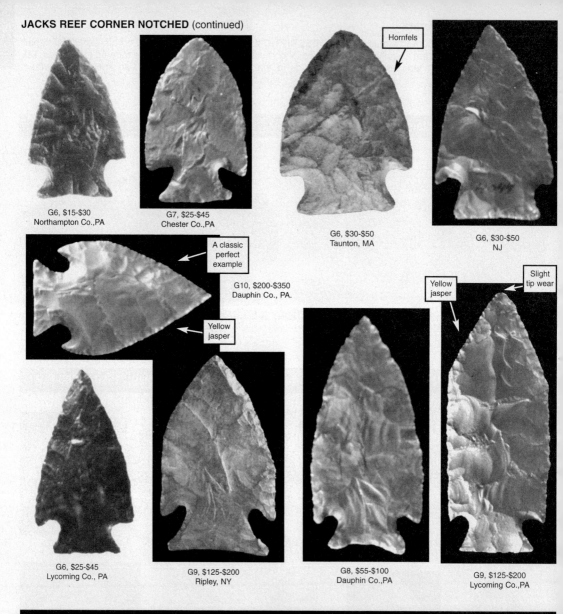

Hornfels

G6, $15-$30
Northampton Co.,PA

G7, $25-$45
Chester Co.,PA

G6, $30-$50
Taunton, MA

G6, $30-$50
NJ

A classic perfect example

G10, $200-$350
Dauphin Co., PA.

Yellow jasper

Yellow jasper

Slight tip wear

G6, $25-$45
Lycoming Co., PA

G9, $125-$200
Ripley, NY

G8, $55-$100
Dauphin Co.,PA

G9, $125-$200
Lycoming Co.,PA

JACKS REEF PENTAGONAL - Late Woodland to Mississippian, 1500 - 1000 B.P.

(Also see Erie Triangle, Levanna, Madison, Susquehannock Triangle)

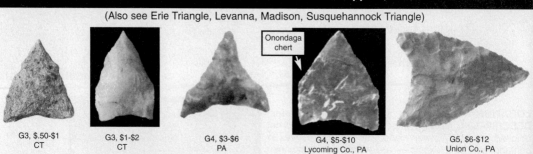

Onondaga chert

G3, $.50-$1
CT

G3, $1-$2
CT

G4, $3-$6
PA

G4, $5-$10
Lycoming Co., PA

G5, $6-$12
Union Co., PA

LOCATION: Southeastern to Northeastern states. **DESCRIPTION:** A small to large size, very thin, five sided point with a sharp tip. The hafting area is usually contracted with a slightly concave to straight base. This type is called *Pee Dee* in North and South Carolina. **I.D. KEY:** Pentagonal form.

JACKS REEF PENTAGONAL (continued)

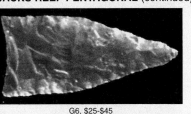

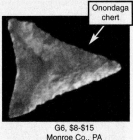

Onondaga chert

G6, $25-$45
Lycoming Co., PA

G6, $8-$15
Monroe Co., PA

G6, $25-$45
Centre Co., PA

Slight tip nick

JIM THORPE - Archaic, 6000 - 4000 B.P.

(Also see Brodhead and Piedmont)

LOCATION: Pennsylvania. **DESCRIPTION:** A medium size, side notched point with tapered to square shoulders and a bulbous stem. The base is convex and the side notches are broad. Random flaking was employed. **I.D. KEY:** Bulbous stem.

G6, $25-$40
PA

KANAWHA - Early Archaic, 9000 - 5000 B.P.

(Also see Kirk Serrated, Lake Erie, LeCroy, MacCorkle, St. Albans, Stanly, Susquehanna Birfurcate)

G5, $12-$20
Union Co., PA

G6, $18-$30
Chester Co., PA

LOCATION: Southeastern to Northeastern states. Type site is in Kanawha Co., WVA. **DESCRIPTION:** A small to medium size, fairly thick, shallowly bifurcated stemmed point. The basal lobes are usually rounded and the shoulders are tapered. Believed to be the ancestor to the *Stanly* type. Very similar to the *Fox Valley* point found in Illinois. Shoulders can be clipped wing, turning towards the tip. **I.D. KEY:** Archaic flaking, weak basal lobes.

KESSEL - Early Archaic, 10,000 - 8000 B.P.

(Also see Cache River, Goddard, Hellgramite, Meadowood, Raccoon Notched)

Black chert

G8, $35-$65
W. PA

LOCATION: Northeastern states. **DESCRIPTION:** A medium to large size, thin, triangular side notched point. Notches are close to the base, are very narrow and angle in from the sides. The base is concave. Almost identical in form and age to the *Cache River* type from Arkansas. **I.D. KEY:** Basal notches, thinness.

G7, $60-$100
Burlington Co., NJ

KIRK CORNER NOTCHED - Early to mid-Archaic, 9000 - 6000 B.P.

(Also see Amos, Brewerton, Charleston Pine Tree, Crooked Creek, Kline & Palmer)

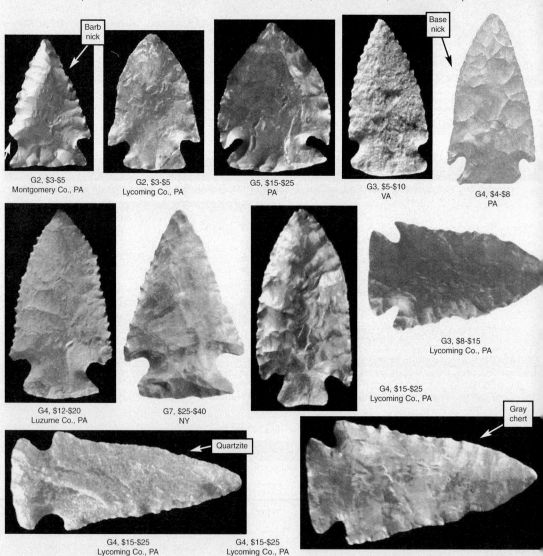

Barb nick

G2, $3-$5
Montgomery Co., PA

G2, $3-$5
Lycoming Co., PA

G5, $15-$25
PA

Base nick

G3, $5-$10
VA

G4, $4-$8
PA

G4, $12-$20
Luzurne Co., PA

G7, $25-$40
NY

G3, $8-$15
Lycoming Co., PA

G4, $15-$25
Lycoming Co., PA

Gray chert

Quartzite

G4, $15-$25
Lycoming Co., PA

G4, $15-$25
Lycoming Co., PA

LOCATION: Southeastern to Northeastern states. **DESCRIPTION:** A medium to large size, corner notched point. Blade edges can be convex to recurved and are finely serrated on many examples. The base can be convex, concave, straight, bifurcated or auriculate. Points that are beveled on one side of each face would fall under the *Lost Lake* or *Hardin* type. **I.D. KEY:** Secondary edgework.

KIRK CORNER NOTCHED (continued)

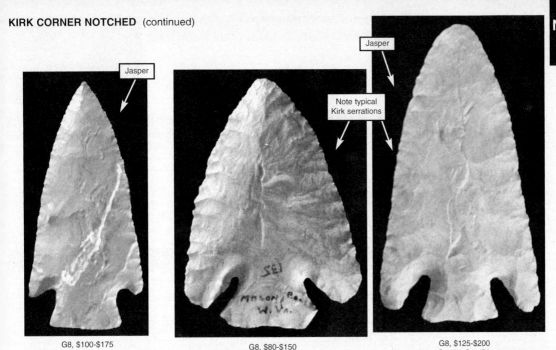

G8, $100-$175
Montgomery Co., PA

G8, $80-$150
Mason Co., WVA

G8, $125-$200
Snyder Co., PA

KIRK STEMMED - Early to mid-Archaic, 9000 - 6000 B.P.

(Also see Bare Island, Duncan's Island, Fountain Creek, Genesee, Heavy Duty, Lackawaxen, Neville, Newmanstown)

G3, $2-$5
Luzurne Co., PA

G5, $8-$15
MD

G6, $8-$15
Montour Co., PA

G6, $5-$10
Northumberland Co., PA

G5, $10-$20
Cent. PA

LOCATION: Eastern states. **DESCRIPTION:** A medium to large size, barbed, stemmed point with deep notches or fine serrations along the blade edges. The stem is parallel, contracting or expanding. The base can be concave, convex or straight, and can be very short. The shoulders are usually strongly barbed. This form is believed to have evolved into *Stanly* and other types. **I.D. KEY:** Serrations.

G6, $40-$75
Lycoming Co., PA

KISKI NOTCHED - Late Woodland, 2000 - 1400 B.P.

(Also see Brewerton, Crooked Creek, Jacks Reef, Lycoming Co., Palmer)

LOCATION: Northeastern states. **DESCRIPTION:** A small size side or corner notched point. **I.D. KEY:** Notching and size.

G4, $5-$10
Lycoming Co., PA

KITTATINY - Middle Archaic, 6000 - 5000 B.P.

(Also see Brewerton Eared, Jacks Reef Pentagonal, Levanna)

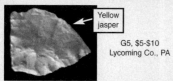

Yellow jasper

G5, $5-$10
Lycoming Co., PA

LOCATION: Northeastern states. **DESCRIPTION:** A small size lanceolate blade with recurved side edges. The base is straight, with the corners forming tiny ears. The stem is square to expanding. The *Nolichucky* type found in the Southeast is similar in outline. **I.D. KEY:** Triangular and basal form.

KLINE - Early Archaic, 9000 - 7000 B.P.

(Also see Brodhead Side Notched, Kirk, Lycoming Co., St. Charles, Susquehanna Broad)

Restored tip

Note early archaic parallel flaking

LOCATION: Northeastern states. **DESCRIPTION:** A medium to large size corner notched point with a convex base that is ground. Shoulders are strong and are horizontal to slightly barbed. Basal corners are rounded. **I.D. KEY:** Corner notching, early flaking.

G3, $8-$15
Lycoming Co., PA

G5, $25-$40
Lycoming Co., PA

KOENS CRISPIN - Late Archaic, 4000 - 3000 B.P.

(Also see Adena, Atlantic Phase Blade, Lehigh, Morrow Mountain, Poplar Island, Schuylkill, Virginsville)

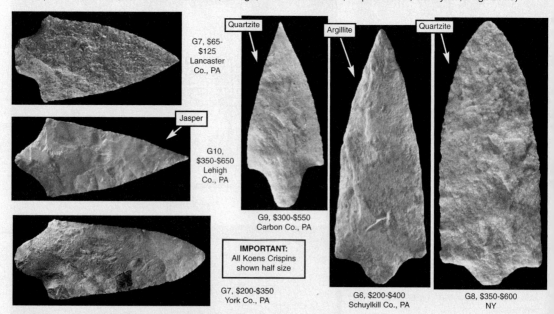

G7, $65-$125
Lancaster Co., PA

Quartzite

Argillite

Quartzite

Jasper

G10, $350-$650
Lehigh Co., PA

G9, $300-$550
Carbon Co., PA

IMPORTANT:
All Koens Crispins shown half size

G7, $200-$350
York Co., PA

G6, $200-$400
Schuylkill Co., PA

G8, $350-$600
NY

LOCATION: Northeastern states. **DESCRIPTION:** A medium to large size, broad, contracted stem point with a rounded base. Shoulders are tapered to straight. Generally poorer quality than the *Lehigh* type. **I.D. KEY:** Contracted stem, strong shoulders.

LACKAWAXEN - Archaic, 6000 - 4000 B.P.

(Also see Bare Island, Duncan's Island, Neville, Piedmont, Tocks Island)

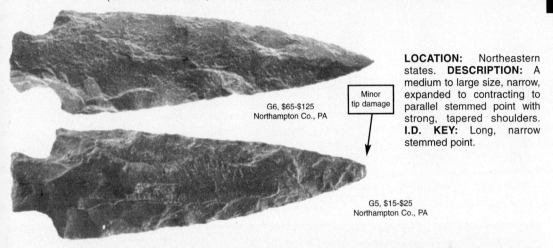

G6, $65-$125
Northampton Co., PA

Minor tip damage

LOCATION: Northeastern states. **DESCRIPTION:** A medium to large size, narrow, expanded to contracting to parallel stemmed point with strong, tapered shoulders. **I.D. KEY:** Long, narrow stemmed point.

G5, $15-$25
Northampton Co., PA

LAKE ERIE - Early to mid-Archaic, 9000 - 5000 B.P.

(Also see Erie Triangle, Fox Valley, Kirk-Bifurcated, LeCroy, MacCorkle, Penn's Creek, St. Albans, Stanly, Susquehanna Bifurcate)

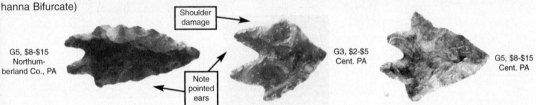

Shoulder damage

G5, $8-$15
Northumberland Co., PA

Note pointed ears

G3, $2-$5
Cent. PA

G5, $8-$15
Cent. PA

LOCATION: Northeastern states. **DESCRIPTION:** A small to medium size, thin, deeply notched or bifurcated stemmed point. The basal lobes are parallel with a tendency to turn inward and are pointed. The outward sides of the basal lobes are usually fractured from the base towards the tip and can be ground. **I.D. KEY:** Pointed basal lobes.

LAMOKA - Middle Archaic, 5500 - 4500 B.P.

(Also see Dewart Stemmed, Duncan's Island, Garver's Ferry, Merrimack, Neville, Piney Island, Randolph, Sandhill Stemmed, Wading River)

G4, $2-$4
Lycoming Co. PA

G4, $2-$4
Lycoming Co. PA

G4, $3-$6
Lycoming Co. PA

G4, $4-$8
Lycoming Co. PA

G6, $6-$12
Lycoming Co. PA

G5, $4-$8
NY

G6, $4-$8
NY

G6, $6-$12
Columbia Co., NY

LOCATION: Northeastern states. **DESCRIPTION:** A small to medium size, narrow, thick, spike point. The shoulders are tapered and the stem is square to contracting to expanding. The base on some examples shows the natural rind of the native material used. Called *Bradley Spike* in the Southeast. **I.D. KEY:** Thin, spike point.

G5, $6-$12
NJ

G6, $8-$15
Lycoming Co. PA

G6, $8-$15
Lycoming Co. PA

G6, $12-$20
PA

G8, $12-$20
Lycoming Co., PA

G8, $15-$25
PA

G8, $15-$25
Lycoming Co., PA

LECROY - Early to mid-Archaic, 9000 - 5000 B.P.

(Also see Decatur, Kanawha, Kirk Serrated, Lake Erie, MacCorkle, Charleston Pine Tree, St. Albans, Stanly, Susquehanna Bifurcate & Taunton River Bifurcate)

Resharpened many times

G5, $12-$20
Union Co., PA

G3, $4-$8
Northum. Co., PA

Jasper

G3, $4-$8
Lycoming Co., PA

Milky quartz

G3, $4-$8
Montgomery Co., PA

Tip wear

G5, $8-$15
Dauphin Co., PA

G6, $12-$20
Lycoming Co., PA

G6, $12-$20
Lycoming Co., PA

Jasper

G8, $15-$30
Monmouth Co., NJ

Serrated edge

G7, $15-$25
Union Co., PA

G6, $12-$20, NY

G5, $8-$15
Union Co., PA

Tip wear

G4, $5-$10
Lycoming Co., PA

G3, $5-$10
Northumb. Co., PA

Yellow jasper

G8, $15-$30
MD

Vein quartz

G7, $12-$20
Lancaster Co., PA

G7, $15-$30
Union Co., PA

LOCATION: Eastern states. Type site is in Hamilton Co., Tennessee. **DESCRIPTION:** A small to medium size, thin, bifurcated point with deeply notched or serrated blade edges. Basal ears can either droop or expand out. The base is usually large in comparison to the blade size. Bases can be ground. **I.D. KEY:** Basal form, thinness.

LEHIGH BROADPOINT - Late Archaic, 4000 - 3000 B.P.

(Also see Adena, Koens Crispin, Morrow Mountain, Poplar Island, Schuylkill, Virginsville)

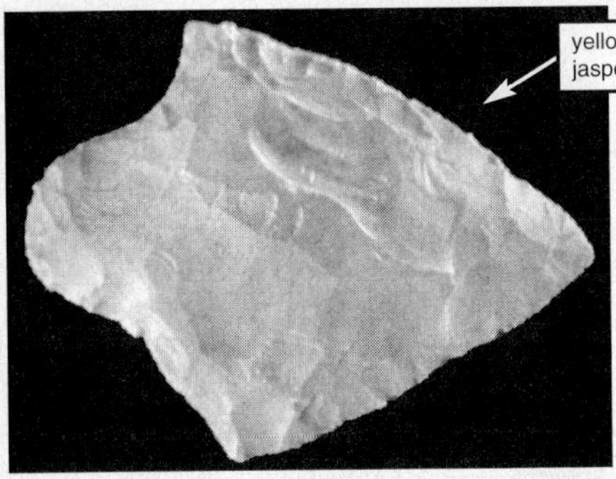
yellow
jasper

G5, $25-$40
Luzurne Co., PA

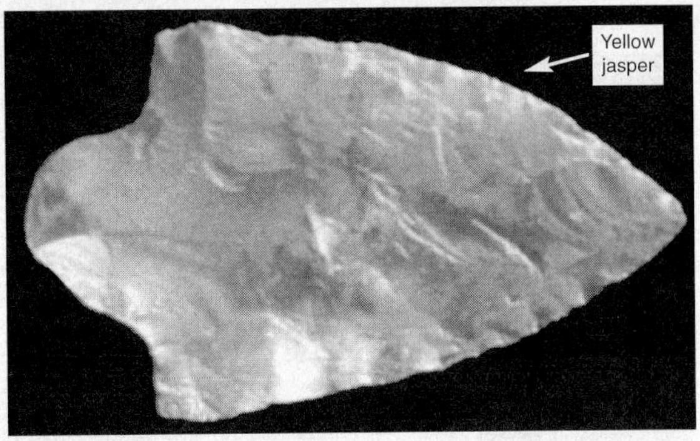
Yellow
jasper

G6, $65-$125
Lycoming Co., PA

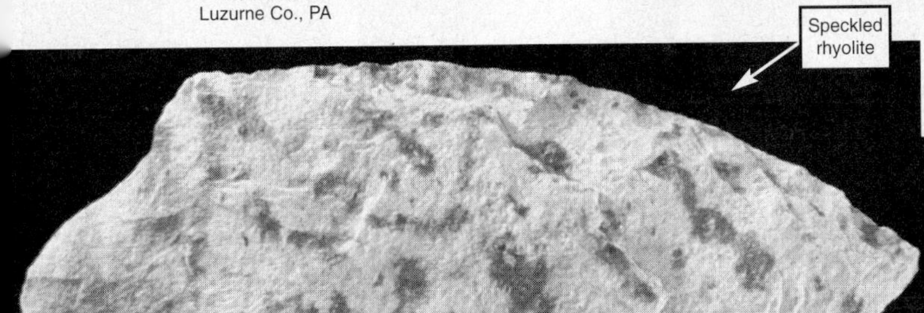
Speckled
rhyolite

G9, $150-$275
Lancaster Co., PA

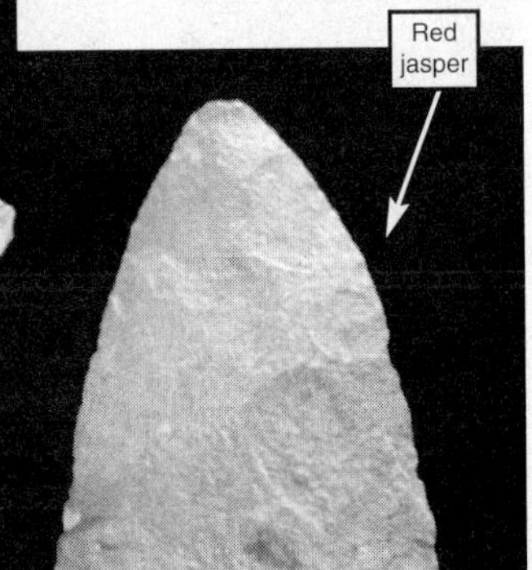
Red
jasper

G9, $125-$200
York Co., PA

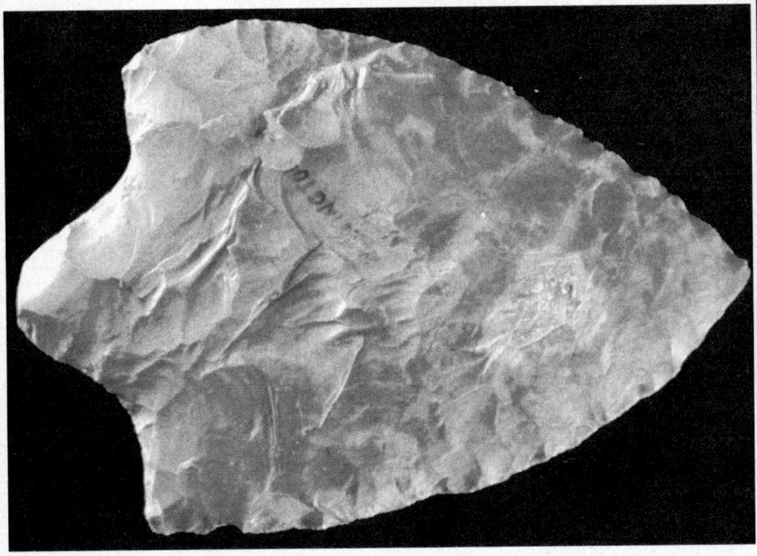

G9, $125-$200
Burlington Co., NJ

LOCATION: Northeastern states. **DESCRIPTION:** A medium to large size, broad, contracted to square stemmed point. Shoulders are horizontal to contracting. The base is straight to rounded. **I.D. KEY:** Broad, contracting stem.

LEVANNA - Late Woodland to Mississippian, 1300 - 600 B.P.

(Also see Madison, Susquehannock Triangle)

G4, $3-$6
NJ

G5, $4-$8
PA

Milky
quartz

G5, $4-$8
NJ

G6, $8-$15
PA

Tip
wear

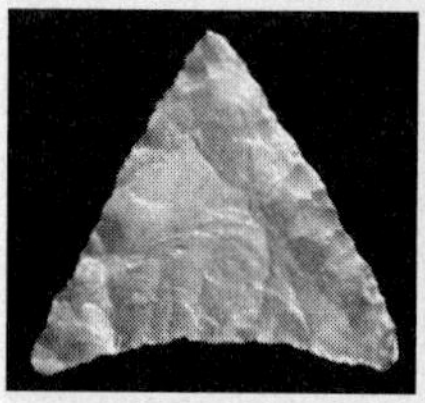

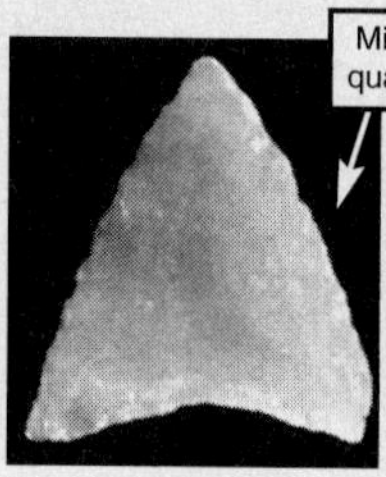

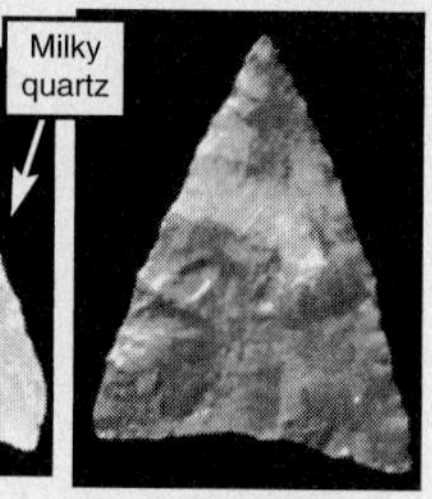

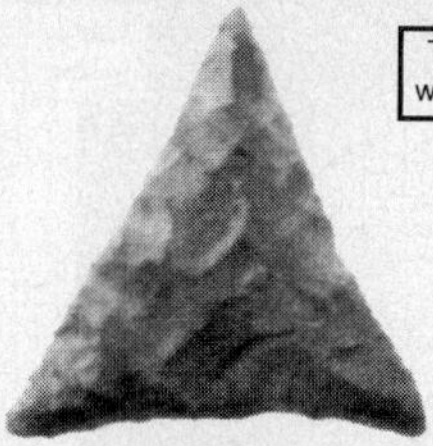

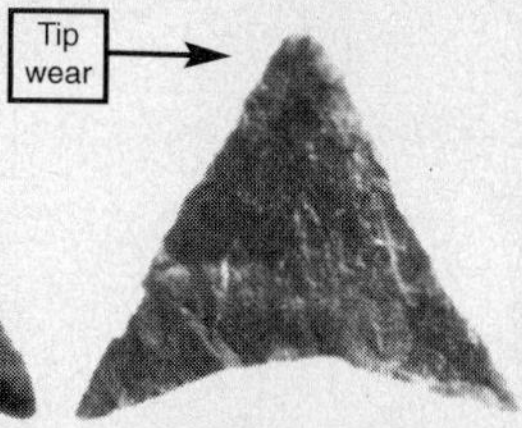

G3, $5-$10
Northumberland Co., PA

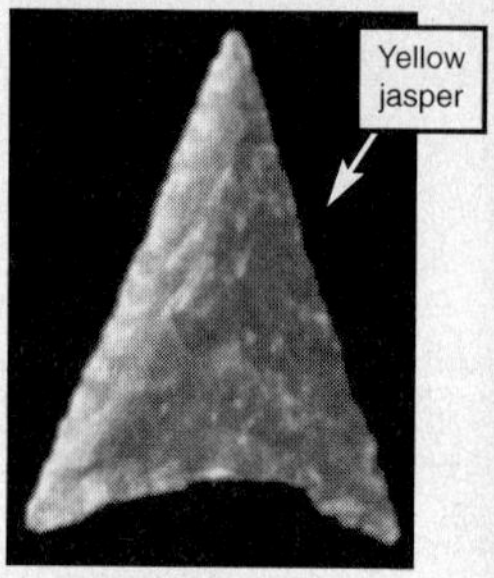

Yellow
jasper

G7, $15-$15
Lehigh Co., PA

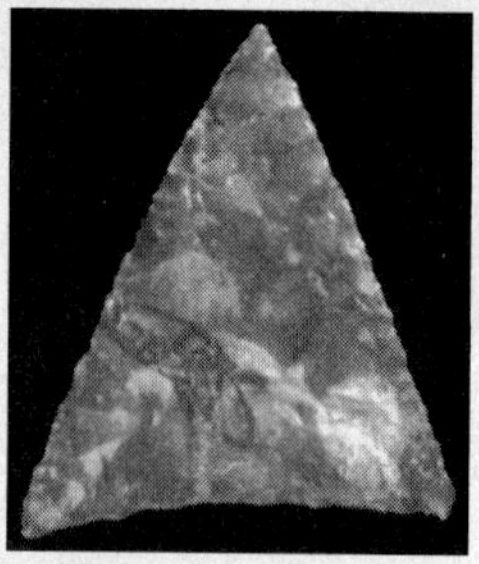

G7, $15-$20
Montgomery Co., PA

Quartzite

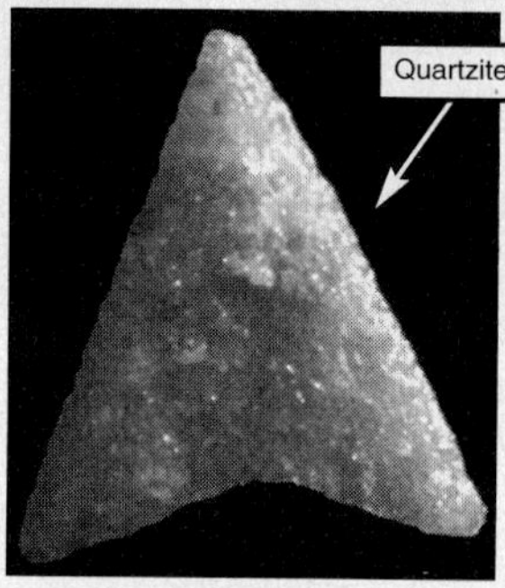

G7, $15-$30
Montgomery Co., PA

Yellow
jasper

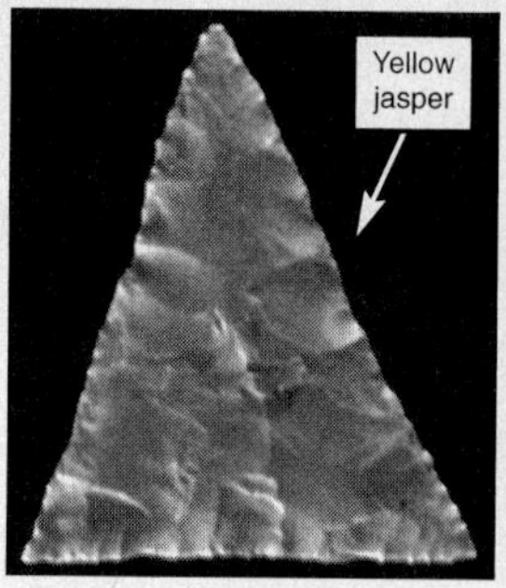

G8, $25-$40
Montgomery Co., PA

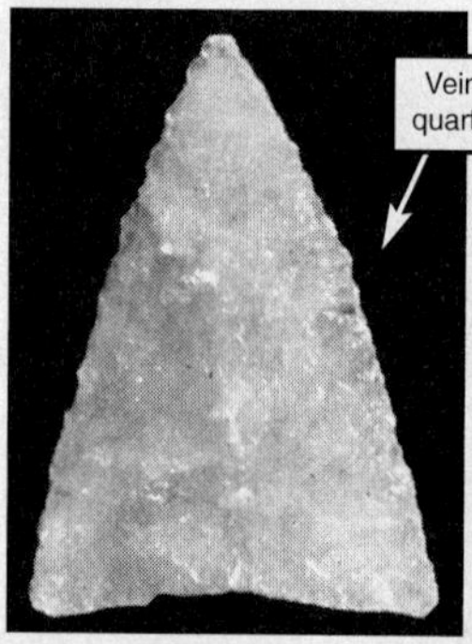

Vein
quartz

G8, $25-$40
MD

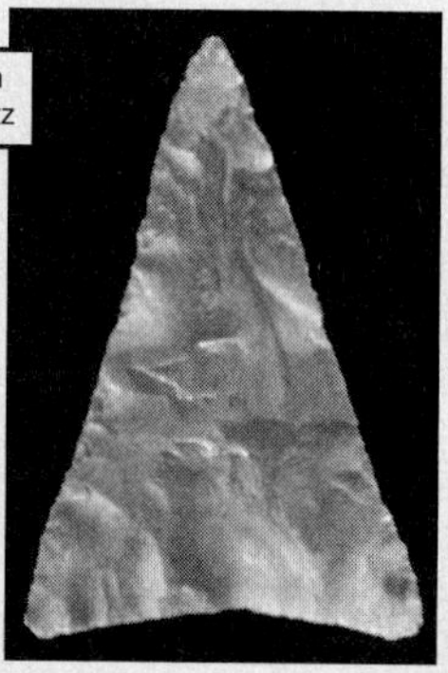

G8, $25-$40
Warren Co., NJ

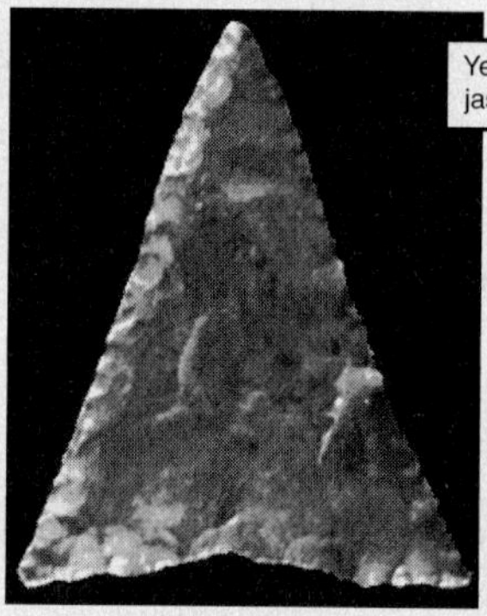

G9, $30-$50
Oswego Co., NY

Yellow
jasper

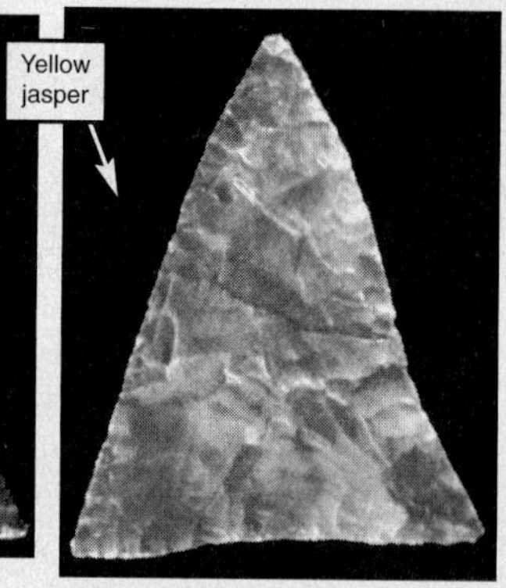

G9, $30-$50
Montgomery Co., PA

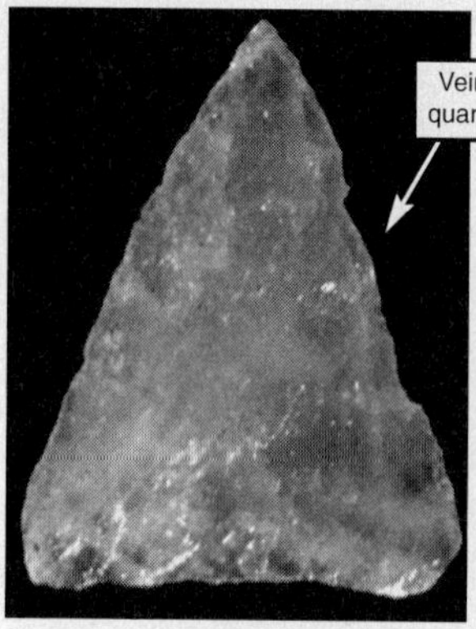

Vein
quartz

G5, $15-$25
Chester Co., PA

Vein
quartz

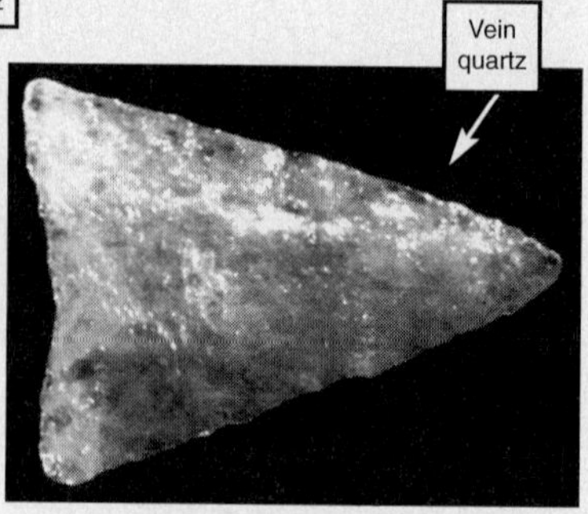

G6, $18-$30
Montgomery Co., PA

Felsite

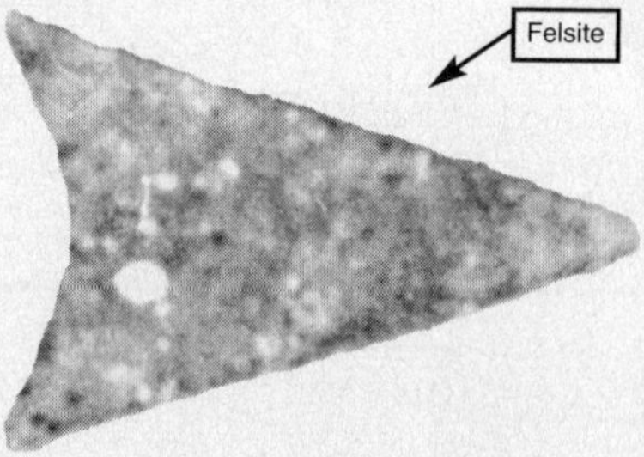

G7, $25-$40
Plymouth Co., MA

LOCATION: Northeastern states. **DESCRIPTION:** A small to medium size, thin, triangular point with a concave to straight base. Believed to be replaced by *Madison* points in later times. Some examples have the basal corners fractured. Called *Yadkin* in North Carolina. **I.D. KEY:** Medium thick cross section triangle.

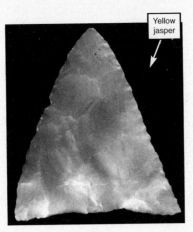

Yellow jasper

Side nick

G6, $30-$50
Montgomery Co., PA

G8, $65-$120
Burlington Co., NJ

G6, $30-$50
Columbia Co., PA

LOST LAKE - Early Archaic, 9000 - 6000 B.P.

(Also see Charleston Pine Tree, Decatur, Kirk, St. Charles and Thebes)

Beveled edge

Beveled edge

Note bevel on left side of each face

Resharpened many times

G6, $40-$75
W. PA

G6, $20-$35
NY

G6, $15-$25
NY

LOCATION: Southeastern, Midwestern to Northeastern states. **DESCRIPTION:** A medium to large size, broad, corner notched point that is beveled on one side of each face. Some examples are finely serrated. Bases are ground. Unbeveled examples would fall into the *Kirk Corner Notched* type. **I.D. KEY:** Notching and opposite beveled blade edge.

LYCOMING COUNTY SERIES - Middle Archaic, 6000 - 4000 B.P.

(Also see Brewerton, Crooked Creek, Garver's Ferry, Otter Creek, Penn's Creek)

LOCATION: Pennsylvania. **DESCRIPTION:** A local variation of the Brewerton type. A small to medium size point with strong shoulders. The series occurs as side notched, corner notched and stemmed forms.

Tip nick

Jasper

G3, $4-$8
Lycoming Co., PA

MacCORKLE - Early Archaic, 8000 - 6000 B.P.

(Also see Kanawha, Kirk Serrated, Lake Erie, LeCroy, St. Albans, Stanly, Susquehanna Bifurcate)

LOCATION: Midwestern to Eastern states. **DESCRIPTION:** A medium to large size, thin, usually serrated, widely corner notched point with large round ears and a deep notch in the center of the base. Bases are usually ground. Called *Nottoway River Bifurcate* in Virginia. **I.D. KEY:** Basal notching, early Archaic flaking.

MACCORKLE (continued)

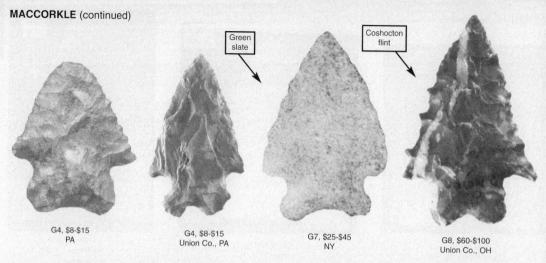

Green slate

Coshocton flint

G4, $8-$15
PA

G4, $8-$15
Union Co., PA

G7, $25-$45
NY

G8, $60-$100
Union Co., OH

MADISON - Mississippian, 1100 - 200 B.P.

(Also see Jacks Reef, Levanna, Squibnocket Triangle, Susquehannock triangle)

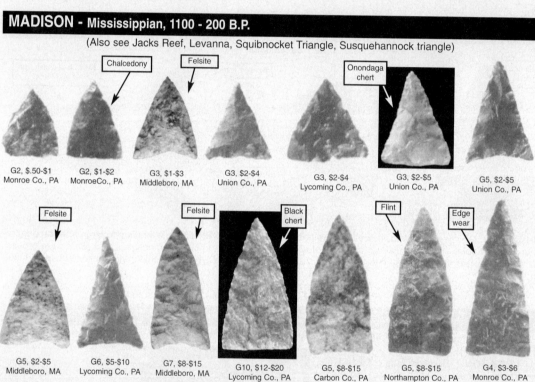

Chalcedony

Felsite

Onondaga chert

G2, $.50-$1
Monroe Co., PA

G2, $1-$2
MonroeCo., PA

G3, $1-$3
Middleboro, MA

G3, $2-$4
Union Co., PA

G3, $2-$4
Lycoming Co., PA

G3, $2-$5
Union Co., PA

G5, $2-$5
Union Co., PA

Felsite

Felsite

Black chert

Flint

Edge wear

G5, $2-$5
Middleboro, MA

G6, $5-$10
Lycoming Co., PA

G7, $8-$15
Middleboro, MA

G10, $12-$20
Lycoming Co., PA

G5, $8-$15
Carbon Co., PA

G5, $8-$15
Northampton Co., PA

G4, $3-$6
Monroe Co., PA

LOCATION: Midwestern to Eastern states. Type site is in Madison Co., IL. Found at Cahokia Mounds (un-notched Cahokias). Used by the Kaskaskia tribe into the 1700s. **DESCRIPTION:** A small to medium size, thin, triangular point with usually straight sides and base. Some examples are notched on two to three sides. Many are of high quality and some are finely serrated. **I.D. KEY:** Thin triangle.

MANSION INN BLADE - Early Woodland, 3700 - 2700 B.P.

(Also see Koens Crispin, Greene, Lehigh, Morrow Mountain, Schuylkill, Virginsville, Wayland Notched & Web Blade)

LOCATION: Maine southward into New Jersey. Type site is in Massachusetts. **DESCRIPTION:** A medium to large size, broad, blade with a short, contracting stem. Believed to be preforms related to the *Perkiomen* and *Susquehanna* types. Three forms have been identified: Coburn, Dudley and Watertown. **I.D. KEY:** Size and base form.

MANSION INN BLADE (continued)

Felsite

Dudley form

Classic form

G5, $15-$25
Plymouth Co., MA

G5, $15-$25
Plymouth Co., MA

G9, $250-$450
MA

Purple felsite

G6, $25-$40
Plymouth Co., MA

IMPORTANT: All Mansion Inn's shown half size

Watertown form

Argillite

G9, $275-$500
NJ

G8, $175-$300
Burlington Co., NJ

Coburn form

Felsite

Dudley form

Watertown form

Watertown form

G9, $250-$400
Bridgewater, MA

G9, $250-$450
Burlington Co., NJ

G9, $250-$450
Burlington Co., NJ

G9, $250-$500
Eastern NY

MEADOWOOD - Late Archaic to early Woodland, 4000 - 2500 B.P.

(Also see Kessel, Otter Creek, Wapanucket)

Onondaga chert

G4, $8-$15
Union Co., PA

G5, $25-$40
NJ

G6, $35-$60
Luzerne Co., PA

G6, $30-$50
PA

LOCATION: Northeastern states. **DESCRIPTION:** A medium to large size point with shallow side notches near the base. The base can be straight to slightly convex. Blade edges can be straight to slightly convex to recurved. Some specimens show a lot of reworking and may be used up and asymmetrical.

139

MEADOWOOD (continued)

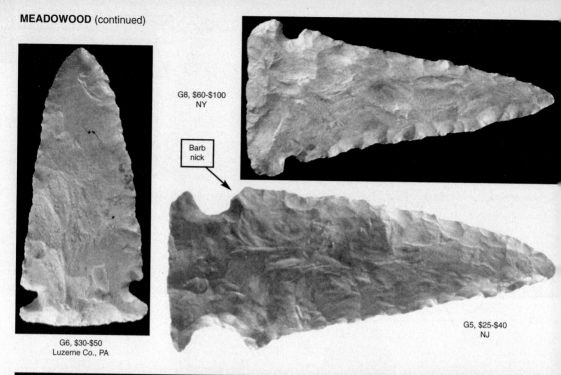

G8, $60-$100
NY

Barb
nick

G6, $30-$50
Luzerne Co., PA

G5, $25-$40
NJ

MERRIMACK STEMMED - Mid-Archaic, 6000 - 5000 B.P.

(Also see Dewart Stemmed, Lamoka, Taconic Stemmed, Wading River)

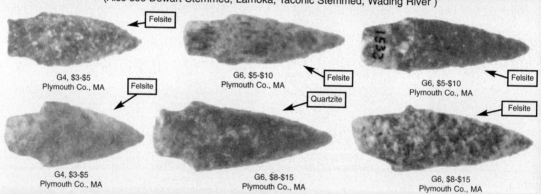

Felsite

G4, $3-$5
Plymouth Co., MA

Felsite

G6, $5-$10
Plymouth Co., MA

Felsite

G6, $5-$10
Plymouth Co., MA

Felsite

Felsite

Quartzite

Felsite

G4, $3-$5
Plymouth Co., MA

G6, $8-$15
Plymouth Co., MA

G6, $8-$15
Plymouth Co., MA

LOCATION: Pennsylvania into New York and Massachusetts. **DESCRIPTION:** A small to medium size, narrow, stemmed point with slight, tapered shoulders. The stem expands, contracts or is parallel sided. **I.D. KEY:** Base form.

MORROW MOUNTAIN - Mid-Archaic, 7000 - 5000 B.P.

(Also see Koens Crispin, Lehigh, Piscataway, Poplar Island, Stark, Swatara/Long, Virginsville)

Jasper

G4, $8-$15
PA

G4, $8-$15
PA

LOCATION: Northeastern states. **DESCRIPTION:** A medium to large size, broad, triangular point with a very short, contracting to rounded stem. Shoulders are usually weak but can be barbed. The blade edges on some examples are serrated with needle points. **I.D. KEY:** Contracted base and Archaic parallel flaking.

G5, $15-$30
Lancaster Co., PA

G6, $25-$40
Lancaster Co., PA

G4, $12-$20
Carbon Co., PA

G5, $15-$30
PA

MUNCY BIFURCATE - Archaic, 8500 - 7000 B.P.

(Also see Fox Valley, Kanawha, Neville and Stanly)

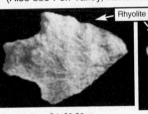

G6, $5-$10
Lycoming Co., PA

G4, $3-$6
Lycoming Co., PA

G5, $4-$8
Union Co., PA

LOCATION: North eastern states. **DESCRIPTION:** A small to medium point with prominent shoulders and a contracting to parallel sided stem. The Base has a shallow notch. Possibly related to *Neville.* **I.D. KEY:** Base form.

NEVILLE - Archaic, 7000 - 6000 B.P.

(Also see Adena Robbins, Bare Island, Duncan's Island, Genesee, Merrimack, Muncy Bifurcate, Newmanstown, Snook Kill, Stark)

G7, $15-$25
Chester Co., PA

G7, $15-$25
Plymouth Co., MA

G6, $15-$25
PA

LOCATION: Northeastern states. **DESCRIPTION:** A medium size, triangular point with barbed to horizontal shoulders and a short, square to contracting stem. **I.D. KEY:** Stem form.

141

NEVILLE (continued)

Felsite

G8, $30-$50
Plymouth Co., MA

Felsite

G9, $35-$60
Plymouth Co., MA

Felsite

G9, $35-$60
Plymouth Co., MA

G5, $8-$15
CT

Quartzite

G8, $30-$50
Montgomery Co., PA

NEWMANSTOWN - Archaic, 7000 - 5000 B.P.

(Also see Bare Island, Duncan's Island, Lackawaxen, Neville, Piedmont, Taconic Stemmed, Tocks Island)

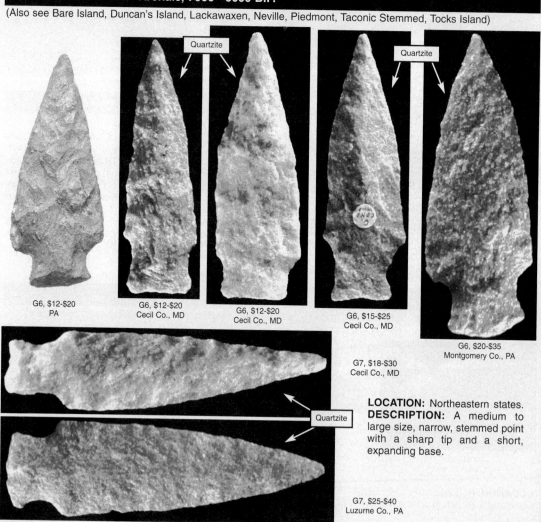

Quartzite

G6, $12-$20
PA

G6, $12-$20
Cecil Co., MD

G6, $12-$20
Cecil Co., MD

Quartzite

G6, $15-$25
Cecil Co., MD

G6, $20-$35
Montgomery Co., PA

G7, $18-$30
Cecil Co., MD

Quartzite

G7, $25-$40
Luzurne Co., PA

LOCATION: Northeastern states.
DESCRIPTION: A medium to large size, narrow, stemmed point with a sharp tip and a short, expanding base.

NORMANSKILL - Late Archaic to early Woodland, 4000 - 2500 B.P.

NE

(Also see Brewerton Corner Notched, Drybrook, Meadowood, Orient, Susquehanna Broad, Tocks Island)

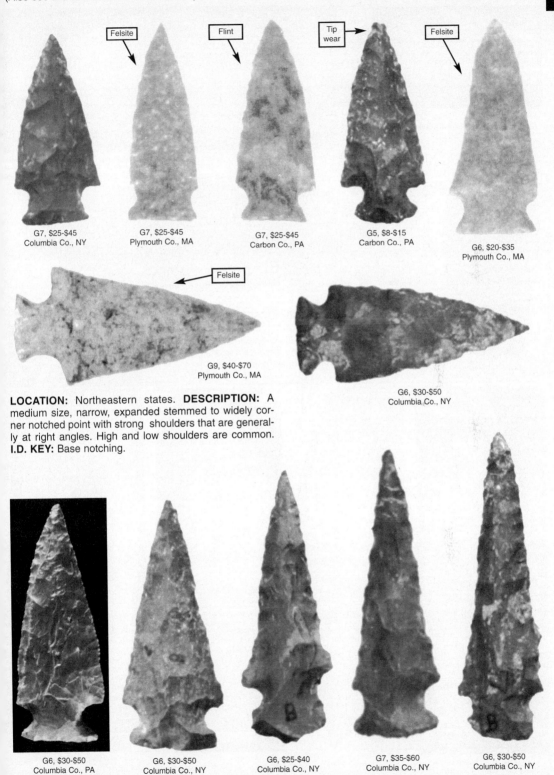

Felsite

Flint

Tip wear

Felsite

G7, $25-$45
Columbia Co., NY

G7, $25-$45
Plymouth Co., MA

G7, $25-$45
Carbon Co., PA

G5, $8-$15
Carbon Co., PA

G6, $20-$35
Plymouth Co., MA

Felsite

G9, $40-$70
Plymouth Co., MA

G6, $30-$50
Columbia Co., NY

LOCATION: Northeastern states. **DESCRIPTION:** A medium size, narrow, expanded stemmed to widely corner notched point with strong shoulders that are generally at right angles. High and low shoulders are common. **I.D. KEY:** Base notching.

G6, $30-$50
Columbia Co., PA

G6, $30-$50
Columbia Co., NY

G6, $25-$40
Columbia Co., NY

G7, $35-$60
Columbia Co., NY

G6, $30-$50
Columbia Co., NY

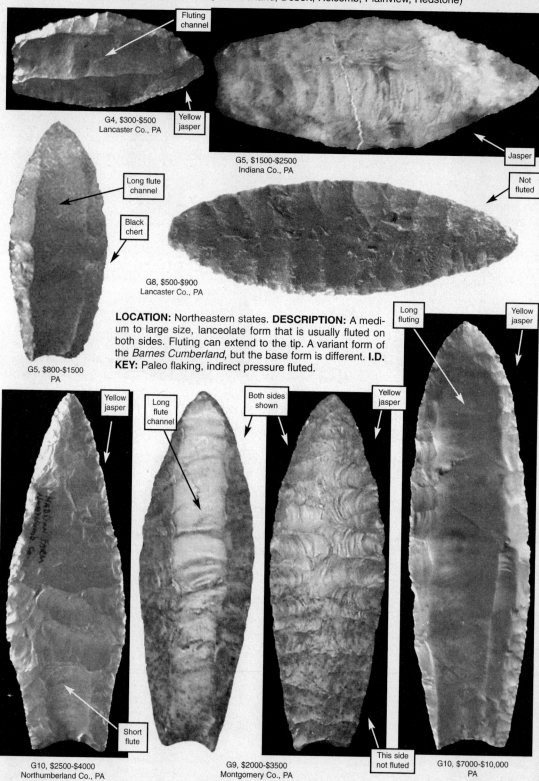

NORTHUMBERLAND FLUTED KNIFE - Paleo, 11,250 - 10,000 B. P.

(Also see Clovis, Crowfield, Cumberland, Debert, Holcomb, Plainview, Redstone)

Fluting channel

G4, $300-$500
Lancaster Co., PA

Yellow jasper

Jasper

G5, $1500-$2500
Indiana Co., PA

Not fluted

Long flute channel

Black chert

G8, $500-$900
Lancaster Co., PA

G5, $800-$1500
PA

LOCATION: Northeastern states. **DESCRIPTION:** A medium to large size, lanceolate form that is usually fluted on both sides. Fluting can extend to the tip. A variant form of the *Barnes Cumberland*, but the base form is different. **I.D. KEY:** Paleo flaking, indirect pressure fluted.

Long fluting

Yellow jasper

Yellow jasper

Long flute channel

Both sides shown

Yellow jasper

Short flute

G10, $2500-$4000
Northumberland Co., PA

G9, $2000-$3500
Montgomery Co., PA

This side not fluted

G10, $7000-$10,000
PA

OHIO LANCEOLATE - Late Paleo, 10,500 - 7000 B.P.

(Also see Angostura, Beaver Lake, Clovis, Dalton, Cumberland & Parallel Lanceolate)

LOCATION: Ohio into W. Pennsylvania. **DESCRIPTION:** A medium to large size lanceolate point with parallel to convex sides and a concave base that is ground. Flaking is early collateral to oblique transverse. Base has light grinding, not fluted or basally thinned. Thinner than *Clovis* or *Agate Basin*. **I.D. KEY:** Base form and parallel flaking.

Side nick

G5, $80-$150
Western PA

OLEY - Woodland, 2200 - 1500 B. P.

(Also see Charleston Pine Tree, Erb Basal Notched, Eshbach, Vestal Notched)

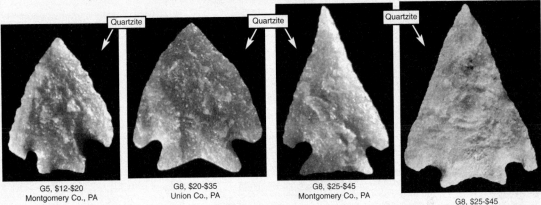

Quartzite

Quartzite

Quartzite

G5, $12-$20
Montgomery Co., PA

G8, $20-$35
Union Co., PA

G8, $25-$45
Montgomery Co., PA

G8, $25-$45
Lancaster Co., PA

LOCATION: Southeast Pennsylvania. **DESCRIPTION:** A small to medium size corner notched barbed point with an expanding base. Blade edges are concave to recurved. Base is concave. **I.D. KEY:** Base form and barbs.

ORIENT FISHTAIL - Late Archaic to Woodland, 4000 - 2500 B. P.

(Also see Drybrook, Forest Notched, Frost Island, Susquehanna Broad, Perkiomen & Taconic Stemmed)

Flint

Jasper

Jasper

G4, $8-$15
Northampton Co., PA

G5, $15-$25
Northampton Co., PA

G6, $15-$30
Northampton Co., PA

G4, $12-$20
Bainbridge, PA

G6, $25-$40
Northampton Co., PA

G6, $25-$40
Northampton Co., PA

Jasper

G6, $35-$60
Lancaster Co., PA

LOCATION: Northeastern states. **DESCRIPTION:** A small to medium size point with broad side notches, rounded shoulders and an expanding base. The base on some examples form auricles. **I.D. KEY:** Base form and rounded shoulders.

ORIENT FISHTAIL(continued)

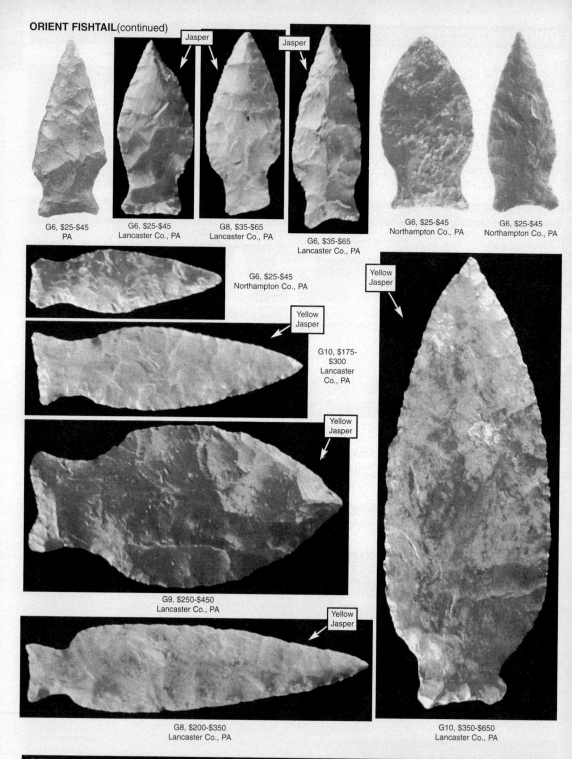

Jasper

Jasper

G6, $25-$45
PA

G6, $25-$45
Lancaster Co., PA

G8, $35-$65
Lancaster Co., PA

G6, $35-$65
Lancaster Co., PA

G6, $25-$45
Northampton Co., PA

G6, $25-$45
Northampton Co., PA

G6, $25-$45
Northampton Co., PA

Yellow Jasper

G10, $175-
$300
Lancaster
Co., PA

Yellow Jasper

Yellow
Jasper

G9, $250-$450
Lancaster Co., PA

Yellow
Jasper

G8, $200-$350
Lancaster Co., PA

G10, $350-$650
Lancaster Co., PA

OTTER CREEK - Mid to late Archaic, 5000 - 3500 B.P.

(Also see Brewerton Side Notched, Goddard, Perkiomen, Raccoon Notched, Susquehanna Broad)

LOCATION: Northeastern states. **DESCRIPTION:** A medium to large size, side notched point with a straight, concave or convex base. Notching is prominent, shoulders are tapered to barbed. Bases are ground. **I.D. KEY:** Side notching.

OTTER CREEK (continued)

G4, $5-$10
Bainbridge, PA

Gray chert

G5, $12-$20
Monroe Co., PA

G5, $12-$20
Lycoming Co., PA

G8, $20-$35
Milton, VT

G5, $20-$35
PA

Gray chert

G7, $30-$50
Lycoming Co., PA

G7, $30-$50
Union Co., PA

Black chert

G7, $30-$50
Union Co., PA

Quartzite

Black flint

G7, $25-$40
Monroe Co., PA

G7, $30-$55
Columbia Co., NY

G7, $45-$80
Wayne Co., PA

G7, $150-$250
Middleboro, MA

OVATES - Woodland, 3000 - 2000 B.P.

(Also see Nodena (Arkansas), Strike-A-Lite Type II)

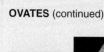

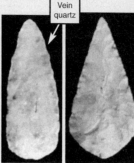

Vein quartz

Vein quartz

| G4, $5-$10 | G5, $8-$15 | G5, $8-$15 | G5, $8-$15 | G6, $12-$20 | G6, $15-$25 | G6, $15-$25 |
| Berks Co., PA | Chester Co., PA | Lycoming Co., PA | Chester Co., PA | Berks Co., PA | Berks Co., PA | Montgomery Co., PA |

LOCATION: Northeastern states. **DESCRIPTION:** A small size tear-drop shaped point with rounded shoulders and base. **I.D. KEY:** Ovoid form.

PALMER - Early Archaic, 9000 - 8000 B.P.

(Also see Amos, Brewerton, Charleston Pine Tree, Kirk Corner Notched, Kiski, Kline)

Jasper

| G5, $15-$25 | G6, $20-$35 | G6, $20-$35 | G5, $15-$25 | G5, $15-$25 | G6, $20-$35 |
| Union Co., PA | Monroer Co., PA | Lycoming Co., PA | Luzurne Co., PA | Lycoming Co., PA | Union Co., PA |

G6, $25-$40
Luzurne Co., PA

LOCATION: Eastern states. **DESCRIPTION:** A small to medium size, corner-notched point with a ground concave, convex, or straight base. Shoulders are barbed to contracting. Many are serrated and large examples would fall under the *Charleston Pine Tree* or *Kirk* Type. **I.D. KEY:** Basal form and notching.

PATUXENT - Late Archaic, 4000 - 3000 B.P.

(Also see Bare Island, Duncan's Island, Frost Island, Orient, Piedmont)

LOCATION: Southeastern PA., MD., VA. **DESCRIPTION:** A small to medium size point with weak, tapered shoulders and an expanding base. The base is concave forming ears. **I.D. KEY:** Basal form and weak shoulders.

G6, $15-$30
Montgomery Co., PA

Quartzite

PENN'S CREEK BIFURCATE - Early Archaic, 9000 - 7000 B.P.

(Also see Culpepper, Kirk Stemmed, LeCroy, MacCorkle, St. Albans, Susquehanna Bifurcate)

LOCATION: Pennsylvania. **DESCRIPTION:** A small size bifurcated point with Archaic flaking. Shoulders are weakly barbed and the base expands to ears. **I.D. KEY:** Basal form and early flaking.

G4, $12-$20
Northumberland Co., PA

PENN'S CREEK SERIES - Early Archaic, 9000 - 7000 B.P.

(Also see Lycoming County Series)

G4, $4-$8
Peach Bottom, PA

LOCATION: Central Pennsylvania.
DESCRIPTION: A small size point that is stemmed, corner or side notched.

PENTAGONAL KNIFE - Mid-Archaic, 6500 - 4000 B.P.

(Also see Jacks Reef Corner Notched)

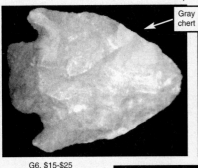

Gray chert

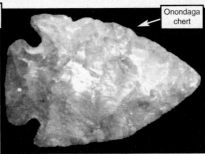

Onondaga chert

LOCATION: Pennsylvania into Ohio, Kentucky, Tennessee and Alabama. **DESCRIPTION:** A medium to large size pentagonal shaped point with a flaring or corner notched stem. Some examples are base notched. Similar to but older than the *Afton* point found in the Midwest. Similar to *Jacks Reef* but thicker. **I.D. KEY:** Blade form.

G6, $15-$25
Crawford Co., PA

G6, $25-$40
Crawford Co., PA

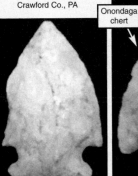

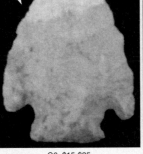

Onondaga chert

Brown chert

G6, $8-$15
Crawford Co., PA

G6, $15-$25
Crawford Co., PA

G6, $35-$50
Crawford Co., PA

PERKIOMEN - Late Archaic to early Woodland, 4000 - 2500 B.P.

(Also see Ashtabula, Frost Island, Manson Inn, Susquehanna Broad, Waratan)

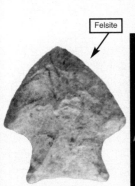

Felsite

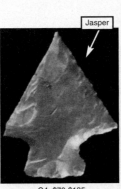

Jasper

Variegated jasper

Rhyolite

G3, $30-$50
Bridgewater, MA

G4, $70-$135
Lancaster Co., PA

G8, $275-$500
Montgomery Co., PA

G6, $65-$125
Lancaster Co., PA

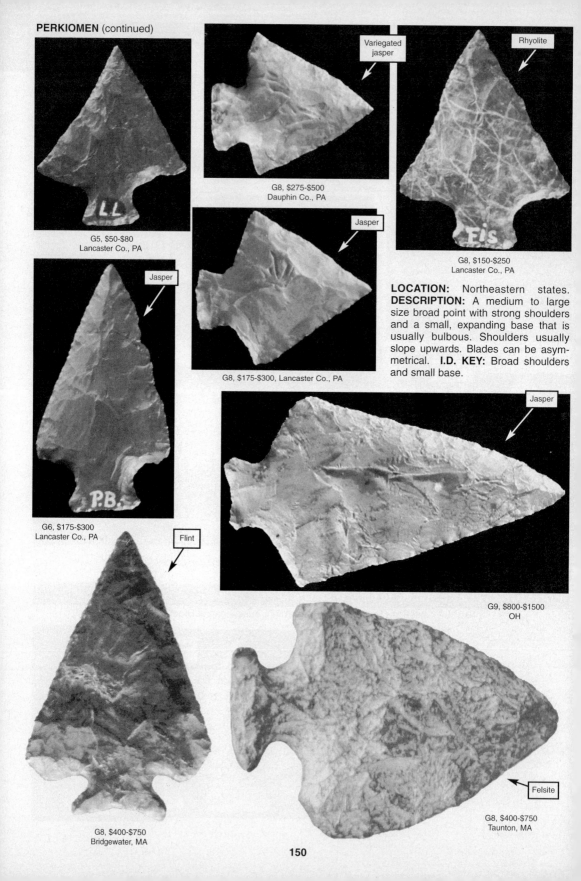

PERKIOMEN (continued)

G5, $50-$80
Lancaster Co., PA

Variegated jasper

G8, $275-$500
Dauphin Co., PA

Rhyolite

G8, $150-$250
Lancaster Co., PA

Jasper

G8, $175-$300, Lancaster Co., PA

Jasper

G6, $175-$300
Lancaster Co., PA

LOCATION: Northeastern states. **DESCRIPTION:** A medium to large size broad point with strong shoulders and a small, expanding base that is usually bulbous. Shoulders usually slope upwards. Blades can be asymmetrical. **I.D. KEY:** Broad shoulders and small base.

Jasper

G9, $800-$1500
OH

Flint

G8, $400-$750
Bridgewater, MA

Felsite

G8, $400-$750
Taunton, MA

PIEDMONT-NORTHERN VARIETY - Archaic, 6000 - 4000 B.P.

(Also see Bare Island, Duncan's Island, Genesee, Hoover's Island, Neville, Lackawaxen, Newmanstown, Patuxent, Piney Island, Tocks Island)

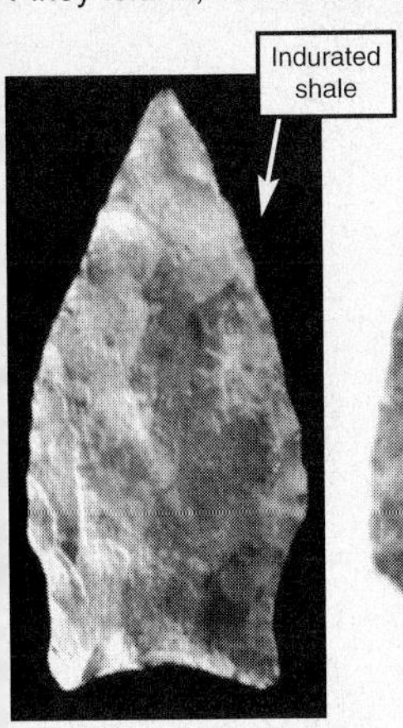

Indurated shale

Black flint

Argillite

Indurated shale

G3, $5-$10
Lycoming Co., PA

G4, $8-$15
Lycoming Co., PA

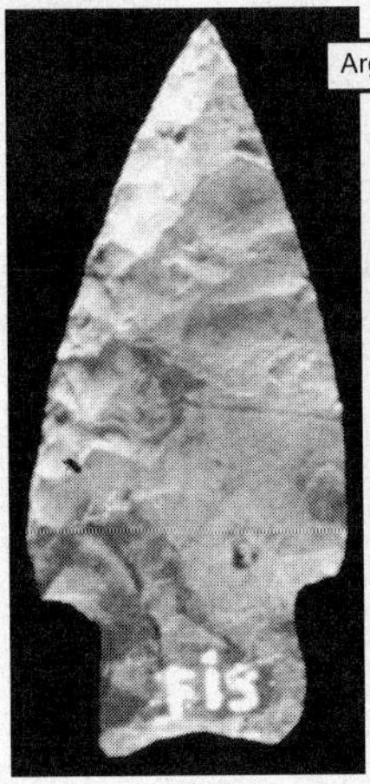

G4, $8-$15
Lancaster Co., PA

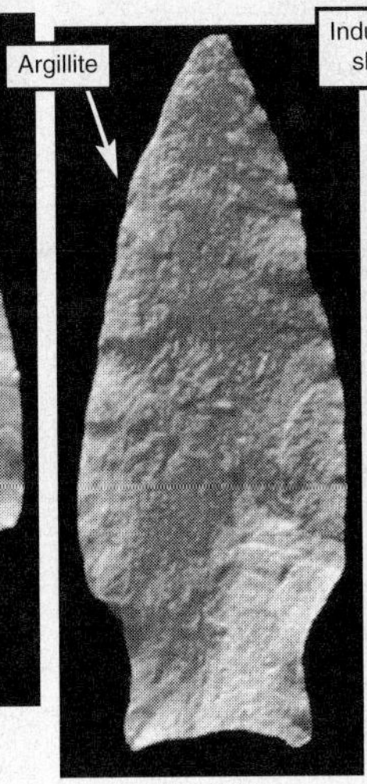

G5, $12-$20
Luzurne Co., PA

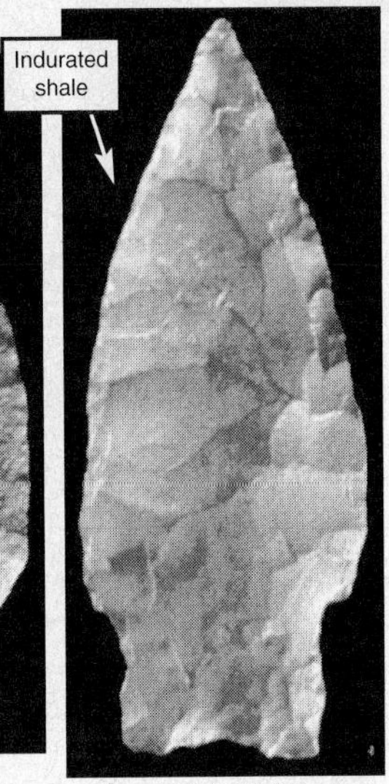

G7, $25-$40
Lycoming Co., PA

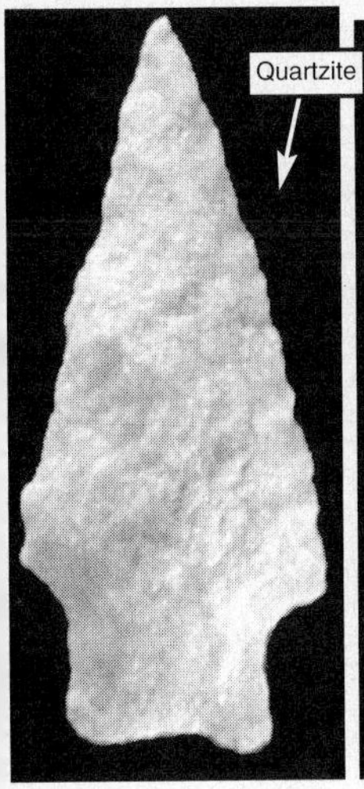

Quartzite

Indurated shale

Indurated shale

G6, $12-$20
Cent. PA

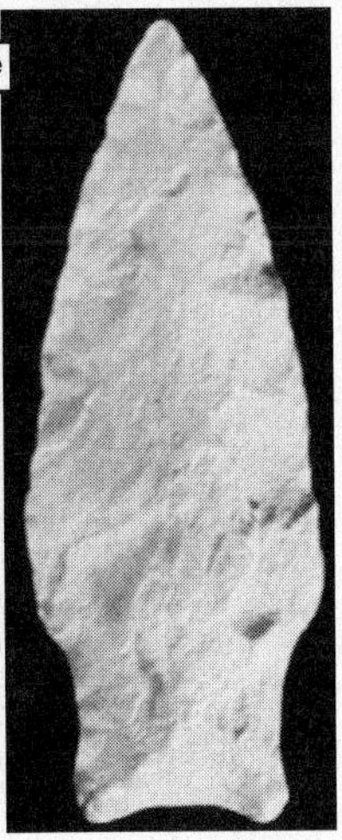

G5, $8-$15
Luzurne Co., PA

G8, $25-$40
PA

G6, $15-$25
Lycoming Co., PA

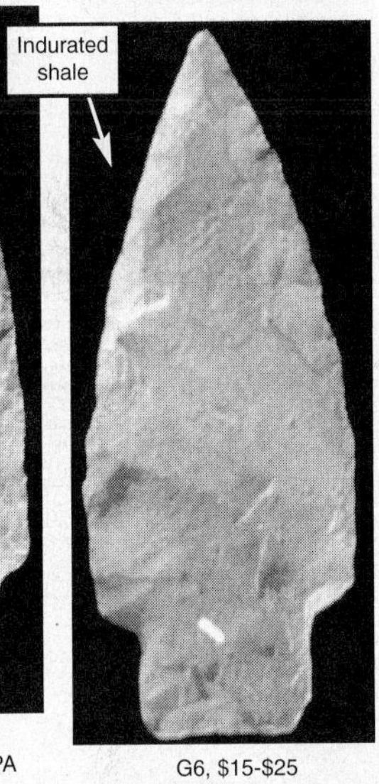

G6, $15-$25
Lycoming Co., PA

G7, $15-$30
Columbia Co., PA

G7, $15-$30
Lycoming Co., PA

G8, $15-$30
Columbia Co., PA

LOCATION: Central Pennsylvania northward. **DESCRIPTION:** A medium to large size, narrow stemmed point. Base varies from straight to convex, from square to expanding or contracting. Shoulders are usually tapered. Named by Fogelman. Usually made of siltstone and indurated shale. **I.D. KEY:** Base form and narrow width.

151

Siltstone

Siltstone

Indurated shale

Quartzite

Quartzite

Quartzite

Quartzite

G8, $25-$45
Northumberland Co., PA

G8, $25-$45
Northumberland Co., PA

G8, $30-$50
Northumberton, Co., PA

G7, $25-$40
Luzurne, Co., PA

G5, $12-$20
PA

G6, $15-$25
Lycoming Co., PA

G8, $30-$50
Montgomery Co., PA

G6, $12-$20
PA

G6, $12-$20
PA

G8, $25-$60
Northumberton Co., PA

G6, $15-$30
PA

PINEY ISLAND - Late Archaic, 6000 - 2000 B.P.

(Also see Bare Island, Duncan's Island, Lamoka, Patuxent, Piedmont, Squibnocket Stemmed)

G6, $20-$35
Northampton Co., PA

G6, $20-$35
Northampton Co., PA

G8, $25-$40
Columbia Co., PA

Black chert

G8, $35-$60
Carbon Co., PA

G8, $40-$70
Lycoming Co., PA

LOCATION: Northeastern states. **DESCRIPTION:** A medium size, narrow, long stemmed point with tapered shoulders. **I.D. KEY:** Basal form and narrow width.

PISCATAWAY - Mid to late Woodland, 2500 - 500 B.P.

(Also see Morrow Mountain, Poplar Island, Schuylkill, Stark, Virginsville)

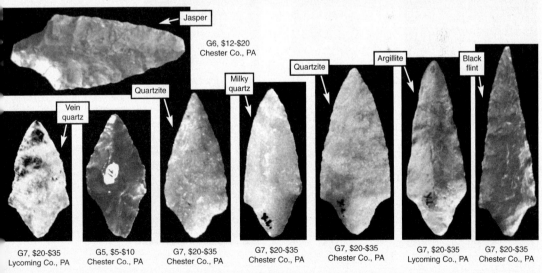

Jasper

G6, $12-$20
Chester Co., PA

Argillite

Black flint

Quartzite

Milky quartz

Quartzite

Vein quartz

G7, $20-$35
Lycoming Co., PA

G5, $5-$10
Chester Co., PA

G7, $20-$35
Chester Co., PA

G7, $20-$35
Chester Co., PA

G7, $20-$35
Chester Co., PA

G7, $20-$35
Lycoming Co., PA

G7, $20-$35
Chester Co., PA

LOCATION: Eastern to Northeastern states. **DESCRIPTION:** A small to medium size, very narrow triangular point with tapered shoulders and a short tapered stem. The base is pointed to rounded. **I.D. KEY:** Basal form and narrow width.

POPLAR ISLAND - Mid-Archaic, 6000 - 4000 B.P.

(Also see Koens Crispin, Morrow Mountain, Piscataway, Schuylkill, Stark, Virginsville)

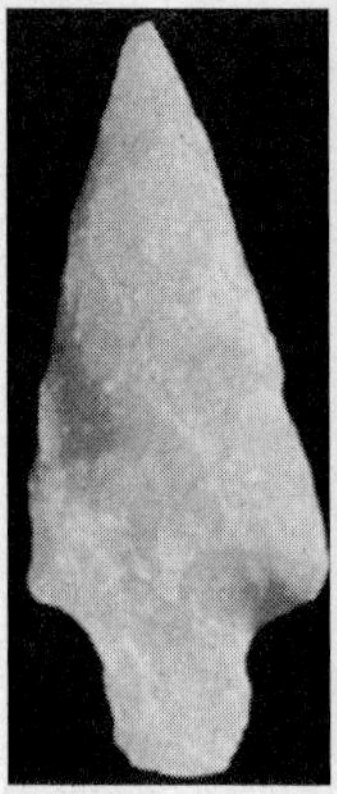

G4, $8-$15
Carbon Co., PA

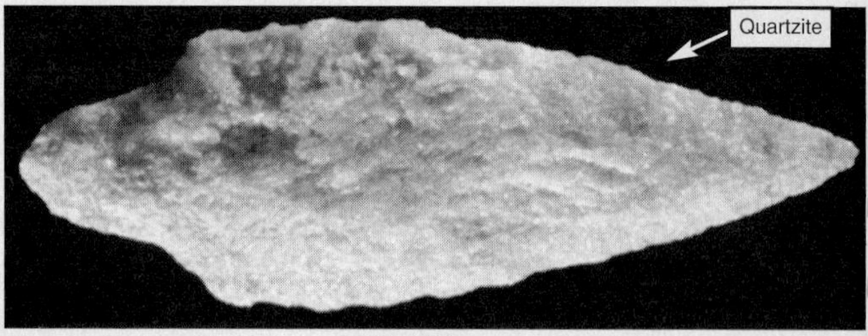

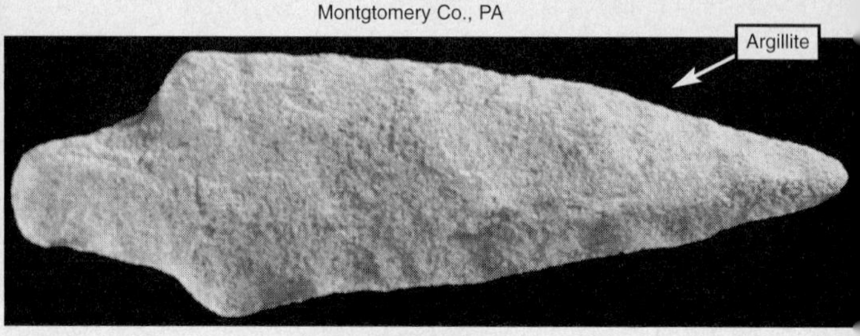

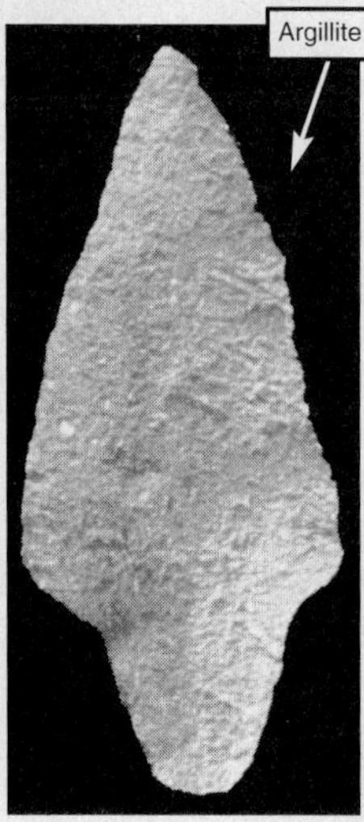

Argillite

G5, $15-$30
NJ

Quartzite

G8, $40-$75
Montgtomery Co., PA

Argillite

G5, $30-$50
Columbia Co., PA

Quartzite

G7, $90-$165
York Co., PA

Argillite

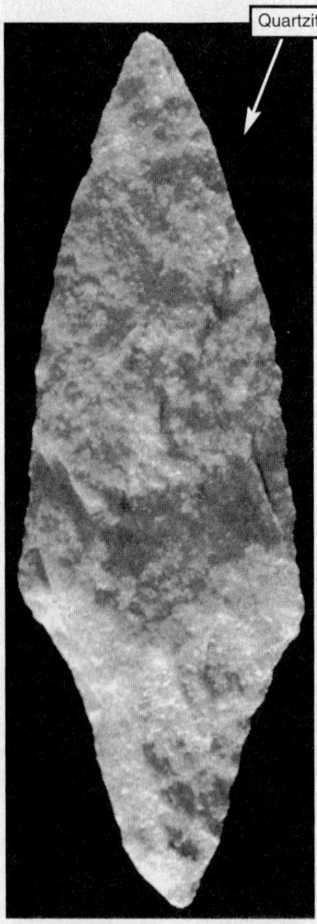

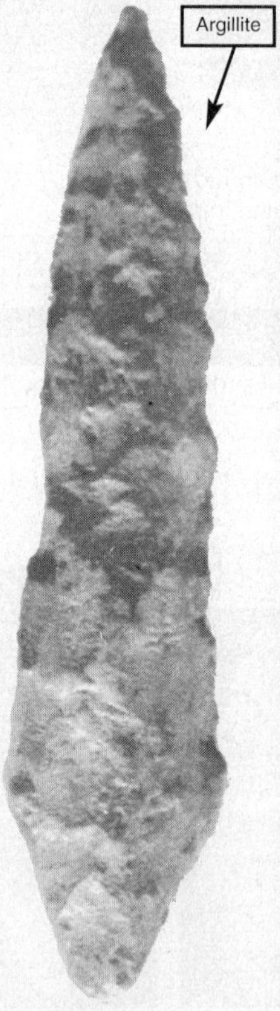

G4, $30-$50
Middleboro, MA

Argillite

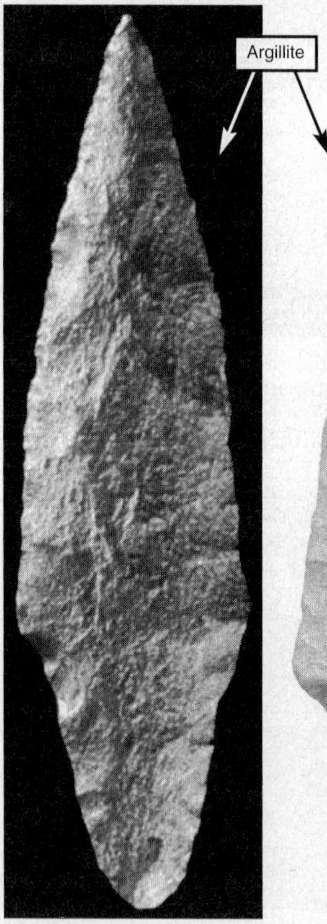

G9, $125-$200
Lancaster Co., PA

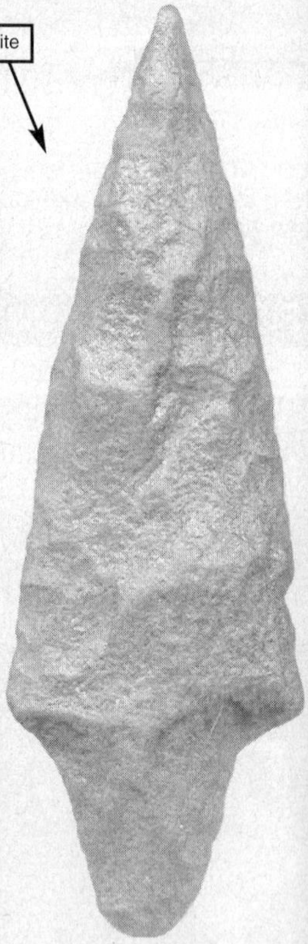

G8, $125-$200
PA

LOCATION: Northeastern states. **DESCRIPTION:** A medium to large size, narrow, triangular point with tapered shoulders and a long contracting base. The base can be pointed to rounded. **I.D. KEY:** Basal form and narrow width.

PORT MAITLAND - Mid-Woodland, 2500 - 1400 B.P.

(Also see Brewerton, Goddard, Raccoon Notched)

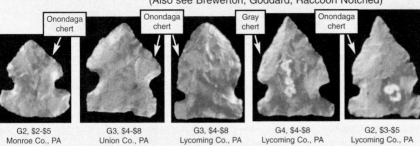

Onondaga chert

Onondaga chert

Gray chert

Onondaga chert

G2, $2-$5
Monroe Co., PA

G3, $4-$8
Union Co., PA

G3, $4-$8
Lycoming Co., PA

G4, $4-$8
Lycoming Co., PA

G2, $3-$5
Lycoming Co., PA

LOCATION: North eastern states. **DESCRIPTION:** A small size side notched point with a straight to slightly concave base. Side notches form square corners at the base. **I.D. KEY:** Notching form and small size.

RACCOON NOTCHED - Late Woodland, 1500 - 1000 B.P.

(Also see Brewerton, Goddard, Jacks Reef, Port Maitland)

Onondaga flint

Red jasper

G4, $12-$20
NY

G5, $25-$40
Union Co., PA

LOCATION: Northeastern states. **DESCRIPTION:** A small to medium size, thin, side notched point. Blade edges are convex to pentagonal shape. Known as *Knight Island* in Southeast. **I.D. KEY:** Side notching and thinness.

RANDOLPH - Woodland to Historic, 2000 - 200 B.P.

(Also see Dewart Stemmed, Lamoka, Merrimack, Wading River)

G7, $5-$10
Union Co., PA

G5, $3-$7
Union Co., PA

LOCATION: Eastern to Northeastern states. **DESCRIPTION:** A medium size, narrow, thick, spike point with tapered shoulders and a short to medium, contracted, rounded stem. Many examples have exaggerated spikes along the blade edges. **I.D. KEY:** Blade form and spikes.

REDSTONE - Paleo, 13,000 - 9000 B.P.

(Also see Clovis, Crowfield, Cumberland, Debert, Holcomb)

LOCATION: Southeastern to Northeastern states. **DESCRIPTION:** A small to large size, thin, auriculate, fluted point with convex sides expanding to a wide, deeply concave base. Fluting can extend most of the way down each face. Multiple flutes are usual. A very rare type. **I.D. KEY:** Batan fluted, edgework on the hafting area.

Restored tip

Fluting channel

G7, $350-$600
Lycoming Co., PA. Coshocton chert.

ROSSVILLE - Late Woodland, 1500 - 1100 B.P.

(Also see Ovates, Morrow Mountain, Piscataway and Stark)

G3, $2-$5
Middleboro, MA

G4, $3-$6
Middleboro, MA

G5, $5-$10
Middleboro, MA

ROSSVILLE (continued)

G3, $5-$10
Middleboro, MA

G7, $15-$25
Middleboro, MA

G6, $12-$20
Middleboro, MA

LOCATION: Southern New England into New Jersey, E. Penn., Maryland and Virginia. **DESCRIPTION:** A small diamond shaped, lanceolate point with a pointed, to rounded, tapered stem. Tips are sharp and blade edges are straight to convex. **I.D. KEY:** Long tapered stem.

ST. ALBANS - Early to mid-Archaic, 9000 - 5000 B.P.

(Also see Charleston Pine Tree, Decatur, Kanawha, Kirk Serrated, Lake Erie, LeCroy, MacCorkle, Stanly & Susquehanna Bifurcate)

G5, $8-$15
Snyder Co., PA

G4, $8-$15
Lycoming Co., PA

G5, $15-$25
Lycoming Co., PA

Milky quartz

G5, $15-$25
MD

G8, $25-$40
Lycoming Co., PA

Serrated edges

G8, $30-$50
Lycoming Co., PA.

Classic form

G9, $35-$65
Union Co., PA

Chert

G6, $15-$30
Montour Co., PA

LOCATION: Eastern to Northeastern states. Type site is in Kanawha Co., WVA. **DESCRIPTION:** A small to medium size, usually serrated, bifurcated point. Basal lobes usually flare outward, and are weakly bifurcated. **I.D. KEY:** Weak bifurcation, base more narrow than shoulders.

ST. ANNE - Early Archaic, 9000 - 8000 B.P.

(Also see Agate Basin, Angostura, Plainview and Scottsbluff)

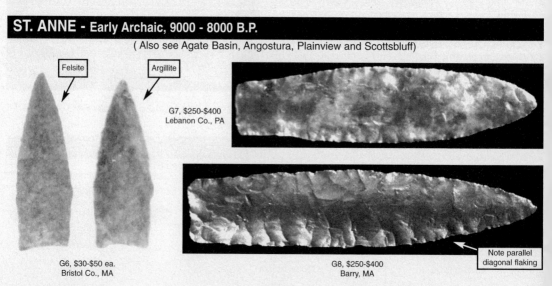

Felsite

Argillite

G7, $250-$400
Lebanon Co., PA

G6, $30-$50 ea.
Bristol Co., MA

G8, $250-$400
Barry, MA

Note parallel diagonal flaking

ST. ANNE (continued)

G3, $30-$50
PA

Green chert

Notched variety

Restored base →

Gray chert

G6, $80-$150
NY

Tip wear

LOCATION: Northeastern states into eastern Canada. **DESCRIPTION:** A small to medium size, narrow, lanceolate point with very weak shoulders. The base is rectangular shaped and is ground. Similar to *Eden* points found further west. **I.D. KEY:** Weak shoulders, narrow blade.

ST. CHARLES - Early Archaic, 9500 - 8000 B.P.

(Also see Brodhead Side Notched, Decatur, Kirk, Kline, Lost Lake & Thebes)

LOCATION: Midwest to Eastern states. **DESCRIPTION:** Also known as *Dovetail*. A medium to large size, corner notched, dovetailed base point. The blade is beveled on one side of each face when resharpened. Bases are straight, convex or bifurcated and are ground and can be fractured from both corners of the base. **I.D. KEY:** Dovetailed base.

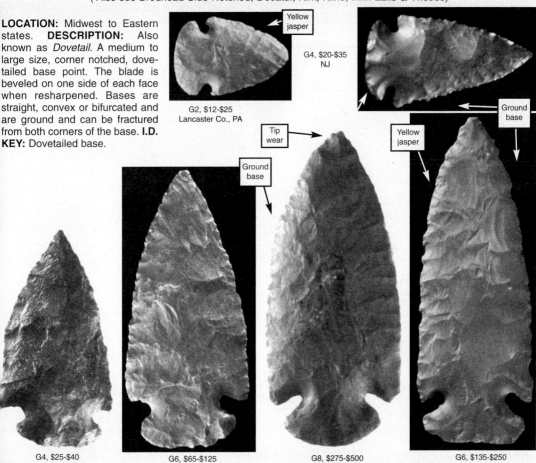

Yellow jasper

G4, $20-$35
NJ

G2, $12-$25
Lancaster Co., PA

Ground base

Tip wear

Ground base

Yellow jasper

G4, $25-$40
PA

G6, $65-$125
MD

G8, $275-$500
Monmouth Co., NJ

G6, $135-$250
Lancaster Co., PA

SANDHILL STEMMED - Mid-Woodland, 2200 - 1700 B.P.

(Also see Dewart Stemmed, Garver's Ferry, Lamoka, Merrimack, Wading River)

LOCATION: Northeastern states. **DESCRIPTION:** A small point with a straight to contracting base. Shoulders are tapered to slightly barbed.

SANDHILL STEMMED (continued)

White chert

G7, $6-$12
Lycoming Co., PA

Red jasper

G5, $6-$12
Monroe Co., PA

Gray chert

Gray flint

G5, $4-$8
Lycoming Co., PA

Red jasper

G8, $8-$15
Lycoming Co., PA

G7, $8-$15
Lycoming Co., PA

G3, $5-$10
Lycoming Co., PA

SAVANNAH RIVER - Mid Archaic to Woodland, 5000 - 2000 B.P.

(Also see Atlantic Phase Blades, Fox Creek, Genesee, Piedmont)

Tip nick

Quartzite

G4, $5-$10
PA

G4, $8-$15
Northumberland Co., PA

G5 $12-$20
PA

G7, $25-$45
PA

G6, $15-$25
PA

LOCATION: Southeastern to Eastern states. **DESCRIPTION:** A medium to large size, straight to contracting stemmed point with a concave, straight or bifurcated base. The shoulders are tapered to square. The stems are narrow to broad. Believed to be related to the earlier Stanly point.

SCHUYLKILL - Late Archaic, 4000 - 2000 B.P.

(Also see Adena, Atlantic Phase Blades, Condoquinet Canfield, Koens Crispin, Lehigh, Morrow Mountain Piscataway, Poplar Island, Stark, Virginsville)

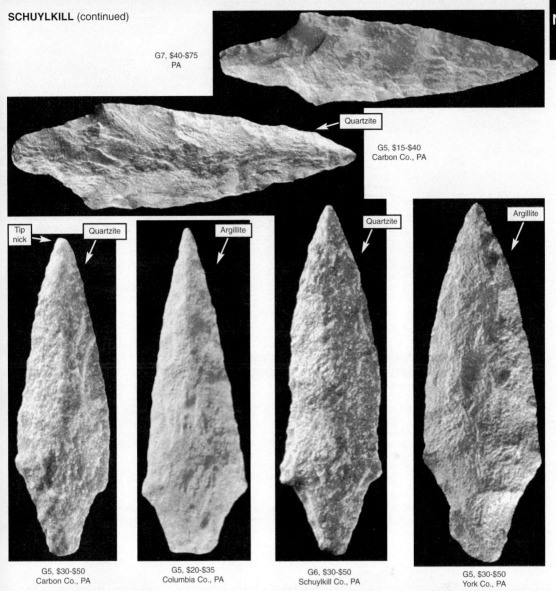

G7, $40-$75
PA

Quartzite

G5, $15-$40
Carbon Co., PA

Tip nick

Quartzite

Argillite

Quartzite

Argillite

G5, $30-$50
Carbon Co., PA

G5, $20-$35
Columbia Co., PA

G6, $30-$50
Schuylkill Co., PA

G5, $30-$50
York Co., PA

LOCATION: Northeastern states. **DESCRIPTION:** A medium to large size, narrow point with a long, tapered, rounded stem. Shoulders are usually at a sharper angle than Poplar Island. **I.D. KEY:** Sharp corners, narrow blade, long tapering stem.

SCRAPER - Paleo to Archaic, 14,000 - 5000 B.P.

(Also see Drill, Graver, Strike-A-Lite)

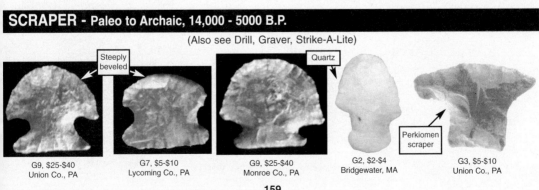

Steeply beveled

Quartz

Perkiomen scraper

G9, $25-$40
Union Co., PA

G7, $5-$10
Lycoming Co., PA

G9, $25-$40
Monroe Co., PA

G2, $2-$4
Bridgewater, MA

G3, $5-$10
Union Co., PA

SCRAPER (continued)

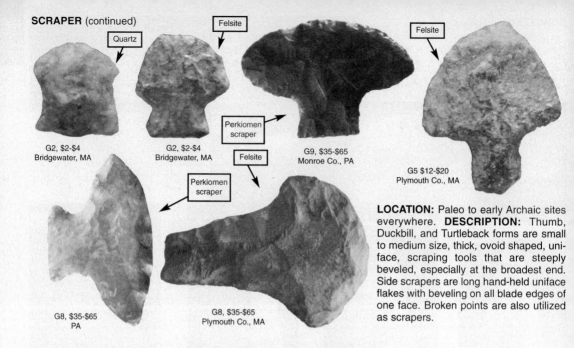

Quartz

Felsite

Felsite

Perkiomen scraper

Felsite

Perkiomen scraper

Felsite

G2, $2-$4
Bridgewater, MA

G2, $2-$4
Bridgewater, MA

G9, $35-$65
Monroe Co., PA

G5 $12-$20
Plymouth Co., MA

G8, $35-$65
PA

G8, $35-$65
Plymouth Co., MA

LOCATION: Paleo to early Archaic sites everywhere. **DESCRIPTION:** Thumb, Duckbill, and Turtleback forms are small to medium size, thick, ovoid shaped, uniface, scraping tools that are steeply beveled, especially at the broadest end. Side scrapers are long hand-held uniface flakes with beveling on all blade edges of one face. Broken points are also utilized as scrapers.

SHARK'S TOOTH - Woodland to Historic, 2000 - 100 B.P.

(Also see Bone/Antler)

LOCATION: Coastal states from Maine to Florida. **DESCRIPTION:** Salvaged from Shark remains and as fossilized teeth found along the shoreline. Used as arrowpoints by Woodland Indians into historic times.

G5, $6-$12
Seaver farm, MA

G6, $6-$15
Seaver farm, MA

G7, $12-$20
Seaver farm, MA

G7, $15-$25
Seaver farm, MA

SNOOK KILL - Late Archaic, 4000 - 2000 B.P.

(Also see Atlantic Phase Blades, Dewart Stemmed, Koens Crispin, Lehigh, Merrimack, Sandhill Stemmed, Stark & Taconic Stemmed)

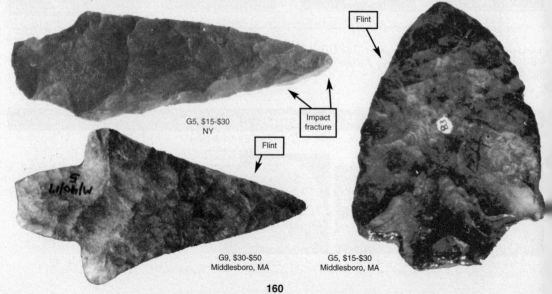

Flint

G5, $15-$30
NY

Impact fracture

Flint

Flint

G9, $30-$50
Middlesboro, MA

G5, $15-$30
Middlesboro, MA

SNOOK KILL (continued)

LOCATION: New York and adjoining states. **DESCRIPTION:** A medium size point with tapered shoulders and a short, contracting to parallel sided stem. Base can be straight to convex. Believed to be related to *Koens Crispin* and *Lehigh*. **I.D. KEY:** Short stem, tapered tangs.

SNYDERS - Woodland, 2500 - 1500 B.P.

(Also see Brewerton and Lycoming County)

LOCATION: West. New York eastward into Ohio. **DESCRIPTION:** A medium to large size, broad, thin, wide corner notched point. Made by the Hopewell culture. **I.D. KEY:** Size and broad corner notches.

> **IMPORTANT:**
> Snyders point shown half size

G7, $80-$150
W. NY

SQUIBNOCKET STEMMED - Mid-late Archaic, 4200 - 4000 B.P.

(Also see Lamoka, Merrimack, Piney Island, Snook Kill, Taconic Stemmed)

| G6, $6-$12 | G7, $8-$15 | G5, $5-$10 | G7, $8-$15 | G8, $12-$20 | G5, $5-$10 | G5, $5-$10 |
| Bridgewater, MA | Bridgewater, MA | Bridgewater, MA | Bridgewater, MA | Bridgewater, MA | Bridgewater, MA | Bridgewater, MA |

LOCATION: Conn., Massachusetts into New York. **DESCRIPTION:** A medium size, narrow, stemmed point with very weak shoulders and a rounded stem. **I.D. KEY:** Narrowness and weak shoulders.

SQUIBNOCKET TRIANGLE - Mid-late Archaic, 4500 - 4000 B.P.

(Also see Levanna, Madison and Susquehannock Triangle)

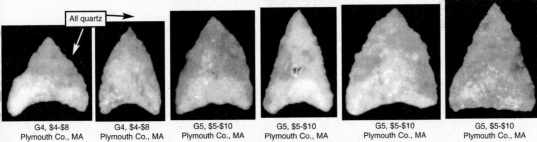

| G4, $4-$8 | G4, $4-$8 | G5, $5-$10 | G5, $5-$10 | G5, $5-$10 | G5, $5-$10 |
| Plymouth Co., MA | Plymouth Co., MA | Plymouth Co., MA | Plymouth Co., MA | Plymouth Co., MA | Plymouth Co., MA |

LOCATION: Conn., Massachusetts into New York. **DESCRIPTION:** A small size, broad, triangular point with excurvate sides and an incurvate base. Basal corners turn inward. **I.D. KEY:** Narrowness and weak shoulders.

STANLY - Early Archaic, 8000 - 5000 B.P.

(Also see Kanawha, Kirk-Bifurcated, LeCroy, Muncy, Savannah River)

STANLY (continued)

G5, $20-$35
Union Co., PA

G9, $25-$40
NJ

Yellow jasper

G5, $15-$25
Lycoming Co., PA

G6, $20-$35
Union Co., PA

G6, $20-$35
Lycoming Co., PA

Called Stanly Narrow Blade in North Carolina

G6, $15-$25
MD

G8, $35-$60
Lancaster Co., PA

Classic form

LOCATION: Southeastern to Northeastern states. **DESCRIPTION:** A small to medium size, broad shoulder point with a small birfurcated stem. Some examples are serrated and show high quality flaking. The shoulders are very prominent and can be tapered, horizontal or barbed. **I.D. KEY:** Tiny bifurcated base.

STARK - Early Archaic, 7000 - 6500 B.P.

(Also see Adena, Koens Crispin, Lehigh, Morrow Mountain, Neville, Piscatawa, Poplar Island, Schuylkill & Stark)

Felsite

Felsite

Felsite

G6, $12-$20
Middleboro, MA

G5, $12-$20
Plymouth Co., MA

G4, $5-$10
CT

G5, $12-$20
Plymouth Co., MA

G5, $12-$20
Plymouth Co., MA

Quartzite

Felsite

G7, $25-$40
Plymouth Co., MA

G7, $25-$40
Plymouth Co., MA

Felsite

LOCATION: Conn., Mass. into New York. **DESCRIPTION:** A small to medium size, narrow, contracted stemmed point with tapering shoulders and a rounded to pointed stem. Similar to *Piscataway* and *Rossville* points found further south.

G7, $25-$45
Plymouth Co., MA

STARK (Continued)

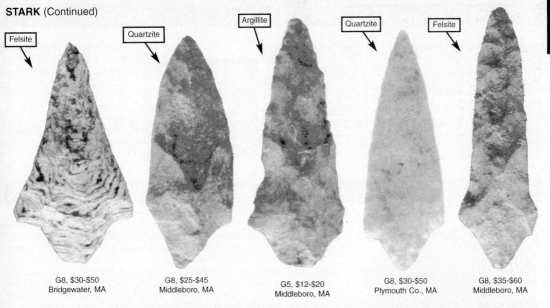

Felsite

Quartzite

Argillite

Quartzite

Felsite

G8, $30-$50
Bridgewater, MA

G8, $25-$45
Middleboro, MA

G5, $12-$20
Middleboro, MA

G8, $30-$50
Plymouth Co., MA

G8, $35-$60
Middleboro, MA

STRIKE-A-LITE, type I - Early to late Archaic, 9000 - 4000 B.P.

(Also see Drill, Scraper)

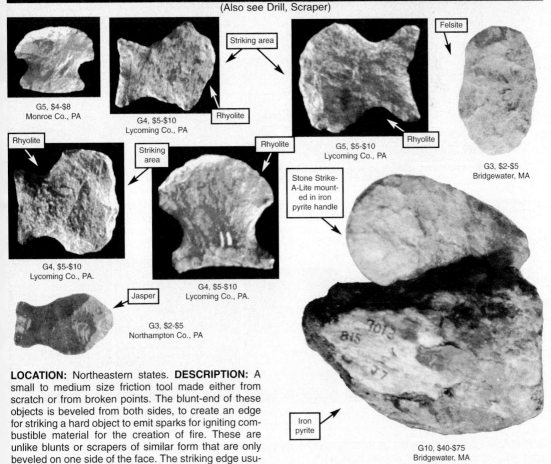

G5, $4-$8
Monroe Co., PA

Striking area

Rhyolite

G4, $5-$10
Lycoming Co., PA

Felsite

G5, $5-$10
Lycoming Co., PA

Rhyolite

G3, $2-$5
Bridgewater, MA

Rhyolite

Striking area

Rhyolite

Stone Strike-
A-Lite mount-
ed in iron
pyrite handle

G4, $5-$10
Lycoming Co., PA.

Jasper

G4, $5-$10
Lycoming Co., PA.

G3, $2-$5
Northampton Co., PA

Iron
pyrite

G10, $40-$75
Bridgewater, MA

LOCATION: Northeastern states. **DESCRIPTION:** A small to medium size friction tool made either from scratch or from broken points. The blunt-end of these objects is beveled from both sides, to create an edge for striking a hard object to emit sparks for igniting combustible material for the creation of fire. These are unlike blunts or scrapers of similar form that are only beveled on one side of the face. The striking edge usually shows extreme wear.

STRIKE-A-LITE, type II - Woodland, 3000 - 1000 B.P.

(Also see Drill, Ovates)

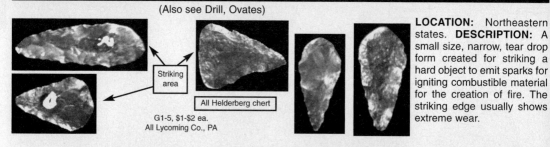

Striking area

All Helderberg chert

G1-5, $1-$2 ea.
All Lycoming Co., PA

LOCATION: Northeastern states. **DESCRIPTION:** A small size, narrow, tear drop form created for striking a hard object to emit sparks for igniting combustible material for the creation of fire. The striking edge usually shows extreme wear.

STRINGTOWN - Early Archaic, 9500 - 7000 B.P.

(Also see Scottsbluff)

G8, $30-$50
Geauga, OH

LOCATION: Pennsylvania, Ohio westward.. **DESCRIPTION:** A medium to large size, broad stemmed point with convex to parallel sides and square shoulders. The stem is parallel sided to slightly expanding. The base is eared and the hafting area is ground. Most examples have horizontal to oblique parallel flaking and are of high quality and thinness. The Eastern form of the *Scottsbluff* type made by the Cody Complex people. The *Eastern Stemmed Lanceolate* is a variation of this form. **I.D. KEY:** Base form and ground stem.

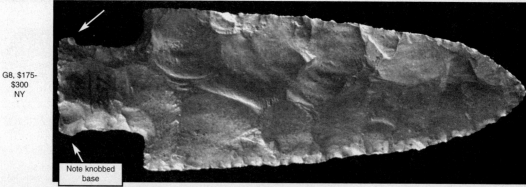

G8, $175-$300
NY

Note knobbed base

SUSQUEHANNA BIFURCATE - Early Archaic, 9000 - 6000 B.P.

(Also see Kanawha, Kirk Stemmed, Lake Erie, LeCroy, MacCorkle, Muncy, Penn's Creek, St. Albans, Stanly, and Taunton River Bifurcate)

Serrated edge

| G4, $8-$15 MD | G7, $12-$20 Centre Co., PA | G7, $12-$20 Lycoming Co., PA | G8, $15-$25 Union Co., PA | G8, $15-$30 MD |

LOCATION: Northeastern states. **DESCRIPTION:** A small to medium size bifurcated point with barbed shoulders and squared basal ears. **I.D. KEY:** Square basal ears.

SUSQUEHANNA BIFURCATE (Continued)

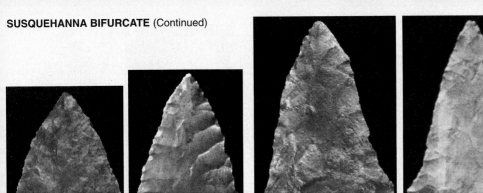

Yellow jasper

G7, $25-$40
Berks Co., PA

G8, $30-$50
Centre Co., PA

G8, $45-$80
Central PA

G9, $65-$125
Columbia Co., MA

SUSQUEHANNA BROAD POINT - Early Woodland, 3700 - 2700 B.P.

(Also see Ashtabula, Drybrook, Frost Island, Orient, Patuxent, Perkiomen and Waratan)

Felsite

Rhyolite

Tip wear

G4, $8-$15
Plymouth Co., MA

G4, $8-$15
Plymouth Co., MA

G5, $12-$20
Columbia Co., NY

G5, $15-$25
Lycoming Co., PA

G4, $12-$20
Lycoming Co., PA

G4, $12-$20
Columbia Co., NY

G6, $15-$30
Luzurne Co., PA

G6, $20-$35
Northumberland Co., PA

G6, $25-$40
Dauphin Co., PA

LOCATION: Northeastern states. **DESCRIPTION:** A medium to large size, broad, expanded stem point with tapered to clipped wing shoulders. The blade width varies from narrow to broad. Many examples are asymmetrical. Early forms have ground bases. An extremely popular type in the collecting area.

SUSQUEHANNA BROAD (Continued)

Rhyolite

Rhyolite

Rhyolite

Jasper

G9, $30-$50
Lycoming Co., PA

G6, $30-$50
Lycoming Co., PA

G9, $30-$50
Lycoming Co., PA

G9, $25-$40
Bridgewater, MA

Clipped wing form

G8, $65-$125
NY

Note heavy patina

Rhyolite

G8, $55-$100
York Co., PA

G9, $80-$150
Cent. OH

Clipped wing form

G10, $300-$500
Lancaster Co., PA

SUSQUEHANNOCK TRIANGLE - Late Woodland, 1500 - 400 B.P.

(Also see Erie Triangle, Levanna, Madison, Squibnocket Triangle, Yadkin)

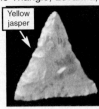

LOCATION: Pennsylvania.
DESCRIPTION: A small to medium size triangle. Some examples can be serrated. **I.D. KEY:** Triangle.

Yellow jasper

G6, $15-$25
Lycoming Co., PA

Serrated edge

Yellow jasper

G7, $25-$40
NJ

SWATARA-LONG - Archaic, 5000 - 4000 B.P.

(Also see Koens Crispin, Lehigh, Morrow Mountain, Poplar Island & Virginsville)

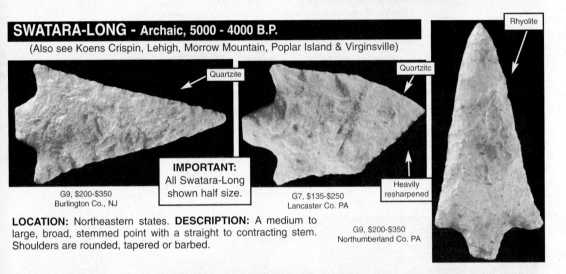

Quartzite

Quartzite

Rhyolite

IMPORTANT:
All Swatara-Long shown half size.

Heavily resharpened

G9, $200-$350
Burlington Co., NJ

G7, $135-$250
Lancaster Co. PA

G9, $200-$350
Northumberland Co. PA

LOCATION: Northeastern states. **DESCRIPTION:** A medium to large, broad, stemmed point with a straight to contracting stem. Shoulders are rounded, tapered or barbed.

TACONIC STEMMED - Mid-Archaic, 5000 - 4000 B.P.

(Also Drybrook, Lamoka, Merrimack, Newmanstown, Orient)

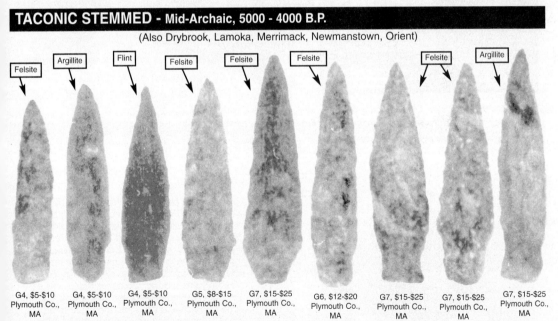

Felsite

Argillite

Flint

Felsite

Felsite

Felsite

Felsite

Argillite

G4, $5-$10	G4, $5-$10	G4, $5-$10	G5, $8-$15	G7, $15-$25	G6, $12-$20	G7, $15-$25	G7, $15-$25	G7, $15-$25
Plymouth Co., MA	Plymouth Co., MA	Plymouth Co., MA	Plymouth Co., MA	Plymouth Co., MA	Plymouth Co., MA	Plymouth Co., MA	Plymouth Co., MA	Plymouth Co., MA

LOCATION: Easterm Penn. into New Jersey, New York and Mass. **DESCRIPTION:** A medium to large, narrow, stemmed point with a straight, or contracting or expanding stem. Shoulders are weak and are tapered.

TAUNTON RIVER BIFURCATE - Early Archaic, 9000 - 8000 B.P.

(Also see LeCroy, MacCorkle, Susquehanna Bifurcate)

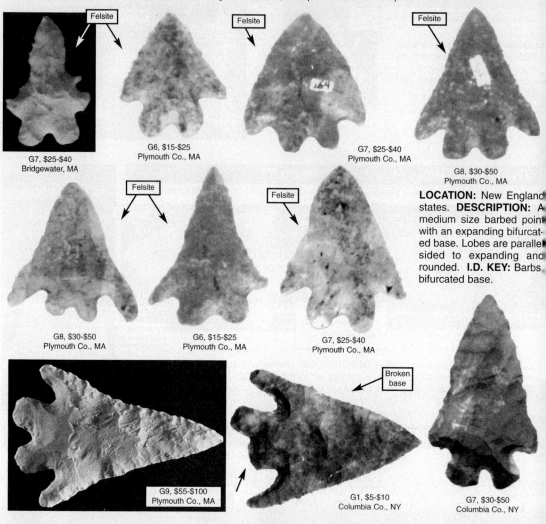

G7, $25-$40
Bridgewater, MA

Felsite

G6, $15-$25
Plymouth Co., MA

Felsite

G7, $25-$40
Plymouth Co., MA

Felsite

G8, $30-$50
Plymouth Co., MA

LOCATION: New England states. **DESCRIPTION:** A medium size barbed point with an expanding bifurcated base. Lobes are parallel sided to expanding and rounded. **I.D. KEY:** Barbs, bifurcated base.

Felsite

G8, $30-$50
Plymouth Co., MA

Felsite

G6, $15-$25
Plymouth Co., MA

Felsite

G7, $25-$40
Plymouth Co., MA

G9, $55-$100
Plymouth Co., MA

Broken base

G1, $5-$10
Columbia Co., NY

G7, $30-$50
Columbia Co., NY

THEBES - Early Archaic, 10,000 - 8000 B.P.

(Also see Lost Lake and St. Charles)

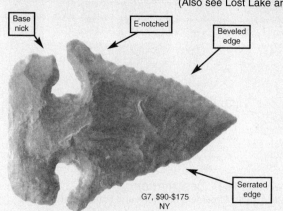

Base nick

E-notched

Beveled edge

Serrated edge

G7, $90-$175
NY

LOCATION: New York eastward into Ohio. **DESCRIPTION:** A medium to large size, wide blade with deep, angled side notches that are parallel sided and squared. Resharpened examples have beveling on one side of each face. The bases have broad proportions and are concave, straight or convex and are ground. Some examples have unusual side notches called *Key notch.* This type of notch is angled into the blade to produce a high point in the center, forming the letter E.

THEBES (Continued)

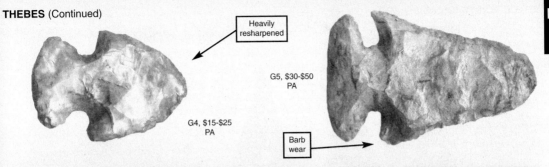

Heavily resharpened

G5, $30-$50
PA

G4, $15-$25
PA

Barb wear

TOCKS ISLAND - Early to mid-Woodland, 1700 - 1500 B.P.

(Also see Bare Island, Duncan's Island, Lackawaxen, Merrimack, Susquehanna Broad)

LOCATION: Lower Hudson river area. **DESCRIPTION:** A small to medium size stem- med point with a small, expanding base. Shoulders are barbed. **I.D. KEY:** Short expanding stem.

G5, $45-$80
Monmouth Co., NJ

White quartz

TRADE POINTS - Historic, 400 - 170 B.P.

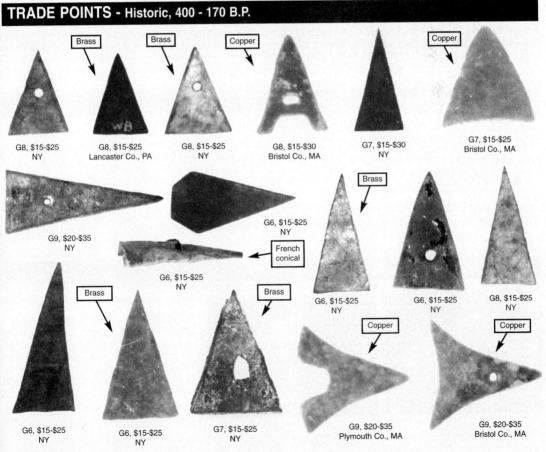

Brass

Brass

Copper

Copper

G8, $15-$25
NY

G8, $15-$25
Lancaster Co., PA

G8, $15-$25
NY

G8, $15-$30
Bristol Co., MA

G7, $15-$30
NY

G7, $15-$25
Bristol Co., MA

G9, $20-$35
NY

G6, $15-$25
NY

French conical

Brass

G6, $15-$25
NY

Brass

G6, $15-$25
NY

G6, $15-$25
NY

G8, $15-$25
NY

Brass

Brass

Copper

Copper

G6, $15-$25
NY

G6, $15-$25
NY

G7, $15-$25
NY

G9, $20-$35
Plymouth Co., MA

G9, $20-$35
Bristol Co., MA

TRADE POINTS (Continued)

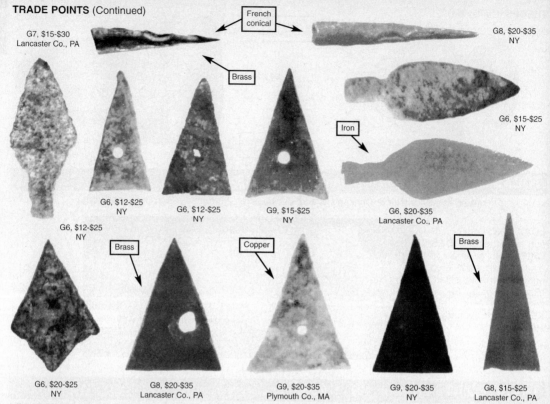

French conical

G7, $15-$30
Lancaster Co., PA

Brass

G8, $20-$35
NY

G6, $12-$25
NY

G6, $12-$25
NY

G9, $15-$25
NY

Iron

G6, $15-$25
NY

G6, $20-$35
Lancaster Co., PA

G6, $12-$25
NY

Brass

Copper

Brass

G6, $20-$25
NY

G8, $20-$35
Lancaster Co., PA

G9, $20-$35
Plymouth Co., MA

G9, $20-$35
NY

G8, $15-$25
Lancaster Co., PA

LOCATION: All States. These points were made of copper, iron and steel and were traded to the Indians by the French, British and others from the 1600s to the 1800s. Examples have been found all over the United States. Similar points were used against Custer at the battle of the Little Big Horn.

VERNON - Early Woodland, 2800 - 2500 B.P.

(Also see Brewerton, Kiski, Kline, Lycoming Co.)

G4, $3-$6
Long Level, PA

LOCATION: Northeastern states. **DESCRIPTION:** A small to medium size triangular point with a short, expanding stem. The base has rounded corners and the shoulders are usually barbed. **I.D. KEY:** Expanded base, barbed shoulders.

VESTAL NOTCHED - Late Archaic, 4500 - 4000 B.P.

(Also see Brewerton, Kiski, Kline, Lycoming Co.)

G6, $5-$15
Luzurne Co., PA

G6, $5-$15
Luzurne Co., PA

LOCATION: Northeastern states. **DESCRIPTION:** A small to medium size triangular point with a short, expanding stem. The base has rounded corners and the shoulders are usually barbed. **I.D. KEY:** Expanded base, barbed shoulders.

(Also see Adena, Conodoquinet Canfield, Lehigh, Koens-Crispin, Morrow Mountain, Piscataway, Poplar Island, Schuylkill)

G4, $8-$15
PA

Quartzite

G4, $12-$20
Montgomery Co., PA

Quartzite

G6, $15-$25
PA

G6, $15-$25
Lancaster Co., PA

Rhyolite

G7, $20-$35
Lancaster Co., PA

Tip nick

G7, $25-$40
Lancaster Co., PA

Rhyolite

G7, $25-$40
Berks Co., PA

G7, $30-$50
Lancaster Co., PA

LOCATION: Northeastern states. **DESCRIPTION:** A medium to large size triangular point with contracting shoulders and base that is usually rounded. **I.D. KEY:** Diamond shape.

VOSBURG - Archaic, 5000 - 4000 B.P.

(Also see Brewerton, Crooked Creek, Goddard, Jacks Reef, Kiski)

G7, $20-$35
Lycoming Co., PA

G5, $12-$20
Lycoming Co., PA

G7, $20-$35
Lycoming Co., PA

G5, $12-$20
Lycoming Co., PA

G7, $20-$35
Lycoming Co., PA

G7, $20-$35
Lycoming Co., PA

Gray chert

G5, $15-$25
Union Co., PA

G7, $20-$35
Union Co., PA

G7, $20-$35
Northampton Co., PA

Tip nick

G7, $20-$35
Union Co., PA

G10, $150-$250
Columbia Co., NY

LOCATION: Northeastern states. **DESCRIPTION:** A small to medium size corner notched point with a short, expanding base that is sometimes eared. **I.D. KEY:** Broad expanding base.

WADING RIVER - Archaic, 4200 - 4000 B.P.

(Also see Dewart Stemmed, Garver's Ferry, Lamoka, Merrimack, Sandhill Stemmed,)

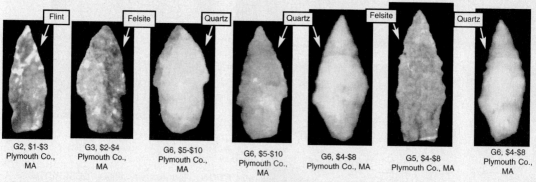

Flint

Felsite

Quartz

Quartz

Felsite

Quartz

G2, $1-$3
Plymouth Co.,
MA

G3, $2-$4
Plymouth Co.,
MA

G6, $5-$10
Plymouth Co.,
MA

G6, $5-$10
Plymouth Co.,
MA

G6, $4-$8
Plymouth Co., MA

G5, $4-$8
Plymouth Co., MA

G6, $4-$8
Plymouth Co.,
MA

LOCATION: Massachusetts and surrounding states. **DESCRIPTION:** A small size, thick, stemmed point. Stem can be contracting, expanding or parallel sided. Base is straight to rounded. **I.D. KEY:** Small size and thick cross section.

WAPANUCKET - Mid-Archaic, 6000 - 4000 B.P.

(Also see Bare Island, Benton (Central East), Genesee, Lackawaxen, Meadowood, New- manstown, Piedmont, Tocks Island)

IMPORTANT: All Wapanuckets shown half size

Jasper

G8, $200-$350
Monmouth Co., NJ

G7, $125-$200
Burlington Co., NJ

G10, $350-$600
MA

LOCATION: Northeastern states. **DESCRIPTION:** A medium to very large size short stemmed point. Bases can be corner or side notched, knobbed, bifurcated or expanded. Found in caches and closely resembles the *Benton* point found further south. **I.D. KEY:** Large size, notched blade.

WARATAN - Woodland, 3000 - 1000 B.P.

(Also see Drybrook, Perkiomen, Susquehanna Broad)

LOCATION: Eastern states. **DESCRIPTION:** A small to medium size point with usually broad, tapered shoulders, weak corner notches and a very short, broad, concave base. The base expands on some examples giving the appearance of ears or auricles. **I.D. KEY:** Short, broad, eared base.

Vein quartz

G6, $20-$35
Montgomery Co., PA

WAYLAND NOTCHED - Late Archaic, 3700 - 2700 B.P.

(Also see Ashtabula, Frost Island, Mansion Inn, Orient, Perkiomen, Susquehanna Broad)

Felsite

G7, $30-$50
Plymouth Co., MA

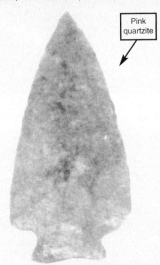

Pink quartzite

G9, $80-$150
Plymouth Co., MA

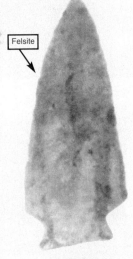

Felsite

G8, $60-$100
Plymouth Co., MA

WAYLAND NOTCHED (Continued)

Felsite

G8, $300-$500
Bridgewater, MA

G9, $150-$250
Norfolk Co., MA

LOCATION: Maine southward into New Jersey. **DESCRIP-TION:** A large size, broad, expanding stem point with tapered shoulders. Similar in form to the *Susquehanna Broad* point in which it is related. See *Mansion Inn* points which represent the preform for this type. **I.D. KEY:** Large size, broad, tapered shoulders.

WEB BLADE - Woodland, 1500 - 500 B.P.

(Also see Adena Blade)

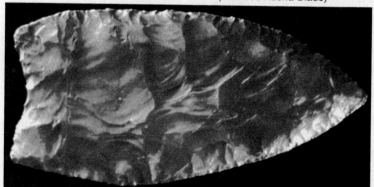

LOCATION: Northeastern states. **DESCRIPTION:** A large size, lanceolate blade with a thin cross section. Bases can be concave to straight. Believed to be related to the Adena culture. **I.D. KEY:** Large, thin blade.

G8, $350-$500
NJ

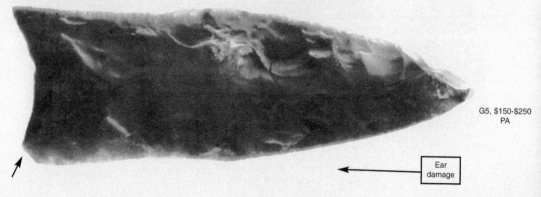

G5, $150-$250
PA

Ear damage

EASTERN SEABOARD SECTION:

This section includes point types from the following states:
North Carolina, South Carolina, Virginia and West Virginia

The points in this section are arranged in alphabetical order and are shown **actual size**. All types are listed that were available for photographing. Any missing types will be added to future editions as photographs become available. We are always interested in receiving sharp, black and white or color glossy photos, color slides or high resolution (300 pixels/inch) digital pictures of your collection. Be sure to include a ruler in the photograph so that proper scale can be determined.

Lithics: Argillite, crystal, chalcedony, chert, Coastal Plain Chert, flint, jasper, limestone, quartz, quartzite, rhyolite, shale, siltstone, slate, vein quartz.

Important sites: Baucom site, Union Co., N.C., Hardaway site in Stanly Co., NC., St. Albans site, Kanawha Co., WVA., Williamson site, Dinwiddie Co., VA.

Regional Consultants:
David Abbott, Ron L. Harris
Rodney Peck, Jack Willhoit
Warner Williams

Special Advisors:
Tommy Beutell
Tom Davis

EASTERN SEABOARD POINT TYPES
(Archaeological Periods)

PALEO (11,500 B. P. - 10,500 B. P.)

Clovis
Clovis Unfluted

Drill
Redstone

LATE PALEO (10,500 B. P. - 10,000 B. P.)

Alamance

Quad

Simpson

EARLY ARCHAIC (10,000 B. P. - 7,000 B. P.)

Amos	Fountain Creek	Kirk Stemmed	Stanly Narrow Stem
Big Sandy	Garth Slough	Kirk Stemmed-Bifurcated	Taylor
Bolen Bevel	Guilford Yuma	Lecroy	Thebes
Bolen Plain	Hardaway	Lost Lake	Van Lott
Charleston Pine Tree	Hardaway Blade	Palmer	Waller Knife
Dalton	Hardaway Dalton	Patrick Henry	
Dalton Greenbrier	Hardaway-Palmer	Rowan	
Decatur	Hardin	St. Albans	
Ecusta	Jude	St. Charles	
Edgefield Scraper	Kanawha Stemmed	Southampton	
Fishspear	Kirk Corner Notched	Stanly	

MIDDLE ARCHAIC (7,500 B. P. - 5,000 B. P.)

Appalachian	Buffalo Stemmed	Guilford Staright Base	Morrow Mountain Straight Base
Benton	Conerly	Halifax	Otter Creek
Brewerton Eared	Guilford Round Base	Heavy Duty	Pentagonal Knife
Brewerton Side Notched	Guilford Stemmed	Morrow Mountain	Pickwick

LATE ARCHAIC (5,000 B. P. - 3,000 B. P.)

Dismal Swamp
Exotic Forms
Holmes

Meadowood
Savannah River

EARLY WOODLAND (3,000 B. P. - 2,100 B. P.)

Adena	Fox Creek	Snyders	Yadkin
Adena Robbins	Greeneville	Waratan	Yadkin Eared
Armstrong	Gypsy	Wateree	
Dickson	Potts	Will's Cove	

MIDDLE WOODLAND (2,100 B. P. - 1,500 B. P.)

Randolph

LATE WOODLAND (1,600 B. P. - 1,000 B. P.)

Jack's Reef Corner Notched
Pee Dee

Uwharrie

LATE PREHISTORIC (1,000 B. P. - 500 B. P.)

Badin
Caraway

Clarksville
Occaneechee

HISTORIC (450 B. P. - 170 B. P.)

Hillsboro

Trade Points

EASTERN SEABOARD
THUMBNAIL GUIDE SECTION

The following references are provided to aid the collector in easier and quicker identification of point types. All photos are exactly 30% of actual size and are proportional to each other. Each point pictured in this section represents a classic form for the type. When a match is found, go to the alphabetical location of that type for more examples in actual size.

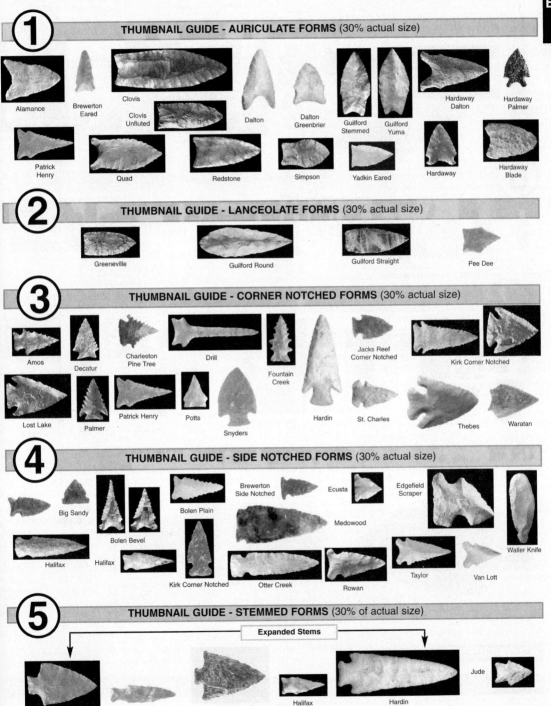

① THUMBNAIL GUIDE - AURICULATE FORMS (30% actual size)

Alamance · Brewerton Eared · Clovis · Clovis Unfluted · Dalton · Dalton Greenbrier · Guilford Stemmed · Guilford Yuma · Hardaway Dalton · Hardaway Palmer · Patrick Henry · Quad · Redstone · Simpson · Yadkin Eared · Hardaway · Hardaway Blade

② THUMBNAIL GUIDE - LANCEOLATE FORMS (30% actual size)

Greeneville · Guilford Round · Guilford Straight · Pee Dee

③ THUMBNAIL GUIDE - CORNER NOTCHED FORMS (30% actual size)

Amos · Decatur · Charleston Pine Tree · Drill · Fountain Creek · Jacks Reef Corner Notched · Kirk Corner Notched · Lost Lake · Palmer · Patrick Henry · Potts · Snyders · Hardin · St. Charles · Thebes · Waratan

④ THUMBNAIL GUIDE - SIDE NOTCHED FORMS (30% actual size)

Big Sandy · Bolen Plain · Brewerton Side Notched · Ecusta · Edgefield Scraper · Medowood · Waller Knife · Bolen Bevel · Halifax · Halifax · Kirk Corner Notched · Otter Creek · Rowan · Taylor · Van Lott

⑤ THUMBNAIL GUIDE - STEMMED FORMS (30% of actual size)

Expanded Stems

Dismal Swamp · Fishspear · Garth Slough · Halifax · Hardin · Jude

177

THUMBNAIL GUIDE- Stemmed Forms (continued)

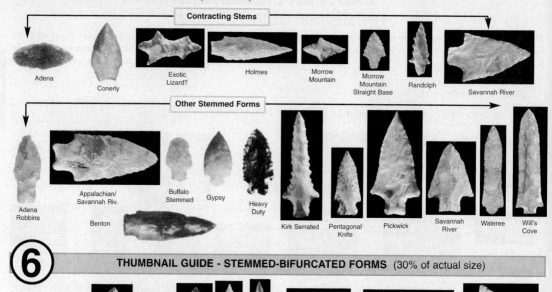

Contracting Stems

Adena

Conerly

Exotic Lizard?

Holmes

Morrow Mountain

Morrow Mountain Straight Base

Randolph

Savannah River

Other Stemmed Forms

Adena Robbins

Appalachian/ Savannah Riv.

Benton

Buffalo Stemmed

Gypsy

Heavy Duty

Kirk Serrated

Pentagonal Knife

Pickwick

Savannah River

Wateree

Will's Cove

⑥ THUMBNAIL GUIDE - STEMMED-BIFURCATED FORMS (30% of actual size)

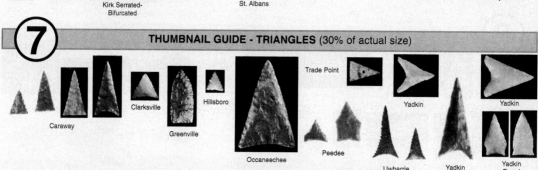

Kanawha

Kanawha

Kirk Serrated-Bifurcated

Lecroy

St. Albans

Southampton

Stanly Narrow Blade

Stanly

⑦ THUMBNAIL GUIDE - TRIANGLES (30% of actual size)

Caraway

Clarksville

Hillsboro

Greenville

Occaneechee

Trade Point

Peedee

Yadkin

Uwharrie

Yadkin

Yadkin

Yadkin Eared

ADENA - Late Archaic to early Woodland, 3000 - 1200 B. P.

(Also see Dickson)

G4, $2-$4
Kanawha Co., WVA

G4, $2-$4
Kanawha Co., WVA

LOCATION: Tenn. into Ohio and West Virginia. **DESCRIPTION:** A medium to large, thin, narrow, triangular blade that is sometimes serrated, and with a medium to long, narrow to broad rounded "beaver tail" stem. Most examples are from average to excellent quality. Bases can be ground. **I.D. KEY:** Rounded base, woodland flaking.

ADENA-DICKSON (see Dickson)

ADENA ROBBINS - Late Archaic to early Woodland, 3000 - 1200 B. P.

(Also see Savannah River)

ADENA ROBBINS (continued)

Tip damage

G3, $2-$4
Putnam Co., WVA

G4, $3-$5
Putnam Co., WVA

ES

LOCATION: Tenn. into Ohio and West Virginia. **DESCRIPTION:** A medium to large, thin, narrow, triangular blade that is sometimes serrated, and with a medium to long, narrow to broad stem that is parallel sided. Base can be straight to rounded. Most examples are from average to excellent quality. Bases can be ground. **I.D. KEY:** Rounded base, woodland flaking.

ALAMANCE - Late Paleo, 10,000 - 8000 B. P.

(Also see Hardaway & Hardaway Dalton)

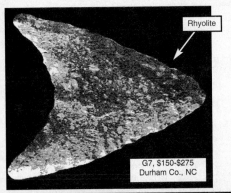

Rhyolite

G7, $150-$275
Durham Co., NC

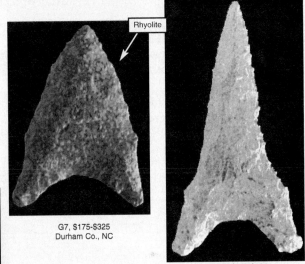

Rhyolite

G7, $175-$325
Durham Co., NC

G8, $250-$400
Surry Co., NC

G8, $275-$500
Chesterfield Co., NC

LOCATION: Coastal states from Virginia to Florida. **DESCRIPTION:** A broad, short, auriculate point with a deeply concave base. The broad basal area is usually ground and can be expanding to parallel sided. A variant form of the *Dalton-Greenbrier* evolving later into the *Hardaway* type. **I.D. KEY:** Width of base and strong shoulder form.

AMOS - Early Archaic, 9900 - 8900 B. P.

(Also see Decatur, Kirk Corner Notched and Palmer)

All-black
Kanawha
chert

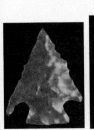 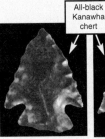    

G5, $15-$25
Putnam Co., WVA

G6, $18-$30
Putnam Co., WVA

G6, $18-$30
Putnam Co., WVA

G6, $20-$35
Putnam Co., WVA

G7, $25-$45
Putnam Co., WVA

G6, $20-$35
Putnam Co., WVA

AMOS (continued)

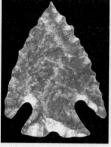

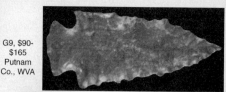

G9, $90-$165
Putnam Co., WVA

G9, $90-$165
Putnam Co., WVA

G7, $30-$50
Putnam Co., WVA

G8, $40-$75
Putnam Co., WVA

G8, $35-$65
Putnam Co., WVA

LOCATION: West Virginia into Pennsylvania and New York. Type site is in Kanawha Co., WVA. **DESCRIPTION:** A medium size, serrated, corner notched point with an expanding stem. Bases are straight, concave or convex and are ground. Basal corners are sharp to rounded. **I.D. KEY:** Deep serrations and expanding stem.

ANGELICO CORNER-NOTCHED (See Decatur)

APPALACHIAN - Middle Archaic, 6000 - 3000 B. P.

(Also see Rowan, Savannah River and Southampton)

Quartzite

G7, $65-$125
McDowell Co., NC

LOCATION: East Tennessee and Georgia into the Carolinas. **DESCRIPTION:** A medium to large size, rather crudely made stemmed point with a concave, straight or convex base. Most examples are made of quartzite. Shoulders are tapered and the base is usually ground. This point was named by Lewis & Kneberg for examples found in East Tenn. and Western North Carolina which were made of quartzite. However, this is the same type as *Savannah River*. **I.D. KEY:** Material Quartzite used.

ARMSTRONG - Woodland, 2450 - 1600 B. P.

(Also see Brewerton, Ecusta, Palmer, Patrick Henry and Potts)

LOCATION: West Virginia and neighboring states. **DESCRIPTION:** A small, short, corner notched point with barbed shoulders. Base is straight to convex and expands. **I.D. KEY:** Tangs and broad notches.

G4, $4-$8
Kanawha Co., WVA

BADIN - Late Prehistoric, 1000 - 800 B. P.

(Also see Caraway, Fox Creek, Guilford and Hillsboro)

LOCATION: Carolinas to Virginia. **DESCRIPTION:** A medium size triangular point that is larger and thicker than Hillsboro. Sides are convex with straight to slightly convex or concave bases. **I.D. KEY:** Thickness and crudeness.

G5, $6-$10
Montgomery Co., NC

BENTON - Middle Archaic, 6000 - 4000 B. P.

(Also see Savannah River, Stanly)

LOCATION: Eastern to midwestern states. **DESCRIPTION:** A medium to very large size, broad, stemmed point with straight to convex sides. Bases can be corner or side notched, double notched, knobbed, bifurcated or expanded. **I.D. KEY:** Wide squared, eared or notched base.

G6, $25-$40
Beaufort Co., SC

ES

BIG SANDY - Early to Late Archaic, 10,000 - 3000 B. P.

(Also see Bolen, Pine Tree, Rowan and Taylor)

Milky quartz

G5, $4-$8
Moore Co., NC

G2, $3-$6
Mason Co., WVA

G4, $6-$12
VA

Restored

G4, $6-$12
South-hampton
Co., VA

G6, $8-$15
Putnam Co., WVA

Quartzite

G5, $12-$20
Randolph Co., NC

LOCATION: Southeastern states. **DESCRIPTION:** A small to medium size, side notched point with early forms showing heavy basal grinding, serrations, and horizontal flaking. **I.D. KEY:** Basal form and blade flaking.

BOLEN BEVEL - Early Archaic, 10,000 - 7000 B. P.

(Also see Big Sandy, Patrick Henry and Taylor)

Beveled edge

Beveled edge

Beveled edge

Beveled edge

G4, $8-$15
Spartanburg Co.,SC

G5, $20-$35
Edgefield Co.,SC

G3, $5-$10
Beaufort Co.,SC

Barb nick

G6, $55-$100
Lexington Co.,SC

G6, $50-$90
Lexington Co., SC

G5 $25-$40
Randolph Co., NC

LOCATION: Coastal states into South Carolina. **DESCRIPTION:** A small to medium size, side-notched point with early forms showing basal grinding, beveling on one side of each face, and serrations. Bases can be straight, concave or convex. The side notch is usually broader than in *Big Sandy* points. E-notched or expanded notching also occurs on early forms. **I.D. KEY:** Basal form and notching.

181

BREWERTON EARED - Middle Archaic, 6000 - 4000 B. P.

(Also see Hardaway, Yadkin Eared)

G3, $3-$5
Kanawha Co., WVA

LOCATION: Eastern to midwestern states. **DESCRIPTION:** A small size, triangular, eared point with a concave base. Shoulders are weak and tapered. Ears are the widest part of the point. **I.D. KEY:** Small ears, weak shoulders.

BREWERTON SIDE NOTCHED - Middle Archaic, 6000 - 4000 B. P.

(Also see Big Sandy, Hardaway and Palmer)

LOCATION: Eastern to midwestern states. **DESCRIPTION:** A small to medium size triangular point with broad side notches. Bases are straight to convex to concave. **I.D. KEY:** Thickness and width.

G4, $5-$9
Mason Co., WVA

G5, $8-$15
Mason Co., WVA

BUFFALO STEMMED - Middle Archaic, 6000 - 4000 B. P.

(Also see Holmes and Savannah River)

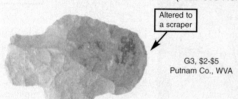

Altered to a scraper

G3, $2-$5
Putnam Co., WVA

LOCATION: West Virginia. **DESCRIPTION:** A medium size, broad, parallel stemmed point with tapered shoulders. **I.D. KEY:** Width, squared stem.

CARAWAY - Late Prehistoric, 1000 - 200 B. P.

(Also see Clarksville, Hillsboro, Uwharrie and Yadkin)

Serrated edge

Serrated on one side only

G4, $5-$10 Randolph Co., NC	G4, $5-$10 Randolph Co., NC	G4, $5-$10 Randolph Co., NC	G5, $8-$15 Randolph Co., NC	G6, $12-$20 Randolph Co., NC	G5, $8-$15 Randolph Co., NC	G6, $12-$20 Randolph Co., NC

Serrated edge

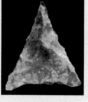

G7, $12-$20 Montgomery Co., NC	G6, $12-$20 Randolph Co., NC	G3, $3-$6 Randolph Co., NC	G6, $12-$20 Randolph Co., NC	G7, $12-$25 Randolph Co., NC	G7, $12-$25 Randolph Co., NC

LOCATION: Coincides with the Mississippian culture in the Eastern states. **DESCRIPTION:** A small to medium size, thin, triangular point with usually straight sides and base, although concave bases are common. Some examples are notched on two to three sides. Many are of high quality and some are finely serrated. Similar to *Madison* found elsewhere.

CARAWAY (continued)

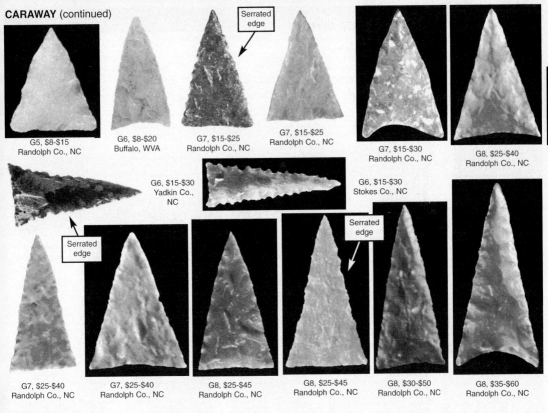

Serrated edge

G5, $8-$15
Randolph Co., NC

G6, $8-$20
Buffalo, WVA

G7, $15-$25
Randolph Co., NC

G7, $15-$25
Randolph Co., NC

G7, $15-$30
Randolph Co., NC

G8, $25-$40
Randolph Co., NC

ES

G6, $15-$30
Yadkin Co., NC

G6, $15-$30
Stokes Co., NC

Serrated edge

Serrated edge

G7, $25-$40
Randolph Co., NC

G7, $25-$40
Randolph Co., NC

G8, $25-$45
Randolph Co., NC

G8, $25-$45
Randolph Co., NC

G8, $30-$50
Randolph Co., NC

G8, $35-$60
Randolph Co., NC

CACTUS HILL (This small triangular point was dated approx. 15,000 B.P. in Virginia but verification is needed from other sites.)

CHARLESTON PINE TREE - Early Archaic, 8000 - 5000 B. P.

(Also see Kirk and Palmer)

LOCATION: Southeastern states. **DESCRIPTION:** A medium to large size, side notched, sometimes corner notched, usually serrated point with parallel flaking to the center of the blade forming a median ridge. The bases are ground and can be concave, convex, straight, or auriculate. Small examples would fall into the Palmer type. **I.D. KEY:** Archaic flaking with long flakes to the center of the blade.

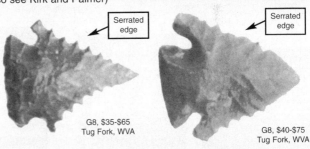

Serrated edge

Serrated edge

G8, $35-$65
Tug Fork, WVA

G8, $40-$75
Tug Fork, WVA

CLARKSVILLE - Late Prehistoric, 1000 - 500 A. D.

(Also see Caraway, Hillsboro, Uwharrie and Yadkin)

G5, $5-$10
Randolph Co., NC

G4, $4-$8
Randolph Co., NC

G3, $3-$6
Union Co., SC

G4, $3-$6
Randolph Co., NC

G3, $2-$5
Newberry Co., SC

LOCATION: Far Eastern states. **DESCRIPTION:** A small size triangular point with all three sides approximately the same width. The base is straight to slightly concave. Examples made from quartzite and quartz tend to be thick in cross section.

183

(Also see Redstone, Quad and Simpson)

Green rhyolite

Ridge & Valley chert

Coastal Plain chert

Petrified wood

G5, $125-$225
Randolph Co., NC

G6, $150-$250
Madison Co., NC

G5, $200-$350
Madison Co., NC

G5, $200-$350
Edgefield Co., SC

G5, $200-$350
Johnston Co., NC

Ridge & Valley chert

Long fluting channel

Slate

G5, $200-$350
Brunswick Co., VA

G5, $250-$450
Buncombe Co., NC

G6, $300-$550
Mecklenburg Co., VA

G7, $350-$600
Moore Co., NC

G6, $350-$600
Randolph Co., NC

All have ground basal areas

G7, $600-$1000
Coeburn Co., VA

Quartz crystal

G5, $250-$400
Randolph Co., NC

G6, $450-$800
Dinwiddie Co., VA

G6, $1000-$1800
Granville Co., NC

CLOVIS (continued)

Tip wear

Fluting channel

Long fluting channel

G8, $800-$1500
Saluda Co., SC

G5, $600-$1000
Clay Co., NC

G8, $800-$1500
Orangeburg Co., SC

G9 $1000-$1800
Mason Co., WVA

LOCATION: All of North America. **DESCRIPTION:** A medium to large size, auriculate, fluted, lanceolate point with convex sides and a concave base that is ground. Most examples are fluted on both sides about 1/3 the way up from the base. The flaking can be random to parallel. *Clovis* is the earliest point type in the hemisphere. *Clovis* technology more closely matches European *Solutrean* forms than anything else. There is no pre-*Clovis* evidence here (crude forms that would pre-date *Clovis*). **I.D. KEY:** Paleo flaking, shoulders, baton or billet fluting instead of indirect style.

CLOVIS-UNFLUTED - Paleo, 11,500 - 10,600 B. P.

(Also see Dalton, Fox Creek and Simpson)

G5, $150-$250
Sussex Co., VA.
Basal thinning.

LOCATION: All of North America. **DESCRIPTION:** A medium to large size, auriculate point identical to fluted *Clovis,* but not fluted. A very rare type.

CONERLY - Middle Archaic, 7500 - 4500 B. P.

(Also see Guilford)

Coastal Plain chert

G7, $80-$150
Edgefield Co., SC

LOCATION: Southern southeastern states including South Carolina. **DESCRIPTION:** A medium to large size, auriculate point with a contracting, concave base which can be ground. On some examples, the hafting area can be seen with the presence of very weak shoulders. The base is usually thinned. Believed to be related to the *Guilford* type. **I.D. KEY:** Base concave, thickness, flaking.

DALTON - Early Archaic, 10,000 - 9200 B. P.

(Also see Hardaway)

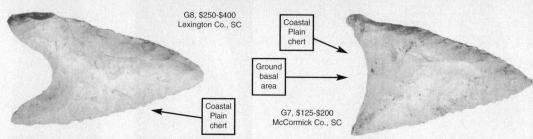

G8, $250-$400
Lexington Co., SC

Coastal Plain chert

Ground basal area

Coastal Plain chert

G7, $125-$200
McCormick Co., SC

LOCATION: Southeastern states including South & North Carolina. **DESCRIPTION:** A medium to large size, auriculate fishtailed point. Many examples are finely serrated and exhibit excellent flaking. Beveling may occur on one side of each face but is usually on the right side. All have basal grinding. This early type spread over most of the Eastern and Midwestern U.S. and strongly influenced many other types to follow. **I.D. KEY:** Concave base with auricles.

DALTON-GREENBRIER - Early Archaic, 10,000 - 9200 B. P.

(Also see Hardaway)

LOCATION: Southeastern states including South & North Carolina. **DESCRIPTION:** A medium size, auriculate form with a concave base and drooping to expanding auricles. Many examples are serrated, some are fluted on both sides, and all have basal grinding. **I.D. KEY:** Expanded auricles.

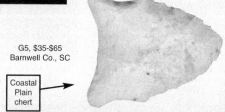

G5, $35-$65
Barnwell Co., SC

Coastal Plain chert

DECATUR - Early Archaic, 9000 - 3000 B. P.

(Also see Amos, Charleston Pine Tree, Dalton, Ecusta, Palmer and St. Charles)

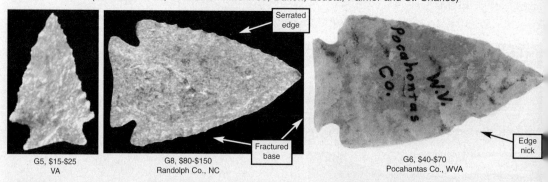

Serrated edge

G5, $15-$25
VA

G8, $80-$150
Randolph Co., NC

Fractured base

Edge nick

G6, $40-$70
Pocahantas Co., WVA

LOCATION: Eastern states. **DESCRIPTION:** A small to medium size, serrated, corner notched point that is usually beveled on one side of each face. The base is usually broken off (fractured) by a blow inward from each corner of the stem. Sometimes the side of the stem and backs of the tangs are also fractured, and rarely the tip may be fractured by a blow on each side directed towards the base. Bases are usually ground and flaking is high quality. Basal and shoulder fracturing also occurs in *Abbey, Dovetail, Eva, Kirk, Motley* and *Snyders*. Unfractured forms are called *Angelico Corner-Notched* in Virginia.

DICKSON - Woodland, 2500 - 1600 B. P.

(Also see Adena)

LOCATION: W. Virginia to Missouri. **DESCRIPTION:** A small to large size point with tapered shoulders and a contracting stem. High quality flaking and thinness is evident on most examples. **I.D. KEY:** Basal form.

Resharpened many times

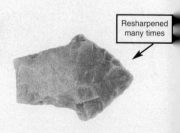

G4, $4-$8
Putnam Co., WVA

186

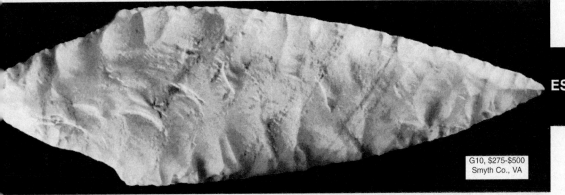

ES

G10, $275-$500
Smyth Co., VA

DISMAL SWAMP - Late Archaic to early Woodland, 3500 - 2000 B. P.

(Also see Garth Slough, Savannah River and Waratan)

LOCATION: North Carolina to Virginia. Similar to *Perkiomen* found in Pennsylvania. **DESCRIPTION:** A medium to large size, broad point with strong shoulders and a small, expanding base that is usually bulbous, blades can be asymmetrical. **I.D. KEY:** Broad shoulders and small base.

G6, $20-$35
Bethany, WVA

DOVETAIL (See St. Charles)

DRILL - Paleo to Historic, 11,500 - 200 B. P.

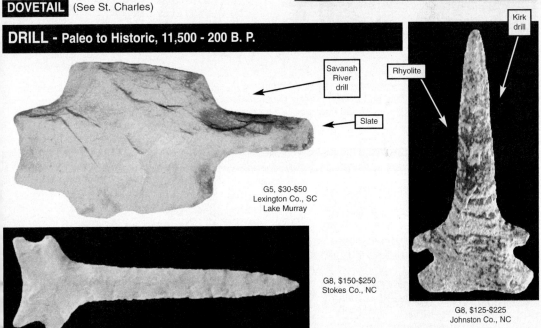

Savanah
River
drill

Slate

G5, $30-$50
Lexington Co., SC
Lake Murray

G8, $150-$250
Stokes Co., NC

Kirk
drill

Rhyolite

G8, $125-$225
Johnston Co., NC

LOCATION: All of North America. **DESCRIPTION:** Although many drills were made from scratch, all point types were made into the drill form. Usually, heavily resharpened and broken points were salvaged and rechipped into drills. These objects were certainly used as drills (evidence of extreme edge wear), but there is speculation that some of these forms may have been used as pins for clothing, ornaments, ear plugs and other uses.

ECUSTA - Early Archaic, 8000 - 5000 B. P.

(Also see Bolen Plain, Palmer and Potts)

G4, $8-$15
Bethany, WVA

G5, $10-$18
Bethany, WVA

G6, $10-$18
Bethany, WVA

LOCATION: Southeastern states. **DESCRIPTION:** A small size, serrated, side-notched point with usually one side of each face steeply beveled, although examples exist with all four sides beveled and flaked to a median ridge. The base and notches are ground. Very similar to *Autauga*, with the latter being corner-notched.

EDGEFIELD SCRAPER - Early Archaic, 9000 - 6000 B. P.

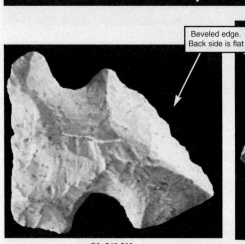

Beveled edge. Back side is flat

G8, $45-$80
Edgefield Co., SC

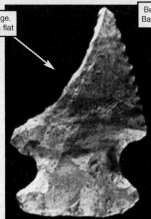

G8, $45-$80
Edgefield Co., SC

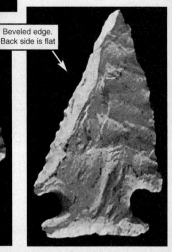

Beveled edge. Back side is flat

G8, $55-$100
Edgefield Co., SC

LOCATION: Southern Atlantic coast states. **DESCRIPTION:** A medium to large size corner notched point that is asymmetrical. Many are uniface and usually steeply beveled along the diagonal side. The blade on all examples leans heavily to one side. Used as a hafted scraper.

EXOTIC FORMS - Late Archaic to Mississippian, 5000 - 1000 B. P.

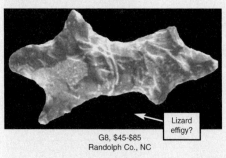

Lizard effigy?

G8, $45-$85
Randolph Co., NC

LOCATION: Everywhere. **DESCRIPTION:** The forms illustrated here are very rare. Some are definitely effigy forms while others may be no more than unfinished and unintentional doodles.

G8, $45-$85
Granville Co., NC

FISHSPEAR - Early to Mid-Archaic, 9000 - 6000 B.P.

(Also see Randolph)

FISH SPEAR (continued)

LOCATION: Northeastern states. **DESCRIPTION:** A medium to large size, narrow, thick, stemmed point with broad side notches to an expanding stem. Bases are usually ground and blade edges can be serrated. Named due to its appearance that resembles a fish. **I.D. KEY:** Narrowness, thickness and long stem.

G3, $8-$15
Kanawha Co., WVA

FOUNTAIN CREEK - Early Archaic, 9000 - 7000 B. P.

(Also see Kirk Stemmed)

G6, $15-$25
Wayne Co., NC

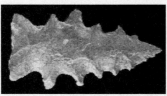

G7, $30-$50
Chatham Co., NC

Note strong barbs

G7, $30-$50
Nash Co., NC

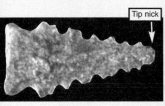

Tip nick

G4, $10-$18
Randolph Co., NC

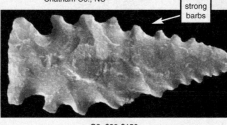

G9, $80-$150
Randolph Co., NC

LOCATION: Eastern states. **DESCRIPTION:** A medium size, narrow corner notched to expanded stemmed point with notched blade edges and a short, rounded base which is ground. **I.D. KEY:** Exaggerated barbs.

FOX CREEK - Woodland, 2500 - 1200 B. P.

(Also see Badin, Clovis Unfluted and Guilford Stemmed)

G6, $12-$20
Bethany, WVA

LOCATION: Northeastern states. **DESCRIPTION:** A medium size blade with a squared to tapered hafting area and a straight to slightly concave base. Shoulders, when present are very weak and tapered.

FOX VALLEY (See Kanawha Stemmed; See N. Central section for Fox Valley points)

GARTH SLOUGH - Early Archaic, 9000 - 4000 B. P.

(Also see Kanawha Stemmed and Stanly)

LOCATION: Southeastern states. **DESCRIPTION:** A small size point with wide, expanded barbs and a small squared base. Rare examples have the tangs clipped (called clipped wing). The blade edges are convex with fine serrations. A similar type of a later time period, called *Catahoula*, is found in the Midwestern states. A bifurcated base would place it into the *Kanawha Stemmed* type. **I.D. KEY:** Expanded barbs, early flaking.

G6, $30-$50
Pearson Co., NC

189

GREENEVILLE - Woodland, 3000 - 1500 B.P.

(Also see Caraway, Clarksville, Madison)

G8, $20-$35
Davidson Co., NC

LOCATION: Southeast to eastern states. **DESCRIPTION:** A small to medium size lanceolate point with convex sides becoming contracting to parallel at the base. The basal edge is slightly concave, convex or straight. This point is usually wider and thicker than *Guntersville*, and is believed to be related to *Camp Creek*, *Ebenezer* and *Nolichucky* points.

GUILFORD-ROUND BASE - Middle Archaic, 6500 - 5000 B. P.

(Also see Cobbs and Lerma in other sections)

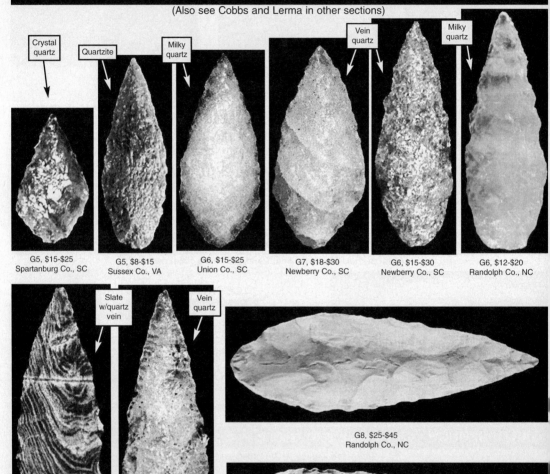

Crystal quartz

Quartzite

Milky quartz

Vein quartz

Milky quartz

G5, $15-$25
Spartanburg Co., SC

G5, $8-$15
Sussex Co., VA

G6, $15-$25
Union Co., SC

G7, $18-$30
Newberry Co., SC

G6, $15-$30
Newberry Co., SC

G6, $12-$20
Randolph Co., NC

Slate w/quartz vein

Vein quartz

G8, $25-$45
Randolph Co., NC

G6, $25-$45
Chester Co., SC

G6, $15-$25
Fairfield Co., SC

G8, $25-$45
Anderson Co., SC

LOCATION: North Carolina and surrounding areas. **DESCRIPTION:** A medium to large size, thick, narrow, lanceolate point with a convex, contracting base. This type is usually made of Quartzite or other poor quality flaking material which results in a more crudely chipped form than *Lerma* (its ancestor). **I.D. KEY:** Thickness, archaic blade flaking.

GUILFORD-ROUND BASE (continued)

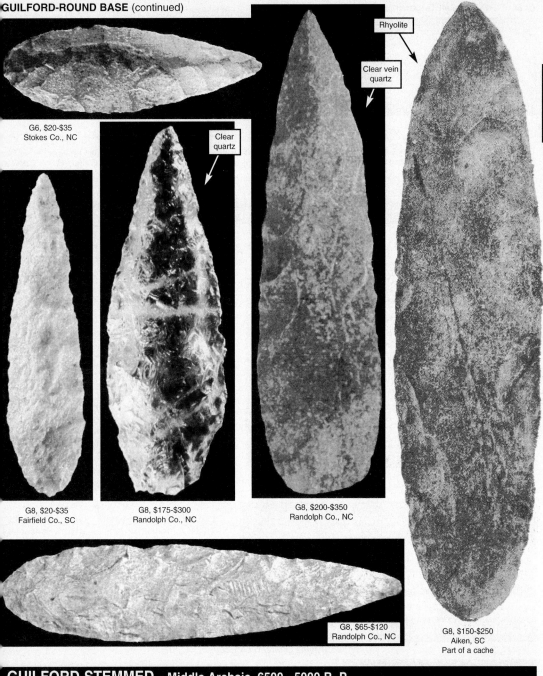

G6, $20-$35
Stokes Co., NC

Clear quartz

G8, $20-$35
Fairfield Co., SC

G8, $175-$300
Randolph Co., NC

Rhyolite

Clear vein quartz

G8, $200-$350
Randolph Co., NC

G8, $65-$120
Randolph Co., NC

G8, $150-$250
Aiken, SC
Part of a cache

ES

GUILFORD-STEMMED - Middle Archaic, 6500 - 5000 B. P.

(Also see Stanly Narrow Stem, Waratan and Yadkin Eared)

G5, $6-$12
Stokes Co., NC

G6, $20-$35
Orangeburg Co., SC

GUILFORD STEMMED (continued)

G4, $12-$20
Newberry Co., SC

G8, $125-$225
Charleston, SC, Ashley River

Coastal
Plain
chert

LOCATION: Far Eastern states. **DESCRIPTION:** A medium size, thick, narrow, lanceolate point with a straight to concave, contracting base. All examples have weak, tapered shoulders. Some bases are ground. Called *Brier Creek* in Georgia.

GUILFORD-STRAIGHT BASE - Middle Archaic, 6500 - 5000 B. P.

(Also see Fox Creek)

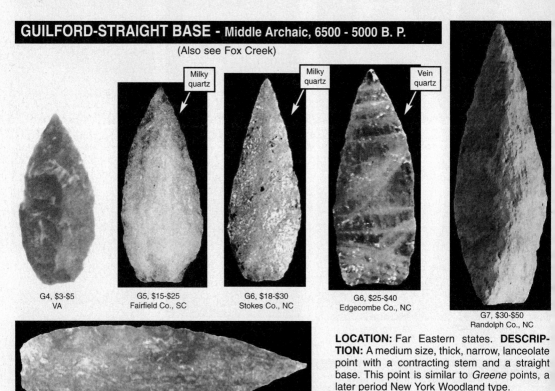

Milky
quartz

Milky
quartz

Vein
quartz

G4, $3-$5
VA

G5, $15-$25
Fairfield Co., SC

G6, $18-$30
Stokes Co., NC

G6, $25-$40
Edgecombe Co., NC

G7, $30-$50
Randolph Co., NC

LOCATION: Far Eastern states. **DESCRIPTION:** A medium size, thick, narrow, lanceolate point with a contracting stem and a straight base. This point is similar to *Greene* points, a later period New York Woodland type.

G8, $35-$60
Randolph Co., NC

GUILFORD-YUMA - Early Archaic, 7500 - 5000 B. P.

(Also see Clovis Unfluted and Yadkin Eared)

Milky
quartz

G5, $18-$30
NC

G6, $22-$35
Stokes Co., NC

Milky
quartz

LOCATION: Far Eastern states. **DESCRIPTION:** A medium to slightly large size, thick, narrow, lanceolate point with a contracting stem and a concave base. Quality of flaking is governed by the type of material, usually quartzite, slate, rhyolite and shale. Bases can be ground. Believed to be an early form for the type and may be related to the *Conerly* type.

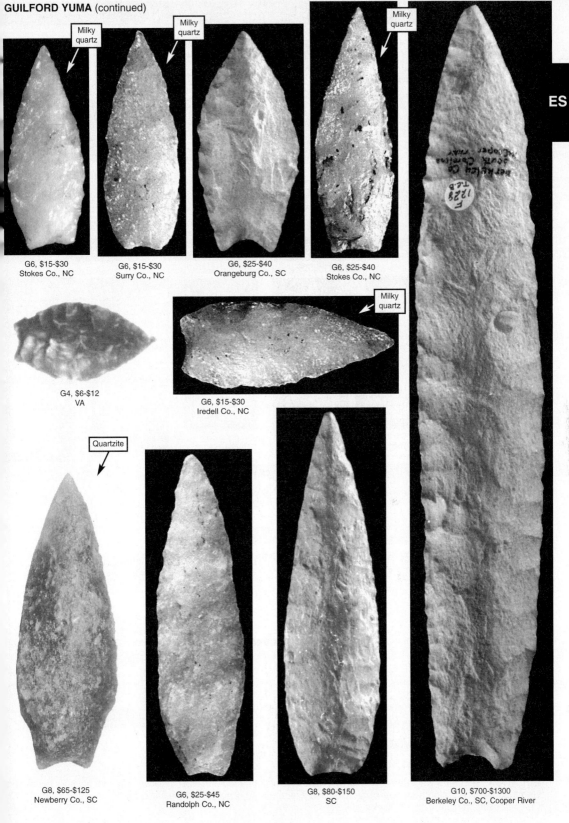

Milky quartz

G6, $15-$30
Stokes Co., NC

Milky quartz

G6, $15-$30
Surry Co., NC

G6, $25-$40
Orangeburg Co., SC

Milky quartz

G6, $25-$40
Stokes Co., NC

ES

G4, $6-$12
VA

Milky quartz

G6, $15-$30
Iredell Co., NC

Quartzite

G8, $65-$125
Newberry Co., SC

G6, $25-$45
Randolph Co., NC

G8, $80-$150
SC

G10, $700-$1300
Berkeley Co., SC, Cooper River

GYPSY - Woodland, 2500 - 1500 B. P.

(Also see St. Charles)

G8, $20-$35
Surry Co., NC

G7, $15-$25
Randolph Co., NC

LOCATION: North Carolina. **DESCRIPTION:** A small to medium size triangular point with a bulbous stem. Shoulders are usually well defined and can be barbed. **I.D. KEY:** Bulbous base.

HALIFAX - Middle to Late Archaic, 6000 - 3000 B. P.

(Also see Holmes, Rowan and Southampton)

Milky quartz

Milky quartz

Quartzite

Milky quartz

G3, $2-$5
Southampton Co., VA

G4, $4-$8
Sussex Co., VA

G4, $4-$8
Southampton Co., VA

G4, $4-$8
Sussex Co., VA

G4, $4-$8
Sussex Co., VA

G6, $5-$10
Sussex Co., VA

G3, $2-$5
Mason Co., WVA

G6, $15-$25
Dinwiddie Co., VA

Milky quartz

G8, $15-$30
Southampton Co., VA

Shale

G7, $15-$30
Disputanta, VA

G6, $4-$10
Sussex Co., VA

G6, $15-$25
Sussex Co., VA

LOCATION: Southeastern states. **DESCRIPTION:** A small to medium size, narrow, side notched to expanded stemmed point. Shoulders can be weak to strongly tapered. Typically one shoulder is higher than the other. North Carolina examples are made of quartz, rhyolite and shale.

HARDAWAY - Early Archaic, 9500 - 8000 B. P.

(Also see Alamance, Hardaway-Dalton, Patrick Henry and Taylor)

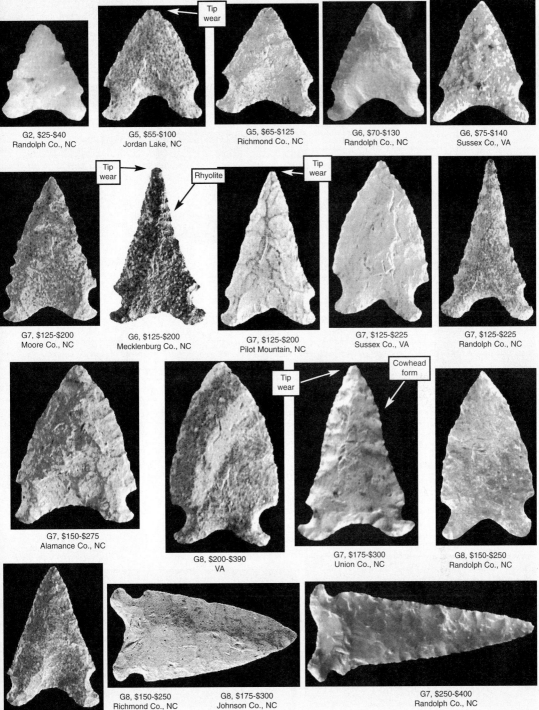

G2, $25-$40
Randolph Co., NC

G5, $55-$100
Jordan Lake, NC

Tip wear

G5, $65-$125
Richmond Co., NC

G6, $70-$130
Randolph Co., NC

G6, $75-$140
Sussex Co., VA

Tip wear

Rhyolite

Tip wear

G7, $125-$200
Moore Co., NC

G6, $125-$200
Mecklenburg Co., NC

G7, $125-$200
Pilot Mountain, NC

G7, $125-$225
Sussex Co., VA

G7, $125-$225
Randolph Co., NC

G7, $150-$275
Alamance Co., NC

Tip wear

Cowhead form

G8, $200-$390
VA

G7, $175-$300
Union Co., NC

G8, $150-$250
Randolph Co., NC

G8, $150-$250
Richmond Co., NC

G8, $175-$300
Johnson Co., NC

G7, $250-$400
Randolph Co., NC

LOCATION: Southeastern states, especially North Carolina. Type site is Stanly Co. NC, Yadkin River. **DESCRIPTION:** A small to medium size point with shallow side notches and expanded auricles forming a wide, deeply concave base. Wide specimens are called *Cow Head Hardaways* in North Carolina by some collectors. Ears and base are usually heavily ground. This type evolved from the *Dalton* point. **I.D. KEY:** Heavy grinding in shoulders, paleo flaking.

HARDAWAY BLADE - Early Archaic, 9500 - 9000 B. P.

(Also see Alamance)

LOCATION: North Carolina. **DESCRIPTION:** A small to medium size, thin, broad, blade with a concave base. The base usually is ground and has thinning strikes. A preform for the *Hardaway* point.

G4, $20-$35
Cent. NC

HARDAWAY-DALTON - Early Archaic, 9500 - 8000 B. P.

(Also see Alamance and Hardaway)

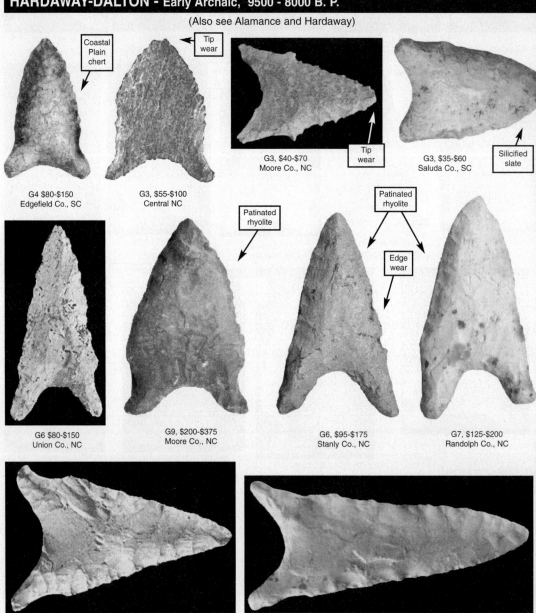

Coastal Plain chert

Tip wear

Tip wear

Silicified slate

G4 $80-$150
Edgefield Co., SC

G3, $55-$100
Central NC

G3, $40-$70
Moore Co., NC

G3, $35-$60
Saluda Co., SC

Patinated rhyolite

Patinated rhyolite

Edge wear

G6 $80-$150
Union Co., NC

G9, $200-$375
Moore Co., NC

G6, $95-$175
Stanly Co., NC

G7, $125-$200
Randolph Co., NC

G7, $250-$400
Johnston Co., NC

G8, $250-$450
Randolph Co., NC

LOCATION: Southeastern states. **DESCRIPTION:** A small to medium size, serrated, auriculate point with a concave base. Basal fluting or thinning is common. Bases are ground. Ears turn outward or have parallel sides. A cross between *Hardaway* and *Dalton*. **I.D. KEY:** Width of base, location found.

HARDAWAY PALMER - Early Archaic, 9500 - 8000 B. P.

(Also see Hardaway and Palmer)

LOCATION: Southeastern states. **DESCRIPTION:** A cross between *Hardaway* and *Palmer* with expanded auricles and a concave base that is ground.

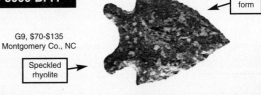

G9, $70-$135
Montgomery Co., NC

Classic form

Speckled rhyolite

HARDIN - Early Archaic, 9000 - 6000 B. P.

(Also see Kirk and Lost Lake)

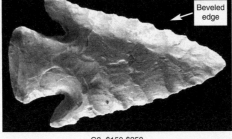

Coastal Plain chert

Beveled edge

G8, $150-$250
Orangeburg Co., SC

LOCATION: Midwestern to Eastern states. **DESCRIPTION:** A large size, well made triangular barbed point with an expanded base that is usually ground. Resharpened examples have one beveled edge on each face. This type is believed to have evolved from the *Scottsbluff* type. **I.D. KEY:** Notches and stem form.

G6, $80-$150
Charleston Co., SC
Cooper River

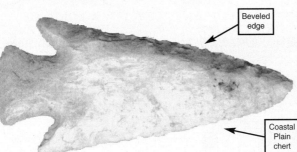

Beveled edge

G8, $200-$350
Brunswick Co., NC

Coastal Plain chert

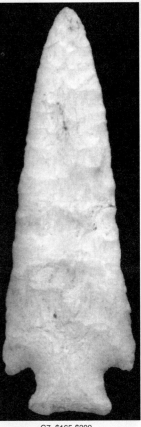

G7, $165-$300
Tyler Co., WVA

HEAVY DUTY - Middle Archaic, 7000 - 5000 B. P.

(Also see Appalachian, Kirk Stemmed and Southampton)

LOCATION: Ohio into West Virginia. **DESCRIPTION:** A medium to large size, thick, serrated point with a parallel stem and straight to slightly concave base. A variant of *Kirk Stemmed* found in the Southeast. **I.D. KEY:** Base, thickness, flaking.

G4, $12-$20
Bethany, WVA

HILLSBORO - Historic, 300 - 200 B. P.

(Also see Caraway and Clarksville)

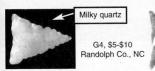

Milky quartz

G4, $5-$10
Randolph Co., NC

Serrated edge

G5, $7-$12
Randolph Co., NC

G5, $8-$15
Randolph Co., NC

Milky quartz

G6, $10-$18
Randolph Co., NC

HILLSBORO (continued)   **LOCATION:** North Carolina. **DESCRIPTION:** A small size, thin, triangular, arrow point with a straight to concave base. Blade edges can be serrated. Smaller than Badin to very small size.

HOLMES - Late Archaic, 4000 - 3000 B. P.

(Also see Savannah River, Southampton and Stanly Narrow Blade)

LOCATION: Far Eastern states. **DESCRIPTION:** A medium size, narrow point with weak, tapered shoulders and a slight concave base.

G4, $8-$15
Sussex Co., VA

Quartzite

JACKS REEF CORNER NOTCHED - Late Woodland to Mississippian, 1500 - 1000 B. P.

(Also see Kirk Corner Notched and Peedee)

Black flint

Tip wear

Tip wear

G4, $15-$25
Ashe Co., NC

G6, $25-$45
Ashe Co., NC

G3, $8-$15
Mason Co., WVA

G3, $8-$15
Mason Co., WVA

G6, $25-$45
Bethany, WVA

Barb nick

LOCATION: Southeastern states. **DESCRIPTION:** A small to medium size, very thin, corner notched point that is well made. The blade is convex to pentagonal. Some examples are widely corner notched and appear to be expanded stem points with barbed shoulders. Rarely, they are basal notched. **I.D. KEY:** Thinness, made by the birdpoint people.

G6, $25-$45
Mason Co., WVA

JACKS REEF PENTAGONAL   (See Peedee)

JUDE - Early Archaic, 9000 - 6000 B. P.

(Also see Garth Slough and Halifax)

G5, $8-$15
Montgomery Co., NC

LOCATION: Southeastern states. **DESCRIPTION:** A small size, short, barbed, expanded to parallel stemmed point. Stems can be as large as the blade. Rare in this area. **I.D. KEY:** Basal form and flaking.

KANAWHA STEMMED - Early Archaic, 8200 - 5000 B. P.

(Also see Kirk Stemmed-Bifurcated, LeCroy, St. Albans, Southampton and Stanly)

KANAWHA STEMMED (continued)

G3, $8-$15
Kanawha Co., WVA

G3, $5-$12
Kanawha Co., WVA

G8, $25-$40
Putnam Co., WVA

G5, $12-$20
Kanawha Co., WVA

G8, $30-$45
Mecklenburg Co., VA

ES

LOCATION: Eastern to Southeastern states. Type site is in Kanawha Co., WVA. **DESCRIPTION:** A small to medium size, fairly thick, shallowly bifurcated stemmed point. The basal lobes are usually rounded and the shoulders tapered or clipped wing turning towards the tip. Believed to be the ancestor to the *Stanly* type. The St. Albans site dated *Kanawha* to 8,200 B.P. Similar to *Fox Valley* found in Illinois.

KIRK CORNER NOTCHED - Early to Middle Archaic, 9000 - 6000 B. P.

(Also see Amos, Bolen, Hardin, Jacks Reef, Lost Lake, St. Charles, Taylor and Thebes)

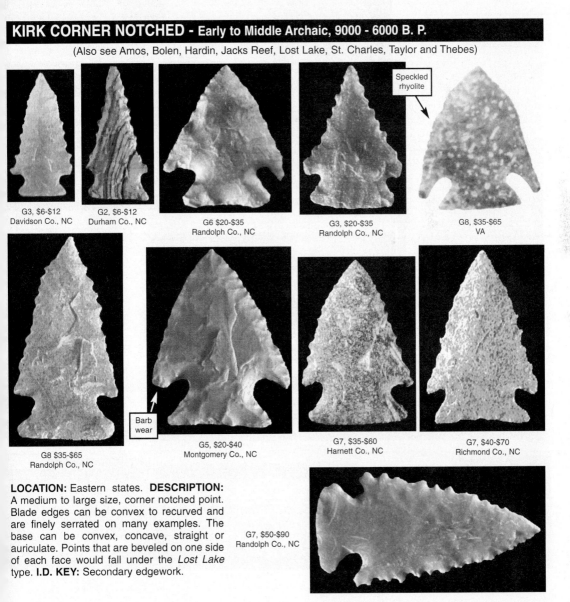

G3, $6-$12
Davidson Co., NC

G2, $6-$12
Durham Co., NC

G6 $20-$35
Randolph Co., NC

G3, $20-$35
Randolph Co., NC

G8, $35-$65
VA

G8 $35-$65
Randolph Co., NC

G5, $20-$40
Montgomery Co., NC

G7, $35-$60
Harnett Co., NC

G7, $40-$70
Richmond Co., NC

G7, $50-$90
Randolph Co., NC

LOCATION: Eastern states. **DESCRIPTION:** A medium to large size, corner notched point. Blade edges can be convex to recurved and are finely serrated on many examples. The base can be convex, concave, straight or auriculate. Points that are beveled on one side of each face would fall under the *Lost Lake* type. **I.D. KEY:** Secondary edgework.

199

KIRK CORNER NOTCHED (continued)

Black Kanawha chert

Barb nick

Green rhyolite

Serrated edge

Green speckled rhyolite

G6, $35-$65
Kanawha Co., WVA, St. Albans

G6, $30-$50
Randolph Co., NC

G8, $150-$250
Randolph Co., NC

G8, $55-$100
Randolph Co., NC

G6, $65-$125
Wilson Co., NC

G8, $175-$300
Surry Co., NC

G10+, $1800-$3000
Surry Co., NC

KIRK STEMMED - Early to Middle Archaic, 9000 - 6000 B. P.

(Also see Bolen, Fountain Creek, Heavy Duty, and Stanly)

Quartzite

G3, $4-$8
Cent. NC

G4, $6-$10
Kanawha Co., WVA

G5, $10-$18
Bethany, WVA

G3, $4-$8
Green Co., VA

ES

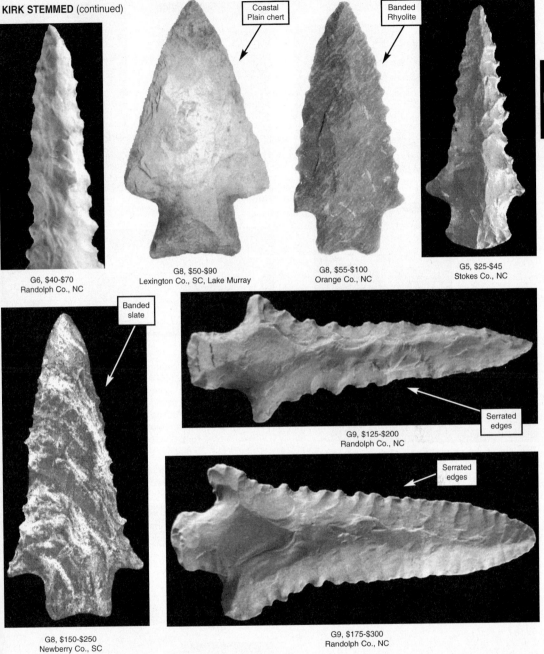

Coastal
Plain chert

Banded
Rhyolite

G6, $40-$70
Randolph Co., NC

G8, $50-$90
Lexington Co., SC, Lake Murray

G8, $55-$100
Orange Co., NC

G5, $25-$45
Stokes Co., NC

Banded
slate

Serrated
edges

G9, $125-$200
Randolph Co., NC

Serrated
edges

G8, $150-$250
Newberry Co., SC

G9, $175-$300
Randolph Co., NC

LOCATION: Southeastern to Eastern states. **DESCRIPTION:** A medium to large size, barbed, stemmed point with deep notches or fine serrations along the blade edges. The stem is parallel to expanding. The stem sides may be steeply beveled on opposite faces. Some examples also have a distinct bevel on the right side of each blade edge. The base can be concave, convex or straight, and can be very short. The shoulders are usually strongly barbed. Believed to have evolved into *Stanly* and other types. The St. Albans site dated this type from 8,850 to 8,980 B.P. **I.D. KEY:** Serrations.

KIRK STEMMED-BIFURCATED - Early Archaic, 9000 - 7000 B. P.

(Also see Cave Spring, Fox Valley, LeCroy, St. Albans, Southhampton and Stanly)

KIRK STEMMED BIFURCATED (continued)

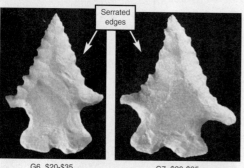

Serrated edges

G6, $20-$35
Randolph Co., NC

G7, $20-$35
Randolph Co., NC

Slate

G4, $12-$20
Saluda Co., SC

G5, $18-$30
Johnson Co., NC

G5, $15-$30
Randolph Co., NC

Serrated edges

G7, $30-$55
Randolph Co., NC

Serrated edges

G6, $25-$45
Randolph Co., NC

LOCATION: Southeastern to Eastern states. **DESCRIPTION:** A medium to large point with deep notches or fine serrations along the blade edges. The stem is parallel sided to expanded and is bifurcated. Believed to be an early form for the type which later developed into *Stanly* and others. Tennessee examples have a steep bevel on the right side of each blade edge.

LECROY - Early to Middle Archaic, 9000 - 5000 B. P.

(Also see Decatur, Kanawha Stemmed, Kirk Stemmed-Bifurcated, St. Albans, Southampton and Stanly)

G4, $10-$20
Wilkes Co., NC

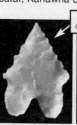

Milky quartz

G5, $10-$20
Wayne Co., NC

G5, $15-$30
Stokes Co., NC

G4, $10-$20
Madison Co., NC

Milky quartz

G5, $20-$35
Sussex Co., VA

Milky quartz

G8, $25-$45
Emporia Co., VA

G4, $12-20
Ashe Co., NC

Milky quartz

G8, $25-$40
Randolph Co., NC

G7, $20-$35
Randolph Co., NC

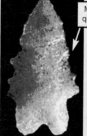

Milky quartz

G7, $25-$40
Emporia Co., VA

Milky quartz

G6, $25-$40
Randolph Co., NC

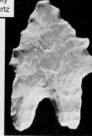

G3, $12-$20
Bethany, WVA

202

LECROY (continued)

G8, $25-$40
Randolph Co., NC

Nice serrations

G7, $25-$40
Randolph Co., NC

ES

G5, $20-$35
Randolph Co., NC

G9, $30-$50
Alleghany Co., NC

Milky quartz

G7, $20-$35
Randolph Co., NC

G5, $15-$30
Guilford Co., NC

G8, $20-$40
Emporia Co., VA

G8, $50-$90
Rowan Co., NC

LOCATION: Southeastern into northeastern states. Type site-Hamilton Co., TN. **DESCRIPTION:** A small to medium size, thin, usually broad point with deeply notched or serrated blade edges and a deeply bifurcated base. Basal ears can either droop or expand out. The stem is usually large in comparison to the blade size. Some stem sides are fractured in Northern examples *(Lake Erie)*. Bases are usually ground. St. Albans site dated *LeCroy* to 8,300 B.P. **I.D. KEY:** Basal form.

LOST LAKE - Early Archaic, 9000 - 6000 B. P.

(Also see Bolen, Decatur, Hardin, Kirk, Palmer, St. Charles, Taylor and Thebes)

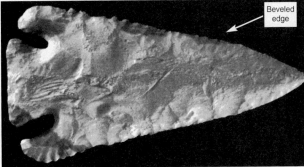

Beveled edge

Beveled edge

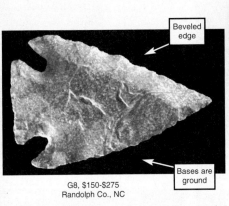

Beveled edge

Bases are ground

G8, $150-$275
Randolph Co., NC

G9, $350-$650
Pitt Co., NC

Beveled edge

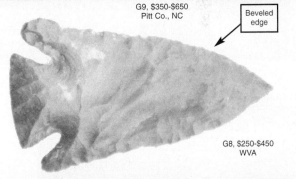

G8, $250-$450
WVA

LOCATION: Southeastern states. **DESCRIPTION:** A medium to large size, broad, corner notched point that is beveled on one side of each face. The beveling continues when resharpened and creates a flat rhomboid cross section. Most examples are finely serrated and exhibit high quality flaking and symmetry. Also known as *Deep Notch.* **I.D. KEY:** Notching, secondary edgework is always opposite creating at least slight beveling.

MEADOWOOD - Late Archaic to early Woodland, 4000 - 2500 B. P.

(Also see Otter Creek and Rowan)

MEADOWOOD (Continued)

LOCATION: Northeastern states into Virginia. **DESCRIPTION:** A medium to large size point with shallow side notches near the base. The base can be straight to slightly convex. Blade edges can be straight to slightly convex to recurved. Some specimens show a lot of reworking and my be used up and asymmetrical. **I.D. KEY:** Notches close to base

G7, $25-$45
VA

MORROW MOUNTAIN - Middle Archaic, 7000 - 5000 B. P.

(Also see Adena and Randolph)

G5, $8-$15
Moore Co., NC, Type I

G5, $8-$15
Sussex Co., VA, Type I

G7, $8-$15
Randolph Co., NC, Type I

G7, $12-$20
Randolphl Co., NC, Type II

G7, $25-$40
Randolph Co., NC, Type I

Rhyolite

G7, $40-$75
Randolph Co., NC, Type I

G6, $20-$35
Randolph Co., NC, Type II

G7, $25-$45
Randolph Co., NC, Type I

G6, $15-$25
Stokes Co., NC, Type II

Rhyolite

Very thin

G7 $25-$45
Randolph Co., NC, Type II

G7 $25-$45
Randolph Co., NC, Type I

LOCATION: Midwestern to Southeastern states. **DESCRIPTION:** A medium to large size, triangular point with a very short contracting to rounded stem. Shoulders are usually weak but can be barbed. The blade edges on some examples are serrated with needle points. **I.D. KEY:** Contracted base and Archaic parallel flaking.

Rhyolite

Flow banded rhyolite

ES

G8, $35-$65
Montgomery Co., NC, Type II

G7, $80-$150
Richland Co., SC, Type I

Slate

G6, $30-$50
Randolph Co., NC, Type II

G7, $350-$650
Newberry Co., SC, Type I, Lake Murray

MORROW MOUNTAIN STRAIGHT BASE - Middle Archaic, 7000 - 5000 B. P.

(Also see Adena and Savannah River)

G7, $8-$15
Bristol, VA

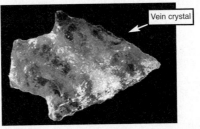

Vein crystal

G9, $65-$125
Johnson Co., NC

LOCATION: Southeastern states. **DESCRIPTION:** A medium size, thin, strongly barbed point with a contracting stem and a straight base. Some examples are serrated and have a needle tip. Look for Archaic parallel flaking.

OCCANEECHEE - Mississippian to Historic, 600 - 400 B. P.

(Also see Yadkin)

OCCANEECHEE (Continued)

Tip damage

LOCATION: North Carolina. **DESCRIPTION:** A large size triangular point with a concave base. Base corners can be sharp to rounded.

G5, $45-$75
Randolph Co.,
NC

OTTER CREEK - Middle to Late Archaic, 6000 - 3500 B. P.
(Also see Big Sandy, Meadowood and Rowan)

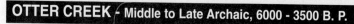

G6, $25-$40
Bethany, WVA

G6, $40-$70
WVA

G5, $15-$25
Bethany, WVA

LOCATION: Northeastern states. **DESCRIPTION:** A medium to large size, narrow side-notched point with a straight, concave or convex base. Notching is prominent, shoulders are tapered to barbed. Bases are ground. **I.D. KEY:** Side notching.

PALMER - Early Archaic, 9000 - 6000 B. P.
(Also see Amos, Ecusta, Hardaway-Palmer, Kirk Corner Notched and Taylor)

Vein quartz

Vein quartz

Vein quartz

Milky quartz

G5, $20-$35
Lexington Co., SC

G5, $20-$35
Lexington Co., SC

G5, $20-$35
Lexington Co., SC

G5, $20-$35
Lexington Co., SC

G5, $20-$35
Lexington Co., SC

G5, $25-$45
Lexington Co., SC

Crystal

Vein quartz

G5, $55-$85
Anderson Co., SC

G5, $20-$35
Lexington Co., SC

Milky quartz

G5, $20-$35
Lexington Co., SC

LOCATION: Southeastern to Eastern states. **DESCRIPTION:** A small size, corner notched, triangular point with a ground concave, convex or straight base. Many are serrated and large examples would fall under the *Pine Tree* or *Kirk* type. This type developed from *Hardaway* in North Carolina where cross types are found.

Crystal

G6, $50-$85
Union Co., SC

G6, $12-$20
Wayne Co., NC

G5, $12-$20
Randolph Co., NC

G6, $15-$30
Rockingham Co., NC

Milky quartz

G4, $8-$15
Onslow Co., NC

G6, $15-$30
Randolph Co., NC

ES

G8, $40-$75
Surry Co., NC

G10+ $250-$400
Randolph Co., NC

G6, $15-$25
Randolph Co., NC

G8, $40-$75
Randolph Co., NC

G8, $50-$90
Stanly Co., NC

G8, $55-$100
Randolph Co., NC

Serrated edges

Crystal

G4, $12-$20
Bethany, WVA

G9, $65-$125
Rockingham Co., NC

G7, $55-$100
Chatham Co., NC

G5, 25-$40
Montgomery Co., NC

G7, $55-$100
Randolph Co., NC

PATRICK HENRY - Early Archaic, 9500 - 8500 B. P.

(Also see Bolen, Decatur, Palmer and Taylor)

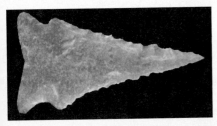

G8, $60-$100
Randolph Co., NC

G8, $65-$125
NC

LOCATION: Eastern seaboard states. **DESCRIPTION:** A medium size corner notched point with a fish-tailed base. Blade edges can be serrated and the basal area is ground.

PEE DEE - Late Woodland to Mississippian, 1500 - 1000 B. P.

(Also see Caraway and Jacks Reef)

LOCATION: Eastern seaboard states. **DESCRIPTION:** A small to large size, very thin, five sided point with a sharp tip. The hafting area is usually contracted with a slightly concave to straight base. Called *Jacks Reef* elsewhere.

G2, $3-$5
Smyth Co., VA

G3, $5-$10
Smyth Co., VA

G4, $5-$10
Wilkes Co., NC

G4, $5-$10
Randolph Co., NC

G3, $8-$15
Rancolph Co., NC

G5, $15-$30
Randolph Co., NC

G6, $15-$25
Wilkes Co., NC

G4, $12-$20
Surry Co., NC

G7, $15-$30
Randolph Co., NC

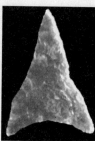
G6, $15-$30
Randolph Co., NC

G6, $25-$40
Randolph Co., NC

G5, $15-$30
Wilkes Co., NC

PENTAGONAL KNIFE - Mid-Archaic, 6500 - 4000 B. P.

(Also see Kirk)

G8, $35-$65
Surry Co., VA

G8, $125-$200
Rockingham Co., NC

LOCATION: Ohio into Kentucky, Tennessee, North Carolina & Alabama. **DESCRIPTION:** A medium to large size pentagonal shaped point with a flaring or corner notched stem. Some examples are base notched. Similar to but older than the *Afton* point found in the Midwest. Similar to *Jacks Reef* but thicker. **I.D. KEY:** Blade form.

PICKWICK - Middle to Late Archaic, 6000 - 3500 B. P.

(Also see Savannah River and Stanly)

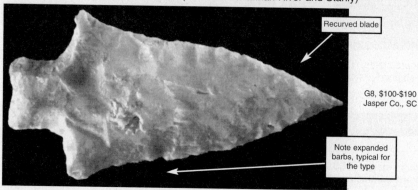

Recurved blade

G8, $100-$190
Jasper Co., SC

Note expanded
barbs, typical for
the type

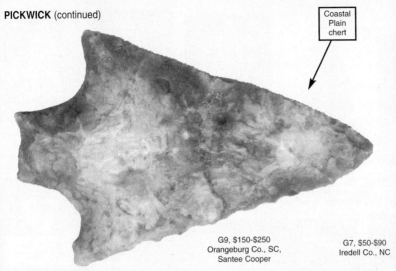

Coastal Plain chert

G9, $150-$250
Orangeburg Co., SC,
Santee Cooper

G7, $50-$90
Iredell Co., NC

LOCATION: Southeastern states into North and South Carolina. **DESCRIPTION:** A medium to large size, expanded shoulder, contracted to expanded stem point. Blade edges are recurved, and many examples show fine secondary flaking with serrations. Some are beveled on one side of each face. The bevel is steep and shallow. Shoulders are horizontal, tapered or barbed and form sharp angles. Some stems are snapped off or may show original rind. **I.D. KEY:** Barbs and blade form.

PINETREE (see Charleston Pine Tree)

POTTS - Woodland, 3000 - 1000 B. P.
(Also see Ecusta and Waratan)

LOCATION: Far Eastern states. **DESCRIPTION:** A medium size triangular point with a short, straight base that has shallow corner notches.

G5, $8-$15
Rockingham Co., NC

QUAD - Late Paleo, 10,000 - 6000 B. P.
(Also see Simpson and Waratan)

G5, $125-$200
Myrtle Beach, SC

G7, $175-$300
Orangeburg Co., SC

LOCATION: Southeastern states. **DESCRIPTION:** A medium to large size lanceolate point with flaring "squared" auricles and a concave base which is ground. Most examples show basal thinning and some are fluted. **I.D. KEY:** Paleo flaking, squarish auricles.

RANDOLPH - Woodland to Historic, 2000 - 200 B. P.
(Also see Morrow Mountain)

LOCATION: Far Eastern states. Type site is Randolph Co., NC. **DESCRIPTION:** A medium size, narrow, thick, spike point with tapered shoulders and a short to medium contracted, rounded stem. Many examples from North Carolina have exaggerated spikes along the blade edges.

RANDOLPH (continued)

G3, $3-$6
Guilford Co., NC

G4, $5-$10
Randolph Co., NC

G6, $5-$10
Randolph Co., NC

G4 $5-$10
Randolph Co., NC

G5 $8-$15
Randolph Co., NC

G7, $15-$25
Randolph Co., NC

G6, $12-$20
Randolph Co., NC

G6, $12-$20
Randolph Co., NC

G7, $20-$35
Randolph Co., NC

G3, $4-$8
Randolph Co., NC

G7, $20-$35
Randolph Co., NC

G8, $30-$55
Guilford Co., NC

G8, $30-$55
Randolph Co., NC

G9, $40-$75
Randolph Co., NC

REDSTONE - Paleo, 11,500 - 10,600 B. P.

(Also see Clovis)

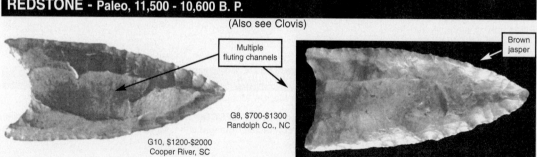

Multiple
fluting channels

Brown
jasper

G8, $700-$1300
Randolph Co., NC

G10, $1200-$2000
Cooper River, SC

REDSTONE (continued)

LOCATION: Southeastern states. **DESCRIPTION:** A medium to large size, thin, auriculate, fluted point with convex sides expanding to a wide, deeply concave base. The hafting area is ground. This point is widest at the base. Fluting can extend most of the way down each face. Multiple flutes are usual. (**Warning:** The more common resharpened *Clovis* point is often sold as this type. *Redstones* are extrememly rare and are almost never offered for sale.) **I.D. KEY:** Baton fluted, edgework on the hafting area.

ROWAN - Early Archaic, 9500 - 8000 B. P.

(Also see Big Sandy and Bolen)

G3, $12-$20
Montgomery Co., NC

G4, $15-$25
Ashe Co., NC

G6, $15-$25
Yadkin Co., NC

G7, $20-$35
Randolph Co., NC

Crystal

Milky quartz

G6, $65-$125
Randolph Co., NC

G7, $15-$25
Randolph Co., NC

Rhyolite

G7, $35-$60
Randolph Co., NC

G7, $25-$45
Randolph Co., NC

G8, $35-$60
Montgomery Co., NC

G6, $20-$35
Randolph Co., NC

G8, $90-$175
Moore Co., NC

LOCATION: Far Eastern states. Type site is Rowan Co., North Carolina. **DESCRIPTION:** A medium to large size, side-notched point that can be easily confused with the *Big Sandy* type. The basal area is usually wider than the blade. Some examples have expanded ears, and grinding commonly occurs around the basal area. Believed to be an intermediate form developing from *Dalton, Quad, Greenbrier* or *Hardaway* and changing into *Big Sandy* and other later side notched forms.

ST. ALBANS - Early to Middle Archaic, 9000 - 5000 B. P.

(Also see Decatur, Kanawha, Kirk Stemmed-Bifurcated, LeCroy, Southampton and Stanly)

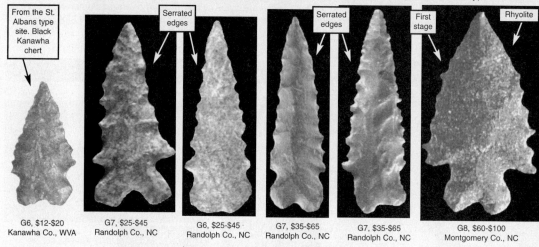

From the St. Albans type site. Black Kanawha chert

Serrated edges

Serrated edges

First stage

Rhyolite

G6, $12-$20
Kanawha Co., WVA

G7, $25-$45
Randolph Co., NC

G6, $25-$45
Randolph Co., NC

G7, $35-$65
Randolph Co., NC

G7, $35-$65
Randolph Co., NC

G8, $60-$100
Montgomery Co., NC

LOCATION: Eastern states. Type site is in Kanawha Co., WVA. **DESCRIPTION:** A small to medium size, narrow, usually serrated, bifurcated point. Basal lobes usually flare outward and most examples are sharply barbed. The basal lobes are more shallow than in the *LeCroy* type, otherwise they are easily confused. St. Albans site dated this type to 8,850 B.P. **I.D. KEY:** Shallow basal lobes and narrowness.

ST. CHARLES - Early Archaic, 9500 - 8000 B. P.

(Also see Bolen Beveled, Decatur, Lost Lake and Thebes)

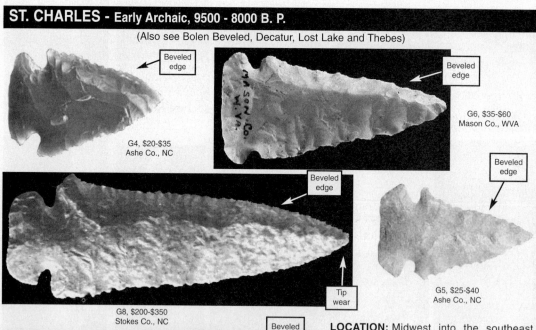

Beveled edge

G4, $20-$35
Ashe Co., NC

Beveled edge

G6, $35-$60
Mason Co., WVA

Beveled edge

Beveled edge

G5, $25-$40
Ashe Co., NC

Tip wear

G8, $200-$350
Stokes Co., NC

Beveled edge

LOCATION: Midwest into the southeast. **DESCRIPTION:** Also known as *Dovetail* and *Plevna*. A medium to large size, corner notched, dovetailed base point. The blade is beveled on one side of each face (usually the left side) on resharpened examples. Bases are always convex. Straight bases would place a point into the *Lost Lake* type. Bases are ground and can be fractured on both sides or center notched on some examples. **I.D. KEY:** Dovetailed base.

G8, $175-$300
Randolph Co., NC

(Also see Appalachian, Kirk and Stanly)

ES

Slate

G6, $30-$55
Orange Co., NC

Banded rhyolite

G7, $65-$125
Alamance Co., NC

Slate

G2, $5-$10
Newberry Co., SC

Slate

G3, $8-$15
Union Co., SC

Coastal Plain chert

G6, $55-$100
Beaufort Co., SC, Combahee River

Rhyolite

G8, $150-$250
Randolph Co., NC

Very thin

G7, $80-$150
Randolph Co., NC

LOCATION: Southeastern to Eastern states. **DESCRIPTION:** A medium to large size, straight to contracting stemmed point with a straight or concave to bifurcated base. The shoulders are tapered to square. The stems are narrow to broad. Believed to be related to the earlier *Stanly* point. Aka *Appalachian* points in East Tenn. & Western North Carolina.

Slate

G6, $65-$125
Fairfield Co., SC

G8, $80-$150
Granville Co., NC

Drill form

Rhyolite

Slate

G8, $150-$250
Cent. NC

G9, $200-$350
NC

G6, $125-$200
Montgomery Co., NC, Pee Dee River

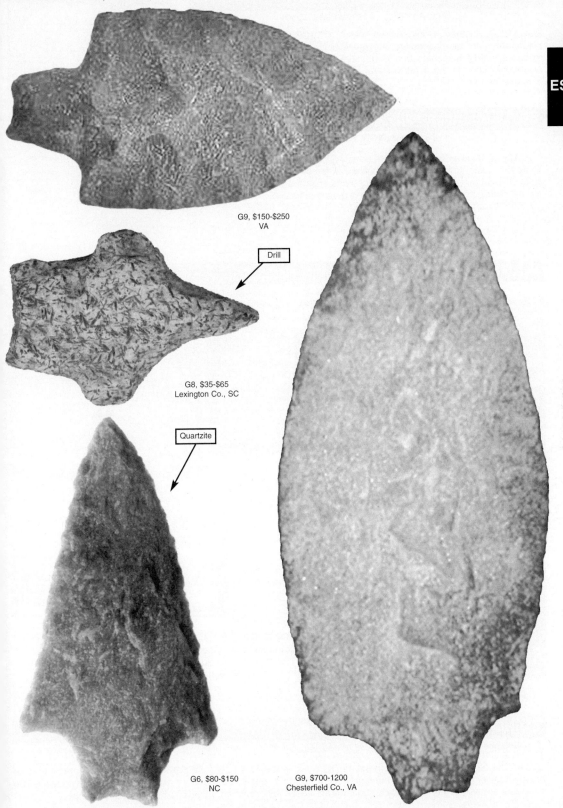

ES

G9, $150-$250
VA

Drill

G8, $35-$65
Lexington Co., SC

Quartzite

G6, $80-$150
NC

G9, $700-1200
Chesterfield Co., VA

SIMPSON - Late Paleo, 10,000 - 9000 B. P.

(Also see Clovis-unfluted and Quad)

LOCATION: Southern Southeastern states. **DESCRIPTION:** A medium to large size lanceolate, auriculate blade with recurved sides, outward flaring ears and a concave base. The hafting area constriction is more narrow than in the *Suwannee* type. Fluting is absent.

G8, $150-$250
Edgefield Co.,
SC

SNYDERS (Hopewell) - Woodland, 2500 - 1500 B. P.

(Also see Jack's Reef)

LOCATION: Midwestern to eastern states. **DESCRIPTION:** A medium to large size, broad, thin, wide corner notched point of high quality. Blade edges and base are convex. This point has been reproduced in recent years. I.D. KEY: Size and broad corner notches.

G8, $35-$65
VA

SOUTHAMPTON - Early Archaic, 8000 - 6000 B. P.

(Also see Kanawha, St. Albans and Stanly)

G3, $3-$5
Sussex Co., VA

Milky quartz

Milky quartz

Quartzite

G3, $4-$8
Southampton Co., VA

G2, $2-$5
Sussex Co., VA

G3, $5-$10
Cent. NC

G3, $5-$10
Dinwiddie Co., VA

G3, $5-$10
Sussex Co., VA

Quartzite

G5, $6-$12
Sussex Co., VA

Quartzite

G4, $6-$12
Dinwiddie Co., VA

G4, $6-$12
Sussex Co., VA

LOCATION: Far Eastern states. **DESCRIPTION:** A medium to large size, narrow, thick, bifurcated stemmed point. The basal lobes can expand and the center notch is shallow. Bases are usually ground.

STANLY - Early Archaic, 8000 - 5000 B. P.

(Also see Garth Slough, Kanawha Stemmed, Kirk Stemmed-Bifurcated, Savannah River and Southampton)

LOCATION: Southeastern to Eastern states. Type site is Stanly Co., NC. **DESCRIPTION:** A small to medium size, broad shoulder point with a small bifurcated stem. Some examples are serrated and show high quality flaking. The shoulders are very prominent and can be tapered, horizontal or barbed. **I.D. KEY:** Small bifurcated base.

Green rhyolite

Worn tip

ES

G8, $40-$75
Randolph Co., NC

G4, $30-$50
Cent. NC

G3, $25-$40
Pearson Co., NC

G7, $50-$90
Stanly Co., NC

G7, $50-$90
Rockingham Co., NC

G6, $30-$55
Cent. NC

G5, $35-$60
Montgomery Co., NC

Rhyolite

Shale

G8, $40-$75
Newberry Co., SC

G5, $30-$55
Wayne Co., NC

G8, $40-$75
Randolph Co., NC

G6, $35-$60
Randolph Co., NC

217

STANLY NARROW STEM - Early Archaic, 8000 - 5000 B. P.

(Also see Kirk Stemmed-Bifurcated, St. Albans, Savannah River & Southampton)

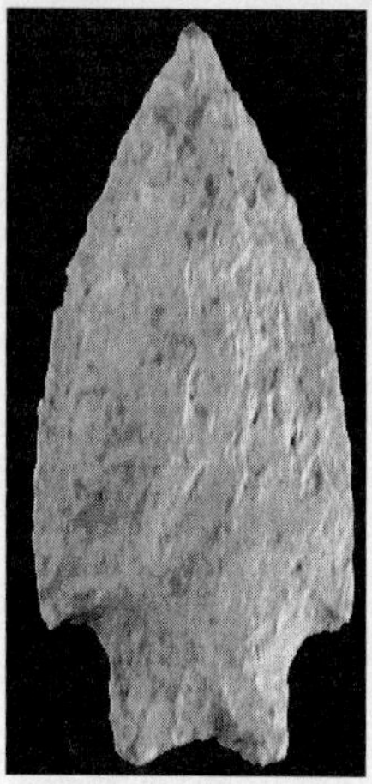

G6, $25-$40
Chatham Co., NC

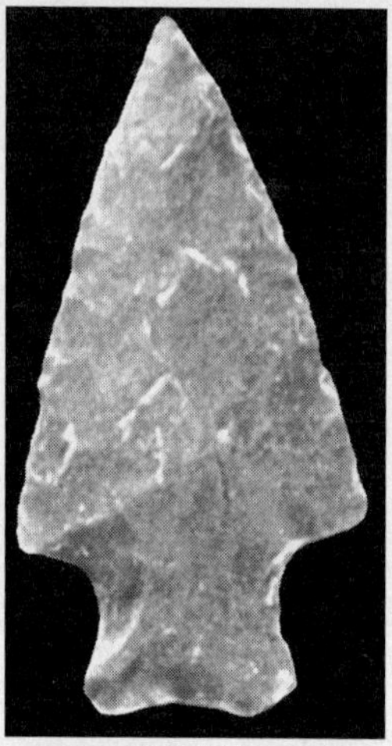

G5, $25-$40
Randolph Co., NC

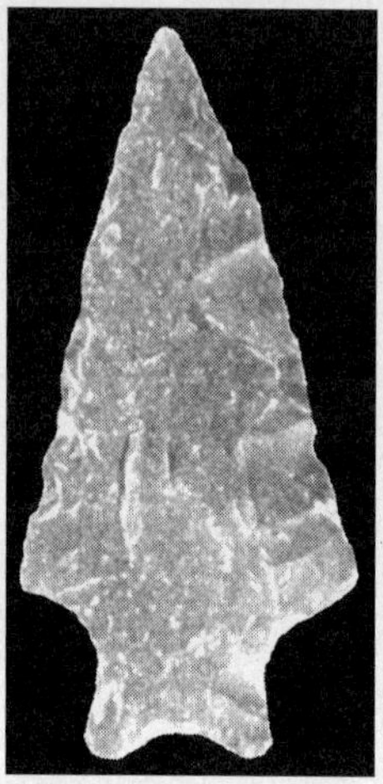

G5, $20-$35
Randolph Co., NC

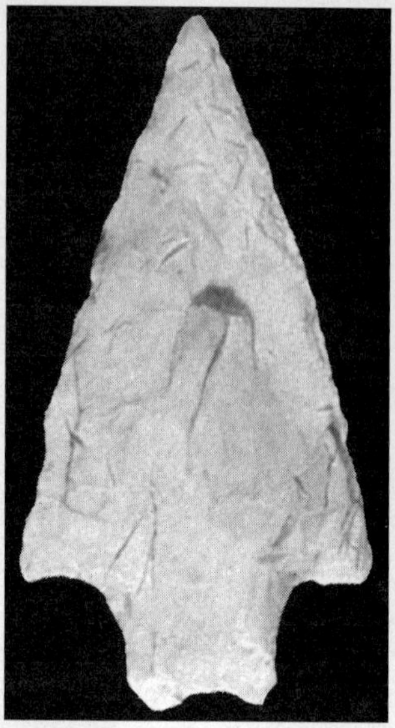

G4, $12-$20
Randolph Co., NC

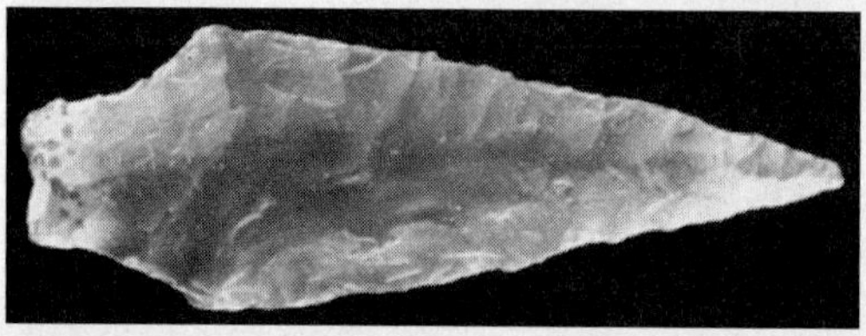

G6, $15-$25
Randolph Co., NC

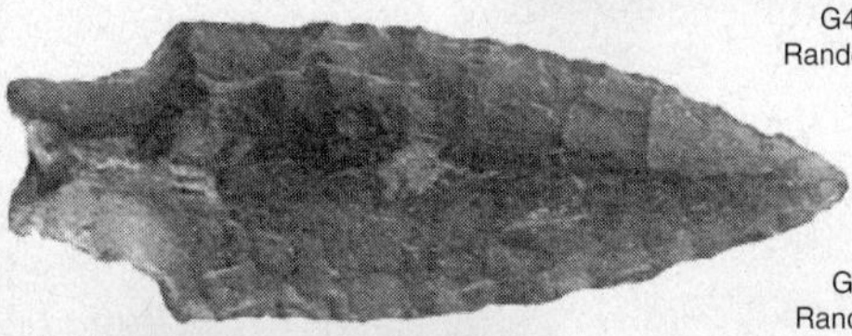

G6, $25-$40
Randolph Co., NC

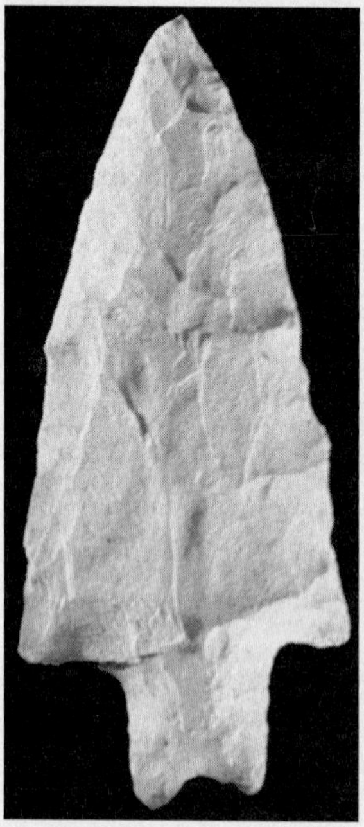

G8, $65-$125
Randolph Co., NC

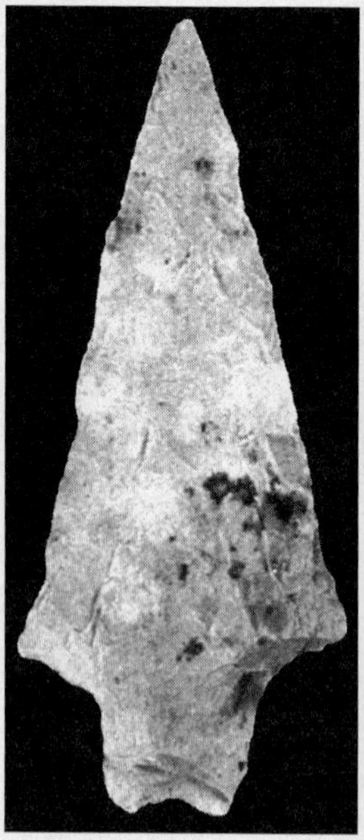

G6, $35-$65
Randolph Co., NC

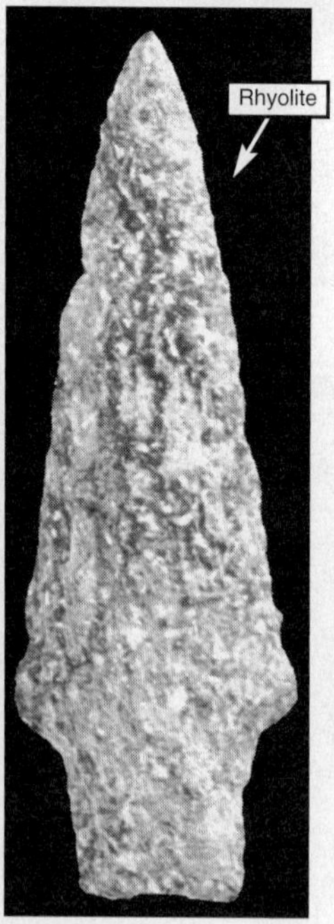
Rhyolite

G5, $20-$35
Randolph Co., NC

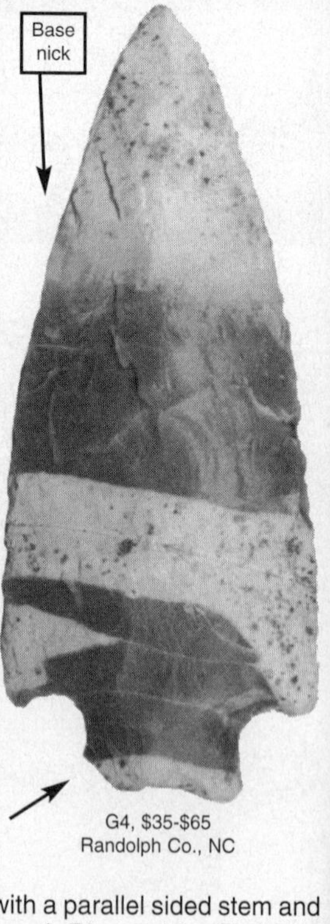
Base nick

G4, $35-$65
Randolph Co., NC

LOCATION: Far Eastern states. **DESCRIPTION:** A medium size, narrow shoulder point with a parallel sided stem and a concave base. Believed to have evolved from *Kirk* points and later evolved into *Savannah River* points. Similar to *Northern Piedmont* in Penn.

ES

G6, $55-$100
Randolph Co., NC

G8, $80-$150
Randolph Co., NC

Very thin

G7, $50-$80
Randolph Co., NC

G10, $175-$300
Montgomery Co., NC

TAYLOR - Early Archaic, 9000 - 6000 B. P.

(Also see Big Sandy, Bolen, Ecusta, Hardaway, Kirk and Palmer)

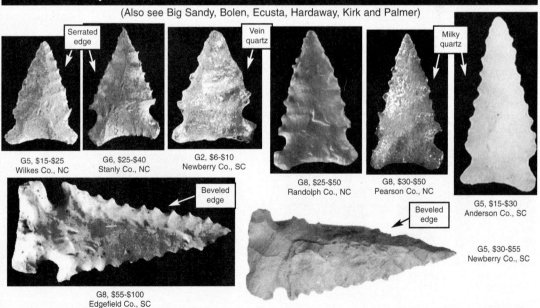

Serrated edge

G5, $15-$25
Wilkes Co., NC

G6, $25-$40
Stanly Co., NC

Vein quartz

G2, $6-$10
Newberry Co., SC

G8, $25-$50
Randolph Co., NC

Milky quartz

G8, $30-$50
Pearson Co., NC

G5, $15-$30
Anderson Co., SC

Beveled edge

G8, $55-$100
Edgefield Co., SC

Beveled edge

G5, $30-$55
Newberry Co., SC

LOCATION: Far Eastern states. **DESCRIPTION:** A medium to large size, side notched to auriculate point with a concave base. Basal areas are ground. Blade edges can be serrated. A cross between *Hardaway* and *Palmer*. Called *Van Lott* in South Carolina.

THEBES - Early Archaic, 10,000 - 8000 B. P.

(Also see Big Sandy, Bolen, Kirk Corner Notched, Lost Lake and St. Charles)

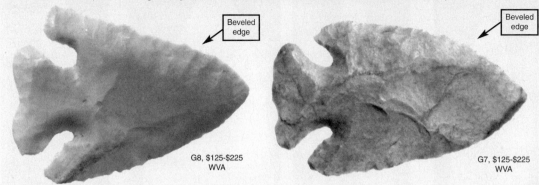

Beveled edge

Beveled edge

G8, $125-$225
WVA

G7, $125-$225
WVA

LOCATION: Midwestern to Eastern states. **DESCRIPTION:** A medium to large size, wide, blade with deep, angled side notches that are parallel sided and squared. Resharpened examples have beveling on one side of each face. The bases of this type have broad proportions and are concave, straight or convex and are ground. Some examples have unusual side notches called Key Notches. This type of notch is angled into the blade to produce a high point in the center, forming the letter E.

TRADE POINTS - Historic, 400 - 170 B. P.

$12-$20
NC, Copper.

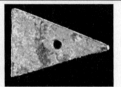

$15-$30
NC, Copper,
circa 1800.

These points were made of copper, iron, and steel and were traded to the Indians by the French, British and others from the 1600s through the 1800s. Examples have been found all over the United States.

UWHARRIE - Late Woodland, 1600 - 1000 B. P.

(Also see Caraway, Clarksville, Hillsboro, Pee Dee and Yadkin)

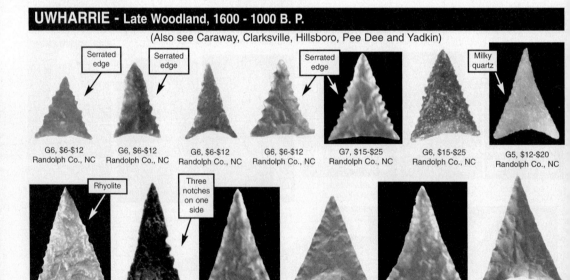

Serrated edge

Serrated edge

Serrated edge

Milky quartz

G6, $6-$12
Randolph Co., NC

G6, $6-$12
Randolph Co., NC

G6, $6-$12
Randolph Co., NC

G6, $6-$12
Randolph Co., NC

G7, $15-$25
Randolph Co., NC

G6, $15-$25
Randolph Co., NC

G5, $12-$20
Randolph Co., NC

Rhyolite

Three notches on one side

G6, $25-$40
Randolph Co., NC

G7, $25-$45
Yadkin Co., NC

G7, $25-$40
Randolph Co., NC

G6, $15-$30
Randolph Co., NC

G7, $25-$45
Randolph Co., NC

G8, $30-$50
Randolph Co., NC

LOCATION: North and South Carolina. **DESCRIPTION:** A small to medium size, thin, triangular arrow point with concave sides and base. Tips and corners can be very sharp. Side edges are straight to concave. Called *Hamilton* in Tennessee. Some examples have special constricted tips called *Donnaha Tips*. Smaller than *Yadkin*.

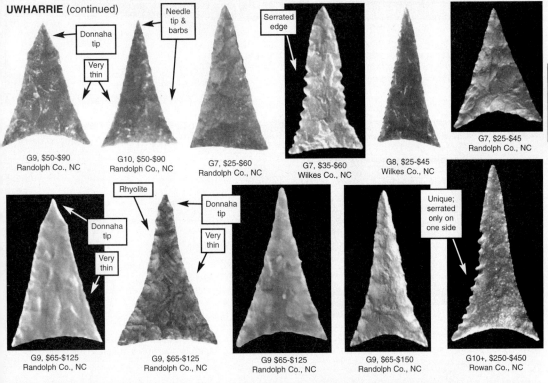

Donnaha tip

Very thin

Needle tip & barbs

Serrated edge

G9, $50-$90
Randolph Co., NC

G10, $50-$90
Randolph Co., NC

G7, $25-$60
Randolph Co., NC

G7, $35-$60
Wilkes Co., NC

G8, $25-$45
Wilkes Co., NC

G7, $25-$45
Randolph Co., NC

Rhyolite

Donnaha tip

Very thin

Donnaha tip

Very thin

Unique; serrated only on one side

G9, $65-$125
Randolph Co., NC

G9, $65-$125
Randolph Co., NC

G9 $65-$125
Randolph Co., NC

G9, $65-$150
Randolph Co., NC

G10+, $250-$450
Rowan Co., NC

ES

VAN LOTT - Early Archaic, 9000 - 8000 B. P.

(Also Palmer & Taylor Side Notched)

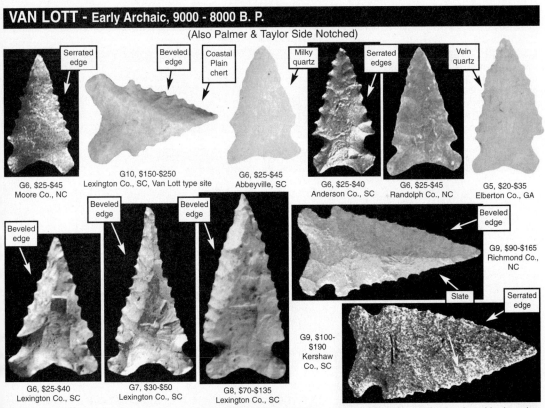

Serrated edge

Beveled edge

Coastal Plain chert

Milky quartz

Serrated edges

Vein quartz

G6, $25-$45
Moore Co., NC

G10, $150-$250
Lexington Co., SC, Van Lott type site

G6, $25-$45
Abbeyville, SC

G6, $25-$40
Anderson Co., SC

G6, $25-$45
Randolph Co., NC

G5, $20-$35
Elberton Co., GA

Beveled edge

Beveled edge

Beveled edge

Beveled edge

Slate

Serrated edge

G6, $25-$40
Lexington Co., SC

G7, $30-$50
Lexington Co., SC

G8, $70-$135
Lexington Co., SC

G9, $90-$165
Richmond Co., NC

G9, $100-$190
Kershaw Co., SC

LOCATION: Eastern Seaboard states. **DESCRIPTION:** A small to medium size, side notched point with drooping basal ears and a deeply concave base. Some examples are beveled on opposite faces when resharpened and are serrated. Bases and ears are ground. **I.D. KEY:** Expanded auricles.

WALLER KNIFE - Early Archaic, 9000 - 5000 B. P.
(Also see Edgefield Scraper)

LOCATION: Southern Southeastern states.
DESCRIPTION: A medium size double uniface knife with a short, notched base, made from a flake. Only the cutting edges have been pressure flaked.

G7, $25-$40
SC

WARATAN - Woodland, 3000 - 1000 B. P.
(Also see Potts and Yadkin)

Quartzite

Vein quartz

Tip wear

Quartzite

G4, $8-$15
Southampton Co., VA

G5, $12-$20
Sussex Co., VA

G6, $20-$35
Davidson Co., NC

G5, $6-$12
Sussex Co., VA

LOCATION: Far Eastern states. **DESCRIPTION:** A medium to large size point with usually broad, tapered shoulders, weak corner notches and a very short, broad, concave base. The base expands on some examples giving the appearance of ears or auricles.

WATEREE - Woodland, 3000 - 1500 B. P.
(Also see Will's Cove)

LOCATION: Far Eastern states.
DESCRIPTION: A medium size, narrow point with a recurvate blade, horizontal shoulders and a very short stem. Similar to North Carolina's *Will's Cove*.

G5, $20-$35
Fairfield Co., SC

WILL'S COVE - Woodland, 3000 - 1000 B. P.
(Also see Wateree)

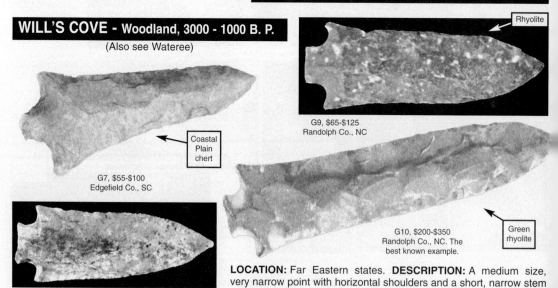

Rhyolite

Coastal Plain chert

G9, $65-$125
Randolph Co., NC

G7, $55-$100
Edgefield Co., SC

G10, $200-$350
Randolph Co., NC. The best known example.

Green rhyolite

G6, $35-$60
Randolph Co., NC

LOCATION: Far Eastern states. **DESCRIPTION:** A medium size, very narrow point with horizontal shoulders and a short, narrow stem with parallel sides and a straight base.

YADKIN - Woodland to Mississippian, 2500 - 500 B. P.

(Also see Caraway, Clarksville, Hillsboro, Occaneechee, Peedee, Uwharrie and Yadkin)

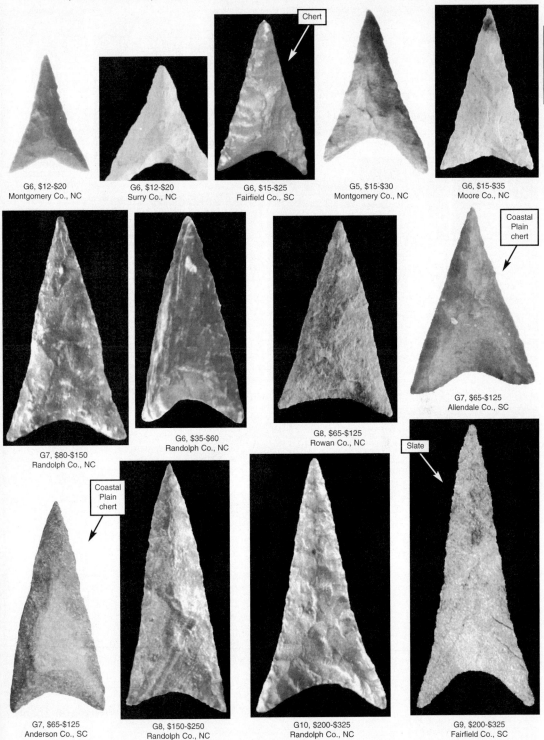

Chert

G6, $12-$20
Montgomery Co., NC

G6, $12-$20
Surry Co., NC

G6, $15-$25
Fairfield Co., SC

G5, $15-$30
Montgomery Co., NC

G6, $15-$35
Moore Co., NC

Coastal
Plain
chert

G7, $80-$150
Randolph Co., NC

G6, $35-$60
Randolph Co., NC

G8, $65-$125
Rowan Co., NC

G7, $65-$125
Allendale Co., SC

Coastal
Plain
chert

Slate

G7, $65-$125
Anderson Co., SC

G8, $150-$250
Randolph Co., NC

G10, $200-$325
Randolph Co., NC

G9, $200-$325
Fairfield Co., SC

LOCATION: Southeastern and Eastern states. Type site is Yadkin River in central North Carolina. **DESCRIPTION:** A small to medium size, broad based, fairly thick, triangular point with a broad, concave base and straight to convex to recurved side edges. Called *Levanna* in New York.

223

(Also see Guilford-Yuma, Hardaway, Potts, and Waratan)

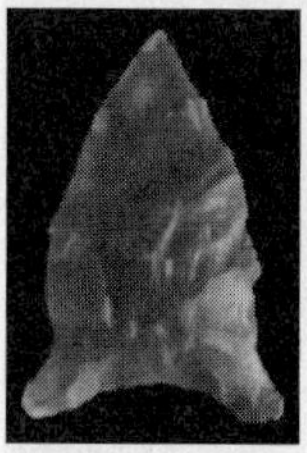

G2, $3-$6
Alleghany Co., NC

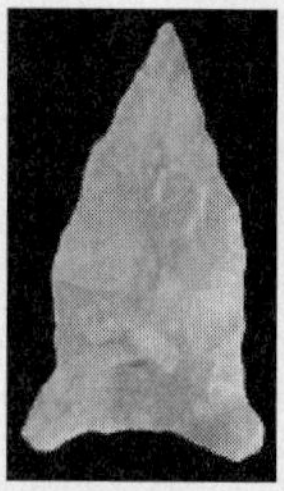

G3, $5-$10
Pearson Co., NC

G4, $8-$15
Central NC

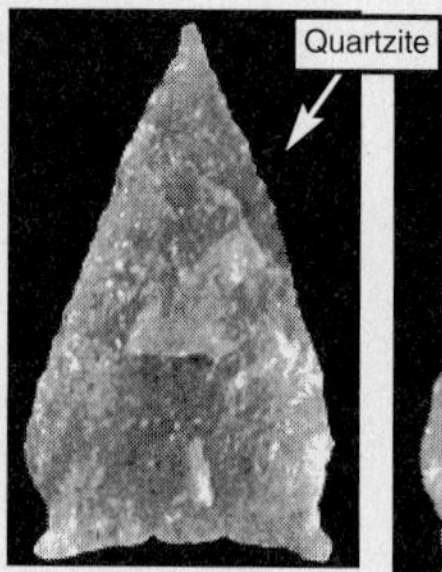

Quartzite

G5, $12-$20
Sussex Co., VA

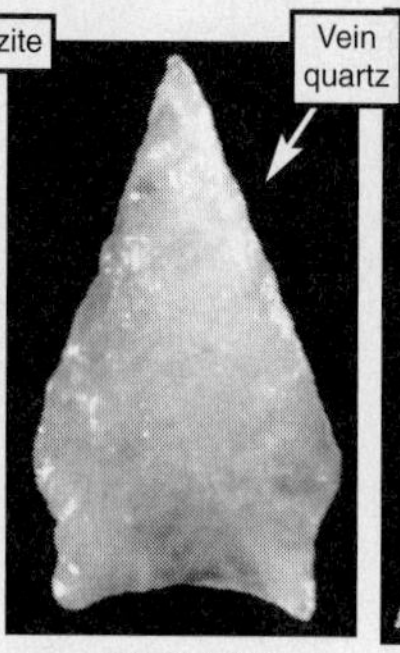

Vein quartz

G6, $15-$25
Randolph Co., NC

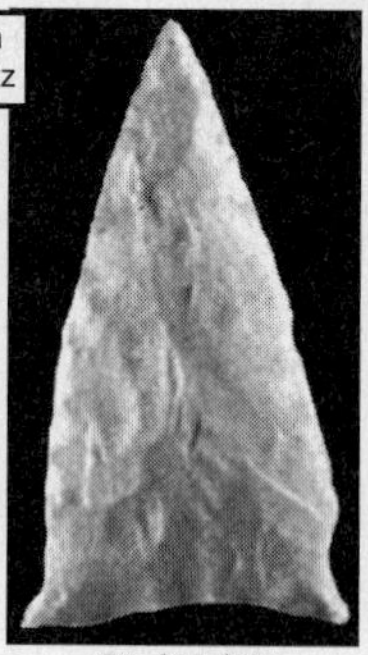

G6, $15-$25
Randolph Co., NC

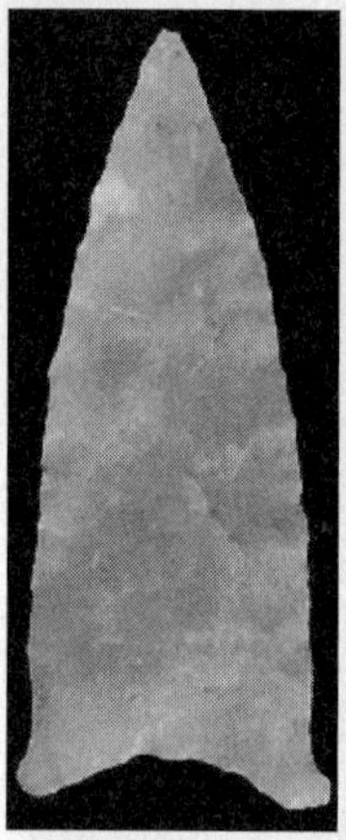

G7, $40-$75
Allendale Co., SC

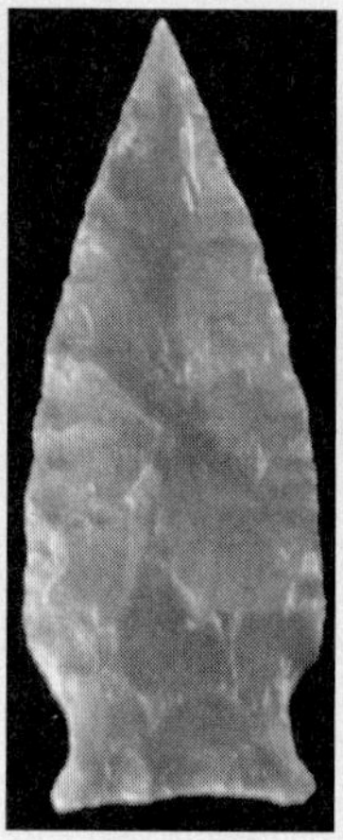

G8, $55-$100
Randolph Co., NC

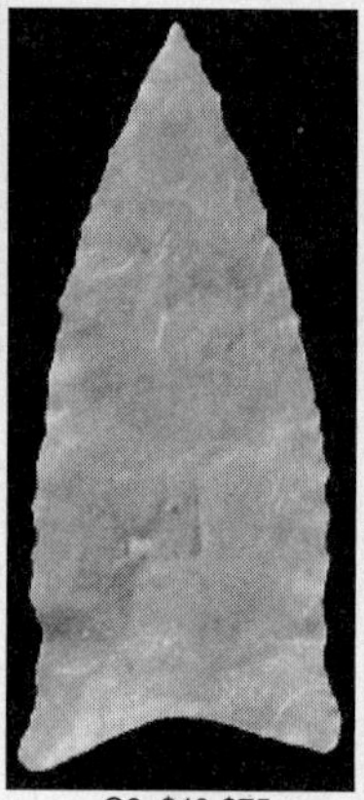

G8, $40-$75
Allendale Co., SC

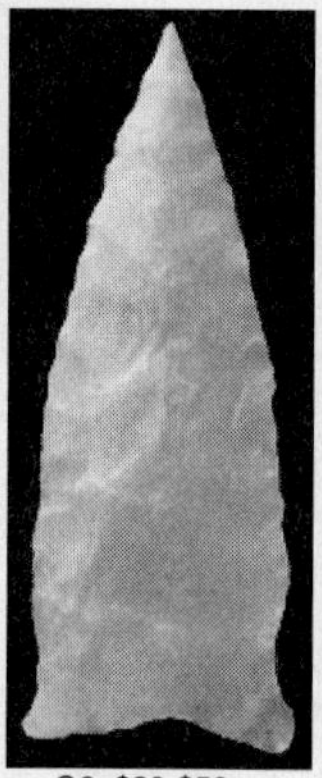

G6, $30-$50
Allendale Co., SC

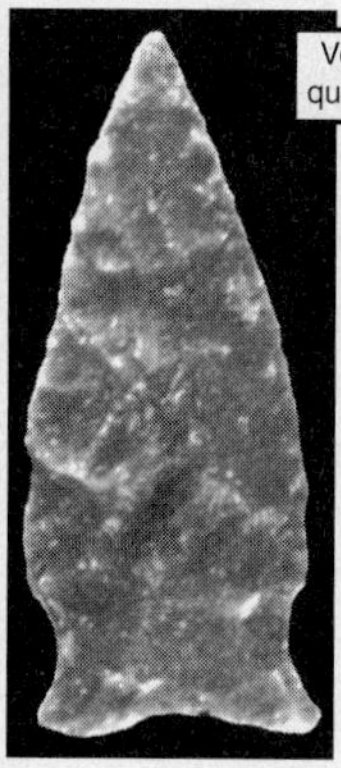

G6, $25-$40
Randolph Co., NC

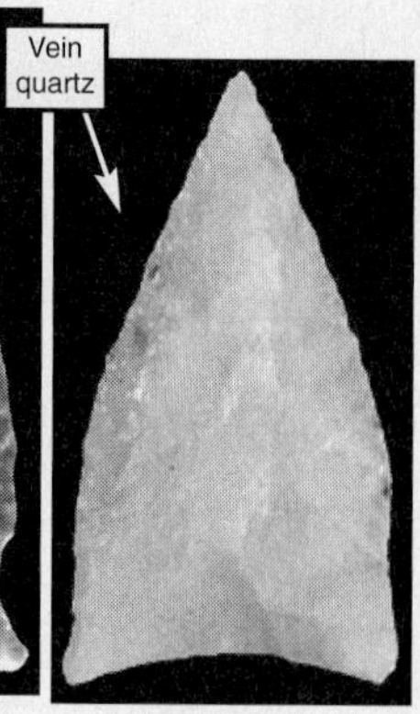

Vein quartz

G5, $25-$40
Randolph Co., NC

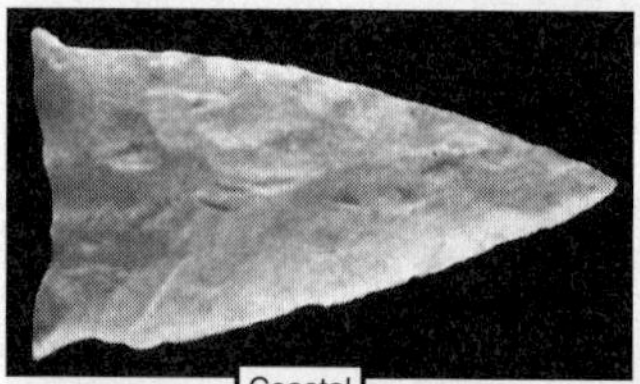

G6, $15-$25
Randolph Co., NC

G6, $15-$25
Stanly Co., NC

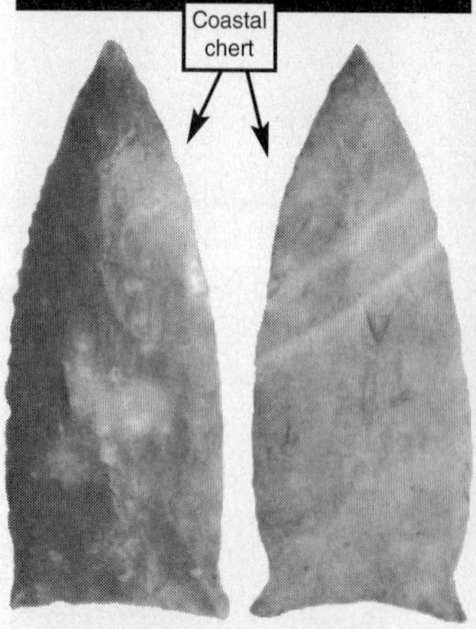

Coastal chert

Quartzite

G8, $80-$150
Allendale Co., SC

G9, $125-$225
Allendale Co., SC

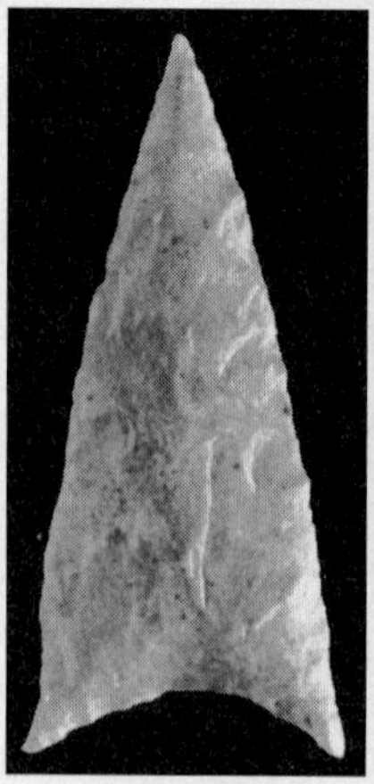

G9, $125-$235
Iredell Co., NC

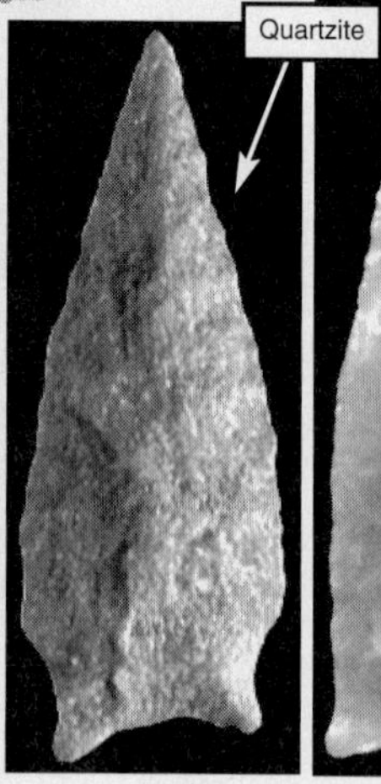

G6, $25-$40
Sussex Co., VA

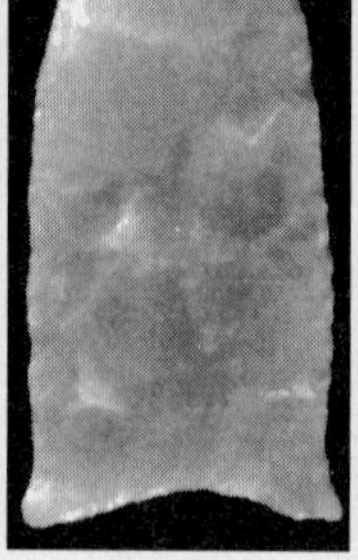

G10, $`150-$250
Allendale Co., SC

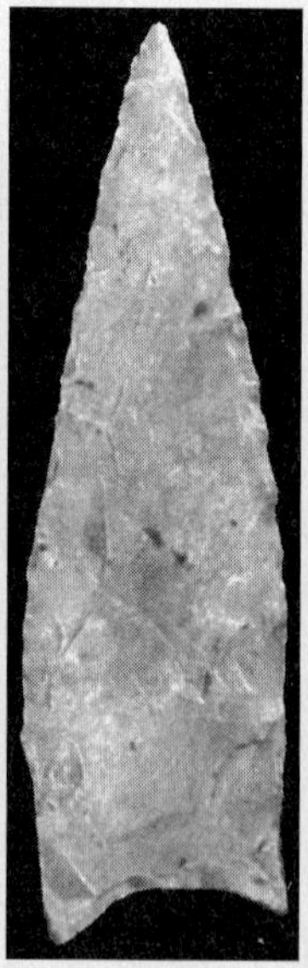

G8, $50-$90
Randolph Co., NC

LOCATION: Eastern Seaboard states, esp. North Carolina. **DESCRIPTION:** A small to medium size triangular, auriculate point with a concave base. The ears are produced by a shallow constriction or notching near the base. The notches are steeply beveled on one edge of each face on some examples.

GULF COASTAL SECTION:

This section includes point types from the following states:
Florida, S. Alabama, S. Georgia, S. Mississippi, S. South Carolina and
S.E. Louisiana.

The points in this section are arranged in alphabetical order and are shown **actual size**. All types are listed that were available for photographing. Any missing types will be added to future editions as photographs become available. We are always interested in receiving sharp, black and white, color glossy photos, color slides or high resolution (300 pixels/inch) digital pictures of your collection. Be sure to include a ruler in the photograph so that proper scale can be determined.

Lithics: Agate, agatized coral, agate, chalcedony, chert, Coastal Plain chert, conglomerate, crystal quartz, flint, hematite, petrified palmwood, quartzite, Tallahatta quartzite and vein quartz.

Special note: Points that are clear, colorful, made of coral, fossilized palmwood or other exotic material will bring a premium price when offered for sale. Exotic materials are pointed out where known.

Regional Consultants:
Tommy Beutell, Gary Davis
Jacky Fuller, Carlos Tatum
Jim Tatum, Jack Willhoit

GULF COASTAL
(Archaeological Periods)

PALEO - LATE PALEO (11,500 B. P. - 10,000 B. P.)

Beaver Lake	Drill	Scraper	Suwannee
Bone Pin	Paleo Knife	Simpson	Withlacoochie
Clovis	Redstone	Simpson-Mustache	
		Simpson-Mustache	

TRANSITIONAL PALEO (10,500 B. P. - 9,000 B. P.)

Cowhouse Slough	Stanfield	Wheeler
Marianna	Union Side Notched	

EARLY ARCHAIC (10,500 B. P. - 7,000 B. P.)

Boggy Branch	Dalton	Kirk Corner Notched	Wacissa
Bolen Beveled	Edgefield Scraper	Kirk Stemmed	Waller Knife
Bolen Plain	Gilchrist	Lost Lake	
Chipola	Hamilton	Osceola Greenbrier	
Cobbs	Hardaway	Taylor Side Notched	
Conerly	Hardin	Thonotosassa	

MIDDLE ARCHAIC (7,500 B. P. - 4,000 B. P.)

Abbey	Cottonbridge	Marion	Sumter
Alachua	Cypress Creek	Morrow Mountain	Westo
Arredondo	Elora	Newnan	
Bascom	Hardee Beveled	Pickwick	
Benton	Hillsborough	Putnam	
Buzzard Roost	Ledbetter	Savannah River	
Clay	Maples	Six Mile Creek	

LATE ARCHAIC (5,000 B. P. - 3,000 B. P.)

Citrus	Lafayette	South Prong Creek
Culbreath	Levy	Tallhassee
Evans	Santa Fe	
Hernando	Seminole	

WOODLAND (3,000 B. P. - 1,300 B. P.)

Adena	Copena	Manasota	Taylor
Bradford	Durant's Bend	Ocala	Weeden Island
Broad River	Duval	O'leno	Yadkin
Broward	Jackson	Sarasota	
Columbia	Leon	Sting Ray Barb	

MISSISSIPPIAN (1300 B. P. - 400 B. P.)

Harahey	Pinellas	Tampa
Ichetucknee	Safety Harbor	Trade

GULF COASTAL
THUMBNAIL GUIDE SECTION

The following references are provided to aid the collector in easier and quicker identification of point types. All photos are exactly 30% of actual size and are proportional to each other. Each point pictured in this section represents a classic form for the type. When a match is found, go to the alphabetical location of that type for more examples in actual size.

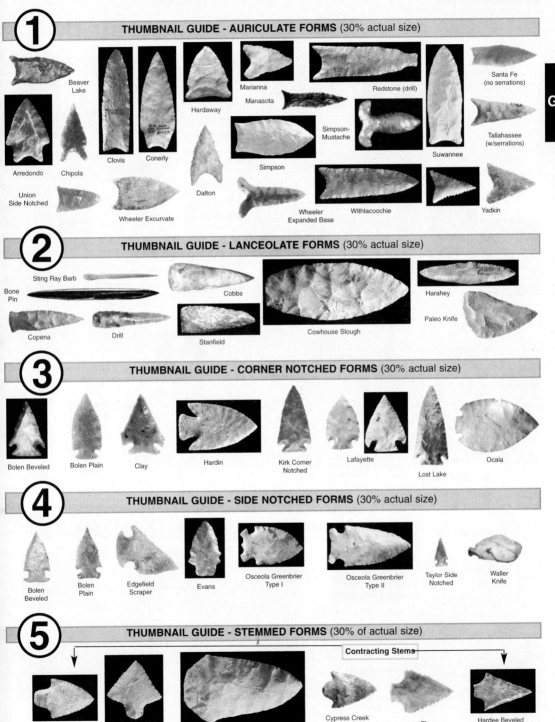

① THUMBNAIL GUIDE - AURICULATE FORMS (30% actual size)

GC

Beaver Lake
Marianna
Manasota
Redstone (drill)
Santa Fe (no serrations)
Hardaway
Clovis
Conerly
Simpson-Mustache
Suwannee
Tallahassee (w/serrations)
Arredondo
Chipola
Dalton
Simpson
Union Side Notched
Wheeler Excurvate
Wheeler Expanded Base
Withlacoochie
Yadkin

② THUMBNAIL GUIDE - LANCEOLATE FORMS (30% actual size)

Sting Ray Barb
Bone Pin
Cobbs
Harahey
Copena
Drill
Stanfield
Cowhouse Slough
Paleo Knife

③ THUMBNAIL GUIDE - CORNER NOTCHED FORMS (30% actual size)

Bolen Beveled
Bolen Plain
Clay
Hardin
Kirk Corner Notched
Lafayette
Lost Lake
Ocala

④ THUMBNAIL GUIDE - SIDE NOTCHED FORMS (30% actual size)

Bolen Beveled
Bolen Plain
Edgefield Scraper
Evans
Osceola Greenbrier Type I
Osceola Greenbrier Type II
Taylor Side Notched
Waller Knife

⑤ THUMBNAIL GUIDE - STEMMED FORMS (30% of actual size)

Contracting Stems

Adena
Cottonbridge
Bascom
Cypress Creek
Elora
Hardee Beveled

227

THUMBNAIL GUIDE - Stemmed Forms (continued)

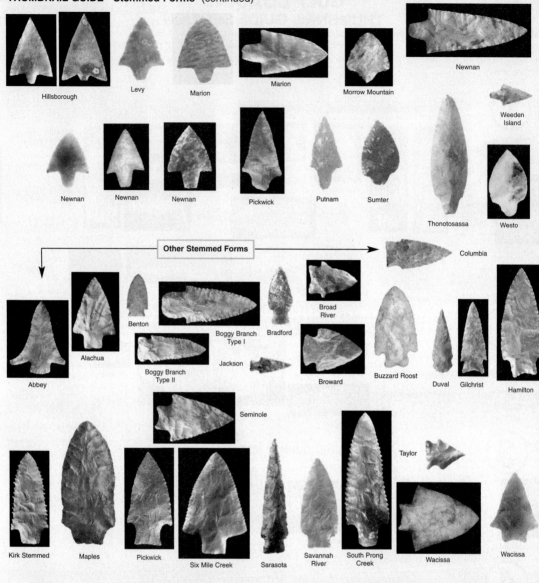

Hillsborough

Levy

Marion

Marion

Morrow Mountain

Newnan

Weeden Island

Newnan

Newnan

Newnan

Pickwick

Putnam

Sumter

Thonotosassa

Westo

Other Stemmed Forms

Columbia

Abbey

Alachua

Benton

Boggy Branch Type I

Bradford

Broad River

Boggy Branch Type II

Jackson

Broward

Buzzard Roost

Duval

Gilchrist

Hamilton

Seminole

Taylor

Kirk Stemmed

Maples

Pickwick

Six Mile Creek

Sarasota

Savannah River

South Prong Creek

Wacissa

Wacissa

 THUMBNAIL GUIDE - BASAL NOTCHED FORMS (30% of actual size)

Citrus

Clay

Culbreath

Hernando

Lafayette

 THUMBNAIL GUIDE - ARROW POINTS (30% of actual size)

Durant's Bend

Ichetucknee

O'leno

Pinellas

Safety Harbor

Tampa

(Also see Alachua, Cottonbridge, Elora, Levy, Notchaway, Pickwick, Savannah River, Six Mile Creek, South Prong Creek and Wacissa)

GC

G3, $8-$15
Decatur Co., GA

G5, $20-$35
Escambia Co., AL

Classic form

G9, $60-$100
Mitchell Co., GA

Serrated edge

G10, $175-$300
Mitchell Co., GA

G7, $30-$50
FL

Serrated edge

G6, $35-$55
Decatur Co., GA

G8, $250-$450
Jefferson Co., FL

LOCATION: GA, AL, FL. **DESCRIPTION:** A medium sized, broad, stemmed point that is fairly thick and is steeply beveled on all four sides of each face. Blade edges are concave to straight. Shoulders are broad and tapered. A relationship to *Elora, Maples* and *Pickwick* has been suggested. **I.D. KEY:** Expanded barbs & fine edgework.

ADENA - Late Archaic to late Woodland, 3000 - 1200 B. P.

(Also see Cypress Creek, Elora, Levy, Pickwick, Putnam, Sumter & Thonotosassa)

LOCATION: Eastern to Southeastern states. **DESCRIPTION:** A medium to large, thin, narrow, triangular blade that is sometimes serrated, and with a medium to long, narrow to broad rounded "beaver tail" stem. Most examples are from average to excellent quality. **I.D. KEY:** Rounded base, woodland flaking.

G5, $30-$50
Suwannee Co., FL

ALACHUA - Middle Archaic, 5500 - 4000 B. P.

(Also see Abbey, Cypress Creek, Hardee Beveled, Levy, Marion, Morrow Mountain, Newnan, Putnam, Six Mile Creek)

Tallahatta quartzite

Florida chert

G9, $80-$150
Sou. AL

LOCATION: Gulf Coastal states. **DESCRIPTION:** A rare type with straight horizontal shoulders and straight stems that don't contract as much. **I.D. KEY:** Squared base, one barb shoulder.

G8, $60-$100
Alachua Co., FL

G9, $150-$225
Chipola Riv., FL

G6, $60-$100
Miller Co., GA

Florida chert

G9, $100-$175
Suwannee Riv., FL

ARREDONDO - Middle to Late Archaic, 6000 - 3500 B. P.

(Also see Buzzard Roost Creek, Hamilton, Kirk Stemmed, Savannah River, Seminole and Wacissa)

LOCATION: AL, GA, FL. **DESCRIPTION:** A thick, medium to large size point with a short, broad blade and a wide, concave to bifurcated base which can be thinned. Basal ears are rounded to pointed. Could be related to *Hamilton* points. **I.D. KEY:** Basal form and thickness.

ARREDONDO (continued)

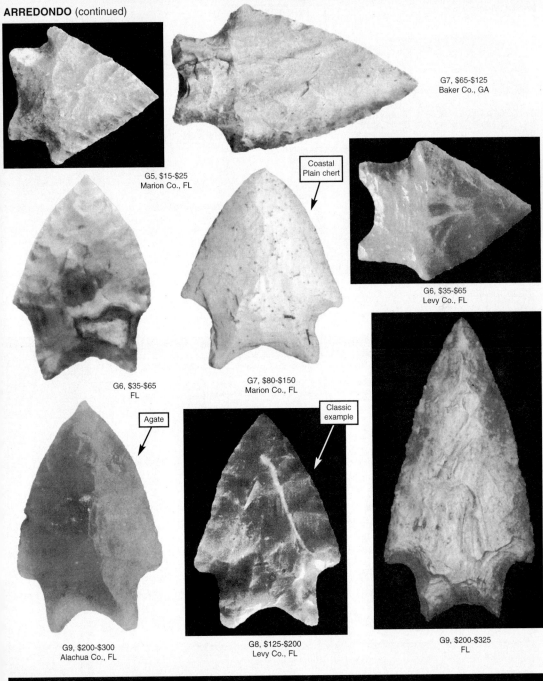

G5, $15-$25
Marion Co., FL

G7, $65-$125
Baker Co., GA

Coastal
Plain chert

GC

G6, $35-$65
Levy Co., FL

G6, $35-$65
FL

G7, $80-$150
Marion Co., FL

Classic
example

Agate

G9, $200-$300
Alachua Co., FL

G8, $125-$200
Levy Co., FL

G9, $200-$325
FL

BASCOM - Middle to Late Archaic, 4500 - 3500 B. P.

(Also see Morrow Mountain and Savannah River)

IMPORTANT:
All Bascoms shown
half size.

G10, $150-$275
Savannah, GA

LOCATION: AL, GA. & SC. **DESCRIPTION:** A large size, broad point with weak shoulders tapering to the base which is usually straight but can be convex. A preform for the *Savannah River* point. A cache of *Bascom* and *Savannah River* were found together. **I.D.KEY:** Basal form.

BASCOM (continued)

IMPORTANT:
All Bascoms
shown half size.

G9, $80-$150
SC coast cache.

G7, $100-$175
Burke Co., GA

G9, $65-$125
SC coast cache.

G10, $90-$150
SC coast cache.

BEAVER LAKE - Paleo & Woodland, 11,250 - 1500 B. P.

(Also see Dalton, Manasota, Santa Fe, Simpson, Suwannee and Tallahassee)

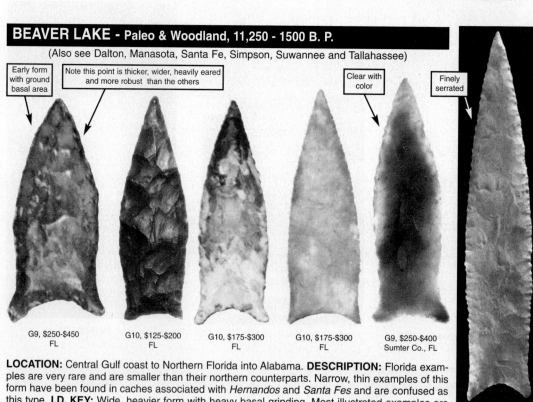

Early form
with ground
basal area

Note this point is thicker, wider, heavily eared
and more robust than the others

Clear with
color

Finely
serrated

G9, $250-$450
FL

G10, $125-$200
FL

G10, $175-$300
FL

G10, $175-$300
FL

G9, $250-$400
Sumter Co., FL

G10+, $1500-$2200
Jackson Co., FL

LOCATION: Central Gulf coast to Northern Florida into Alabama. **DESCRIPTION:** Florida examples are very rare and are smaller than their northern counterparts. Narrow, thin examples of this form have been found in caches associated with *Hernandos* and *Santa Fes* and are confused as this type. **I.D. KEY:** Wide, heavier form with heavy basal grinding. Most illustrated examples are probably the Woodland variety and are priced as such.

BENTON - Middle Archaic, 6000 - 4000 B. P.

(Also see Buzzard Roost Creek, Hamilton, Savannah River)

BENTON (continued)

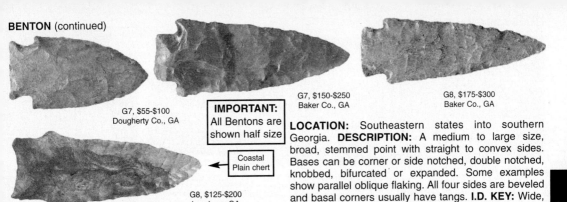

G7, $55-$100
Dougherty Co., GA

G7, $150-$250
Baker Co., GA

G8, $175-$300
Baker Co., GA

IMPORTANT: All Bentons are shown half size

Coastal Plain chert

G8, $125-$200
Leesburg, GA

LOCATION: Southeastern states into southern Georgia. **DESCRIPTION:** A medium to large size, broad, stemmed point with straight to convex sides. Bases can be corner or side notched, double notched, knobbed, bifurcated or expanded. Some examples show parallel oblique flaking. All four sides are beveled and basal corners usually have tangs. **I.D. KEY:** Wide, squared, eared or notched base.

GC

BOGGY BRANCH-TYPE I - Early to Middle Archaic, 9000 - 6000 B. P.
(Also see Kirk Stemmed and South Prong Creek)

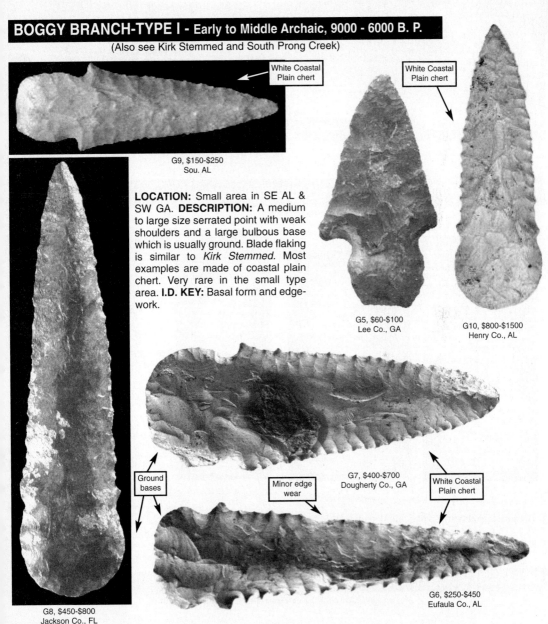

White Coastal Plain chert

G9, $150-$250
Sou. AL

White Coastal Plain chert

White Coastal Plain chert

LOCATION: Small area in SE AL & SW GA. **DESCRIPTION:** A medium to large size serrated point with weak shoulders and a large bulbous base which is usually ground. Blade flaking is similar to *Kirk Stemmed.* Most examples are made of coastal plain chert. Very rare in the small type area. **I.D. KEY:** Basal form and edge-work.

G5, $60-$100
Lee Co., GA

G10, $800-$1500
Henry Co., AL

Ground bases

Minor edge wear

G7, $400-$700
Dougherty Co., GA

White Coastal Plain chert

G6, $250-$450
Eufaula Co., AL

G8, $450-$800
Jackson Co., FL

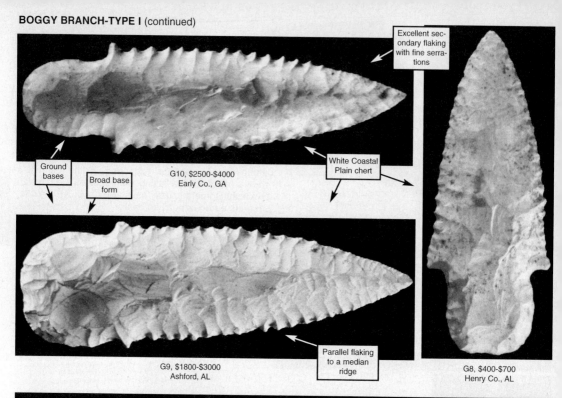

Excellent secondary flaking with fine serrations

Ground bases

Broad base form

G10, $2500-$4000
Early Co., GA

White Coastal Plain chert

Parallel flaking to a median ridge

G9, $1800-$3000
Ashford, AL

G8, $400-$700
Henry Co., AL

BOGGY BRANCH-TYPE II - Early to Middle Archaic, 9000 - 6000 B. P.

(Also see Kirk Stemmed and South Prong Creek)

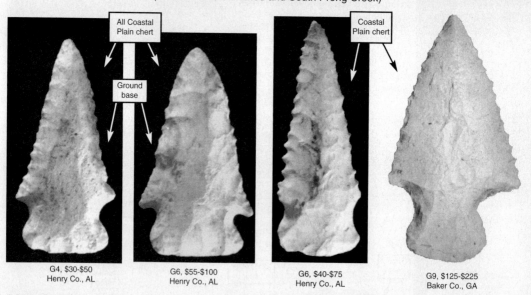

All Coastal Plain chert

Ground base

Coastal Plain chert

G4, $30-$50
Henry Co., AL

G6, $55-$100
Henry Co., AL

G6, $40-$75
Henry Co., AL

G9, $125-$225
Baker Co., GA

LOCATION: Southern Southeastern states. **DESCRIPTION:** A small to medium size serrated point with weak shoulders and a bulbous base which is usually ground. The base is shorter and smaller than in type I. **I.D. KEY:** Basal form and early flaking.

BOLEN BEVELED - Early Archaic, 10,500 - 8000 B. P.

(Also Clay, Lafayette, Lost Lake and Osceola Greenbriar)

BOLEN BEVELED (contin

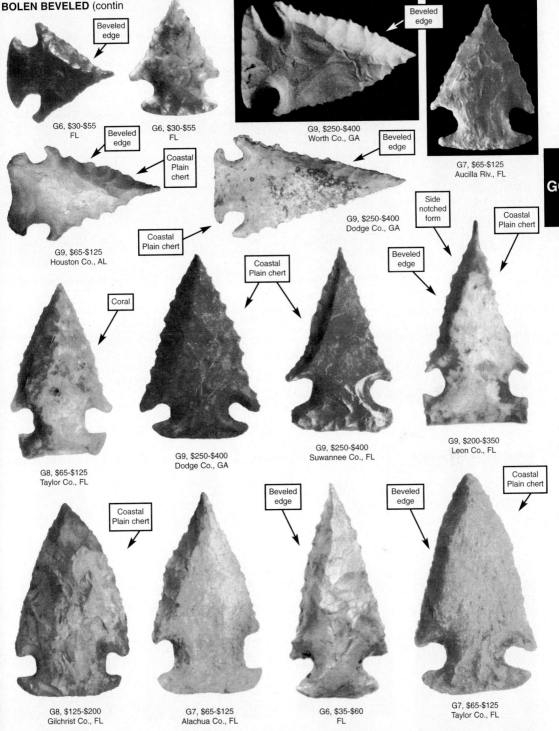

Beveled edge

G6, $30-$55
FL

Beveled edge

G6, $30-$55
FL

Beveled edge

G9, $250-$400
Worth Co., GA

G7, $65-$125
Aucilla Riv., FL

GC

Beveled edge

Coastal Plain chert

Coastal Plain chert

G9, $65-$125
Houston Co., AL

Beveled edge

G9, $250-$400
Dodge Co., GA

Side notched form

Coastal Plain chert

Beveled edge

Coral

Coastal Plain chert

Coastal Plain chert

G8, $65-$125
Taylor Co., FL

G9, $250-$400
Dodge Co., GA

G9, $250-$400
Suwannee Co., FL

G9, $200-$350
Leon Co., FL

Coastal Plain chert

Beveled edge

Beveled edge

Coastal Plain chert

G8, $125-$200
Gilchrist Co., FL

G7, $65-$125
Alachua Co., FL

G6, $35-$60
FL

G7, $65-$125
Taylor Co., FL

LOCATION: Southeastern states including Florida. **DESCRIPTION:** A small to medium size, side to corner notched point with early forms showing basal grinding, beveling on one side of each face, and serrations. Bases can be straight, concave or convex. The side notch is usually broader than in *Big Sandy* points. E-notched or expanded notching also occurs on early forms. **Note:** *Bolens* have been found with horse remains in Florida indicating use in killing the horse which was probably hunted into extinction in the U.S. about 7,000 years ago. **I.D. KEY:** Basal form and notching.

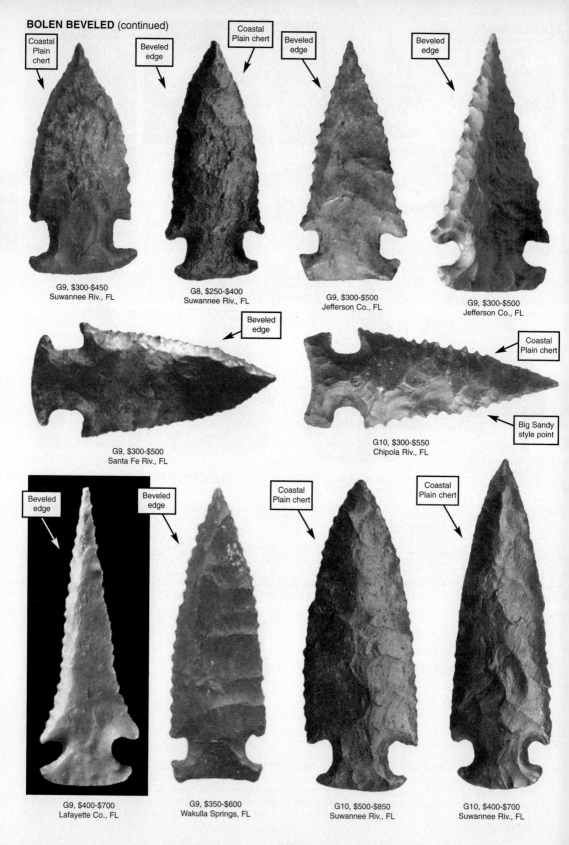

Coastal Plain chert

Beveled edge

Coastal Plain chert

Beveled edge

Beveled edge

G9, $300-$450
Suwannee Riv., FL

G8, $250-$400
Suwannee Riv., FL

G9, $300-$500
Jefferson Co., FL

G9, $300-$500
Jefferson Co., FL

Beveled edge

G9, $300-$500
Santa Fe Riv., FL

Coastal Plain chert

Big Sandy style point

G10, $300-$550
Chipola Riv., FL

Beveled edge

Beveled edge

Coastal Plain chert

Coastal Plain chert

G9, $400-$700
Lafayette Co., FL

G9, $350-$600
Wakulla Springs, FL

G10, $500-$850
Suwannee Riv., FL

G10, $400-$700
Suwannee Riv., FL

BOLEN PLAIN - Early Archaic, 9000 - 7000 B. P.

(Also see Kirk Corner Notched, Lafayette, Osceola Greenbriar and Taylor)

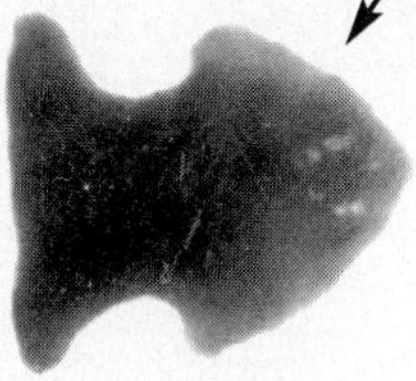
Clear

G5, $12-$20
FL

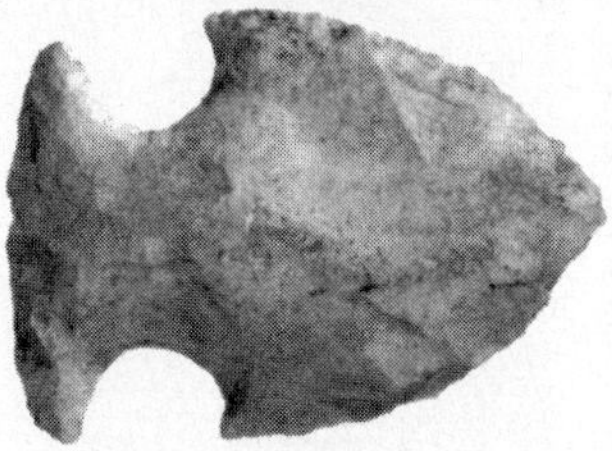

G6, $25-$45
FL

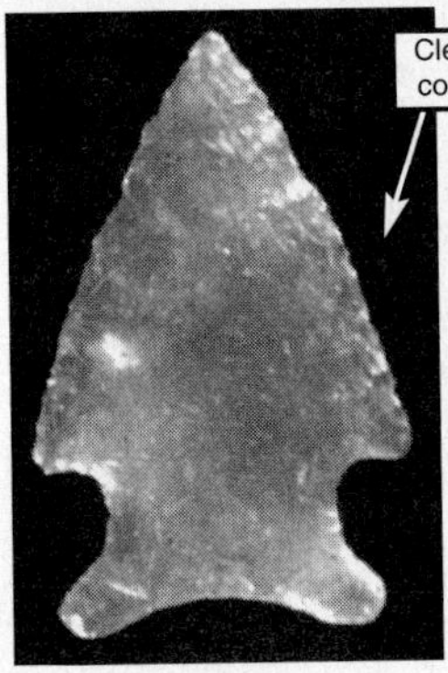
Clear
coral

G6, $100-$175
Santa Fe Riv., FL

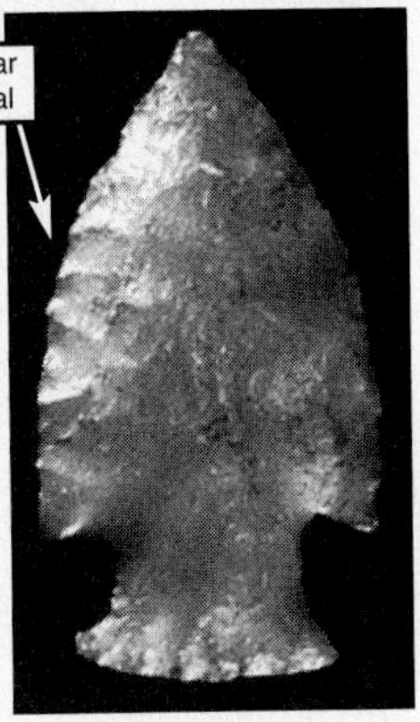

G8, $125-$225
Suwannee Co., FL

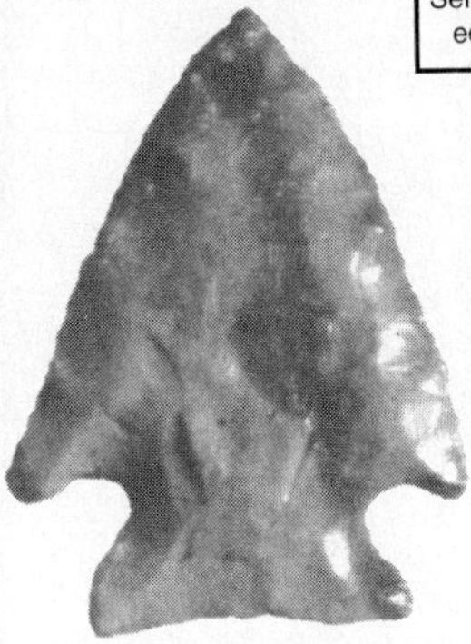

G7, $40-$75
FL

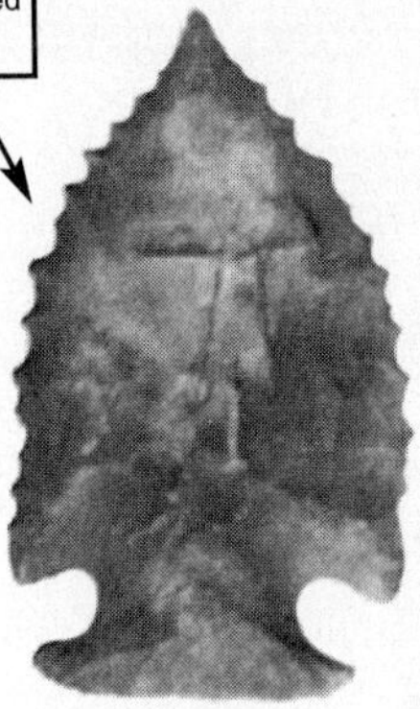
Serrated
edge

G8, $65-$125
Jefferson Co., FL

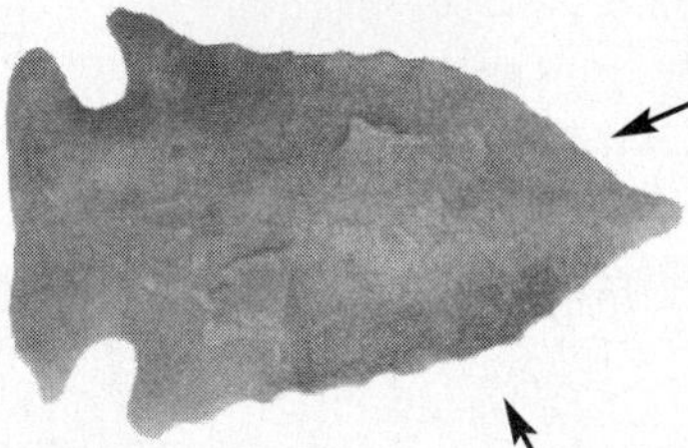
Coastal
Plain
chert
Serrated
edge

G7, $125-$200
Dodge Co., GA

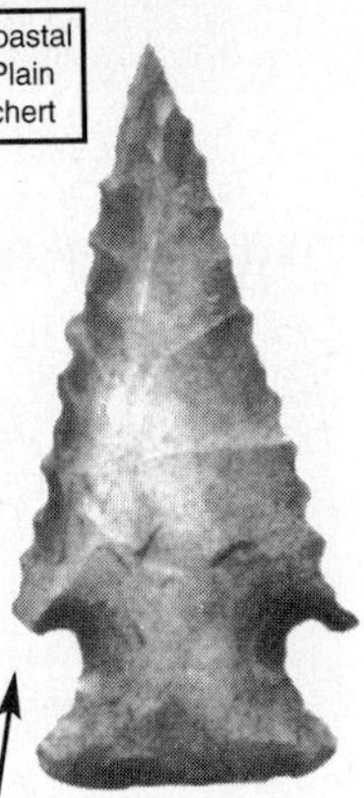
Barb
nick

G7, $65-$125
FL

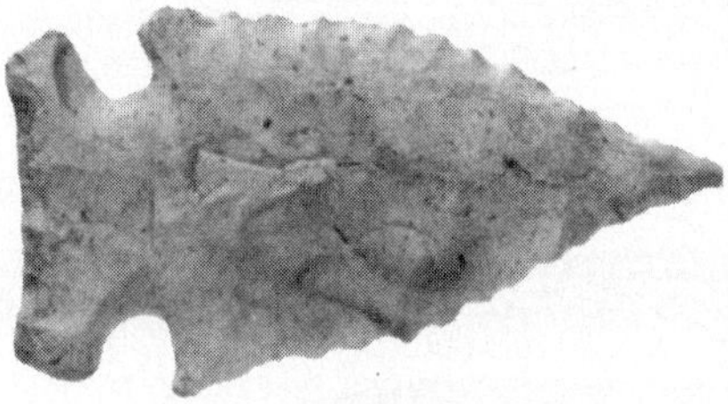

G8, $80-$150
FL

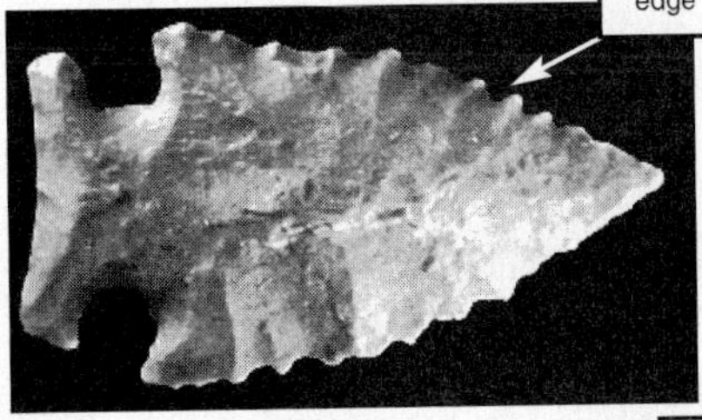

G7, $40-$75
Aucilla Riv., FL

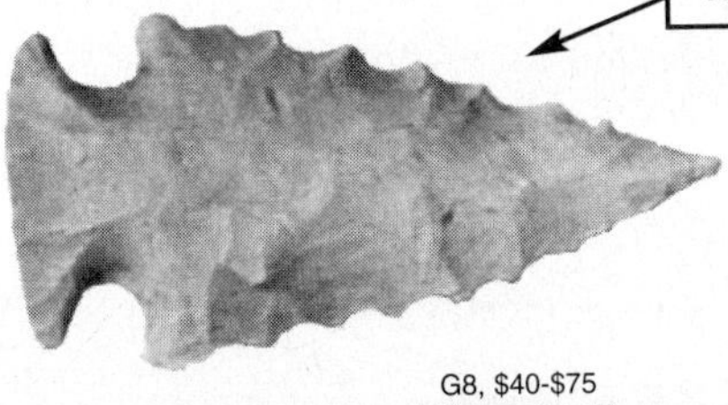
Serrated
edge

G8, $40-$75
Jefferson Co., FL

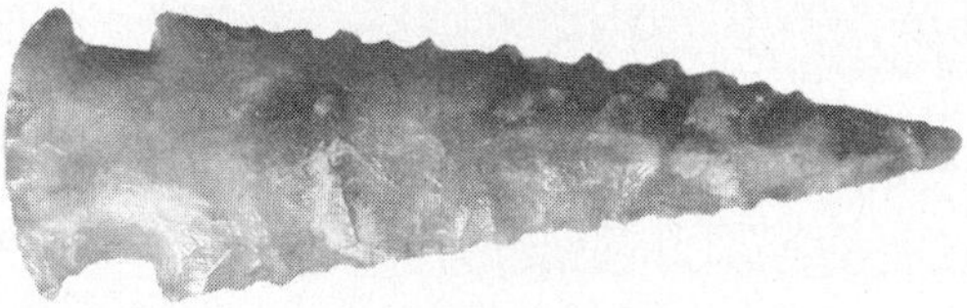

G8, $80-$150
Hillsborough Co., FL

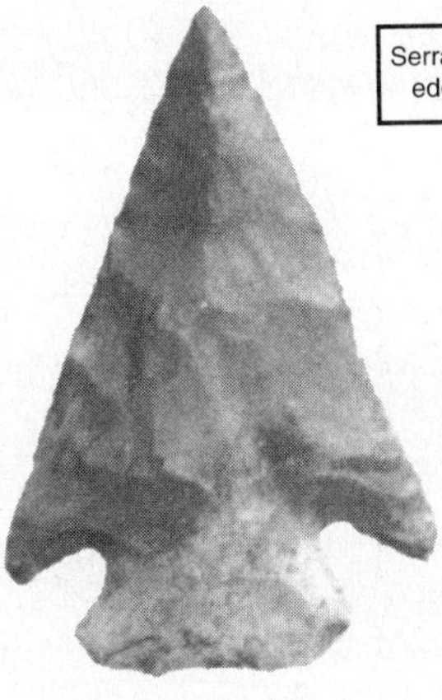

G7, $40-$75
FL

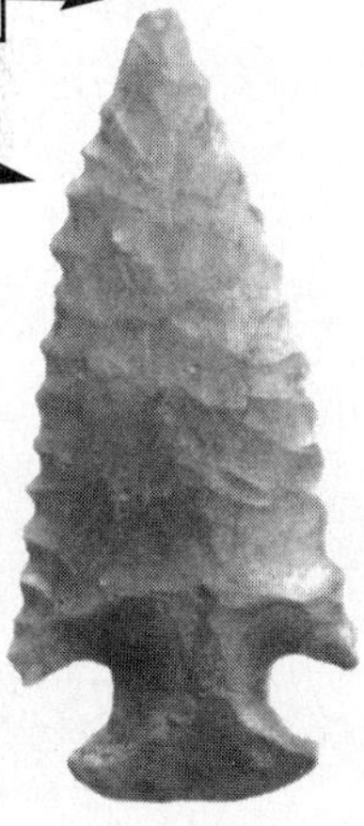
Tip
nick
Serrated
edge

G7, $40-$75
GA

BOLEN PLAIN (continued)

E-notch

Serrated edge

E-notch

Serrated edge

G9 $300-$550
Jefferson Co., FL

G9, $300-$550
Jefferson Co., FL

G10, $300-$550
SC

G7, $150-$275
Jackson Co., FL

G9, $350-$650
FL

LOCATION: Eastern states. **DESCRIPTION:** A small to medium size, side to corner notched point with early forms showing basal grinding and serrations. Bases are straight, concave or convex. The side notches are usually broader than in the *Big Sandy* type, and can be expanded to E-notched on some examples. **I.D. KEY:** Basal form and flaking on blade.

BONE PIN - Paleo to Historic, 11,500 - 200 B. P.

G6, $12-$20
FL

G6, $12-$20
Hillsborough Co., FL

G7, $15-$30
FL

G8, $40-$75
Aucilla Riv., FL

G8, $40-$75
Wakulla Co., FL

G10, $70-$120
Wakulla Co., FL

LOCATION: Florida. **DESCRIPTION:** Medium to large size, slender, double pointed spear pins made from deer leg bone, some camel and rarely mammoth. Less than 1% are mammoth ivory. The bone is usually blackened with age.

BRADFORD - Woodland to Mississippian, 2000 - 800 B. P.

(Also see Broward, Columbia and Sarasota)

LOCATION: Southern Southeastern states. **DESCRIPTION:** A medium size, narrow, expanded stem point with tapered to rounded shoulders. Basal corners can also be rounded. Bases are straight to slightly convex.

G3, $3-$6
Hillsborough Co., FL

G6, $15-$30
FL

G8, $35-$60
Suwannee Co., FL

BROAD RIVER - Woodland, 3000 - 1500 B. P.

(Also see Broward, Columbia, Sarasota, Savannah River and Wacissa)

LOCATION: Southern Southeastern states. **DESCRIPTION:** A small size, thick point with small shoulder barbs, a parallel sided stem and a straight to concave base.

G5, $8-$12
Beaufort Co., SC

G6, $10-$15
Henry Co., AL

BROWARD - Woodland to Mississippian, 2000 - 800 B. P.

(Also see Bradford, Broad River, Columbia and Sarasota)

G5, $10-$15
Seminole Co., GA

G8, $35-$65
FL

G6, $15-$25
FL

G8, $25-$45
FL

BROWARD (continued)

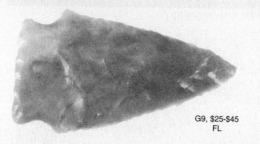

G9, $25-$45
FL

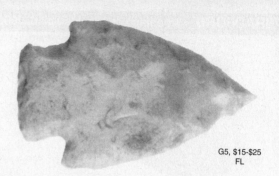

G5, $15-$25
FL

LOCATION: Southern Southeastern states. **DESCRIPTION:** A medium to large size triangular point with tapered to square shoulders and a short expanding stem. The base can be straight, concave or convex. Basal corners are usually rounded. An uncommon type. **I.D. KEY:** High and low barbs.

BUZZARD ROOST- Middle Archaic, 6000 - 4000 B. P.

(Also see Benton)

Coastal Plain chert

G8, $150-$300
Dodge Co., GA

LOCATION: Southeastern states. **DESCRIPTION:** A medium to large size, stemmed point with a bifurcated base. Believed to be related to the *Benton* point. **I.D. KEY:** Bifurcated base and basal width. Found with *Benton* points. A notched base *Benton*.

CHIPOLA - Early Archaic, 10,000 - 8000 B. P.

(Also see Dalton, Gilchrist and Hardaway)

Clear

G8, $200-$375
Chipola River, FL

G9, $350-$650
Hamilton Co., FL

Rare Chipola variant

G10, $550-$900
Pasco Co., FL

LOCATION: Southern southeastern states. **DESCRIPTION:** A small to medium size triangular point with long, expanding auricles and a tapered shoulder. Bases are deeply concave and are thinned. A *Dalton* variant form. Similar to *San Patrice* points found in Louisiana and Texas. May be related to *Gilchrist.* Rare in type area.

(Also see Culbreath and Hernando)

G5, $30-$50
FL

G7, $150-$250
Citrus Co., FL

GC

G8, $90-$150
FL

Clear

G8, $350-$600
NW Cent. FL

G9, $400-$750
Columbia Co., FL

Color
& clear

G10, $450-$850
FL

G8, $350-$600
Hillsborough Co., FL

G10, $1200-$2000
Levy Co., FL

LOCATION: Southern Southeastern states including Florida. **DESCRIPTION:** A medium to large size basal-notched point. The stem is wider than *Hernando*. The base and tangs usually forms an arc on most examples. **I.D. KEY:** Notches and random flaking on blade.

CITRUS (continued)

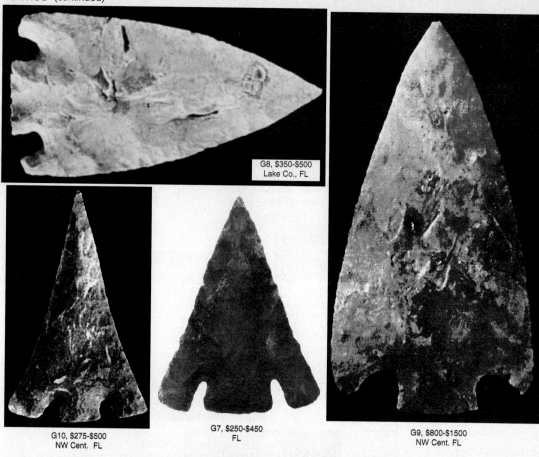

G8, $350-$500
Lake Co., FL

G10, $275-$500
NW Cent. FL

G7, $250-$450
FL

G9, $800-$1500
NW Cent. FL

CLAY - Middle to Late Archaic, 5000 - 3500 B. P.

(Also see Kirk Corner Notched and Lafayette)

G6, $40-$70
FL

G8, $200-$350
Suwannee Co., FL

G5, $40-$75
Decatur Co., GA

G8, $80-$150
FL

LOCATION: Southern Southeastern states including Florida. **DESCRIPTION:** A medium to large size basal-notched point with outward-flaring, squared shoulders (clipped wing). Blades are recurvate. Related to *Lafayette* points. **I.D. KEY:** Deep notches and squared barbs. Asymmetrical examples with one squared and one pointed or rounded barb also occur.

GC

G8, $175-$300
Cent. FL

G9, $550-$1000
Dougherty Co., GA

G6, $175-$300
Suwannee Co., FL

G7, $250-$400
NW Cent. FL

G7, $400-$750
Gougherty Co., GA

G8, $175-$300
FL

CLOVIS - Early Paleo, 11,500 - 10,600 B. P.

(Also see Chipola, Redstone, Simpson, Suwannee and Withlacoochie)

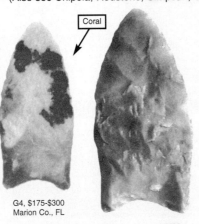

LOCATION: All of North America. **DESCRIPTION:** A medium to large size, auriculate, fluted, lanceolate point with convex sides and a concave base that is ground. Most examples are fluted on both sides about 1/3 the way up from the base. The flaking can be random to parallel. *Clovis* is the earliest point type in the hemisphere. The origin of *Clovis* is unknown. *Clovis* technology more closely matches European *Solutrean* forms than anything else. **I.D. KEY:** Paleo flaking, shoulders, batan fluting instead of indirect style.

G4, $175-$300
Suwannee Riv., FL

G4, $175-$300
Marion Co., FL

G7, $400-$650
FL

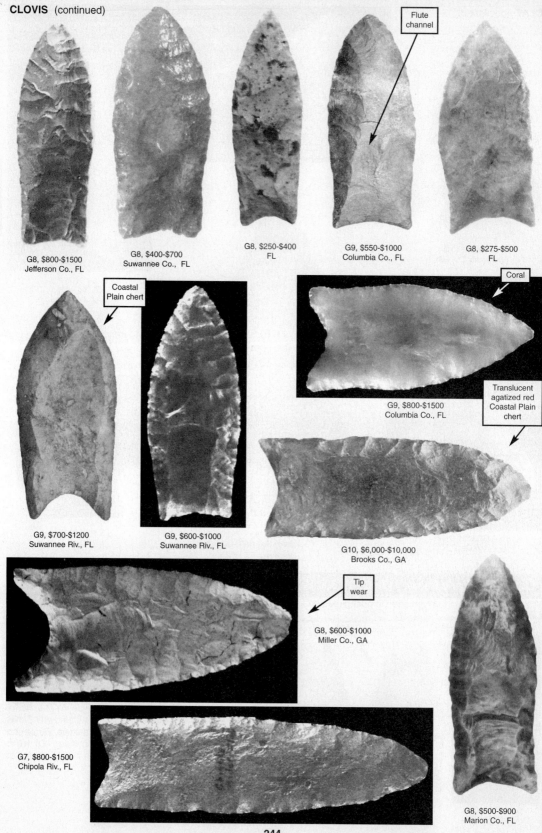

Flute channel

G8, $800-$1500
Jefferson Co., FL

G8, $400-$700
Suwannee Co., FL

G8, $250-$400
FL

G9, $550-$1000
Columbia Co., FL

G8, $275-$500
FL

Coastal Plain chert

Coral

G9, $700-$1200
Suwannee Riv., FL

G9, $600-$1000
Suwannee Riv., FL

G9, $800-$1500
Columbia Co., FL

Translucent agatized red Coastal Plain chert

G10, $6,000-$10,000
Brooks Co., GA

Tip wear

G8, $600-$1000
Miller Co., GA

G7, $800-$1500
Chipola Riv., FL

G8, $500-$900
Marion Co., FL

COBBS - Early Archaic, 9000 - 5000 B. P.

(Also see Bolen Beveled, Hardin and Lost Lake)

GC

G10, $350-$600
Jackson Co., FL

LOCATION: Southeastern states. **DESCRIPTION:** A medium to large size , lanceolate blade with a broad, rounded to square base. One side of each face is usually steeply beveled. These are un-notched preforms for early Archaic beveled types.

COLUMBIA - Woodland, 2000 - 1000 B. P.

(Also see Bradford, Hamilton, Ledbetter, Sarasota and Thonotosassa)

G8, $80-$150
FL

G8, $125-$200
FL

G4, $12-$20
FL

G7, $25-$45
FL

LOCATION: Southern Southeastern states. **DESCRIPTION:** A medium to large size stemmed point. Shoulders are tapered to horizontal and are weak. Stem is short and slightly expanding. Base is straight.

Stem wear

G7, $80-$150
FL

CONERLY - Middle Archaic, 7500 - 4500 B. P.

(Also see Beaver Lake, Simpson and Suwannee)

Coastal Plain chert

Coastal Plain chert

G7, $125-$200
Burke Co., GA

G10, $225-$400
Burke Co., GA

G10, $250-$450
Savannah River, GA
Brier Creek

G6, $40-$75
Burke Co., GA

G6, $250-$400
Dodge Co., GA

LOCATION: Southern Southeastern states, especially Tennessee and Georgia. **DESCRIPTION:** A medium to large auriculate point with a contracting, concave base which can be ground. On some examples, the hafting area can be seen with the presence of very weak shoulders. The base is usually thinned. Believed to be related to the *Guilford* type. **I.D. KEY:** Base concave, thickness, flaking.

COPENA - Woodland, 2500 - 1500 B. P.

(Also see Duval and Safety Harborl)

Serrated edge

G7, $65-$125
Brooks Co., GA

LOCATION: Southern Gulf states. **DESCRIPTION:** A medium size lanceolate point with recurved blade edges and a straight to slightly convex base. Florida Copenas are usually smaller than those found further north. **I.D. KEY:** Recurved blade edges.

COTTONBRIDGE - Middle Archaic, 6000 - 4000 B. P.

(Also see Abbey and Elora)

LOCATION: Southern Gulf states. **DESCRIPTION:** A medium size, broad, stemmed point that is fairly thick and beveled on all four sides. Shoulders are tapered and blade edges are straight. Base is small and rounded with contracting sides. **I.D. KEY:** Small, round base, broad shoulders.

COTTONBRIDGE (continued)

G7, $35-$60
Henry Co., AL

G7, $25-$45
FL

GC

COWHOUSE SLOUGH - Transitional Paleo, 10,000 - 6000 B. P.

(Also see Stanfield)

G8, $65-$125
Brooks Co., GA

G6, $80-$150
Hillsborough Co., FL

Beautiful random percussion flaking

Classic example

G9, $800-$1500
Gilchrist Co., FL

LOCATION: Gulf Coastal states. **DESCRIPTION:** A medium to large size, broad, lanceolate blade with a contracting, straight to slightly convex base which may be ground as well as fluted or thinned. This type may possibly be a preform. **I.D. KEY:** Paleo flaking.

CULBREATH - Late Archaic to Woodland, 5000 - 3000 B. P.

(Also see Citrus, Clay, Hernando, Kirk Corner Notched and Lafayette)

LOCATION: Southern Gulf states. **DESCRIPTION:** A medium to large size, broad, basal notched point, barbs are rounded and blade edges are convex. On some examples, the barbs do not reach the base. The earlier *Eva* point found in Kentucky and Tennessee could be a Northern cousin. **I.D. KEY:** Notching. Barb is always straight or contracting, never expanding.

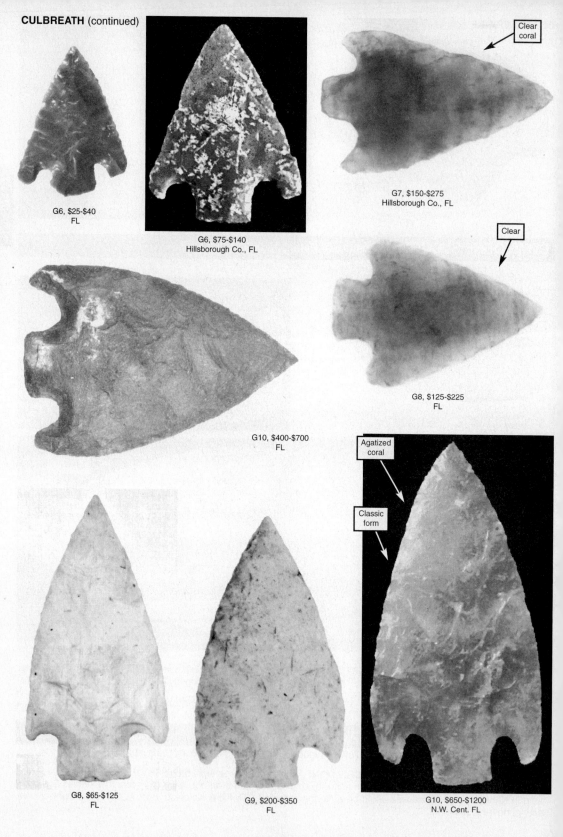

G6, $25-$40
FL

G6, $75-$140
Hillsborough Co., FL

Clear coral

G7, $150-$275
Hillsborough Co., FL

Clear

G8, $125-$225
FL

G10, $400-$700
FL

Agatized coral

Classic form

G8, $65-$125
FL

G9, $200-$350
FL

G10, $650-$1200
N.W. Cent. FL

CYPRESS CREEK - Middle Archaic, 5500 - 3000 B. P.

(Also see Alachua, Hillsborough, Levy, Morrow Mountain, Putnam and Sumter)

Clear

G4, $5 -$10
FL

G10, $150-$250
FL

G7, $25-$40
FL

G7, $35-$60
Hillsborough Co., FL

GC

LOCATION: Southern South eastern states. **DESCRIPTION:** A medium size point with a short, pointed to rounded contracting base. Shoulders have short barbs and can be asymmetrical with one barbed and the other tapered.

G7, $40-$75
Pasco Co., FL

G8, $65-$125
Pasco Co., FL

DALTON - Early Archaic, 10,000 - 9200 B. P.

(Also see Beaver Lake, Chipola, Hardaway, Safety Harbor, Santa Fe, Tallahassee & Withlacoochie)

G8, $150-$250
Warner Robbins, GA

Shoulders become more prominent due to resharpening

G10, $700-$1200
Blakely, GA

First stage, unsharpened form

LOCATION: North Florida into Georgia and Alabama. **DESCRIPTION:** A medium to large size, auriculate, fishtailed point. Resharpened examples are serrated and exhibit excellent flaking. Beveling does not usually occur on Florida examples. All have heavier basal grinding and most are thicker and wider than the look-alike *Santa Fe* and *Tallahassee* points. **I.D. KEY:** Thicker cross section, broader, heavier grinding than *Santa Fe* and *Tallahassees*.

249

DALTON (continued)

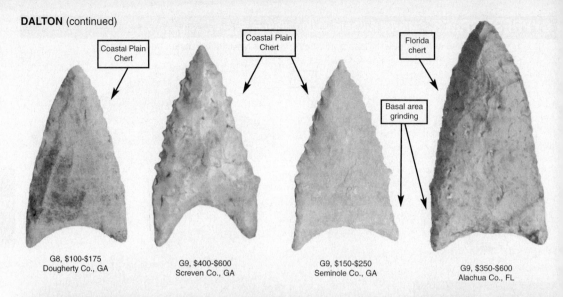

Coastal Plain Chert

Coastal Plain Chert

Florida chert

Basal area grinding

G8, $100-$175
Dougherty Co., GA

G9, $400-$600
Screven Co., GA

G9, $150-$250
Seminole Co., GA

G9, $350-$600
Alachua Co., FL

DRILL - Paleo to Historic, 11,500 - 200 B. P.

(Also see Edgefield Scraper)

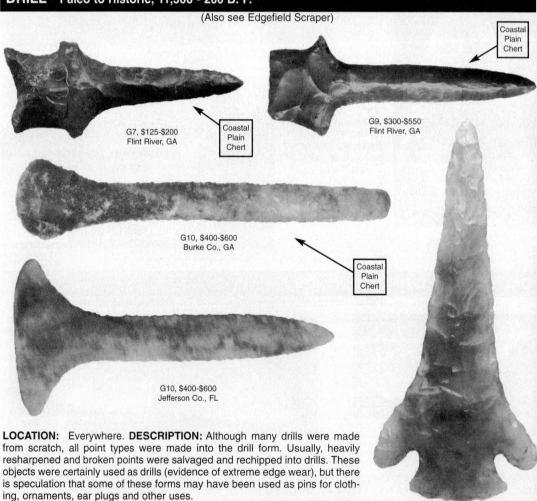

Coastal Plain Chert

G7, $125-$200
Flint River, GA

Coastal Plain Chert

G9, $300-$550
Flint River, GA

G10, $400-$600
Burke Co., GA

Coastal Plain Chert

G10, $400-$600
Jefferson Co., FL

LOCATION: Everywhere. **DESCRIPTION:** Although many drills were made from scratch, all point types were made into the drill form. Usually, heavily resharpened and broken points were salvaged and rechipped into drills. These objects were certainly used as drills (evidence of extreme edge wear), but there is speculation that some of these forms may have been used as pins for clothing, ornaments, ear plugs and other uses.

G9, $400-$600
FL

DURANT'S BEND - Woodland-Mississippian, 1600 - 1000 B. P.

(Also see Pinellas)

G7, $8-$15
Dallas Co., AL

G8, $12-$20
Dallas Co., AL

G8, $12-$20
Dallas Co., AL

G8, $12-$20
Dallas Co., AL

G8, $15-$30
Dallas Co., AL

G10, $55-$100
Dallas Co., AL

LOCATION: Southern Alabama. **DESCRIPTION:** A small size, narrow, triangular point with flaring ears and a serrated blade. Made from nodular black chert or milky quartz.

G9, $25-$40
Dallas Co., AL.

G10, $35-$65
Sou. AL

DUVAL - Late Woodland, 2000 - 1000 B. P.

(Also see Bradford, Copena, Jackson and Westo)

Coastal Plain chert

G7, 12-$20
FL

G7, $15-$30
Jefferson Co., FL

G6, $15-$25
Marion Co., FL

G5, $12-$20
Marion Co., FL

G8, $25-$40
Marion Co., FL

G7, $30-$50
Marion Co., FL

G9, $35-$65
FL

G9, $40-$75
FL

LOCATION: Gulf states. **DESCRIPTION:** A small to medium size, narrow, spike point with shallow side notches, an expanding stem and a straight to convex base. The stem can be slight to moderate. Similar to *Bradley Spike* points from Tennessee.

EDGEFIELD SCRAPER - Early Archaic, 10,500 - 8000 B. P.

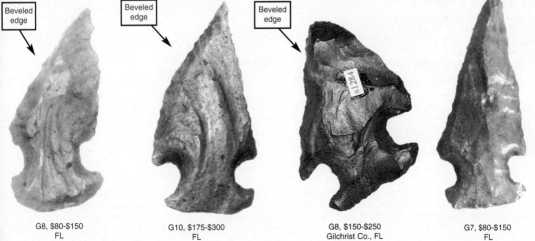

Beveled edge

Beveled edge

Beveled edge

G8, $80-$150
FL

G10, $175-$300
FL

G8, $150-$250
Gilchrist Co., FL

G7, $80-$150
FL

EDGEFIELD SCRAPER (continued)

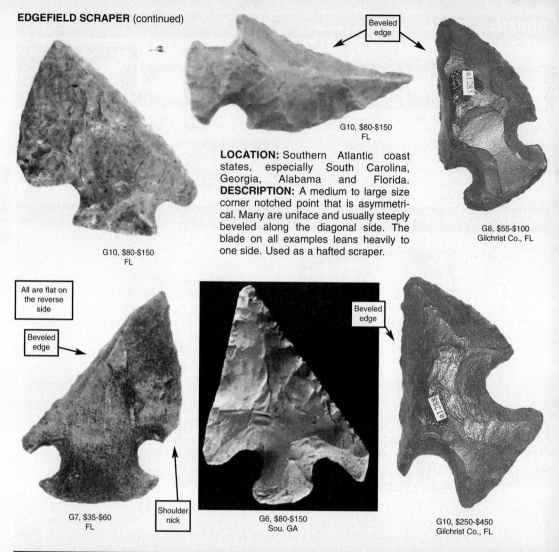

Beveled edge

G10, $80-$150
FL

G8, $55-$100
Gilchrist Co., FL

LOCATION: Southern Atlantic coast states, especially South Carolina, Georgia, Alabama and Florida. **DESCRIPTION:** A medium to large size corner notched point that is asymmetrical. Many are uniface and usually steeply beveled along the diagonal side. The blade on all examples leans heavily to one side. Used as a hafted scraper.

G10, $80-$150
FL

All are flat on the reverse side

Beveled edge

Beveled edge

Shoulder nick

G7, $35-$60
FL

G6, $80-$150
Sou. GA

G10, $250-$450
Gilchrist Co., FL

ELORA - Middle to Late Archaic, 6000 - 3000 B. P.

(Also see Abbey, Alachua, Cottonbridge, Kirk Stemmed, Levy, Newnan, Notchaway, Pickwick, Putnam, Savannah River, Six Mile Creek and South Prong Creek)

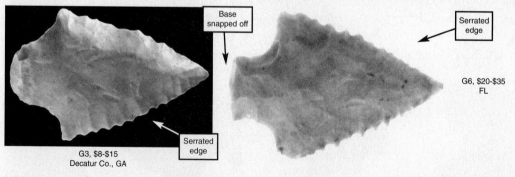

Base snapped off

Serrated edge

Serrated edge

G3, $8-$15
Decatur Co., GA

G6, $20-$35
FL

LOCATION: Southeastern states. **DESCRIPTION:** A medium size, broad, thick point with tapered shoulders and a short, contracting stem that is sometimes fractured or snapped off. However, some examples have finished bases. Early examples are serrated. **I.D. KEY:** One barb sharper, edgework.

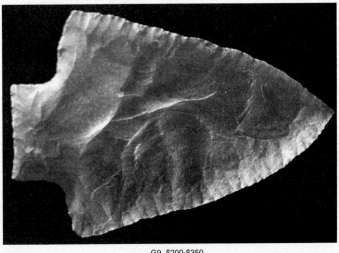

GC

G7, $30-$50
FL

G9, $200-$350
Taylor Co., FL

EVANS - Late Archaic to Woodland, 4000 - 2000 B. P.

(Also see Merkle)

G5, $12-$20
Natchez, MS

G6, $20-$35
Suwannee Riv., FL

G6, $20-$35
Natchez, MS

G5, $15-$25
Natchez, MS

G5, $18-$30
Natchez, MS

LOCATION: Southeastern states into southern Alabama and Mississippi. **DESCRIPTION:** A medium to large size stemmed point that is notched on each side somewhere between the point and shoulder. **I.D. KEY:** Side notches with stem.

GILCHRIST - Early Archaic, 10,000? - 7000 B. P.

(Also see Chipola, Beaver Lake and Taylor)

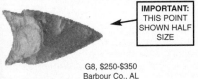

IMPORTANT:
THIS POINT
SHOWN HALF
SIZE

LOCATION: Southern Southeastern states. **DESCRIPTION:** A small to medium size, broad point with a short stem that is square, bifurcated or auriculate. Shoulders are weak and can be tapered, horizontal or slightly barbed. The blade can be straight or concave and could be ground. Early forms may be related to *Suwannee.*

G8, $250-$350
Barbour Co., AL

GILCHRIST (continued)

G7, $15-$30
Aiken, SC

G6, $15-$30
FL

G8, $80-$150
Marion Co., FL

Clear

Clear

G7, $15-$25
FL

G8, $275-$500
FL

G9, $450-$800
FL

GREENBRIAR (See Osceola Greenbriar)

HAMILTON - Early Archaic, 8000 - 5000 B. P.

(Also see Columbia, Kirk, Savannah River, Seminole and Thonotosassa)

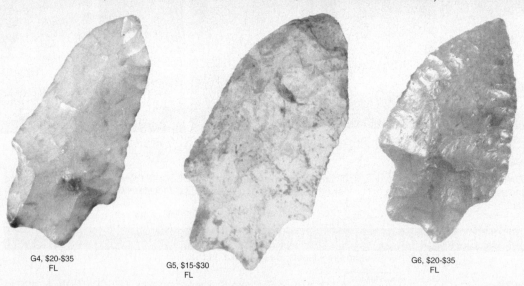

G4, $20-$35
FL

G5, $15-$30
FL

G6, $20-$35
FL

LOCATION: Southern Southeastern states. **DESCRIPTION:** A large size, thick, broad stemmed point with a concave base. Shoulders are horizontal to slightly tapered to barbed and are weaker than *Savannah River* points. Basal corners are slightly rounded **I.D. KEY:** Broad shoulders, basal form; i.e. short, wide tangs with a concave base. Confused with *Savannah Rivers* which have straight to concave bases, stronger shoulders and are not as old. Related to *Arredondo* points.

254

Barb nick

G7, $40-$75
Hamilton Co., FL

GC

Hand held to show translucency

G7, $65-$125
FL

G10, $250-$450
Jefferson Co., FL

Quartzite

G7, $80-$150
Burke Co., GA

G7, $125-$200
FL

255

HARAHEY - Mississippian, 700 - 350 B. P.

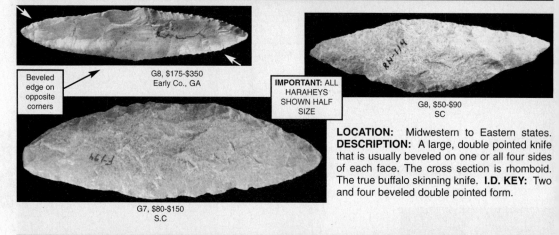

Beveled edge on opposite corners

G8, $175-$350
Early Co., GA

IMPORTANT: ALL HARAHEYS SHOWN HALF SIZE

G8, $50-$90
SC

G7, $80-$150
S.C

LOCATION: Midwestern to Eastern states. **DESCRIPTION:** A large, double pointed knife that is usually beveled on one or all four sides of each face. The cross section is rhomboid. The true buffalo skinning knife. **I.D. KEY:** Two and four beveled double pointed form.

HARDAWAY - Early Archaic, 9500 - 8000 B. P.

(Also see Chipola, Dalton, Santa Fe, Tallahassee and Union Side Notched)

Coastal Plain chert

Coastal Plain chert

Ground ears & base

Coastal Plain chert

G7, $70-$125
Gilchrist Co., FL

G7, $80-$150
Dougherty Co., GA

G8, $80-$150
Suwannee Co., FL

G8, $70-$125
Suwannee Co., FL

G8, $80-$150
Suwannee Co., FL

G5, $40-$75
Columbia Co., FL

G6, $80-$150
FL

G6, $75-$140
Marion Co., FL

LOCATION: The Carolinas into Florida. **DESCRIPTION:** A small to medium size point with shallow side notches and expanding auricles forming a wide, deeply concave base. Ears and base are usually heavily ground. This type evolved from the *Dalton* point. **I.D. KEY:** Heavy grinding in shoulders, paleo flaking.

HARDEE BEVELED - Middle Archaic, 5500 - 3000 B. P.

(Also see Alachua, Levy, Marion and Putnam)

LOCATION: Southern Southeastern states. **DESCRIPTION:** A small to medium size stemmed point that occurs in two forms. One has a distinct bevel on the right side of each face. The other has the typical bifacial beveling. Shoulders are tapered to horizontal and are sharp. This type resembles the other Florida Archaic stemmed points (see above) except for the bevel and may be their ancestor. Found mostly in Tampa Bay vicinity. **I.D. KEY:** Beveling on right side of each face and sharp shoulders.

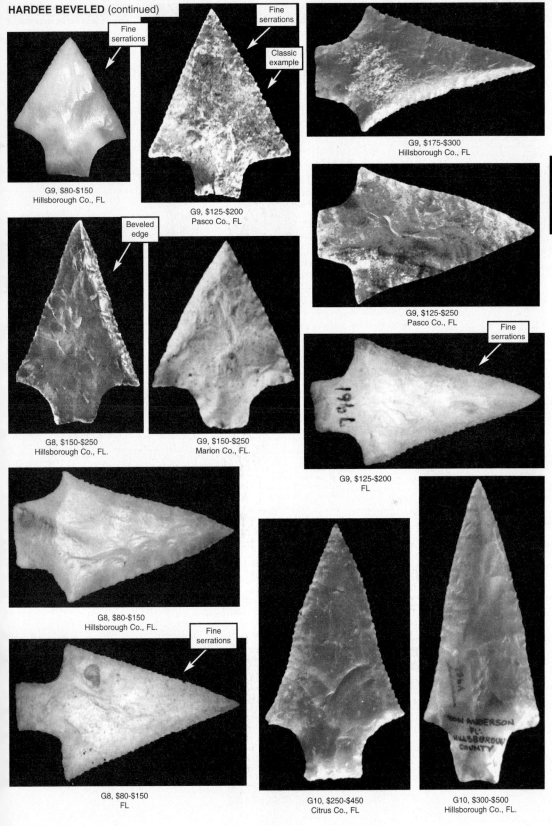

HARDEE BEVELED (continued)

Fine serrations

G9, $80-$150
Hillsborough Co., FL

Fine serrations

Classic example

G9, $125-$200
Pasco Co., FL

G9, $175-$300
Hillsborough Co., FL

GC

G9, $125-$250
Pasco Co., FL

Beveled edge

G8, $150-$250
Hillsborough Co., FL.

G9, $150-$250
Marion Co., FL.

Fine serrations

G9, $125-$200
FL

G8, $80-$150
Hillsborough Co., FL.

Fine serrations

G8, $80-$150
FL

G10, $250-$450
Citrus Co., FL

G10, $300-$500
Hillsborough Co., FL.

257

HARDIN - Early Archaic, 9000 - 6000 B. P.

(Also see Cypress Creek, Kirk Corner Notched, Lafayette and Ocala)

Bay Bottom Agate

G8, $250-$400
Hillsborough Co., FL

G8, $175-$275
Madison Co., FL

G8, $200-$350
Tampa, FL

G10, $1200-$2000
Dougherty Co., GA

LOCATION: Mid western to Eastern states. **DESCRIPTION:** A large, well made triangular barbed point with an expanded base that is usually ground. Resharpened examples have one beveled edge on each face. This type is believed to have evolved from the *Scottsbluff* type. **I.D. KEY:** Notches and stem form.

jasper

G9, $500-$850
Dodge Co., GA

G9, $500-$850
Jefferson Co., FL

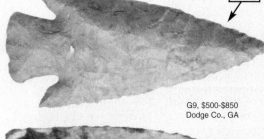

G8, $500-$850
Bulloch Co., GA

HERNANDO - Late Archaic, 4000 - 2500 B. P.

(Also see Citrus and Culbreath)

Agate

G9, $200-$300
Dodge Co., GA

G7, $65-$125
Marion Co., FL

LOCATION: Georgia, Alabama and Florida. **DESCRIPTION:** A medium to large size, basal notched, triangular point with wide flaring tangs that may extend beyond the base. Side edges are straight to concave. Similar in outline only to the much earlier *Eva* type. Has been found in cache with *Santa Fe* and *Tallahassee* types as well as *Beaver Lake* style points. **I.D. KEY:** Narrow stem.

G7, $65-$125
Jefferson Co., FL

G9, $200-$350
NW Cent. FL

GC

G9, $250-$450
FL

G9, $250-$400
FL

G7, $80-$150
NW Cent. FL

Clear

G8, $250-$400
Dougherty Co., GA

G9, $250-$400
NW Cent. FL

G10, $400-$700
Hillsborough Co., FL

G7, $170-$300
NW Cent. FL

G10, $400-$700
NW Cent. FL

G9, $300-$500
NW Cent. FL

HILLSBOROUGH - Middle Archaic, 5500 - 3000 B. P.

(Also see Marion and Newnan)

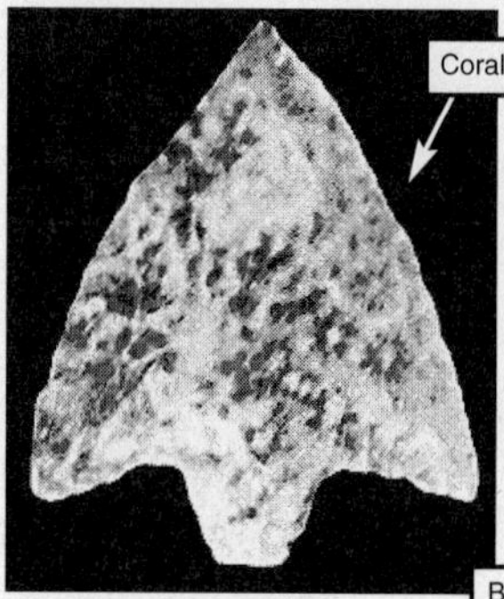
Coral

G5, $125-$200
NW Cent., FL

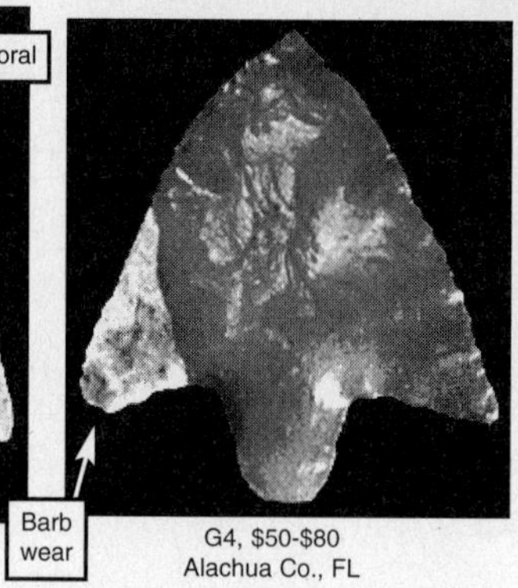
Barb
wear

G4, $50-$80
Alachua Co., FL

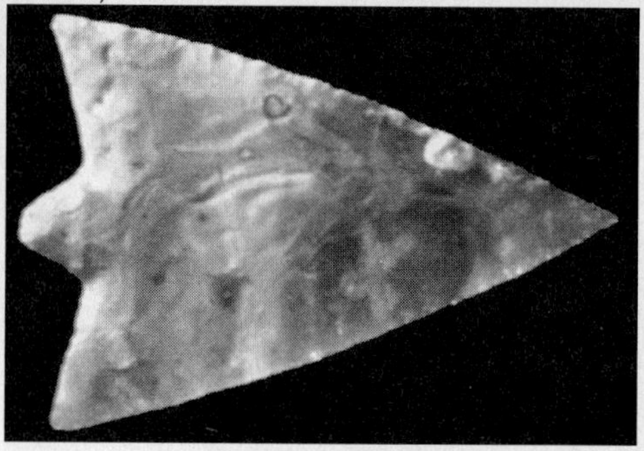

G10, $550-$1000
FL

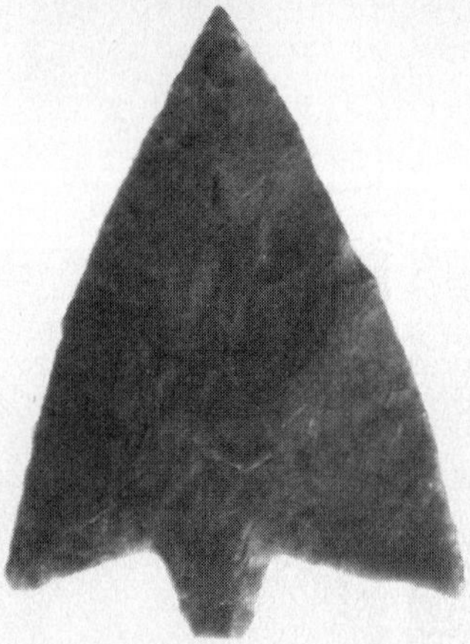

G8, $350-$600
FL

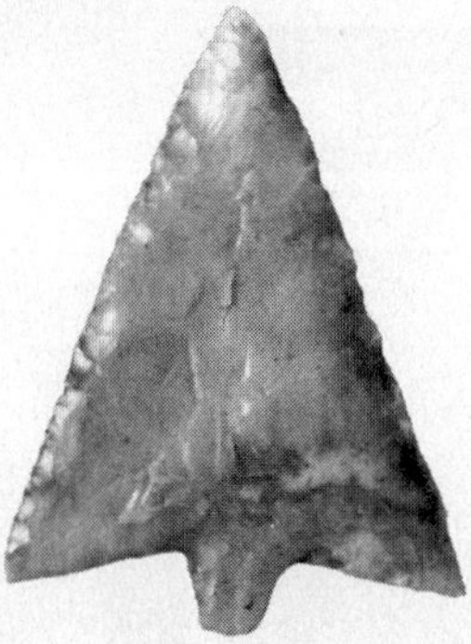

G10, $275-$500
Hillsborough Co., FL

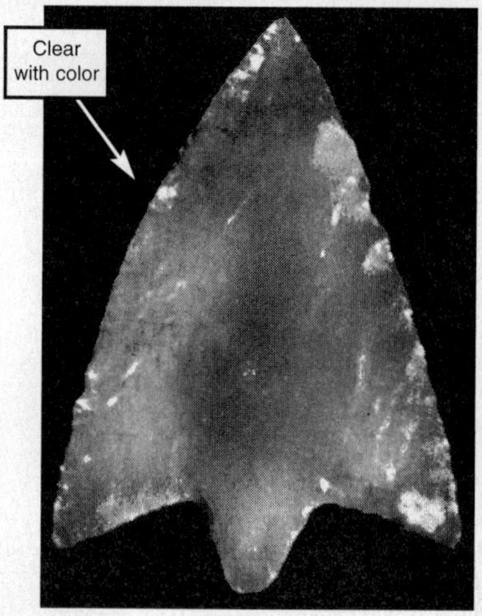
Clear
with color

G8, $550-$1000
NW Cent., FL

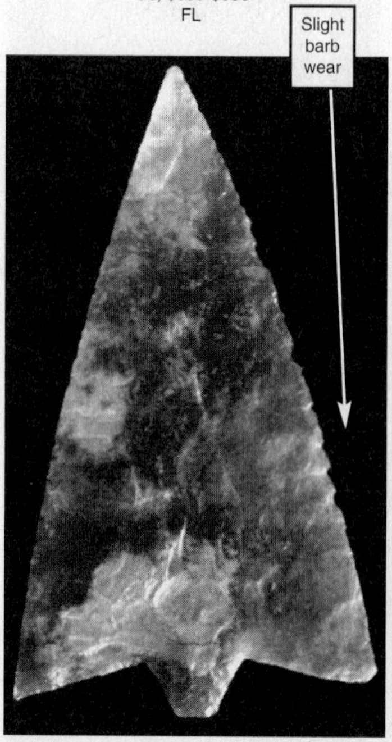
Slight
barb
wear

G9, $550-$1000
Polk Co., FL

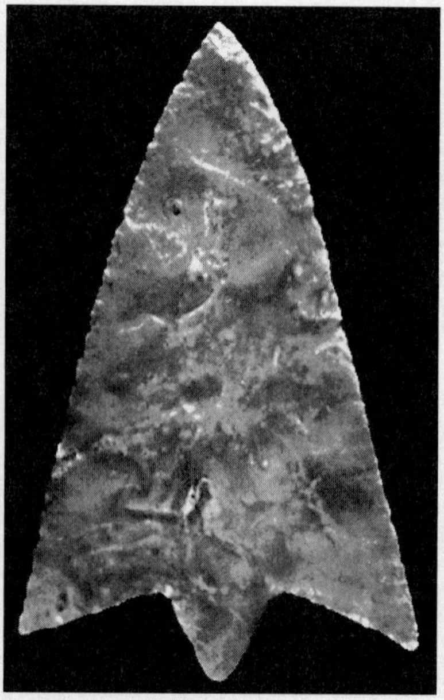

G10, $1000-$1800
FL

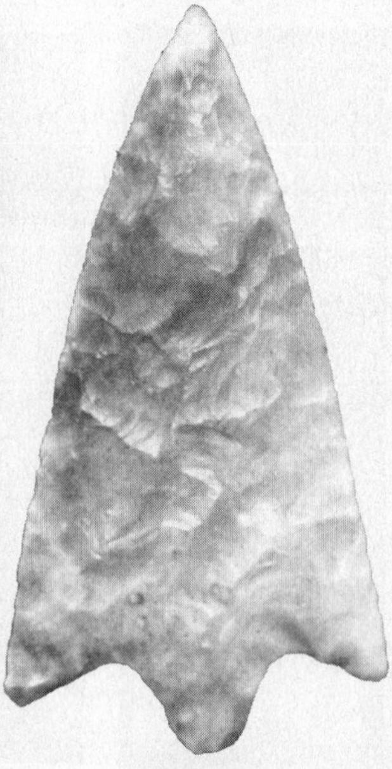

G8, $275-$500
Marion Co., FL

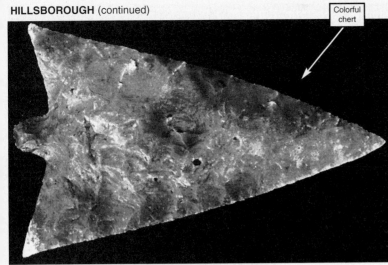

Colorful chert

G10+, $4000-$7500
N. W. Cent. FL.
Cache point

GC

G8, $150-$250
Gainesville, FL

Colorful chert

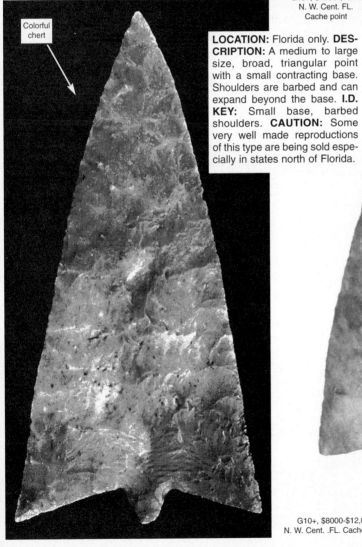

LOCATION: Florida only. **DESCRIPTION:** A medium to large size, broad, triangular point with a small contracting base. Shoulders are barbed and can expand beyond the base. **I.D. KEY:** Small base, barbed shoulders. **CAUTION:** Some very well made reproductions of this type are being sold especially in states north of Florida.

G8, $800-$1500
FL

G10+, $8000-$12,000
N. W. Cent. .FL. Cache point.

261

ICHETUCKNEE - Mississippian to Historic, 700 - 200 B. P.

(Also see Pinellas)

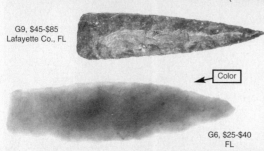

G9, $45-$85
Lafayette Co., FL

G7, $50-$75
Marion Co., FL

Color

G6, $25-$40
FL

LOCATION: Southeastern states. **DESCRIPTION:** A small to medium size, thin, narrow, lanceolate point with usually a straight base. Flaking quality is excellent. This point is called *Guntersville* to the north. **I.D. KEY:** Narrowness and blade expansion; blade edges curve inward at base.

JACKSON - Late Woodland to Mississippian, 2000 - 700 B. P.

(Also see Duval)

G10, $20-$35
FL

G5, $8-$15
FL.

LOCATION: Coastal states. **DESCRIPTION:** A small size, thick, narrow, triangular point with wide, shallow side notches. Some examples have an unfinished rind or base. Called *Swan Lake* in upper Southeastern states

KASKASKIA POINT   (See Trade Points)

KIRK CORNER NOTCHED - Early to Middle Archaic, 9000 - 6000 B. P.

(Also see Bolen, Hardin, Lafayette and Ocala)

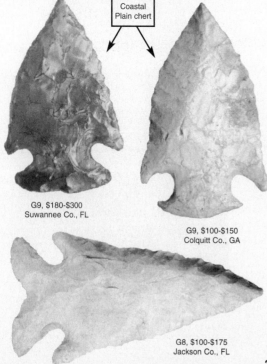

Coastal Plain chert

Coastal Plain chert

G9, $180-$300
Suwannee Co., FL

G9, $100-$150
Colquitt Co., GA

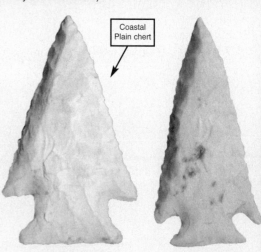

G8, $80-$150
Seminole Co., GA

G8, $125-$200
Chatham Co., GA

G8, $100-$175
Jackson Co., FL

LOCATION: Southeastern states. **DESCRIPTION:** A medium to large size, corner notched point. Blade edges can be convex to recurved and are finely serrated on many examples. The base can be concave, convex, straight or auriculate. **I.D. KEY:** Secondary edgework.

(Also see Abbey, Arredondo, Boggy Branch, Bolen, Elora, Hamilton and Six Mile Creek)

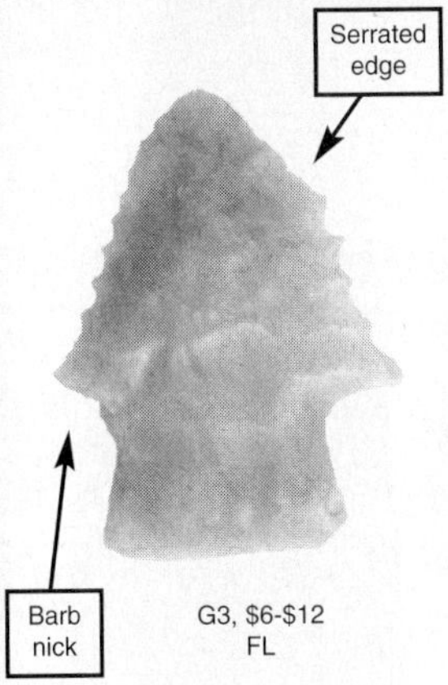

Serrated edge

Serrated edge

GC

Barb nick

G3, $6-$12
FL

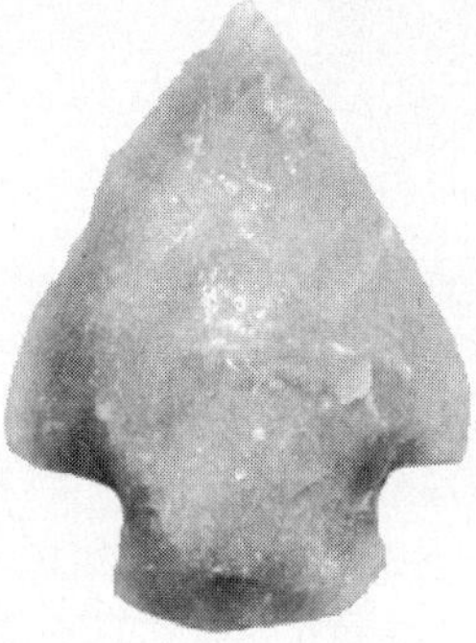

G5, $8-$15
Jefferson Co., FL

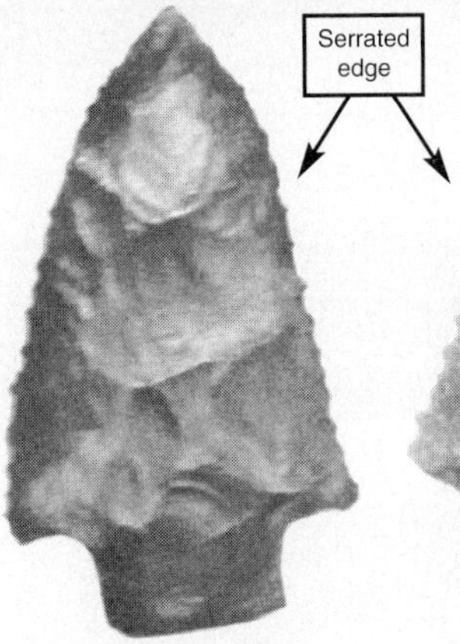

G5, $18-$30
Jefferson Co., FL

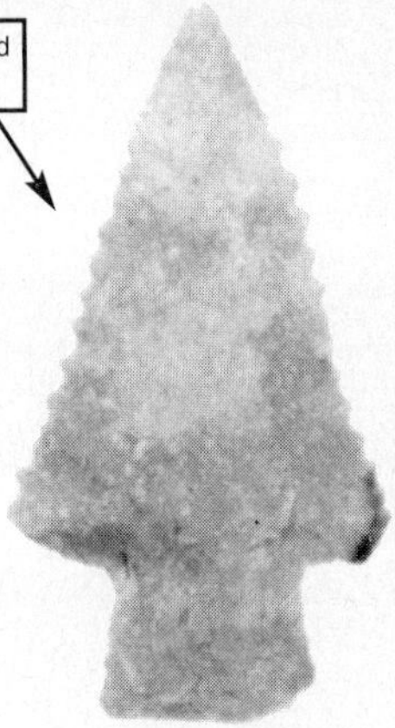

G5, $20-$35
FL, cache point

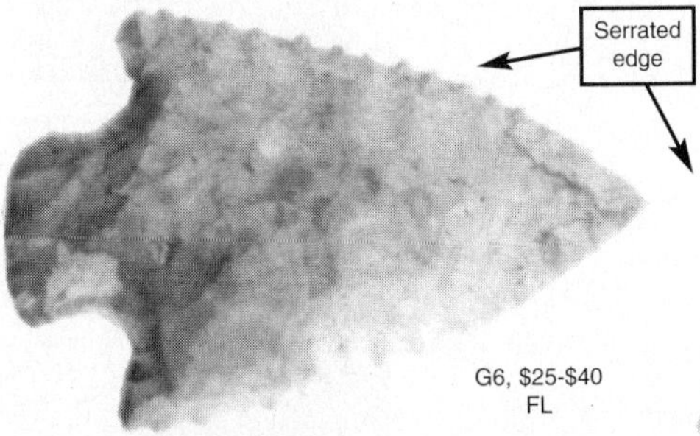

Serrated edge

Translucent

G6, $25-$40
FL

Agate

G8, $40-$75
FL

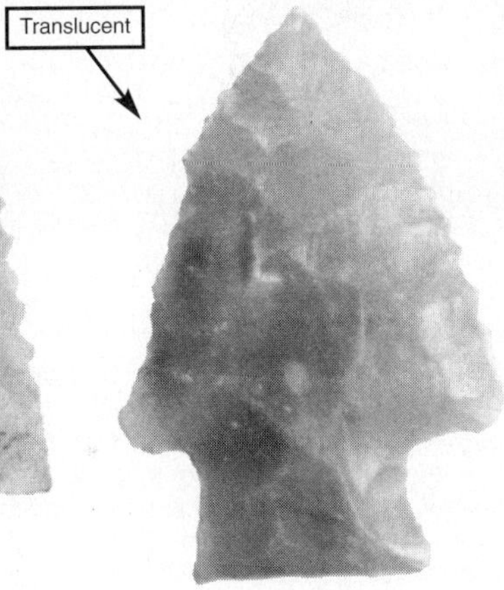

G6, $35-$50
FL

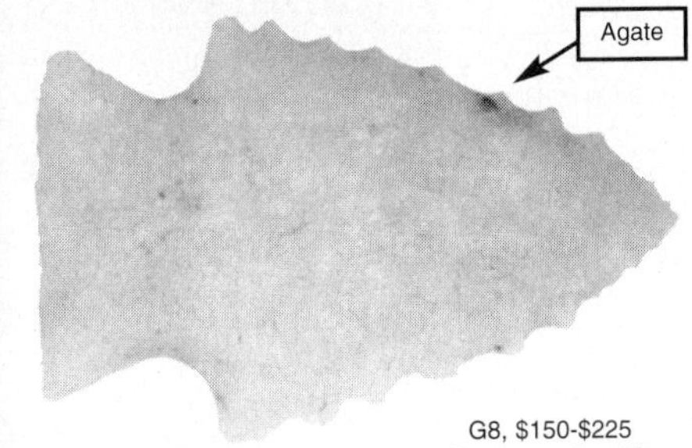

G8, $150-$225
Suwannee Co., FL

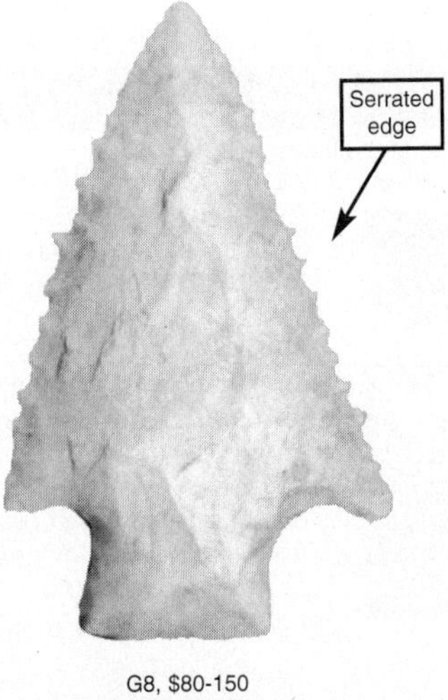

Serrated edge

Florida chert

Serrated edge

Florida chert

G8, $80-150
Early Co., GA

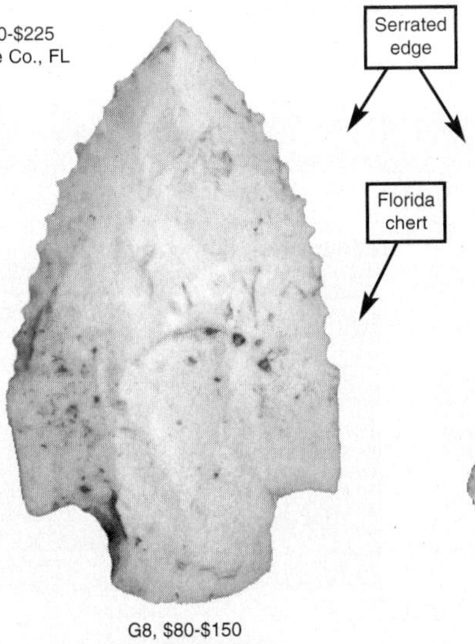

G8, $80-$150
Rainbow Riv., FL

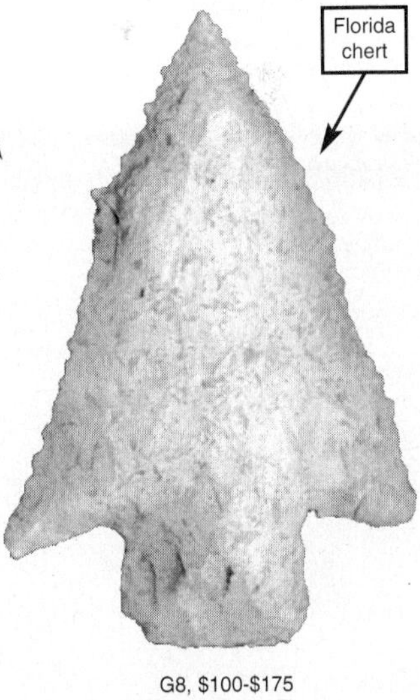

G8, $100-$175
Lake Tarpon, FL

KIRK STEMMED (continued)

Quartzite

G9, $150-$250
AL

Tallahatta quartzite

G10, $175-$300
AL

Serrated edge

Coastal Plain chert

Rind

G10, $300-$475
Marion Co., FL, Orange Lake

G9, $550-$850
St. Johns Riv., FL

LOCATION: Eastern to Gulf Coastal states.
DESCRIPTION: A medium to large size, barbed, stemmed point with deep notches or fine serrations along the blade edges. The stem is parallel, contracting or expanding. The base can be concave, convex or straight, and can be very short. The shoulders are usually strongly barbed. **I.D. KEY:** Serrations.

LAFAYETTE - Late Archaic, 4000 - 3000 B. P.

(Also see Bolen Plain, Clay, Culbreath, Kirk Corner Notched and Ocala)

G6, $35-$60
FL

G8, $80-$150
Marion Co., FL

LOCATION: Southern to Southeastern states. **DESCRIPTION:** A medium size, broad, corner-notched point with a straight to concave base. Barbs and basal corners are more rounded than pointed. Related to *Clay* points. Previously shown (in error) as *Ocala* points. Barbs expand.

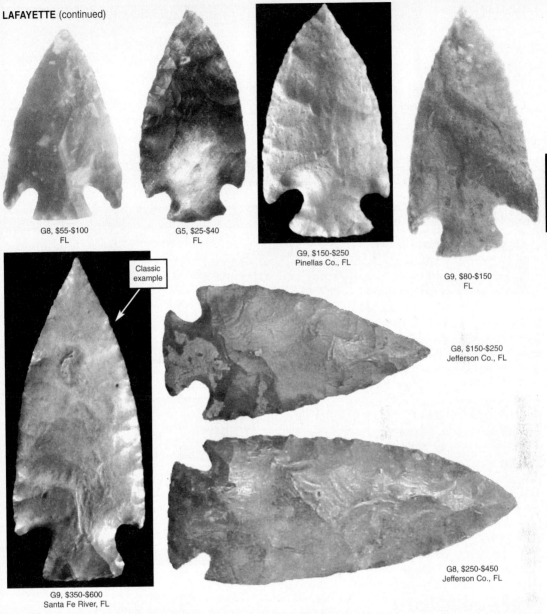

GC

G8, $55-$100
FL

G5, $25-$40
FL

G9, $150-$250
Pinellas Co., FL

G9, $80-$150
FL

Classic example

G8, $150-$250
Jefferson Co., FL

G8, $250-$450
Jefferson Co., FL

G9, $350-$600
Santa Fe River, FL

LEDBETTER - Mid to late Archaic, 6,000 - 3500 B. P.

(Also see Pickwick and Levy)

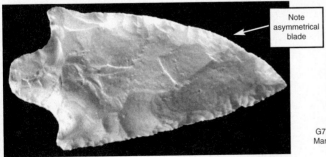

Note asymmetrical blade

LOCATION: Southeastern into the Gulf states. **DESCRIPTION:** A medium to large size *Pickwick* point that is asymmetrical with one side of the blade curving to the tip more than the other. Bases are contracting to expanding. Blade edges can be serrated. **I.D. KEY:** Asymmetrical blade.

G7, $80-$150
Marion Co., FL

LEDBETTER (continued)

G7, $175-$300
Leesburg, GA

LEON - Woodland - Mississippian, 1500 - 1000 B. P.

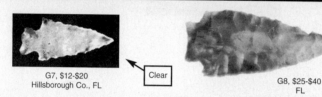

G7, $12-$20
Hillsborough Co., FL

Clear

G8, $25-$40
FL

LOCATION: Southern to Southeastern states. **DESCRIPTION:** A small size coner notched point. Blade edges are straight to convex. Bases expand with sharp to rounded basal corners. **I.D. KEY:** Size and corner notching.

LEVY - Late Archaic, 5000 - 3000 B. P.

(Also see Abbey, Alachua, Cypress Creek, Elora, Hardee Beveled, Ledbetter, Marion, Newnan, Putnam, Savannah River and Sumter)

Colorful purple coral

Clear coral

G8, $200-$350
Pasco Co., FL

G6, $150-$250
Hillsborough co., FL

G6, $15-$25
FL

Levy with Newnan stem

G8, $55-$100
FL

G9, $125-$200
FL

LOCATION: Southern to Southeastern states. **DESCRIPTION:** A medium size, broad, contracted stemmed point with wide, tapered to slightly barbed shoulders. May have evolved from the earlier *Newnan* form. **I.D. KEY:** Edgework and one ear is stronger. *Levy* shoulders have concave edges connecting base and shoulder corners.

LEVY (continued)

GC

Colorful coral

Tallahatta quartzite

G8, $80-$150
FL

G9, $400-$700
Hillsborough Co., FL

G10, $200-$350
FL

G10, $250-$400
FL

G7, $40-$70
FL

G7, $80-$150
Sou. AL

G5, $25-$40
FL

G10, $300-$550
Madison Co., FL

267

(Also see Bolen Beveled, Kirk Corner Notched)

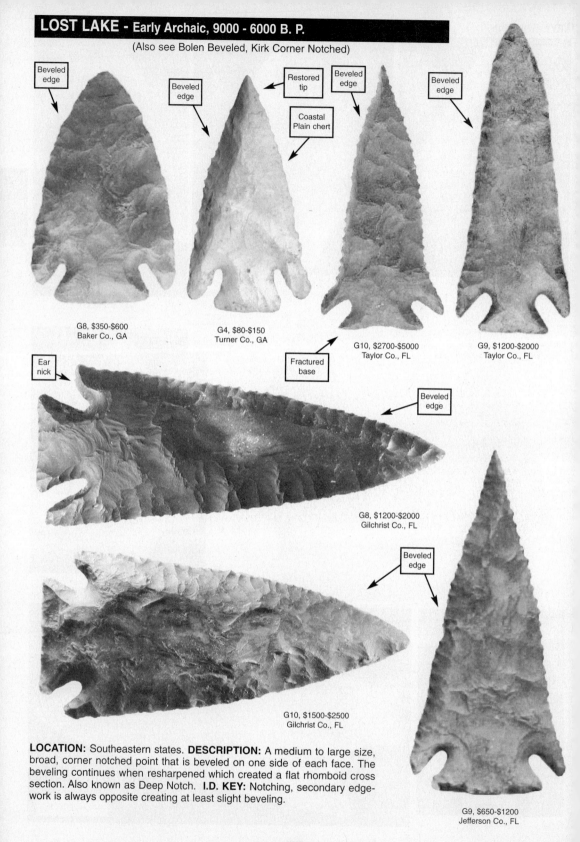

Beveled edge

Beveled edge

Restored tip

Coastal Plain chert

Beveled edge

Beveled edge

G8, $350-$600
Baker Co., GA

G4, $80-$150
Turner Co., GA

Fractured base

G10, $2700-$5000
Taylor Co., FL

G9, $1200-$2000
Taylor Co., FL

Ear nick

Beveled edge

G8, $1200-$2000
Gilchrist Co., FL

Beveled edge

G10, $1500-$2500
Gilchrist Co., FL

Beveled edge

G9, $650-$1200
Jefferson Co., FL

LOCATION: Southeastern states. **DESCRIPTION:** A medium to large size, broad, corner notched point that is beveled on one side of each face. The beveling continues when resharpened which created a flat rhomboid cross section. Also known as Deep Notch. **I.D. KEY:** Notching, secondary edge-work is always opposite creating at least slight beveling.

MANASOTA - Woodland 3,000 - 1500 B. P.

(Also see Beaver Lake and Safety Harbor)

No grinding in hafting area

Very thin in cross section

G10, $125-$200
Sumter Co., FL

LOCATION: Tampa Bay area into the Florida panhandle. **DESCRIPTION:** A medium size, thin, narrow, auriculate point with recurved blade edges and a sharp tip. Similar to the much earlier *Beaver Lake* point but usually smaller and narrower and the stem is not ground. **I.D. KEY:** Narrowness and no grinding. See Schroder, pg. 194, The Anthropology of Florida Points and Blades.

MAPLES - Middle Archaic, 4500 - 3500 B. P.

(Also see Elora, Morrow Mountain and Savannah River)

GC

Jasper

G7, $150-$250
Dodge Co., GA

LOCATION: N. Florida into Georgia. **DESCRIPTION:** A very large, broad, thick, short stemmed blade. Shoulders are tapered and the stem is contracting with a concave to straight base. Usually thick and crudely made, but fine quality examples have been found. Not to be confused with Morrow Mountain which has Archaic parallel flaking.

MARIANNA - Transitional Paleo, 10,000 - 8500 B. P.

(Also see Conerly)

G5, $8-$15
FL

LOCATION: Southern to Southeastern states. **DESCRIPTION:** A rare type. A medium size lanceolate point with a constricted, concave base. Look for parallel to oblique flaking.

MARION - Middle Archaic, 7000 - 3000 B. P.

(Also see Adena, Alachua, Cottonbridge, Cypress Creek, Hardee Beveled, Levy, Morrow Mountain, Newnan, Pickwick and Putnam)

G6, $30-$50
Dale Co., AL

G7, $40-$75
Hillsborough Co., FL

269

Clear coral

G7, $65-$120
Hillsborough Co., FL

G7, $30-$50
FL

G8, $550-$1000
Pasco Co., FL

G8, $350-$600
NW Cent., FL

Agatized coral

Coral

G9, $450-$800
Pasco Co., FL

G9, $700-$1300
Hillsborough Co., FL

G8, $800-$1200
Lake Co., FL

Florida chert

G7, $150-$225
Santa Fe Riv., FL

G8, $80-$150
FL

GC

Clear

G8, $150-$250
Polk Co., FL

Colorful chert

LOCATION: Southern to South eastern states. **DESCRIPTION:** A medium to large size, broad, contracted stemmed point with slightly <u>tapered shoulders</u> and rounded basal corners. *Marions* with *Newnan* type squarish bases represent a *Marion/Newnan* cross type. **I.D. KEY:** Tapered shoulders, rounded stem.

Clear coral

G9, $350-$600
FL

G10, $2500-$4000
Hillsborough Co., FL

G9, $700-$1200
Pasco Co., FL

(Also see Bascom, Cypress Creek, Eva, Maples, Marion, Putnam and Thonotosassa)

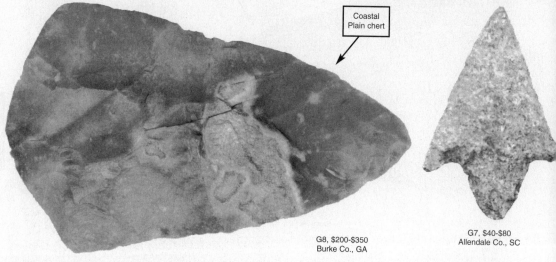

Coastal Plain chert

G8, $200-$350
Burke Co., GA

G7, $40-$80
Allendale Co., SC

Tallahatta quartzite

G6, $250-$400
Sou. AL

LOCATION: Midwestern to Southeastern states. **DESCRIPTION:** A medium to large size, triangular point with a very short contracting to rounded stem. Shoulders are usually weak, but can be barbed. The blade edges on some examples are serrated with needle points. **I.D. KEY:** Contracted base and Archaic parallel flaking.

(Also see Adena, Alachua, Cypress Creek, Hardee Beveled, Hillsborough, Levy, Marion, Morrow Mountain, and Putnam)

Clear coral

G5, $25-$45
Alachua Co., FL

G9 $200-$350
FL

LOCATION: Southern Southeastern states. **DESCRIPTION:** A medium to large size, broad, stemmed point with a short to long contracting base. Shoulders form a straight line and are horizontal to downward and outward sloping. Stems have contracted, straight sides and a straight to rounded base. *Newnans* with *Marion*-type rounded bases represent a *Newnan/Marion* cross type and would fall under *Marion* if the shoulders slope up.

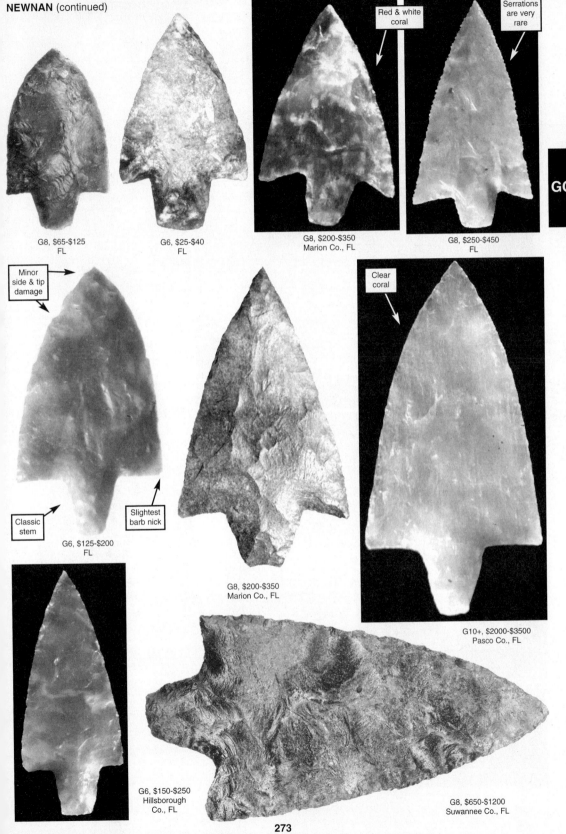

GC

G8, $65-$125
FL

G6, $25-$40
FL

Red & white coral

G8, $200-$350
Marion Co., FL

Serrations are very rare

G8, $250-$450
FL

Minor side & tip damage

Classic stem

Slightest barb nick

G6, $125-$200
FL

G8, $200-$350
Marion Co., FL

Clear coral

G10+, $2000-$3500
Pasco Co., FL

G6, $150-$250
Hillsborough Co., FL

G8, $650-$1200
Suwannee Co., FL

Clear

G10, $650-$1200
Hillsborough Co., FL

Shoulder wear

Coral polyps

G9, $1000-$1800
Marion Co., FL

G7, $200-$350
Marion Co., FL

Newnan barbs & Marion style base. Found in a Newnan cache. Subtype: Pasco Point

Red & white chert

Classic form

G9, $400-$750
Marion Co., FL

G9, $450-$800
Pasco Co., FL

G10, $2500-$4000
Dixie Co., FL

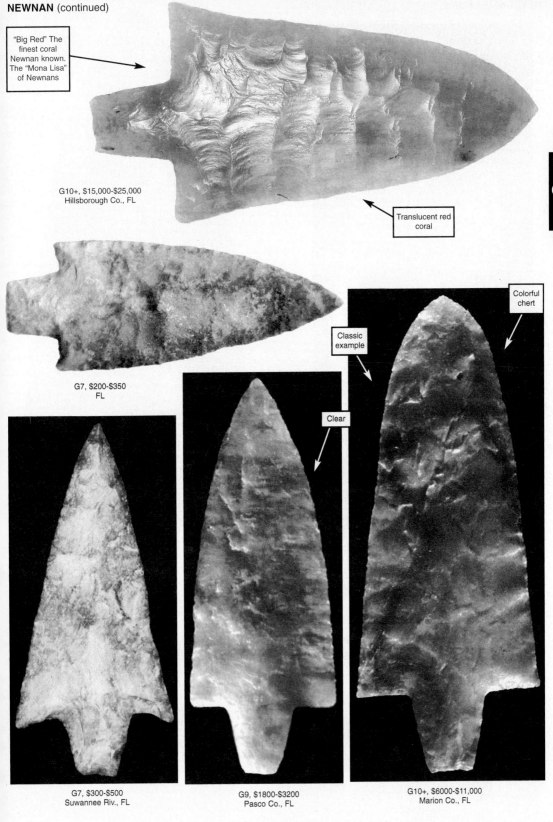

"Big Red" The finest coral Newnan known. The "Mona Lisa" of Newnans

G10+, $15,000-$25,000
Hillsborough Co., FL

Translucent red coral

GC

G7, $200-$350
FL

Classic example

Colorful chert

Clear

G7, $300-$500
Suwannee Riv., FL

G9, $1800-$3200
Pasco Co., FL

G10+, $6000-$11,000
Marion Co., FL

Classic stem &
shoulder form.
Good symmetry

G9, $2500-$4000
Alachua Co., FL

G10+, $9000-$16,000
Jefferson Co., FL

OCALA - Woodland, 2500 - 1500 B. P.

(Also see Bolen, Clay, Culbreath, Kirk Corner Notched & Lafayette)

LOCATION: Gulf Coastal states. **DESCRIPTION:** A medium to large size broad corner-notched point with a straight to convex base. Some examples have a base similar to *Dovetails*. Barbs and basal corners are sharp to rounded. Barbs curve inward. Rare in Florida. According to Bullen this type is larger and better crafted than *Bolens* or *Lafayettes* and dates to 2500 B.P. **I.D. KEY:** Size and corner notching.

G8, $35-$65
FL

Broken & glued

G7, $250-$400
Marion Co., AL

GC

O'LENO - Woodland, 2000 - 800 B. P.

(Also see Pinellas, Tampa and Yadkin)

G7, $20-$35
Henry Co., AL

G6, $15-$25
Marion Co., FL

G6, $15-$25
N.W. FL

LOCATION: Southern Southeastern states. **DESCRIPTION:** A medium size, broad, triangle point with a straight to slightly concave base.

OSCEOLA-GREENBRIAR - Early Archaic, 9500 - 6000 B. P.

(Also see Bolen)

Clear

Tip nick

Clear

G7, $80-$150, type I
FL

G6, $125-$200, type I
FL

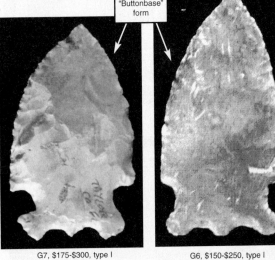

"Buttonbase" form

G7, $175-$300, type I
Taylor Co., FL

G6, $150-$250, type I
NW Cent. FL

277

G7, $55-$100, type I
FL

G9, $175-$300, type I
FL

G8, $275-$500, type I
N. W. Cent. FL

G7, $80-$150, type II
FL

G8, $80-$150, type II
FL

G9, $150-$250, type II
FL

G7, $80-$150, type II
Marion Co., FL

G6, $65-$125, type I
FL

G6, $80-$150, type II
NW Cent., FL

G7, $175-$300, type II
Pasco Co., FL

G7, $150-$250, type II
Santa Fe Riv., FL

LOCATION: Gulf Coastal states. **DESCRIPTION:** A medium to large size, broad, side-notched point with two base variations. The base is either concave or has two shallow notches creating a high point in the center. Bases and notches are usually heavily ground. This type is found in the same layer with *Bolen* points in Florida.

G6, $175-$300, type II
Santa Fe Riv., FL

OSCEOLA GREENBRIAR (continued)

G9, $250-$450, type II
Jefferson Co., FL

G10, $400-$750, type II
NW Cent. FL

PALEO KNIFE - Paleo, 10,000 B. P.

(Also see Scraper)

G8, $15-$25
Suwannee Co., FL

G6, $20-$35
Suwannee Co., FL

Flat side
shown

G10, $125-$200
Suwannee Co., FL

LOCATION: Florida. **DESCRIPTION:** A medium to large size, uniface blade found with bison, mammoth and mastodon remains. Flat on one face and steeply beveled on the opposing face. **I.D. KEY:** Uniface and steep beveling.

279

PICKWICK - Middle to Late Archaic, 6000 - 3500 B. P.

(Also see Elora, Ledbetter and Savannah River)

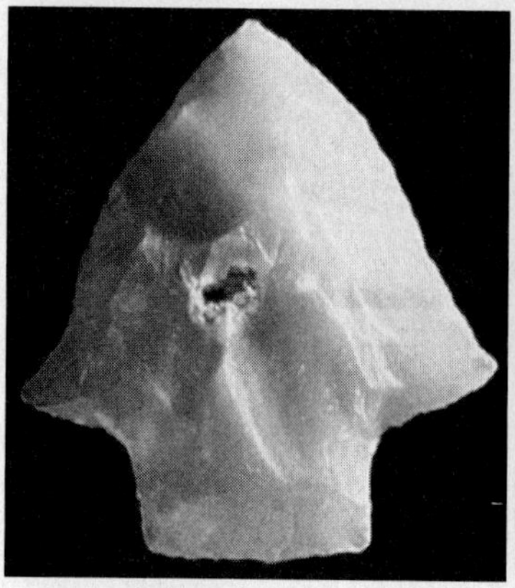

G5, $12-$20
Burke Co., GA

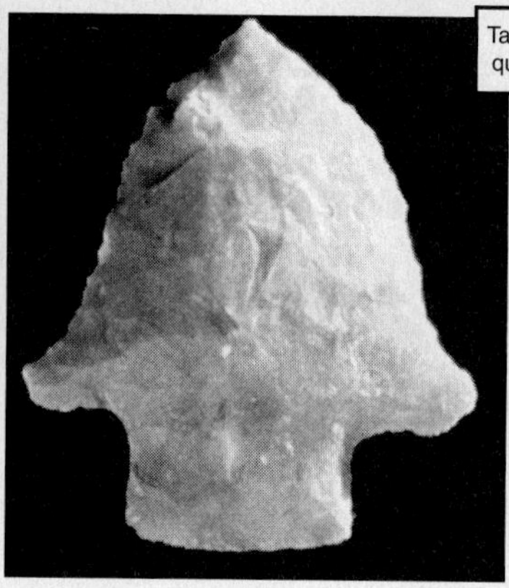

G5, $12-$20
Burke Co., GA

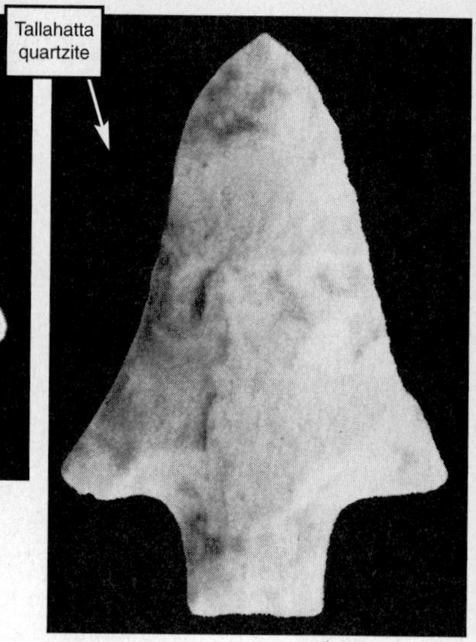
Tallahatta quartzite

G9, $150-$250
Sou. AL

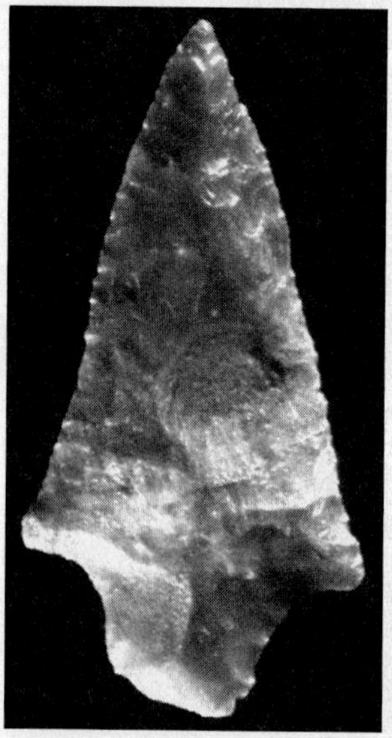

G6, $80-$150
Marion Co., FL

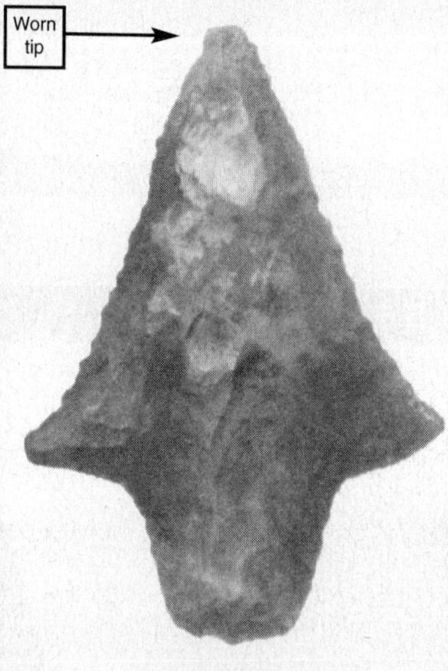
Worn tip

G7, $80-$150
FL

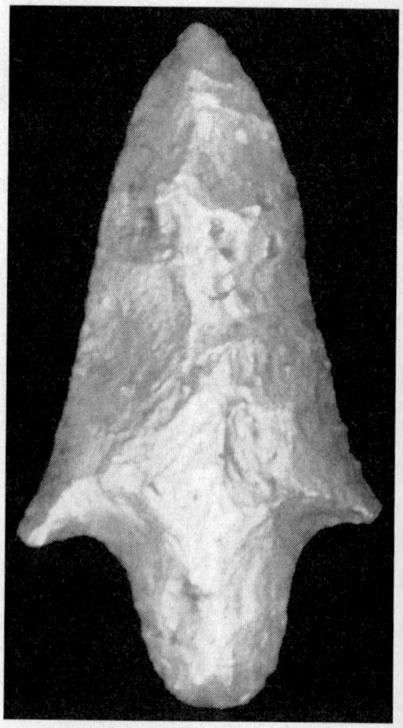

G8, $150-$250
Albany, GA

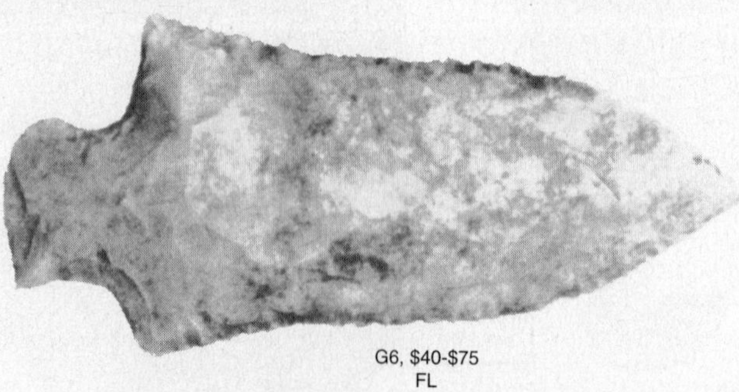

G6, $40-$75
FL

LOCATION: Found North of the Suwannee River into Georgia and Alabama. **DESCRIPTION:** A medium to large size, expanded shoulder, contracted to expanded stem point. Blade edges are recurved, and many examples show fine secondary flaking with serrations. Alabama and Tennessee examples are beveled on one side of each face. The bevel is steep and shallow. Shoulders are horizontal, tapered or barbed and form sharp angles. Some stems are snapped off or may show original rind.

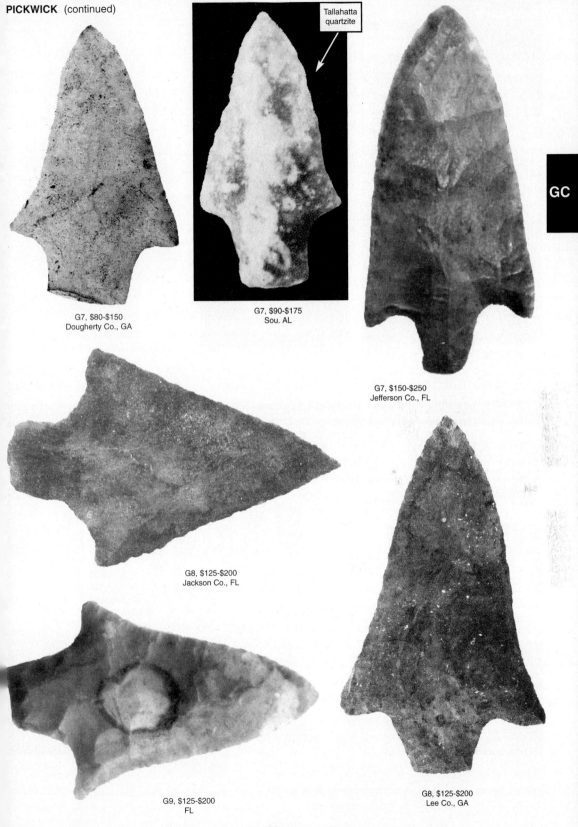

PICKWICK (continued)

Tallahatta quartzite

GC

G7, $80-$150
Dougherty Co., GA

G7, $90-$175
Sou. AL

G7, $150-$250
Jefferson Co., FL

G8, $125-$200
Jackson Co., FL

G9, $125-$200
FL

G8, $125-$200
Lee Co., GA

281

PICKWICK (continued)

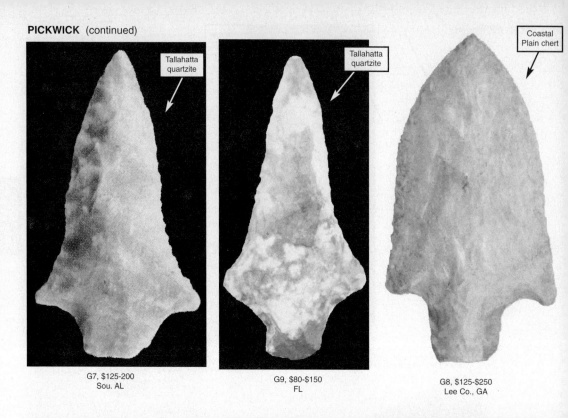

Tallahatta quartzite

Tallahatta quartzite

Coastal Plain chert

G7, $125-200
Sou. AL

G9, $80-$150
FL

G8, $125-$250
Lee Co., GA

PINELLAS - Mississippian, 800 - 400 B. P.

(Also see O'Leno, Safety Harbor, Tallahassee and Yadkin)

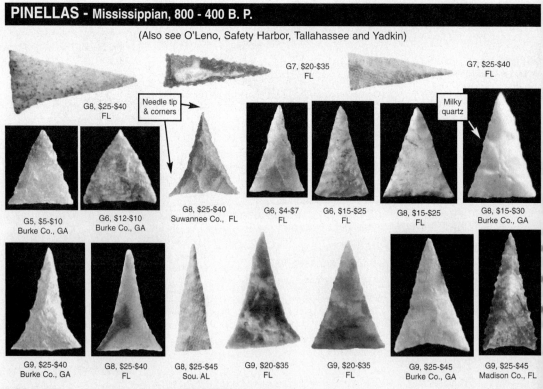

G7, $20-$35
FL

G7, $25-$40
FL

G8, $25-$40
FL

Needle tip & corners

Milky quartz

G5, $5-$10
Burke Co., GA

G6, $12-$10
Burke Co., GA

G8, $25-$40
Suwannee Co., FL

G6, $4-$7
FL

G6, $15-$25
FL

G8, $15-$25
FL

G8, $15-$30
Burke Co., GA

G9, $25-$40
Burke Co., GA

G8, $25-$40
FL

G8, $25-$45
Sou. AL

G9, $20-$35
FL

G9, $20-$35
FL

G9, $25-$45
Burke Co., GA

G9, $25-$45
Madison Co., FL

LOCATION: Gulf Coastal states. **DESCRIPTION:** A small, narrow, thick to thin, triangular point with a straight to slightly concave base. Blade edges can be serrated.

PINELLAS (continued)

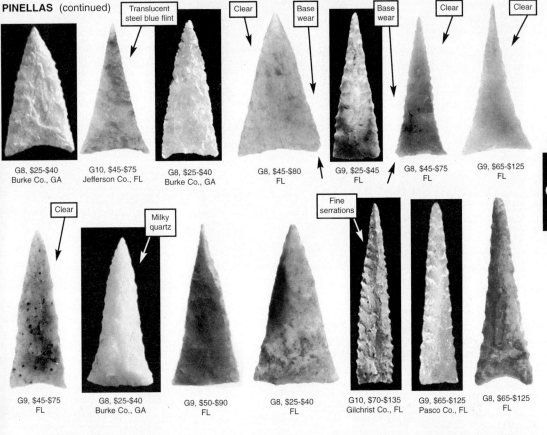

Translucent steel blue flint

Clear

Base wear

Base wear

Clear

Clear

G8, $25-$40
Burke Co., GA

G10, $45-$75
Jefferson Co., FL

G8, $25-$40
Burke Co., GA

G8, $45-$80
FL

G9, $25-$45
FL

G8, $45-$75
FL

G9, $65-$125
FL

GC

Clear

Milky quartz

Fine serrations

G9, $45-$75
FL

G8, $25-$40
Burke Co., GA

G9, $50-$90
FL

G8, $25-$40
FL

G10, $70-$135
Gilchrist Co., FL

G9, $65-$125
Pasco Co., FL

G8, $65-$125
FL

PUTNAM - Middle Archaic, 6500 - 3000 B. P.

(Also see Cypress Creek, Hardee Beveled, Levy, Marion, Morrow Mountain, Newnan, Sumter and Thonotosassa)

Classic example

G6, $20-$35
FL

Coral

G6, $12-$20
FL

G5, $20-$35
FL

Coral

G8, $25-$40
FL

G7, $25-$40
FL

LOCATION: Southern Southeastern states. **DESCRIPTION:** A medium to large size, broad, contracted stemmed point with rounded to sharp shoulders. The stem is short to long with a convex base. The shoulders are tapered and can be rounded. Believed to have evolved from the *Marion* type. **I.D. KEY:** Weak shoulders, rounded barbs formed by continuous recurved edges.

G7, $25-$40
FL

G6, $25-$40
FL

G6, $30-$50
FL

G10, $350-$600
FL

G9, $175-$300
FL

Semi-clear

Miinor
edge
nick

G9, $800-$1400
Aucilla Riv., FL

REDSTONE - Paleo, 11,500 - 10,500 B. P.

(Also see Clovis, Simpson and Suwannee)

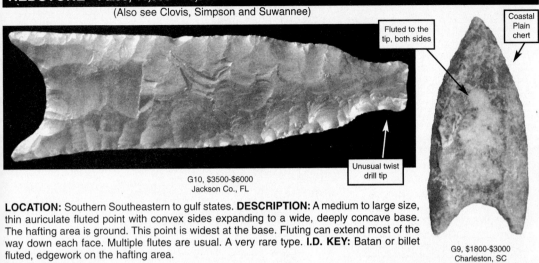

Fluted to the tip, both sides

Coastal Plain chert

Unusual twist drill tip

G10, $3500-$6000
Jackson Co., FL

GC

G9, $1800-$3000
Charleston, SC

LOCATION: Southern Southeastern to gulf states. **DESCRIPTION:** A medium to large size, thin auriculate fluted point with convex sides expanding to a wide, deeply concave base. The hafting area is ground. This point is widest at the base. Fluting can extend most of the way down each face. Multiple flutes are usual. A very rare type. **I.D. KEY:** Batan or billet fluted, edgework on the hafting area.

SAFETY HARBOR - Mississippian to Historic, 1100 - 300 B. P.

(Also see Manasota, O'Leno, Pinellas, Santa Fe, Tallahassee and Yadkin)

G5, $15-$25
Sumter Co., FL

Serrated edge

G9, $90-$175
Sumter Co., FL

G10, $150-$275
Sumter Co., FL

G9, $90-$175
Sumter Co., FL

LOCATION: The Tampa Bay area of Florida. Named in the 1960s by Jarl Malwin. **DESCRIPTION:** A medium size, narrow, thin, triangular point with a concave base. Basal corners are sharp. Blade edges can be serrated. These are similar points to *Santa Fe* and *Tallahassee* found in other areas but are not as old. Basal edges of *Safety Harbor* points are not ground.

SANTA FE - Late Archaic to Woodland 4000 - 1500 B.P

(Also see Beaver Lake, Dalton, Hardaway, Safety Harbor and Tallahassee)

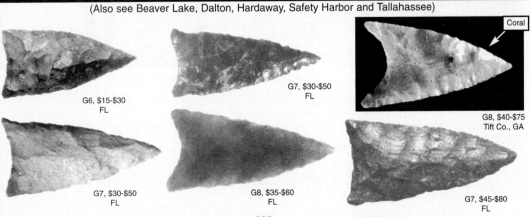

Coral

G6, $15-$30
FL

G7, $30-$50
FL

G8, $40-$75
Tift Co., GA

G7, $30-$50
FL

G8, $35-$60
FL

G7, $45-$80
FL

285

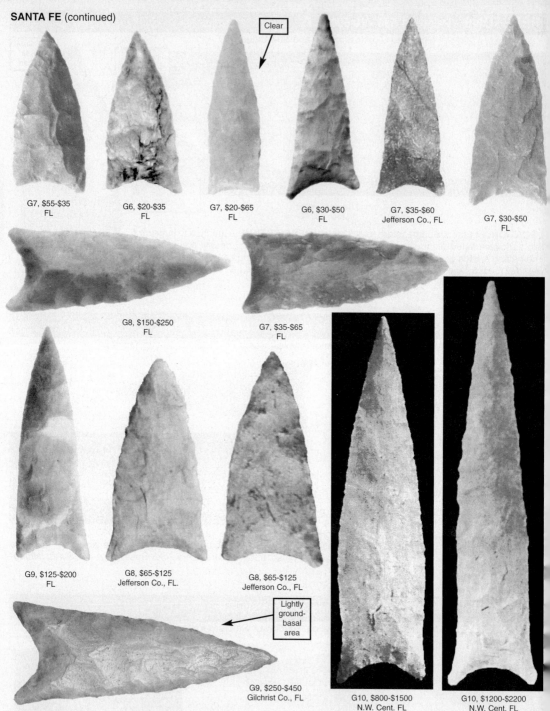

Clear

G7, $55-$35
FL

G6, $20-$35
FL

G7, $20-$65
FL

G6, $30-$50
FL

G7, $35-$60
Jefferson Co., FL

G7, $30-$50
FL

G8, $150-$250
FL

G7, $35-$65
FL

G9, $125-$200
FL

G8, $65-$125
Jefferson Co., FL.

G8, $65-$125
Jefferson Co., FL

Lightly ground-basal area

G9, $250-$450
Gilchrist Co., FL

G10, $800-$1500
N.W. Cent. FL

G10, $1200-$2200
N.W. Cent. FL

LOCATION: From the Tampa Bay area of Florida northward into southern Alabama, Georgia and South Carolina. **DESCRIPTION:** A medium size, thin, narrow, auriculate point with expanding auricules and a concave base. Hafting area is not well defined and can be lightly ground although many examples are not ground. Blade edges are not serrated as in *Tallahassee* which is the serrated form of the two types. **Note:** This type along with the *Tallahassee* point have been confused with a much earlier *Dalton* type found in Northern Florida into Southern Alabama, Georgia and South Carolina. Compared to the *Dalton* type, the *Santa Fe* and the *Tallahassee* points are narrower and much thinner and have less patination. The *Dalton* is a heavier point being thicker and wider with heavy grinding around the entire basal area. the blade edge serrations are also formed differently on *Dalton* points. **I.D. KEY:** Thinness, narrowness, light grinding around base.

SARASOTA - Woodland, 3000 - 1500 B. P.

(Also see Bradford, Columbia, Ledbetter and Pickwick)

G5, $12-$20
FL

LOCATION: Southern Southeastern states.
DESCRIPTION: A medium to large size stemmed point with horizontal shoulders. The stem can be parallel sided to slightly expanding or contracting. Blade edges are slightly convex to recurved. Similar to the northern *Pickwick* type.

G6, $45-$80
FL

SAVANNAH RIVER - Middle Archaic to Woodland, 5000 - 2000 B. P.

(Also see Abbey, Arredondo, Bascom, Elora, Hamilton, Kirk, Levy, Seminole, Thonotosassa and Wacissa)

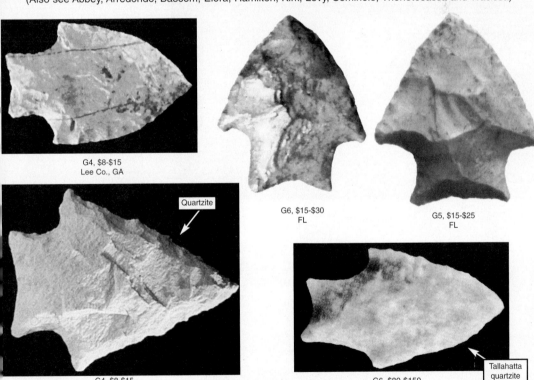

G4, $8-$15
Lee Co., GA

Quartzite

G4, $8-$15
Burke Co., GA

G6, $15-$30
FL

G5, $15-$25
FL

Tallahatta quartzite

G6, $80-$150
Sou. AL

LOCATION: Southeastern to Eastern states. **DESCRIPTION:** A medium to large size, straight to contracting stemmed point with a straight to concave base. The shoulders are tapered to square and are strong. The stems are narrow to broad. Believed to be related to the earlier *Stanly* point. The preform is called *Bascom*. A large cache of *Bascom* and *Savannah River* points were found together in South Carolina. **KEY:** Stems have straight to concave bases, shoulders are strong, *Savannah River* points are usually large. Similar to *Hamilton* points which are much older and have concave bases and weaker shoulders.

287

G6, $125-$200
Sou. AL

G8, $175-$300
Suwannee Riv., FL

Coastal
Plain chert

G7, $175-$300
Dodge Co., GA

G9, $250-$450
Suwannee Riv., FL

G9, $200-$350
Luraville, FL

G10, $700-$1200
Lee Co., GA

G8, $150-$250
Suwannee Riv., FL

Coastal
Plain chert

GC

G9, $350-$600
Dodge Co., GA

G8, $200-$350
Dodge Co., GA

G9, $250-$450
Albany, GA

Slight
tip nick

G9, $350-$600
Miller Co., GA

Finely
serrated
edge

G8, $150-$300
Jackson Co., FL

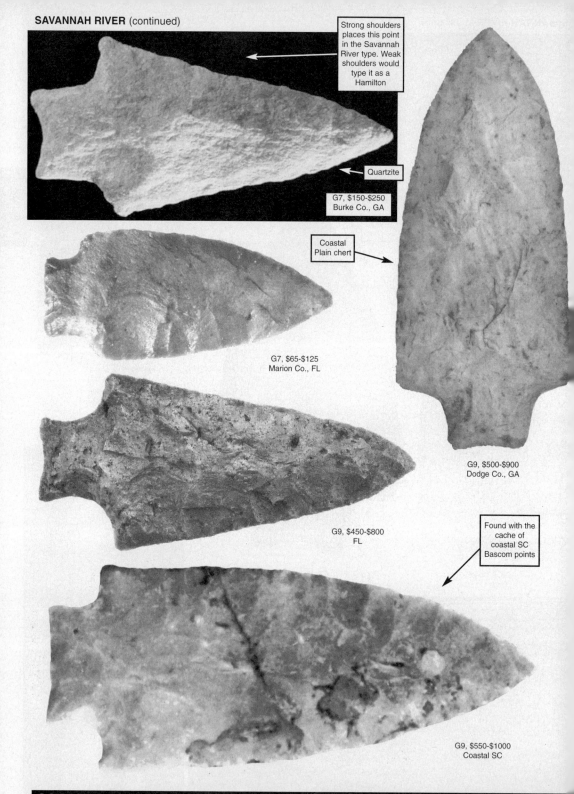

Strong shoulders places this point in the Savannah River type. Weak shoulders would type it as a Hamilton

Quartzite

G7, $150-$250
Burke Co., GA

Coastal Plain chert

G7, $65-$125
Marion Co., FL

G9, $500-$900
Dodge Co., GA

G9, $450-$800
FL

Found with the cache of coastal SC Bascom points

G9, $550-$1000
Coastal SC

SCRAPER - Paleo to Historic, 11,500 - 200 B. P.

(Also see Abbey, Elora, Hamilton, Levy, Paleo Knife, Savannah River and Wacissa)

SCRAPER (continued)

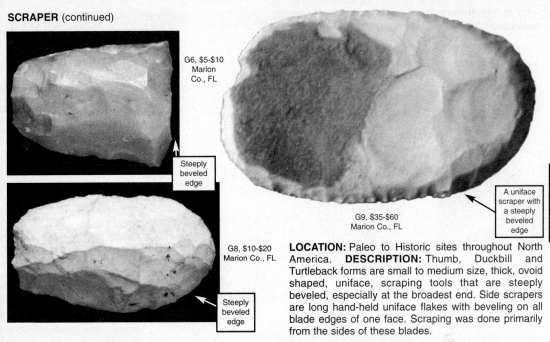

G6, $5-$10
Marion Co., FL

Steeply beveled edge

G9, $35-$60
Marion Co., FL

A uniface scraper with a steeply beveled edge

G8, $10-$20
Marion Co., FL

Steeply beveled edge

LOCATION: Paleo to Historic sites throughout North America. **DESCRIPTION:** Thumb, Duckbill and Turtleback forms are small to medium size, thick, ovoid shaped, uniface, scraping tools that are steeply beveled, especially at the broadest end. Side scrapers are long hand-held uniface flakes with beveling on all blade edges of one face. Scraping was done primarily from the sides of these blades.

SEMINOLE - Late Archaic, 5000 - 3500 B. P.

(Also see Abbey, Elora, Hamilton, Levy, Savannah River and Wacissa)

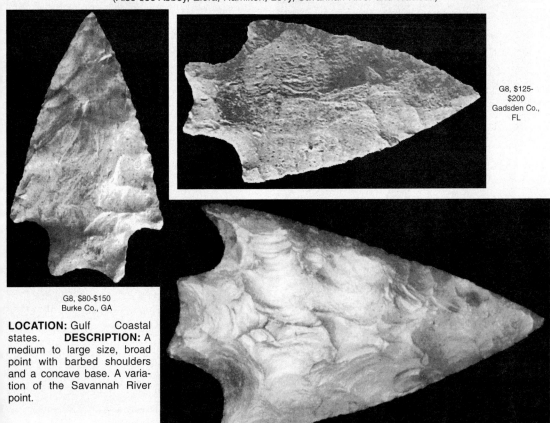

G8, $125-$200
Gadsden Co., FL

G8, $80-$150
Burke Co., GA

LOCATION: Gulf Coastal states. **DESCRIPTION:** A medium to large size, broad point with barbed shoulders and a concave base. A variation of the Savannah River point.

G9, $250-$450
Albany, GA

291

SIMPSON - Late Paleo, 10,000 - 9000 B. P.

(Also see Beaver Lake, Clovis, Conerly, Simpson-Mustache, Suwannee & Withlacoochie)

G5, $150-$275
Southern AL

G8, $450-$800
FL

G5, $200-$350
Jefferson Co., FL

G9, $700-$1200
FL

Coral

G9, $1200-$2000
Suwannee Co., FL

G9, $900-$1600
Gilchrist Co., FL

G9, $700-$1200
Jefferson Co., FL

G7, $800-$1500
NW Cent. FL

G9, $900-$1600
FL

G8, $800-$1400
Hillsborough Co., FL

SIMPSON (continued)

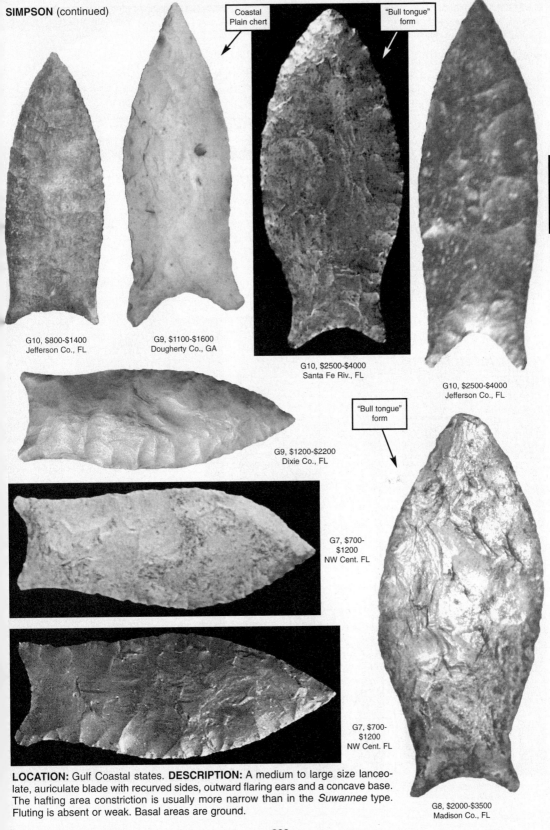

Coastal Plain chert

"Bull tongue" form

GC

G10, $800-$1400
Jefferson Co., FL

G9, $1100-$1600
Dougherty Co., GA

G10, $2500-$4000
Santa Fe Riv., FL

G10, $2500-$4000
Jefferson Co., FL

"Bull tongue" form

G9, $1200-$2200
Dixie Co., FL

G7, $700-$1200
NW Cent. FL

G7, $700-$1200
NW Cent. FL

G8, $2000-$3500
Madison Co., FL

LOCATION: Gulf Coastal states. **DESCRIPTION:** A medium to large size lanceolate, auriculate blade with recurved sides, outward flaring ears and a concave base. The hafting area constriction is usually more narrow than in the *Suwannee* type. Fluting is absent or weak. Basal areas are ground.

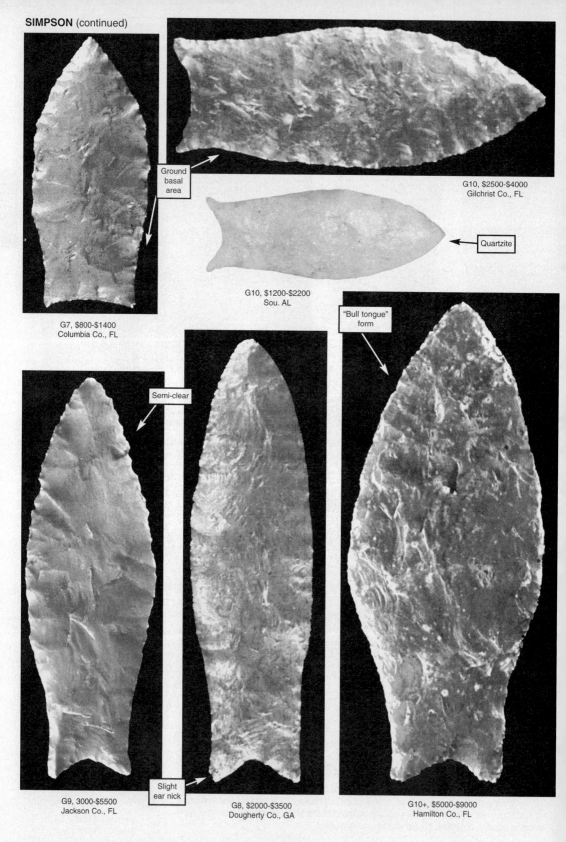

Ground basal area

G10, $2500-$4000
Gilchrist Co., FL

Quartzite

G10, $1200-$2200
Sou. AL

"Bull tongue" form

G7, $800-$1400
Columbia Co., FL

Semi-clear

Slight ear nick

G9, 3000-$5500
Jackson Co., FL

G8, $2000-$3500
Dougherty Co., GA

G10+, $5000-$9000
Hamilton Co., FL

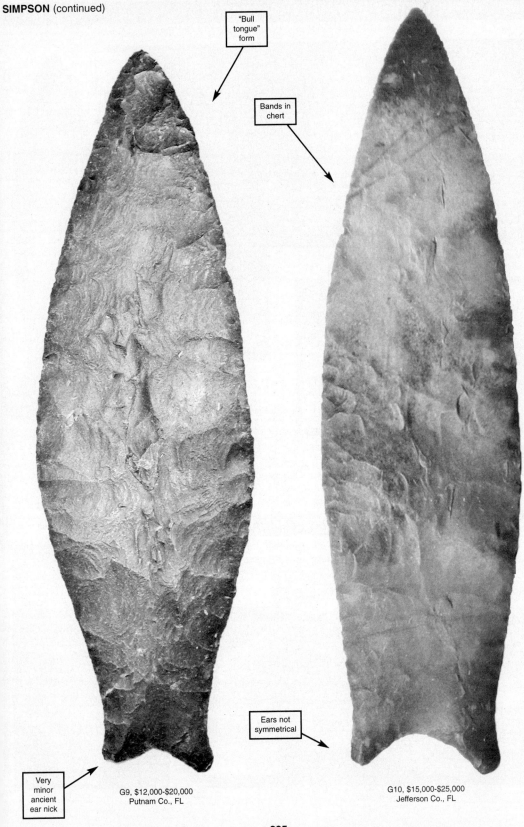

"Bull tongue" form

Bands in chert

GC

Ears not symmetrical

Very minor ancient ear nick

G9, $12,000-$20,000
Putnam Co., FL

G10, $15,000-$25,000
Jefferson Co., FL

SIMPSON-MUSTACHE - Late Paleo, 12,000 - 8000 B. P.

(Also see Beaver Lake, Conerly, Suwannee and Wheeler Expanded Base)

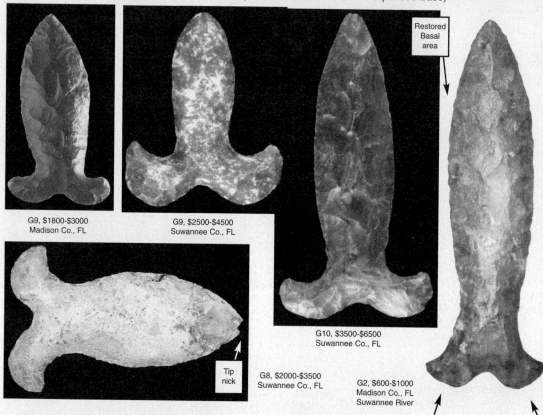

G9, $1800-$3000
Madison Co., FL

G9, $2500-$4500
Suwannee Co., FL

Restored
Basal
area

G10, $3500-$6500
Suwannee Co., FL

Tip
nick

G8, $2000-$3500
Suwannee Co., FL

G2, $600-$1000
Madison Co., FL
Suwannee River

LOCATION: Florida. **DESCRIPTION:** A small to medium size, narrow point with large up-turning ears and a convex base. Very rare in the type area. Fluting is absent. Only about 40-50 including broken ones are known. A very rare type.

SIX MILE CREEK - Middle Archaic, 7500 - 5000 B. P.

(Also see Cottonbridge, Elora, Kirk Serrated and South Prong Creek)

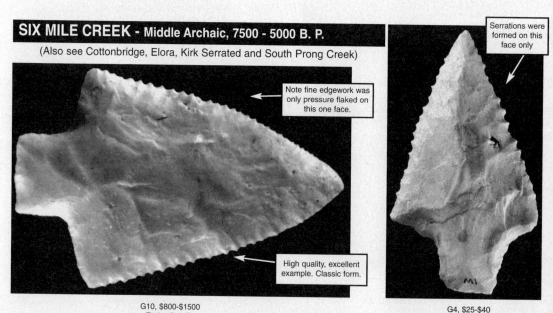

Note fine edgework was
only pressure flaked on
this one face.

Serrations were
formed on this
face only

High quality, excellent
example. Classic form.

G10, $800-$1500
Taylor Co., FL

G4, $25-$40
Decatur Co., GA

SIX MILE CREEK (continued)

LOCATION: Gulf Coastal states. **DESCRIPTION:** A medium to large size, broad, stemmed, serrated point. The serrations are uniquely formed by careful pressure flaking applied from the side of only one face. Normal *Kirk* serrations are pressure flaked alternately from both faces. Believed to be a later *Kirk* variant.

SOUTH PRONG CREEK - Late Archaic, 5000 - 3000 B. P.

(Also see Abbey, Cottonbridge, Elora, Savannah River and Six Mile Creek)

Broad serrations on this type

GC

G8, $150-$250
Burke Co., GA

G7, $65-$125
Seminole Co., GA

G7, $40-$75
Henry Co., AL

G5, $20-$35
Decatur Co., GA

G8, $125-$200
FL

Note how serrations end here

G9, $1000-$1800
Early Co., GA

Clear

LOCATION: Southern Southeastern states. **DESCRIPTION:** A large size, broad shouldered point with a small rectangular stem. Blade edges are usually bifacially serrated beginning at each shoulder and terminating about 1/3 the way from the tip.

STANFIELD - Transitional Paleo, 10,000 - 8000 B. P.

(Also see Cottonbridge, Elora, Kirk Serrated and South Prong Creek)

G10, $150-$250
FL

IMPORTANT:
Stanfields
shown half size

G10, $350-$600
Madison Co., FL

G9, $175-$300
Madison Co., FL

G9, $250-$400
Henry Co., AL

LOCATION: Southeastern states. **DESCRIPTION:** A medium to large size, narrow, lanceolate point with parallel sides and a straight base. Some rare examples are fluted. Bases are ground.

STING RAY BARB - Woodland-Historic, 2500 - 400 B. P.

LOCATION: Florida. **DESCRIPTION:** Not only bone and wood were utilized as arrow points. These barbs taken from rays were hafted to shafts as well. Found on coastal occupation sites.

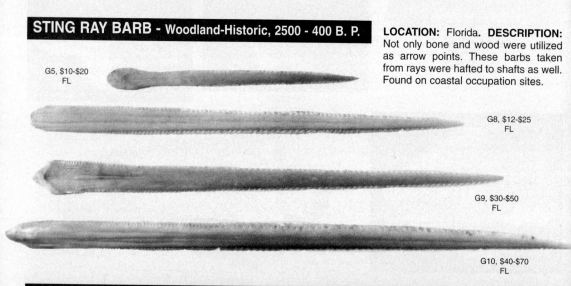

G5, $10-$20
FL

G8, $12-$25
FL

G9, $30-$50
FL

G10, $40-$70
FL

SUMTER - Middle Archaic, 7000 - 5000 B. P.

(Also see Adena, Elora, Kirk, Levy, Putnam, Thonotosassa & Westo)

G6, $15-$25
Marion Co., FL

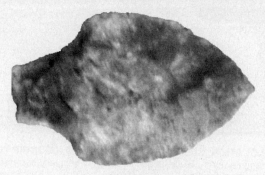

G8, $30-$50
Jefferson Co., FL

SUMTER (continued)

LOCATION: Southern Southeastern states.
DESCRIPTION: A medium to large size, broad, thick point with weak, tapered shoulders and a contracting stem. These may be small versions of the *Thonotosassa* type and are believed to be related.

GC

G6, $18-$30
FL

G5, $20-$35
Decatur Co., GA

G6, $30-$50
Hillsborough Co., FL

SUWANNEE - Late Paleo, 10,000 - 9000 B. P.

(Also see Beaver Lake, Clovis, Conerly, Simpson, Union Side Notched & Withlacoochie)

G7, $200-$350
Allendale Co., SC

LOCATION: Southern Southeastern states. **DESCRIPTION:** A medium to large size, fairly thick, broad, auriculate point. The basal constriction is not as narrow as in *Simpson* points. Most examples have ground bases and are usually unfluted. **I.D. KEY:** Thickness and broad hafting area, expanding ears, less waisted than *Simpsons*.

G7, $350-$600
FL

G7, $350-$600
FL

G5, $250-$450
FL

Florida chert

Coastal Plain chert

G9, $450-$750
Suwannee Riv., FL

G9, $800-$1200
Dooley Co., GA

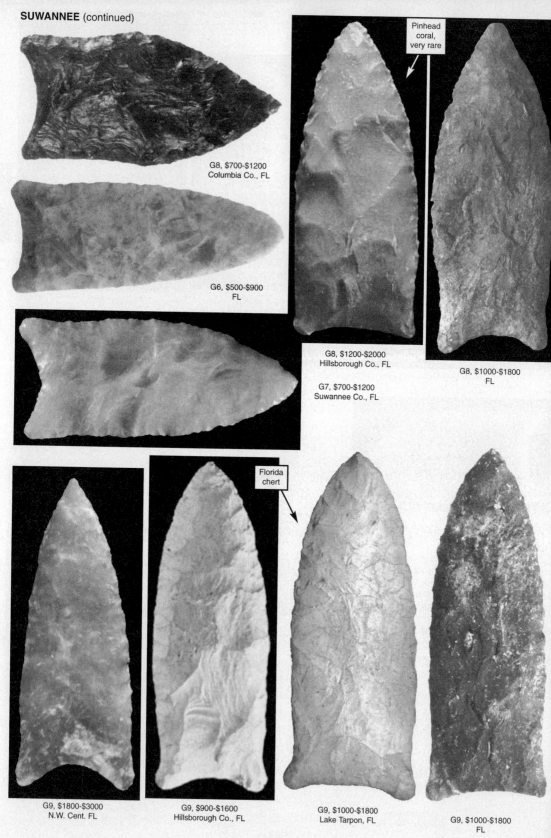

G8, $700-$1200
Columbia Co., FL

G6, $500-$900
FL

Pinhead coral, very rare

G8, $1200-$2000
Hillsborough Co., FL

G7, $700-$1200
Suwannee Co., FL

G8, $1000-$1800
FL

Florida chert

G9, $1800-$3000
N.W. Cent. FL

G9, $900-$1600
Hillsborough Co., FL

G9, $1000-$1800
Lake Tarpon, FL

G9, $1000-$1800
FL

(Also see Beaver Lake, Dalton, Hardaway, Safety Harbor, Pinellas, Santa Fe and Yadkin)

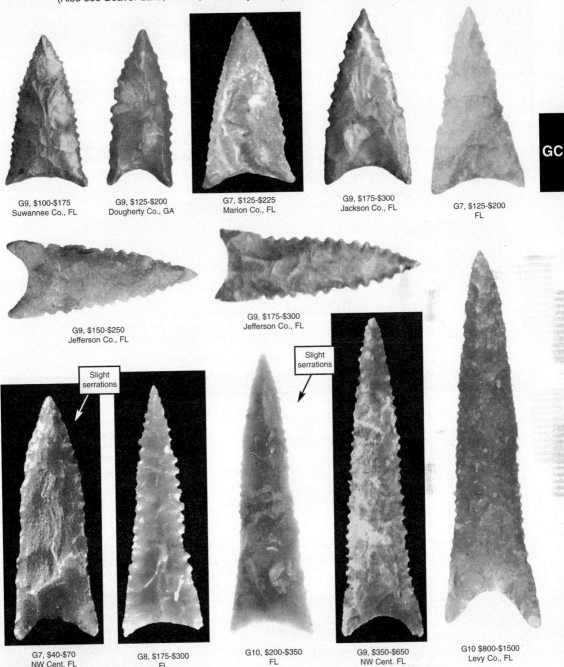

GC

G9, $100-$175
Suwannee Co., FL

G9, $125-$200
Dougherty Co., GA

G7, $125-$225
Marion Co., FL

G9, $175-$300
Jackson Co., FL

G7, $125-$200
FL

G9, $150-$250
Jefferson Co., FL

G9, $175-$300
Jefferson Co., FL

Slight serrations

Slight serrations

G7, $40-$70
NW Cent. FL

G8, $175-$300
FL

G10, $200-$350
FL

G9, $350-$650
NW Cent. FL

G10 $800-$1500
Levy Co., FL

LOCATION: Tampa Bay Area northward into Alabama, Georgia and South Carolina. **DESCRIPTION:** A medium size, thin, narrow, auriculate, serrated, triangular point with expanding auricules and a concave base. Hafting area is not well defined and can be lightly ground. Blade edges are serrated (see *Santa Fe*) and are resharpened on each face rather than the usual *Dalton* procedure of beveling on opposite faces. **Note:** This type along with the *Santa Fe* point have been confused with a much earlier *Dalton* type found in Northern Florida into southern Alabama, Georgia and South Carolina. Compared to the *Dalton* type, the *Tallahassee* is narrower and much thinner and has less patination. The Dalton is a heavier point being thicker and wider with heavy grinding around the entire basal area. The blade edge serrations are formed differently than on *Dalton* points. **I.D. KEY:** Thinness, narrowness and light grinding.

TAMPA - Mississippian, 800 - 400 B. P.

(Also see O'Leno and Pinellas)

G10, $90-$175
FL

G10, $175-$300
FL

G7, $35-$65
Hillsborough Co., FL

G9, $35-$65
FL

G9, $35-$65
FL

G10, $200-$350
Hernando Co., FL

G10, $150-$225
Hernando Co., FL

LOCATION: Gulf Coastal states. **DESCRIPTION:** A small size, narrow to broad, tear drop shaped point with a rounded base. Similar to the *Nodena* type found further north and west. A rare point.

TAYLOR - Woodland, 2500 - 2200 B. P.

(Also see Bolen Plain and Kirk)

G5, $8-$15
FL

G7, $15-$25
FL

LOCATION: Gulf Coastal states. **DESCRIPTION:** A small to medium size, corner notched point with a straight to incurvate base. Basal areas are not ground. Blade edges are straight to excurvate and shoulders are weak.

TAYLOR SIDE-NOTCHED - Early Archaic, 9000 - 8000 B. P.

(Also see Bolen Beveled Plain and Osceola Greenbrier)

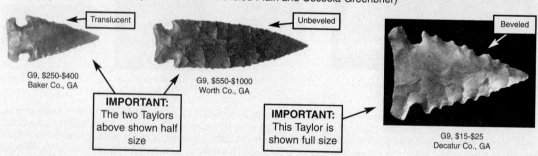

Translucent

G9, $250-$400
Baker Co., GA

Unbeveled

G9, $550-$1000
Worth Co., GA

Beveled

IMPORTANT:
The two Taylors above shown half size

IMPORTANT:
This Taylor is shown full size

G9, $15-$25
Decatur Co., GA

LOCATION: South Carolina into southern Georgia. **DESCRIPTION:** A medium size, side-notched point with a slightly concave base. Some examples are beveled and serrated. Base and notches are ground. Shoulders are pointed. Blade edges are straight to slightly concave or convex.

(Also see Hamilton, Morrow Mountain, Putnam, Savannah River and Sumter)

G6, $15-$30
Hillsborough
Co., FL

G7, $25-$45
FL

GC

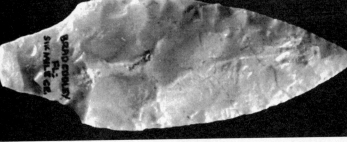

G8, $80-$150
Hillsborough Co., FL

G10, $400-$700
Six Mile Creek, FL

LOCATION: Florida only. **DESCRIPTION:** A large size, narrow, usually heavy, crudely made blade with weak shoulders and a stem that can be parallel sided to contracting. The base can be straight to rounded. Believed to be related to the smaller *Sumter* type. Also believed to be the first Florida point with heated stone. Found almost exclusively in Central Florida.

G9, $200-$350
Hillsborough Co., FL

G9, $300-$500
Hillsborough Co., FL

TRADE POINTS - Historic, 400 - 170 B. P.

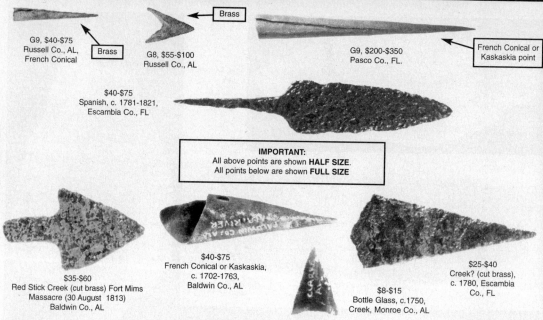

G9, $40-$75
Russell Co., AL,
French Conical

Brass

G8, $55-$100
Russell Co., AL

Brass

G9, $200-$350
Pasco Co., FL.

French Conical or
Kaskaskia point

$40-$75
Spanish, c. 1781-1821,
Escambia Co., FL

IMPORTANT:
All above points are shown **HALF SIZE**.
All points below are shown **FULL SIZE**

$35-$60
Red Stick Creek (cut brass) Fort Mims
Massacre (30 August 1813)
Baldwin Co., AL

$40-$75
French Conical or Kaskaskia,
c. 1702-1763,
Baldwin Co., AL

$8-$15
Bottle Glass, c.1750,
Creek, Monroe Co., AL

$25-$40
Creek? (cut brass),
c. 1780, Escambia
Co., FL

LOCATION: All of United States and Canada. **DESCRIPTION:** Trade points were made of copper, iron and steel and were traded to the Indians by the French, British and others from the 1600s to the 1800s. The French Conical point (above) is known as Kaskaskia in the midwest.

UNION SIDE NOTCHED - Trans. Paleo, 10,000 - 9000 B. P.

(Also see Beaver Lake, Hardaway, Osceola Greenbrier and Suwannee)

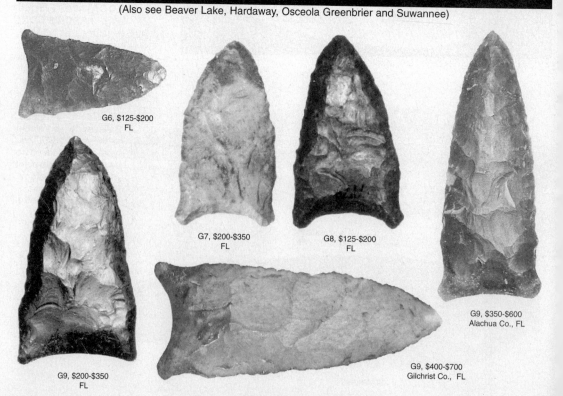

G6, $125-$200
FL

G7, $200-$350
FL

G8, $125-$200
FL

G9, $350-$600
Alachua Co., FL

G9, $200-$350
FL

G9, $400-$700
Gilchrist Co., FL

UNION SIDE NOTCHED (continued)

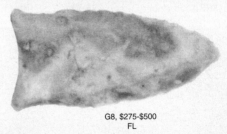

G8, $275-$500
FL

G9, $400-$700
FL

LOCATION: Gulf Coastal states. **DESCRIPTION:** A medium to large size, broad blade with weak side notches expanding into auricles. Base can be straight to slightly concave or convex and is usually heavily ground all around the basal area.

WACISSA - Early Archaic, 9000 - 6000 B. P.

(Also see Abbey, Arredondo, Bolen, Elora, Hamilton, Kirk Stemmed, Savannah River and Seminole)

G8, $30-$50
Allendale Co., SC

G5, $12-$20
Henry Co., AL

G9, $40-$75
S. GA

Serrated edge

G9, $200-$350
Worth Co., GA

Serrated edge

G9, $125-$200
Dodge Co., GA

LOCATION: Gulf Coastal states. **DESCRIPTION:** A small to medium size, thick, short, broad stemmed point that is beveled on all four sides. Shoulders are moderate to weak and horizontal to slightly barbed. Some examples are serrated.

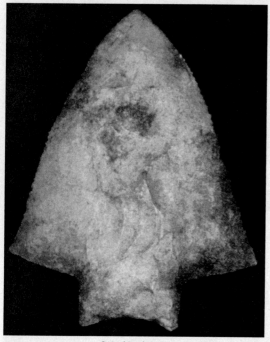

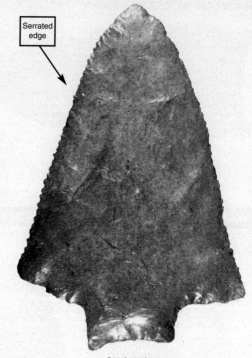

Serrated edge

G10+ $550-$1000
Jackson Co., FL

G10 $450-$650
Decatur Co., GA

WALLER KNIFE - Early Archaic, 9000 - 5000 B. P.
(Also see Edgefield Scraper)

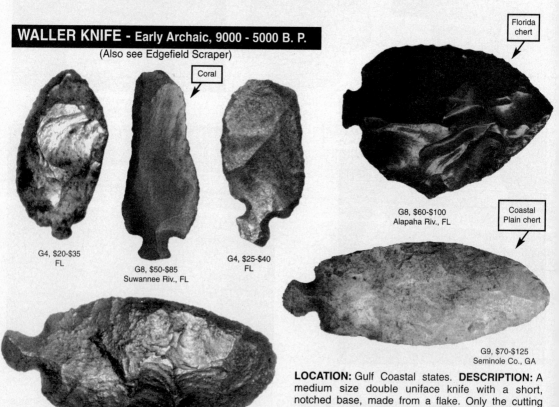

Coral

Florida chert

Coastal Plain chert

G4, $20-$35
FL

G8, $50-$85
Suwannee Riv., FL

G4, $25-$40
FL

G8, $60-$100
Alapaha Riv., FL

G9, $65-$125
Dixie Co., FL

G9, $70-$125
Seminole Co., GA

LOCATION: Gulf Coastal states. **DESCRIPTION:** A medium size double uniface knife with a short, notched base, made from a flake. Only the cutting edges have been pressure flaked. The classical Waller exhibits a dorsal ridge.

WEEDEN ISLAND - Woodland, 2500 - 1000 B. P.

(Also see Jackson)

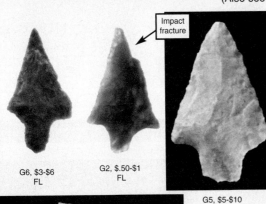

Impact fracture

G6, $3-$6
FL

G2, $.50-$1
FL

G5, $5-$10
Marion Co., FL

G7 $8-$15
Marion Co., FL

GC

G7 $10-$20
Marion Co., FL

G7, $10-$20
Marion Co., FL

LOCATION: Gulf Coastal states. **DESCRIPTION:** A small size triangular point with a contracting stem. Shoulders can be tapered to barbed. Bases are straight to rounded.

WESTO - Middle Archaic, 5000 - 4000 B. P.

(Also see Duval, Sumter)

G7, $30-$50
FL

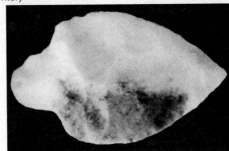

G9, $50-$90
FL

LOCATION: Northern Florida into Georgia. **DESCRIPTION:** A small to medium size, narrow to broad point with a straight to convex blade edge and a short, rounded stem. Shoulders are tapered and many examples are made of quartz and are relatively thick in cross section. **I.D. KEY:** Thickness & short, rounded stem.

WHEELER - Transitional Paleo, 10,000 - 8000 B. P.

(Also see Beaver Lake and Simpson-Mustache)

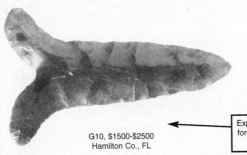

G10, $1500-$2500
Hamilton Co., FL

Expanded base form. Collateral flaking

LOCATION: Southeastern states to Florida. **DESCRIPTION:** A small to medium size triangular, auriculate point with a concave base. The ears are produced by a shallow constriction or notching near the base. This form occurs in three forms: Excurvate, recurvate and expanded base. Excurvate and expanded base forms are shown. A very rare type in Florida.

307

WHEELER (continued)

G7, $250-$400
FL

Excurvate form

Excurvate form

G9, $250-$400
Dodge Co., GA

Agate

WITHLACOOCHIE - Late Paleo, 10,500 - 10,000 B. P.

(Also see Clovis, Dalton, Simpson and Suwannee)

LOCATION: Withlacoochie Riv. area of Northern Florida, sou. Alabama and Georgia. **DESCRIPTION:** A small to medium size triangular, auriculate point with a concave base. Believed to be a cross between *Clovis* and *Dalton*. Thinner and much better made than Suwannee and not waisted like Simpson. Entire hafting area is ground. Blade edges can have fine serrations.

Translucent

G10 $1800-$3200
Wakulla Co., FL

YADKIN - Woodland to Mississippian, 2500 - 500 B. P.

(Also see Pinellas, Safety Harbor, Santa Fe and Tallahassee)

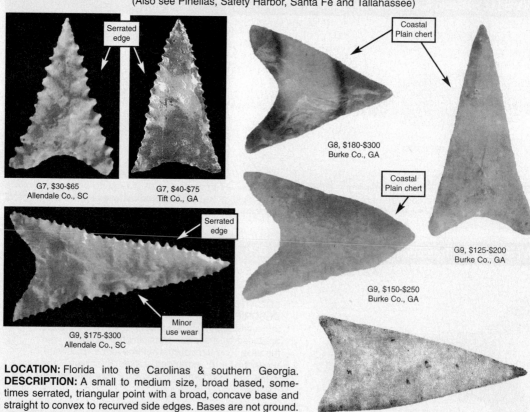

Serrated edge

G7, $30-$65
Allendale Co., SC

G7, $40-$75
Tift Co., GA

Coastal Plain chert

G8, $180-$300
Burke Co., GA

Coastal Plain chert

Serrated edge

Minor use wear

G9, $175-$300
Allendale Co., SC

G9, $150-$250
Burke Co., GA

G9, $125-$200
Burke Co., GA

G9, $40-$75
Bulloch Co., GA

LOCATION: Florida into the Carolinas & southern Georgia. **DESCRIPTION:** A small to medium size, broad based, sometimes serrated, triangular point with a broad, concave base and straight to convex to recurved side edges. Bases are not ground. **I.D. KEY:** Broadness of base tangs, lack of grinding.

EASTERN CENTRAL SECTION:

This section includes point types from the following states:
Alabama, Georgia, Indiana, Kentucky, Michigan, Mississippi, Ohio and Tennessee.

The points in this section are arranged in alphabetical order and are shown **actual size**. All types are listed that were available for photographing. Any missing types will be added to future editions as photographs become available. We are always interested in receiving sharp, black and white or color glossy photos, color slides or high resolution (300 pixels/inch) digital pictures of your collection. Be sure to include a ruler in the photograph so that proper scale can be determined.

Lithics: Materials employed in the manufacture of projectile points from this region include: agate, chalcedony, chert, coshocton, crystal, flint, jasper, limestone, quartz, quartzite, silicified sandstone and upper mercer.

Important Sites: Nuckolls, Humphreys Co., TN.; Cotaco, Cotaco Creek, Morgan Co., AL.; Cumberland, Cumberland River Valley, TN.; Damron, Lincoln Co., TN.; Elk River, Limestone Co., AL.; Eva, Benton Co., TN.; Quad, Limestone Co., AL.; Pine Tree, Limestone Co., AL.; Dover Flint, Humphreys Co., TN.; Redstone, Madison Co., AL.; Plevna (Dovetail), Madison Co., AL.; Stone Pipe, Wheeler Reservoir, Limestone Co., AL. for Wheeler and Decatur points.

EC

Regional Consultants:
Tom Davis,
John T. Pafford and Eric C. Wagner

EASTERN CENTRAL
(Archaeological Periods)

PALEO (11,500 B. P. - 10,000 B. P.)

Beaver Lake
Clovis

Clovis-Hazel
Clovis Unfluted

Cumberland
Debert

Graver
Lancet

Redstone
Scraper

TRANSITIONAL PALEO (10,500 B. P. - 9,000 B. P.)

Agate Basin
Early Ovoid Knife
Haw River
Hi-Lo

Hinds
Jeff
Marianna
Ohio Lanceolate

Paint Rock Valley
Pelican
Plainview
Quad

Square Knife
Stanfield
Wheeler Excurvate
Wheeler Expanded

Wheeler Recurvate
Wheeler Triangular

EARLY ARCHAIC (10,000 B. P. - 7,000 B. P.)

Alamance
Alberta
Angostura
Autauga
Big Sandy
Big Sandy Broad Base
Big Sandt Contracted Base
Big Sandy E-Notched
Big Sandy Leighton Base
Cave Spring
Cobbs Triangular
Coldwater
Conerly
Crawford Creek
Dalton Classic
Dalton Colbert
Dalton Greenbrier

Dalton Hemphill
Dalton Nuckolls
Damron
Decatur
Decatur Blade
Eastern Stemmed Lanceolate
Ecusta
Elk River
Eva
Fishspear
Fountain Creek
Frederick
Garth Slough
Graham Cave
Greenbrier
Hardaway
Hardaway Dalton

Hardin
Harpeth River
Heavy Duty
Hidden Valley
Holland
Johnson
Jude
Kanawha Stemmed
Kirk Corner Notched
Kirk Snapped Base
Kirk Stemmed
Kirk Stemmed-Bifur.
Lake Erie
Lecroy
Leighton
Lerma
Limeton Bifurcate

Lost Lake
MacCorkle
Meserve
Neuberger
Newton Falls
Palmer
Perforator
Pine Tree
Pine Tree Corner
Notched
Rice Lobbed
Russel Cave
San Patrice-Hope
St. Albans
St. Charles
St. Helena
St. Tammany

Stanly
Steubenville
Stilwell
Stringtown
Tennessee River
Tennessee Saw
Thebes
Warrick
Watts Cave
White Springs

MIDDLE ARCHAIC (7,500 B. P. - 4,000 B. P.)

Appalachian
Benton
Benton Blade
Benton Bottle Neck
Benton Double Notched
Benton Narrow Blade
Big Slough
Brewerton Corner Notched
Brewerton Eared Triangular
Brewerton Side Notched
Brunswick

Buck Creek
Buggs Island
Buzzard Roost Creek
Copena Auriculate
Cypress Creek
Elora
Epps
Exotic Forms
Frazier
Guilford Round Base
Halifax

Kays
Ledbetter
Limestone
Maples
Matanzas
McIntire
McWhinney Heavy Stemmed
Morrow Mountain
Morrow Mountain Round Base
Morrow Mountain Straight Base
Motley

Mountain Fork
Mulberry Creek
Patrick
Pentagonal Knife
Pickwick
Ramey Knife
Savage Cave
Savannah River
Searcy
Smith
Sykes

Tortugas
Turkeytail Tupelo
Wade
Warito

LATE ARCHAIC (5,000 B. P. - 3,000 B. P.)

Ashtabula
Bakers Creek
Beacon Island
Bradley Spike
Copena Classic
Copena Round Base
Copena Triangular

Dagger
Etley
Evans
Flint Creek
Little Bear Creek
Meadowood
Merkle

Merom
Mud Creek
Orient
Pontchartrain Type I & II
Rankin
Rheems Creek
Shoals Creek

Smithsonia
Snake Creek
Square-end Knife
Sublet Ferry
Swan Lake
Table Rock
Turkeytail-Fulton

Turkeytail-Harrison
Turkeytail-Hebron

WOODLAND (3,000 B. P. - 1,300 B. P.)

Addison Micro-Drill
Adena
Adena Blade
Adena-Narrow Stem
Adena-Notched Base
Adena Robbins
Adena Vanishing Stem
Alba
Benjamin
Camp Creek
Candy Creek

Chesser
Coosa
Cotaco Creek
Cotaco Creek Blade
Cotaco-Wright
Cresap
Dickson
Duval
Ebenezer
Fairland
Gibson

Greeneville
Hamilton
Hamilton Stemmed
Hopewell
Intrusive Mound
Jacks Reef Corner Notched
Jacks Reef Pentagonal
Knight Island
Lowe
Montgomery
Morse Knife

Mouse Creek
New Market
Nolichucky
North
Nova
Ohio Double Notched
Red Ochre
Ross
Sand Mountain
Snyders
Spokeshave

Tear Drop
Vallina
Washington
Waubesa
Yadkin

MISSISSIPPIAN (1300 B. P. - 400 B. P.)

Duck River Sword
Fort Ancient
Fort Ancient Blade
Guntersville

Harahey
Keota
Levanna
Lozenge

Mace
Madison
Nodena
Pipe Creek

Sun Disc
Washita

HISTORIC (450 B. P. - 170 B. P.)

Trade Points

EASTERN CENTRAL
THUMBNAIL GUIDE SECTION

The following references are provided to aid the collector in easier and quicker identification of point types. All photos are exactly 30% of actual size and are proportional to each other. Each point pictured in this section represents a classic form for the type. When a match is found, go to the alphabetical location of that type for more examples in actual size.

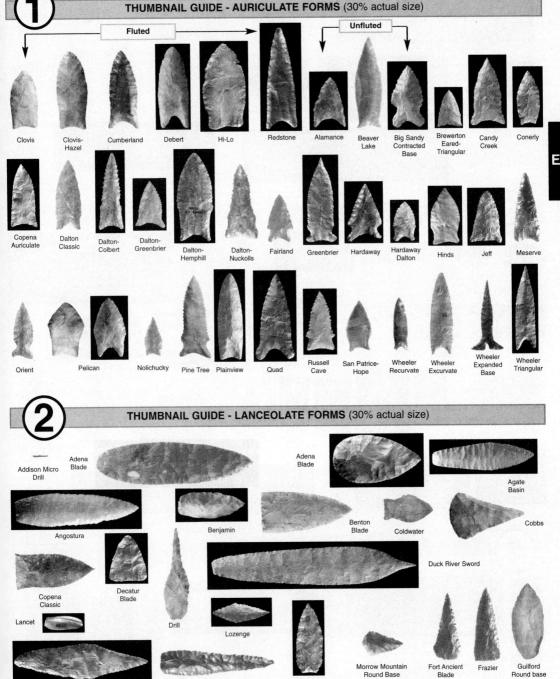

① THUMBNAIL GUIDE - AURICULATE FORMS (30% actual size)

Fluted

Unfluted

Clovis · Clovis-Hazel · Cumberland · Debert · Hi-Lo · Redstone · Alamance · Beaver Lake · Big Sandy Contracted Base · Brewerton Eared-Triangular · Candy Creek · Conerly

Copena Auriculate · Dalton Classic · Dalton-Colbert · Dalton-Greenbrier · Dalton-Hemphill · Dalton-Nuckolls · Fairland · Greenbrier · Hardaway · Hardaway Dalton · Hinds · Jeff · Meserve

Orient · Pelican · Nolichucky · Pine Tree · Plainview · Quad · Russell Cave · San Patrice-Hope · Wheeler Recurvate · Wheeler Excurvate · Wheeler Expanded Base · Wheeler Triangular

② THUMBNAIL GUIDE - LANCEOLATE FORMS (30% actual size)

Addison Micro Drill · Adena Blade · Adena Blade · Agate Basin

Angostura · Benjamin · Benton Blade · Coldwater · Cobbs

Duck River Sword

Copena Classic · Decatur Blade · Lancet · Drill · Lozenge · Morrow Mountain Round Base · Fort Ancient Blade · Frazier · Guilford Round base

Harahey · Lerma Rounded Base · Marianna

EC

311

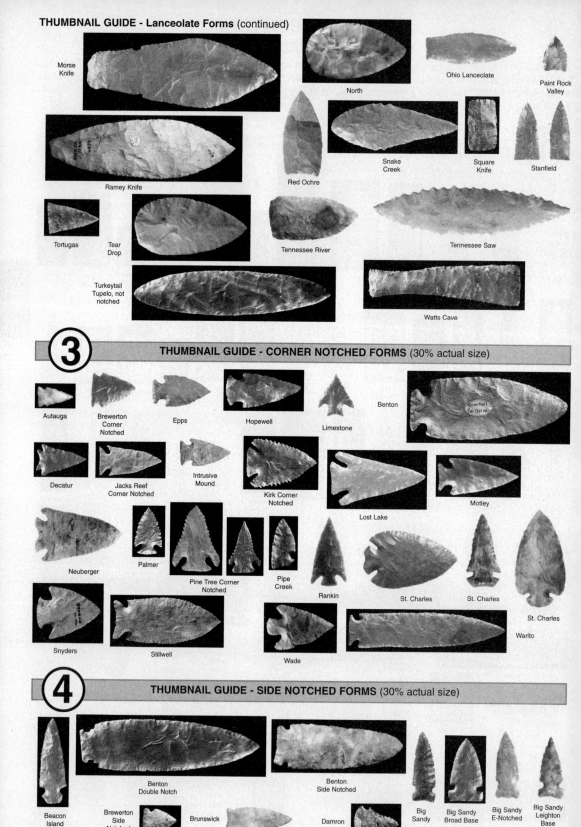

THUMBNAIL GUIDE - Lanceolate Forms (continued)

Morse Knife

North

Ohio Lanceolate

Paint Rock Valley

Ramey Knife

Red Ochre

Snake Creek

Square Knife

Stanfield

Tortugas

Tear Drop

Tennessee River

Tennessee Saw

Turkeytail Tupelo, not notched

Watts Cave

③ THUMBNAIL GUIDE - CORNER NOTCHED FORMS (30% actual size)

Autauga

Brewerton Corner Notched

Epps

Hopewell

Limestone

Benton

Decatur

Jacks Reef Corner Notched

Intrusive Mound

Kirk Corner Notched

Lost Lake

Motley

Neuberger

Palmer

Pine Tree Corner Notched

Pipe Creek

Rankin

St. Charles

St. Charles

St. Charles

Warito

Snyders

Stillwell

Wade

④ THUMBNAIL GUIDE - SIDE NOTCHED FORMS (30% actual size)

Beacon Island

Benton Double Notch

Benton Side Notched

Brewerton Side Notched

Brunswick

Damron

Big Sandy

Big Sandy Broad Base

Big Sandy E-Notched

Big Sandy Leighton Base

THUMBNAIL GUIDE - Side Notched Forms (continued)

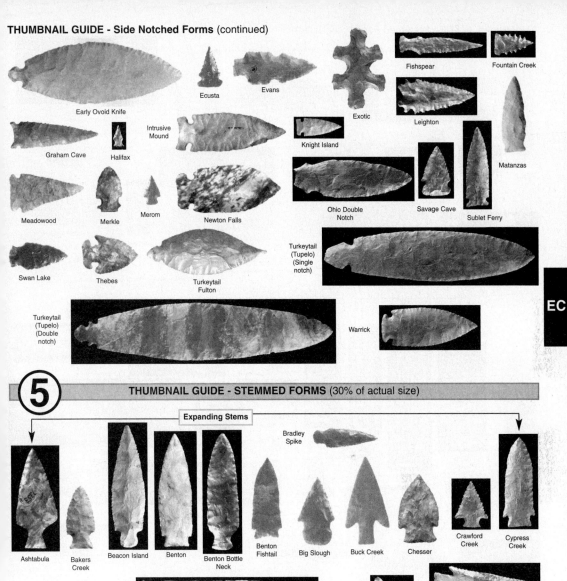

Early Ovoid Knife

Ecusta

Evans

Exotic

Fishspear

Fountain Creek

Leighton

Graham Cave

Halifax

Intrusive Mound

Knight Island

Matanzas

Meadowood

Merkle

Merom

Newton Falls

Ohio Double Notch

Savage Cave

Sublet Ferry

Swan Lake

Thebes

Turkeytail Fulton

Turkeytail (Tupelo) (Single notch)

Turkeytail (Tupelo) (Double notch)

Warrick

EC

(5) THUMBNAIL GUIDE - STEMMED FORMS (30% of actual size)

Expanding Stems

Bradley Spike

Ashtabula

Bakers Creek

Beacon Island

Benton

Benton Bottle Neck

Benton Fishtail

Big Slough

Buck Creek

Chesser

Crawford Creek

Cypress Creek

Duval

Etley

Garth Slough

Hardin

Harpeth River

Johnson

Flint Creek

Hamilton Stemmed

Jude

Lowe

McIntire

Mountain Fork

Mud Creek

Pentagonal Knife

Pentagonal Knife

Rankin

Shoals Creek

Spokeshave

Sykes

Table Rock

Turkeytail-Harrison

313

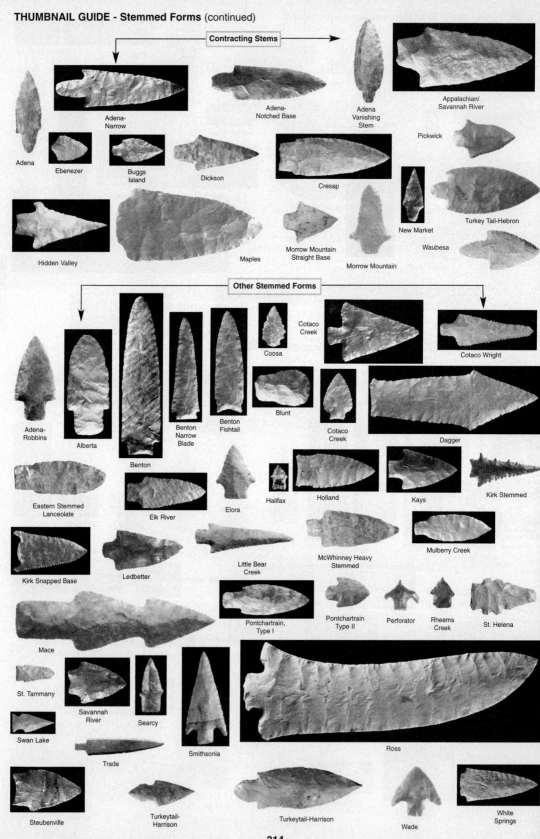

Contracting Stems

Adena-Narrow

Adena-Notched Base

Adena Vanishing Stem

Appalachian/ Savannah River

Adena

Ebenezer

Buggs Island

Dickson

Cresap

Pickwick

New Market

Turkey Tail-Hebron

Waubesa

Hidden Valley

Maples

Morrow Mountain Straight Base

Morrow Mountain

Other Stemmed Forms

Adena-Robbins

Alberta

Benton Narrow Blade

Benton Fishtail

Coosa

Cotaco Creek

Blunt

Cotaco Creek

Cotaco Wright

Dagger

Benton

Eastern Stemmed Lanceolate

Elk River

Elora

Halifax

Holland

Kays

Kirk Stemmed

Kirk Snapped Base

Ledbetter

Little Bear Creek

McWhinney Heavy Stemmed

Mulberry Creek

Mace

Pontchartrain, Type I

Pontchartrain Type II

Perforator

Rheems Creek

St. Helena

St. Tammany

Savannah River

Searcy

Swan Lake

Smithsonia

Ross

Trade

Steubenville

Turkeytail-Harrison

Turkeytail-Harrison

Wade

White Springs

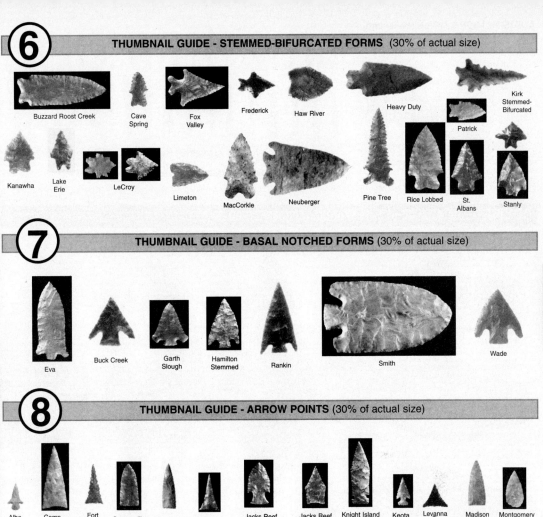

⑥ THUMBNAIL GUIDE - STEMMED-BIFURCATED FORMS (30% of actual size)

Buzzard Roost Creek • Cave Spring • Fox Valley • Frederick • Haw River • Heavy Duty • Kirk Stemmed-Bifurcated • Patrick • Kanawha • Lake Erie • LeCroy • Limeton • MacCorkle • Neuberger • Pine Tree • Rice Lobbed • St. Albans • Stanly

⑦ THUMBNAIL GUIDE - BASAL NOTCHED FORMS (30% of actual size)

Eva • Buck Creek • Garth Slough • Hamilton Stemmed • Rankin • Smith • Wade

EC

⑧ THUMBNAIL GUIDE - ARROW POINTS (30% of actual size)

Alba • Camp Creek • Fort Ancient • Greeneville • Guntersville • Hamilton • Jacks Reef Corner Notched • Jacks Reef Pentagonal • Knight Island • Keota • Levanna • Madison • Montgomery

Mouse Creek • Nodena • Nova • Sand Mountain • Valina • Washington • Washita • Yadkin

---

ADDISON MICRO-DRILL - Late Woodland to Mississippian, 2000 - 1000 B. P.

(Also see Drill, Flint River Spike and Schild Spike)

LOCATION: Examples have been found in Alabama, Kentucky, Illinois, North Carolina, North Georgia and Tennessee. Named after the late Steve Addison who collected hundreds of examples. **DESCRIPTION:** Very small to medium size, narrow, slivers, flattened to rectangular in cross section. Theory is that this is the final form of a drilling process. The original form was flint slivers with sharp edges that were used as drills. As the sliver was turned in the drilling process, the opposite edges in the direction of movement began to flake off. As the drilling operation proceeded, the edges became steeper as more and more of each side was flaked. Eventually a thin, steeply flaked, rectangular drill form was left and discarded. Unique in that these micro artifacts are not made and then used, but are created by use, and discarded as the edges became eroded away by extremely fine flaking, thus reducing their effectiveness as a cutting edge.

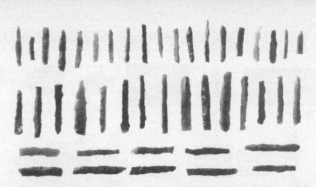

$4-$8 each
Shown actual size. All found
in Bradley & Hamilton Co.,
TN.

ADENA - Late Archaic to Late Woodland, 3000 - 1200 B. P.

(Also see Adena Blade, Bakers Creek, Dickson, Kays, Little Bear Creek, Turkeytail and Waubesa)

G3, $5-$10
Jessamine Co., KY

G3, $8-$15
NW AL

G6, $12-$20
KY

G6, $15-$25
KY

G6, $15-$25
TN

G7, $20-$35
TN

G6, $25-$45
Decatur Co., AL

G6, $20-$35
Wood Co., OH

G6, $20-$35
KY

LOCATION: Eastern to Southeastern states.
DESCRIPTION: A medium to large, thin, narrow, triangular blade that is sometimes serrated, and with a medium to long, narrow to broad rounded "beaver tail" stem. Most examples are from average to excellent quality. Bases can be ground. Has been found with *Nolichucky, Camp Creek, Candy Creek, Ebenezer* and *Greeneville* points (Rankin site, Cocke Co., TN). **I.D. KEY:** Rounded base, woodland flaking.

ADENA (continued)

Red jasper

G8, $35-$60
Hardin Co., TN

G7, $25-$40
KY

Dover chert

G5, $15-$30
TN

Dover chert

EC

G7, $55-$100
Camden, TN

Sonora flint

G9, $150-$250
White Co., TN

G7, $30-$50
AL

G7, $30-$50
KY

G8, $80-$150
TN

G8, $65-$125
TN

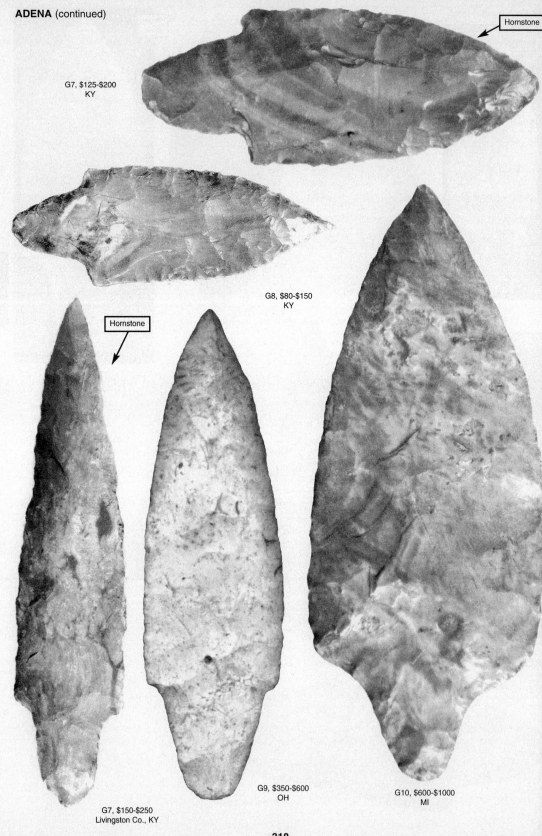

Hornstone

G7, $125-$200
KY

G8, $80-$150
KY

Hornstone

G7, $150-$250
Livingston Co., KY

G9, $350-$600
OH

G10, $600-$1000
MI

ADENA BLADE - Late Archaic to Woodland, 3000-1200 B. P.

(Also see Copena, North, Tear Drop and Tennessee River)

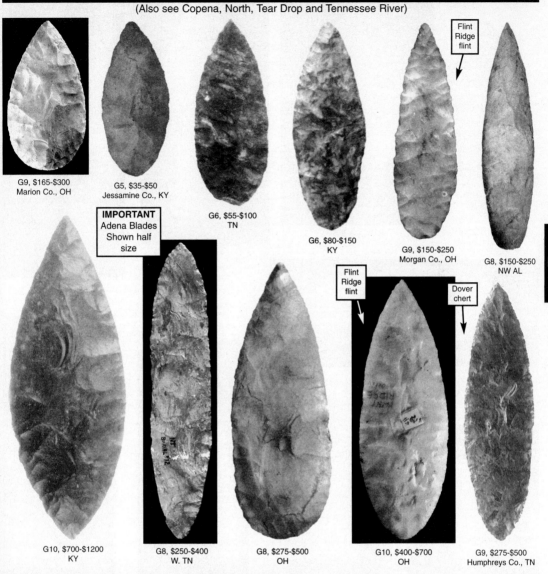

G9, $165-$300
Marion Co., OH

G5, $35-$50
Jessamine Co., KY

G6, $55-$100
TN

IMPORTANT
Adena Blades
Shown half
size

G6, $80-$150
KY

Flint
Ridge
flint

G9, $150-$250
Morgan Co., OH

G8, $150-$250
NW AL

EC

G10, $700-$1200
KY

G8, $250-$400
W. TN

G8, $275-$500
OH

Flint
Ridge
flint

Dover
chert

G10, $400-$700
OH

G9, $275-$500
Humphreys Co., TN

LOCATION: Midwestern to Eastern states. **DESCRIPTION:** A large size, thin, broad to narrow, ovate blade with a rounded to pointed base. Blade edgework can be very fine. Usually found in caches. **I.D. KEY:** Woodland flaking, large direct primary strikes.

ADENA-DICKSON   (see Dickson)

ADENA-NARROW STEM - Late Archaic-Woodland, 3000 - 1200 B. P.

(Also see Little Bear Creek and Waubesa)

G7, $25-$40
Humphreys Co., TN

LOCATION: Eastern to Southeastern states. **DESCRIPTION:** A medium to large, thin, narrow triangular blade that is sometimes serrated, with a medium to long, narrow, rounded stem. Most examples are well made. **I.D. KEY:** Narrow rounded base with more secondary work than ordinary *Adena*.

319

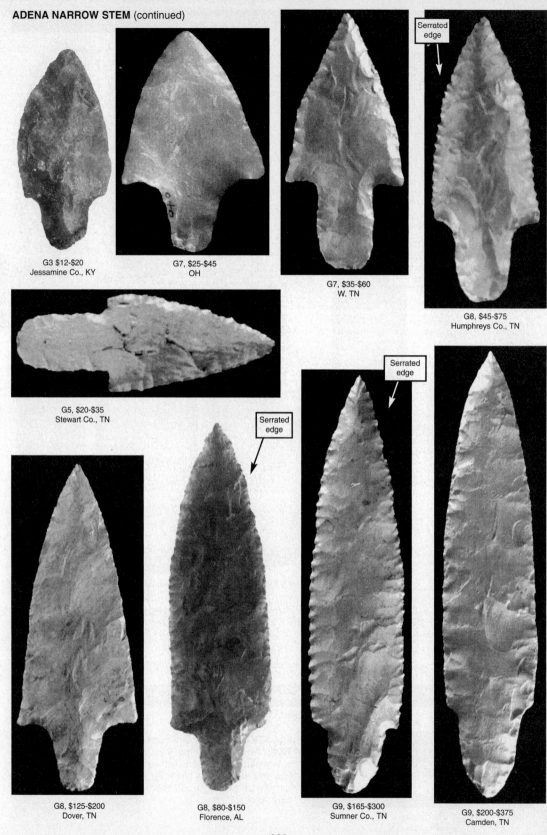

G3 $12-$20
Jessamine Co., KY

G7, $25-$45
OH

G7, $35-$60
W. TN

Serrated edge

G8, $45-$75
Humphreys Co., TN

G5, $20-$35
Stewart Co., TN

Serrated edge

Serrated edge

G8, $125-$200
Dover, TN

G8, $80-$150
Florence, AL

G9, $165-$300
Sumner Co., TN

G9, $200-$375
Camden, TN

ADENA-NOTCHED BASE - Late Archaic-Woodland, 3000 - 1200 B. P.

(Also see Adena and Little Bear Creek)

LOCATION: Southeastern states. **DESCRIPTION:** Identical to *Adena*, but with a notched or snapped-off concave base. **I.D. KEY:** Basal form different.

G8, $30-$50
Coffee Lake, AL

ADENA-ROBBINS - Late Archaic to Woodland, 3000 - 1800 B. P.

(See Alberta, Cresap, Dickson, Kays, Little Bear Creek, Mulberry Creek and Pontchartrain)

EC

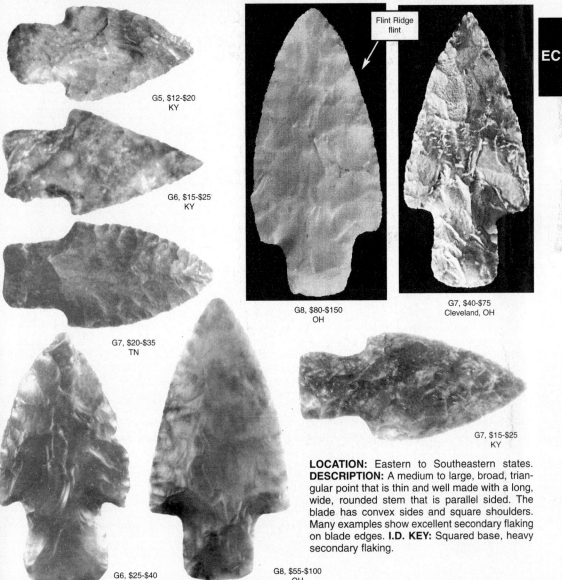

G5, $12-$20
KY

G6, $15-$25
KY

Flint Ridge flint

G7, $20-$35
TN

G8, $80-$150
OH

G7, $40-$75
Cleveland, OH

G7, $15-$25
KY

G6, $25-$40
KY

G8, $55-$100
OH

LOCATION: Eastern to Southeastern states. **DESCRIPTION:** A medium to large, broad, triangular point that is thin and well made with a long, wide, rounded stem that is parallel sided. The blade has convex sides and square shoulders. Many examples show excellent secondary flaking on blade edges. **I.D. KEY:** Squared base, heavy secondary flaking.

321

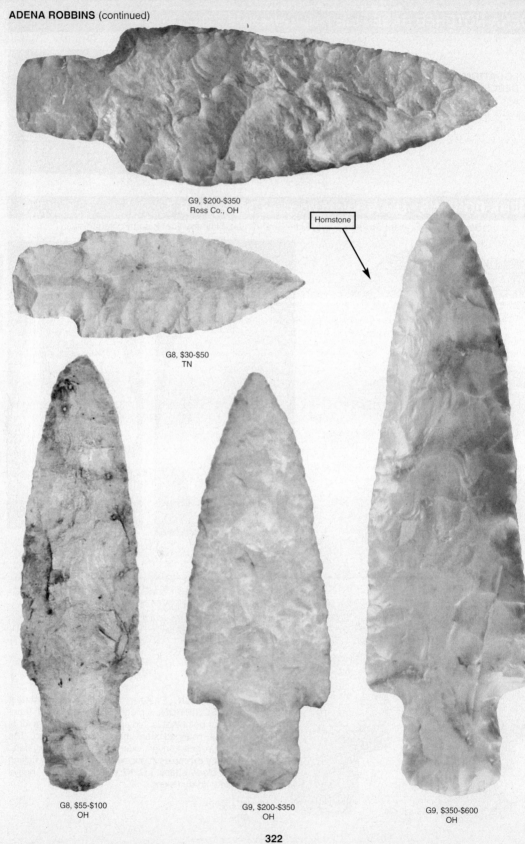

G9, $200-$350
Ross Co., OH

Hornstone

G8, $30-$50
TN

G8, $55-$100
OH

G9, $200-$350
OH

G9, $350-$600
OH

ADENA-VANISHING STEM - Late Archaic to Woodland, 3000 - 1800 B. P.

(See Cresap, Dickson, Little Bear Creek, Mulberry Creek and Pontchartrain)

Boyle chert

G4, $12-$20
Jessamine Co., KY

G3, $8-$15
Jessamine Co., KY

LOCATION: Eastern to Southeastern states.
DESCRIPTION: A medium to large size point with a small, narrow, short stem that is rounded. **I.D. KEY:** Small stem.

G8, $35-$65
Jessamine Co., KY

G6, $20-$35
KY

G8, $65-$125
Madison Co., KY

ADENA-WAUBESA (see Waubesa)

AFTON (see Pentagonal Knife)

EC

AGATE BASIN - Transitional Paleo to Early Archaic, 10,500 - 8000 B. P.

(Also see Angostura, Lerma, Ohio Lanceolate and Sedalia)

G5, $25-$40
TN

G8, $150-$250
Geauga Co., OH

Ground
basal area

G5, $55-$100
Geauga Co., OH

G8, $200-$350
Holmes Co., OH

G8, $250-$400
IN

323

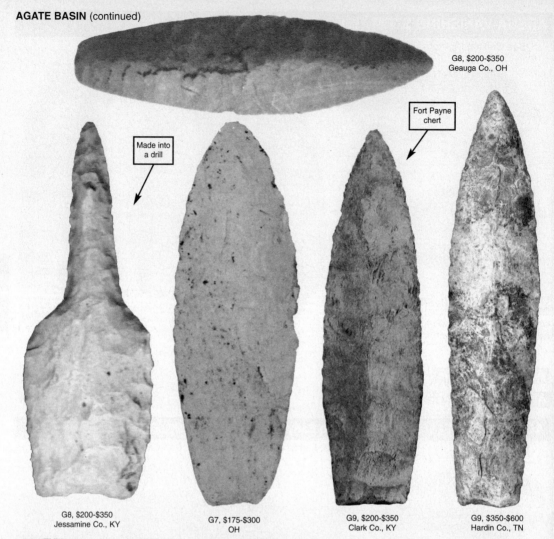

G8, $200-$350
Geauga Co., OH

Made into
a drill

Fort Payne
chert

G8, $200-$350
Jessamine Co., KY

G7, $175-$300
OH

G9, $200-$350
Clark Co., KY

G9, $350-$600
Hardin Co., TN

LOCATION: Pennsylvania to Texas to Montana   **DESCRIPTION:** A medium to large size lanceolate blade of high quality. Bases are either convex, concave or straight and are usually ground. Some examples are median ridged and have random to parallel collateral flaking. Thicker than the *Ohio Lanceolate*. **I.D. KEY:** Basal form and flaking style.

ALAMANCE - Early Archaic, 10,000 - 8000 B. P.
(Also see Dalton, Hardaway and Haw River)

LOCATION: Coastal states from Virginia to Florida. **DESCRIPTION:** A broad, short, auriculate point with a deeply concave base. The broad basal area is usually ground and can be expanding to parallel sided. A variant form of the *Dalton-Greenbrier* evolving later into the *Hardaway* type. **ID. KEY:** Width of base and strong shoulder form.

G6, $55-$100
Autauga Co.,
AL

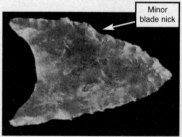

Minor
blade nick

ALBERTA - Early Archaic, 9500 - 8000 B. P.
(Also see Eastern Stemmed Lanceolate, Holland, Scottsbluff and Stringtown)

LOCATION: Northern states and Canada from Pennsylvania, Michigan to Montana. **DESCRIPTION:** A medium to large size point with a broad, long, parallel stem and weak shoulders. Believed to belong to the *Cody Complex* and is related to the *Scottsbluff* type. **I.D. KEY:** Long stem, short blade.

ALBERTA (continued)

Very rare in the Eastern U.S. →

G6, $350-$600
MI

ALBA - Woodland to Mississippian, 2000 - 400 B. P.

(Also see Agee, Bonham, Colbert, Cuney, Hayes, Homan, Keota, Perdiz, Scallorn and Sequoyah in SC section)

LOCATION: Eastern Texas, Arkansas and Louisiana. **DESCRIPTION:** A small to medium size, narrow, well made point with prominent tangs, a recurved blade and a bulbous stem. Some examples are serrated. **I.D. KEY:** Rounded base and expanded barbs.

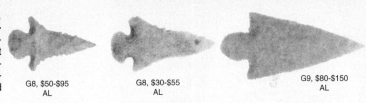

G8, $50-$95
AL

G8, $30-$55
AL

G9, $80-$150
AL

EC

ANGOSTURA - Early Archaic, 9000 - 8000 B. P.

(Also see Browns Valley, Clovis-Unfluted, Paint Rock Valley, Plainview and Wheeler)

G7, $80-$150
Huntsville, AL, Paleo site

Fine serrations

LOCATION: South Dakota southward to Texas and W. Tenn. **DESCRIPTION:** A medium to large size lanceolate blade with a contracting, concave base. Both broad and narrow forms occur. Flaking can be parallel oblique to random. Bases are not usually ground but are thinned. **I.D. KEY:** Basal form, early flaking on blade.

G6, $125-$200
Union Co., OH

Diagonal flaking

G9, $200-$350
Humphreys Co., TN

G6, $80-$150
Humphreys Co., TN

APPALACHIAN - Mid-Archaic, 6000 - 3000 B. P.

(Also see Ashtabula, Hamilton and Savannah River)

Quartzite

Quartzite

G3, $20-$35
Polk Co., GA

G8, $125-$200
Norris Lake, TN

G6, $55-$100
Paulding Co., GA

LOCATION: Southeastern states. **DESCRIPTION:** A medium to large size, rather crudely made stemmed point with a concave base. Most examples are made of quartzite. Shoulders are tapered and the base is usually ground. This form was named by Lewis & Kneberg for examples found in East Tenn. and Western North Carolina which were made of quartzite. However, this is the same type as *Savannah River*. **I.D. KEY:** Basal form.

ASHTABULA - Late Archaic, 4000 - 1500 B. P.

(Also see Appalachian and Table Rock)

G5, $30-$50
OH

IMPORTANT:
All Ashtabulas
shown half size

G7, $200-$350
OH

G6, $150-$275
OH

LOCATION: Northeastern states, especially Northeastern Ohio and Western Penn. **DESCRIPTION:** A medium to large size, broad, thick, expanded stem point with tapered shoulders. **I.D. KEY:** Basal form, one barb round and the other stronger.

326

ASHTABULA (continued)

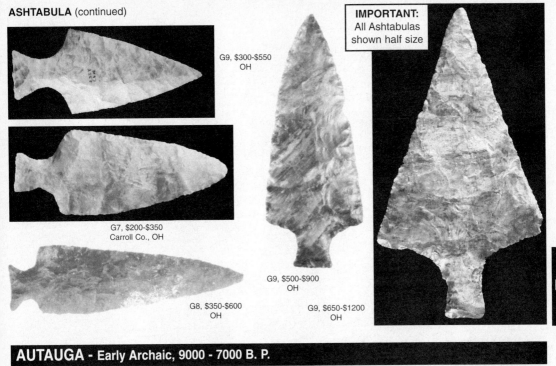

G9, $300-$550
OH

G7, $200-$350
Carroll Co., OH

G8, $350-$600
OH

G9, $500-$900
OH

G9, $650-$1200
OH

EC

AUTAUGA - Early Archaic, 9000 - 7000 B. P.

(Also see Brewerton, Ecusta and Palmer)

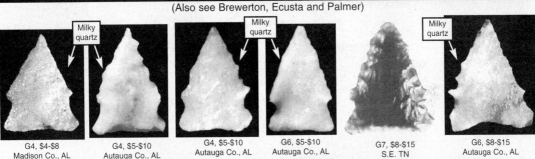

Milky quartz

Milky quartz

Milky quartz

G4, $4-$8
Madison Co., AL

G4, $5-$10
Autauga Co., AL

G4, $5-$10
Autauga Co., AL

G6, $5-$10
Autauga Co., AL

G7, $8-$15
S.E. TN

G6, $8-$15
Autauga Co., AL

LOCATION: Southeastern states. **DESCRIPTION:** A small, weakly corner notched point with a straight base, that is usually ground, and straight blade edges that are serrated. Blades can be beveled on one side of each face. **I.D. KEY:** Archaic flaking on blade.

Milky quartz

Classic form

Classic form

G8, $12-$20
Dalton, GA

G8, $15-$30
Dalton, GA

G10, $35-$65
Humphreys Co., TN

G10, $35-$65
Tishimingo Co., MS

BAKERS CREEK - Late Archaic to Woodland, 4000 - 1300 B. P.

(Also see Chesser, Copena, Harpeth River, Lowe, Mud Creek, Swan Lake & Table Rock)

LOCATION: Southeastern states. **DESCRIPTION:** A small to large size expanded stem point with tapered or barbed shoulders. Bases are concave to convex to straight. Related to *Copena* (found with them in caches) and are called Stemmed *Copenas* by some collectors. Called *Lowe* and *Steuben* in Illinois. **I.D. KEY:** Expanded base, usually thin.

Edge wear

G3, $2-$5
W. TN

G4, $3-$6
W. TN

G4, $3-$6
W. TN

G5, $8-$15
OH

G4, $8-$15
W. TN

G6 $12-$20
OH

G4, $8-$15
Sullivan Co., TN

G6, $15-$30
AL

G6, $20-$35
S. E. TN

G5, $15-$30
Florence, AL

Hornstone

G8, $40-$75
Livingston Co., KY

G5, $25-$40
Florence, AL

G8, $30-$50
Parsons, TN

G7, $35-$60
Parsons, TN

G9, $80-$150
Humphreys Co., TN

G7, $25-$45
Florence, AL

BAKERS CREEK (continued)

Needle tip →

Needle tip →

EC

G8, $65-$125 Clifton, TN	G8, $90-$175 KY	G9, $125-$200 Humphryes Co., TN	G10, $125-$225 Lauderdale Co., AL	G10, $150-$250 KY

BEACON ISLAND - Late Archaic, 4000 - 3000 B. P.
(Also see Big Slough and Flint Creek)

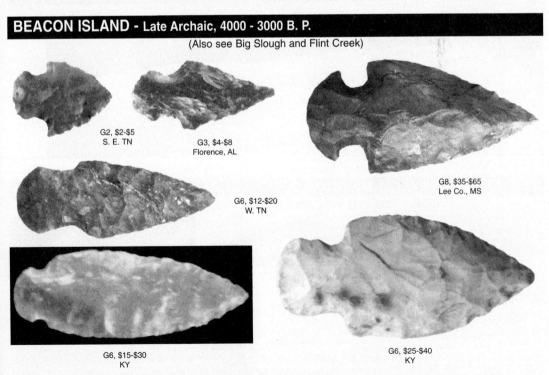

G2, $2-$5
S. E. TN

G3, $4-$8
Florence, AL

G8, $35-$65
Lee Co., MS

G6, $12-$20
W. TN

G6, $15-$30
KY

G6, $25-$40
KY

LOCATION: Southeastern states. **DESCRIPTION:** A small to large size triangular point with a bulbous stem. Shoulders are usually well defined and can be barbed. Similar to *Palmillas* in Texas. **I.D. KEY:** Bulbous base.

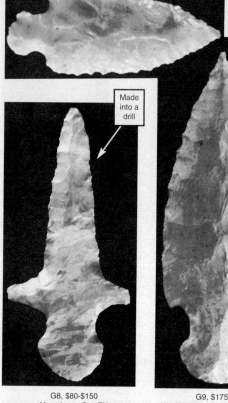

G6, $12-$20
White Co., TN

Classic
example

Made
into a
drill

G8, $80-$150
Humphreys Co., TN

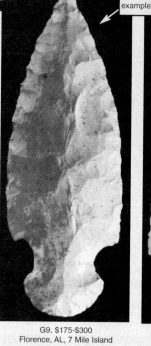

G9, $175-$300
Florence, AL, 7 Mile Island

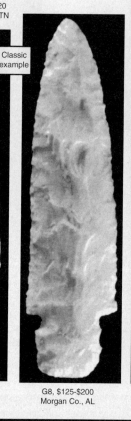

G8, $125-$200
Morgan Co., AL

G8, $150-$250
Florence, AL

G7,
$150-
$250
Jackson
Co., AL

BEAVER LAKE - Paleo, 11,250 - 8000 B. P.

(Also see Candy Creek, Cumberland, Dalton, Golondrina and Quad)

G7, $80-$150
N.W. AL

G6, $100-$175
Lauderdale Co., AL

Fort
Payne
chert

G7, $100-$175
Giles Co., TN

LOCATION: Southeastern states. **DESCRIPTION:** A medium to large size lanceolate blade with flaring ears and a concave base. Contemporaneous and associated with *Cumberland*, but thinner than unfluted *Cumberlands*. Bases are ground and blade edges are recurved. Has been found in deeper layers than *Dalton*. **I.D. KEY:** Paleo flaking, shoulder area.

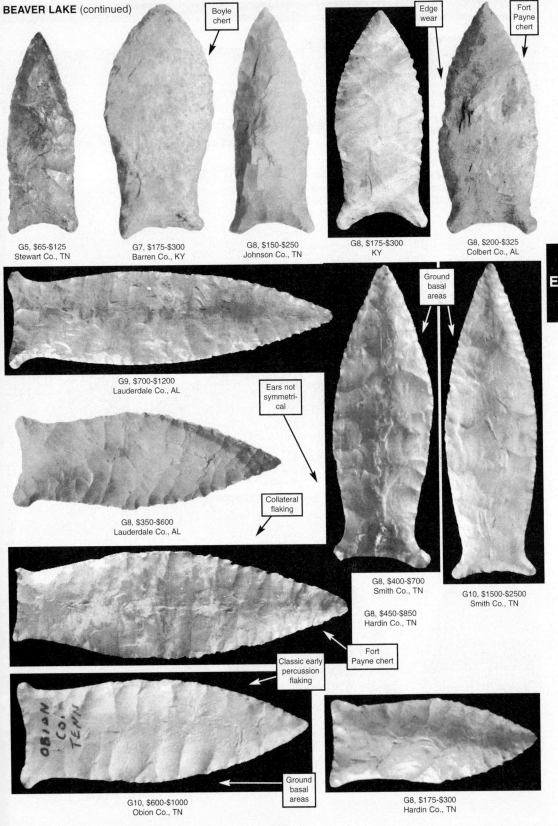

Boyle chert

Edge wear

Fort Payne chert

G5, $65-$125
Stewart Co., TN

G7, $175-$300
Barren Co., KY

G8, $150-$250
Johnson Co., TN

G8, $175-$300
KY

G8, $200-$325
Colbert Co., AL

EC

Ground basal areas

G9, $700-$1200
Lauderdale Co., AL

Ears not symmetri-cal

Collateral flaking

G8, $350-$600
Lauderdale Co., AL

G8, $400-$700
Smith Co., TN

G10, $1500-$2500
Smith Co., TN

G8, $450-$850
Hardin Co., TN

Fort Payne chert

Classic early percussion flaking

G10, $600-$1000
Obion Co., TN

Ground basal areas

G8, $175-$300
Hardin Co., TN

BENJAMIN - Woodland, 3000 - 1600 B. P.

(Also see Copena Round Base and Montgomery)

G5, $6-$10
Limestone Co., AL

G5, $8-$15
Morgan Co., AL

LOCATION: Southeastern states. **DESCRIPTION:** A medium to large size, thin, narrow, lanceolate point with random flaking and a rounded base. This point has been found in association with *Copena*.

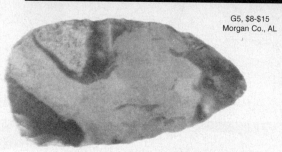

G7, $12-$20
TN

BENTON - Middle Archaic, 6000 - 4000 B. P.

(Also see Buzzard Roost Creek, Cresap, Elk River, Sykes, Turkeytail and Warito)

G3, $4-$8
Jessamine Co., KY

G4, $5-$10
N.W. AL

G5, $12-$20
N. W. AL

G4, $5-$10
Burke Co., GA

G7, $25-$45
Florence, AL

G7, $20-$35
N.W. AL

G5, $12-$20
N.W. AL

G6, $15-$25
N.W. AL

332

BENTON (continued)

Tallahatta quartzite

Diagonal flaking

EC

G6, $25-$40
N.W. AL

G3, $12-$20
N.W. AL

G6, $30-$50
N. W. AL

G6, $80-$150
Clark Co., AL

G6, $30-$100
Gray Co., MS

G7, $150-$250
KY

G6, $50-$100
Florence, AL

G8, $175-$300
N.W. AL

LOCATION: Southeastern to Midwestern states. **DESCRIPTION:** A medium to very large size, broad, stemmed point with straight to convex sides. Bases can be corner or side notched, double notched, knobbed, bifurcated or expanded. Some examples show parallel oblique flaking. All four sides are beveled and basal corners usually have tangs. Examples have been found in Arkansas with a steeply beveled edge on one side of each face (Transition form?). Found in caches with *Turkeytail* points in Mississippi on *Benton* sites. *Bentons* and *Turkeytails* as long as 16-3/4 inches were found together on this site and dated to about 4750 B.P. **I.D. KEY:** Wide squared, eared or notched base.

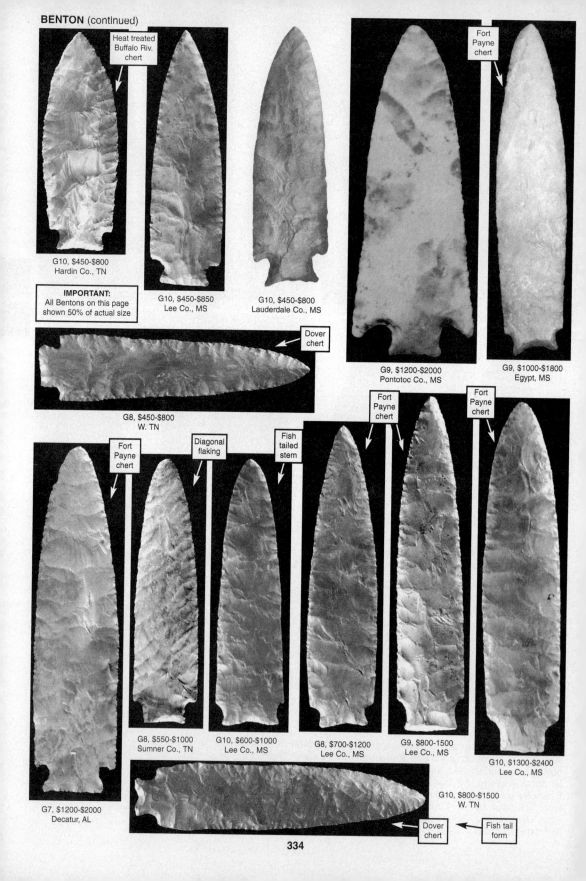

Heat treated
Buffalo Riv.
chert

G10, $450-$800
Hardin Co., TN

IMPORTANT:
All Bentons on this page
shown 50% of actual size

G10, $450-$850
Lee Co., MS

G10, $450-$800
Lauderdale Co., MS

Fort
Payne
chert

Fort
Payne
chert

G9, $1200-$2000
Pontotoc Co., MS

G9, $1000-$1800
Egypt, MS

Dover
chert

G8, $450-$800
W. TN

Fort
Payne
chert

Diagonal
flaking

Fish
tailed
stem

Fort
Payne
chert

Fort
Payne
chert

G8, $550-$1000
Sumner Co., TN

G10, $600-$1000
Lee Co., MS

G8, $700-$1200
Lee Co., MS

G9, $800-1500
Lee Co., MS

G10, $1300-$2400
Lee Co., MS

G7, $1200-$2000
Decatur, AL

G10, $800-$1500
W. TN

Dover
chert

Fish tail
form

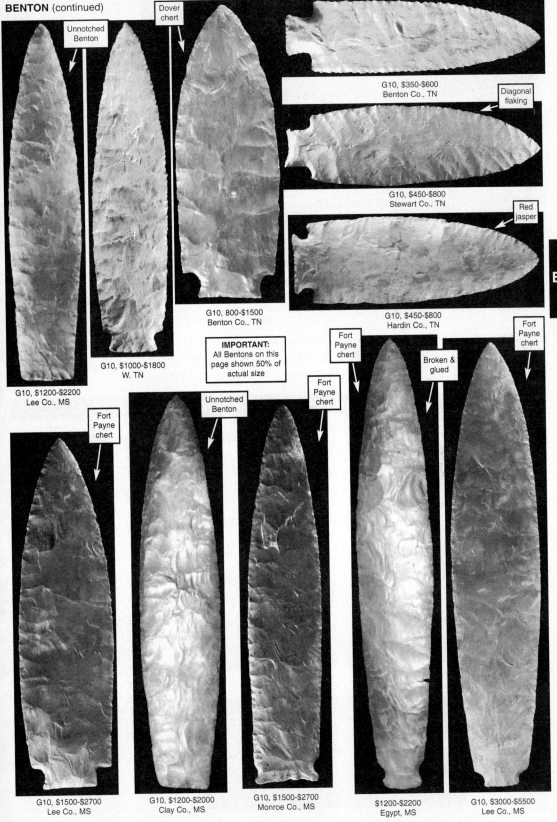

BENTON (continued)

Unnotched Benton

Dover chert

G10, $350-$600
Benton Co., TN

Diagonal flaking

G10, $450-$800
Stewart Co., TN

Red jasper

G10, $450-$800
Hardin Co., TN

EC

G10, 800-$1500
Benton Co., TN

G10, $1000-$1800
W. TN

IMPORTANT:
All Bentons on this page shown 50% of actual size

G10, $1200-$2200
Lee Co., MS

Fort Payne chert

Fort Payne chert

Fort Payne chert

Broken & glued

Fort Payne chert

Unnotched Benton

Fort Payne chert

G10, $1500-$2700
Lee Co., MS

G10, $1200-$2000
Clay Co., MS

G10, $1500-$2700
Monroe Co., MS

$1200-$2200
Egypt, MS

G10, $3000-$5500
Lee Co., MS

335

BENTON BLADE - Middle Archaic, 6000 - 4000 B. P.

(Also see Benton and Copena)

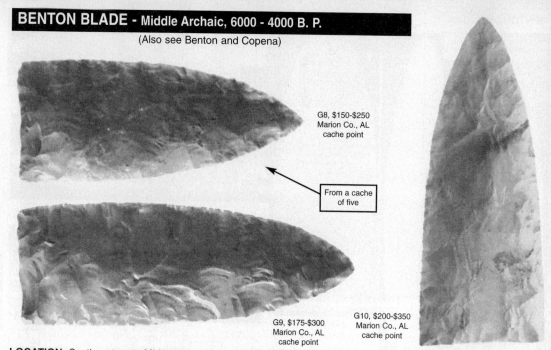

G8, $150-$250
Marion Co., AL
cache point

From a cache
of five

G9, $175-$300
Marion Co., AL
cache point

G10, $200-$350
Marion Co., AL
cache point

LOCATION: Southeastern to Midwestern states. **DESCRIPTION:** A medium to very large size, broad, finished blade used either as a knife or as a preform for later knapping into a *Benton* point. Usually found in caches. **I.D. KEY:** Archaic flaking similar to the *Benton* type.

BENTON-BOTTLE NECK - Middle Archaic, 6000 - 4000 B. P.

(Also see Benton and Table Rock)

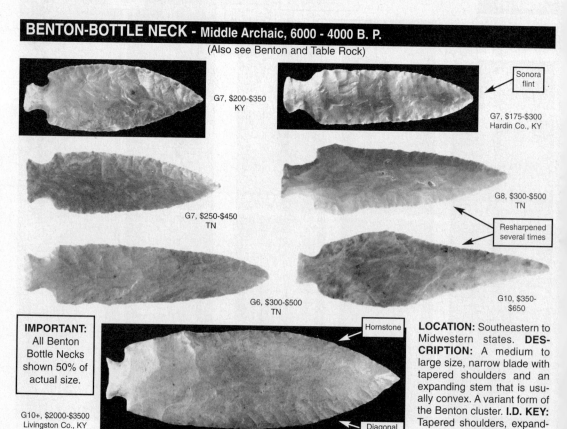

G7, $200-$350
KY

Sonora
flint

G7, $175-$300
Hardin Co., KY

G7, $250-$450
TN

G8, $300-$500
TN

Resharpened
several times

G6, $300-$500
TN

G10, $350-$650

IMPORTANT:
All Benton
Bottle Necks
shown 50% of
actual size.

G10+, $2000-$3500
Livingston Co., KY

Hornstone

Diagonal
flaking

LOCATION: Southeastern to Midwestern states. **DESCRIPTION:** A medium to large size, narrow blade with tapered shoulders and an expanding stem that is usually convex. A variant form of the Benton cluster. **I.D. KEY:** Tapered shoulders, expanding stem.

336

BENTON DOUBLE-NOTCHED - Middle Archaic, 6000 - 4000 B. P.

(Also see Benton and Turkeytail)

Fort Payne chert

G10, $3000-$5500
Lee Co., MS

IMPORTANT:
All double notched Bentons shown 50% of actual size

Fort Payne chert

Ground base

G10, $2000-$3500
Monroe Co., MS

LOCATION: Southeastern to Midwestern states. **DESCRIPTION:** A medium to very large size, broad, finished blade with double notches on each side of the blade at the base. Used as a knife and usually found in caches. Has been found associated with un-notched and double to triple-notched *Turkeytail* blades in Mississippi. Unique and rare. **I.D. KEY:** Multiple notching at base.

EC

G9, $1200-$2200
W. TN

G9, $1500-$2800
Lee Co., MS

BENTON-NARROW BLADE - Middle Archaic, 6000 - 4000 B. P.

(Also see Elk River, Kays and Little Bear Creek)

G8, $250-$450
Hamilton Co. TN

LOCATION: Southeastern to Midwestern states. **DESCRIPTION:** A medium to large size, narrow, stemmed variant of the *Benton* form.

BIG SANDY - Early to Late Archaic, 10,000 - 3000 B. P.

(Also see Cache River, Graham Cave, Newton Falls, Pine Tree and Savage Cave)

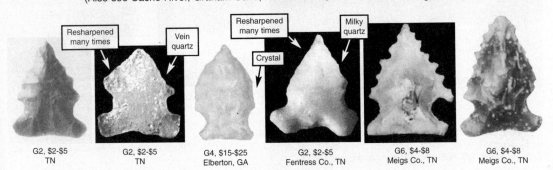

Resharpened many times

Vein quartz

Resharpened many times

Milky quartz

Crystal

G2, $2-$5
TN

G2, $2-$5
TN

G4, $15-$25
Elberton, GA

G2, $2-$5
Fentress Co., TN

G6, $4-$8
Meigs Co., TN

G6, $4-$8
Meigs Co., TN

337

BIG SANDY (continued)

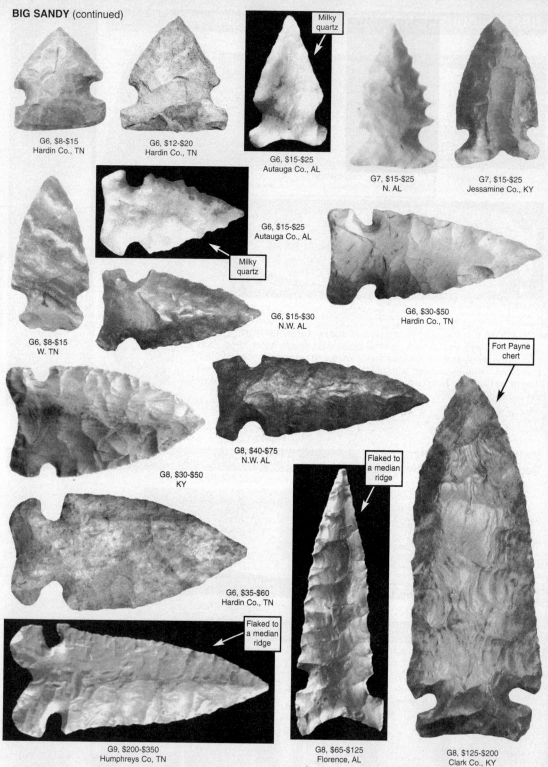

G6, $8-$15
Hardin Co., TN

G6, $12-$20
Hardin Co., TN

Milky quartz

G6, $15-$25
Autauga Co., AL

G7, $15-$25
N. AL

G7, $15-$25
Jessamine Co., KY

G6, $15-$25
Autauga Co., AL

Milky quartz

G6, $8-$15
W. TN

G6, $15-$30
N.W. AL

G6, $30-$50
Hardin Co., TN

Fort Payne chert

G8, $30-$50
KY

G8, $40-$75
N.W. AL

Flaked to a median ridge

G6, $35-$60
Hardin Co., TN

Flaked to a median ridge

G9, $200-$350
Humphreys Co, TN

G8, $65-$125
Florence, AL

G8, $125-$200
Clark Co., KY

LOCATION: Southeastern states. **DESCRIPTION:** A small to medium size, side-notched point with early forms showing heavy basal grinding, serrations, and horizontal flaking. This type may be associated with the *Frazier* point, being an unnotched form. Some examples have been carbon dated to 10,000 B.P., but most are associated with Mid-Archaic times. **I.D. KEY:** Basal form and blade flaking.

338

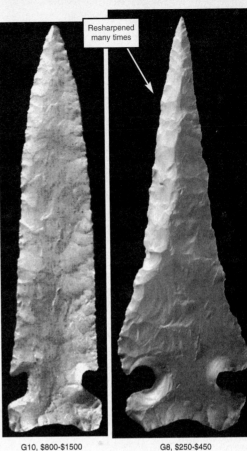

Resharpened many times

EC

G8, $500-$800
Morgan Co., AL

G8, $175-$300
Florence, AL

G10, $800-$1500
Decatur Co., TN

G8, $250-$450
N. AL

BIG SANDY-BROAD BASE - Early Archaic, 10,000 - 7000 B. P.

(Also see Cache River, Newton Falls and Savage Cave)

G8, $20-$35
TN

G7, $15-$25
OH

G8, $25-$40
Hardin Co., KY

Black chert

G8, $25-$40
Colbert Co., AL

G6, $20-$35
TN/KY

LOCATION: Southeastern states.
DESCRIPTION: A small to medium size, side notched point with a broad base that is usually ground. The base is wider than the blade.

339

BIG SANDY BROAD-BASE (continued)

Jasper

G9, $60-$100
Breathitt Co., KY

G6, $25-$40
KY

G6, $35-$60
Humphryes Co., TN

G6, $35-$60
KY

G9, $100-$175
Humphreys Co., TN

G9, $150-$275
Humphreys Co., TN

G7, $45-$80
Humphreys Co., TN

G9, $150-$250
KY

BIG SANDY-CONTRACTED BASE - Early Archaic, 10,000 - 7000 B. P.

(Also see MacCorkle, Pine Tree and Quad)

G5, $5-$10
Hamilton Co., TN

G5, $5-$10
Meigs Co., TN

G5, $8-$15
Hamilton Co., TN

G6, $12-$20
Humphreys Co., TN

BIG SANDY CONTRACTED BASE (continued)

LOCATION: Southeastern states. **DESCRIPTION:** A small to medium size, side notched point with a deeply concave ground base, and drooping ears. Some examples exhibit nice parallel flaking.

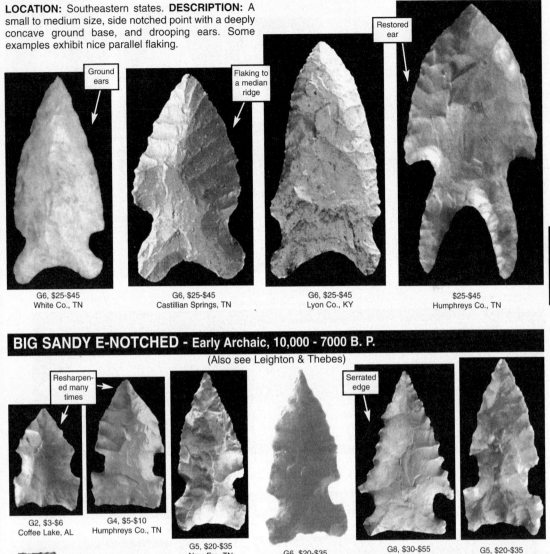

G6, $25-$45
White Co., TN

G6, $25-$45
Castillian Springs, TN

G6, $25-$45
Lyon Co., KY

$25-$45
Humphreys Co., TN

BIG SANDY E-NOTCHED - Early Archaic, 10,000 - 7000 B. P.
(Also see Leighton & Thebes)

G2, $3-$6
Coffee Lake, AL

G4, $5-$10
Humphreys Co., TN

G5, $20-$35
New Era, TN

G6, $20-$35
Coffee Lake, AL

G8, $30-$55
N. AL

G5, $20-$35
Humphreys Co., TN

G7, $40-$75
Humphreys Co., TN

G8, $65-$125
Coffee Lake, AL

G9, $80-$150
Humphreys Co., TN

LOCATION: Southeastern states. **DESCRIPTION:** A small to medium size expanded side-notched point. The notching is unique and quite rare for the type. This type of notch is angled into the blade to produce a high point or nipple in the center, forming the letter E. Also called key-notched. Rarely, the base is also E-notched. The same notching occurs in the *Bolen* and *Thebes* types. **I.D. KEY:** Two flake notching system.

BIG SANDY E-NOTCH (continued)

Purple & beige Buffalo River chert

Prominent E-notches

Prominent E-notches, sides & base

G8, $125-$200
Humphreys Co., TN

G9, $150-$250
N.W. AL

G10, $400-$750
Humphreys Co., TN

G10, $250-$400
Humphreys Co., TN

G7, $65-$125
Humphreys Co., TN

G10, $1250-$2250
Clarksville, TN

BIG SANDY-LEIGHTON BASE - Early Archaic, 10,000 - 7000 B. P.

(Also see Leighton and Thebes)

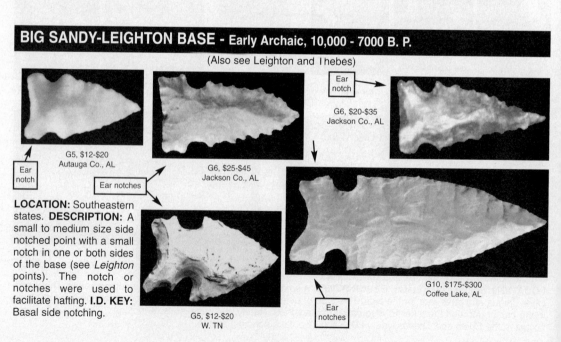

Ear notch

G6, $20-$35
Jackson Co., AL

G5, $12-$20
Autauga Co., AL

Ear notch

G6, $25-$45
Jackson Co., AL

Ear notches

LOCATION: Southeastern states. **DESCRIPTION:** A small to medium size side notched point with a small notch in one or both sides of the base (see *Leighton* points). The notch or notches were used to facilitate hafting. **I.D. KEY:** Basal side notching.

G5, $12-$20
W. TN

Ear notches

G10, $175-$300
Coffee Lake, AL

(Also see Beacon Island and Elk River)

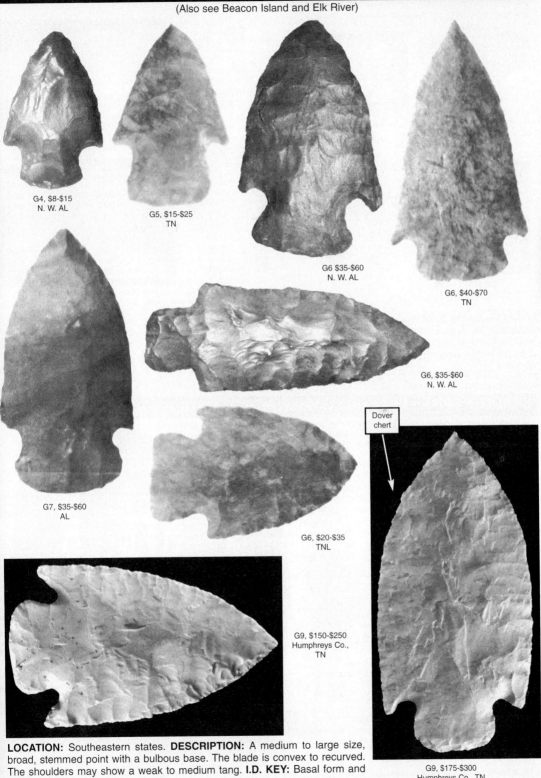

EC

G4, $8-$15
N. W. AL

G5, $15-$25
TN

G6 $35-$60
N. W. AL

G6, $40-$70
TN

G6, $35-$60
N. W. AL

G7, $35-$60
AL

G6, $20-$35
TNL

Dover chert

G9, $150-$250
Humphreys Co.,
TN

G9, $175-$300
Humphreys Co., TN

LOCATION: Southeastern states. **DESCRIPTION:** A medium to large size, broad, stemmed point with a bulbous base. The blade is convex to recurved. The shoulders may show a weak to medium tang. **I.D. KEY:** Basal form and barbs.

BLUNT - Paleo to Woodland, 11,500 - 1000 B. P.

(Also see Drill, Perforator and Scraper)

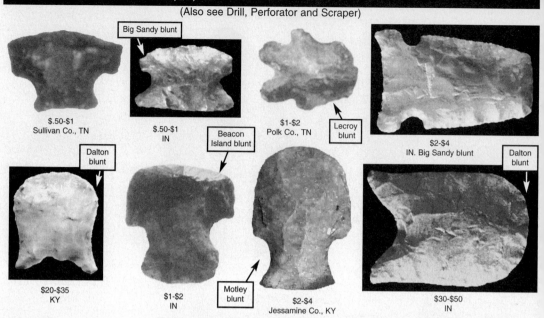

Big Sandy blunt

$.50-$1
Sullivan Co., TN

$.50-$1
IN

Beacon
Island blunt

$1-$2
Polk Co., TN

Lecroy
blunt

$2-$4
IN. Big Sandy blunt

Dalton
blunt

Dalton
blunt

$20-$35
KY

$1-$2
IN

Motley
blunt

$2-$4
Jessamine Co., KY

$30-$50
IN

LOCATION: Throughout North America. **DESCRIPTION:** Blunts are usually made from broken points that are rechipped into this form, but can be made from scratch. All point types can occur as blunts. Some collectors call this form Stunners believing they were made to stun animals, not to kill. However, most archaeologists think they were used as knives and for scraping hides. Many blunts show excessive wear on the blunt edge proving their use as scrapers.

BRADLEY SPIKE - Late Archaic to Woodland, 4000 - 1800 B. P.

(Also see Buggs Island, Mountain Fork, New Market and Schild Spike)

G5, $4-$8
S. E. TN

G5, $4-$8
Jackson Co., AL

G6, $5-$10
Jackson Co., AL

G6, $6-$12
Meigs Co., TN

G6, $8-$15
Nickajack
Lake, TN

G6, $8-$15
S. E. TN

G7, $15-$25
Limestone Co., AL

G8, $20-$35
Dayton, TN

G7, $12-$20
Jessamine Co., KY

G7, $8-$15
Limestone Co., AL

Black chert

G10, $35-$60
Madison Co., AL

LOCATION: Southeastern states. **DESCRIPTION:** A small to medium size, narrow, thick, spike point. The shoulders are tapered and the stem contracts. The base on some examples shows the natural rind of the native material used.

BREWERTON CORNER NOTCHED - Middle to Late Archaic, 6000 - 4000 B. P.

(Also see Autauga)

G3, $2-$5
S.E. TN

G3, $2-$4
S.E. TN

G3, $2-$4
W. KY

G3, $2-$5
W. KY

G6, $8-$15
W. KY

G8, $15-$30
N. AL

G10, $35-$60
Humphreys Co., TN

EC

G8, $15-$30
Seymor, IN

LOCATION: Eastern to Midwestern states. **DESCRIPTION:** A small size, triangular point with faint corner notches and a straight to concave base. Called *Freeheley* in Michigan. **I.D. KEY:** Width, thickness.

BREWERTON EARED-TRIANGULAR - Mid-Archaic, 6000 - 4000 B. P.

(Also see Autauga, Camp Creek, Candy Creek, Nolichucky and Yadkin)

G3, $2-$4
Polk Co., TN

G3, $2-$4
Sullivan Co., TN

G3, $2-$4
Jessamine Co., KY

G3, $2-$5
Walker Co., AL

G3, $2-$4
W. KY

G5, $3-$6
Jessamine Co., KY

G6, $8-$15
Trimble Co., KY

LOCATION: Eastern to Midwestern states. **DESCRIPTION:** A small size, triangular, eared point with a concave base. Shoulders are weak and tapered. Ears are widest part of point.

BREWERTON SIDE NOTCHED - Mid-Archaic, 6000 - 4000 B. P.

(Also see Big Sandy, Brunswick, Hardaway and Matanzas)

LOCATION: Eastern to Midwestern states. **DESCRIPTION:** A small to medium size, triangular point with shallow side notches and a concave to straight base.

G3, $1-$2
Trimble Co., KY

G4, $1-$3
Walker Co., GA

G4, $1-$3
Jessamine Co., KY

G3, $1-$2
Dallas Isle, TN

345

BREWERTON SIDE NOTCHED (continued)

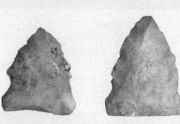

G4, $1-$3
Jessamine Co., KY

G4, $1-$3
Jessamine Co., KY

G5, $2-$5
Harrison Co., IN

G5, $2-$5
Jessamine Co., KY

G7, $8-$15
Jessamine Co., KY

BRUNSWICK - Middle Archaic, 5000 - 4500 B. P.

(Also see Brewerton, Greenbrier and Matanzas)

G7, $40-$75
KY

G6, $35-$65
KY

LOCATION: Kentucky, Indiana. **DESCRIPTION:** A medium sized point with weak side notches. The base can be slightly concave to straight. **I.D. KEY:** Weak notching.

BUCK CREEK - Middle to Late Archaic, 6000 - 3500 B. P.

(Also see Hamilton, Motley, Rankin, Smithsonia, Table Rock and Wade)

Red, yellow & blue
Horse Creek chert

G8, $150-$250
MS

G6, $35-$65
Dickson Co., TN

G5, $15-$25
KY

G6, $35-$65
KY

G7, $55-$100
IN

G6, $25-$40
TN

LOCATION: Kentucky and surrounding states. **DESCRIPTION:** A large, thin, broad, stemmed point with strong barbs and high quality flaking. Some have needle tips, blade edges are convex to recurved. Blade width can be narrow to broad. **I.D. KEY:** Barb expansion and notching.

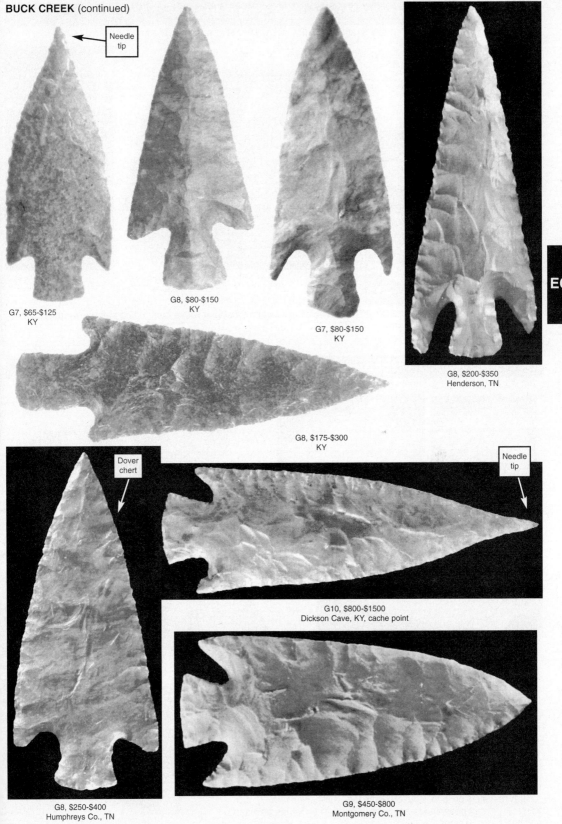

BUCK CREEK (continued)

Needle tip

G7, $65-$125
KY

G8, $80-$150
KY

G7, $80-$150
KY

EC

G8, $200-$350
Henderson, TN

G8, $175-$300
KY

Dover chert

Needle tip

G10, $800-$1500
Dickson Cave, KY, cache point

G8, $250-$400
Humphreys Co., TN

G9, $450-$800
Montgomery Co., TN

BUGGS ISLAND - Mid to Late Archaic, 5500 - 3500 B. P.

(Also see Bradley Spike, Coosa, Ebenezer and New Market)

G3, $2-$4
S.E. TN

G4, $2-$4
Whitwell, TN

G5, $3-$6
Dunlap, TN

G6, $6-$12
Meigs Co., TN

G6, $6-$12
S.E. TN

Milky quartz

G5, $4-$8
S.E. TN

LOCATION: Eastern states. **DESCRIPTION:** A small to medium size point with a contracting stem and tapered shoulders. The base is usually straight.

BUZZARD ROOST CREEK - Middle Archaic, 6000 - 4000 B. P.

(Also see Benton and Kirk Stemmed)

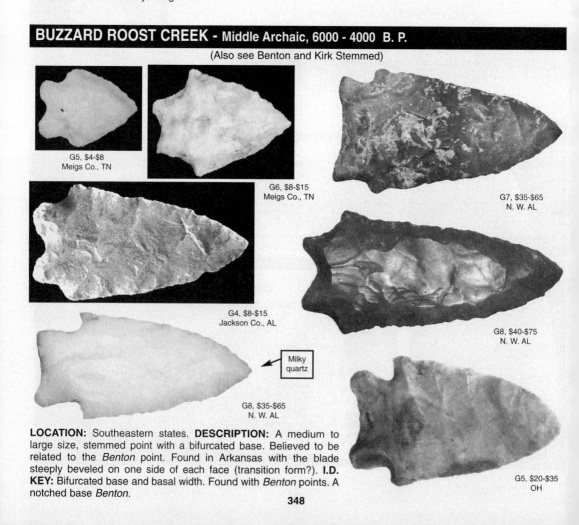

G5, $4-$8
Meigs Co., TN

G6, $8-$15
Meigs Co., TN

G7, $35-$65
N. W. AL

G4, $8-$15
Jackson Co., AL

G8, $40-$75
N. W. AL

Milky quartz

G8, $35-$65
N. W. AL

G5, $20-$35
OH

LOCATION: Southeastern states. **DESCRIPTION:** A medium to large size, stemmed point with a bifurcated base. Believed to be related to the *Benton* point. Found in Arkansas with the blade steeply beveled on one side of each face (transition form?). **I.D. KEY:** Bifurcated base and basal width. Found with *Benton* points. A notched base *Benton*.

348

Drill form

G8, $65-$125
TN

G5, $25-$45
TN

EC

G8, $40-$75
N. W. AL

G5, $25-$45
Florence, AL

G8, $55-$100
N. W. AL

G8, $65-$125
N. W. AL

G8, $80-$150
N. W. AL

G10, $700-$1200
Clifton, TN

CAMP CREEK - Woodland, 3000 - 1500 B. P.

(Also see Copena, Greeneville, Hamilton, Madison, Nolichucky and Yadkin)

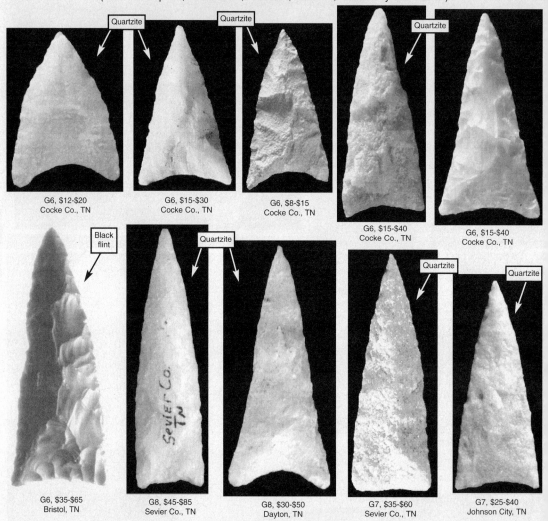

Quartzite

G6, $12-$20
Cocke Co., TN

Quartzite

G6, $15-$30
Cocke Co., TN

Quartzite

G6, $8-$15
Cocke Co., TN

Quartzite

G6, $15-$40
Cocke Co., TN

G6, $15-$40
Cocke Co., TN

Black flint

G6, $35-$65
Bristol, TN

Quartzite

G8, $45-$85
Sevier Co., TN

G8, $30-$50
Dayton, TN

Quartzite

G7, $35-$60
Sevier Co., TN

Quartzite

G7, $25-$40
Johnson City, TN

LOCATION: Southeastern states. **DESCRIPTION:** A small to medium size triangular point with straight to convex sides and a concave base. Believed to have evolved into Hamilton points; related to Greeneville and Nolichucky points. Has been found with Adena stemmed in caches (Rankin site, Cocke Co.,TN).

CANDY CREEK - Early Woodland, 3000 - 1500 B. P.

(Also see Beaver Lake, Brewerton, Camp Creek, Copena, Dalton, Nolichucky and Quad)

G3, $4-$8
Dayton, TN

G4, $5-$10
W. TN

G7, $30-$50
Nickajack Lake, TN

CANDY CREEK (continued)

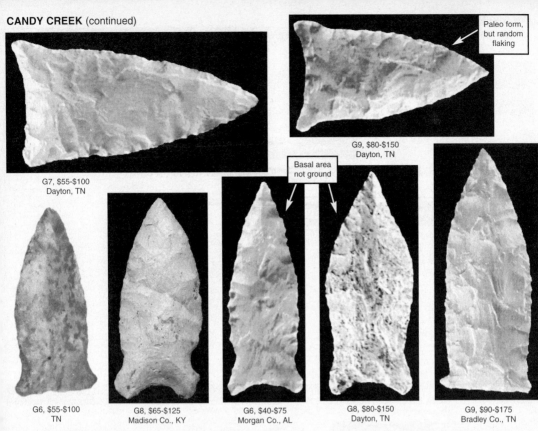

Paleo form, but random flaking

Basal area not ground

G7, $55-$100
Dayton, TN

G9, $80-$150
Dayton, TN

EC

G6, $55-$100
TN

G8, $65-$125
Madison Co., KY

G6, $40-$75
Morgan Co., AL

G8, $80-$150
Dayton, TN

G9, $90-$175
Bradley Co., TN

LOCATION: Southeastern states. **DESCRIPTION:** A medium size, lanceolate, eared point with a concave base and recurved blade edges. Bases may be thinned or fluted and lightly ground. Flaking is of the random Woodland type and should not be confused with the earlier auriculate forms that have the parallel flaking. These points are similar to *Cumberland, Beaver Lake, Dalton* and *Quad*, but are shorter and of poorer quality. It is believed that Paleo people survived in East Tennessee to 3,000 B.P., and influenced the style of the *Candy Creek* point. Believed to be related to *Copena, Camp Creek, Ebenezer, Greenville* and *Nolichucky* points. **I.D. KEY:** Ears, thickness and Woodland flaking.

CAVE SPRING - Early Archaic, 9000 - 8000 B. P.

(Also see Frederick, Jude, LeCroy and Patrick)

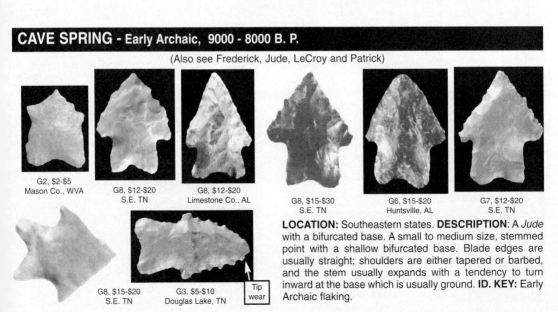

G2, $2-$5
Mason Co., WVA

G8, $12-$20
S.E. TN

G8, $12-$20
Limestone Co., AL

G8, $15-$30
S.E. TN

G6, $15-$20
Huntsville, AL

G7, $12-$20
S.E. TN

G8, $15-$20
S.E. TN

G3, $5-$10
Douglas Lake, TN

Tip wear

LOCATION: Southeastern states. **DESCRIPTION**: A *Jude* with a bifurcated base. A small to medium size, stemmed point with a shallow bifurcated base. Blade edges are usually straight; shoulders are either tapered or barbed, and the stem usually expands with a tendency to turn inward at the base which is usually ground. **ID. KEY:** Early Archaic flaking.

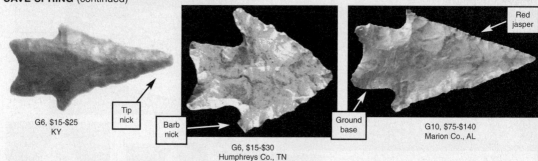

G6, $15-$25
KY

Tip nick

Barb nick

G6, $15-$30
Humphreys Co., TN

Ground base

Red jasper

G10, $75-$140
Marion Co., AL

CHESSER - Late Woodland-Miss., 1600 - 1200 B. P.

(Also see Bakers Creek, Lowe, McIntire, Mud Creek)

LOCATION: Ohio into Pennsylvania.
DESCRIPTION: A medium size, broad point with a short, expanding stem. Bases are generally straight. Blade edges are convex to recurved and the shoulders are slightly barbed to tapered. **ID. KEY:** Broad, expanding stem.

G9, $80-$150
Hocking Co., OH

Coshocton chert

CLOVIS - Early Paleo, 11,500 - 10,600 B. P.

(Also see Angostura, Browns Valley, Cumberland, Dalton, Folsom and Redstone)

Broken ear

G3, $50-$100
Meigs Co., TN

G5, $250-$400
Castillian Springs, TN

Ridge & Valley chert

G7, $350-$600
Jefferson Co., TN

G7, $300-$500
IN

Fluting channel

G7, $325-$600
AL

G7, $350-$650
MS

G7, $350-$650
E. TN

G8, $350-600
IN

G4, $275-$350
AL

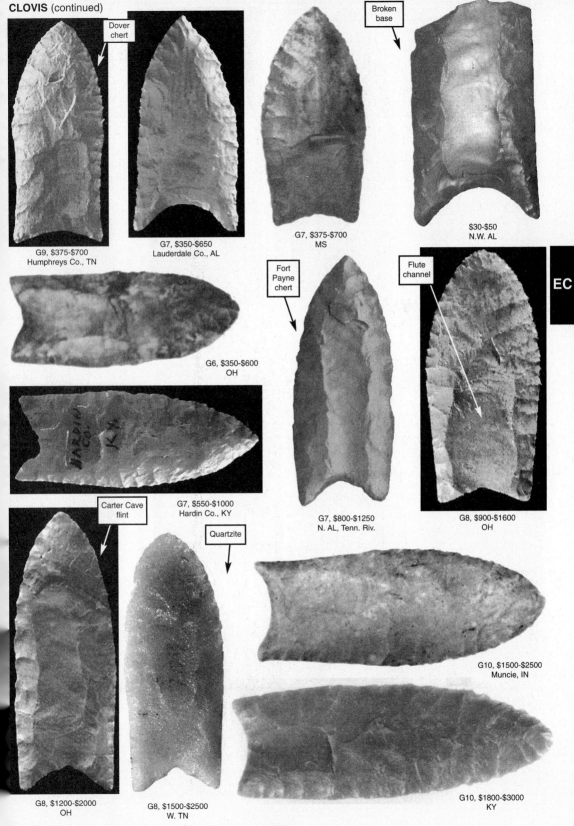

Dover chert

Broken base

G9, $375-$700
Humphreys Co., TN

G7, $350-$650
Lauderdale Co., AL

G7, $375-$700
MS

$30-$50
N.W. AL

EC

Fort Payne chert

Flute channel

G6, $350-$600
OH

G7, $550-$1000
Hardin Co., KY

G7, $800-$1250
N. AL, Tenn. Riv.

G8, $900-$1600
OH

Carter Cave flint

Quartzite

G10, $1500-$2500
Muncie, IN

G8, $1200-$2000
OH

G8, $1500-$2500
W. TN

G10, $1800-$3000
KY

CLOVIS (continued)

Tyrone chert

Petrified wood

Flute channel

Fort Payne chert

G6, $800-$1500
Clark Co., KY

G7, $1200-$2000
Blount Co., AL

G9, $1200-$2000
Humphreys Co., TN

G8, $1000-$1700
N. AL, Tenn. Riv.

Patinated hornstone

Fluted to the tip, both sides

Dover chert

Flute channel

G8, $1600-$3000
IN

G9, $1600-$3000
Humphreys Co., TN

G8, $1500-$2500
Humphreys Co., TN

G9, $1600-$3000
Hardin Co., TN

LOCATION: All of North America. **DESCRIPTION:** A medium to large size, auriculate, fluted, lanceolate point with convex sides and a concave base that is ground. Most examples are fluted on both sides about 1/3 the way up from the base. The flaking can be random to parallel. *Clovis* is the earliest point type in the hemisphere. *Clovis* technology more closely matches European Solutrean forms than anywhere else. There is no pre-*Clovis* evidence here (crude forms that would pre-date *Clovis*). The first *Clovis* find associated with Mastodons was in 1979 at Mastodon State Park, Jefferson Co., MO. in the Kimmswick bone bed dated to 12,000 B.P. carbon years. **I.D. KEY:** Paleo flaking, shoulders, baton or billet fluting instead of indirect style.

CLOVIS (continued)

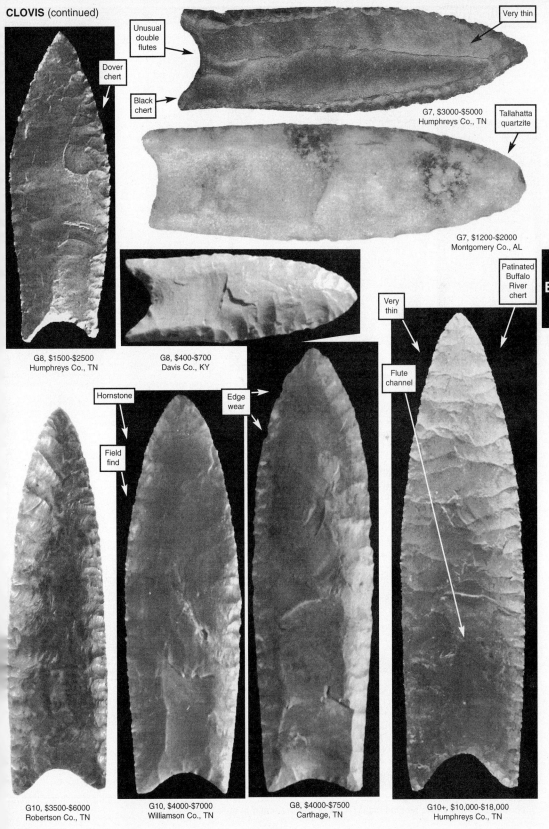

Unusual double flutes

Very thin

Black chert

G7, $3000-$5000
Humphreys Co., TN

Tallahatta quartzite

Dover chert

G7, $1200-$2000
Montgomery Co., AL

Patinated Buffalo River chert

EC

Very thin

Flute channel

G8, $1500-$2500
Humphreys Co., TN

G8, $400-$700
Davis Co., KY

Hornstone

Edge wear

Field find

G10, $3500-$6000
Robertson Co., TN

G10, $4000-$7000
Williamson Co., TN

G8, $4000-$7500
Carthage, TN

G10+, $10,000-$18,000
Humphreys Co., TN

CLOVIS-HAZEL - Paleo, 11,500 - 10,600 B. P.

(Also see Angostura, Beaver Lake, Candy Creek, Golondrina and Plainview)

Flute channel

Tip wear

G9, $700-$1200
Lewis Co., KY

G10, $1200-$2000
KY

G10, $1500-$2500
KY

G8, $800-$1500
KY

G7, $700-$1200
KY

LOCATION: Eastern U.S. from Florida, Alabama, Tennessee, Kentucky, Ohio westward. **DESCRIPTION:** A medium to large size, auriculate point that has similarities to the Ross County variety, but with a more fishtailed appearance and a longer hafting area.

CLOVIS-UNFLUTED - Paleo, 11,500 - 10,600 B. P.

(Also see Angostura, Beaver Lake, Candy Creek, Golondrina and Plainview)

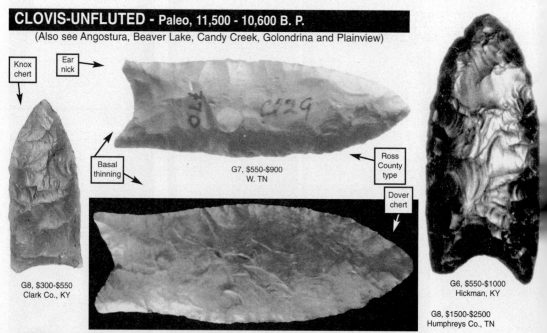

Knox chert

Ear nick

Basal thinning

G7, $550-$900
W. TN

Ross County type

Dover chert

G8, $300-$550
Clark Co., KY

G6, $550-$1000
Hickman, KY

G8, $1500-$2500
Humphreys Co., TN

LOCATION: All of North America. **DESCRIPTION:** A medium to large size, auriculate point identical to fluted *Clovis*, but not fluted. A very rare type as most *Clovis* points are fluted in their finished form.

(Also see Abasolo, Decatur, Lerma, Lost Lake and St. Charles)

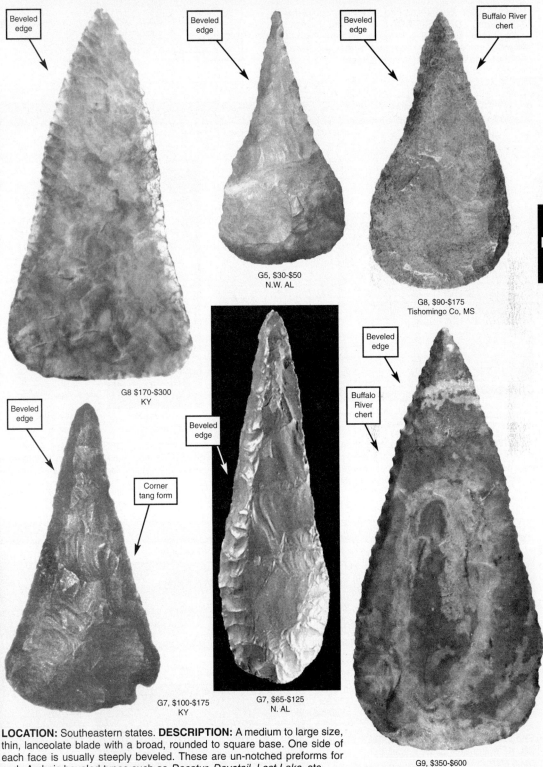

Beveled edge

Beveled edge

Beveled edge

Buffalo River chert

EC

G5, $30-$50
N.W. AL

G8, $90-$175
Tishomingo Co, MS

G8 $170-$300
KY

Beveled edge

Beveled edge

Corner tang form

Beveled edge

Buffalo River chert

G7, $100-$175
KY

G7, $65-$125
N. AL

G9, $350-$600
Livingston Co., KY

LOCATION: Southeastern states. **DESCRIPTION:** A medium to large size, thin, lanceolate blade with a broad, rounded to square base. One side of each face is usually steeply beveled. These are un-notched preforms for early Archaic beveled types such as *Decatur, Dovetail, Lost Lake,* etc.

COLDWATER - Trans. Paleo, 10,000 - 8000 B. P.

(Also see Hinds and Pelican)

LOCATION: East Texas into Arkansas, Louisiana & Tenn. **DESCRIPTION:** A medium size, Lanceolate point with a longer waist than *Pelican* and a straight to concave base which is ground. The blade expands up from the base.

G6, $150-$250
AL

Ground stem →

CONERLY - Middle Archaic, 7500 - 4500 B. P.

(Also see Beaver Lake and Copena)

Fairly thick cross section

G7, $25-$45
Nickajack Lake, TN

G7, $25-$45
Putnam Co., TN

G10, $65-$125
Bradley Co., TN

G7, $30-$60
TN

G8, $40-$75
KY

LOCATION: Southern Southeastern states, especially Tennessee, Georgia and Florida. **DESCRIPTION:** A medium to large auriculate point with a contracting, concave base which can be ground. On some examples, the hafting area can be seen with the presence of very weak shoulders. The base is usually thinned. Believed to be related to the *Guilford* type. **I.D. KEY:** Base concave, thickness, flaking.

COOSA - Woodland, 2000 - 1500 B. P.

(Also see Buggs Island and Crawford Creek)

G5, $1-$2
Nickajack Lake, TN

G5, $1-$3
Meigs Co., TN

G5, $1-$3
Jackson Co., AL

LOCATION: Southeastern states. **DESCRIPTION:** A medium size, usually serrated medium grade point with a short stem. Some examples are shallowly side-notched. Shoulders are roughly horizontal. **I.D. KEY:** Serrated blade edges, bulbous stem.

G5, $2-$4
Jackson Co., AL

G5, $1-$3
Jackson Co., AL

358

COPENA-AURICULATE - Middle Archaic-Woodland, 5000 - 2500 B. P.

(Also see Beaver Lake, Camp Creek, Candy Creek, Clovis, Quad and Yadkin)

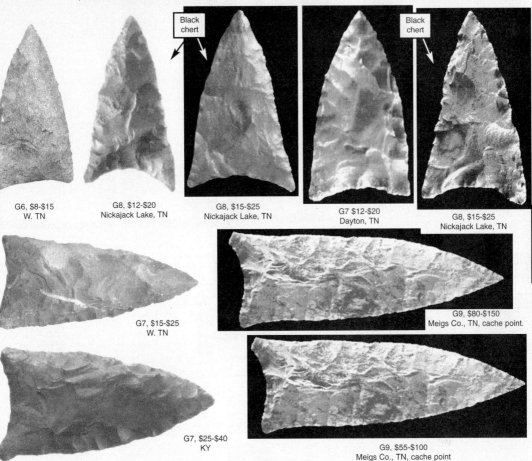

G6, $8-$15
W. TN

G8, $12-$20
Nickajack Lake, TN

Black chert

G8, $15-$25
Nickajack Lake, TN

Black chert

G7 $12-$20
Dayton, TN

G8, $15-$25
Nickajack Lake, TN

EC

G7, $15-$25
W. TN

G9, $80-$150
Meigs Co., TN, cache point.

G7, $25-$40
KY

G9, $55-$100
Meigs Co., TN, cache point

LOCATION: Southeastern states. **DESCRIPTION:** A medium to large size, lanceolate point with convex, straight to recurved blade edges and a concave, auriculate base. Could be confused with *Beaver Lake, Candy Creek, Clovis, Cumberland* or other auriculate forms. Look for the random Woodland flaking on this type. Stems are not ground. **I.D. KEY:** Concave base.

COPENA-CLASSIC (Shield form) - Late Archaic to Woodland, 4000 - 1200 B. P.

(Also see Bakers Creek & Nolichucky)

Corner nick

G4, $5-$10
TN

Edge wear

G6, $15-$25
TN

G3, $2-$5
Meigs Co., TN

G4, $5-$10
TN

LOCATION: Southeastern states. **DESCRIPTION:** A medium to large size, lanceolate point with recurved blade edges and a straight to slightly convex base. This point usually occurs in Woodland burial mounds, but is also found in late Archaic sites in Tennessee. The Alabama and Tennessee forms are usually very thin with high quality primary and secondary flaking.

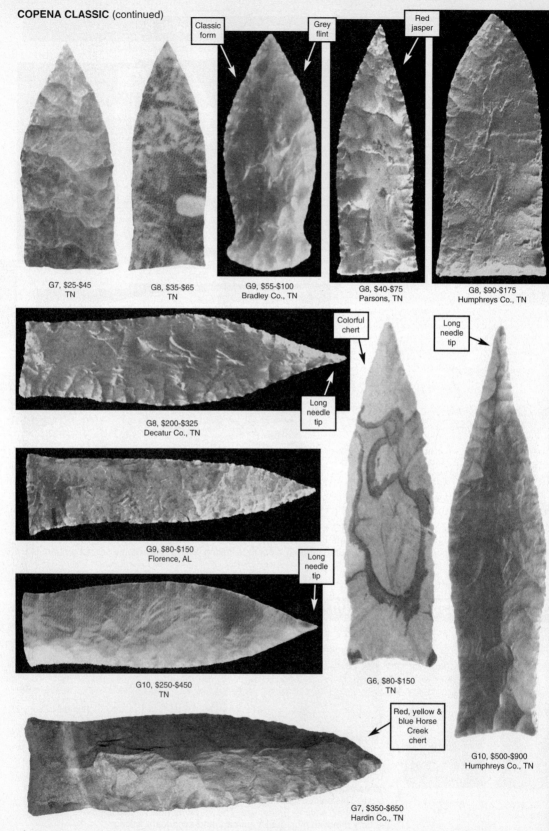

Classic form

Grey flint

Red jasper

G7, $25-$45
TN

G8, $35-$65
TN

G9, $55-$100
Bradley Co., TN

G8, $40-$75
Parsons, TN

G8, $90-$175
Humphreys Co., TN

Colorful chert

Long needle tip

Long needle tip

G8, $200-$325
Decatur Co., TN

Long needle tip

G9, $80-$150
Florence, AL

Long needle tip

G10, $250-$450
TN

G6, $80-$150
TN

Red, yellow & blue Horse Creek chert

G10, $500-$900
Humphreys Co., TN

G7, $350-$650
Hardin Co., TN

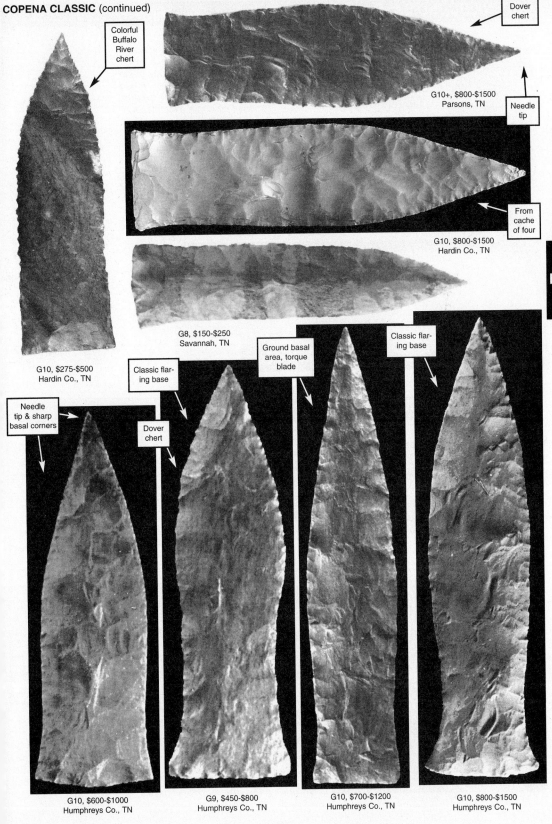

Colorful Buffalo River chert

Dover chert

G10+, $800-$1500
Parsons, TN

Needle tip

From cache of four

G10, $800-$1500
Hardin Co., TN

G8, $150-$250
Savannah, TN

EC

G10, $275-$500
Hardin Co., TN

Needle tip & sharp basal corners

Dover chert

Classic flaring base

Ground basal area, torque blade

Classic flaring base

G10, $600-$1000
Humphreys Co., TN

G9, $450-$800
Humphreys Co., TN

G10, $700-$1200
Humphreys Co., TN

G10, $800-$1500
Humphreys Co., TN

COPENA-ROUND BASE - Late Archaic to Woodland, 4000 - 1200 B. P.

(Also see Frazier & Tennessee River)

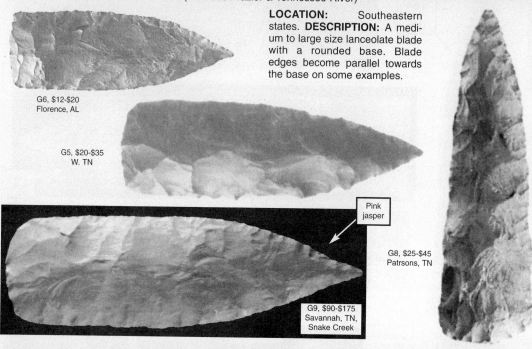

LOCATION: Southeastern states. **DESCRIPTION:** A medium to large size lanceolate blade with a rounded base. Blade edges become parallel towards the base on some examples.

G6, $12-$20
Florence, AL

G5, $20-$35
W. TN

Pink jasper

G8, $25-$45
Patrsons, TN

G9, $90-$175
Savannah, TN,
Snake Creek

COPENA-TRIANGULAR - Late Archaic to Woodland, 4000 - 1800 B. P.

(See Benton Blade, Frazier and Stanfield)

G3, $2-$5
Walker Co., AL

G8, $35-$60
Greene Co., OH

G7, $20-$35
Patrsons, TN

G5, $20-$35
Bristol, TN

G5, $15-$25
N.W. AL

G8, $30-$50
Dayton, TN

G8, $30-$50
New Era, TN

LOCATION: Southeastern states. **DESCRIPTION:** A medium to large size lanceolate blade with a straight base. Blade edges become parallel towards the base. Some examples show a distinct hafting area near the base where the blade edges form a very weak shoulder and become slightly concave.

COPENA TRIANGULAR (continued)

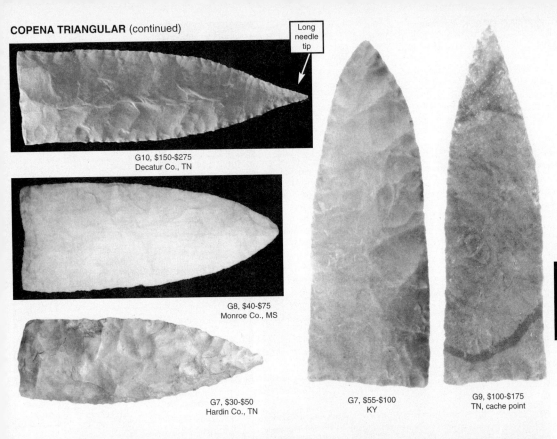

Long needle tip

G10, $150-$275
Decatur Co., TN

G8, $40-$75
Monroe Co., MS

G7, $30-$50
Hardin Co., TN

G7, $55-$100
KY

G9, $100-$175
TN, cache point

COTACO CREEK - Woodland, 2500 - 2000 B. P.

(Also see Flint Creek, Little Bear Creek, Smithsonia and Table Rock)

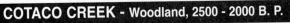

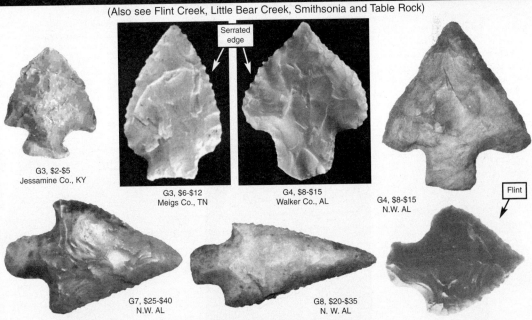

Serrated edge

G3, $2-$5
Jessamine Co., KY

G3, $6-$12
Meigs Co., TN

G4, $8-$15
Walker Co., AL

G4, $8-$15
N.W. AL

Flint

G7, $25-$40
N.W. AL

G8, $20-$35
N. W. AL

G3, $5-$12
Walker Co., AL

LOCATION: Southeastern states. **DESCRIPTION:** A small to medium size, well made, broad, triangular stemmed point with wide rounded to square shoulders. Blade edges are usually finely serrated and some examples have blunt tips. **I.D. KEY:** Edgework and rounded shoulders.

363

Serrated edge

G5, $15-$25
N.W. AL

G7, $35-$65
Jackson Co., AL

G8, $35-$65
TN

G6, $30-$50
TN

Classic form

G9, $250-$450
Florence, AL

Note fine sec-
ondary flaking
along edge &
at tip

G7, $35-$65
Savannah, TN

Classic
"blunt" tip

Classic
"blunt" tip

Colorful
Buffalo
River chert

G9, $150-$250
TN

G8, $200-$350
Clifton, TN

G10, $300-$550
N. AL

COTACO CREEK BLADE - Woodland, 2500 - 2000 B. P.

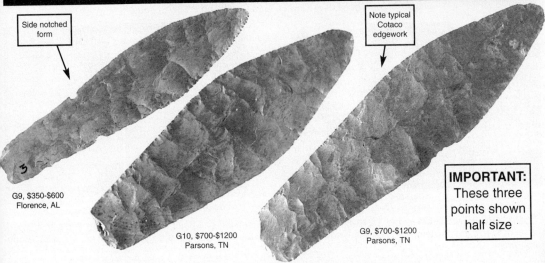

Side notched form

Note typical Cotaco edgework

G9, $350-$600
Florence, AL

G10, $700-$1200
Parsons, TN

G9, $700-$1200
Parsons, TN

IMPORTANT:
These three points shown half size

EC

LOCATION: Southeastern states. **DESCRIPTION:** A medium to large size lanceolate blade with a rounded base. Blade edges expand past mid-section. Some examples are side notched for hafting.

COTACO-WRIGHT - Woodland, 2500 - 1800 B. P.

(Also see Flint Creek and Little Bear Creek)

G9, $80-$150
Florence, AL

G5, $12-$20
N. W. AL

G6, $18-$35
Morgan Co., AL

G6, $15-$30
Morgan Co., AL

G9, $65-$125
N.W. AL

LOCATION: Southeastern states. **DESCRIPTION:** A small to medium size, well made, narrow, triangular stemmed point with rounded to square shoulders. Blade edges are usually finely serrated and some have blunt tips.

G9, $55-$100
N. W. AL

365

CRAWFORD CREEK - Early Archaic, 8000 - 5000 B. P.

(Also see Coosa, Kirk Corner, Mud Creek and White Springs)

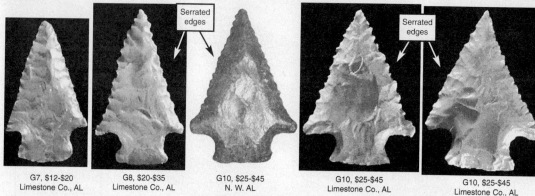

Serrated edges

Serrated edges

| G7, $12-$20 Limestone Co., AL | G8, $20-$35 Limestone Co., AL | G10, $25-$45 N. W. AL | G10, $25-$45 Limestone Co., AL | G10, $25-$45 Limestone Co., AL |

LOCATION: Southeastern states. **DESCRIPTION:** A small to medium size point that is usually serrated with a short, straight to expanding stem. Shoulders are square to tapered. Blade edges are straight to recurved. **I.D. KEY:** Early edgework.

CRESAP - Late Archaic to Woodland, 3000 - 2500 B. P.

(Also see Adena, Benton, Dickson)

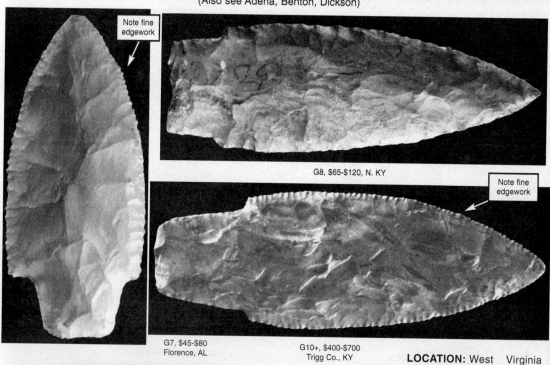

Note fine edgework

Note fine edgework

G8, $65-$120, N. KY

G7, $45-$80 Florence, AL

G10+, $400-$700 Trigg Co., KY

G9, $175-$300 W. KY

LOCATION: West Virginia into Kentucky. **DESCRIPTION:** A medium to large size point that has a medium-long contracting stem and slight shoulders. The base is usually straight. Stems can be ground. Associated with the early Adena culture. **I.D. KEY:** Long "squarish" tapered stem.

(Also see Beaver Lake, Clovis, Copena Auriculate and Quad)

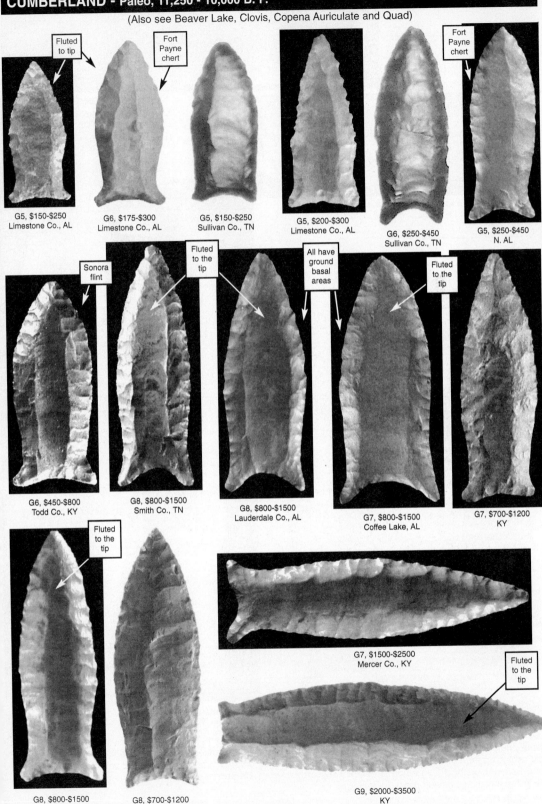

Fluted to tip

Fort Payne chert

EC

G5, $150-$250
Limestone Co., AL

G6, $175-$300
Limestone Co., AL

G5, $150-$250
Sullivan Co., TN

G5, $200-$300
Limestone Co., AL

G6, $250-$450
Sullivan Co., TN

Fort Payne chert

G5, $250-$450
N. AL

Sonora flint

Fluted to the tip

All have ground basal areas

Fluted to the tip

G6, $450-$800
Todd Co., KY

G8, $800-$1500
Smith Co., TN

G8, $800-$1500
Lauderdale Co., AL

G7, $800-$1500
Coffee Lake, AL

G7, $700-$1200
KY

Fluted to the tip

G7, $1500-$2500
Mercer Co., KY

Fluted to the tip

G8, $800-$1500
Taylor Co., KY

G8, $700-$1200
W. KY

G9, $2000-$3500
KY

367

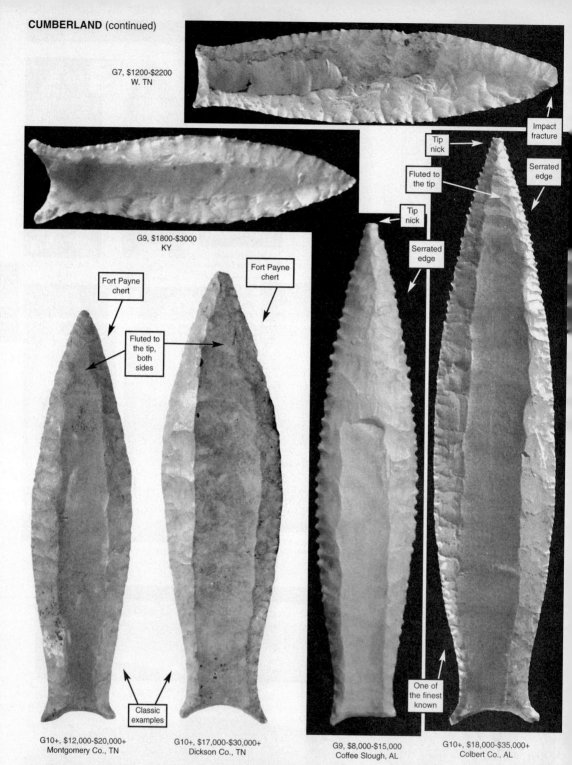

G7, $1200-$2200
W. TN

G9, $1800-$3000
KY

Tip nick

Fluted to the tip

Impact fracture

Serrated edge

Tip nick

Serrated edge

Fort Payne chert

Fort Payne chert

Fluted to the tip, both sides

Classic examples

One of the finest known

G10+, $12,000-$20,000+
Montgomery Co., TN

G10+, $17,000-$30,000+
Dickson Co., TN

G9, $8,000-$15,000
Coffee Slough, AL

G10+, $18,000-$35,000+
Colbert Co., AL

LOCATION: Southeastern states to Canada. **DESCRIPTION:** A medium to large size, lanceolate, eared form that is usually fluted on both faces. The fluting and flaking technique is an advanced form as in *Folsom*, with the flutes usually extending the entire length of the blade. Bases are ground on all examples. An unfluted variant which is thicker than *Beaver Lake* has been found. This point is scarce everywhere and has been reproduced in large numbers. **I.D. KEY:** Paleo flaking, indirect pressure fluting.

CYPRESS CREEK - Middle to Late Archaic, 5000 - 3000 B. P.

(Also see Benton, Hardin, Kirk Corner Notched, Harpeth River, Lost Lake & McIntire)

Dover

G8, $60-$100 Humphreys Co., TN

Classic drooping shoulders

Classic drooping shoulders

G5, $35-$60 Humphreys Co., TN

G6, $40-$70 Giles Co., TN

EC

G9, $650-$1200 Benton Co., TN

LOCATION: Southeastern states. **DESCRIPTION:** A medium to large size, broad stemmed point with an expanded base and drooping "umbrella" shoulder tangs. A cross between Lost Lake and Kirk Corner Notched. The blade is beveled on all four sides. **I.D. KEY:** Archaic flaking, shoulders droop.

DAGGER - Late Archaic to Woodland, 4000 - 1500 B. P.

(Also see Duck River Sword and Mace)

Dover chert

G8, $1000-$1800 Humphreys Co., TN

IMPORTANT: Daggers shown half size

G8, $600-$1000 Hickman Co., TN

DAGGER (continued)

LOCATION: Southeastern states. **DESCRIPTION:** A large size knife with a handle fashioned for holding or for hafting. Most examples have a very thick cross section and are rare everywhere. Beware of counterfeits.

DALTON-CLASSIC - Early Archaic, 10,000 - 9200 B. P.

(Also see Clovis, Debert and Hardaway)

Red jasper

Beveled edge

Fort Payne chert

Made into a perforator

G2, $5-$10
Polk Co., TN

G5, $20-$35
MS

G5, $30-$50
Coffee Lake, AL

G6, $30-$50
TN

G6, $65-$125
AL

Made into a blunt

G5, $20-$35
IN

G5, $25-$45
KY

G8, $80-$150
KY

G8, $100-$175
TN

G9, $125-$200
Monroe Co., MS

G8, $65-$125
TN

G8, $100-$175
TN

LOCATION: Midwestern to Southeastern states. **DESCRIPTION:** A medium to large size, thin, auriculate, fishtailed point. Many examples are finely serrated and exhibit excellent flaking. Beveling may occur on one side of each face but is usually on the right side. All have basal grinding. This early type spread over most of the Eastern and Midwestern U.S. and strongly influenced many other types to follow.

DALTON CLASSIC (continued)

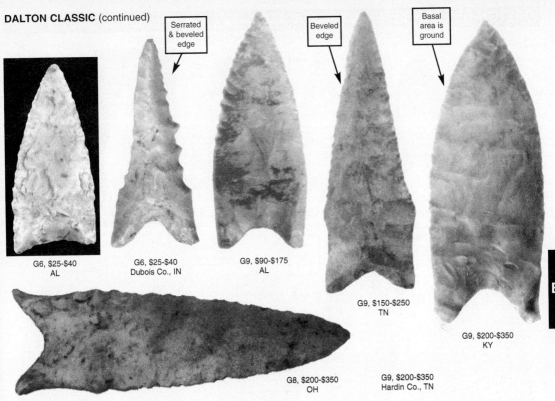

Serrated & beveled edge

Beveled edge

Basal area is ground

G6, $25-$40
AL

G6, $25-$40
Dubois Co., IN

G9, $90-$175
AL

G9, $150-$250
TN

G9, $200-$350
KY

G8, $200-$350
OH

G9, $200-$350
Hardin Co., TN

EC

DALTON-COLBERT - Early Archaic, 10,000 - 9200 B. P.

(Also see Beaver Lake, Dalton-Nuckolls, Plainview and Searcy)

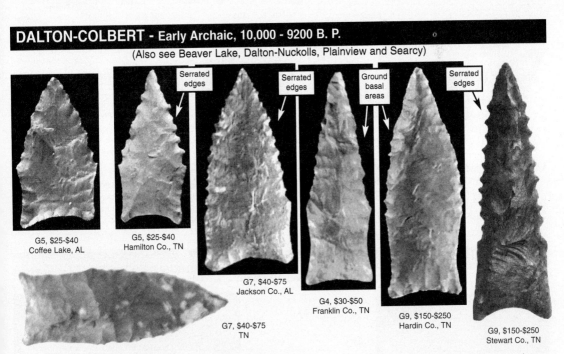

Serrated edges

Serrated edges

Ground basal areas

Serrated edges

G5, $25-$40
Coffee Lake, AL

G5, $25-$40
Hamilton Co., TN

G7, $40-$75
Jackson Co., AL

G7, $40-$75
TN

G4, $30-$50
Franklin Co., TN

G9, $150-$250
Hardin Co., TN

G9, $150-$250
Stewart Co., TN

LOCATION: Midwestern to Southeastern states. **DESCRIPTION:** A medium size, auriculate form with a squared stem and a weakly defined hafting area which is ground. Some examples are serrated and exhibit parallel flaking of the highest quality. **I.D. KEY:** Squarish basal area.

DALTON-GREENBRIER - Early Archaic, 10,000 - 9200 B. P.

(Also see Beaver Lake, Greenbrier, Hardaway and Haw River)

Tip wear

G6, $12-$20
TN

G6, $20-$35
Meigs Co., TN

G5 $25-$40
KY

G6, $25-$40
Adams Co., MS

G8, $40-$75
Hamilton Co., TN

G6, $30-$50
TN

Petrified wood

Ground basal area

Serrated edge

Tip wear

G9, $150-$250
Pontotac Co., MS

G9, $80-$150
Alcorn Co., MS

G8, $55-$100
Pontotac Co., MS

G9, $80-$150
TN

G6, $30-$50
Meigs Co., TN

Serrated edge

G8, $55-$100
TN

G9, $200-$350
Cumberland Riv., TN

Serrated edge

LOCATION: Midwestern to Eastern states and Florida. **DESCRIPTION:** A medium to large size, auriculate form with a concave base and drooping to expanding auricles. Many examples are serrated, some are fluted on both sides, and all have basal grinding. Resharpened examples are usually beveled on the right side of each face although left side beveling does occur. Thinness and high quality flaking is evident on many examples. This early type spread over most the U.S. and strongly influenced many other types to follow. **I.D. KEY:** Expanded auricles.

DALTON-HEMPHILL - Early Archaic, 10,000 - 9200 B. P.

(Also see Cave Spring, Hardaway and Holland)

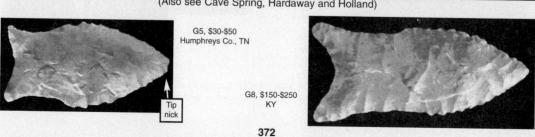

G5, $30-$50
Humphreys Co., TN

G8, $150-$250
KY

Tip nick

372

DALTON HEMPHILL (continued)

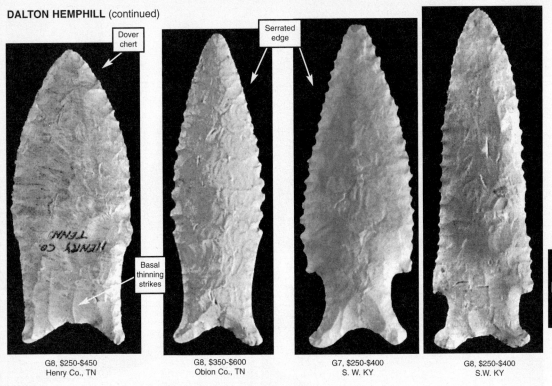

Dover chert

Serrated edge

Basal thinning strikes

HENRY CO. TENN

G8, $250-$450
Henry Co., TN

G8, $350-$600
Obion Co., TN

G7, $250-$400
S. W. KY

G8, $250-$400
S.W. KY

LOCATION: Midwestern to Eastern states. **DESCRIPTION:** A medium to large size point with expanded auricles and horizontal, tapered to weak shoulders. Blade edges are usually serrated and bases are ground. In later times, this variant developed into the *Hemphill* point. **I.D. KEY:** Straightened extended shoulders.

DALTON-NUCKOLLS - Early Archaic, 10,000 - 9200 B. P.

(Also see Dalton-Colbert and Hardaway)

Collateral flaking

G5, $15-$25
KY

Dover chert

G5, $30-$40
KY

G6, $40-$75
KY

G8, $45-$85
Humphreys Co., TN

G6, $30-$50
Humphreys Co., TN

LOCATION: Midwestern to Southeastern states. Type site is in Humphreys Co., TN. **DESCRIPTION:** A medium to large size variant form, probably occuring from resharpening the Greenbrier Dalton. Bases are squared to lobbed to eared, and have a shallow concavity. **I.D. KEY:** Broad base and shoulders, flaking on blade.

373

DALTON-NUCKOLLS (continued)

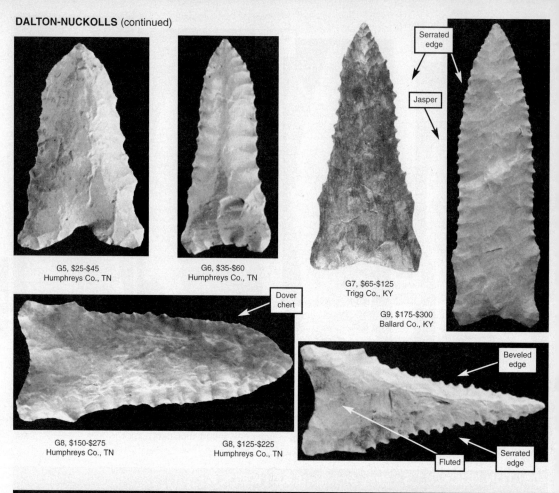

G5, $25-$45
Humphreys Co., TN

G6, $35-$60
Humphreys Co., TN

Serrated edge

Jasper

G7, $65-$125
Trigg Co., KY

G9, $175-$300
Ballard Co., KY

Dover chert

G8, $150-$275
Humphreys Co., TN

G8, $125-$225
Humphreys Co., TN

Beveled edge

Fluted

Serrated edge

DAMRON - Early to Middle Archaic, 8000 - 4000 B. P.

(Also see Autauga, Ecusta, Gibson, Palmer and St. Charles)

G6, $8-$15
S.E. TN

G7, $15-$25
Limestone Co., AL

G7, $15-$25
Humphreys Co., TN

G5, $6-$12
Limestone Co., AL

G9, $35-$60
Florence, AL

LOCATION: Southeastern states. **DESCRIPTION:** A small to medium size, triangular, side-notched point with a wide, prominent, convex to straight base. **I.D. KEY:** Basal form.

374

DEBERT- Paleo, 11,000 - 9500 B. P.

(Also see Clovis and Dalton)

LOCATION: Northeastern to Eastern states.
DESCRIPTION: A medium to large size, thin, auriculate point that evolved from *Clovis.* Most examples are fluted twice on each face resulting in a deep basal concavity. The second flute usually removed traces of the first fluting. A very rare form of late *Clovis.* **I.D. KEY:** Deep basal notch.

G8, $800-$1500
KY

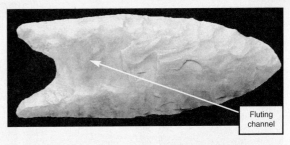

Fluting channel

DECATUR - Early Archaic, 9000 - 3000 B. P.

(Also see Cobbs Triangular, Ecusta, Hardin, Kirk, Lost Lake, Palmer and St. Charles)

EC

Beveled edge

Burinated tip

All Decaturs have ground basal areas

Fractured shoulders and basal sides

Fractured base

Base not fractured

G8, $55-$100
Hamilton Co., TN

Actual size photos of an excellent example found in Hamilton Co., TN. These oblique photos illustrate the fractured tangs, stem sides and base that occur on this type. In rare cases the tip is also fractured on both sides. Shoulder and base fracturing also occurs in Abbey, Dovetail, Kirk and other Archaic forms.

Beveled edge

Beveled edge

Beveled edge

Beveled edge

Beveled edge

G3, $12-$20
Sullivan Co., TN

G6, $35-$60
Florence, AL

G6, $35-$60
Dayton, TN

G5, $20-$35
Walker Co., AL

G6, $35-$60
S. E. TN

G7, $40-$75
Colbert Co., AL

LOCATION: Eastern states. **DESCRIPTION:** A small to medium size, serrated, corner notched point that is usually beveled on one side of each face. The base is usually broken off (fractured) by a blow inward from each corner of the stem. Sometimes the sides of the stem and backs of the tangs are also fractured, and rarely the tip may be fractured by a blow on each side directed towards the base. Bases are usually ground and flaking is of high quality. Basal/shoulder fracturing also occurs in *Dovetail, Eva, Kirk, Motley* and *Snyders.* Unfractured forms are called *Angelico Corner-Notched* in Virginia.

Beveled edge

G6, $65-$125
Coffee Lake, AL

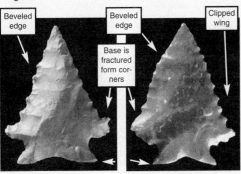

Beveled edge

Beveled edge

Clipped wing

Base is fractured form corners

G9, $125-$200
Humphreys Co., TN

G9, $125-$200
Huntsville, AL

Beveled edge

Beveled edge

G9, $150-$250
Coffee Slough, AL

G7, $125-$100
Sullivan Co., TN

375

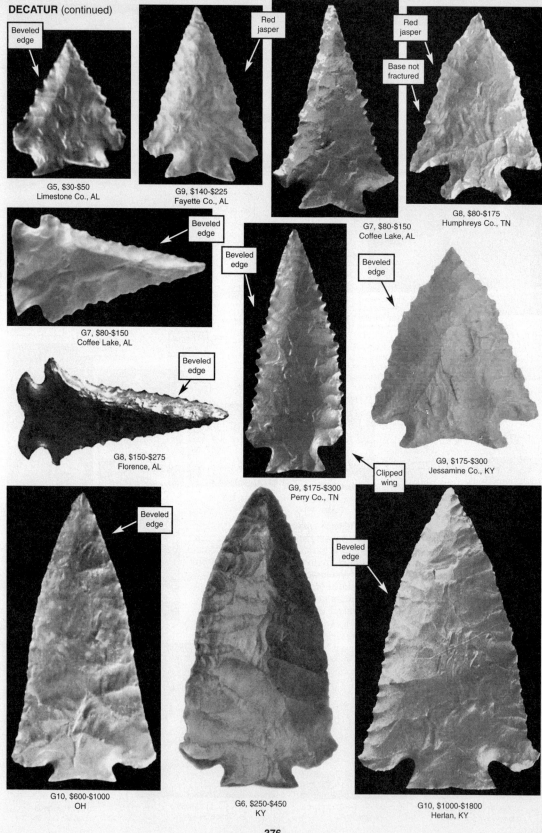

Beveled edge

G5, $30-$50
Limestone Co., AL

Red jasper

G9, $140-$225
Fayette Co., AL

Red jasper

Base not fractured

G7, $80-$150
Coffee Lake, AL

G8, $80-$175
Humphreys Co., TN

Beveled edge

G7, $80-$150
Coffee Lake, AL

Beveled edge

Beveled edge

Beveled edge

G9, $175-$300
Jessamine Co., KY

Beveled edge

G8, $150-$275
Florence, AL

Clipped wing

G9, $175-$300
Perry Co., TN

Beveled edge

Beveled edge

G10, $600-$1000
OH

G6, $250-$450
KY

G10, $1000-$1800
Herlan, KY

376

DECATUR BLADE - Early Archaic, 9000 - 3000 B. P.

(Also see Hardaway Blade)

LOCATION: Eastern states. **DESCRIPTION:** A medium to large size, broad triangular blade with rounded corners and a straight base. A preform for *Decatur* points found on Decatur chipping sites.

G7, $5-$10
Morgan Co., AL. Found on a Decatur chipping site along with dozens of Decatur points.

DICKSON - Woodland, 2500 - 1500 B. P.

(Also see Adena, Cresap, Gary, Morrow Mountain and Waubesa)

G5, $8-$15
KY

G7, $25-$45
KY

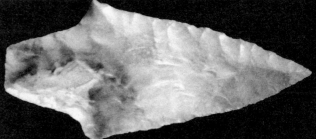

G8, $125-$225
OH

G9, $80-$150
KY

G8, $125-$225
OH

LOCATION: Midwestern states. Type site: Fulton Co., MO., Dickson mounds, Don F. Dickson, 1927. **DESCRIPTION:** A medium to large size point with tapered shoulders and a contracting stem. High quality flaking and thinness is evident on most examples. **I.D. KEY:** Basal form.

G8, $125-$225
OH

EC

DOVETAIL (See St. Charles)

DRILL - Paleo to Historic, 14,000 - 200 B. P.

(Also see Addison Micro-Drill and Scraper)

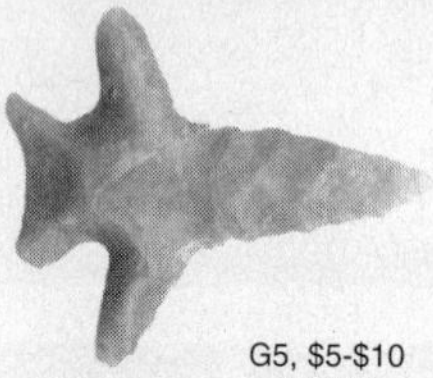

G5, $5-$10
W. TN

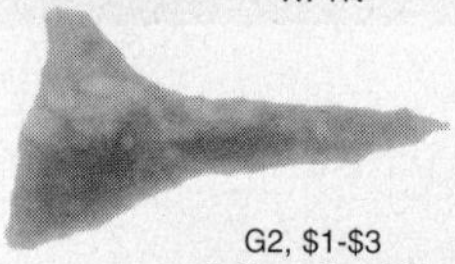

G2, $1-$3
Sullivan Co., TN

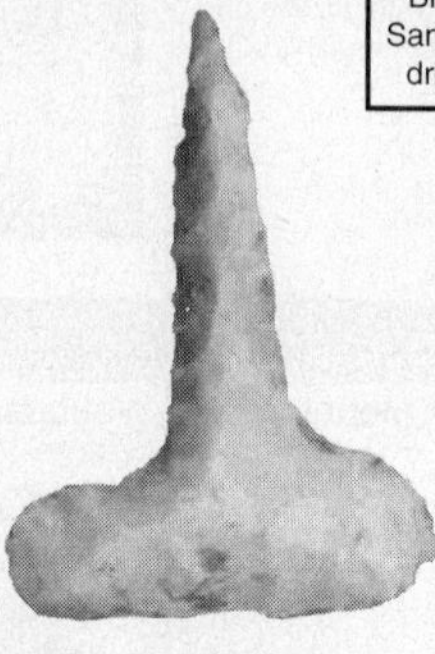

G4, $5-$15
Jessamine Co., KY

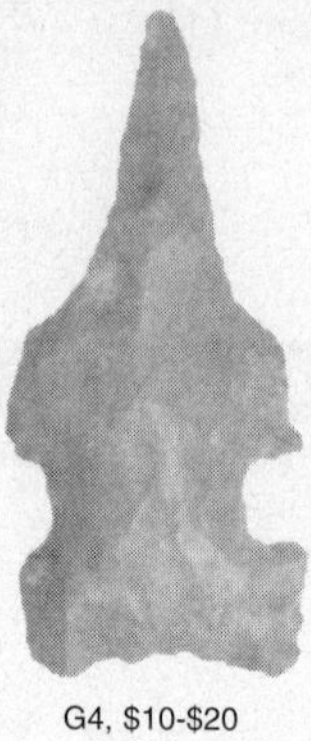
Big Sandy drill

G4, $10-$20
KY

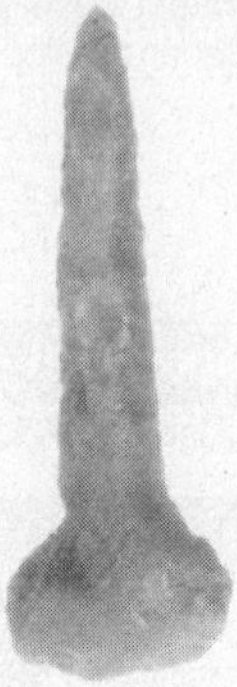

G4, $10-$20
KY

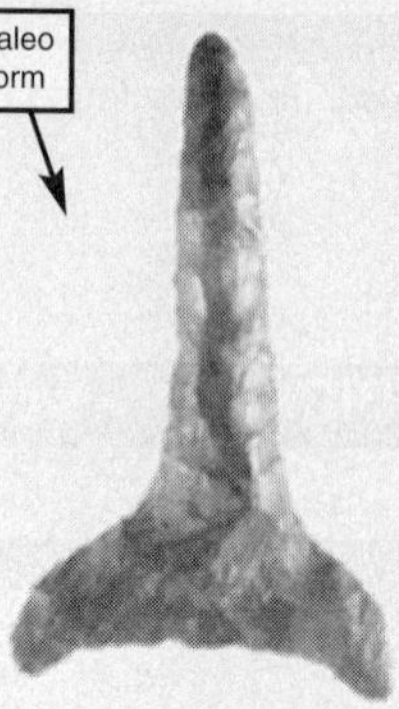
Paleo form

G5, $25-$40
OH

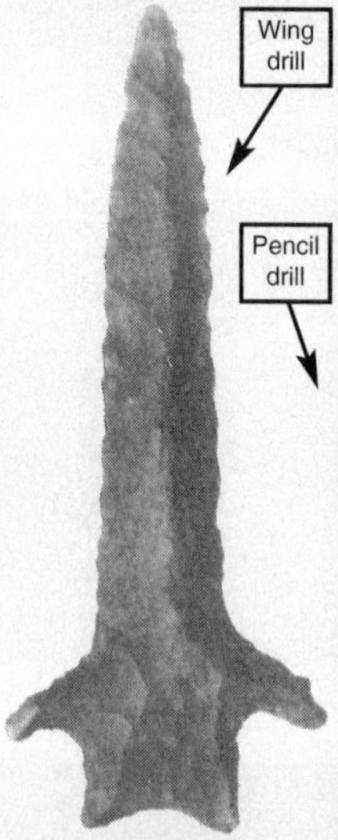
Wing drill
Pencil drill

G9, $150-$250
KY

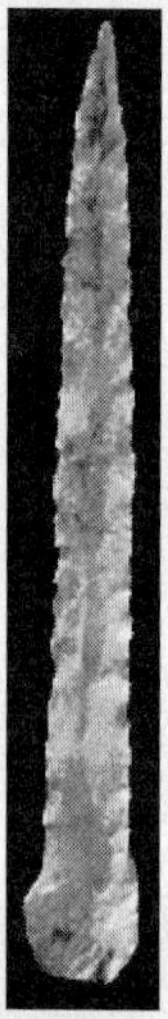

G8, $35-$60
OH

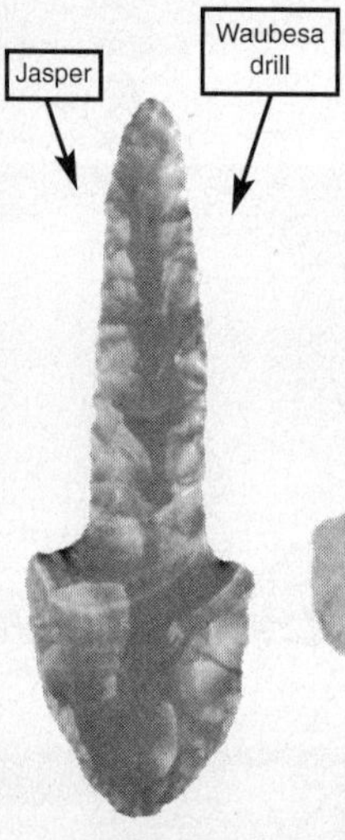
Jasper
Waubesa drill

G8, $45-$80
TN

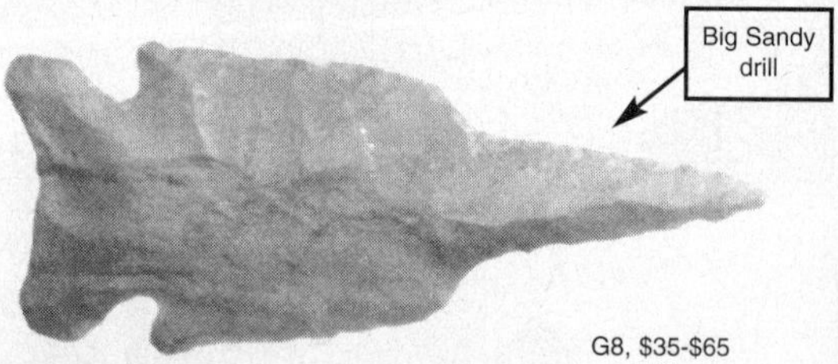
Big Sandy drill

G8, $35-$65
KY

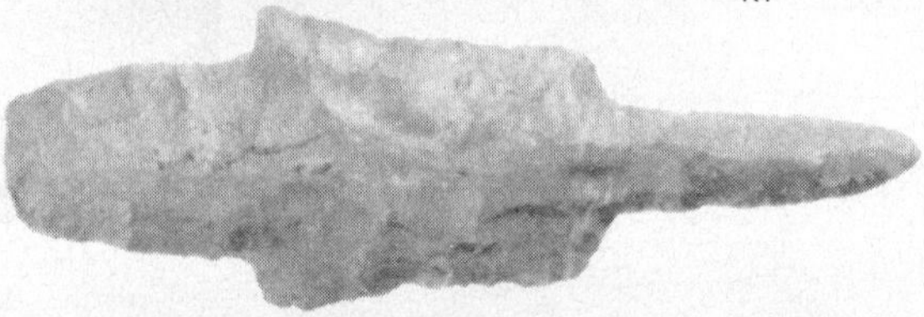

G9, $45-$80
AL

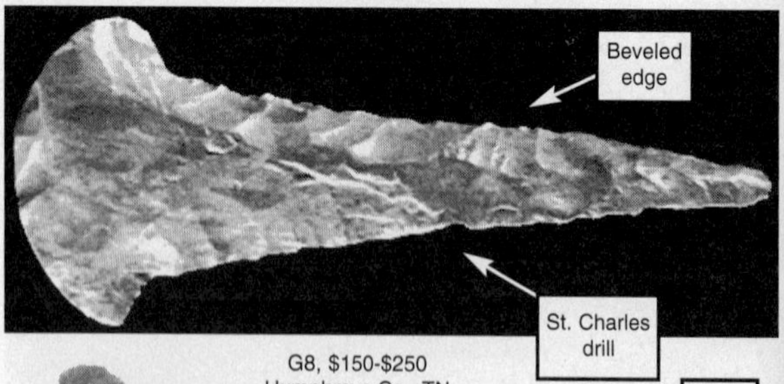
Beveled edge
St. Charles drill

G8, $150-$250
Humphreys Co., TN

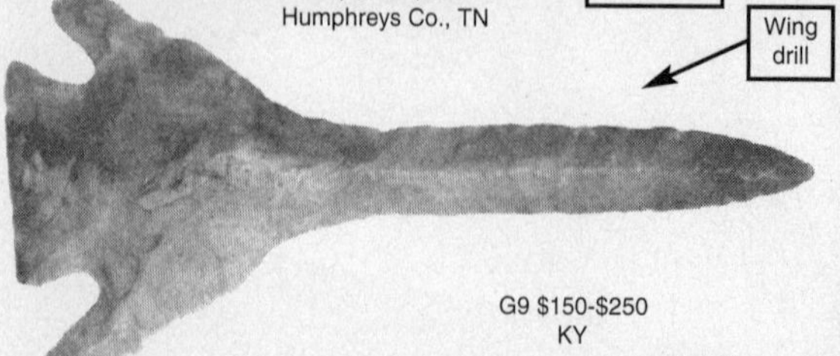
Wing drill

G9 $150-$250
KY

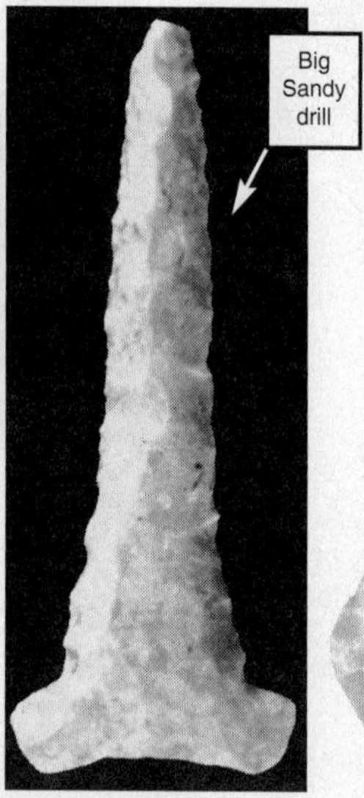
Big Sandy drill

G7, $35-$60
KY

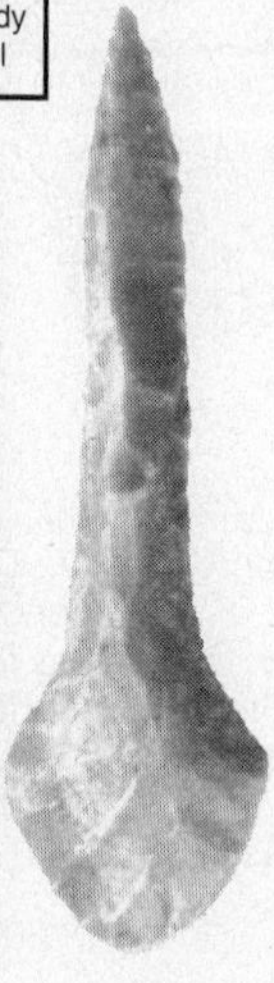

G8, $30-$50
TN

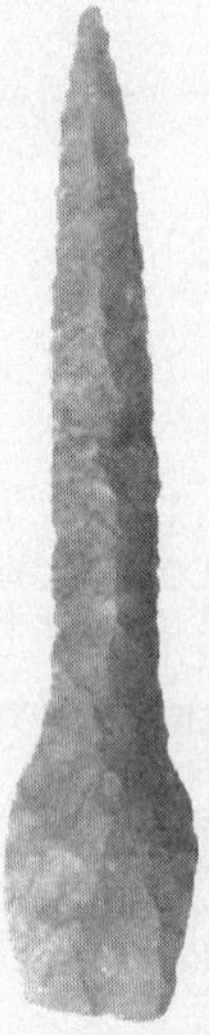

G8 $30-$50
KY

DRILL (continued)

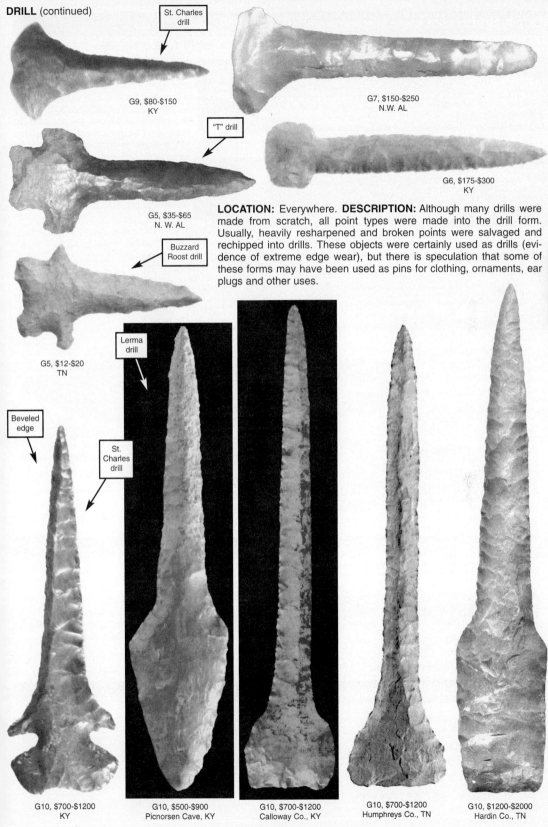

St. Charles drill

G9, $80-$150
KY

G7, $150-$250
N.W. AL

"T" drill

G6, $175-$300
KY

G5, $35-$65
N. W. AL

Buzzard Roost drill

LOCATION: Everywhere. **DESCRIPTION:** Although many drills were made from scratch, all point types were made into the drill form. Usually, heavily resharpened and broken points were salvaged and rechipped into drills. These objects were certainly used as drills (evidence of extreme edge wear), but there is speculation that some of these forms may have been used as pins for clothing, ornaments, ear plugs and other uses.

EC

G5, $12-$20
TN

Lerma drill

Beveled edge

St. Charles drill

G10, $700-$1200
KY

G10, $500-$900
Picnorsen Cave, KY

G10, $700-$1200
Calloway Co., KY

G10, $700-$1200
Humphreys Co., TN

G10, $1200-$2000
Hardin Co., TN

379

DUCK RIVER SWORD - Mississippian, 1100 - 600 B. P.

(Also see Adena Blade, Dagger, Mace, Morse Knife, Sun Disk and Tear Drop)

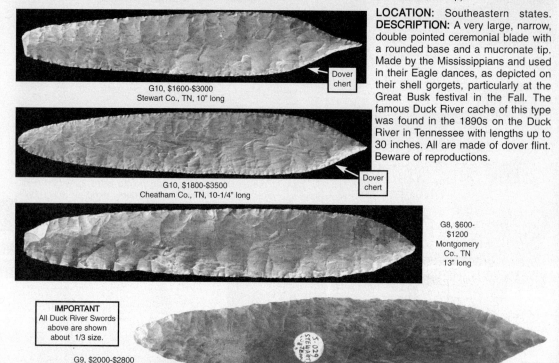

LOCATION: Southeastern states.
DESCRIPTION: A very large, narrow, double pointed ceremonial blade with a rounded base and a mucronate tip. Made by the Mississippians and used in their Eagle dances, as depicted on their shell gorgets, particularly at the Great Busk festival in the Fall. The famous Duck River cache of this type was found in the 1890s on the Duck River in Tennessee with lengths up to 30 inches. All are made of dover flint. Beware of reproductions.

G10, $1600-$3000
Stewart Co., TN, 10" long

Dover chert

G10, $1800-$3500
Cheatham Co., TN, 10-1/4" long

Dover chert

G8, $600-$1200
Montgomery Co., TN
13" long

IMPORTANT
All Duck River Swords above are shown about 1/3 size.

G9, $2000-$2800
Stewart Co., TN

Dover chert

G10, $3000-$4800
TN

DUVAL - Late Woodland, 2000 - 1000 B. P.

(Also see Bradley Spike, Fishspear & Mountain Fork)

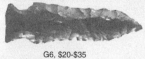

G6, $20-$35
Bristol, TN

G6, $20-$35
Catoosa Co.,GA

LOCATION: Southeastern states.
DESCRIPTION: A small to medium size, narrow, spike point with shallow side notches and a straight to concave base. The base can be slight to moderate.

EARLY OVOID KNIFE - Trans. Paleo-early Archaic, 11,000 - 8000 B. P.

(Also see Turkeytail)

LOCATION: Midwestern states from Kentucky, Arkansas north to Wisconsin and Michigan. **DESCRIPTION:** A medium to very large size, broad, thin blade that comes in two forms. It can be bi-pointed or it can have a small, rounded stem created by side notches. **I.D. KEY:** Stem size and blade form.

IMPORTANT
All Early Ovoid Knives are shown 1/2 size.

G10, $400-$700
KY

EARLY OVOID KNIFE (continued)

G9, $550-$1000
KY

G9, $800-$1500
KY

G10, $350-$600
KY

> **IMPORTANT**
> All Early Ovoid Knives
> are shown 1/2 size.

EASTERN STEMMED LANCEOLATE - Early Archaic, 9500 - 7000 B. P.
(Also see Alberta and Stringtown)

Upper Mercer chert

Impact fracture

Ground stem

Coshocton chert

G6, $150-$250
Washington Co., OH

G7, $150-$275
OH

G7, $200-$350
Delaware Co., OH

EC

LOCATION: Pennsylvania, Ohio westward. **DESCRIPTION:** A medium to large size, broad stemmed point with convex to parallel sides and square shoulders. The stem is parallel sided to slightly expanding. The hafting area is ground. Most examples have horizontal to oblique parallel flaking and are of high quality and thinness. The Eastern form of the *Scottsbluff* type made by the Cody Complex people. The *Stringtown* is an eared version of this type. **I.D. KEY:** Base form and parallel flaking.

EBENEZER - Woodland, 2000 - 1500 B. P.
(Also see Buggs Island, Gary, Montgomery and Morrow Mountain)

Milky quartz

Milky quartz

LOCATION: Southeastern states. **DESCRIPTION:** A small size, broad, triangular point with a short, rounded stem. Some are round base triangles with no stem. Shoulders are tapered to square. Very similar to the earlier *Morrow Mountain Round Base* but with random Woodland chipping. Related to *Candy Creek, Camp Creek* and *Nolichucky.*

G5, $2-$4
Morgan Co., AL

G4, $2-$4
Dallas Co., AL

G4, $2-$4
Dallas Co., AL

G4, $2-$4
Dallas Co., AL

ECUSTA - Early Archaic, 8000 - 5000 B. P.

(Also see Autauga, Brewerton, Damron, Decatur and Palmer)

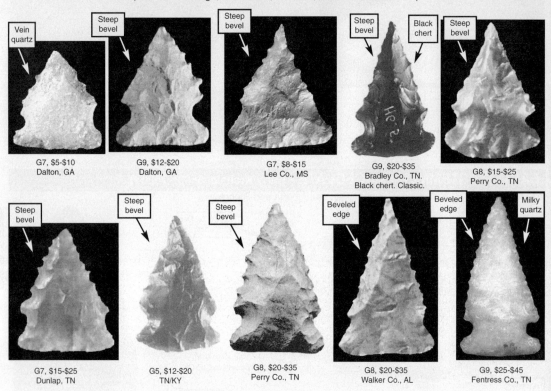

G7, $5-$10
Dalton, GA

G9, $12-$20
Dalton, GA

G7, $8-$15
Lee Co., MS

G9, $20-$35
Bradley Co., TN.
Black chert. Classic.

G8, $15-$25
Perry Co., TN

G7, $15-$25
Dunlap, TN

G5, $12-$20
TN/KY

G8, $20-$35
Perry Co., TN

G8, $20-$35
Walker Co., AL

G9, $25-$45
Fentress Co., TN

LOCATION: Southeastern states. **DESCRIPTION:** A small size, serrated, side-notched point with usually one side of each face steeply beveled. Although examples exist with all four sides beveled and flaked to a median ridge. The base and notches are ground. Very similar to *Autauga*, with the latter being corner-notched and not beveled.

ELK RIVER - Early Archaic, 8000 - 5000 B. P.

(Also see Benton and Buzzard Roost Creek)

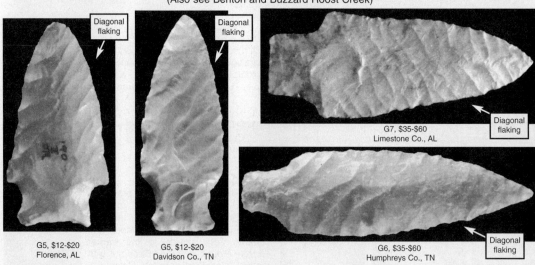

G7, $35-$60
Limestone Co., AL

G5, $12-$20
Florence, AL

G5, $12-$20
Davidson Co., TN

G6, $35-$60
Humphreys Co., TN

LOCATION: Southeastern states. **DESCRIPTION:** A medium to large size, narrow, stemmed blade with oblique parallel flaking. Shoulders are tapered, straight or barbed. Stems are parallel, contracting, expanding, bulbous or bifurcated. Believed to be related to *Benton* points. **I.D. KEY:** Squared base, diagonal parallel flaking.

EC

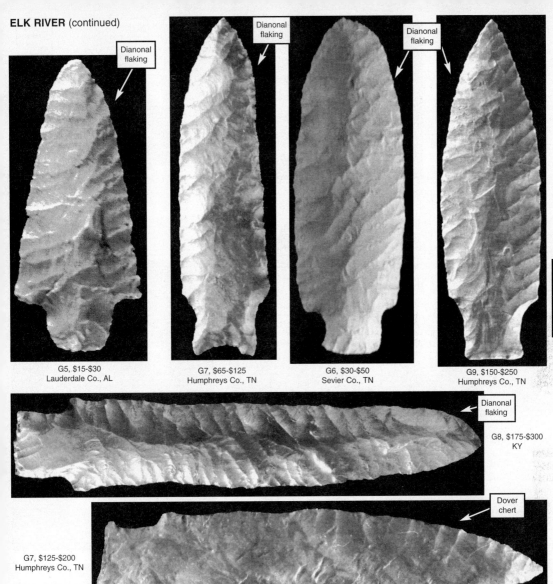

G5, $15-$30
Lauderdale Co., AL

G7, $65-$125
Humphreys Co., TN

G6, $30-$50
Sevier Co., TN

G9, $150-$250
Humphreys Co., TN

Dianonal flaking

Dianonal flaking

Dianonal flaking

Dianonal flaking

Dianonal flaking

G8, $175-$300
KY

Dover chert

G7, $125-$200
Humphreys Co., TN

ELORA - Middle to Late Archaic, 6000 - 3000 B. P.

(Also see Maples, Morrow Mountain, Pickwick, Savannah River and Shoals Creek)

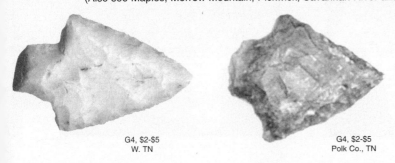

G4, $2-$5
W. TN

G4, $2-$5
Polk Co., TN

LOCATION: Southeastern states. **DESCRIPTION:** A medium size, broad, thick point with tapered shoulders and a short, contracting stem that is sometimes fractured or snapped off. However, some examples have finished bases. Early examples are serrated. **I.D. KEY:** One barb sharper, edgework.

Conglomerate

G3, $2-$5
Polk Co., TN

G5, $8-$15
Colbert Co., AL

Classic rind base

G5, $5-$10
Jackson Co., AL

Classic rind base

Note fine serrations

Serrated edge

G6, $25-$40
GA

G6, $25-$40
GA

Serrated edge

G7, $30-$50
Andersonville, GA

Serrated edge

G9, $80-$150
Warner Robbins, GA

Serrated edge

G9, $65-$125
Lee Co., GA

384

EPPS - Late Archaic to Woodland, 4500 - 2500 B. P.

(Also see Buck Creek, Smithsonia, Motley, Snyders)

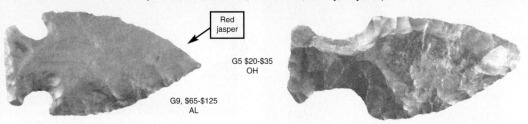

Red jasper

G5 $20-$35
OH

G9, $65-$125
AL

LOCATION: Southeastern states. **DESCRIPTION:** A Motley variant. A medium to large size, expanded stemmed to widely corner notched point with strong barbs. The blade edges and the base are convex to straight. Has been found associated with *Wade* points in caches. Similar to *Epps* found in Louisiana which has a straight base; *Motley*s are more barbed than *Epps*.

ETLEY - Late Archaic, 4000 - 2500 B. P.

(Also see Hardin, Mehlville, Pickwick and Stilwell)

LOCATION: Midwestern states. **DESCRIPTION:** A large size, narrow point with barbed shoulders, recurved blade edges and an expanding stem. **I.D. KEY:** One barb sharper, edgework.

IMPORTANT:
Etley shown
half size

G7, $150-$250
Warren Co., OH

G8, $200-$350
Dekalb Co., IN

EVA - Early to Middle Archaic, 8000 - 5000 B. P.

(Also see Hamilton Stemmed and Wade)

Black Dover chert

G4, $12-$20
TN

G3, $12-$20
W. TN

G4, $15-$25
Humphreys Co., TN

G8, $30-$50
W. TN

G6, $15-$30
KY

G6, $20-$35
TN

G7, $30-$50
KY

LOCATION: West Tennessee to SW Kentucky. Type site, Eva island in Humphreys Co., TN. **DESCRIPTION:** A medium to large size, triangular point with shallow basal notches, recurved sides and sometimes flaring barbs. Early examples show parallel flaking. A large Eva cache was found that included a Pickwick point. **I.D. KEY:** Basal notches, Archaic flaking.

385

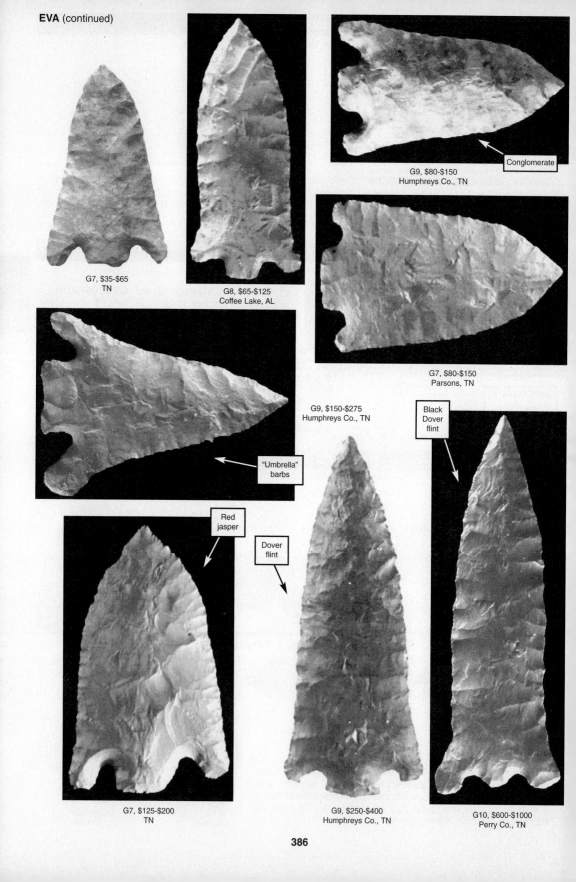

G9, $80-$150
Humphreys Co., TN

Conglomerate

G7, $35-$65
TN

G8, $65-$125
Coffee Lake, AL

G7, $80-$150
Parsons, TN

G9, $150-$275
Humphreys Co., TN

"Umbrella" barbs

Black Dover flint

Red jasper

Dover flint

G7, $125-$200
TN

G9, $250-$400
Humphreys Co., TN

G10, $600-$1000
Perry Co., TN

EVANS - Late Archaic to Woodland, 4000 - 2000 B. P.

(Also see Benton, Leighton, Merkle, Ohio Double-Notched, St. Helena, St. Tammany & Turkeytail)

Red jasper

G5, $15-$25
MS

G5, $15-$25
MS

G6, $20-$35
MS

G5, $12-$20
W. TN

G6, $25-$45
Natchez, MS

EC

G9, $65-$125
Choctaw Co., AL

G6, $20-$35
Natchez, MS

G5, $12-$20
Florence, AL

G9, $40-$75
Adams Co., MS

G6, $25-$40
Natchez, MS

LOCATION: Midwestern to Southeastern states. **DESCRIPTION:** A medium to large size stemmed point that is notched on each side somewhere between the point and shoulders. A similar form is found in Ohio and called *Ohio Double-Notched*.

EXOTIC FORMS - Mid-Archaic to Mississippian, 5000 - 1000 B. P.

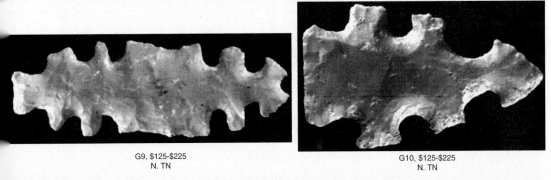

G9, $125-$225
N. TN

G10, $125-$225
N. TN

LOCATION: Throughout North America. **DESCRIPTION:** The forms illustrated on this and the following pages are very rare. Some are definitely effigy forms while others may be no more than unfinished and unintentional doodles.

FAIRLAND - Woodland, 3000 - 1500 B. P.

(Also see Bakers Creek, Hardaway, Johnson, Limestone and Steubenville)

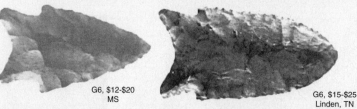

G6, $12-$20
MS

G6, $15-$25
Linden, TN

LOCATION: Texas, Arkansas, and Mississippi. **DESCRIPTION:** A small to medium size, thin, expanded stem point with a concave base that is usually thinned. Shoulders can be weak and tapered to sightly barbed. **I.D. KEY:** Basal form, systematic form of flaking.

FISHSPEAR - Early to Middle Archaic, 9000 - 4000 B. P.

(Also see Duval and Table Rock)

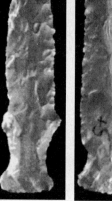

G5, $12-$20
S.E. TN

G5, $12-$20
TN

G7, $30-$50
W. TN

G8, $35-$60
OH

G9, $65-$125
Tallahatchie Co., MS

G9, $80-$150
Parsons, TN

G9, $125-$200
West TN

LOCATION: Eastern states. **DESCRIPTION:** A medium to large size, narrow, thick, point with wide side notches. Bases are usually ground and blade edges can be serrated. Named due to its appearance that resembles a fish.

FLINT CREEK - Late Archaic to Woodland, 3500 - 1000 B. P.

(Also see Cotaco Creek, Elora, Kirk Stemmed, Mud Creek and Pontchartrain)

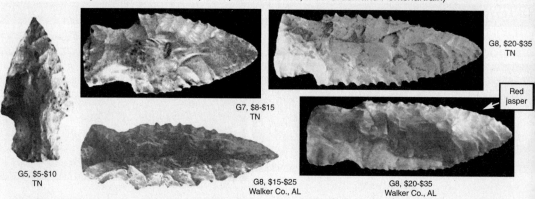

G5, $5-$10
TN

G7, $8-$15
TN

G8, $15-$25
Walker Co., AL

G8, $20-$35
TN

Red jasper

G8, $20-$35
Walker Co., AL

LOCATION: Southeastern and Gulf states. **DESCRIPTION:** A medium to large size, narrow, thick, serrated, expanded stem point. Shoulders can be horizontal, tapered or barbed. Base can be expanded, parallel sided or rounded. **I.D. KEY:** Thickness and flaking near point.

G6, $8-$15
Walker Co., AL

G6, $12-$20
Walker Co., AL

G6, $20-$35
Walker Co., AL

G6, $20-$35
Fayette, AL

Black & gray

EC

G9, $40-$75
Humphreys Co., TN

G7, $25-$45
Walker Co., AL

G8, $30-$55
Hardin Co., TN

G10, $100-$175
Florence, AL

G9, $90-$150
Florence, AL

FLINT RIVER SPIKE   (see McWhinney Heavy Stemmed)

FORT ANCIENT - Mississippian to Historic, 800 - 400 B. P.

(Also see Hamilton, Madison and Sand Mountain)

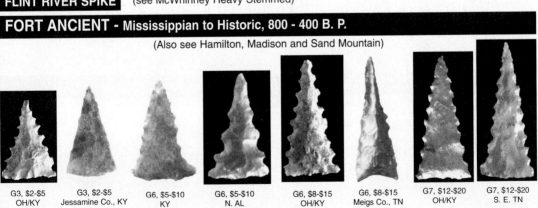

G3, $2-$5
OH/KY

G3, $2-$5
Jessamine Co., KY

G6, $5-$10
KY

G6, $5-$10
N. AL

G6, $8-$15
OH/KY

G6, $8-$15
Meigs Co., TN

G7, $12-$20
OH/KY

G7, $12-$20
S. E. TN

LOCATION: Southeastern states into Ohio. **DESCRIPTION:** A small to medium size, thin, narrow, long, triangular point with concave sides and a straight to slightly convex or concave base. Some examples are strongly serrated or notched. **I.D. KEY:** Edgework.

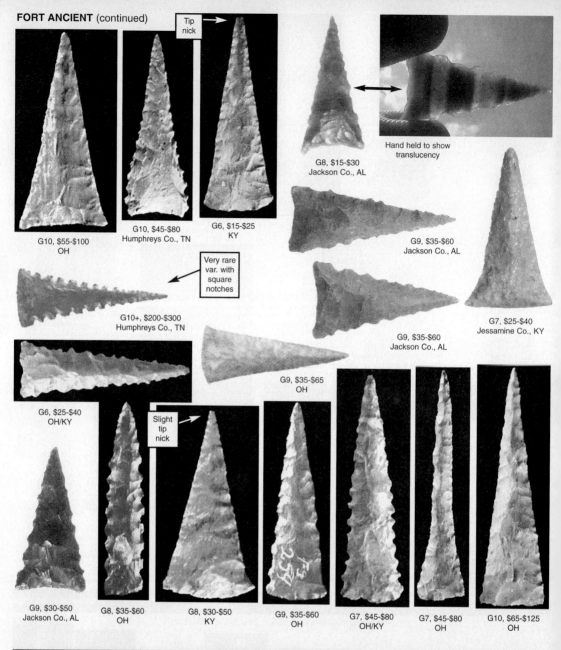

Tip
nick

G8, $15-$30
Jackson Co., AL

Hand held to show
translucency

G10, $55-$100
OH

G10, $45-$80
Humphreys Co., TN

G6, $15-$25
KY

G9, $35-$60
Jackson Co., AL

Very rare
var. with
square
notches

G10+, $200-$300
Humphreys Co., TN

G9, $35-$60
Jackson Co., AL

G7, $25-$40
Jessamine Co., KY

G6, $25-$40
OH/KY

G9, $35-$65
OH

Slight
tip
nick

G9, $30-$50
Jackson Co., AL

G8, $35-$60
OH

G8, $30-$50
KY

G9, $35-$60
OH

G7, $45-$80
OH/KY

G7, $45-$80
OH

G10, $65-$125
OH

FORT ANCIENT BLADE - Mississippian to Historic, 800 - 400 B. P.

(Also see Copena)

G8, $35-$65
KY

G8, $40-$75
Mason Co., KY

LOCATION: Eastern to Southeastern states. **DESCRIPTION:** A medium size triangular blade with a squared base. Blade edges expand to meet the base **I.D. KEY:** Basal form.

FORT ANCIENT BLADE (continued)

G5 $15-$30
N.E. AL

Thin
cross
section

G8, $45-$85
Whitwell, TN

FOUNTAIN CREEK - Early Archaic, 9000 - 7000 B. P.

(Also see Kirk Stemmed)

LOCATION: North Carolina into east Tennessee.
DESCRIPTION: A medium size, narrow point with notched blade edges and a short, rounded base which is ground. **I.D. KEY:** Edgework.

G10, $20-$35
Dayton, TN

Barbed edge

FOX VALLEY (See Kanawha for a similar type found in Ky, TN, AL to WVA)

EC

FRAZIER - Middle to Late Archaic, 7000 - 3000 B. P.

(Also see Big Sandy, Copena and Stanfield)

Black
flint

G9, $25-$40
W. TN

LOCATION: Southeastern states. **DESCRIPTION:** A generally narrow, medium to large size lanceolate blade with a slightly concave to straight base. Flaking technique and shape is identical to that of *Big Sandy* points (minus the notches) and is found on *Big Sandy* sites. Could this type be unnotched *Big Sandy's*? **I.D. KEY:** Archaic flaking.

FREDERICK - Early to Middle Archaic, 9000 - 4000 B. P.

(Also see Cave Spring, Fox Valley, Garth Slough, Jude, Kanawha, Kirk, LeCroy, Rice Lobbed and Stanly)

LOCATION: Southeastern states. **DESCRIPTION:** A small to medium size point with flaring, up-lifting shoulders and an extended narrow bifurcated base. A variation of the *Fox Valley* type. In the classic form, shoulders are almost bulbous and exaggerated.

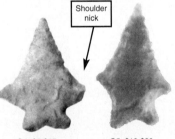

Shoulder
nick

G4, $8-$15
TN

G5, $12-$20
Walker Co., GA

G6, $20-$35
Cookeville, TN. Classic form.

G7, $35-$65
S.E. TN. Classic form.

GARTH SLOUGH - Early Archaic, 9000 - 4000 B. P.

(Also see Frederick, Jude, Kanawha and Stanly)

LOCATION: Southeastern states. **DESCRIPTION:** A small size point with wide, expanded barbs and a small squared base. Rare examples have the tangs clipped (called clipped wing). The blade edges are concave with fine serrations. A similar type of a later time period, called *Catahoula,* is found in Louisiana. A bifurcated base would place it into the *Kanawha* type. **I.D. KEY:** Expanded barbs, early flaking.

391

GARTH SLOUGH (continued)

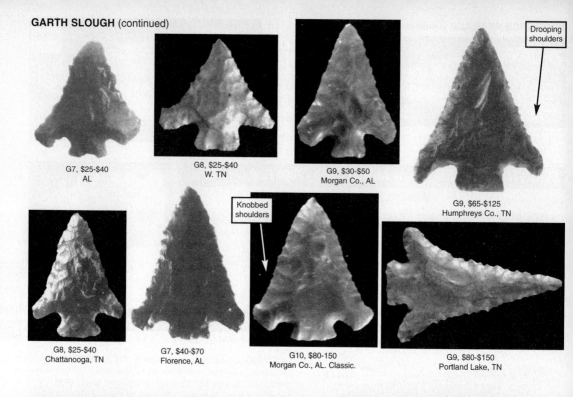

G7, $25-$40
AL

G8, $25-$40
W. TN

G9, $30-$50
Morgan Co., AL

Drooping
shoulders

G9, $65-$125
Humphreys Co., TN

G8, $25-$40
Chattanooga, TN

G7, $40-$70
Florence, AL

Knobbed
shoulders

G10, $80-150
Morgan Co., AL. Classic.

G9, $80-$150
Portland Lake, TN

GIBSON - Woodland, 2000 - 1500 B. P.

(Also see Hopewell, St. Charles and Snyders)

Hornstone
with
"bullesye"
pattern

G6, $35-$65
Trimble Co., KY

G7, $25-$45
KY

G7, $35-$65
KY

G7, $35-$65
OH

LOCATION: Midwestern to Eastern states. Type site is in Calhoun Co., Illinois. **DESCRIPTION:** A medium to large size side to corner notched point with a large, convex base. The base is typically broader than the blade. Made by the *Snyders* people. **I.D. KEY:** Short, broad base.

GRAHAM CAVE - Early to Mid-Archaic, 9000 - 5000 B. P.

(Also see Big Sandy, Newton Falls)

G6, $25-$40
TN

G5, $35-$60
KY

Very rare. Made from a fluted point

G9, $150-$250
KY

Note drooping ears

Jasper

Long channel flute

G7, $80-$150
W. KY

G9, $250-$450
Florence, AL

EC

G10 $400-$750
KY

LOCATION: Kentucky into midwestern states. **DESCRIPTION:** A medium to large size narrow, side-notched point with recurved sides, pointed auricles, and a concave base. Similar to White River points found in Ark. and OK. **I.D. KEY:** Drooping, pointed ears.

GRAVER - Paleo to Archaic, 11,500 - 4000 B. P.

(Also see Perforator and Scraper)

Graver points

G5, $8-$15
Humphreys Co., TN

G6 $20-$40
Humphreys Co., TN

Graver points

G3, $1-$2
Sullivan Co., TN

LOCATION: Found on Paleo and Archaic sites throughout North America. **DESCRIPTION:** An irregular shaped uniface tool with sharp, pointed projections used for puncturing, incising, tattooing, etc. Some examples served a dual purpose for scraping as well. In later times, *Perforators* took the place of *Gravers*.

393

GREENBRIER - Early Archaic, 9500 - 6000 B. P.

(Also see Brunswick, Dalton-Greenbrier, Hardaway and Pine Tree)

G5, $30-$50
Barkely Lake, KY

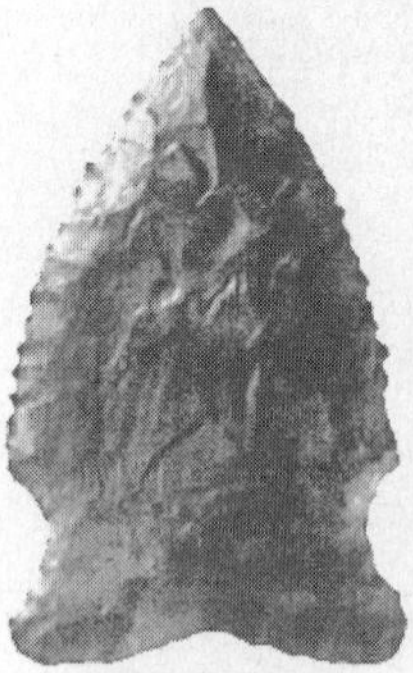

Buffalo River chert

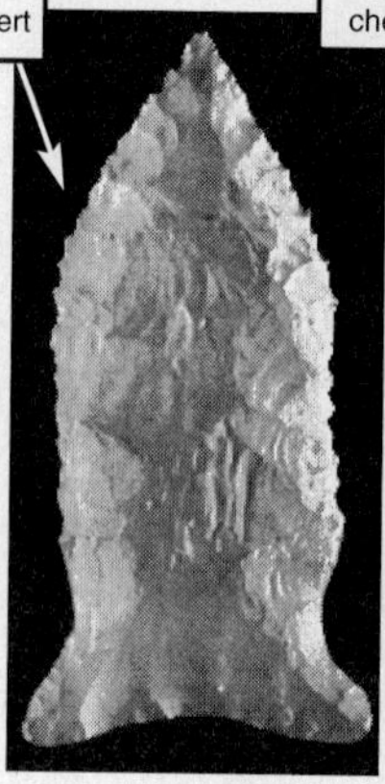

G6, $80-$150
Parsons, TN

Dover chert

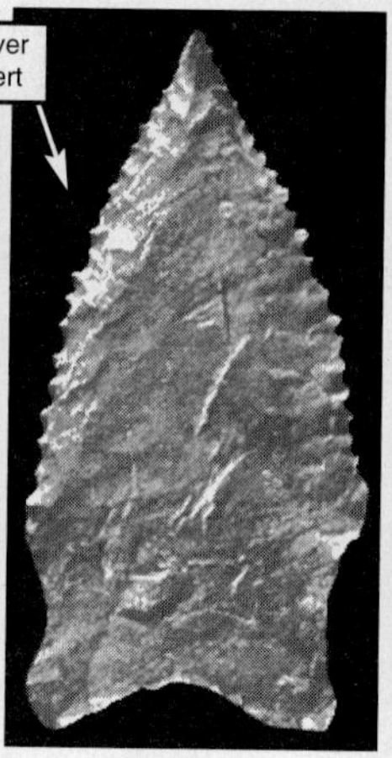

G6, $55-$100
Humphreys Co., TN

Dover chert

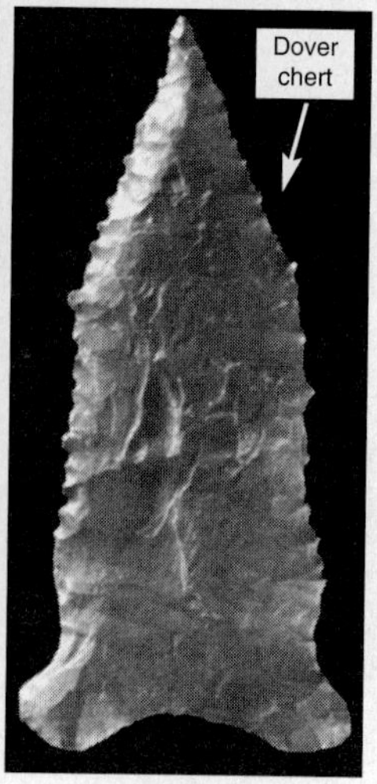

G7, $90-$175
Humphreys Co., TN

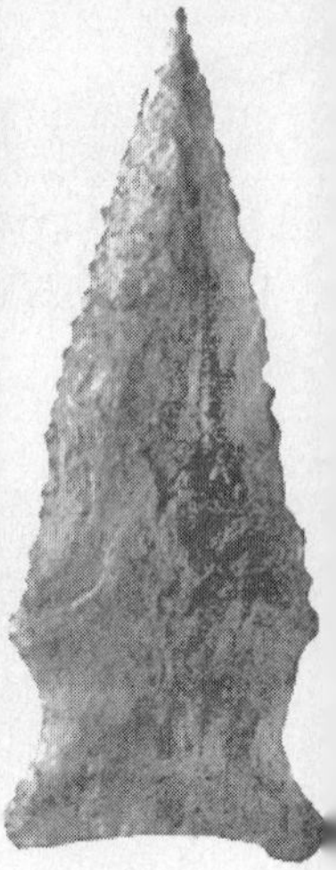

G6, $65-$125
Parsons, TN

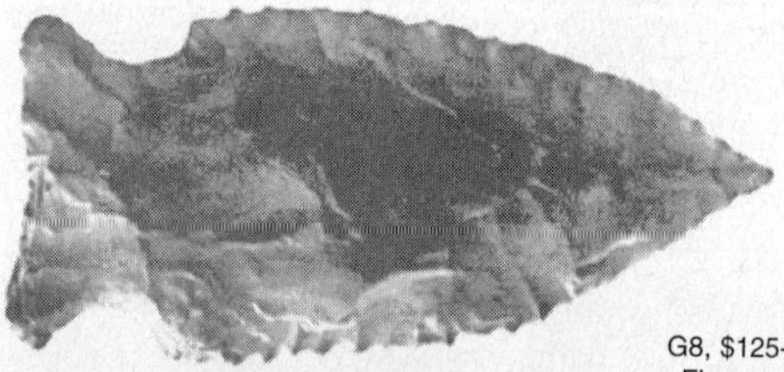

Needle tip & nice serrations

G8, $125-$200
Florence, AL

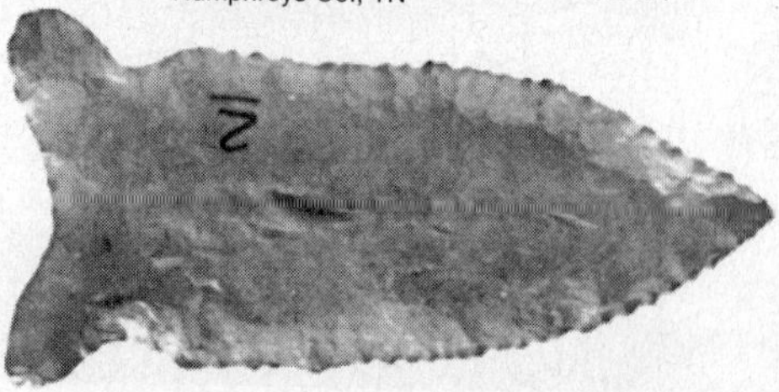

G10, $150-$250
Florence, AL

G10, $225-$400
Florence, AL

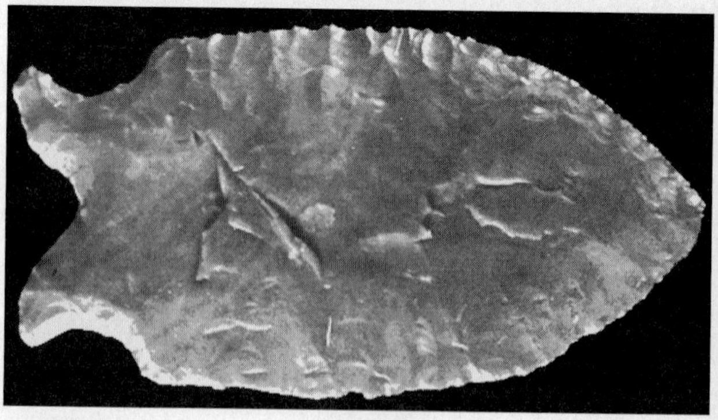

G8, $250-$500
Humphreys Co., TN

Vertical yellow streak adds value

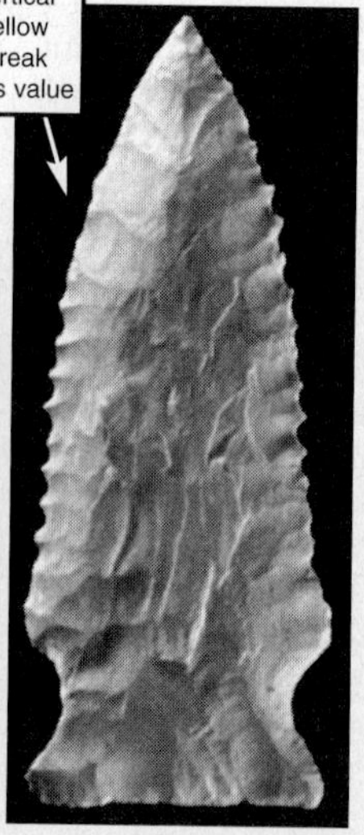

G6, $275-$500
Humphreys Co., TN

Black, heat treated Dover chert

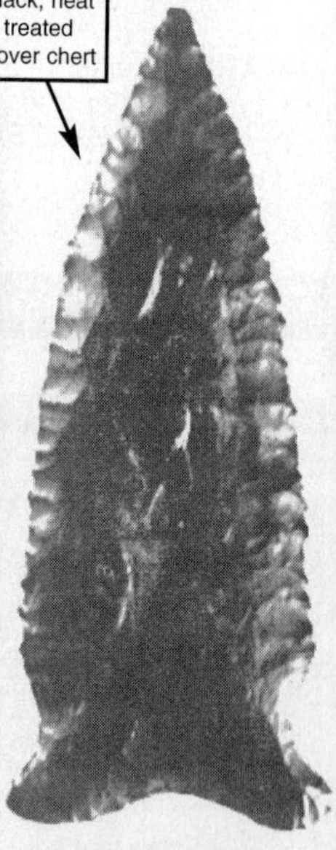

G9, $350-$600
Humphreys Co., TN

LOCATION: Southeastern states. **DESCRIPTION:** A medium to large size, auriculate point with tapered shoulders and broad, weak side notches. Blade edges are usually finely serrated. The base can be concave, lobbed, eared, straight or bifurcated and is ground. Early examples can be fluted. This type developed from the *Dalton* point and later evolved into other types such as the *Pine Tree* point. **I.D. KEY:** Heavy grinding in shoulders, good secondary edge-work.

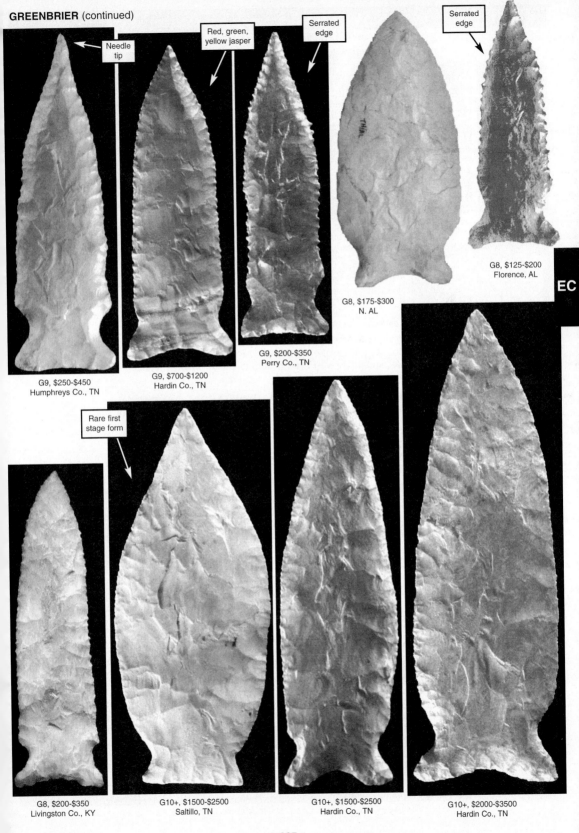

GREENBRIER (continued)

Needle tip

Red, green, yellow jasper

Serrated edge

Serrated edge

G8, $125-$200
Florence, AL

EC

G8, $175-$300
N. AL

G9, $250-$450
Humphreys Co., TN

G9, $700-$1200
Hardin Co., TN

G9, $200-$350
Perry Co., TN

Rare first stage form

G8, $200-$350
Livingston Co., KY

G10+, $1500-$2500
Saltillo, TN

G10+, $1500-$2500
Hardin Co., TN

G10+, $2000-$3500
Hardin Co., TN

395

GREENEVILLE - Woodland, 3000 - 1500 B. P.

(Also see Camp Creek, Guntersville, Madison and Nolichucky)

G6, $12-$20
E. KY

G6, $12-$20
Hamilton Co., TN

G8, $20-$35
E. TN

G8, $20-$35
Parsons, TN

G8, $20-$35
Dayton, TN

G9, $40-$75
Humphreys Co., TN

G6, $12-$20
Coffee Lake, AL

G6, $8-$15
S. E. TN

LOCATION: Southeastern states. **DESCRIPTION:** A small to medium size lanceolate point with convex sides becoming contracting to parallel at the base. The basal edge is slightly concave, convex, or straight. This point is usually wider and thicker than *Guntersville*, and is believed to be related to *Camp Creek, Ebenezer* and *Nolichucky* points.

GUILFORD-ROUND BASE - Middle Archaic, 6500 - 5000 B. P.

(Also see Cobbs, Copena Round, Lerma & Morrow Mountain Round)

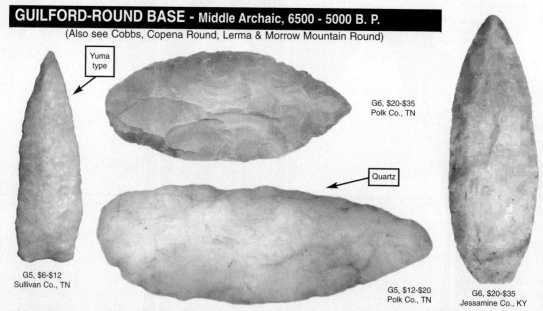

Yuma type

G6, $20-$35
Polk Co., TN

Quartz

G5, $6-$12
Sullivan Co., TN

G5, $12-$20
Polk Co., TN

G6, $20-$35
Jessamine Co., KY

LOCATION: North Carolina and surrounding areas into East Tennessee and Georgia. **DESCRIPTION:** A medium to large size, thick, narrow, lanceolate point with a convex, contracting base. This type is usually made of Quartzite or other poor quality flaking material which results in a more crudely chipped form than *Lerma* (its ancestor). **I.D. KEY:** Thickness, archaic blade flaking.

GUNTERSVILLE - Mississippian to Historic, 700 - 200 B. P.

(Also see Camp Creek, Greeneville, Madison and Nodena)

GUNTERSVILLE (continued)

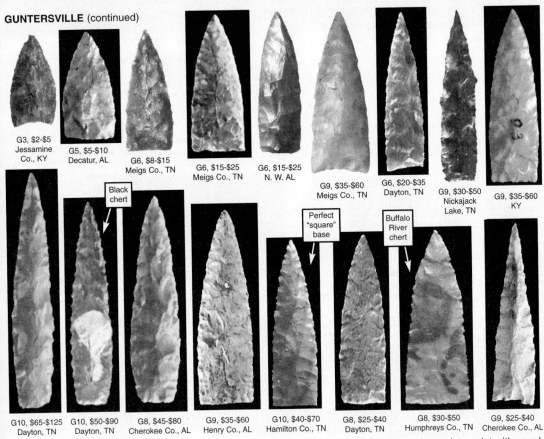

G3, $2-$5
Jessamine
Co., KY

G5, $5-$10
Decatur, AL

G6, $8-$15
Meigs Co., TN

G6, $15-$25
Meigs Co., TN

G6, $15-$25
N. W. AL

G9, $35-$60
Meigs Co., TN

G6, $20-$35
Dayton, TN

G9, $30-$50
Nickajack
Lake, TN

G9, $35-$60
KY

Black chert

Perfect "square" base

Buffalo River chert

G10, $65-$125
Dayton, TN

G10, $50-$90
Dayton, TN

G8, $45-$80
Cherokee Co., AL

G9, $35-$60
Henry Co., AL

G10, $40-$70
Hamilton Co., TN

G8, $25-$40
Dayton, TN

G8, $30-$50
Humphreys Co., TN

G9, $25-$40
Cherokee Co., AL

LOCATION: Southeastern states. **DESCRIPTION:** A small to medium size, thin, narrow, lanceolate point with usually a straight base. Flaking quality is excellent. Formerly called *Dallas* points. **I.D. KEY:** Narrowness & blade expansion.

HALIFAX - Middle to Late Archaic, 6000 - 3000 B. P.

(Also see Bakers Creek, Jude, Rheems Creek and Swan Lake)

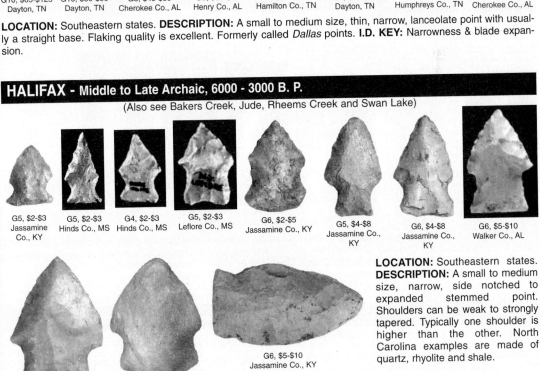

G5, $2-$3
Jassamine
Co., KY

G5, $2-$3
Hinds Co., MS

G4, $2-$3
Hinds Co., MS

G5, $2-$3
Leflore Co., MS

G6, $2-$5
Jassamine Co., KY

G5, $4-$8
Jassamine Co.,
KY

G6, $4-$8
Jassamine Co.,
KY

G6, $5-$10
Walker Co., AL

G6, $5-$10
Jassamine Co., KY

LOCATION: Southeastern states. **DESCRIPTION:** A small to medium size, narrow, side notched to expanded stemmed point. Shoulders can be weak to strongly tapered. Typically one shoulder is higher than the other. North Carolina examples are made of quartz, rhyolite and shale.

G6, $5-$10
Jassamine Co., KY

G6, $5-$10
Jassamine Co., KY

HAMILTON - Woodland to Mississippian, 1600 - 1000 B. P.

(Also see Camp Creek, Fort Ancient, Madison and Sand Mountain)

Serrated on one side

Donaha tip

G4, $5-$10
Jackson Co., AL

G5, $5-$10
Jackson Co., AL

G5, $5-$10
Jackson Co., AL

G8, $12-$20
Jackson Co., AL

G5, $8-$15
Bradley Co., TN

G6, $12-$20
Limestone Co., AL

G6, $5-$15
Jackson Co., AL

G6, $5-$15
Sullivan Co., TN

Red/white agate

Needle tip

G6, $5-$10
Hamilton Co., TN

G8, $8-$15
W. TN

G8, $12-$20
Bradley Co., TN

G8, $15-$25
Sullivan Co., TN

G8, $20-$35
S. E. TN

G8, $20-$35
Hamilton Co., TN

G9, $20-$35
Hamilton Co., TN

G10, $25-$45
Morgan Co., AL

Milky quartz

G8, $15-$30
Limestone Co., AL

G10, $15-$30
Burke Co., GA

G10, $15-$30
Burke Co., GA

G10, $50-$90
Bradley Co., TN

G8, $35-$65
KY

G8, $35-$65
Hamilton Co., TN

G10, $35-$65
TN

Needle tip

Donaha tip

G10, $40-$75
Bristol, TN

G10, $40-$75
Bristol, TN

G10, $55-$100
Dayton, TN

G9, $35-$65
Hamilton Co., TN

G10, $40-$75
Hamilton Co., TN

G9, $40-$75
KY

G10, $55-$100
KY

LOCATION: Southeastern states. **DESCRIPTION:** A small to medium size triangular point with concave sides and base. Many examples are very thin, of the highest quality, and with serrated edges. Side edges can also be straight. This type is believed to have evolved from *Camp Creek* points. Called *Uwharrie* in North Carolina. Some North Carolina and Tennessee examples have special constricted tips called *Donnaha Tips*.

HAMILTON-STEMMED - Late Woodland to Mississippian, 3000 - 1000 B. P.

(Also see Buck Creek, Motley, Rankin, Smithsonia and Wade)

LOCATION: Southeastern states. **DESCRIPTION:** A medium to large size, barbed, expanded stem point. Most examples have a sharp needle like point, and the blade edges are convex to recurved. Called *Rankin* in Northeast Tenn.

398

HAMILTON STEMMED (continued)

G6, $30-$50
Fentress Co., TN

G8, $20-$35
Putnam Co., TN

G7, $45-$80
Meigs Co., TN

G7, $40-$70
Meigs Co., TN

G8, $65-$125
Dayton, TN

G10, $90-$150
Fentress Co., TN

Classic

EC

G10+, $200-$350
Meigs Co., TN

G6, $55-$100
W. TN

HARAHEY - Mississippian, 700 - 350 B. P.
(Also see Lerma, Ramey Knife and Snake Creek)

G8, $125-$200
KY

G9, $55-$100
TN

G9, $35-$65
TN

LOCATION: Kentucky to Texas, Arkansas and Missouri. **DESCRIPTION:** A large size, double pointed knife that is usually beveled on one side of each face. The cross section is rhomboid.

G7, $80-$150
KY

HARDAWAY - Early Archaic, 9500 - 8000 B. P.

(Also see Alamance, Dalton-Greenbrier, Haw River, Russel Cave, San Patrice and Wheeler)

Crystal

G7, $125-$200
Lee Co., AL

G7, $30-$55
Fort Payne, AL

Ground basal area

G7, $125-$200
Lake Seminole, GA

G6, $80-$150
Sullivan Co., TN

Serrated edge

G7, $65-$125
Fort Payne, AL

Serrated edge

G7, $80-$150
Huntsville, AL

Colorful Carter Cave chert

Ground basal area

G8, $175-$300
Cent. KY

G6, $150-$250
Sullivan Co., TN

LOCATION: Southeastern states. **DESCRIPTION:** A small to medium size point with shallow side notches and expanded auricles forming a wide, deeply concave base. Wide specimens are called *Cow Head Hardaways* by some collectors in North Carolina. Ears and base are usually heavily ground. This type evolved from the *Dalton* point. **I.D. KEY:** Heavy grinding in shoulders, paleo flaking.

HARDAWAY-DALTON - Early Archaic, 9500 - 8000 B. P.

(Also see Alamance and Dalton)

G5, $12-$20
Winston Co., AL

G6, $35-$60
Sevier Co., TN

G6, $35-$60
Nickajack Lake, TN

LOCATION: Southeastern states. **DESCRIPTION:** A small to medium size, serrated, auriculate point with a concave base. Basal fluting or thinning is common. Bases are ground. Ears turn outward or have parallel sides. A cross between *Hardaway* and *Dalton*. **I.D. KEY:** Width of base, location found.

HARDAWAY DALTON (continued)

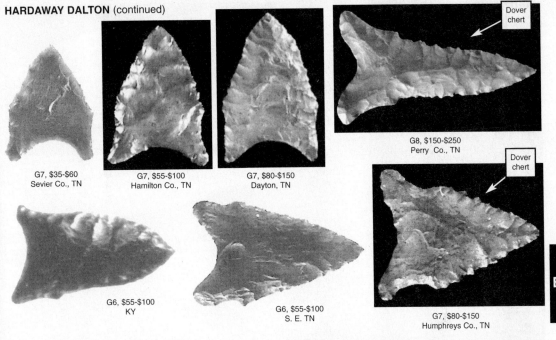

G7, $35-$60
Sevier Co., TN

G7, $55-$100
Hamilton Co., TN

G7, $80-$150
Dayton, TN

Dover chert

G8, $150-$250
Perry Co., TN

Dover chert

G6, $55-$100
KY

G6, $55-$100
S. E. TN

G7, $80-$150
Humphreys Co., TN

EC

HARDIN - Early Archaic, 9000 - 6000 B. P.

(Also see Buck Creek, Cypress Creek, Kirk, Lost Lake, Scottsbluff, St. Charles & Stilwell)

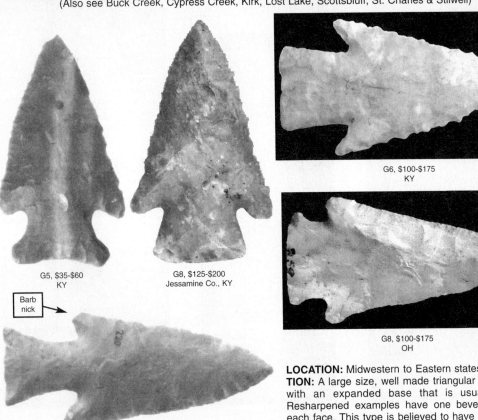

G5, $35-$60
KY

G8, $125-$200
Jessamine Co., KY

Barb nick

G5, $35-$60
IN

G6, $100-$175
KY

G8, $100-$175
OH

LOCATION: Midwestern to Eastern states. **DESCRIPTION:** A large size, well made triangular barbed point with an expanded base that is usually ground. Resharpened examples have one beveled edge on each face. This type is believed to have evolved from the *Scottsbluff* type. **I.D. KEY:** Notches and stem form.

401

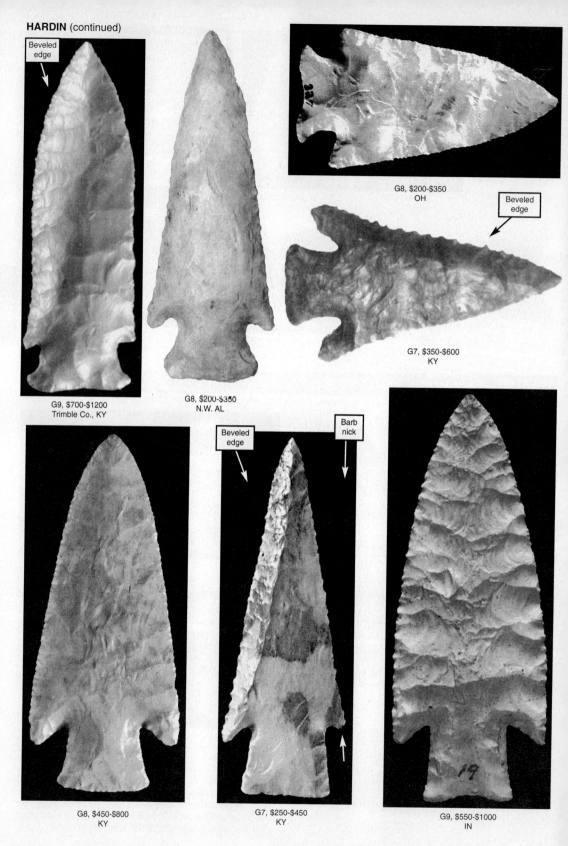

Beveled edge

G9, $700-$1200
Trimble Co., KY

G8, $200-$350
N.W. AL

G8, $200-$350
OH

Beveled edge

G7, $350-$600
KY

G8, $450-$800
KY

Beveled edge

Barb nick

G7, $250-$450
KY

G9, $550-$1000
IN

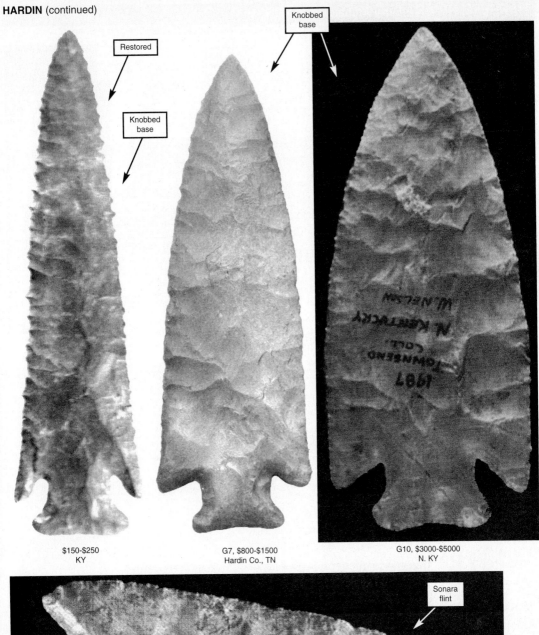

Restored

Knobbed base

Knobbed base

Knobbed base

Restored
KY
$150-$250

G7, $800-$1500
Hardin Co., TN

G10, $3000-$5000
N. KY

EC

Sonara flint

G8, $1500-$2500
Clay Co., TN

G2, $12-$20
Humphreys Co., TN

G3, $15-$25
Davidson Co., TN

Dover chert

G6, $35-$65
Lime Co., TN

G8, $65-$125
Humphreys Co., TN

Buffalo River chert

G8, $80-$150
Humphreys Co., TN

Ground stem

Edge wear

G6, $45-$80
Dickson Co., TN

Cache point

G9, $250-$450
Davidson Co., TN

Dover chert

G6, $150-$250
Davidson Co., TN

G6, $65-$125
TN

G7, $175-$300
Clarksville, TN

G9, $350-$600
Humphreys Co., TN

LOCATION: Southwestern Kentucky into the Southeastern states. **DESCRIPTION:** A medium to large size, narrow, thick, serrated stemmed point that is steeply beveled on all four sides. The hafting area either has shallow side notches or an expanding stem. The base is usually thinned and ground. Rarely, the base is bifurcated. **I.D. KEY:** Weak notches, edgework.

HAW RIVER - Transitional Paleo, 11,000 - 8000 B. P.

(Also see Golondrina and Hardaway)

G10, $2500-$4000
Grayson Co., KY

LOCATION: AL, KY, NC, PA & VA. **DES-CRIPTION:** A medium to large size, thin, broad, elliptical blade with a basal notch and usually, rounded barbs that turn inward. Believed to be ancestral to the *Alamance* point. **I.D. KEY:** Notched base.

G8, $800-$1500
Coffee Lake, AL

EC

HEAVY DUTY - Early to Middle Archaic, 7000 - 5000 B. P.

(Also see Harpeth River and Kirk Stemmed, McWhinney and Russell Cave)

Coshocton chert

G5, $12-$20
KY

G8, $80-$150
OH

G7, $55-$100
Harrison Co., KY

G6, $45-$80
OH

G6, $45-$80
Bath Co., KY

G7, $65-$125
Russell Co., KY

G6, $35-$65
Clark Co., KY

LOCATION: Eastern states. **DESCRIPTION:** A medium to large size, thick, serrated point with a parallel stem and a straight to slightly concave to lobbed base. Basal areas are ground. A variant of *Kirk Stemmed* found in the Southeast. **I.D. KEY:** Base, thickness, flaking.

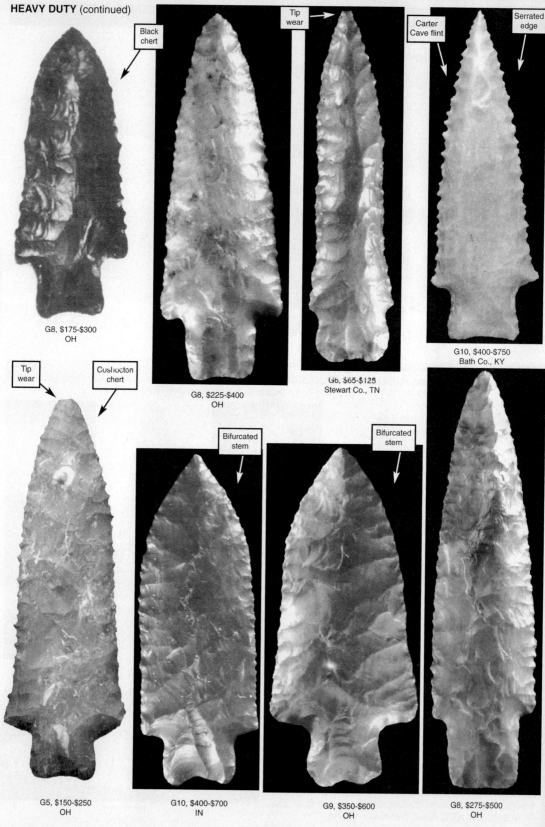

Black chert

Tip wear

Carter Cave flint

Serrated edge

G8, $175-$300
OH

Tip wear

Coshocton chert

Bifurcated stem

Bifurcated stem

G8, $225-$400
OH

Tip wear

G6, $65-$125
Stewart Co., TN

G10, $400-$750
Bath Co., KY

G5, $150-$250
OH

G10, $400-$700
IN

G9, $350-$600
OH

G8, $275-$500
OH

HI-LO - Transitional Paleo, 10,000 - 8000 B. P.

(Also see Angostura, Golondrina, Jeff, Johnson and Paint Rock Valley)

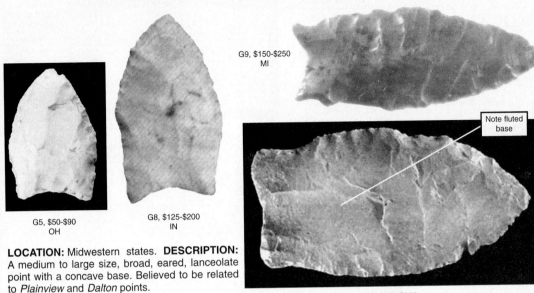

G9, $150-$250
MI

Note fluted base

G5, $50-$90
OH

G8, $125-$200
IN

EC

LOCATION: Midwestern states. **DESCRIPTION:** A medium to large size, broad, eared, lanceolate point with a concave base. Believed to be related to *Plainview* and *Dalton* points.

G6, $150-$250
Barren Co., KY

HIDDEN VALLEY - Early to Middle Archaic, 8000 - 6000 B. P.

(also see Dickson and Morrow Mountain)

LOCATION: Arkansas, West Tennessee to Wisconsin. **DESCRIPTION:** A medium size point with square to tapered shoulders and a contracting base that can be pointed to straight. Flaking is earlier and more parallel than on *Gary* points. Called *Rice Contracted Stemmed* in Missouri.

G10, $150-$250
TN

HINDS - Transitional Paleo, 10,000 - 6000 B. P.

(Also see Pelican and Quad)

Classic form

Serrated edge

Fine serrations

G6, $125-$200
Dyersburg, TN

G8, $150-$250
Lee Co., MS

LOCATION: Tennessee, N. Alabama, Mississippi, Louisiana and Arkansas. **DESCRIPTION:** A short, broad, auriculate point with basal grinding. Shoulders taper into a short expanding stem. Some examples are basally thinned or fluted. Related to *Pelican* and *Coldwater* points found in Texas.

407

HOLLAND - Early Archaic, 9500 - 7500 B. P.

(Also see Dalton, Hardin and Scottsbluff)

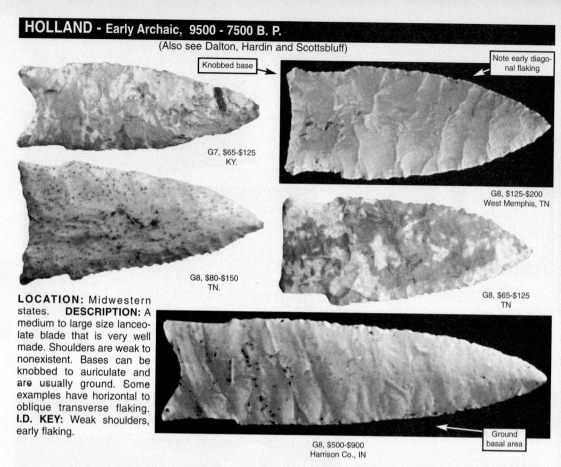

Knobbed base

Note early diagonal flaking

G7, $65-$125
KY.

G8, $125-$200
West Memphis, TN

G8, $80-$150
TN.

G8, $65-$125
TN

Ground basal area

G8, $500-$900
Harrison Co., IN

LOCATION: Midwestern states. **DESCRIPTION:** A medium to large size lanceolate blade that is very well made. Shoulders are weak to nonexistent. Bases can be knobbed to auriculate and are usually ground. Some examples have horizontal to oblique transverse flaking. **I.D. KEY:** Weak shoulders, early flaking.

HOPEWELL - Woodland, 2500 - 1500 B. P.

(Also see Dickson, Gibson, North, St. Charles and Snyders)

Flintridge flint

G6, $20-$35
OH

G6, $15-$25
OH

G5, $15-$30
KY

G6, $20-$35
Jackson Co., IN

G6, $30-$50
OH

LOCATION: Midwestern to Eastern states. **DESCRIPTION:** A large size, broad, corner notched point that is similar to *Snyders*. Made by the Hopewell culture.

Tip wear

EC

G5, $25-$40
OH

G6, $35-$60
Carroll Co., OH

G5, $35-$60
OH

G9, $80-$150
KY

HOWARD COUNTY - Early Archaic., 7500 - 6500 B. P.

(also see Big Sandy, Gibson & St. Charles)

G6, $150-$250
Boyd Co., KY

LOCATION: Missouri, Illinois into Kentucky. **DESCRIPTION:** A small to medium size, thin, well-made point, The blade is long and triangular with slightly convex edges. Notches are narrow and fairly low on the sides, entering at a slight diagonally upward angle. The basal edge may range from straight to slightly convex or concave. Basal edge has light grinding to none.

INTRUSIVE MOUND - Late Woodland-Miss., 1500 - 1000 B. P.

(also see Jacks Reef, Knight Island)

Barb nick

Tip nick

Base skewed

Tip nick

G8, $25-$45
OH

G2, $2-$5
OH

G3, $5-$10
OH

G4, $12-$20
OH

LOCATION: Ohio Valley area. **DESCRIPTION:** A very thin, narrow, medium size side to corner-notched point with a concave to straight base and slightly barbed shoulders. Notching angles towards the tip. Contemporaneous with *Knight Island* & Jacks Reef points found in Kentucky, Tenn. and Alabama. **I.D. KEY:** Thinness of blade.

INTRUSIVE MOUND (continued)

Tip wear

Edgewear

G8, $20-$35
OH

G8, $25-$45
OH

G5, $8-$15
OH

G8, $35-$65
OH

G8, $35-$65
OH

JACKS REEF CORNER NOTCHED - Late Woodland to Mississippian, 1500 - 1000 B. P.

(Also see Intrusive Mound, Knight Island & Pentagonal Knife)

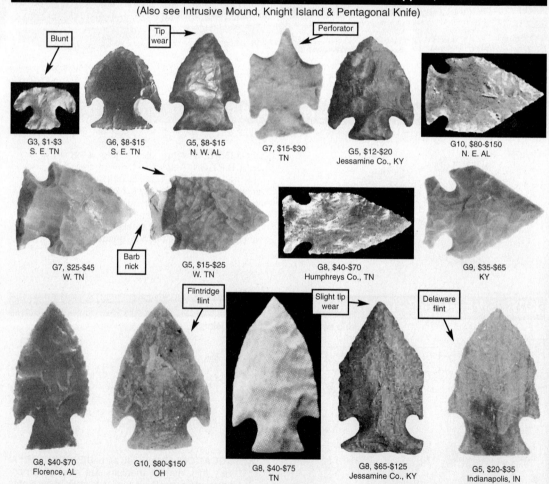

Blunt

Tip wear

Perforator

G3, $1-$3
S. E. TN

G6, $8-$15
S. E. TN

G5, $8-$15
N. W. AL

G7, $15-$30
TN

G5, $12-$20
Jessamine Co., KY

G10, $80-$150
N. E. AL

G7, $25-$45
W. TN

Barb nick

G5, $15-$25
W. TN

G8, $40-$70
Humphreys Co., TN

G9, $35-$65
KY

Flintridge flint

Slight tip wear

Delaware flint

G8, $40-$70
Florence, AL

G10, $80-$150
OH

G8, $40-$75
TN

G8, $65-$125
Jessamine Co., KY

G5, $20-$35
Indianapolis, IN

LOCATION: Southeastern states. **DESCRIPTION:** A small to medium size, very thin, corner notched point that is well made. The blade is convex to pentagonal. Some examples are widely corner notched and appear to be expanded stem points with barbed shoulders. Rarely, they are basal notched. **I.D. KEY:** Thinness, made by the birdpoint people.

JACKS REEF CORNER NOTCHED (continued)

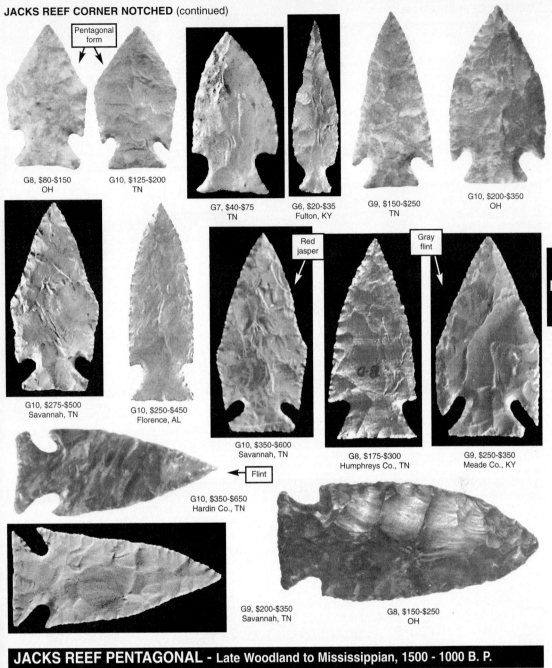

Pentagonal form

G8, $80-$150
OH

G10, $125-$200
TN

G7, $40-$75
TN

G6, $20-$35
Fulton, KY

G9, $150-$250
TN

G10, $200-$350
OH

G10, $275-$500
Savannah, TN

G10, $250-$450
Florence, AL

Red jasper

Gray flint

EC

G10, $350-$600
Savannah, TN

G8, $175-$300
Humphreys Co., TN

G9, $250-$350
Meade Co., KY

Flint

G10, $350-$650
Hardin Co., TN

G9, $200-$350
Savannah, TN

G8, $150-$250
OH

JACKS REEF PENTAGONAL - Late Woodland to Mississippian, 1500 - 1000 B. P.

(Also see Madison and Mouse Creek)

G2, $1-$3
Jackson Co., AL

G2, $2-$4
Sullivan Co., TN

G6, $5-$10
KY

G3, $2-$4
Jackson Co., AL

G6, $5-$10
Florence, AL

G5, $5-$10
N. E. AL

G5, $5-$10
W. TN

411

JACKS REEF PENTAGONAL (continued)

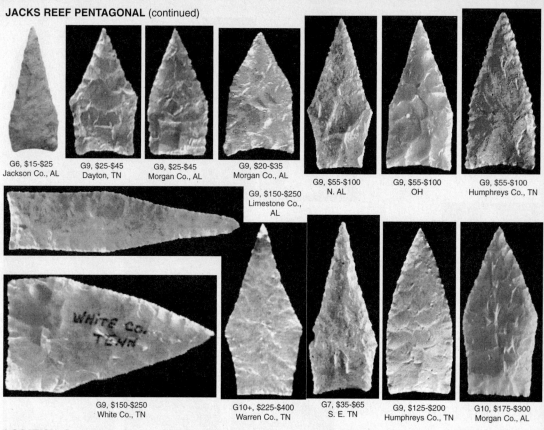

G6, $15-$25
Jackson Co., AL

G9, $25-$45
Dayton, TN

G9, $25-$45
Morgan Co., AL

G9, $20-$35
Morgan Co., AL

G9, $55-$100
N. AL

G9, $55-$100
OH

G9, $55-$100
Humphreys Co., TN

G9, $150-$250
Limestone Co., AL

G9, $150-$250
White Co., TN

G10+, $225-$400
Warren Co., TN

G7, $35-$65
S. E. TN

G9, $125-$200
Humphreys Co., TN

G10, $175-$300
Morgan Co., AL

LOCATION: Southeastern states. **DESCRIPTION:** A small to large size, very thin, five sided point with a sharp tip. The hafting area is usually contracted with a slightly concave to straight base. This type is called *Pee Dee* in North and South Carolina.

JEFF - Late Paleo, 10,000 - 8000 B. P.

(Also see Angostura, Browns Valley, Golondrina, Hi-Lo, Paint Rock Valley and Quad)

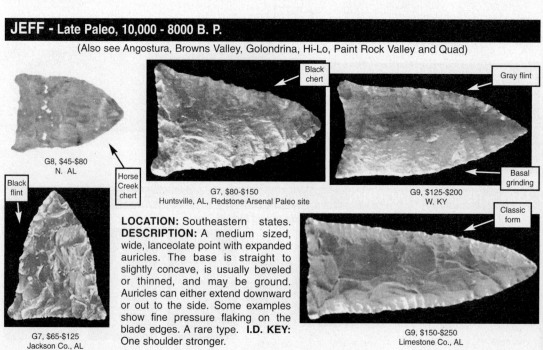

G8, $45-$80
N. AL

Black chert

Horse Creek chert

Black flint

G7, $80-$150
Huntsville, AL, Redstone Arsenal Paleo site

Gray flint

Basal grinding

G9, $125-$200
W. KY

Classic form

G7, $65-$125
Jackson Co., AL

LOCATION: Southeastern states. **DESCRIPTION:** A medium sized, wide, lanceolate point with expanded auricles. The base is straight to slightly concave, is usually beveled or thinned, and may be ground. Auricles can either extend downward or out to the side. Some examples show fine pressure flaking on the blade edges. A rare type. **I.D. KEY:** One shoulder stronger.

G9, $150-$250
Limestone Co., AL

JOHNSON - Early to Middle Archaic, 9000 - 5000 B. P.

(Also see Fairland, Hi-Lo, Limestone, McIntire, Savannah River and Steubenville)

G5, $15-$30
Natchez, MS

G5, $15-$30
W. TN

G5, $15-$30
N.E. AL

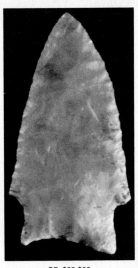
G7, $35-$60
Huntsville, AL

EC

LOCATION: Midwestern to Southeastern states. **DESCRIPTION:** A medium size, thick, well made, expanded stem point with a broad, concave base. Shoulders can be slightly barbed, straight or tapered. Basal corners are rounded to pointed to auriculate. Bases are thinned and ground. **I.D. KEY:** Pointed ears and thickness.

JUDE - Early Archaic, 9000 - 6000 B. P.

(Also see Cave Spring, Garth Slough, Halifax, Kanawha Stemmed, LeCroy, McIntire and Rheems Creek)

Red jasper

Diagonal flaking

Carter Cave flint

G5, $8-$15
Walker Co., AL

G5, $12-$20
Christian Co., KY

G6, $12-$20
S. E. TN

G9, $35-$65
Colbert Co., AL

G6, $15-$30
Dickson, TN

G8, $25-$45
Marion Co., KY

Milky quartz

Classic form

G6, $8-$15
Walker Co., AL

G9, $35-$65
N. AL

G6, $15-$25
Humphreys Co., TN

LOCATION: Southeastern states. **DESCRIPTION:** A small size, short, barbed, expanded to parallel stemmed point with straight to convex blade edges. Stems are usually as large or larger than the blade. Bases are straight, concave, convex or bifurcated. Shoulders are either square, tapered or barbed. This is one of the earliest stemmed points along with *Pelican*. Some examples have serrated blade edges that may be beveled on one side of each face. **I.D. KEY:** Basal form and flaking.

KANAWHA STEMMED - Early Archaic, 8200 - 5000 B. P.

(Also see Frederick, Jude, Kirk Stemmed-Bifurcated, LeCroy, St. Albans and Stanly)

KANAWHA STEMMED (continued)

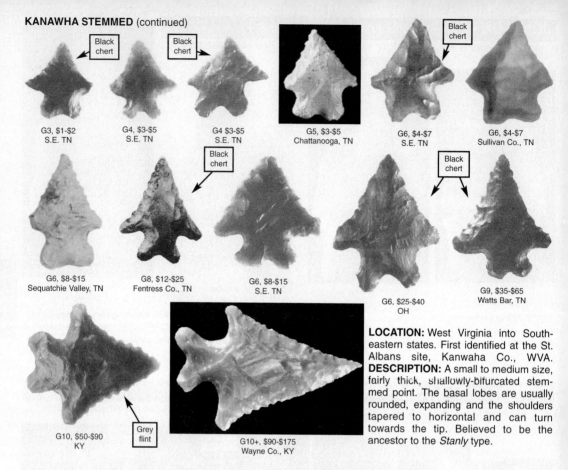

Black chert

G3, $1-$2
S.E. TN

Black chert

G4, $3-$5
S.E. TN

G4 $3-$5
S.E. TN

Black chert

G5, $3-$5
Chattanooga, TN

Black chert

G6, $4-$7
S.E. TN

G6, $4-$7
Sullivan Co., TN

G6, $8-$15
Sequatchie Valley, TN

G8, $12-$25
Fentress Co., TN

Black chert

G6, $8-$15
S.E. TN

Black chert

G6, $25-$40
OH

G9, $35-$65
Watts Bar, TN

G10, $50-$90
KY

Grey flint

G10+, $90-$175
Wayne Co., KY

LOCATION: West Virginia into Southeastern states. First identified at the St. Albans site, Kanwaha Co., WVA. **DESCRIPTION:** A small to medium size, fairly thick, shallowly-bifurcated stemmed point. The basal lobes are usually rounded, expanding and the shoulders tapered to horizontal and can turn towards the tip. Believed to be the ancestor to the *Stanly* type.

KAYS - Middle Archaic to Woodland, 5000 - 2000 B. P.

(Also see Adena Robbins, Cresap, Little Bear Creek, McIntire and Pontchartrain)

G5, $8-$15
Limestone Co., AL

G5, $8-$15
S. E. TN

G6, $12-$20
Limestone Co., AL

G5, $8-$15
TN

G6, $12-$20
Morgan Co., AL

LOCATION: Southeastern states. **DESCRIPTION:** A medium to large size, narrow, parallel sided stemmed point with a straight base. Shoulders are tapered to square. The blade is straight to convex. **I.D. KEY:** One barb is higher.

414

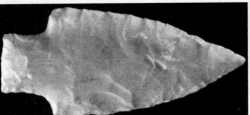

G7, $15-$30
Decatur, AL

G6, $15-$25
Decatur, AL

G8, $30-$50
Decatur, AL

G9, $30-$55
Morgan Co., AL

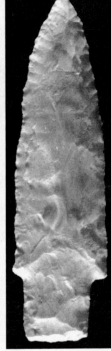

G8, $65-$125
Decatur, AL

G9, $80-$150
Megis Co., TN, Hiwassee River.

EC

KEOTA - Mississippian, 800 - 600 B. P.

(Also see Merom)

LOCATION: Okla, Ark, S.E. TN. & N. AL. **DESCRIPTION:** A small size, thin, triangular, side to corner-notched point with a rounded base.

G4, $1-$2
Meigs Co., TN

G4, $1-$2
Meigs Co., TN

G5, $5-$10
Wash. Co., AL

KIRK CORNER NOTCHED - Early to Middle Archaic, 9000 - 6000 B. P.

(Also see Crawford Creek, Cypress Creek, Lost Lake, Neuberger, Pine Tree and St. Charles)

LOCATION: Southeastern states. **DESCRIPTION:** A medium to large size, corner notched point. Blade edges can be convex to recurved and are finely serrated on many examples. The base can be convex, concave, straight or auriculate. Points that are beveled on one side of each face would fall under the *Lost Lake* type. **I.D. KEY:** Secondary edgework.

G4, $3-$5
Jessamine Co., KY

G4, $3-$6
W. TN

G4, $3-$6
Walker Co., AL

415

Base nick

Serrated edge

G4, $3-$5
KY

G4, $3-$5
KY

G5, $5-$10
KY

G7, $125-$200
KY

Banded chert

Serrated edge

Serrated edge

G8, $55-$100
Dunlap, TN

G8, $125-$200
Spencer Co., OH

G8, $80-$150
White Co., TN

G8, $80-$150
KY

Serrated edge

Serrated edge

G8, $150-$275
Florence, AL

G9, $150-$275
Wayne Co., TN

G9, $175-$350
KY

All have ground basal areas

Serrated edge

Serrated edge

G9, $350-$600
KY

G8, $150-$250
W. KY

416

KIRK CORNER NOTCHED (continued)

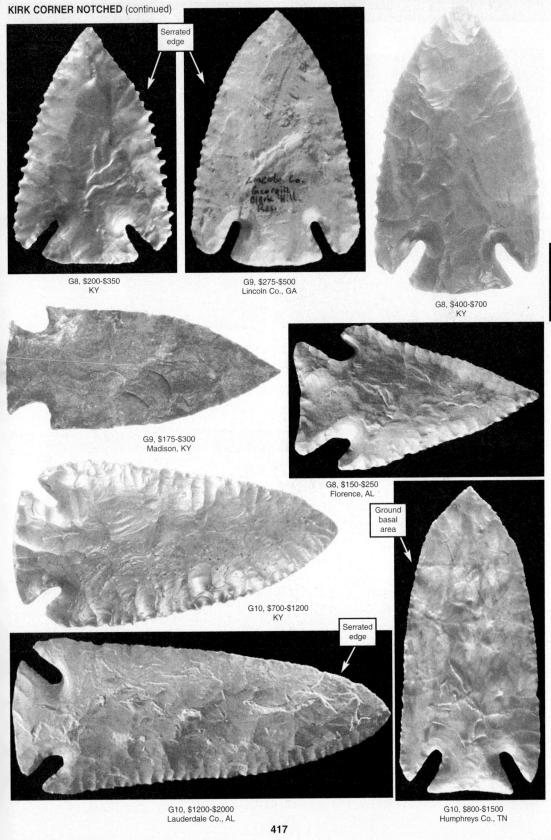

Serrated edge

G8, $200-$350
KY

G9, $275-$500
Lincoln Co., GA

G8, $400-$700
KY

EC

G9, $175-$300
Madison, KY

G8, $150-$250
Florence, AL

G10, $700-$1200
KY

Ground basal area

Serrated edge

G10, $1200-$2000
Lauderdale Co., AL

G10, $800-$1500
Humphreys Co., TN

KIRK SNAPPED BASE - Early to Middle Archaic, 9000 - 6000 B. P.

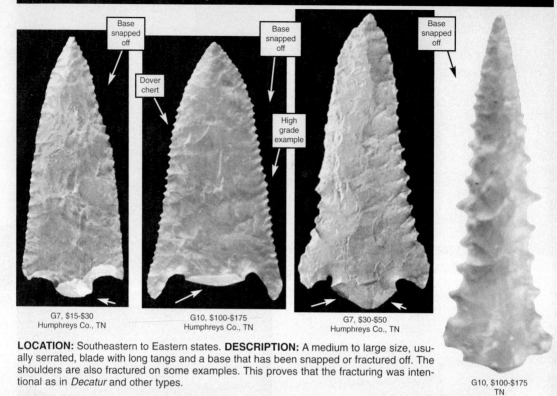

Base snapped off

Dover chert

Base snapped off

High grade example

Base snapped off

G7, $15-$30
Humphreys Co., TN

G10, $100-$175
Humphreys Co., TN

G7, $30-$50
Humphreys Co., TN

G10, $100-$175
TN

LOCATION: Southeastern to Eastern states. **DESCRIPTION:** A medium to large size, usually serrated, blade with long tangs and a base that has been snapped or fractured off. The shoulders are also fractured on some examples. This proves that the fracturing was intentional as in *Decatur* and other types.

KIRK STEMMED - Early to Middle Archaic, 9000 - 6000 B. P.

(Also see Elora, Flint Creek, Hamilton, Heavy Duty, St. Tammany and Stanly)

G2, $1-$3
Sullivan Co., TN

G3, $5-$10
KY

G4, $5-$10
TN

Serrated edge

G6, $12-$20
KY

Serrated edge

G4, $2-$5
Jessamine Co., KY

G6, $6-$12
AL

G5, $6-$12
KY

G6, $12-$20
KY

LOCATION: Southeastern to Eastern states. **DESCRIPTION:** A medium to large size, barbed, stemmed point with deep notches or fine serrations along the blade edges. The stem is parallel to expanding. The stem sides may be steeply beveled on opposite faces. Some examples also have a distinct bevel on the right side of each blade edge. The base can be concave, convex or straight, and can be very short. The shoulders are usually strongly barbed. Believed to have evolved into *Stanly* and other types. **I.D. KEY:** Serrations.

KIRK STEMMED (continued)

G5, $12-$20
OH

G6, $25-$45
KY/TN

Serrated edge

G5, $20-$35
OH

Serrated edge

G6, $25-$45
Marshall Co., KY

EC

Serrated edge

G9, $80-$150
Benton Co., TN

G8, $30-$50
W. TN

G8, $30-$50
Hardin Co., KY

G9, $80-$150
Hardin Co., KY

Serrated edge

G9, $125-$200
Mason Co., KY

Serrated edge

G9, $150-$250
Lyon Co., KY

Serrated edge

G9, $150-$250
Lyon Co., KY

Serrated edge

G9, $150-$250
Marshall Co., KY

419

Black heat treated Dover chert

Black heat treated Dover chert

Serrated edge

G9, $175-$300
Humphreys Co., TN

G10+, $250-$400
Humphreys Co., TN

G8, $150-$250
Crittenden Co., KY

G9, $175-$300
Humphreys Co., TN

Drill form

G10, $200-$350
Lyon co., KY

Black heat treated Dover chert

Serrated edge

Serrated edge

G9, $225-$400
Humphreys Co., TN

G9, $175-$300
Marshall Co., KY

G9, $225-$400
Humphreys Co., TN

G8, $125-$200
Marshall Co., KY

KIRK STEMMED-BIFURCATED - Early Archaic, 9000 - 7000 B. P.

(Also see Cave Spring, Fox Valley, Heavy Duty, LeCroy, St. Albans and Stanly)

Hooked barb

G4, $5-$10
KY

G4, $5-$10
KY

G6, $12-$20
S.E. TN

G6, $20-$35
KY

G4, $6-$12
KY

Serrated edge

Serrated edge

EC

G6, $25-$40
GA

G6, $15-$30
Garrard Co., KY

G5, $15-$25
KY

G9, $50-$90
KY

G6, $20-$35
Stewart Co., TN

G9, $150-$250
KY

LOCATION: Southeastern to Eastern states. **DESCRIPTION:** A medium to large size point with deep notches or fine serrations along the blade edges. The stem is parallel sided to expanded and is bifurcated. Believed to be an early form for the type which later developed into *Stanly* and other types. Some examples have a steep bevel on the right side of each blade edge.

KNIGHT ISLAND - Late Woodland, 1500 - 1000 B. P.

(Also see Cache River, Intrusive Mound and Jacks Reef)

G5, $20-$35
Humphreys Co., TN

G5, $20-$35
Humphreys Co., TN

G5, $20-$35
Humphreys Co., TN

G5, $20-$35
S. E. TN

G5, $12-$20
TN

G8, $25-$45
Jessamine Co., KY

LOCATION: Southeastern states. **DESCRIPTION:** A small to medium size, very thin, narrow, side-notched point with a straight base. Longer examples can have a pentagonal apperarance. Called *Raccoon Creek* in Ohio. A side-notched Jacks Reef. **I.D. KEY:** Thinness, basal form. Made by the bird point people.

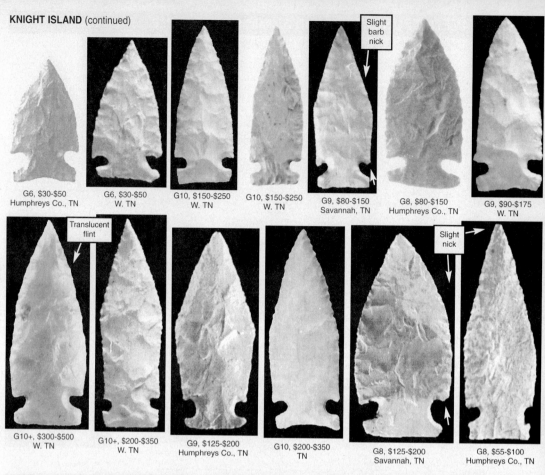

G6, $30-$50
Humphreys Co., TN

G6, $30-$50
W. TN

G10, $150-$250
W. TN

G10, $150-$250
W. TN

Slight barb nick

G9, $80-$150
Savannah, TN

G8, $80-$150
Humphreys Co., TN

G9, $90-$175
W. TN

Translucent flint

G10+, $300-$500
W. TN

G10+, $200-$350
W. TN

G9, $125-$200
Humphreys Co., TN

G10, $200-$350
TN

Slight nick

G8, $125-$200
Savannah, TN

G8, $55-$100
Humphreys Co., TN

LAKE ERIE - Early to Middle Archaic, 9000 - 5000 B. P.

(Also see Jude, Kanawha, Kirk Stemmed-Bifurcated, LeCroy, MacCorkle, St. Albans and   Stanly)

G5, $4-$8
Carroll, Co., OH

G6, $8-$15
Cleveland, OH

G5, $4-$8
OH

Coshocton chert

Black chert

Coshocton chert

G8, $40-$75
Carroll Co., OH

G9, $20-$35
Ross Co., OH. Classic

Basal sides are fractured

G9, $30-$50
Cleveland, OH

Coshocton chert

G9, $80-$150
Cleveland, OH

G9, $80-$150
Cleveland, OH

LOCATION: Northeastern states. **DESCRIPTION:** A small to medium size, thin, deeply notched or serrated, bifurcated stemmed point. The basal lobes are parallel with a tendency to turn inward and are pointed. The outward sides of the basal lobes are usually fractured from the base towards the tip and can be ground.

LANCET - Paleo to Archaic, 11,500 - 5000 B. P.

(Also see Drill and Scraper)

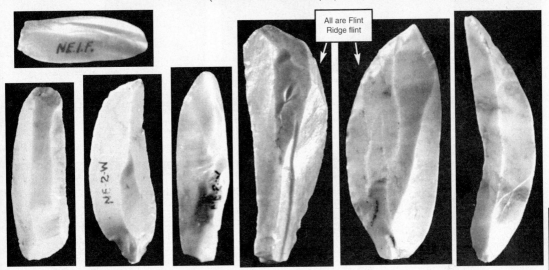

All are Flint Ridge flint

$3-$5 ea.
All from Flint Ridge, OH

LOCATION: Found on all early man sites. **DESCRIPTION:** A medium to large size sliver used as a knife for cutting. Recent experiments proved that these knives were sharper than a surgeon's scalpel. Similar to *Burins* which are fractured at one end to produce a sharp point.

LECROY - Early to Middle Archaic, 9000 - 5000 B. P.

(Also see Decatur, Jude, Kanawha Stemmed, Kirk Stemmed-Bifurcated, Lake Erie, MacCorkle, Pine Tree, Rice Lobbed, St. Albans and Stanly)

Black Kanawha flint

Crystal

Fort Payne chert

G8, $5-$10
Mason Co., WVA

G4, $5-$10
Fentress Co., TN

G4, $12-$20
Elberton, GA

G6, $5-$10
Pikeville, TN

G5, $8-$15
S. E. TN

G8, $8-$15
Meigs Co., TN

G6, $8-$15
Jessamine Co., KY

Serrated edge

G4, $8-$15
S. E. TN

G6, $12-$20
Monteray, TN

G8, $12-$20
S. E. TN

G7, $12-$20
Citico, TN

G6, $12-$20
Meigs Co., TN

G7, $15-$25
Jessamine Co., KY

G8, $20-$35
Jackson Co., AL

G6, $12-$20
Moccasin Bend, TN

LOCATION: Southeastern states. Type site-Hamilton Co., TN. Named after Archie LeCroy. **DESCRIPTION:** A small to medium size, thin, usually broad point with deeply notched or serrated blade edges and a deeply bifurcated base. Basal ears can either droop or expand out. The stem is usually large in comparison to the blade size. Some stem sides are fractured in Northern examples *(Lake Erie)*. Bases are usually ground. **I.D. KEY:** Basal form.

423

LECROY (continued)

G8, $15-$25
Dayton, TN

G9, $25-$40
W. TN

G6, $15-$30
Hamilton Co., TN
Type site

G10+, $40-$70
Dayton, TN

G9, $25-$40
W. E. TN

Serrated edge

G9, $30-$50
S. E. TN

G10, $80-$150
KY

G8, $40-$70
Jackson Co., AL

LEDBETTER - Middle to Late Archaic, 6000 - 3500 B. P.

(Also see Little Bear Creek, Mulberry Creek, Pickwick and Shoals Creek)

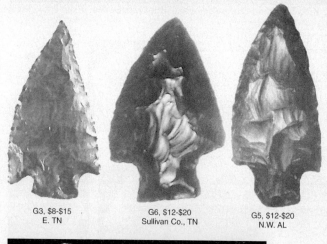

G4, $12-$20
E. TN

G3, $8-$15
E. TN

G6, $12-$20
Sullivan Co., TN

G5, $12-$20
N.W. AL

LOCATION: Southeastern states. **DESCRIPTION:** A medium to large size asymmetrical point with a short, usually fractured or snapped base. One blade edge is curved more than the other. Shoulders are tapered, squared or slightly barbed. Some examples show fine pressure flaking along the blade edges. Believed to be *Pickwick* knives. **I.D. KEY:** Blade form.

G7, $30-$50
Florence, AL

G9, $25-$40
Florence, AL

LEDBETTER (continued)

Buffalo River chert

Red, yellow & blue Horse Creek chert

EC

G5, $12-$20
N. AL

G5, $40-$70
Jessamine Co., KY

G6, $30-$50
N. W. AL

G8, $700-$1200
Hardin Co., TN

G6, $15-$30
TN

Serrated edge

G8, $150-$250
Coffee Lake, AL

G8, $150-$250
E. TN

G9, $200-$350
Humphreys Co., TN

LEIGHTON - Early Archaic, 8000 - 5000 B. P.

(Also see Benton, Big Sandy, Evans, Merkle, Ohio Double Notched and St. Helena)

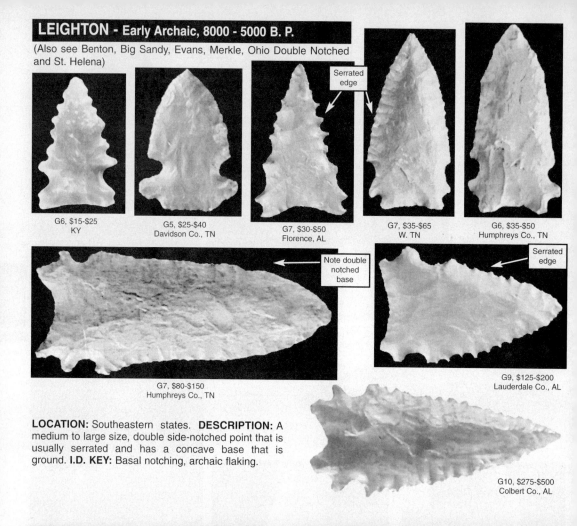

Serrated edge

G6, $15-$25
KY

G5, $25-$40
Davidson Co., TN

G7, $30-$50
Florence, AL

G7, $35-$65
W. TN

G6, $35-$50
Humphreys Co., TN

Note double notched base

Serrated edge

G7, $80-$150
Humphreys Co., TN

G9, $125-$200
Lauderdale Co., AL

LOCATION: Southeastern states. **DESCRIPTION:** A medium to large size, double side-notched point that is usually serrated and has a concave base that is ground. **I.D. KEY:** Basal notching, archaic flaking.

G10, $275-$500
Colbert Co., AL

LERMA - Early to Mid-Archaic, 10,000 - 5000 B. P.

(Also see Adena Blade, Harahey, North, Paleo Knife, Snake Creek, Tear Drop & Tenn. Saw)

LOCATION: Siberia to Alaska, Canada, Mexico, South America, and across the U.S. **DESCRIPTION:** A large size, narrow, thick, lanceolate blade with a rounded base. Some Western examples are beveled on one side of each face. Flaking tends to be collateral and finer examples are thin in cross section.

G6, $25-$40
Benton Co., KY

Resharpened many times

Note long hafting area

IMPORTANT:
This Lerma shown half size

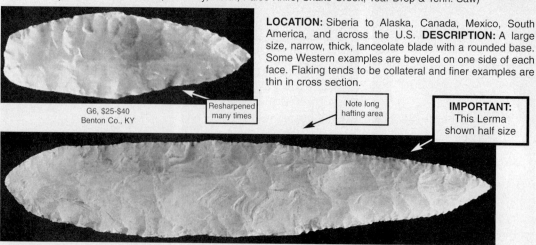

G10+, $700-$1200
Parsons, TN, 10-1/4" long

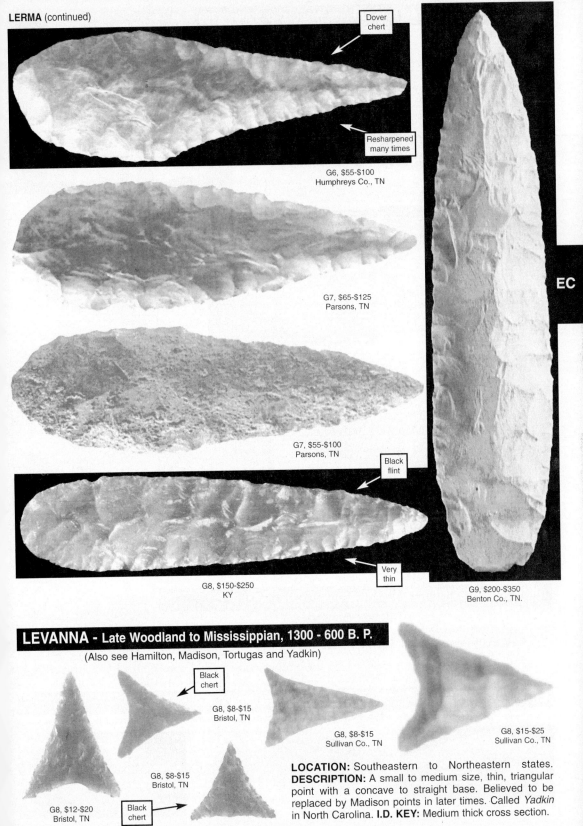

LERMA (continued)

Dover chert

Resharpened many times

G6, $55-$100
Humphreys Co., TN

G7, $65-$125
Parsons, TN

G7, $55-$100
Parsons, TN

Black flint

Very thin

G8, $150-$250
KY

EC

G9, $200-$350
Benton Co., TN.

LEVANNA - Late Woodland to Mississippian, 1300 - 600 B. P.

(Also see Hamilton, Madison, Tortugas and Yadkin)

Black chert

G8, $8-$15
Bristol, TN

G8, $8-$15
Sullivan Co., TN

G8, $15-$25
Sullivan Co., TN

G8, $8-$15
Bristol, TN

Black chert

G8, $12-$20
Bristol, TN

LOCATION: Southeastern to Northeastern states. **DESCRIPTION:** A small to medium size, thin, triangular point with a concave to straight base. Believed to be replaced by Madison points in later times. Called *Yadkin* in North Carolina. **I.D. KEY:** Medium thick cross section.

427

LIMESTONE - Late Archaic to Early Woodland, 5000 - 2000 B. P.

(Also see Fairland, Johnson, McIntire)

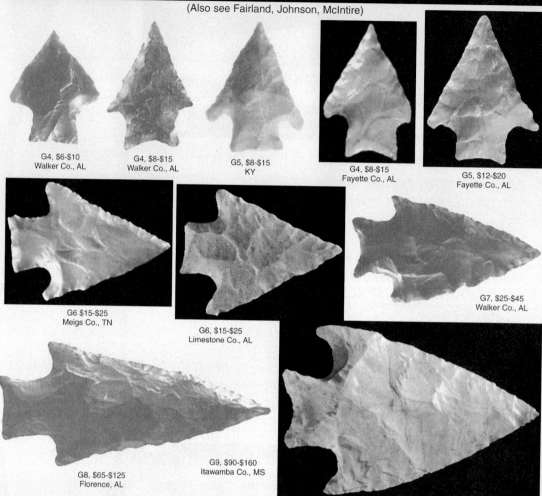

G4, $6-$10
Walker Co., AL

G4, $8-$15
Walker Co., AL

G5, $8-$15
KY

G4, $8-$15
Fayette Co., AL

G5, $12-$20
Fayette Co., AL

G6 $15-$25
Meigs Co., TN

G6, $15-$25
Limestone Co., AL

G7, $25-$45
Walker Co., AL

G8, $65-$125
Florence, AL

G9, $90-$160
Itawamba Co., MS

LOCATION: Southeastern states. **DESCRIPTION:** A small to medium size, triangular stemmed point with an expanded, concave base and barbed to tapered shoulders. Blade edges are concave, convex or straight. **I.D. KEY:** Concave base, one barb is higher.

LIMETON BIFURCATE - Early Archaic, 9000 - 6000 B. P.

(Also see Haw River)

LOCATION: Eastern states. **DESCRIPTION:** A medium size, crudely made, broad, lanceolate blade with a central notch in the base.

G6, $5-$10
Southeast, TN

LITTLE BEAR CREEK - Late Archaic to late Woodland, 4000 - 1500 B. P.

(Also see Adena, Kays, McWhinney, Mulberry Creek, Pickwick and Ponchartrain)

Red jasper

G6 $12-$20
Madison Co., AL

G6, $15-$25
W. TN

G6, $6-$12
N. E. MS

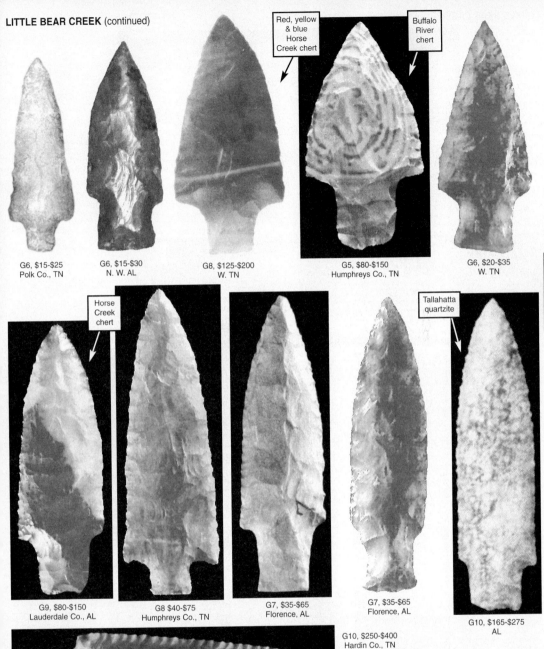

Red, yellow & blue Horse Creek chert

Buffalo River chert

G6, $15-$25
Polk Co., TN

G6, $15-$30
N. W. AL

G8, $125-$200
W. TN

G5, $80-$150
Humphreys Co., TN

G6, $20-$35
W. TN

EC

Horse Creek chert

Tallahatta quartzite

G9, $80-$150
Lauderdale Co., AL

G8 $40-$75
Humphreys Co., TN

G7, $35-$65
Florence, AL

G7, $35-$65
Florence, AL

G10, $165-$275
AL

G10, $250-$400
Hardin Co., TN

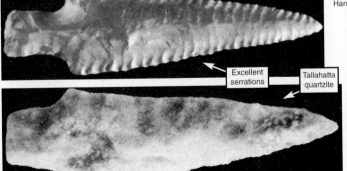

Excellent serrations

Tallahatta quartzite

LOCATION: Southeastern states. **DESCRIPTION:** A medium to large size, narrow point with a long parallel stem that may contract or expand slightly. Blade edges are slightly convex. Shoulders are usually squared, tapered or slightly barbed. The base can be fractured or snapped off. Blade edges can be beveled on one side of each face and finely serrated. Called *Sarasota* in Florida. **I.D. KEY:** Straight base, woodland flaking.

G10, $200-$350
AL

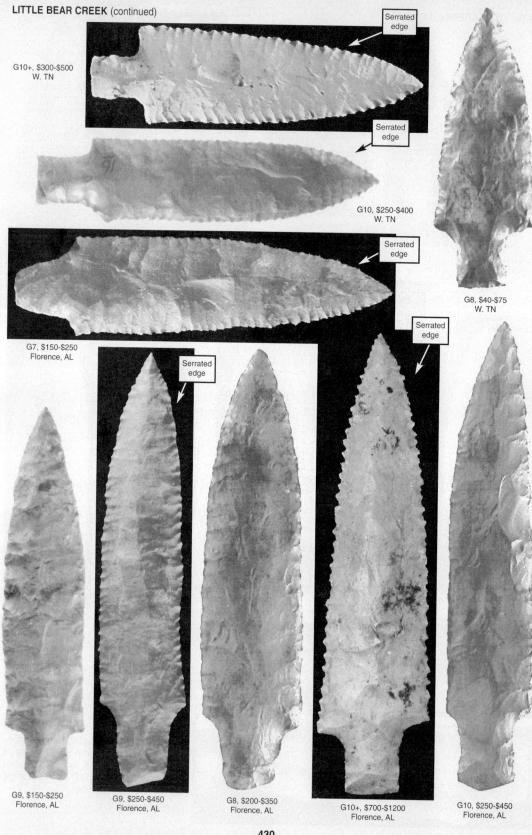

Serrated edge

Serrated edge

G10+, $300-$500
W. TN

G10, $250-$400
W. TN

Serrated edge

G8, $40-$75
W. TN

Serrated edge

G7, $150-$250
Florence, AL

Serrated edge

Serrated edge

G9, $150-$250
Florence, AL

G9, $250-$450
Florence, AL

G8, $200-$350
Florence, AL

G10+, $700-$1200
Florence, AL

G10, $250-$450
Florence, AL

(Also see Cobbs, Cypress Creek, Hardin, Kirk Corner Notched, St. Charles and Thebes)

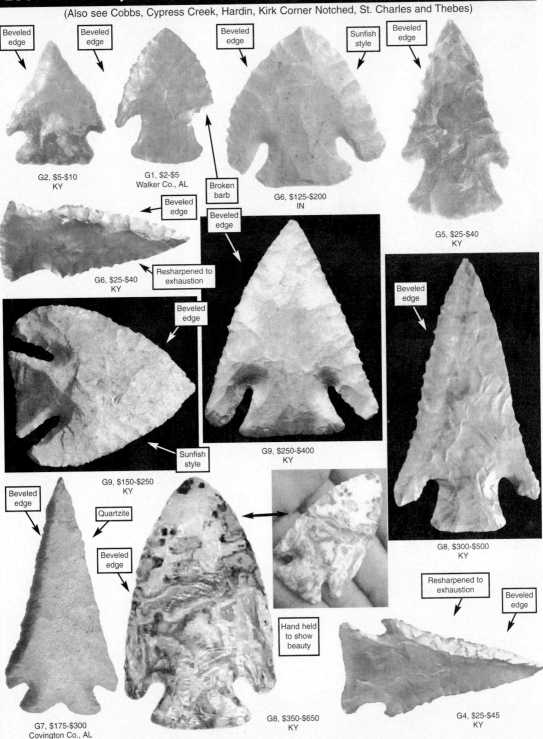

Beveled edge

Beveled edge

Beveled edge

Sunfish style

Beveled edge

G2, $5-$10
KY

G1, $2-$5
Walker Co., AL

Beveled edge

Broken barb

G6, $125-$200
IN

Beveled edge

G6, $25-$40
KY

Resharpened to exhaustion

Beveled edge

G5, $25-$40
KY

Beveled edge

Beveled edge

Sunfish style

G9, $250-$400
KY

G9, $150-$250
KY

G8, $300-$500
KY

Beveled edge

Quartzite

Beveled edge

Hand held to show beauty

Resharpened to exhaustion

Beveled edge

G7, $175-$300
Covington Co., AL

G8, $350-$650
KY

G4, $25-$45
KY

EC

LOCATION: Southeastern states. **DESCRIPTION:** A medium to large size, broad, corner notched point that is beveled on one side of each face. The beveling continues when resharpened which created a flat rhomboid cross section. Most examples are finely serrated and exhibit high quality flaking and symmetry. Also known as *Deep Notch,* and typed as *Bolen Bevel Corner Notched* in Florida. **I.D. KEY:** Notching, secondary edgework is always opposite creating at least slight beveling.

Beveled edge

Beveled edge

Beveled edge

G8, $450-$800
KY

G6, $175-$300
Coffee Lake, AL

G10, $1500-$2500
Crossville, TN

Beveled edge

Beveled edge

Beveled edge

G7, $300-$500
Florence, AL

G8, 700-$1200
Florence, AL

Beveled edge

G9, $1500-$2500
Florence, AL

G10+, $2000-$3500
Giles Co., TN

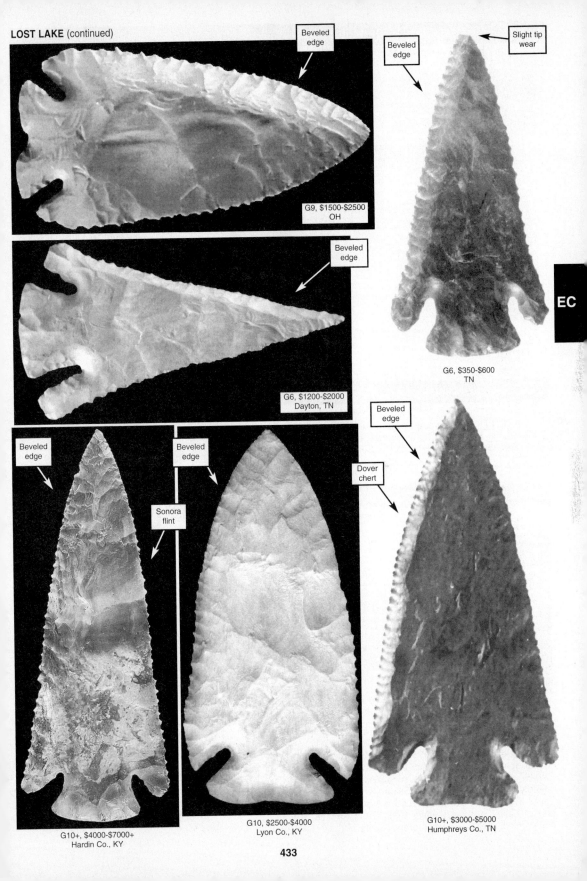

LOST LAKE (continued)

Beveled edge

G9, $1500-$2500
OH

Beveled edge

G6, $1200-$2000
Dayton, TN

Beveled edge

Slight tip wear

G6, $350-$600
TN

EC

Beveled edge

Sonora flint

G10+, $4000-$7000+
Hardin Co., KY

Beveled edge

G10, $2500-$4000
Lyon Co., KY

Beveled edge

Dover chert

G10+, $3000-$5000
Humphreys Co., TN

433

LOWE - Mississippian, 1650 - 1450 B. P.

(Also see Bakers Creek, Chesser, McIntire, Mud Creek and Table Rock)

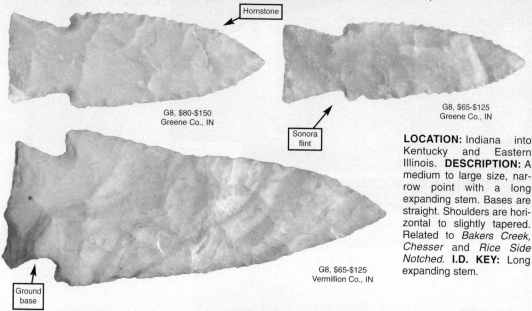

Hornstone

G8, $80-$150
Greene Co., IN

G8, $65-$125
Greene Co., IN

Sonora flint

Ground base

G8, $65-$125
Vermillion Co., IN

LOCATION: Indiana into Kentucky and Eastern Illinois. **DESCRIPTION:** A medium to large size, narrow point with a long expanding stem. Bases are straight. Shoulders are horizontal to slightly tapered. Related to *Bakers Creek, Chesser* and *Rice Side Notched.* **I.D. KEY:** Long expanding stem.

LOZENGE - Mississippian, 1000 - 400 B. P.

(Also see Nodena)

LOCATION: Midwestern to Southeastern states. **DESCRIPTION:** A small size, narrow, thin, double pointed arrow point.

G8, $8-$15
KY

MACCORKLE - Early Archaic, 8000 - 6000 B. P.

(Also see Kanawha Stemmed, Kirk Stemmed-Bifurcated, LeCroy, Rice Lobbed and St. Albans)

G5, $20-$35
Dayton, TN

G6, $15-$25
S. E. TN

G6, $20-$35
S. E. TN

Serrated edge

G8, $35-$60
Benton Co., KY

LOCATION: Midwestern to Southeastern states. **DESCRIPTION:** A medium to large size, thin, usually serrated, widely corner notched point with large round ears and a deep notch in the center of the base. Bases are usually ground. The smaller examples can be easily confused with the *LeCroy* point. Shoulders and blade expand more towards the base than *LeCroy*, but only in some cases. Called *Nottoway River Bifurcate* in Virginia. **I.D. KEY:** Basal notching, early Archaic flaking.

G6, $25-$40
Florence, AL

MACCORKLE (continued)

Coshocton chert

Serrated edge

G9, $30-$55
OH

G9, $40-$75
Union Co., OH

G10, $125-$200
KY

Serrated edge

G6, $25-$40
S. E. TN

G9, $150-$250
Florence, AL

G5, $12-$20
S. E. TN

G8, $80-$150
OH

Knife form

Serrated edge

Buffalo River chert

Serrated edge

Serrated edge

G9, $150-$250
Sumner Co., TN

G10, $200-$350
Humphreys Co., TN

G10, $300-$550
Hardin Co., KY

EC

MACE - Mississippian, 1100 - 600 B. P.

(Also see Dagger and Sun Disc)

All Maces shown half size

G10, $2000-$3500
Henry Co., TN

G8, $1500-$2500
Stewart Co., TN

G8, $1200-$2000
Montgomery Co., TN

LOCATION: Southeastern states. **DESCRIPTION:** A very large, thick, hand-held barbed dagger used in the Sun dance ceremony along with the Duck River Swords, Sun Discs and shell gorgets by the Mississippian culture. Such dances are depicted on the shell gorgets themselves. These objects are made from high grade flint and are flaked to perfection. **Warning:** Absolute provinence is needed to prove authenticity. Very rare, existing mostly in museum collections. **I.D. KEY:** Thickness, notching, flaking.

MADISON - Mississippian, 1100 - 200 B. P.

(Also see Camp Creek, Fort Ancient, Guntersville, Hamilton, Levanna, Sand Mountain and Valina)

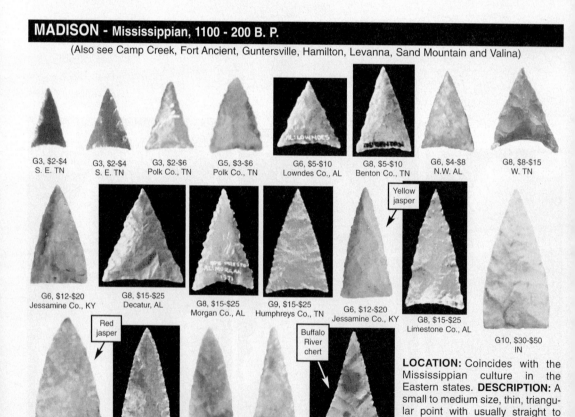

G3, $2-$4
S. E. TN

G3, $2-$4
S. E. TN

G3, $2-$6
Polk Co., TN

G5, $3-$6
Polk Co., TN

G6, $5-$10
Lowndes Co., AL

G8, $5-$10
Benton Co., TN

G6, $4-$8
N.W. AL

G8, $8-$15
W. TN

G6, $12-$20
Jessamine Co., KY

G8, $15-$25
Decatur, AL

G8, $15-$25
Morgan Co., AL

G9, $15-$25
Humphreys Co., TN

G6, $12-$20
Jessamine Co., KY

Yellow jasper

G8, $15-$25
Limestone Co., AL

G10, $30-$50
IN

Red jasper

G10, $35-$65
KY

G8, $30-$50
Humphreys Co., TN

G6, $15-$25
KY

G10, $35-$65
TN

Buffalo River chert

G9, $35-$65
Humphreys Co., TN

LOCATION: Coincides with the Mississippian culture in the Eastern states. **DESCRIPTION:** A small to medium size, thin, triangular point with usually straight to convex sides. Bases are straight to concave. Some examples are notched on one to two sides. Many are of high quality and some are finely serrated.

MADISON (continued)

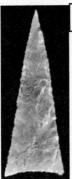
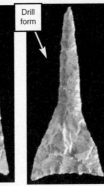
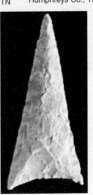

G9, $35-$65 Meigs Co., TN	G10, $35-$65 TN	G8, $35-$65 Dayton, TN	G9, $45-$80 Humphreys Co., TN	G10, $45-$80 Humphreys Co., TN	G9, $45-$80 Humphreys Co., TN	G10, $45-$80 Morgan Co., AL

Drill
form

G8, $45-$80 Humphreys Co., TN	G10, $55-$100 Humphreys Co., TN	G10, $45-$80 Hamilton Co., TN	G10, $55-$100 Humphreys Co., TN	G9, $45-$80 Humphreys Co., TN	G9, $45-$80 Humphreys Co., TN

EC

MAPLES - Middle Archaic, 4500 - 3500 B. P.

(Also see Elora, Morrow Mountain and Savannah River)

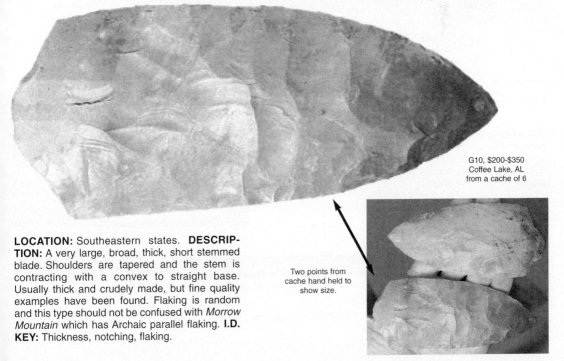

G10, $200-$350
Coffee Lake, AL
from a cache of 6

Two points from
cache hand held to
show size.

LOCATION: Southeastern states. **DESCRIP-TION:** A very large, broad, thick, short stemmed blade. Shoulders are tapered and the stem is contracting with a convex to straight base. Usually thick and crudely made, but fine quality examples have been found. Flaking is random and this type should not be confused with *Morrow Mountain* which has Archaic parallel flaking. **I.D. KEY:** Thickness, notching, flaking.

437

Two points from
cache hand held to
show size.

G7, $150-$250
Coffee Lake, AL
from a cache of 6

G9, $175-$300
Coffee Lake, AL
from a cache of 6

MARIANNA - Transitional Paleo, 10,000 - 8500 B. P.

(Also see Angostura, Browns Valley and Conerly)

LOCATION: Southern to Southeastern states. **DESCRIPTION:** A medium size lanceolate point with a constricted, concave base. Look for parallel to oblique flaking.

G7, $15-$25
Dayton, TN. Note
diagonal flaking.

MATANZAS - Mid-Archaic to Woodland, 4500 - 2500 B. P.

(Also see Brewerton Side Notched, Brunswick and Swan Lake)

LOCATION: Ohio westward to Iowa. **DESCRIPTION:** A narrow, medium size point with broad side notches to an expanding stem.

MATANZAS (continued)

G6, $15-$25
KY

Base
nick

G4, $4-$8
KY

MCINTIRE - Middle to Late Archaic, 6000 - 4000 B. P.

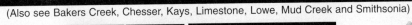

(Also see Bakers Creek, Chesser, Kays, Limestone, Lowe, Mud Creek and Smithsonia)

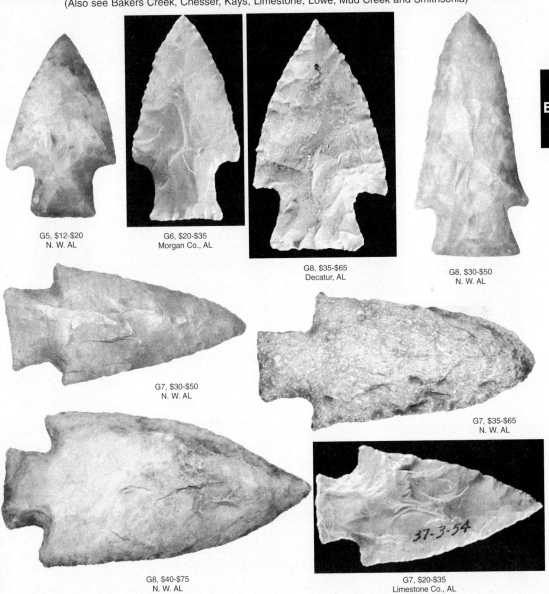

G5, $12-$20
N. W. AL

G6, $20-$35
Morgan Co., AL

G8, $35-$65
Decatur, AL

G8, $30-$50
N. W. AL

G7, $30-$50
N. W. AL

G7, $35-$65
N. W. AL

G8, $40-$75
N. W. AL

G7, $20-$35
Limestone Co., AL

LOCATION: Southeastern states. **DESCRIPTION:** A medium to large point with straight to convex blade edges and a broad parallel to expanding stem. Shoulders are square to slightly barbed and the base is usually straight.

MCWHINNEY HEAVY STEMMED - Mid-Late Archaic, 6000 - 3000 B. P.

(Also see Heavy Duty, Little Bear Creek, Mud Creek, Mulberry Creek and Pickwick)

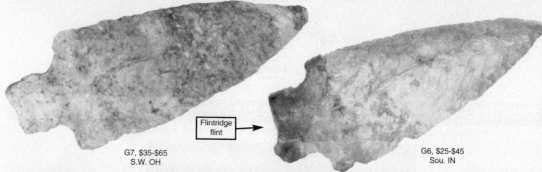

Flintridge flint →

G7, $35-$65
S.W. OH

G6, $25-$45
Sou. IN

LOCATION: Illinois, Ohio into Kentucky. **DESCRIPTION:** A medium size, fairly thick point with a short stem and squared shoulders. Stems can be bulbous, straight to expanding. On some examples side notches occur where the stem and shoulders intersect. Previously known as the *Flint River Spike* point.

MEADOWOOD - Late Archaic to Woodland, 4000 - 2000 B. P.

(Also see Big Sandy and Newton Falls)

G6, $25-$45
OH

G7, $35-$65
OH

G7, $40-$75
KY

G7, $35-$65
N. W. AL

G6, $55-$100
OH

LOCATION: Northeastern to Eastern states. **DESCRIPTION:** Medium to large size, thick, broad side notched point. Notches occur close to the base. This point is found from Indiana to New York.

MEADOWOOD (continued)

Coshocton chert

G6, $80-$150
Fayette Co., KY

G8, $150-$275
Dearborne Co., IN

G8, $150-$275
Shelby Co., IN

EC

MERKLE - Late Archaic to Woodland, 4000 - 2000 B. P.
(Also see Evans and Leighton)

G4, $12-$20
Polk Co., TN

G6, $25-$45
Hamilton Co., TN

G6, $20-$35
KY

G6, $25-$45
Hamilton Co., TN

G5, $25-$40
Nickajack Lake, TN

G10, $65-$125
Humphreys Co., TN

G9, $35-$65
KY

LOCATION: Midwestern states into Tennessee. **DESCRIPTION:** A medium size point with a short stem and broad side notches and corner notches at the base. Bases are usually straight to convex. **I.D. KEY:** Double notching.

441

MEROM - Late Archaic, 4000 - 3000 B. P.
(Also see Keota)

G7, $4-$8
Polk Co., TN

G5, $1-$3
Meigs Co., TN

G7, $3-$5
TN

G6, $3-$5
Polk Co., TN

LOCATION: Illinois into Tenn. & Kent. **DESCRIPTION:** A small size, triangular, point with wide side notches and a convex base. Some examples have fine serrations.

MESERVE - Early to Middle Archaic, 9500 - 4000 B. P.
(Also see Dalton)

G8, $60-$100
OH

G9, $65-$125
TN

LOCATION: Midwestern states, rarely into Ohio & Tennessee. **DESCRIPTION:** A medium size, auriculate form with a blade that is beveled on one side of each face. Beveling extends into the basal area. This type is related to *Dalton* points.

MONTGOMERY - Woodland, 2500 - 1000 B. P.
(Also see Benjamin, Ebenezer and Morrow Mountain)

Milky quartz

Milky quartz

Milky quartz

G5, $1-$2
Montgomery Co., AL

G5, $1-$2
Montgomery Co., AL

G5, $1-$3
Montgomery Co., AL

G5, $1-$3
Montgomery Co., AL

G5, $1-$3
Autauga Co., AL

G5, $1-$3
Jackson Co., AL

G8, $2-$4
Autauga Co., AL

LOCATION: Southeastern states. **DESCRIPTION:** A small, broad, tear-drop shaped point with a rounded base. Flaking is random. This type is similar to *Catan* found in Texas.

MORROW MOUNTAIN - Middle Archaic, 7000 - 5000 B. P.
(Also see Buggs Island, Cypress Creek, Ebenezer, Elora, Eva and Maples)

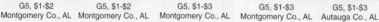

Milky quartz

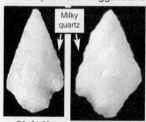

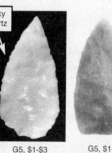

G2, $1-$2
Burke Co., GA

G2, $1-$2
Burke Co., GA

G4, $2-$4
Jessamine Co., KY

G6, $8-$15
Polk Co., TN

G4, $3-$6
Jessamine Co., KY

LOCATION: Midwestern to Southeastern states. **DESCRIPTION:** A medium to large size, triangular point with a very short contracting to rounded stem. Shoulders are usually weak but can be barbed. The blade edges on some examples are serrated with needle points. **I.D. KEY:** Contracted base and Archaic parallel flaking.

MORROW MOUNTAIN (continued)

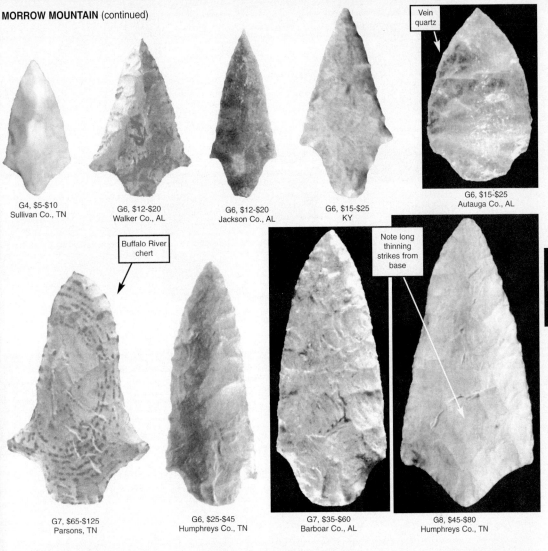

G4, $5-$10
Sullivan Co., TN

G6, $12-$20
Walker Co., AL

G6, $12-$20
Jackson Co., AL

G6, $15-$25
KY

Vein quartz

G6, $15-$25
Autauga Co., AL

Buffalo River chert

Note long thinning strikes from base

EC

G7, $65-$125
Parsons, TN

G6, $25-$45
Humphreys Co., TN

G7, $35-$60
Barboar Co., AL

G8, $45-$80
Humphreys Co., TN

MORROW MOUNTAIN ROUNDED BASE - Middle Archaic, 7000 - 5000 B. P.

(Also see Ebenezer, Guilford Round Base and Montgomery)

Crystal

G3, $1-$2
Polk Co., TN

G3, $1-$2
S. E. TN

G4, $5-$10
Burke Co., GA

G5, $2-$4
Jessamine Co., KY

G5, $2-$4
Dunlap, TN

Crystal

G6, $12-$20
Burke Co., GA

LOCATION: Midwestern to Southeastern states. **DESCRIPTION:** A small to medium size tear-drop point with a pronounced, short, rounded base and no shoulders. Some examples have a straight to slightly convex base. This type has similarities to Gypsum Cave points found in the Western states.

MORROW MOUNTAIN ROUND BASE (continued)

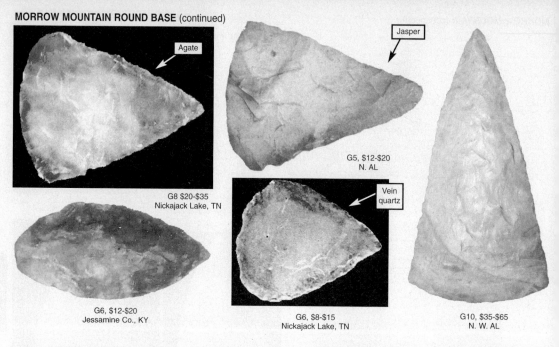

Agate

Jasper

G8 $20-$35
Nickajack Lake, TN

G5, $12-$20
N. AL

Vein quartz

G6, $12-$20
Jessamine Co., KY

G6, $8-$15
Nickajack Lake, TN

G10, $35-$65
N. W. AL

MORROW MOUNTAIN STRAIGHT BASE - Middle Archaic, 7000 - 5000 B. P.

(Also see Hidden Valley, Mud Creek)

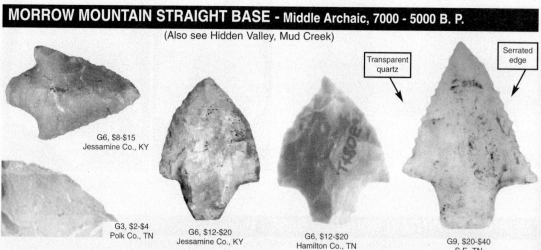

Transparent quartz

Serrated edge

G6, $8-$15
Jessamine Co., KY

G3, $2-$4
Polk Co., TN

G6, $12-$20
Jessamine Co., KY

G6, $12-$20
Hamilton Co., TN

G9, $20-$40
S.E. TN

LOCATION: Southeastern states. **DESCRIPTION:** A medium size, thin, strongly barbed point with a contracting stem and a straight base. Some examples are serrated and have a needle tip. Look for Archaic parallel flaking.

MORSE KNIFE - Woodland, 3000 - 1500 B. P.

(Also see Cotaco Creek, Duck River Sword, Ramey Knife and Snake Creek)

Rind showing at base

IMPORTANT:
Morse Knives are shown half size

G7, $450-$800
W. TN

LOCATION: Midwestern to Southeastern states. **DESCRIPTION:** A large lanceolate blade with a long contracting stem and a rounded base. The widest part of the blade is towards the tip.

444

MORSE KNIFE (continued)

IMPORTANT: Morse Knives are shown half size

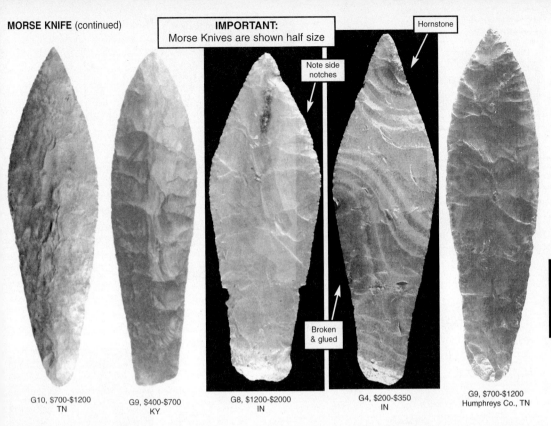

Hornstone

Note side notches

Broken & glued

EC

G10, $700-$1200
TN

G9, $400-$700
KY

G8, $1200-$2000
IN

G4, $200-$350
IN

G9, $700-$1200
Humphreys Co., TN

MOTLEY - Late Archaic to Woodland, 4500 - 2500 B. P.

(Also see Buck Creek, Epps, Hamilton, Smithsonia, Snyders and Wade)

G5, $8-$15
Jessamine Co., KY

G4, $8-$15
Jessamine Co., KY

G6, $15-$30
KY

G6, $20-$35
IN

G5 $15-$25
OG

G5 $15-$25
Meigs Co., TN

G7, $25-$45
KY

LOCATION: Southeastern states. **DESCRIPTION:** A medium to large size, expanded stemmed to widely corner notched point with strong barbs. The blade edges and the base are convex to straight. Has been found associated with *Wade* points in caches. Similar to *Epps* found in Louisiana which has a straight base; *Motley*s are more barbed than *Epps*.

445

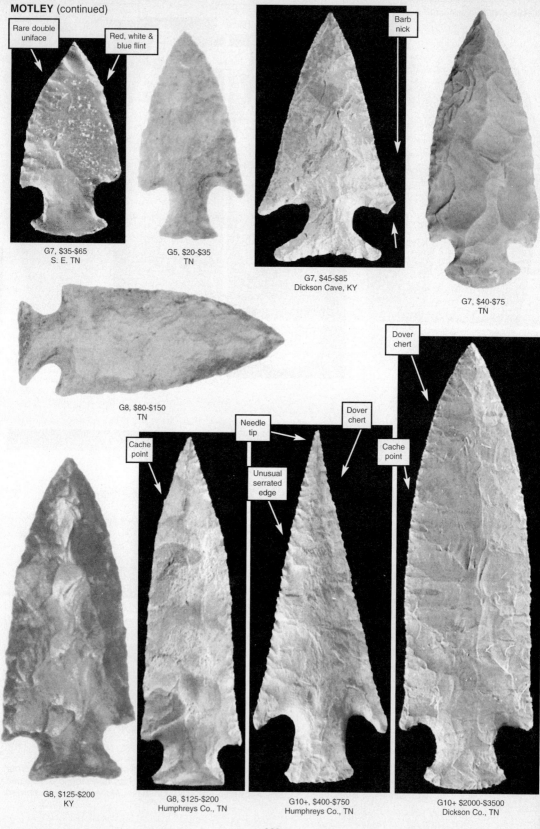

MOTLEY (continued)

Rare double uniface

Red, white & blue flint

G7, $35-$65
S. E. TN

G5, $20-$35
TN

Barb nick

G7, $45-$85
Dickson Cave, KY

G7, $40-$75
TN

G8, $80-$150
TN

Dover chert

Cache point

Needle tip

Unusual serrated edge

Dover chert

Cache point

G8, $125-$200
KY

G8, $125-$200
Humphreys Co., TN

G10+, $400-$750
Humphreys Co., TN

G10+ 2000-$3500
Dickson Co., TN

MOUNTAIN FORK - Middle Archaic to Woodland, 6000 - 2000 B. P.

(Also see Bradley Spike, Duval and New Market)

G4, $8-$15
Decatur, AL

G6, $15-$25
S.E. TN

G4, $8-$15
Ft. Payne, AL

G4, $8-$15
Decatur, AL

G6, $20-$35
Limestone Co., AL

G6, $12-$20
W. TN

LOCATION: Southeastern states. **DESCRIPTION:** A small to medium size, narrow, thick, stemmed point with tapered shoulders.

MOUSE CREEK - Woodland, 1500 - 1000 B. P.

EC

(Also see Jacks Reef Pentagonal)

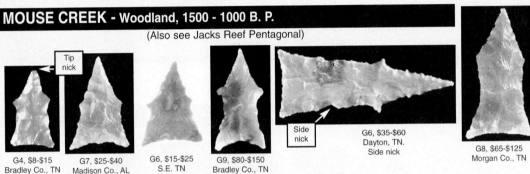

Tip nick

G4, $8-$15
Bradley Co., TN

G7, $25-$40
Madison Co., AL

G6, $15-$25
S.E. TN

G9, $80-$150
Bradley Co., TN

Side nick

G6, $35-$60
Dayton, TN.
Side nick

G8, $65-$125
Morgan Co., TN

LOCATION: Southeastern states. **DESCRIPTION:** A small to medium size, thin, pentagonal point with prominent shoulders, a short pointed blade and a long, expanding stem. The base is concave with pointed ears. The hafting area is over half the length of the point. This type is **very rare** and could be related to Jacks Reef. A similar form is found in OK, TX, & LA called "Snow Lake."

MUD CREEK - Late Archaic to Woodland, 4000 - 2000 B. P.

(Also see Bakers Creek, Beacon Island, Chesser, Flint Creek, Little Bear Creek, Lowe, McIntire, McWhinney and Mulberry Creek)

G6, $3-$6
W. TN

G5, $2-$5
W. TN

G2, $1-$2
Jessamine Co., KY

G4, $2-$4
Sullivan Co., TN

G5, $2-$5
E. TN

G5 $4-$8
Dunlap, TN

G7, $12-$20
Decatur, AL

LOCATION: Southeastern states. **DESCRIPTION:** A medium size point with slightly recurved blade edges, a narrow, needle like tip, square to tapered shoulders and an expanded stem. Called *Patuxent* in Virginia. **I.D. KEY:** Thickness, point form, high barb.

MUD CREEK (continued)

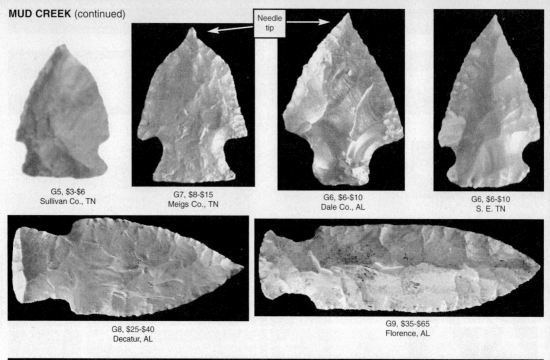

Needle tip

G5, $3-$6
Sullivan Co., TN

G7, $8-$15
Meigs Co., TN

G6, $6-$10
Dale Co., AL

G6, $6-$10
S. E. TN

G8, $25-$40
Decatur, AL

G9, $35-$65
Florence, AL

MULBERRY CREEK - Mid-Archaic to Woodland, 5000 - 3000 B. P.

(Also see Little Bear Creek, McWhinney and Pickwick)

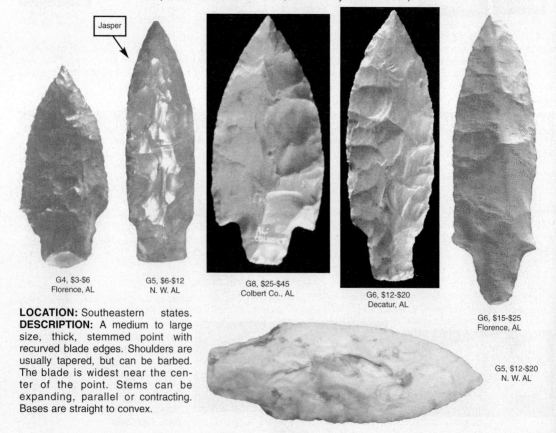

Jasper

G4, $3-$6
Florence, AL

G5, $6-$12
N. W. AL

G8, $25-$45
Colbert Co., AL

G6, $12-$20
Decatur, AL

G6, $15-$25
Florence, AL

G5, $12-$20
N. W. AL

LOCATION: Southeastern states.
DESCRIPTION: A medium to large size, thick, stemmed point with recurved blade edges. Shoulders are usually tapered, but can be barbed. The blade is widest near the center of the point. Stems can be expanding, parallel or contracting. Bases are straight to convex.

448

MULBERRY CREEK (continued)

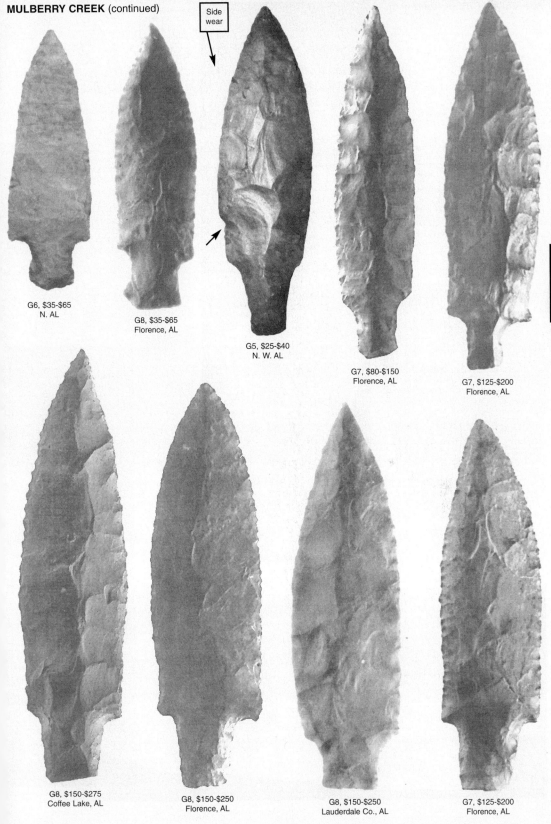

Side wear

G6, $35-$65
N. AL

G8, $35-$65
Florence, AL

G5, $25-$40
N. W. AL

G7, $80-$150
Florence, AL

G7, $125-$200
Florence, AL

EC

G8, $150-$275
Coffee Lake, AL

G8, $150-$250
Florence, AL

G8, $150-$250
Lauderdale Co., AL

G7, $125-$200
Florence, AL

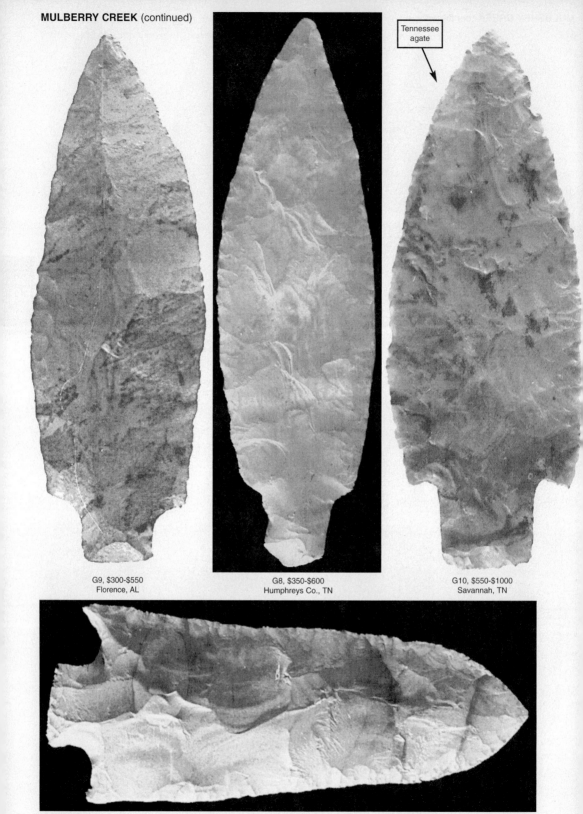

Tennessee agate

G9, $300-$550
Florence, AL

G8, $350-$600
Humphreys Co., TN

G10, $550-$1000
Savannah, TN

G9, $350-$600
Hamilton Co., TN

NEUBERGER - Early-Mid Archaic, 9000 - 6000 B. P.

(Also see Kirk Corner Notched and Pine Tree)

LOCATION: Tennessee, Kentucky, Ohio to Illinois. **DESCRIPTION:** A medium to large size, broad, corner notched point with a short, auriculated base. Blade edges are recurved and the base is indented. Shoulders curve in towards the base.

G10, $275-$500
TN

G10, $400-$750
KY

EC

NEW MARKET - Woodland, 3000 - 1000 B. P.

(Also see Bradley Spike, Buggs Island, Duval and Flint River)

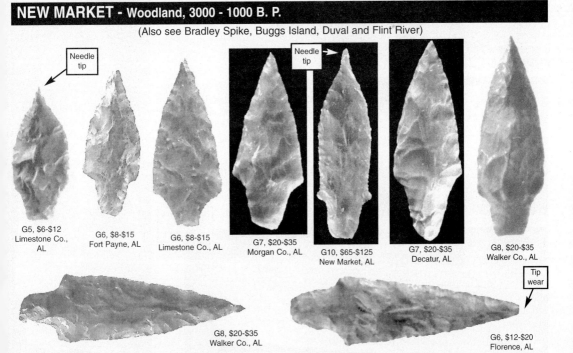

Needle tip

Needle tip

Tip wear

G5, $6-$12
Limestone Co.,
AL

G6, $8-$15
Fort Payne, AL

G6, $8-$15
Limestone Co., AL

G7, $20-$35
Morgan Co., AL

G10, $65-$125
New Market, AL

G7, $20-$35
Decatur, AL

G8, $20-$35
Walker Co., AL

G8, $20-$35
Walker Co., AL

G6, $12-$20
Florence, AL

LOCATION: Southeastern states. **DESCRIPTION:** A small to medium size point with tapered shoulders and an extended, rounded base. Shoulders are usually asymmetrical with one higher than the other.

(Also see Benton, Big Sandy, Cache River, Graham Cave and Meadowood)

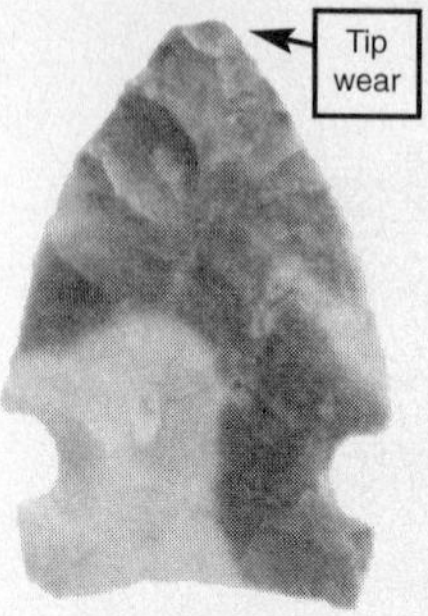

Tip wear

G6, $15-$25
OH

Burlington chert

G7, $65-$125
OH

G9, $350-$650
Alexander, OH

G9, $250-$400
IN

G8, $65-$150
OH

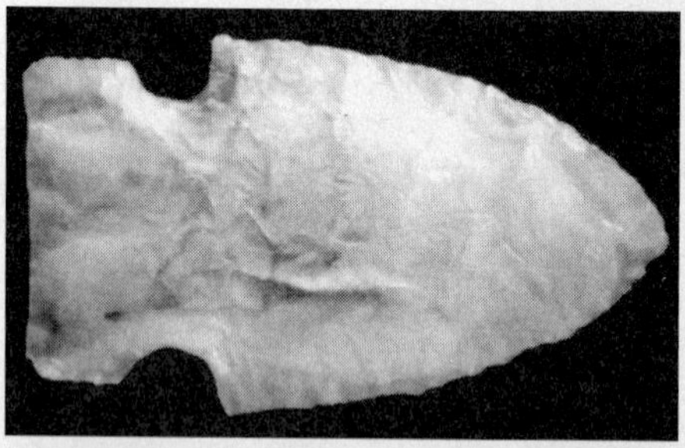

LOCATION: Ohio and surrounding states. **DESCRIPTION:** A medium to large size, narrow, side notched point with paralled sides on longer examples and a straight to concave base which could be ground. Similar to *Big Sandy, Godar, Hemphill* and *Osceola* found in other areas. **I.D. KEY:** Size and narrowness.

G8, $30-$60
OH

Red, yellow & blue Horse Creek chert

Tip wear

G6, $90-$175
TN

G6, $65-$125
Union Co., OH

NODENA - Mississippian to Historic, 600 - 400 B. P.

(Also see Guntersville and Lozenge)

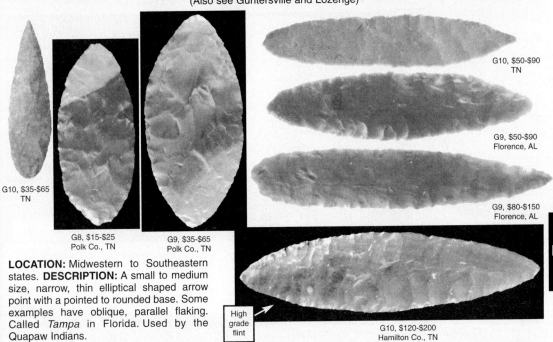

G10, $50-$90
TN

G9, $50-$90
Florence, AL

G9, $80-$150
Florence, AL

G10, $35-$65
TN

G8, $15-$25
Polk Co., TN

G9, $35-$65
Polk Co., TN

High
grade
flint

G10, $120-$200
Hamilton Co., TN

EC

LOCATION: Midwestern to Southeastern states. **DESCRIPTION:** A small to medium size, narrow, thin elliptical shaped arrow point with a pointed to rounded base. Some examples have oblique, parallel flaking. Called *Tampa* in Florida. Used by the Quapaw Indians.

NOLICHUCKY - Woodland, 3000 - 1500 B. P.

(Also see Camp Creek, Candy Creek, Copena Auriculate, Greeneville and Yadkin)

G5, $2-$5
Bristol, TN

G6, $5-$10
Bristol, TN

G5, $4-$8
Bristol, TN

G6, $5-$10
Sullivan Co., TN

G9, $30-$50
Clarksville, TN

G10, $80-$150
Bristol, TN

G10, $80-$150
Dunlap, TN

G6, $12-$20
Sullivan Co., TN

H7

Needle
tip

G6, $8-$15
Bradley Co., TN

G9, $30-$50
Bradley Co., TN

G5, $5-$10
Sullivan Co., TN

LOCATION: Southeastern states. **DESCRIPTION:** A small to medium size, triangular point with recurved blade edges and a straight to concave base. Most examples have small pointed ears at the basal corners. Bases could be ground. Believed to have evolved from *Candy Creek* points and later developed into *Camp Creek*, *Greeneville* and *Guntersville* points. Found with *Ebenezer*, *Camp Creek*, *Candy Creek* and *Greeneville* in caches (Rankin site, Cocke Co. TN.) **I.D. KEY:** Thickness and hafting area.

NORTH - Woodland, 2200 - 1600 B. P.

(Also see Adena Blade, Hopewell, Snyders and Tear Drop)

Flint Ridge flint

G6, $40-$75
OH

G8, $200-$350
Sidney, OH

LOCATION: Midwestern to Eastern states. **DESCRIPTION:** A large, thin, elliptical, broad, well made blade with a concave blade. This type is usually found in caches and is related to the Snyders point of the Hopewell culture. Believed to be unnotched Snyders points.

NOVA - Woodland to Mississippian, 1600 - 1000 B. P.

(Also see Durant's Bend and Washington)

LOCATION: Southeastern states. **DESCRIPTION:** A small point shaped like a five pointed star.

G8, $3-$5
Dallas Co., AL

G5, $1-$2
Dallas Co., AL

G6, $1-$3
Dallas Co., AL

G2, $1-$2
Dallas Co., AL

OHIO DOUBLE NOTCHED - Woodland, 3000 - 2000 B. P.

(Also see Benton, Evans, Leighton and St. Helena)

G9, $350-$600
OH

G5, $35-$60
OH

LOCATION: Ohio and surrounding states. **DESCRIPTION:** A medium to large size, narrow, rather crude, point with side notches on both sides and a short base that is usually notched.

OHIO LANCEOLATE - Trans. Paleo-Early Archaic, 10,500 - 8000 B. P.

(Also see Agate Basin, Angostura, Browns Valley, Sedalia)

OHIO LANCEOLATE (continued)

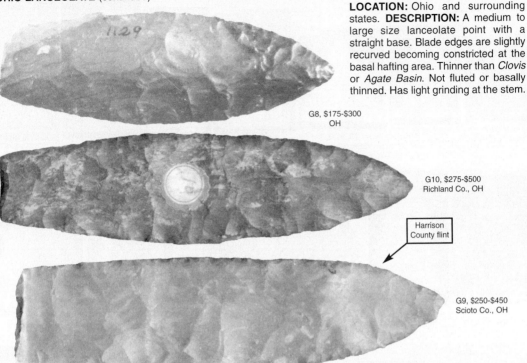

LOCATION: Ohio and surrounding states. **DESCRIPTION:** A medium to large size lanceolate point with a straight base. Blade edges are slightly recurved becoming constricted at the basal hafting area. Thinner than *Clovis* or *Agate Basin*. Not fluted or basally thinned. Has light grinding at the stem.

G8, $175-$300
OH

G10, $275-$500
Richland Co., OH

Harrison County flint

G9, $250-$450
Scioto Co., OH

EC

PAINT ROCK VALLEY - Transitional Paleo, 10,000 - 6000 B. P.

(Also see Angostura, Browns Valley, Frazier, Hardaway Blade, Jeff and Tortugas)

Basal thinning

G7, $35-$65
Colbert Co., AL

G6, $30-$50
Fort Payne, AL

G6, $30-$50
Warren Co., TN

G7, $35-$65
Decatur Co., AL

G9, $65-$125
Walker Co., AL

LOCATION: Southeastern states. **DESCRIPTION:** A medium size, wide, lanceolate point with a concave base. Flaking is usually parallel with fine secondary work on the blade edges. The bases may be multiple fluted, thinned or beveled.

PALMER - Early Archaic, 9000 - 6000 B. P.

(Also see Autauga, Decatur, Ecusta, Kirk Corner Notched and Pine Tree)

LOCATION: Southeastern to Eastern states. **DESCRIPTION:** A small size, corner notched, triangular point with a ground concave, convex or straight base. Many are serrated and large examples would fall under the *Pine Tree* or *Kirk* type. This type developed from *Hardaway* in North Carolina where cross types are found.

PALMER (continued)

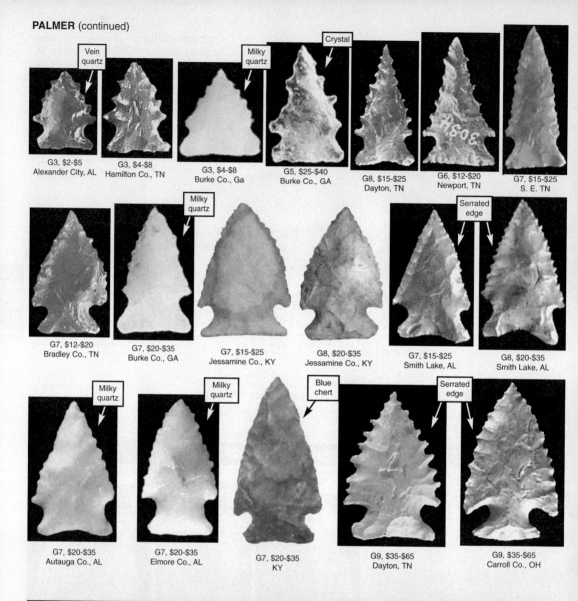

Vein quartz

G3, $2-$5
Alexander City, AL

G3, $4-$8
Hamilton Co., TN

Milky quartz

G3, $4-$8
Burke Co., Ga

Crystal

G5, $25-$40
Burke Co., GA

G8, $15-$25
Dayton, TN

G6, $12-$20
Newport, TN

G7, $15-$25
S. E. TN

G7, $12-$20
Bradley Co., TN

Milky quartz

G7, $20-$35
Burke Co., GA

G7, $15-$25
Jessamine Co., KY

G8, $20-$35
Jessamine Co., KY

Serrated edge

G7, $15-$25
Smith Lake, AL

G8, $20-$35
Smith Lake, AL

Milky quartz

G7, $20-$35
Autauga Co., AL

Milky quartz

G7, $20-$35
Elmore Co., AL

Blue chert

G7, $20-$35
KY

Serrated edge

G9, $35-$65
Dayton, TN

G9, $35-$65
Carroll Co., OH

PATRICK - Mid-Archaic, 5000 - 3000 B. P.

(Also see Cave Spring, Fox Valley, Kanawha Stemmed, LeCroy, Stanly and Wheeler)

G5, $3-$6
Sequatchie Valley, TN

G5, $5-$10
KY

G7, $8-$15
Dunlap., TN

LOCATION: Eastern states. **DESCRIPTION:** A small to medium size, narrow point with very weak shoulders and a long, parallel sided, bifurcated stem.

PELICAN - Transitional Paleo, 10,000 - 6000 B. P.

(Also see Hinds and Arkabutla and Coldwater in SW Section)

PELICAN (continued)

Ground basal area

G9, $225-$400
Sou. MS

G9, $200-$350
Sou. MS

G8, $150-$250
Blueskin Creek, MS

G9, $250-$450
Sou. MS

EC

LOCATION: Mississippi, Tennessee westward intro Texas and Arkansas. **DESCRIPTION:** A short, broad, usually auriculate point with basal grinding. Shoulders taper into a long contracting stem. Some examples are basally thinned or fluted. **I.D. KEY:** Basal contraction, small size.

PENTAGONAL KNIFE - Mid-Archaic, 6500 - 4000 B. P.

(Also see Jacks Reef Corner Notched)

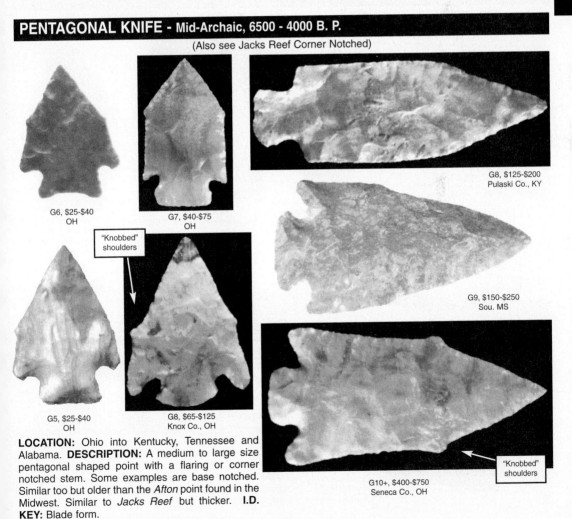

G6, $25-$40
OH

G7, $40-$75
OH

"Knobbed" shoulders

G5, $25-$40
OH

G8, $65-$125
Knox Co., OH

G8, $125-$200
Pulaski Co., KY

G9, $150-$250
Sou. MS

G10+, $400-$750
Seneca Co., OH

"Knobbed" shoulders

LOCATION: Ohio into Kentucky, Tennessee and Alabama. **DESCRIPTION:** A medium to large size pentagonal shaped point with a flaring or corner notched stem. Some examples are base notched. Similar too but older than the *Afton* point found in the Midwest. Similar to *Jacks Reef* but thicker. **I.D. KEY:** Blade form.

457

PERFORATOR - Archaic to Mississippian, 9000 - 400 B. P.

(Also see Drill, Graver and Lancet)

Made from a Pickwick point

Made from a Pickwick point

G3, $2-$5
Sullivan Co., TN

G7, $6-$12
KY

G7, $8-$15
Meigs Co., TN

G7, $8-$15
KY

G7, $12-$20
TN

LOCATION: Archaic and Woodland sites everywhere. **DESCRIPTION:** A jabbing projection at the tip would qualify for the type. It is believed that *perforators* were used for tattooing, incising or to punch holes in leather or other materials or objects. Paleo peoples used *Gravers* for the same purpose. All Archaic and Woodland cultures converted their points into this type. Therefore, most point types could occur in this form.

PICKWICK - Middle to Late Archaic, 6000 - 3500 B. P.

(Also see Elora, Ledbetter, Little Bear Creek, McWhinney, Mulberry Creek and Shoals Creek)

G5, $2-$5
Sullivan Co., TN

G5, $4-$8
Sullivan Co., TN

G6, $12-$20
Sullivan Co., TN

G6, $12-$20
Meigs Co., TN

G7, $15-$30
Meigs Co., TN

G7, $25-$45
N. W. AL

G8, $25-$45
N. W. AL

G8, $25-$45
N. W. AL

LOCATION: Southeastern states. **DESCRIPTION:** A medium to large size, expanded shoulder, contracted to expanded stem point. Blade edges are recurved, and many examples show fine secondary flaking with serrations. Some are beveled on one side of each face. The bevel is steep and shallow. Shoulders are horizontal, tapered or barbed and form sharp angles. Some stems are snapped off or may show original rind.

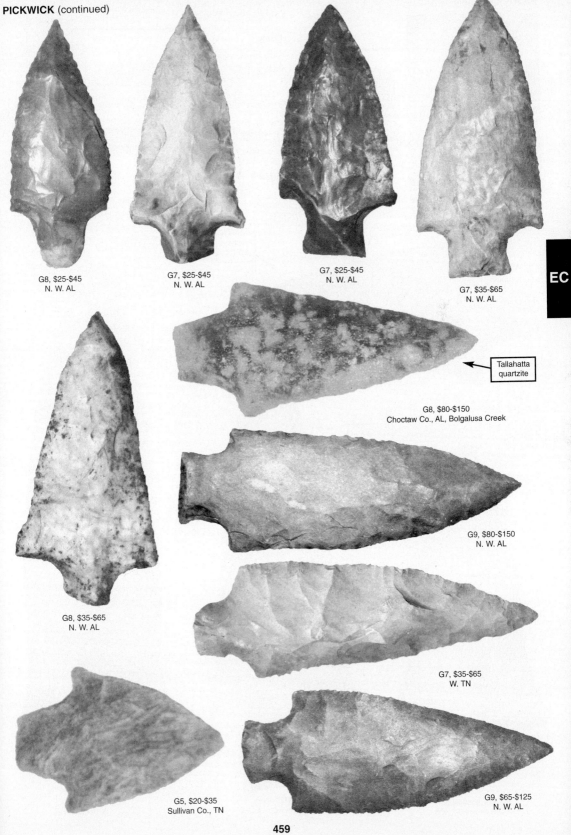

EC

G8, $25-$45
N. W. AL

G7, $25-$45
N. W. AL

G7, $25-$45
N. W. AL

G7, $35-$65
N. W. AL

Tallahatta quartzite

G8, $80-$150
Choctaw Co., AL, Bolgalusa Creek

G9, $80-$150
N. W. AL

G8, $35-$65
N. W. AL

G7, $35-$65
W. TN

G5, $20-$35
Sullivan Co., TN

G9, $65-$125
N. W. AL

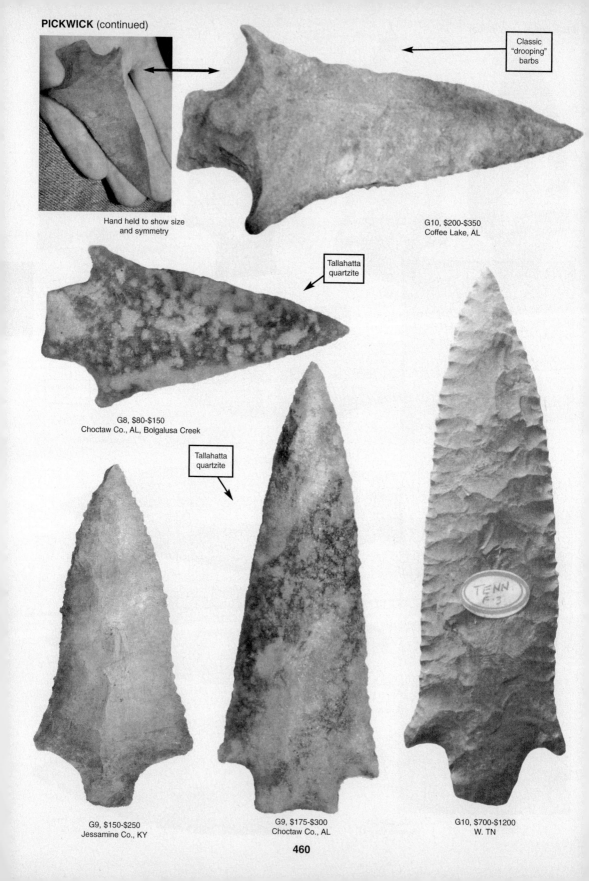

PICKWICK (continued)

Hand held to show size
and symmetry

Classic "drooping" barbs

G10, $200-$350
Coffee Lake, AL

Tallahatta quartzite

G8, $80-$150
Choctaw Co., AL, Bolgalusa Creek

Tallahatta quartzite

TENN.
F-3

G9, $150-$250
Jessamine Co., KY

G9, $175-$300
Choctaw Co., AL

G10, $700-$1200
W. TN

(Also see Big Sandy, Decatur, Greenbrier, Kirk and Palmer)

Tip wear

G3, $2-$5
Jessamine Co., KY

G2, $2-$4
Jessamine Co., KY

G4, $8-$15
Lauderdale Co., AL

G3, $5-$10
Lawrence Co., AL

G8, $15-$25
Dayton, TN

G8, $40-$75
Sullivan Co., TN

Heavily resharpened

Serrated edge

EC

G3, $5-$10
Humphreys Co., TN

G3, $12-$20
Humphreys Co., TN

G8, $15-$25
Hamilton Co., TN

G6, $35-$50
Humphreys Co., TN

G6, $15-$25
N. W. AL

Bifurcated base

Lobbed base

Bifurcated base

Bifurcated base

G5, $25-$40
N. AL

G9, $35-$65
KY

G8, $35-$65
KY

G5, $25-$40
N. AL

G6, $25-$40
TN

Lobbed base

G9, $80-$150
Coffee Lake, AL

LOCATION: Southeastern states. **DESCRIPTION:** A medium to large size, side notched, usually serrated point with parallel flaking to the center of the blade forming a median ridge. The bases are ground and can be concave, convex, straight, or auriculate. This type developed from the earlier *Greenbrier* point. Small examples would fall into the *Palmer* type. **I.D. KEY:** Archaic flaking with long flakes to the center of the blade.

461

PINE TREE (continued)

Serrated edge

Lobbed base

Eared base

Dover chert

G6, $30-$50
Jackson Co., AL

Dover chert

Dover chert

G8, $125-$200
Coffee Lake, AL

G8, $200-$350
Humphreys Co., TN

G6, $80-$150
W. TN

G9, $400-$750
W. KY

G9, $250-$400
Florence, AL

Red, yellow & blue Horse Creek chert

Fort Payne chert

Bifurcated base

Note how pressure flaking goes to the center, typical of the type

G9, $350-$600
Lauderdale Co., AL

G9, $250-$400
Humphreys Co., TN

G10, $650-$1200
IN

G10, $1000-$1800
Coffee Lake, AL

(Also see Kirk, Neuberger and Palmer)

G6, $25-$45
TN

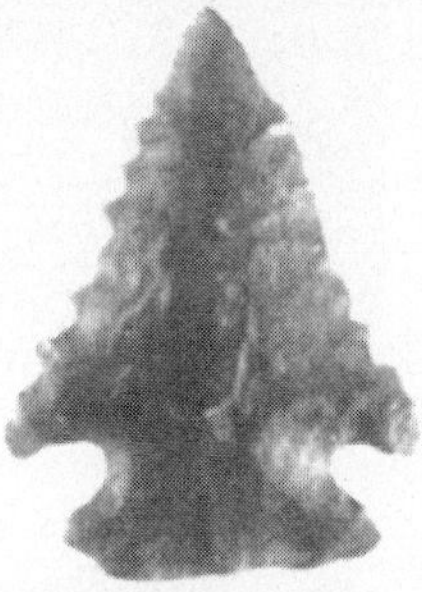

G6, $25-$45
Johnson City, TN

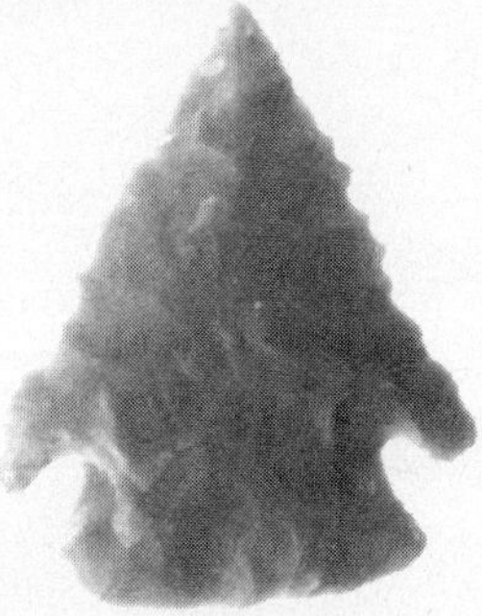

G6, $25-$45
KY

G8, $40-$70
KY

EC

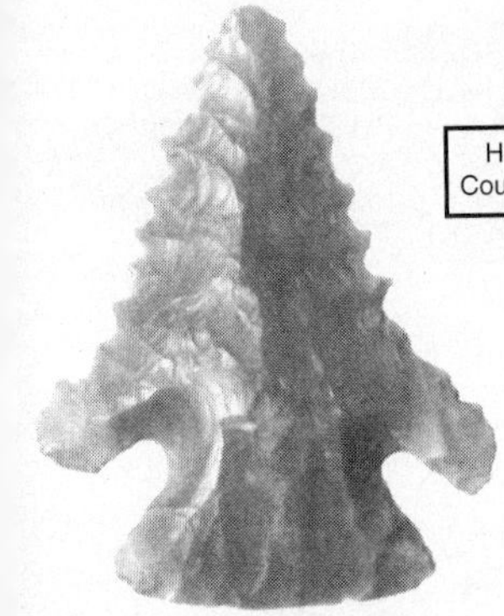

G7, $80-$150
KY

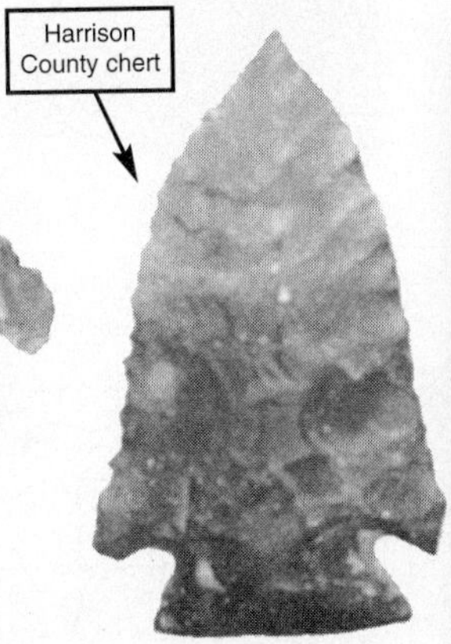

Harrison
County chert

G9, $65-$125
Harrison Co., IN

G8, $125-$200
KY

G10, $175-$300
Coffee Lake, AL

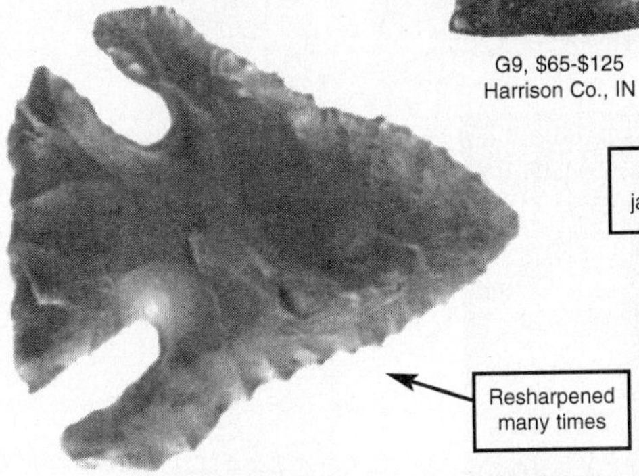

Red
jasper

Serrated
edge

Resharpened
many times

G8, $200-$350
Coffee Lake, AL

Boyle
chert

G9, $300-$550
Clark Co., KY

G9, $200-$350
Clifton, TN

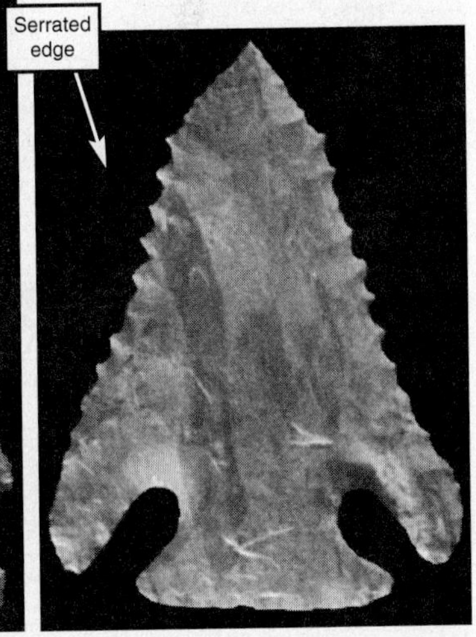

G10, $275-$500
Florence, AL

LOCATION: Southeastern States. **DESCRIPTION:** A small to medium size, thin, corner notched point with a concave, convex, straight, bifurcated or auriculate base. Blade edges are usually serrated and flaking is parallel to the center of the blade. The shoulders expand and are barbed. The base is ground. Small examples would fall under the *Palmer* type. **I.D. KEY:** Archaic flaking to the center of each blade.

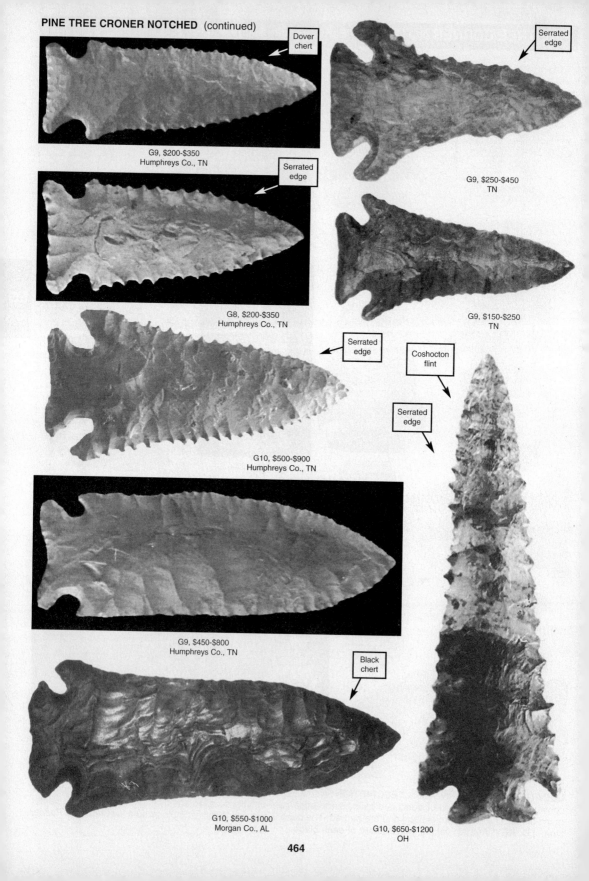

PINE TREE CRONER NOTCHED (continued)

Dover chert

G9, $200-$350
Humphreys Co., TN

Serrated edge

G8, $200-$350
Humphreys Co., TN

Serrated edge

G10, $500-$900
Humphreys Co., TN

G9, $450-$800
Humphreys Co., TN

Serrated edge

G9, $250-$450
TN

G9, $150-$250
TN

Serrated edge

Coshocton flint

Serrated edge

Black chert

G10, $550-$1000
Morgan Co., AL

G10, $650-$1200
OH

PIPE CREEK - Mississippian, 1200 - 1000 B. P.

G7, $15-$25
Portland Lake, TN

G9, $25-$40
W. TN

G8, $20-$35
W. TN

G8, $30-$50
W. TN

LOCATION: Texas to Southeastern states. **DESCRIPTION:** An unusual knife form having a single corner notch at one basal corner. The base is straight to slightly convex and can be lopsided. Perino and others speculate that this tool was used by early arrow makers in preparing feathers for use on arrow shafts.

PLAINVIEW- Late Paleo, 10,000 - 7000 B. P.

(Also see Angostura, Browns Valley, Clovis and Dalton)

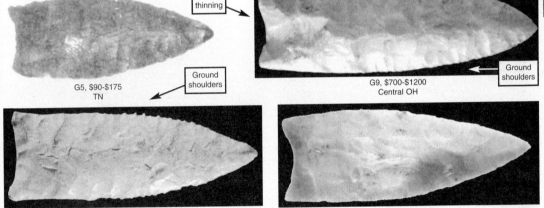

Basal thinning

Ground shoulders

G5, $90-$175
TN

Ground shoulders

G9, $700-$1200
Central OH

G6, $150-$250
W,. Memphis, TN

G8, $250-$450
KY

LOCATION: DESCRIPTION: A medium size, thin, lanceolate point with usually parallel sides and a concave base that is ground. Some examples are thinned or fluted and are believed to be related to the earlier *Clovis* and contemporary *Dalton* type. Flaking is of high quality and can be collateral to oblique transverse.

PLEVNA (See St. Charles)

PONTCHARTRAIN (Type I) - Late Archaic-Woodland, 4000 - 2000 B. P.

(Also see Kays, Little Bear Creek and Mulberry Creek)

G6, $20-$40
Clarksville, TN

G6, $20-$40
TN

LOCATION: Mid-southeastern states. **DESCRIPTION:** A medium to large size, thick, narrow, stemmed point with weak, tapered or barbed shoulders. The stem is parallel sided with a convex base. Some examples are finely serrated and are related and similar to the *Flint Creek* type.

465

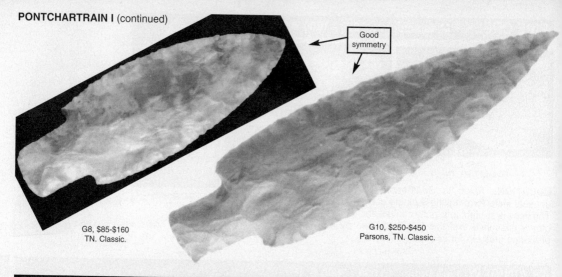

Good symmetry

G8, $85-$160
TN. Classic.

G10, $250-$450
Parsons, TN. Classic.

PONTCHARTRAIN (Type II) - Woodland, 3400 - 2000 B. P.

(Also see Buck Creek, Hardin and Hamilton Stemmed)

Note drooping shoulders

G7, $20-$35
TN

G9, $125-$200
West TN

G8, $35-$60
Noxubee Co., MS

G9, $200-$350
West TN

LOCATION: Mid-southeastern states. **DESCRIPTION:** A medium to large size, broad, stemmed point with barbed shoulders. The stem is parallel to slightly contracting and the base is straight to convex.

QUAD - Late Paleo, 10,000 - 6000 B. P.

(Also see Beaver Lake, Candy Creek, Cumberland, Golondrina and Hinds)

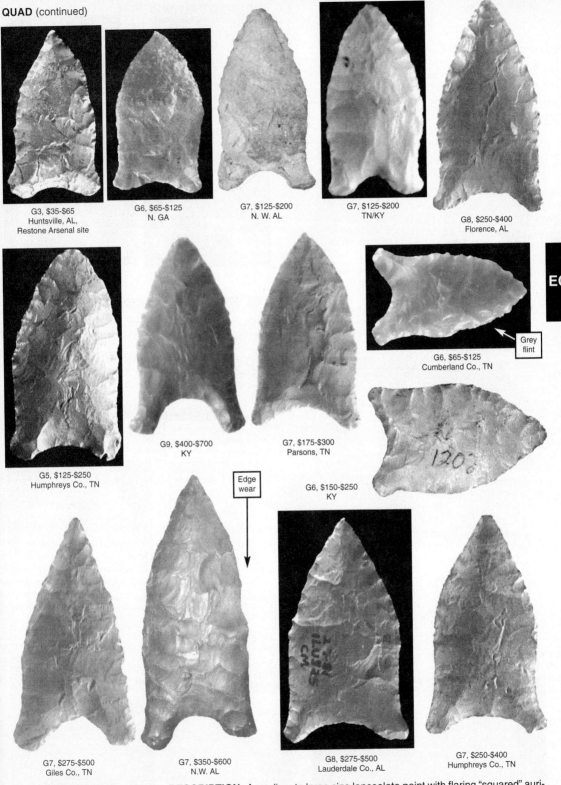

G3, $35-$65
Huntsville, AL,
Restone Arsenal site

G6, $65-$125
N. GA

G7, $125-$200
N. W. AL

G7, $125-$200
TN/KY

G8, $250-$400
Florence, AL

EC

G6, $65-$125
Cumberland Co., TN

Grey flint

G5, $125-$250
Humphreys Co., TN

G9, $400-$700
KY

G7, $175-$300
Parsons, TN

G6, $150-$250
KY

Edge wear

G7, $275-$500
Giles Co., TN

G7, $350-$600
N.W. AL

G8, $275-$500
Lauderdale Co., AL

G7, $250-$400
Humphreys Co., TN

LOCATION: Southeastern states. **DESCRIPTION:** A medium to large size lanceolate point with flaring "squared" auricles and a concave base which is ground. Most examples show basal thinning and some are fluted. Believed to be related to the earlier *Cumberland* point. **I.D. KEY:** Paleo flaking, squarish auricles.

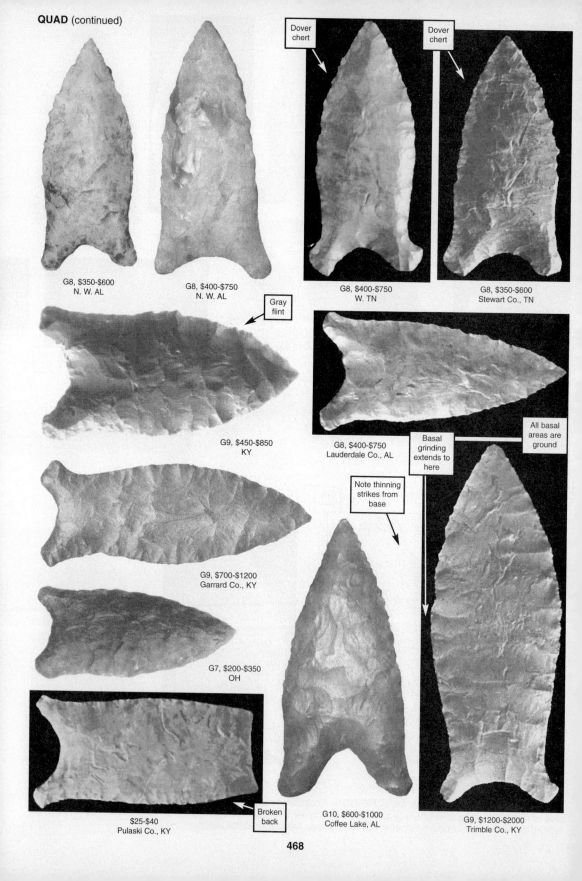

QUAD (continued)

Dover chert

Dover chert

G8, $350-$600
N. W. AL

G8, $400-$750
N. W. AL

G8, $400-$750
W. TN

G8, $350-$600
Stewart Co., TN

Gray flint

G9, $450-$850
KY

G8, $400-$750
Lauderdale Co., AL

Basal grinding extends to here

All basal areas are ground

Note thinning strikes from base

G9, $700-$1200
Garrard Co., KY

G7, $200-$350
OH

Broken back

$25-$40
Pulaski Co., KY

G10, $600-$1000
Coffee Lake, AL

G9, $1200-$2000
Trimble Co., KY

RAMEY KNIFE - Middle Archaic, 5000 - 4000 B. P.

(Also see Cotaco Creek, Morse Knife and Snake Creek)

Note side notches

IMPORTANT:
Shown 50% actual size.

G8, $450-$800
KY

LOCATION: Type site is at the Cahokia Mounds in IL. **DESCRIPTION:** A large size broad, lanceolate blade with a rounded base and high quality flaking. The Tenn. form is similar to the Illinois form.

G8, $450-$800
KY

RHEA CO.
TENN.
L-483

RANKIN - Late Archaic-Woodland, 4000 - 2500 B. P.

(Also see Buck Creek, Hamilton Stemmed and Wade)

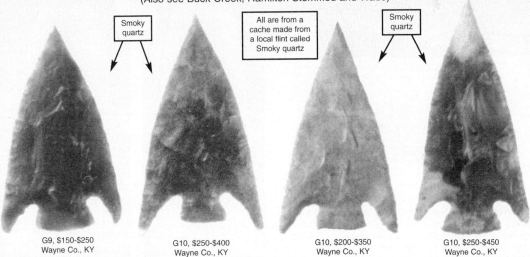

Smoky quartz

All are from a cache made from a local flint called Smoky quartz

Smoky quartz

G9, $150-$250
Wayne Co., KY

G10, $250-$400
Wayne Co., KY

G10, $200-$350
Wayne Co., KY

G10, $250-$450
Wayne Co., KY

LOCATION: Tennessee into Kentucky. **DESCRIPTION:** A medium size, thin, well made barbed dart point with a short, expanding stem. Barbs are pointed and can extend beyond the base. Blade is recurved with a needle tip. **I.D. KEY:** Drooping barbs, short base.

RED OCHRE - Woodland, 3000 - 1500 B. P.

G8, $125-$200
KY

IMPORTANT: This Red Ochre point is shown full size

LOCATION: Mid-western states into Ohio and Kentucky. **DESCRIPTION:** A large, thin, broad blade with a contracting basal area. The base is convex to straight. Very similar to *Wadlow* which has parallel sides. Possibly related to the *Turkeytail* type.

RED OCHRE (continued)
(Also see Adena Blade, Copena Round Base and Tennessee River)

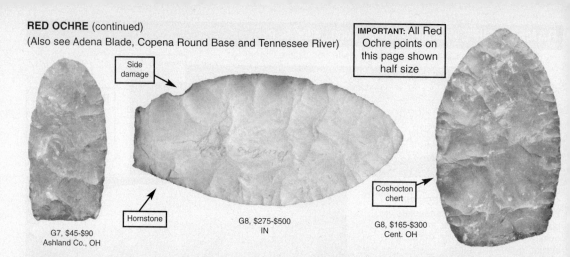

IMPORTANT: All Red Ochre points on this page shown half size

Side damage

Hornstone

G7, $45-$90
Ashland Co., OH

G8, $275-$500
IN

Coshocton chert

G8, $165-$300
Cent. OH

REDSTONE - Paleo, 13,000 - 9000 B. P.

(Also see Clovis and Cumberland)

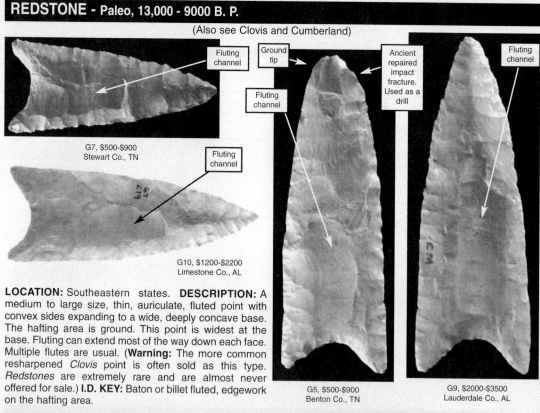

Fluting channel

G7, $500-$900
Stewart Co., TN

Fluting channel

G10, $1200-$2200
Limestone Co., AL

Ground tip

Fluting channel

Ancient repaired impact fracture. Used as a drill

Fluting channel

G5, $500-$900
Benton Co., TN

G9, $2000-$3500
Lauderdale Co., AL

LOCATION: Southeastern states. **DESCRIPTION:** A medium to large size, thin, auriculate, fluted point with convex sides expanding to a wide, deeply concave base. The hafting area is ground. This point is widest at the base. Fluting can extend most of the way down each face. Multiple flutes are usual. (**Warning:** The more common resharpened *Clovis* point is often sold as this type. *Redstones* are extremely rare and are almost never offered for sale.) **I.D. KEY:** Baton or billet fluted, edgework on the hafting area.

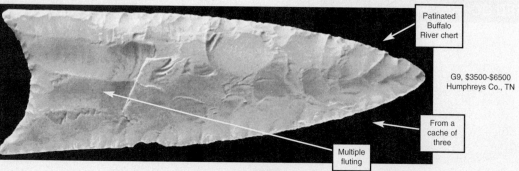

Patinated Buffalo River chert

G9, $3500-$6500
Humphreys Co., TN

From a cache of three

Multiple fluting

470

RHEEMS CREEK - Late Archaic to Woodland, 4000 - 2000 B. P.

(Also see Halifax and Jude)

G2, $1-$2
Meigs Co., TN

G2, $1-$2
N. AL

G3, $2-$4
Huntsville, AL

G5, $3-$6
Meigs Co., TN

G5, $3$6
N. AL

G3, $2-$4
Jessamine Co., KY

LOCATION: Southeastern states. **DESCRIPTION:** A small size, stubby, parallel sided, stemmed point with straight shoulders. Similar to *Halifax* which expands at the base.

RICE LOBBED - Early Archaic, 9000 - 5000 B. P.

(Also see Kanawha, LeCroy, MacCorkle and Pine Tree)

EC

Basal lobes are ground

Barb nick

Serrated edge

G8, $60-$100
OH

G5, $12-$20
OH

G8, $80-$150
Salt Lick, KY

G8, $80-$150
Salt Lick, KY

LOCATION: Midwestern to Northeastern states. **DESCRIPTION:** A medium to large size bifurcated to lobbed base point with serrated blade edges. The base has a shallow indentation compared to the other bifurcated types. Shoulders are sharp and prominent. Called *Culpepper Bifurcate* in Virginia.

ROSS - Woodland, 2500 - 1500 B. P.

(Also see Hopewell, North & Snyders)

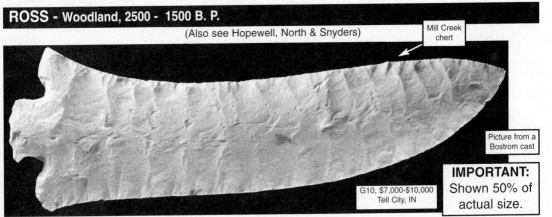

Mill Creek chert

Picture from a Bostrom cast

G10, $7,000-$10,000
Tell City, IN

IMPORTANT: Shown 50% of actual size.

ROSS (continued)

LOCATION: Midwestern to Eastern states. **DESCRIPTION:** A very large size blade with an expanded, rounded base. Some examples have a contracting "V" shaped base. **I.D. KEY:** Size, base form.

RUSSELL CAVE - Early Archaic, 9000 - 7000 B. P.

(Also see Hardaway, Harpeth River, Heavy Duty, Pine Tree and Searcy)

Bifurcated base

Note fine serrations

G5, $12-$20
S.E. TN

G6, $20-$35
Davidson Co., TN

G6, $20-$35
W. TN

G6, $20-$35
Clarksville, TN

G9, $50-$90
Huntsville, AL

Bifurcated base

Dover chert

G8, $55-$100
Humphreys Co., TN

G9, $70-$135
Camden, TN

G6, $20-$35
Limestone Co., AL

LOCATION: Southeastern states. **DESCRIPTION:** A medium size, triangular point with weak shoulders and an expanding to auriculate base. The stem appears to be an extension of the blade edges, expanding to the base. Most examples are serrated and beveled on one side of each face, although some examples are beveled on all four sides. The base is straight, concave, bifurcated or auriculate. **I.D. KEY:** Notched base and edgework.

ST. ALBANS - Early to Middle Archaic, 8900 - 8000 B. P.

(Also see Decatur, Jude, Kanawha Stemmed, Kirk Stemmed-Bifurcated, Lake Erie, LeCroy, MacCorkle, Pine Tree, Rice Lobbed and Stanly)

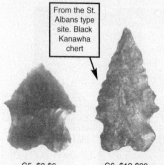

From the St. Albans type site. Black Kanawha chert

G4, $4-$8
E. TN

G5, $5-$10
GA

G5, $3-$6
Hamilton Co., TN

G6, $12-$20
Kanawha Co., WVA

LOCATION: A West Virginia type that extends into Pennsylvania, Virginia, Tennessee and the Carolinas. **DESCRIPTION:** Called *St. Albans Side Notched* in type site report. A small to medium size, usually serrated, narrow, bifurcated point. Basal lobes usually flare outwards. Weak shoulders are formed by slight side notches producing basal lobes or ears. The basal lobes are more shallow than in the *LeCroy* type, otherwise they are easily confused. **I.D. KEY:** Shallow basal lobes.

ST. CHARLES - Early Archaic, 9500 - 8000 B. P.

(Also see Decatur, Gibson, Kirk Corner Notched, Thebes and Warrick)

Tip wear

G4, $5-$10
Jessamine Co., KY

G2, $6-$12
S. E. TN

G4, $12-$20
OH

Beveled edge

G7, $30-$50
Jessamine Co., KY

Beveled edge

G8, $35-$60
Hamilton Co., TN

Beveled edge

Tip wear

G4, $15-$25
KY

Beveled edge

G7, $55-$100
KY

Resharpened many times

G2, $15-$25
KY

Beveled edge

Hornstone

G7, $80-$150
Clark Co., KY

EC

Beveled edge

G8, $45-$85
KY

Beveled edge

Barb wear

G5, $30-$50
KY

Beveled edge

G7, $80-$150
Jessamine Co., KY

Beveled edge

G7, $45-$85
OH

LOCATION: Midwestern to Eastern states. **DESCRIPTION:** A medium to large size, broad, thin, elliptical, corner notched point with a dovetail base. First stage forms are not beveled. Beveling on opposite sides of each face occurs during the resharpening process. The base is convex and most examples exhibit high quality flaking. There is a rare variant that has the barbs clipped (clipped wing) as in the *Decatur* type. There are many variations on base style from bifurcated to eared, rounded or squared. Base size varies from small to very large. Contemporary with the *Hardin* and *Decatur* points. Formally called *Dovetail* and *Plevna* which were the resharpened (beveled) forms. It was previously reported in error that the unbeveled forms were from the late Archaic when actually all are the same type from the early Archaic period. **I.D. KEY:** Dovetail base.

473

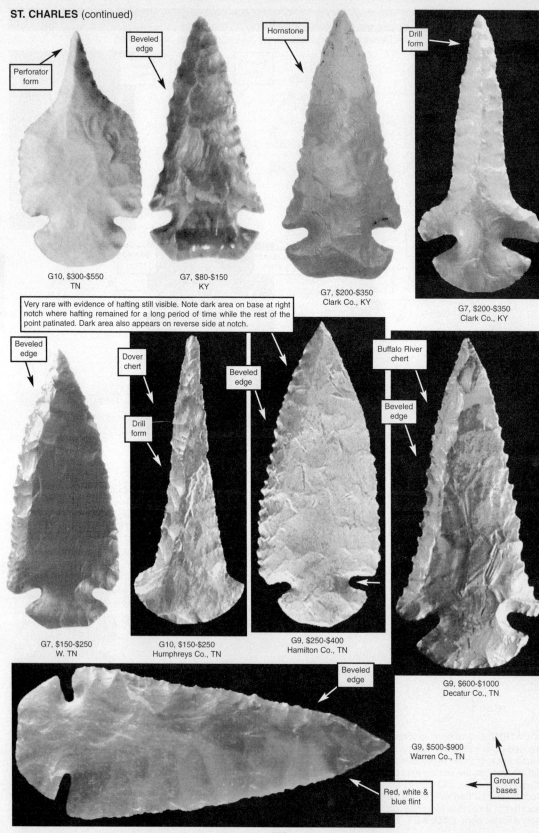

Perforator form

Beveled edge

Hornstone

Drill form

G10, $300-$550
TN

G7, $80-$150
KY

G7, $200-$350
Clark Co., KY

G7, $200-$350
Clark Co., KY

Very rare with evidence of hafting still visible. Note dark area on base at right notch where hafting remained for a long period of time while the rest of the point patinated. Dark area also appears on reverse side at notch.

Beveled edge

Dover chert

Drill form

Beveled edge

Buffalo River chert

Beveled edge

G7, $150-$250
W. TN

G10, $150-$250
Humphreys Co., TN

G9, $250-$400
Hamilton Co., TN

G9, $600-$1000
Decatur Co., TN

Beveled edge

G9, $500-$900
Warren Co., TN

Red, white & blue flint

Ground bases

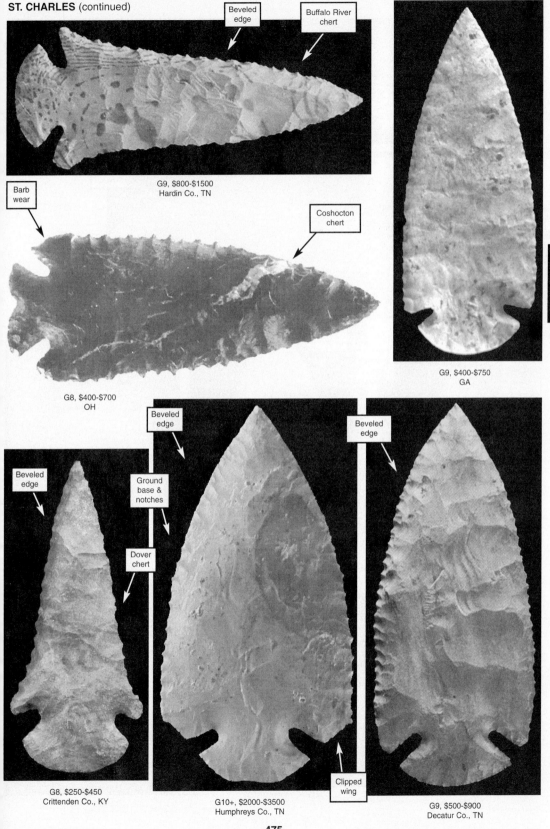

Beveled edge

Buffalo River chert

G9, $800-$1500
Hardin Co., TN

Barb wear

Coshocton chert

G8, $400-$700
OH

G9, $400-$750
GA

EC

Beveled edge

Beveled edge

Ground base & notches

Beveled edge

Dover chert

Clipped wing

G8, $250-$450
Crittenden Co., KY

G10+, $2000-$3500
Humphreys Co., TN

G9, $500-$900
Decatur Co., TN

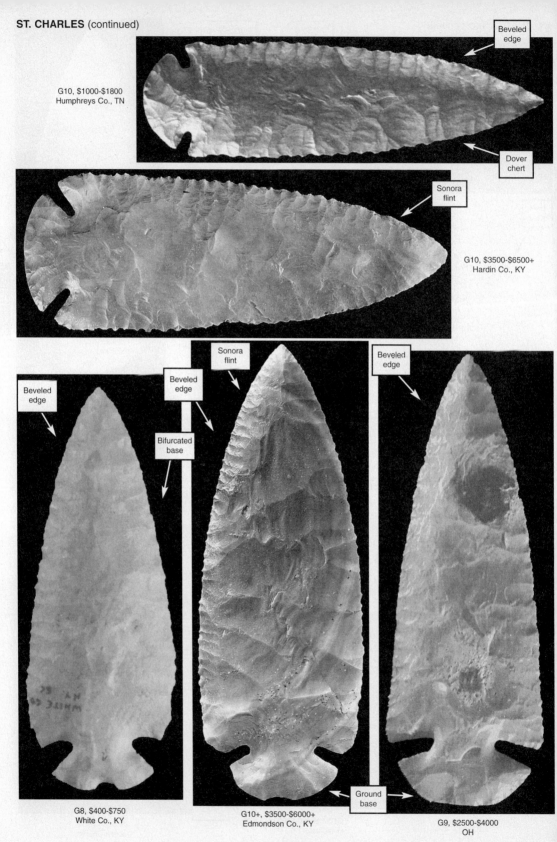

Beveled edge

G10, $1000-$1800
Humphreys Co., TN

Dover chert

Sonora flint

G10, $3500-$6500+
Hardin Co., KY

Beveled edge

Beveled edge

Sonora flint

Beveled edge

Bifurcated base

Ground base

G8, $400-$750
White Co., KY

G10+, $3500-$6000+
Edmondson Co., KY

G9, $2500-$4000
OH

ST. HELENA - Early to Mid-Archaic, 8000 - 5000 B. P.

(Also see Benton, Evans, Leighton and Ohio Double Notched)

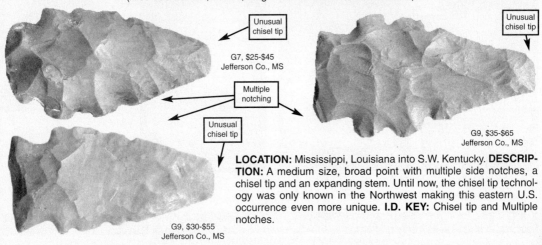

Unusual chisel tip

Unusual chisel tip

G7, $25-$45
Jefferson Co., MS

Multiple notching

Unusual chisel tip

G9, $35-$65
Jefferson Co., MS

LOCATION: Mississippi, Louisiana into S.W. Kentucky. **DESCRIPTION:** A medium size, broad point with multiple side notches, a chisel tip and an expanding stem. Until now, the chisel tip technology was only known in the Northwest making this eastern U.S. occurrence even more unique. **I.D. KEY:** Chisel tip and Multiple notches.

G9, $30-$55
Jefferson Co., MS

ST. TAMMANY - Early to Mid-Archaic, 8000 - 5000 B. P.

(Also see Evans, Kirk Stemmed and St. Helena)

Unique apiculate tip

G5, $25-$45
W. TN

Notched edges

G8, $50-$90
Jefferson Co., MS

Unique apiculate tip

Unique chisel tip

G8, $40-$70
Jefferson Co., MS

G8, $45-$80
Jefferson Co., MS

LOCATION: Mississippi into LA. **DESCRIPTION:** A medium size, expanded stem point with broad serrations on the blade edges. Base is straight to convex and an apiculate distal end. Some examples have a chisel tip. **I.D. KEY:** Apiculate distal end, blade notching.

SAN PATRICE - Early Archaic, 10,000 - 8000 B. P.

(Also see Coldwater, Dalton, Hinds, Palmer, Pelican)

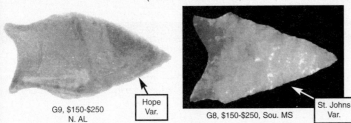

G9, $150-$250
N. AL

Hope Var.

St. Johns Var.

G8, $150-$250, Sou. MS

LOCATION: W. Alabama to Louisiana into Oklahoma. **DESCRIPTION:** A small size, thin, auriculate point with a concave base. Some examples are thinned from the base. Basal area is longer than the "St. Johns" variety and is usually ground. **I.D. KEY:** Extended auriculate base and small size.

EC

477

SAN PATRICE (continued)

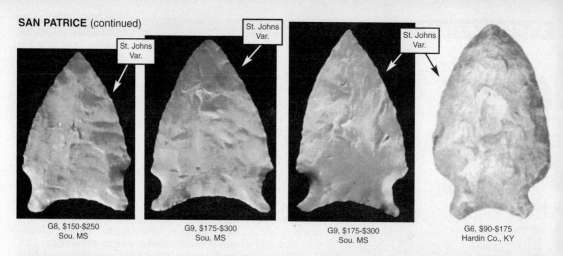

G8, $150-$250
Sou. MS

St. Johns Var.

St. Johns Var.

G9, $175-$300
Sou. MS

St. Johns Var.

G9, $175-$300
Sou. MS

G6, $90-$175
Hardin Co., KY

SAND MOUNTAIN - Late Woodland to Mississippian, 1500 - 400 B. P.

(Also see Durant's Bend, Fort Ancient and Madison)

G3, $3-$6
S. E. TN

G4, $4-$8
Morgan Co., AL

Serrated edge

G6, $8-$15
S. E. TN

G6, $8-$15
Limestone Co., AL

G6, $10-$20
Limestone Co., AL

G7, $25-$40
Morgan Co., AL

G7, $25-$40
Limestone Co., AL

G8, $25-$40
Limestone Co., AL

LOCATION: Southeastern states. **DESCRIPTION:** A small size, triangular point with serrated blade edges and a concave base. A straight base would place it in the *Fort Ancient* type. **I.D. KEY:** Basal corners are not symmetrical.

SAVAGE CAVE - Early to Middle Archaic, 7000 - 4000 B. P.

(Also see Big Sandy and Newton Falls)

G5, $8-$15
Meigs Co., TN

G6, $10-$20
Henry Co., AL

LOCATION: Kentucky and surrounding states. **DESCRIPTION:** A medium to large size, broad, side notched point that is usually serrated. Bases are generally straight but can be slightly concave or convex.

SAVANNAH RIVER - Middle Archaic to Woodland, 5000 - 2000 B. P.

(Also see Appalachian, Elora, Hamilton, Johnson, Kirk, Maples and Stanly)

LOCATION: Southeastern to Eastern states. **DESCRIPTION:** A medium to large size, straight to contracting stemmed point with a straight, concave or bifurcated base. The shoulders are tapered to square. The stems are narrow to broad. Believed to be related to the earlier *Stanly* point.

Milky quartz

G6, $6-$12
Polk Co., TN

G6, $8-$15
Athens, GA

G5, $2-$4
Dayton, TN

Tallahatta quartzite

EC

Tallahatta quartzite

G3, $125-$200
Choctaw Co., AL, Bogalusa Creek

G7, $80-$150
Choctaw Co., AL, Bogalusa Creek

G6, $55-$100
Dodge Co., GA

Triasic diabase

G5, $20-$35
GA

G7, $80-$150
Choctaw Co., AL

479

(Also see Drill, Graver, Lancet and Spokeshave)

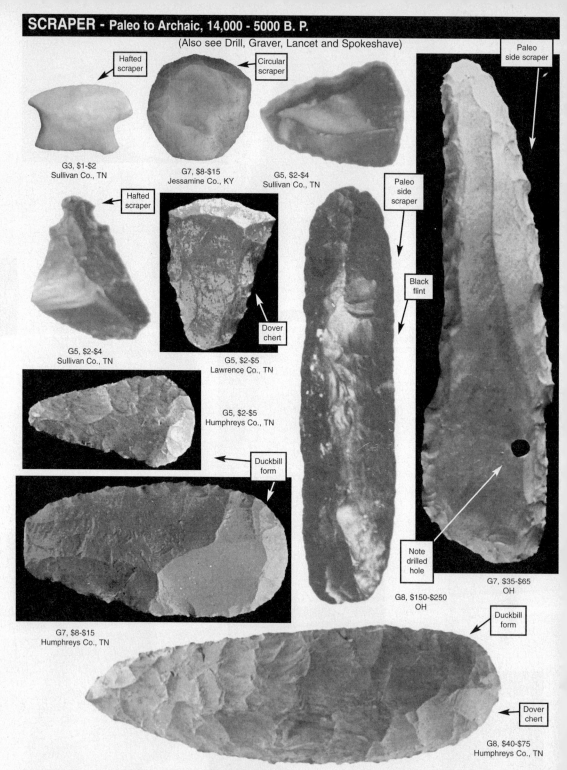

Hafted scraper

G3, $1-$2
Sullivan Co., TN

Circular scraper

G7, $8-$15
Jessamine Co., KY

G5, $2-$4
Sullivan Co., TN

Paleo side scraper

Hafted scraper

G5, $2-$4
Sullivan Co., TN

Dover chert

G5, $2-$5
Lawrence Co., TN

G5, $2-$5
Humphreys Co., TN

Paleo side scraper

Black flint

Note drilled hole

G7, $35-$65
OH

Duckbill form

G7, $8-$15
Humphreys Co., TN

G8, $150-$250
OH

Duckbill form

Dover chert

G8, $40-$75
Humphreys Co., TN

LOCATION: Paleo to early Archaic sites throughout North America. **DESCRIPTION:** Thumb, duckbill and turtleback forms are small to medium size, thick, ovoid shaped, uniface, scraping tools that are steeply beveled, especially at the broadest end. Side scrapers are long hand-held uniface flakes with beveling on all blade edges of one face. Scraping was done primarily from the sides of these blades.

SEARCY - Early to Middle Archaic, 7000 - 5000 B. P.

(Also see Dalton-Colbert, Harpeth River, Kirk Stemmed and Russell Cave)

G6, $15-$25
W. TN

G7, $35-$65
New Market, AL

LOCATION: Midwestern states. **DESCRIPTION:** A small to medium size, thin, lanceolate point with a squared hafting area that (usually) has concave sides and base which is ground. Many examples are serrated.

G5, $15-$25
Meigs Co., TN

SHOALS CREEK - Late Archaic to Woodland, 4000 - 2000 B. P.

(Also see Elora, Kirk Stemmed, Ledbetter, Little Bear Creek, Pickwick and Smithsonia)

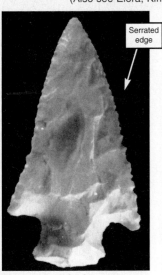

Serrated edge

G6, $18-$30
Lawrence Co., AL

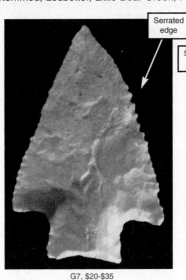

Serrated edge

G7, $20-$35
Lawrence Co., AL

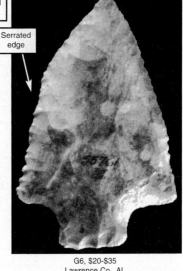

Serrated edge

G6, $20-$35
Lawrence Co., AL

LOCATION: Southeastern states. **DESCRIPTION:** A medium to large size point with serrated edges, an expanded base and sharp barbs.

SMITH - Middle Archaic, 7000 - 4000 B. P.

(Also see Eva, Hamilton, Rankin and Wade)

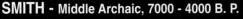

G7, $185-$350
OH

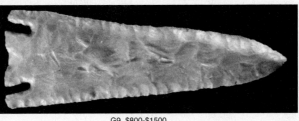

G9, $800-$1500
OH

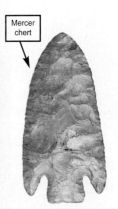

Mercer chert

G9, $400-$750
IN

IMPORTANT:
Smith Points Shown 50% actual size.

481

SMITH (continued)

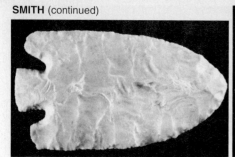

G7, $250-$400
OH

G9, $600-$1000
IN

IMPORTANT:
Smith Points
Shown 50%
actual size.

LOCATION: Midwestern states into Ohio. **DESCRIPTION:** A very large size, broad, point with long parallel shoulders and a squared to slightly expanding base. Some examples may appear to be basally notched due to the long barbs.

SMITHSONIA - Late Archaic to Woodland, 4000 - 1500 B. P.

(See Buck Creek, Cotaco Cr., Hamilton, Motley, Shoals Creek, Table Rock and Wade)

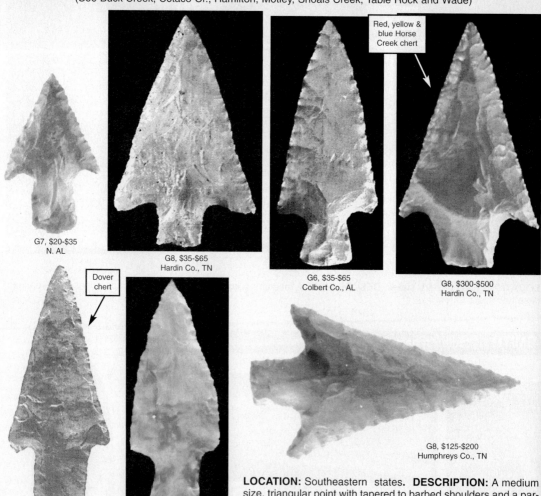

G7, $20-$35
N. AL

G8, $35-$65
Hardin Co., TN

Red, yellow & blue Horse Creek chert

G6, $35-$65
Colbert Co., AL

G8, $300-$500
Hardin Co., TN

Dover chert

G6, $25-$45
Humphreys Co., TN

G5, $15-$25
Putnam Co., TN

G8, $125-$200
Humphreys Co., TN

LOCATION: Southeastern states. **DESCRIPTION:** A medium size, triangular point with tapered to barbed shoulders and a parallel sided stem with a straight base. Many examples have finely serrated blade edges which are usually straight. **I.D. KEY:** High barb on one side and fine edgework.

482

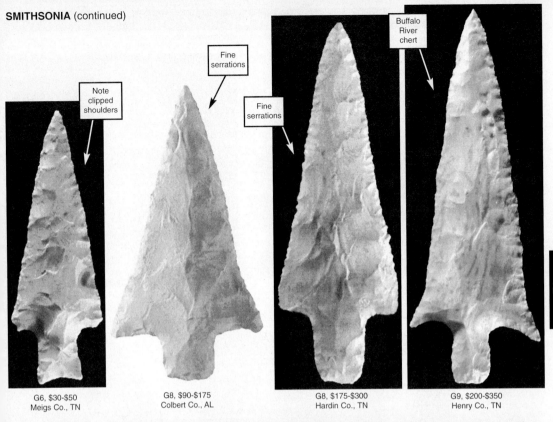

Note clipped shoulders

Fine serrations

Fine serrations

Buffalo River chert

EC

G6, $30-$50
Meigs Co., TN

G8, $90-$175
Colbert Co., AL

G8, $175-$300
Hardin Co., TN

G9, $200-$350
Henry Co., TN

SNAKE CREEK - Late Archaic, 4000 - 3000 B. P.

(Also see Harahey, Lerma, Morse, Ramey Knife and Tear Drop)

Double and single side notches

G9, $350-$600
Hardin Co., TN.
Snake Creek.

Double side notches

G9, $350-$600
Hardin Co., TN. Snake Creek.

LOCATION: Tennessee and Kentucky **DESCRIPTION:** A large size, broad, ovoid blade with shallow side notches about 30 to 40% of the way between the base and tip. Double side notches are common. The stem contracts to a rounded base.

(Also see Buck Creek, Hopewell, Motley and North)

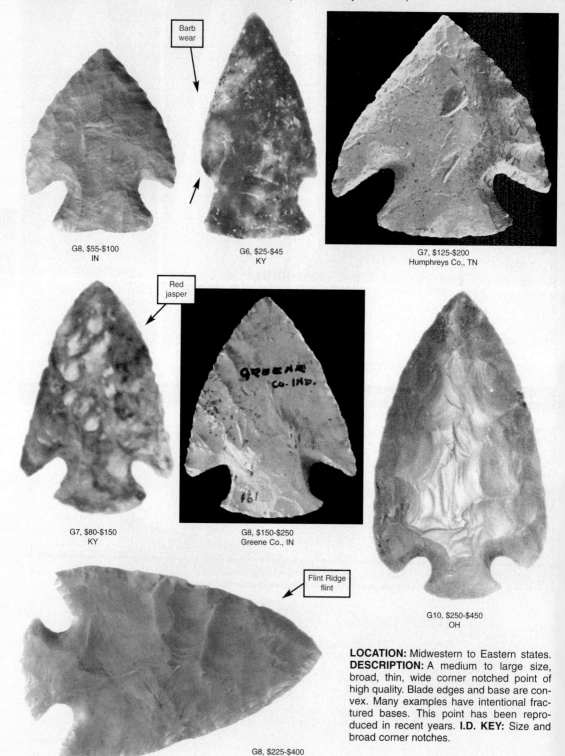

Barb wear

Red jasper

Flint Ridge flint

G8, $55-$100
IN

G6, $25-$45
KY

G7, $125-$200
Humphreys Co., TN

G7, $80-$150
KY

G8, $150-$250
Greene Co., IN

G10, $250-$450
OH

G8, $225-$400
OH

LOCATION: Midwestern to Eastern states. **DESCRIPTION:** A medium to large size, broad, thin, wide corner notched point of high quality. Blade edges and base are convex. Many examples have intentional fractured bases. This point has been reproduced in recent years. **I.D. KEY:** Size and broad corner notches.

SPOKESHAVE - Woodland, 3000 -1500 B. P.

LOCATION: Kentucky, Ohio into Indiana. **DESCRIPTION:** A medium to large size stemmed tool used for scraping. The blade is asymmetrical with one edge convex and the other concave.

G8, $55-$100
OH

G8, $55-$100
IN

SQUARE-END KNIFE - Late Archaic to Historic, 3500 - 400 B. P.

(Also see Angostura, Fort Ancient Blade, Frazier and Watts Cave Knife)

LOCATION: Midwestern states. **DESCRIPTION:** A medium to large size rectangular blade. Edges are generally straight to slightly convex.

G7, $65-$125
Humphreys Co., TN

EC

G8, $80-$150
TN

G7, $80-$150
TN

STANFIELD - Transitional Paleo, 10,000 - 8000 B. P.

(Also see Angostura, Copena, Fort Ancient Blade, Frazier and Tennessee River)

G6, $25-$40
Colbert Co., AL

G8, $25-$45
Colbert Co., AL

Basal grinding

G6, $30-$50
Colbert Co., AL.

G8, $25-$45
Colbert Co., AL

LOCATION: Southeastern states. Type site is in Colbert Co., AL. **DESCRIPTION:** A medium size, narrow, lanceolate point with parallel sides and a straight base. Some rare examples are fluted. Bases are usually ground and flattened. Flaking is to the center of the blade. This point has been confused with the *Tennessee River* point which is simply a preform for early non-beveled Archaic types. This type is smaller, narrowerer and is flaked to the center of the blade and is much rarer than the type with which it is often confused.

485

STANLY - Early Archaic, 8000 - 5000 B. P.

(Also see Frederick, Garth Slough, Kanawha Stemmed, Kirk Stemmed -Bifurcated and Savannah River)

G5, $3-$5
KY

G5, $3-$5
S.E. TN

G7, $12-$20
KY

G4, $2-$5
S.E. TN

G3, $2-$5
TN

G5, $4-$8
KY

G8 $15-$25
Nickajack Lake, TN

G6, $8-$15
S.E. TN

G7, $12-$20
KY

Grey flint

G10, $50-$90
KY

G5, $8-$15
Dayton, TN

G10, $35-$60
S.E. TN

G6, $12-$20
McMinn Co., TN

G6, $12-$20
S.E. TN

G7, $15-$30
Jessamine Co., KY

LOCATION: Southeastern to Eastern states. Type site is Stanly Co., N.C. **DESCRIPTION:** A small to medium size, broad shoulder point with a small bifurcated stem. Some examples are serrated and show high quality flaking. The shoulders are very prominent and can be tapered, horizontal or barbed. **I.D. KEY:** Tiny bifurcated base.

STEUBENVILLE - Early Archaic, 9000 - 6000 B. P.

(Also see Holland and Johnson)

G6, $35-$65
OH

G7, $60-$100
OH

486

LOCATION: Ohio into the Northeast. **DESCRIPTION:** A medium to large size, broad, triangular point with weak tapered shoulders, a wide parallel sided stem and a concave base. The basal area is ground. Believed to be developed from the *Scottsbluff* type.

STILWELL - Early Archaic, 9000 - 7000 B. P.

(Also see Kirk Corner Notched, Neuberger and Pine Tree)

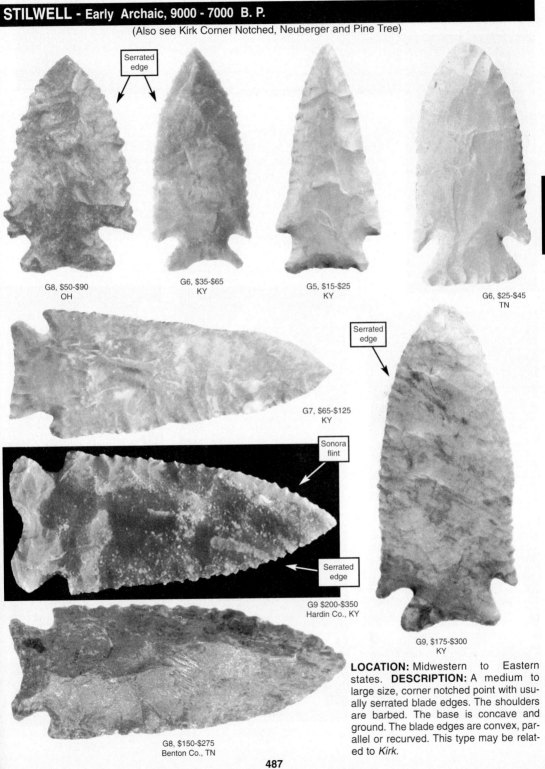

Serrated edge

G8, $50-$90
OH

G6, $35-$65
KY

G5, $15-$25
KY

G6, $25-$45
TN

EC

G7, $65-$125
KY

Serrated edge

Sonora flint

Serrated edge

G9 $200-$350
Hardin Co., KY

G9, $175-$300
KY

G8, $150-$275
Benton Co., TN

LOCATION: Midwestern to Eastern states. **DESCRIPTION:** A medium to large size, corner notched point with usually serrated blade edges. The shoulders are barbed. The base is concave and ground. The blade edges are convex, parallel or recurved. This type may be related to *Kirk*.

STILWELL (continued)

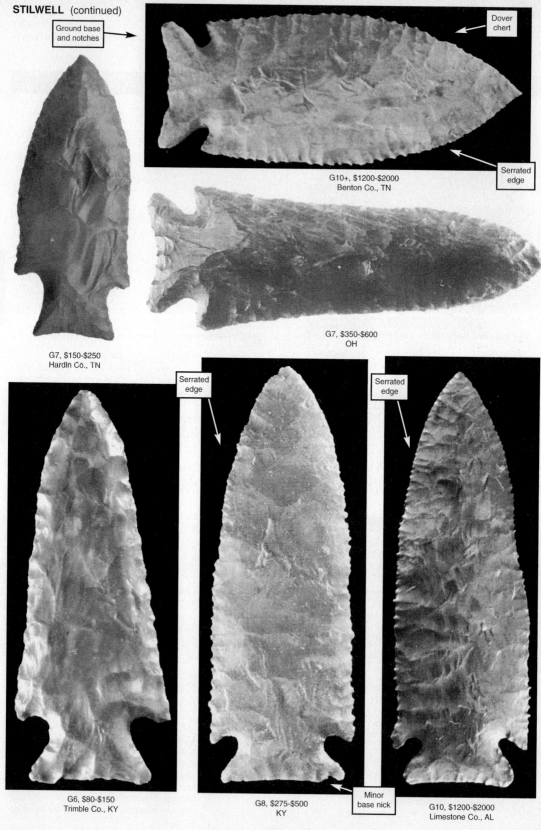

Ground base and notches

Dover chert

Serrated edge

G10+, $1200-$2000
Benton Co., TN

G7, $150-$250
Hardln Co., TN

G7, $350-$600
OH

Serrated edge

Serrated edge

G6, $80-$150
Trimble Co., KY

G8, $275-$500
KY

Minor base nick

G10, $1200-$2000
Limestone Co., AL

STRINGTOWN - Early Archaic, 9500 - 7000 B. P.

(Also see Alberta and Eastern Stemmed Lanceolate)

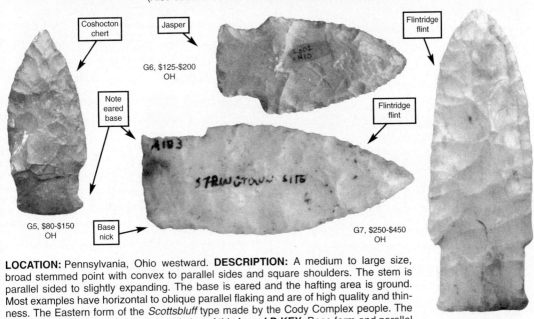

Coshocton chert

Jasper

G6, $125-$200
OH

Flintridge flint

Note eared base

Flintridge flint

G5, $80-$150
OH

Base nick

G7, $250-$450
OH

EC

LOCATION: Pennsylvania, Ohio westward. **DESCRIPTION:** A medium to large size, broad stemmed point with convex to parallel sides and square shoulders. The stem is parallel sided to slightly expanding. The base is eared and the hafting area is ground. Most examples have horizontal to oblique parallel flaking and are of high quality and thinness. The Eastern form of the *Scottsbluff* type made by the Cody Complex people. The Eastern Stemmed Lanceolate is a variation of this form. **I.D.KEY:** Base form and parallel flaking.

G8, $750-$1200
Licking Co., OH

SUBLET FERRY - Late Archaic to Woodland, 4000 - 2000 B. P.

(Also see Big Sandy, Brewerton Side Notched, Coosa and Meadowood)

LOCATION: Southeastern states. **DESCRIPTION:** A small to medium size point with side notches that are very close to the base. The base is straight to slightly convex. Blade edges are straight to convex and may be serrated.

G6, $8-$15
Trimble Co., KY

Dover chert

Dover chert

Notching occurs close to the base

G8, $18-$30
Humphreys Co., TN

G6, $12-$20
Putnam Co., TN

G6, $15-$25
Dayton, TN

G9, $40-$70
TN

G9, $45-$80
Humphreys Co., TN

G8, $30-$50
Humphreys Co., TN

SUN DISC - Mississippian, 1100 - 600 B. P.

(Also see Duck River Sword and Mace)

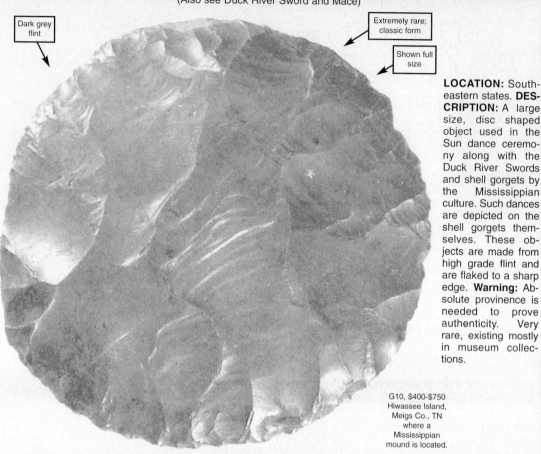

Dark grey flint

Extremely rare; classic form

Shown full size

LOCATION: Southeastern states. **DESCRIPTION:** A large size, disc shaped object used in the Sun dance ceremony along with the Duck River Swords and shell gorgets by the Mississippian culture. Such dances are depicted on the shell gorgets themselves. These objects are made from high grade flint and are flaked to a sharp edge. **Warning:** Absolute provenience is needed to prove authenticity. Very rare, existing mostly in museum collections.

G10, $400-$750
Hiwassee Island,
Meigs Co., TN
where a
Mississippian
mound is located.

SWAN LAKE - Late Archaic to Woodland, 3500 - 2000 B. P.

(Also see Bakers Creek, Brewerton, Durst, Halifax and Matanzas)

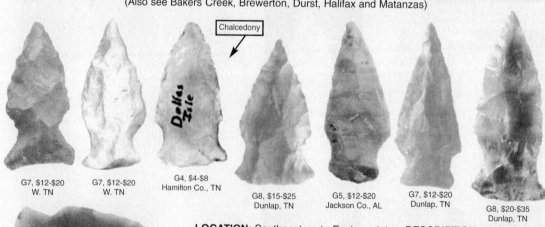

Chalcedony

G7, $12-$20
W. TN

G7, $12-$20
W. TN

G4, $4-$8
Hamilton Co., TN

G8, $15-$25
Dunlap, TN

G5, $12-$20
Jackson Co., AL

G7, $12-$20
Dunlap, TN

G8, $20-$35
Dunlap, TN

G7, $12-$20
Dunlap, TN

LOCATION: Southeastern to Eastern states. **DESCRIPTION:** A small size, thick, triangular point with wide, shallow side notches. Some examples have an unfinished rind or base. Similar to the side-notched *Lamoka* in New York. Called *Jackson* in Florida.

490

SYKES - Early to Late Archaic, 6000 - 5000 B. P.

(Also see Benton)

G6, $15-$25
KY

G5, $12-$20
TN

G8, $15-$25
Limestone Co., AL

G7, $25-$45
N. W. AL

EC

LOCATION: Southeastern states. **DESCRIPTION:** Believed to be related to *Benton* points. A medium size, point with a broad blade and a very short, broad stem. Bases are straight to concave. The stem is formed by corner notches. **I.D. KEY:** Short stem and broadness.

TABLE ROCK - Late Archaic, 4000 - 3000 B. P.

(Also see Bakers Creek, Buck Creek, Cotaco Creek, Fishspear, Motley and Smithsonia)

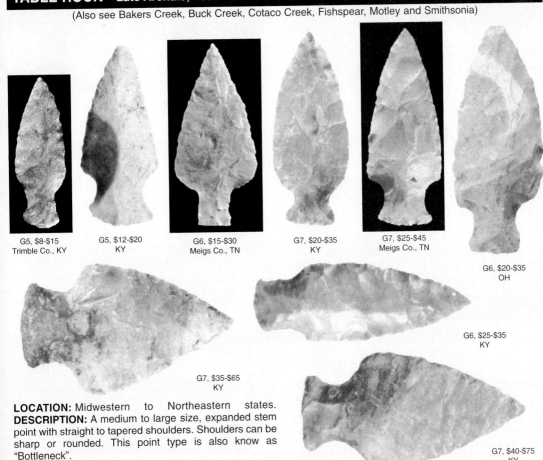

G5, $8-$15
Trimble Co., KY

G5, $12-$20
KY

G6, $15-$30
Meigs Co., TN

G7, $20-$35
KY

G7, $25-$45
Meigs Co., TN

G6, $20-$35
OH

G6, $25-$35
KY

G7, $35-$65
KY

G7, $40-$75
KY

LOCATION: Midwestern to Northeastern states. **DESCRIPTION:** A medium to large size, expanded stem point with straight to tapered shoulders. Shoulders can be sharp or rounded. This point type is also know as "Bottleneck".

491

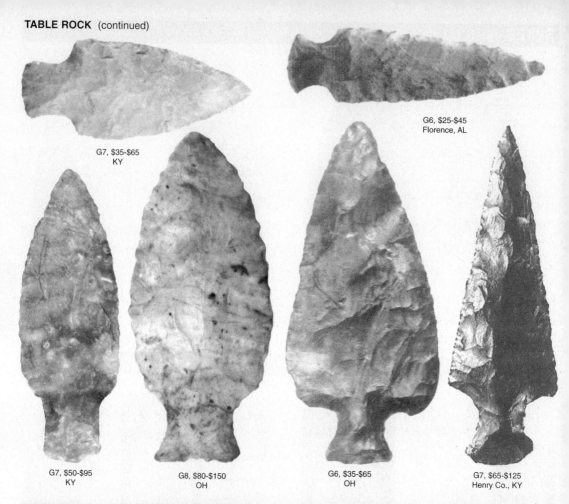

G7, $35-$65
KY

G6, $25-$45
Florence, AL

G7, $50-$95
KY

G8, $80-$150
OH

G6, $35-$65
OH

G7, $65-$125
Henry Co., KY

TEAR DROP - Woodland, 2000 - 1000 B. P.

(Also see Adena Blade and Red Ochre)

Made from white chert

G10, $700-$1200
Humphreys Co., TN
Cache blade

G10, $800-$1500
TN

IMPORTANT: Tear Drop points shown half size.

G10, $600-$1000
Humphreys Co., TN
Cache blade

Made from white chert

LOCATION: Southeastern states. **DESCRIPTION:** A large size, broad, thin, elliptical blade with a rounded to straight base. Usually found in caches and are believed to be a little later than the *Adena* blades. Usually made from a special white chert. Some examples have been found stained with red ochre.

(Also see Adena Blade, Cobbs Triangular, Kirk, Red Ochre and Stanfield)

Kirk preform

Eva preform

EC

G7, $40-$75
Lauderdale Co., AL

G7, $20-$35
KY

G7, $40-$75
Florence, AL

G8, $125-$225
Parsons, TN

G8, $65-$125
TN

G8, $150-$250
Dickson Co., TN

LOCATION: Southeastern states. **DESCRIPTION:** These are unnotched preforms for early Archaic types such as *Kirk, Eva*, etc. and would have the same description as that type without the notches. Bases can be straight, concave or convex. **I.D. KEY:** Archaic style edgework. **NOTE:** This type has been confused with the *Stanfield* point which is a medium size, narrow, thicker point. A beveled edge would place your point under the *Cobbs Triangular* type

TENNESSEE SAW - Early Archaic, 8000 - 6000 B. P.

(Also see Lerma)

G10, $600-$1000
TN

LOCATION: Tennessee and Kentucky. **DESCRIPTION:** A very large by-pointed, serrated blade that was probably used as a knife. Very rare in collecting area. **I.D. KEY:** Size and serrations.

IMPORTANT: THIS POINT SHOWN HALF SIZE

TENNESSEE SWORD (See Duck River Sword)

THEBES - Early Archaic, 10,000 - 8000 B. P.

(Also see Big Sandy E-Notched, Lost Lake and St. Charles)

Barb & base wear

Beveled edge

"E" notch

Barb & base nick

Beveled edge

G4, $30-$50
OH

G7, $175-$300
OH

G5, $40-$75
OH

G8, $180-$350
Knox Co., OH

Barb & base nick

G7, $80-$150
OH

"E" notch

Coshocton flint

G6, $80-$150
OH

G8, $175-$325
OH

G8, $175-$325
IN

494

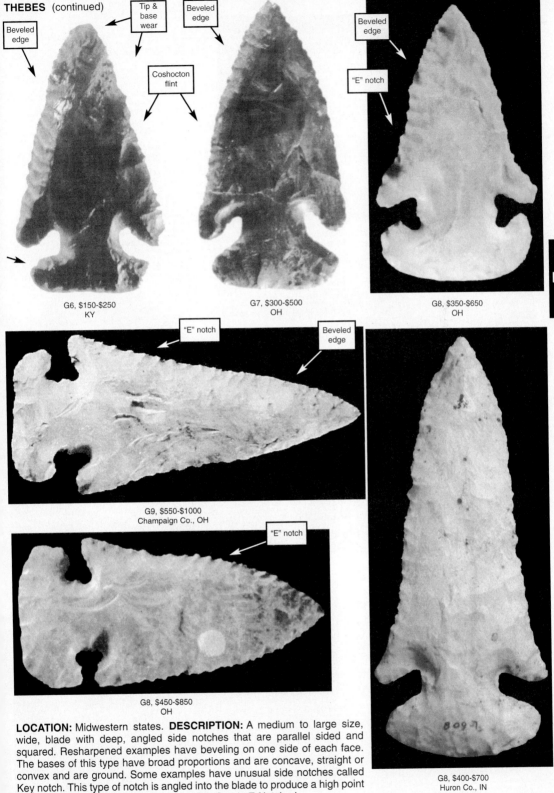

THEBES (continued)

Beveled edge

Tip & base wear

Beveled edge

Coshocton flint

Beveled edge

"E" notch

G6, $150-$250
KY

G7, $300-$500
OH

G8, $350-$650
OH

EC

"E" notch

Beveled edge

G9, $550-$1000
Champaign Co., OH

"E" notch

G8, $450-$850
OH

G8, $400-$700
Huron Co., IN

LOCATION: Midwestern states. **DESCRIPTION:** A medium to large size, wide, blade with deep, angled side notches that are parallel sided and squared. Resharpened examples have beveling on one side of each face. The bases of this type have broad proportions and are concave, straight or convex and are ground. Some examples have unusual side notches called Key notch. This type of notch is angled into the blade to produce a high point in the center, forming the letter E. See *Big Sandy E-Notched*.

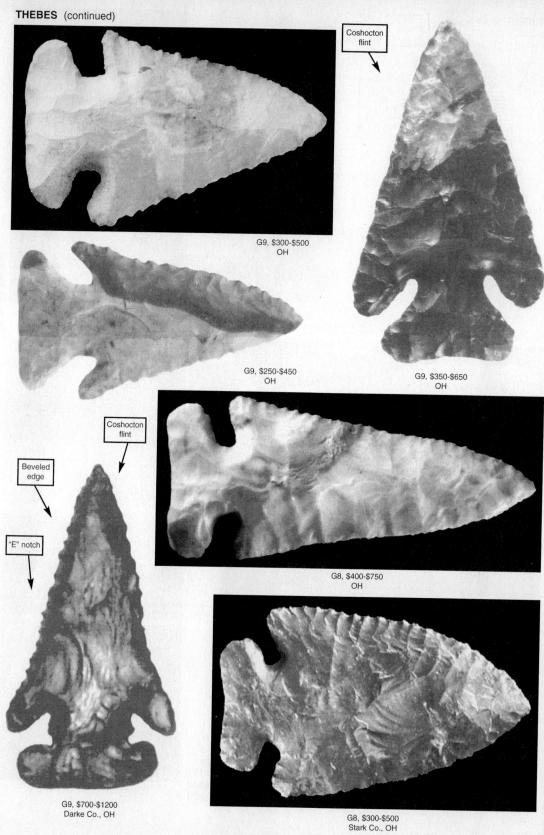

Coshocton flint

G9, $300-$500
OH

G9, $250-$450
OH

G9, $350-$650
OH

Coshocton flint

Beveled edge

"E" notch

G8, $400-$750
OH

G9, $700-$1200
Darke Co., OH

G8, $300-$500
Stark Co., OH

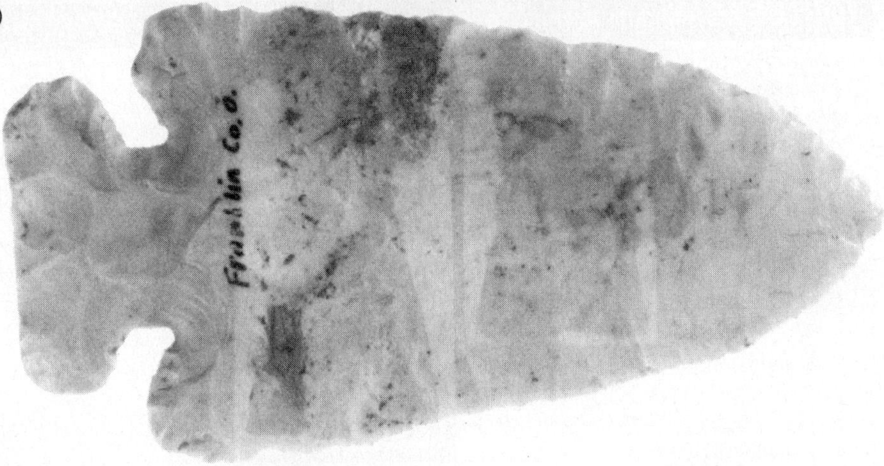

G8, $250-$450
Franklin Co., OH

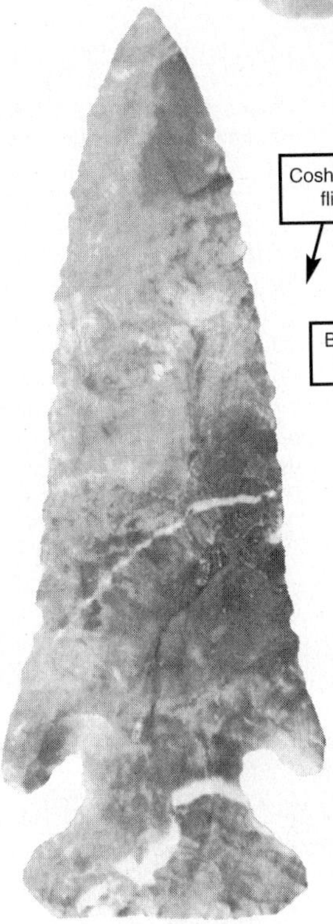

Coshocton
flint

Beveled
edge

EC

G10, $300-$550
OH

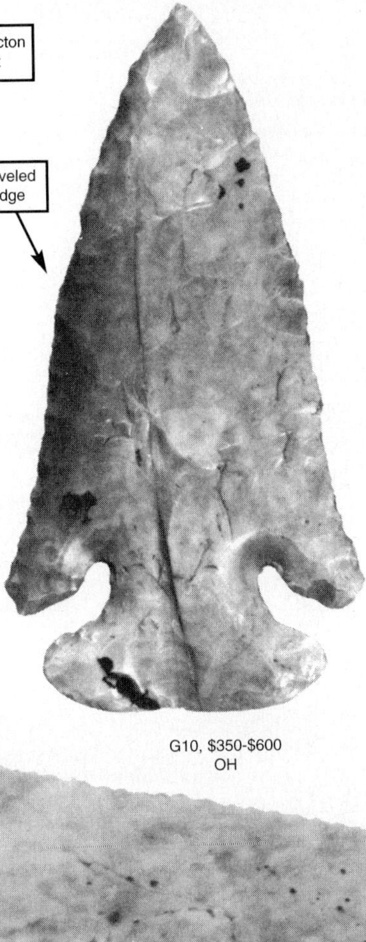

G10, $350-$600
OH

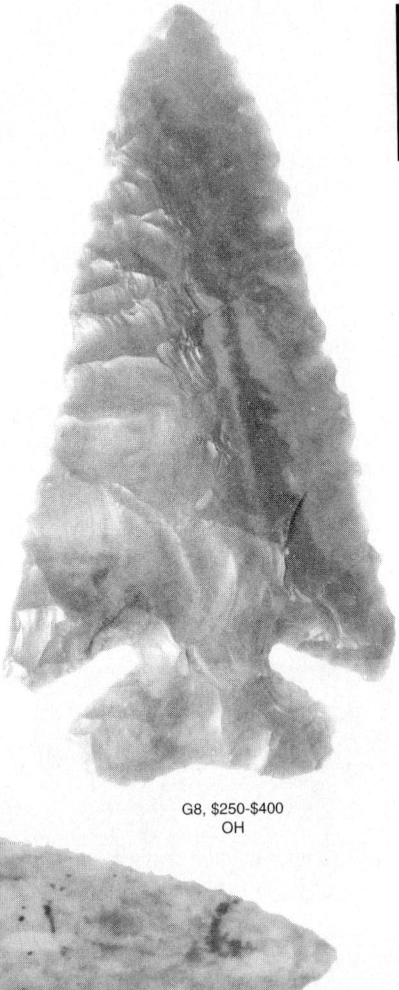

G8, $250-$400
OH

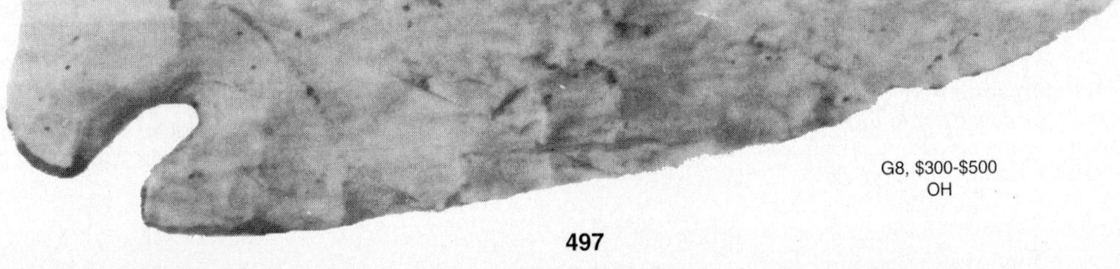

G8, $300-$500
OH

TORTUGAS - Middle Archaic to Woodland, 6000 - 1000 B. P.

(Also see Frazier, Levanna and Paint Rock Valley)

G5, $4-$8
Tishomingo Co., MS

G5, $4-$8
Decatur, AL

G7, $12-$20
Florence, AL

G8, $20-$35
Parsons, TN

Dover chert

G7, $12-$20
W. TN

G9, $25-$45
Camden, TN

LOCATION: Typically found in northern Mexico into southern Texas. Similar points (shown here) are also found in Mississippi, Alabama and western Tenn. **DESCRIPTION:** A medium size, fairly thick, triangular point with straight to convex sides and base. Some examples are beveled on one side of each face. Bases are usually thinned. This type is much thicker than *Madison* points and are more triangular than *Frazier* points.

TRADE POINTS - Historic, 400 - 170 B. P.

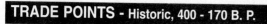

$10-$20
Tellico Plains, TN
Cherokee

$15-$25, Tn, Cherokee
c. 1810-1830 (cut sheet iron)

$65-$125, Tn, Cherokee
c. 1810-1830 (cut sheet iron)

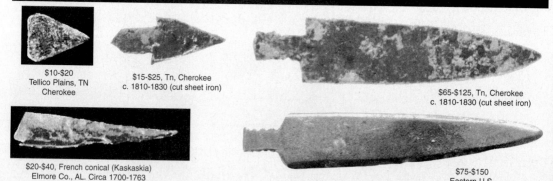

$20-$40, French conical (Kaskaskia)
Elmore Co., AL. Circa 1700-1763

$75-$150
Eastern U.S.

These points were made of copper, iron, and steel and were traded to the Indians by the French, British and others from the 1600s to the 1800s. Examples have been found all over the United States.

TURKEYTAIL-FULTON - Late Archaic to Woodland, 4000 - 2500 B. P.

(Also see Adena, Early Ovoid Knife and Turkeytail-Tupelo)

LOCATION: Midwestern to Eastern states. **DESCRIPTION:** A medium to large size, wide, thin, elliptical blade with shallow notches very close to the base. This type is usually found in caches and has been reproduced in recent years. Made by the Adena culture. A similar form, but much earlier, is found in late *Benton* caches in Mississippi. **I.D. KEY:** Smaller base than the Harrison Var.

TURKEYTAIL-FULTON (continued)

G3, $12-$20
Cookeville, TN

Minor side wear

Minor side wear

G7 $200-$350
Jay Co., IN

G4, $350-$650
KY

G5, $150-$250
TN

EC

G7, $350-$650
KY

Restored tip

Restored edge

Small notches at base

G5, $450-$850
KY

G9, $1500-$2500
KY

(Alse see Adena)

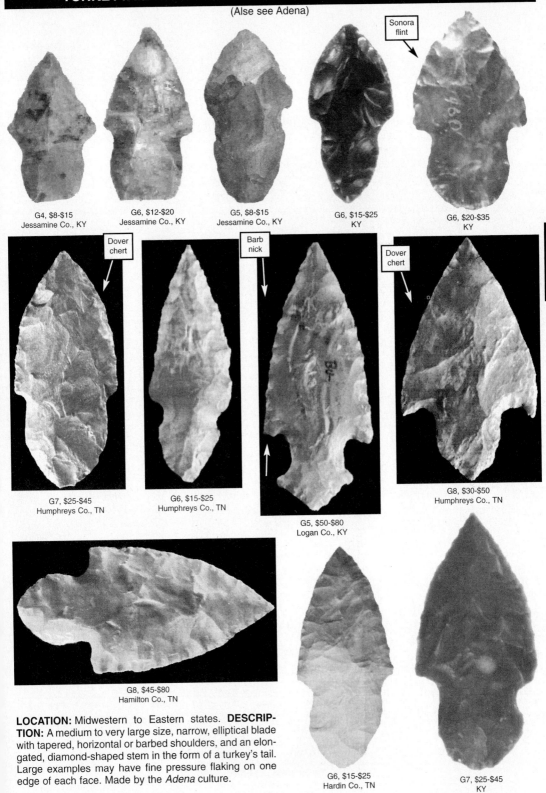

Sonora flint

G4, $8-$15
Jessamine Co., KY

G6, $12-$20
Jessamine Co., KY

G5, $8-$15
Jessamine Co., KY

G6, $15-$25
KY

G6, $20-$35
KY

EC

Dover chert

Barb nick

Dover chert

G7, $25-$45
Humphreys Co., TN

G6, $15-$25
Humphreys Co., TN

G5, $50-$80
Logan Co., KY

G8, $30-$50
Humphreys Co., TN

G8, $45-$80
Hamilton Co., TN

G6, $15-$25
Hardin Co., TN

G7, $25-$45
KY

LOCATION: Midwestern to Eastern states. **DESCRIPTION:** A medium to very large size, narrow, elliptical blade with tapered, horizontal or barbed shoulders, and an elongated, diamond-shaped stem in the form of a turkey's tail. Large examples may have fine pressure flaking on one edge of each face. Made by the *Adena* culture.

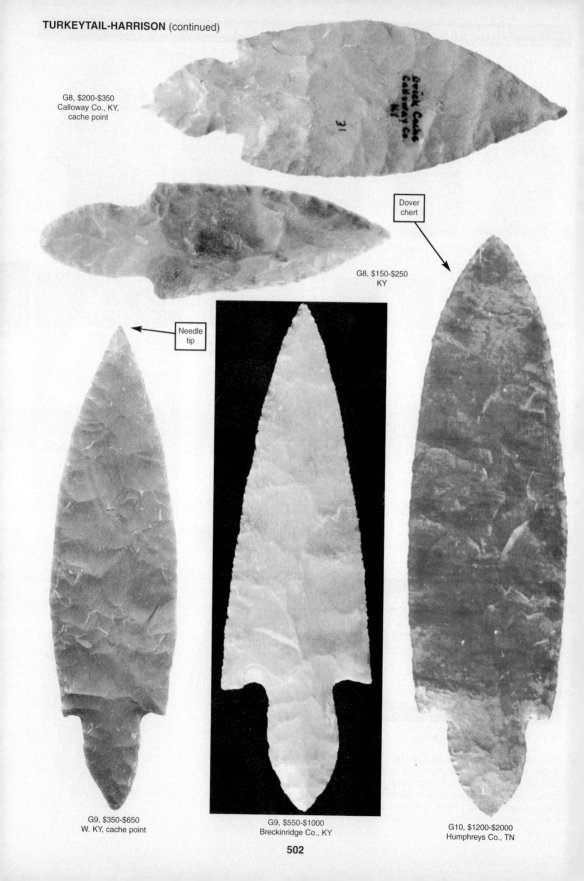

G8, $200-$350
Calloway Co., KY,
cache point

Dover chert

G8, $150-$250
KY

Needle tip

G9, $350-$650
W. KY, cache point

G9, $550-$1000
Breckinridge Co., KY

G10, $1200-$2000
Humphreys Co., TN

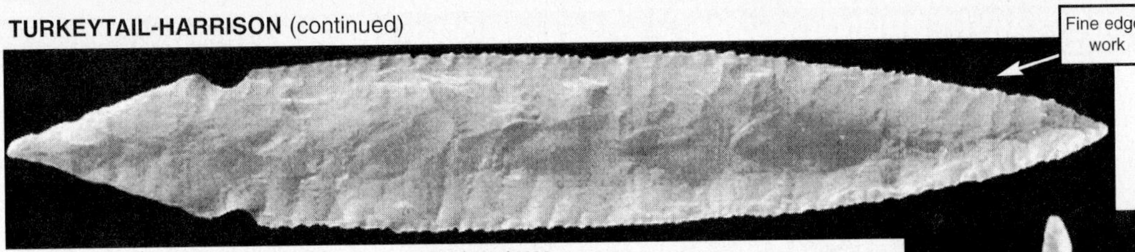

Fine edge-work

G9, $800-$1500
Hardin Co., TN

G9, $250-$450
Nashville, TN

Dover chert

Thin cross section

G6, $150-$250
W. KY

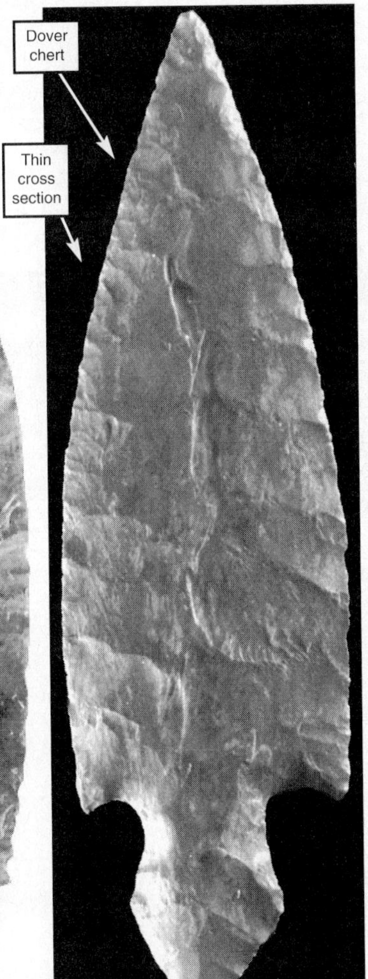

G10+, $1200-$2000
KY

G10, $550-$1000
W. KY, cache point

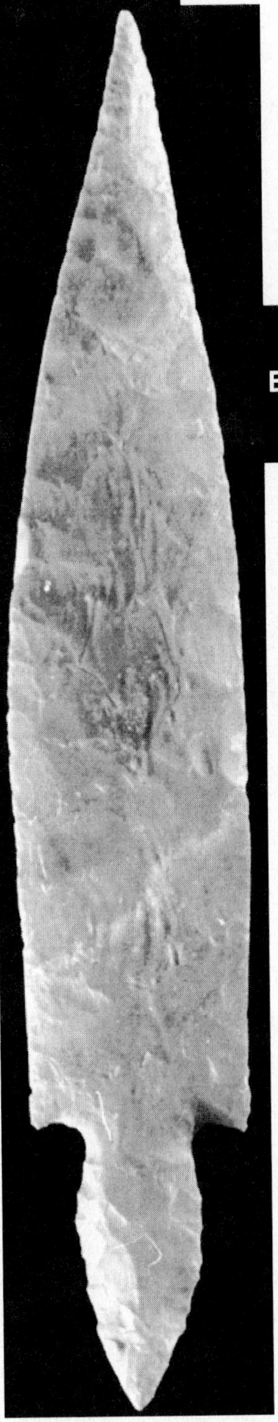

G10+, $3500-$6000
KY, cache point

EC

TURKEYTAIL-HEBRON - Late Archaic to Woodland, 3500 - 2500 B. P.

(Also see Waubesa)

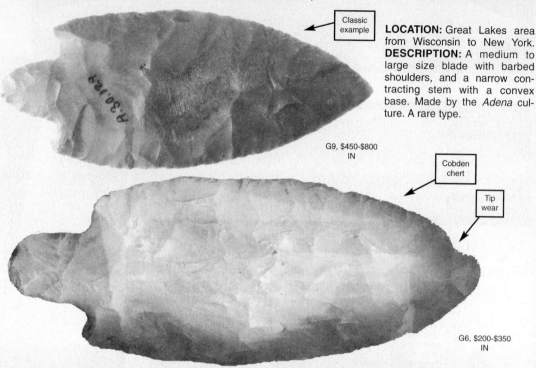

Classic example

LOCATION: Great Lakes area from Wisconsin to New York. **DESCRIPTION:** A medium to large size blade with barbed shoulders, and a narrow contracting stem with a convex base. Made by the *Adena* culture. A rare type.

G9, $450-$800
IN

Cobden chert

Tip wear

G6, $200-$350
IN

TURKEYTAIL-TUPELO - Late Archaic, 4750 - 3900 B. P.

(Also see Benton and Warito)

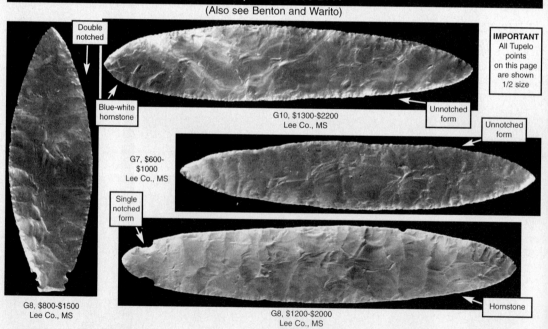

Double notched

Blue-white hornstone

IMPORTANT
All Tupelo points on this page are shown 1/2 size

Unnotched form

Unnotched form

G10, $1300-$2200
Lee Co., MS

G7, $600-$1000
Lee Co., MS

Single notched form

G8, $800-$1500
Lee Co., MS

G8, $1200-$2000
Lee Co., MS

Hornstone

LOCATION: Mississippi, Alabama and Tennessee. **DESCRIPTION:** A large size, thin, well-made blade that is found in caches with large *Benton* and *Warito* points. Some are not notched, but most have single, double or triple notches. Polishing occurs on the edges and surfaces of a few examples, possibly used as dance blades. These are unique and 1000 years older than the northern type.

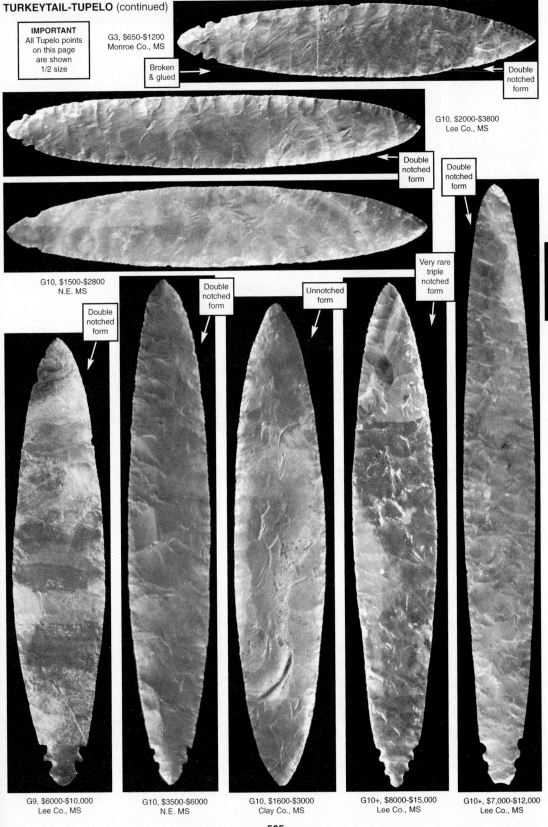

TURKEYTAIL-TUPELO (continued)

IMPORTANT
All Tupelo points
on this page
are shown
1/2 size

G3, $650-$1200
Monroe Co., MS

Broken
& glued

Double
notched
form

G10, $2000-$3800
Lee Co., MS

Double
notched
form

Double
notched
form

G10, $1500-$2800
N.E. MS

Double
notched
form

Double
notched
form

Unnotched
form

Very rare
triple
notched
form

EC

G9, $6000-$10,000
Lee Co., MS

G10, $3500-$6000
N.E. MS

G10, $1600-$3000
Clay Co., MS

G10+, $8000-$15,000
Lee Co., MS

G10+, $7,000-$12,000
Lee Co., MS

VALINA - Woodland, 2500 - 1000 B. P.

(Also see Madison and Morrow Mountain)

G5, $1-$2
Sequatchie Valley, TN

G5, $1-$2
Meigs Co., TN

G7, $1-$3
Meigs Co., TN

G7, $1-$3
S. E. TN

LOCATION: Eastern states. **DESCRIPTION:** A small size, broad triangle with rounded basal corners and a convex base.

WADE - Late Archaic to Woodland, 4500 - 2500 B. P.

(Also see Buck Creek, Eva, Hamilton Stemmed, Motley, Rankin, Smith and Smithsonia)

Resharpening into shoulder

G3, $12-$20
Decatur, AL

G7, $35-$50
W. TN

G2, $8-$15
E. TN

G5 $25-$40
Florence, AL

G8, $30-$50
KY

G6, $40-$75
Walker Co., AL

G8, $100-$175
Dayton, TN

LOCATION: Southern states. **DESCRIPTION:** A medium to large size, broad, well barbed, stemmed point. Some examples appear to be basal notched. The blade is straight to convex. The stem is straight to expanding or contracting. On some examples, the barbs almost reach the base and are rounded to pointed. Has been found with *Motley* points in caches.

G8, $80-$150
Dayton, TN

G8, $90-$175

G6 $55-$100
Clarksville, TN

EC

WARITO - Mid-Archaic, 5500 - 4500 B. P.

(Also see Benton and Turkeytail)

G10, $700-$1200, Hardin Co., TN

Pink jasper

Minor edge wear

G6, $350-$600
Sumner Co., TN

Ground basal area

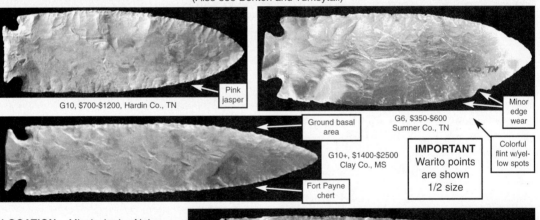

Colorful flint w/yellow spots

G10+, $1400-$2500
Clay Co., MS

IMPORTANT
Warito points
are shown
1/2 size

Fort Payne chert

LOCATION: Mississippi, Alabama and Tennessee. **DESCRIPTION:** A medium to very large size corner notched point. Bases are ground. Found in caches with *Benton* and *Turkeytail Tupelo* points. **I.D. KEY:** Large corner notched point.

G9, $700-$1200
Decatur, AL

WARRICK - Early Archaic, 9000 - 5000 B. P.

(Also see Hardin and St. Charles)

LOCATION: Ohio and adjacent states. **DESCRIPTION:** A medium to large size, fairly thick, sturdy side notched point. Notching is very close to the base. Bases are ground and flaking is of high quality.

WARRICK (continued)

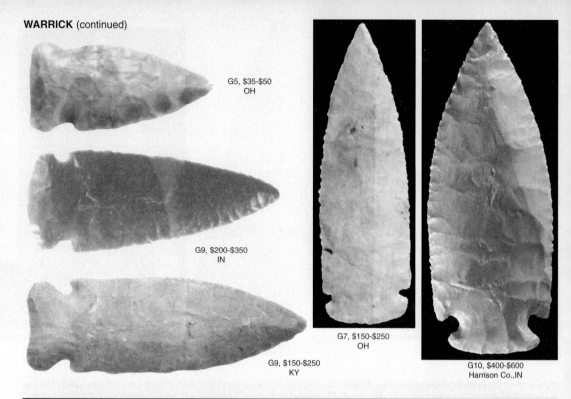

G5, $35-$50
OH

G9, $200-$350
IN

G9, $150-$250
KY

G7, $150-$250
OH

G10, $400-$600
Harrison Co.,IN

WASHINGTON - Woodland, 3000 - 1500 B. P.

(Also see Durant's Bend and Nova)

LOCATION: Southeastern states. **DESCRIPTION:** A small size, serrated, corner to side notched point with a concave, expanded base.

G5, $8-$15
Dallas Co., AL. Classic.

WASHITA - Mississippian, 800 - 400 B. P.

(Also see Keota)

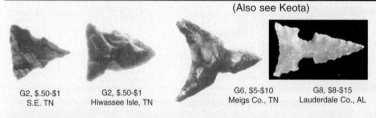

G2, $.50-$1
S.E. TN

G2, $.50-$1
Hiwassee Isle, TN

G6, $5-$10
Meigs Co., TN

G8, $8-$15
Lauderdale Co., AL

LOCATION: Midwestern states into Tenn. and Ala **DESCRIPTION:** A small size, thin, triangular side notched arrow point with a concave base. Basal area is usually large in proportion to the blade size. A Mississippian point probably transported between the Mississippian sites.

WATTS CAVE - Trans. Paleo to Early Archaic, 10,000 - 8000 B. P.

(Also see Square End Knife)

Finely serrated edge

IMPORTANT
This knife shown 1/2 size

G10, $400-$700
Dickson Cave, KY

LOCATION: Tennessee into Kentucky and Ohio. **DESCRIPTION:** A large size, serrated, knife form with squared corners and the blade expanding towards both ends. First recognized as a type from Watts Cave in Kentucky. Some examples are fluted.

WAUBESA - Woodland, 2500 - 1500 B. P.

(Also see Adena, Dickson and Turkeytail-Hebron)

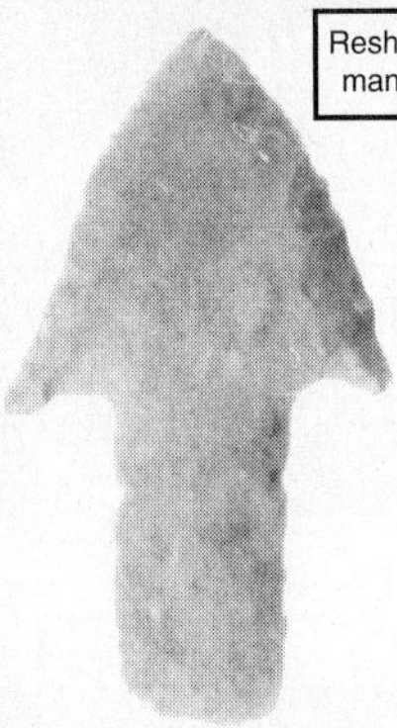

G7, $20-$35
TN

Resharpened many times

G5, $8-$15
KY

G4 $5-$10
KY

Resharpened many times

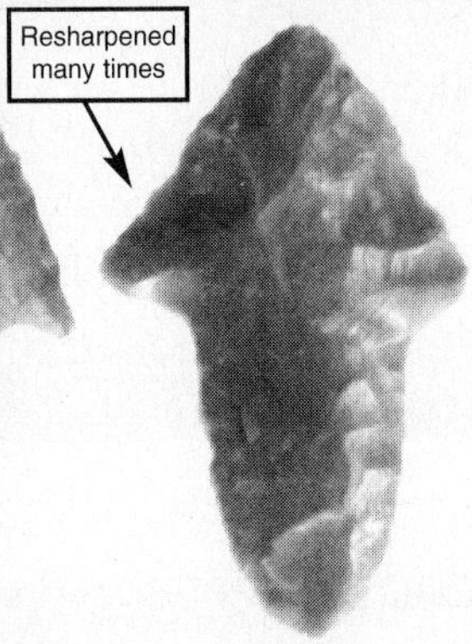

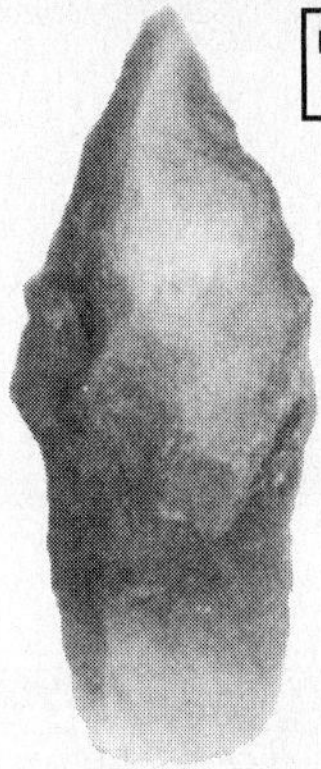

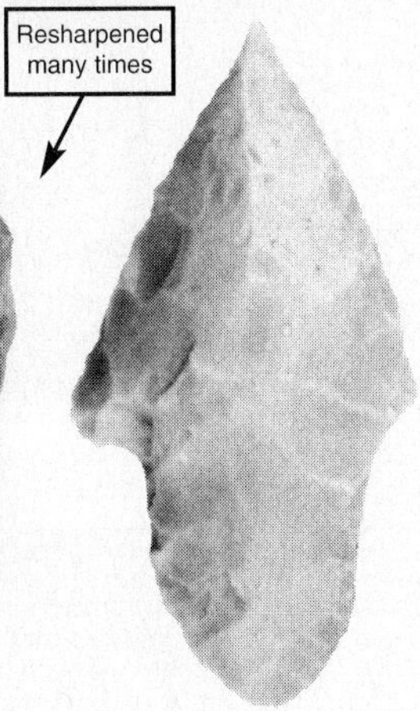

G6, $15-$25
KY

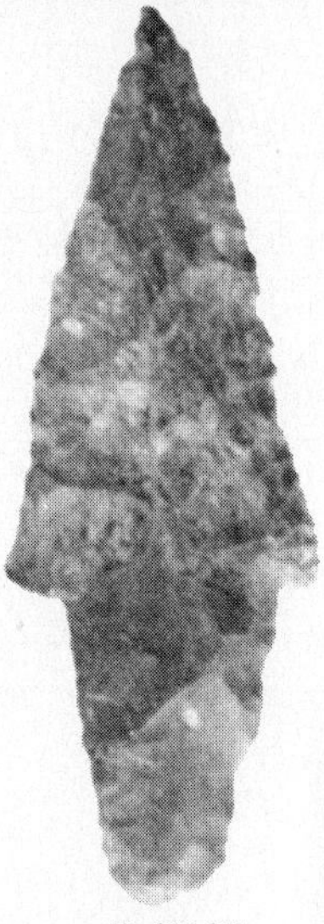

G6, $20-$35
KY

EC

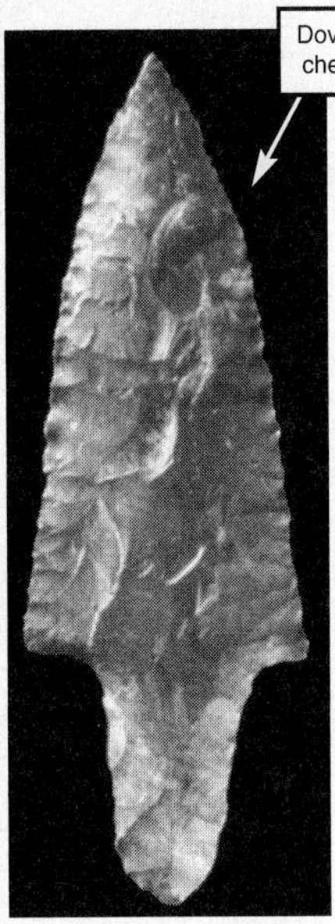

Dover chert

G8, $40-$75
Benton Co., TN

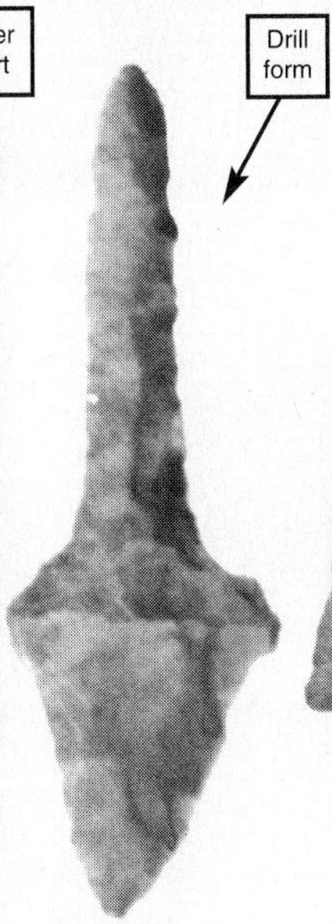

Drill form

G7, $20-$45
TN

Drill form

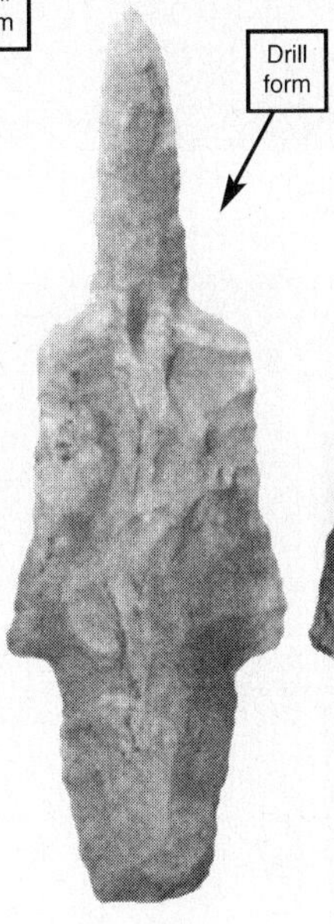

G7, $35-$65
TN

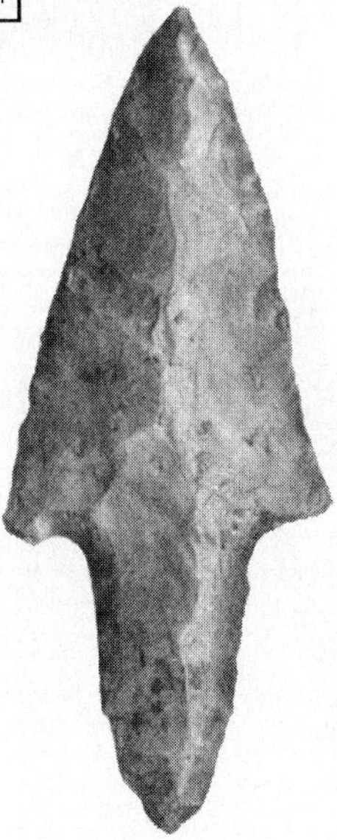

G7, $65-$125
Benton Co., TN

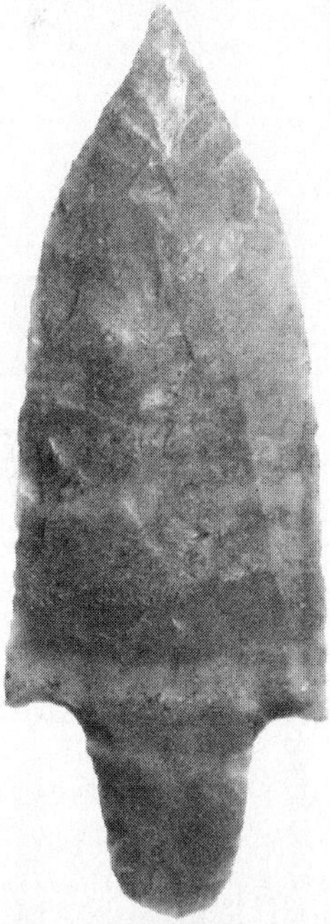

G9, $80-$150
KY

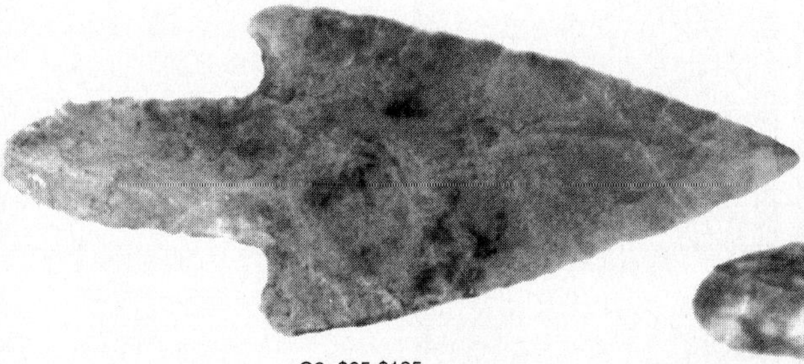

G9, $65-$125
TN

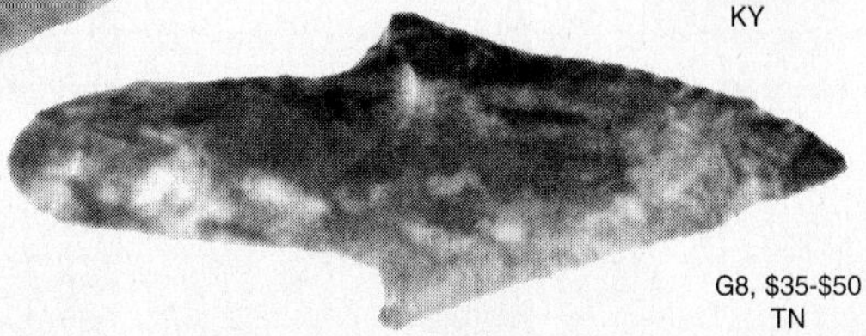

G8, $35-$50
TN

LOCATION: Eastern to Southeastern states. **DESCRIPTION:** A medium to large, narrow, thin, well made point with a contracting stem that is rounded or pointed. Some examples exhibit unusually high quality flaking and saw-tooth serrations. Blades are convex to recurved. Shoulders are squared to barbed. **I.D. KEY:** Basal form pointed or near pointed, good secondary flaking and thin. **NOTE:** Believed to be associated with the Hopewell culture.

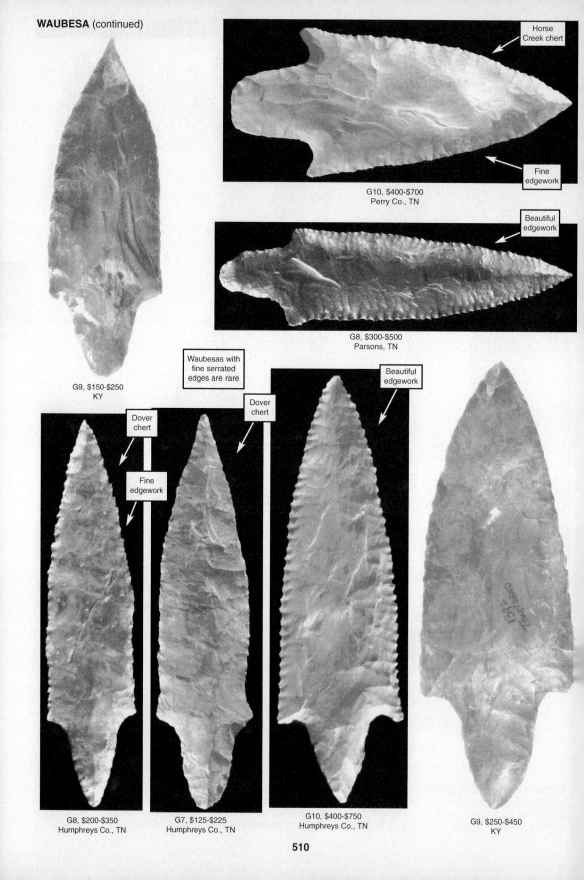

WAUBESA (continued)

Horse Creek chert

Fine edgework

G10, $400-$700
Perry Co., TN

Beautiful edgework

G8, $300-$500
Parsons, TN

G9, $150-$250
KY

Waubesas with fine serrated edges are rare

Dover chert

Dover chert

Beautiful edgework

Fine edgework

G8, $200-$350
Humphreys Co., TN

G7, $125-$225
Humphreys Co., TN

G10, $400-$750
Humphreys Co., TN

G9, $250-$450
KY

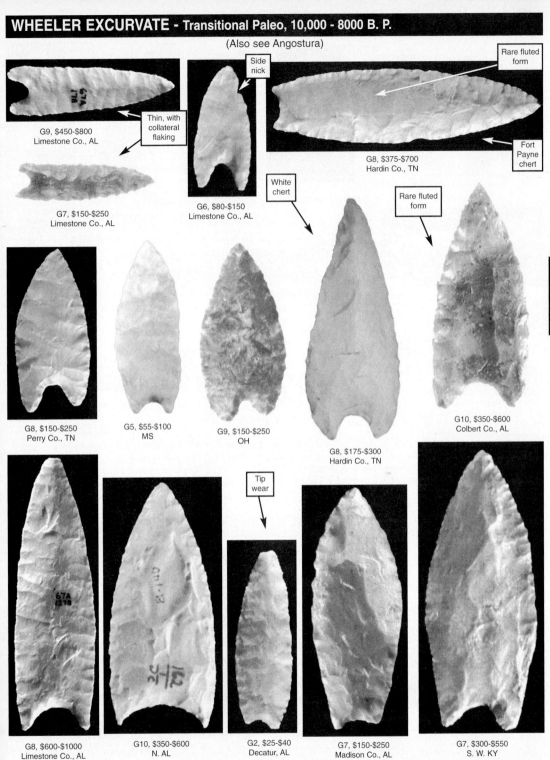

WHEELER EXCURVATE - Transitional Paleo, 10,000 - 8000 B. P.

(Also see Angostura)

G9, $450-$800
Limestone Co., AL

Thin, with collateral flaking

G7, $150-$250
Limestone Co., AL

Side nick

G6, $80-$150
Limestone Co., AL

Rare fluted form

Fort Payne chert

G8, $375-$700
Hardin Co., TN

White chert

Rare fluted form

G8, $150-$250
Perry Co., TN

G5, $55-$100
MS

G9, $150-$250
OH

G8, $175-$300
Hardin Co., TN

G10, $350-$600
Colbert Co., AL

EC

Tip wear

G8, $600-$1000
Limestone Co., AL

G10, $350-$600
N. AL

G2, $25-$40
Decatur, AL

G7, $150-$250
Madison Co., AL

G7, $300-$550
S. W. KY

LOCATION: Southeastern states. **DESCRIPTION:** A small to medium size, lanceolate point with a deep concave base that is steeply beveled. Some examples are fluted, others are finely serrated and show excellent quality collateral flaking. Most bases are deeply notched but some examples have a more shallow concavity. Basal grinding does occur but is usually absent. The ears on some examples turn inward. Blade edges are excurvate. **I.D. KEY:** Base form and flaking style.

511

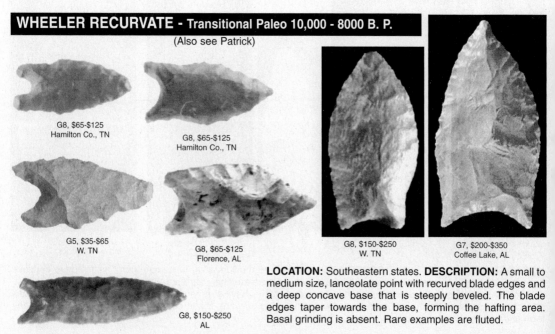

Broken back

$2-$5
Sullivan Co., TN

G6, $55-$100
Sullivan Co., TN

Broken back

Tip gone

G2, $12-$20
Lincoln Co., TN

G2, $12-$20
Coffee Lake, AL

Tip wear

G5, $80-$150
Savannah, TN

Buffalo River chert

G5, $55-$100
W. TN

G10, $185-$350
Lawrence Co., AL

Collateral flaking

Ground base

G10, $1000-$1800
Middle TN/AL.

Black flint; collateral flaking

G10+, $1600-$3000
Hardin Co., TN. The finest example known.

Patinated Dover chert

Thin cross section

G10, $800-$1500
Kanawha Co., WVA, St. Albans site

Ground basal area & entire blade edges

Black Zaleski chert

LOCATION: Northwest Alabama and southern Tennessee. **DESCRIPTION:** A small to medium size, very narrow, thin, lanceolate point with expanding, squared ears forming a "Y" at the base which is "V" notched. Most examples have high quality collateral flaking. This very rare type has been found on *Wheeler* sites in the type area. Scarcity of this type suggests that it was not in use but for a short period of time. **I.D. KEY:** Notch and ears.

WHEELER RECURVATE - Transitional Paleo 10,000 - 8000 B. P.

(Also see Patrick)

G8, $65-$125
Hamilton Co., TN

G8, $65-$125
Hamilton Co., TN

G5, $35-$65
W. TN

G8, $65-$125
Florence, AL

G8, $150-$250
W. TN

G7, $200-$350
Coffee Lake, AL

G8, $150-$250
AL

LOCATION: Southeastern states. **DESCRIPTION:** A small to medium size, lanceolate point with recurved blade edges and a deep concave base that is steeply beveled. The blade edges taper towards the base, forming the hafting area. Basal grinding is absent. Rare examples are fluted.

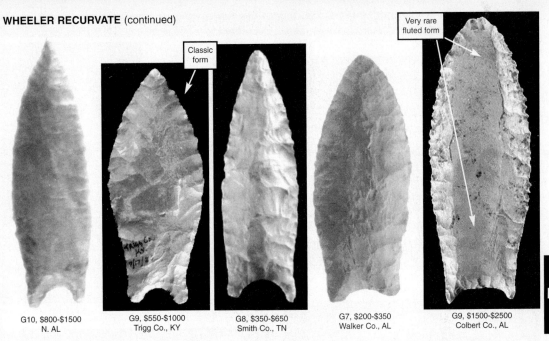

Very rare
fluted form

Classic
form

EC

G10, $800-$1500
N. AL

G9, $550-$1000
Trigg Co., KY

G8, $350-$650
Smith Co., TN

G7, $200-$350
Walker Co., AL

G9, $1500-$2500
Colbert Co., AL

WHEELER TRIANGULAR - Transitional Paleo 10,000 - 8000 B. P.

(Also see Camp Creek, Copena, Madison and Sand Mountain)

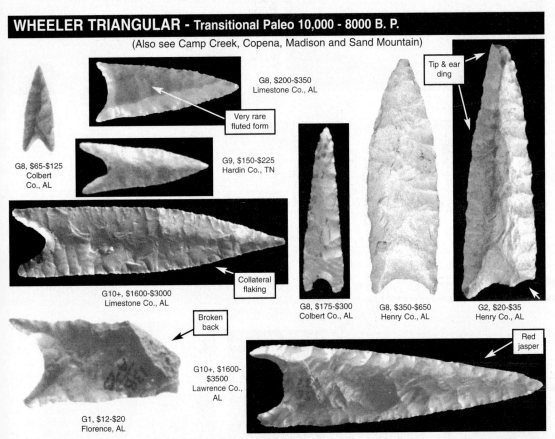

G8, $200-$350
Limestone Co., AL

Very rare
fluted form

Tip & ear
ding

G8, $65-$125
Colbert
Co., AL

G9, $150-$225
Hardin Co., TN

G10+, $1600-$3000
Limestone Co., AL

Collateral
flaking

G8, $175-$300
Colbert Co., AL

G8, $350-$650
Henry Co., AL

G2, $20-$35
Henry Co., AL

Broken
back

G10+, $1600-
$3500
Lawrence Co.,
AL

Red
jasper

G1, $12-$20
Florence, AL

LOCATION: Southeastern states. **DESCRIPTION:** A small to medium size, lanceolate point with straight sides and a deep concave base that is steeply beveled. On some examples, the ears point inward toward the base. This is a rare form and few examples exist. **I.D. KEY:** Beveled base and Paleo flaking.

WHITE SPRINGS - Early to Middle Archaic, 8000 - 6000 B. P.

(Also see Benton)

Fort Payne chert

G5, $8-$15
Limestone Co., AL

G6, $15-$25
Limestone Co., AL

G5, $15-$25
Limestone Co., AL

G8, $25-$40
Limestone Co., AL

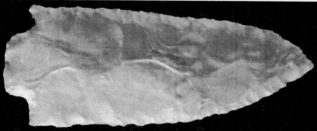

G8, $20-$35
Limestone Co., AL

Early parallel flaking

G10, $55-$100
Colbert Co., AL

LOCATION: Southeastern states. **DESCRIPTION:** A medium size, broad, triangular point with a medium to wide very short straight stem. Shoulders are usually square and the base is straight, slightly convex or concave. **I.D. KEY:** Short base and early flaking.

G9, $55-$100
Limestone Co., AL

YADKIN - Woodland to Mississippian, 2500 - 500 B. P.

(Also see Camp Creek, Hamilton, Levanna and Nolichucky)

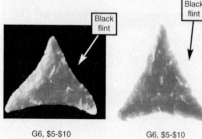

Black flint

Black flint

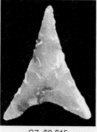

LOCATION: Southeastern and Eastern states. **DESCRIPTION:** A small to medium size, broad based, fairly thick, triangular point with a broad, concave base and straight to convex to recurved side edges.

G6, $5-$10
Bristol, TN

G6, $5-$10
Bristol, TN

G7, $8-$15
Bristol, TN

G6, $8-$15
Bradley Co., TN

514

SOUTHERN CENTRAL SECTION:

This section includes point types from the following states:
Arkansas, Louisiana, Oklahoma, Texas

The points in this section are arranged in alphabetical order and are shown **actual size**. All types are listed that were available for photographing. Any missing types will be added to future editions as photographs become available. We are always interested in receiving sharp, black and white or color glossy photos, color slides or high resolution (300 pixels/inch) digital pictures of your collection. Be sure and include a ruler in the photograph so that proper scale can be determined.

Lithics: Materials employed in the manufacture of projectile points from this region are: basalt, chalcedony, chert, conglomerate, crystal, flint, novaculite, obsidian, quartz, quartzite with lesser amounts of agate, jasper, and petrified wood.

Regional Consultant:
Dwain Rogers

Special Advisors:
Tom Davis, Glen Kizzia, Bob McWilliams, Donald Meador,
Lyle Nickel, Michael Speer, Art Tatum, Sam Williams

SOUTHERN CENTRAL
(Archaeological Periods)

PALEO (11,500 B.P. - 10,600 B.P.)

Chopper	Clovis	Drill	Graver	Scraper

LATE PALEO (11,250 B.P. - 9,000 B.P.)

Folsom	Frederick	Goshen	Midland	Milnesand	Plainview

TRANSITIONAL PALEO (10,700 B.P. - 8,000 B.P.)

Agate Basin	Arkabutla	Coldwater	Hell Gap	Pelican
Allen	Barber	Crescent Knife	Mahaffey	Plainview
Archaic Knife	Browns Valley	Golondrina	Paleo Knife	

EARLY ARCHAIC (10,000 B.P. - 7,000 B.P.)

Albany Knife	Dalton Classic	Frederick	Lerma Rounded	San Patrice-Hope Var.
Alberta	Dalton Colbert	Gower	Martindale	San Patrice-Keithville Var.
Andice	Dalton Greenbrier	Graham Cave	Meserve	San Patrice-St. Johns Var.
Angostura	Dalton Hemphill	Hardin	Perforator	Scottsbluff I & II
Baker	Dalton Hempstead	Hidden Valley	Pike County	Victoria
Bandy	Darl Stemmed	Holland	Red River Knife	Wells
Big Sandy	Early Stemmed	Hoxie	Rice Lobbed	Zella
Cache River	Early Stemmed Lanceolate	Jakie Stemmed	Rio Grande	Zephyr
Calf Creek	Early Triangular	Jetta	Rodgers Side Hollowed	
Cosotat River	Eden	Johnson	St. Charles	
Dalton Breckenridge	Firstview	Lerma Pointed	San Patrice-Geneill	

MIDDLE ARCHAIC (7,000 B.P. - 4,000 B.P.)

Abasolo	Coryell	Lange	Travis
Afton	Dawoon	Langtry	Uvalde
Almagre	Exotic	Langtry-Arenosa	Val Verde
Axtel	Frio	Little River	White River
Bell	Hemphill	Marshall	Williams
Brewerton Eared	Hickory Ridge	Matanzas	Zorra
Brewerton Side Notched	Kerrville Knife	McKean	
Bulverde	Kings	Merkle	
Carrizo	Kinney	Montell	
Carrolton	La Jita	Motley	
		Nolan	
		Paisano	
		Palmillas	
		Pandale	
		Pedernales	
		San Jacinto	
		Savage Cave	
		Savannah River	
		Searcy	
		Tortugas	

LATE ARCHAIC (4,000 B.P. - 3,000 B.P.)

Base Tang Knife	Delhi	Gahagan	Refugio
Big Creek	Desmuke	Gary	Sabine
Castroville	Elam	Hale	Smith
Catan	Ellis	Marshall	Table Rock
Coahuila	Ensor	Marcos	Trinity
Conejo	Ensor Split-Base	Mid-Back Tang	Turkeytail
Corner Tang Knife	Epps	Morhiss	
Covington	Evans	Pandora	
Dallas	Friday	Pontchartrain I, II	

WOODLAND (3,000 B.P. - 1,300 B.P.)

Adena Blade	Dickson	Gibson	Oauchita	Shumla
Adena-Robbins	Duran	Godley	Peisker Diamond	Sinner
Burkett	Edgewood	Grand	Pogo	Spokeshave
Charcos	Edwards	Hare Biface	Reed	Steuben
Cupp	Fairland	Kent	Rice Shallow Side Notched	Yarbrough
Darl	Figueroa	Knight Island	Rockwall	
Darl Blade	Friley	Matamoros	San Gabriel	
Deadman's	Gar Scale	Morill	San Saba	

MISSISSIPPIAN (1300 B.P. - 400 B.P.)

Agee	Caracara	Harrell	Keota	Nodena	Starr
Alba	Catahoula	Haskell	LeFlore Blade	Perdiz	Steiner
Antler	Clifton	Hayes	Livermore	Round-End Knife	Talco
Bassett	Colbert	Homan	Lott	Sabinal	Toyah
Bayogoula	Dardanelle	Howard	Maud	Sallisaw	Turner
Blevins	Fresno	Huffaker	Mineral Springs	Scallorn	Washita
Bonham	Garza	Hughes	Moran	Schustorm	Washita-Peno
Caddoan Blade	Harahey	Kay Blade	Morris	Sequoyah	Young

HISTORIC (450 B.P. - 170 B.P.)

Cuney	Guerrero	Trade Points

SOUTHERN CENTRAL
THUMBNAIL GUIDE SECTION

The following references are provided to aid the collector in easier and quicker identification of point types. All photos are exactly 30% of actual size and are proportional to each other. Each point pictured in this section represents a classic form for the type. When a match is found, go to the alphabetical location of that type for more examples in true actual size.

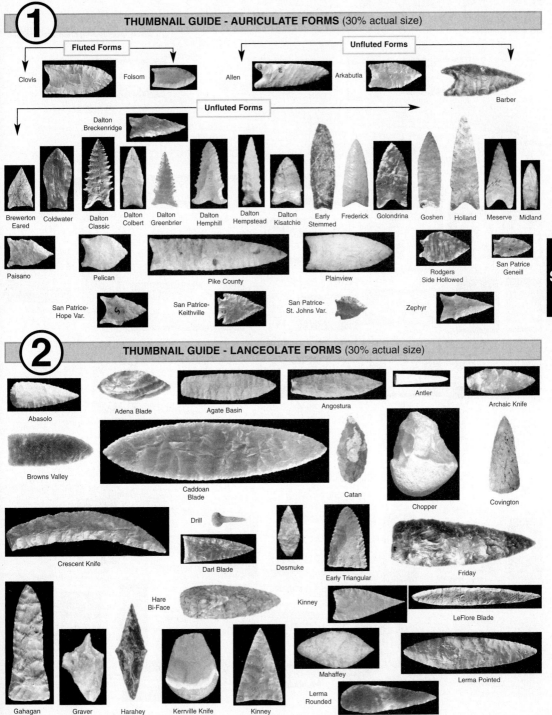

① THUMBNAIL GUIDE - AURICULATE FORMS (30% actual size)

Fluted Forms

Clovis · Folsom

Unfluted Forms

Allen · Arkabutla · Barber

Unfluted Forms

Dalton Breckenridge

Brewerton Eared · Coldwater · Dalton Classic · Dalton Colbert · Dalton Greenbrier · Dalton Hemphill · Dalton Hempstead · Dalton Kisatchie · Early Stemmed · Frederick · Golondrina · Goshen · Holland · Meserve · Midland

Paisano · Pelican · Pike County · Plainview · Rodgers Side Hollowed · San Patrice Geneill

San Patrice-Hope Var. · San Patrice-Keithville · San Patrice-St. Johns Var. · Zephyr

SC

② THUMBNAIL GUIDE - LANCEOLATE FORMS (30% actual size)

Abasolo · Adena Blade · Agate Basin · Angostura · Antler · Archaic Knife

Browns Valley · Caddoan Blade · Catan · Chopper · Covington

Crescent Knife · Drill · Darl Blade · Desmuke · Early Triangular · Friday

Hare Bi-Face · Kinney · LeFlore Blade

Gahagan · Graver · Harahey · Kerrville Knife · Kinney · Mahaffey · Lerma Rounded · Lerma Pointed

517

THUMBNAIL GUIDE - Lanceolate Forms (continued)

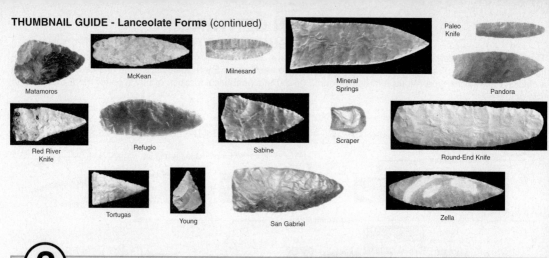

Matamoros

McKean

Milnesand

Mineral Springs

Paleo Knife

Pandora

Red River Knife

Refugio

Sabine

Scraper

Round-End Knife

Tortugas

Young

San Gabriel

Zella

③ THUMBNAIL GUIDE - CORNER NOTCHED FORMS (30% actual size)

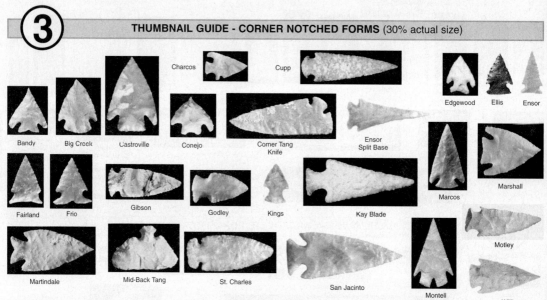

Charcos

Cupp

Edgewood

Ellis

Ensor

Bandy

Big Creek

Castroville

Conejo

Corner Tang Knife

Ensor Split Base

Fairland

Frio

Gibson

Godley

Kings

Kay Blade

Marcos

Marshall

Martindale

Mid-Back Tang

St. Charles

San Jacinto

Montell

Motley

Williams

④ THUMBNAIL GUIDE - SIDE NOTCHED FORMS (30% actual size)

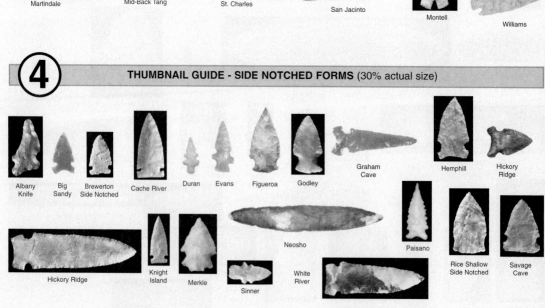

Albany Knife

Big Sandy

Brewerton Side Notched

Cache River

Duran

Evans

Figueroa

Godley

Graham Cave

Hemphill

Hickory Ridge

Hickory Ridge

Knight Island

Merkle

Sinner

Neosho

White River

Paisano

Rice Shallow Side Notched

Savage Cave

518

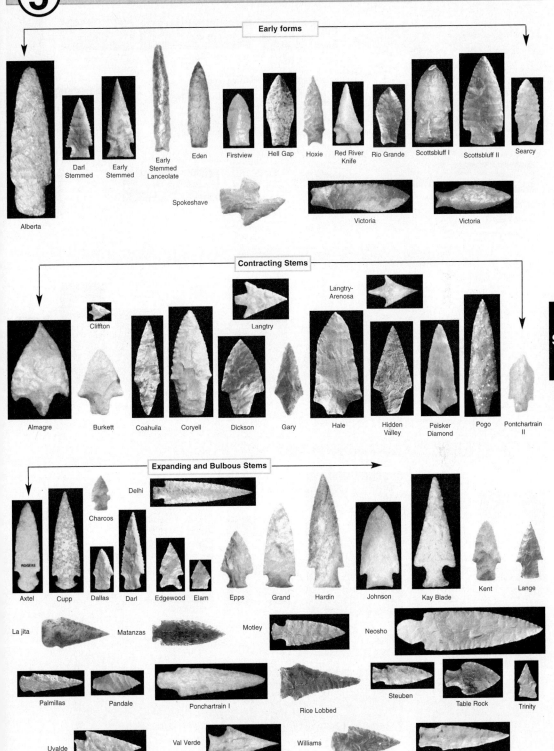

Early forms

Alberta

Darl Stemmed

Early Stemmed

Early Stemmed Lanceolate

Eden

Firstview

Hell Gap

Hoxie

Red River Knife

Rio Grande

Scottsbluff I

Scottsbluff II

Searcy

Spokeshave

Victoria

Victoria

Contracting Stems

Cliffton

Langtry

Langtry-Arenosa

Almagre

Burkett

Coahuila

Coryell

Dickson

Gary

Hale

Hidden Valley

Peisker Diamond

Pogo

Pontchartrain II

SC

Expanding and Bulbous Stems

Delhi

Charcos

Axtel

Cupp

Dallas

Darl

Edgewood

Elam

Epps

Grand

Hardin

Johnson

Kay Blade

Kent

Lange

La jita

Matanzas

Motley

Neosho

Palmillas

Pandale

Ponchartrain I

Rice Lobbed

Steuben

Table Rock

Trinity

Uvalde

Val Verde

Williams

Yarbrough

THUMBNAIL GUIDE - Stemmed Forms (continued)

Long Stemmed Forms

Adena Robbins

Bulverde

Carrolton

Dawson

Morrill

Morhiss

Nolan

Perforator

Oauchita

Savannah River

Travis

Trade

Wells

Zorra

EXOTIC FORMS

Exotic

---

⑥ THUMBNAIL GUIDE - STEMMED-BIFURCATED FORMS (30% of actual size)

Baker

Conejo

Cosotat River

Ensor Split Base

Frio

Gower

Jakie Stemmed

Jetta

Montell

Pedernales

Uvalde

---

⑦ THUMBNAIL GUIDE - BASAL NOTCHED FORMS (30% of actual size)

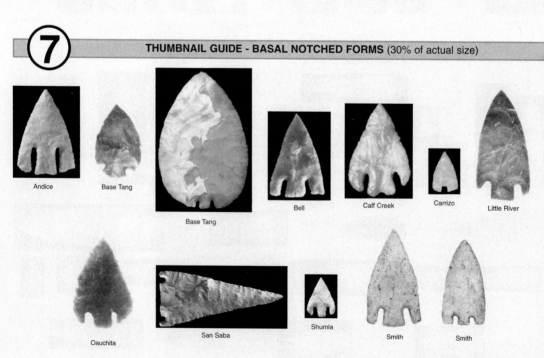

Andice

Base Tang

Base Tang

Bell

Calf Creek

Carrizo

Little River

Oauchita

San Saba

Shumla

Smith

Smith

Agee   Alba   Basset   Bayogoula   Blevins   Bonham   Caracara   Colbert   Catahoula   Cuney   Deadman's   Dardanelle   Edwards   Fresno   Friley

Garza   Guerrero   Harrell   Haskell   Homan   Hayes   Howard   Huffaker   Hughes   Keota   Knight Island   Livermore   Lott   Maud   Moran   Morris   Nodena

Perdiz   Reed   Rockwall   Sabinal   Sallisaw   Scallorn   Schustorm   Sequoyah   Starr   Steiner   Talco   Toyah   Turner   Washita   Washita-Peno

ABASOLO - Early to Middle Archaic, 7000 - 5000 B. P.

(Also see Catan and Matamoros)

SC

G7, $1-$2
S. TX

G7, $2-$4
Nuevo Leon, MX

G7, $2-$5
Starr Co., TX

G6, $2-$5
S. TX

G7, $4-$8
Zapata Co., TX

G5, $3-$6
Travis Co., TX

G5, $3-$6
TX

G6, $5-$10
TX

G7, $5-$10
Bell Co., TX

LOCATION: Southern Midwestern states and Mexico. **DESCRIPTION:** A medium to large size, broad, lanceolate point with a rounded base. The blade can be beveled on one side of each face and the base can be thinned. **I.D. KEY:** Early form of flaking on blade with good secondary edgework and rounded base.

ADENA BLADE - Late Archaic to Late Woodland, 3000 - 1200 B. P.

(Also see Harahey, Lerma, Pandora)

G7, $12-$20
AR

LOCATION: Arkansas eastward. **DESCRIPTION:** A large size, thin, broad, ovate blade with a rounded to pointed base and is usually found in caches. **I.D. KEY:** Woodland flaking, large direct strikes.

ADENA-DICKSON (See Dickson)

ADENA-ROBBINS - Late Archaic to Woodland, 3000 - 1800 B. P.

(Also see Bulverde, Carrolton, kent and Wells)

G5, $25-$45
AR

LOCATION: Arkansas eastward. **DESCRIPTION:** A large, broad, triangular point that is thin and well made with a long, wide, rounded to rectangular stem that is parallel sided. The blade has convex sides and square shoulders. Many examples show excellent secondary flaking on blade edges. **I.D. KEY:** Squared base, heavy secondary flaking.

G5, $12-$20
AR

G5, $15-$25
AR

AFTON - Middle Archaic to early Woodland, 5000 - 2000 B. P.

(Also see Apple Creek, Ferry and Helton)

Kay County chert

G6, $90-$175
N.E. OK

G9, $175-$300
N.E. OK

LOCATION: Midwestern states and is rarely found in some Eastern and Southeastern states. **DESCRIPTION:** A medium to large size pentagonal shaped point with a flaring or corner notched stem. Some examples are base notched and some are stemmed. **I.D. KEY:** Blade form.

AFTON (continued)

G7, $15-$25
Coryell Co., TX

G10+, $1500-$2500
OK

AGATE BASIN - Transitional Paleo to Early Archaic, 10,200 - 8500 B. P.

(Also see Allen, Angostura, Hell Gap, Lerma, Mahaffey and Sedalia)

Tip wear

Basal area is ground

Collateral flaking

Collateral flaking

SC

G4, $55-$100
Tulsa Co., OK

G4, $55-$100
Tulsa Co., OK

G5, $80-$150
Tulsa Co., OK

G8, $200-$350
Wagoner Co., OK

G7, $200-$350
Union Parrish, LA

Basal area is ground

Heavily resharpened

G8, $250-$400
TX

G4, $35-$65
N.E. OK

LOCATION: New Mexico to Montana eastward to Pennsylvania. **DESCRIPTION:** A medium to large size lanceolate blade of usually high quality. Bases are either convex, concave or straight, and are normally ground. Some examples are median ridged and have random to parallel flaking. **I.D. KEY:** Basal form and flaking style.

AGEE - Mississippian, 1200 - 700 B. P.

(Also see Alba, Dardanelle, Hayes, Homan and Keota)

G6, $50-$90
AR

G8, $80-$150
AR

G8, $90-$175
AR

G8, $55-$100
AR

G7, $125-$200
AR

G8, $55-$100
AR

Glued

G6, $30-$50
AR

G6, $65-$125
AR

G6, $125-$225
AR

G5, $50-$90
AR

Glued

G8, $80-$150
AR

G9, $200-$350
AR

G9, $200-$350
AR

Brown
chert

G8, $150-$250
AR

G9, $200-$350
Little Riv. Co., AR

G9, $250-$450
Little Riv. Co., AR

G9, $300-$550
Pike Co., AR

Novaculite

Glued

G9, $350-$600
Pike Co., AR

G10, $275-$500
Pike Co., AR

Red & white novaculite

Novaculite

Glued

Red novaculite

Novaculite

Glued

Very rare preform

Red novaculite

G10+, $1000-$1800
Pike Co., AR

G7, $450-$800
Pike Co., AR

G9, $800-$1400
Pike Co., AR

G9, $1000-$1800
Pike Co., AR

G10, $1200-$2000
Pike Co., AR

G10+, $1000-$1800
Pike Co., AR

LOCATION: Arkansas Caddo sites. **DESCRIPTION:** The finest, most exquisite arrow point made in the United States. A small to medium size, narrow, very thin, expanded barbed, corner notched point. Tips are needle sharp. Some examples are double notched at the base. A rare type that has only been found on a few sites. Total estimated known examples are 1100 to 1200. **I.D. KEY:** Basal form and barb expansion.

ALBA - Woodland to Mississippian, 1100 - 800 B. P.

(Also see Agee, Bonham, Colbert, Cuney, Hayes, Homan, Keota, Perdiz, Scallorn and Sequoyah)

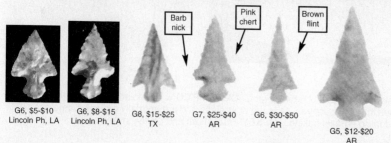

G6, $5-$10
Lincoln Ph, LA

G6, $8-$15
Lincoln Ph, LA

Barb
nick

G8, $15-$25
TX

Pink
chert

G7, $25-$40
AR

Brown
flint

G6, $30-$50
AR

G5, $12-$20
AR

LOCATION: Eastern Texas, Arkansas and Louisiana. **DESCRIPTION:** A small to medium size, narrow, well made point with prominent barbs, a recurved blade and a bulbous stem. Some examples are serrated. **I.D. KEY:** Rounded base and expanded barbs.

ALBA (continued)

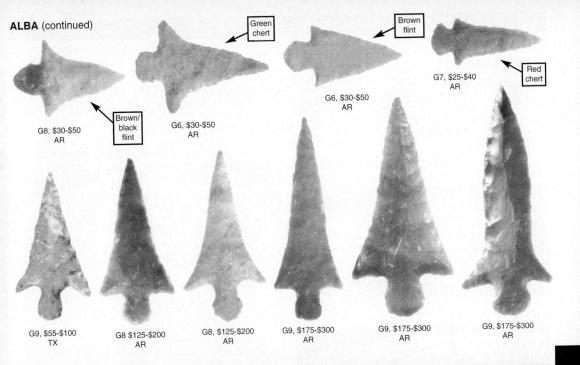

Green chert

Brown flint

Brown/ black flint

Red chert

G8, $30-$50
AR

G6, $30-$50
AR

G6, $30-$50
AR

G7, $25-$40
AR

G9, $55-$100
TX

G8 $125-$200
AR

G8, $125-$200
AR

G9, $175-$300
AR

G9, $175-$300
AR

G9, $175-$300
AR

SC

ALBANY KNIFE - Early Archaic 10,000 - 8000 B. P.

(Also see Red River Knife and San Patrice)

Beveled edge

Jasper

G6, $15-$30
Angelina Co., TX

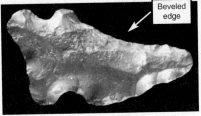

Beveled edge

G7, $40-$75
Angelina Co., TX

LOCATION: Louisiana, E. Texas and Arkansas. **DESCRIPTION:** A small to medium size knife form of the *San Patrice* point. Form is asymmetrical with a steeply beveled edge on the diagonal side. Bases are ground. Similar to the Edgefield Scraper found in Florida. **I.D. KEY:** Symmetry & beveling.

ALBERTA - Early Archaic, 10,000 - 8500 B. P.

(Also see Angostura, Brown's Valley, Clovis, Plainview and Scottsbluff)

G9, $1200-$2000
N.E. OK

G7, $200-$350
N. OK

LOCATION: Oklahoma northward to Canada and eastward to Michigan. **DESCRIPTION:** A medium to large size, broad stemmed point with weak, horizontal to tapered shoulders. Made by the Cody Complex people who made *Scottsbluff* points. A very rare type. Basal corners are rounded and the tip is blunt. **I.D. KEY:** Long, broad stem and blunted tip.

ALLEN - Transitional Paleo to Early Archaic, 8500 - 7500 B. P.

(Also see Angostura, Barber, Brown's Valley, Clovis, Golondrina, Goshen, McKean and Plainview)

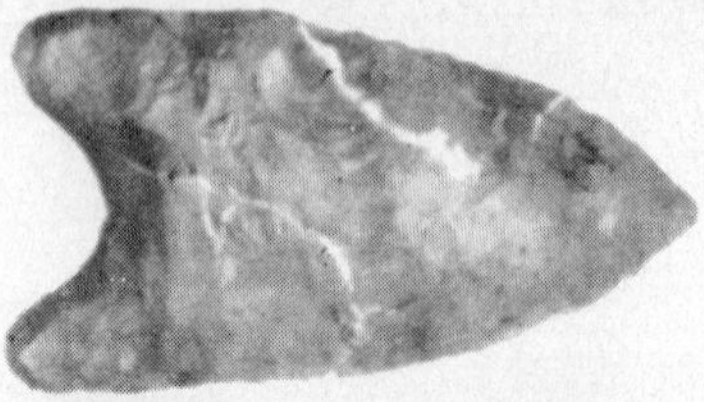

G5, $125-$200
Comanche Co., TX

Translucent
Alibates
dolomite

G10, $800-$1500
N. OK

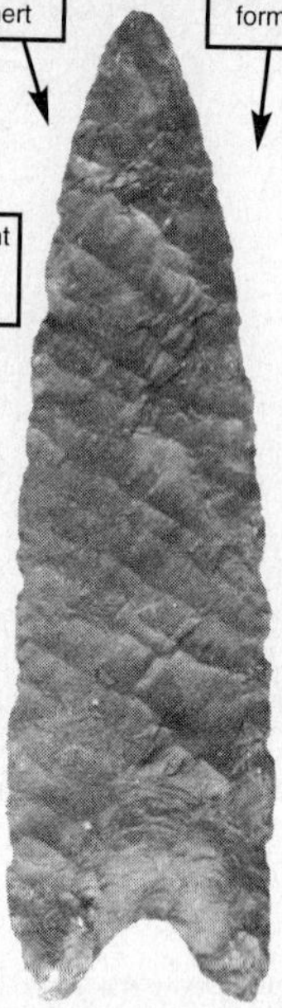

Florence
chert
Classic
form

G10, $800-$1500
N. OK

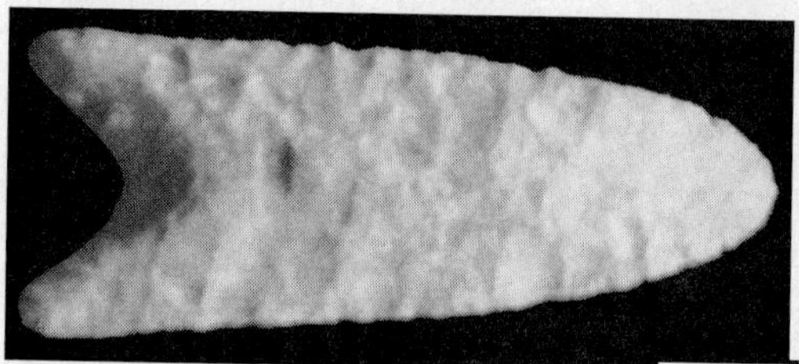

G8, $400-$750
N. OK

Oblique
transverse
flaking

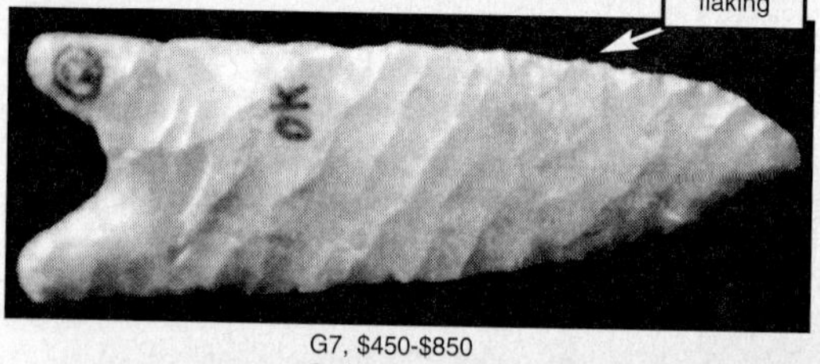

G7, $450-$850
Osage Co., OK

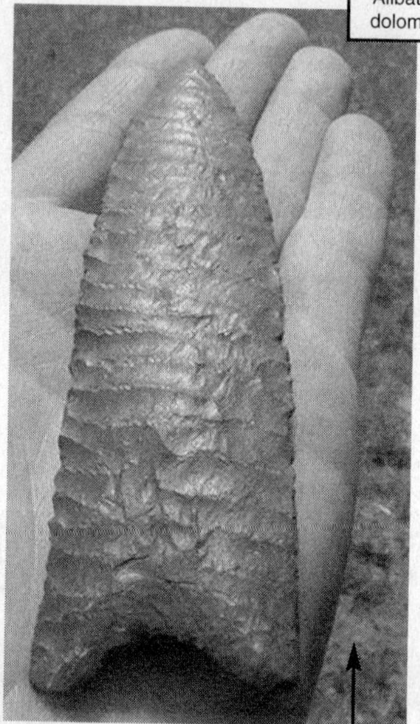

Hand held to
show size
and beauty

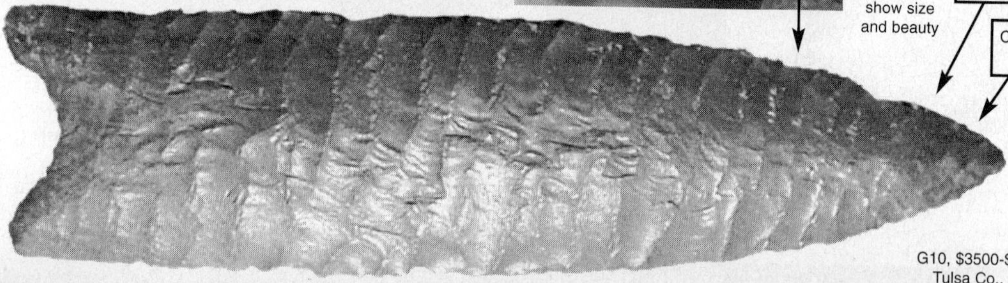

Oblique
transverse
flaking
Classic
form

G10, $3500-$6000
Tulsa Co., OK

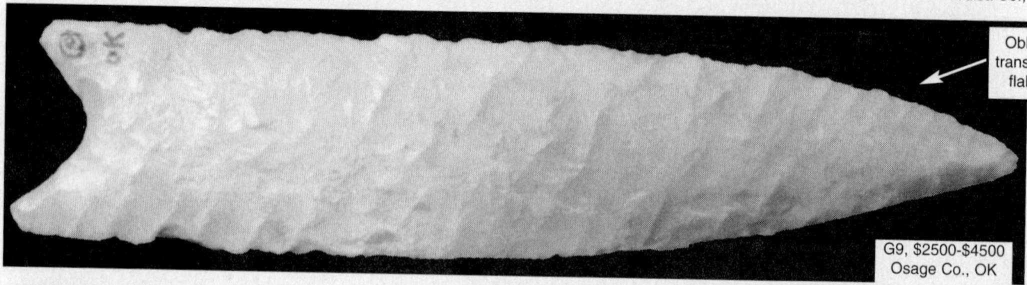

Oblique
transverse
flaking

G9, $2500-$4500
Osage Co., OK

LOCATION: Midwestern states to Canada. Named after Jimmy Allen of Wyoming. **DESCRIPTION:** A medium to large size, narrow, lanceolate point that has oblique tranverse flaking and a concave base. Basal ears tend to be rounded and the base is ground. **I.D. KEY:** Flaking style and blade form.

ALMAGRE - Early Archaic, 6000 - 4500 B. P.

(Also see Gary, Hidden Valley, Langtry-Arenosa and Morrow Mountain)

ALMAGRE (continued)

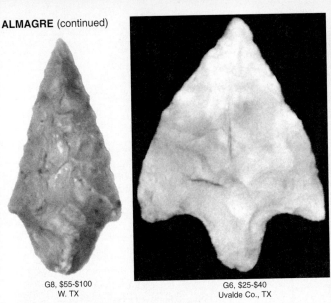

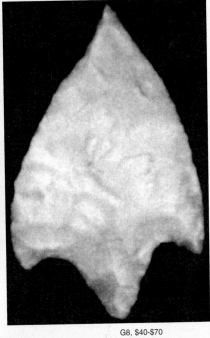

G8, $55-$100
W. TX

G6, $25-$40
Uvalde Co., TX

G8, $40-$70
Uvalde Co., TX

LOCATION: Midwestern states. **DESCRIPTION:** A broad, triangular point with pointed barbs and a long contracted pointed to rounded base. This point could be a preform for the *Langtry-Arenosa* type.

G4, $8-$15
Val Verde Co., TX

G9, $125-$200
Waco, TX

ANDICE - Early Archaic, 8000 - 5000 B. P.
(Also see Bell, Calf Creek and Little River)

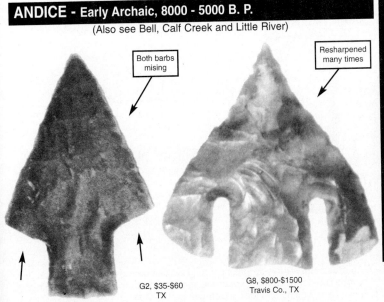

Both barbs mising

Resharpened many times

Deep notching producing drooping barbs

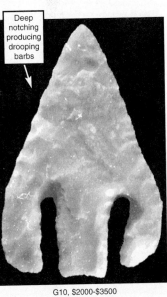

G2, $35-$60
TX

G8, $800-$1500
Travis Co., TX

G10, $2000-$3500
Comanche Co., TX

ANDICE (continued)

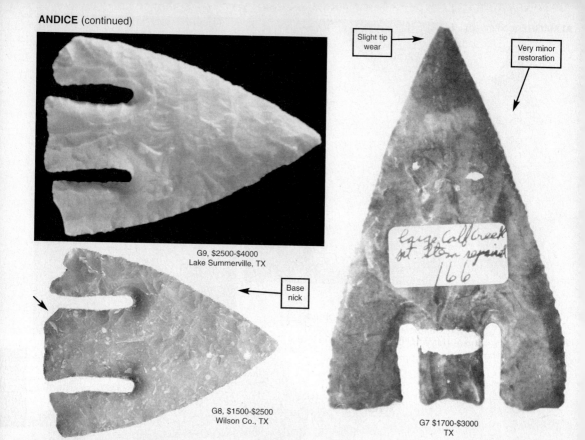

Slight tip wear

Very minor restoration

G9, $2500-$4000
Lake Summerville, TX

Base nick

G8, $1500-$2500
Wilson Co., TX

*large Calf Creek
pat. Stem repair*
166

G7 $1700-$3000
TX

LOCATION: Southern to Central Texas, Oklahoma and Kansas. **DESCRIPTION:** A broad, thin, large, triangular point with very deep, parallel basal notches. Larger than *Bell* or *Calf Creek* Points. Barbs reach the base. Because of the deep notches, barbs were easily broken off making complete, unbroken specimens rare. Found in a cave hafted to a wooden handle with pitch adhesive; used as a knife. **I.D. KEY:** Location and deep parallel basal notches.

ANGOSTURA - Early Archaic, 8800 - 7500 B. P.

(Also see Agate Basin, Allen, Archaic Knife, Hell Gap, Lerma, Midland, Milnesand, Plainview, Victoria & Zella)

Beveled edge

Beveled edge

Beveled edge

G8, $125-$200
Taylor Co., TX

G4, $25-$40
TX

G6, $40-$75
Taylor Co., TX

G8, $65-$125
Bell Co., TX

G9, $80-$150
TX

G6, $65-$125
Bexar Co., TX

LOCATION: Midwest to Western states. **DESCRIPTION:** A medium to large size, lanceolate blade with a contracting, concave, straight or convex base. Both broad and narrow forms occur. Flaking can be parallel oblique to random. Blades are commonly steeply beveled on one side of each face; some are serrated and most have basal grinding. Formerly called Long points. **I.D. KEY:** Basal form, flaking on blade which can be beveled.

ANGOSTURA (continued)

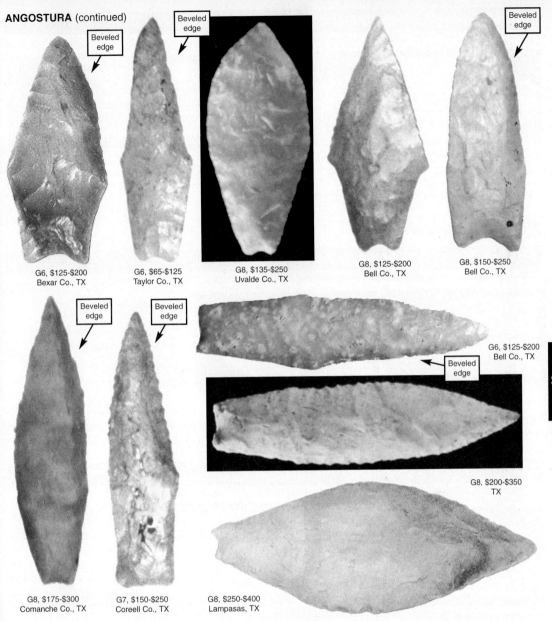

Beveled edge

Beveled edge

Beveled edge

Beveled edge

G6, $125-$200
Bexar Co., TX

G6, $65-$125
Taylor Co., TX

G8, $135-$250
Uvalde Co., TX

G8, $125-$200
Bell Co., TX

G8, $150-$250
Bell Co., TX

Beveled edge

Beveled edge

Beveled edge

G6, $125-$200
Bell Co., TX

SC

G8, $200-$350
TX

G8, $175-$300
Comanche Co., TX

G7, $150-$250
Coreell Co., TX

G8, $250-$400
Lampasas, TX

ANTLER - Mississippian, 1300 - 400 B. P.

(Also see Angostura, Golondrina, Midland, Pelican and Plainview)

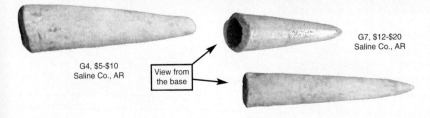

G4, $5-$10
Saline Co., AR

View from the base

G7, $12-$20
Saline Co., AR

LOCATION: Most of United States. **DESCRIPTION:** A medium size, conical shaped point made from deer antler.

ARCHAIC KNIFE - Transitional Paleo, 10,000 - 5000 B. P.

(Also see Angostura, Darl Stemmed, Early Stemmed and Victoria)

G6, $15-$25
Comal Co., TX

G6, $15-$30
Comal Co., TX

LOCATION: Texas, Oklahoma and Arkansas. **DESCRIPTION:** A medium to large size, lanceolate point with a contracting basal area. Shoulders are weakly tapered to non-existant.

ARENOSA   (See Langtry-Arenosa)

ARKABUTLA - Transitional Paleo, 10,000 - 8000 B. P.

(Also see Angostura, Coldwater, Golondrina, Midland, Pelican, Plainview, Rodgers Side Hollowed and San Patrice)

G7, $125-$225
Mineola, TX

G8, $165-$300
Cent. TX

G9, $275-$500
AR

LOCATION: AR, LA, MS, TN. **DESCRIPTION:** A small to medium size, broad, thin, lanceolate point with expanded auricles. Blade edges recurve into the base which is concave. **I.D. KEY:** Eared basal form.

AXTEL - Early-mid Archaic 7,000 - 3500 B. P.

(Also see Godley, Lajita, Palmillas and Williams)

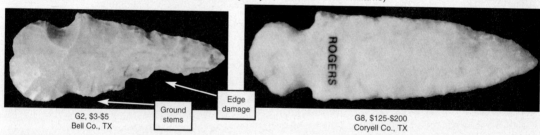

Ground
stems

Edge
damage

ROGERS

G2, $3-$5
Bell Co., TX

G8, $125-$200
Coryell Co., TX

LOCATION: Central Texas. **DESCRIPTION:** A medium size, narrow point with barbed shoulders and a bulbous stem. Called "Penny Points" by local collectors. Stem edges are usually ground. **I.D. KEY:** Bulbous stem that is ground. See Prewitt, p.90, Tex. Arc. Society 66, 1995 and *Field Guide to Stone Artifacts of Texas*, Turner & Hester, p.75, 1993

BAKER - Early Archaic, 7500 - 6000 B. P.

(Also see Bandy, Pedernales and Uvalde)

G7, $12-$20
W. TX

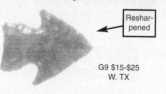

Reshar-
pened

G9 $15-$25
W. TX

G7, $7-$12
W. TX

BAKER (continued)

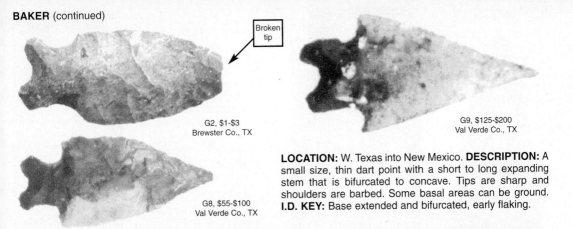

Broken tip

G2, $1-$3
Brewster Co., TX

G9, $125-$200
Val Verde Co., TX

G8, $55-$100
Val Verde Co., TX

LOCATION: W. Texas into New Mexico. **DESCRIPTION:** A small size, thin dart point with a short to long expanding stem that is bifurcated to concave. Tips are sharp and shoulders are barbed. Some basal areas can be ground. **I.D. KEY:** Base extended and bifurcated, early flaking.

BANDY - Early Archaic, 7500 - 5000 B. P.

(Also see Baker, Marcos, Marshall and Martindale)

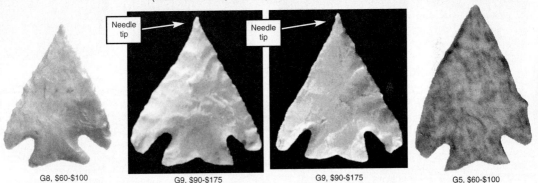

Needle tip

Needle tip

SC

G8, $60-$100
Comanche Co., TX

G9, $90-$175
Austin, TX

G9, $90-$175
Comanche Co., TX

G5, $60-$100
S. TX

LOCATION: Southern Texas. **DESCRIPTION:** A small sized *Martindale* more commonly found in southern Texas. A corner notched to expanded stemmed point. The base is usually formed by two curves meeting at the center but can be straight to concave. **I.D. KEY:** Basal form, early flaking.

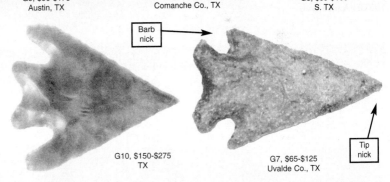

Barb nick

Tip nick

G10, $150-$275
TX

G7, $65-$125
Uvalde Co., TX

BARBER - Transitional Paleo, 10,000 - 9000 B. P.

(Also see Allen, Angostura, Clovis, Golondrina, Goshen, Kinney, McKean and Plainview)

G7, $275-$500
Llano Co., TX

G5, $150-$250
Llano Co., TX

531

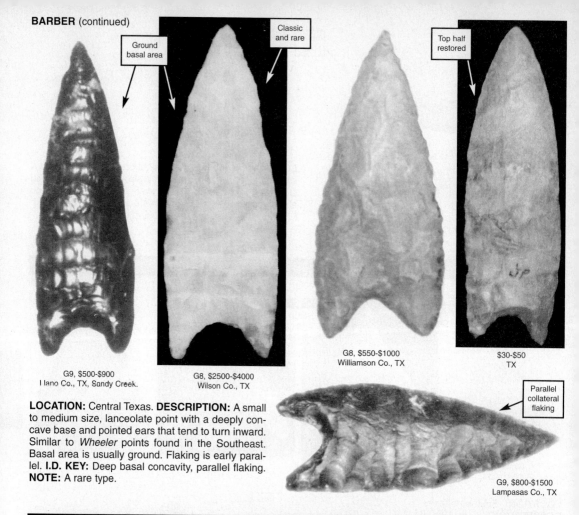

Ground basal area

Classic and rare

Top half restored

G9, $500-$900
Llano Co., TX, Sandy Creek.

G8, $2500-$4000
Wilson Co., TX

G8, $550-$1000
Williamson Co., TX

$30-$50
TX

LOCATION: Central Texas. **DESCRIPTION:** A small to medium size, lanceolate point with a deeply concave base and pointed ears that tend to turn inward. Similar to *Wheeler* points found in the Southeast. Basal area is usually ground. Flaking is early parallel. **I.D. KEY:** Deep basal concavity, parallel flaking. **NOTE:** A rare type.

Parallel collateral flaking

G9, $800-$1500
Lampasas Co., TX

BASE TANG KNIFE - Late Archaic to Woodland, 4000 - 2000 B. P.

(Also see Corner Tang, Mid-Back Tang and San Saba)

G6, $35-$60
Travis Co., TX

IMPORTANT:
All Shown half size

Black chert

G7, $225-$400
Abilene, TX

G7, $275-$500
Travis Co., TX

G9, $450-$800
Coryell Co., TX

G8, $300-$500
TX

G5, $175-$300
Coryell Co., TX

G8, $400-$700
Coryell Co., TX

BASE TANG KNIFE (continued)

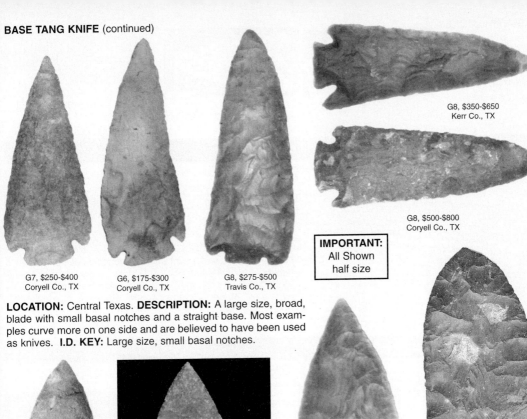

G8, $350-$650
Kerr Co., TX

G8, $500-$800
Coryell Co., TX

IMPORTANT:
All Shown
half size

G7, $250-$400
Coryell Co., TX

G6, $175-$300
Coryell Co., TX

G8, $275-$500
Travis Co., TX

LOCATION: Central Texas. **DESCRIPTION:** A large size, broad, blade with small basal notches and a straight base. Most examples curve more on one side and are believed to have been used as knives. **I.D. KEY:** Large size, small basal notches.

G9, $700-$1200
Coryell Co., TX

G10, $800-$1500
Kerr Co., TX

G9, $700-$1200
Gillespie Co., TX

G9, $1500-$2500
TX

SC

BASSETT - Mississippian, 800 - 400 B. P.

(Also see Cliffton, Perdiz, Rockwall and Steiner)

G8, $25-$40
Smith Co., TX

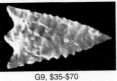

G9, $35-$70
Smith Co., TX

G7, $25-$45
Smith Co., TX

G6, $20-$35
Smith Co., TX

LOCATION: Midwestern states. **DESCRIPTION:** A small size, thin, triangular point with pointed tangs and a small pointed base. High quality flaking is evident on most examples. **I.D. KEY:** Small pointed base.

BASSETT (continued)

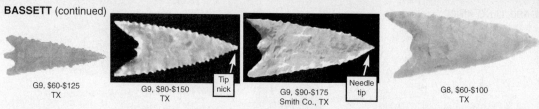

G9, $60-$125
TX

G9, $80-$150
TX

Tip nick

G9, $90-$175
Smith Co., TX

Needle tip

G8, $60-$100
TX

BAYOGOULA - Mississippian, 800 - 400 B. P.

(Also see Edwards, Friley)

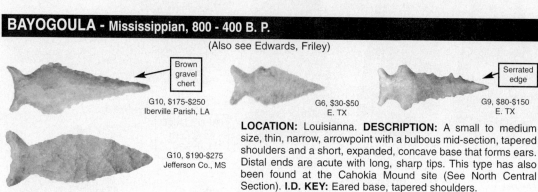

Brown gravel chert

G10, $175-$250
Iberville Parish, LA

G6, $30-$50
E. TX

Serrated edge

G9, $80-$150
E. TX

G10, $190-$275
Jefferson Co., MS

LOCATION: Louisianna. **DESCRIPTION:** A small to medium size, thin, narrow, arrowpoint with a bulbous mid-section, tapered shoulders and a short, expanded, concave base that forms ears. Distal ends are acute with long, sharp tips. This type has also been found at the Cahokia Mound site (See North Central Section). **I.D. KEY:** Eared base, tapered shoulders.

BELL - Middle Archaic, 7000 - 5000 B. P.

(Also see Andice and Calf Creek).

Broken barb & stem

G5, $45-$80
Wilson Co., TX

Broken barb

G3, $30-$50
TX

G1, $5-$10
Val Verde Co., TX

Broken barb & stem

G8, $200-$350
TX

G2, $35-$60
Bexar Co., TX

G7, $200-$375
Williamson Co., TX

LOCATION: Central Texas. **DESCRIPTION:** A small to medium size point with medium-deep parallel basal notches, but not as deep as in *Andice*. Larger examples usually would fall under *Andice*. Found primarily in Texas. Tangs can turn inward at the base. **I.D. KEY:** Shorter barbs and notching.

BELL (continued)

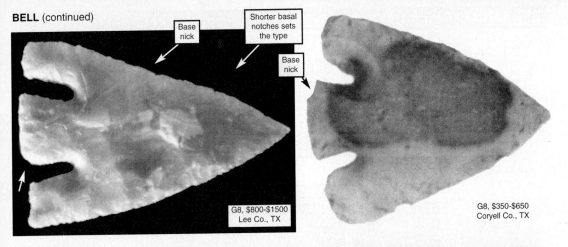

Base nick

Shorter basal notches sets the type

Base nick

G8, $800-$1500
Lee Co., TX

G8, $350-$650
Coryell Co., TX

BIG CREEK - Late Archaic to early Woodland, 3500 - 2500 B. P.

(Also see Ellis, Grand, Kings, Marcos and Williams)

Made into a blunt; used as a hafted scraper

Conglomerate

SC

G4, $5-$8
AR

G3, $2-$5
AR

G5, $8-$15
AR

G4, $8-$15
AR

G5, $8-$15
AR

G5 $8-$15
AR

G7, $15-$25
AR

G8, $25-$40
AR

LOCATION: Arkansas and surrounding states. **DESCRIPTION:** A small to medium size, short, broad, corner notched point with a bulbous base. Believed to be related to *Marcos* points. The tips are needle sharp on some examples, similar to *Mud Creek* points from Alabama. Barbs can be weak to very long. Small *Big Sloughs* of the Southeast would be indistinguishable to this type. **I.D. KEY:** Rounded base and barbs drop.

535

BIG SANDY - Early to Late Archaic, 10,000 - 3000 B. P.

(Also see Cache River, Ensor, Frio, Hickory Ridge and Savage Cave)

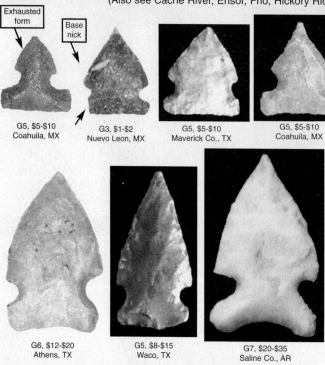

Exhausted form

Base nick

G5, $5-$10
Coahuila, MX

G3, $1-$2
Nuevo Leon, MX

G5, $5-$10
Maverick Co., TX

G5, $5-$10
Coahuila, MX

G4, $5-$10
Val Verde Co., TX

G6, $12-$20
Athens, TX

G5, $8-$15
Waco, TX

G7, $20-$35
Saline Co., AR

Resharpened

G7, $80-$150
Travis Co., TX

G9, $150-$250
TX

LOCATION: Eastern Texas eastward. **DESCRIPTION:** A small to medium size, side notched point with early forms showing basal grinding, serrations and horizontal flaking. Bases are straight to concave. Deeply concave bases form ears. **I.D. KEY:** Basal form.

BLEVINS - Mississippian, 1200 - 600 B. P.

(Also see Hayes, Howard and Sequoyah)

G8, $35-$60
W. AR.

LOCATION: Midwestern states. **DESCRIPTION:** A small size, narrow spike point with two or more notches on each blade side. The base is diamond shaped. A cross between *Hayes* and *Howard*. **I.D. KEY:** Diamond shaped base.

BONHAM - Woodland to Mississippian, 1200 - 600 B. P.

(Also see Alba, Bulbar Stemmed, Cuney, Hayes, Moran, Perdiz, Rockwall & Sabinal)

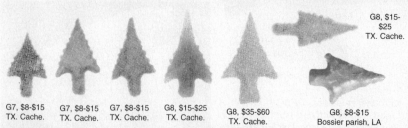

G8, $15-$25
TX. Cache.

G7, $8-$15
TX. Cache.

G7, $8-$15
TX. Cache.

G7, $8-$15
TX. Cache.

G8, $15-$25
TX. Cache.

G8, $35-$60
TX. Cache.

G8, $8-$15
Bossier parish, LA

G9, $35-$60
TX. Cache

G8, $35-$60
Comanche Co., TX

LOCATION: Texas and Oklahoma. **DESCRIPTION:** A small to medium size, thin, well made triangular point with a short to long squared or rounded, narrow stem. Many examples are finely serrated. Blade edges are straight, concave, or convex or recurved. Shoulders are squared to barbed. **I.D. KEY:** Long straight base, expanded barbs.

Bonham (continued)

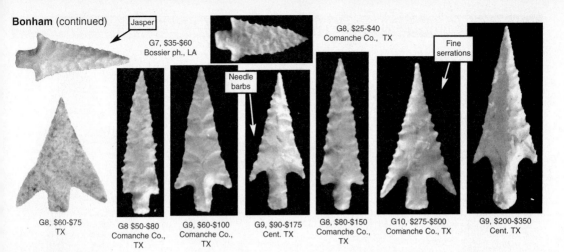

Jasper

G7, $35-$60
Bossier ph., LA

Needle barbs

G8, $25-$40
Comanche Co., TX

Fine serrations

G8, $60-$75
TX

G8 $50-$80
Comanche Co.,
TX

G9, $60-$100
Comanche Co.,
TX

G9, $90-$175
Cent. TX

G8, $80-$150
Comanche Co.,
TX

G10, $275-$500
Comanche Co., TX

G9, $200-$350
Cent. TX

BRAZOS (See Darl Stemmed)

BREWERTON EARED - Middle to Late Archaic, 6000 - 4000 B. P.

(Also see Rice Shallow Side Notched)

LOCATION: Northeast Texas eastward. **DESCRIPTION:** A small size, triangular point with shallow side notches and a concave base.

G4, $1-$2
Nuevo Leon, MX

G4, $1-$2
Saline Co., AR

G7, $3-$5
AR

SC

BREWERTON SIDE NOTCHED - Middle to Late Archaic, 6000 - 4000 B. P.

(Also see Big Sandy)

G2, $1-$2
Friendship Co., AR

G6, $2-$3
Waco, TX

LOCATION: Northeast Texas eastward. **DESCRIPTION:** A small size, triangular point with shallow side notches and a concave base.

BROWNS VALLEY - Transitional Paleo, 10,000 - 8000 B. P.

(Also see Agate Basin, Allen, Angostura, Barber, Clovis, Firstview, Midland and Plainview)

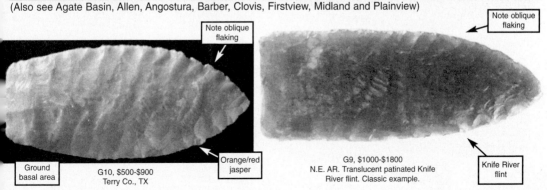

Note oblique flaking

Note oblique flaking

Ground basal area

Orange/red jasper

G10, $500-$900
Terry Co., TX

G9, $1000-$1800
N.E. AR. Translucent patinated Knife River flint. Classic example.

Knife River flint

LOCATION: A Minnesota type that has been found in Arkansas and W. Texas. **DESCRIPTION:** A medium to large, thin, lanceolate blade with usually oblique to horizontal transverse flaking and a concave to straight base which can be ground. A very rare type. **I.D. KEY:** Paleo transverse flaking.

BULVERDE - Middle Archaic to Woodland, 5000 - 1000 B. P.

(Also see Carrolton, Delhi and Wells)

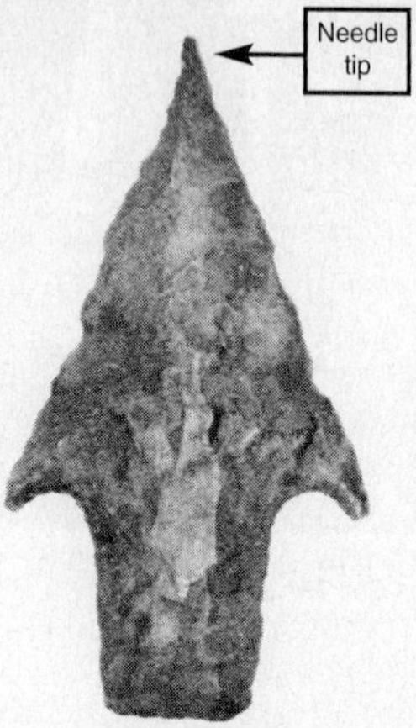

Needle tip

G8, $30-$50
Bell Co., TX

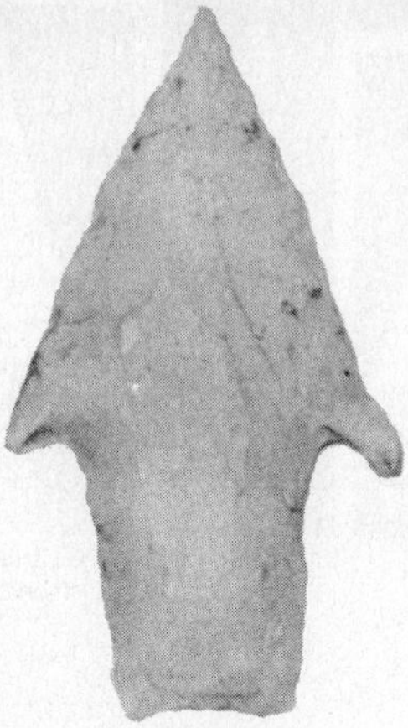

G8, $35-$65
Bell Co., TX

Barb nick

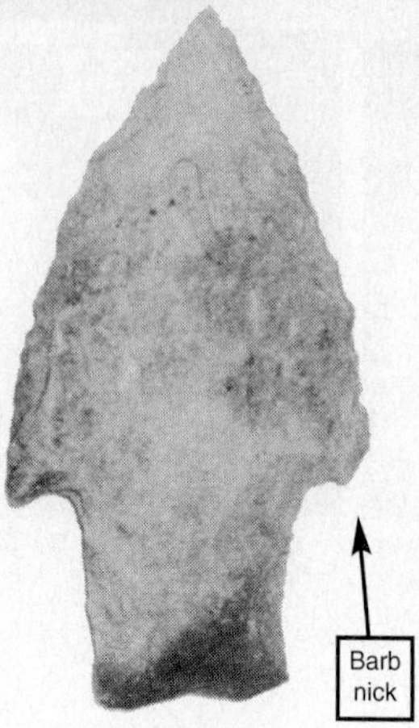

G4, $20-$35
TX

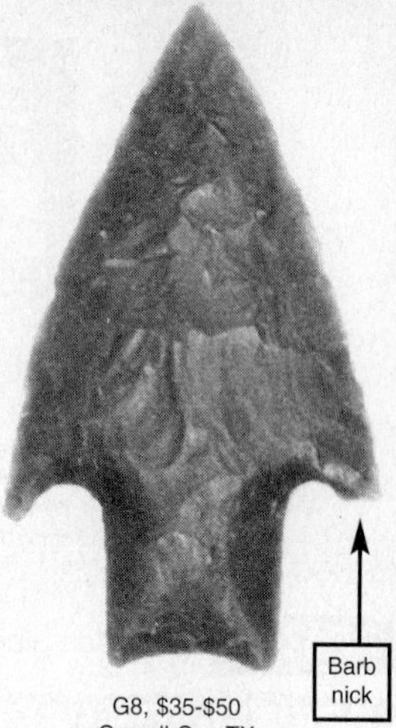

Barb nick

G8, $35-$50
Coryell Co., TX

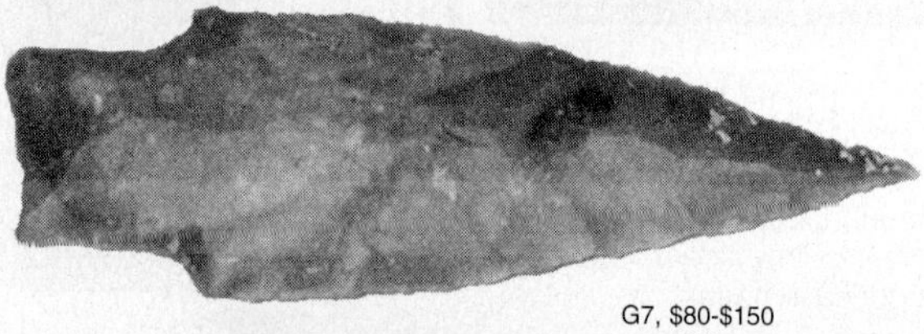

G7, $80-$150
TX

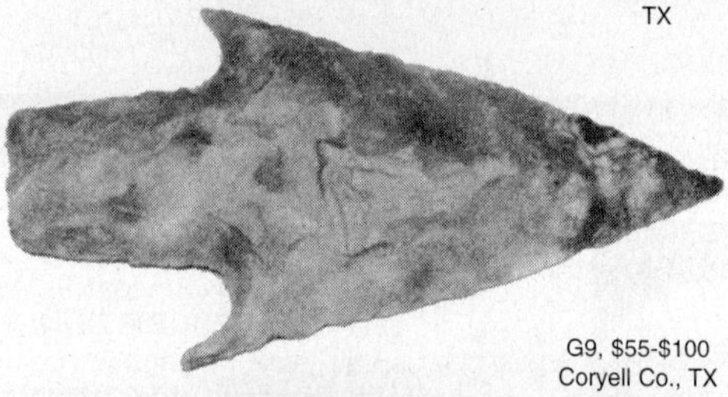

G9, $55-$100
Coryell Co., TX

Slight tip wear

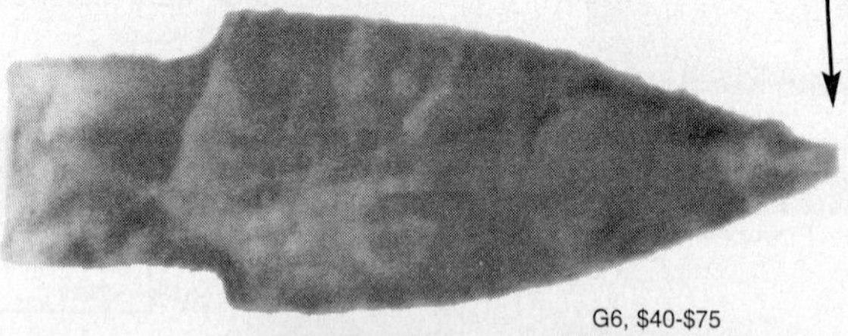

G6, $40-$75
Williamson Co., TX

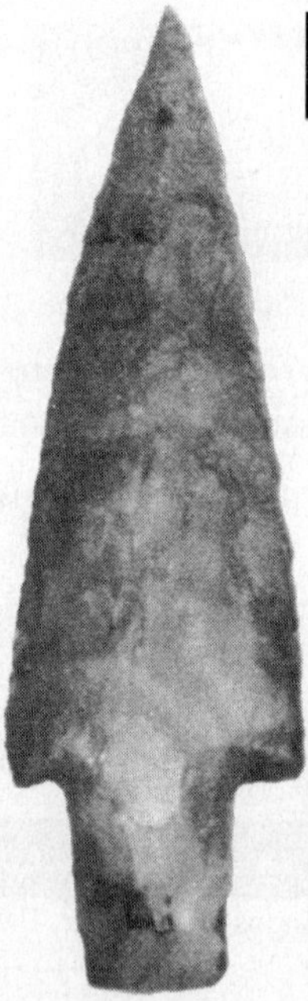

G9, $150-$275
Coryell Co., TX

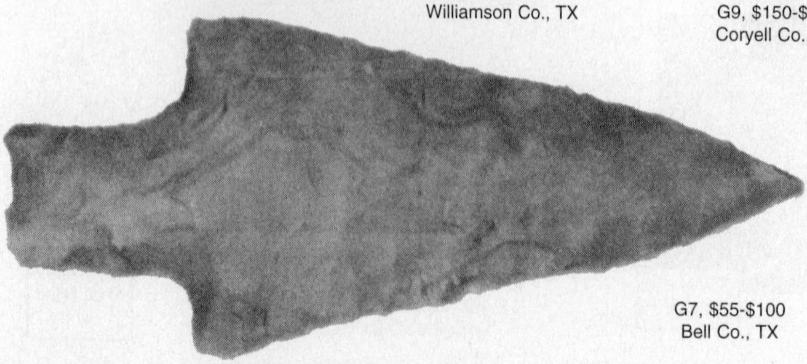

G7, $55-$100
Bell Co., TX

Slight tip wear

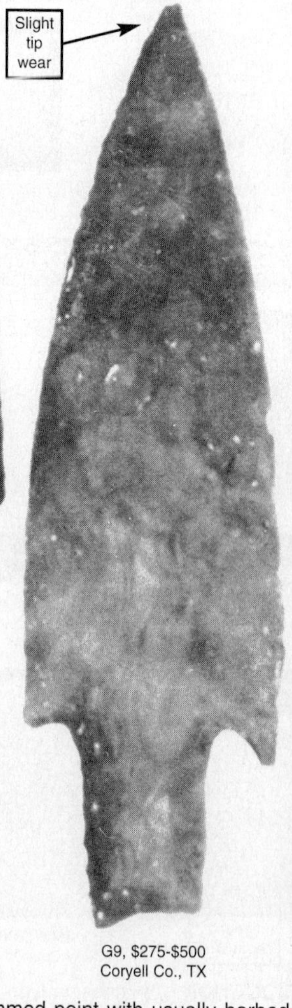

G9, $275-$500
Coryell Co., TX

LOCATION: Texas. **DESCRIPTION:** A medium to large size, long, rectangular stemmed point with usually barbed shoulders. Believed to be related to Carrolton. **I.D. KEY:** Long, squared base and barbed shoulders.

BURKETT - Woodland, 2300 - 2000 B. P.

(Also see Dickson and Gary)

Serrated edge

G7, $15-$25
AR

G6, $8-$15
Saline Co., AR

LOCATION: Arkansas into Missouri. **DESCRIPTION:** A broad, medium size point with a contracting to parallel sided stem and barbed to horizontal shoulders.

CACHE RIVER - Early to Late Archaic, 10,000 - 5000 B. P.

(Also see Big Sandy, Hickory Ridge, Knight Island and White River)

Cobble chert

Fossil chert

G7, $125-$200
AR

Jasper

G6, $80-$150
W. Carroll Ph, LA

G7, $125-$200
Richland Ph, LA

G7, $125-$200
AR

Agate

G9, $250-$450
Pike Co., AR

G9, $275-$500
Greene Co., AR

G10, $400-$700
AR

G10, $500-$900
Greene Co., AR

SC

LOCATION: Arkansas to Ohio, West Virginia and Pennsylvania. **DESCRIPTION:** A small to medium size, fairly thin, side-notched, triangular point with a concave base. Blade flaking is of the early parallel type. Could be related to *Big Sandy* points. Called *Kessell* in West Virginia. **I.D. KEY:** Base form, narrow notched & flaking of blade.

CADDOAN BLADE - Mississippian, 800 - 600 B. P.

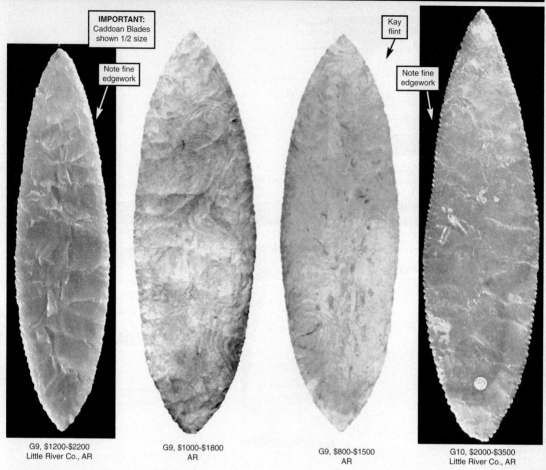

IMPORTANT:
Caddoan Blades
shown 1/2 size

Note fine
edgework

Kay
flint

Note fine
edgework

G9, $1200-$2200
Little River Co., AR

G9, $1000-$1800
AR

G9, $800-$1500
AR

G10, $2000-$3500
Little River Co., AR

LOCATION: Texas and Arkansas on Caddo culture sites. **DESCRIPTION:** A large size, thin, double pointed, elliptical blade with serrated edges. Examples with basal side notches have been found in Texas. Beware of fakes. **I.D. KEY:** Edgework, flaking style on blade.

CALF CREEK - Early to Middle Archaic, 8000 - 5000 B. P.

(Also see Andice and Bell)

Bifurcated
base

G8, $150-$250
N.E. OK

G7, $175-$300
TX/AR

G6, $55-$100
TX

CALF CREEK (continued)

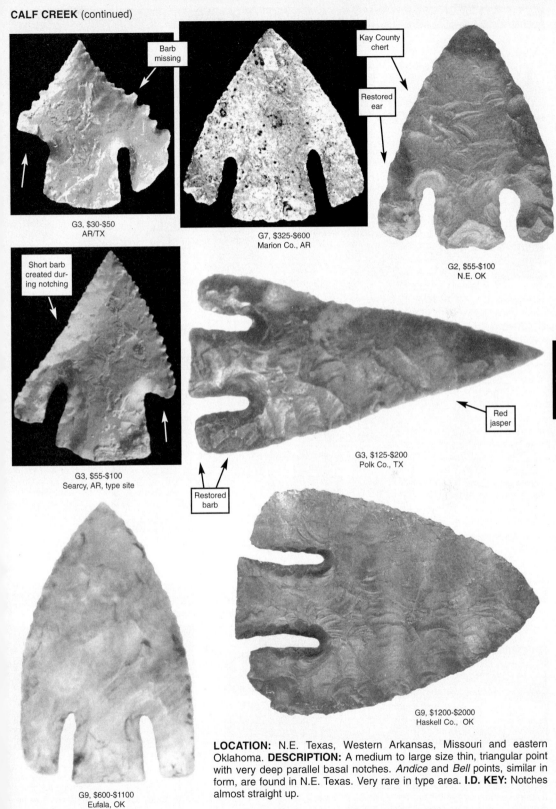

Barb missing

G3, $30-$50
AR/TX

Kay County chert

Restored ear

G7, $325-$600
Marion Co., AR

G2, $55-$100
N.E. OK

Short barb created during notching

G3, $55-$100
Searcy, AR, type site

Restored barb

Red jasper

G3, $125-$200
Polk Co., TX

G9, $1200-$2000
Haskell Co., OK

G9, $600-$1100
Eufala, OK

LOCATION: N.E. Texas, Western Arkansas, Missouri and eastern Oklahoma. **DESCRIPTION:** A medium to large size thin, triangular point with very deep parallel basal notches. *Andice* and *Bell* points, similar in form, are found in N.E. Texas. Very rare in type area. **I.D. KEY:** Notches almost straight up.

541

CARACARA - Mississippian to Historic, 600 - 400 B. P.

(Also see Huffaker, Reed and Washita)

Calcedony

G9, $15-$35
MX

G3, $2-$5
S. TX

G5, $10-$18
Nuevo Leon, MX

G7, $15-$25
TX

G5, $10-$18
Nuevo Leon, MX

G8, $20-$35
TX

G9, $20-$35
MX

G6, $15-$25
TX

G9, $50-$90
TX

Serrated tip

Serrated tip

Serrated tip

Serrated tip

G8, $35-$60
S. TX

G9, $45-$80
S. W. TX

G9, $45-$80
S. W. TX

G10, $55-$100
TX

G10, $55-$100
TX

G10, $55-$100
TX

G6, $15-$25
TX

G10, $55-$100
TX

LOCATION: Texas. **DESCRIPTION:** A small size, thin, side notched point with a straight, concave or convex base. Side notches can be deep and occur close to the base.

Serrated tip

Calcedony

Black chert

Calcedony

G8, $35-$65
TX

G10, $90-$175
TX

G7, $40-$75
S. W. TX

G9, $65-$125
TX

G10, $150-$250
TX

G10, $175-$350
Zapata Co., TX

G9, $90-$175
Coahuila, MX

CARRIZO - Middle Archaic, 7000 - 4000 B. P.

(Also see Early Triangle, Montell and Tortugas)

Rare double tip

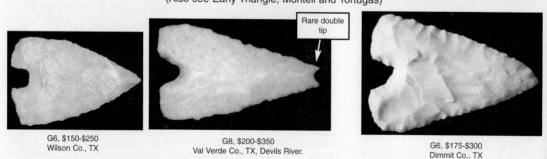

G6, $150-$250
Wilson Co., TX

G8, $200-$350
Val Verde Co., TX, Devils River.

G6, $175-$300
Dimmit Co., TX

LOCATION: Texas to Colorado. **DESCRIPTION:** A small to medium size, triangular point with a deep single notch or a concave indention in the center of the base. Flaking is parallel to random. Blade edges are rarely serrated. Can be confused with resharpened *Montells*. **I.D. KEY:** Basal notch.

CARRIZO (continued)

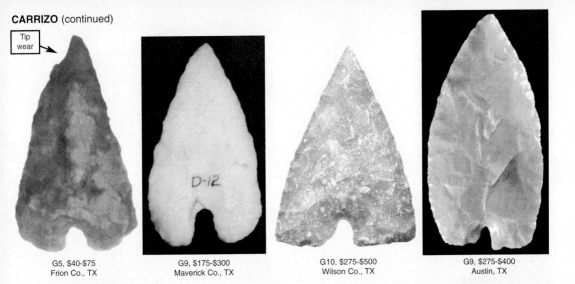

Tip wear →

G5, $40-$75
Frion Co., TX

G9, $175-$300
Maverick Co., TX

G10, $275-$500
Wilson Co., TX

G9, $275-$400
Austin, TX

CARROLTON - Middle to Late Archaic, 5000 - 3000 B. P.

(Also see Adena, Bulverde, Dallas, Morrill and Wells)

G2, $1-$2
Cent. TX

G6, $5-$10
Eufaula Lake, OK

G7, $15-$30
Coryell Co., TX

G6, $12-$20
Comanche Co., TX

G6, $12-$20
Bell Co., TX

G7, $25-$40
Central TX

LOCATION: North Texas. **DESCRIPTION:** A medium to large size, long parallel stemmed point with a square base. Shoulders are usually tapered. Workmanship is crude to medium grade. Believed to be related to *Bulverde* points.

CASTROVILLE - Late Archaic to Woodland, 4000 - 1500 B. P.

(Also see Lange, Marcos, Marshall and San Jacinto)

G7, $30-$50
TX

Tip wear

G6, $25-$40
TX

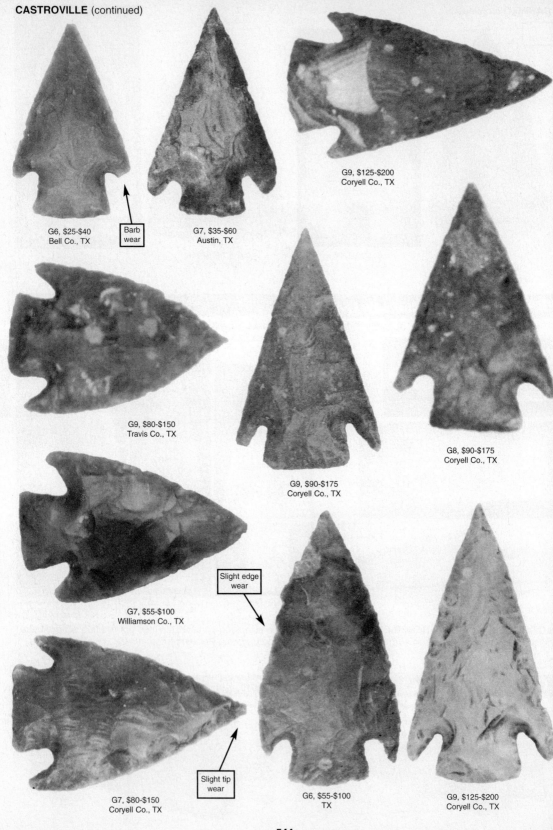

G9, $125-$200
Coryell Co., TX

G6, $25-$40
Bell Co., TX

Barb
wear

G7, $35-$60
Austin, TX

G9, $80-$150
Travis Co., TX

G9, $90-$175
Coryell Co., TX

G8, $90-$175
Coryell Co., TX

G7, $55-$100
Williamson Co., TX

Slight edge
wear

Slight tip
wear

G7, $80-$150
Coryell Co., TX

G6, $55-$100
TX

G9, $125-$200
Coryell Co., TX

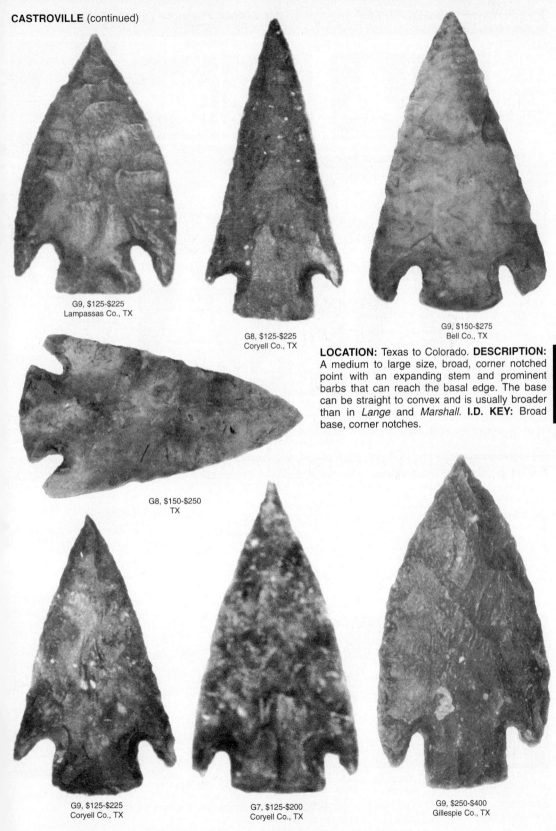

G9, $125-$225
Lampassas Co., TX

G8, $125-$225
Coryell Co., TX

G9, $150-$275
Bell Co., TX

LOCATION: Texas to Colorado. **DESCRIPTION:** A medium to large size, broad, corner notched point with an expanding stem and prominent barbs that can reach the basal edge. The base can be straight to convex and is usually broader than in *Lange* and *Marshall*. **I.D. KEY:** Broad base, corner notches.

SC

G8, $150-$250
TX

G9, $125-$225
Coryell Co., TX

G7, $125-$200
Coryell Co., TX

G9, $250-$400
Gillespie Co., TX

CATAHOULA - Mississippian, 800 - 400 B. P.

(Also see Friley, Rockwall and Scallorn)

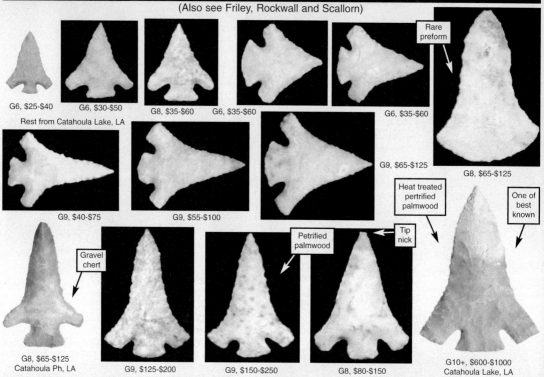

G6, $25-$40

G6, $30-$50

G8, $35-$60

G6, $35-$60

Rest from Catahoula Lake, LA

G6, $35-$60

G9, $65-$125

G8, $65-$125

Rare preform

Heat treated pertrified palmwood

One of best known

G9, $40-$75

G9, $55-$100

Petrified palmwood

Tip nick

Gravel chert

G8, $65-$125
Catahoula Ph, LA

G9, $125-$200

G9, $150-$250

G8, $80-$150

G10+, $600-$1000
Catahoula Lake, LA

LOCATION: East Texas, Louisiana to Arkansas. **DESCRIPTION**: A small size, thin, point with broad, flaring, squared tangs. The stem is parallel sided to expanding. The base is straight to convex. **I.D. KEY:** Expanded barbs.

CATAN - Late Archaic to Mississippian, 4000 - 300 B. P.

(Also see Abasolo, Matamoros and Young)

G5, $1-$2
Nuevo Leon, MX

G6, $1-$2
Nuevo Leon, MX

G6, $1-$3
Nuevo Leon, MX

G7, $1-$3
Starr Co., TX

G7, $2-$5
Nuevo Leon, MX

G6, $2-$5
Starr Co., TX

G9, $4-$8
Nuevo Leon, MX

G7, $2-$5
Starr Co., TX

G9, $5-$10
Nuevo Leon, MX

LOCATION: Southern Texas and New Mexico. **DESCRIPTION**: A small, thin, lanceolate point with a rounded base. Large examples would fall under the *Abasolo* type.

CHARCOS - Woodland, 3000 - 2000 B. P.

(Also see Duran, Evans and Sinner)

G8, $35-$65
TX

G7, $15-$25
MX

G6, $12-$20
TX

G10, $65-$125
TX

G8, $40-$70
TX

G8, $80-$150
TX

LOCATION: Northern Mexico into south Texas & Colorado. **DESCRIPTION:** A small size, thin, single barbed point with a notch near the opposite shoulder. Stem is rectangular. **I.D. KEY:** Asymmetrical form. Some are double notched. Beware of resharpened *Shumla* points with notches added in modern times to look like *Charcos*.

CHOPPER - Paleo to Archaic, 11,500 - 6000 B. P.

(Also see Kerrville Knife)

LOCATION: Paleo sites everywhere. **DESCRIPTION:** A medium to large size, thick, ovoid hand axe made from local creek or river stones. Used in the butchering process. Also known as Butted knife.

Chopper shown
half size

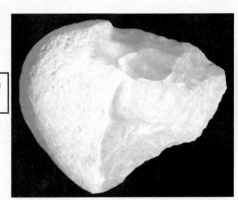

G8, $30-$50
Kimble Co., TX

CLIFFTON - Mississippian, 1200 - 500 B. P.

(Also see Bassett)

LOCATION: Central Texas. **DESCRIPTION:** A small size, crude point that is usually made from a flake and is uniface. The base is sharply contracting to pointed. Preforms for *Perdiz*?

G9, $5-$10
TX

G1, $.50-$1
Waco, TX

G6, $4-$8
TX

G6, $1-$2
TX

CLOVIS - Early Paleo, 11,500 - 10,600 B. P.

(Also see Allen, Angostura, Barber, Browns Valley, Dalton, Golondrina and Plainview)

LOCATION: All of North America. **DESCRIPTION:** A medium to large size, auriculate, fluted, lanceolate point with convex sides and a concave base that is ground. Most examples are fluted on both sides about 1/3 the way up from the base. The flaking can be random to parallel. *Clovis* is the earliest point type in the hemisphere. There is no pre-*Clovis* evidence here in the U.S.(no crude forms that pre-date *Clovis*). The origin of *Clovis* is unknown. It may have developed from earlier forms brought here from the old world. *Clovis*-like fluted points have been reported found in China dating to 11-12,000 B.P. *Clovis* has also been found in Alaska and southern Chile in South America. **I.D. KEY:** Paleo flaking, shoulders, batan fluting instead of indirect style. Basal form and fluting.

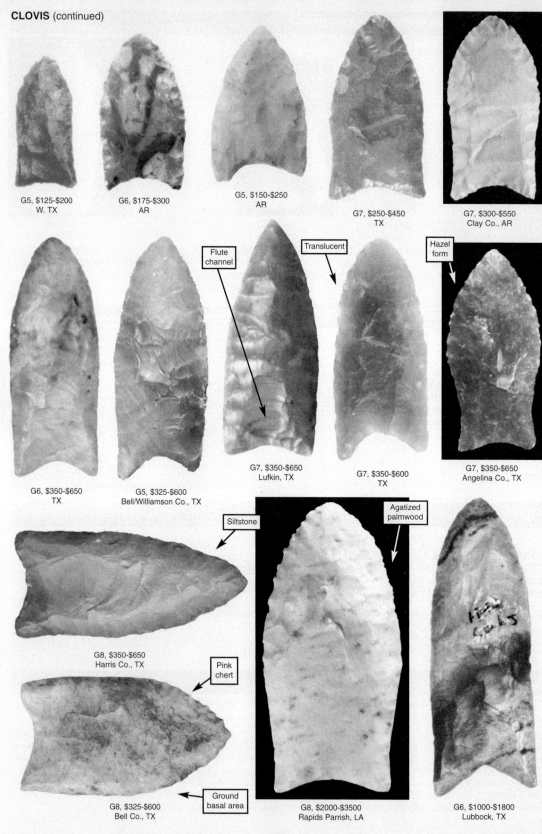

G5, $125-$200
W. TX

G6, $175-$300
AR

G5, $150-$250
AR

G7, $250-$450
TX

G7, $300-$550
Clay Co., AR

Flute channel

Translucent

Hazel form

G6, $350-$650
TX

G5, $325-$600
Bell/Williamson Co., TX

G7, $350-$650
Lufkin, TX

G7, $350-$600
TX

G7, $350-$650
Angelina Co., TX

Siltstone

Agatized palmwood

G8, $350-$650
Harris Co., TX

Pink chert

Ground basal area

G8, $325-$600
Bell Co., TX

G8, $2000-$3500
Rapids Parrish, LA

G6, $1000-$1800
Lubbock, TX

CLOVIS (continued)

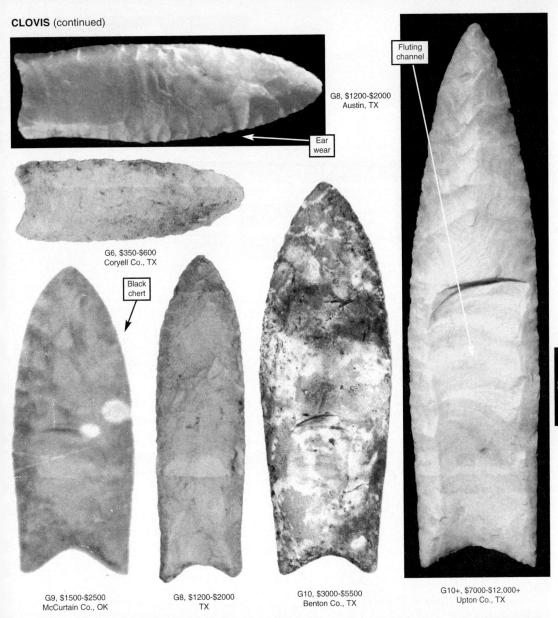

G8, $1200-$2000
Austin, TX

Ear wear

Fluting channel

G6, $350-$600
Coryell Co., TX

Black chert

SC

G9, $1500-$2500
McCurtain Co., OK

G8, $1200-$2000
TX

G10, $3000-$5500
Benton Co., TX

G10+, $7000-$12,000+
Upton Co., TX

COAHUILA - Late Archaic to Woodland, 4000 - 2000 B. P.

(Also see Adena, Gary, Hidden Valley and Langtry)

LOCATION: Central Texas. **DESCRIPTION:** A medium to large size, narrow point with tapered shoulders and a long, pointed, contracting stem. A scarce type. **I.D. KEY:** Long, pointed stem. Rare type. Also known as *Jora* points.

G5, $12-$20
Comanche Co., TX

G8, $35-$65
Comanche Co., TX

549

COAHUILA (continued)

G7, $35-$60
TX

G7, $12-$20
Val Verde Co., TX

CODY KNIFE (See Red River Knife)

COLBERT - Mississippian, 1100 - 800 B. P.

(Also see Alba, Homan, Hughes and Keota)

G5, $2-$4
Ellis Co., TX

Serrated edges

G5, $3-$6
Ellis Co., TX

G6, $5-$10
Ellis Co., TX

G5, $3-$6
Saline Co., AR

G7, $25-$40
TX

Very large for type

G8, $12-$20
TX

G9, $175-$300
Tulsa Co., OK

LOCATION: Louisiana to E. Oklahoma. **DESCRIPTION:** A small to medium size, arrow point with wide corner notches. Stems expand and bases can be straight to rounded. Reported to be related to *Alba* points. Also known as *Massard* points.

COLDWATER - Trans. Paleo, 10,000 - 8000 B. P.

(Also see Arkabutla, Pelican and San Patrice)

Petrified wood

G10, $200-$350
San Augustine Co., TX

LOCATION: East Texas into Arkansas & Louisiana. **DESCRIPTION:** A medium size, Lanceolate point with a longer waist than *Pelican* and a straight to concave base which is ground. The blade expands up from the base.

CONEJO - Late Archaic, 4000 - 3000 B. P.

(Also see Bandy, Ellis, Fairland and Marshall)

LOCATION: Texas and New Mexico **DESCRIPTION:** A medium size, corner notched point with an expanding, concave base and shoulder tangs that turn towards the base.

G4, $3-$5
Comanche Co., TX

G5, $8-$15
Schleicher Co., TX

CORNER TANG KNIFE - Late Archaic to Woodland, 4000 - 2000 B. P.

(Also see Base Tang, Crescent Knife and Mid-Back Tang Knife)

Made into a drill

G7, $350-$600
Comanche Co., TX

G7, $350-$650
Travis Co., TX

Tip wear

Caliche on surface

G7, $350-$600
W. TX

G9, $1000-$1800
Comanche Co., TX

G6, $300-$550
Lagrance Co., TX

G7, $250-$450
Williamson Co., TX

LOCATION: Texas to Oklahoma. **DESCRIPTION:** This knife is notched producing a tang at a corner for hafting to a handle. Tang knives are very rare and have been reproduced in recent years. **I.D. KEY:** Angle of hafting.

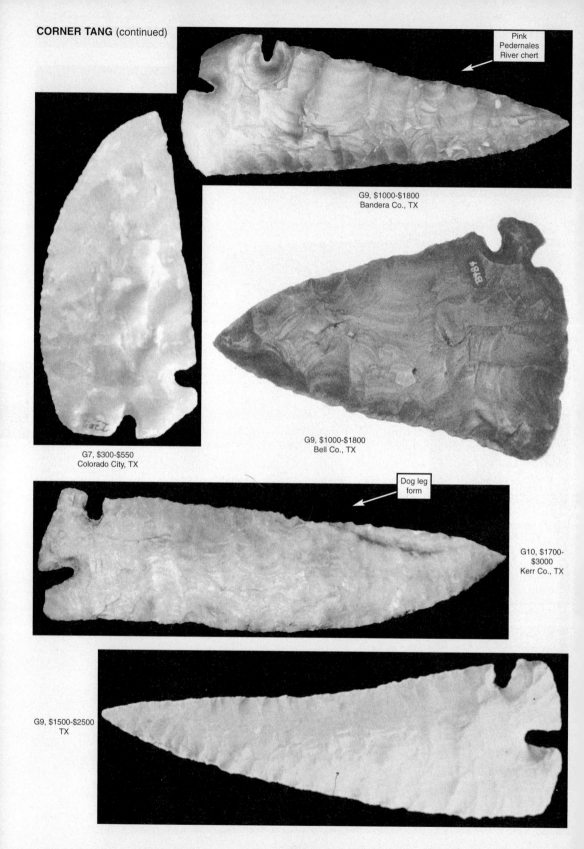

Pink
Pedernales
River chert

G9, $1000-$1800
Bandera Co., TX

G9, $1000-$1800
Bell Co., TX

G7, $300-$550
Colorado City, TX

Dog leg
form

G10, $1700-
$3000
Kerr Co., TX

G9, $1500-$2500
TX

(Also see Searcy and Wells)

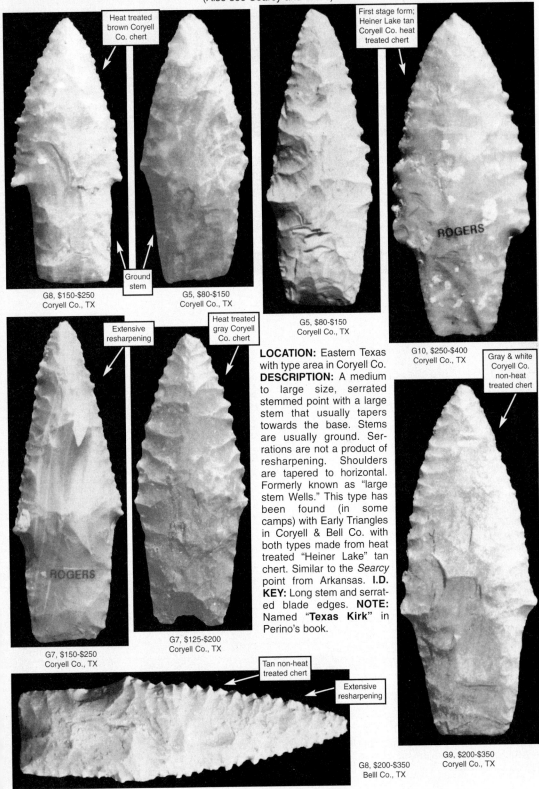

Heat treated brown Coryell Co. chert

First stage form; Heiner Lake tan Coryell Co. heat treated chert

Ground stem

G8, $150-$250
Coryell Co., TX

G5, $80-$150
Coryell Co., TX

G5, $80-$150
Coryell Co., TX

ROGERS

SC

G10, $250-$400
Coryell Co., TX

Gray & white Coryell Co. non-heat treated chert

Extensive resharpening

Heat treated gray Coryell Co. chert

ROGERS

G7, $150-$250
Coryell Co., TX

G7, $125-$200
Coryell Co., TX

LOCATION: Eastern Texas with type area in Coryell Co. **DESCRIPTION:** A medium to large size, serrated stemmed point with a large stem that usually tapers towards the base. Stems are usually ground. Serrations are not a product of resharpening. Shoulders are tapered to horizontal. Formerly known as "large stem Wells." This type has been found (in some camps) with Early Triangles in Coryell & Bell Co. with both types made from heat treated "Heiner Lake" tan chert. Similar to the *Searcy* point from Arkansas. **I.D. KEY:** Long stem and serrated blade edges. **NOTE:** Named **"Texas Kirk"** in Perino's book.

Tan non-heat treated chert

Extensive resharpening

G8, $200-$350
Belll Co., TX

G9, $200-$350
Coryell Co., TX

COSOTAT RIVER - Early Archaic, 9500 - 8000 B. P.

(Also see Ensor Split Base and Frio)

G8, $150-$250
AR

LOCATION: Texas into Oklahoma, Arkansas and Missouri. **DESCRIPTION:** A medium to large size, thin, usually serrated, widely corner notched point with large round to square ears and a shallow to deep notch in the center of the base. Bases are usually ground. **I.D. KEY:** Basal notching and early Archaic flaking.

G8, $65-$125
Lake Eufaula, OK

COVINGTON - Late Archaic, 4000 - 3000 B. P.

(Also see Crescent Knife, Friday, Gahagan, Sabine, San Saba and San Gabriel)

G6, $20-$35
Hill Co., TX

G8, $20-$45
TX

G6, $35-$65
Williamson Co., TX

G7, $55-$80
Gray Co., TX

G7, $45-$80
Travis Co., TX

G9, $65-$125
TX

> **IMPORTANT:**
> All Covingtons
> Shown 50% actual size.

G9, $250-$400
Burnet Co., TX

G9, $175-$300
TX

Edge wear

G9, $150-$250
Bell Co., TX

G6, $175-$300
Gillespie Co., TX

G8, $275-$500
TX

LOCATION: Texas into Oklahoma. **DESCRIPTION:** A medium to large size, thin, lanceolate blade with a broad, rounded base.

554

CRESCENT - Mid-Archaic, 5000 - 4500 B. P.

(Also see Drill and Scraper)

G7, $12-$20
Nuevo Leon, MX,
chalcedony

G7, $15-$25
Nuevo Leon, MX

G6, $8-$15
Nuevo Leon, MX **Hafted**

G6, $8-$15
Nuevo Leon, MX

G7, $15-$30
Nuevo Leon, MX

G6, $15-$30
Nuevo Leon, MX

 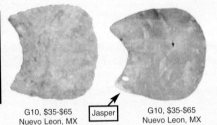

G9, $25-$40
Nuevo Leon, MX

G10, $35-$65
Nuevo Leon, MX **Jasper**

G10, $35-$65
Nuevo Leon, MX

LOCATION: Central Mexico into sou. Texas.
DESCRIPTION: A thin, uniface tool, convex on one side and concave on the opposite side with sharp corners. Long strikes were taken off with delicate presure flaking. Chalcedony, agates, jaspers, cherts and flints were used. Different than the Crescents from the Northwest which are not uniface. **I.D. KEY:** Crescent form.

CRESCENT KNIFE - Trans. Paleo to Early Archaic, 10,200 - 8000 B. P.

(Also see Base Tang, Corner Tang, Covington)

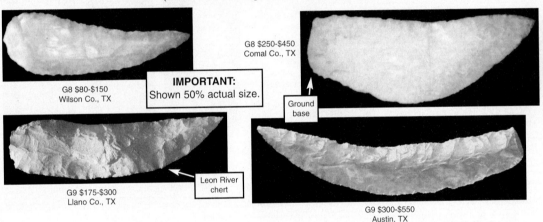

G8 $250-$450
Comal Co., TX

IMPORTANT:
Shown 50% actual size.

G8 $80-$150
Wilson Co., TX

Ground base

G9 $175-$300
Llano Co., TX

Leon River chert

G9 $300-$550
Austin, TX

LOCATION: Texas. **DESCRIPTION:** A large size, crescent shaped knife with a square to rounded stem. The basal area is usually ground. Found below and older than *Angostura* (10,000 B.P.) in Texas.

CUNEY - Historic, 400 - 200 B. P.

(Also see Bonham, Edwards, Morris, Perdiz, Rockwall and Scallorn)

G5, $12-$20
Comanche Co., TX

G9, $30-$50
TX

G9, $40-$75
Comanche Co., TX

G8, $30-$50
Hill Co., TX

G5, $12-$20
Comanche Co., TX

G7, $30-$50
Comanche Co., TX

G10, $60-$100
AR. Tan chert.

LOCATION: Midwestern states. **DESCRIPTION:** A small size, well made, barbed, triangular point with a very short, small, expanding base that is bifurcated.

CUPP - Late Woodland to Mississippian, 1500 - 600 B. P.

(Also see Epps, Gibson, Grand and Motley)

Stone material sparkles with mica

Classic "textbook" example

LOCATION: Northern Texas, Arkansas and Oklahoma. **DESCRIPTION**: A medium to large size, narrow barbed point with a short, expanding stem, broad corner notches and a convex base. Basal corners can be asymmetrical. Similar to *Motley*, but the base stem is shorter. *Epps* has square to tapered shoulders, otherwise is identical to *Motley*.

G9, $275-$500
Osage Co., OK

DALLAS - Late Archaic to Woodland, 4000 - 1500 B. P.

(Also see Carrolton, Dawson, Elam, kent, Travis and Wells)

G4, $1-$2
Waco, TX

G3, $1-$2
Hill Co., TX

G4, $1-$2
Waco, TX

Knife form

G8, $25-$40
TX

G5, $3-$6
Comanche Co., TX

G5, $3-$6
Waco, TX

G5, $3-$6
Comanche Co., TX

LOCATION: Texas to Oklahoma. **DESCRIPTION**: A small to medium size point with a short blade, weak shoulders, and a long squared stem. Stem can be half the length of the point. Basal area can be ground. **I.D. KEY**: Size, squared stem.

DALTON-BRECKENRIDGE - Early Archaic, 10,000 - 9200 B. P.

(Also see Dalton Classic and Meserve)

G4, $20-$35
AR

LOCATION: Midwestern states, **DESCRIPTION**: A medium to large size, auriculate point with an obvious bevel extending the entire length of the point from tip to base. Similar in form to the *Dalton-Greenbrier*. Basal area is usually ground.

DALTON CLASSIC - Early Archaic, 10,000 - 9200 B. P.

(Also see Angostura, Barber, Clovis, Golondrina, Meserve, Plainview and San Patrice)

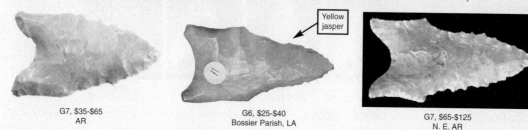

Yellow jasper

G7, $35-$65
AR

G6, $25-$40
Bossier Parish, LA

G7, $65-$125
N. E. AR

556

DALTON CLASSIC (continued)

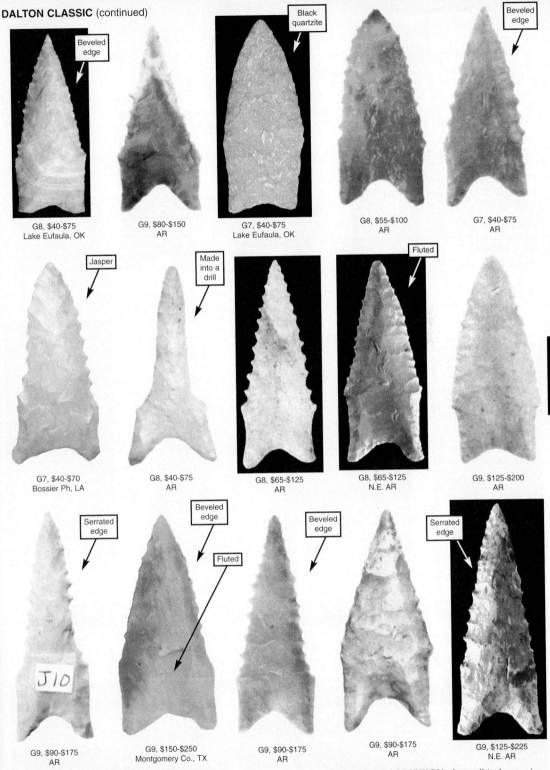

G8, $40-$75
Lake Eufaula, OK

G9, $80-$150
AR

Black quartzite

G7, $40-$75
Lake Eufaula, OK

G8, $55-$100
AR

Beveled edge

G7, $40-$75
AR

SC

Jasper

G7, $40-$70
Bossier Ph, LA

Made into a drill

G8, $40-$75
AR

G8, $65-$125
AR

Fluted

G8, $65-$125
N.E. AR

G9, $125-$200
AR

Serrated edge

G9, $90-$175
AR

Beveled edge

Fluted

G9, $150-$250
Montgomery Co., TX

Beveled edge

G9, $90-$175
AR

G9, $90-$175
AR

Serrated edge

G9, $125-$225
N.E. AR

LOCATION: Midwestern to Southeastern states. First recognized in Missouri. **DESCRIPTION:** A small to large size, thin, auriculate, fishtailed point. Many examples are finely serrated and exhibit excellent flaking. Some are fluted. Beveling may occur on one side of each face but is usually on the right side. All have basal grinding. This early type spread over most of the Eastern and Midwestern U.S. and strongly influenced many other types to follow.

557

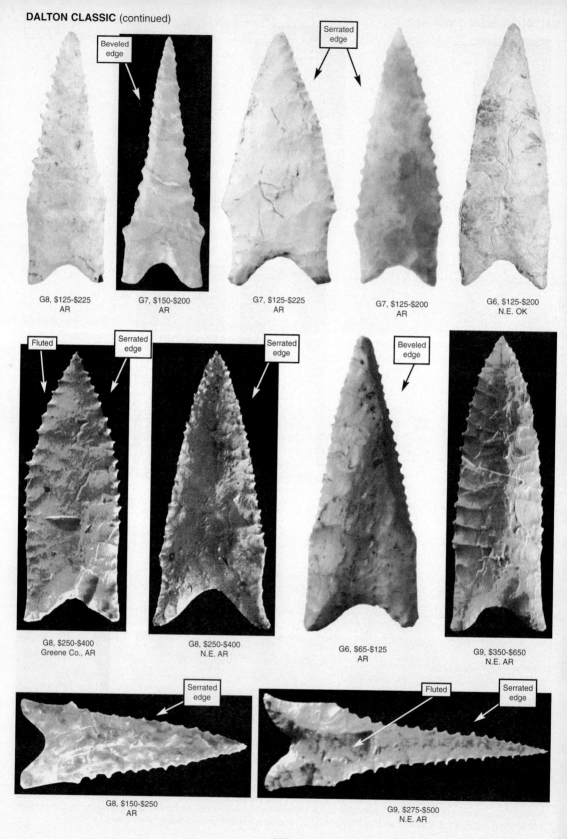

Beveled edge

Serrated edge

G8, $125-$225
AR

G7, $150-$200
AR

G7, $125-$225
AR

G7, $125-$200
AR

G6, $125-$200
N.E. OK

Fluted

Serrated edge

Serrated edge

Beveled edge

G8, $250-$400
Greene Co., AR

G8, $250-$400
N.E. AR

G6, $65-$125
AR

G9, $350-$650
N.E. AR

Serrated edge

Fluted

Serrated edge

G8, $150-$250
AR

G9, $275-$500
N.E. AR

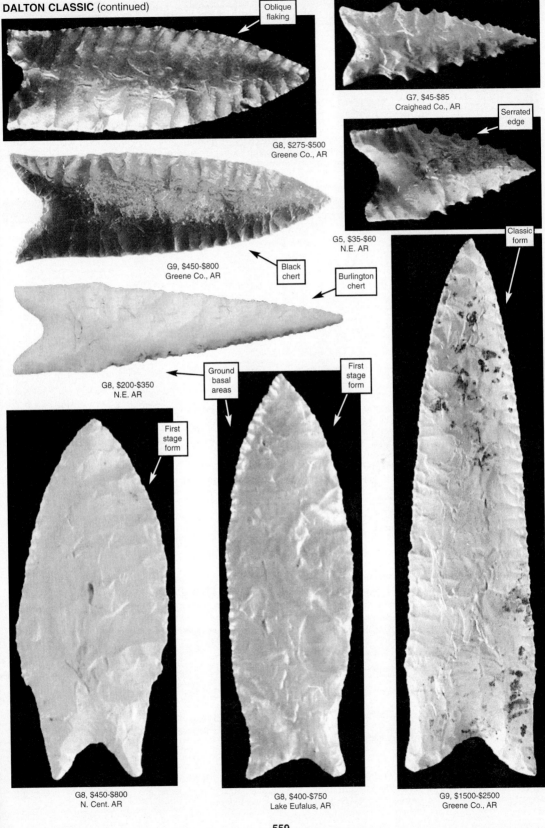

DALTON CLASSIC (continued)

Oblique flaking

G8, $275-$500
Greene Co., AR

G7, $45-$85
Craighead Co., AR

Serrated edge

G9, $450-$800
Greene Co., AR

Black chert

G5, $35-$60
N.E. AR

Burlington chert

Classic form

G8, $200-$350
N.E. AR

Ground basal areas

First stage form

First stage form

First stage form

G8, $450-$800
N. Cent. AR

G8, $400-$750
Lake Eufalus, AR

G9, $1500-$2500
Greene Co., AR

SC

DALTON-COLBERT - Early Archaic, 10,000 - 9200 B. P.

(Also see Beaver Lake, Dalton-Nuckolls, Plainview and Searcy)

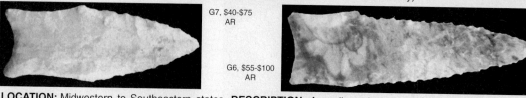

G7, $40-$75
AR

G6, $55-$100
AR

LOCATION: Midwestern to Southeastern states. **DESCRIPTION:** A medium size, auriculate form with a squared base and a weakly defined hafting area which is ground. Some examples are serrated and exhibit parallel flaking of the highest quality. **I.D. KEY:** Squarish basal area.

DALTON-GREENBRIER - Early Archaic, 10,000 - 9200 B. P.

(Also see Dalton Breckenridge, Golondrina, Meserve, Pelican and Plainview)

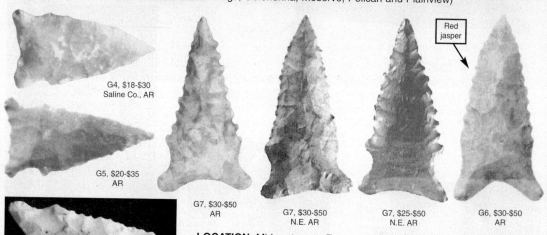

Red jasper

G4, $18-$30
Saline Co., AR

G5, $20-$35
AR

G7, $30-$50
AR

G7, $30-$50
N.E. AR

G7, $25-$50
N.E. AR

G6, $30-$50
AR

G6, $25-$40
AR

LOCATION: Midwestern to Eastern states and Florida. **DESCRIPTION:** A medium to large size, auriculate form with a concave base and drooping to expanding auricles. Many examples are serrated, some are fluted on both sides, and all have basal grinding. Resharpened examples are usually beveled on the right side of each face although left side beveling does occur. Thinness and high quality flaking is evident on many examples. This early variation developed in the Arkansas/Kentucky/Tennessee area. **I.D. KEY:** Expanded auricles.

DALTON-HEMPHILL - Early Archaic, 10,000 - 9200 B. P.

(Also see Firstview, Hardin, Holland and Scottsbluff)

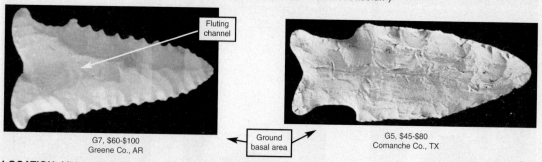

Fluting channel

G7, $60-$100
Greene Co., AR

Ground basal area

G5, $45-$80
Comanche Co., TX

LOCATION: Midwestern to Eastern states. **DESCRIPTION:** A medium to large size point with expanded auricles and horizontal, tapered to weak shoulders. Blade edges are usually serrated and bases are ground. In later times, this variant developed into the *Hemphill* point. **I.D. KEY:** Straightened extended shoulders.

DALTON HEMPHILL (continued)

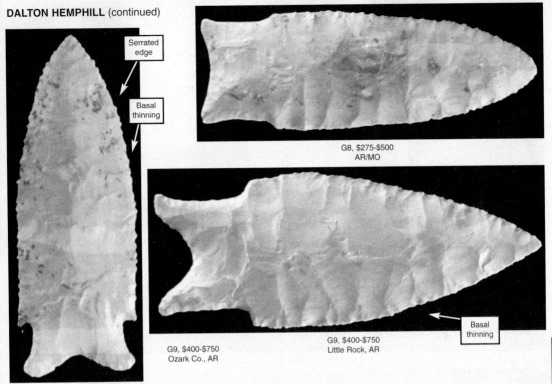

Serrated edge

Basal thinning

G8, $275-$500
AR/MO

G9, $400-$750
Ozark Co., AR

G9, $400-$750
Little Rock, AR

Basal thinning

SC

DALTON-HEMPSTEAD - Early Archaic, 10,000 - 9200 B. P.

(Also see Dalton Breckenridge and Meserve)

G7, $45-80
Saline Co., AR

LOCATION: Arkansas. **DESCRIPTION:** A medium size, narrow, auriculate, fishtailed point with wide side notches and a hafting area that is shorter than the classic *Dalton*. The base is concave and is ground. Blade edges can be serrated.

DALTON-KISATCHIE - Early Archaic, 10,000 - 9200 B. P.

(Also see Breckenridge, Dalton Classic, and Meserve)

G5, $35-$60
LA

G8, $55-$100
LA

G5, $40-$75
LA

G8, $80-$150
LA

G3, $35-$60
LA

DALTON-KISATCHIE (continued)

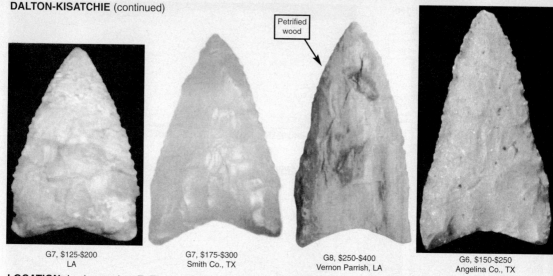

Petrified wood

G7, $125-$200
LA

G7, $175-$300
Smith Co., TX

G8, $250-$400
Vernon Parrish, LA

G6, $150-$250
Angelina Co., TX

LOCATION: Louisanna into E. Texas, Arkansas & Oklahoma. **DESCRIPTION:** A medium size, fishtailed point with a shorter hafting area than the traditional *Dalton*. Stem sides and bases are gound. Blade edges can be serrated. The base is concave and can be thinned. **I.D. KEY:** Shorter hafting area.

DARDANELLE - Mississippian, 600 - 400 B. P.

(Also see Agee, Keota and Nodena)

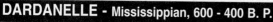

G5, $30-$50
TX

G10, $125-$200
Spiro Mound, OK

G8, $125-$200
Spiro Mound, OK

G10, $175-$300
Yell Co., OK

G10, $175-$300
Spiro Mound, OK

G10, $175-$300
OK

G10, $200-$350
Spiro Mound, OK

G10, $200-$350
Spiro Mound, OK

G10, $200-$350
Spiro Mound, OK

LOCATION: Arkansas to Oklahoma. **DESCRIPTION:** A small to medium size, narrow, thin, serrated, corner or side notched arrow point. Bases can be rounded or square. A *Nodena* variant form with basal notches. This type has been found in caches from the Spiro mound in Oklahoma and from Arkansas. **I.D. KEY:** Basal form.

DARL - Woodland, 2500 - 1000 B. P.

(Also see Darl Stemmed, Dawson, Hoxie, kent & Zephyr)

G8, $15-$25
Coryell Co., TX

G9, $25-$40
Bell Co., TX

G8, $35-$60
Bell Co., TX

G8, $25-$45
Coryell Co., TX

G9, $55-$100
Austin, TX

Beveled edge

Beveled edge

562

DARL (continued)

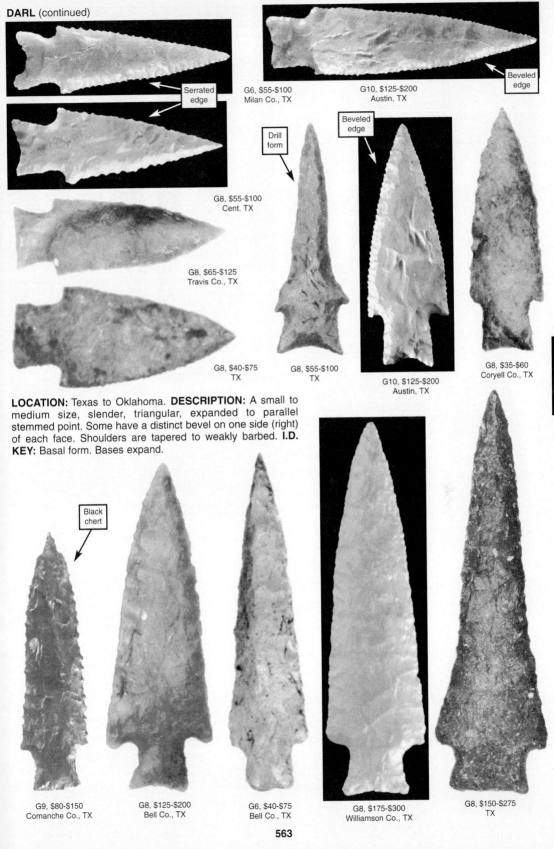

G6, $55-$100
Milan Co., TX

Serrated edge

G10, $125-$200
Austin, TX

Beveled edge

G8, $55-$100
Cent. TX

Drill form

Beveled edge

G8, $65-$125
Travis Co., TX

G8, $40-$75
TX

G8, $55-$100
TX

G10, $125-$200
Austin, TX

G8, $35-$60
Coryell Co., TX

SC

LOCATION: Texas to Oklahoma. **DESCRIPTION:** A small to medium size, slender, triangular, expanded to parallel stemmed point. Some have a distinct bevel on one side (right) of each face. Shoulders are tapered to weakly barbed. **I.D. KEY:** Basal form. Bases expand.

Black chert

G9, $80-$150
Comanche Co., TX

G8, $125-$200
Bell Co., TX

G6, $40-$75
Bell Co., TX

G8, $175-$300
Williamson Co., TX

G8, $150-$275
TX

(Also see Covington, Friday, Gahagan and Kinney)

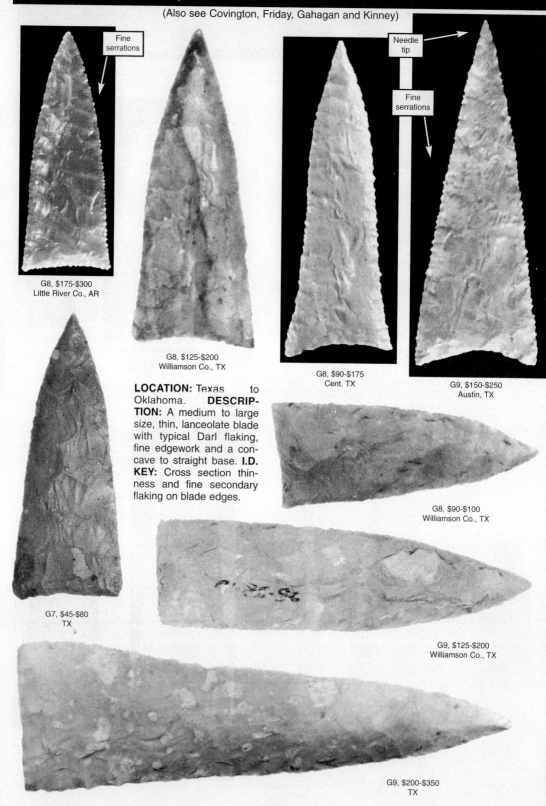

Fine serrations

Needle tip

Fine serrations

G8, $175-$300
Little River Co., AR

G8, $125-$200
Williamson Co., TX

G8, $90-$175
Cent. TX

G9, $150-$250
Austin, TX

LOCATION: Texas to Oklahoma. **DESCRIPTION:** A medium to large size, thin, lanceolate blade with typical Darl flaking, fine edgework and a concave to straight base. **I.D. KEY:** Cross section thinness and fine secondary flaking on blade edges.

G8, $90-$100
Williamson Co., TX

G7, $45-$80
TX

G9, $125-$200
Williamson Co., TX

G9, $200-$350
TX

DARL FRACTURED BASE - Woodland, 2500 - 1000 B. P.

(Also see Darl Stemmed, Dawson, Hoxie & Zephyr)

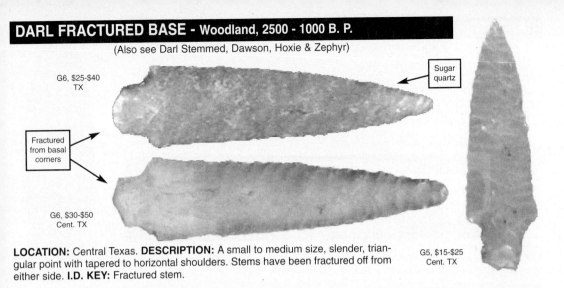

G6, $25-$40
TX

Sugar
quartz

Fractured
from basal
corners

G6, $30-$50
Cent. TX

G5, $15-$25
Cent. TX

LOCATION: Central Texas. **DESCRIPTION:** A small to medium size, slender, triangular point with tapered to horizontal shoulders. Stems have been fractured off from either side. **I.D. KEY:** Fractured stem.

DARL STEMMED - Early Archaic, 8000 - 5000 B. P.

(Formerly Brazos; also see Darl, Hoxie, and Zephyr)

SC

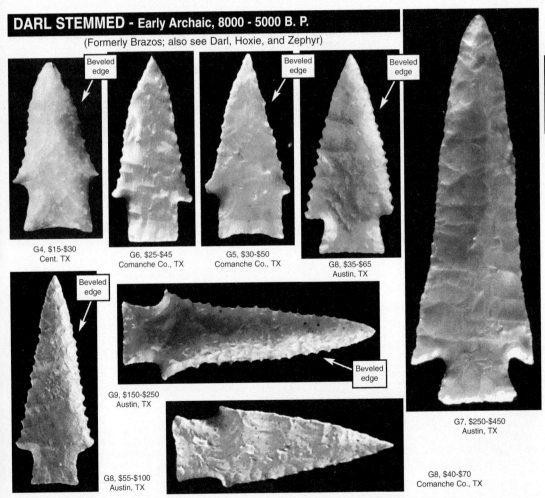

Beveled
edge

Beveled
edge

Beveled
edge

G4, $15-$30
Cent. TX

G6, $25-$45
Comanche Co., TX

G5, $30-$50
Comanche Co., TX

G8, $35-$65
Austin, TX

Beveled
edge

Beveled
edge

G9, $150-$250
Austin, TX

G7, $250-$450
Austin, TX

G8, $55-$100
Austin, TX

G8, $40-$70
Comanche Co., TX

LOCATION: Central Texas. **DESCRIPTION:** A medium to large size, narrow point with horizontally barbed shoulders and an expanding to square stem. The blades on most examples are steeply beveled on one side of each face. Flaking is early parallel and is of much higher quality than *Darl*. **I.D. KEY:** Early flaking, straight base.

565

DAWSON - Middle Archaic, 7000 - 4000 B. P.

(Also see Adena, Carrolton, Darl and Wells)

G8, $65-$125
N.E. OK

G9, $125-
$200
Austin, TX

LOCATION: Texas. **DESCRIPTION:** A medium size, narrow, stemmed point with strong, tapered shoulders. The base is rounded to square.

G8, $60-$100
N.E. OK

DEADMAN'S - Desert Traditions-Developmental Phase, 1600 - 1300 B. P.

(Also see Perdiz, Rockwall and Scallorn)

G8, $50-$90
TX

G9, $70-$120
TX

G9, $70-$120
TX

G9, $35-$65
TX

G10, $80-$150
TX

G10, $125-$200
TX

LOCATION: Southeastern Arizona, southern New Mexico and western Texas. **DESCRIPTION:** A small arrow point with very deep basal notches creating a long, straight to slightly bulbous stem with a rounded basal edge. The blade is triangular. **I.D. KEY:** Long stem and barbs.

DELHI - Late Archaic, 3500 - 2000 B. P.

(Also see Darl, Kent, Pogo and Pontchartrain)

G6, $25-$40
TX

Gravel
chert

G8, $125-$200
Houston, TX

LOCATION: Louisiana into E. Texas. **DESCRIPTION:** A medium to large size, narrow, stemmed point with strong, barbed shoulders. The stem can be square or expands and the base is straight to slightly convex.

G7, $55-$100
Richland, Ph, LA, Macon Ridge

566

G9, $150-$250
LA

G10, $350-$600
LA

G8, $80-$150
Comanche Co., TX

G7, $175-$300
E. TX

G6, $90-$175
Bell Co., TX

SC

DESMUKE - Late Archaic to Woodland, 4000 - 2000 B. P.

(Also see Lerma)

G5, $2-$5
Nuevo Leon, MX

G5, $3-$6
Nuevo Leon, MX

G10, $25-$40
Austin, TX

Petrified wood

G8, $6-$12
S. TX

G5, $4-$8
Val Verde Co., TX

LOCATION: Central to southern Texas. **DESCRIPTION:** A medium size lanceolate point with a recurved to convex blade and a contracting stem that is usually rounded. **I.D. KEY:** Stem form.

DICKSON - Late Archaic to Woodland, 2500 - 1600 B. P.

(Also see Burkett, Gary, Hidden Valley and Morrow Mountain)

LOCATION: Midwestern states. **DESCRIPTION:** A medium to large size point with tapered shoulders and a contracting stem. High quality flaking and thinness is evident on most examples. **I.D. KEY:** Basal form.

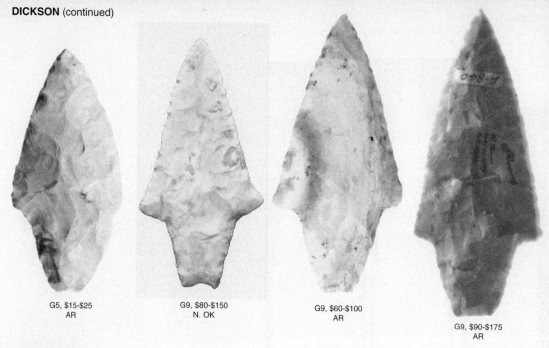

G5, $15-$25
AR

G9, $80-$150
N. OK

G9, $60-$100
AR

G9, $90-$175
AR

DOUBLE TIP (Occurs in Carrizo and Pedernales types)

DOVETAIL (See St. Charles)

DRILL - Paleo to Historic, 11,500 - 200 B. P.

(Also see Perforator and Scraper)

Castroville
drill

Georgetown
flint

G6, $30-$50
TX

Agate

G5, $5-$10
Pike Co., AR

G10, $80-$150
TX

G8, $40-$75
Coryell Co., TX

Holland
drill

G8, $80-$150
McIntosh Co., OK

LOCATION: Everywhere. **DESCRIPTION:** Although many drills were made from scratch, all point types were made into the drill form. Usually, heavily resharpened and broken points were salvaged and rechipped into drills. These objects were certainly used as drills (evidence of extreme edge wear), but there is speculation that some of these forms may have been used as pins for clothing, ornaments, ear plugs and other uses.

DRILL (continued)

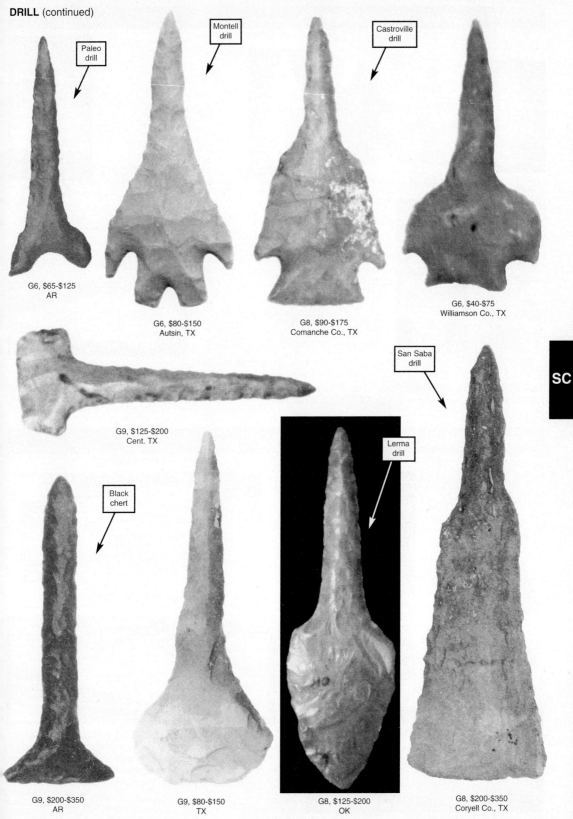

Paleo drill

Montell drill

Castroville drill

G6, $65-$125
AR

G6, $80-$150
Autsin, TX

G8, $90-$175
Comanche Co., TX

G6, $40-$75
Williamson Co., TX

San Saba drill

SC

G9, $125-$200
Cent. TX

Black chert

Lerma drill

G9, $200-$350
AR

G9, $80-$150
TX

G8, $125-$200
OK

G8, $200-$350
Coryell Co., TX

569

DURAN - Woodland, 3000 - 2000 B. P.

(Also see Charcos, Evans and Sinner)

G5, $12-$20
Coahila, MX

G10, $50-$90
TX

G8, $25-$45
TX

G9, $40-$70
Nuevo Leon, MX

G9, $40-$70
TX

G9, $45-$85
TX

G10, $45-$85
TX

Barb nick

Quartzite

G6, $25-$45
TX

G5, $15-$25
TX

G6, $25-$45
Zapata Co., TX

G9, $40-$70
W. TX

G9, $45-$85
TX

G9, $40-$70
W. TX

G8, $35-$65
TX

LOCATION: Texas. **DESCRIPTION:** A small size, narrow, stemmed point with double notches on each side. Base can be parallel sided to tapered. **I.D. KEY:** Double notches.

EARLY STEMMED - Early Archaic, 9000 - 7000 B. P.

(Also see Castroville, Darl Stemmed, King, Lange, Scottsbluff and Zephyr)

Barb nick

G7, $125-$225
Milan Co., TX

G9, $175-$300
Wilson Co., TX

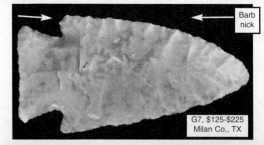

G7, $60-$100
Bell Co., TX

G7, $80-$150
Angelina Co., TX

Barb nick

LOCATION: Texas to Oklahoma. **DESCRIPTION:** A medium to large size, broad point with a medium to long expanded stem and shoulder barbs. Stems are ground. Often confused with *Lange* points which do not have ground stems. Also known as *Wilson* points from the Wilson-Leonard site in Bell Co.

G7, $90-$175
Wilson Co., TX

EARLY STEMMED LANCEOLATE - Early Archaic, 9000 - 7000 B. P.

(Also see Angostura, Archaic Knife, Castroville, Darl Stemmed, Pontchartrain, Rio Grande, Victoria & Zephyr)

G5, $12-$20
TX

G6, $55-$100
Bell Co., TX

G9, $55-$100
TX

G6, $40-$75
Bell Co., TX

LOCATION: Texas to Oklahoma. **DESCRIPTION:** A medium to large size, narrow lanceolate stemmed point with weak, tapered shoulders.

EARLY TRIANGULAR - Early Archaic, 9000 - 7000 B. P.

(Also see Angostura, Carrizo, Clovis, Kinney and Tortugas)

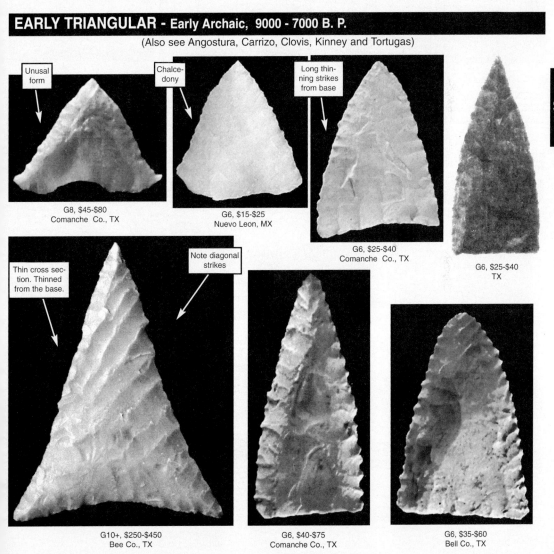

Unusal form

Chalce-dony

Long thinning strikes from base

G8, $45-$80
Comanche Co., TX

G6, $15-$25
Nuevo Leon, MX

G6, $25-$40
Comanche Co., TX

G6, $25-$40
TX

Thin cross section. Thinned from the base.

Note diagonal strikes

G10+, $250-$450
Bee Co., TX

G6, $40-$75
Comanche Co., TX

G6, $35-$60
Bell Co., TX

SC

571

EARLY TRIANGULAR (continued)

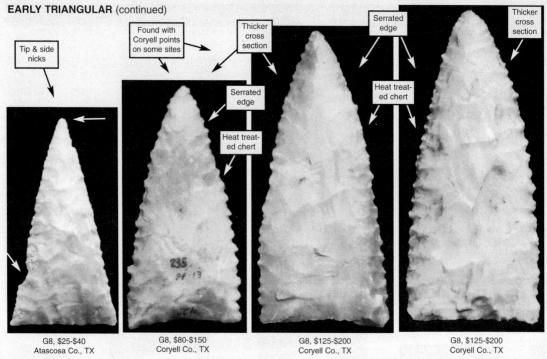

Tip & side nicks

Found with Coryell points on some sites

Thicker cross section

Serrated edge

Heat treated chert

Serrated edge

Heat treated chert

Thicker cross section

| G8, $25-$40 Atascosa Co., TX | G8, $80-$150 Coryell Co., TX | G8, $125-$200 Coryell Co., TX | G8, $125-$200 Coryell Co., TX |

LOCATION: Texas. **DESCRIPTION:** A medium to large size, broad, triangle that is usually serrated. The base is either fluted or has long thinning strikes. Quality is excellent with early oblique transverse flaking and possible right hand beveling. **I.D. KEY:** Basal thinning and edgework.

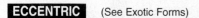

ECCENTRIC (See Exotic Forms)

EDEN - Early Archaic, 10,000 - 8000 B. P.

(Also see Firstview and Scottsbluff)

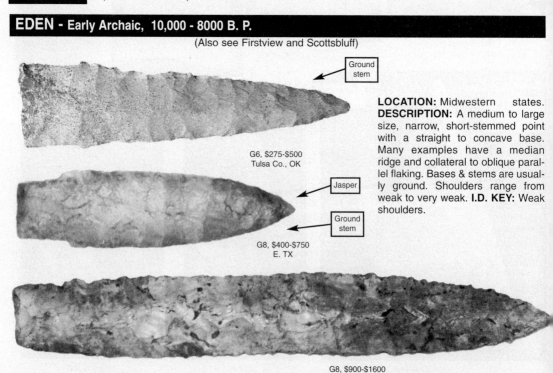

Ground stem

G6, $275-$500
Tulsa Co., OK

Jasper

Ground stem

G8, $400-$750
E. TX

LOCATION: Midwestern states. **DESCRIPTION:** A medium to large size, narrow, short-stemmed point with a straight to concave base. Many examples have a median ridge and collateral to oblique parallel flaking. Bases & stems are usually ground. Shoulders range from weak to very weak. **I.D. KEY:** Weak shoulders.

G8, $900-$1600
Bailey Co., TX

EDGEWOOD - Woodland, 3000 - 1500 B. P.

(Also see Ellis and Fairland)

G9, $25-$40
TX

G4, $2-$5
Saline Co., AR

G6, $12-$20
Saline Co., AR

G4, $3-$5
Concho Co., TX

G8, $25-$45
McIntosh Co., OK

G4, $5-$8
Killeen, TX

LOCATION: Texas to Oklahoma. **DESCRIPTION:** A small to medium size, expanded stem point with a concave base. Shoulders are barbed to tapered and the base is usually as wide as the shoulders.

SC

G6, $12-$20
McCulloch Co., TX

G7, $12-$20
Comanche Co., TX

G4, $3-$5
Comanche Co., TX

EDWARDS - Woodland to Mississippian, 2000 - 1000 B. P.

(Also see Bayogoula, Cuney, Haskell and Sallisaw)

G4, $2-$5
S. TX

Tip nick →

G4, $12-$20
Coman. Co., TX

G10, $20-$35
TX

G9, $18-$30
TX

G8, $65-$125
Spiro Mound, OK

G9, $20-$35
TX

G5, $15-$25
TX

G9, $80-$150
Spiro Mound, OK

G10, $450-$850
Comanche Co., TX

G8, $65-$125
Spiro Mound, OK

G8, $65-$125
Comanche Co., TX

G9, $150-$250
Spiro Mound, OK

G8, $40-$75
Spiro Mound, OK

G9, $150-$250
Spiro Mound, OK

LOCATION: Texas to Oklahoma. **DESCRIPTION:** A small size, thin, barbed arrow point with long, flaring ears at the base. Some examples are finely serrated. **I.D. KEY:** Basal form and flaking.

ELAM - Late Archaic to Woodland, 4000 - 2000 B. P.

(Also see Dallas, Darl and Ellis)

G6, $3-$5
Comanche Co., TX

G4, $3-$5
Comanche Co., TX

G4, $3-$5
Waco, TX

LOCATION: Texas. **DESCRIPTION:** A small size exhausted point with a squared base and weak shoulders. A resharpened point almost to exhaustion.

ELLIS - Late Archaic, 4000 - 2000 B. P.

(Also see Edgewood, Ensor, Godley, Marcos and Scallorn)

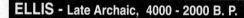

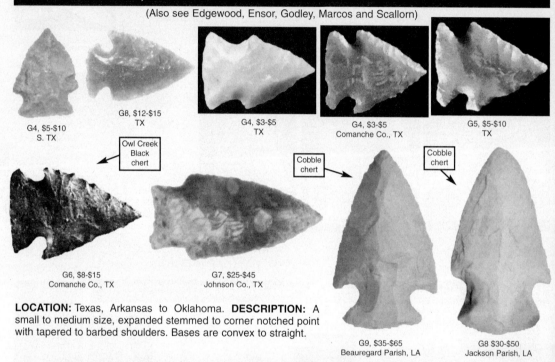

G4, $5-$10
S. TX

G8, $12-$15
TX

G4, $3-$5
TX

G4, $3-$5
Comanche Co., TX

G5, $5-$10
TX

Owl Creek Black chert

Cobble chert

Cobble chert

G6, $8-$15
Comanche Co., TX

G7, $25-$45
Johnson Co., TX

G9, $35-$65
Beauregard Parish, LA

G8 $30-$50
Jackson Parish, LA

LOCATION: Texas, Arkansas to Oklahoma. **DESCRIPTION:** A small to medium size, expanded stemmed to corner notched point with tapered to barbed shoulders. Bases are convex to straight.

ENSOR - Late Archaic to Early Woodland, 4000 - 1500 B. P.

(Also see Ellis, Frio, Marcos, Marshall and San Jacintol)

G5, $15-$30
Bell Co., TX

G6, $25-$40
TX

G6, $25-$40
TX

Black chert

G7, $30-$50
Bell Co., TX

G8, $30-$50
TX

G8, $30-$50
TX

ENSOR (continued)

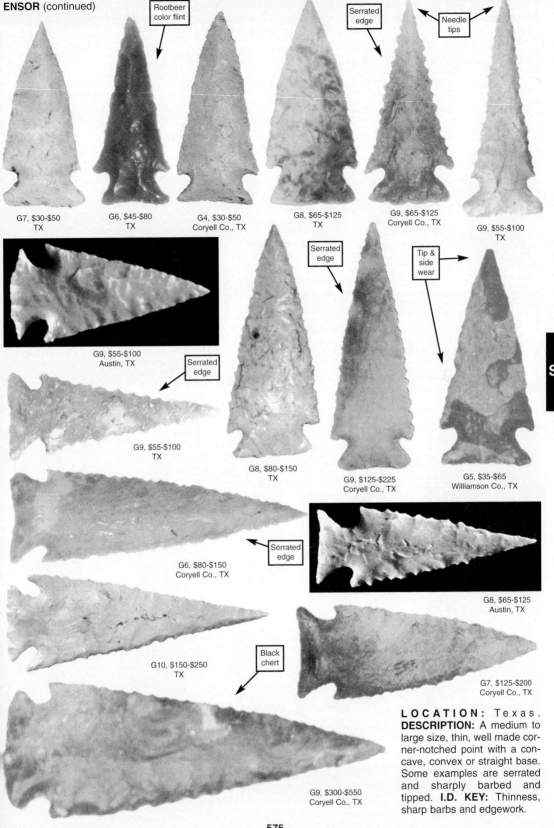

Rootbeer color flint

Serrated edge

Needle tips

G7, $30-$50
TX

G6, $45-$80
TX

G4, $30-$50
Coryell Co., TX

G8, $65-$125
TX

G9, $65-$125
Coryell Co., TX

G9, $55-$100
TX

G9, $55-$100
Austin, TX

Serrated edge

Serrated edge

Tip & side wear

G9, $55-$100
TX

G8, $80-$150
TX

G9, $125-$225
Coryell Co., TX

G5, $35-$65
Williamson Co., TX

Serrated edge

G6, $80-$150
Coryell Co., TX

G8, $65-$125
Austin, TX

G10, $150-$250
TX

Black chert

G7, $125-$200
Coryell Co., TX

G9, $300-$550
Coryell Co., TX

LOCATION: Texas.
DESCRIPTION: A medium to large size, thin, well made corner-notched point with a concave, convex or straight base. Some examples are serrated and sharply barbed and tipped. **I.D. KEY:** Thinness, sharp barbs and edgework.

SC

575

ENSOR SPLIT-BASE - Late Archaic to Early Woodland, 4000 - 1500 B. P.

(Also see Cosotat River, Edgewood, Frio and Martindale)

G6, $35-$65
TX

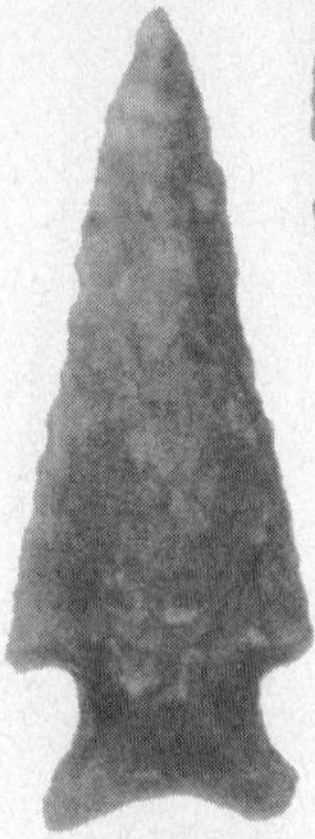

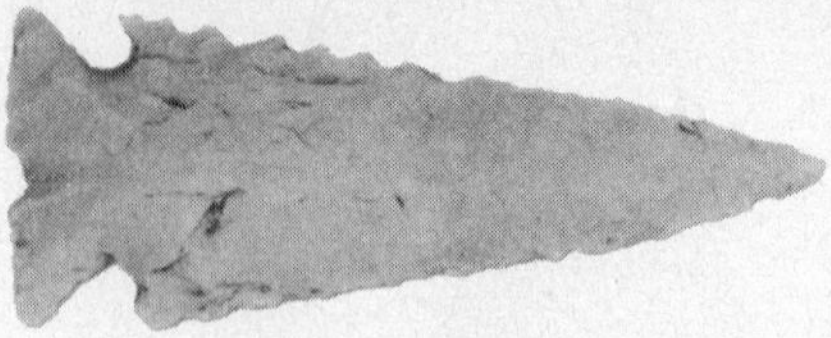

G6, $50-$90
Coryell Co., TX

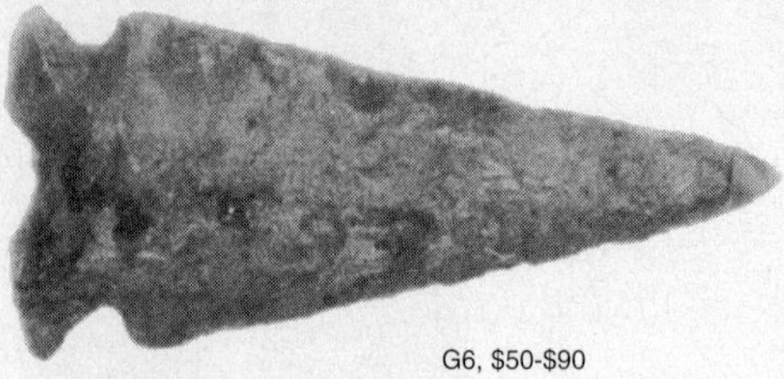

G6, $50-$90
TX

LOCATION: Texas. **DESCRIPTION:** Identical to *Ensor* except for the bifurcated base. Look for *Ensor* flaking style. A cross type linking *Frio* with *Ensor*. **I.D. KEY:** Sharp barbs, thinness, edgework and split base.

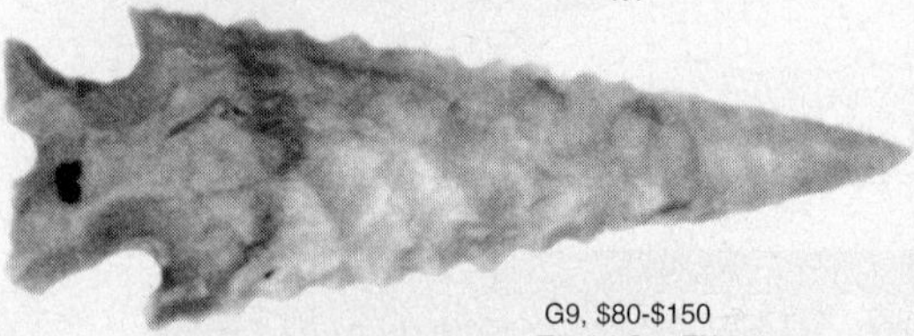

G9, $80-$150
Travisl Co., TX

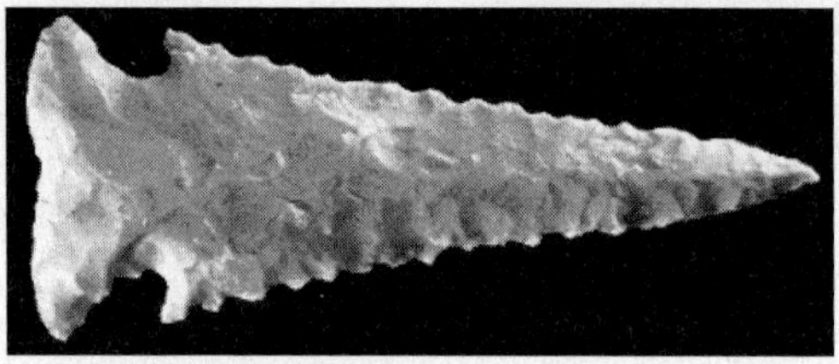

G9, $125-$200
Austin, TX

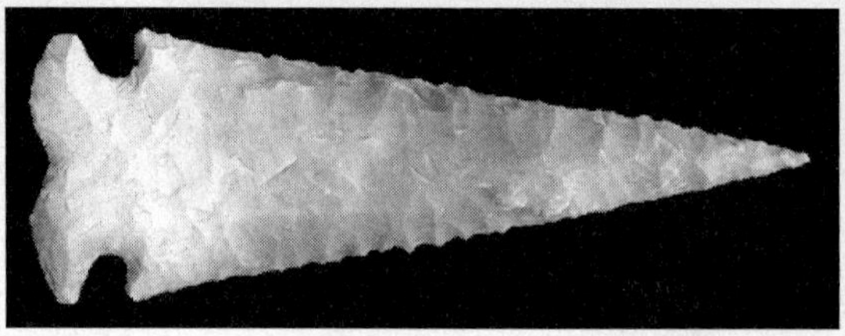

G10+, $200-$350
Kerr Co., TX

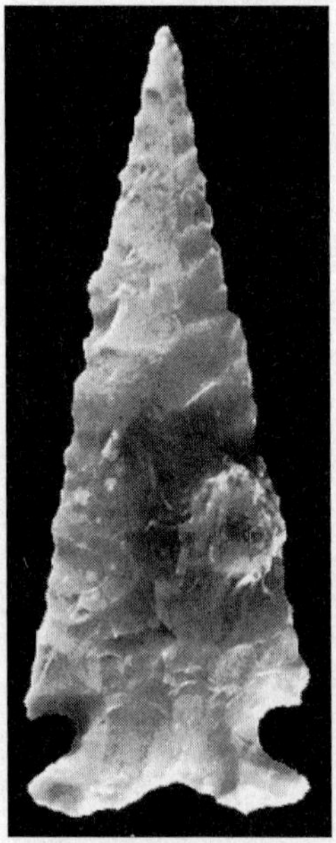

G8, $150-$250
Comanche Co., TX

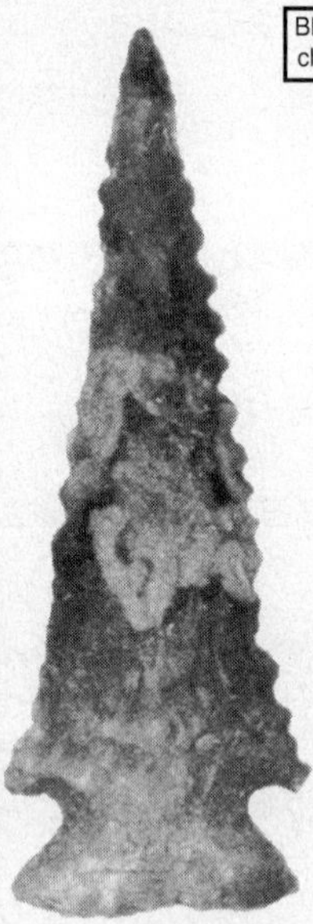

G10, $150-$275
Coryell Co., TX

Black chert

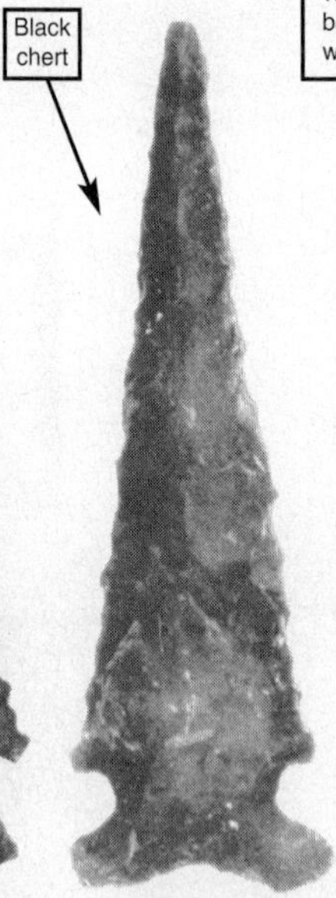

G7, $90-$175
Coryell Co., TX

Tip & base wear

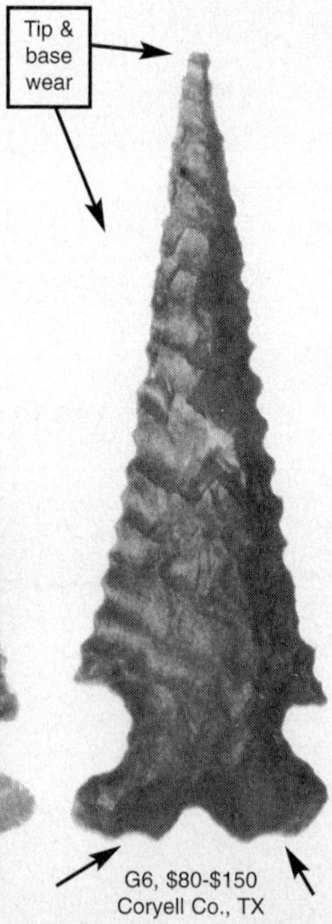

G6, $80-$150
Coryell Co., TX

Barb wear

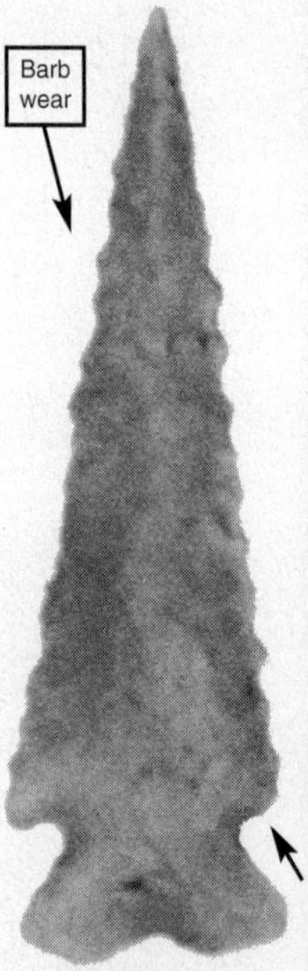

G6, $125-$200
TX

EPPS - Late Archaic to Woodland, 3500 - 2000 B. P.

(Also see Cupp, Grand, Kay Blade & Motley)

EPPS (continued)

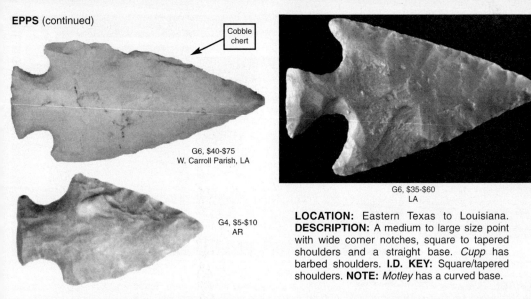

Cobble chert

G6, $40-$75
W. Carroll Parish, LA

G6, $35-$60
LA

G4, $5-$10
AR

LOCATION: Eastern Texas to Louisiana. **DESCRIPTION:** A medium to large size point with wide corner notches, square to tapered shoulders and a straight base. *Cupp* has barbed shoulders. **I.D. KEY:** Square/tapered shoulders. **NOTE:** *Motley* has a curved base.

SC

EVANS - Late Archaic To Woodland, 4000 - 2000 B. P.

(Also see Charcos, Duran and Sinner)

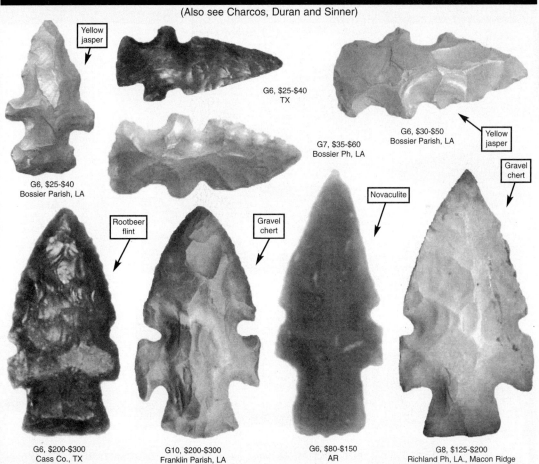

Yellow jasper

G6, $25-$40
TX

G6, $30-$50
Bossier Parish, LA

Yellow jasper

G7, $35-$60
Bossier Ph, LA

G6, $25-$40
Bossier Parish, LA

Gravel chert

Rootbeer flint

Gravel chert

Novaculite

G6, $200-$300
Cass Co., TX

G10, $200-$300
Franklin Parish, LA

G6, $80-$150
AR

G8, $125-$200
Richland Ph, LA., Macon Ridge

LOCATION: Eastern Texas Eastward to Tennessee. **DESCRIPTION:** A medium to large size stemmed double notched point. The notching occurs somewhere between the tip and shoulders. **I.D. KEY:** Expanding stem and side notches.

EXOTIC FORMS - Mid Archaic to Mississippian, 5000 - 1000 B. P.

(Also see Double Tip)

G5, $12-$20
Saline Co., AR

G7, 25-$40
Coleman Co., TX

Exotic
Marshall
point

G9, $150-$250
Kerr Co., TX

LOCATION: Everywhere **DESCRIPTION:** The forms illustrated here are very rare. Some are definitely effigy forms while others may be no more than the result of practicing how to notch, or unfinished and unintentional doodles.

FAIRLAND - Woodland, 3000 - 1500 B. P.

(Also see Edgewood, Ellis, Marcos and Marshall)

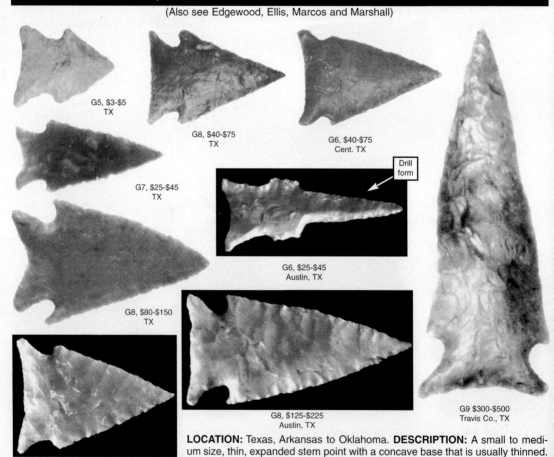

G5, $3-$5
TX

G8, $40-$75
TX

G6, $40-$75
Cent. TX

G7, $25-$45
TX

Drill
form

G6, $25-$45
Austin, TX

G8, $80-$150
TX

G8, $125-$225
Austin, TX

G9 $300-$500
Travis Co., TX

G9, $40-$75
Bell Co., TX

LOCATION: Texas, Arkansas to Oklahoma. **DESCRIPTION:** A small to medium size, thin, expanded stem point with a concave base that is usually thinned. Shoulders can be weak and tapered to slightly barbed. The base is broad. **I.D. KEY:** Basal form, systematic form of flaking.

FAIRLAND (continued)

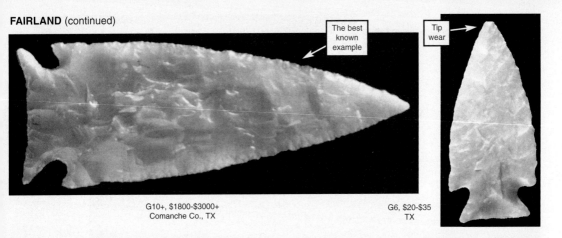

The best known example

Tip wear

G10+, $1800-$3000+
Comanche Co., TX

G6, $20-$35
TX

SC

FIGUEROA - Woodland, 3000 - 1500 B. P.

(Also see Big Sandy, Brewerton, Ensor, Gibson and Zorra)

G3, $2-$5
Nuevo Leon, MX

G4, $8-$5
Val Verde Co., TX

G6, $8-$15
Val Verde Co., TX

G6, $8-$15
Nuevo Leon, MX

G3, $3-$6
Nuevo Leon, MX

G3, $3-$6
Nuevo Leon, MX

Tip wear

G5, $5-$10
Val Verde Co., TX

G5, $5-$10
Val Verde Co., TX

G5, $5-$10
Val Verde Co., TX

G6, $8-$15
Comanche Co., TX

G9, $20-$35
Val Verde Co., TX

LOCATION: Texas. **DESCRIPTION:** A small to medium size side notched to expanded base point with a convex to straight base. Basal corners are sharp to rounded. **I.D. KEY:** Basal form, wide notches.

FIRSTVIEW - Early Archaic, 10,000 - 8000 B. P.

(Also see Alberta, Dalton, Eden, Red River and Scottsbluff)

Ground basal area

Base nick

G7, $800-$1500
Winkler Co., TX

Resharpened many times

G5, $175-325
Reeves Co., TX

579

FIRSTVIEW (continued)

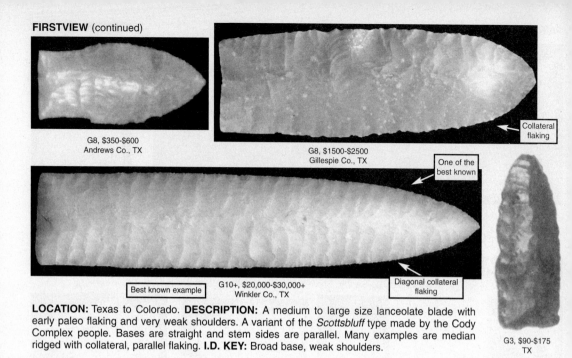

G8, $350-$600
Andrews Co., TX

G8, $1500-$2500
Gillespie Co., TX

Collateral flaking

One of the best known

Best known example

G10+, $20,000-$30,000+
Winkler Co., TX

Diagonal collateral flaking

G3, $90-$175
TX

LOCATION: Texas to Colorado. **DESCRIPTION:** A medium to large size lanceolate blade with early paleo flaking and very weak shoulders. A variant of the *Scottsbluff* type made by the Cody Complex people. Bases are straight and stem sides are parallel. Many examples are median ridged with collateral, parallel flaking. **I.D. KEY:** Broad base, weak shoulders.

FOLSOM - Late Paleo, 11,000 - 10,000 B. P.

(Also see Arkabutla, Clovis, Coldwater, Golondrina, Goshen, McKean, Midland and Plainview)

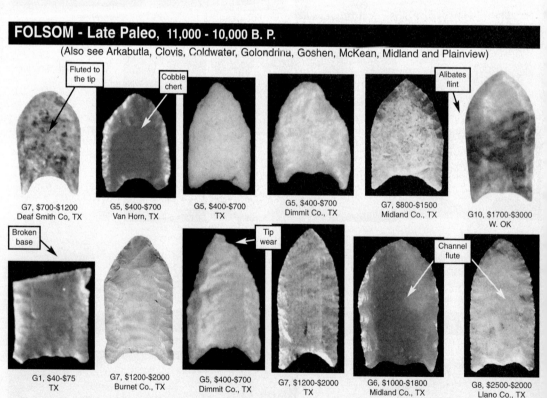

Fluted to the tip

Cobble chert

Alibates flint

G7, $700-$1200
Deaf Smith Co, TX

G5, $400-$700
Van Horn, TX

G5, $400-$700
TX

G5, $400-$700
Dimmit Co., TX

G7, $800-$1500
Midland Co., TX

G10, $1700-$3000
W. OK

Broken base

Tip wear

Channel flute

G1, $40-$75
TX

G7, $1200-$2000
Burnet Co., TX

G5, $400-$700
Dimmit Co., TX

G7, $1200-$2000
TX

G6, $1000-$1800
Midland Co., TX

G8, $2500-$2000
Llano Co., TX

LOCATION: Texas to Montana to Canada. **DESCRIPTION:** A small to medium size, very thin, high quality, fluted point with contracted, pointed auricles and a concave base. Fluting usually extends the entire length of each face. Blade flaking is extremely fine. The hafting area is ground. A very rare type, even in area of highest incidence. Modern reproductions have been made and extreme caution should be exercised in acquiring an original specimen. Usually found in association with extinct bison fossil remains. **I.D. KEY:** Flaking style (Excessive secondary flaking)

FOLSOM (continued)

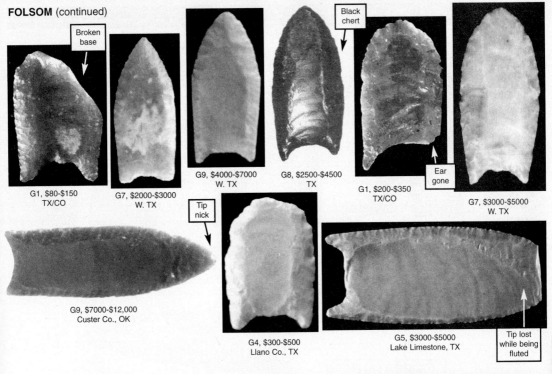

G1, $80-$150
TX/CO

G7, $2000-$3000
W. TX

G9, $4000-$7000
W. TX

Black chert

G8, $2500-$4500
TX

G1, $200-$350
TX/CO

Ear gone

Broken base

G7, $3000-$5000
W. TX

Tip nick

G9, $7000-$12,000
Custer Co., OK

G4, $300-$500
Llano Co., TX

G5, $3000-$5000
Lake Limestone, TX

Tip lost while being fluted

SC

FREDERICK - Late Paleo-Early Archaic, 9000 - 8000 B. P.

(Also see Angostura, Clovis, Dalton, Golondrina, and Plainview)

Ground stem

G10, $350-$650
N.E. OK

LOCATION: Texas, Oklahoma, Montana, Nebraska and Kansas.
DESCRIPTION: A medium size, thin, lanceolate blade with early diagonal to collateral flaking and a concave base. Basal area is ground.
I.D. KEY: Broad base, deep concavity.

FRESNO - Mississippian, 1200 - 250 B. P.

(Also see Bassett, Friley, Huffaker, Maud and Talco)

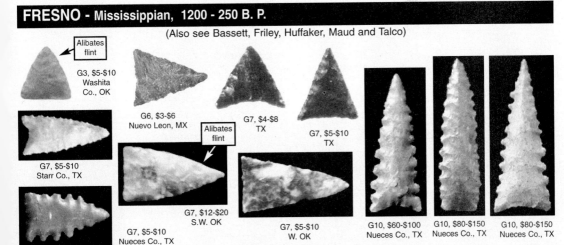

Alibates flint

G3, $5-$10
Washita Co., OK

G6, $3-$6
Nuevo Leon, MX

G7, $4-$8
TX

G7, $5-$10
TX

G7, $5-$10
Starr Co., TX

Alibates flint

G7, $12-$20
S.W. OK

G7, $5-$10
Nueces Co., TX

G7, $5-$10
W. OK

G10, $60-$100
Nueces Co., TX

G10, $80-$150
Nueces Co., TX

G10, $80-$150
Nueces Co., TX

LOCATION: Texas, Arkansas, Oklahoma and New Mexico. **DESCRIPTION:** A small, thin, triangular point with convex to straight sides and a concave to straight base. Many examples are deeply serrated and some are side notched.

581

G8, $150-$275
Williamson Co., TX

G7, $125-$200
TX

G6, $65-$125
TX

G7, $150-$275
Bell Co., TX

G8, $150-$250
Coryell Co., TX

G9, $175-$300
Coryell Co., TX

G9, $250-$450
TX

G9, $200-$350
Milam Co., TX

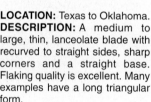

G8, $150-$250
Bell Co., TX

IMPORTANT:
All Fridays shown
half size

Black
chert

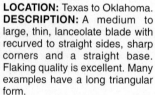

G9, $300-$500
TX

LOCATION: Texas to Oklahoma.
DESCRIPTION: A medium to large, thin, lanceolate blade with recurved to straight sides, sharp corners and a straight base. Flaking quality is excellent. Many examples have a long triangular form.

G8, $125-$200
Bell Co., TX

G9, $300-$500
Kerrville, TX

G7, $250-$400
Bell Co., TX

G9, $450-$800
Bexar Co., TX

G8, $600-$1000
Coryell Co., TX

FRILEY - Late Woodland, 1500 - 1000 B. P.

(Also see Bayogoula, Edwards, Fresno, Morris and Steiner)

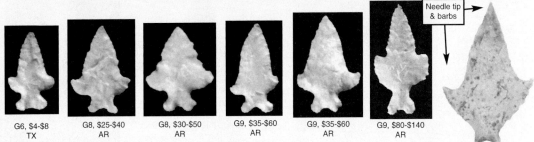

Needle tip & barbs →

G6, $4-$8
TX

G8, $25-$40
AR

G8, $30-$50
AR

G9, $35-$60
AR

G9, $35-$60
AR

G9, $80-$140
AR

G10+, $450-$700
Vernon Parish, LA

LOCATION: East Texas, Arkansas to Louisiana. **DESCRIPTION:** A small size, thin, triangular point with exaggerated shoulders that flare outward and towards the tip. The base can be rounded to eared.

FRIO - Middle Archaic to Woodland, 5000 - 1500 B. P.

(Also see Big Sandy, Cosotat River, Ensor Split-Base, Fairland, Montell and Uvalde)

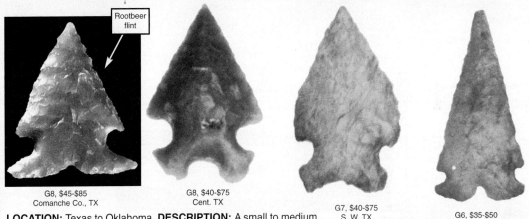

Rootbeer flint

G8, $45-$85
Comanche Co., TX

G8, $40-$75
Cent. TX

G7, $40-$75
S. W. TX

G6, $35-$50
Frio Co., TX

LOCATION: Texas to Oklahoma. **DESCRIPTION:** A small to medium size, side to corner-notched point with a concave to notched base that has squared to rounded ears that flare. Some examples can be confused with *Big Sandy Auriculate* forms. **I.D. KEY:** Flaring ears.

G10, $150-$250
Bell Co., TX

G7, $55-$100
Bandera Co., TX

G6, $55-$100
Frio Co., TX

G7, $80-$150
AR

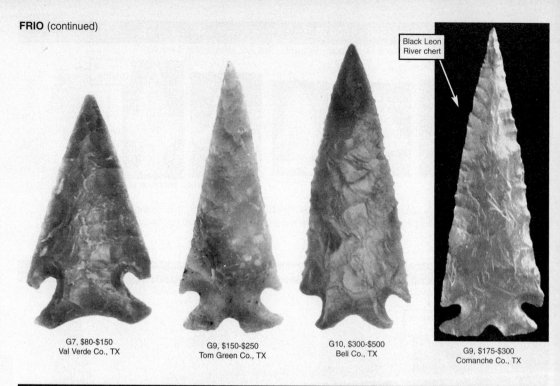

Black Leon
River chert

G7, $80-$150
Val Verde Co., TX

G9, $150-$250
Tom Green Co., TX

G10, $300-$500
Bell Co., TX

G9, $175-$300
Comanche Co., TX

GAHAGAN - Woodland, 4000 - 1500 B. P.

(Also see Covington, Darl Blade, Friday, Kinney, Mineral Springs, Sabine and San Gabriel)

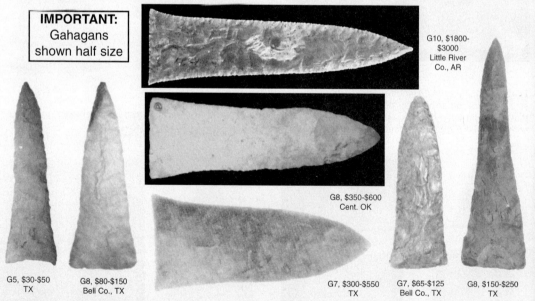

IMPORTANT:
Gahagans
shown half size

G10, $1800-
$3000
Little River
Co., AR

G8, $350-$600
Cent. OK

G5, $30-$50
TX

G8, $80-$150
Bell Co., TX

G7, $300-$550
TX

G7, $65-$125
Bell Co., TX

G8, $150-$250
TX

LOCATION: Texas. **DESCRIPTION:** A large size, broad, thin, triangular blade with recurved sides and a straight base.

GAR SCALE - Late Woodland to Mississippian, 1800 - 400 B. P.

LOCATION: Sites along large rivers in the Southeast such as the Tennessee River and the Mississippi. **DESCRIPTION:** Scales from Garfish were utilized as arrow points. These scales are hard and are naturally bipointed which was easily adapted as tips for arrows. Some examples altered into more symmetrical forms by the Indians.

GAR SCALE (continued)

G5, $1-$2
LA/TX

G5, $1-$2
LA/TX

G5, $1-$2
LA/TX

G7, $2-$5
LA/TX

G7, $1-$2
LA/TX

GARY - Late Archaic to early Woodland, 3200 - 1000 B. P.

(Also see Adena, Almagre, Burkett, Dickson, Hidden Valley, Kent, Langtry, Morrow Mountain and Waubesa)

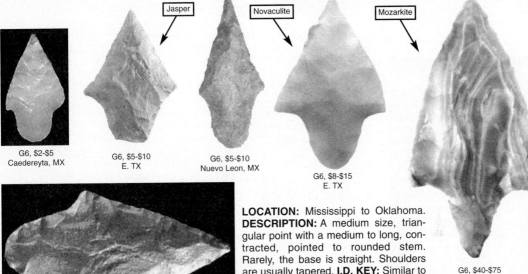

Jasper

Novaculite

Mozarkite

G6, $2-$5
Caedereyta, MX

G6, $5-$10
E. TX

G6, $5-$10
Nuevo Leon, MX

G6, $8-$15
E. TX

G6, $40-$75
AR

SC

LOCATION: Mississippi to Oklahoma. **DESCRIPTION:** A medium size, triangular point with a medium to long, contracted, pointed to rounded stem. Rarely, the base is straight. Shoulders are usually tapered. **I.D. KEY:** Similar to *Adena,* but thinned more. Another similar form, *Morrow Mountain* has earlier parallel flaking. **I.D. KEY:** Long contracted stem.

G4, $25-$40
McIntosh Co., OK

Translucent
novaculite

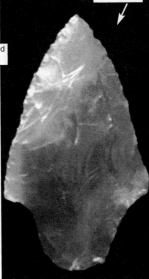

Translucent
novaculite

G9, $30-$50
AR

Banded
chert

G8, $30-$50
Eufaula Lake, OK

G5, $15-$25
Nuevo Leon, MX

G6, $20-$35
Comanche Co., TX

585

GARY (continued)

Chickachock chert

G9, $150-$250
McIntosh Co., OK

Quartzite

G7, $40-$75
Eufaula Lake, OK

G7, $125-$200
Davis, OK

G9, $175-$300
AR

Black quartzite

G10, $300-$500
Bossier Parish., LA

GARZA - Mississippian to Historic, 500 - 300 B. P.

(Also see Harrell, Lott, Starr and Toyah)

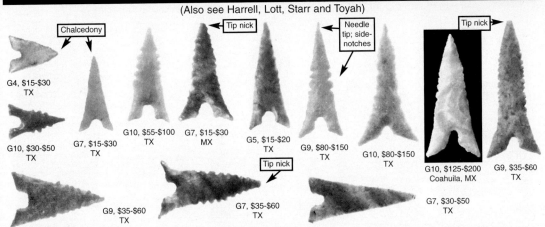

Chalcedony

Tip nick

Needle tip; side-notches

Tip nick

Tip nick

G4, $15-$30
TX

G10, $30-$50
TX

G7, $15-$30
TX

G10, $55-$100
TX

G7, $15-$30
MX

G5, $15-$20
TX

G9, $80-$150
TX

G10, $80-$150
TX

G10, $125-$200
Coahuila, MX

G9, $35-$60
TX

G9, $35-$60
TX

G7, $35-$60
TX

G7, $30-$50
TX

LOCATION: Northern Mexico to Oklahoma. **DESCRIPTION:** A small size, thin, triangular point with concave to convex sides and base that has a single notch in the center. Many examples are serrated. See *Soto* in SW Section.

GIBSON - Mid to Late Woodland, 2000 - 1500 B. P.

(Also see Cupp, Epps, Grand, Motley and St. Charles)

SC

LOCATION: Midwestern to Eastern states. **DESCRIPTION:** A medium to large size side to corner notched point with a large, convex base.

G8, $50-$90
AR

GODLEY - Woodland, 2500 - 1500 B. P.

(Also see Ellis and Palmillas)

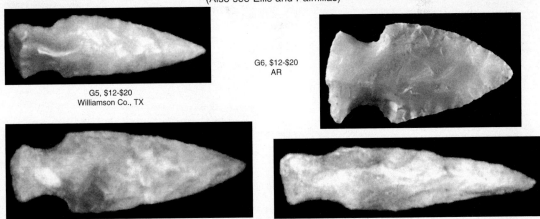

G5, $12-$20
Williamson Co., TX

G6, $12-$20
AR

G6, $15-$30
Williamson Co., TX

G6, $15-$30
Williamson Co., TX

LOCATION: Texas. **DESCRIPTION:** A small to medium size point with broad, expanding side-notches, tapered shoulders and a convex base. Basal area can be ground. Many specimens show unique beveling at the stem, usually from the same side.

587

(Also see Angostura, Arkabutla, Dalton, Midland, Pelican, Plainview & San Patrice)

G5, $55-$100
Medina, TX

G6, $80-$150
Cass Co., TX

G5, $125-$200
Medina Co., TX

G5, $55-$100
Lubbock, TX

G6, $40-$75
TX

G5, $55-$100
Lubbock, TX

G7, $90-$175
TX

G8, $150-$250
Midland, TX

G8, $175-$300
Bell Co., TX

G8, $200-$350
Wilson Co., TX

G7, $125-$200
Wilson Co., TX

G8, $150-$250
TX

G8, $275-$500
Waller Co., TX

LOCATION: Texas, Arkansas to Oklahoma. **DESCRIPTION:** A medium to large size auriculate unfluted point with rounded ears that flare and a deeply concave base. Basal areas are ground. Believed to be related to *Dalton*. **I.D. KEY:** Expanded ears, paleo flaking.

(Also see Clovis, Midland, Milnesand)

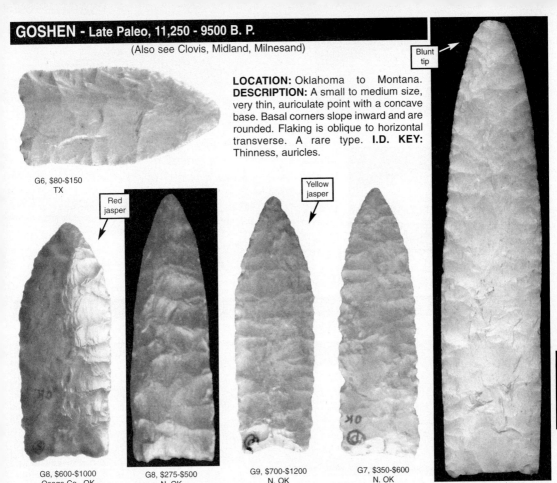

LOCATION: Oklahoma to Montana. **DESCRIPTION:** A small to medium size, very thin, auriculate point with a concave base. Basal corners slope inward and are rounded. Flaking is oblique to horizontal transverse. A rare type. **I.D. KEY:** Thinness, auricles.

Blunt tip

Red jasper

Yellow jasper

G6, $80-$150
TX

G8, $600-$1000
Osage Co., OK

G8, $275-$500
N. OK

G9, $700-$1200
N. OK

G7, $350-$600
N. OK

G10, $3000-$5000
Comanche Co., TX

SC

GOWER - Early Archaic, 8000 - 5000 B. P.

(Also see Barber, Jetta, Pedernales and Uvalde)

G7, $15-$25
Cent. TX

G6, $40-$75
TX

G10, $175-$325
Williamson Co., TX

G6, $15-$30
Comanche Co., TX

LOCATION: Texas. **DESCRIPTION:** A medium size, narrow point with weak shoulders and a long, deeply bifurcated stem. One or both basal ears turn inward on some examples or flare outward on others. **I.D. KEY:** Narrowness, base form.

GOWER (continued)

G6, $15-$30
Comanche Co., TX

G6, $80-$150
Travis Co., TX

G6, $25-$40
Comanche Co., TX

G5, $30-$50
Williamson Co., TX

GRAHAM CAVE - Early to Middle Archaic, 9000 - 5000 B. P.

(Also see Big Sandy, Hickory Ridge and White River)

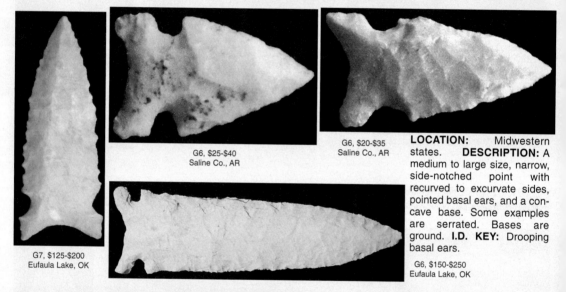

G6, $25-$40
Saline Co., AR

G6, $20-$35
Saline Co., AR

G7, $125-$200
Eufaula Lake, OK

G6, $150-$250
Eufaula Lake, OK

LOCATION: Midwestern states. **DESCRIPTION:** A medium to large size, narrow, side-notched point with recurved to excurvate sides, pointed basal ears, and a concave base. Some examples are serrated. Bases are ground. **I.D. KEY:** Drooping basal ears.

GRAND - Mid-Woodland, 1800 - 1600 B. P.

(Also see Big Creek, Cupp, Epps, Gibson and Motley)

G9, $150-$250
Cherokee Co., OK

G6, $30-$50
N.E. OK

LOCATION: Oklahoma into Kansas. **DESCRIPTION:** A medium sized, broad, corner notched point with barbed shoulders and an expanding, convex base. Basal corners can be sharp. **I.D. KEY:** Width of blade, corner notches.

GRAVER - Paleo to Archaic, 11,500 - 4000 B. P.

(Also see Drill, Perforator and Scraper)

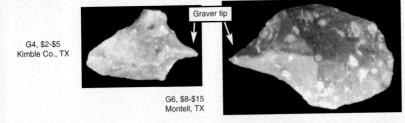

Graver tip

G4, $2-$5
Kimble Co., TX

G6, $8-$15
Montell, TX

LOCATION: Early man sites everywhere. **DESCRIPTION:** An irregular shaped uniface tool with sharp, pointed projections used for puncturing, incising, tattooing, etc. Some examples served a dual purpose for scraping as well. In later times.

GUERRERO - Historic, 300 - 100 B. P.

(Also see Maud and Nodena)

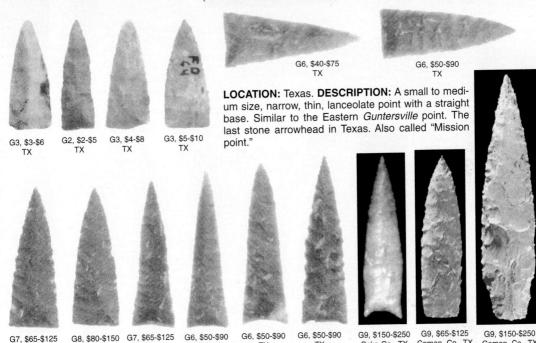

G6, $40-$75
TX

G6, $50-$90
TX

LOCATION: Texas. **DESCRIPTION:** A small to medium size, narrow, thin, lanceolate point with a straight base. Similar to the Eastern *Guntersville* point. The last stone arrowhead in Texas. Also called "Mission point."

G3, $3-$6
TX

G2, $2-$5
TX

G3, $4-$8
TX

G3, $5-$10
TX

G7, $65-$125
TX

G8, $80-$150
TX

G7, $65-$125
TX

G6, $50-$90
TX

G6, $50-$90
TX

G6, $50-$90
TX

G9, $150-$250
Coke Co., TX

G9, $65-$125
Coman. Co., TX

G9, $150-$250
Coman. Co., TX

SC

HALE (Bascom) - Late Archaic, 4000 - 3500 B. P.

(Also see Peisker Diamond)

G7, $25-$40
AR

LOCATION: Arkansas into Mississippi. **DESCRIPTION:** A large size, broad point with shoulders tapering to the base which is straight to rounded. Similar to the *Bascom* form found in Alabama and Georgia.

HARAHEY - Mississippian, 700 - 400 B. P.

(Also see Covington, Friday, Lerma and Refugio)

Alibates dolomite

G6, $65-$125
N. E. OK

G6, $65-125
Deaf Smith Co.,
TX

G5, $55-$100
Tulsa, OK

G8, $80-$150
Austin, TX

G8, $200-$350
N. OK

G7, $125-$200
Comanche Co.,
TX

G8, $175-$300
Bexar Co., TX

G9, $175-$300
Austin, TX

Edwards Plateau chert

G9, $275-$500
Garza Co., TX

IMPORTANT: All Haraheys shown 50% actual size

First stage form

G8, $150-$250
TX

G7, $150-$250
Bell Co., TX

G10, $450-$800
Uvalde Co., TX

G9, $350-$600
Coryell Co., TX

G10, $400-$700
TX

G9, $275-$500
AR

LOCATION: Texas to Colorado. **DESCRIPTION:** A large size, double pointed knife that is usually beveled on one or all four sides of each face. The cross section is rhomboid. The true buffalo skinning knife. Found associated with small arrow points in Texas. **I.D. KEY:** Four beveled double pointed form. See *Neosho* for the two beveled form.

HARDIN - Early Archaic, 9000 - 6000 B. P.

(Also see Alberta, Kirk, St. Charles and Scottsbluff)

LOCATION: Midwestern to Eastern states. **DESCRIPTION:** A large size, well made triangular barbed point with an expanded base that is usually ground. Resharpened examples have one beveled edge on each face. *Hardin* points are believed to have evolved from the *Scottsbluff* type. **I.D. KEY:** Notches and stem form.

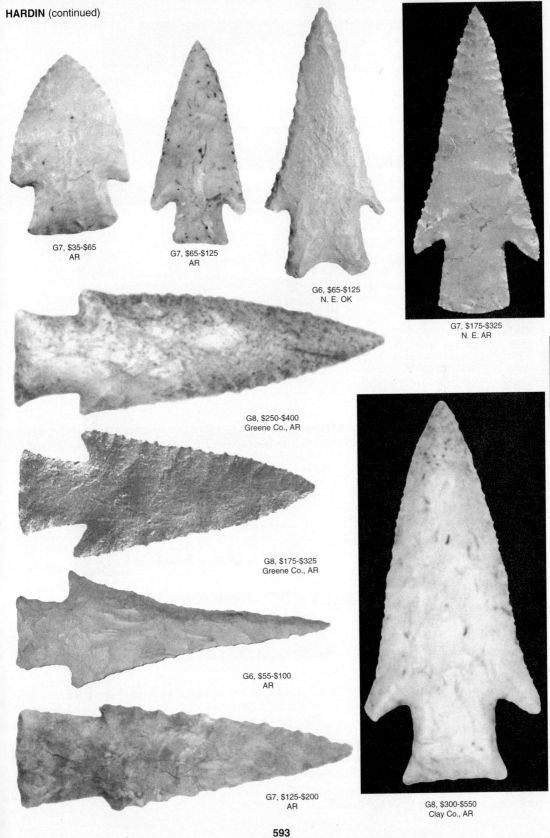

G7, $35-$65
AR

G7, $65-$125
AR

G6, $65-$125
N. E. OK

G7, $175-$325
N. E. AR

SC

G8, $250-$400
Greene Co., AR

G8, $175-$325
Greene Co., AR

G6, $55-$100
AR

G7, $125-$200
AR

G8, $300-$550
Clay Co., AR

HARDIN (continued)

Serrated edge

G9, $500-$900
AR

HARE BIFACE - Late Archaic to Woodland, 3000 - 2000 B. P.

(Also see Covington, Friday, Pandora and San Gabriel)

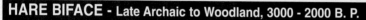

Petrified wood

G6, $12-$20
TX

LOCATION: Texas. **DESCRIPTION:** A medium to large size knife with excurvate sides and a rounded base. Made primarily by the percussion flake method. Bases can be beveled to thinned.

G6, $25-$40
Bell Co., TX

HARRELL - Mississippian to Historic, 900 - 500 B. P.

(Also see Toyah and Washita)

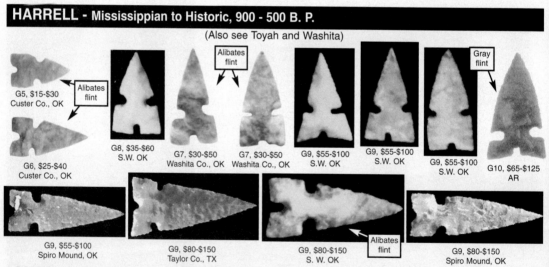

Alibates flint

Gray flint

G5, $15-$30
Custer Co., OK

Alibates flint

G8, $35-$60
S.W. OK

G7, $30-$50
Washita Co., OK

G7, $30-$50
Washita Co., OK

G9, $55-$100
S.W. OK

G9, $55-$100
S.W. OK

G9, $55-$100
S.W. OK

G10, $65-$125
AR

G6, $25-$40
Custer Co., OK

G9, $55-$100
Spiro Mound, OK

G9, $80-$150
Taylor Co., TX

G9, $80-$150
S. W. OK

Alibates flint

G9, $80-$150
Spiro Mound, OK

LOCATION: Texas to Oklahoma. **DESCRIPTION:** A small size, thin, triangular arrow point with side and a basal notch. Basal lobes are squared.

HASKELL - Mississippian to Historic, 800 - 600 B. P.

(Also see Edwards, Huffaker, Reed, Toyah and Washita)

LOCATION: Oklahoma to Arkansas. **DESCRIPTION:** A small size, thin, narrow, triangular, side notched point with a concave base. Rarely, basal tangs are notched.

HASKELL (continued)

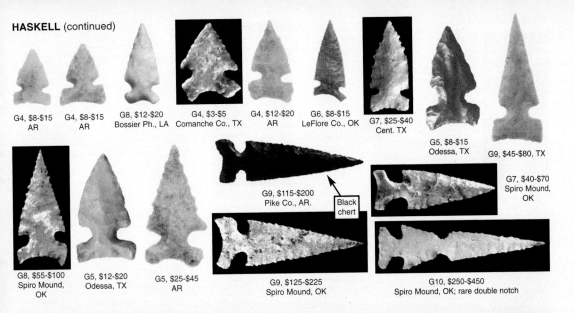

G4, $8-$15
AR

G4, $8-$15
AR

G8, $12-$20
Bossier Ph., LA

G4, $3-$5
Comanche Co., TX

G4, $12-$20
AR

G6, $8-$15
LeFlore Co., OK

G7, $25-$40
Cent. TX

G5, $8-$15
Odessa, TX

G9, $45-$80, TX

G8, $55-$100
Spiro Mound,
OK

G5, $12-$20
Odessa, TX

G5, $25-$45
AR

G9, $115-$200
Pike Co., AR.

Black
chert

G7, $40-$70
Spiro Mound,
OK

G9, $125-$225
Spiro Mound, OK

G10, $250-$450
Spiro Mound, OK; rare double notch

HAYES - Mississippian, 1200 - 600 B. P.

(Also see Alba, Blevins, Homan, Howard, Perdiz, Sequoya and Turner)

SC

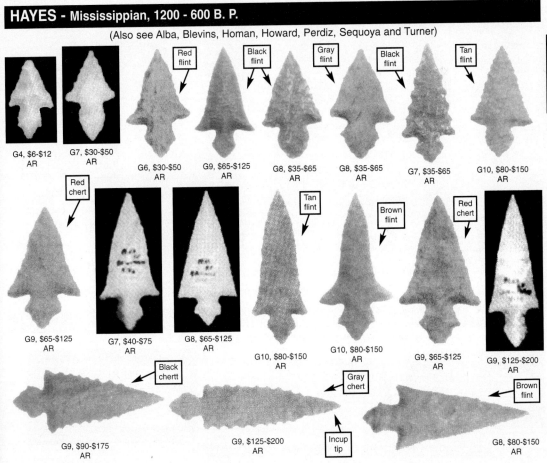

G4, $6-$12
AR

G7, $30-$50
AR

Red
flint

G6, $30-$50
AR

Black
flint

G9, $65-$125
AR

Gray
flint

G8, $35-$65
AR

Black
flint

G8, $35-$65
AR

Tan
flint

G7, $35-$65
AR

G10, $80-$150
AR

Red
chert

G9, $65-$125
AR

G7, $40-$75
AR

G8, $65-$125
AR

Tan
flint

G10, $80-$150
AR

Brown
flint

G10, $80-$150
AR

Red
chert

G9, $65-$125
AR

G9, $125-$200
AR

Black
chertt

G9, $90-$175
AR

G9, $125-$200
AR

Gray
chert

Incup
tip

Brown
flint

G8, $80-$150
AR

LOCATION: Louisiana to Oklahoma. **DESCRIPTION:** A small to medium size, narrow, expanded tang arrow point with a turkeytail base. Blade edges are usually strongly recurved forming sharp pointed barbs. Base is pointed and can be double notched. Some examples are serrated. Has been found in caches. **I.D. KEY:** Diamond shaped base and flaking style.

HAYES (continued)

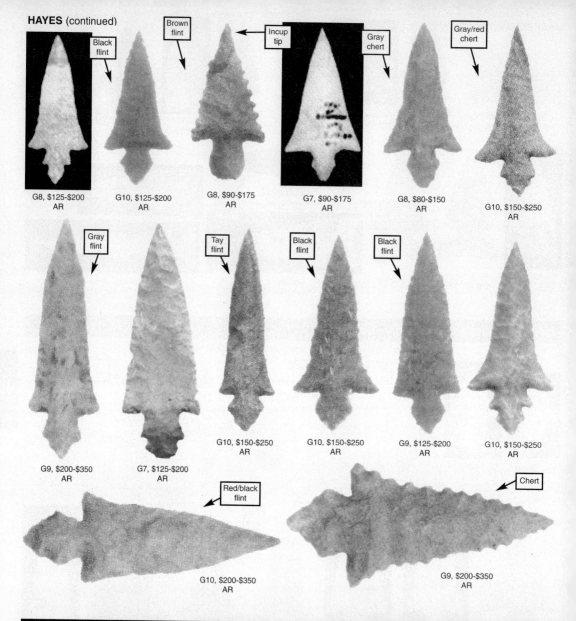

Black flint

Brown flint

Incup tip

Gray chert

Gray/red chert

G8, $125-$200
AR

G10, $125-$200
AR

G8, $90-$175
AR

G7, $90-$175
AR

G8, $80-$150
AR

G10, $150-$250
AR

Gray flint

Tay flint

Black flint

Black flint

G9, $200-$350
AR

G7, $125-$200
AR

G10, $150-$250
AR

G10, $150-$250
AR

G9, $125-$200
AR

G10, $150-$250
AR

Red/black flint

Chert

G10, $200-$350
AR

G9, $200-$350
AR

HELL GAP - Transitional Paleo, 10,300 - 9500 B. P.

(Also see Agate Basin, Angostura, Midland, Pelican and Rio Grande)

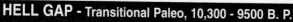

G3, $12-$20
Val Verde Co., TX

Petrified Palmwood

G6, $80-$150
TX

G6, $35-$60
Schleicher Co., TX

LOCATION: Texas northward to Canada. **DESCRIPTION:** A medium to large size, lanceolate point with a long, contracting stem. The widest part of the blade is above mid-section. The base is straight to slightly concave and the stem edges are usually ground. **I.D. KEY:** Very high up blade stems.

Ground
stem

G7, $80-$150
Tom Greene Co., TX

G8, $150-$275
Travis Co., TX

Ground
stem

G5, $80-$150
Osage Co., OK

Ground
stem

G8, $150-$275
Muskogee Co., OK

G6, $65-$125
N. E. OK

SC

Tip
damage

G7, $80-$150
McIntosh Co., OK

Ground
stem

Needle
tip

Rootbeer
colored
flint

G10, $250-$400
TX

G2, $55-$100
W. TX

G7, $125-$200
N. OK

Alibates
flint

Collateral
flaking

G10, $350-$600
TX

G7, $150-$275
N. OK

HEMPHILL - Middle Archaic, 7000 - 4000 B. P.

(Also see Big Sandy, Dalton-Hemphill, Graham Cave, Hemphill and
Hickory Ridge)

LOCATION: Missouri, Illinois into Wisconsin.
DESCRIPTION: A medium to large size side-
notched point with a concave base and parallel to
convex sides. These points are usually thinner and
of higher quality than the similar *Osceola* type found
in Wisconsin.

G4, $15-$30
Jonesboro, AR

597

HICKORY RIDGE - Middle Archaic, 7000 - 4000 B. P.

(Also see Big Sandy, Cache River and Hemphill)

Novaculite

G6, $12-$20
Saline Co., AR

G6, $20-$35
Saline Co., AR

G9, $200-$350
Greene Co., AR

G7, $80-$150
AR

G4, $8-$15
AR

Red jasper

G10, $300-$550
AR

LOCATION: Arkansas. **DESCRIPTION:** A medium to large size side-notched point. The base is straight to concave and early forms are ground. Basal corners are rounded to square. Side notches are usually wide. **I.D. KEY:** Broad, large side notched point.

HIDDEN VALLEY - Early to Middle Archaic, 8000 - 6000 B. P.

(Also see Burkett, Dickson, Gary, Langtry and Morrow Mountain)

LOCATION: Arkansas to Wisconsin. **DESCRIPTION:** A medium size point with square to tapered shoulders and a contracting base that can be pointed to straight. Flaking is earlier and more parallel than on *Gary* points. Called *Rice Contracted Stemmed* in Missouri.

G6, $45-$80
Craighead, AR

G7, $35-$60
Craighead, AR

G6, $45-$80
Craighead, AR

HOLLAND - Early Archaic, 10,000 - 7500 B. P.

(Also see Alberta, Dalton, Eden, Hardin and Scottsbluff)

G6, $80-$150
AR

SC

G9, $225-$400
AR

G8, $150-$250
N. OK

LOCATION: Midwestern to Northeastern states. **DESCRIPTION:** A medium to large size broad stemmed point of high quality. Shoulders are weak to nonexistant. Bases can be knobbed to auriculate and are usually ground. Some examples have horizontal to oblique transverse flaking. **I.D. KEY:** Weak shoulders, concave base.

G8, $200-$350
Bowie Co., TX

G9, $225-$400
AR

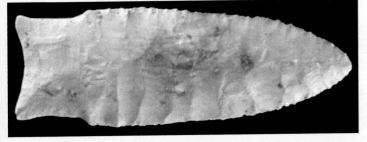

G8, $325-$500
AR/MO

G10, $1000-$1800
Broken Bow, OK

HOMAN - Mississippian, 1000 - 700 B. P.

(Also see Agee, Alba, Colbert, Hayes, Hughes, Keota, Perdiz and Scallorn)

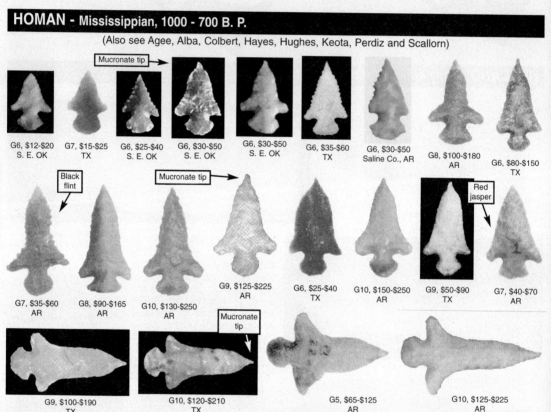

Mucronate tip

G6, $12-$20
S. E. OK

G7, $15-$25
TX

G6, $25-$40
S. E. OK

G6, $30-$50
S. E. OK

G6, $30-$50
S. E. OK

G6, $35-$60
TX

G6, $30-$50
Saline Co., AR

G8, $100-$180
AR

G6, $80-$150
TX

Black flint

Mucronate tip

Red jasper

G7, $35-$60
AR

G8, $90-$165
AR

G10, $130-$250
AR

G9, $125-$225
AR

G6, $25-$40
TX

G10, $150-$250
AR

G9, $50-$90
TX

G7, $40-$70
AR

Mucronate tip

G9, $100-$190
TX

G10, $120-$210
TX

G5, $65-$125
AR

G10, $125-$225
AR

LOCATION: Oklahoma to Arkansas. **DESCRIPTION:** A small size expanded barbed arrow point with a bulbous stem. Some tips are mucronate or apiculate. **I.D. KEY:** Bulbous stem.

HOWARD - Mississippian, 700 - 500 B. P.

(Also see Blevins, Hayes and Sequoyah)

G7, $30-$50
AR

Black flint

G7, $50-$90
AR

G9, $50-$90
AR

G10, $125-$200
AR

LOCATION: Louisiana to Oklahoma. **DESCRIPTION:** A small size, narrow, spike point with two or more barbs on each side, restricted to the lower part of the point and a parallel to expanding, rounded stem. A diamond shaped base places the point in the *Blevins* type. **I.D. KEY:** Multiple serrations near the base.

HOWARD (continued)

G7, $45-$80
W. AR

G8, $90-$175
W. AR

G8, $80-$150
W. AR

G7, $55-$100
W. AR

G7, $80-$125
W. AR

G8, $80-$125
W. AR

G8, $80-$150
W. AR

G8, $80-$150
W. AR

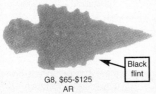

Black flint

G8, $65-$125
AR

G9, $175-$325
W. AR

MS-I

G9, $200-$350
Howard Co., AR, Mineral Springs

HOXIE - Early Archaic, 8000 - 5000 B. P.

(Also see Bulverde, Darl, Darl Stemmed, Early Stemmed Lanceolate, Gower and Zephyr)

Beveled edge

Translucent

G7, $12-$20
Comanche Co., TX

G6, $15-$25
Comanche Co., TX

G8, $55-$100
Austin, TX

G6, $35-$60
Cent. TX

Black chert

G8, $125-$200
Austin, TX

G8, $200-$350
Hood Co., TX

LOCATION: Texas. **DESCRIPTION:** A medium to large size, narrow point with weak shoulders and a parallel sided, concave base that is ground. Believed to be an early form of *Darl*.

HUFFAKER - Mississippian, 1000 - 500 B. P.

(Also see Duran, Evans, Fresno, Harrell, Haskell, Sinner and Washita)

G3, $5-$10
Cent. TX

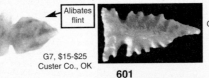

Alibates flint

G7, $15-$25
Custer Co., OK

G7, $30-$55
Comanche Co., TX

G8, $25-$45
TX

HUFFAKER (continued)

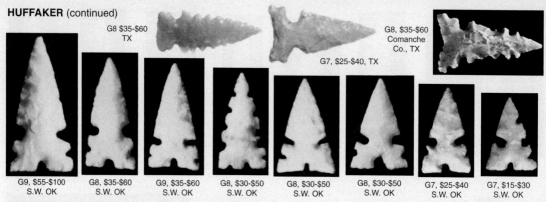

G8 $35-$60
TX

G8, $35-$60
Comanche
Co., TX

G7, $25-$40, TX

G9, $55-$100
S.W. OK

G8, $35-$60
S.W. OK

G9, $35-$60
S.W. OK

G8, $30-$50
S.W. OK

G8, $30-$50
S.W. OK

G8, $30-$50
S.W. OK

G7, $25-$40
S.W. OK

G7, $15-$30
S.W. OK

LOCATION: Texas northward to Canada. **DESCRIPTION:** A small size triangular point with a straight to concave base and double side notches. Blade edges can be heavily barbed. Bases can have a single notch. **I.D. KEY:** Double notches.

HUGHES - Mississippian, 1200 - 600 B. P.

(Also see Alba, Colbert, Hayes, Homan, Keota)

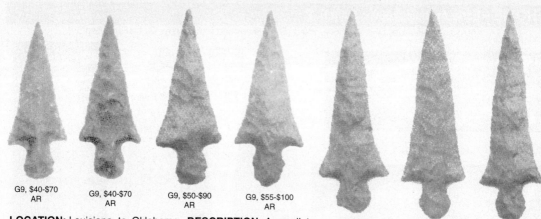

G9, $40-$70
AR

G9, $40-$70
AR

G9, $50-$90
AR

G9, $55-$100
AR

G9, $65-$125
AR

G9, $65-$125
AR

G10, $80-$150
AR

LOCATION: Louisiana to Oklahoma. **DESCRIPTION:** A small to medium size, thin, narrow point with a sharp tip, horizontal to slightly barbed shoulders and an expanding, bulbous stem. **I.D. KEY:** Bulbous stem.

JAKIE STEMMED - Early Archaic, 8000 - 5000 B. P.

(Also see Cosatot River, Gower, Pedernales and Uvalde)

G7, $15-$30
Saline Co., AR

G8, $20-$35
Saline Co., AR

LOCATION: Oklahoma, AR., MO. **DESCRIPTION:** A medium size point with an expanded to parallel sided, auriculate to bifurcated stem. Blade edges are serrated and the base is ground with rounded lobes.

G7, $25-$40
Saline Co., AR

602

JETTA - Early Archaic, 8000 - 5000 B. P.

(Also see Gower, Pedernales and Uvalde)

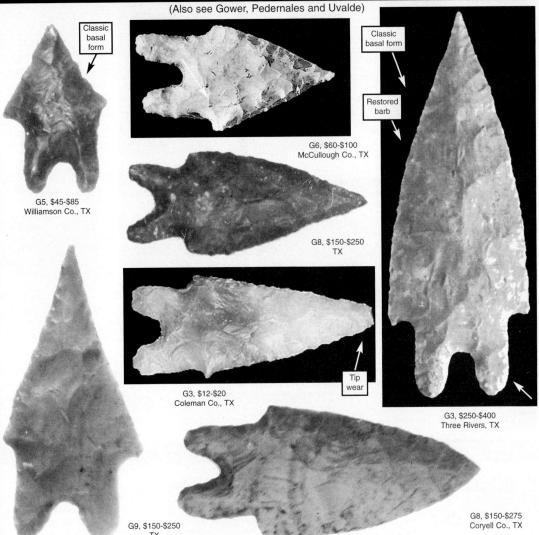

Classic basal form

G5, $45-$85
Williamson Co., TX

G6, $60-$100
McCullough Co., TX

G8, $150-$250
TX

G3, $12-$20
Coleman Co., TX

Tip wear

Classic basal form

Restored barb

SC

G3, $250-$400
Three Rivers, TX

G9, $150-$250
TX

G8, $150-$275
Coryell Co., TX

LOCATION: Texas to Oklahoma. **DESCRIPTION:** A medium to large size point with tapered, horizontal or short pointed shoulders and a deeply notched base. Basal tangs are rounded and the stem is more squared and wider than *Pedernalis*. A very rare type.

JOHNSON - Early to Middle Archaic, 9000 - 5000 B. P.

(Also see Bulverde and Savannah River)

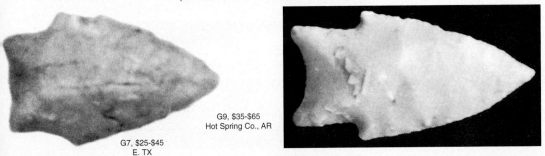

G9, $35-$65
Hot Spring Co., AR

G7, $25-$45
E. TX

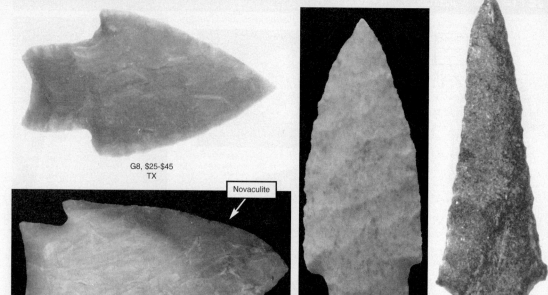

G8, $25-$45
TX

Novaculite

G8, $65-$125
Cent. AR. Novaculite.

G8, $40-$70
Hot Spring, AR

G7, $55-$100
AR

LOCATION: Mississippi to Oklahoma. **DESCRIPTION:** A medium size, thick, well made, expanded stem point with a broad, short, concave base. Bases are usually thinned and grinding appears on some specimens. Shoulders can be slight and are roughly horizontal. **I.D. KEY:** Broad stem that is thinned.

JORA (see Coahuila)

KAY BLADE - Mississippian, 1000 - 600 B. P.

(Also see Cupp, Epps, Motley)

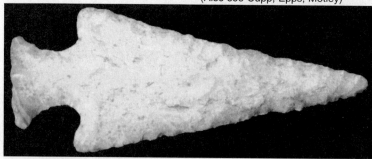

LOCATION: Oklahoma into midwestern states. **DESCRIPTION:** A medium to large size corner notched point with a long expanding stem and barbed shoulders. Bases are straight to almost convex. Used by the Mississippian, Caddoan people. **I.D. KEY:** Broad corner notches.

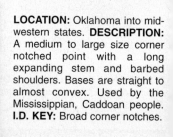

G8, $200-$350
N. OK

G8, $200-$350
N. OK

KENT- Woodland, 3000 - 2800 B. P.

(Also see Adena-Robbins, Dallas, Darl, Delhi, Gary, Morrill, Travis)

G2, $2-$3
E. TX

G4, $2-$5
E. TX

G7, $8-$15
E. TX

G7, $12-$20
E. TX

LOCATION: NW Louisiana into Arkansas, Texas & Oklahoma. **DESCRIPTION:** A small to medium size, narrow point with a parallel sided stem and a base that is straight to convex. Shoulders are usually tapered.

KEOTA - Mississippian, 800 - 600 B. P.

(Also see Agee, Alba, Colbert, Dardanelle, Hayes, Homan, Hughes and Sequoyah)

G3, $5-$10
Comanche
Co., TX

G9, $80-$140
TX

LOCATION: Texas, Arkansas to Oklahoma. **DESCRIPTION:** A small size, thin, triangular, side to corner-notched point with a rounded, bulbous base. The basal area is large on some specimens. **I.D. KEY:** Large bulbous base.

G8, $35-$125
Spiro Mound, OK

G9, $90-$175 ea.
Spiro Mound, OK

KERRVILLE KNIFE - Middle to Late Archaic, 5000 - 3000 B. P.

(Also see Chopper and Scraper)

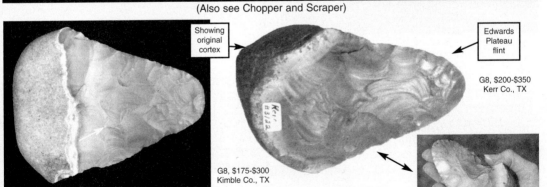

Showing original cortex

Edwards Plateau flint

G8, $200-$350
Kerr Co., TX

G8, $175-$300
Kimble Co., TX

Showing original cortex

LOCATION: Midwestern states. **DESCRIPTION:** A large size, thick, triangular cutting or chopping tool with straight to slightly convex edges. The original rind occurs at the base. Also called fist axes.

Kerrvilles shown half size

Hand-held to show size & structure

SC

KINGS - Middle Archaic, 5000 - 2000 B. P.

(Also see Big Creek, Cupp, Epps and Motley)

G3, $12-$20
TX

G9, $125-$200
N.E. OK

LOCATION: Arkansas, Oklahoma into Missouri and Kansas. **DESCRIPTION:** A medium to large size, corner notched point with strong, sharp shoulders and an expanding base. Bases are straight, concave or convex.

KINNEY - Middle Archaic-Woodland, 5000 - 2000 B. P.

(Also see Darl Blade, Early Triangular, Gahagan, Pandora and Tortugas)

G7, $80-$150
Coryell Co., TX

Rootbeer colored Georgetown flint

G6, $35-$60
Cent. TX

G9, $125-$200
Austin, TX

G6, $40-$75
Coryell Co., TX

G3, $8-$15
TX

G9, $175-$300
Coryell Co., TX

LOCATION: Texas. **DESCRIPTION:** A medium to large size, thin, broad, lanceolate, well made blade with convex to straight blade edges and a concave base. Basal corners are pointed to rounded. **I.D. KEY:** Broad, concave base.

G8, $400-$700
Burleson Co., TX

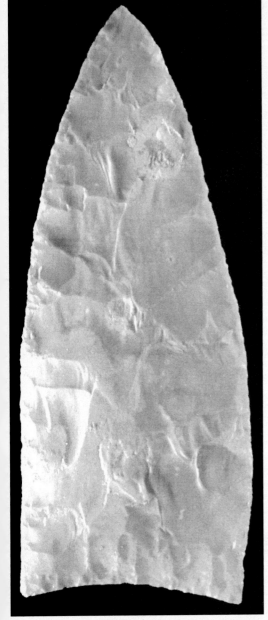

G10+, $700-$1200
Cent. TX

Heavy
patination

G10, $600-$1000
Waco, TX

SC

KNIGHT ISLAND - Late Woodland, 1500 - 1000 B. P.

(Also see Brewerton, Cache River, Hickory Ridge, Reed, Schustorm and White River)

G10, $150-$250
N.E. AR

G8, $65-$125
N.E., AR

LOCATION: Arkansas to Southeastern states. **DESCRIPTION:** A small to medium size, very thin, narrow, side-notched point with a straight base. Longer examples can have a pentagonal appearance. Called *Racoon Creek* in Ohio. A side-notched Jacks Reef. **I.D. KEY:** Thinness, basal form. Made by the small triangle point people.

LA JITA - Middle Archaic, 7000 - 4000 B. P.

(Also see Axtel, Palmillas and Williams)

LOCATION: Texas. **DESCRIPTION:** A medium to large size, broad point with weak shoulders and a broad, bulbous base that expands and has rounded basal corners. **I.D. KEY:** Large bulbous base.

G7, $45-$80
Coryell Co., TX

White patination

G8, $55-$100
Bandera Co., TX

G6, $45-$80
Coryell Co., TX

G9, $80-$150
Kerr Co., TX

G7, $80-$150
Bandera Co., TX

LAMPASAS (See Zephyr)

LANGE - Middle Archaic to Woodland, 6000 - 1000 B. P.

(Also see Bulverde, Castorville, Morrill, Nolan and Travis)

LOCATION: Louisiana to Texas to Oklahoma. **DESCRIPTION:** A medium to large size, narrow, expanded stem dart point with tapered to horizontal, barbed shoulders and a straight to convex base. **I.D. KEY:** Expanding base, tapered to horizontal shoulders.

LANGE (continued)

G2, $2-$5
Val Verde Co., TX

G3, $5-$10
Comanche Co., TX

G6, $20-$35
Comanche Co., TX

Brown
quartzite

G9, $90-$175
Bossier Ph., LA

G8, $125-$200
Bell Co., TX

G9, $125-$200
Coryell Co., TX

SC

G9, $150-$250
Austin, TX

G3, $8-$15
Comanche Co., TX

G9, $150-$250
Waco, TX

Black
chert

G7, $65-$125
Williamson Co., TX

G10, $200-$350
Eufaula Lake, OK

Barb nicks

G4, $8-$15
Val Verde Co., TX

G3, $2-$5
Zapata Co., TX

G6, $15-$30
Coryell Co., TX

G8, $55-$100
Val Verde Co., TX

Needle tip & barbs

G9, $150-$250
Frio Co., TX

G10, $125-$200
Webb Co., TX

G8, $80-$150
W. TX

G8, $55-$100
W. TX

G8, $65-$125
TX

G5, $30-$50
Bell Co., TX

G7, $80-$150
Comanche Co., TX

G10, $275-$500
Coryell Co., TX

LOCATION: Texas to Oklahoma. **DESCRIPTION:** A medium size triangular dart point with a short to long contracting to straight stem. Shoulders can be square, tapered or strongly barbed. Bases are concave to straight. Found in a cave hafted to a wooden forshaft with pitch. **I.D. KEY:** Strong barbs, tapered stem.

LANGTRY-ARENOSA - Middle Archaic to Woodland, 5000 - 2000 B. P.

(Also see Almagre, Coahuila and Gary)

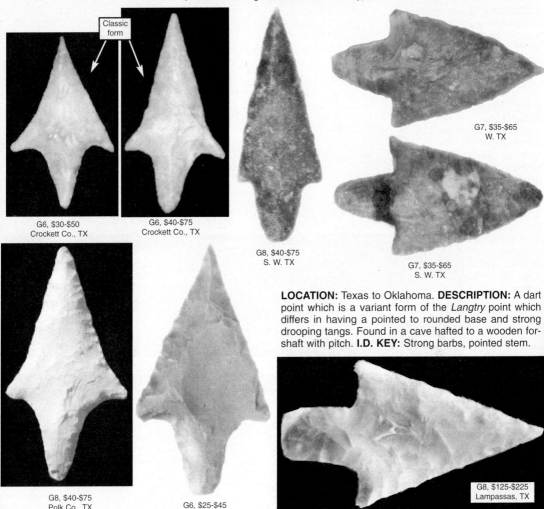

Classic form

G6, $30-$50
Crockett Co., TX

G6, $40-$75
Crockett Co., TX

G8, $40-$75
S. W. TX

G7, $35-$65
W. TX

G7, $35-$65
S. W. TX

G8, $40-$75
Polk Co., TX

G6, $25-$45
TX

G8, $125-$225
Lampassas, TX

LOCATION: Texas to Oklahoma. **DESCRIPTION:** A dart point which is a variant form of the *Langtry* point which differs in having a pointed to rounded base and strong drooping tangs. Found in a cave hafted to a wooden forshaft with pitch. **I.D. KEY:** Strong barbs, pointed stem.

SC

LEFLORE BLADE - Mississippian-Historic, 500 - 250 B. P.

(Also see Agate Basin, Lerma)

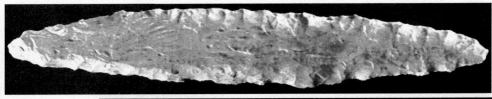

G8, $175-$300
McIntosh Co., OK

G8, $150-$275
McIntosh Co., OK

LOCATION: Oklahoma to N. Texas and Kansas. **DESCRIPTION:** A large size, narrow lanceolate, bi-pointed blade. Blade edges are usually smoothed. Much more narrow than *Lerma* points. **I.D. KEY:** Narrow width in relation to length.

LERMA POINTED BASE - Early Archaic, 9000 - 8000 B. P.

(Also see Agate Basin, Angostura, Desmuke, Harahey & LeFlore Blade)

LOCATION: Siberia to Alaska, Canada, Mexico, South America and across the U.S. **DESCRIPTION:** A large size, narrow, lanceolate blade with a pointed base. Most are fairly thick in cross section but finer examples can be thin. Flaking tends to be collateral. Basal areas can be ground. Western forms are beveled on one side of each face. Similar forms have been found in Europe and Africa dating back to 20,000 - 40,000 B.P., but didn't enter the U.S. until after the advent of *Clovis*.
NOTE: Lerma may be much older.

G6, $80-$150
TX

G10, $175-$325
Wilson Co., TX

G9, $175-$325
Comanche Co., TX

LERMA ROUNDED BASE - Early Archaic, 9000 - 8000 B. P.

(Also see Agate Basin, Angostura, Covington and Harahey)

Resharpened with serrations

Petrified wood

G8, $35-$50
Cent. TX

G8, $35-$50
Comanche Co., TX

G6, $35-$65
TX

G8, $40-$75
TX

G9, $55-$100
Bell Co., TX

LOCATION: Same as pointed base Lerma.
DESCRIPTION: A large size, narrow, thick, lanceolate blade with a rounded base. Some Western examples are beveled on one side of each face. Flaking tends to be collateral and finer examples are thin in cross section.

LERMA ROUND BASE (continued)

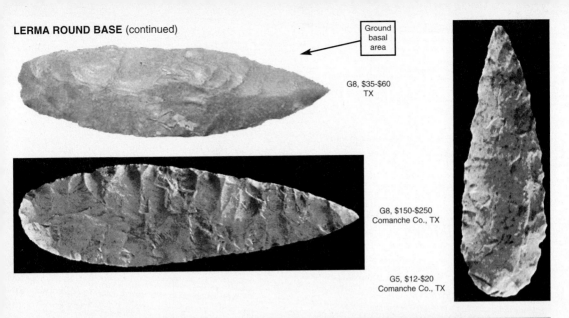

Ground basal area

G8, $35-$60
TX

G8, $150-$250
Comanche Co., TX

G5, $12-$20
Comanche Co., TX

SC

LITTLE RIVER - Mid to Late Archaic, 5000 -3000 B. P.

(Also see Smith)

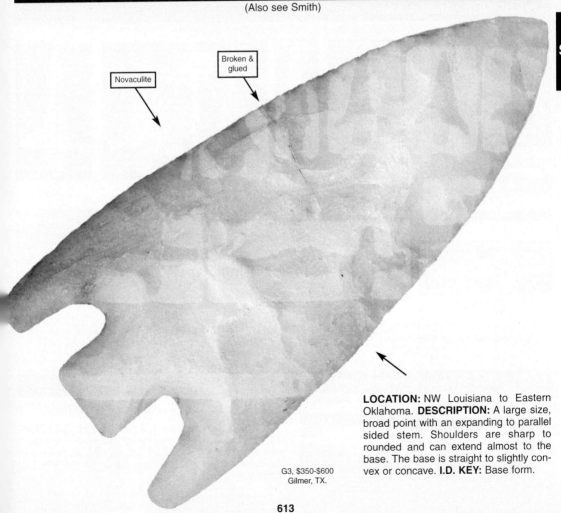

Novaculite

Broken & glued

LOCATION: NW Louisiana to Eastern Oklahoma. **DESCRIPTION:** A large size, broad point with an expanding to parallel sided stem. Shoulders are sharp to rounded and can extend almost to the base. The base is straight to slightly convex or concave. **I.D. KEY:** Base form.

G3, $350-$600
Gilmer, TX.

613

LITTLE RIVER (continued)

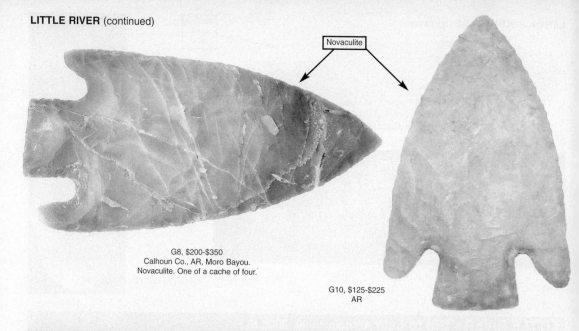

Novaculite

G8, $200-$350
Calhoun Co., AR, Moro Bayou.
Novaculite. One of a cache of four.

G10, $125-$225
AR

LIVERMORE - Mississippian, 1200 - 600 B. P.

(Also see Bassett, Drill, Howard and Sequoyah)

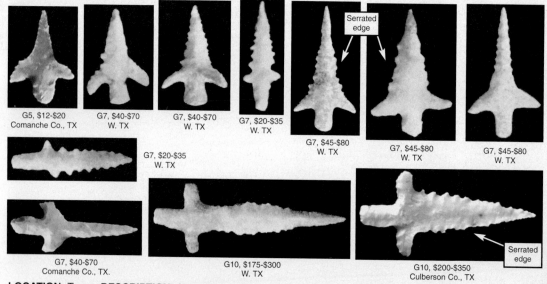

Serrated edge

G5, $12-$20
Comanche Co., TX

G7, $40-$70
W. TX

G7, $40-$70
W. TX

G7, $20-$35
W. TX

G7, $45-$80
W. TX

G7, $45-$80
W. TX

G7, $45-$80
W. TX

G7, $20-$35
W. TX

G7, $40-$70
Comanche Co., TX.

G10, $175-$300
W. TX

G10, $200-$350
Culberson Co., TX

Serrated edge

LOCATION: Texas. **DESCRIPTION:** A small to medium size, very narrow, spike point with wide flaring barbs and a narrow stem that can be short to long. Some examples are serrated. **I.D. KEY:** Extreme narrowness of blade.

LOTT - Mississippian to Historic, 500 - 300 B. P.

(Also see Garza and Harrell)

G9, $55-$100
Garza Co., TX

G10, $80-$150
Garza Co., TX

LOCATION: Texas to Arizona. A rare type. **DESCRIPTION:** A medium size, weakly barbed, thin, arrow point with a bifurcated base. Ears can be long and flare outward. Basal sides and the base are usually straight. **I.D. KEY:** Form of ears.

MAHAFFEY - Transitional Paleo-Early Archaic, 10,500 - 8000 B. P.

(Also see Agate Basin and Angostura)

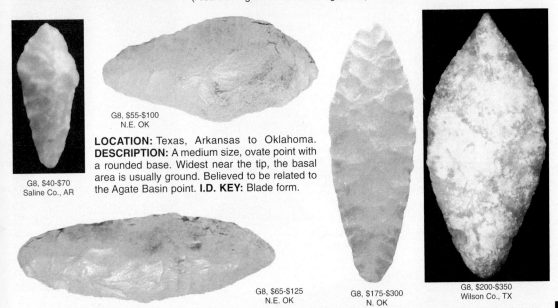

G8, $55-$100
N.E. OK

G8, $40-$70
Saline Co., AR

LOCATION: Texas, Arkansas to Oklahoma. **DESCRIPTION:** A medium size, ovate point with a rounded base. Widest near the tip, the basal area is usually ground. Believed to be related to the Agate Basin point. **I.D. KEY:** Blade form.

G8, $65-$125
N.E. OK

G8, $175-$300
N. OK

G8, $200-$350
Wilson Co., TX

MARCOS - Late Archaic to Woodland, 3500 - 1800 B. P.

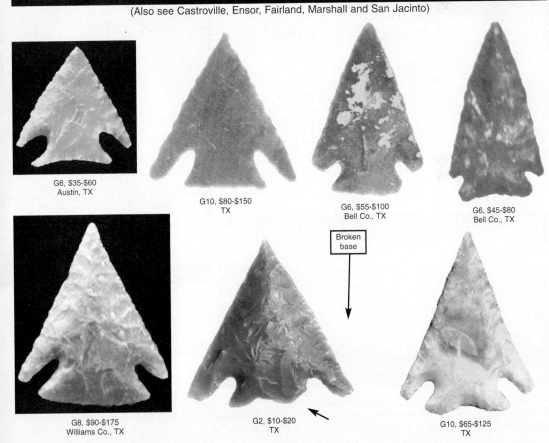

(Also see Castroville, Ensor, Fairland, Marshall and San Jacinto)

SC

G6, $35-$60
Austin, TX

G10, $80-$150
TX

G6, $55-$100
Bell Co., TX

G6, $45-$80
Bell Co., TX

G8, $90-$175
Williams Co., TX

Broken
base

G2, $10-$20
TX

G10, $65-$125
TX

MARCOS (continued)

Leon River black chert

G8, $45-$85
Austin, TX

G8, $35-$150
Coryell Co., TX

G8, $80-$150
Wilson Co., TX

G10+ $550-$1000
Wilson Co., TX

G8, $200-$350
Wilson Co., TX

G8, $250-$400
Bell Co., TX

ROGERS

G9, $250-$450
Comanche Co., TX

G10+, $1500-$2500
Coryell Co., TX

LOCATION: Texas to Oklahoma. **DESCRIPTION:** A small to medium size, broad, corner notched point with an expanded stem. The blade edges are straight to recurved. Many examples have long barbs and a sharp pointed tip. Bases are convex, straight or concave. **I.D. KEY:** Angle of corner notches.

616

MARSHALL - Middle Archaic to Woodland, 6000 - 2000 B. P.

(Also see Castroville, Ensor, Marcos and San Jacinto)

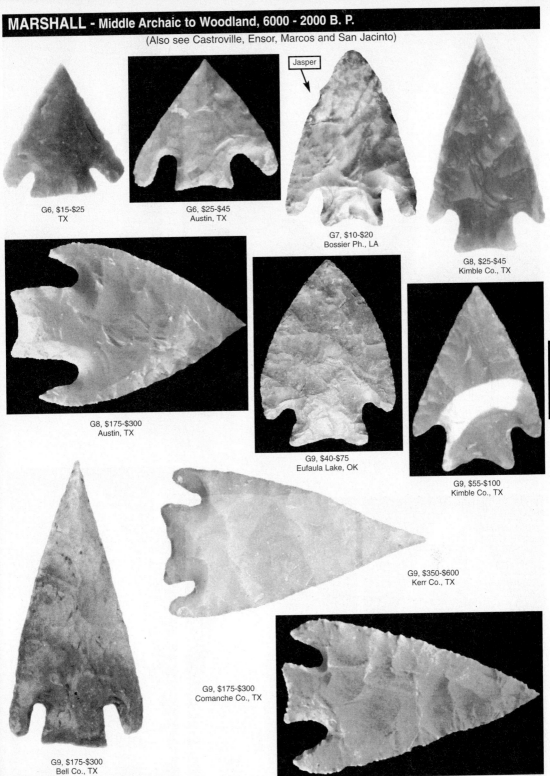

Jasper

G6, $15-$25
TX

G6, $25-$45
Austin, TX

G7, $10-$20
Bossier Ph., LA

G8, $25-$45
Kimble Co., TX

G8, $175-$300
Austin, TX

G9, $40-$75
Eufaula Lake, OK

G9, $55-$100
Kimble Co., TX

SC

G9, $350-$600
Kerr Co., TX

G9, $175-$300
Comanche Co., TX

G9, $175-$300
Bell Co., TX

LOCATION: Texas to Colorado. **DESCRIPTION:** A medium to large size, broad, high quality, corner to basal notched point with long barbs that turn inward towards the base. Notching is less angled than in *Marcos*. Bases are straight to concave to bifurcated. **I.D. KEY:** Drooping tangs.

617

Note side notches

G7, $125-$200
Austin, TX

G9, $250-$400
Austin, TX

G8, $150-$300
Austin, TX

G7, $125-$200
Bell Co., TX

G7, $30-$50
Llano Co., TX

Very thin cross section

G9, $250-$400
TX

G9, $250-$450
Austin, TX

G9, $350-$600
Comanche Co., TX

MARTINDALE - Early Archaic, 8000 - 5000 B. P.

(Also see Bandy, Marcos and Marshall)

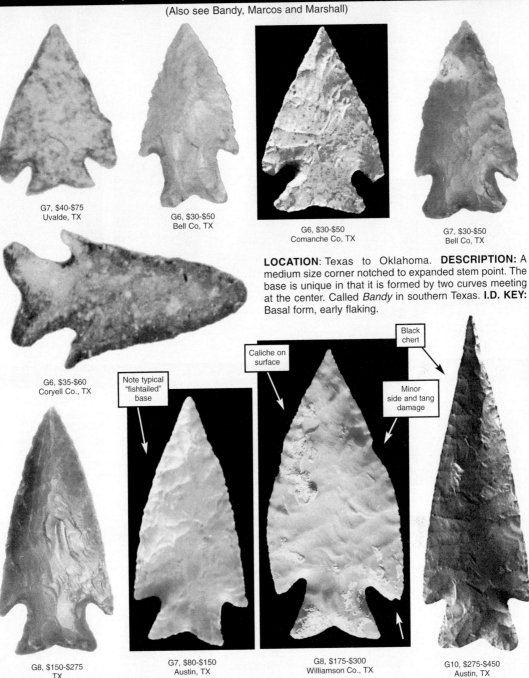

G7, $40-$75
Uvalde, TX

G6, $30-$50
Bell Co, TX

G6, $30-$50
Comanche Co, TX

G7, $30-$50
Bell Co, TX

G6, $35-$60
Coryell Co., TX

LOCATION: Texas to Oklahoma. **DESCRIPTION**: A medium size corner notched to expanded stem point. The base is unique in that it is formed by two curves meeting at the center. Called *Bandy* in southern Texas. **I.D. KEY:** Basal form, early flaking.

Black chert

Caliche on surface

Note typical "fishtailed" base

Minor side and tang damage

G8, $150-$275
TX

G7, $80-$150
Austin, TX

G8, $175-$300
Williamson Co., TX

G10, $275-$450
Austin, TX

SC

MASSARD   (see Colbert)

MATAMOROS - Late Archaic to Mississippian, 3000 - 300 B. P.

(Also see Abasolo, Catan and Tortugas)

LOCATION: Texas. **DESCRIPTION**: A small to medium size, broad, triangular point with concave, straight, or convex base. On some examples, beveling occurs on one side of each face as in *Tortugas* points. Larger points would fall under the *Tortugas* type.

MATAMOROS (continued)

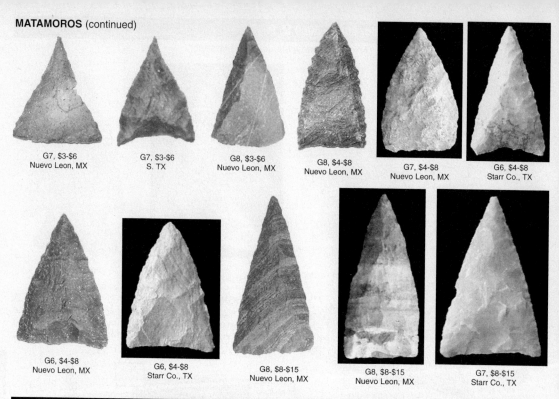

G7, $3-$6
Nuevo Leon, MX

G7, $3-$6
S. TX

G8, $3-$6
Nuevo Leon, MX

G8, $4-$8
Nuevo Leon, MX

G7, $4-$8
Nuevo Leon, MX

G6, $4-$8
Starr Co., TX

G6, $4-$8
Nuevo Leon, MX

G6, $4-$8
Starr Co., TX

G8, $8-$15
Nuevo Leon, MX

G8, $8-$15
Nuevo Leon, MX

G7, $8-$15
Starr Co., TX

MATANZAS - Mid-Archaic to Mississippian, 4500 - 3000 B. P.

(Also see Palmillas)

G7, $30-$50
AR

LOCATION: Arkansas to Missouri. **DESCRIPTION:** A medium size, narrow, side notched dart point with an expanding stem and a straight base.

MAUD - Mississippian, 800 - 500 B. P.

(Also see Fresno, Starr and Talco)

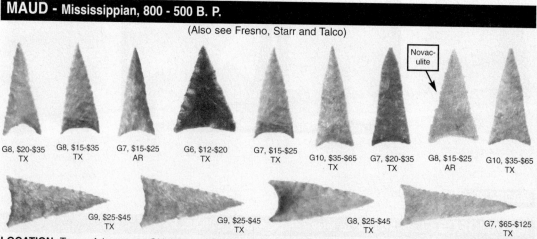

Novac-ulite

G8, $20-$35
TX

G8, $15-$35
TX

G7, $15-$25
AR

G6, $12-$20
TX

G7, $15-$25
TX

G10, $35-$65
TX

G7, $20-$35
TX

G8, $15-$25
AR

G10, $35-$65
TX

G9, $25-$45
TX

G9, $25-$45
TX

G8, $25-$45
TX

G7, $65-$125
TX

LOCATION: Texas, Arkansas to Oklahoma. **DESCRIPTION:** A small size, thin, triangular arrow point with straight to convex sides and a concave base. Basal corners are sharp. Associated with the Caddo culture in the Midwest. Blades are usually very finely serrated. **I.D. KEY:** Convex sides, sharp basal corners.

MAUD (continued)

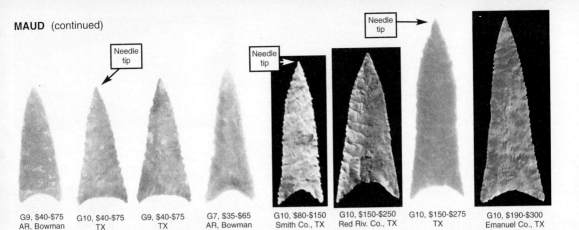

Needle tip

Needle tip

Needle tip

G9, $40-$75
AR, Bowman
site

G10, $40-$75
TX

G9, $40-$75
TX

G7, $35-$65
AR, Bowman
site

G10, $80-$150
Smith Co., TX

G10, $150-$250
Red Riv. Co., TX

G10, $150-$275
TX

G10, $190-$300
Emanuel Co., TX

MCKEAN - Middle to Late Archaic, 4500 - 2500 B. P.

(Also see Angostura, Folsom, Goshen)

G9, $250-$450
N. OK

LOCATION: N. Plains into Oklahoma. **DESCRIPTION:** A small to medium size, narrow, basal notched point. No basal grinding is evident. Similar to the much earlier *Wheeler* points of the Southeast. Basal ears are rounded to pointed. Flaking is more random although earlier examples can have parallel flaking. **I.D. KEY:** Narrow lanceolate with notched base.

SC

MERKLE - Mid-Archaic to Mississippian, 4500 - 3000 B. P.

(Also see Duran, Evans, Sinner)

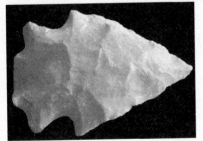

G6, $25-$50
Saline Co., AR

G7, $35-$60
N. OK

LOCATION: Arkansas to Missouri. **DESCRIPTION:** A medium size, side notched dart point with a short stem formed by corner notches. The base is straight. **I.D. KEY:** Straight base and double notches.

MESERVE - Early Archaic, 9500 - 4000 B. P.

(Also see Angostura, Dalton and Plainview)

Alibates dolomite

G6, $90-$175
OK

G8, $65-$125
OK

MESERVE (continued)

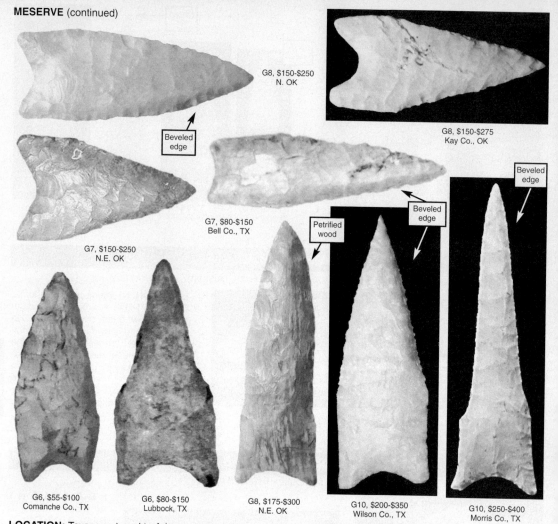

G8, $150-$250
N. OK

Beveled edge

G8, $150-$275
Kay Co., OK

Beveled edge

Beveled edge

G7, $80-$150
Bell Co., TX

Petrified wood

Beveled edge

G7, $150-$250
N.E. OK

G6, $55-$100
Comanche Co., TX

G6, $80-$150
Lubbock, TX

G8, $175-$300
N.E. OK

G10, $200-$350
Wilson Co., TX

G10, $250-$400
Morris Co., TX

LOCATION: Texas westward to Arizona and northward to Montana. **DESCRIPTION:** A medium size, auriculate point with a blade that is beveled on one side of each face. Beveling extends into the basal area. This type is the western form of *Dalton* points.

MID-BACK TANG - Late Archaic to Woodland, 4000 - 2000 B. P.

(Also see Base Tang Knife and Corner Tang)

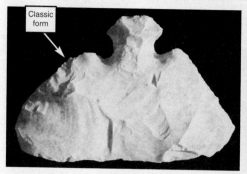

Classic form

G6, $200-$350
Coleman Co., TX

Leon River chert

G7, $250-$475
Coryell Co., TX.

622

MID-BACK TANG (continued)

LOCATION: Texas. **DESCRIPTION:** A variation of the corner tang knife with the hafting area occuring near the center of one side of the blade. A very rare type.

MIDLAND - Late Paleo, 11,000 - 10,000 B. P.

(Also see Angostura, Arkabutla, Clovis, Folsom, Goshen, Milnesand and Plainview)

Translucent

G6, $250-$400
Winkler Co., TX

G5, $175-$300
TX

G6, $175-$300
OK

Black chert

G5, $125-$200
Lubbock, TX

G5, $250-$400
Plainview, TX

Translucent flint

G7, $400-$700
Crane Co., TX

Tip wear

G6, $200-$350
TX

G6, $250-$400
Midland Co., TX

G7, $700-$1200
Andrews Co., TX

Ground basal sides

G5, $200-$350
Wise Co., TX

Tip impact

G5, $225-$400
Midland Co., TX

Collateral flaking

G10, $1500-$2500
Lubbock, TX

LOCATION: Texas northward to Canada. **DESCRIPTION:** An unfluted *Folsom*. A small to medium size, thin, unfluted lanceolate point with parallel to convex sides. Basal thinning is weak and the blades exhibit fine micro edgework. Bases usually have a shallow concavity and are ground most of the way to the tip.

MILNESAND - Late Paleo, 11,000 - 10,000 B. P.

(Also see Agate Basin, Angostura, Browns Valley, Firstview, Hell Gap and Rio Grande)

Edge impact

G5, $80-$150
W. TX

Ground base & sides

G7, $250-$400
Comanche Co., TX

G6, $175-$350
Bandera Co., TX

LOCATION: Texas, New Mexico, northward to Canada and Alaska. **DESCRIPTION:** A medium size unfluted lanceolate point that becomes thicker and wider towards the tip. The base is basically square and ground. Thicker than *Midland*. **I.D. KEY:** Square base and Paleo flaking.

SC

623

MILNESAND (continued)

Basal grinding to here

Impact fracture

Collateral flaking

G9, $500-$800
Bell Co., TX

G6, $350-$600
Zapata Co., TX

G10, $900-$1700
W. TX

G8, $350-$600
Red River, AR

G6, $250-$450
Cent. TX

MINERAL SPRINGS - Mississippian, 1300 - 1000 B. P.

(Also see Gahagan)

G9, $575-$1100
TX

IMPORTANT:
Both Mineral
Springs shown
half size

LOCATION: Texas, Oklahoma, Arkansas and Louisiana. **DESCRIPTION:** A broad, large size knife with recurved sides, sharp basal corners and a concave base. Some examples have notches at the basal corners.

G10+, $2500-$4000
Little River
Co., AR.
Outstanding quality.

MONTELL - Mid-Archaic to late Woodland, 5000 - 1000 B. P.

(Also see Ensor Split-Base and Uvalde)

G3, $4-$8
Val Verde Co., TX

G6, $15-$25
TX

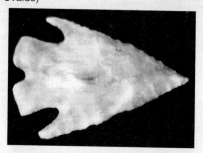

G8, $60-$100
Llano Co., TX

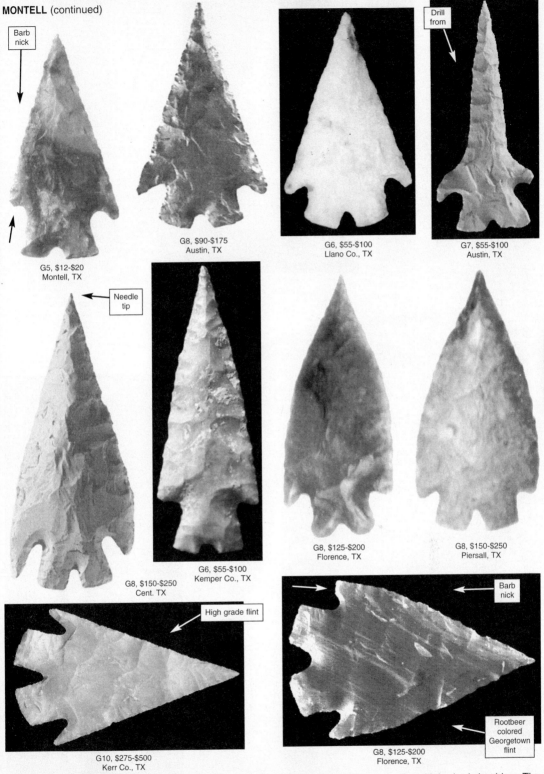

Barb
nick

G5, $12-$20
Montell, TX

G8, $90-$175
Austin, TX

Drill
from

G6, $55-$100
Llano Co., TX

G7, $55-$100
Austin, TX

Needle
tip

G8, $150-$250
Cent. TX

G6, $55-$100
Kemper Co., TX

G8, $125-$200
Florence, TX

G8, $150-$250
Piersall, TX

SC

High grade flint

G10, $275-$500
Kerr Co., TX

Barb
nick

Rootbeer
colored
Georgetown
flint

G8, $125-$200
Florence, TX

LOCATION: Midwestern states. **DESCRIPTION:** A small to medium size, bifurcated point with barbed shoulders. The ears are usually squared and some examples are beveled on one side of each face and are serrated. The deep basal notch "buck tooth" form is the preferred style. **I.D. KEY:** Square basal lobes.

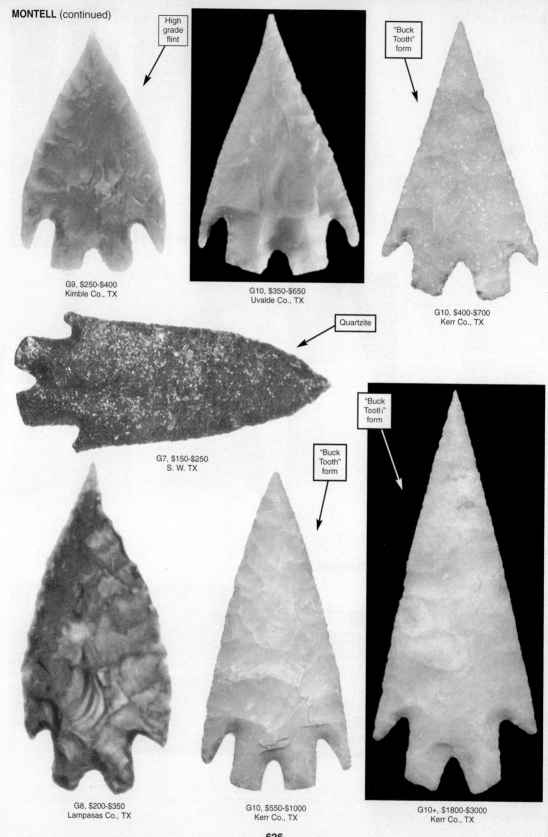

High grade flint

"Buck Tooth" form

G9, $250-$400
Kimble Co., TX

G10, $350-$650
Uvalde Co., TX

G10, $400-$700
Kerr Co., TX

Quartzite

G7, $150-$250
S. W. TX

"Buck Tooth" form

"Buck Tooth" form

G8, $200-$350
Lampasas Co., TX

G10, $550-$1000
Kerr Co., TX

G10+, $1800-$3000
Kerr Co., TX

MORAN - Woodland-Mississippian, 1200 - 600 B. P.

(Also see Bonham, Colbert, Rockwall, Sabinal and Scallorn)

G9, $30-$50
TX

G8, $65-$125
S. W. TX

LOCATION: Central Texas. **DESCRIPTION:** A small, thin, barbed arrow point with a narrow, rectangular base. Shoulder barbs are usually sharp. Very limited distributional area.

MORHISS - Late Archaic to Woodland, 4000 - 1000 B. P.

(Also see Adena, Bulverde, Carrolton and Morrill)

G3, $2-$4
Hill Co., TX

G3, $2-$4
Nuevo Leon, MX

LOCATION: Texas to Oklahoma. **DESCRIPTION:** A medium to large size, thick, long stemmed point with weak shoulders and a convex base.

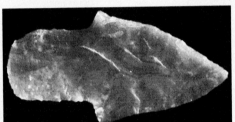

G5, $20-$35
Comanche Co., TX

G9, $125-$200
E. TX

G9, $175-$300
Calhoun Co., TX

SC

MORRILL - Woodland, 3000 - 1000 B. P.

(Also see Carrolton, Kent, Lange, Morhiss, Pontchartrain, Wells and Yarbrough)

G5, $8-$15
Coryell Co., TX

G5, $8-$15
TX

G6, $20-$35
Bowie, TX

LOCATION: Texas. **DESCRIPTION:** A medium size, thick, narrow, triangular point with weak, squared shoulders and a long rectangular stem. Bases are usually straight.

G6, $30-$50
Saline Co., AR

G7, $35-$60
Llano Co., TX

G8, $55-$100
Bell Co., TX

G9, $150-$250
Bell Co., TX

G9, $175-$300
TX

MORRIS - Mississippian, 1200 - 400 B. P.

(Also see Cuney, Friley and Sallisaw)

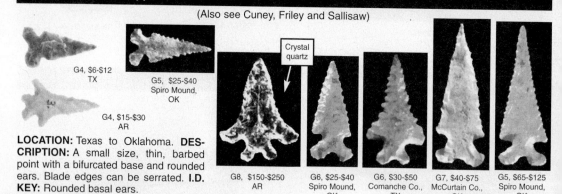

G4, $6-$12
TX

G5, $25-$40
Spiro Mound,
OK

G4, $15-$30
AR

Crystal
quartz

G8, $150-$250
AR

G6, $25-$40
Spiro Mound,
OK

G6, $30-$50
Comanche Co.,
TX

G7, $40-$75
McCurtain Co.,
OK

G5, $65-$125
Spiro Mound,
OK

LOCATION: Texas to Oklahoma. **DESCRIPTION:** A small size, thin, barbed point with a bifurcated base and rounded ears. Blade edges can be serrated. **I.D. KEY:** Rounded basal ears.

MORROW MOUNTAIN (See Hale and Peisker Diamond)

MOTLEY - Middle Archaic to Woodland, 4500 - 2500 B. P.

(Also see Cupp, Epps, Gibson, Grand and Kings)

LOCATION: Eastern Texas into Arkansas and Louisiana. **DESCRIPTION:** A medium to large size, expanded stemmed to widely corner notched point with strong barbs. The blade edges and the base are convex. **I.D. KEY:** Long, expanding base, convex base.

MOTLEY (continued)

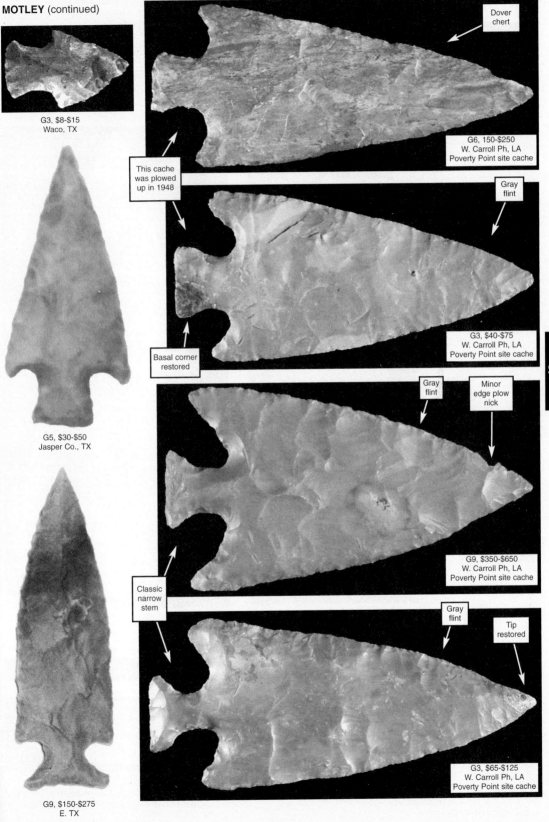

G3, $8-$15
Waco, TX

G5, $30-$50
Jasper Co., TX

G9, $150-$275
E. TX

Dover chert

G6, 150-$250
W. Carroll Ph, LA
Poverty Point site cache

This cache was plowed up in 1948

Gray flint

Basal corner restored

G3, $40-$75
W. Carroll Ph, LA
Poverty Point site cache

SC

Gray flint

Minor edge plow nick

G9, $350-$650
W. Carroll Ph, LA
Poverty Point site cache

Classic narrow stem

Gray flint

Tip restored

G3, $65-$125
W. Carroll Ph, LA
Poverty Point site cache

MOTLEY (continued)

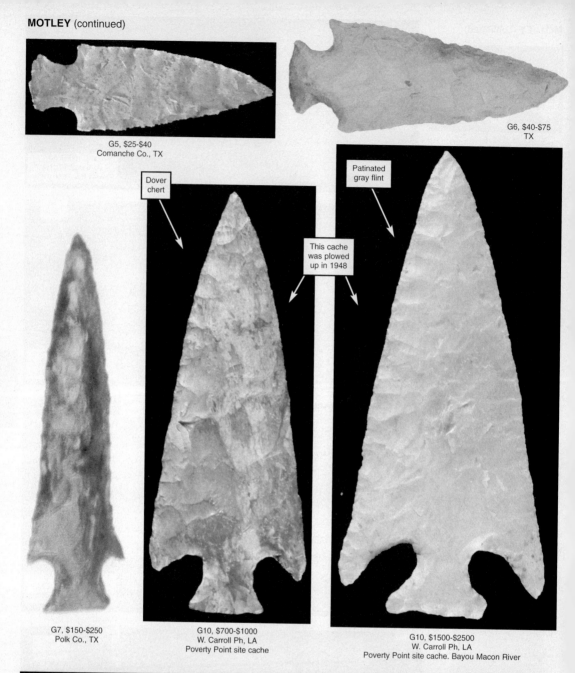

G5, $25-$40
Comanche Co., TX

G6, $40-$75
TX

Dover chert

Patinated gray flint

This cache was plowed up in 1948

G7, $150-$250
Polk Co., TX

G10, $700-$1000
W. Carroll Ph, LA
Poverty Point site cache

G10, $1500-$2500
W. Carroll Ph, LA
Poverty Point site cache. Bayou Macon River

NEOSHO - Late Archaic, 400 - 250 B. P.

(Also see Palmillas)

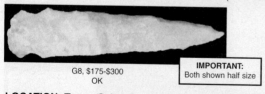

G8, $175-$300
OK

IMPORTANT:
Both shown half size

G7, $165-$300, Cache Riv., AR, Harrison form.

LOCATION: Texas, Colorado, Oklahoma, into Arkansas & Missouri. **DESCRIPTION:** A large size, narrow knife form with broad to narrow side notches and a short, convex to a long tapered stem that can be pointed to rounded. Related to the *Harahey* Knife.

630

G7, $350-$600
S.W. TX

NODENA - Mississippian to Historic, 600 - 400 B. P.

(Also see Dardanelle, Guerrero and Guntersville)

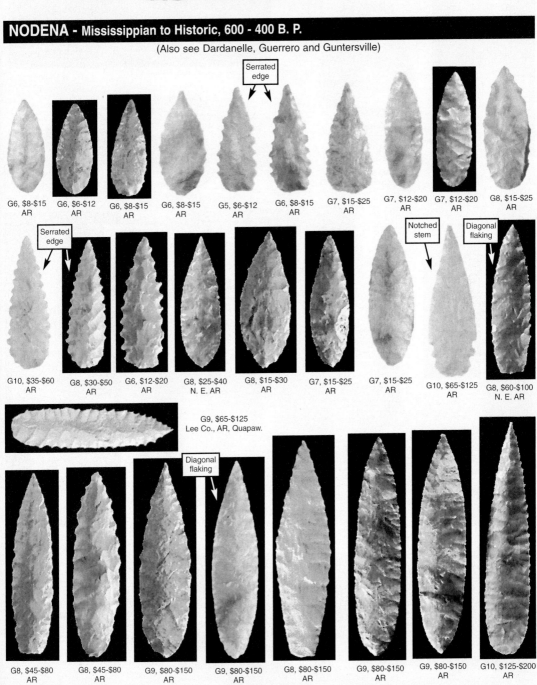

Serrated edge

G6, $8-$15
AR

G6, $6-$12
AR

G6, $8-$15
AR

G6, $8-$15
AR

G5, $6-$12
AR

G6, $8-$15
AR

G7, $15-$25
AR

G7, $12-$20
AR

G7, $12-$20
AR

G8, $15-$25
AR

Serrated edge

Notched stem

Diagonal flaking

SC

G10, $35-$60
AR

G8, $30-$50
AR

G6, $12-$20
AR

G8, $25-$40
N. E. AR

G8, $15-$30
AR

G7, $15-$25
AR

G7, $15-$25
AR

G10, $65-$125
AR

G8, $60-$100
N. E. AR

G9, $65-$125
Lee Co., AR, Quapaw.

Diagonal flaking

G8, $45-$80
AR

G8, $45-$80
AR

G9, $80-$150
AR

G9, $80-$150
AR

G8, $80-$150
AR

G9, $80-$150
AR

G9, $80-$150
AR

G10, $125-$200
AR

LOCATION: Arkansas and Tennessee. **DESCRIPTION:** A small to medium size, narrow, thin, elliptical shaped arrow point with a pointed to rounded base. Some examples have oblique, parallel flaking. Called *Tampa* in Florida. Used by the Quapaw Indians.

(Also see Bulverde, Lange, Travis and Zorra)

Beveled stem on opposite faces

G4, $8-$15
S. TX

G8, $20-$35
Coryell Co., TX

G7, $65-$125
Bell Co., TX

G7, $40-$75
TX

Rootbeer colored flint

Beveled stem on opposite faces

Beveled stem on opposite faces

G8, $125-$200
Williamson Co., TX

G7, $15-$175
Williamson Co., TX

G6, $65-$125
TX

G9, $165-$300
Bell Co., TX

Beveled stem on opposite faces

G9, $200-$350
Austin, TX

LOCATION: Texas to Oklahoma. **DESCRIPTION:** A medium to large size, stemmed point with a needle like point. Shoulders are tapered to rounded. The stem is unique in that it is steeply beveled on one side of each face. **I.D. KEY:** Beveled stem.

NOLAN (continued)

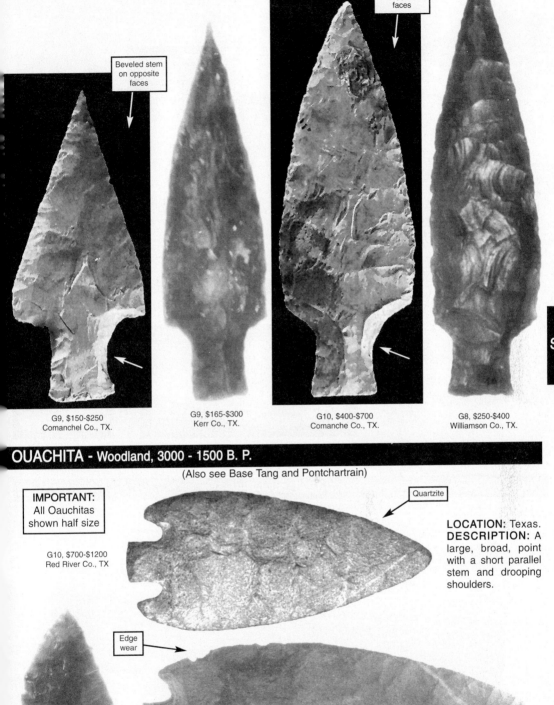

Beveled stem on opposite faces

Beveled stem on opposite faces

Beveled stem on opposite faces

SC

G9, $150-$250
Comanchel Co., TX.

G9, $165-$300
Kerr Co., TX.

G10, $400-$700
Comanche Co., TX.

G8, $250-$400
Williamson Co., TX.

OUACHITA - Woodland, 3000 - 1500 B. P.

(Also see Base Tang and Pontchartrain)

IMPORTANT:
All Ouachitas
shown half size

Quartzite

G10, $700-$1200
Red River Co., TX

LOCATION: Texas.
DESCRIPTION: A
large, broad, point
with a short parallel
stem and drooping
shoulders.

Edge wear

G6, $125-$200
TX

G9, $700-$1200
Tyler, TX

633

PAISANO - Mid-Archaic, 6000 - 5000 B. P.

(Also see Big Sandy, Dalton, San Patrice)

LOCATION: Texas. **DESCRIPTION:** A medium size point with broad side notches forming a squared to auriculate base that is concave. Some examples have notched/serrated edges.

Needle tip →

Notched edge →

G5, $15-$30
W. TX

G6, $30-$50
W. TX

G6, $25-$40
Pecos Co., TX

G7, $30-$50
Val Verde Co., TX

G8, $80-$150
Reeves Co., TX

G9, $150-$250
Val Verde Co., TX

G7, $30-$50
W. TX

G6, $25-$40
Comanche Co., TX

G8, $60-$100
McIntosh Co., OK

PALEO KNIFE - Transitional Paleo, 10,000 - 8000 B. P.

(Also see Scraper, Round-End Knife and Square Knife)

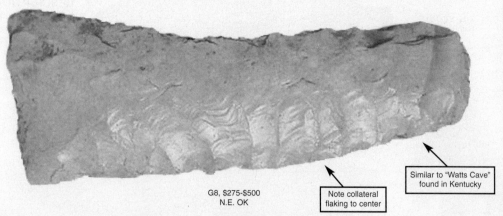

G8, $275-$500
N.E. OK

Note collateral flaking to center

Similar to "Watts Cave" found in Kentucky

LOCATION: All of North America. **DESCRIPTION:** A large size lanceolate blade finished with broad parallel flakes. These are found on Paleo sites and were probably used as knives.

634

PALEO KNIFE (continued)

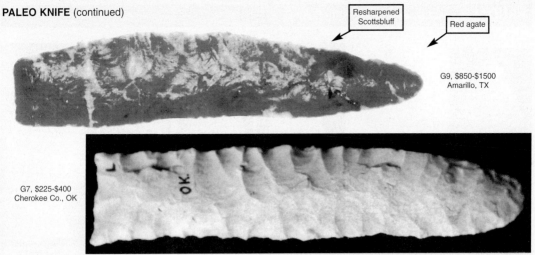

Resharpened
Scottsbluff

Red agate

G9, $850-$1500
Amarillo, TX

G7, $225-$400
Cherokee Co., OK

PALMILLAS - Middle to Late Archaic, 6000 - 3000 B. P.

(Also see Axtel, Godley and Williams)

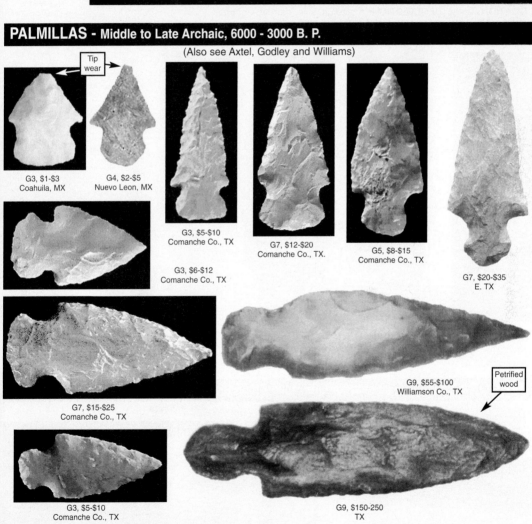

SC

Tip
wear

G3, $1-$3
Coahuila, MX

G4, $2-$5
Nuevo Leon, MX

G3, $5-$10
Comanche Co., TX

G3, $6-$12
Comanche Co., TX

G7, $12-$20
Comanche Co., TX.

G5, $8-$15
Comanche Co., TX

G7, $20-$35
E. TX

G7, $15-$25
Comanche Co., TX

G9, $55-$100
Williamson Co., TX

Petrified
wood

G3, $5-$10
Comanche Co., TX

G9, $150-250
TX

LOCATION: Texas to Oklahoma. **DESCRIPTION:** A small to medium size triangular point with a bulbous stem. Shoulders are prominent and can be horizontal to barbed or weak and tapered. Stems expand and are rounded. **I.D. KEY:** Bulbous stem.

PANDALE - Middle Archaic, 6000 - 3000 B. P.

(Also see Darl and Travis)

G6, $25-$40
Val Verde Co., TX

G4, $15-$25
W. TX

G6, $35-$50
Val Verde Co., TX

G6, $25-$40
Val Verde Co., TX

G6, $35-$65
Val Verde Co., TX

G8, $40-$75
Val Verde Co., TX

LOCATION: Texas. **DESCRIPTION:** A medium size, narrow, stemmed point or spike with a steepy beveled or torque blade. Some examples show oblique parallel flaking.

G9, $80-$150
Val Verde Co., TX

G7, $35-$60
Lynn Co., TX

G6, $65-$125
S. W. TX

G9, $125-$200
TX

G8, $90-$175
Val Verde Co., TX

PANDORA - Late Archaic to Woodland, 4000 - 1000 B. P.

(Also see Adena Blade, Friday, Kinney and Refugio)

G5, $12-$20
Val Verde Co., TX

G9, $35-$60
Comache Co., TX

Classic form

PANDORA (continued)

LOCATION: Central Texas southward. **DESCRIPTION:** A medium to large size, lanceolate blade with basically a straight base. Blade edges can be parallel to convex.

G8, $65-$125
Cent. TX

PEDERNALES - Middle Archaic to Woodland, 6000 - 2000 B. P.

(Also see Hoxie, Jetta, Langtry, Montell, Uvalde and Val Verde)

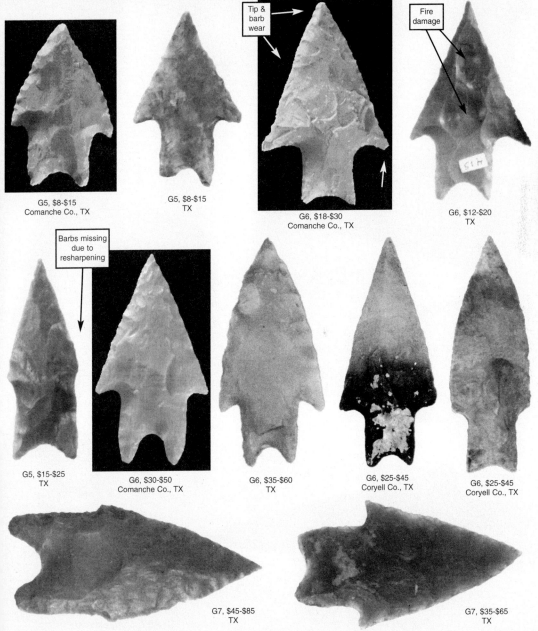

Tip & barb wear

Fire damage

G5, $8-$15
Comanche Co., TX

G5, $8-$15
TX

G6, $18-$30
Comanche Co., TX

G6, $12-$20
TX

SC

Barbs missing due to resharpening

G5, $15-$25
TX

G6, $30-$50
Comanche Co., TX

G6, $35-$60
TX

G6, $25-$45
Coryell Co., TX

G6, $25-$45
Coryell Co., TX

G7, $45-$85
TX

G7, $35-$65
TX

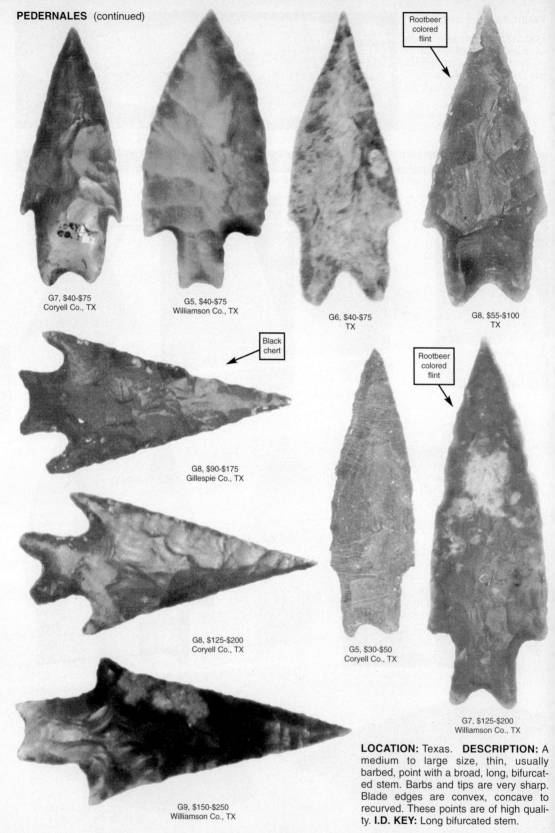

Rootbeer colored flint

G7, $40-$75
Coryell Co., TX

G5, $40-$75
Williamson Co., TX

G6, $40-$75
TX

G8, $55-$100
TX

Black chert

G8, $90-$175
Gillespie Co., TX

Rootbeer colored flint

G8, $125-$200
Coryell Co., TX

G5, $30-$50
Coryell Co., TX

G9, $150-$250
Williamson Co., TX

G7, $125-$200
Williamson Co., TX

LOCATION: Texas. **DESCRIPTION:** A medium to large size, thin, usually barbed, point with a broad, long, bifurcated stem. Barbs and tips are very sharp. Blade edges are convex, concave to recurved. These points are of high quality. **I.D. KEY:** Long bifurcated stem.

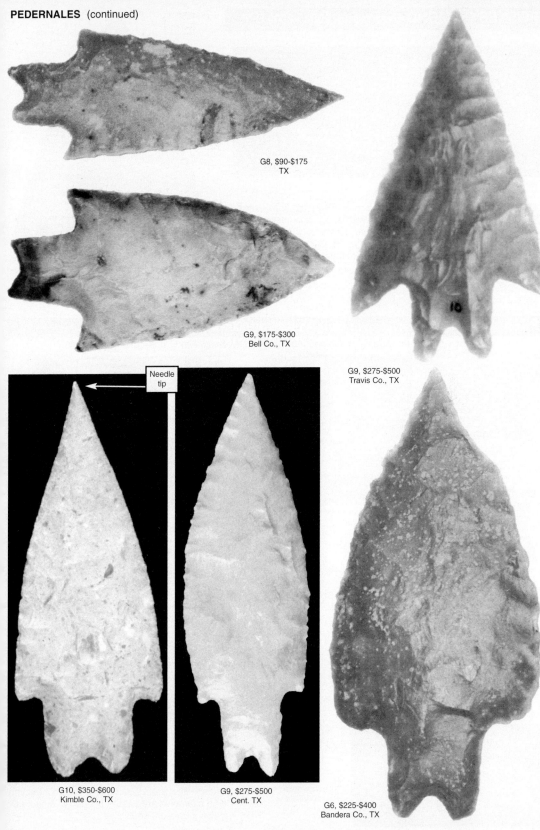

G8, $90-$175
TX

G9, $175-$300
Bell Co., TX

G9, $275-$500
Travis Co., TX

SC

Needle
tip

G10, $350-$600
Kimble Co., TX

G9, $275-$500
Cent. TX

G6, $225-$400
Bandera Co., TX

PEISKER DIAMOND - Woodland, 2500 - 2000 B. P.

(Also see Gary and Hale)

Translucent novaculite

Black chert

G7, $30-$50
Howard Co., AR

LOCATION: Illinois, Missouri, Arkansas, Kansas into Iowa.
DESCRIPTION: A large, broad blade with sharp shoulders and a short to moderate contracting base that comes to a point. Blade edges are recurved, convex or straight. Similar in form to the *Morrow Mountain* point found in the Southeast, but not as old. **I.D.KEY:** Contracted "v" base.

G9, $125-$200
OK

PELICAN - Transitional Paleo to Early Archaic, 10,000 - 8000 B. P.

(Also see Arkabutla, Coldwater, Golondrina, Hell Gap, Midland, Rio Grande and San Patrice)

Yellow jasper

Tan jasper

Petrified wood

G3, $35-$65
Vernon Parrish, LA

G8, $150-$250
Shelby Co., TX

G8, $80-$150
Sabine Co., TX

G7, $150-$250
Angelina Co., TX

G8, $125-$200
TX

G7, $80-$150
Newton Co., TX

Cobble chert

Red jasper

G6, $55-$100
E. TX

G6, $65-$125
Richland Parish, LA

G8, $125-$200
TX

G8, $150-$250
Vernon Parish, LA

Chert

G10, $200-$350
Sabine Co., TX

LOCATION: West Tennessee to Texas. **DESCRIPTION:** A short, broad, usually auriculate point with basal grinding. Shoulders taper into a long contracting stem. Some examples are basally thinned or fluted. **I.D. KEY:** Basal contraction, small size.

PELICAN (continued)

Thinned from base

Petrified wood

Cobble chert

G8, $150-$250
LA

G7, $125-$200
AR

G6, $65-$125
Catahoula Parish, LA

G5, $80-$150
Richland Parish, LA

PERDIZ - Mississippian, 1000 - 500 B. P.

(Also see Alba, Bassett, Bonham, Cliffton, Cuney, Hayes, Homan and Keota)

SC

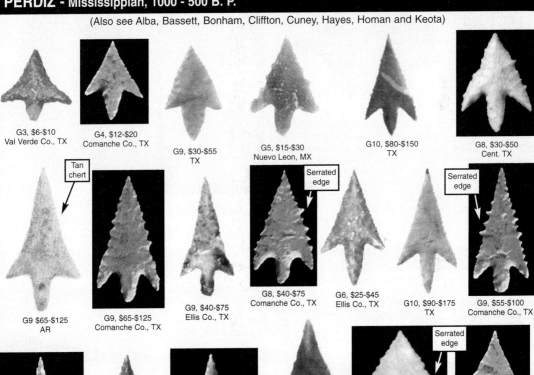

G3, $6-$10
Val Verde Co., TX

G4, $12-$20
Comanche Co., TX

G9, $30-$55
TX

G5, $15-$30
Nuevo Leon, MX

G10, $80-$150
TX

G8, $30-$50
Cent. TX

Tan chert

Serrated edge

Serrated edge

G9 $65-$125
AR

G9, $65-$125
Comanche Co., TX

G9, $40-$75
Ellis Co., TX

G8, $40-$75
Comanche Co., TX

G6, $25-$45
Ellis Co., TX

G10, $90-$175
TX

G9, $55-$100
Comanche Co., TX

Serrated edge

G7, $30-$50
E. TX

G6, $35-$65
Ellis Co., TX

G8, $30-$50
Comanche Co., TX

G10, $150-$250
Emanuel Co., TX

G8, $65-$125
TX

G10, $80-$150
Nueces Co., TX

LOCATION: Texas to Oklahoma. **DESCRIPTION:** A small to medium size, thin, narrow, triangular arrow point with pointed barbs and a long, pointed to near pointed stem. Some examples are serrated. Barbs and tips are sharp. **I.D. KEY:** Long pointed stem and barbs.

641

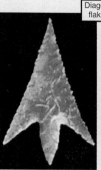

Diagonal flaking

G9, $175-$300
Emanuel Co., TX

G10, $250-$450
Emanuel Co., TX

G10, $250-$450
Comanche Co., TX

G9, $175-$300
Val Verde Co., TX

G9, $175-$300
Comanche Co., TX

G10, $300-$550
Emanuel Co., TX

PERFORATOR - Archaic to Mississippian, 9000 - 400 B. P.

(Also see Drill, Graver and Scraper)

G3, $1-$3
Nuevo Leon, MX

G5, $5-$10
Bell Co., TX

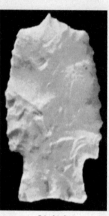

LOCATION: Archaic and Woodland sites everywhere. **DESCRIPTION:** A jabbing projection at the tip would qualify for the type. It is believed that *perforators* were used for tattooing, incising or to punch holes in leather or other materials or objects. Paleo peoples used *Gravers* for the same purpose. All Archaic and Woodland cultures converted their points into this type. Therefore, most point types could occur in this form.

G6, $8-$15
Comanche Co., TX.

G9, $65-$125
Kimble Co., TX.

PIKE COUNTY - Early Archaic, 10,000 - 9200 B. P.

(Also see Dalton and Plainview)

IMPORTANT:
All shown half size

G9, $250-$450
McIntosh Co., OK

Agate

G9+, $1700-$3000
McIntosh Co., OK

Classic form

G10, $800-$1500
AR

LOCATION: Oklahoma, Arkansas into Missouri and Illinois. **DESCRIPTION:** A large size, lanceolate blade with an eared, concave base. Basal area is ground. Related To *Dalton*. **I.D. KEY:** Fishtailed base.

PIPE CREEK - Mississippian, 1200 - 1000 B. P.

(Also see Corner Tang Knife)

PIPE CREEK (continued)

G9, $50-$90
TX

G8, $40-$75
S. W. TX

LOCATION: Texas into the southeastern states. **DESCRIPTION:** An unusual knife form having a single corner notch at one basal corner. The base is straight to slightly convex and can be lopsided. Perino and others speculate that this tool was used by early arrow makers in preparing feathers for use on arrow shafts. **I.D. KEY:** Single notch at base.

PLAINVIEW - Late Paleo, 11,250 - 9500 B. P.

(Also see Angostura, Barber, Brown's Valley, Clovis, Dalton, Frederick, Golondrina, Gosen and Midland)

G5, $55-$100
W. TX

G6, $90-$175
Comanche Co., TX

Impact fracture →

G6, $125-$225
E. TX

Tip wear →

G5, $55-$100
TX

SC

G8, $175-$300
Llano Co., TX

G7, $175-$300
Trinidad, TX

G8, $200-$350
Comanche Co., TX

G7, $200-$350
TX

G8, $200-$350
Irion Co., TX

G7, $125-$225
TX

← Resharpened several times

G8, $250-$400
N. OK

LOCATION: Mexico northward to Canada and Alaska. **DESCRIPTION:** A medium size, thin, lanceolate point with usually parallel sides and a concave base that is ground. Some examples are thinned or fluted and is believed to be related to the earlier *Clovis* and contemporary *Dalton* type. Flaking is of high quality and can be collateral to oblique transverse.

643

G7, $350-$600
N. OK

G7, $350-$600
Wilson Co., TX

G6, $175-$300
TX

G6, $150-$250
TX

G6, $175-$300
TX

Diagonal
flaking

G9, $800-$1500
Wilson Co., TX

Diagonal
flaking

G9, $175-$300
McIntosh Co., OK

Miniature
form

Side
wear

Fluted

Fluted

G7, $275-$500
Bell Co., TX

G8, $400-$700
Montgomery Co., TX

G8, $350-$650
TX

G9, $800-$1500
N. OK

G7, $800-$1500
Wilson Co., TX

POGO - Woodland to Mississippian, 2000 - 500 B. P.

(Also see Darl, Dickson, Hidden Valley, Lange, Morhiss, Pontchartrain and Travis)

LOCATION: Texas. **DESCRIPTION:** A medium to large size contracted stem point with small, tapered shoulders. The base is usually straight. Also known as *Morhiss.*

G9, $90-$175
Montgomery Co., TX

G10, $200-$350
Trinity Co., TX

PONTCHARTRAIN (Type I) - Late Archaic to Woodland, 3400 - 2000 B. P.

(Also see Lange, Morrill, Morhiss, Pogo and Travis)

G7, $15-$30
E. TX

LOCATION: Alabama to Texas. **DESCRIPTION:** A medium to large size, thick, narrow, stemmed point with weak, tapered or barbed shoulders. The stem is parallel sided with a convex to straight base. Some examples are finely serrated and are related and similar to the *Flint Creek* type.

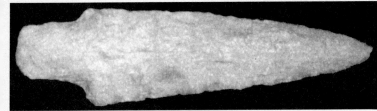

G9, $60-$100
E. TX

PONTCHARTRAIN (Type II) - Late Archaic to Woodland, 3400 - 2000 B. P.

(Also see Lange, Morrill and Morhiss)

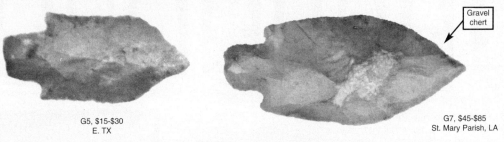

Gravel chert

G5, $15-$30
E. TX

G7, $45-$85
St. Mary Parish, LA

LOCATION: Alabama to Texas. **DESCRIPTION:** A medium to large size, thick, broad, stemmed point with barbed shoulders. The stem is parallel sided to tapered with a convex to straight base.

RED RIVER KNIFE - Early Archaic, 9500 - 7000 B. P.

(Also see Albany Knife, Alberta, Eden, Firstview and Scottsbluff)

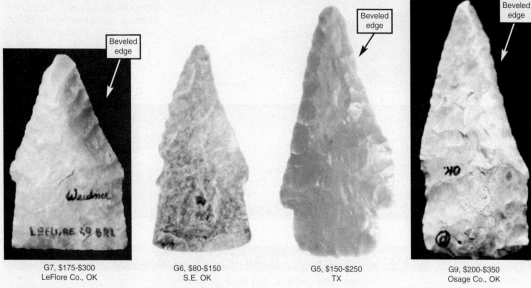

Beveled edge

Beveled edge

Beveled edge

Beveled edge

G7, $175-$300
LeFlore Co., OK

G6, $80-$150
S.E. OK

G5, $150-$250
TX

G9, $200-$350
Osage Co., OK

LOCATION: Texas to Colorado. **DESCRIPTION:** A medium size, asymmetrical blade with weak shoulders and a short, expanding to squared stem. Bases are straight to slightly convex. It has been reported that these knifes were made by the Cody Complex people from *Scottsbluff* points. Look for early parallel flaking and stem grinding.

REED - Woodland to Mississippian, 1500 - 500 B. P.

(Also see Haskell, Knight Island, Schustorm and Washita)

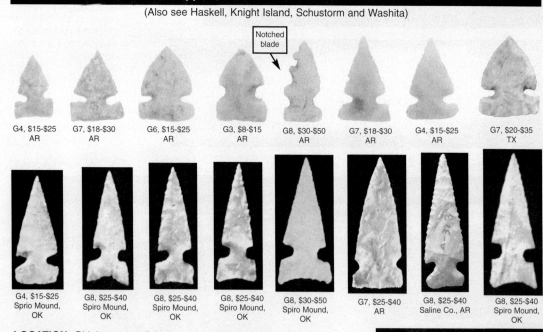

Notched blade

G4, $15-$25
AR

G7, $18-$30
AR

G6, $15-$25
AR

G3, $8-$15
AR

G8, $30-$50
AR

G7, $18-$30
AR

G4, $15-$25
AR

G7, $20-$35
TX

G4, $15-$25
Sprio Mound,
OK

G8, $25-$40
Spiro Mound,
OK

G8, $25-$40
Spiro Mound,
OK

G8, $25-$40
Spiro Mound,
OK

G8, $30-$50
Spiro Mound,
OK

G7, $25-$40
AR

G8, $25-$40
Saline Co., AR

G8, $25-$40
Spiro Mound,
OK

LOCATION: Oklahoma to Arkansas. **DESCRIPTION:** A small size, thin, triangular, side notched point with a straight to concave base. Rarely, serrations occur.

G8, $55-$100
AR

G9, $45-$80
Spiro Mound, OK

REFUGIO - Late Archaic, 4000 - 2000 B. P.

(Also see Gahagan, Pandora and Sabine)

LOCATION: S.W. to central Texas. **DESCRIPTION:** A medium to large size, narrow, lanceolate blade with a rounded base.

G6, $40-$75
Comanche Co., TX

RICE CONTRACTED STEM   (See Hidden Valley)

RICE LOBBED - Early Archaic, 9000 - 5000 B. P.

(Also see Uvalde)

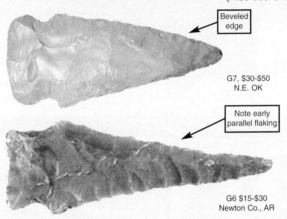

Beveled edge

G7, $30-$50
N.E. OK

Note early parallel flaking

G6 $15-$30
Newton Co., AR

G6, $20-$35
AR

LOCATION: Oklahoma to Missouri. **DESCRIPTION:** A medium to large size bifurcated to lobed base point with serrated blade edges. The base has a shallow indentation compared to the other bifurcated types. Shoulders are sharp and prominent. Called *Culpepper Bifurcate* in Virginia.

RICE SHALLOW SIDE NOTCHED - Woodland, 1600 - 1400 B. P.

(Also see Brewerton Eared & Jakie Stemmed)

G4, $6-$10
Saline Co., AR

G4, $6-$10
Saline Co., AR

LOCATION: Oklahoma to Missouri. **DESCRIPTION:** A medium size, broad point with shallow side notches and a convex base.

RIO GRANDE - Early Archaic, 7500 - 6000 B. P.

(Also see Agate Basin, Angostura, Hell Gap and Pelican)

LOCATION: New Mexico, Texas to Colorado. **DESCRIPTION:** A medium to large size, lanceolate point with tapered shoulders and a long parallel sided to contracting stem. The base can be straight, concave or convex. **I.D. KEY:** Long contracting stem.

SC

RIO GRANDE (continued)

Rootbeer colored flint

Ground basal area

G5, $55-$125
TX

G7, $55-$150
W. TX

G7, $80-$150
Bailey Co., TX

G7, $80-$150
Comanche Co., TX

G6, $65-$125
Uvalde, TX

Rootbeer colored flint

G8, $150-$275
W. TX

Ground basal area

G7, $90-$175
Amarillo, TX

ROCKWALL - Late Woodland, 1400 - 1000 B. P.

(Also see Alba, Colbert, Moran, Sabinal, Scallorn and Shumla)

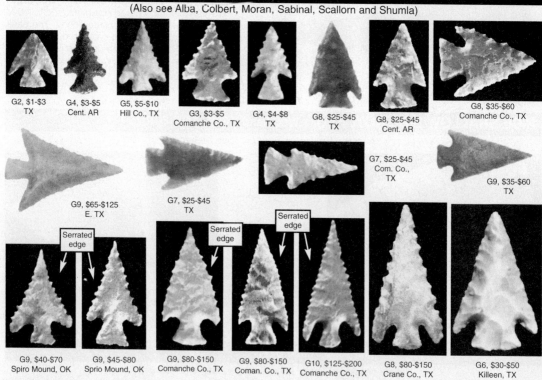

G2, $1-$3
TX

G4, $3-$5
Cent. AR

G5, $5-$10
Hill Co., TX

G3, $3-$5
Comanche Co., TX

G4, $4-$8
TX

G8, $25-$45
TX

G8, $25-$45
Cent. AR

G8, $35-$60
Comanche Co., TX

G9, $65-$125
E. TX

G7, $25-$45
TX

G7, $25-$45
Com. Co., TX

G9, $35-$60
TX

Serrated edge

G9, $40-$70
Spiro Mound, OK

G9, $45-$80
Sprio Mound, OK

Serrated edge

G9, $80-$150
Comanche Co., TX

Serrated edge

G9, $80-$150
Coman. Co., TX

G10, $125-$200
Comanche Co., TX

G8, $80-$150
Crane Co., TX

G6, $30-$50
Killeen, TX

LOCATION: Louisiana to Oklahoma. **DESCRIPTION:** A small, thin, triangular arrow point with corner notches. Shoulders are barbed and usually extend almost to the base. Many examples are serrated. Tips and barbs are sharp. **I.D. KEY:** Broad corner notches

RODGERS SIDE HOLLOWED - Early Archaic, 10,000 - 8000 B. P.

(Also see Arkabutla, Dalton, Golondrina, Pelican and San Patrice)

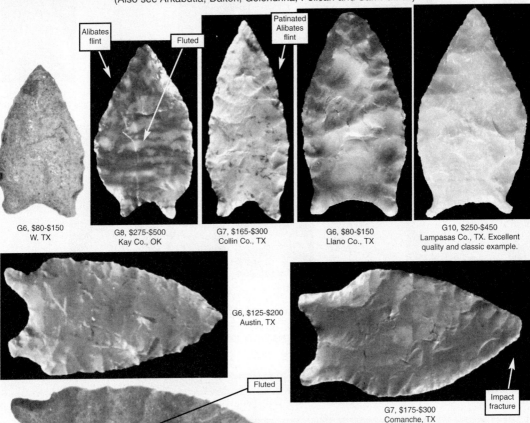

Alibates flint

Fluted

Patinated Alibates flint

G6, $80-$150
W. TX

G8, $275-$500
Kay Co., OK

G7, $165-$300
Collin Co., TX

G6, $80-$150
Llano Co., TX

G10, $250-$450
Lampasas Co., TX. Excellent quality and classic example.

G6, $125-$200
Austin, TX

SC

Fluted

G8, $200-$350
AR

G7, $175-$300
Comanche, TX

Impact fracture

LOCATION: Texas into Arkansas. **DESCRIPTION:** A medium size, broad, unfluted auriculate point which is a variant form of the *San Patrice* type. Also known as *Brazos Fishtail*. Base is concave and is ground. Some examples are fluted. **I.D. KEY:** Expanding auricles.

ROSS COUNTY   (See Clovis)

ROUND-END KNIFE - Historic 1000 - 300 B. P.

(Also see Archaic Knife, Paleo Knife and Square-End Knife)

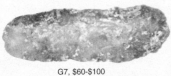

IMPORTANT:
Shown half size

G7, $60-$100
Victoria, TX

G9, $400-$700
Travis Co., TX

LOCATION: Texas. **DESCRIPTION:** A large, narrow knife form with rounded ends. This form was hafted along one side leaving a cutting edge on the opposite side.

SABINAL - Mississippian, 1000 - 700 B. P.

(Also see Bonham & Rockwall)

SABINAL (continued)

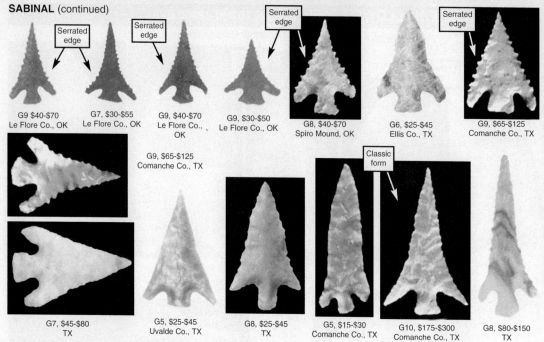

Serrated edge

Serrated edge

Serrated edge

Serrated edge

G9, $40-$70
Le Flore Co., OK

G7, $30-$55
Le Flore Co., OK

G9, $40-$70
Le Flore Co., OK

G9, $30-$50
Le Flore Co., OK

G8, $40-$70
Spiro Mound, OK

G6, $25-$45
Ellis Co., TX

G9, $65-$125
Comanche Co., TX

G9, $65-$125
Comanche Co., TX

Classic form

G7, $45-$80
TX

G5, $25-$45
Uvalde Co., TX

G8, $25-$45
TX

G5, $15-$30
Comanche Co., TX

G10, $175-$300
Comanche Co., TX

G8, $80-$150
TX

LOCATION: Southern Texas. **DESCRIPTION:** A small size, thin basal notched point with shoulders that flare outward and a short expanding to parallel sided stem. Bases are usually straight but can be slightly convex or concave. Blade edges are usually concave or recurved but can be straight. **I.D. KEY:** Flaring barbs.

SABINE - Late Archaic to Woodland, 4000 - 2000 B. P.

(Also see Covington, Friday, Gahagan, Refugio and San Gabriel)

G4, $12-$20
Comanche Co., TX

LOCATION: Mid- western states. **DESCRIPTION:** A medium to large size, thin, lanceolate blade with a contracting, rounded to "V" base. Blade edges can be serrated.

ST. CHARLES - Early Archaic, 9500 - 8000 B. P.

(Also see Gibson and Thebes)

LOCATION: East Texas Eastward. **DESCRIPTION:** Also known as *Dovetail* medium to large size, corner notched, dovetailed base point. The blade is beveled on one side of each face on resharpened examples. Bases are ground and can be fractured on both sides or center notched on some examples as found in Ohio. **I.D. KEY:** Dovetailed base, early flaking.

G6, $275-$500
Cherokee Co., TX

SAINT CHARLES (continued)

Rarity in area increases value

G9, $800-$1500
Cass Co., TX

G8, $200-$375
AR

G9, $450-$800
Taylor Co., TX

SALLISAW - Mississippian, 800 - 600 B. P.

(Also see Edwards, Haskell and Morris)

G8, $65-$125
Spiro Mound, OK

G9, $200-$350
Le Flore Co., OK

G10+, $600-$1000
Comanche Co., TX. very thin and excellent quality.

LOCATION: Oklahoma to Arkansas and Texas. **DESCRIPTION:** A small size, thin, serrated, barbed point with long drooping basal tangs and a deeply concave base. A very rare type. **I.D. KEY:** Long drooping ears.

SAN GABRIEL - Woodland 2000 - 1500 B. P.

(Also see Covington, Friday, Gahagan, Kinney and Sabine)

Edwards Plateau chert

G7, $125-$225
Comanche Co., TX

IMPORTANT:
All San Gabriels shown half size

LOCATION: Central Texas. **DESCRIPTION:** A large size, broad blade with a straight to slightly convex base.

G10, $350-$600
Kimble Co., TX

G6, $125-$200
TX

G6, $175-$300
Zapata Co., TX

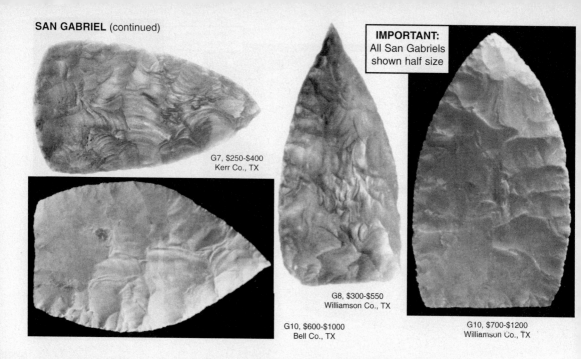

SAN GABRIEL (continued)

IMPORTANT:
All San Gabriels
shown half size

G7, $250-$400
Kerr Co., TX

G8, $300-$550
Williamson Co., TX

G10, $600-$1000
Bell Co., TX

G10, $700-$1200
Williamson Co., TX

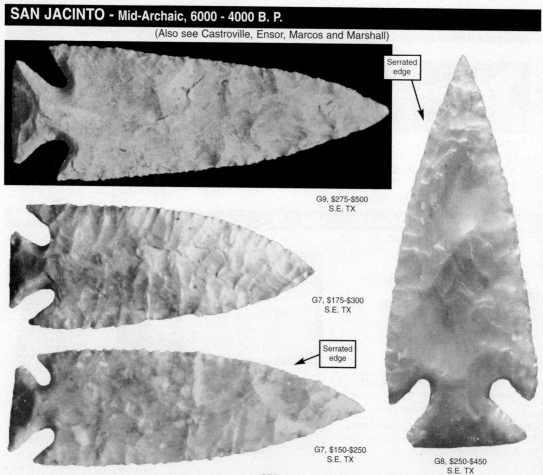

SAN JACINTO - Mid-Archaic, 6000 - 4000 B. P.

(Also see Castroville, Ensor, Marcos and Marshall)

Serrated edge

G9, $275-$500
S.E. TX

G7, $175-$300
S.E. TX

Serrated edge

G7, $150-$250
S.E. TX

G8, $250-$450
S.E. TX

SAN JACINTO (continued)

G8, $250-$450
S.E. TX

LOCATION: Texas S.E. Gulf Coast and Coastal Plain areas. **DESCRIPTION:** A medium to large size, thin, corner notched knife with a straight base. Notches are deep and angular creating a broad expanding stem. Base width is less than shoulder width. Some examples are finely serrated. **I.D. KEY:** Deep corner notches. Named by Dwain Rogers.

SAN PATRICE-GENEILL - Early Archaic, 10,000 - 8000 B. P.

(Also see Dalton, Palmer, Pelican and Rodgers Side Hollowed)

Red chert

G5, $60-$100
AR

G8, $175-$300
TX

LOCATION: Louisiana to Oklahoma. **DESCRIPTION:** A scarce, small size, thin, stemmed point with a short, expanding concave base that forms small ears. Shoulders can be strong and sharp. Some examples are thinned from the base. Basal area is usually ground. **I.D. KEY:** Extended auriculate base and small size.

SC

SAN PATRICE-HOPE VARIETY - Early Archaic, 10,000 - 8000 B. P.

(Also see Coldwater, Dalton, Hinds, Palmer, Pelican, Rodgers Side Hollowed and Zephyr)

Yellow jasper

Petrified wood

Petrified wood

G6, $55-$100
Cent. TX

G8, $55-$100
E. TX

G8, $55-$100
E. TX

G7, $90-$175
Angelina Co., TX

G7, $150-$250
Gregg Co., TX

Petrified palmwood

Petrified wood

Deeply fluted

Translucent novaculite

G8, $150-$250
Jasper Co., TX

G7, $125-$200
Jasper Co., TX

G8, $150-$250
Harris Co., TX

LOCATION: Louisiana to Oklahoma. **DESCRIPTION:** A small size, thin, auriculate point with a concave base. Some examples are thinned from the base. Basal area is longer than the "St. Johns" variety and is usually ground. **I.D. KEY:** Extended auriculate base and small size.

653

SAN PATRICE-HOPE (continued)

Petrified palmwood

G8, $150-$275
Vernon Parish, LA

G8, $150-$275
Vernon Parish, LA

Petrified palmwood

Deeply fluted

G10, $200-$350
N. E. TX

G8, $175-$300
Angelina Co., TX

G6, $150-$250
E. TX

G10, $275-$500
Lufkin, TX

Petrified palmwood

SAN PATRICE-KEITHVILLE - Early Archaic, 10,000 - 8000 B. P.

(Also see Albany Knife, Dalton, Palmer, Pelican and Rodgers Side Hollowed)

Serrated edge

Serrated edge

G2, $8-$15
Val Verde Co., TX

G6, $30-$50
E. TX

G4, $15-$30
Val Verde Co., TX

G7, $80-$150
Lufkin, TX

G7, $45-$80
E. TX

G5, $35-$60
Val Verde Co., TX

LOCATION: Louisiana to Oklahoma. **DESCRIPTION:** A small size, thin, auriculate to side notched point forming a lobed base. Basal area is usually ground. Blade edges can be serrated. **I.D. KEY:** Lobbed base.

Yellow jasper

G6, $55-$100
Lincoln Parish, LA

G9, $125-$200
Montgomery Co,, TX

G7, $55-$100
Angelina Co., TX

Novaculite

G8, $150-$250
N. E. TX

G7, $125-$200
AR

G9, 175-$300
Harris Co., TX

(Also see Dalton, Palmer, Pelican and Rodgers Side Hollowed)

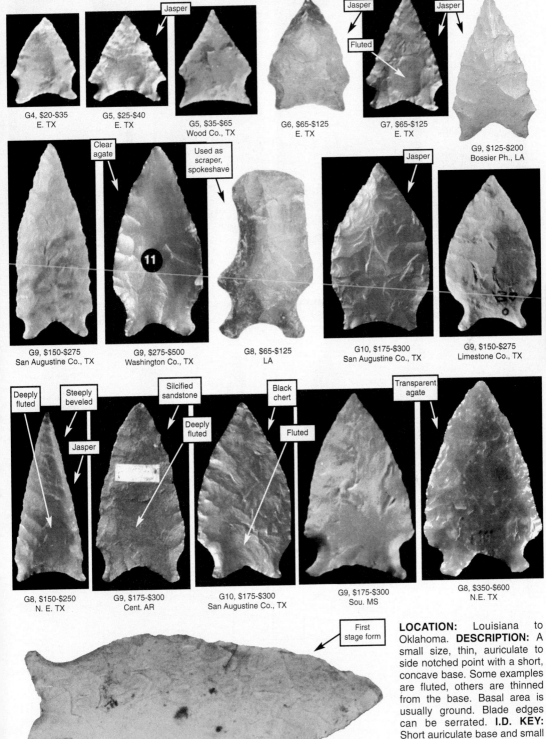

Jasper

G4, $20-$35
E. TX

G5, $25-$40
E. TX

G5, $35-$65
Wood Co., TX

G6, $65-$125
E. TX

Jasper

Jasper

Fluted

G7, $65-$125
E. TX

Jasper

G9, $125-$200
Bossier Ph., LA

Clear agate

Used as scraper, spokeshave

Jasper

G9, $150-$275
San Augustine Co., TX

G9, $275-$500
Washington Co., TX

G8, $65-$125
LA

G10, $175-$300
San Augustine Co., TX

G9, $150-$275
Limestone Co., TX

SC

Deeply fluted

Steeply beveled

Silcified sandstone

Deeply fluted

Black chert

Fluted

Transparent agate

Jasper

G8, $150-$250
N. E. TX

G9, $175-$300
Cent. AR

G10, $175-$300
San Augustine Co., TX

G9, $175-$300
Sou. MS

G8, $350-$600
N.E. TX

First stage form

G5, $175-$300
AR

LOCATION: Louisiana to Oklahoma. **DESCRIPTION:** A small size, thin, auriculate to side notched point with a short, concave base. Some examples are fluted, others are thinned from the base. Basal area is usually ground. Blade edges can be serrated. **I.D. KEY:** Short auriculate base and small size.

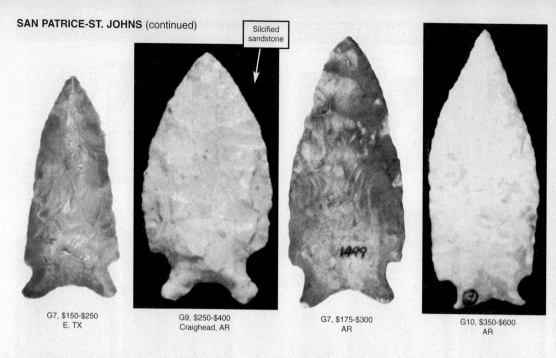

Silcified sandstone

G7, $150-$250
E. TX

G9, $250-$400
Craighead, AR

G7, $175-$300
AR

G10, $350-$600
AR

SAN SABA - Woodland, 3000 - 2000 B. P.

(Also see Base Tang, Corner Tang and Mid-Back Tang)

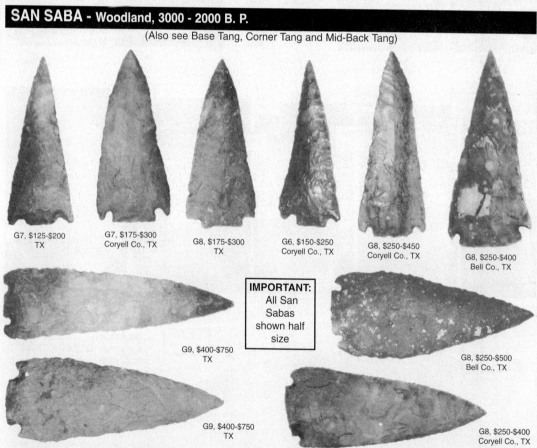

G7, $125-$200
TX

G7, $175-$300
Coryell Co., TX

G8, $175-$300
TX

G6, $150-$250
Coryell Co., TX

G8, $250-$450
Coryell Co., TX

G8, $250-$400
Bell Co., TX

G9, $400-$750
TX

IMPORTANT:
All San Sabas shown half size

G8, $250-$500
Bell Co., TX

G9, $400-$750
TX

G8, $250-$400
Coryell Co., TX

LOCATION: Texas. **DESCRIPTION:** A large size, triangular blade with shallow, narrow, basal notches. Bases usually are straight. **I.D. KEY:** Small basal notches.

SAVAGE CAVE - Early to Middle Archaic, 7000 - 4000 B. P.

(Also see Big Sandy, Cache River, Hemphill, Hickory Ridge and White River)

G7, $15-$25
N.E. AR

G6, $8-$15
Jonesboro, AR

G3, $3-$6
N.E. AR

LOCATION: Kentucky, Tennessee to Arkansas. **DESCRIPTION:** A medium to large size, broad, side notched point that is usually serrated. Bases are generally straight but can be slightly concave or convex.

SAVANNAH RIVER - Middle Archaic to Woodland, 5000 - 2000 B. P.

(Also see Johnson)

G5, $12-$20
Jonesboro, AR

G5, $15-$25
Jonesboro, AR

LOCATION: Arkansas to Eastern states. **DESCRIPTION:** A medium to large size, straight to contracting stemmed point with a Straight or concave to bifurcated base. The shoulders are tapered to square. The stems are narrow to broad. Believed to be related to the earlier *Stanly* point. **I.D. KEY:** Broad, concave base.

G5, $20-$35
Jonesboro, AR

SC

SCALLORN - Woodland to Mississippian, 1300 - 500 B. P.

(Also see Alba, Catahoula, Cuney, Ellis, Homan, Keota, Rockwall, Sequoyah and Steiner)

Tan chert

G6, $15-$25
TX

G6, $15-$25
Comanche
Co., TX

G6, $15-$25
Comanche
Co., TX

G6, $15-$25
Comanche
Co., TX

G8, $25-$45
Comanche
Co., TX

G6, $20-$35
Comanche
Co., TX

G8, $25-$45
AR

G8, $25-$45
AR

G9, $25-$45
TX

LOCATION: Texas, Oklahoma. **DESCRIPTION:** A small size, corner notched arrow point with a flaring stem. Bases and blade edges are straight, concave or convex and many examples are serrated. Not to be confused with *Sequoyah* not found in Texas. **I.D. KEY:** Small corner notched point with sharp barbs and tip.

657

SCALLORN (continued)

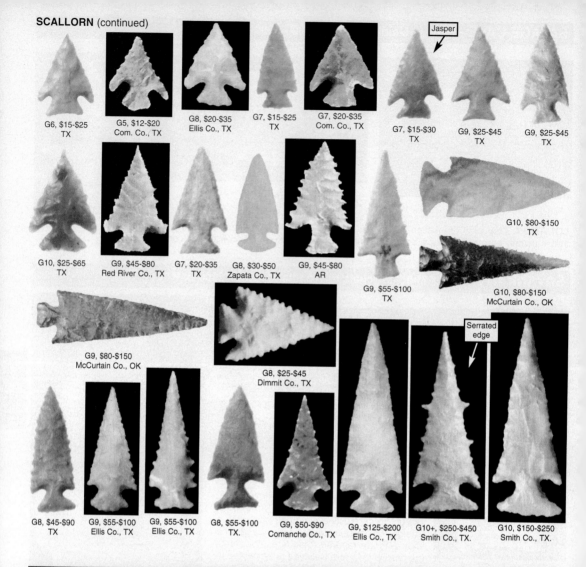

G6, $15-$25
TX

G5, $12-$20
Com. Co., TX

G8, $20-$35
Ellis Co., TX

G7, $15-$25
TX

G7, $20-$35
Com. Co., TX

Jasper

G7, $15-$30
TX

G9, $25-$45
TX

G9, $25-$45
TX

G10, $25-$65
TX

G9, $45-$80
Red River Co., TX

G7, $20-$35
TX

G8, $30-$50
Zapata Co., TX

G9, $45-$80
AR

G9, $55-$100
TX

G10, $80-$150
TX

G10, $80-$150
McCurtain Co., OK

G9, $80-$150
McCurtain Co., OK

G8, $25-$45
Dimmit Co., TX

Serrated
edge

G8, $45-$90
TX

G9, $55-$100
Ellis Co., TX

G9, $55-$100
Ellis Co., TX

G8, $55-$100
TX.

G9, $50-$90
Comanche Co., TX

G9, $125-$200
Ellis Co., TX

G10+, $250-$450
Smith Co., TX.

G10, $150-$250
Smith Co., TX.

SCHUSTORM - Mississippian, 1200 - 600 B. P.

(Also see Knight Island, Reed and Washita)

G9, $60-$100
AR., Bowman site.

LOCATION: Arkansas into Texas. **DESCRIPTION:** A small size, thin, triangular arrow point with small, weak side notches high up from the base. The base is concave **I.D. KEY:** Weak notches.

SCOTTSBLUFF I - Early Archaic, 10,000 - 8000 B. P.

(Also see Alberta, Cody Knife, Eden, Hardin, Holland and Red River)

LOCATION: Louisiana to New Mexico to Canada and the Northwest coast. **DESCRIPTION:** A medium to large size, broad stemmed point with convex to parallel sides and weak shoulders. The stem is parallel to expanding. The basal area is ground. Most examples have horizontal to oblique parallel flaking and are of high quality and thinness. Made by the Cody Complex people. Believed to have evolved into *Hardin* in later times. **I.D. KEY:** Broad stem, weak shoulders, collateral flaking.

Resharpened many times removing the shoulders

Tip wear

G3, $40-$75
Sabine Co., TX

G3, $55-$100
Lufkin, TX

G4, $55-$100
TX

G6, $80-$150
E. TX

SC

G7, $175-$300
TX

G7, $175-$300
Sabine Co., TX

G9, $250-$450
McIntosh Co., OK

G9, $400-$750
McLennan Co., TX

G5, $125-$200
Eufaula Lake, OK

Tip wear

Ground basal area

G8, $225-$400
Upshur Co., TX

G6, $200-$375
E. TX

G8, $225-$400
Sabine Co., TX

G7, $275-$500
Toledo Bend, TX

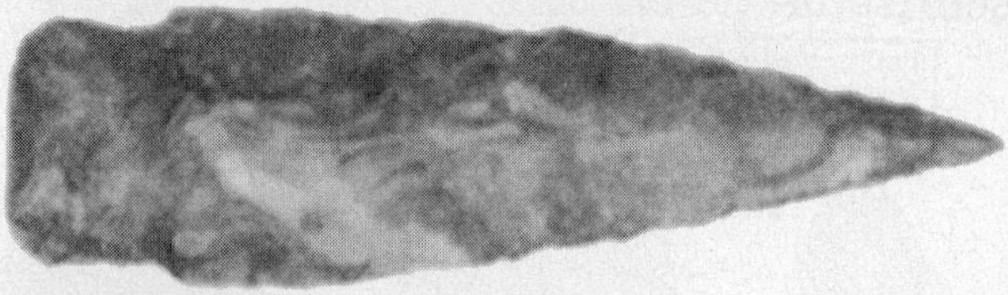

G7, $125-$200
Coryell Co., TX

G8, $500-$900
OK

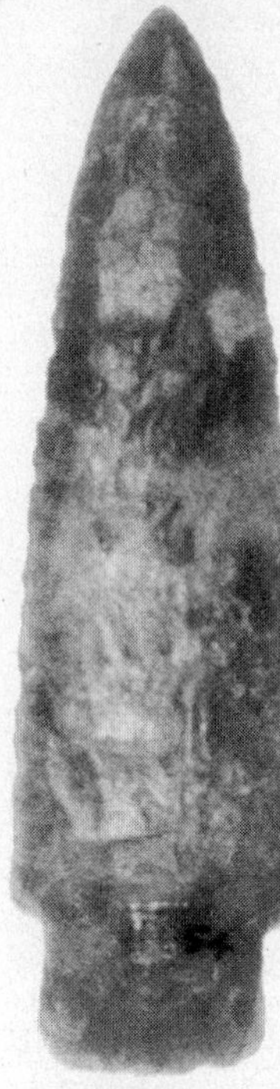

G9, $500-$900
Shelby Co., TX

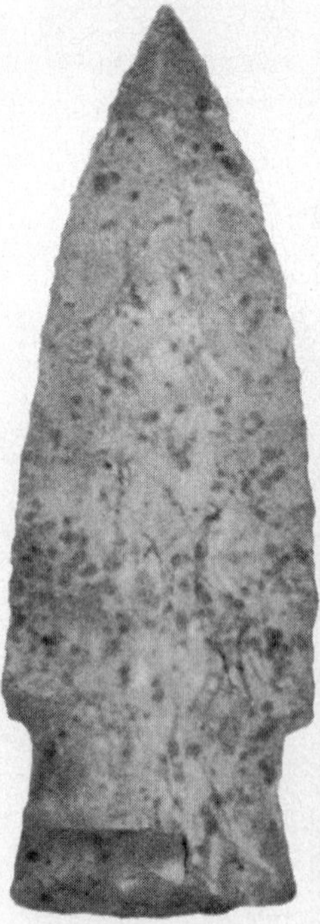

Ground basal area

Collateral flaking

Minor base nick

G9, $550-$1000
Sabine Co., TX

G8, $1200-$2000
Anderson Co., TX

G9, $2500-$4000
Polk Co., TX

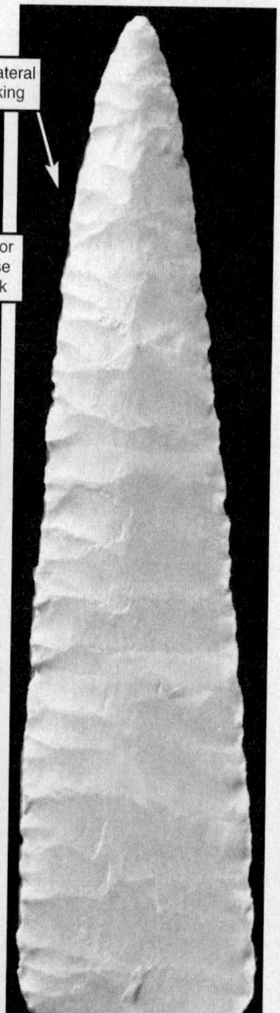

G9, $3000-$5000+
N. E. TX

660

(Also see Alberta, Cody Knife, Eden, Hardin, Holland and Red River)

G3, $80-$150
Sabine Co., TX

G4, $90-$175
Harrison Co., TX

G6, $150-$250
Sabine Co., TX

G4, $90-$175
TX

G7, $175-$300
Montgomery Co., TX

G5, $150-$275
E. TX

G7, $275-$500
Tulsa Co., OK

SC

Ground basal area

Edwards Plateau flint

G8, $450-$800
McLennan Co., TX

G7, $275-$500
Bossier Parish., LA

G7, $350-$650
Montgomery Co., TX

G8, $450-$800
AR

LOCATION: Louisiana to New Mexico to Canada to the Northwest coast. **DESCRIPTION:** A medium to large size, broad stemmed point with convex to parallel sides and stronger shoulders than type I. The stem is parallel sided to slightly expanding. The hafting area is ground. Most examples have horizontal to oblique parallel flaking and are of high quality and thinness. Made by the Cody Complex people. **I.D. KEY:** Stronger shoulders.

Basal corner wear

G7, $200-$375
Waco, TX

G8, $450-$800
Montgomery Co., TX

G9, $900-$1600
Angelina Co., TX

G8, $800-$1500
N. E. OK

SCRAPER - Paleo to Archaic, 11,500 - 5000 B. P.

(Also see Drill, Graver, Perforator and Paleo Knife)

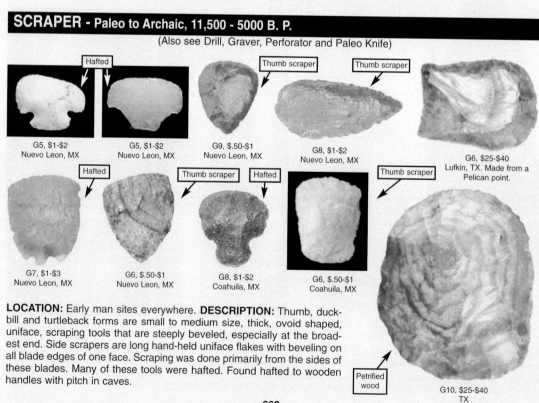

Hafted

G5, $1-$2
Nuevo Leon, MX

G5, $1-$2
Nuevo Leon, MX

Thumb scraper

G9, $.50-$1
Nuevo Leon, MX

Thumb scraper

G8, $1-$2
Nuevo Leon, MX

Thumb scraper

G6, $25-$40
Lufkin, TX. Made from a
Pelican point.

Hafted

G7, $1-$3
Nuevo Leon, MX

Thumb scraper

G6, $.50-$1
Nuevo Leon, MX

Hafted

G8, $1-$2
Coahuila, MX

Thumb scraper

G6, $.50-$1
Coahuila, MX

Thumb scraper

Petrified wood

G10, $25-$40
TX

LOCATION: Early man sites everywhere. **DESCRIPTION:** Thumb, duck-bill and turtleback forms are small to medium size, thick, ovoid shaped, uniface, scraping tools that are steeply beveled, especially at the broadest end. Side scrapers are long hand-held uniface flakes with beveling on all blade edges of one face. Scraping was done primarily from the sides of these blades. Many of these tools were hafted. Found hafted to wooden handles with pitch in caves.

SEARCY - Early to Middle Archaic, 7000 - 5000 B. P.

(Also see Coryell, Dalton, Early Stemmed, Hoxie, Rio Grande, Victoria & Wells)

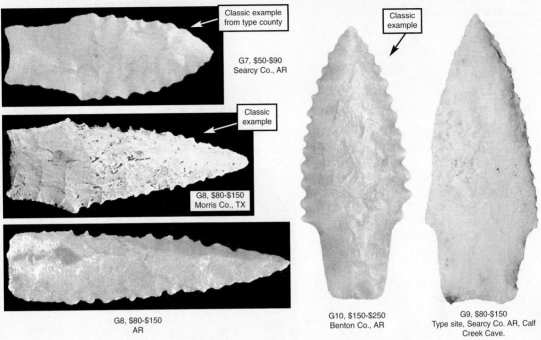

Classic example from type county

G7, $50-$90
Searcy Co., AR

Classic example

G8, $80-$150
Morris Co., TX

G8, $80-$150
AR

Classic example

G10, $150-$250
Benton Co., AR

G9, $80-$150
Type site, Searcy Co. AR, Calf Creek Cave.

SC

LOCATION: Texas, Oklahoma to Missouri to Tennessee. **DESCRIPTION:** A small to medium size, thin, lanceolate point with a squared hafting area. Blade edges are serrated. The base is straight to concave and is usually ground. **I.D. KEY:** Long squared stem, serrations.

SEQUOYAH - Mississippian, 1000 - 600 B. P.

(Also see Alba, Blevins, Hayes, Homan, Livermore, Scallorn and Steiner)

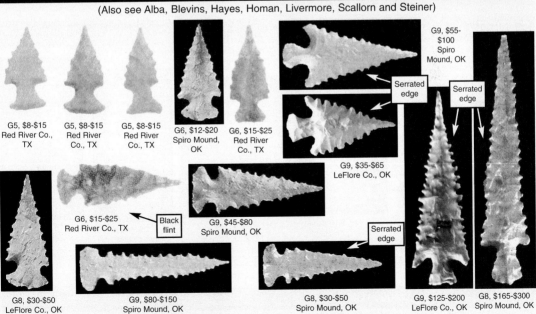

G5, $8-$15
Red River Co.,
TX

G5, $8-$15
Red River
Co., TX

G5, $8-$15
Red River
Co., TX

G6, $12-$20
Spiro Mound,
OK

G6, $15-$25
Red River
Co., TX

G9, $55-$100
Spiro Mound, OK

Serrated edge

Serrated edge

G9, $35-$65
LeFlore Co., OK

G6, $15-$25
Red River Co., TX

Black flint

G9, $45-$80
Spiro Mound, OK

Serrated edge

G8, $30-$50
LeFlore Co., OK

G9, $80-$150
Spiro Mound, OK

G8, $30-$50
Spiro Mound, OK

G9, $125-$200
LeFlore Co., OK

G8, $165-$300
Spiro Mound, OK

LOCATION: IL, OK, AR, MO. **DESCRIPTION:** A small size, thin, narrow point with coarse serrations and an expanded, bulbous stem. Believed to have been made by Caddo and other people. Named after the famous Cherokee of the same name. **I.D. KEY:** Bulbous base, coarse serrations.

SHUMLA - Woodland, 3000 - 1000 B. P.

(Also see Bell, Calf Creek, Marshall and Rockwall)

LOCATION: Louisiana to Texas. **DESCRIPTION:** A medium size, expanded stemmed point with several barbs occurring above the shoulders. **I.D. KEY:** Barbed edges.

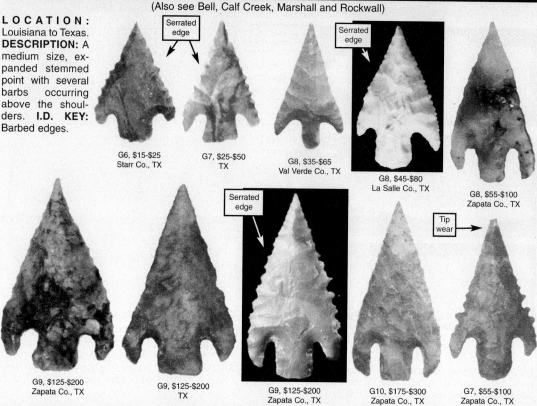

Serrated edge

Serrated edge

Serrated edge

Tip wear

G6, $15-$25
Starr Co., TX

G7, $25-$50
TX

G8, $35-$65
Val Verde Co., TX

G8, $45-$80
La Salle Co., TX

G8, $55-$100
Zapata Co., TX

G9, $125-$200
Zapata Co., TX

G9, $125-$200
TX

G9, $125-$200
Zapata Co., TX

G10, $175-$300
Zapata Co., TX

G7, $55-$100
Zapata Co., TX

LOCATION: Texas to Oklahoma. **DESCRIPTION:** A small size, basal notched point with convex, straight or recurved sides. Barbs turn in towards and usually extend to the base.

SINNER - Woodland, 3000 - 2000 B. P.

(Also see Charcos, Duran, Evans and Huffaker)

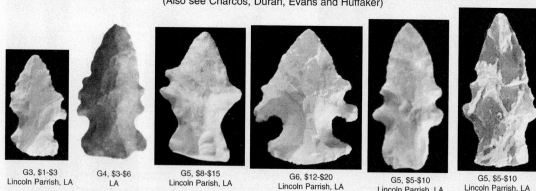

G3, $1-$3
Lincoln Parrish, LA

G4, $3-$6
LA

G5, $8-$15
Lincoln Parish, LA

G6, $12-$20
Lincoln Parrish, LA

G5, $5-$10
Lincoln Parrish, LA

G5, $5-$10
Lincoln Parrish, LA

LOCATION: Louisianna to Texas. **DESCRIPTION:** A medium size, expanded stemmed point with several barbs occurring above the shoulders. **I.D. KEY:** Barbed edges.

SMITH - Late Archaic, 4000 - 3000 B. P.

(Also see Bell, Castroville, Calf Creek, Little River, San Saba, Shumla)

LOCATION: Arkansas into Missouri and Illinois. **DESCRIPTION:** A very large size, broad, point with long parallel shoulders and a squared to slightly expanding base. Some examples may appear to be basally notched due to the long barbs.

SMITH (continued)

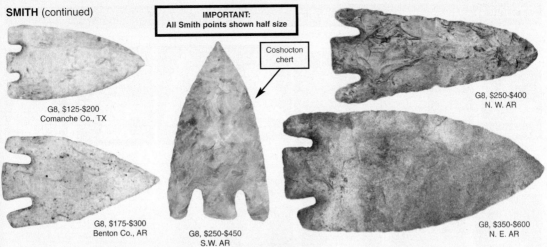

> **IMPORTANT:**
> All Smith points shown half size

G8, $125-$200
Comanche Co., TX

G8, $250-$400
N. W. AR

Coshocton chert

G8, $175-$300
Benton Co., AR

G8, $250-$450
S.W. AR

G8, $350-$600
N. E. AR

SPOKESHAVE - Woodland, 3000 -1500 B. P.

(Also see Scraper)

LOCATION: Tennessee, Kentucky, Ohio, Indiana into Texas. **DESCRIPTION:** A medium to large size stemmed tool used for scraping. The blade is asymmetrical with one edge convex or notched and the other concave.

G10, $65-$120
TX

SC

STARR - Mississippian to Historic, 1000 - 250 B. P.

(Also see Maud and Talco)

G5, $20-$35
Starr Co., TX

G9, $40-$75
TX

G8, $55-$100
L. Amstad, TX

G7, $40-$75
S. W. TX

G7, $35-$60
TX

G8, $55-$100
Val Verde Co., TX

G10, $55-$100
E. TX

G9, $55-$100
L. Amstad, TX

Needle tip

G9, $70-$135
TX

G7, $40-$75
TX

G8, $55-$100
Val Verde Co., TX

G10, $80-$150
Nueces Co., TX

G10, $125-$200
Zapata Co., TX

LOCATION: Texas westward. **DESCRIPTION:** A small size, thin, triangular point with a "V" base concavity. Blade edges can be concave to straight. An eccentric form of Starr is call "New Form" found near the Mexican border. **I.D. KEY:** "V" base.

STEINER - Mississippian, 1000 - 400 B. P.

(Also see Friley, Scallorn and Sequoyah)

Notched edge

G4, $8-$15
Comanche Co.,
TX

G3, $8-$15
Comanche
Co., TX

G8, $25-$40
AR

G6, $15-$30
Waco, TX

G8, $25-$40
Comanche
Co., TX

G6, $25-$40
Waco, TX

G6, $30-$50
Waco, TX

G6, $30-$50
Waco, TX

G6, $30-$50
Comanche Co., TX

G6, $30-$50
Comanche Co., TX

G7, $35-$60
AR

G6, $30-$50
Comanche Co., TX

Classic form

G9, $60-$100
TX

Brown chert

G6, $25-$45
AR

Tan chert

G9, $45-$80
AR

Bifurcated stem

Classic form

Red quartz

Red/gray chert

Brown chert

G6, $30-$50
Comanche Co., TX

G9, $60-$110
TX

G8, $35-$65
TX

G8, $35-$65
AR

G8, $40-$75
Comanche Co., TX

G10, $65-$125
AR

G10, $65-$125
TX

LOCATION: Mexico, E. Texas into Arkansas. **DESCRIPTION:** A small to medium size, thin, barbed arrow point with strong shoulders. The stem is short and may be horizontal or expanded to bifurcated. Believed to be related to the *Friley* point. **I.D. KEY:** Strong barbs.

STEUBEN - Woodland, 2000 - 1000 B. P.

(Also see Lange, Palmillas and Table Rock)

G4, $4-$8
Saline Co., AR

G5, $5-$10
Saline Co., AR

G7, $12-$20
AR

LOCATION: Arkansas to Illinois. **DESCRIPTION:** A medium to large size, narrow, expanded stem point. shoulders can be tapered to straight. The base is straight to convex. This type is very similar to *Bakers Creek* in the Southeast.

666

STEUBEN (continued)

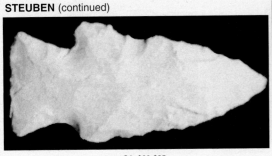 

G6, $20-$35
Saline Co., AR

G6, $20-$35
Saline Co., AR

TABLE ROCK - Late Archaic, 4000 - 3000 B. P.

(Also see Lange, Matanzas, Motley and Steuben)

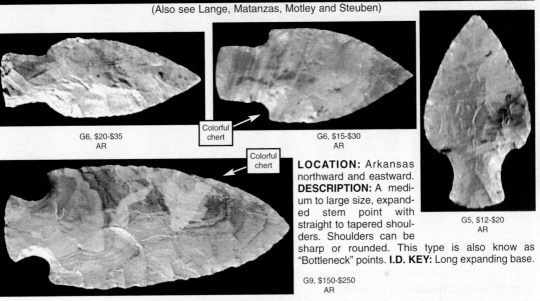

G6, $20-$35
AR

Colorful chert

G6, $15-$30
AR

G5, $12-$20
AR

Colorful chert

LOCATION: Arkansas northward and eastward. **DESCRIPTION:** A medium to large size, expanded stem point with straight to tapered shoulders. Shoulders can be sharp or rounded. This type is also know as "Bottleneck" points. **I.D. KEY:** Long expanding base.

G9, $150-$250
AR

SC

TALCO - Mississippian to Historic, 800 - 500 B. P.

(Also see Guerrero, Maud and Starr)

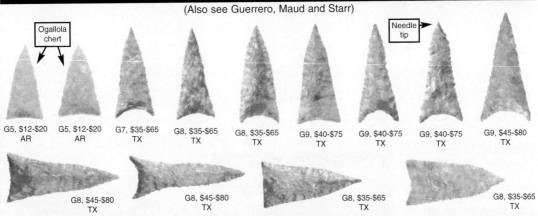

Ogallola chert

Needle tip

G5, $12-$20
AR

G5, $12-$20
AR

G7, $35-$65
TX

G8, $35-$65
TX

G8, $35-$65
TX

G9, $40-$75
TX

G9, $40-$75
TX

G9, $40-$75
TX

G9, $45-$80
TX

G8, $45-$80
TX

G8, $45-$80
TX

G8, $35-$65
TX

G8, $35-$65
TX

LOCATION: Texas to Oklahoma. **DESCRIPTION:** A small to medium size, thin, narrow, triangular arrow point with recurved sides and a concave base. Blade edges are very finely serrated. On classic examples, tips are more angled than *Maud*. Tips and corners are sharp. This type is found on Caddo and related sites. **I.D. KEY:** Angled tip.

TALCO (continued)

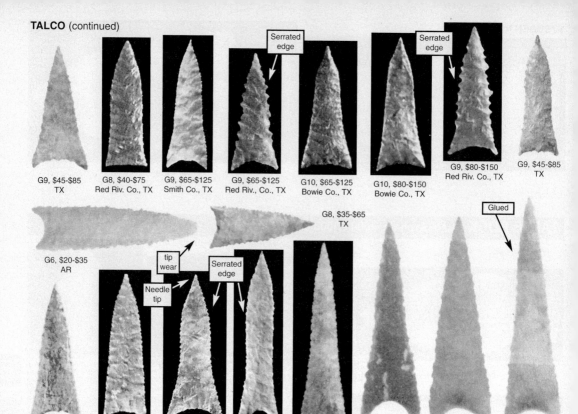

G9, $45-$85
TX

G8, $40-$75
Red Riv. Co., TX

G9, $65-$125
Smith Co., TX

Serrated edge

G9, $65-$125
Red Riv., Co., TX

G10, $65-$125
Bowie Co., TX

G10, $80-$150
Bowie Co., TX

Serrated edge

G9, $80-$150
Red Riv. Co., TX

G9, $45-$85
TX

G6, $20-$35
AR

G8, $35-$65
TX

Glued

tip wear

Needle tip

Serrated edge

G10, $175-$300
Bowie Co., TX

G10, $175-$300
Comanche Co., TX

G10, $175-$300
Emanuel Co., TX

G10, $175-$300
Smith Co., TX

G10, $150-$275
Pike Co., AR.
Terrell site.

G10, $175-$300
AR

G10, $150-$250
AR

G5, $65-$125
AR

TEXAS KIRK   (see Coryell)

TORTUGAS - Middle Archaic to Woodland, 6000 - 1000 B. P.

(Also see Kinney, Early Triangular and Matamoros)

G4, $1-$3
Nuevo Leon, MX

G4, $1-$3
Nuevo Leon, MX

G5, $2-$4
S. TX

G7, $3-$6
Nuevo Leon, MX

G7, $4-$8
Nuevo Leon, MX

LOCATION: Oklahoma to Tennessee. **DESCRIPTION:** A medium size, fairly thick, triangular point with straight to convex sides and base. Some examples are beveled on one side of each face. Bases are usually thinned. Smaller examples would fall in the *Matamoros* type.

G5, $6-$12
Cent. TX

G6, $3-$6
Nuevo Leon, MX

TORTUGAS (continued)

G7, $8-$15
Starr Co., TX

G7, $12-$20
TX

G8, $15-$25
McCulloch Co., TX

G8, $20-$35
Maverick Co., TX

TOYAH - Mississippian to Historic, 600 - 400 B. P.

(Also see Garza, Harrell, Huffaker, Morris and Washita)

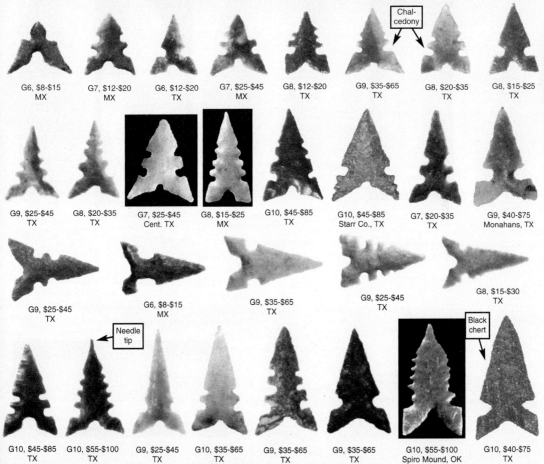

G6, $8-$15
MX

G7, $12-$20
MX

G6, $12-$20
TX

G7, $25-$45
MX

G8, $12-$20
TX

G9, $35-$65
TX

Chalcedony

G8, $20-$35
TX

G8, $15-$25
TX

G9, $25-$45
TX

G8, $20-$35
TX

G7, $25-$45
Cent. TX

G8, $15-$25
MX

G10, $45-$85
TX

G10, $45-$85
Starr Co., TX

G7, $20-$35
TX

G9, $40-$75
Monahans, TX

G9, $25-$45
TX

G6, $8-$15
MX

G9, $35-$65
TX

G9, $25-$45
TX

G8, $15-$30
TX

Needle tip

G10, $45-$85
TX

G10, $55-$100
TX

G9, $25-$45
TX

G10, $35-$65
TX

G9, $35-$65
TX

G9, $35-$65
TX

Black chert

G10, $55-$100
Spiro Mound, OK

G10, $40-$75
TX

LOCATION: Northern Mexico to Texas. **DESCRIPTION:** A small size, thin, triangular point with expanded barbs and one or more notches on each side and a basal notch. **I.D. KEY:** Has drooping, pointed barbs.

669

TRADE POINTS - Historic, 400 - 170 B. P.

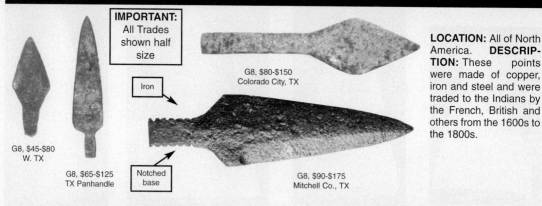

IMPORTANT: All Trades shown half size

Iron

Notched base

G8, $45-$80
W. TX

G8, $65-$125
TX Panhandle

G8, $80-$150
Colorado City, TX

G8, $90-$175
Mitchell Co., TX

LOCATION: All of North America. **DESCRIPTION:** These points were made of copper, iron and steel and were traded to the Indians by the French, British and others from the 1600s to the 1800s.

TRAVIS - Middle-Archaic to Woodland, 5500 - 1000 B. P.

(Also see Darl, Gary, Kent, Lange, Nolan and Pandale)

G4, $8-$15
TX

G7, $15-$25
Comanche Co., TX

G6, $8-$15
Concho Co., TX

G6, $15-$30
Comanche Co., TX

G6, $15-$30
Austin, TX

G9, $35-$60
Comanche Co., TX

G5 $20-$35
Amarillo, TX

G8, $25-$45
TX

G9, $40-$75
TX

G4, $8-$15
Comanche Co., TX

LOCATION: Texas to Oklahoma. **DESCRIPTION:** A small to medium size, narrow point with weak, tapered shoulders and a parallel sided to expanded or contracting stem. The base is straight to convex. Some examples have sharp needle-like tips. **I.D. KEY:** Weak, tapered shoulders.

TRAVIS (continued)

G5, $12-$20
Austin, TX

G8, $40-$75
Coryell Co., TX

G10, $150-$250
Coryell Co., TX

G8, $65-$125
Bell Co., TX

G6, $55-$100
TX

G10, $170-$325
Austin, TX

TRINITY - Late Archaic, 4000 - 2000 B. P.

(Also see Ellis, Godley and Travis)

G6, $12-$20
Waco, TX

G4, $1-$2
Comanche Co., TX

LOCATION: Texas to Oklahoma. **DESCRIPTION:** A small to medium size point with broad side notches, weak shoulders and a broad convex base which is usually ground.

G4, $5-$10
Comanche Co., TX

TURNER - Mississippian, 1000 - 800 B. P.

(Also see Alba, Blevins, Hayes, Homan, Howard, Perdiz and Sequoyah)

Incup tip

Incup tip

G8, $60-$100
Bell Co., TX

G8, $60-$100
Bell Co., TX

G8, $60-$100
Bell Co., TX

LOCATION: Louisiana to Oklahoma. **DESCRIPTION:** Related to *Hayes* points and is a later variety. A small size, narrow, expanded barb arrow point with a turkeytail base. The tip is inset about 1/4th the distance. Blade edges are usually incurved forming sharp, "squarish" pointed barbs. Base is pointed and can be double notched. Some examples are serrated. Has been found in caches. **I.D. KEY:** Diamond shaped base and flaking style.

671

UVALDE - Middle Archaic to Woodland, 6000 - 1500 B. P.

(Also see Frio, Hoxie, Langtry, Pedernales, Rice Lobbed and Val Verde)

G6, $3-$5
Coahuilla, MX

G4, $2-$5
Val Verde Co., TX

G5, $5-$10
Val Verde Co., TX

G4, $4-$8
Val Verde Co., TX

G7, $35-$60
Comanche Co., TX

G8, $60-$100
Comanche Co., TX

G7, $30-$55
TX

G7, $35-$65
Comanche Co., TX

G8, $45-$85
Coryell Co., TX

G6, $35-$60
Kerr Co., TX.

G8, $60-$125
Comanche Co., TX.

G9, $90-$175
TX.

G6 $55-$100
TX.

LOCATION: Texas to Oklahoma. **DESCRIPTION:** A medium size, bifurcated stemmed point with barbed to tapered shoulders. Some examples are serrated. The *Frio* point is similar but is usually broader and the ears flare outward more than this type. **I.D. KEY:** Narrow bifurcated stem.

UVALDE (continued)

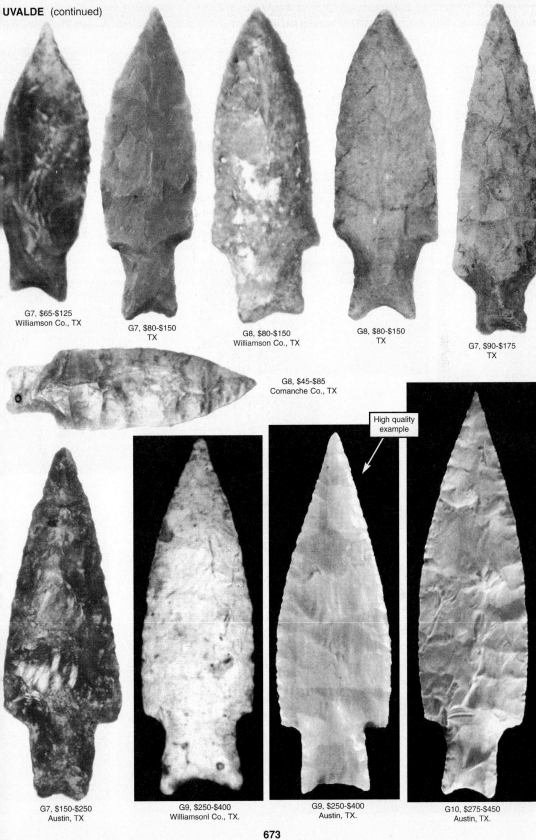

G7, $65-$125
Williamson Co., TX

G7, $80-$150
TX

G8, $80-$150
Williamson Co., TX

G8, $80-$150
TX

G7, $90-$175
TX

SC

G8, $45-$85
Comanche Co., TX

High quality
example

G7, $150-$250
Austin, TX

G9, $250-$400
Williamsonl Co., TX.

G9, $250-$400
Austin, TX.

G10, $275-$450
Austin, TX.

673

(Also see Langtry, Pedernales and Uvalde)

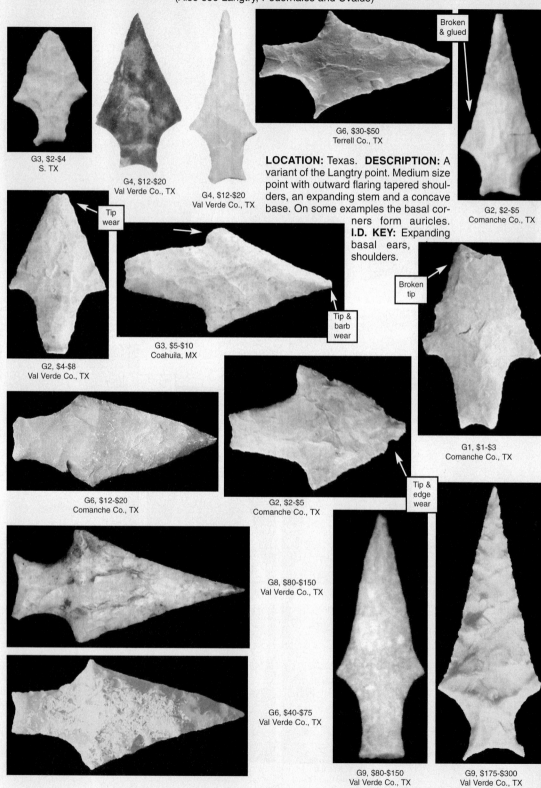

G3, $2-$4
S. TX

G4, $12-$20
Val Verde Co., TX

G4, $12-$20
Val Verde Co., TX

G6, $30-$50
Terrell Co., TX

Broken & glued

LOCATION: Texas. **DESCRIPTION:** A variant of the Langtry point. Medium size point with outward flaring tapered shoulders, an expanding stem and a concave base. On some examples the basal corners form auricles. **I.D. KEY:** Expanding basal ears, shoulders.

G2, $2-$5
Comanche Co., TX

Tip wear

Tip & barb wear

G3, $5-$10
Coahuila, MX

G2, $4-$8
Val Verde Co., TX

Broken tip

G1, $1-$3
Comanche Co., TX

G6, $12-$20
Comanche Co., TX

G2, $2-$5
Comanche Co., TX

Tip & edge wear

G8, $80-$150
Val Verde Co., TX

G6, $40-$75
Val Verde Co., TX

G9, $80-$150
Val Verde Co., TX

G9, $175-$300
Val Verde Co., TX

674

VICTORIA - Early Archaic, 8000 - 6000 B. P.

(Also see Angostura, Early Stemmed Lanceolate, Hell Gap, Rio Grande and Searcy)

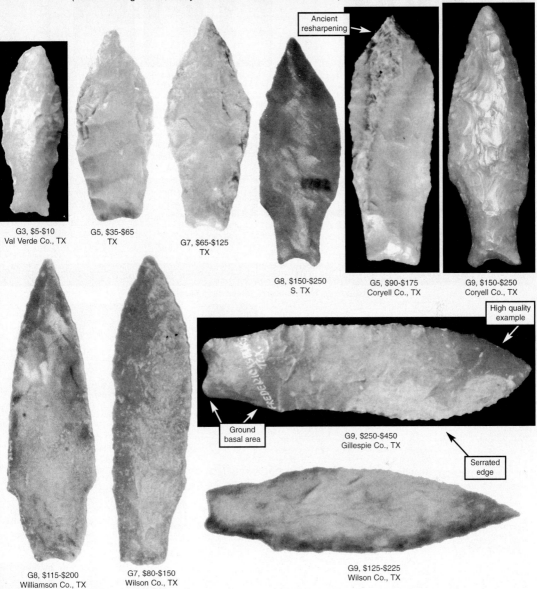

G3, $5-$10
Val Verde Co., TX

G5, $35-$65
TX

G7, $65-$125
TX

Ancient resharpening

G8, $150-$250
S. TX

G5, $90-$175
Coryell Co., TX

G9, $150-$250
Coryell Co., TX

SC

High quality example

Ground basal area

G9, $250-$450
Gillespie Co., TX

Serrated edge

G8, $115-$200
Williamson Co., TX

G7, $80-$150
Wilson Co., TX

G9, $125-$225
Wilson Co., TX

LOCATION: Texas. **DESCRIPTION:** A medium to large size, narrow, lanceolate blade with an incurvate base. The hafting area is separated from the blade by weak, tapered shoulders. Bases are ground. **I.D. KEY:** Base form.

WASHITA - Mississippian, 800 - 400 B. P.

(Also see Harrell, Haskell, Keota, Reed, Schustorm and Toyah)

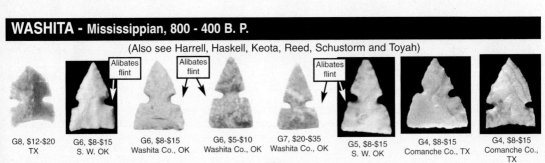

G8, $12-$20
TX

G6, $8-$15
S. W. OK

Alibates flint

G6, $8-$15
Washita Co., OK

Alibates flint

G6, $5-$10
Washita Co., OK

G7, $20-$35
Washita Co., OK

Alibates flint

G5, $8-$15
S. W. OK

G4, $8-$15
Comanche Co., TX

G4, $8-$15
Comanche Co., TX

675

WASHITA (continued)

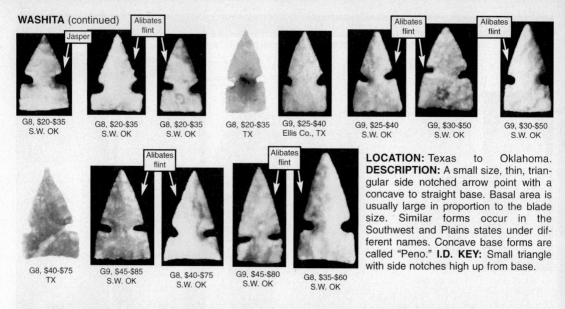

G8, $20-$35
S.W. OK

G8, $20-$35
S.W. OK

G8, $20-$35
S.W. OK

G8, $20-$35
TX

G9, $25-$40
Ellis Co., TX

G9, $25-$40
S.W. OK

G9, $30-$50
S.W. OK

G9, $30-$50
S.W. OK

G8, $40-$75
TX

G9, $45-$85
S.W. OK

G8, $40-$75
S.W. OK

G9, $45-$80
S.W. OK

G8, $35-$60
S.W. OK

LOCATION: Texas to Oklahoma. **DESCRIPTION:** A small size, thin, triangular side notched arrow point with a concave to straight base. Basal area is usually large in proportion to the blade size. Similar forms occur in the Southwest and Plains states under different names. Concave base forms are called "Peno." **I.D. KEY:** Small triangle with side notches high up from base.

WASHITA-PENO - Mississippian, 800 - 400 B. P.

(Also see Harrell, Keota, Reed and Toyah)

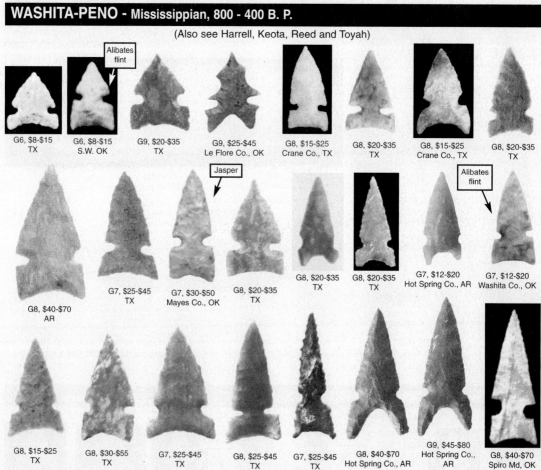

G6, $8-$15
TX

G6, $8-$15
S.W. OK

G9, $20-$35
TX

G9, $25-$45
Le Flore Co., OK

G8, $15-$25
Crane Co., TX

G8, $20-$35
TX

G8, $15-$25
Crane Co., TX

G8, $20-$35
TX

G8, $40-$70
AR

G7, $25-$45
TX

G7, $30-$50
Mayes Co., OK

G8, $20-$35
TX

G8, $20-$35
TX

G8, $20-$35
TX

G7, $12-$20
Hot Spring Co., AR

G7, $12-$20
Washita Co., OK

G8, $15-$25
TX

G8, $30-$55
TX

G7, $25-$45
TX

G8, $25-$45
TX

G7, $25-$45
TX

G8, $40-$70
Hot Spring Co., AR

G9, $45-$80
Hot Spring Co., AR

G8, $40-$70
Spiro Md, OK

LOCATION: Texas to Oklahoma. **DESCRIPTION:** A variant form with side notches one third to one half the distance up from the base and the base is concave to eared. Basal concavity can be slight to very deep. **I.D. KEY:** Base form and notch placement.

(Also see Adena, Bulverde, Carrolton, Coryell, Dawson & Searcy)

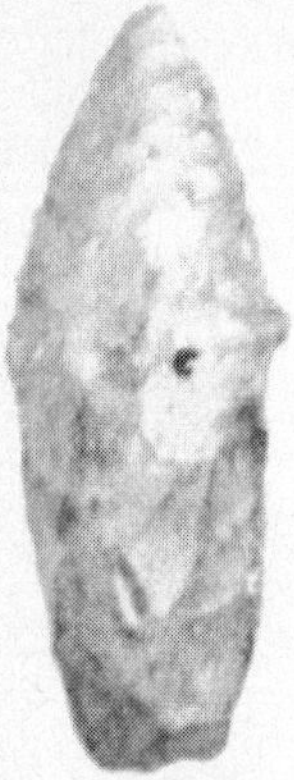

Serrated edge

G8, $65-$125
Bell Co., TX

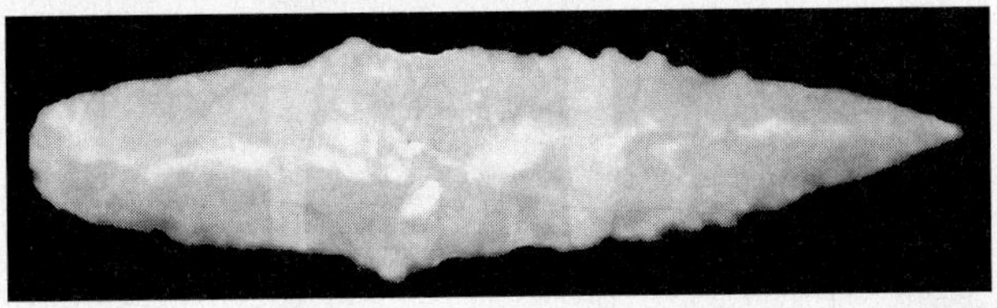

Barbed shoulders

SC

G3, $12-$20
Comanche Co., TX

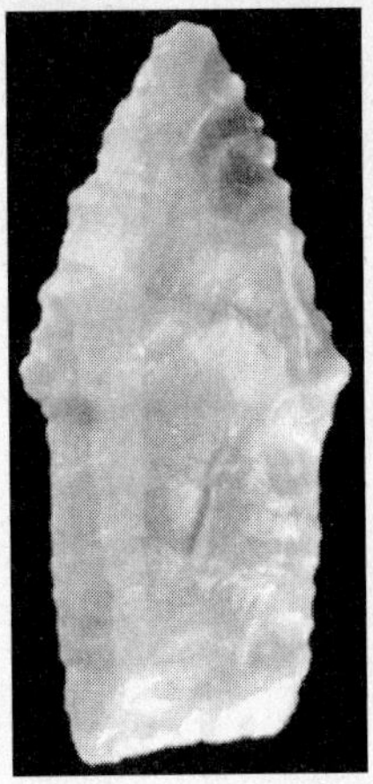

G5, $15-$40
Austin, TX

G9, $65-$125
Williamsonl Co., TX

G8, $45-$85
Georgetown Co., TX

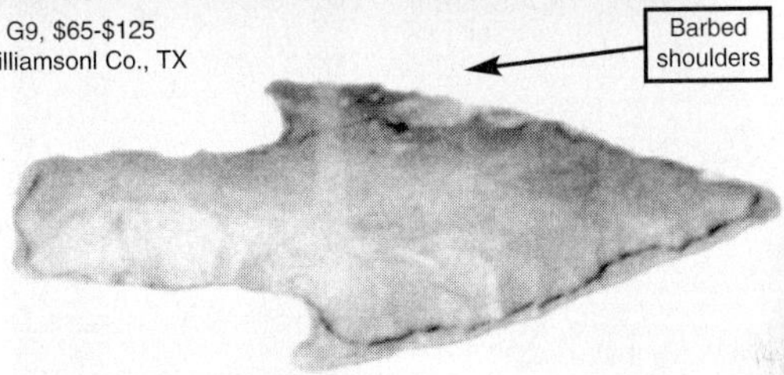

G7, $30-$50
Llanol Co., TX

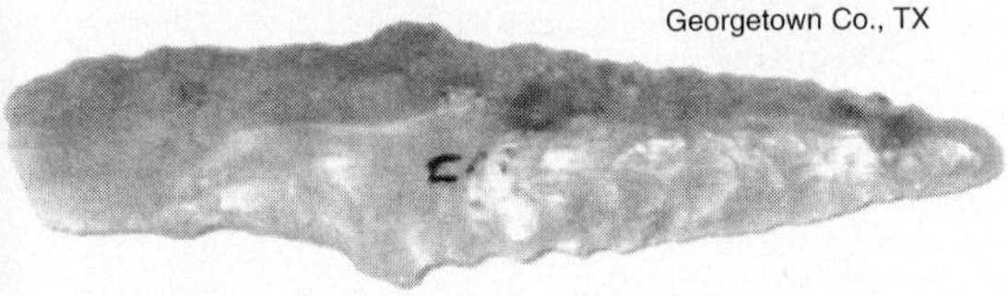

Serrated edge

G6, $30-$50
Travis Co., TX

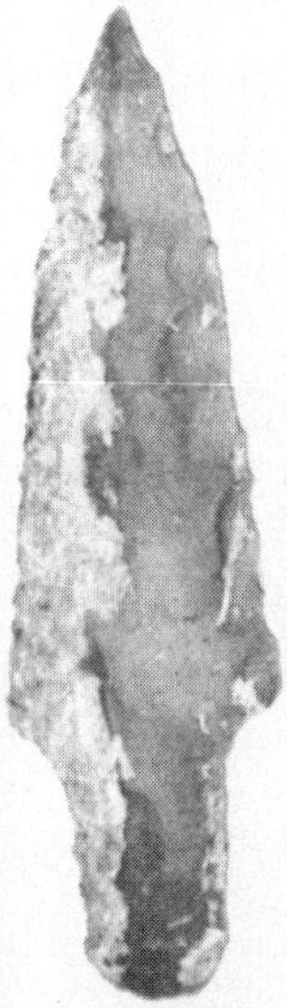

G7, $35-$65
Bell Co., TX

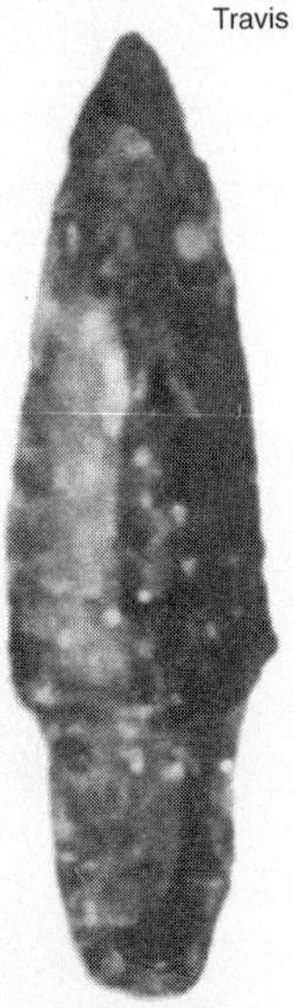

G8, $40-$75
Bell Co., TX

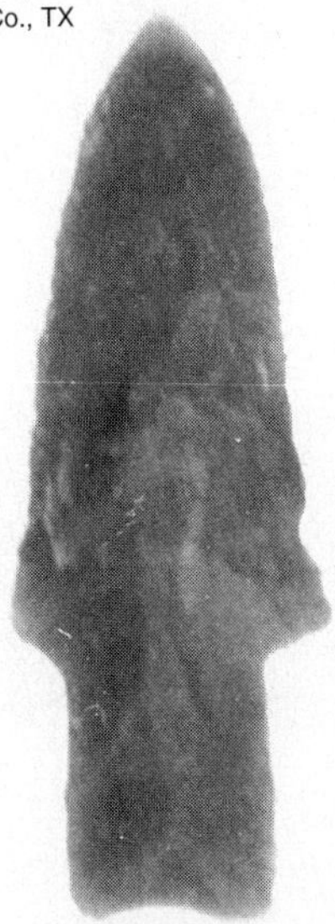

G8, $40-$75
Williamson Co., TX

G8, $75-$135
Cent. TX

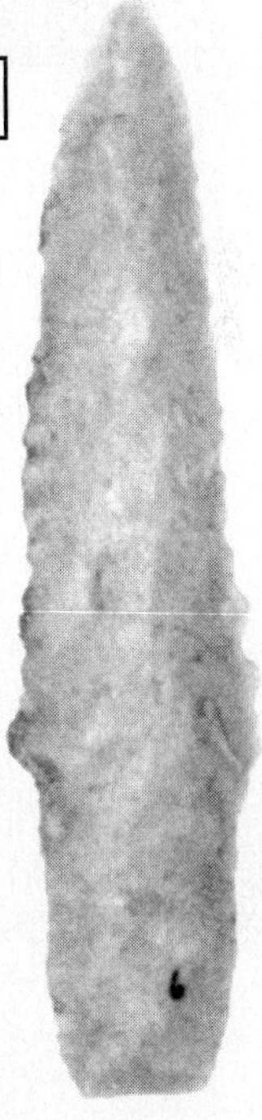

G3, $90-$175
Burnet, TX

G8, $40-$75
Williamson Co., TX

LOCATION: Eastern Texas and Oklahoma. **DESCRIPTION:** A medium to large size, thin, usually serrated point with a long, narrow, contracting to parallel stem that has a rounded to straight base. Shoulders are weak and can be tapered, horizontal or barbed. **I.D. KEY:** Basal form, extended and squared up. Early flaking style.

Serrated edge

G7, $150-$250
TX

G8, $125-$200
N. OK

G6, $80-$150
Georegtown Co., TX

Serrated edge

G7, $65-$125
Austin, TX

Serrated edge

ROGERS

G9, $125-$225
Bell Co., TX

G7, $80-$150
Comanche Co., TX

G7, $65-$125
Travis Co., TX

G8, $175-$300
Waller Co., TX

WHITE RIVER - Middle Archaic to Woodland, 6000 - 1000 B. P.

(Also see Big Sandy and Hickory Ridge)

LOCATION: Arkansas, Missouri. **DESCRIPTION:** A medium to large size, narrow, side notched point with a straight to concave base. Blade edges can be beveled and serrated. Similar to *Graham Cave* points found further north.

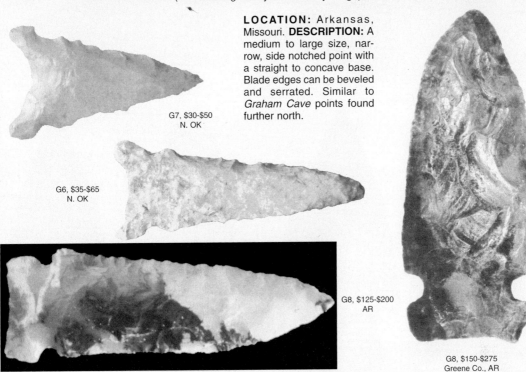

G7, $30-$50
N. OK

G6, $35-$65
N. OK

G8, $125-$200
AR

G8, $150-$275
Greene Co., AR

WILLIAMS - Middle Archaic to Woodland, 6000 - 1000 B. P.

(Also see Axtel, Castroville, Marcos, Marshall, Palmillas and Shumla)

Yellow jasper

G8, $12-$20
TX

G9, $25-$45
TX

G9, $25-$45
TX

G6, $20-$35
Bossier Parish., LA

G6, $15-$25
Comanche Co., TX

G6, $35-$65
Comanche Co., TX

G6 $15-$25
Coryell Co., TX

LOCATION: Texas to Oklahoma. **DESCRIPTION:** A medium to large size, barbed point with an expanded, rounded base. Resharpened examples have tapered shoulders. **I.D. KEY:** Base form, barbs.

G8, $30-$50
Florence, TX

G8, $30-$50
Belton, TX

G4, $12-$20
Bell Co., TX

G9, $40-$80
TX

G9, $65-$120
Bell Co., TX

G7, $35-$60
Lampassas, TX

G8, $40-$75
TX

G8, $125-$200
Coryell Co., TX

G9, $175-$300
Travis Co., TX

G9, $175-$325
Waco, TX

YARBROUGH - Woodland, 2500 - 1000 B. P.

(Also see Darl, Hoxie, Lange, Travis and Zorra)

G5, $8-$15
Comanche Co., TX

G6, $15-$25
Bell Co., TX

G5, $12-$20
Bell Co., TX

G7, $60-$110
Bell Co., TX

G7, $55-$100
Ellis Co., TX

G6, $50-$90
Comanche Co., TX

G6, $55-$100
Williamson Co., TX

LOCATION: Texas to Oklahoma. **DESCRIPTION:** A medium size, narrow point with a long, expanding, rectangular stem that has slightly concave sides. The shoulders are very weak and tapered. The stem edges are usually ground. **I.D. KEY:** Expanding stem.

YOUNG - Mississippian, 1000 - 400 B. P.

(Also see Catan and Clifton)

LOCATION: Texas. **DESCRIPTION:** A small size, crudely chipped, elliptical shaped, usually round base point made from a flake. One side is commonly uniface. **I.D. KEY:** Base form, uniface.

G1, $.50-$1
Waco, TX

G5, $.50-$1
Comanche Co., TX

G3, $.50-$1
Comanche Co., TX

(Also see Agate Basin, Angostura, Lerma and Mahaffey)

G9, $125-$225
TX

LOCATION: Texas.
DESCRIPTION: A large size, narrow, lanceolate blade with a rounded to small straight base. Bases are ground. Believed to be a form of Angostura.

Petrified wood

G9, $275-$500
Wilson Co., TX

(Formerly Lampasos; also see Darl Stemmed, Darl, Hoxie and Uvalde)

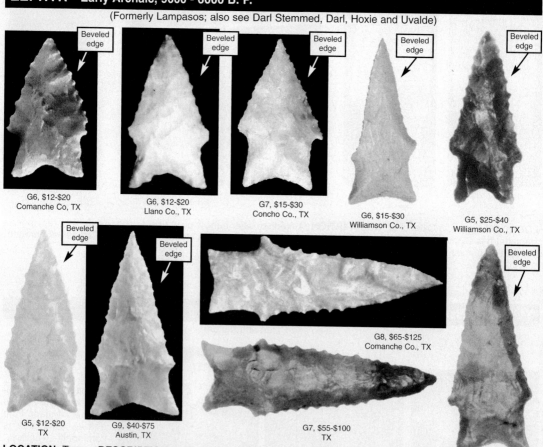

Beveled edge

G6, $12-$20
Comanche Co, TX

Beveled edge

G6, $12-$20
Llano Co., TX

Beveled edge

G7, $15-$30
Concho Co., TX

Beveled edge

G6, $15-$30
Williamson Co., TX

Beveled edge

G5, $25-$40
Williamson Co., TX

Beveled edge

G5, $12-$20
TX

Beveled edge

G9, $40-$75
Austin, TX

G8, $65-$125
Comanche Co., TX

G7, $55-$100
TX

Beveled edge

G8, $55-$100
Coryell Co., TX

LOCATION: Texas. **DESCRIPTION:** A medium to large size, narrow, serrated point with square to tapered, barbed shoulders and an eared base. Blade edges are beveled on one side of each face on resharpened forms. Flaking is of high quality. These points were classified with *Darl* in the past. Also known as *Mahomet* locally. **I.D. KEY:** Fishtail base and serrations.

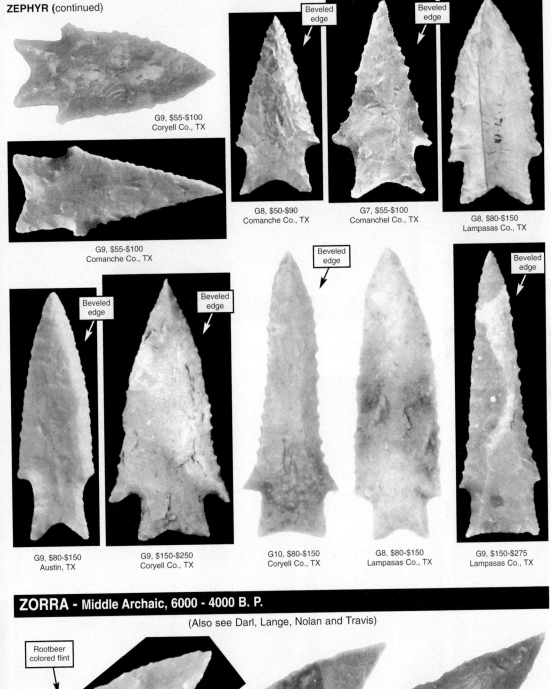

G9, $55-$100
Coryell Co., TX

Beveled edge

Beveled edge

G8, $50-$90
Comanche Co., TX

G7, $55-$100
Comanchel Co., TX

G8, $80-$150
Lampasas Co., TX

G9, $55-$100
Comanche Co., TX

Beveled edge

Beveled edge

Beveled edge

Beveled edge

SC

G9, $80-$150
Austin, TX

G9, $150-$250
Coryell Co., TX

G10, $80-$150
Coryell Co., TX

G8, $80-$150
Lampasas Co., TX

G9, $150-$275
Lampasas Co., TX

ZORRA - Middle Archaic, 6000 - 4000 B. P.

(Also see Darl, Lange, Nolan and Travis)

Rootbeer colored flint

G6, $12-$20
Austin, TX

G8, $20-$35
Williamson Co., TX

G8, $25-$40
Coryell Co., TX

G8, $55-$100
Williamson Co., TX

Note patination
of rind showing
at base

G7, $35-$60
Austin, TX

G8, $90-$175
TX

G8, $125-$200
Austin, TX. Classic

G9, $175-$300
Austin Co., TX

G9, $150-$250
TX

G10, $350-$600
Austin, TX. Excellent quality.

LOCATION: Texas. **DESCRIPTION:** A medium to large size point with tapered shoulders and stem that is usually flat on one face and beveled on both sides of the opposite face. Otherwise identical to *Nolan*. Most have needle tips and good quality flaking. **I.D. KEY:** Base beveling.

NORTHERN CENTRAL SECTION:

This section includes point types from the following states:
Eastern Colorado, Kansas, Illinois, Iowa, Minnesota, Missouri, Nebraska and Wisconsin.

The points in this section are arranged in alphabetical order and are shown **actual size**. All types are listed that were available for photographing. Any missing types will be added to future editions as photographs become available. We are always interested in receiving sharp, black and white or color glossy photos, color slides or high resolution (300 pixels/inch) digital pictures of your collection. Be sure to include a ruler in the photograph so that proper scale can be determined.

Lithics: Materials employed in the manufacture of point types from this region include: agate, Burlington, chalcedony, chert, conglomerate, crystal, flint, jasper, kaolin, Knife River, hornstone, novaculite, petrified wood, quartzite, silicified sandstone and vein quartz.

Regional Consultant:
Roy Motley and Dave Church

Special Advisors:
Tom Davis, Bill Jackson
Glenn Leesman, Floyd Ritter,
Larry Troman, Michael Troman, Brian Wrage

NORTHERN CENTRAL
(Archaeological Periods)

PALEO-LATE PALEO (11,500 B.P. - 10,000 B.P.)

Beaver Lake
Clovis
Clovis-Hazel
Clovis-St. Louis

Cumberland
Cumberland Unfluted
Drill
Folsom

Goshen
Plainview
Redstone

TRANSITIONAL PALEO (11,000 B.P. - 9,000 B.P.)

Agate Basin
Allen
Angostura
Browns Valley

Early Ovoid Knife
Eden
Hell Gap
Hi-Lo

Paleo Knife
Pelican
Quad
Scottsbluff Type I & 2

Wheeler

EARLY ARCHAIC (10,000 B.P. - 7,000 B.P.)

Allen
Angostura
Burroughs
Cache River
Calf Creek
Cobbs Triangular
Cossatot River
Dalton Breckenridge
Dalton Classic
Dalton-Colbert
Dalton-Hemphill
Dalton-Nuckolls
Dalton-Sloan

Decatur
Dovetail
Firstview
Fox Valley
Graham Cave
Greenbrier
Hardin
Heavy Duty
Hickory Ridge
Hidden Valley
Holland
Hollenberg Stemmed
Howard County

Johnson
Kirk Corner Notched
Lake Erie
Lerma
Lost Lake
Meserve
Nebo Hill
Neuberger
Osceola
Pike County
Pine Tree Corner Notched
Rice Lobbed
Rochester

St. Charles
Stilwell
Tennessee River
Thebes
Turin
Warrick

MIDDLE ARCHAIC (7,000 B.P. - 4,000 B.P.)

Afton
Epps
Exotic Forms
Ferry

Hemphill
Kings
Lamine Knife
Matanzas

Motley
Munker's Creek
Raddatz
Ramey Knife

Red Ochre
Sedalia
Smith
Stone Square Stem

LATE ARCHAIC (4,000 B.P. - 3,000 B.P.)

Copena Classic
Corner Tang Knife
Delhi
Etley
Evans

Gary
Godar
Hatten Knife
Helton
Knight Island

Mehlville
Merkle
Pelican Lake
Robinson
Square Knife

Table Rock
Turkeytail-Fulton
Turkeytail-Harrison
Turkeytail-Hebron
Wadlow

WOODLAND (3,000 B.P. - 1,300 B.P.)

Adena
Adena Blade
Adena-Narrow Stem
Adena-Notched Base
Alba
Apple Creek
Burkett

Carter
Collins
Cupp
Dickson
Gibson
Grand
Hopewell

Jacks Reef Corner Notched
Kampsville
Kramer
Lehigh
Morse Knife
North
Peisker Diamond

Rice Side-Notched
Ross
Snyders
Steuben
Waubesa

MISSISSIPPIAN (1300 B.P. - 400 B.P.)

Agee
Bayogoula
Cahokia
Harahey
Harrell

Haskell
Hayes
Homan
Huffaker
Kay Blade

Lundy
Madison
Nodena
Scallorn
Sequoyah

Washita

HISTORIC (450 B.P. - 170 B.P.)

Neosho

NORTHERN CENTRAL
THUMBNAIL GUIDE SECTION

The following references are provided to aid the collector in easier and quicker identification of point types. All photos are exactly 30% of actual size and are proportional to each other. Each point pictured in this section represents a classic form for the type. When a match is found, go to the alphabetical location of that type for more examples in actual size.

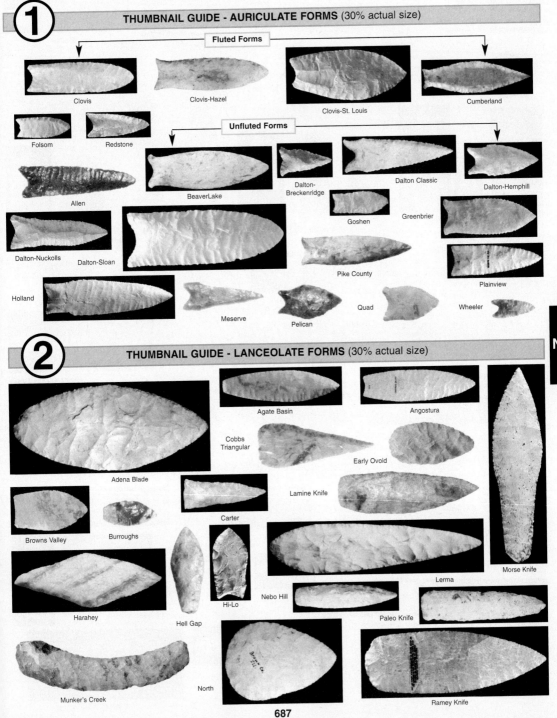

① THUMBNAIL GUIDE - AURICULATE FORMS (30% actual size)

Fluted Forms

Clovis

Clovis-Hazel

Clovis-St. Louis

Cumberland

Folsom

Redstone

Unfluted Forms

Allen

BeaverLake

Dalton-Breckenridge

Dalton Classic

Dalton-Hemphill

Goshen

Greenbrier

Dalton-Nuckolls

Dalton-Sloan

Pike County

Plainview

Holland

Meserve

Pelican

Quad

Wheeler

② THUMBNAIL GUIDE - LANCEOLATE FORMS (30% actual size)

Agate Basin

Angostura

Cobbs Triangular

Early Ovoid

Adena Blade

Lamine Knife

Carter

Browns Valley

Burroughs

Morse Knife

Lerma

Harahey

Hi-Lo

Nebo Hill

Paleo Knife

Hell Gap

Munker's Creek

North

Ramey Knife

NC

687

THUMBNAIL GUIDE - Lanceolate forms (continued)

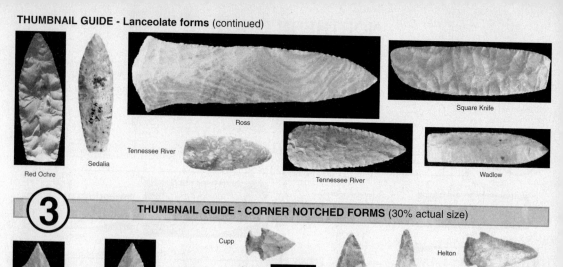

Red Ochre

Sedalia

Ross

Tennessee River

Tennessee River

Square Knife

Wadlow

③ THUMBNAIL GUIDE - CORNER NOTCHED FORMS (30% actual size)

Afton

Apple Creek

Cupp

Carter

Corner Tang Knife

Decatur

Epps

Gibson

Helton

Grand

Hopewell

Kay Blade

Kings

Kirk Corner Notched

Lost Lake

Lundy

Motley

Neuberger

Pelican Lake

Pine Tree

Rice Lobbed

St. Charles showing different base forms

Snyders

Stilwell

Thebes

④ THUMBNAIL GUIDE - SIDE NOTCHED FORMS (30% actual size)

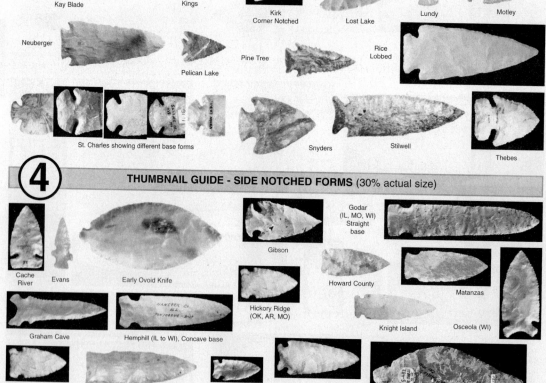

Cache River

Evans

Early Ovoid Knife

Gibson

Godar (IL, MO, WI) Straight base

Howard County

Matanzas

Hickory Ridge (OK, AR, MO)

Knight Island

Osceola (WI)

Graham Cave

Hemphill (IL to WI), Concave base

Raddatz (WI)

Rice Side-Notched

Robinson (MO, IL, IN)

Turin

Turkeytail-Fulton

688

Neosho

Turkeytail-Harrison

Warrick

⑤ THUMBNAIL GUIDE - STEMMED FORMS (30% of actual size)

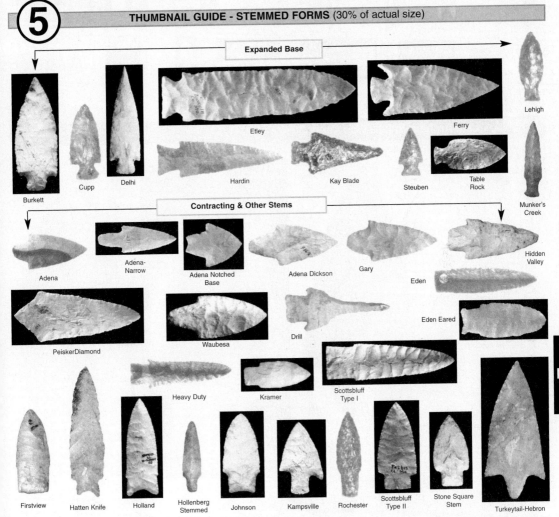

Expanded Base

Lehigh

Etley

Ferry

Cupp

Delhi

Hardin

Kay Blade

Steuben

Table Rock

Burkett

Munker's Creek

Contracting & Other Stems

Adena

Adena-Narrow

Adena Notched Base

Adena Dickson

Gary

Hidden Valley

Eden

PeiskerDiamond

Waubesa

Drill

Eden Eared

Heavy Duty

Kramer

Scottsbluff Type I

NC

Firstview

Hatten Knife

Holland

Hollenberg Stemmed

Johnson

Kampsville

Rochester

Scottsbluff Type II

Stone Square Stem

Turkeytail-Hebron

⑥ THUMBNAIL GUIDE - STEMMED-BIFURCATED FORMS (30% of actual size)

Fox Valley

Lake Erie

Cossatot River

⑦ THUMBNAIL GUIDE - BASAL NOTCHED FORMS (30% of actual size)

Calf Creek

Mehlville

Smith

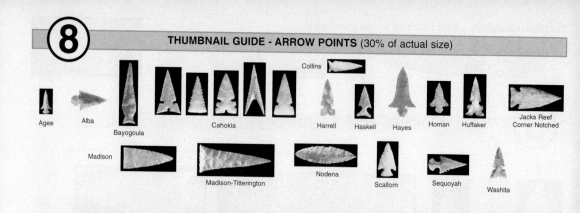

Agee   Alba   Bayogoula   Cahokia   Collins   Harrell   Haskell   Hayes   Homan   Huffaker   Jacks Reef Corner Notched

Madison   Madison-Titterington   Nodena   Scallorn   Sequoyah   Washita

ADENA - Late Archaic to late Woodland, 3000 - 1200 B. P.

(see Burkett, Dickson, Gary, Kramer, Hidden Valley, Rochester and Waubesa)

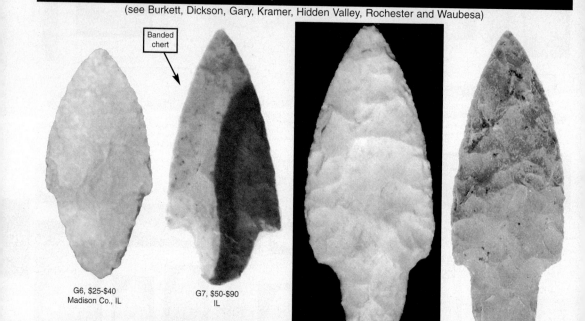

Banded chert

G6, $25-$40
Madison Co., IL

G7, $50-$90
IL

G6, $40-$75
Illinois Riv., IL

G7, $65-$125
Alexandra Co., IL

G9, $90-$175
IL

Red jasper

G9, $250-$400
IL

ADENA (continued)

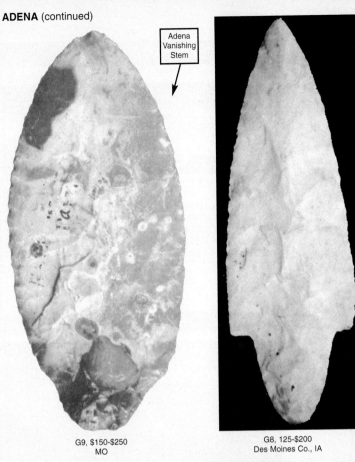

Adena
Vanishing
Stem

G9, $150-$250
MO

G8, 125-$200
Des Moines Co., IA

LOCATION: Eastern to Southeastern states. **DESCRIPTION:** A medium to large, thin, narrow, triangular blade that is sometimes serrated, and with a medium to long, narrow to broad rounded "beaver tail" stem. Most examples are from average to excellent quality. Base can be ground. **I.D. KEY:** Rounded base, Woodland random flaking.

G9, $300-$500
IL

ADENA BLADE - Late Archaic to Woodland, 3000 - 1200 B. P.

(Also see Lerma, North, Red Ochre & Stenfield)

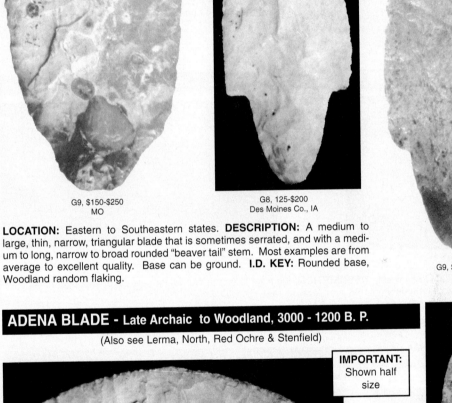

IMPORTANT:
Shown half
size

G8, $275-$500
McLean Co., IL

G7, $175-$300
WI

LOCATION: Midwestern to Eastern states. **DESCRIPTION:** A large size, thin, broad, ovate blade with a rounded base and is often found in caches. **I.D. KEY:** Random flaking.

691

ADENA-NARROW STEM - Late Archaic to Woodland, 3000 - 1200 B. P.

(Also see Adena, Dickson, Rochester and Waubesa)

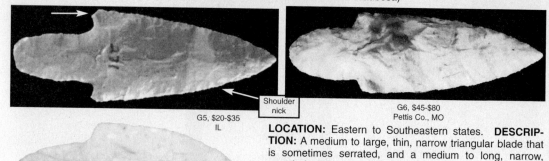

Shoulder nick

G5, $20-$35
IL

G6, $45-$80
Pettis Co., MO

LOCATION: Eastern to Southeastern states. **DESCRIPTION:** A medium to large, thin, narrow triangular blade that is sometimes serrated, and a medium to long, narrow, rounded stem. Most examples are well made. **I.D. KEY:** Narrow rounded base with more secondary work than ordinary Adena.

G5, $12-$20
Macoupin Co., IL

ADENA-NOTCHED BASE - Late Archaic to Woodland, 3000 - 1200 B. P.

G5, $15-$25
MO

G5, $30-$50
MO

LOCATION: Southeast to Midwest. **DESCRIPTION:** Identical to Adena, but with a notched or snapped-off concave base. **I.D. KEY:** Basal form different.

ADENA-WAUBESA (See Waubesa)

AFTON - Middle Archaic to early Woodland, 5000 - 2000 B. P.

(Also see Apple Creek, Ferry and Helton)

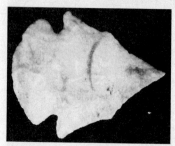

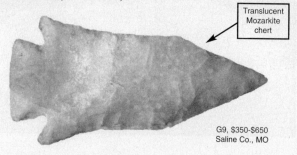

Translucent Mozarkite chert

G8, $80-$150
Cooper Co., MO

G9, $350-$650
Saline Co., MO

LOCATION: Midwestern states and is rarely found in some Eastern and Southeastern states. **DESCRIPTION:** A medium to large size pentagonal shaped point with a flaring or corner notched stem. Some examples are base notched and some are stemmed. **I.D. KEY:** Blade form.

AFTON (continued)

Black chert

G8, $200-$350
IL

G8, $250-$400
MO

G10, $550-$1000
Cherokee Co., OK

G9, $550-$1000
Webster Co., MO

NC

AGATE BASIN - Transitional Paleo to Early Archaic, 10,200 - 8500 B. P.

(Also see Allen, Angostura, Burroughs, Eden, Lerma, Nebo Hill and Sedalia)

LOCATION: Midwestern states. **DESCRIPTION:** A medium to large size lanceolate blade of unusually high quality. Bases are either convex, concave or straight, and are usually ground. Some examples are median ridged and have random to parallel flaking. **I.D. KEY:** Basal form and flaking style.

G5, $65-$125
MO.

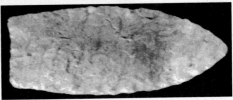

693

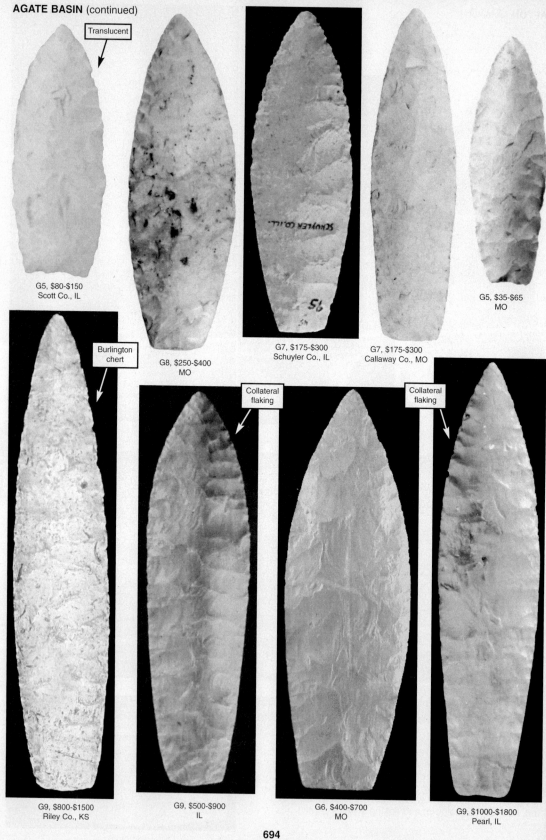

AGATE BASIN (continued)

Translucent

G5, $80-$150
Scott Co., IL

G8, $250-$400
MO

G7, $175-$300
Schuyler Co., IL

G7, $175-$300
Callaway Co., MO

G5, $35-$65
MO

Burlington chert

Collateral flaking

Collateral flaking

G9, $800-$1500
Riley Co., KS

G9, $500-$900
IL

G6, $400-$700
MO

G9, $1000-$1800
Pearl, IL

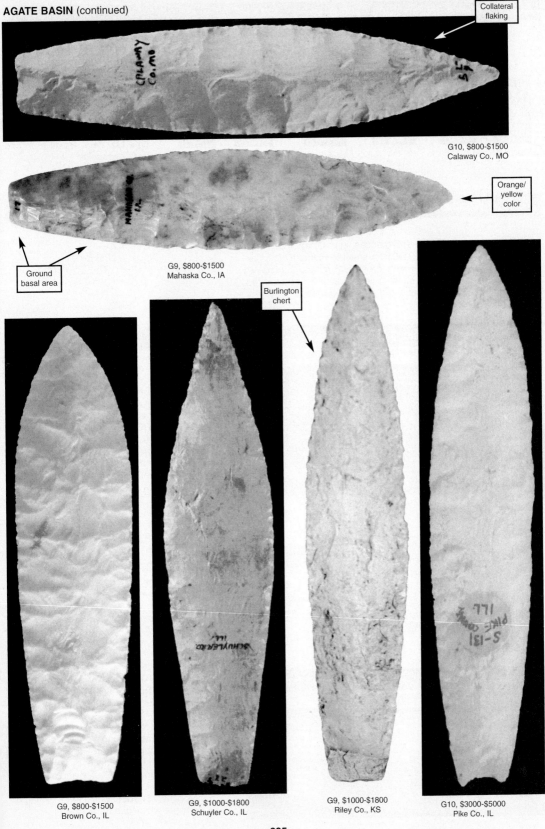

Collateral flaking

G10, $800-$1500
Calaway Co., MO

Orange/ yellow color

Ground basal area

G9, $800-$1500
Mahaska Co., IA

Burlington chert

NC

G9, $800-$1500
Brown Co., IL

G9, $1000-$1800
Schuyler Co., IL

G9, $1000-$1800
Riley Co., KS

G10, $3000-$5000
Pike Co., IL

AGEE - Mississippian, 1200 - 700 B. P.

(Also see Alba, Hayes, Homan)

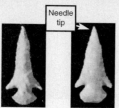

Needle tip

Shoulder nick

LOCATION: Arkansas; rarely into Missouri and Illinois. **DESCRIPTION:** A small to medium size, narrow, expanded barbed, corner notched point. Tips are needle sharp. Some examples are double notched at the base. A rare type **I.D. KEY:** Basal form and barb expansion.

G5, $90-$150 Cent., MO

G6, $125-$200 Cent., MO

G5, $165-$300 Cent., MO

G6, $165-$300 Cent., MO

G6, $165-$300 Cent., MO

G6, $125-$200 Cent., MO

ALBA - Woodland to Mississippian, 2000 - 400 B. P.

(Also see Agee, Hayes, Homan and Sequoyah)

LOCATION: Louisiana, Arkansas into Oklahoma; rarely into Illinois. **DESCRIPTION:** A small to medium size, narrow, well made point with prominent tangs, a recurved blade and a bulbous stem. Some examples are serrated. **I.D. KEY:** Rounded base and expanded barbs.

G7, $80-$150 IL

ALLEN - Early Archaic, 8,500 - 7500 B. P.

(Also see Angostura, Browns Valley, Clovis, Goshen and Plainview)

Tip nick

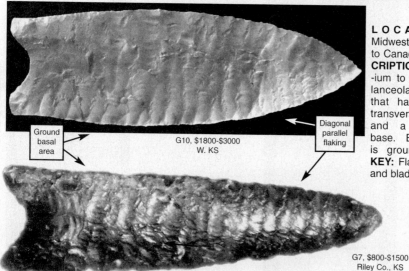

LOCATION: Midwestern states to Canada. **DESCRIPTION:** A medium to large size lanceolate point that has oblique transverse flaking and a concave base. Basal area is ground. **I.D. KEY:** Flaking style and blade form.

Ground basal area

Diagonal parallel flaking

G10, $1800-$3000 W. KS

G7, $800-$1500 Riley Co., KS

G5, $250-$450 Pottowatomie Co., KS

ANGOSTURA - Early to Middle Archaic, 8,800 - 7500 B. P.

(Also see Agate Basin, Allen, Eden & Wheeler Excurvate)

G9, $350-$600 Sou. Platt Riv., NB

LOCATION: Midwest to Western states. **DESCRIPTION:** A medium to large size lanceolate blade with a contracting, concave, straight or convex base. Both broad and narrow forms occur. Flaking can be parallel oblique to random. Blades are commonly steeply beveled on one side of each face; some are serrated and most have basal grinding. Formerly called *Long* points. **I.D. KEY:** Basal form, flaking on blade which can be beveled.

696

ANGOSTURA (continued)

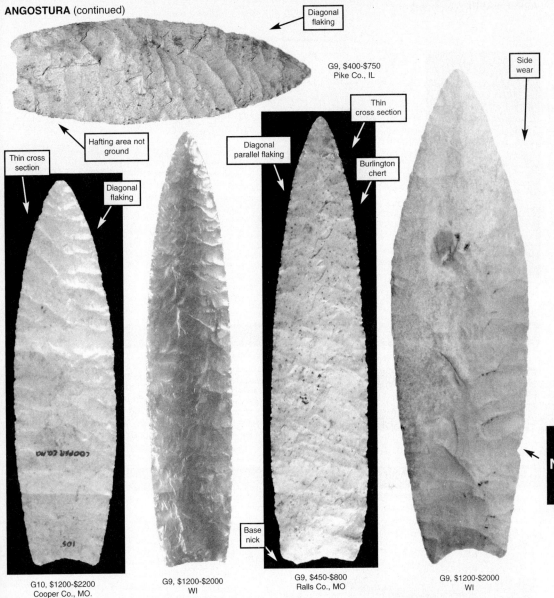

Diagonal flaking

G9, $400-$750
Pike Co., IL

Hafting area not ground

Side wear

Thin cross section

Thin cross section

Diagonal parallel flaking

Diagonal flaking

Burlington chert

NC

Base nick

G10, $1200-$2200
Cooper Co., MO.

G9, $1200-$2000
WI

G9, $450-$800
Ralls Co., MO

G9, $1200-$2000
WI

APPLE CREEK - Late Woodland, 1700 - 1500 B. P.

(Also see Helton, Jacks Reef, Kirk Corner Notched, Lundy and Pine Tree)

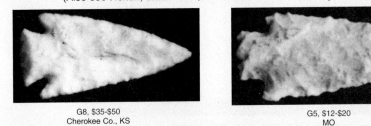

G8, $35-$50
Cherokee Co., KS

G5, $12-$20
MO

LOCATION: Kansas, Missouri & Illinois. **DESCRIPTION:** A medium to large size, broad, corner notched point with an expanded stem. Barbs are short to moderate. Bases are convex, straight or concave. **I.D. KEY:** Angle of corner notches.

Burlington chert

G6, $20-$35
Miller Co., MO

G5, $40-$75
Greene Co., IL

G8, $80-$150
Madison Co., IL

G9, $125-$200
Madison Co., IL

BAYOGOULA - Mississippian, 800 - 400 B. P.

(Also see Cahokia, Madison)

This point was brought up to Cahokia from Louisianna, possibly on a trading trip

G1, $40-$70
Cahokia Mound site, IL

Restored base

LOCATION: Louisiana. **DESCRIPTION:** A small to medium size, thin, narrow, arrowpoint with tapered shoulders and a short, expanded base that is concave. A Louisiana type that has been found at Cahokia Mound site.

BEAVER LAKE - Paleo, 11,250 - 8000 B. P.

(Also see Clovis, Cumberland, Greenbrier, Pike County and Quad)

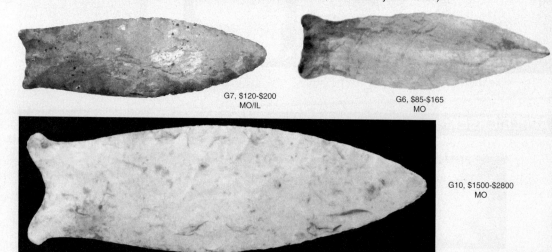

G7, $120-$200
MO/IL

G6, $85-$165
MO

G10, $1500-$2800
MO

LOCATION: Alabama, Tennessee into Illinois and Missouri. **DESCRIPTION:** A medium to large size lanceolate blade with flaring ears. Contemporaneous and associated with *Cumberland,* but thinner than unfluted *Cumberlands.* Bases are ground and blade edges are recurved. **I.D. KEY:** Paleo flaking, shoulder area.

BREWERTON CORNER NOTCHED - Mid-late Archaic, 6000 - 4000 B. P.

(Also see Apple Creek, Helton, Kirk, Lundy)

G5, $12-$20
MO

G6, $15-$25
MO

G5, $15-$30
MO

LOCATION: Midwestern states into the Northeast. **DESCRIPTION:** A small size triangular point with faint corner notches and a convex base. Called *Freeheley* in Michigan.

BREWERTON SIDE NOTCHED - Mid-late Archaic, 6000 - 4000 B. P.

(Also see Godar, Graham Cave, Hickory Ridge, Howard County, Raddatz and Robinson)

LOCATION: Midwestern states into the Northeast. **DESCRIPTION:** A small to medium size, triangular point with weak side notches and a concave to straight base.

G5, $12-$20
MO

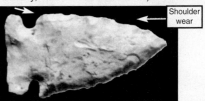

Shoulder wear

BROWNS VALLEY - Transitional Paleo, 10,000 - 8000 B. P.

(Also see Agate Basin, Allen, Angostura, Burroughs, Clovis, Plainview and Sedalia)

Diagonal flaking

G7, $300-$550
Cent. IL. Note oblique parallel flaking which is characteristic of the type.

LOCATION: Upper Midwestern states. **DESCRIPTION:** A medium to large, thin, lanceolate blade with usually oblique to horizontal transverse flaking and a concave to straight base which can be ground. **I.D. KEY:** Paleo transverse flaking.

BURKETT - Woodland, 2300 - 1800 B. P.

(Also see Adena, Dickson, Gary)

LOCATION: Missouri into Arkansas. **DESCRIPTION:** A medium to large size point with a short rectangular to contracting stem. The base can be straight to rounded. Shoulders can be tapered to barbed.

G7, $65-$125
Stockton Lake, MO

BURROUGHS - Early Archaic, 8000 - 6000 B. P.

(Also see Agate Basin and Browns Valley

G6, $45-$80
Riley Co., KS

LOCATION: Northern Midwestern states.
DESCRIPTION: A small to medium size, lanceolate point with convex sides and a straight to slightly concave base.

CACHE RIVER - Early to Middle Archaic, 10,000 - 5000 B. P.

(Also see Godar, Graham Cave, Hickory Ridge, Howard County, Raddatz and Robinson)

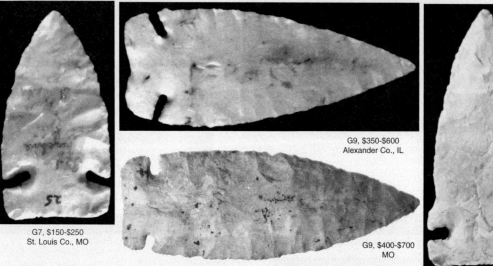

G9, $350-$600
Alexander Co., IL

G7, $150-$250
St. Louis Co., MO

G9, $400-$700
MO

G7, $80-$150
Alexander Co., IL

LOCATION: Midwestern states. **DESCRIPTION:** A small to medium size, fairly thin, side-notched, triangular point with a concave base. Could be related to *Big Sandy* points.
I.D. KEY: Base form, narrow notched & flaking of blade.

CAHOKIA - Mississippian, 1000 - 500 B. P.

(Also see Harrell, Huffaker, Madison and Washita)

Very thin

Four notches

G8, $40-$70
MO

G8, $80-$150
St. Clair Co., IL

G9, $125-$200
IL

G8, $80-$150
Madison Co., IL

Tri-notched

Five notches

G10, $80-$150
IL

G6, $45-$85
MO

Very thin

G10, $300-$500
Madison Co., IL

G6, $80-$150
IL

G6, $35-$65
Madison Co., IL

Tri-notched

G10, $250-$400
IL

Serrated edge

G8, $80-$150
IL

Tri-notched

G10, $250-$400
IL

Four notches

G7, $35-$65
Madison Co., IL

CAHOKIA (continued)

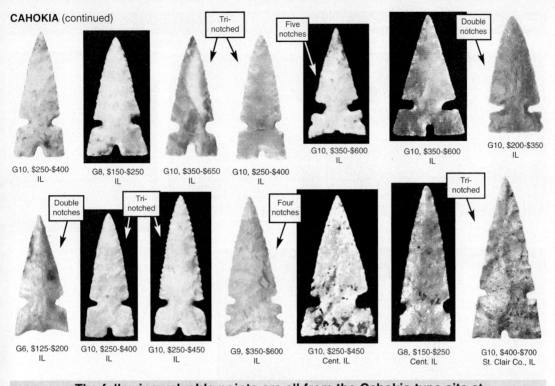

Tri-notched

Five notches

Double notches

G10, $250-$400
IL

G8, $150-$250
IL

G10, $350-$650
IL

G10, $250-$400
IL

G10, $350-$600
IL

G10, $350-$600
IL

G10, $200-$350
IL

Double notches

Tri-notched

Four notches

Tri-notched

G6, $125-$200
IL

G10, $250-$400
IL

G10, $250-$450
IL

G9, $350-$600
IL

G10, $250-$450
Cent. IL

G8, $150-$250
Cent. IL

G10, $400-$700
St. Clair Co., IL

The following valuable points are all from the Cahokia type site at the Cahokia Mounds location in St. Clair Co., IL

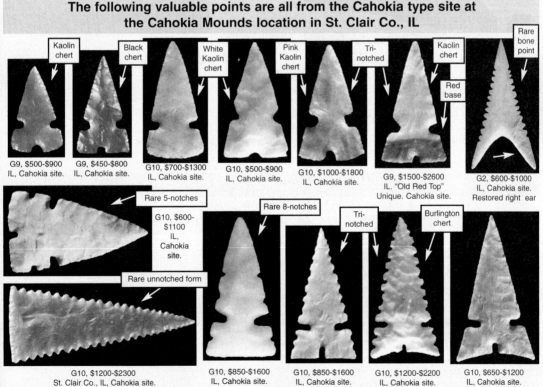

Kaolin chert

Black chert

White Kaolin chert

Pink Kaolin chert

Tri-notched

Kaolin chert

Red base

Rare bone point

NC

G9, $500-$900
IL, Cahokia site.

G9, $450-$800
IL, Cahokia site.

G10, $700-$1300
IL, Cahokia site.

G10, $500-$900
IL, Cahokia site.

G10, $1000-$1800
IL, Cahokia site.

G9, $1500-$2600
IL. "Old Red Top"
Unique. Cahokia site.

G2, $600-$1000
IL, Cahokia site.
Restored right ear

Rare 5-notches

G10, $600-$1100
IL, Cahokia site.

Rare 8-notches

Tri-notched

Burlington chert

Rare unnotched form

G10, $1200-$2300
St. Clair Co., IL, Cahokia site.

G10, $850-$1600
IL, Cahokia site.

G10, $850-$1600
IL, Cahokia site.

G10, $1200-$2200
IL, Cahokia site.

G10, $650-$1200
IL, Cahokia site.

LOCATION: Midwestern states. The famous Cahokia mounds are located in Illinois close to the Mississippi River in St. Clair Co. **DESCRIPTION:** A small to medium size, thin, triangular point that can have one or more notches on each blade edge. A rare unnotched serrated form also occurs on the Cahokia site. The base is either plain, has a center notch or is deeply concave. Rarely, they are made of bone. Associated with the Caddo culture.

CALF CREEK - Early to Middle Archaic, 8000 - 5000 B. P.

(Also see Andice and Bell in Southern Central Section)

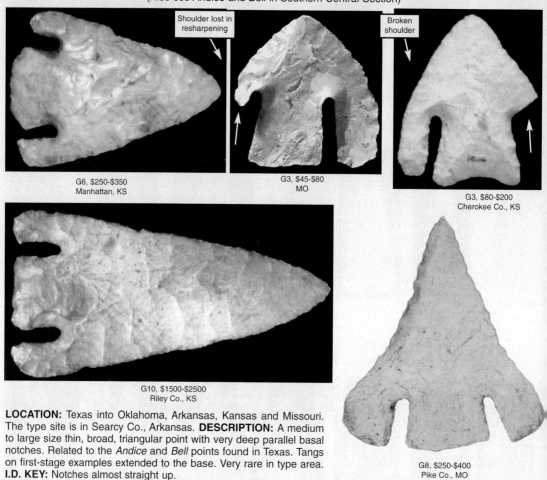

Shoulder lost in resharpening

Broken shoulder

G6, $250-$350
Manhattan, KS

G3, $45-$80
MO

G3, $80-$200
Cherokee Co., KS

G10, $1500-$2500
Riley Co., KS

G8, $250-$400
Pike Co., MO

LOCATION: Texas into Oklahoma, Arkansas, Kansas and Missouri. The type site is in Searcy Co., Arkansas. **DESCRIPTION:** A medium to large size thin, broad, triangular point with very deep parallel basal notches. Related to the *Andice* and *Bell* points found in Texas. Tangs on first-stage examples extended to the base. Very rare in type area. **I.D. KEY:** Notches almost straight up.

CARTER - (Hopewell) - Woodland, 2500 - 1500 B. P.

(Also see Grand and Snyders)

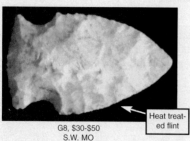

Heat treated flint

G8, $30-$50
S.W. MO

Blade form

G7, $25-$45
Madison Co., IL

G7, $25-$45
MO

LOCATION: Illinois. **DESCRIPTION:** A medium to large size, narrow, wide corner to side notched point with a convex base. Shoulders are rounded, weak to non-existent. The Blade form has no shoulders and is similar in appearance to *Copena* found in Tennessee and Alabama. Related to the *Snyders* point.

G5, $20-$35
IL

G10, $150-$250
IL

CLOVIS - Early Paleo, 11,500 - 10,600 B. P.

(Also see Allen, Angostura, Browns Valley, Cumberland, Dalton, Folsom and Plainview)

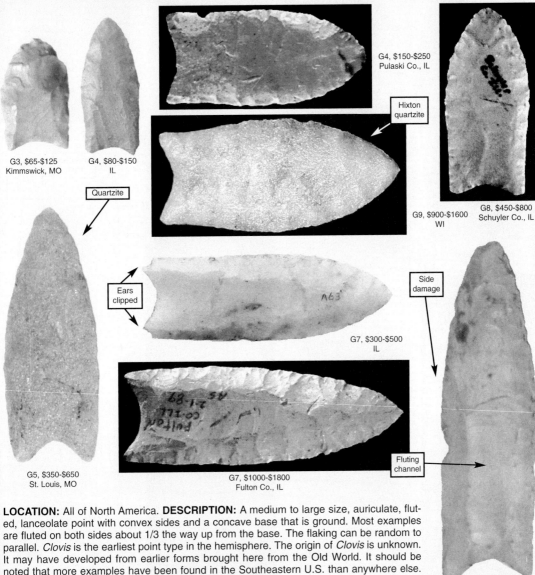

G3, $65-$125
Kimmswick, MO

G4, $80-$150
IL

Quartzite

G4, $150-$250
Pulaski Co., IL

Hixton
quartzite

G9, $900-$1600
WI

G8, $450-$800
Schuyler Co., IL

NC

Ears
clipped

A63

G7, $300-$500
IL

Side
damage

G5, $350-$650
St. Louis, MO

G7, $1000-$1800
Fulton Co., IL

Fluting
channel

G5, $600-$1000
IL

LOCATION: All of North America. **DESCRIPTION:** A medium to large size, auriculate, fluted, lanceolate point with convex sides and a concave base that is ground. Most examples are fluted on both sides about 1/3 the way up from the base. The flaking can be random to parallel. *Clovis* is the earliest point type in the hemisphere. The origin of *Clovis* is unknown. It may have developed from earlier forms brought here from the Old World. It should be noted that more examples have been found in the Southeastern U.S. than anywhere else. *Clovis* is known from South America as well. **I.D. KEY:** Paleo flaking, shoulders, billet or baton fluting instead of indirect style.

G8, $1500-$2500
IL

Knife River
flint

Upper
Mercer
flint

G6, $700-$1200
DeMoines, IA

Fluting
channel

G8, $2000-$3500
IL

G8, $700-$1200
Nemaha Co., KS

Burlington
chert

Basal
grinding

G7, $500-$900
Pike Co., IL

Knife
River
flint

Pink
Burlington
chert

Long
flute
channel

G9, $1800-$3000
St. Joseph, MO

G9, $700-$1200
Boulder, IL

G10, $2500-$4000
Fulton Co., IL

G10, $2500-$4000
Mills Co., IA

CLOVIS (continued)

G9, $1500-$2500
Kimmswick, MO

Burlington chert

G9, $1000-$1800
IL

G8, 1000-$1800
St. Louis Co., MO

Silicified sandstone

Photo from a Pete Bostrom cast

Fluting channel

G8, $3000-$5000
Fulton Co., IL

G10, $4000-$7500
Adams Co., IL

NC

CLOVIS-HAZEL - Early Paleo, 11,500 - 10,600 B. P.

Flute channel

G8, $400-$700
IL

G8, $900-$1700
IL

CLOVIS-HAZEL (continued)

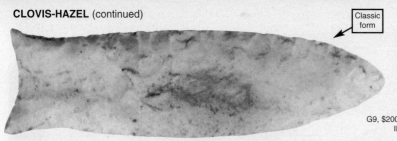

Classic form

LOCATION: Midwestern states eastward. **DESCRIPTION:** A small to large size auriculate point with recurved blade edges and a fishtailed base that is concave. **I.D. KEY:** Fishtailed base.

G9, $2000-$3500
IL

CLOVIS-ST. LOUIS - Early Paleo, 11,500 - 10,600 B. P.

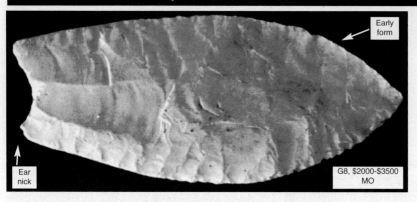

Early form

Ear nick

G8, $2000-$3500
MO

LOCATION: The Dakotas, Wisconsin southward to Arkansas and eastward to Michigan. **DESCRIPTION:** A large size, broad, auriculate, fluted, lanceolate point with convex sides and a concave base that is ground. Most examples are fluted on both sides 1/3 or more up from the base. The flaking can be random to parallel. One of the Earliest *Clovis* forms. **I.D. KEY:** Size and broadness.

COBBS TRIANGULAR - Early Archaic, 8000 - 5000 B. P.

(Also see Decatur, Dovetail, Lerma and Lost Lake)

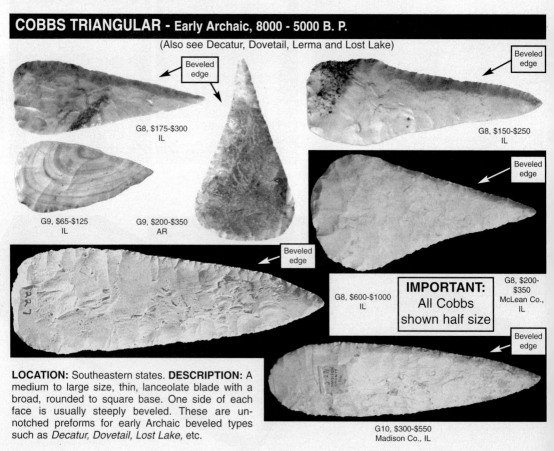

Beveled edge

Beveled edge

G8, $175-$300
IL

Beveled edge

G8, $150-$250
IL

G9, $65-$125
IL

G9, $200-$350
AR

Beveled edge

Beveled edge

IMPORTANT: All Cobbs shown half size

G8, $600-$1000
IL

G8, $200-$350
McLean Co., IL

Beveled edge

G10, $300-$550
Madison Co., IL

LOCATION: Southeastern states. **DESCRIPTION:** A medium to large size, thin, lanceolate blade with a broad, rounded to square base. One side of each face is usually steeply beveled. These are unnotched preforms for early Archaic beveled types such as *Decatur, Dovetail, Lost Lake,* etc.

COLLINS - Woodland, 1500 - 1200 B. P.

(Also see Haskell, Scallorn)

G8, $35-$65
Cherokee
Co., KS

LOCATION: Arkansas into Kansas. **DESCRIPTION:** A small, narrow arrowpoint with broad side notches. Bases can be straight, to eared to convex.

CORNER TANG KNIFE- Late Archaic to Woodland, 4000 - 2000 B. P.

Winterset
chert

LOCATION: Missouri, Kansas, Arkansas, Texas, Oklahoma. **DESCRIPTION:** This knife is notched producing a tang at a corner for hafting to a handle. Tang knives are very rare and have been reproduced in recent years. **I.D. KEY:** Angle of hafting.

G9, $350-$650
Jackson Co., MO

Knife River
flint

G9, $3500-$5500
Pottawatomie Co., KS

COSSATOT RIVER - Early Archaic, 9500 - 8000 B. P.

(Also see Fox Valley and Lake Erie)

Hornstone

G6, $40-$75
Madison Co., IL

G4, $12-$20
Logan Co., IL

G6, $15-$30
Madison Co., IL

G8, $15-$30
Logan Co., IL

Serrated
edge

G9, $65-$125, Logan Co., IL.

G8, $40-$75
Logan Co., IL

G6, $20-$35
Logan Co., IL

COSSATOT RIVER (continued)

Serrated edge

G6, $55-$100
McLean Co., IL

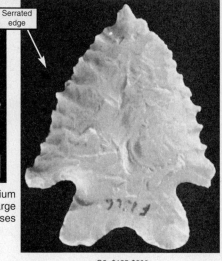

Serrated edge

G9, $125-$200
Adams Co., IL

LOCATION: Illinois, Missouri into Oklahoma. **DESCRIPTION:** A medium to large size, thin, usually serrated, widely corner notched point with large round to square ears and a deep notch in the center of the base. Bases are usually ground. **I.D. KEY:** Basal notching, early Archaic flaking.

CRESCENT KNIFE   (see Munker/s Creek)

CUMBERLAND - Paleo, 11,250 - 10,000 B. P.

(Also see Beaver Lake, Clovis, Dalton and Quad)

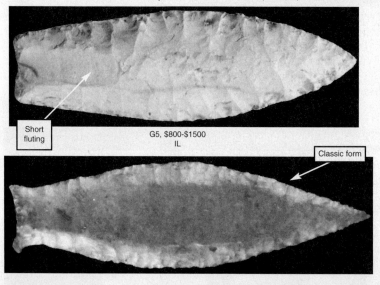

Short fluting

G5, $800-$1500
IL

Classic form

G9, $3500-$6000
Cent. IL

LOCATION: Southeastern states into Illinois. Called *Barnes Cumberland* in the Northeast. **DESCRIPTION:** A medium to large size, lanceolate, eared form that is usually fluted on both faces. The fluting and flaking technique is an advanced form as in *Folsom*, with the flutes usually extending the entire length of the blade. Bases are ground on all examples. An unfluted variant which is thicker than *Beaver Lake* has been found. This point is scarce everywhere and has been reproduced in large numbers. **I.D. KEY:** Paleo flaking, indirect pressure fluted.

CUMBERLAND UNFLUTED - Paleo, 11,500 - 10,000 B. P.

(Also see Beaver Lake, Clovis, Pike County and Quad)

G10, $3500-$6000
St. Clair Co., IL

DESCRIPTION: Identical to fluted *Cumberland*, but without the fluting. **Very rare** in the type area. Cross section is thicker than *Beaver Lake*.

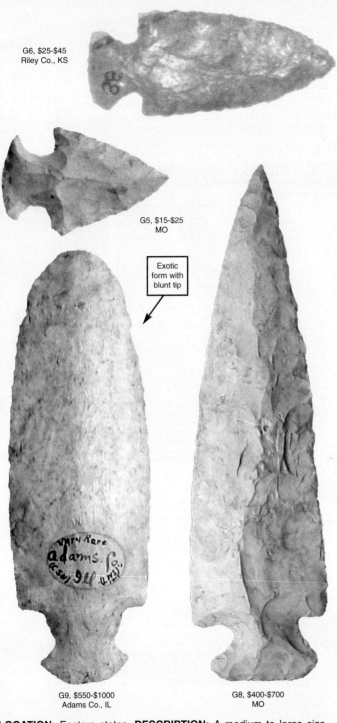

G6, $25-$45
Riley Co., KS

G5, $15-$25
MO

Exotic form with blunt tip

G9, $550-$1000
Adams Co., IL

G8, $400-$700
MO

NC

G8, $1500-$2500
MO

LOCATION: Eastern states. **DESCRIPTION:** A medium to large size, narrow point with wide corner notches, shoulder barbs and a convex base. Similar to *Motley,* but the base stem is shorter and broader. *Epps* has square to tapered shoulders and a straight base, otherwise is identical to *Motley.*

DALTON-BRECKENRIDGE - Early Archaic, 10,00 - 9200 B. P.

(Also see Dalton and Meserve)

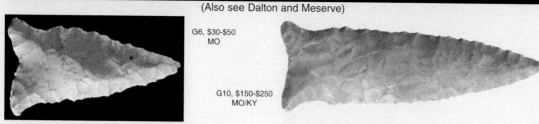

G6, $30-$50
MO

G10, $150-$250
MO/KY

LOCATION: Midwestern states, **DESCRIPTION:** A medium to large size, auriculate point with an obvious bevel extending the entire length of the point from tip to base. Similar in form to the *Dalton-Greenbrier*. Basal area is usually ground.

DALTON CLASSIC - Early Archaic, 10,000 - 9200 B. P.

(Also see Beaver Lake, Greenbrier, Holland, Meserve, Pelican, Plainview and Quad)

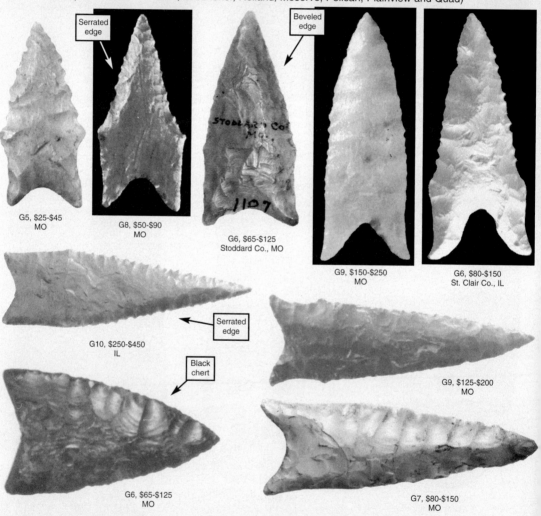

Serrated edge

Beveled edge

G5, $25-$45
MO

G8, $50-$90
MO

G6, $65-$125
Stoddard Co., MO

G9, $150-$250
MO

G6, $80-$150
St. Clair Co., IL

Serrated edge

G10, $250-$450
IL

Black chert

G9, $125-$200
MO

G6, $65-$125
MO

G7, $80-$150
MO

LOCATION: Midwestern to Southeastern states. **DESCRIPTION:** A medium to large size, thin, auriculate, fishtailed point. Many examples are finely serrated and exhibit excellent flaking. Beveling may occur on one side of each face but is usually on the right side. All have basal grinding. This early type spread over most of the Eastern and Midwestern U.S. and strongly influenced many types to follow.

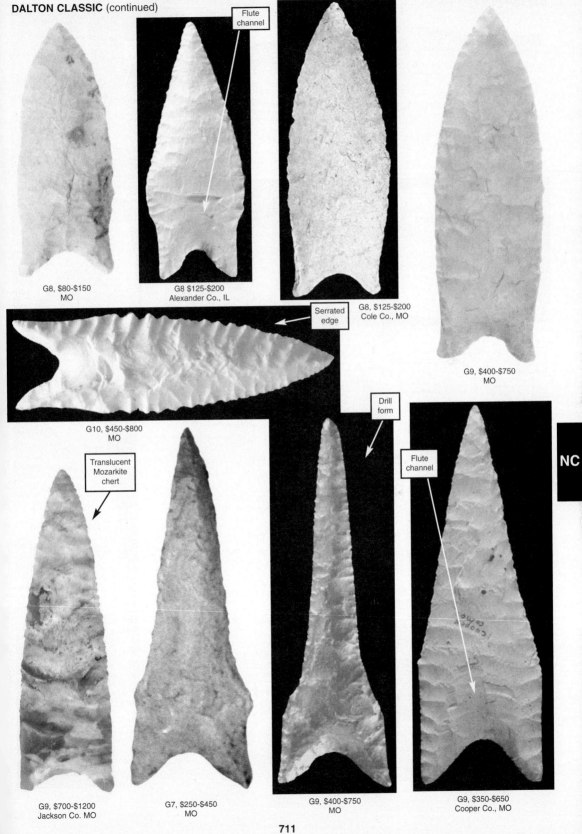

Flute channel

G8, $80-$150
MO

G8 $125-$200
Alexander Co., IL

Serrated edge

G8, $125-$200
Cole Co., MO

G9, $400-$750
MO

G10, $450-$800
MO

NC

Translucent Mozarkite chert

Drill form

Flute channel

G9, $700-$1200
Jackson Co. MO

G7, $250-$450
MO

G9, $400-$750
MO

G9, $350-$650
Cooper Co., MO

711

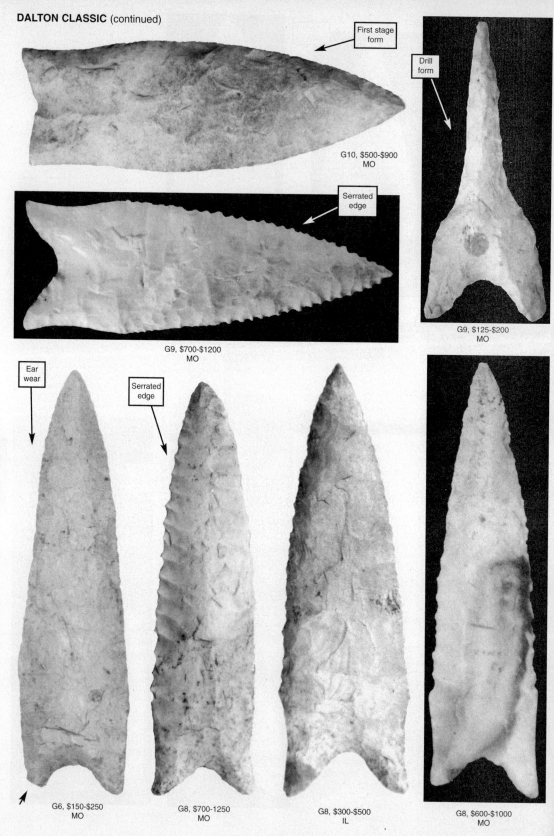

DALTON CLASSIC (continued)

First stage form

G10, $500-$900
MO

Drill form

G9, $125-$200
MO

Serrated edge

G9, $700-$1200
MO

Ear wear

Serrated edge

G6, $150-$250
MO

G8, $700-1250
MO

G8, $300-$500
IL

G8, $600-$1000
MO

DALTON CLASSIC (continued)

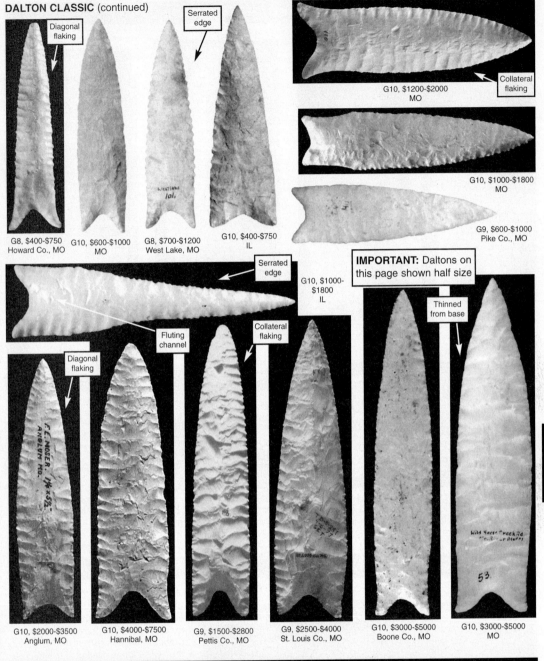

Diagonal flaking

Serrated edge

Collateral flaking

G10, $1200-$2000
MO

G10, $1000-$1800
MO

G9, $600-$1000
Pike Co., MO

G8, $400-$750
Howard Co., MO

G10, $600-$1000
MO

G8, $700-$1200
West Lake, MO

G10, $400-$750
IL

IMPORTANT: Daltons on this page shown half size

Serrated edge

G10, $1000-$1800
IL

Fluting channel

Collateral flaking

Thinned from base

Diagonal flaking

G10, $2000-$3500
Anglum, MO

G10, $4000-$7500
Hannibal, MO

G9, $1500-$2800
Pettis Co., MO

G9, $2500-$4000
St. Louis Co., MO

G10, $3000-$5000
Boone Co., MO

G10, $3000-$5000
MO

NC

DALTON-COLBERT - Early Archaic, 10,000 - 9200 B. P.

(Also see Beaver Lake, Greenbrier, Meserve)

Serrated

Black agate

LOCATION: Midwestern to Eastern states. **DESCRIPTION:** A medium size auriculate form with a squared stem and a weakly defined hafting area which is ground. Some examples are serrated and exhibit parallel flaking of the highest quality. **I.D. KEY:** Squarish basal area.

G8, $200-$350
N.E. KS

DALTON-HEMPHILL - Early Archaic, 10,000 - 9200 B. P.

(Also see Holland and Scottsbluff)

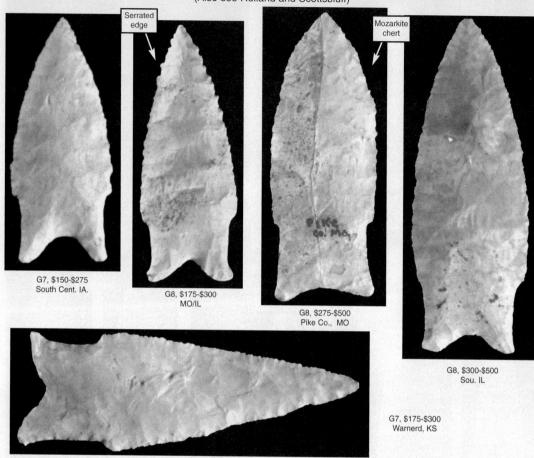

Serrated edge

Mozarkite chert

G7, $150-$275
South Cent. IA.

G8, $175-$300
MO/IL

G8, $275-$500
Pike Co., MO

G8, $300-$500
Sou. IL

G7, $175-$300
Warnerd, KS

LOCATION: Midwestern to Eastern states. **DESCRIPTION:** A medium to large size point with expanded auricles and horizontal, tapered to weak shoulders. Blade edges are usually serrated and bases are ground. In later times, this variant developed into the *Hemphill* point. **I.D. KEY:** Straightened extended shoulders.

DALTON-NUCKOLLS - Early Archaic, 10,000 - 9200 B. P.

(Also see Dalton and Holland)

Collateral flaking

LOCATION: Midwestern to Southeastern states. **DESCRIPTION:** A medium to large size variant form, probably occurring from resharpening the *Greenbrier Dalton*. Bases are squared to lobbed to eared, and have a shallow concavity. **I.D. KEY:** Broad base and shoulders, flaking on blade.

G8, $250-$400
Graves Co., IL

DALTON-SLOAN - Early Archaic, 10,000 - 9200 B. P.

(Also see Allen, Angostura, Dalton, Greenbrier, Holland and Plainview)

DALTON-SLOAN (continued)

LOCATION: Midwestern states. **DESCRIPTION:** A large size variant of the *Dalton* point. This point is usually serrated, lacking shoulders and has a concave, fishtail base. Flaking is typically of the Dalton parallel style. **I.D. KEY:** No shoulders, serrations, fishtail base.

> **IMPORTANT:**
> All Sloans shown half size

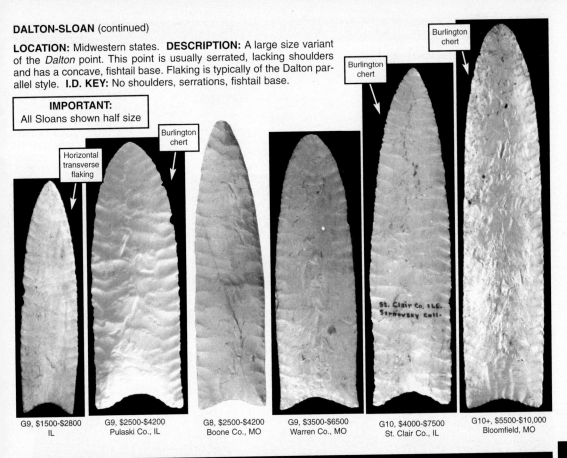

G9, $1500-$2800
IL

G9, $2500-$4200
Pulaski Co., IL

G8, $2500-$4200
Boone Co., MO

G9, $3500-$6500
Warren Co., MO

G10, $4000-$7500
St. Clair Co., IL

G10+, $5500-$10,000
Bloomfield, MO

DECATUR - Early Archaic, 9000 - 3000 B. P.

(Also see Cobbs Triangular, Hardin, Kirk, Lost Lake and St. Charles)

NC

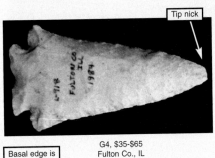

G4, $35-$65
Fulton Co., IL

G9, $225-$400
IL

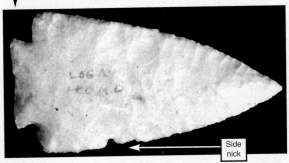

LOCATION: Eastern to Midwestern states. **DESCRIPTION:** A small to medium size, serrated, corner notched point that is usually beveled on one side of each face. The base is usually broken off (fractured) by a blow inward from each corner of the stem. Sometimes the sides of the stem and backs of the tangs are also fractured, and in rare cases, the tip may be fractured by a blow on each side directed towards the base. Bases are usually ground and flaking is of high quality. Basal fracturing also occurs in *Kirk, Motley, St. Charles* and *Snyders*.

G5, $90-$175
Logan Co., IL

715

DELHI - Late Archaic, 3500 - 2000 B. P.

(Also see Helton)

G8, $65-$125
Cooper Co., MO

G9, $80-$150
Cooper Co., MO

LOCATION: Louisiana into Missouri. **DESCRIPTION:** A medium to large size, narrow, stemmed point with a long blade and strong, barbed shoulders. The stem can be square but usually expands and the base is straight to slightly convex. **I.D. KEY:** Base form, narrowness of blade.

DICKSON - Woodland, 2500 - 1600 B. P.

(Also see Adena, Burkett, Gary, Hidden Valley and Waubesa)

G5, $12-$20
AR

G6, $15-$25
WI

G6, $15-$25
IL

G9, $65-$125
MO

Heat treated
Burlington
chert

G6, $35-$65
St. Louis Co., MO

G6, $25-$45
AR

716

DICKSON (continued)

G6, $40-$75
AR

G7, $125-$200
AR

G7, $55-$100
AR

LOCATION: Midwestern states. **DESCRIPTION:** Associated with the Hopewell culture. A medium to large size point with tapered shoulders and a contracting stem. High quality flaking and thinness is evident on most examples. **I.D. KEY:** Basal form.

G7, $150-$250
IL

G9, $200-$350
IL

G8, $250-$450
Cooper Co., MO

717

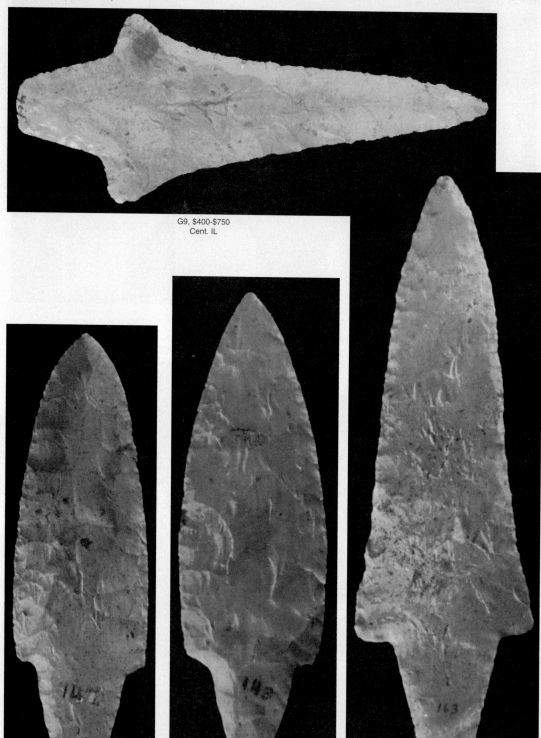

G9, $400-$750
Cent. IL

G8, $400-$700
IL

G9, $350-$650
MO

G9, $1000-$1800
Cole Co., MO

DRILL - Paleo to Historic, 11,500 - 200 B. P.

(Also see Scraper)

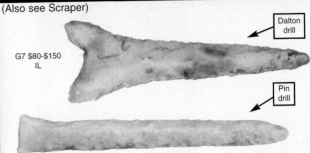

G7 $80-$150
IL

> Dalton drill

> Pin drill

G10, $65-$125
Madison Co., IL

G6, $20-$35
Logan Co., IL

G8, $20-$35
Lasalle Co., IL

LOCATION: Everywhere. **DESCRIPTION:** Although many drills were made from scratch, all point types were made into the drill form. Usually, heavily resharpened and broken points were salvaged and rechipped into drills. These objects were certainly used as drills (evidence of extreme edge wear), but there is speculation that some of these forms may have been used as pins for clothing, ornaments, ear plugs and other uses.

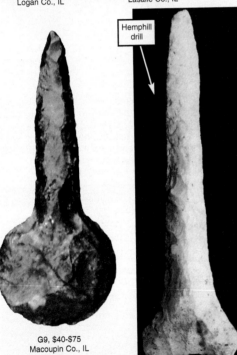

G9, $40-$75
Macoupin Co., IL

> Hemphill drill

G8, $175-$300
Cooper Co., MO

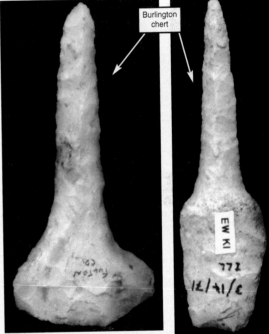

> Burlington chert

G8, $65-$125
Fulton Co., IL

G8, $65-$125
IL

NC

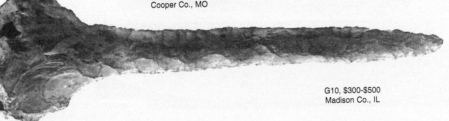

G10, $300-$500
Madison Co., IL

EARLY OVOID KNIFE - Trans. Paleo-Early Archaic, 11,000 - 9000 B. P.

(Also see Turkeytail)

Kaolin chert

G10, $3500-$6000
MO. Rare

G10, $3000-$5000
Madison Co., IL.. Rare

G8, $100-$195
Jackson Co., MO

Burlington chert

G9, $3500-$6000
IL. Rare

G9, $400-$750
Fulton Co., IL. Rare

G7, $125-$225
Jackson Co., MO

Winerset chert

IMPORTANT:
All Early Ovoids shown half size

LOCATION: Arkansas, Missouri to Wisconsin.
DESCRIPTION: A medium to large size, broad, thin, flat ovoid knife. Usually occurs as a double pointed blade but examples have been found with a small, notched stem. A very rare type. **I.D. KEY:** Broad blade, small stem to ovoid shape.

EDEN - Transitional Paleo, 10,000 - 8000 B. P.

(Also see Agate Basin, Angostura, Hardin, Holland, Hollenberg Stemmed, Nebo Hill, Scottsbluff)

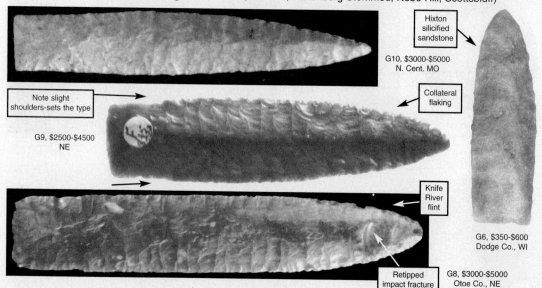

Hixton silicified sandstone

G10, $3000-$5000
N. Cent. MO

Note slight shoulders-sets the type

Collateral flaking

G9, $2500-$4500
NE

Knife River flint

G6, $350-$600
Dodge Co., WI

Retipped impact fracture

G8, $3000-$5000
Otoe Co., NE

EDEN (continued)

Impact fracture

Collateral flaking

Hixton silicified sandstone

G6, $350-$650
W. MO

Eden Eared form
G7, $19,000-$30,0000+
Jackson Co., WI

Note knobbed base

Eden Eared form
G5, $550-$1000
Rock Co., WI

LOCATION: Midwestern states. **DESCRIPTION:** A medium to large size, narrow, lanceolate blade with a straight to concave base. Many examples have a median ridge and collateral to oblique parallel flaking. Bases are usually ground. **I.D. KEY:** Weak shoulders.

EPPS - Late Archaic to Woodland, 3500 - 2000 B. P.

(Also see Cupp, Kay Blade and Motley)

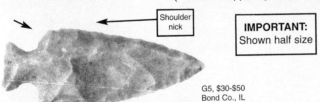

Shoulder nick

IMPORTANT:
Shown half size

LOCATION: Louisiana, Arkansas into Illinois. **DESCRIPTION:** A medium to large broadly corner notched to expanded stemmed point. Base is straight. Shoulders are not as strongly barbed as *Motley* points which also have a convex base.

G5, $30-$50
Bond Co., IL

ETLEY - Late Archaic, 4000 - 2500 B. P.

(Also see Hardin, Mehlville, Smith, Stilwell, Stone Square Stem and Wadlow)

G6, $40-$75
MO

Burlington chert

G8, $125-$200
Madison Co., IL

G8, $150-$250
Morgan Co. MO

G8, $200-$350
St. Charles Co., MO

G8, $150-$250
MO

G9, $200-$350
MO

ETLEY (continued)

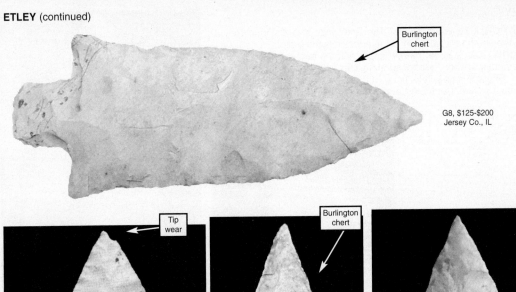

Burlington chert

G8, $125-$200
Jersey Co., IL

Tip wear

Burlington chert

G8, $200-$325
Pike Co., IL

G8, $400-$750
Fulton Co., IL

G9, $550-$1000
St. Clair Co., IL

NC

ETLEY (continued)

LOCATION: Midwestern states. The Etley site is in Calhoun Co., IL. Many *Wadlow* points were found there which is the preform for this type. **DESCRIPTION:** A large, narrow, blade with an angular point, recurved blade edges, a short, expanded stem and a straight to slightly convex base. Shoulders usually expand but have a tendency to point inward towards the base. **I.D. KEY:** Large size, barbs, narrow blade.

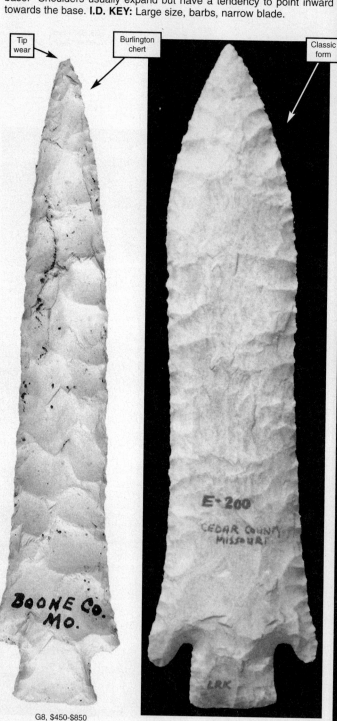

Tip wear

Burlington chert

Classic form

G8, $450-$850
Boone Co., MO

G10, $800-$1500
Cedar Co., MO

G10, $1600-$3000
Montgomery Co., MO

EVANS - Late Archaic to Woodland, 4000 - 2000 B. P.

(Also see Hickory Ridge, Merkle and Turkeytail)

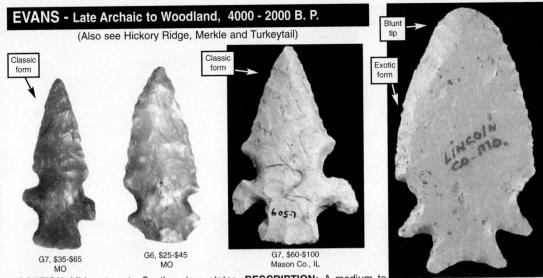

Classic form

Classic form

Blunt tip

Exotic form

G7, $35-$65
MO

G6, $25-$45
MO

G7, $60-$100
Mason Co., IL

G8, $175-$300
Cent. IL

LOCATION: Midwestern to Southeastern states. **DESCRIPTION:** A medium to large size stemmed point that is notched on each side somewhere between the point and shoulders. A similar form is found in Ohio and called *Ohio Double-Notched.*

EXOTIC FORMS - Archaic-Mississippian, 5000 - 1000 B. P.

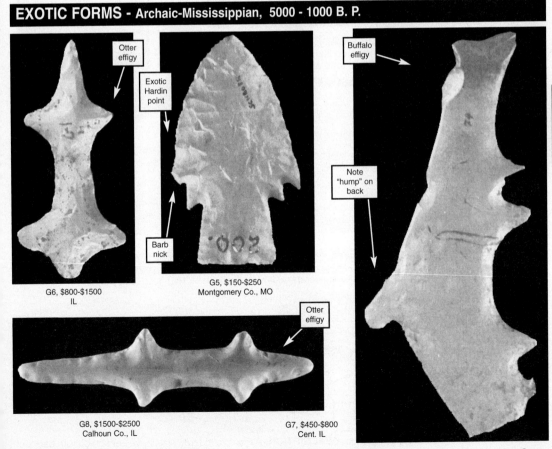

Otter effigy

Exotic Hardin point

Buffalo effigy

Note "hump" on back

Barb nick

G6, $800-$1500
IL

G5, $150-$250
Montgomery Co., MO

Otter effigy

G8, $1500-$2500
Calhoun Co., IL

G7, $450-$800
Cent. IL

LOCATION: Everywhere. **DESCRIPTION:** The forms illustrated on this and the following pages are very rare. Some are definitely effigy forms while others may be no more than unfinished and unintentional doodles.

725

FERRY - Middle to late Archaic, 5500 - 4500 B. P.

(Also see Grand, Hardin, Kay Blade, Kirk Corner Notched and Stilwell)

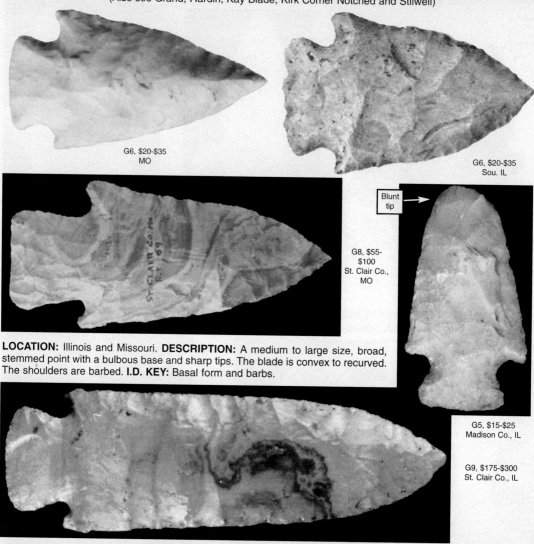

G6, $20-$35
MO

G6, $20-$35
Sou. IL

Blunt tip

G8, $55-$100
St. Clair Co., MO

LOCATION: Illinois and Missouri. **DESCRIPTION:** A medium to large size, broad, stemmed point with a bulbous base and sharp tips. The blade is convex to recurved. The shoulders are barbed. **I.D. KEY:** Basal form and barbs.

G5, $15-$25
Madison Co., IL

G9, $175-$300
St. Clair Co., IL

FIRSTVIEW - Transitional Paleo, 10,000 - 8000 B. P.

(Also see agate Basin, Angostura, Eden, Holland, Nebo Hill, Scottsbluff)

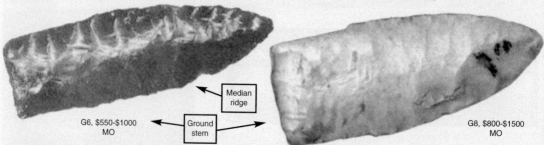

Median ridge

Ground stem

G6, $550-$1000
MO

G8, $800-$1500
MO

LOCATION: Missouri into Texas to Colorado. **DESCRIPTION:** A medium to large size lanceolate blade with early collateral flaking and very weak shoulders. A variant of the *Scottsbluff* type made by the Cody Complex people. Bases are straight and stem sides are parallel. Many examples are median ridged with collateral, parallel flaking. **I.D. KEY:** Broad base, weak shoulders.

FOLSOM - Paleo, 11,000 - 10,000 B. P.

(Also see Clovis, Cumberland and Goshen)

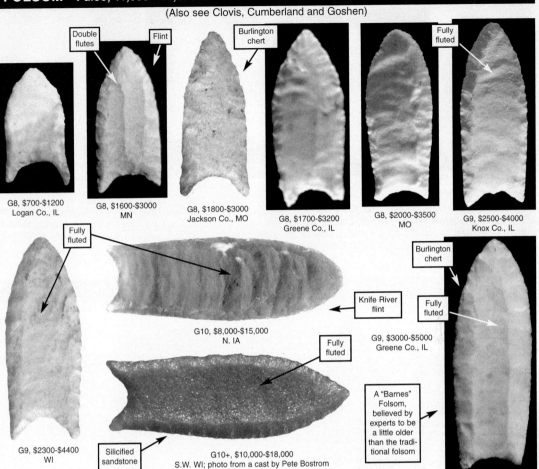

Double flutes | Flint

G8, $700-$1200
Logan Co., IL

G8, $1600-$3000
MN

Burlington chert

G8, $1800-$3000
Jackson Co., MO

G8, $1700-$3200
Greene Co., IL

G8, $2000-$3500
MO

Fully fluted

G9, $2500-$4000
Knox Co., IL

Fully fluted

G10, $8,000-$15,000
N. IA

Knife River flint

G9, $2300-$4400
WI

Silicified sandstone

Fully fluted

G10+, $10,000-$18,000
S.W. WI; photo from a cast by Pete Bostrom

Burlington chert

Fully fluted

G9, $3000-$5000
Greene Co., IL

A "Barnes" Folsom, believed by experts to be a little older than the traditional folsom

NC

LOCATION: N. Indiana Westward to Texas, northward to the Dakotas and West to Montana. **DESCRIPTION:** A small to medium size, thin, high quality, fluted point with contracted to slightly expanding, pointed auricles and a concave base. Fluting usually extends the entire length of each face. Blade flaking is extremely fine. The hafting area is ground. A very rare type, even in area of highest incidence. Modern reproductions have been made and extreme caution should be exercised in acquiring an original specimen. Often found in association with extinct bison fossil remains. **I.D. KEY:** Thinness and flaking style (Excessive secondary flaking). **NOTE:** A *Folsom* site was recently found on the Tippecanoe River in N. Indiana. *Clovis* and *Beaver Lake* were also found there.

FOX VALLEY - Early to Middle Archaic, 9000 - 4000 B. P.

(Also see Kirk, Lake Erie and Cossatot River)

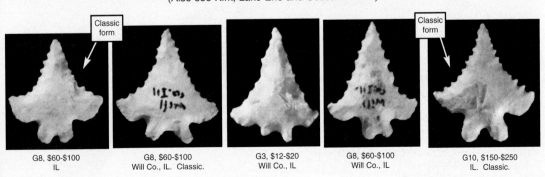

Classic form

Classic form

G8, $60-$100
IL

G8, $60-$100
Will Co., IL. Classic.

G3, $12-$20
Will Co., IL

G8, $60-$100
Will Co., IL

G10, $150-$250
IL. Classic.

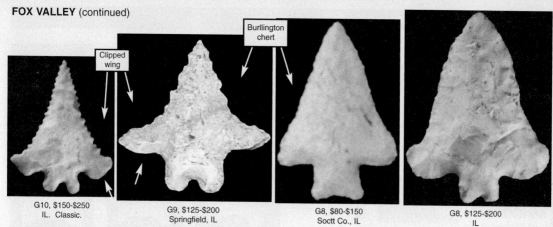

G10, $150-$250
IL. Classic.

Clipped wing

Burllington chert

G9, $125-$200
Springfield, IL

G8, $80-$150
Soctt Co., IL

G8, $125-$200
IL

LOCATION: Midwestern states. **DESCRIPTION:** A small size, triangular point with flaring shoulders and a short bifurcated stem. Shoulders are sometimes clipped winged and have a tendency to turn towards the tip. Blades exhibit early parallel flaking and the edges are usually serrated. An identical point is found in TN, KY to WV to New York known as *Kanawha Stemmed*. **I.D. KEY:** Bifurcated base and barbs.

GARY - Late Archaic to Early Woodland, 3200 - 300 B. P.

(Also see Adena, Burkett, Dickson, Hidden Valley, Peisker Diamond and Waubesa)

Mozarkite

G9, $125-$200
MO

G5, $8-$15
KS

G7, $12-$20
IL

G9, $150-$250
Anglum, MO

G8, $30-$50
MO

LOCATION: Midwestern to Southwestern states. **DESCRIPTION:** A medium size, triangular point with a medium to long, contracted, pointed to rounded base. Shoulders are usually tapered. **I.D. KEY:** Similar to *Adena*, but thinned more.

GARY (continued)

G10, $250-$450
MO

GIBSON - Mid to late Woodland, 2000 - 1500 B. P.

(Also see Cupp, Grand, Motley and St. Charles)

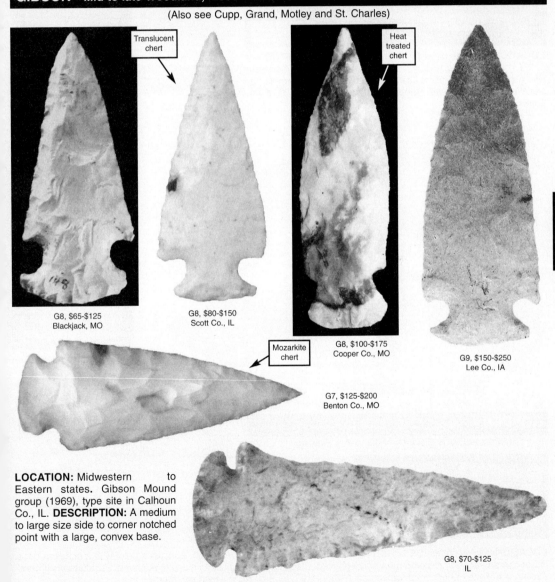

Translucent chert

Heat treated chert

NC

G8, $65-$125
Blackjack, MO

G8, $80-$150
Scott Co., IL

G8, $100-$175
Cooper Co., MO

G9, $150-$250
Lee Co., IA

Mozarkite chert

G7, $125-$200
Benton Co., MO

LOCATION: Midwestern to Eastern states. Gibson Mound group (1969), type site in Calhoun Co., IL. **DESCRIPTION:** A medium to large size side to corner notched point with a large, convex base.

G8, $70-$125
IL

GODAR - Late Archaic, 4500 - 3500 B. P.

(Also see Hemphill, Hickory Ridge, Osceola and Raddatz)

G7, $50-$80
Madison Co., IL

Burlington chert

Heavily resharpened

G7, $80-$150
Morgan Co., MO

LOCATION: Illinois, Missouri into Wisconsin. **DESCRIPTION:** A medium to large size, sturdy, narrow to wide, side-notched point with a straight base and parallel sides. Some examples show parallel flaking. **Note:** *Black Sand* points are now typed as *Godar* points.

G8, $125-$200
Macoupin Co., IL

G8, $150-$275
Clinton Co., IL

Purple chert

G10, $400-$700
Herman, MO

G9, $175-$300
MO

GOSHEN - Paleo, 11,250 - 9500 B. P.

(Also see Clovis, Folsom, Midland and Plainview)

G7, $200-$350
S.E. KS

Heat treated Burlington chert

G9, $600-$1000
E. KS

LOCATION: Plains states. **DESCRIPTION:** A small to medium size, very thin, auriculate point with a concave base. Basal corners range from being rounded to pointed. Blade edges are parallel sided to recurved. Basal area is ground. Flaking is oblique to horizontal transverse. A very rare type. **I.D. KEY:** Thinness, auricles

GRAHAM CAVE - Early to Middle Archaic, 9000 - 5000 B. P.

(Also see Godar, Hemphill, Howard County, Osceola and Raddatz)

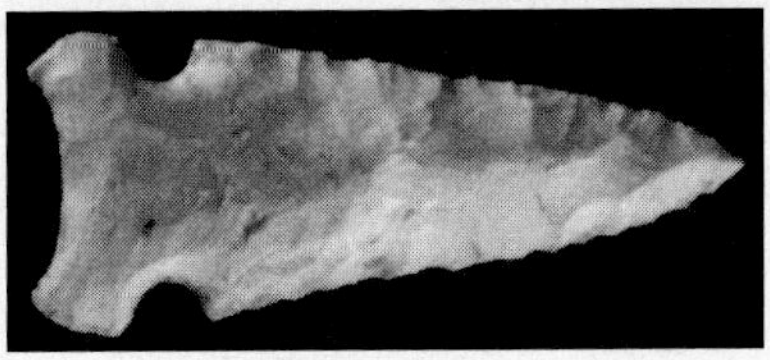

G5, $35-$65
Graham, MO

Morgan
Co. Mo.

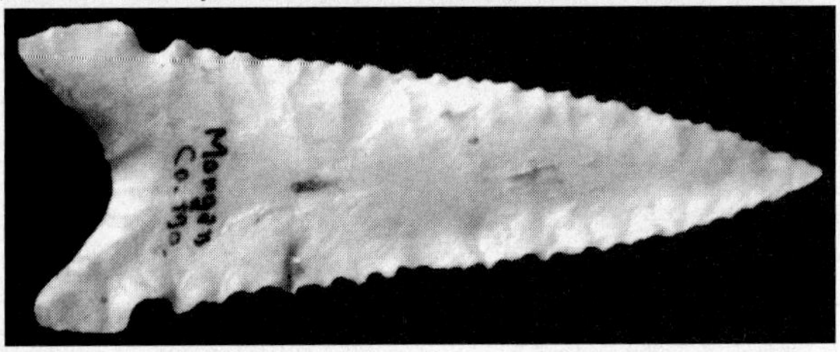

G10, $250-$450
Morgan Co., MO

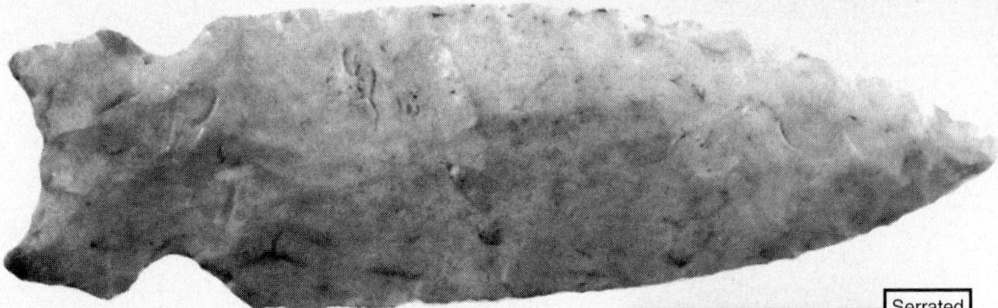

G7, $200-$350
IL

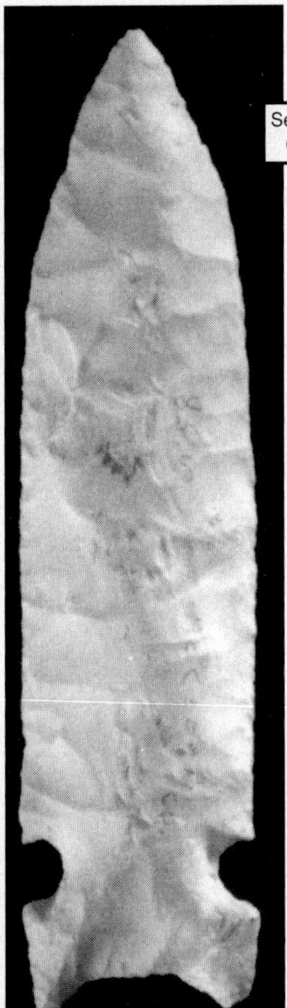

Serrated
edge

G8, $350-$650
McClean Co., IL

Mozarkite
chert

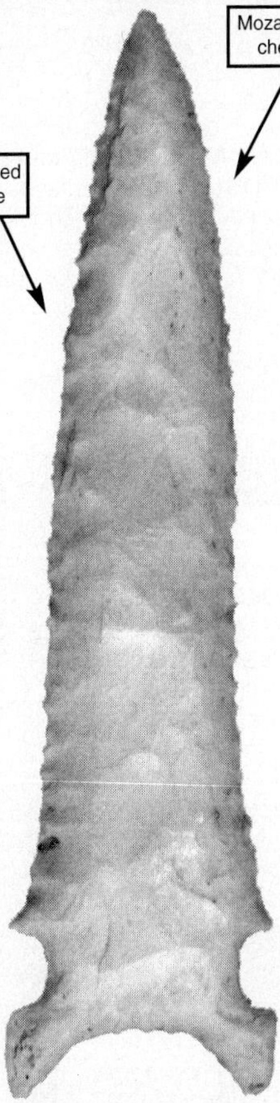

G10, $1000-$1750
Saline Co., MO

Serrated
edge

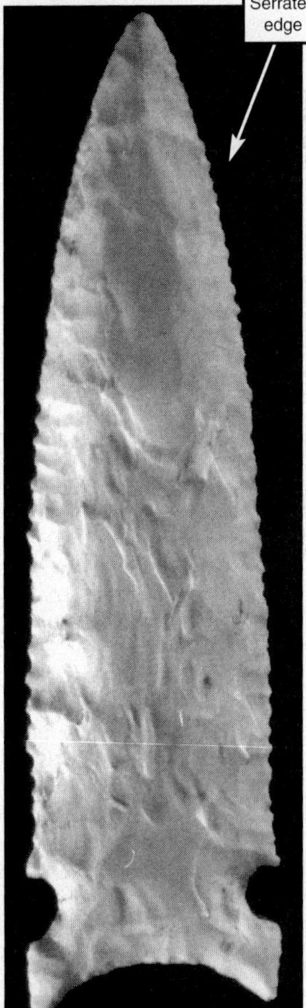

G9, $550-$1000
Lincoln Co., MO

Burlington
chert

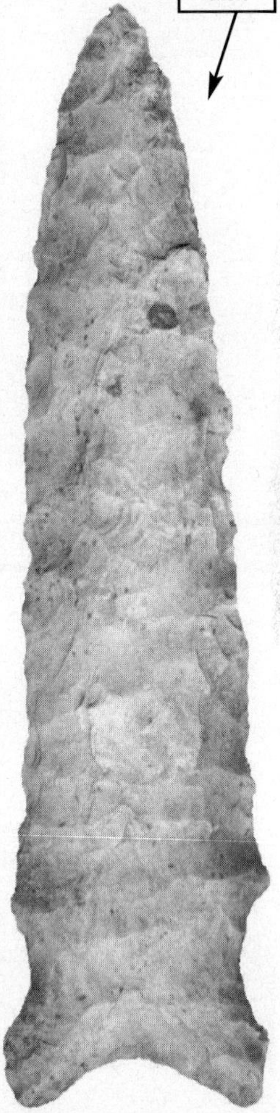

G6, $250-$450
Jackson Co., MO

LOCATION: Midwestern states. **DESCRIPTION:** A medium to large size, narrow, side-notched point with recurved sides, pointed auricles, and a concave base. Rarely, examples have been found fully fluted. Similar to *White River* points found in Ark. & OK.

GRAND- Mid-Woodland, 1800 - 1600 B. P.

(Also see Carter, Ferry, Gibson, Helton, Kirk Corner Notched, Lost Lake, Lundy and Snyders)

G6, $25-$40
Burlington, IL

G5, $15-$25
MO

G10, $65-$125
MO

G9, $80-$150
MO

G8, $65-$125
Riley Co., KS

LOCATION: Oklahoma, Kansas. **DESCRIPTION:** A medium sized, broad, corner notched point with barbed shoulders and an expanding, convex base. Basal corners can be sharp. **I.D. KEY:** Width of blade, corner notching.

GREENBRIER - Early Archaic 9500 - 6000 B. P.

(Also see Dalton, Pike County and Pine Tree)

Banded chert

G10, $250-$450
MO

LOCATION: Southeastern to Midwestern states. **DESCRIPTION:** A medium to large size, auriculate point with tapered shoulders and broad, weak side notches. Blade edges are usually finely serrated. The base can be concave, lobbed, eared, straight or bifurcated and is ground. Early examples can be fluted. This type developed from the *Dalton* point and later evolved into other types such as the *Pine Tree* point. **I.D. KEY:** Heavy grinding in shoulders, good secondary edgework.

G10, $700-$1200
IL

G8, $400-$750
Adams Co., IL

732

GREENBRIER (continued)

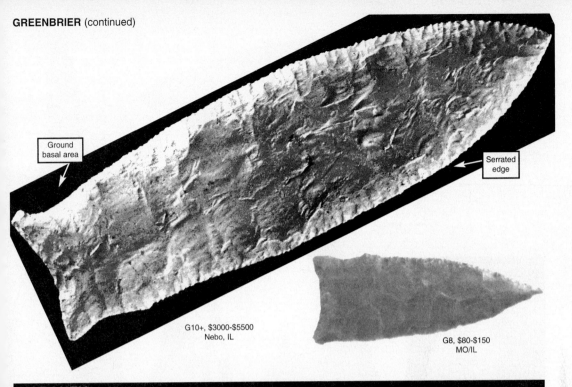

Ground basal area

Serrated edge

G10+, $3000-$5500
Nebo, IL

G8, $80-$150
MO/IL

HARAHEY - Mississippian, 700 - 350 B. P.

(Also see Lerma and Morse Knife)

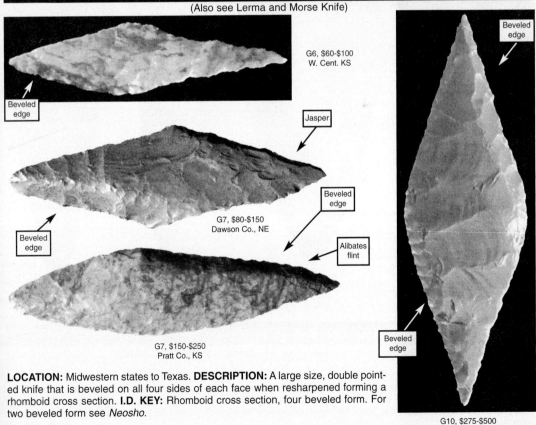

Beveled edge

G6, $60-$100
W. Cent. KS

Jasper

Beveled edge

Beveled edge

G7, $80-$150
Dawson Co., NE

Alibates flint

Beveled edge

G7, $150-$250
Pratt Co., KS

Beveled edge

NC

Beveled edge

G10, $275-$500
E. CO

LOCATION: Midwestern states to Texas. **DESCRIPTION:** A large size, double point-ed knife that is beveled on all four sides of each face when resharpened forming a rhomboid cross section. **I.D. KEY:** Rhomboid cross section, four beveled form. For two beveled form see *Neosho*.

G7, $150-$275
Laclede, MO

Beveled edge

Alibates chert

Beveled edge

Beveled edge

Beveled edge

Beveled edge

G6, $175-$300
Brown Co., IL

G9, $350-$600
Hamilton Co., KS

G9, $350-$600
Comanche Co., KS

G9, $450-$850
S. W. MO

HARDIN - Early Archaic, 9000 - 6000 B. P.

(Also see Ferry, Kirk, Lost Lake, St. Charles, Scottsbluff and Stilwell)

LOCATION: Midwestern to Eastern states. **DESCRIPTION:** A large size, well made triangular barbed point with an expanded base that is usually ground. Resharpened examples have one beveled edge on each face. This type is believed to have evolved from the *Scottsbluff* type. Examples have occurred with fluted bases **I.D. KEY:** Notches and stem form.

G5, $40-$75
Stod Co., MO

G5, $45-$85
MO

G6, $40-$75
IL

Banded chert

G6, $65-$125
IL

Serrated edge

G8, $65-$125
IL

G8, $175-$300
MO

G5, $40-$75
IL

NC

G9, $65-$125
IL

Mozarkite chert

Winterset chert

G6, $50-$100
Greene Co., IL

G8, $250-$400
Miller Co., MO

G7, $65-$125
IL

G8, $200-$350
Jackson Co., MO

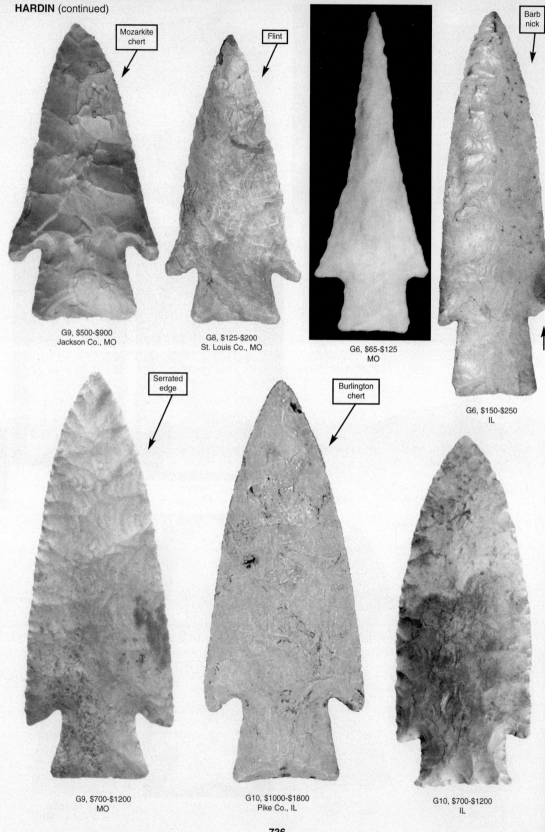

Mozarkite chert

Flint

Barb nick

Serrated edge

Burlington chert

G9, $500-$900
Jackson Co., MO

G8, $125-$200
St. Louis Co., MO

G6, $65-$125
MO

G6, $150-$250
IL

G9, $700-$1200
MO

G10, $1000-$1800
Pike Co., IL

G10, $700-$1200
IL

HARDIN (continued)

Mozarkite chert

Serrated edge

G10, $700-$1200
St. Louis Co., MO

G8, $250-$450
Boone Co., MO

G9, $550-$1000
Jackson Co., MO

Chert

Edwards Plateau chert

Short stemmed, knobbed hardin

NC

G10+, $1800-$3000
Greene Co., IL

G8, $700-$1200
Cass Co., IL

G10, $1000-$1800
Brown Co., IL

HARRELL- Mississippian, 900 - 500 B. P.

(Also see Cahokia, Huffaker and Washita)

G5, $25-$40
IL

G5, $25-$40
IL

G8, $50-$95
Pottowatomie Co., KS

G4, $25-$40
IL

G4, $15-$25
IL

Tip
damage

G7, $45-$80
Howard Co., MO

G7, $45-$80
Riley Co., KS

LOCATION: Midwestern states. **DESCRIPTION:** A small, thin, triangular arrow point with side and basal notches. Basal ears can be pointed. Bases are usually slighly concave with a basal notch. **I.D. KEY:** Triple notching.

HASKELL- Mississippian to Historic, 800 - 600 B. P.

(Also see Bayogoula, Collins and Washita)

G6, $20-$35
Cherokee Co., KS

G7, $25-$45
Cherokee Co., KS

G9, $35-$60
IL

G9, $65-$125
IL

LOCATION: Midwestern states. **DESCRIPTION:** A small, thin, triangular arrow point with upward sloping side notches. The base is concave and on some examples, basal ears can be extreme. **I.D. KEY:** Broad basal ears.

HATTEN KNIFE - Late Archaic, 3000 - 2800 B. P.

(Also see Hardin)

G7, $200-$350
Tulsa Co., OK

LOCATION: Oklahoma into Wisconsin. **DESCRIPTION:** A large size, narrow, stemmed knife with short shoulders that can be horizontal to slightly barbed and side notches angled in towards the tip. Bases are concave and the stem is usually ground. **I.D. KEY:** Small side notches.

HAYES - Mississippian, 1200 - 600 B. P.

(Also see Alba, Homan and Sequoyah)

G7, $65-$125
Central, MO

Serrated
edge

G10, $125-$225
IL

Serrated
edge

G9, $90-$175
IL

LOCATION: Midwestern states. **DESCRIPTION:** A small to medium size, narrow, expanded tang point with a turkeytail base. Blade edges are usually strongly recurved forming sharp pointed barbs. Base is pointed and can be double notched. Some examples are serrated. **I.D. KEY:** Pointed base and flaking style.

HAYES (continued)

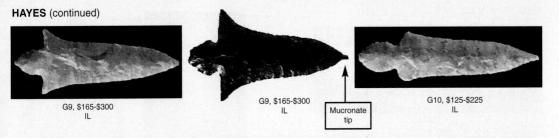

G9, $165-$300
IL

G9, $165-$300
IL

Mucronate tip

G10, $125-$225
IL

HEAVY DUTY - Early to Middle Archaic, 7000 - 5000 B. P.

(Also see Rochester, Stone Square Stem)

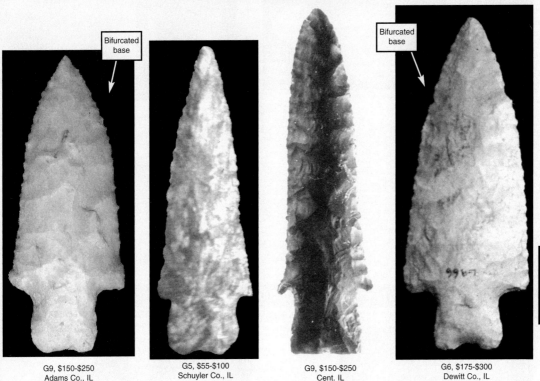

Bifurcated base

Bifurcated base

G9, $150-$250
Adams Co., IL

G5, $55-$100
Schuyler Co., IL

G9, $150-$250
Cent. IL

G6, $175-$300
Dewitt Co., IL

NC

LOCATION: Eastern to Midwestern states. **DESCRIPTION:** A medium to large size, thick, serrated point with a parallel stem and a straight to slightly concave base. **I.D. KEY:** Base, thickness, flaking.

HELL GAP - Transitional Paleo, 10,300 - 9500 B. P.

(Also see Agate Basin, Angostura and Burroughs)

G8, $200-$350
MO

LOCATION: Midwestern to Western states. **DESCRIPTION:** A medium to large size, lanceolate point with a long, contracting stem. The widest part of the blade is above the midsection. The base is straight to slightly concave and the stem edges are usually ground. **I.D. KEY:** Early flaking and base form.

HELL GAP (continued)

G7, $150-$250
MO

Westerville chert

G7, $55-$100
Adams Co., IL

G7, $65-$125
S.E. KS

G10, $800-$1500
Clay Co., MO

G9, $400-$750
MO

HELTON - Late Archaic to early Woodland, 4000 - 2500 B. P.

(Also see Apple Creek, Delhi, Kay Blade, Lehigh, Lundy and Motley)

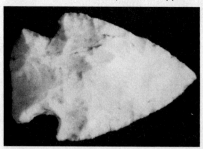

G6, $25-$40
Riley Co., KS

G8, $30-$50
Cherokee Co., KS

LOCATION: Midwestern states.
DESCRIPTION: A medium to large size, broad point with a short, expanding stem. Shoulders are horizontal to barbed, and the base is convex. **I.D. KEY:** Base form.

G8, $30-$50
Cherokee Co., KS

HEMPHILL - Mid to Late Archaic, 7000 - 5000 B. P.

(Also see Godar, Graham Cave, Howard County, Osceola, Raddatz and Turin)

Translucent chert

Purple/white chert

G5, $12-$20
Bond Co., IL

G7, $40-$75
Jersey Co., IL

G7, $40-$75
Macoupin Co., MO

G6, $35-$60
MO

G9, $80-$150
Cooper Co., MO

Long impact fracture

LOCATION: Illinois, Missouri into Wisc. Type site-Brown Co., IL. Associated with the Old Copper & Red Ochre culture. **DESCRIPTION:** A medium to large size side-notched point with a concave base and parallel to convex sides. These points are usually thinner and of higher quality than the similar *Osceola* type.

Heat treated Burlington

NC

G9, $275-$500
Saline Co., MO

G6, $55-$100
Macoupin Co., IL

G3, $55-$100
Jersey Co., IL

G10+, $5500-$10,000
Cass Co., IL

741

G8, $200-$350
MO

HI-LO - Transitional Paleo, 10,000 - 8000 B. P.

(Also see Angostura, Browns Valley and Burroughs)

G7, $150-$250
MO

LOCATION: Midwestern states. **DESCRIPTION:** A medium to large size, broad, eared, lanceolate point with a concave base. Believed to be related to *Plainview* and *Dalton* points.

HICKORY RIDGE - Early Archaic, 7000 - 5000 B.P.

(Also see Godar, Hemphill, Osceola, Raddatz, Robinson and Turin)

Maroon chert

G6, $25-$40
MO

G6, $30-$50
Cent. MO

G9, $225-$400
MO

Barb nick

G6, $30-$50
Greene Co., IL

LOCATION: Oklahoma, Arkansas into Missouri. **DESCRIPTION:** A medium to large size side notched point with a straight to slightly concave base

G8, $175-$300
MO

(Also see Adena, Dickson, Gary and Waubesa)

LOCATION: Oklahoma, Missouri, Illinois into Indiana. **DESCRIPTION:** A medium to large size point with square to barbed shoulders and a contracting stem that can be pointed to straight. Flaking is earlier and more parallel than on *Gary* points. Basal areas are ground. Called *Rice Contracted Stemmed* in Missouri.

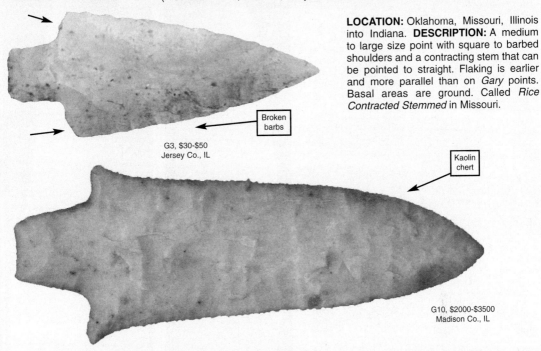

Broken barbs

G3, $30-$50
Jersey Co., IL

Kaolin chert

G10, $2000-$3500
Madison Co., IL

(Also see Dalton, Dalton-Sloan, Eden, Hardin, Johnson, Pike County and Scottsbluff)

NC

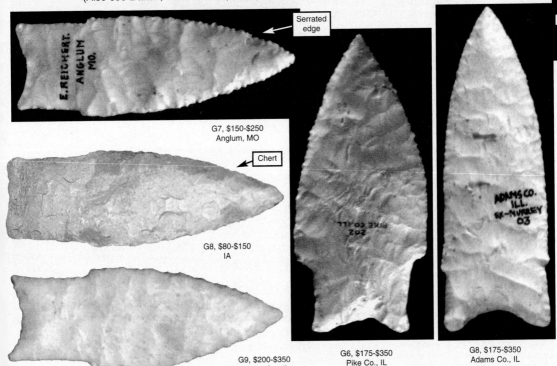

Serrated edge

E. REICHERT. ANGLUM MO.

G7, $150-$250
Anglum, MO

Chert

G8, $80-$150
IA

G9, $200-$350
Adams Co., IL

G6, $175-$350
Pike Co., IL

G8, $175-$350
Adams Co., IL

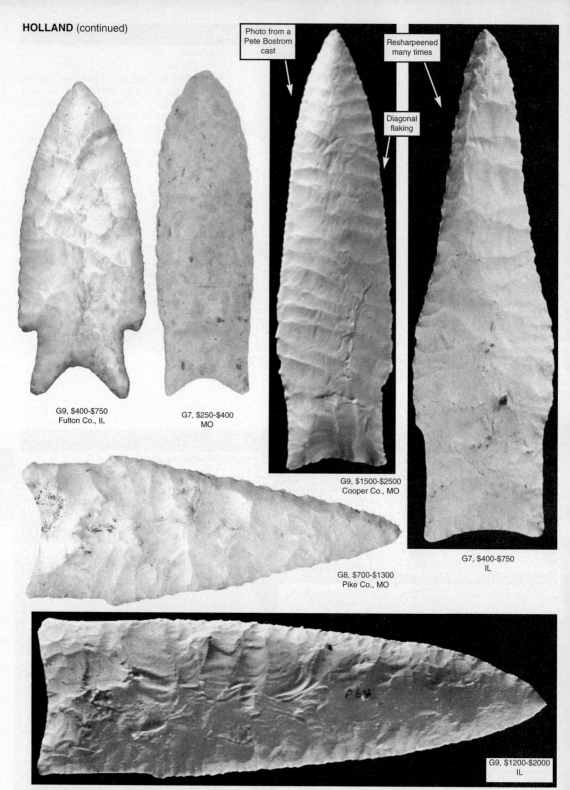

Photo from a Pete Bostrom cast

Resharpeened many times

Diagonal flaking

G9, $400-$750
Fulton Co., IL

G7, $250-$400
MO

G9, $1500-$2500
Cooper Co., MO

G8, $700-$1300
Pike Co., MO

G7, $400-$750
IL

G9, $1200-$2000
IL

LOCATION: Midwestern states. **DESCRIPTION:** A medium to large size lanceolate blade that is very well made. Shoulders are weak to nonexistent. Bases can be knobbed to auriculate and are usually ground. Some examples have horizontal to oblique transverse flaking. Related to Dalton Sloan points. **I.D. KEY:** Weak shoulders, concave base.

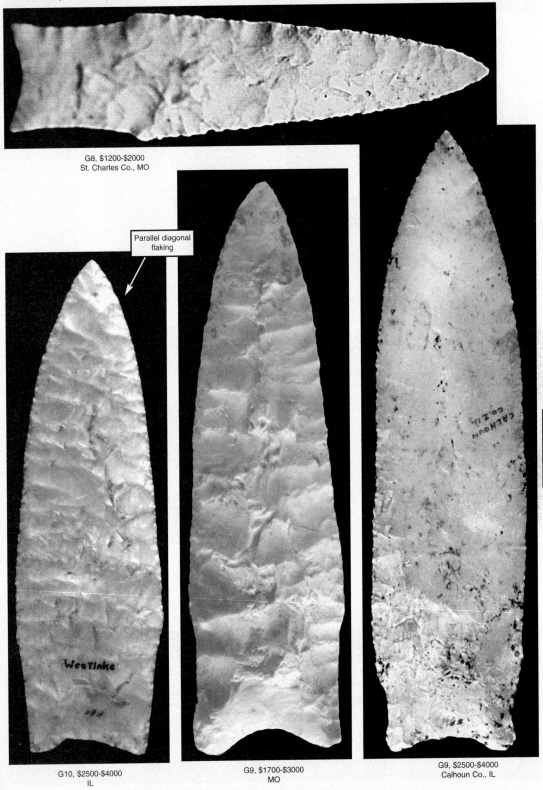

G8, $1200-$2000
St. Charles Co., MO

Parallel diagonal flaking

G10, $2500-$4000
IL

G9, $1700-$3000
MO

G9, $2500-$4000
Calhoun Co., IL

NC

HOLLENBERG STEMMED - Early Archaic, 9000 - 7500 B. P.

(Also see Eden, Munker's Creek and Scottsbluff)

G7, $55-$100
Washington Co., KS

G7, $55-$100
Jefferson Co., NE

G7, $150-$250
Washington Co., KS

G6, $40-$75
Washington Co., KS

G6, $55-$100
Washington Co., KS

G8, $150-$250
Nuckolls Co., NE

G8, $150-$250
Washington Co., KS

G7, $125-$200
Jefferson Co., NE

Tip
wear

G6, $55-$100
Gage Co., NE

G6, $80-$150
Jefferson Co., KS

G8, $150-$250
Washington Co., KS

LOCATION: Central to Eastern Nebraska and Kansas. **DESCRIPTION:** A medium to large size, narrow, stemmed point with tapered shoulders and a straight to convex base. Related to *Eden* and *Eden Eared*. Stem sides are parallel to slightly expanding and are ground.

HOMAN - Mississippian, 1000 - 700 B. P.

(Also see Agee, Alba, Hayes and Sequoyah)

G6, $35-$65
IL

LOCATION: Northwest to Midwestern states. **DESCRIPTION:** A small size expanded barb point with a bulbous stem. Some tips are mucronate or apiculate.

HOPEWELL - Woodland, 2500 - 1500 B. P.

(Also see Carter, Dickson, Gibson, Motley, North, St. Charles, Snyders & Waubesa)

HOPEWELL (continued)

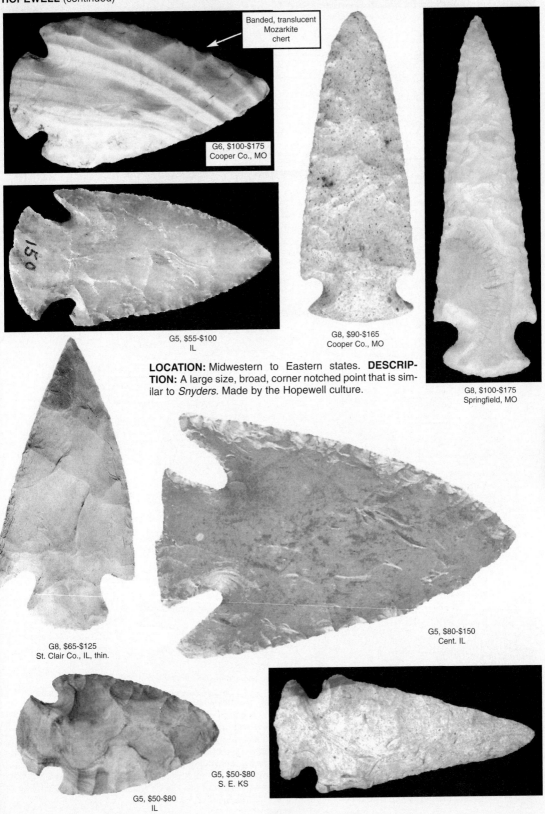

Banded, translucent Mozarkite chert

G6, $100-$175
Cooper Co., MO

G5, $55-$100
IL

G8, $90-$165
Cooper Co., MO

G8, $100-$175
Springfield, MO

LOCATION: Midwestern to Eastern states. **DESCRIPTION:** A large size, broad, corner notched point that is similar to *Snyders*. Made by the Hopewell culture.

NC

G8, $65-$125
St. Clair Co., IL, thin.

G5, $80-$150
Cent. IL

G5, $50-$80
S. E. KS

G5, $50-$80
IL

(Also see Cache River, Gibson, Grand, Helton, St. Charles)

Burlington chert

Mozarkite chert

G8, $55-$100
Calhoun, Co., IL

G10, $125-$200
Pettis Co., MO

Jefferson City chert

Burlington chert

G9, $450-$800
Jersey, Co., IL

G9, $65-$125
Howard Co., MO

Fort Payne chert

Burlington chert

Burlington chert

St. Louis Co., Mo.

525

G9, $200-$350
St. Louis Co., MO

G8, $125-$200
Madison Co., IL

G8, $350-$600
Johnson Co., IL

G9, $400-$700
Jersey Co., IL

LOCATION: Illinois and Missouri. **DESCRIPTION:** A small to medium size, thin, well-made point. The blade is long and triangular with slightly convex edges. Notches are narrow and fairly low on the sides, entering at a slight diagonally upward angle. The basal edge may range from slightly incurvate to slightly convex. It has squared basal corners on straight-based points and rounded basal corners on convex-based points. Basal edge has light grinding to none. If grinding is absent, light crushing of the basal edge is noted. A peculiarity of this point is that it has been recognized primarily for its like-new, unused condition with little to no evidence of resharpening, as has been noted on *Cache River* and *Kessel* points. For years this has been an un-named variant of the *Cache River* points. **I.D. KEY:** Lack of basal grinding and resharpening. Can be much larger than *Cache River* or *Kessel* points.

HUFFAKER - Mississippian, 1000 - 500 B. P.

(Also see Cahokia, Evans and Washita)

 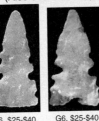    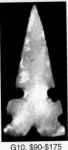 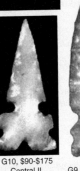

G8, $40-$75
Cooper Co., MO

G6, $25-$40
IL

G6, $25-$40
IL

G6, $25-$40
IL

G6, $25-$40
IL

G7, $30-$50
Pottowatomie Co., KS

G10, $90-$175
Central IL

G9, $60-$100
Geary Co., KS

G10 $55-$100
Cooper Co., MO

G8, $65-$125
Pottowatomie Co., KS

G9, $50-$80
Cooper Co., MO

LOCATION: Midwestern states. **DESCRIPTION:** A small size triangular point with a straight to concave base and double side notches. Bases can have a single notch.

JACKS REEF CORNER NOTCHED - Late Woodland to Miss., 1500 - 1000 B. P.

(Also see Afton, Apple Creek, Hopewell, Kirk Corner Notched)

G8, $30-$50
Madison Co., IL

G9, $70-$120
Cooper Co., MO

G9, $80-$150
Cooper Co., MO

G8, $40-$75
Madison Co., IL

NC

LOCATION: Midwestern to Eastern states. **DESCRIPTION:** A small to medium size, thin, corner notched point that is well made. The blade is convex to pentagonal. Some examples are widely corner notched and appear to be expanded stem points with barbed shoulders. Rarely, they are basal notched. **I.D. KEY:** Thinness, made by the birdpoint people.

JOHNSON - Early to Middle Archaic, 9000 - 5000 B. P.

(Also see Hidden Valley, Holland and Stone Square Stem)

G7, $35-$65
Cherokee Co., KS

G9, $65-$125
Washington Co., KS

LOCATION: Mississippi to Kansas. **DESCRIPTION:** A medium size, thick, well made, expanded to contracting stem point with a broad, short, concave base. Bases are usually thinned and grinding appears on some specimens. Shoulders can be slight and are roughly horizontal. **I.D. KEY:** Broad stem that is thinned.

KAMPSVILLE - Late Archaic to Woodland, 3000 - 2500 B. P.

(Also see Cupp, Helton, Kings, Kramer, Lundy, Lehigh and Motley)

LOCATION: Midwestern states.
DESCRIPTION: A medium to large size, point with broad corner notches producing a parallel stem and barbed shoulders. Similar to *Buck Creek* found in Kentucky.

G8, $45-$85
Pettis Co., MO

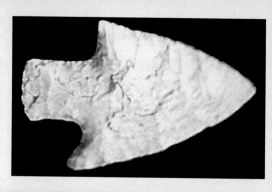

KAY BLADE - Mississippian, 1000 - 600 B. P.

(Also see Cupp, Epps, Helton, Kramer, Lundy, Lehigh and Motley)

G6, $35-$60
Douglas Co., KS

G9, $80-$150
N.E. OK

G7, $150-$300
St. Louis Co., MO

G10, $400-$750
Green Co., MO

IMPORTANT:
Kay Blades shown half size

LOCATION: Midwestern states.
DESCRIPTION: A medium to large size point with a long expanding stem and barbed shoulders. Used by the Mississippian, Caddoan people.

KINGS - Middle Archaic to Woodland, 4500 - 2500 B. P.

(Also see Apple Creek, Hopewell, Kampsville, Kirk Corner and Motley)

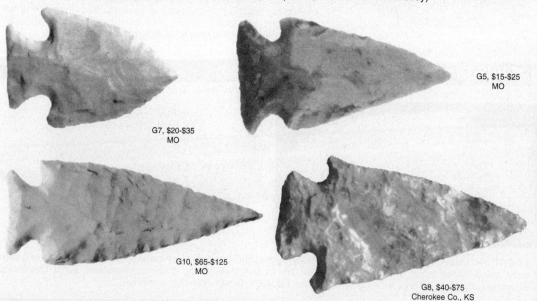

G7, $20-$35
MO

G5, $15-$25
MO

G10, $65-$125
MO

G8, $40-$75
Cherokee Co., KS

LOCATION: Midwestern states. **DESCRIPTION:** A medium size corner notched point with an expanding stem and barbed shoulders. Barbs and basal corners are sharp. Base can be convex, straight or concave.

(Also see Apple Creek, Decatur, Lost Lake, Pine Tree, St. Charles & Stilwell)

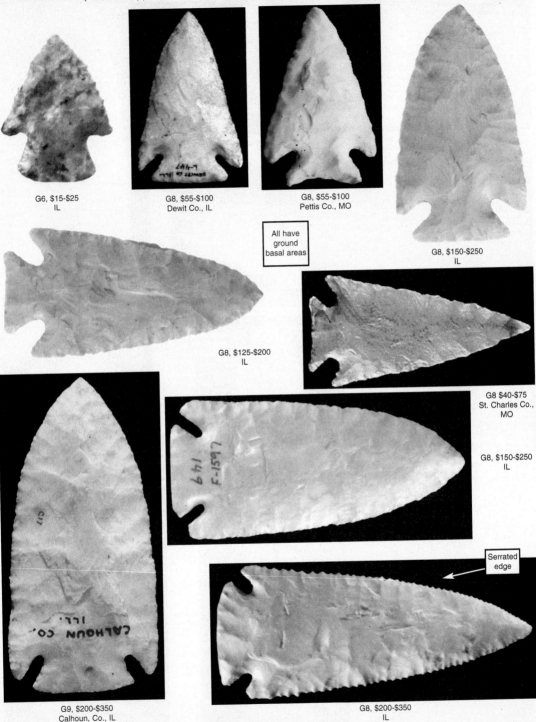

G6, $15-$25
IL

G8, $55-$100
Dewit Co., IL

G8, $55-$100
Pettis Co., MO

All have
ground
basal areas

G8, $150-$250
IL

G8, $125-$200
IL

G8 $40-$75
St. Charles Co.,
MO

G8, $150-$250
IL

NC

Serrated
edge

G9, $200-$350
Calhoun, Co., IL

G8, $200-$350
IL

LOCATION: Midwestern to Southeasten states. **DESCRIPTION:** A medium to large size, corner notched point. Blade edges can be convex to recurved and are finely serrated on many examples. The base can be convex, concave, straight or auriculate. Points that are beveled on one side of each face would fall under the *Lost Lake* type. **I.D. KEY:** Secondary edgework.

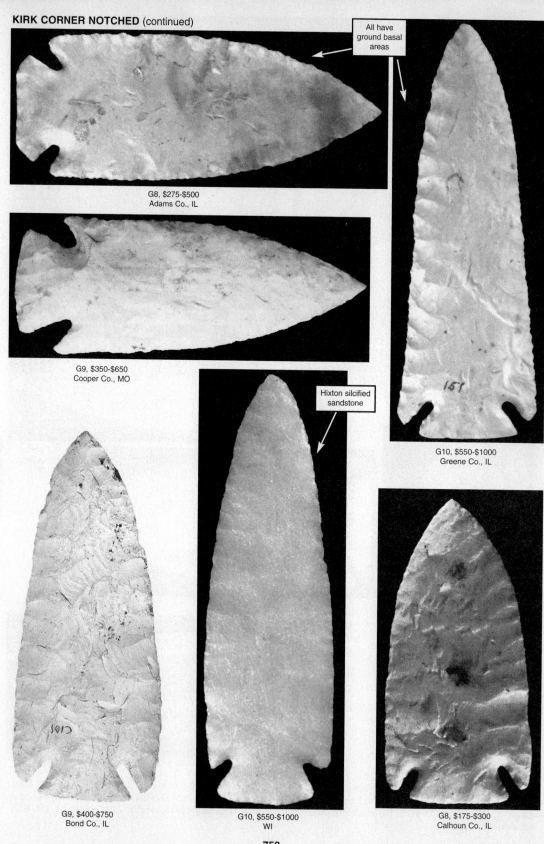

KIRK CORNER NOTCHED (continued)

All have ground basal areas

Hixton silcified sandstone

G8, $275-$500
Adams Co., IL

G9, $350-$650
Cooper Co., MO

G10, $550-$1000
Greene Co., IL

G9, $400-$750
Bond Co., IL

G10, $550-$1000
WI

G8, $175-$300
Calhoun Co., IL

KNIGHT ISLAND - LATE Woodland, 1500 - 1000 B. P.

(Also see Cache River, Jacks Reef and Robinson)

LOCATION: Tennessee, Alabama, Kentucky into Illinois. **DESCRIPTION:** A small to medium size, very thin, narrow, side-notched point with a straight base. Longer examples can have a pentagonal appearance. Called *Raccoon Creek* in Ohio. A side-notched *Jacks Reef*. **I.D. KEY:** Thinness, basal form.

G9, $150-$250
Scott Co., IL

KRAMER - Woodland, 3000 - 2500 B. P.

(Also see Helton, Lehigh, Rochester and Stone Square Stem)

G7, $20-$35
Miller Co., MO

G5, $30-$50
Bond Co., IL

G7, $40-$75
Madison Co., IL

G6, $25-$45
Fayette Co., IL

G7, $55-$100
MO

G9, $350-$600
MO/IL

LOCATION: Midwest. **DESCRIPTION:** A medium size, narrow point with weak shoulders that are tapered to horizontal and a long rectangular stem. Stems are usually ground. **I.D. KEY:** Rectangular stem.

G7, $80-$150
St. Clair Co., IL

LAKE ERIE - Early to Middle Archaic, 9000 - 5000 B. P.

(Also see Cossatot River and Fox Valley)

Tip nick

G5, $3-$6
IL

G5, $8-$15
IL

G4, $2-$5
IL

G6, $12-$20
IL

G6, $12-$20
IL

G7, $15-$25
IL

G5, $8-$15
IL

LOCATION: Northeastern states. **DESCRIPTION:** A small to medium size, thin, deeply notched or serrated, bifurcated stemmed point. The basal lobes are parallel with a tendency to turn inward and are pointed. The outward sides of the basal lobes are usually fractured from the base towards the tip and can be ground. Similar to *LeCroy* found further south.

LAMINE KNIFE - Archaic, 5000 - 3000 B. P.

(Also see Morse Knife, Munker's Creek, Ramey Knife, Sedalia and Wadlow)

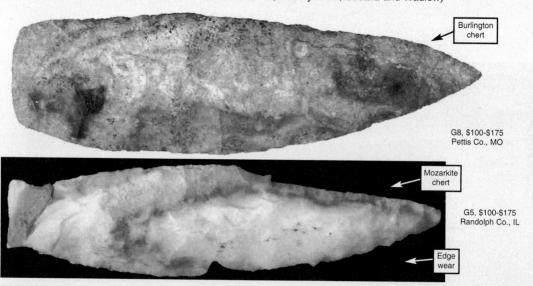

Burlington chert

G8, $100-$175
Pettis Co., MO

Mozarkite chert

G5, $100-$175
Randolph Co., IL

Edge wear

LOCATION: Missouri and adjacent area. **DESCRIPTION:** A large size, narrow knife with an assymmetrical blade with one edge curved more towards the tip. Stem form varies from rounded to expanded. Believed to have been used for cutting thatch since most examples show a polish, usually along the curved, cutting edge. **I.D. KEY:** Size and form.

LAMINE KNIFE (continued)

Burlington chert

(Also see Helton, Kay Blade, Kramer, Lundy and Steuben)

G6, $25-$40
Pottowatomie Co., KS

LOCATION: Midwest. **DESCRIPTION:** A medium to large size, narrow point with tapered shoulders and a long expanding stem. Bases are straight. **I.D. KEY:** Long expanding stem.

LERMA - Early to Middle Archaic, 10,000 - 5000 B. P.

(Also see Agate Basin, Burroughs and Sedalia)

G8, $150-$250
Fulton Co., IL

IMPORTANT: All Lermas shown half size

G7, $175-$300
MO

G10, $300-$550
Cent. MO

NC

LOCATION: Siberia to Alaska, Canada, Mexico, South America and across the U.S. **DESCRIPTION:** A large size, narrow, lanceolate blade with a pointed base. Most are fairly thick in cross section but finer examples can be thin. Flaking tends to be collateral. Basal areas can be ground. Western forms are beveled on one side of each face. Similar forms have been found in Europe and Africa dating back to 20,000 - 40,000 B.P., but didn't appear in the U.S. until after the advent of *Clovis*.

PETTIS
CO MO
$750

PETTIS
Co.Mo.
1758

G7 $300-$575
Pettis Co., MO

G10, $700-$1200
Pettis Co., MO

shown
half size

G8, $450-$800
IL

LOST LAKE - Early Archaic, 9000 - 6000 B. P.

(Also see Hardin, Kirk Corner Notched, St. Charles and Thebes)

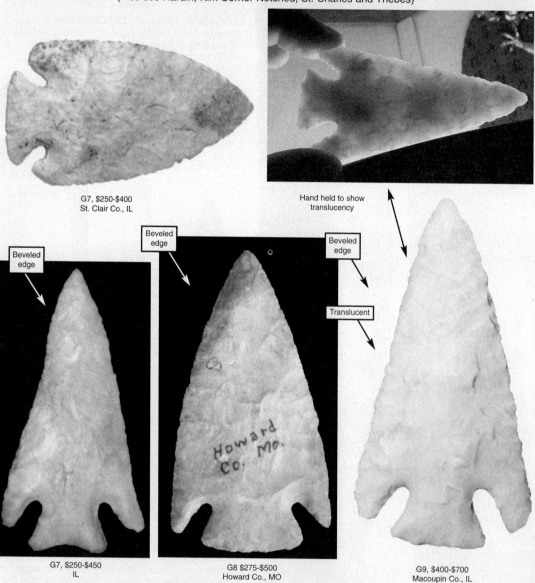

G7, $250-$400
St. Clair Co., IL

Hand held to show
translucency

Beveled
edge

Beveled
edge

Beveled
edge

Translucent

G7, $250-$450
IL

Howard
Co. Mo.

G8 $275-$500
Howard Co., MO

G9, $400-$700
Macoupin Co., IL

LOCATION: DESCRIPTION: A medium to large size, broad, corner notched point that is beveled on one side of each face. The beveling continues when resharpened and creates a flat rhomboid cross section. Most examples are finely serrated and exhibit high quality flaking and symmetry. **I.D. KEY:** Notching, secondary edgework is always opposite creating at least slight beveling on one side of each face.

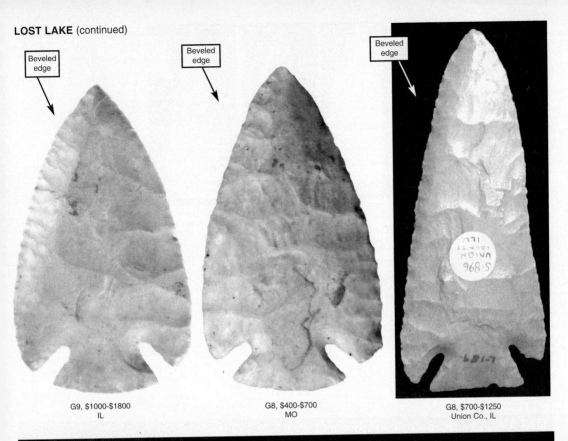

Beveled edge

Beveled edge

Beveled edge

G9, $1000-$1800
IL

G8, $400-$700
MO

G8, $700-$1250
Union Co., IL

LUNDY- Late Caddoan, 800 - 600 B. P.

(Also see Helton, Kay Blade, Lehigh, Motley, Steuben and Table Rock)

G6, $15-$30
Geary Co., KS

LOCATION: Midwestern states. **DESCRIPTION:** A small to medium size, narrow, corner notched point with barbed shoulders and a convex base.

MADISON - Mississippian, 1100 - 200 B. P.

(Also see Cahokia)

Flint

Flint

G3, $1-$2
MN

G3, $4-$8
MN

G5, $5-$8
Madison Co., IL

G5, $5-$8
Minn.

G8, $12-$20
Macoupin Co., IL

G5, $5-$8
Clinton Co., IL

G8, $15-$25
Cooper Co., MO

G6, $8-$15
Clinton Co., IL

LOCATION: Coincides with the Mississippian culture in the Eastern states. Type site-St. Clair Co., IL. Found at Cahokia mounds. Un-notched *Cahokias.* Used by the Kaskaskia tribe into the 1700s. **DESCRIPTION:** A small to medium size, thin, triangular point with usually straight sides and base. Some examples are notched on two to three sides. Many are of high quality and some are finely serrated.

MADISON (continued)

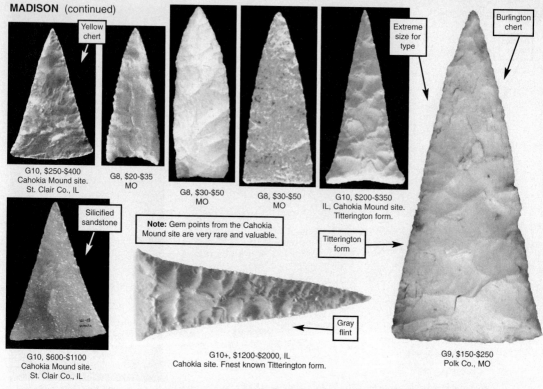

Yellow chert

G10, $250-$400
Cahokia Mound site.
St. Clair Co., IL

G8, $20-$35
MO

G8, $30-$50
MO

G8, $30-$50
MO

Extreme size for type

G10, $200-$350
IL, Cahokia Mound site.
Titterington form.

Burlington chert

Note: Gem points from the Cahokia Mound site are very rare and valuable.

Silicified sandstone

Titterington form

G10, $600-$1100
Cahokia Mound site.
St. Clair Co., IL

Gray flint

G10+, $1200-$2000, IL
Cahokia site. Fnest known Titterington form.

G9, $150-$250
Polk Co., MO

MATANZAS - Mid-Archaic to Woodland, 4500 - 2500 B. P.

(Also see Carter, Cupp, Hickory Ridge, Kirk Corner Notched)

G4, $2-$5
Fayette Co., IL

G5, $5-$10
Clinton Co., IL

G6, $8-$15
Clinton Co., IL

G5, $5-$10
Madison Co., IL

G6, $25-$40
IL

LOCATION: Midwestern states. **DESCRIPTION:** A small to medium size, narrow, side notched point with a concave, convex or straight base.

G6, $25-$45
Cooper Co., MO

G6, $35-$50
Cass Co., IL

(Also see Etley and Smith)

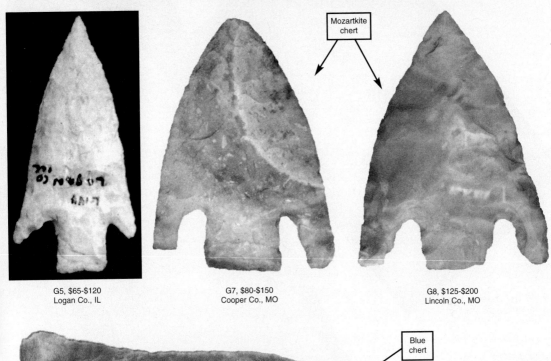

Mozartkite chert

G5, $65-$120
Logan Co., IL

G7, $80-$150
Cooper Co., MO

G8, $125-$200
Lincoln Co., MO

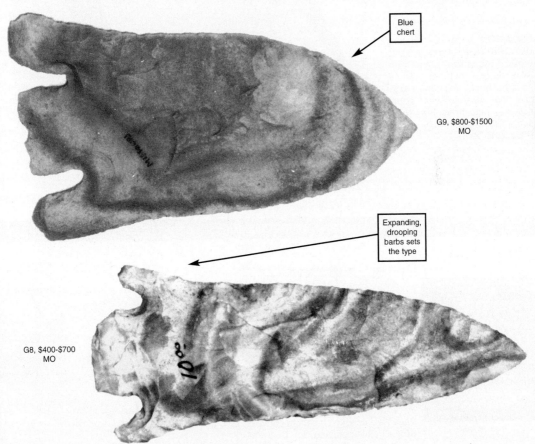

Blue chert

G9, $800-$1500
MO

NC

Expanding, drooping barbs sets the type

G8, $400-$700
MO

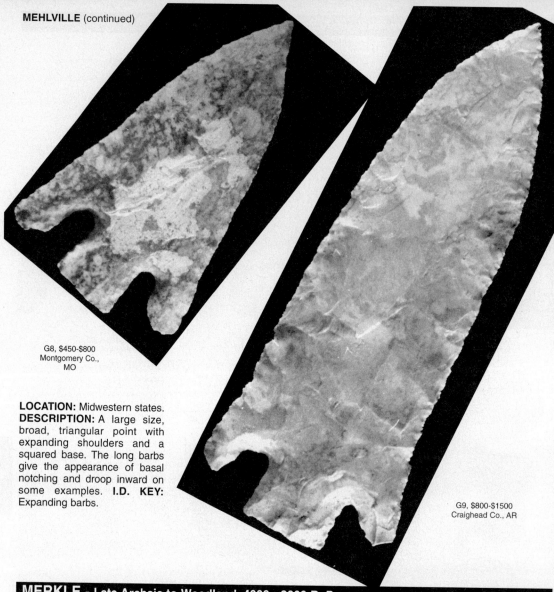

G8, $450-$800
Montgomery Co.,
MO

LOCATION: Midwestern states.
DESCRIPTION: A large size,
broad, triangular point with
expanding shoulders and a
squared base. The long barbs
give the appearance of basal
notching and droop inward on
some examples. **I.D. KEY:**
Expanding barbs.

G9, $800-$1500
Craighead Co., AR

MERKLE - Late Archaic to Woodland, 4000 - 2000 B. P.

(Also see Evans)

G6, $5-$10
MO

G6, $5-$10
IL

LOCATION: Midwestern states. **DES-
CRIPTION:** A medium to large size point
with a short stem and broad side notch-
es and corner notches at the base.
Bases are usually straight to convex. **I.D.
KEY:** Double notching.

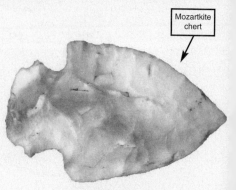

Mozartkite
chert

G7, $80-$150
Saline Co., MO

MERKLE (continued)

G10, $250-$475
IL

Serrated edge

MESERVE - Early Archaic, 9500 - 4000 B. P.

(Also see Dalton, Greenbrier and Plainview)

G8, $80-$150
Manhattan, KS

LOCATION: Midwestern states to Texas and west to Montana. **DESCRIPTION:** A medium size auriculate point with a blade that is beveled on one side of each face. Beveling extends into the basal area. Related to *Dalton* points. **I.D. KEY:** Beveling into the base.

MORSE KNIFE - Woodland, 3000 - 1500 B. P.

(Also see Harahey, Lerma, Ramey Knife and Red Ochre)

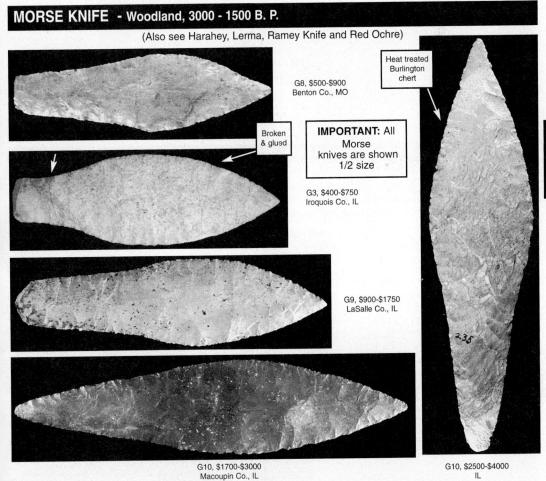

G8, $500-$900
Benton Co., MO

Broken & glued

IMPORTANT: All Morse knives are shown 1/2 size

G3, $400-$750
Iroquois Co., IL

G9, $900-$1750
LaSalle Co., IL

Heat treated Burlington chert

NC

235

G10, $1700-$3000
Macoupin Co., IL

G10, $2500-$4000
IL

LOCATION: Midwestern states. **DESCRIPTION:** A large lanceolate blade with a long contracting stem and a rounded base. The widest part of the blade is towards the tip.

MOTLEY - Late Archaic-Woodland, 4500 - 2500 B. P.

(Also see Cupp, Epps, Helton, Kay Blade, Lundy, Snyders, Steuben, Table Rock)

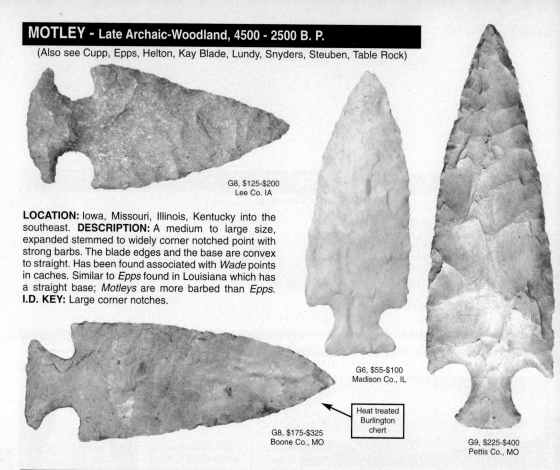

G8, $125-$200
Lee Co. IA

LOCATION: Iowa, Missouri, Illinois, Kentucky into the southeast. **DESCRIPTION:** A medium to large size, expanded stemmed to widely corner notched point with strong barbs. The blade edges and the base are convex to straight. Has been found associated with *Wade* points in caches. Similar to *Epps* found in Louisiana which has a straight base; *Motleys* are more barbed than *Epps*. **I.D. KEY:** Large corner notches.

G6, $55-$100
Madison Co., IL

Heat treated
Burlington
chert

G8, $175-$325
Boone Co., MO

G9, $225-$400
Pettis Co., MO

MUNKER'S CREEK - Early Archaic, 5400 - 3300 B. P.

(Also see Hollenberg Stemmed, Lamine Knife & Tablerock)

LOCATION: Central to eastern Kansas and Nebraska. **DESCRIPTION: Curved Knife:** A large size, thick, curved knife with rounded base and tip. Both knives and points are found together.

DESCRIPTION: Dart/knife form: A medium to large size, narror, stemmed point with a long parallel sided to expanding stem. Bases are straight to slightly concave or convex. Shoulders are weak and tapered. Blade edges are slightly convex to parallel sided.

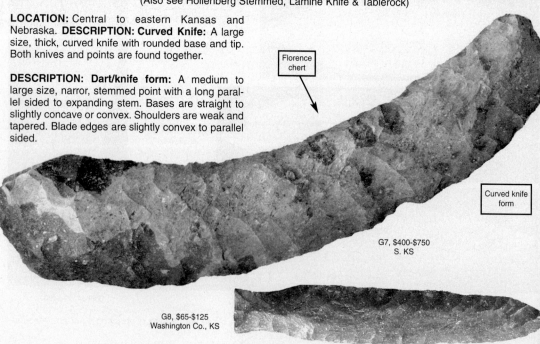

Florence
chert

Curved knife
form

G7, $400-$750
S. KS

G8, $65-$125
Washington Co., KS

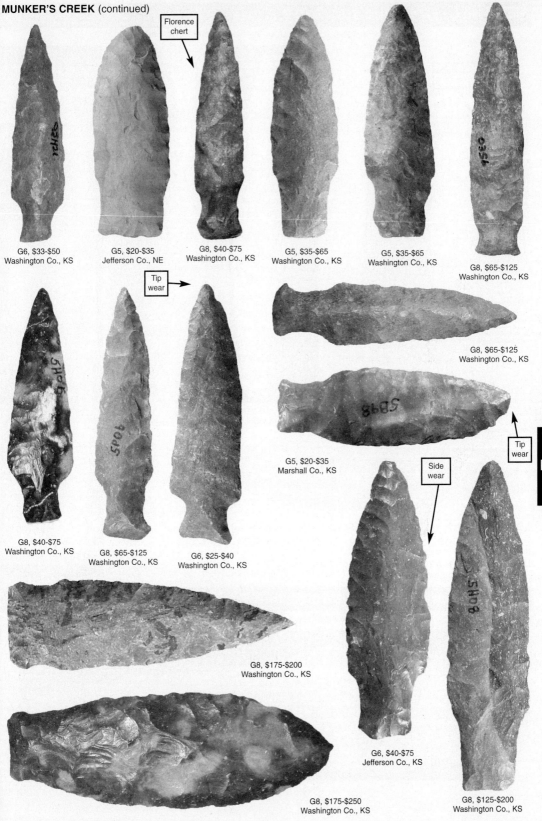

Florence chert

G6, $33-$50
Washington Co., KS

G5, $20-$35
Jefferson Co., NE

G8, $40-$75
Washington Co., KS

G5, $35-$65
Washington Co., KS

G5, $35-$65
Washington Co., KS

G8, $65-$125
Washington Co., KS

Tip wear

G8, $65-$125
Washington Co., KS

Tip wear

NC

G8, $40-$75
Washington Co., KS

G8, $65-$125
Washington Co., KS

G6, $25-$40
Washington Co., KS

G5, $20-$35
Marshall Co., KS

Side wear

G8, $175-$200
Washington Co., KS

G6, $40-$75
Jefferson Co., KS

G8, $175-$250
Washington Co., KS

G8, $125-$200
Washington Co., KS

NEBO HILL - Early Archaic, 7500 - 6000 B. P.

(Also see Agate basin, Burroughs, Eden, Lerma and Sedalia)

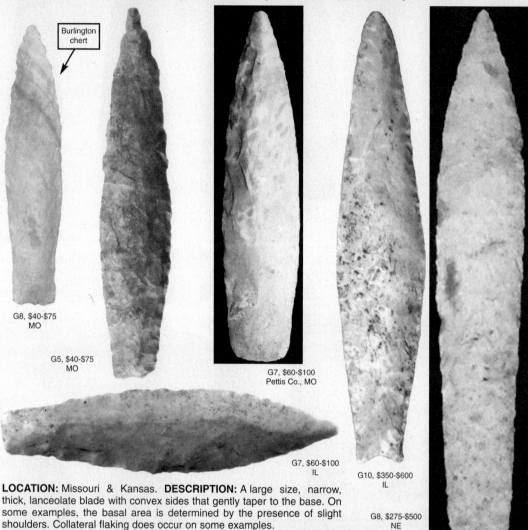

Burlington
chert

G8, $40-$75
MO

G5, $40-$75
MO

G7, $60-$100
Pettis Co., MO

G7, $60-$100
IL

G10, $350-$600
IL

G8, $275-$500
NE

LOCATION: Missouri & Kansas. **DESCRIPTION:** A large size, narrow, thick, lanceolate blade with convex sides that gently taper to the base. On some examples, the basal area is determined by the presence of slight shoulders. Collateral flaking does occur on some examples.

NEOSHO - Early Archaic, 400 - 250 B. P.

(Also see Harahey, Lamine Knife, Munker's Creek)

G6, $80-$150
MO

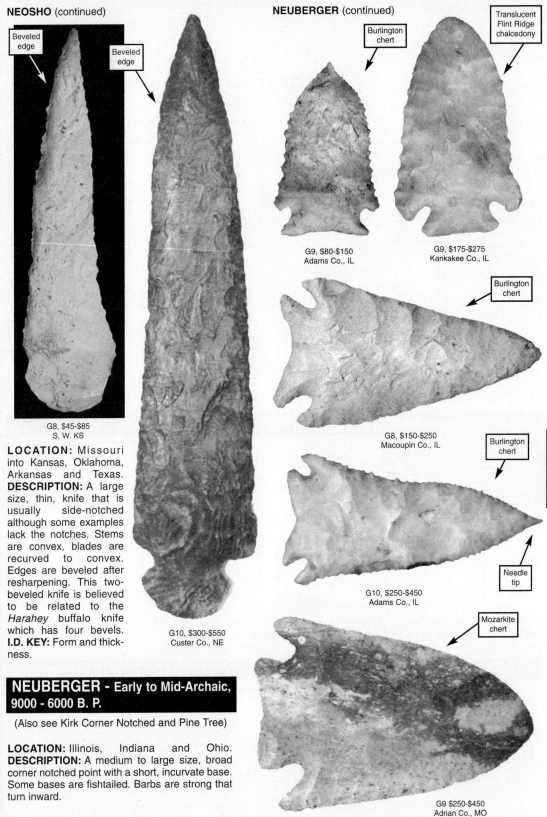

NEOSHO (continued)

Beveled edge

Beveled edge

G8, $45-$85
S. W. KS

LOCATION: Missouri into Kansas, Oklahoma, Arkansas and Texas. **DESCRIPTION:** A large size, thin, knife that is usually side-notched although some examples lack the notches. Stems are convex, blades are recurved to convex. Edges are beveled after resharpening. This two-beveled knife is believed to be related to the *Harahey* buffalo knife which has four bevels. **I.D. KEY:** Form and thickness.

G10, $300-$550
Custer Co., NE

NEUBERGER - Early to Mid-Archaic, 9000 - 6000 B. P.

(Also see Kirk Corner Notched and Pine Tree)

LOCATION: Illinois, Indiana and Ohio. **DESCRIPTION:** A medium to large size, broad corner notched point with a short, incurvate base. Some bases are fishtailed. Barbs are strong that turn inward.

NEUBERGER (continued)

Burlington chert

Translucent Flint Ridge chalcedony

G9, $80-$150
Adams Co., IL

G9, $175-$275
Kankakee Co., IL

Burlington chert

G8, $150-$250
Macoupin Co., IL

Burlington chert

Needle tip

G10, $250-$450
Adams Co., IL

Mozarkite chert

G9 $250-$450
Adrian Co., MO

NC

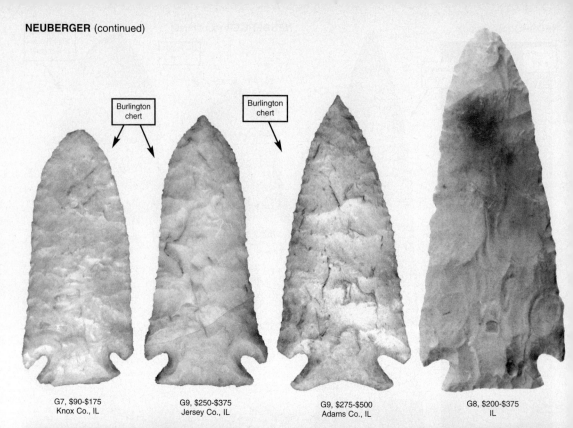

G7, $90-$175
Knox Co., IL

G9, $250-$375
Jersey Co., IL

G9, $275-$500
Adams Co., IL

G8, $200-$375
IL

NODENA - Mississippian to Historic, 600 - 400 B. P.

G7, $30-$50
Pemiscot Co., MO

G7, $30-$50
Washington Co., IL

G7, $35-$60
Pemiscot Co., MO

G7, $40-$75
Pemiscot
Co., MO

G7, $65-$125
IL

LOCATION: Midwestern states. **DESCRIPTION:** A small to medium size, narrow, thin elliptical shaped arrow point with a pointed to rounded base. Some examples have oblique, parallel flaking.

NORTH - Woodland, 2200 - 1600 B. P.

(Also see Hopewell, Snyders and Stenfield)

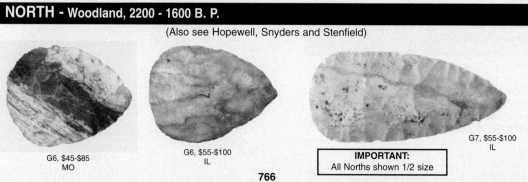

G6, $45-$85
MO

G6, $55-$100
IL

G7, $55-$100
IL

IMPORTANT:
All Norths shown 1/2 size

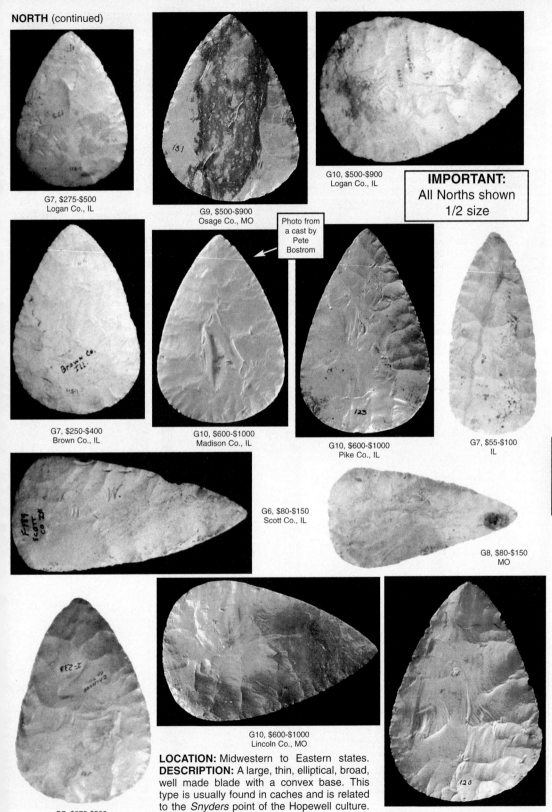

G7, $275-$500
Logan Co., IL

G9, $500-$900
Osage Co., MO

G10, $500-$900
Logan Co., IL

IMPORTANT:
All Norths shown
1/2 size

G7, $250-$400
Brown Co., IL

Photo from
a cast by
Pete
Bostrom

G10, $600-$1000
Madison Co., IL

G10, $600-$1000
Pike Co., IL

G7, $55-$100
IL

NC

G6, $80-$150
Scott Co., IL

G8, $80-$150
MO

G10, $600-$1000
Lincoln Co., MO

LOCATION: Midwestern to Eastern states.
DESCRIPTION: A large, thin, elliptical, broad, well made blade with a convex base. This type is usually found in caches and is related to the *Snyders* point of the Hopewell culture. Believed to be unnotched *Snyders* points.

G7, $275-$500
Calhoun Co., IL

G8, $350-$650
Lincoln Co., MO

767

G8, $250-$450
Keokuk Co., IA

G9, $150-$250
MO

LOCATION: Wisconsin into Iowa. **DESCRIPTION:** A large size, narrow, side notched point with parallel sides on longer examples and a straight to concave to notched base which could be ground. **I.D. KEY:** Always has early flaking to the middle of the blade.

G8, $275-$500
Bourbon Co., KS

G8, $275-$500
IL

G8, $350-$650
Fulton Co., IL

G10, $700-$1200
Calhoun Co., IL

OVOID (see Early Ovoid Knife)

PALEO KNIFE - Transitional Paleo, 10,000 - 8000 B. P.

(Also see Scraper and Square Knife)

Flaked to the center

G6, $150-$250
Pettis Co., MO

LOCATION: All of North America. **DES - CRIPTION:** A large size lanceolate blade finished with broad parallel flakes. These are found on Paleo sites and were probably used as knives.

IMPORTANT: All Paleo Knives shown half size

G9, $800-$1400
Stark Co., IL

PEISKER DIAMOND - Woodland, 2500 - 2000 B. P.

(Also see Adena and Gary)

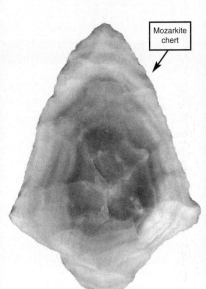

Mozarkite chert

G9, $150-$250
Lincoln Co., MO

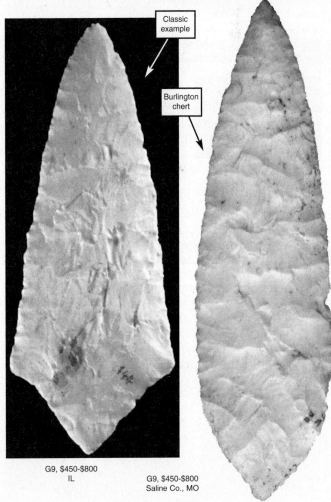

Classic example

Burlington chert

NC

LOCATION: Illinois, Missouri, Kansas into Iowa. **DESCRIPTION:** A large, broad blade with sharp shoulders and a short to moderate contracting base that comes to a point. Blade edges are recurved, convex or straight. Similar in form to the Morrow Mountain point found in the Southeast, but not as old. **I.D.KEY:** Contracted base, pointed base.

G9, $450-$800
IL

G9, $450-$800
Saline Co., MO

PEISKER DIAMOND (continued)

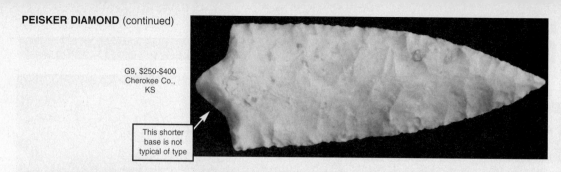

G9, $250-$400
Cherokee Co.,
KS

This shorter
base is not
typical of type

PELICAN - Transitional Paleo, 10,000 - 6000 B. P.

(Also see Beaver Lake, Dalton, Greenbrier and Holland)

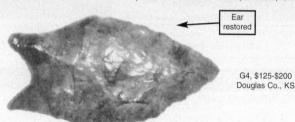

Ear restored

G4, $125-$200
Douglas Co., KS

LOCATION: Louisiana, Texas, Arkansas into Kansas. **DESCRIPTION:** A medium size auriculate point with recurved sides. The base is concave with edge grinding. **I.D. KEY:** Basal contraction.

PELICAN LAKE - Late Archaic to Woodland, 3500 - 2200 B. P.

(Also see Apple Creek, Kirk Corner Notched and Pine Tree)

Tip wear

Winterset chert

G5, $15-$30
E. NE

G7, $35-$65
E. NE

G10, $150-$250
Clay Co., MO

LOCATION: Plains states into Missouri. **DESCRIPTION:** A medium size, thin, corner notched dart point with a straight to concave to convex, expanding base. Tangs are usually pointed. Grinding may occur in notches and around base.

PIKE COUNTY - Early Archaic, 9500 - 7500 B. P.

(Also see Beaver Lake, Dalton, Greenbrier and Holland)

G8, $300-$500
Pike Co., MO

LOCATION: Midwestern states. **DESCRIPTION:** A medium to large size, lanceolate blade with an eared, fishtail base. Basal area is ground. Related to *Dalton*.

Burlington chert

G10, $800-$1500
IL

770

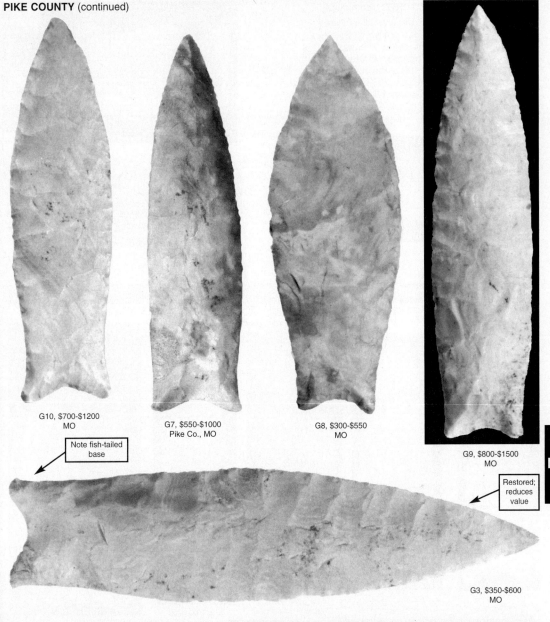

G10, $700-$1200
MO

G7, $550-$1000
Pike Co., MO

G8, $300-$550
MO

G9, $800-$1500
MO

NC

Note fish-tailed base

Restored; reduces value

G3, $350-$600
MO

PINE TREE CORNER NOTCHED - Early Archaic, 8000 - 5000 B. P.

(Also see Kirk and Lost Lake and Stilwell)

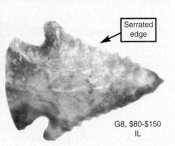

Serrated edge

G9, $25-$40
Cooper Co., MO

G8, $60-$100
Cooper Co., MO

G8, $80-$150
IL

PINE TREE CORNER NOTCHED (continued)

LOCATION: DESCRIPTION: A small to medium size, thin, corner notched point with a concave, convex, straight, bifurcated or auriculate base. Blade edges are usually serrated and flaking is parallel to the center of the blade. The shoulders expand and are barbed. The base is ground. Small examples would fall under the *Palmer* type. **I.D. KEY:** Archaic flaking to the center of each blade.

G9, $250-$450
MO

Needle tip

Serrated edge

Serrated edge

G8, $125-$200
Morgan Co., MO

G8, $165-$300
MO

PLAINVIEW - Late Paleo, 11,250 - 9500 B. P.

(Also see Angostura, Browns Valley, Clovis, Cumberland and Dalton)

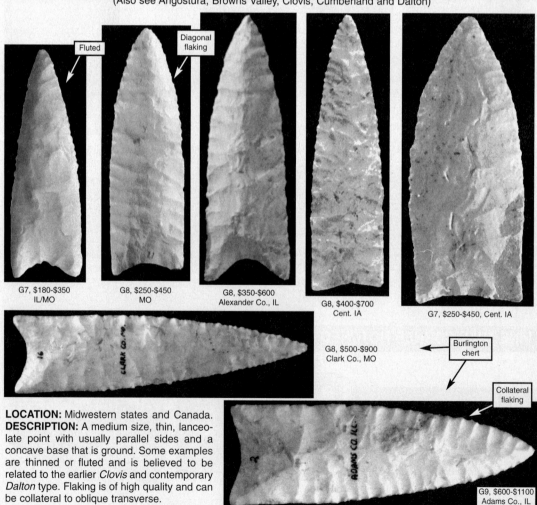

Fluted

Diagonal flaking

G7, $180-$350
IL/MO

G8, $250-$450
MO

G8, $350-$600
Alexander Co., IL

G8, $400-$700
Cent. IA

G7, $250-$450, Cent. IA

G8, $500-$900
Clark Co., MO

Burlington chert

Collateral flaking

G9, $600-$1100
Adams Co., IL

LOCATION: Midwestern states and Canada. **DESCRIPTION:** A medium size, thin, lanceolate point with usually parallel sides and a concave base that is ground. Some examples are thinned or fluted and is believed to be related to the earlier *Clovis* and contemporary *Dalton* type. Flaking is of high quality and can be collateral to oblique transverse.

772

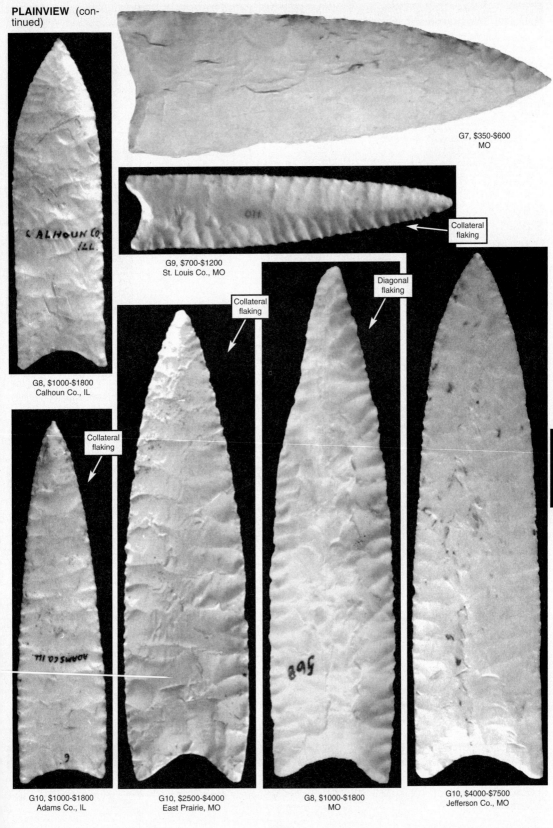

G7, $350-$600
MO

Collateral flaking

G9, $700-$1200
St. Louis Co., MO

G8, $1000-$1800
Calhoun Co., IL

Collateral flaking

Collateral flaking

Diagonal flaking

NC

Collateral flaking

G10, $1000-$1800
Adams Co., IL

G10, $2500-$4000
East Prairie, MO

G8, $1000-$1800
MO

G10, $4000-$7500
Jefferson Co., MO

QUAD - Transitional Paleo, 10,000 - 6000 B. P.

(Also see Beaver Lake, Clovis, Gosen and Cumberland)

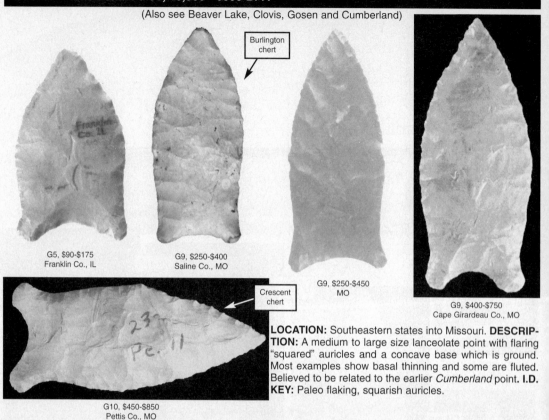

Burlington chert

G5, $90-$175
Franklin Co., IL

G9, $250-$400
Saline Co., MO

G9, $250-$450
MO

G9, $400-$750
Cape Girardeau Co., MO

Crescent chert

G10, $450-$850
Pettis Co., MO

LOCATION: Southeastern states into Missouri. DESCRIPTION: A medium to large size lanceolate point with flaring "squared" auricles and a concave base which is ground. Most examples show basal thinning and some are fluted. Believed to be related to the earlier *Cumberland* point. I.D. KEY: Paleo flaking, squarish auricles.

RADDATZ - Mid-Archaic to Woodland, 5000 - 2000 B. P.

(Also see Godar, Graham Cave, Hemphill, Hickory Ridge and Osceola)

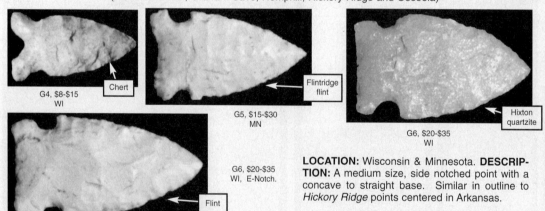

Chert

G4, $8-$15
WI

Flintridge flint

G5, $15-$30
MN

Hixton quartzite

G6, $20-$35
WI

G6, $20-$35
WI, E-Notch.

Flint

LOCATION: Wisconsin & Minnesota. DESCRIPTION: A medium size, side notched point with a concave to straight base. Similar in outline to *Hickory Ridge* points centered in Arkansas.

RAMEY KNIFE- Mid-Archaic, 5000 - 4000 B. P.

(Also see Lerma, Morse Knife and Red Ochre)

LOCATION: Midwestern states. DESCRIPTION: A large size, broad, lanceolate blade with a rounded base and high quality flaking.

RAMEY KNIFE (continued)

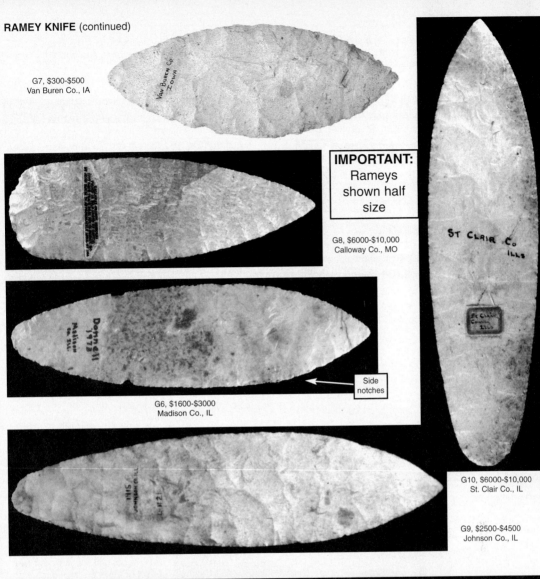

G7, $300-$500
Van Buren Co., IA

IMPORTANT:
Rameys
shown half
size

G8, $6000-$10,000
Calloway Co., MO

Side
notches

G6, $1600-$3000
Madison Co., IL

ST CLAIR CO
ILLS

G10, $6000-$10,000
St. Clair Co., IL

G9, $2500-$4500
Johnson Co., IL

NC

RED OCHRE - Mid to Late Archaic, 5000 - 3000 B. P.

(Also see Adena Blade, Sedalia and Wadlow)

G5, $25-$40
St. Clair Co., IL
One of a cache.

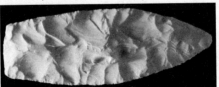

G0, 000-0150
St. Clair Co., IL. One
of a cache

Burlington
chert

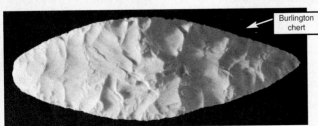

G10, $350-$600
St. Clair Co., IL

Red Ochres
Shown half size

G8, $80-$150
Sikeston, MO

RED OCHRE (continued)

LOCATION: Midwestern states. Type site-St. Louis MO. Named by Scully ('51)-Red Ochre Mound in Fulton Co., MO.
DESCRIPTION: A large, thin, broad blade with a contracting basal area. The base is convex to straight. Very similar to *Wadlow* which has the parallel sides. Possibly related to the *Turkeytail* type.

REDSTONE - Paleo, 11,500 - 10,600 B. P.

(Also see Allen, Angostura, Clovis, Cumberland, Dalton, Folsom & Plainview)

Flute channel

G8, $450-$850
MO

LOCATION: Midwestern to Southeastern states.
DESCRIPTION: A medium to large size, thin, auriculate, fluted point with convex sides expanding to a wide, deeply concave base. The hafting area is ground. This point is widest at the base. Fluting can extend most of the way down each face. Multiple flutes are usual. **I.D. KEY:** Baton or billet fluted, edgework on the hafting area. Very Rare.

RICE LOBBED - Early Archaic, 9000 - 5000 B. P.

(Also see Grand, Helton and Lundy)

G8, $25-$45
Clinton Co., IL

G8, $40-$70
MO

G8, $15-$25
MO

G4, $12-$20
Stone Co., MO

LOCATION: Midwestern to Northeastern states. **DESCRIPTION:** A medium to large size broad point with a straight to lobbed base. Blade edges can be serrated and beveled. The lobbed base variety has a shallow indentation compared to the other bifurcated types. Shoulders are horizontal to tapered and basal corners are rounded.

RICE SIDE-NOTCHED - Late Woodland, 1600 - 1400 B. P.

(Also see Carter, Lehigh, Mantanzas and Steuben)

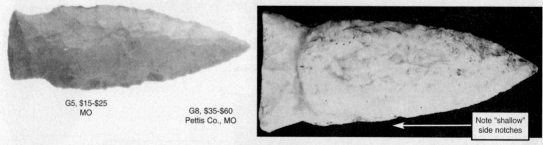

G5, $15-$25
MO

G8, $35-$60
Pettis Co., MO

Note "shallow" side notches

LOCATION: Arkansas into Missouri and Kansas. **DESCRIPTION:** A medium to large size, narrow, point with broad side notches to an expanding stem and weak shoulders. The base is straight but can be slightly concave. **I.D. KEY:** Basal form.

RICE SIDE-NOTCHED
(continued)

G8, $125-$200
Boone Co., MO

ROBINSON - Late Archaic, 4000 - 3000 B. P.

(Also see Cache River, Hickory Ridge, Knight Island and Raddatz)

LOCATION: Missouri & Illinois. **DESCRIPTION:** A small to medium size, narrow, side-notched point with a straight to concave base. **I.D. KEY:** Size, small basal notches.

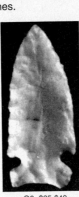

G4, $2-$5
Clinton Co., IL

G6, $12-$20
Clinton Co., IL

G5, $6-$12
Clinton Co., IL

G6, $15-$25
MO

G6, $25-$40
MO

G8, $60-$100
Cooper Co., MO

ROCHESTER - Early Archaic, 8000 - 6000 B. P.

(Also see Kramer)

NC

Blunt tip

G5, $20-$35
Marion Co., KS

G6, $35-$50
Pottowatomie Co., KS

LOCATION: Midwestern states. **DESCRIPTION:** A medium to large size, narrow point with weak, tapered shoulders and a long rectangular stem.

G6, $50-$90
Riley Co., KS

ROSS- Woodland, 2500 - 1500 B. P.

Banded rose quartzite

IMPORTANT:
Shown half size

LOCATION: Midwestern to Eastern states. **DESCRIPTION:** A large size ceremonial blade with an expanded, rounded base. Some examples have a contracting "V" shaped base.

G10+, $12,000-$20,000+
Kent Co., MI. 9-3/4" long

ST. CHARLES - Early Archaic, 9500 - 8000 B. P.

(Also see Gibson, Grand, Helton, Kirk Corner Notched and Lost Lake)

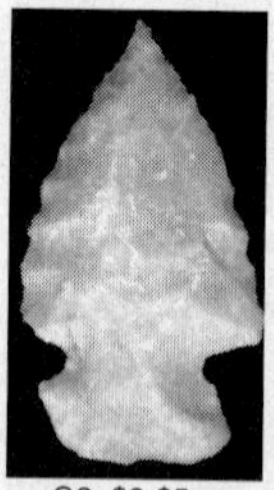

Broken tip

Beveled edge

Beveled edge

Beveled edge

Broken tip

Beveled edge

G3, $2-$5
IL

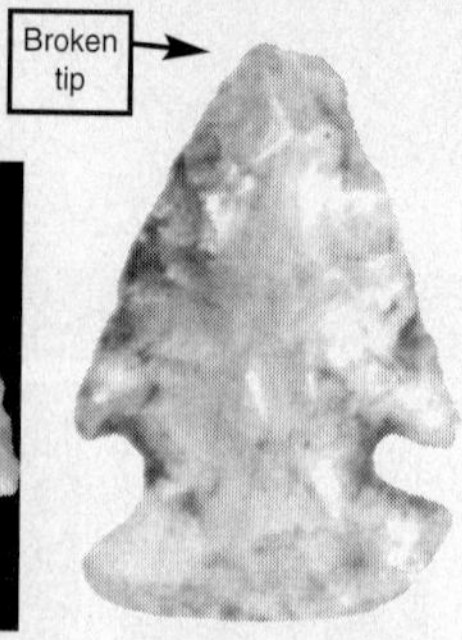

G2, $2-$5
IL

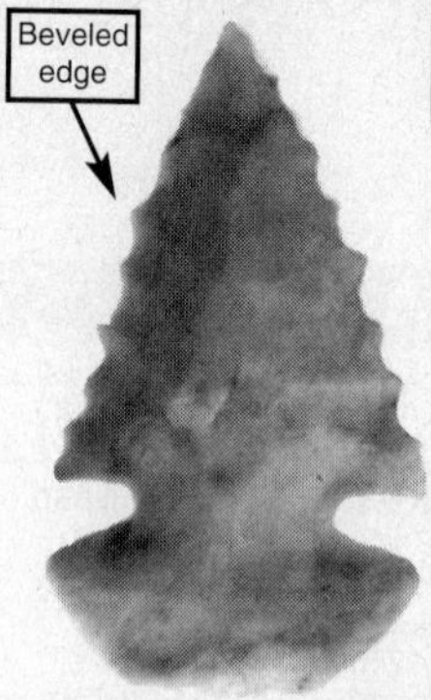

G6, $40-$75
IL

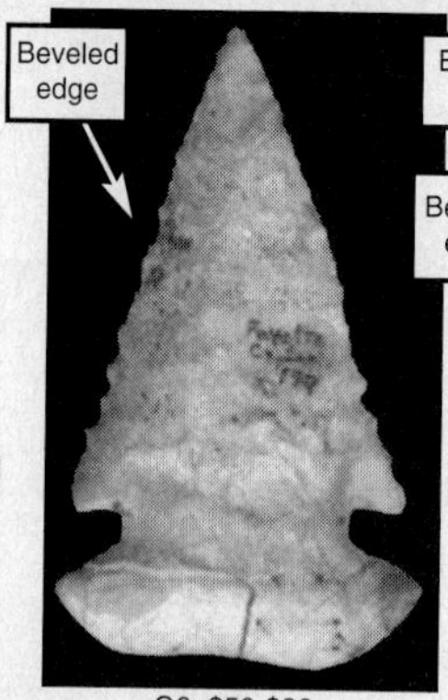

G6, $50-$90
Fayette Co., IL

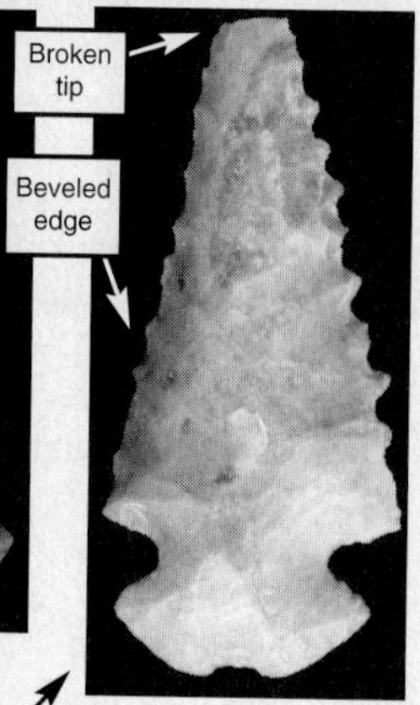

G2, $5-$10
IL

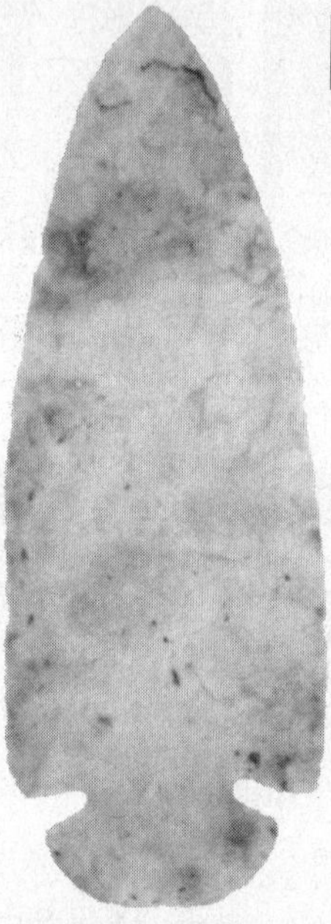

Beveled edge

Beveled edge

Indented base

Beveled edge

G8, $250-$450
IL

G7, $175-$300
IL

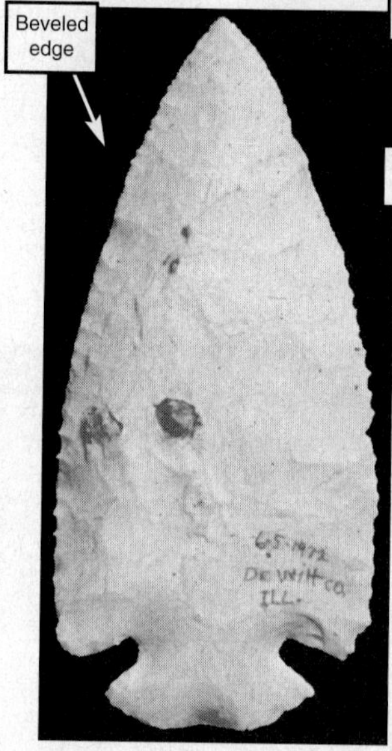

G7, $150-$250
DeWitt Co., IL

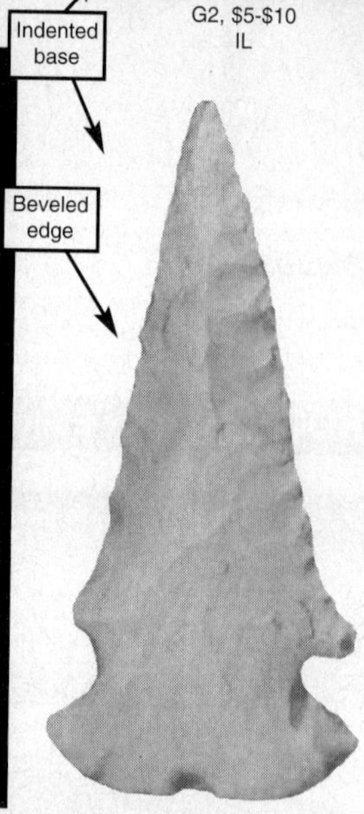

G6, $55-$100
Jersey Co., IL

G7, $90-$175
Scott So., MO

G7, $40-$75
Macoupin Co., IL

LOCATION: Midwestern to Eastern states. **DESCRIPTION:** Also known as *Dovetail.* A medium to large size, broad, thin, elliptical, corner notched point with a dovetail base. Blade edges are beveled on opposite sides when resharpened. The base is convex and most examples exhibit high quality flaking. There is a rare variant that has the barbs clipped (clipped wing) as in the *Decatur* type. There are many variations on base style from bifurcated to eared, rounded or squared. Base size varies from small to very large. **I.D. KEY:** Dovetailed base.

778

Beveled edge

Ground stem →

← Un-notched preform

G8, $65-$125
Macoupin Co., IL

Collateral flaking

G7, $55-$100
IL

G7, $700-$1250
Boone Co., MO

Beveled edge

Tip & barb nick

G10, $500-$900
IL

NC

LaSalle flint

G8, $700-$1200
LaSalle Co., IL

G10, $700-$1200
Madison Co., IL

G8, $250-$450
LaSalle Co., IL

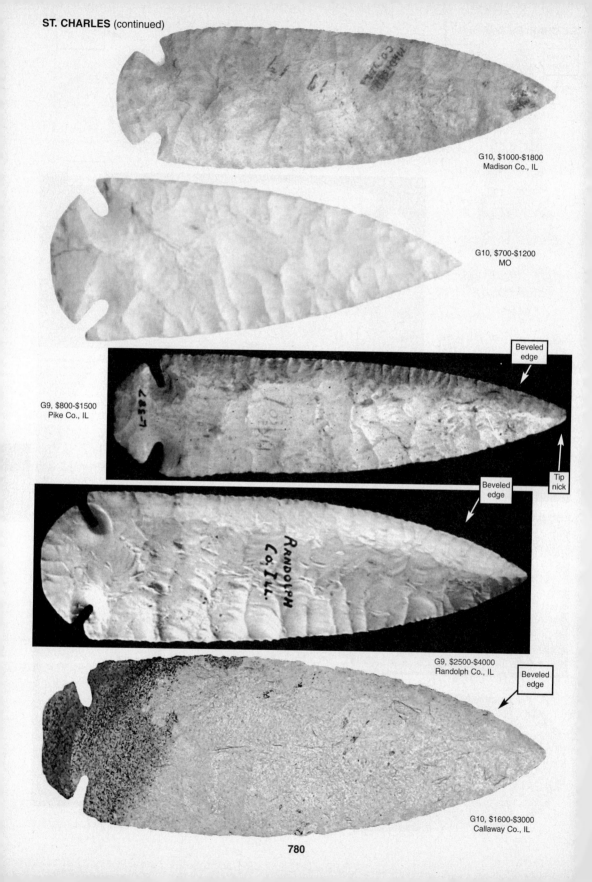

G10, $1000-$1800
Madison Co., IL

G10, $700-$1200
MO

G9, $800-$1500
Pike Co., IL

Beveled edge

Tip nick

Beveled edge

G9, $2500-$4000
Randolph Co., IL

Beveled edge

G10, $1600-$3000
Callaway Co., IL

SCALLORN - Woodland to Mississippian, 1300 - 500 B. P.

(Also see Alba, Collins, Haskell, Jacks Reef and Sequoyah)

G3, $2-$5
IL

G6, $25-$40
IL

G8, $50-$80
Cooper Co., MO

G9, $80-$150
MO

G8, $6-10
Cooper Co., MO

G6, $25-$40
Cooper Co., MO

G8, $50-$95
Cooper Co., MO

LOCATION: Texas, Oklahoma, Arkansas into Missouri. **DESCRIPTION:** A small size, corner notched arrow point with a flaring stem. Bases and bladed edges are straight, concave or convex and many examples are serrated. **I.D. KEY:** Small corner notched point with sharp barbs and tip.

SCOTTSBLUFF I - Transitional Paleo, 10,000 - 8000 B. P.

(Also see Eden, Hardin, Holland, Hollenberg Stemmed and Stone Square Stem)

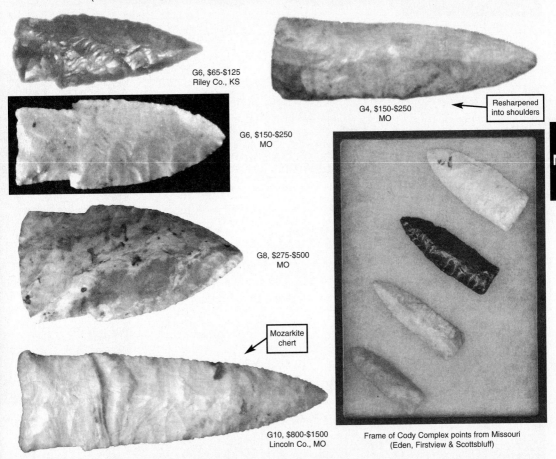

G6, $65-$125
Riley Co., KS

G6, $150-$250
MO

G4, $150-$250
MO

Resharpened into shoulders

NC

G8, $275-$500
MO

Mozarkite chert

G10, $800-$1500
Lincoln Co., MO

Frame of Cody Complex points from Missouri
(Eden, Firstview & Scottsbluff)

LOCATION: Midwestern states. **DESCRIPTION:** A medium to large size, broad stemmed point with convex to parallel sides and weak shoulders. The stem is parallel sided to expanding. The hafting area is ground. Made by the Cody Complex people. Contemporary with *Hardins*. Most examples have horizontal to oblique parallel flaking and are of high quality and thinness.

781

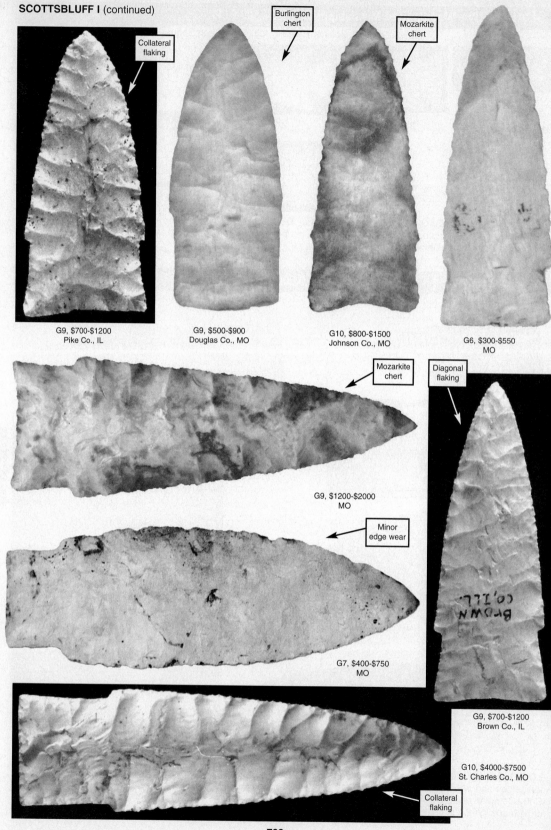

Collateral flaking

Burlington chert

Mozarkite chert

G9, $700-$1200
Pike Co., IL

G9, $500-$900
Douglas Co., MO

G10, $800-$1500
Johnson Co., MO

G6, $300-$550
MO

Mozarkite chert

Diagonal flaking

G9, $1200-$2000
MO

Minor edge wear

G7, $400-$750
MO

G9, $700-$1200
Brown Co., IL

G10, $4000-$7500
St. Charles Co., MO

Collateral flaking

782

SCOTTSBLUFF II - Early Archaic, 9500 - 7000 B. P.

(Also see Hardin, Holland and Hollenberg Stemmed)

Hixton silcified sandstone

Diagonal flaking

G9, $600-$1000
Kansas City, MO.

G3, $40-$75
WI

G5, $80-$150
Moro, IL

Hixton silcified sandstone

G8, $350-$650
Pettis Co., MO

LOCATION: Midwestern states. **DESCRIPTION:** A medium to large size triangular point with shoulders a little stronger than on Type I and a broad parallel sided/expanding stem.

G5, $175-$300
WI, Mississippi Riv.

G7, $175-$300
MO

G8, $800-$1500
Jackson Co., MO

G6, $350-$600
MO

G9, $1600-$3000
Cooper Co., MO

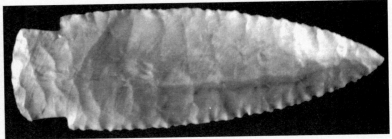

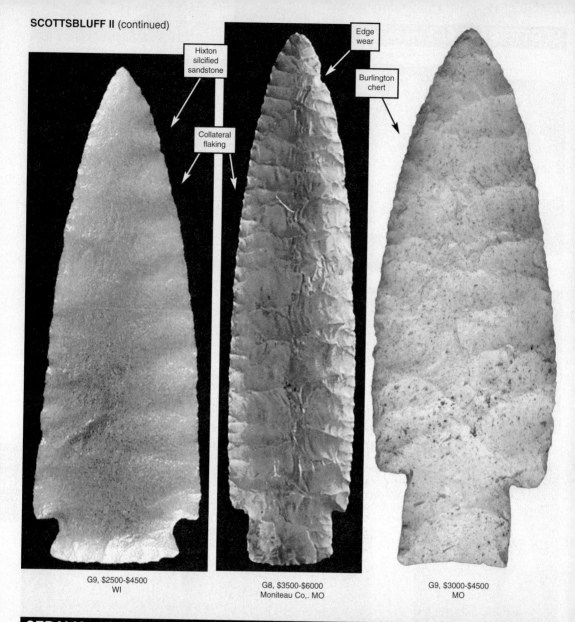

Hixton silcified sandstone

Collateral flaking

Edge wear

Burlington chert

G9, $2500-$4500
WI

G8, $3500-$6000
Moniteau Co,. MO

G9, $3000-$4500
MO

SEDALIA - Mid-Late Archaic, 5000 - 3000 B. P.

(Also see Agate Basin, Burroughs, Lerma, Nebo Hill and Red Ochre)

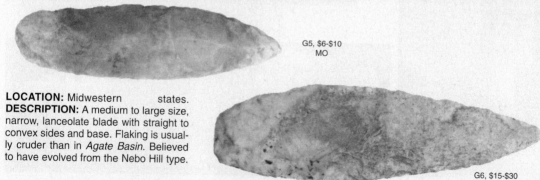

G5, $6-$10
MO

LOCATION: Midwestern states.
DESCRIPTION: A medium to large size, narrow, lanceolate blade with straight to convex sides and base. Flaking is usually cruder than in *Agate Basin*. Believed to have evolved from the Nebo Hill type.

G6, $15-$30
MO

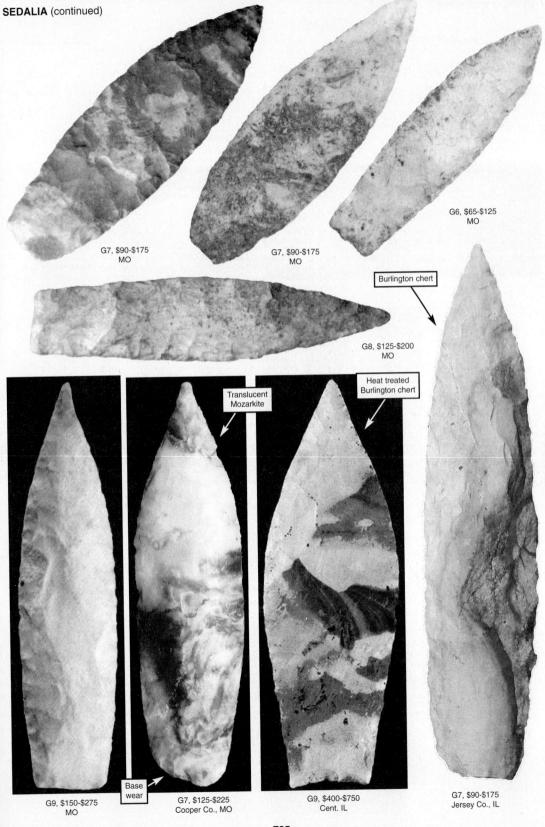

G7, $90-$175
MO

G7, $90-$175
MO

G6, $65-$125
MO

Burlington chert

G8, $125-$200
MO

Heat treated
Burlington chert

Translucent
Mozarkite

NC

Base
wear

G9, $150-$275
MO

G7, $125-$225
Cooper Co., MO

G9, $400-$750
Cent. IL

G7, $90-$175
Jersey Co., IL

Low quality heat treated chert

G7, $175-$300
Pike Co., MO

Tip wear

G6, $150-$250
Pettis Co., MO

Heat treated Burlington chert

G10, $250-$450
MO

G8, $250-$450
Pettis Co., MO

G7, $200-$350
Cooper Co., MO

G9, $600-$1000
MO

SEQUOYAH - Mississippian, 1000 - 600 B. P.

(Also see Alba, Hayes and Homan)

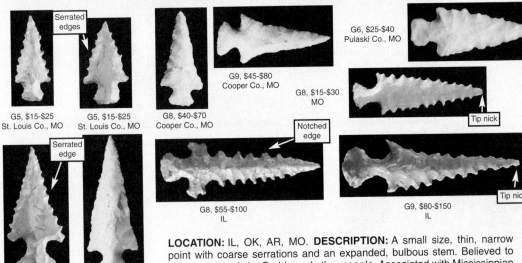

Serrated edges

G5, $15-$25
St. Louis Co., MO

G5, $15-$25
St. Louis Co., MO

G8, $40-$70
Cooper Co., MO

G9, $45-$80
Cooper Co., MO

G6, $25-$40
Pulaski Co., MO

G8, $15-$30
MO

Tip nick

Notched edge

G8, $55-$100
IL

G9, $80-$150
IL

Tip nick

Serrated edge

G8, $50-$90
IL

G9, $45-$80
Cooper Co., MO

LOCATION: IL, OK, AR, MO. **DESCRIPTION:** A small size, thin, narrow point with coarse serrations and an expanded, bulbous stem. Believed to have been made by Caddo and other people. Associated with Mississippian Caddo culture sites. Named after the famous Cherokee chief of the same name. **I.D. KEY:** Bulbous base, coarse serrations.

SMITH - Middle Archaic, 7000 - 4000 B. P.

(Also see Etley and Mehlville)

Only one notch

NC

G8, $125-$200
Cherokee Co., KS

G9, $350-$600
Advance, MO

Banded chert

G6, $125-$200
Miller Co., MO

G7, $150-$250
MO

LOCATION: Midwestern states. **DESCRIPTION:** A very large size, broad, point with long parallel shoulders and a squared to slightly expanding base. Some examples may appear to be basally notched due to the long barbs.

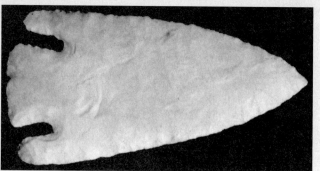

G10, $400-$700
Menard Co., IL

Indiana
hornstone

G7, $400-$750
Howard Co., MO

G8, $350-$600
MO

G8, $150-$250
Macoupin Co., IL

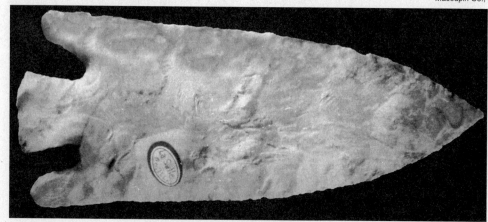

G9, $950-
$1750
La Salle Co.,
IL

SNYDERS - HOPEWELL - Woodland, 2500 - 1500 B. P.

(Also see Carter, Grand, Helton, Hopewell, North and Steuben)

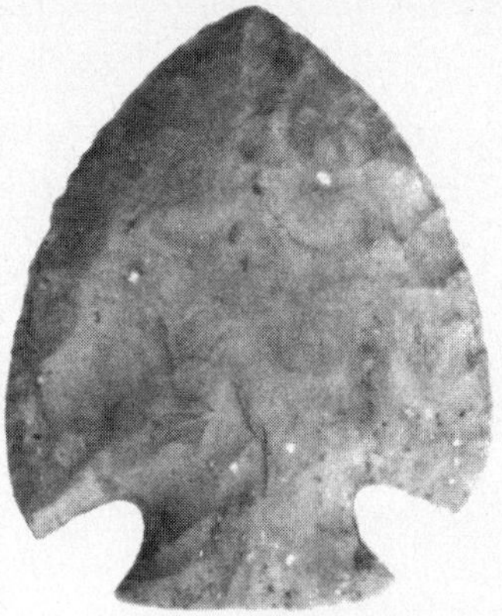

G7, $65-$125
IL

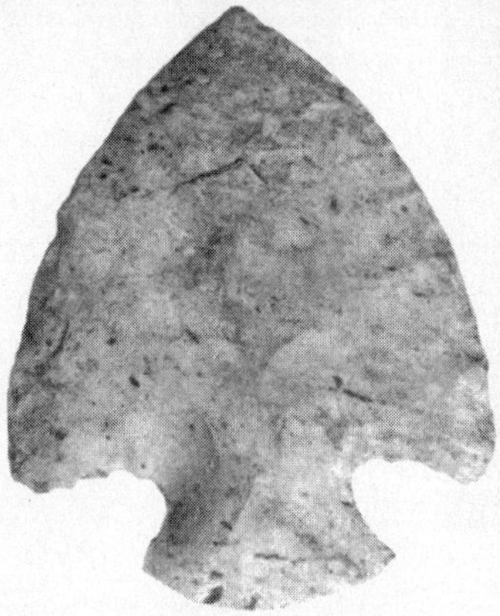

G6, $65-$125
IL

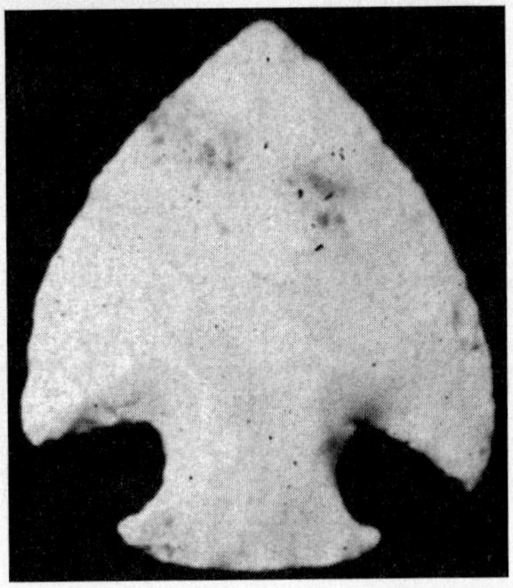

G8, $125-$200
Livingston Co., IL

Burlington chert

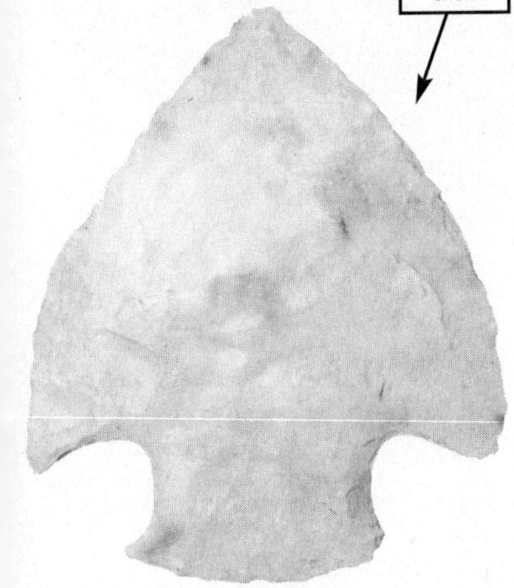

G8, $175-$300
Scott Co., IL

Angel Fish form

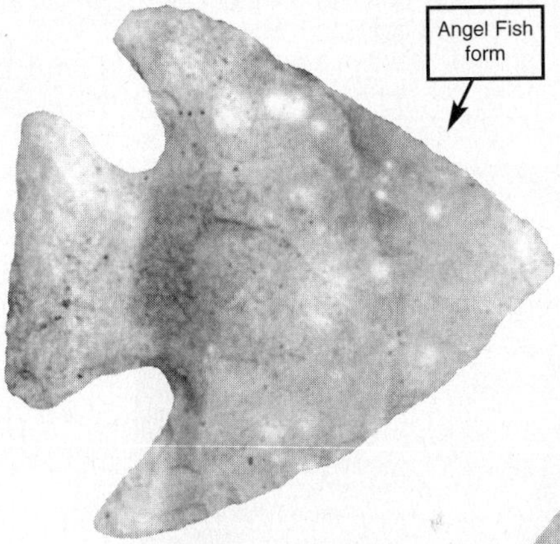

G7, $125-$200
Scott Co., IL

IMPORTANT:
All Snyders points on this page shown actual size

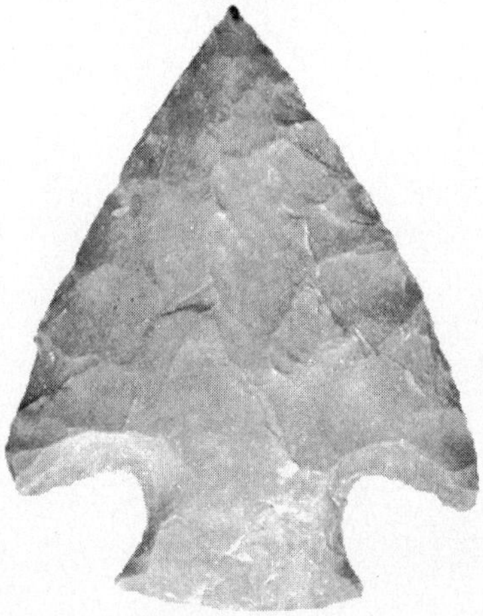

G10, $150-$275
Clinton Co., IL

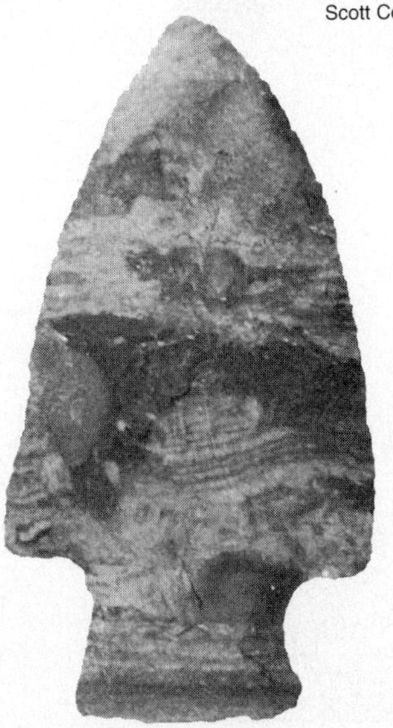

G7, $150-$250
Madison Co., IL

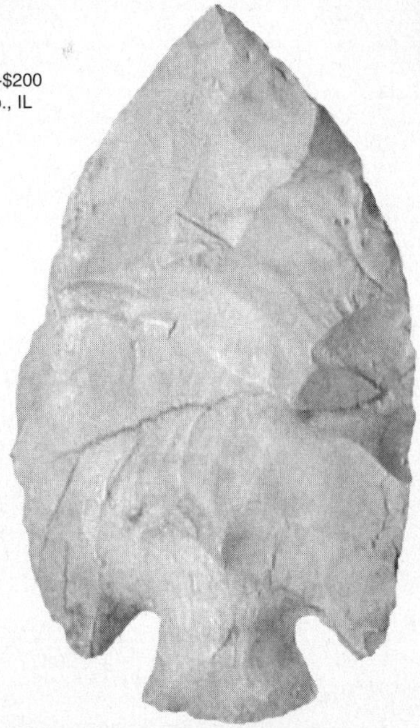

G7, $200-$350
IL

SNYDERS (continued)

G8, $200-$350
Lincoln Co., MO

G10, $500-$800
Greene Co., IL

LOCATION: Midwestern to Eastern states. Type site located in Calhoun Co., IL. **DESCRIPTION:** A medium to large size, broad, thin, wide corner notched point of high quality. Blade edges and base are convex. Many examples have intentional fractured bases. Made by the Hopewell culture. This point has been reproduced in recent years. **I.D. KEY:** Size and broad corner notches.

G8, $450-$800
IL

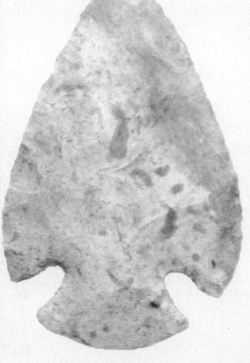

G9, $275-$500
IL

G7, $350-$650
IL

SQUARE KNIFE - Late Archaic to Historic, 3500 - 400 B. P.

(Also see Angostura, Red Ochre and Wadlow)

G6, $150-$250
Morris Co., KS

LOCATION: Midwestern states. **DESCRIPTION:** A medium to large size squared blade with rounded corners.

G10, $800-$1500
Douglas Co., KS. Classic. Cache blade.

G6, $65-$120
Morgan Co., MO

G9, $350-$600
Madison Co., IL

IMPORTANT:
All shown half size

STANFIELD   (see Tennessee River)

STEUBEN- Woodland, 2000 - 1000 B. P.

(Also see Carter, Ferry, Hardin, Lehigh, Matanzas, Motley, Rice Side Notched and Table Rock)

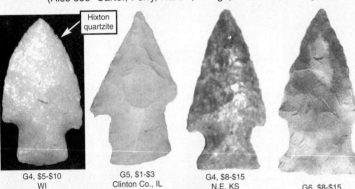

Hixton quartzite

G4, $8-$15
Washington Co., KS

LOCATION: Midwestern states. **DESCRIPTION:** A medium to large size, narrow point with tapered to horizontal shoulders and a medium to long expanding stem. The base is straight. Convex base places it under the *Snyder* type. **I.D. KEY:** Long expanded stem.

G4, $5-$10
WI

G5, $1-$3
Clinton Co., IL

G4, $8-$15
N.E. KS

G6, $8-$15
Madison Co., IL

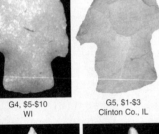

G6, $8-$15
Clinton Co., IL

G4, $8-$15
Miller Co., MO

G6, $15-$25
Washington Co., KS

G6, $25-$45
Washington Co., KS

G6, $25-$40
Madison Co., IL

G7, $25-$45
Madison Co., IL

(Also see Kirk Corner Notched and Pine Tree)

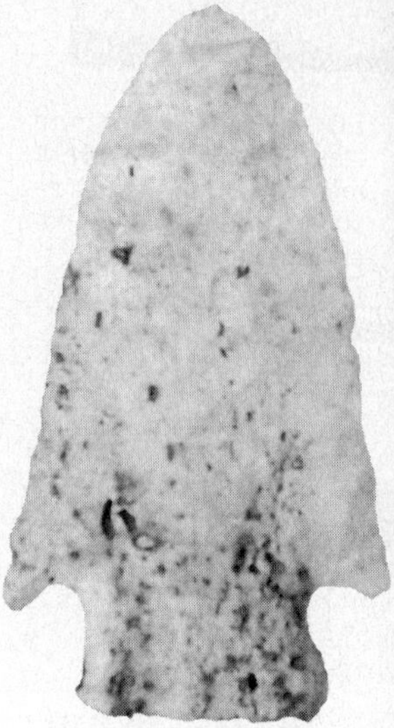

Heat treated Burlington chert

Serrated edge

G6, $65-$125
Madison Co., IL

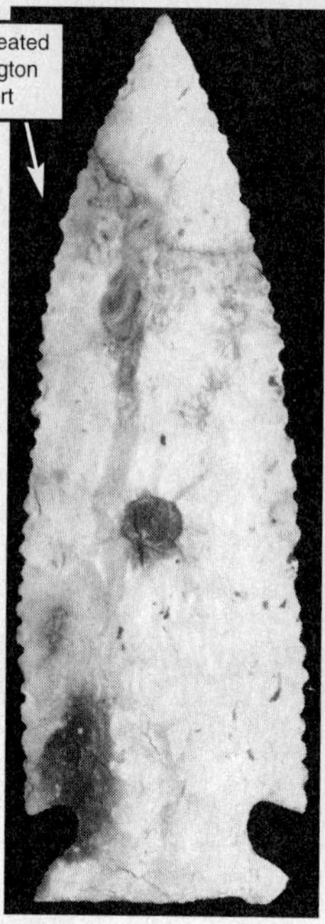

G8, $175-$300
Cooper Co., MO

G8, $125-$200
MO

G9, $175-$300
MO

Barb nick

G7, $80-$150
Brown Co., IL

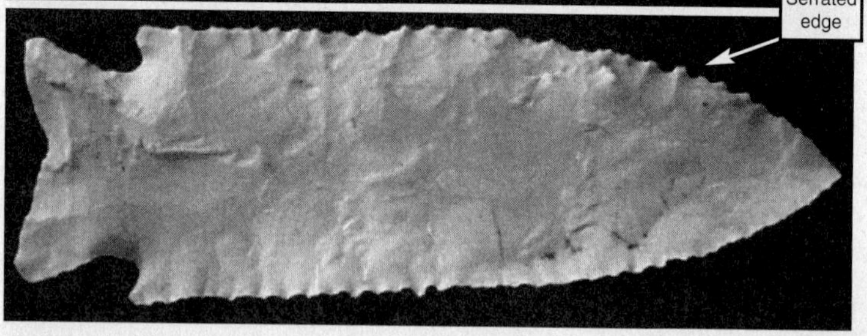

Serrated edge

G8, $250-$400
IL

Serrated edge

G8, $165-$300
Cherokee Co., KS

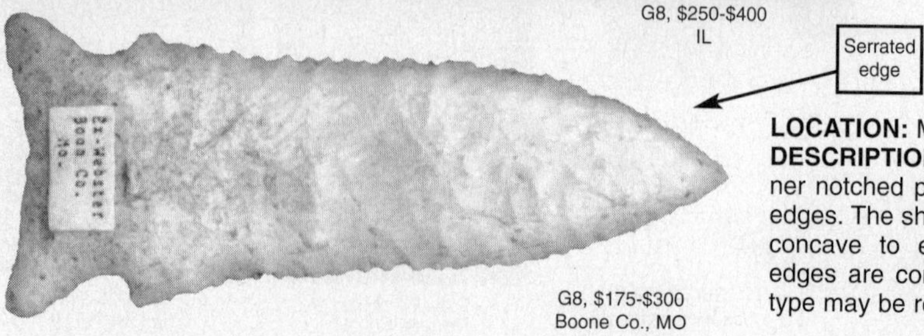

G8, $175-$300
Boone Co., MO

LOCATION: Midwestern to Eastern states. **DESCRIPTION:** A medium to large size, corner notched point with usually serrated blade edges. The shoulders are barbed. The base is concave to eared and ground. The blade edges are convex, parallel or recurved. This type may be related to *Kirk*.

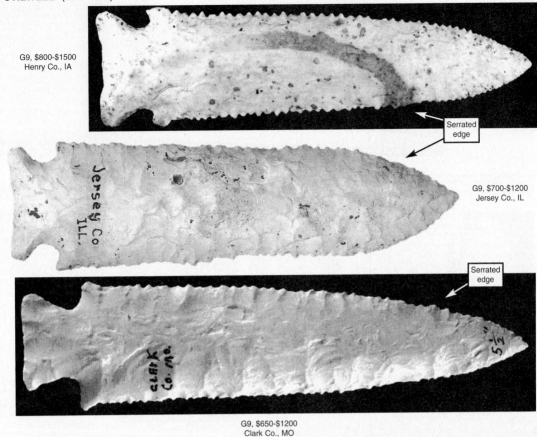

G9, $800-$1500
Henry Co., IA

Serrated edge

G9, $700-$1200
Jersey Co., IL

Serrated edge

G9, $650-$1200
Clark Co., MO

NC

STONE SQUARE STEM - Middle Archaic, 6000 - 4000 B. P.

(Also see Etley, Heavy Duty, Johnson, Kramer and Rochester)

G5, $15-$25
Clinton Co., IL

G6, $25-$45
Cherokee Co., KS

G6, $20-$35
Morgan Co., MO

LOCATION: Midwestern states. Type site is in Stone Co., MO. **DESCRIPTION:** A medium to large size, broad stemmed point. Blade edges are convex to recurved. The shoulders are horizontal to barbed and the base is square to slightly expanding with a prominent, short stem. **I.D. KEY:** Short, square stem.

STONE SQUARE STEM (continued)

G10, $250-$400
Cent. IL

TABLE ROCK - Late Archaic, 4000 - 3000 B. P.

(Also see Kay Blade, Lehigh, Motley, Munker's Creek and Steuben)

Hixton quartzite

G5, $15-$25
WI

G5, $15-$25
MO/IL

G6, $25-$40
WI

G6, $30-$50, MO

G6, $30-$50
IL

G8, $40-$75
Madison Co., IL

G7, $50-$90
IA

G7, $40-$75
Madison Co., IL

G8, $65-$125
Cooper Co., MO

G7, $25-$65
Bureau Co., IL

G6, $25-$50
MO

LOCATION: Midwestern to Northeastern states.
DESCRIPTION: A medium to large size, expanded stem point with straight to tapered shoulders. Shoulders can be sharp or rounded. This type is also known as a "Bottleneck" point.

Tip wear

Base wear

G8, $150-$250
St. Louis Co., MO

G7, $150-$250
St. Louis Co., MO

G9, $150-$275
MO

G7, $55-$100
S. E. MO

TENNESSEE RIVER - Early Archaic, 9000 - 6000 B. P.

(Also see Adena Blade, Cobbs Triangular, Kirk, Red Ochre and Stanfield)

NC

LOCATION: Midwestern to Southeastern states. **DESCRIPTION:** These are unnotched preforms for early Archaic types such as *Kirk, Eva*, etc. and would have the same description as that type without the notches. Bases can be straight, concave or convex. **I.D. KEY:** Archaic style edgework. **NOTE:** This type has been confused with the *Stanfield* point which is a medium size, narrow, thicker point. A beveled edge would place your point under the *Cobbs Triangular* type.

G8, $80-$150
Madison Co., IL

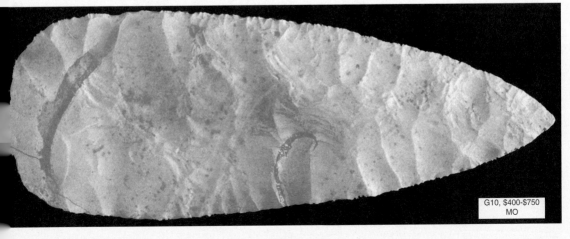

G10, $400-$750
MO

G8, $65-$125
Pemiscott Co., MO

G8, $80-$150
Macoupin Co., IL

THEBES - Early Archaic, 10,000 - 8000 B. P.

(Also see Lost Lake, St. Charles and Stilwell)

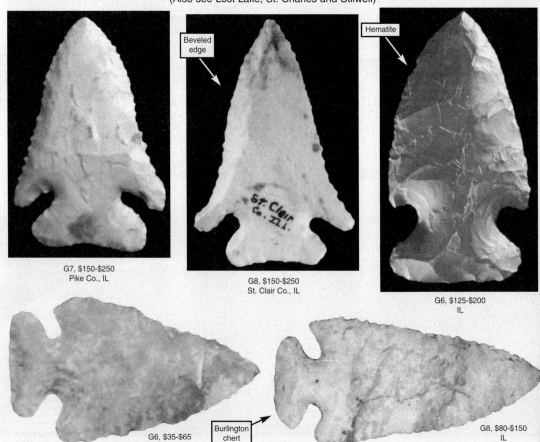

Beveled edge

Hematite

G7, $150-$250
Pike Co., IL

G8, $150-$250
St. Clair Co., IL

St. Clair Co. Ill.

G6, $125-$200
IL

G6, $35-$65
Jersey Co., IL

Burlington chert

G8, $80-$150
IL

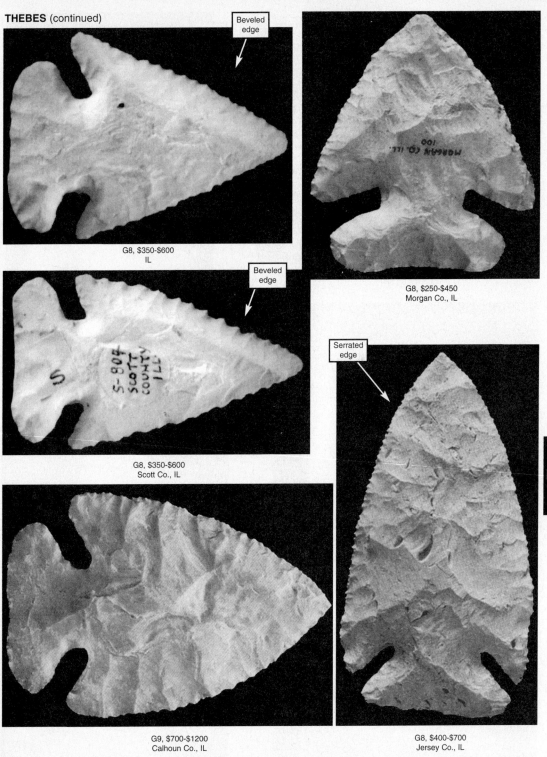

Beveled edge

Beveled edge

Serrated edge

G8, $350-$600
IL

G8, $250-$450
Morgan Co., IL

G8, $350-$600
Scott Co., IL

G9, $700-$1200
Calhoun Co., IL

G8, $400-$700
Jersey Co., IL

LOCATION: Midwestern states. **DESCRIPTION:** A medium to large size, wide blade with deep, angled side notches that are parallel sided and squared. Resharpened examples have beveling on one side of each face. The bases of this type have broad proportions and are concave, straight or convex and are ground. Some examples have unusual side notches called Key or "E" notch. This type of notch is angled into the blade to produce a high point in the center, forming the letter E. See *Big Sandy E-Notched*.

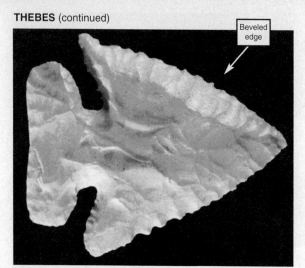

Beveled edge

G8, $350-$600
Randolph Co., IL

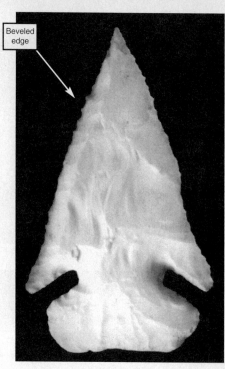

Beveled edge

G8, $400-$700
IL

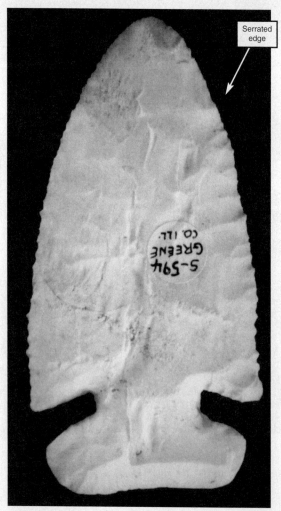

Serrated edge

G10, $1700-$3000
Greene Co., IL

G8, $400-$700
LaSalle Co., IL

Hixton slicified sandstone

Broken & glued

G5, $450-$850
Taswell Co., IL; if not broken $1800-$3000

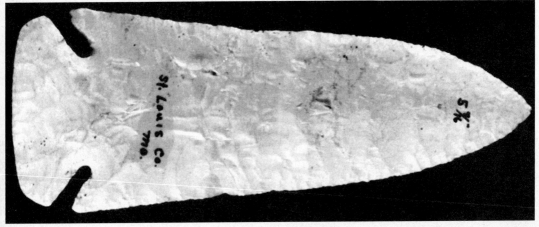

NC

G10, $2500-$4000
St. Louis Co., MO

Beveled edge

G9, $2500-$4000
Scott Co., IL

TURIN - Early Archaic, 8500 - 7500 B. P.

(Also see Godar, Graham Cave, Hemphill, Hickory Ridge, Osceola, Raddatz and Robinson)

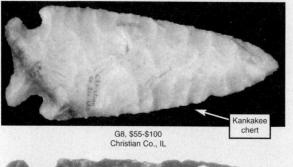

Kankakee chert

G8, $55-$100
Christian Co., IL

LOCATION: Illinois, Missouri, Nebraska northward. **DESCRIPTION:** A small to medium size side-notched point with an auriculate base that is concave. Notching occurs close to the base and the shoulders are barbed. Bases are ground. **I.D. KEY:** Eared base.

G7, $125-$200
S.E. KS

G7, $65-$125
Pottowatomie Co., KS

TURKEYTAIL-FULTON - Late Archaic to Woodland, 4000 - 2500 B. P.

(Also see Early Ovoid Knife)

One of a large cache

G8, $800-$1400
St. Charles Co., MO

G6, $400-$700
MO. Titterington cache.

One of a large cache

G9, $2000-$3500
Morgan Co., IL

G8, $800-$1400
St. Charles Co., MO

One of a large cache

G9, $2500-$4000
St. Charles Co., MO., part of Turkeytail cache.

IMPORTANT:
All Turkeytails shown half size

LOCATION: Midwestern to Eastern states. **DESCRIPTION:** A medium to large size, wide, thin, elliptical blade with shallow notches very close to the base. This type is usually found in caches and has been reproduced in recent years. Made by the Adena culture. An earlier form was found in *Benton* caches in Mississippi carbon dated to about 4700 B.P.

TURKEYTAIL-HARRISON - Late Archaic to Woodland, 4000 - 2500 B. P.

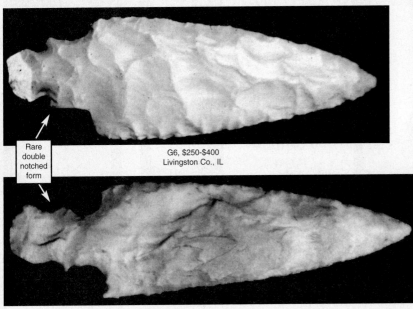

LOCATION: Midwestern to Eastern states. **DESCRIPTION:** A medium to large size, narrow, elliptical tapered, horizontal or barbed shoulders, and an elongated, diamond-shaped stem in the form of a turkey's tail. Large examples may have fine pressure flaking on one edge of each face. Made by the Adena culture. Lengths up to 20 inches known.

Rare double notched form

G6, $250-$400
Livingston Co., IL

G7, $250-$400
Miller Co., MO. Rare.

TURKEYTAIL-HEBRON - Late Archaic to Woodland, 3500 - 2500 B. P.
(Also see Waubesa)

NC

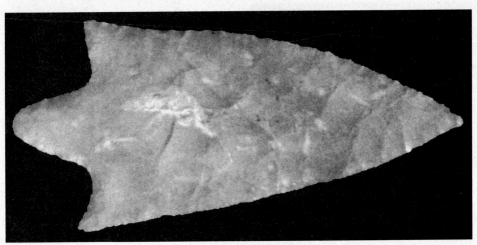

G10, $1500-$2500
Cairo., IL

LOCATION: Around the great lakes region from Wisconsin to New York. **DESCRIPTION:** A medium to large size blade with barbed shoulders, and a narrow, contracting stem with a convex base. Made by the *Adena* culture.

WADLOW - Late Archaic, 4000 - 2500 B. P.
(Also see Cobbs Triangular, Etley and Red Ochre)

G6, $55-$100
IL

G6, $50-$90
MO

G7, $50-$90
IL

G8, $80-$150
Pettis Co., MO

G9, $250-$400
MO

IMPORTANT:
All Wadlows
shown half
size

LOCATION: Midwestern states. Type site-The Etley site, Calhoun Co., IL. Walter Wadlow first discovered this form in 1939, Jersey Co., IL. **DESCRIPTION:** A large to very large size, broad, parallel sided blade with a straight to convex base. The preform for the *Etley* point.

G9, $400-
$750
Ralls Co.,
MO

G8, $250-$400
IL

G8, $200-$350
IL

G10, $4000-$7000
Cooper Co., MO

G9, $450-$800
IL

G5, $350-$600
Cherokee Co., MO

G7, $200-$350
IL

G8, $400-$750
IL

G8, $450-$800
MO

G6, $275-$500
MO

WARRICK - Early Archaic, 9000 - 5000 B. P.

(Also see St. Charles)

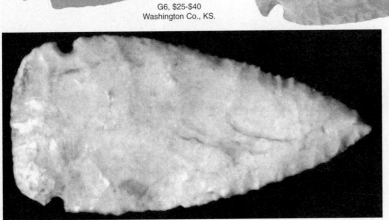

G6, $25-$40
Washington Co., KS.

G8, $135-$250
Washington Co., KS.

LOCATION: Midwestern states. **DESCRIPTION:** A medium to large size, sturdy, side to corner notched point. Notching is close to the base which is ground. Flaking is of high quality.

G8, $275-$500
Camden Co., MO

WASHITA - Mississippian, 800 - 400 B. P.

(Also see Cahokia and Huffaker)

G5, $12-$20
IL

G9, $65-$125
Garden City, KS

Alibates

G9, $50-$95
Pottowatomie Co., KS

G10, $150-$250
Garden City, KS

Alibates

G9, $150-$250
Hooker Co., NE

LOCATION: Midwestern states. **DESCRIPTION:** A small size, thin, triangular side notched arrow point with a concave base. Basal area is usually large in proportion to the blade size.

WAUBESA - Woodland, 2500 - 1500 B. P.

(Also see Adena, Dickson, Gary, Hidden Valley & Turkeytail-Hebron)

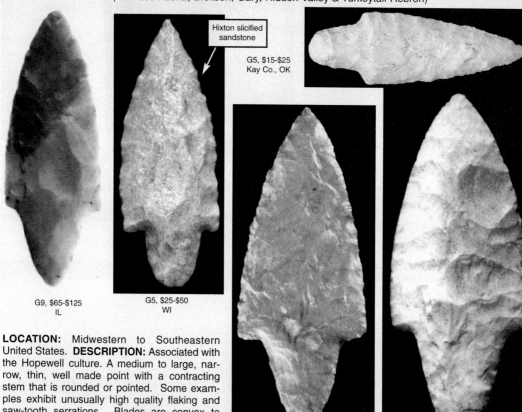

Hixton slicified sandstone

G5, $15-$25
Kay Co., OK

G9, $65-$125
IL

G5, $25-$50
WI

G8, $125-$200
IL

G9, $160-$300
Sedalia, MO

LOCATION: Midwestern to Southeastern United States. **DESCRIPTION:** Associated with the Hopewell culture. A medium to large, narrow, thin, well made point with a contracting stem that is rounded or pointed. Some examples exhibit unusually high quality flaking and saw-tooth serrations. Blades are convex to recurved. Shoulders are squared to barbed. **I.D. KEY:** Basal form pointed or near pointed. Good secondary flaking and thin.

WHEELER EXCURVATE - Transitional Paleo, 10,000 - 8000 B. P.

(Also see Angostura)

G9, $125-$200
S.W. MO

LOCATION: Southeastern states. Rare in Illinois and Missouri. **DESCRIPTION:** A small to medium size, lanceolate point with a deep concave base that is steeply beveled. Some examples are fluted, others are finely serrated and show excellent quality collateral flaking. Most bases are deeply notched but some examples have a more shallow concavity. Basal grinding is usually absent. The ears on some examples turn inward. Blade edges are excurvate. **I.D. KEY:** Base form and flaking style.

DESERT SOUTHWEST SECTION:

This section includes point types from the following states: Arizona, Colorado, Nevada, New Mexico, Texas, Utah and from Mexico

The points in this section are arranged in alphabetical order and are shown **actual size**. All types are listed that were available for photographing. Any missing types will be added to future editions as photographs become available. We are always interested in receiving sharp, black and white or color glossy photos, color slides or high resolution (300 pixels/inch) digital pictures of your collection. Be sure to include a ruler in the photograph so that proper scale can be determined.

Lithics: Materials employed in the manufacture of projectile points from this region are: agate, basalt, chalcedony, chert, jasper, obsidian, petrified wood, quartzite, siltstone.

Important sites: Clovis (Paleo), Blackwater Draw, NM. Folsom (Paleo), Folsom NM. Sandia (Paleo), Sandia Cave, NM.

SPECIAL SENIOR ADVISOR:
Ben Stermer

Other advisors:
Richard E. Bachman, John Byrd
Jim Hogue, Alan L. Phelps,
Art Tatum

In memory of Charles D. Meyer who was instrumental in establishing this section of the guide with his advice, descriptions, and photographs.

DESERT SOUTHWEST POINT TYPES
(Archaeological Periods)

PALEO (13,200 B.P - 9,000 B.P.)

Belen	Folsom	Lake Mohave	Midland
Clovis	Goshen	Lancet	Milnesand
Drill	Graver	Madden Lake	Sandia

EARLY ARCHAIC (10,300 B.P - 5,000 B.P.)

Abasolo	Bell	Escobas	Palmillas	Sudden Series
Agate Basin	Circular Uniface Knife	Firstview	Pelona	Texcoco
Allen	Cody Knife	Golondrina	Perforator	Tortugas
Angostura	Cruciform I	Hell Gap	Pinto Basin	Uvalde
Archaic Knife	Cruciform II	Jay	Plainview	Ventana-Amargosa
Augustin	Darl Stemmed	Lancet	Rio Grande	Zephyr
Augustin Snapped Base	Datil	Marshall	Round-Back Knife	Zorra
Bajada	Early Leaf	Meserve	San Jose	
Baker	Early Triangular	Mount Albion	Scottsbluff	
Barreal	Eden	Moyote	Scraper	
Bat Cave	Embudo	Northern Side Notched	Silver Lake	

MIDDLE ARCHAIC (5,100 B.P - 3,300 B.P.)

Ahumada	Crescent	Frio Transitional	Manzano
Armijo	Dagger	Green River	Neff
Catan	Disc	Gypsum Cave	Refugio
Chiricahua	Duncan	Hanna	San Rafael
Corner Tang Knife	Durango	Kinney	Squaw Mountain
Cortero	Frio	Lerma	Ventana Side Notched

LATE ARCHAIC (3,400 B.P - 2,300 B.P.)

Acatita	Conejo	Gobernadora	Shumla
Amaragosa	Duran	Maljamar	Socorro
Basal Double Tang	Early Stemmed	Martis	Triangular Knife
Carlsbad	Elko Corner Notched	Matamoros	Yavapai
Charcos	Elko Eared	San Pedro	
Cienega	Exotic	Saw	

DESERT TRADITIONS:
TRANSITIONAL (2,300 B.P - 1600 B.P.)

Black Mesa Narrow Neck	Figueroa	Guadalupe	Humboldt

DEVELOPMENTAL (1600 - 700 B.P)

Awatovi Side Notched	Dry Prong	Point Of Pines Side Notched	Snaketown
Basketmaker	Eastgate Split-Stem	Pueblo Alto Side Notched	Snaketown Side Notched
Bonito Notched	Gatlin Side Notched	Pueblo Del Arroyo Side Notched	Snaketown Triangular
Bull Creek	Gila River Corner Notched	Pueblo Side Notched	Soto
Chaco Corner Notrched	Hodges Contracting Stem	Rose Springs Corner Notched	Temporal
Citrus Side Notched	Hohokam Knife	Rose Springs Stemmed	Truxton
Cohonina Stemmed	Kin Kletso Side Notched	Sacaton	Walnut Canyon Side Notched
Convento	Mimbre	Salado	
Deadman's	Nawthis	Salt River Indented Base	
Dolores	Parowan	Santa Cruz	

CLASSIC PHASE (700 - 400 B.P)

Aguaje	Cow's Skull	Desert-Sierra	Sobaipuri
Buck Taylor Notched	Del Carmen	Garza	Toyah
Caracara	Desert-Delta	Harahey	White Mountain Side Notched
Cottonwood Leaf	Desert-General	Mescal Knife	
Cottonwood Triangle	Desert-Redding	San Bruno	

HISTORIC (400 B.P - Present)

Glass	Trade

DESERT SOUTHWEST
THUMBNAIL GUIDE SECTION

The following references are provided to aid the collector in easier and quicker identification of point types. All photos are exactly 30% of actual size and are proportional to each other. Each point pictured in this section represents a classic form for the type. When a match is found, go to the alphabetical location of that type for more examples in true actual size.

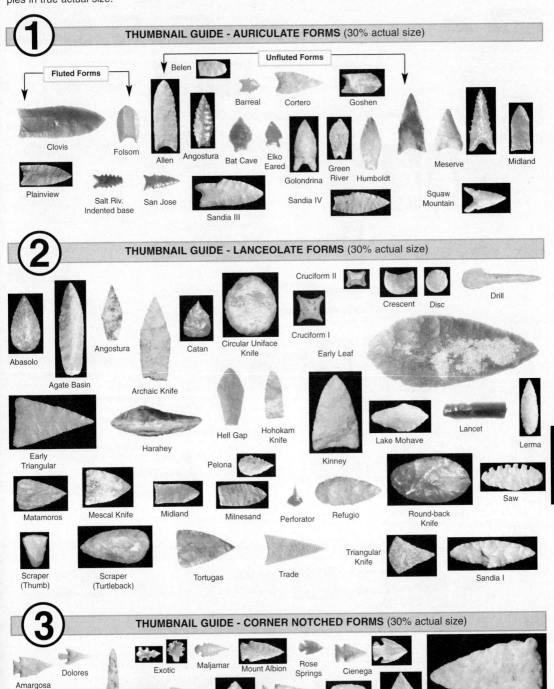

① THUMBNAIL GUIDE - AURICULATE FORMS (30% actual size)

Fluted Forms

Belen

Unfluted Forms

Clovis

Folsom

Allen

Angostura

Bat Cave

Elko Eared

Barreal

Cortero

Goshen

Golondrina

Green River

Humboldt

Meserve

Midland

Plainview

Salt Riv. Indented base

San Jose

Sandia III

Sandia IV

Squaw Mountain

② THUMBNAIL GUIDE - LANCEOLATE FORMS (30% actual size)

Abasolo

Agate Basin

Angostura

Archaic Knife

Catan

Circular Uniface Knife

Cruciform II

Crescent

Disc

Drill

Cruciform I

Early Leaf

Early Triangular

Harahey

Hell Gap

Hohokam Knife

Kinney

Lake Mohave

Lancet

Lerma

Matamoros

Mescal Knife

Midland

Pelona

Milnesand

Perforator

Refugio

Round-back Knife

Saw

Scraper (Thumb)

Scraper (Turtleback)

Tortugas

Trade

Triangular Knife

Sandia I

③ THUMBNAIL GUIDE - CORNER NOTCHED FORMS (30% actual size)

Amargosa

Dolores

Exotic

Maljamar

Mount Albion

Rose Springs

Cienega

Corner Tang

Elko Corner Notched

Drill

Frio

Marshall

Moyote

San Pedro

Scraper (Blunt)

Texcoco

807

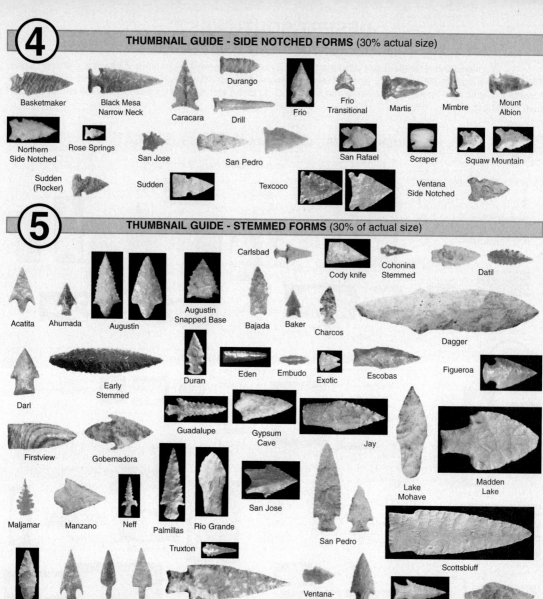

④ THUMBNAIL GUIDE - SIDE NOTCHED FORMS (30% actual size)

Basketmaker

Black Mesa Narrow Neck

Caracara

Durango

Drill

Frio

Frio Transitional

Martis

Mimbre

Mount Albion

Northern Side Notched

Rose Springs

San Jose

San Pedro

San Rafael

Scraper

Squaw Mountain

Sudden (Rocker)

Sudden

Texcoco

Ventana Side Notched

⑤ THUMBNAIL GUIDE - STEMMED FORMS (30% of actual size)

Acatita

Ahumada

Augustin

Augustin Snapped Base

Carlsbad

Cody knife

Cohonina Stemmed

Datil

Bajada

Baker

Charcos

Dagger

Darl

Early Stemmed

Duran

Eden

Embudo

Exotic

Escobas

Figueroa

Firstview

Gobernadora

Guadalupe

Gypsum Cave

Jay

Lake Mohave

Madden Lake

Maljamar

Manzano

Neff

Palmillas

Rio Grande

San Jose

San Pedro

Scottsbluff

Truxton

Ventana-Amargosa

Silver Lake

Socorro

Trade

Trade

Uvalde

Yavapai

Zephyr

Zorra

⑥ THUMBNAIL GUIDE - STEMMED-BIFURCATED FORMS (30% of actual size)

Barreal

Chiricauha

Conejo

Duncan

Eastgate Split Stem

Hanna

San Jose

⑦ THUMBNAIL GUIDE - BASAL NOTCHED FORMS (30% of actual size)

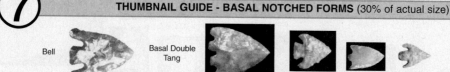

Bell

Basal Double Tang

Moyote

Parowan

Shumla

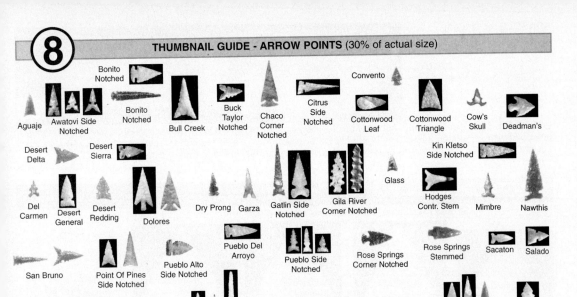

Aguaje | Awatovi Side Notched | Bonito Notched | Bonito Notched | Bull Creek | Buck Taylor Notched | Chaco Corner Notched | Citrus Side Notched | Convento | Cottonwood Leaf | Cottonwood Triangle | Cow's Skull | Deadman's

Desert Delta | Desert Sierra | Del Carmen | Desert General | Desert Redding | Dolores | Dry Prong | Garza | Gatlin Side Notched | Gila River Corner Notched | Glass | Kin Kletso Side Notched | Hodges Contr. Stem | Mimbre | Nawthis

San Bruno | Point Of Pines Side Notched | Pueblo Alto Side Notched | Pueblo Del Arroyo | Pueblo Side Notched | Rose Springs Corner Notched | Rose Springs Stemmed | Sacaton | Salado

Santa Cruz | Snaketown | Snaketown Side Notched | Snaketown Triangular | Sobaipuri | Soto | Temporal | Toyah | Walnut Canyon Side Notched | White Mountain Side Notched

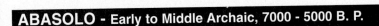

ABASOLO - Early to Middle Archaic, 7000 - 5000 B. P.

(Also see Catan, Matamoros and Refugio)

G2, $5-$10
Otero Co., NM, restored

G9, $20-$35
NW Chih. Mex.

G7, $15-$25
Luna Co., NM

G7, $15-$25
Otero Co., NM

G10, $30-$50
Otero Co. NM

Brown jasper

Red jasper

Gray chert

Red jasper

Restored

Red jasper

SW

Beveled on left side of each face

Chocolate jasper

G9, $40-$70
NW Chih. Mex.

G5, $12-$20
S.W. CO

ABASOLO (continued)

G10, $125-$200
Eddy Co., NM, thin

Tan
jasper

LOCATION: Southern Texas into Mexico and New Mexico. **DESCRIPTION:** A medium to large size, broad, lanceolate point with a rounded base. The blade can be beveled on one side of each face and the base can be thinned. **I.D. KEY:** Early form of flaking on blade with good secondary edgework and rounded base.

ACATITA - Late Archaic, 3000 - 2600 B.P.

(Also see Augustine, Gobernadora, Gypsum Cave, Manzano, Socorro and Shumla)

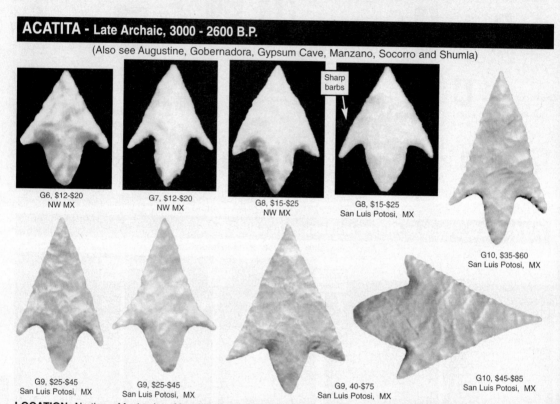

G6, $12-$20
NW MX

G7, $12-$20
NW MX

G8, $15-$25
NW MX

Sharp
barbs

G8, $15-$25
San Luis Potosi, MX

G10, $35-$60
San Luis Potosi, MX

G9, $25-$45
San Luis Potosi, MX

G9, $25-$45
San Luis Potosi, MX

G9, 40-$75
San Luis Potosi, MX

G10, $45-$85
San Luis Potosi, MX

LOCATION: Northern Mexico into New Mexico. **DESCRIPTION:** A small to medium sized, thin dart/knife point with drooping barbs and a pointed to rounded contracting stem. A cross between the *Shumla* and the *Perdiz* point. Formerly known as *Cedral*; given the name *Acatita* by Perino in his Vol. 3. **I.D. KEY:** Barbs and base form.

AGATE BASIN - Early Archaic, 10,200 - 8,500 B.P.

(Also see Allen, Angostura, Archaic Knife, Lerma and Sandia)

G7, $125-$225
NM

G8, $175-$325
Chaves Co., NM

LOCATION: New Mexico eastward to Pennsylvania. **DESCRIPTION:** A medium to large size lanceolate blade of high quality. Bases are either convex, concave or straight and are usually ground. Some examples are median ridged. **I.D. KEY:** Basal form and flaking style.

810

AGATE BASIN (continued)

G9, $200-$375
AZ

AGUAJE - Classic Phase, 600 - 550 B.P.

(Also see Bull Creek, Cottonwood and Sobaipuri)

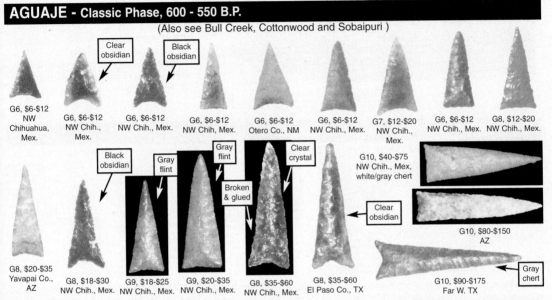

G6, $6-$12
NW
Chihuahua,
Mex.

Clear obsidian

G6, $6-$12
NW Chih.,
Mex.

Black obsidian

G6, $6-$12
NW Chih., Mex.

G6, $6-$12
NW Chih, Mex.

G6, $6-$12
Otero Co., NM

G6, $6-$12
NW Chih., Mex.

G7, $12-$20
NW Chih.,
Mex.

G6, $6-$12
NW Chih., Mex.

G8, $12-$20
NW Chih., Mex.

Black obsidian

Gray flint

Gray flint

Broken & glued

Clear crystal

G10, $40-$75
NW Chih., Mex,
white/gray chert

Clear obsidian

G8, $20-$35
Yavapai Co.,
AZ

G8, $18-$30
NW Chih., Mex.

G9, $18-$25
NW Chih., Mex.

G9, $20-$35
NW Chih., Mex.

G8, $35-$60
NW Chih., Mex.

G8, $35-$60
El Paso Co., TX

G10, $80-$150
AZ

Gray chert

G10, $90-$175
Far W. TX

LOCATION: Northwest Chihuahua, MX. into Sou. New Mexico and far West Texas. **DESCRIPTION:** A small, thin triangular arrow point with a straight to concave base. This type has needle tips and sharp basal corners. Some examples have basal ears. **I.D. KEY:** Small, narrow triangle.

AHUMADA - Mid-Late Archaic, 4000 - 2500 B.P.

(Also see Carlsbad, Cienega, Dolores, Guadalupe, Maljamar, Neff and Truxton)

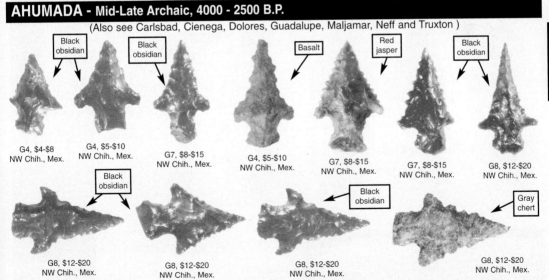

Black obsidian

Black obsidian

Basalt

Red jasper

Black obsidian

G4, $4-$8
NW Chih., Mex.

G4, $5-$10
NW Chih., Mex.

G7, $8-$15
NW Chih., Mex.

G4, $5-$10
NW Chih., Mex.

G7, $8-$15
NW Chih., Mex.

G7, $8-$15
NW Chih., Mex.

G8, $12-$20
NW Chih., Mex.

Black obsidian

Black obsidian

Gray chert

G8, $12-$20
NW Chih., Mex.

G8, $12-$20
NW Chih., Mex.

G8, $12-$20
NW Chih., Mex.

G8, $12-$20
NW Chih., Mex.

LOCATION: Arizona, New Mexico and N.W. Chihuahua, MX. **DESCRIPTION:** A corner notched dart point with a triangular blade; almost always serrated and with an expanding stem. Named "Pindejo" by McNish who reported that most examples are from Villa Ahumada in N.W. Chihuahua, MX. **I.D. KEY:** Fan shaped stem and serrations.

SW

ALLEN - Early Archaic, 8,500 - 7500 B.P.

(Also see Angostura, Clovis, Cortero, Goshen, Humboldt, Meserve, Plainview)

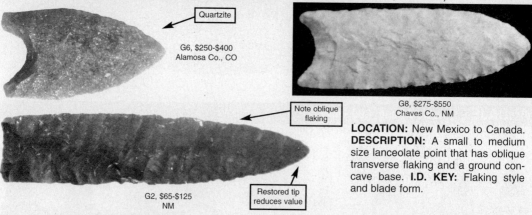

Quartzite

G6, $250-$400
Alamosa Co., CO

Note oblique flaking

G2, $65-$125
NM

Restored tip reduces value

G8, $275-$550
Chaves Co., NM

LOCATION: New Mexico to Canada. **DESCRIPTION:** A small to medium size lanceolate point that has oblique transverse flaking and a ground concave base. **I.D. KEY:** Flaking style and blade form.

AMARGOSA - Middle Archaic, 3000 - 2000 B.P.

(Also see Basketmaker, Cienega, Elko Corner Notched, Figueroa, Mt. Albion, San Pedro)

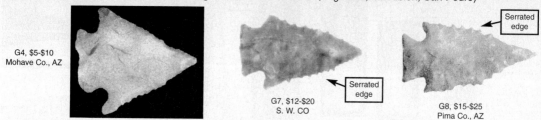

G4, $5-$10
Mohave Co., AZ

Serrated edge

G7, $12-$20
S. W. CO

Serrated edge

G8, $15-$25
Pima Co., AZ

LOCATION: Southeastern California into W. Arizona and W. Nevada. **DESCRIPTION:** A small size, corner notched dart/knife point with a needle tip and sharp tangs. Some examples are serrated. Bases are straight to slightly convex or concave. **I.D. KEY:** Sharp tangs and corners, needle tip.

ANGOSTURA - Early Archaic, 8,800 - 7500 B.P.

(Also see Agate Basin, Allen, Archaic Knife, Clovis and Humboldt)

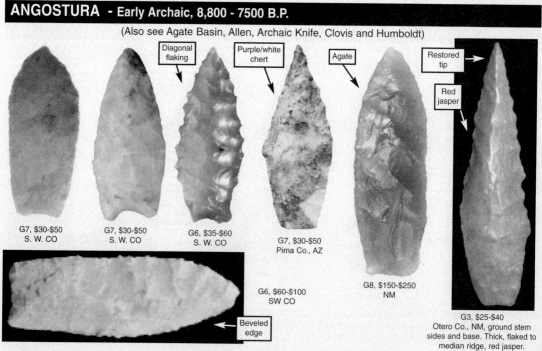

Diagonal flaking

Purple/white chert

Agate

Restored tip

Red jasper

G7, $30-$50
S. W. CO

G7, $30-$50
S. W. CO

G6, $35-$60
S. W. CO

G7, $30-$50
Pima Co., AZ

G8, $150-$250
NM

Beveled edge

G6, $60-$100
SW CO

G3, $25-$40
Otero Co., NM, ground stem sides and base. Thick, flaked to median ridge, red jasper.

ANGOSTURA (continued)

LOCATION: Southwestern states. **DESCRIPTION:** A medium to large size lanceolate blade of unusually high quality. Bases are either convex, concave or straight and are usually ground. Most examples have oblique transverse flaking. **I.D. KEY:** Basal form and flaking style.

G9, $250-$450
W. TX

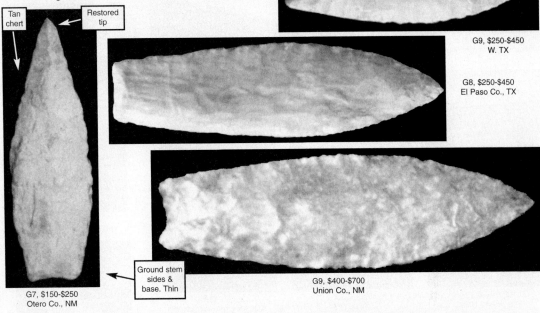

Tan chert

Restored tip

G8, $250-$450
El Paso Co., TX

Ground stem sides & base. Thin

G9, $400-$700
Union Co., NM

G7, $150-$250
Otero Co., NM

ARCHAIC KNIFE - Early to Mid Archaic, 6000 - 4000 B.P.

(Also see Angostura and Early Triangular)

G2, $15-$30
Pima Co., AZ

Broken & glued

Base nick

LOCATION: Arizona into Plains states. **DESCRIPTION:** A medium to large size triangular blade with a concave to straight base. **I.D. KEY:** Large triangle with early flaking.

ARMIJO - Early to Mid Archaic, 3800 - 2800 B.P.

(Also see Meserve, San Jose)

Ground stem & base

G3, $5-$10
NM

LOCATION: Arizona, New Mexico. **DESCRIPTION:** A small size auriculate, serrated point with a ground stem and base that is concave. Related to the earlier *San Jose* type. **I.D. KEY:** Eared base.

AUGUSTIN - Early to Middle Archaic, 7000- 5000 B.P.

(Also see Acatita, Gypsum Cave, Manzano and Santa Cruz)

Basalt

G4, $8-$15
Yavapai Co., AZ

G8, $25-$40
S. W. CO

G8, $25-$40
S. W. CO

AUGUSTIN (continued)

White chert, serrated

G6, $30-$50
SW CO

Red jasper, serrated

G8, $40-$75
NW Chih, Mex., thin, not ground.

Gray chert

G8, $60-$110
Otero Co., NM, ground stem.

Red jasper, serrated

G9, $60-$110
Luna Co., NM

G5, $30-$50
Luna Co., NM

G9, $95-$185
NW Chih, Mex, ground stem, thin.

Pink jasper, serrated.

G10, $250-$425
NW Chih, Mex., thin.

G9, $95-$185
SW CO

LOCATION: The southern portion of the southwestern states and northern Mexico. **DESCRIPTION:** A small to medium sized dart/knife point with a broad triangular blade and a contracting, rounded to pointed stem and obtuse shoulders. The *Gypsum Cave* point may be a westerly and northerly extension of this point. **I.D. KEY:** Contracting base.

AUGUSTIN-SNAPPED BASE - Early to Mid-Archaic, 7000 - 5000 B.P.

(Also see Gypsum Cave)

G6, $12-$20
Otero Co., NM

G6, $12-$20
El Paso Co., TX, snapped base.

LOCATION: E. Arizona to S.W. TX. **DESCRIPTION:** A medium size, serrated, barbed point with a snapped-off base to facilitate hafting. Similar in form to Kirk Snapped Base points found in the southeastern U.S. **I.D. KEY:** Base snapped off.

AUGUSTIN SNAPPED BASE (continued)

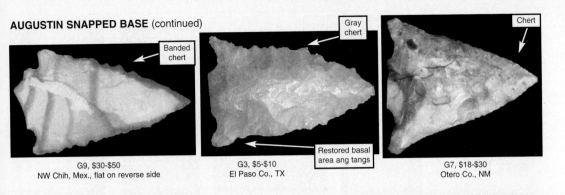

G9, $30-$50
NW Chih., Mex., flat on reverse side

G3, $5-$10
El Paso Co., TX

G7, $18-$30
Otero Co., NM

AWATOVI SIDE NOTCHED - Develop. to Classic Phase, 750 - 600 B.P.

(Also see Buck Taylor Notched, Dell Carmen, Desert Sierra, Pueblo Side, White Mountain)

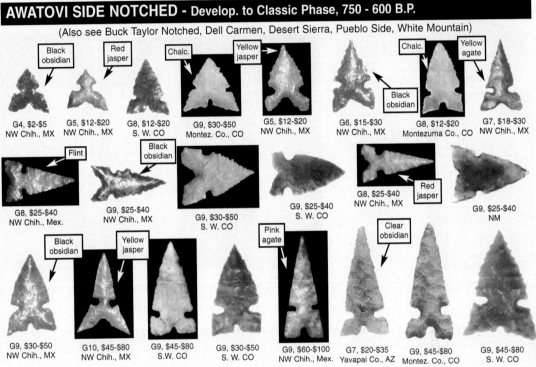

G4, $2-$5
NW Chih., MX

G5, $12-$20
NW Chih., MX

G8, $12-$20
S. W. CO

G9, $30-$50
Montez. Co., CO

G5, $12-$20
NW Chih., MX

G6, $15-$30
NW Chih., MX

G8, $12-$20
Montezuma Co., CO

G7, $18-$30
NW Chih., MX

G8, $25-$40
NW Chih., Mex.

G9, $25-$40
NW Chih., MX

G9, $30-$50
S. W. CO

G9, $25-$40
S. W. CO

G8, $25-$40
NW Chih., MX

G9, $25-$40
NM

G9, $30-$50
NW Chih., MX

G10, $45-$80
NW Chih., MX

G9, $45-$80
S.W. CO

G9, $30-$50
S. W. CO

G9, $60-$100
NW Chih., Mex.

G7, $20-$35
Yavapai Co., AZ

G9, $45-$80
Montez. Co., CO

G9, $45-$80
S. W. CO

LOCATION: Arizona, New Mexico, northern Mexico, southern Utah and S.W. Colorado. **DESCRIPTION:** A small size, narrow, triple-notched, triangular arrow point. Side notches can occur high up from the base. Part of the *Pueblo Side Notched* cluster and similar to the *Harrell* point of the southern Plains. **I.D. KEY:** Tri-notches.

BAJADA - Late Archaic to Developmental Phase, 6000 - 5000 B.P.

(Also see Conejo, Duncan, Escobas, Hanna, Jay and Rio Grande)

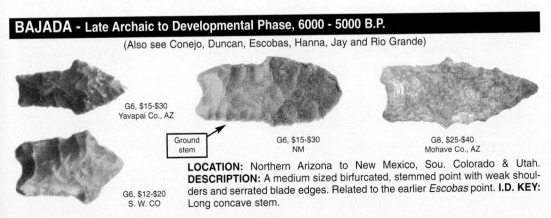

G6, $15-$30
Yavapai Co., AZ

G6, $15-$30
NM

G8, $25-$40
Mohave Co., AZ

G6, $12-$20
S. W. CO

LOCATION: Northern Arizona to New Mexico, Sou. Colorado & Utah. **DESCRIPTION:** A medium sized birfurcated, stemmed point with weak shoulders and serrated blade edges. Related to the earlier *Escobas* point. **I.D. KEY:** Long concave stem.

SW

BAJADA (continued)

G8, $30-$50
S. W. CO

Restored tip

Ground stem

G3, $12-$20
Otero Co., NM

G6, $20-$40
S. W. CO

G6, $30-$55
Montezuma Co., CO

G6, $20-$40
S. W. CO

G6, $15-$30
S. W. CO

G8, $40-$70
S. W. CO

G8, $45-$85
S. W. CO

G10, $80-$150
Montezuma Co., CO

G9, $40-$75
Montezuma Co., CO

G6, $65-$115
Yuma Co., AZ

BAKER - Early Archaic, 7500 - 6000 B. P.

(Also see Bajada, Darl, Datil, San Jose, Uvalde and Zephyr)

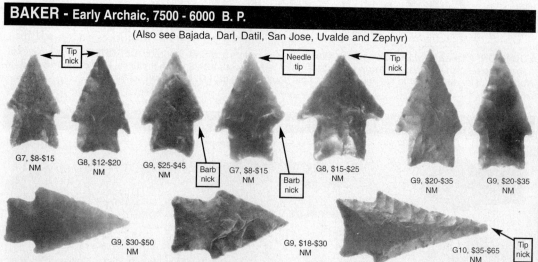

Tip nick

Needle tip

Tip nick

G7, $8-$15
NM

G8, $12-$20
NM

G9, $25-$45
NM

Barb nick

G7, $8-$15
NM

Barb nick

G8, $15-$25
NM

G9, $20-$35
NM

G9, $20-$35
NM

G9, $30-$50
NM

G9, $18-$30
NM

G10, $35-$65
NM

Tip nick

LOCATION: Western Texas into New Mexico. **DESCRIPTION:** A small to medium size, thin, point with a sharp tip and a bifurcated to concave base. Barbs are sharp and the stem expands. The stem length varies from short to long. Similar to the *Bandy* point found in southern Texas. **I.D. KEY:** Base extended and bifurcated.

BAKER (continued)

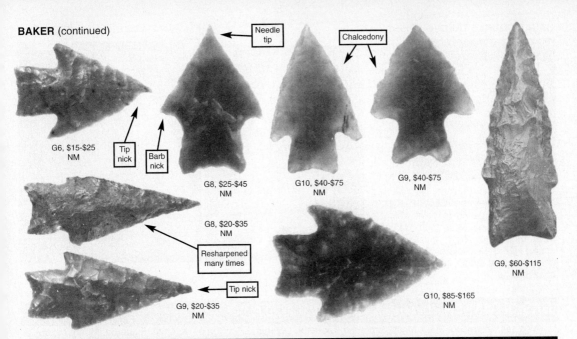

Needle tip

Chalcedony

G6, $15-$25
NM

Tip nick

Barb nick

G8, $25-$45
NM

G10, $40-$75
NM

G9, $40-$75
NM

G8, $20-$35
NM

Resharpened
many times

G9, $60-$115
NM

Tip nick

G9, $20-$35
NM

G10, $85-$165
NM

BARREAL - Early Archaic, 9000 - 7200 B.P.

(Also see Duncan, Hanna, San Jose, Squaw Mountain)

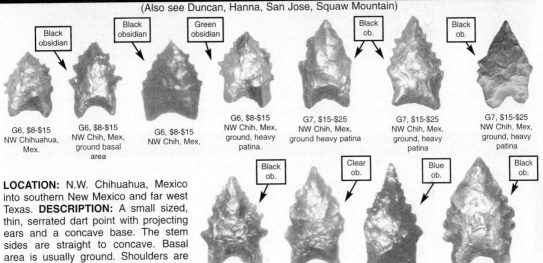

Black obsidian

Black obsidian

Green obsidian

Black ob.

Black ob.

G6, $8-$15
NW Chihuahua,
Mex.

G6, $8-$15
NW Chih, Mex,
ground basal
area

G6, $8-$15
NW Chih, Mex,

G6, $8-$15
NW Chih, Mex,
ground, heavy
patina.

G7, $15-$25
NW Chih, Mex,
ground heavy patina

G7, $15-$25
NW Chih, Mex,
ground, heavy
patina

G7, $15-$25
NW Chih, Mex,
ground, heavy
patina

Black ob.

Clear ob.

Blue ob.

Black ob.

LOCATION: N.W. Chihuahua, Mexico into southern New Mexico and far west Texas. **DESCRIPTION:** A small sized, thin, serrated dart point with projecting ears and a concave base. The stem sides are straight to concave. Basal area is usually ground. Shoulders are weak to non-existent. **I.D. KEY:** Basal form and serrations.

G8, $25-$40
NW Chih, Mex,
ground, heavy patina

G9, $30-$50
NW Chih, Mex,
ground basal area

G7, $15-$25
NW Chih, Mex,
ground basal area

G9, $30-$50
NW Chih, Mex,
ground basal area,
heavy patina

BASAL DOUBLE TANG - Late Archaic, 3500 - 2300 B.P.

(Also see Bell and Parowan)

G5, $10-$20
San Luis Potosi, MX

G4, $10-$20
San Luis Potosi, MX

G3, $4-$8
San Luis Potosi, MX

SW

BASAL DOUBLE TANG (continued)

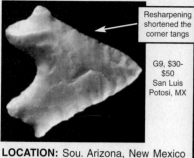

Resharpening shortened the corner tangs

G9, $30-$50
San Luis Potosi, MX

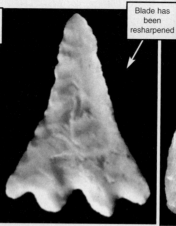

Blade has been resharpened

G8, $40-$75
San Luis Potosi, MX

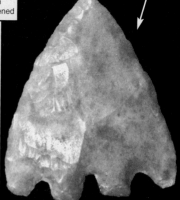

Pristine example

G10, $80-$150
Pinal Co., AZ

LOCATION: Sou. Arizona, New Mexico and northern Mexico. **DESCRIPTION:** A medium sized dart/knife point which is baseally notched, and then with the stem bifurcated. Worn out examples appear as a lanceolate blade with a notched basal edge. **I.D. KEY:** Triple basal notches.

BASKETMAKER - Developmental, 1500 - 1300 B.P.

(Also see Amargosa, Black Mesa, Carlsbad, Cienega, Dolores, Elko Corner Notched, Figueroa, Mount Albion)

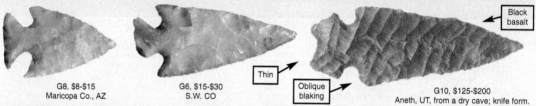

G8, $8-$15
Maricopa Co., AZ

G6, $15-$30
S.W. CO

Thin

Oblique blaking

Black basalt

G10, $125-$200
Aneth, UT, from a dry cave; knife form.

LOCATION: Southern Utah into northern Arizona & N.W. New Mexico. **DESCRIPTION:** A small to medium size, thin, dart/knife point that is side to corner notched. **I.D. KEY:** Corner notching.

BAT CAVE - Early Archaic, 9000 - 8000 B.P.

(Also see Humboldt)

G6, $25-$45
Cochise Co., AZ

G4, $10-$20
Yavapai Co., AZ

G6, $35-$60
Yavapai Co., AZ

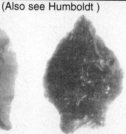

G5, $15-$30
Yavapai Co., AZ

G5, $15-$30
Yavapai Co., AZ

G5, $15-$30
CO

G8, $125-$225
CO

G3, $5-$10
Yavapai Co., AZ

G7, $50-$95
NM

LOCATION: The southwestern states and northern Mexico. **DESCRIPTION:** A small, lanceolate dart/knife with convex blade edges, constricting toward the base to form small, flaring ears. The basal edge is slightly concave and is well thinned. **I.D. KEY:** Waisted appearance and small, flaring ears.

BELEN - Paleo, 10,500 - 8000 B.P.

(Also see Midland, Milnesand)

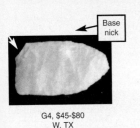

Base nick

G4, $45-$80
W. TX

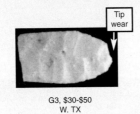

Tip wear

G3, $30-$50
W. TX

LOCATION: E. New Mexico into W. Texas.
DESCRIPTION: A small, thin lanceloate point with ground stem sides and a straight to concave base. Similar to *Midland* points but differ in that *Belen* points have one basal ear that is more prominent.
I.D. KEY: Thinness, prominent single basal ear.

BELL - Middle Archaic, 7000 - 5000 B.P.

(Also see Basal Double Tang, Moyote and Parowan)

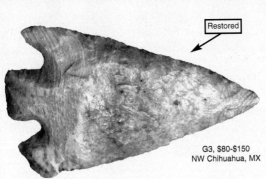

Restored

G3, $80-$150
NW Chihuahua, MX

G6, $250-$400
NW Chihuahua, MX

LOCATION: Cent. Texas into N. Mexico. **DESCRIPTION:** A small to medium size point with medium-deep parallel basal notches, but not as deep as in Andice. Larger examples usually would fall under Andice. Found primarily in Texas. Barbs turn inward at the base. **I.D. KEY:** Shorter barbs and notching.

BLACK MESA NARROW NECK - Trans.-Developmental Phase, 2000 - 1200 B.P.

(Also see Amargosa, Basketmaker, Figueroa and San Pedro)

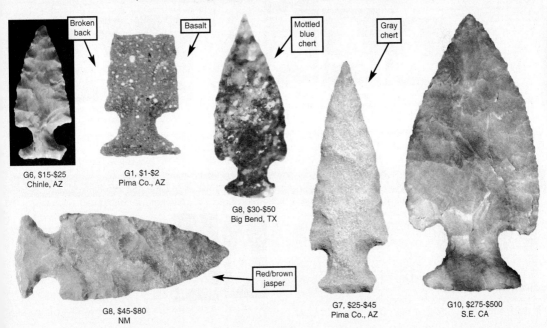

Broken back

Basalt

Mottled blue chert

Gray chert

G6, $15-$25
Chinle, AZ

G1, $1-$2
Pima Co., AZ

G8, $30-$50
Big Bend, TX

Red/brown jasper

G8, $45-$80
NM

G7, $25-$45
Pima Co., AZ

G10, $275-$500
S.E. CA

SW

819

BLACK MESA NARROW NECK (continued)

LOCATION: Sou. California into Arizona and New Mexico. **DESCRIPTION:** A medium to large deeply corner notched dart point with a narrow neck and an expanding stem. Bases are straight to convex. **I.D. KEY:** Very narrow neck.

G10+, $250-$450
Pima Co., AZ

Gray basalt

BONITO NOTCHED - Developmental, 1050 - 850 B.P.

(Also see Chaco Corner Notched, Convento, Desert, Dry Prong, Rose Springs & Temporal)

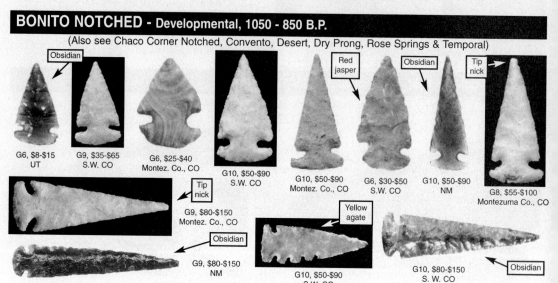

Obsidian

G6, $8-$15
UT

G9, $35-$65
S.W. CO

G6, $25-$40
Montez. Co., CO

G10, $50-$90
S.W. CO

Red jasper

G10, $50-$90
Montez. Co., CO

Obsidian

G6, $30-$50
S.W. CO

G10, $50-$90
NM

Tip nick

G8, $55-$100
Montezuma Co., CO

Tip nick

G9, $80-$150
Montez. Co., CO

Obsidian

G9, $80-$150
NM

Yellow agate

G10, $50-$90
S.W. CO

Obsidian

G10, $80-$150
S. W. CO

LOCATION: Arizona, New Mexico, S.W. Colorado, sou. Utah. **DESCRIPTION:** A small size, narrow, side notched arrow point with a convex base. Some examples are double or triple notched on one side. Part of the Chaco cluster. **I.D. KEY:** Convex base, long, narrow blade.

BUCK TAYLOR NOTCHED - Classic to Historic Phase, 600 - 200 B.P.

(Also see Awatovi Side Notched, Desert, Dell Carmen, Walnut Canyon, Sobaipuri, White Mtn.)

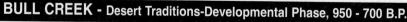

Clear obsidian

Black obsidian

G7, $20-$35
Pima Co., AZ.

G6, $8-$15
Maricopa Co., AZ

G5, $8-$15
Mohave Co., AZ

G4, $6-$12
Mohave Co., AZ

G6, $12-$20
Mohave Co., AZ

G6, $18-$30
NW Chihuahua, Mex.

Clear obsidian

G5, $8-$15
Yavapai Co., AZ

G6, $15-$30
Mohave Co., AZ

Obsidian

G7, $8-$15
Maricopa Co., AZ

LOCATION: Arizona. **DESCRIPTION:** A small, triangular, tri-notched arrow point including a deep basal notch. Part of the *Pueblo Side Notched* cluster. Formerly known as *Red Horn*. **I.D. KEY:** Very narrow neck.

BULL CREEK - Desert Traditions-Developmental Phase, 950 - 700 B.P.

(Also see Aguaje, Cottonwood, Desert, Pueblo Side Notched & Snaketown Triangular)

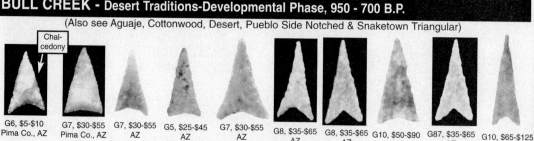

Chalcedony

G6, $5-$10
Pima Co., AZ

G7, $30-$55
Pima Co., AZ

G7, $30-$55
AZ

G5, $25-$45
AZ

G7, $30-$55
AZ

G8, $35-$65
AZ

G8, $35-$65
AZ

G10, $50-$90
AZ

G87, $35-$65
AZ

G10, $65-$125
AZ

BULL CREEK (continued)

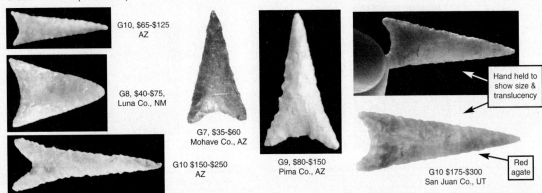

G10, $65-$125
AZ

G8, $40-$75,
Luna Co., NM

G10 $150-$250
AZ

G7, $35-$60
Mohave Co., AZ

G9, $80-$150
Pima Co., AZ

Hand held to show size & translucency

Red agate

G10 $175-$300
San Juan Co., UT

LOCATION: Northern Arizona, southern Utah and northeastern Nevada. **DESCRIPTION:** A long, thin triangular arrow point with a deeply concave basal edge. They are sometimes serrated. Some examples have been shortened by resharpening. **I.D. KEY:** Isosceles triangle shape and concave base.

CARACARA - Mississippian to Historic, 600 - 400 B.P.

(Also see Desert, Frio, Hohokam, Martis, Sacaton, Salado, Ventana Side Notched)

LOCATION: Texas into N.W. Chihuahua, MX. **DESCRIPTION:** A small size, thin, side notched arrow point with a straight, concave or convex base. Shoulders can be tapered to horizontal to barbed. Side notches are shallow to deep.

G10, $80-$150
NM

CARLSBAD - Late Archaic-Transitional, 3000 - 1700 B.P.

(Also see Amargosa, Basketmaker, Black Mesa, Cienega, Dolores and Guadalupe)

Red basalt

Broken tip

G1, $2-$5
Pima Co., AZ

Basalt

Basalt

G6 $20-$35
Alamosa, CO

Worn tip

G3, $15-$25
Pima Co., AZ

LOCATION: Sou. New Mexico into Mexico and Arizona. **DESCRIPTION:** Part of the *Cienega* cluster. A small size, deep basal to corner notched point and a convex base. Most examples have been resharpened to exhaustion reducing the shoulders significantly. Stem sides are concave and expanding.

SW

CATAN - Late Archaic to Mississippian, 4000 - 300 B. P.

(Also see Abasolo and Matamoros)

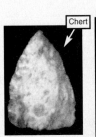
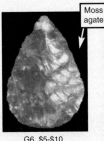

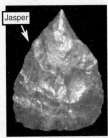

Chert

Moss agate

Jasper

Jasper

G7, $4-$8
El Paso Co., TX

G6, $5-$10
Luna Co., NM, very thin

G7, $6-$12
S. W. CO

G10, $8-$15
NW Chihuahua, Mex,
needle tip

G10, $8-$15
NW Chihuahua, Mex,
needle tip

CATAN (continued)

Red jasper

Jasper

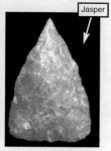

G9, $12-$20
Dona Ana Co., NM

Brown jasper

G10, $8-$15
S. W. CO

G10, $12-$20
NW Chihuahua, Mex,
very thin

G9, $8-$15
Dona Ana Co., NM,
needle tip

LOCATION: Southern Texas, New Mexico into Northern Mexico. **DESCRIPTION**: A small, thin, lanceolate point with a rounded base. Large examples would fall under the *Abasolo* type.

CEDRAL (see Acatita)

CHACO CORNER NOTCHED - Developmental, 1250 - 1050 B.P.

(Also see Bonito Notched, Convento and Rose Springs)

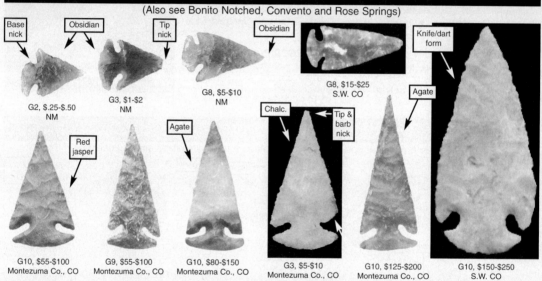

Base nick

Obsidian

Tip nick

Obsidian

Knife/dart form

G8, $15-$25
S.W. CO

Agate

G2, $.25-$.50
NM

G3, $1-$2
NM

G8, $5-$10
NM

Red jasper

Agate

Chalc.

Tip & barb nick

G10, $55-$100
Montezuma Co., CO

G9, $55-$100
Montezuma Co., CO

G10, $80-$150
Montezuma Co., CO

G3, $5-$10
Montezuma Co., CO

G10, $125-$200
Montezuma Co., CO

G10, $150-$250
S.W. CO

LOCATION: Arizona, New Mexico, S.W. Colorado, sou. Utah. **DESCRIPTION:** A small to medium size, thin, corner notched arrow point with a wide convex base. Notches turn upward toward the tip. **I.D. KEY:** Broad convex base, deep, upward sloping notches.

CHARCOS - Late Archaic-Trans., 3000 - 2000 B.P.

G6, $12-$20
Alamosa Co., CO

LOCATION: N. Mexico into New Mexico, Texas and Colorado. **DESCRIPTION:** A small size, thin, single barbed point with a notch near the opposite shoulder. Stem is rectangular or expanding. **I.D. KEY:** Asymmetrical form. Some are double notched.

CHIRICAHUA - Middle Archaic, 5000 - 4000 B.P.

(Also see Duncan, Frio-Transitional, Hanna, San Jose, Squaw Mountain and Ventana Side Notched)

CHIRICAHUA (continued)

Basalt

G3, $2-$4
Alamosa Co., CO

G3, $2-$4
Cochise Co., AZ

G6, $8-$15
Cochise Co., AZ

G5, $6-$12
Cochise Co., AZ

Basalt

G6, $10-$20
Cochise Co., AZ

Basalt

G5, $8-$16
S.W. CO

Double tip

G5, $25-$45
Cochise Co., AZ

G8, $40-$70
AZ

Dinged

G6, $8-$15
Mohave Co., AZ

G9, $40-$70
Cochise Co., AZ

LOCATION: New Mexico, Arizona, southern California and northern Mexico. **DESCRIPTION:** A small to medium sized dart/knife point with side notches and a concave base, producing an eared appearance. **I.D. KEY:** Generally ears are "rounded" in appearance.

CIENEGA - Late Archaic-Transitional, 2800 - 1800 B.P.

(Also see Amargosa, Basketmaker, Black Mesa, Carlsbad, Dolores, Guadalupe and San Pedro)

Agate

Gray basalt

Red basalt

Tip nick

Clear banded agate

G8, $12-$20
NM

G8, $15-$25
N. AZ

G6, $15-$25
Pima Co., AZ

G4, $5-$10
Pima Co., AZ

G7, $8-$15
Pima Co., AZ

G9, $25-$45
NM

G9, $15-$30
NM

Chalcedony

Petrified wood

G7, $15-$30
AZ

G7, $15-$30
S.W. CO

G8, $20-$35
Pima Co., AZ

G7, $25-$45
NM

G9, $70-$135
Bernalillo Co., NM

G9, $70-$135
NM

G9, $45-$80
Montezuma Co., CO

Chalcedony

G9, $45-$85
Playas, NM

Chert

G7, $30-$55
Pima Co., AZ

SW

CIENEGA (continued)

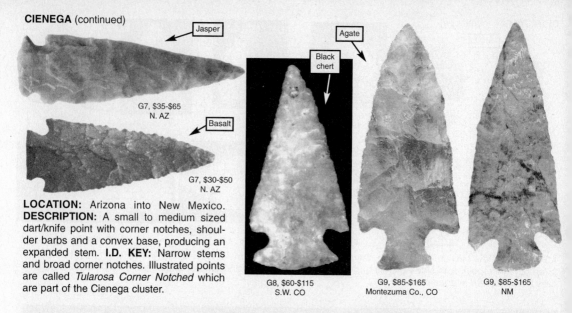

Jasper

G7, $35-$65
N. AZ

Basalt

G7, $30-$50
N. AZ

Black chert

Agate

LOCATION: Arizona into New Mexico.
DESCRIPTION: A small to medium sized
dart/knife point with corner notches, shoulder barbs and a convex base, producing an
expanded stem. **I.D. KEY:** Narrow stems
and broad corner notches. Illustrated points
are called *Tularosa Corner Notched* which
are part of the Cienega cluster.

G8, $60-$115
S.W. CO

G9, $85-$165
Montezuma Co., CO

G9, $85-$165
NM

CIRCULAR UNIFACE KNIFE - Archaic, 6000 - 4000 B.P.

(Also see Disc, Lancet, Scraper)

LOCATION: New Mexico. **DESCRIPTION:** A
medium sized circular knife that is uniface on
one side and steeply flaked on the other
side. **I.D. KEY:** Circular uniface.

G10, $12-$20
NM, knife.

CITRUS SIDE NOTCHED - Develop. to Classic Phase, 800 - 600 B.P.

(Also see Desert, Gatlin Side Notched, Salado)

G7, $30-$50
AZ

Tip nick

G7, $30-$50
AZ

LOCATION: Arizona **DESCRIPTION:** A small size, very thin, triangular, side notched *Hohokam* arrow point with a
straight to slightly convex base which is the widest part of the point. Blade edges are concave, tips are long and slender. **I.D. KEY:** Long, needle tips

CLOVIS - Early Paleo, 11,500 - 10,600 B.P.

(Also see Allen, Angostura, Folsom, Golondrina, Goshen, Madden Lake, Meserve and Sandia)

Brown/beige
banded chert

G8, $200-$350
Eddy Co., NM,
ground basal area.

Gray chert

G3, $125-$200
Hudspeth Co., TX,
ground basal.

CLOVIS (continued)

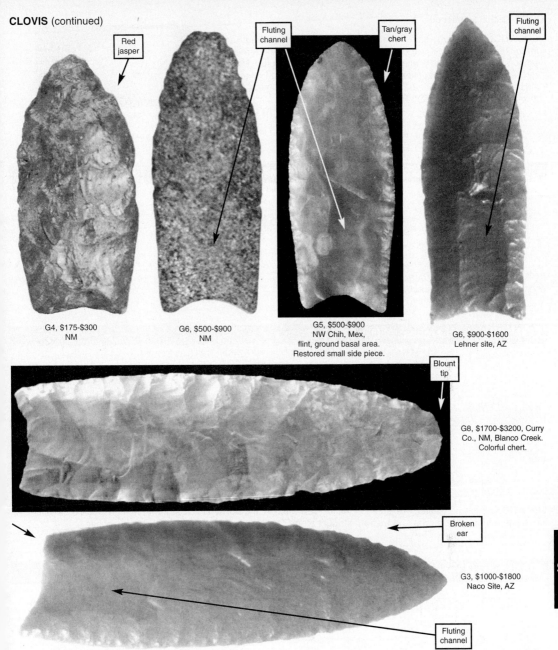

Red jasper

Fluting channel

Tan/gray chert

Fluting channel

G4, $175-$300
NM

G6, $500-$900
NM

G5, $500-$900
NW Chih, Mex,
flint, ground basal area.
Restored small side piece.

G6, $900-$1600
Lehner site, AZ

Blount tip

G8, $1700-$3200, Curry
Co., NM, Blanco Creek.
Colorful chert.

Broken ear

G3, $1000-$1800
Naco Site, AZ

Fluting channel

SW

LOCATION: All of North America. Named after Clovis, New Mexico near where these fluted projectile points were found. **DESCRIPTION:** A medium to large size, auriculate, fluted, lanceolate point with a concave base that is ground. Most examples are fluted on both sides about 1/3 the way up from the base. *Clovis* is the earliest known point type in the hemisphere. The first *Clovis* find associated with Mastodons was in 1979 at Mastodon State Park, Jefferson Co., MO. in the Kimmswick bone bed dated to 11,500 B.P. The origin of Clovis is a mystery as there is no pre-*Clovis* evidence here (crude forms that pre-date Clovis). **I.D. KEY:** Paleo flaking, basal ears, baton or billet fluting instead of indirect style.

CODY KNIFE - Early to Middle Archaic, 10,000 - 8000 B. P.

(Also see Base-Tang Knife, Corner Tang, Eden, Mid-Back Tang and Scottsbluff)

CODY KNIFE (continued)

LOCATION: Northern Plains states. **DESCRIPTION:** A medium to large size asymmetrical blade with one or two shoulders and a medium to short stem. Stem edges are ground on early examples. Made by the Cody complex people who made *Scottsbluff* points. Flaking is similar to the *Scottsbluff* type and some examples were made from *Scottsbluff* points. **I.D. KEY:** Paleo flaking, asymmetrical form.

G5, $350-$600
Luna Co., NM, snapped base,
not ground

COHONINA STEMMED - Developmental Phase, 1300 - 900 B.P.

(Also see Rose Springs)

G4, $2-$4
Coconino Co., AZ

G5, $4-$8
Coconino Co., AZ

G6, $8-$15
Coconino Co., AZ

G7, $8-$15
Coconino Co., AZ

LOCATION: Northern Arizona. **DESCRIPTION:** A small size, narrow, stemmed to corner notched point with tapered shoulders and an expanding stem.

CONEJO - Late Archaic, 3500 - 2300 B.P.

(Also see Bell, Duncan)

Shoulder nick

G6, $8-$15
S. W. CO

G3, $4-$8
Luna Co., NM

G7, $35-$60
Luna Co., NM

LOCATION: Extreme western Texas and most of New Mexico. **DESCRIPTION:** A corner notched dart/knife with convex blade edges, short barbs and a short, straight stem. The basal edge may be straight or concave.

CONVENTO - Developmental Phase, 950 - 850 B. P.

(Also see Chaco Corner Notched, Rose Springs)

Banded obsidian

Black obsidian

Clear obsidian

Black obsidian

G7, $12-$20

G7, $5-$15

G4, $4-$8   G5, $8-$15   G5, $5-$10   G5, $5-$10   G6, $8-$15   G5, $5-$10   G7, $8-$15

All from N.W. Chihuahua, Mexico

Black obsidian

Clear obsidian

Black obsidian

Clear obsidian

Black obsidian

Black obsidian

G7, $8-$15   G7, $5-$15   G8, $12-$20   G8, $12-$20   G8, $12-$20   G7, $5-$20   G7, $12-$20   G8, $15-$25   G8, $15-$25   G9, $20-$35

LOCATION: N.W. Chihuahua, MX into southern New Mexico and far west Texas. **DESCRIPTION:** A small, thin, barbed, corner notched arrow point with an expanding stem and a convex base. **I.D. KEY:** Barbs and base form.

LOCATION: Texas, Oklahoma, New Mexico. **DESCRIPTION:** This knife is notched producing a tang at a corner for hafting to a handle. Tang knives are very rare and have been reproduced in recent years. **I.D. KEY:** Angle of hafting.

G6, $300-$500
San Juan Co., NM

(Also see Clovis, Cottonwood, Golondrina, Goshen, Plainview)

Basalt

Red basalt

G7, $15-$25
Pima Co., AZ

G5, $8-$15
Pima Co., AZ

G6, $15-$25
Pima Co., AZ

G5, $8-$15
Pima Co., AZ

G7, $20-$35
Pima Co., AZ

G8, $20-$35
Pima Co., AZ

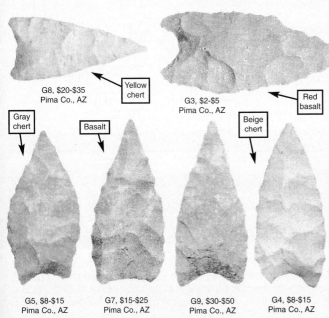

G8, $20-$35
Pima Co., AZ

Yellow chert

G3, $2-$5
Pima Co., AZ

Red basalt

Gray chert

Basalt

Beige chert

G5, $8-$15
Pima Co., AZ

G7, $15-$25
Pima Co., AZ

G9, $30-$50
Pima Co., AZ

G4, $8-$15
Pima Co., AZ

LOCATION: Southern Arizona and S.W. New Mexico. **DESCRIPTION:** A small, fairly thick, triangular point with a concave base. Cross-section is diamond shaped. Bases are not ground. Some examples show pressure flaking along the edges. **I.D. KEY:** Blade form and thickness.

SW

G9, $40-$75
Pima Co., AZ

Basalt

G10, $175-$325
Pima Co., AZ

COTTONWOOD LEAF - Desert Traditions-Classic/Historic Phases, 700 - 200 B.P.

(Also see Catan, Datil and Pelona)

G7, $25-$50
Apache Co., AZ

G2, $.50-$1
Mohave Co., AZ

G8, $30-$50
Pima Co., AZ

G3, $2-$4
Pima Co., AZ

G6, $5-$10
Pima Co., AZ

G7, $20-$40
Yavapai Co., AZ

LOCATION: Arizona and westward into California and Nevada. **DESCRIPTION:** A small, thin, leaf shaped arrow point that resembles a long tear-drop. The base is rounded. **I.D. KEY:** Size and blade form.

COTTONWOOD TRIANGLE - Desert Traditions-Classic and Historic Phases, 700 - 200 B.P.

(Also see Aguaje, Bull Creek, Cottonwood Leaf, Desert, Pueblo Side Notched, Sobaipuri)

G6, $8-$15
Cochise Co., AZ

G4, $3-$5
Cochise Co., AZ

G2, $1-$2
Cochise Co., AZ

G6, $5-$10
Yavapai Co., AZ

G6, $10-$20
Cochise Co., AZ

G4, $3-$5
Pima Co., AZ

G2, $1-$2
Pima Co., AZ

G6, $15-$30
Cochise Co., AZ

G5, $8-$15
Pima Co., AZ

G6, $15-$30
Cochise Co., AZ

LOCATION: Arizona and westward into California and Nevada. **DESCRIPTION:** A small, thin triangular arrow point with a straight to slightly convex basal edge. **I.D. KEY:** Size and blade form.

COW'S SKULL- Classic Phase, 600 - 550 B. P.

(Also see Del Carmen, Desert, Toyah)

LOCATION: Northwest Chihuahua, Mex. **DESCRIPTION:** A small, thin triangular arrow point with a concave base and exaggerated basal ears that are long and swing upwards towards the tip. Shoulders are tapered and the blade is serrated. A very rare form. This may possibly be a Hohokam variant. **I.D. KEY:** Base form.

Black obsidian

G6, $15-$30
Yavapai Co., AZ

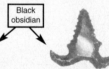

G10, $65-$120
NW Chih, Mex

CRESCENT - Mid-Archaic, 5000 - 4500 B. P.

(Also see Cruciform, Disc, Drill and Lancet)

Chalc.

G8, $18-$30
San Luis Potosi, MX

G7, $18-$30
San Luis Potosi, MX

G8, $25-$40
San Luis Potosi, MX

G8, $25-$40
San Luis Potosi, MX

G8, $25-$40
San Luis Potosi, MX

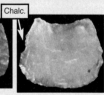

G7, $18-$30
San Luis Potosi, MX

LOCATION: Central Mexico. **DESCRIPTION:** A thin, uniface tool, convex on one side and concave on the opposite side with sharp corners. Long strikes were taken off with delicate pressure flaking. Chalcedony, agates, jaspers, cherts and flints were used. Different than the Crescents from the Northwest which are not uniface. **I.D. KEY:** Crescent form.

CRESCENT (continued)

G7, $25-$40
San Luis Potosi, MX

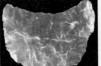

G7, $25-$40
San Luis Potosi, MX

G7, $25-$40
San Luis Potosi, MX

G8, $25-$40
San Luis Potosi, MX

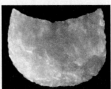

G9, $35-$50
San Luis Potosi, MX

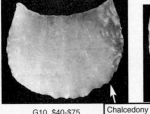

G10, $40-$75
Chihuahua, MX

Chalcedony

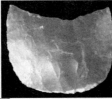

G10, $35-$65
Chihuahua, MX

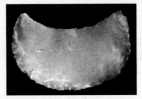

G10, $30-$50
San Luis Potosi, MX.

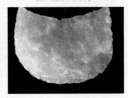

G8, $25-$40
N. Chihuahua, MX.,

CRUCIFORM I- Early to Mid-Archaic, 6000 - 4500 B. P.

(Also see Disc, Drill, Exotic and Lancet)

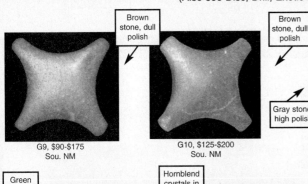

Brown stone, dull polish

Brown stone, dull polish

Gray stone, high polish

Black obsidian, heavy patina

G9, $90-$175
Sou. NM

G10, $125-$200
Sou. NM

G9, $125-$200
Sou. NM

G8, $80-$150
Sou. NM

Green stone, polished

Hornblend crystals in gray stone

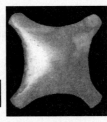

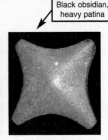

G10, $125-$200
Sou. NM, flattened pyramid form on each face

G9, $90-$175
Sou. NM, polished

LOCATION: W. Texas, Sou. New Mexico, and Sou. Arizona. **DESCRIPTION:** Occurs in two forms. Type one is a medium sized, four pronged object in a pyramidal form on opposing faces. It is hand tooled from hardstone or flaked from obsidian and then ground on both faces and around the edges. Careful attention was given to the quality of the finished form. A pair of these objects were found on both sides of the skull in an excavated grave in Arizona. It is believed that these were used as ear ornaments. These objects were named due to their resemblance to cruciforms. **I.D. KEY:** Form.

SW

CRUCIFORM II- Late to Transitional, 3000 - 2000 B. P.

(Also see Disc, Drill, Exotic and Lancet)

G3, $40-$75
Lordsberg, NM

G6, $40-$75
Sou. NM,
clear obsidian,
ground, heavy patina

G6, $50-$90
Sou. NM,
clear obsidian,
ground, heavy patina

G6, $50-$90
Sou. NM,
black obsidian,
ground, heavy patina

G8, $55-$100
Sou. NM,
clear obsidian,
ground, heavy patina

G9, $55-$100
Sou. NM,
black obsidian, flaked
and not yet ground.

CRUCIFORM II (continued)

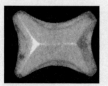

G9 $55-$100
Sou. NM,
black obsidian, ground,
heavy patina

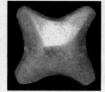

G10, $55-$100
Sou. NM,
clear obsidian, ground,
heavy patina

G10, $55-$100
Sonora, MX, basalt,
ground.

LOCATION: W. Texas, Sou. New Mexico, and Sou. Arizona. **DESCRIPTION:** Occurs in two forms. Type two is a small sized, four pronged object in a slanted roof form on opposing faces. It is flaked from hard stone or black or clear obsidian and then ground on both faces and around the edges. Careful attention was given to the quality of the finished form. These objects' actual use is unknown and were named due to their resemblance to cruciforms. **I.D. KEY:** Form.

DAGGER- Mid-Archaic, 4000 - 2500 B. P.

(Also see Disc, Drill, Early Stemmed and Lancet)

LOCATION: Mexico. **DESCRIPTION:** A large size lanceolate knife with a recurved blade, expanding, tapered tangs and a long contracting stem. Probably hafted to a handle in use. **I.D. KEY:** Size and form.

G9, $300-$575
MX

← Shown half size

DARL STEMMED - Early Archaic, 8000 - 5000 B. P.

(Also see Ahumada, Datil, San Pedro and Ventana Amargosa)

Pink quartz

G6, $3-$6
N.W. MX

G6, $5-$10
Otero Co., NM

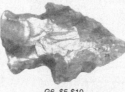

G6, $5-$10
Otero Co., NM

G7, $12-$20
Otero Co., NM

LOCATION: Central Texas into New Mexico and Northern Mexico. **DESCRIPTION:** A medium to large size point with horizontally barbed shoulders and an expanding to square stem. The blades can be steeply beveled on one side of each face. Flaking is early parallel and is of much higher quality than *Darl*. **I.D. KEY:** Early flaking, straight base.

DATIL - Early Archaic, 7000 - 6000 B. P.

(Also see Cottonwood Leaf, Darl, Embudo, Lerma, Pelona, San Pedro and Truxton)

G4, $2-$5
Cochise Co., AZ

G6, $12-$20
Yavapai Co., AZ

G5, $12-$20
Cochise Co., AZ

G6, $15-$25
S. W. CO

G9, $80-$150
San Juan Co., NM

G5, $15-$25
S. W. CO

DATIL (continued)

G5, $12-$20
S. W. CO

Basalt

G5, $5-$10
Yavapai Co., AZ

G7, $25-$40
Yavapai Co., AZ

G4, $5-$10
Yavapai Co., AZ

basalt

G6, $15-$25
Pima Co., AZ

G5, $8-$15
Pima Co., AZ

Banded
purple
chert

G7, $80-$150
Pima Co., AZ

Orange
chert

G5, $8-$15
Pima Co., AZ
trans. point.

G7, $25-$40
Yavapai Co., AZ

Basalt

G10, $120-$200
Yavapai Co., AZ

Serrated
edge

LOCATION: The southern portion of the southwestern states. **DESCRIPTION:** A small dart/knife with long, narrow, heavily serrated blade edges. The stem is short and rectangular to rounded. Shoulders are straight to obtuse and are very small to non-existent in relation to the overall size of the point.

DEADMAN'S - Desert Traditions-Developmental Phase, 1600 - 1300 B. P.

(Also see Hodges Contracting Stem, Gila Butte, Perdiz and Rose Springs)

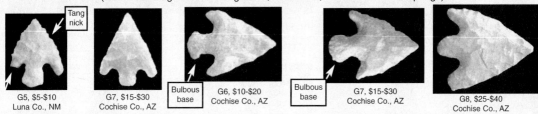

Tang
nick

G5, $5-$10
Luna Co., NM

G7, $15-$30
Cochise Co., AZ

Bulbous
base

G6, $10-$20
Cochise Co., AZ

Bulbous
base

G7, $15-$30
Cochise Co., AZ

G8, $25-$40
Cochise Co., AZ

SW

LOCATION: Southeastern Arizona, southern New Mexico and western Texas. **DESCRIPTION:** A small arrow point with very deep basal notches creating a long, straight to slightly bulbous stem with a rounded basal edge. The blade is triangular. **I.D. KEY:** Bulbous stem and barbs.

DEL CARMEN - Classic Phase, 550 B. P.

(Also see Awatovi Side Notched, Buck Taylor Notched, Desert, Pueblo Side, Soto, Toyah)

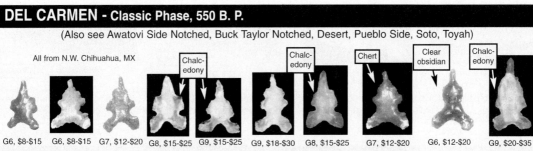

All from N.W. Chihuahua, MX

Chalc-
edony

Chalc-
edony

Chert

Clear
obsidian

Chalc-
edony

G6, $8-$15   G6, $8-$15   G7, $12-$20   G8, $15-$25   G9, $15-$25   G9, $18-$30   G8, $15-$25   G7, $12-$20   G6, $12-$20   G9, $20-$35

LOCATION: N.W. Chihuahua, MX. into sou. New Mexico. **DESCRIPTION:** A small, thin, arrow point with an elongated tip, side notches, expanding ears and a concave base. Some examples are double notched. **I.D. KEY:** Barbs always flare out beyond the base.

DESERT DELTA - Desert Traditions-Classic to Historic, 700 - 200 B. P.

(Also see Pueblo Side Notched, Sacaton, Salado, Temporal, Walnut Canyon)

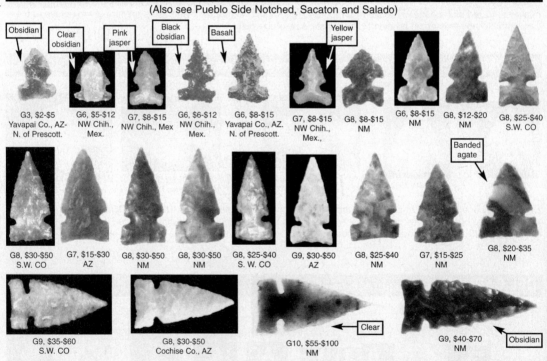

G3, $2-$5
S.W. CO

G3, $2-$5
S.W. CO

G3, $2-$5
S.W. CO

G5, $5-$10
NM

G6, $8-$15
S.W. CO

G6, $8-$15
S.W. CO

G6, $8-$15
S.W. CO

Clear obsidian

G7, $25-$40
AZ

Chalc-edony

Tip nick

Chert

G10, $55-$100
N. AZ

G6, $8-$15
S.W. CO

G8, $30-$50
Yuma Co., AZ

G7, $20-$35
Cochise Co., AZ

G5. $5-$10
N. AZ

G7, $15-$30
AZ

G7, $15-$25
Pima Co., AZ

G9, $20-$35
NM

LOCATION: Most of Arizona and contiguous states to the west. **DESCRIPTION:** A small arrow point with straight blade edges, side notches and a concave, expanding basal edge. **I.D. KEY:** Expanding basal edge..

DESERT GENERAL-Desert Traditions-Classic to Historic,700-200 B. P.

(Also see Pueblo Side Notched, Sacaton and Salado)

Obsidian

Clear obsidian

Pink jasper

Black obsidian

Basalt

Yellow jasper

G3, $2-$5
Yavapai Co., AZ-
N. of Prescott.

G6, $5-$12
NW Chih.,
Mex.

G7, $8-$15
NW Chih., Mex

G6, $6-$12
NW Chih.,
Mex.

G6, $8-$15
Yavapai Co., AZ.
N. of Prescott.

G7, $8-$15
NW Chih.,
Mex.,

G8, $8-$15
NM

G6, $8-$15
NM

G8, $12-$20
NM

G8, $25-$40
S.W. CO

Banded agate

G8, $30-$50
S.W. CO

G7, $15-$30
AZ

G8, $30-$50
NM

G8, $30-$50
NM

G8, $25-$40
S. W. CO

G9, $30-$50
AZ

G8, $25-$40
NM

G7, $15-$25
NM

G8, $20-$35
NM

G9, $35-$60
S.W. CO

G8, $30-$50
Cochise Co., AZ

Clear

G10, $55-$100
NM

G9, $40-$70
NM

Obsidian

LOCATION: Most of Arizona and contiguous states to the west. **DESCRIPTION:** A small arrow point with convex blade edges, side notches and a straight to slightly concave basal edge. **I.D. KEY:** Straight to concave base.

DESERT REDDING-Desert Traditions-Classic to Historic, 700-200 B. P.

(Also see Mimbre, Pueblo Side Notched, Sacaton, Salado and Temporal)

DESERT REDDING (continued)

G4, $5-$10
NM

G6, $8-$15
NM

G5, $6-$10
Pima Co., AZ

G7, $12-$25
Pima Co., AZ

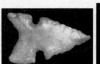
G8, $18-$30
NW Chih., Mex., chalc.

G8, $25-$45
S.W. CO

LOCATION: Most of Arizona and contiguous states to the west. **DESCRIPTION:** A small arrow point with convex sides, diagonal side notches and a concave basal edge which is narrower than the shoulders. **I.D. KEY:** Narrow basal edge.

DESERT SIERRA - Desert Traditions-Classic to Historic, 700-200 B. P.

(Also see Awatovi, Buck Taylor, Notched, Del Carmen, Sacaton, White Mountain)

G4, $2-$5
S.W. CO

G6, $8-$15
S.W. CO

G6, $8-$15
S.W. CO

G6, $8-$15
AZ

G4, $6-$10
Pima Co., AZ

G5, $6-$10
AZ

G6 12-$20
AZ

G6 12-$20
AZ

G6, $12-$20
AZ

G6, $8-$15
AZ

G6, $12-$20
S. W. CO

G6, $12-$20
AZ

G6, $12-$20
AZ

G5, $6-$12
Cochise Co., AZ

G7, $15-$30
S. W. CO

G9, $35-$65
Montez. Co., CO

G7, $25-$40
CO

LOCATION: Most of Arizona and contiguous states to the west. **DESCRIPTION:** A small arrow point with straight sides, a straight basal edge and a basal notch. **I.D. KEY:** Triangular tri-notched point.

DISC - Mid-Archaic, 5000 - 4500 B.P.

(Also see Crescent, Cruciform and Exotic)

All from San Luis Potosi, MX

G7, $8-$15

G8, $12-$20

G9, $12-$20

G9, $12-$20

G9, $12-$25

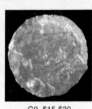
G9, $15-$30

LOCATION: Central Mexico. **DESCRIPTION:** A small circular object pressure flaked to an edge on each face. The purpose of these objects is unknown. These were in use about the same time as the *Crescents*. Examples show good patination. **I.D. KEY:** Circular form.

DOLORES - Developmental Phase, 1400 - 1100 B.P.

(Also see Amargosa, Basketmaker, Carlsbad, Cienega, Guadalupe)

G5, $5-$10
Montezuma Co., CO

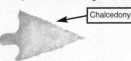
Chalcedony
G8, $12-$20
Yavapai Co., AZ

LOCATION: Northern Arizona & New Mexico into southern Utah and S.W. Colorado. Type area is in S.W. Colorado. **DESCRIPTION:** A small, barbed arrow point with a medium to long, narrow expanding to parallel to slightly contracting stem. Blade edges are concave to recurved and can be serrated. **I.D. KEY:** Barbs and narrow stem.

SW

DOLORES (continued)

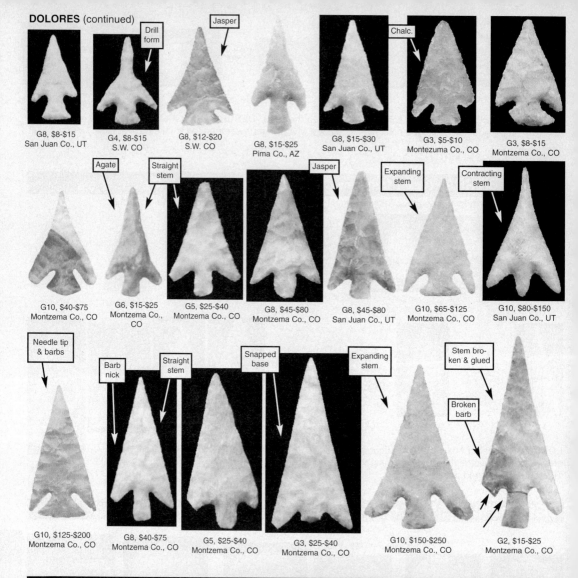

G8, $8-$15
San Juan Co., UT

G4, $8-$15
S.W. CO

Drill form

Jasper

G8, $12-$20
S.W. CO

G8, $15-$25
Pima Co., AZ

G8, $15-$30
San Juan Co., UT

Chalc.

G3, $5-$10
Montezuma Co., CO

G3, $8-$15
Montzema Co., CO

Agate

Straight stem

G10, $40-$75
Montzema Co., CO

G6, $15-$25
Montzema Co., CO

G5, $25-$40
Montzema Co., CO

Jasper

G8, $45-$80
Montzema Co., CO

G8, $45-$80
San Juan Co., UT

Expanding stem

G10, $65-$125
Montzema Co., CO

Contracting stem

G10, $80-$150
San Juan Co., UT

Needle tip & barbs

G10, $125-$200
Montzema Co., CO

Barb nick

Straight stem

G8, $40-$75
Montzema Co., CO

Snapped base

G5, $25-$40
Montzema Co., CO

G3, $25-$40
Montzema Co., CO

Expanding stem

G10, $150-$250
Montzema Co., CO

Stem broken & glued

Broken barb

G2, $15-$25
Montzema Co., CO

DRILL - Paleo to Historic, 11,500 - 850 B.P.

(Also see Circular Uniface Knife, Lancet and Scraper)

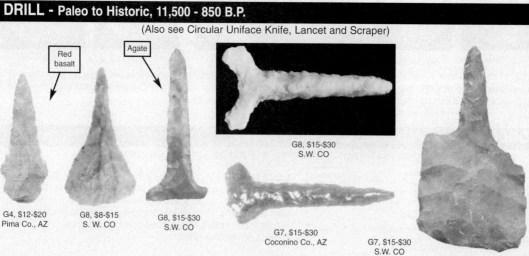

Red basalt

Agate

G4, $12-$20
Pima Co., AZ

G8, $8-$15
S. W. CO

G8, $15-$30
S.W. CO

G8, $15-$30
S.W. CO

G7, $15-$30
Coconino Co., AZ

G7, $15-$30
S.W. CO

DRILL (continued)

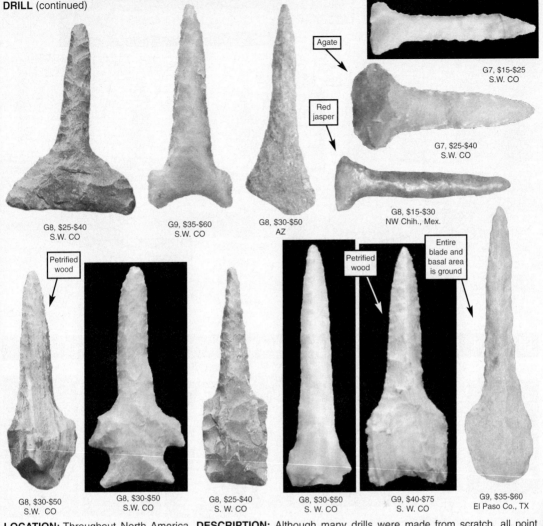

Agate

Red jasper

G7, $15-$25
S.W. CO

G7, $25-$40
S.W. CO

G8, $15-$30
NW Chih., Mex.

G8, $25-$40
S.W. CO

G9, $35-$60
S.W. CO

G8, $30-$50
AZ

Petrified wood

Petrified wood

Entire blade and basal area is ground

G8, $30-$50
S.W. CO

G8, $30-$50
S.W. CO

G8, $25-$40
S. W. CO

G8, $30-$50
S. W. CO

G9, $40-$75
S. W. CO

G9, $35-$60
El Paso Co., TX

LOCATION: Throughout North America. **DESCRIPTION:** Although many drills were made from scratch, all point types were made into the drill form. Usually, heavily resharpened and broken points were salvaged and rechipped into drills. **I.D. KEY:** Narrow blade form.

DRY PRONG - Desert Traditions, 1000 - 850 B.P.

(Also see Desert, Mimbre, Pueblo Side Notched, Sacaton and Temporal)

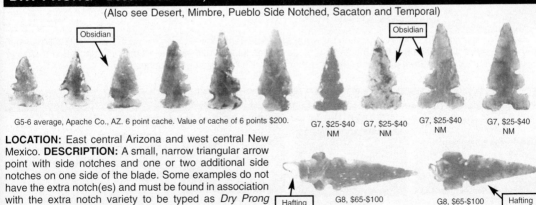

Obsidian

Obsidian

G5-6 average, Apache Co., AZ. 6 point cache. Value of cache of 6 points $200.

G7, $25-$40
NM

G7, $25-$40
NM

G7, $25-$40
NM

G7, $25-$40
NM

LOCATION: East central Arizona and west central New Mexico. **DESCRIPTION:** A small, narrow triangular arrow point with side notches and one or two additional side notches on one side of the blade. Some examples do not have the extra notch(es) and must be found in association with the extra notch variety to be typed as *Dry Prong* points. **I.D. KEY:** The extra side notch(es).

Hafting attached

G8, $65-$100
NM

G8, $65-$100
NM

Hafting attached

835

DRY PRONG (continued)

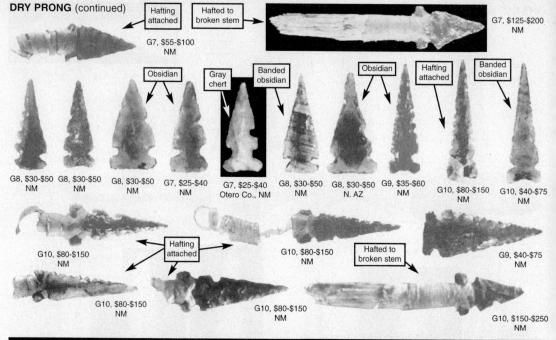

Hafting attached — G7, $55-$100 NM

Hafted to broken stem — G7, $125-$200 NM

Obsidian

Gray chert

Banded obsidian

Obsidian

Hafting attached

Banded obsidian

G8, $30-$50 NM | G8, $30-$50 NM | G8, $30-$50 NM | G7, $25-$40 NM | G7, $25-$40 Otero Co., NM | G8, $30-$50 NM | G8, $30-$50 N. AZ | G9, $35-$60 NM | G10, $80-$150 NM | G10, $40-$75 NM

G10, $80-$150 NM

Hafting attached

G10, $80-$150 NM

Hafted to broken stem

G9, $40-$75 NM

G10, $80-$150 NM

G10, $80-$150 NM

G10, $150-$250 NM

DUNCAN - Middle to Late Archaic, 4500 - 2850 B. P.

(Also see Bajada, Barreal, Chiricahua, Escobas, Hanna and San Jose)

Chalcedony

Tip wear

G7, $15-$30 Apache Co., AZ

G7, $10-$20 Yavapai Co., AZ

G8, $25-$40 Pinal Co., AZ

G6, $10-$20 Cochise Co., AZ

G5, $6-$12 Apache Co., AZ

G6, $6-$12 Santa Fe Co., NM

G8, $25-$40 Yavapai Co., AZ

Tip wear

G5, $15-$30 S. W. CO

G6, $30-$50 S. W. CO

Serrated edge

LOCATION: Northern Arizona to Canada on the north and to eastern Oklahoma on the east. **DESCRIPTION:** A small to medium sized dart/knife point with a triangular blade and angular shoulders. The stem is straight with a V-shaped notch in the basal edge. Stem edges are usually ground. **I.D. KEY:** Straight stem edges.

DURAN - Late Archaic to Transitional Phase, 3000 - 2000 B. P.

(Also see Guadalupe, Maljamar, Neff and Truxton)

G7, $25-$40 Apache Co., AZ

G6, $20-$35 Apache Co., AZ

G6, $20-$35 S.W. CO

LOCATION: Texas into Mexico. **DESCRIPTION:** A small size, narrow, stemmed point with double to multiple notches on each side. Base can be parallel sided to tapered with rounded basal corners. **I.D. KEY:** Double notches, round base.

DURAN (continued)

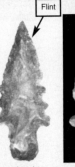

Flint

G2, $10-$20
San Luis Potosi,
Mex.

G2, $10-$20
San Luis Potosi, Mex.

G7, $20-$35
S.W. CO

G7, $20-$35
Dona Ana Co., NM

G7, $20-$35
NW Chih., Mex.

G8, $25-$45
NW Chih., Mex.

G6, $25-$40
San Luis Potosi, MX

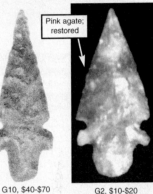

Basalt

Barb nick

Pink agate; restored

G8, $35-$60
Montezuma Co., CO

G9, $65-$125
NM

G9, $35-$60
NW Chihuahua, Mex.

G9, $55-$100
Chaves Co., NM

G10, $40-$70
W. TX

G2, $10-$20
NW Chih., Mex.

DURANGO - Mid to LateArchaic, 4500 - 2500 B. P.

(Also see Basketmaker and San Pedro)

Washington Pass red agate

G9, $25-$40
S.W. CO

LOCATION: Type site in Durango, Colorado.
DESCRIPTION: A small size, narrow point with shallow side notches near the base. Most examples are serrated and the base is either convex or straight. **I.D. KEY:** Weak notches near the base.

EARLY LEAF - Early to Middle Archaic, 8000 - 5000 B. P.

(Also see Early Stemmed, Refugio, Round-back Knife)

SW

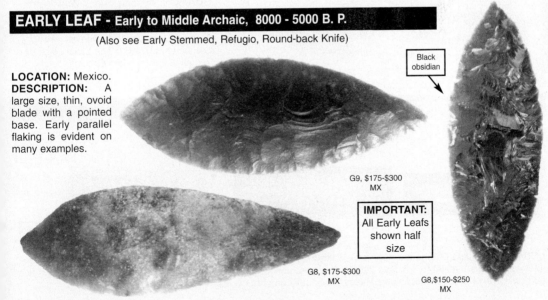

LOCATION: Mexico.
DESCRIPTION: A large size, thin, ovoid blade with a pointed base. Early parallel flaking is evident on many examples.

Black obsidian

G9, $175-$300
MX

IMPORTANT:
All Early Leafs shown half size

G8, $175-$300
MX

G8,$150-$250
MX

837

EARLY STEMMED - Late Archaic to Woodland, 3500 - 2300 B. P.

(Also see Augustin, Early Leaf, Escobas)

G4, $30-$50
Albequerque, NM

Diagonal flaking

Obsidian

Obsidian

G9, $80-$150
MX

LOCATION: Mexico. **DESCRIPTION:** A medium size point with sloping shoulders. Stems are straight to contracting to a straight to convex base. Shoulders are weak and sloping. Stem sides are sometimes ground. Flaking is oblique transverse and the cross section is elliptical. **I.D. KEY:** Base form and size.

EARLY TRIANGULAR - Early Archaic, 9000 - 7000 B. P.

(Also see Angostura, Clovis, Kinney, Mescal Knife, Tortugas & Triangular Knife)

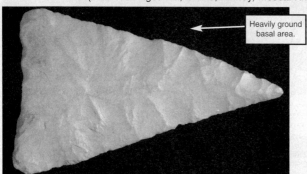

Heavily ground basal area.

G10, $125-$225
Otero Co., NM
Thin.

LOCATION: New Mexico into Texas. **DESCRIPTION:** A medium to large size, broad, thin, trianglular blade that can be serrated. The base is either fluted or has long thinning strikes. Quality is excellent with early oblique transverse and possible right hand beveling when resharpened. Basal areas are ground. **I.D. KEY:** Basal thinning and edgework.

EASTGATE SPLIT-STEM - Desert Traditions-Developmental Phase, 1400 - 1000 B. P.

(Also see Conejo, Duncan, Elko and Hanna)

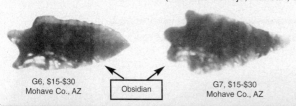

G6, $15-$30
Mohave Co., AZ

Obsidian

G7, $15-$30
Mohave Co., AZ

LOCATION: Arizona to Washington. **DESCRIPTION:** A corner to base notched arrow point with a triangular blade and a straight to slightly expanding stem with a basal notch. **I.D. KEY:** The basal notch differentiates it from other *Eastgate* points.

EDEN - Early Archaic, 9500 - 7500 B. P.

(Also see Firstview and Scottsbluff)

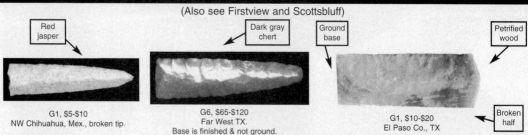

Red jasper

Dark gray chert

Ground base

Petrified wood

G1, $5-$10
NW Chihuahua, Mex., broken tip.

G6, $65-$120
Far West TX.
Base is finished & not ground.

G1, $10-$20
El Paso Co., TX

Broken half

LOCATION: Southwest to northern and midwestern states. **DESCRIPTION:** A medium to large size, narrow, lanceolate blade with a straight to concave base and almost unnoticable shoulders. Many examples have a median ridge and collateral oblique parallel flaking. Bases are usually ground. **I.D. KEY:** Narrowness, weak shoulders.

ELKO CORNER NOTCHED - Mid-Archaic to Developmental Phase, 3500 - 1200 B.P.

(Also see Amargosa, Cienega, Eastgate, Mount Albion, San Pedro)

Yellow agate

Gray chert

Chalc.

G6, $5-$10
Yavapai Co., AZ

G8, $15-$25
S.W. CO

G3, $2-$5
AZ

G8, $30-$50
Otero Co., NM

G7, $12-$20
Montezuma Co., CO

Serrated edge

G10, $25-$40
S.W. CO

Serrated edge

G6, $15-$25
S.W. CO

LOCATION: Great Basin into Arizona. **DESCRIPTION:** A small to large size, thin, corner notched dart point with shoulder barbs and a convex, concave or auriculate base. Shoulders and tips are sharp. Some examples exhibit excellent parallel flaking on blade edges which can be serrated. **I.D. KEY:** Corner notches, sharp tangs.

ELKO EARED - Mid-Archaic to Developmental Phase, 3500 - 1200 B.P.

(Also see Eastgate, Hanna and San Jose)

Tang damage

G5, $5-$10
Mohave Co., AZ

G2, $5-$10
S.W. CO

Barb nick

LOCATION: Great Basin into Arizona. **DESCRIPTION:** A small to large size, thin, corner notched dart point with shoulder tangs and an eared base. Basal ears are usually exaggerated and corners and tips are sharp. Some examples exhibit excellent parallel flaking on blade edges. **I.D. KEY:** Expanding to drooping ears.

EMBUDO - Early Archaic, 7000 - 6000 B. P.

(Also see Cohonina Stemmed, Datil and Pelona)

Obsidian

Black basalt

Obsidian

Obsidian

Black obsidian

G6, $8-$15

G5, $5-$10   G6, $8-$15   G6, $8-$15   G6, $8-$15   G6, $8-$15   G8, $12-$20   G6, $8-$15

G7, $18-$30

Dark gray chert

White chert

G6, $18-$20   G9, $25-$40   All from NW Chihuahua, Mexico   G10, $30-$50

839

EMBUDO (continued)

LOCATION: N.W. Chihuahua, Mex. **DESCRIPTION:** A small to medium sized, narrow, spike dart point with weak, sloping shoulders and a contracting, straight to bulbous stem. Blade edges can have fine serrations. Stem sides are usually ground. Bases are usually convex but can be incurvate to straight. **I.D. KEY:** Spike-like form.

ESCOBAS - Mid-Archaic, 6500 - 5000 B. P.

(Also see Bajada, Duncan, Hanna, Jay, Rio Grande and San Jose)

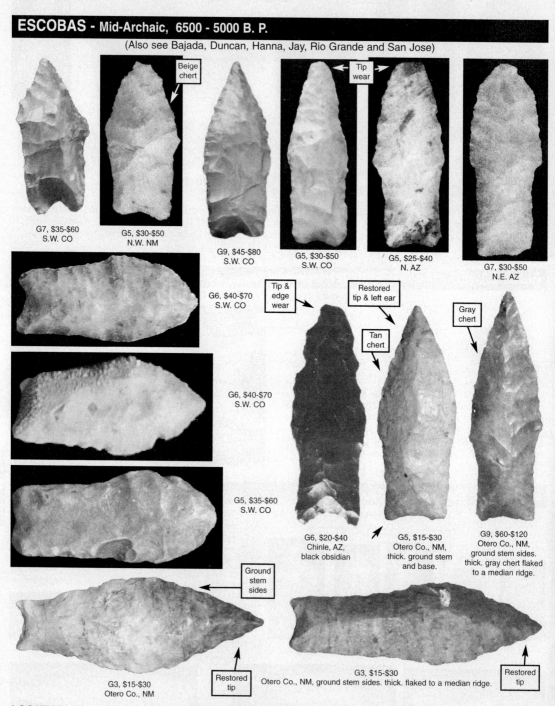

G7, $35-$60
S.W. CO

Beige chert

G5, $30-$50
N.W. NM

G9, $45-$80
S.W. CO

Tip wear

G5, $30-$50
S.W. CO

G5, $25-$40
N. AZ

G7, $30-$50
N.E. AZ

G6, $40-$70
S.W. CO

G6, $40-$70
S.W. CO

G5, $35-$60
S.W. CO

Tip & edge wear

Restored tip & left ear

Tan chert

Gray chert

G6, $20-$40
Chinle, AZ,
black obsidian

G5, $15-$30
Otero Co., NM,
thick. ground stem
and base.

G9, $60-$120
Otero Co., NM,
ground stem sides.
thick. gray chert flaked
to a median ridge.

Ground stem sides

G3, $15-$30
Otero Co., NM

Restored tip

G3, $15-$30
Otero Co., NM, ground stem sides. thick. flaked to a median ridge.

Restored tip

LOCATION: Arizona into New Mexico. **DESCRIPTION:** A medium size, thick, long stemmed point with weak shoulders and a concave base. Basal areas are ground. Flaking is to a median ridge. Develops into the *Bajada* point. Related to the earlier *Rio Grande* type. **I.D. KEY:** Long straight stem; concave base.

840

EXOTIC - Late Archaic to Developmental Phase, 3000 - 1000 B. P.

(Also see Crescent, Cruciform and Disc)

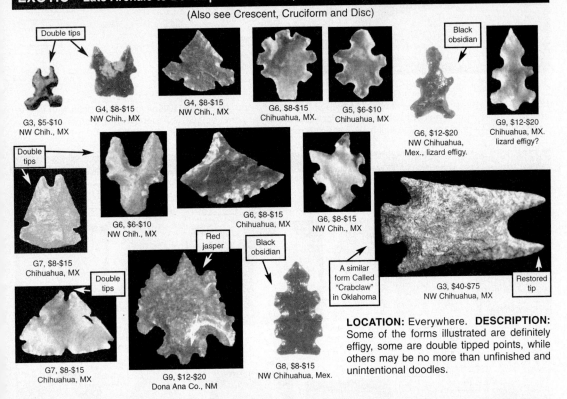

Double tips

G3, $5-$10
NW Chih., MX

G4, $8-$15
NW Chih., MX

G4, $8-$15
NW Chih., MX

G6, $8-$15
Chihuahua, MX.

G5, $6-$10
Chihuahua, MX

Black obsidian

G6, $12-$20
NW Chihuahua,
Mex., lizard effigy.

G9, $12-$20
Chihuahua, MX.
lizard effigy?

Double tips

G6, $6-$10
NW Chih., MX

G6, $8-$15
Chihuahua, MX

G6, $8-$15
NW Chih., MX

G7, $8-$15
Chihuahua, MX

Red jasper

Black obsidian

A similar form Called "Crabclaw" in Oklahoma

Restored tip

G3, $40-$75
NW Chihuahua, MX

Double tips

G7, $8-$15
Chihuahua, MX

G9, $12-$20
Dona Ana Co., NM

G8, $8-$15
NW Chihuahua, Mex.

LOCATION: Everywhere. **DESCRIPTION:** Some of the forms illustrated are definitely effigy, some are double tipped points, while others may be no more than unfinished and unintentional doodles.

FIGUEROA - Transitional Phase, 2200 B. P.

(Also see Amargosa, Black Mesa Narrow Neck, Cienega, Mount Albion, San Pedro)

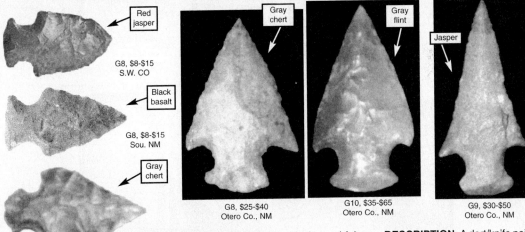

Red jasper

G8, $8-$15
S.W. CO

Black basalt

G8, $8-$15
Sou. NM

Gray chert

Gray chert

Gray flint

Jasper

G8, $25-$40
Otero Co., NM

G10, $35-$65
Otero Co., NM

G9, $30-$50
Otero Co., NM

G6, $15-$25
NW Chih., Mex.

LOCATION: Western Texas, New Mexico and Arizona. **DESCRIPTION:** A dart/knife point with medium-wide side notches, an expanding stem and a convex basal edge. Similar to the *Motley* point found in Louisiana. **I.D. KEY:** Wide side notches, convex base.

SW

FIRSTVIEW - Late Paleo, 10,000 - 8000 B. P.

(Also see Eden, Escobas and Scottsbluff)

G9, $450-$800
Chaves Co., NM

G7, $1500-$2500
El Paso Co., TX

"Fingerprint" jasper

Collateral flaking

Restored tip & base chip

Collateral flaking

LOCATION: Extreme W. Texas into New Mexico and Sou. Colorado. **DESCRIPTION:** A lanceolate point with slightly convex edges, slight shoulders and a rectangular stem. Shoulders are sometimes absent from resharpening. It generally exhibits parallel-transverse flaking. **I.D. KEY:** A diamond shaped cross-section.

FOLSOM - Paleo, 11,000 - 10,000 B. P.

(Also see Allen, Belen, Angostura, Clovis, Goshen, Green River and Midland)

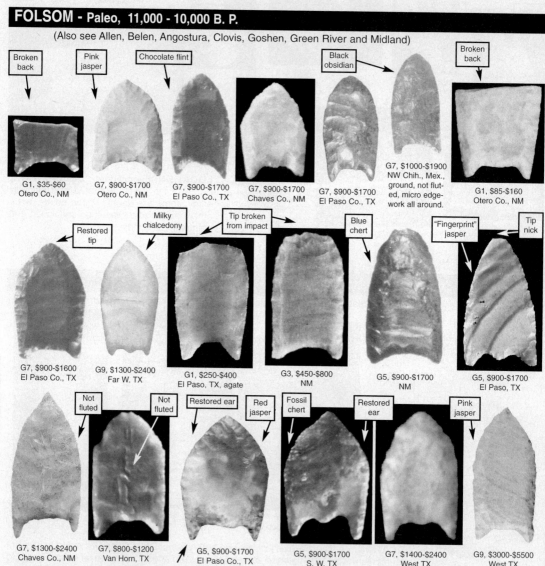

G1, $35-$60
Otero Co., NM

G7, $900-$1700
Otero Co., NM

G7, $900-$1700
El Paso Co., TX

G7, $900-$1700
Chaves Co., NM

G7, $900-$1700
El Paso Co., TX

G7, $1000-$1900
NW Chih., Mex., ground, not fluted, micro edge-work all around.

G1, $85-$160
Otero Co., NM

G7, $900-$1600
El Paso Co., TX

G9, $1300-$2400
Far W. TX

G1, $250-$400
El Paso, TX, agate

G3, $450-$800
NM

G5, $900-$1700
NM

G5, $900-$1700
El Paso, TX

G7, $1300-$2400
Chaves Co., NM

G7, $800-$1200
Van Horn, TX

G5, $900-$1700
El Paso Co., TX

G5, $900-$1700
S. W. TX

G7, $1400-$2400
West TX

G9, $3000-$5500
West TX

Labels: Broken back, Pink jasper, Chocolate flint, Black obsidian, Broken back, Restored tip, Milky chalcedony, Tip broken from impact, Blue chert, "Fingerprint" jasper, Tip nick, Not fluted, Not fluted, Restored ear, Red jasper, Fossil chert, Restored ear, Pink jasper

LOCATION: The southwestern states and as far north as Canada and east to northern Indiana. Type site is a bison kill site near Folsom, NM, where 24 fluted *Folsom* points were excavated in 1926-1928. Being the first fluted point named, for years all fluted points were called *Folsom*. **DESCRIPTION:** A very thin, small to medium sized, lanceolate point with convex to parallel edges and a concave basal edge creating sharp ears or basal corners. Most examples are fluted from the basal edge to nearly the tip of the point. They do rarely occur unfluted. Workmanship is very fine and outstanding. Most examples found have worn out tips or were rebased from longer points that broke at the haft. **I.D. KEY:** Micro secondary flaking, pointed auricles.

FOLSOM (continued)

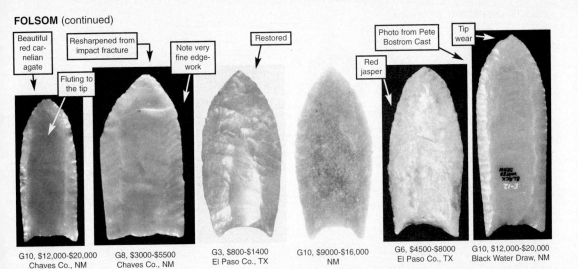

Beautiful red carnelian agate

Fluting to the tip

Resharpened from impact fracture

Note very fine edge-work

Restored

Photo from Pete Bostrom Cast

Tip wear

Red jasper

G10, $12,000-$20,000
Chaves Co., NM

G8, $3000-$5500
Chaves Co., NM

G3, $800-$1400
El Paso Co., TX

G10, $9000-$16,000
NM

G6, $4500-$8000
El Paso Co., TX

G10, $12,000-$20,000
Black Water Draw, NM

FRIO - Early to Middle Archaic, 5000 - 1500 B. P.

(Also see Caracara, Uvalde, Squaw Mountain, Ventana Side Notched)

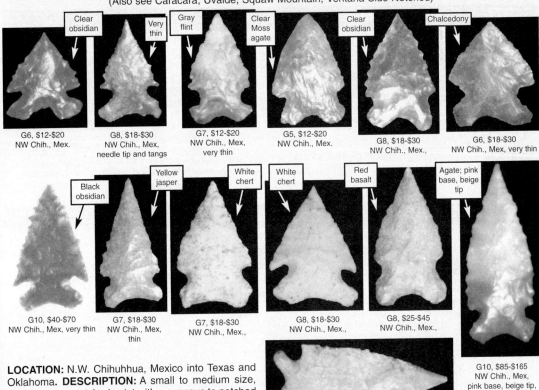

Clear obsidian

Very thin

Gray flint

Clear Moss agate

Clear obsidian

Chalcedony

G6, $12-$20
NW Chih., Mex.

G8, $18-$30
NW Chih., Mex,
needle tip and tangs

G7, $12-$20
NW Chih., Mex,
very thin

G5, $12-$20
NW Chih., Mex.

G8, $18-$30
NW Chih., Mex.,

G6, $18-$30
NW Chih., Mex, very thin

Black obsidian

Yellow jasper

White chert

White chert

Red basalt

Agate; pink base, beige tip

G10, $40-$70
NW Chih., Mex, very thin

G7, $18-$30
NW Chih., Mex,
thin

G7, $18-$30
NW Chih., Mex.,

G8, $18-$30
NW Chih., Mex.,

G8, $25-$45
NW Chih., Mex.,

G10, $85-$165
NW Chih., Mex,
pink base, beige tip
agate, very thin

LOCATION: N.W. Chihuhhua, Mexico into Texas and Oklahoma. **DESCRIPTION:** A small to medium size, side to corner-notched point with a concave to notched base that has squared to rounded ears that flare. Some examples are similar to *Big Sandy Auriculate* forms from Tennessee. **I.D. KEY:** Flaring ears.

G10, $70-$135
NW Chih., Mex, very thin, ground base

SW

FRIO-TRANSITIONAL - Late Archaic to Trans., 3000 - 2000 B. P.

(Also see Barreal, Chiricahua)

FRIO TRANSITIONAL (continued)

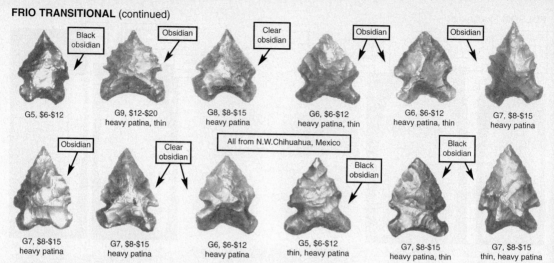

G5, $6-$12

Black obsidian

G9, $12-$20
heavy patina, thin

Obsidian

G8, $8-$15
heavy patina

Clear obsidian

G6, $6-$12
heavy patina, thin

Obsidian

G6, $6-$12
heavy patina, thin

Obsidian

G7, $8-$15
heavy patina

G7, $8-$15
heavy patina

Obsidian

G7, $8-$15
heavy patina

Clear obsidian

G6, $6-$12
heavy patina

All from N.W. Chihuahua, Mexico

G5, $6-$12
thin, heavy patina

Black obsidian

G7, $8-$15
heavy patina, thin

Black obsidian

G7, $8-$15
thin, heavy patina

LOCATION: N.W. Chihuahua, Mexico. **DESCRIPTION:** A small size dart point with side notches and an eared base. Serrations and basal grinding occur. Ears are usually rounded. Shoulders are tapered to horizontal and can be sharp. Very similar to the *Chiricahua* point found in Arizona but not as old. **I.D. KEY:** Short stubby point with flaring ears.

GARZA - Desert Traditions-Classic Phase, 500 - 300 B.P.

(Also see Buck Taylor Notched, Snaketown Triangular, Soto and Toyah)

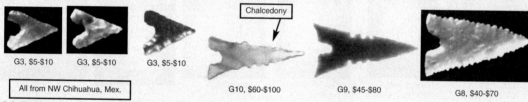

G3, $5-$10

G3, $5-$10

G3, $5-$10

All from NW Chihuahua, Mex.

Chalcedony

G10, $60-$100

G9, $45-$80

G8, $40-$70

LOCATION: NW Chihuahua, Mexico. **DESCRIPTION:** A small, thin, triangular arrow point. Blade edges vary from convex to concave and can be serrated. The basal edge is deeply concave and notched, creating long, thin ears.

GATLIN SIDE NOTCHED Devel. to Classic Phase, 800 - 600 B. P.

(Also see Pueblo Side Notched, Snaketown Triangular)

G2, $5-$10
AZ. Gatlin Variety.

Broken tip

G9, $175-$325
Mohave Co., AZ

Serrated edge

G5, $35-$65
AZ

G9, $125-$225
AZ

Tip nick

LOCATION: Sou. California into Arizona. **DESCRIPTION:** A medium size, thin, triangular *Hohokam* arrow point with broad side notches, a long needle tip and a wide base that can be deeply concave. Some examples are serrated. Basal corners are sharp to rounded. **I.D. KEY:** Long needle tip.

GILA BUTTE (see Hodges Contracting Stem)

GILA RIVER CORNER NOTCHED - Devel. Phase, 1350-1000 B. P.

(Also see Snaketown)

GILA RIVER CORNER NOTCHED (continued)

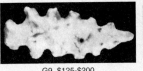

G9, $125-$200
AZ

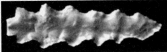

G10, $140-$265
Phoenix, AZ

LOCATION: Arizona. **DESCRIPTION:** A very rare form of *Hohokam* arrow point. The stem is straight to expanded and sometimes concave to bifurcated and has large serrations on both sides of the blade. Some examples are serrated on the lower half of the point. **I.D. KEY:** Narrowness, length, broad serrations.

GLASS- Historic, 400 - 100 B. P.

(Also see Bull Creek, Cottonwood, Sobaipuri and Trade)

Green glass

Green glass

Amber glass

G3, $5-$10
Pima Indian,
Maricopa Co., AZ

G3, $8-$15
Pima Indian,
Maricopa Co., AZ

G6, $20-$25
Pima Iindian,
Maricopa Co., AZ

G6, $20-$25
Pima Indian,
Maricopa Co., AZ

G8, $20-$35
Pima Indian, Maricopa Co., AZ

LOCATION: Historic sites everywhere. **DESCRIPTION:** A small, thin arrow point that can be triangular or side notched fashioned from bottle and telephone insulator glass. Such tribes as Pima, Papago and others utilized glass for this purpose. **I.D. KEY:** Made from glass.

GOBERNADORA - Late Archaic, 3000 B. P.

(Also see Acatita, Augustin, Gypsum Cave and Socorro)

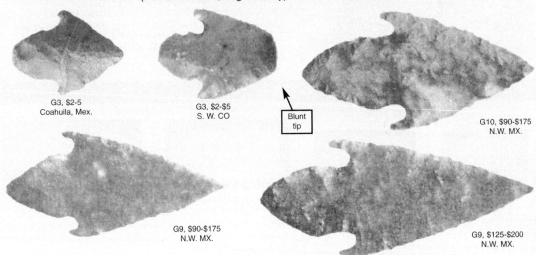

G3, $2-5
Coahuila, Mex.

G3, $2-$5
S. W. CO

Blunt tip

G10, $90-$175
N.W. MX.

G9, $90-$175
N.W. MX.

G9, $125-$200
N.W. MX.

SW

LOCATION: S.E. Arizona into southern New Mexico and N.E. Mexico. **DESCRIPTION:** A medium sized, thin, dart/knife with inward-sloping tangs and a long contracting turkeytail stem. **I.D. KEY:** Stem form.

GOLONDRINA - Transitional Paleo, 9000 - 7000 B. P.

(Also see Angostura, Cortero, Meserve, Midland, Plainview & San Jose)

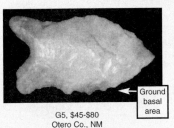

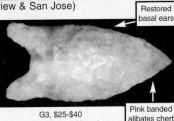

Restored basal ears

White chert

Ground basal area

G5, $45-$80
Otero Co., NM

Restored tip

G3, $25-$40
Otero Co., NM

Pink banded alibates chert

G3, $25-$40
Otero Co., NM, ground basal area.

845

GOLONDRINA (continued)

LOCATION: New Mexico, Texas, Arkansas to Oklahoma.
DESCRIPTION: A medium to large size auriculate unfluted point with rounded ears that flare and a deeply concave base. Basal areas are ground. Believed to be related to Dalton. **I.D. KEY:** Expanded ears, paleo flaking.

Restored

G3, $35-$65
NM

GOSHEN - Paleo, 11,250 - 9,500 B. P.

(Also see Clovis, Folsom, Green River, Meserve, Midland, Milnesand)

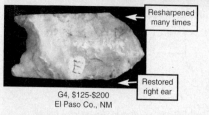

Resharpened
many times

Restored
right ear

G4, $125-$200
El Paso Co., NM

Flaked to a
median ridge

G3, $250-$400
Hudspeth Co., TX

Restored
tip & left
basal ear

LOCATION: Oklahoma to Montana. **DESCRIPTION:** A small to medium size, very thin, auriculate point with a concave base. Basal corners slope inward and are rounded. Flaking is oblique to horizontal transverse. A rare type. **I.D. KEY:** Thinness, auricles.

GRAVER - Paleo to Archaic, 14,000 - 4000 B. P.

(Also see Drill, Perforator and Scraper)

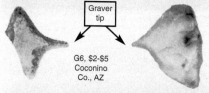

Graver
tip

G6, $2-$5
Coconino
Co., AZ

G6, $4-$8
Coconino Co.,
AZ

LOCATION: Paleo and Archaic sites everywhere. **DESCRIPTION:** An irregular shaped uniface took with one or more sharp, pointed projections used for puncturing, incising, tattooing, etc. Some examples served a dual purpose for scraping as well. **I.D. KEY:** Stem form.

GREEN RIVER - Mid-Archaic, 4500 - 4200 B. P.

(Also see Allen, Bat Cave, Folsom, Goshen, Humboldt and Midland)

G4, $8-$15
Mohave Co., AZ

G6, $25-$40
Mohave Co., AZ

G6, $25-$40
Mohave Co., AZ

G6, $30-$50
Mohave Co., AZ

LOCATION: Central Arizona to Wyoming, Colorado, Montana, New Mexico and Nebraska. **DESCRIPTION:** A small size auriculate point with a concave base. Auricles turn inward and are rounded. Similar to *McKean* found further north. **I.D. KEY:** Stem form.

GUADALUPE - Transitional-Developmental, 1900 - 1200 B. P.

(Also see Ahumada, Carlsbad, Cienega, Dolores and Neff)

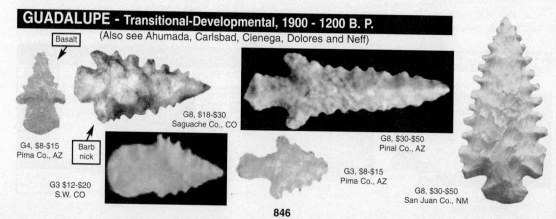

Basalt

G8, $18-$30
Saguache Co., CO

G4, $8-$15
Pima Co., AZ

Barb
nick

G3 $12-$20
S.W. CO

G8, $30-$50
Pinal Co., AZ

G3, $8-$15
Pima Co., AZ

G8, $30-$50
San Juan Co., NM

LOCATION: Arizona, New Mexico into N. Mexico. **DESCRIPTION:** A medium size, barbed, corner notched dart/arrow point with an expanding stem. Blades are serrated and bases are straight to convex. Believed to be part of the Livermore cluster. **I.D. KEY:** Wild serrations, expanded stem with corner notches.

GYPSUM CAVE - Middle Archaic, 5000 - 3300 B. P.

(Also see Augustin, Manzano, Parowan and Santa Cruz)

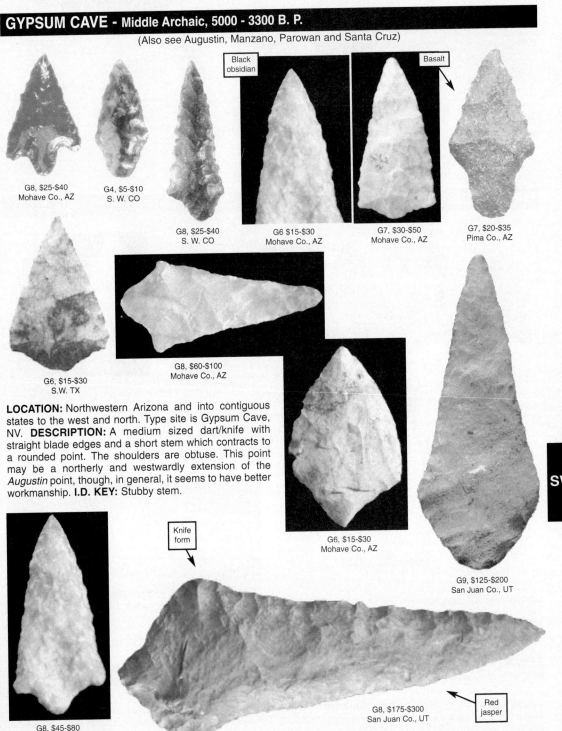

G8, $25-$40
Mohave Co., AZ

G4, $5-$10
S. W. CO

G8, $25-$40
S. W. CO

Black obsidian

G6 $15-$30
Mohave Co., AZ

Basalt

G7, $30-$50
Mohave Co., AZ

G7, $20-$35
Pima Co., AZ

G6, $15-$30
S.W. TX

G8, $60-$100
Mohave Co., AZ

G6, $15-$30
Mohave Co., AZ

G9, $125-$200
San Juan Co., UT

LOCATION: Northwestern Arizona and into contiguous states to the west and north. Type site is Gypsum Cave, NV. **DESCRIPTION:** A medium sized dart/knife with straight blade edges and a short stem which contracts to a rounded point. The shoulders are obtuse. This point may be a northerly and westwardly extension of the *Augustin* point, though, in general, it seems to have better workmanship. **I.D. KEY:** Stubby stem.

Knife form

G8, $45-$80
Mohave Co., AZ

G8, $175-$300
San Juan Co., UT

Red jasper

SW

847

GYPSUM CAVE (continued)

Basalt

G5, $5-$10
Pima Co., AZ

G7, $25-$40
Otero Co., NM

G7, $25-$40
Otero Co., NM

Black obsidian

G9, $30-$65
Mexico

HANNA - Middle to Late Archaic, 4500 - 2850 B. P.

(Also see Barreal, Chiricahua, Duncan and Squaw Mountain)

Basalt

Basalt

Basalt

Basalt

G4, $8-$15
Yavapai Co., AZ

G6, $12-$20
S.W. CO

G4, $8-$15
Yavapai Co., AZ

G5, $15-$30
Yavapai Co., AZ

G4, $8-$15
Yavapai Co., AZ

G6, $18-$30
Mineral Co., CO

G8, $30-$55
S. W. CO

Tip nick

Basalt

G7, $30-$50
Yavapai Co., AZ

Orange mottled agate

G10, $150-$275
NW Chihuahua,
Mex., not
ground.

G7, $30-$50
Otero Co., NM

G6, $30-$50
Mineral Co., CO

LOCATION: Southwestern states and north as far as Canada and east as far as Nebraska. **DESCRIPTION:** A small dart/knife with obtuse shoulders and an expanding stem which is notched to produce diagonally projecting ears. **I.D. KEY:** Expanding stem.

HARAHEY- Classic Phase, 700 - 400 B. P.

(Also see Archaic Knife)

LOCATION: Texas to Colorado. **DESCRIPTION:** A large size, double pointed knife that is usually beveled on one of all four sides of each face. The cross section is rhomboid. The true buffalo skinning knife. Found in association with small arrow points in Texas. **I.D. KEY:** Four beveled double pointed form.

HARAHEY (continued)

Alibates chert

G6, $80-$150
NM

HARRELL (see Awatovi)

HELL GAP - Late Paleo, 10,300 - 8500 B. P.

(Also see Agate Basin, Angostura, Escobas, Jay, Lake Mohave, Rio Grande)

LOCATION: Colorado northward to the Dakotas and Canada and eastward to Texas. **DESCRIPTION:** A medium size lanceolate point with a long, contracting basal stem and a short, stubby tip. Bases are generally straight and are ground. High quality flaking. **I.D. KEY:** Long stem.

Basalt

G7, $125-$200
S.W., CO

HODGES CONTRACTING STEM - Develop. Phase,1500 - 1300 B. P.

(Also see Gila River, Santa Cruz and Snaketown)

G8, $18-$30
Mohave Co.,
AZ

G6, $5-$10
Mohave Co., AZ

G4, $5-$10
Mohave Co., AZ

G4, $8-$15
Yavapai Co., AZ

G4, $8-$15
Hildago Co., NM

G6, $12-$20
Navajo Co., AZ

G4, $8-$15
Hildago Co., NM

G3, $6-$10
Mohave Co.,
AZ

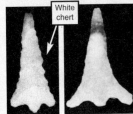

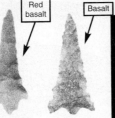

White chert

Red basalt

Basalt

White chert

G7, $12-$20
Tucson, AZ

G7, $25-$40
Mohave Co., AZ

G6, $8-$15
AZ

G8, $15-$25
Pima Co., AZ

G9, $25-$45
Pima Co., AZ

G6, $12-$20
UT

LOCATION: Arizona ranging into adjacent parts of contiguous states. **DESCRIPTION:** A small *Hohokam* arrow point with basal notching which creates barbs ranging from shallow to deep. The stem may be pointed or truncated. part of the *Snaketown* cluster. **I.D. KEY:** Basal notches.

SW

HOHOKAM (see Awatovi Side Notched, Buck Taylor Notched, Citrus Side Notched, Gatlin Side Notched, Gila River Corner Notched, Hodges Contracted Stem, Pueblo Side Notched, Salt River Indented Base, Snaketown Triangular, Sobaipuri, Walnut Canyon Side Notched)

HOHOKAM KNIFE - Desert Trad.-Develop. Phase, 1200 - 1000 B. P.

(Also see Abasolo, Archaic Knife)

Pink/beige chert

G7, $20-$35
Pima Co., AZ

LOCATION: Most of Arizona. **DESCRIPTION:** A medium to large size blade that can be parallel sided to convex and can be side notched. Bases are straight. Random flaking was used.

HOHOKAM KNIFE (continued)

Basalt

G6, $25-$45
Pima Co., AZ

Ground slate, hafted

G8, $35-$60
AZ.

Tchamahia form of Hohokam knife

Purple quartzite

G8, $55-$100
AZ.

HUMBOLDT - Transitional Phase, 2000 - 1500 B. P.

(Also see Allen, Angostura)

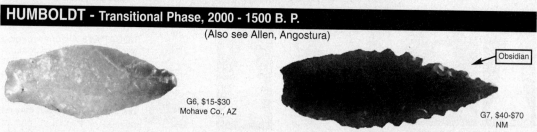

G6, $15-$30
Mohave Co., AZ

Obsidian

G7, $40-$70
NM

LOCATION: Great Basin states, esp. Nevada. **DESCRIPTION:** A small to medium size, narrow, lanceolate point with a constricted, concave base. Basal concavity can be slight to extreme. **I.D. KEY:** Base form.

JAY- Early Archaic, 8000 - 6800 B. P.

(Also see Bajada, Hell Gap, Lake Mohave, Rio Grande, Silver Lake)

LOCATION: Southern Arizona. **DESCRIPTION:** A medium to large size, narrow, long stemmed point with tapered shoulders. The base is convex. Stem sides and base are ground. Similar to the Hell Gap point found further east. **I.D. KEY:** Broad, concave base.

Basalt

G9, $125-$225
Otero Co., NM, ground stem sides & base.

KIN KLETSO SIDE NOTCHED - Late Archaic to Classic Phase, 900 - 750 B. P.

(Also see Bonito, Chaco & Pueblo Alto & Pueblo Del Arroyo Side Notched)

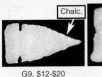

Chalc.

G9, $12-$20
S. W. CO

G8, $15-$30
S. W. CO

Yellow agate

G8, $25-$40
S. W. CO

LOCATION: Chaco Canyon and four corners area. **DESCRIPTION:** A small, thin, side notched arrow point with a straight to slightly concave base. Notching is very narrow. **I.D. KEY:** Triangular form.

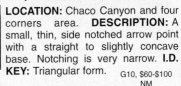

G10, $60-$100
NM

KINNEY - Middle Archaic-Woodland, 5000 - 2000 B. P.

(Also see Early Triangular, Matamoros, Mescal Knife and Tortugas)

LOCATION: Texas into northern Mexico. **DESCRIPTION:** A medium to large size, thin, broad, lanceolate, well made blade with convex to straight blade edges and a concave base. Basal corners are pointed to rounded. **I.D. KEY:** Broad, concave base.

G8, $80-$150
NW Chihuahua, Mex.,
thin

White/orange chert

LAKE MOHAVE - Paleo, 13,200 - 10,000 B.P.

(Also see Hell Gap, Jay, Rio Grande, Silver Lake)

Agate

G6, $35-$60
N. AZ

Ground stem

Conglomerate

Ground stem

G6, $35-$60
Navajo Co., AZ

Ground stem

G7, $35-$60
S.W. CO

Ground stem

G8, $200-$350
S.E. AZ. ground stem.

Ground stem

G9, $45-$85
S.W. CO

Ground stem

Ground stem

Pink jasper

Ground stem

G9, $175-$300
S.W. CO

G6, $80-$150
S.W. CO

SW

LOCATION: Southern California into Arizona and the Great Basin. **DESCRIPTION:** A medium sized, narrow, parallel to contracting stemmed point with weak, tapered to no shoulders. Stem is much longer than the blade. Some experts think these points are worn out *Parman* points. **I.D. KEY:** Long stem, very short blade.

LAKE MOHAVE (continued)

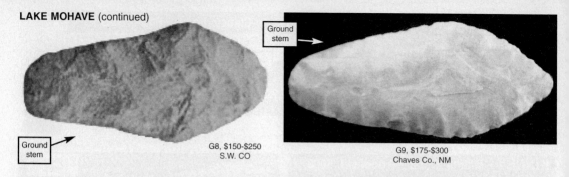

Ground stem

G8, $150-$250
S.W. CO

Ground stem

G9, $175-$300
Chaves Co., NM

LANCET- All Periods from Paleo to Historic

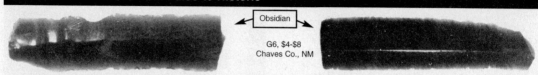

Obsidian

G6, $4-$8
Chaves Co., NM

G6, $4-$8, Chaves Co., NM

LOCATION: Over the entire U.S. **DESCRIPTION:** This artifact is also known as a lammeler flake blade and was produced by knocking a flake or spall off a parent stone. Most of the western examples are of obsidian. Perhaps the best known of the type were those made and used by the Hopewell people in the midwest. **I.D. KEY:** Double uniface and the presence, generally, of the parent stone showing on one face.

LERMA - Middle to Late Archaic, 4000 - 1000 B. P.

(Also see Abasolo, Agate Basin, Angostura, Catan, Datil and Pelona)

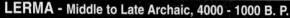

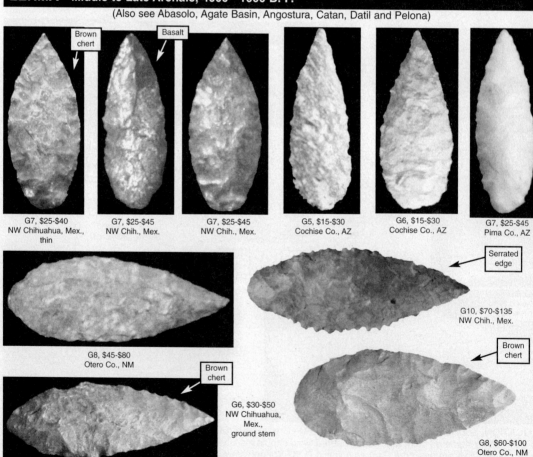

Brown chert

Basalt

G7, $25-$40
NW Chihuahua, Mex.,
thin

G7, $25-$45
NW Chih., Mex.

G7, $25-$45
NW Chih., Mex.

G5, $15-$30
Cochise Co., AZ

G6, $15-$30
Cochise Co., AZ

G7, $25-$45
Pima Co., AZ

Serrated edge

G10, $70-$135
NW Chih., Mex.

G8, $45-$80
Otero Co., NM

Brown chert

Brown chert

G6, $30-$50
NW Chihuahua,
Mex.,
ground stem

G8, $60-$100
Otero Co., NM

852

LERMA (continued)

Basalt

Chalcedony

Tan chert

G9, $50-$90
NW Chihuahua, Mex.,
heavy grinding in basal area

G9, $70-$135
NW Chihuahua, Mex., thin.

G10, $125-$200
Hidalgo Co., NM

G9, $90-$175
S.W. CO

G9, $70-$135
Otero Co., NM,
ground basal area, thin.

G8, $50-$90
S. NV

LOCATION: From central Texas westward through New Mexico, N.W. Chihuahua, Mexico and into eastern Arizona. Examples of *Lerma* points from further east are, most likely, Guilford points. **DESCRIPTION:** A long ovoid with a rounded to somewhat pointed basal edge.

MADDEN LAKE - Paleo, 10,700 B. P.

(Also see Clovis, Rio Grande, San Jose and Sandia)

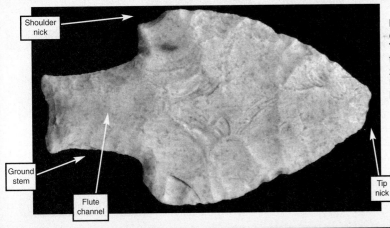

Shoulder nick

Ground stem

Flute channel

Tip nick

LOCATION: Panama to southern South America. **DESCRIPTION:** A medium to large size, fluted stemmed point with horizontal to tapered shoulders. Bases are fishtailed and ground. **I.D. KEY:** Fishtail stem.

G6, $1800-$3000
N. Belize, Fells Creek

SW

MALJAMAR - Late Archaic, 3500 - 2300 B. P.

(Also see Ahumada, Duran, Mount Albion, Neff, San Jose and Truxton)

Barbed edges

Dark gray flint

G8, $55-$100
Otero Co., NM

G8, $60-$100
Gaines Co., TX

G6, $30-$50
NW Chih., Mex.

G6, $30-$50
Ward Co., TX

MALJAMAR (continued)

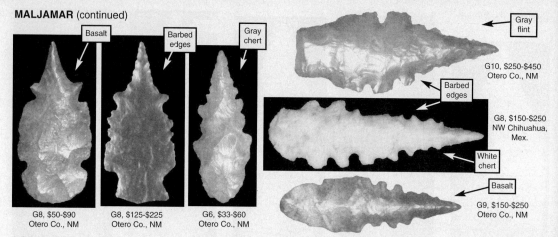

Basalt

Barbed edges

Gray chert

Gray flint

G10, $250-$450
Otero Co., NM

Barbed edges

G8, $150-$250
NW Chihuahua, Mex.

White chert

Basalt

G9, $150-$250
Otero Co., NM

G8, $50-$90
Otero Co., NM

G8, $125-$225
Otero Co., NM

G6, $33-$60
Otero Co., NM

LOCATION: N.W. Chihuahua, Mexico, Southeastern New Mexico and extreme western Texas. **DESCRIPTION:** A small side notched dart point with a rounded to pointed stem. They are serrated, sometimes heavily, and can acquire extra notches along the blade edges. Similar to *Duran* and *Sinner* found in Texas. **I.D. KEY:** Multiple notching.

MANZANO - Mid to Late Archaic, 5000 - 3000 B. P.

(Also see Augustin, Gypsum Cave and Santa Cruz)

Beveled edge

G8, $25-$40
N.W. NM

G6, $25-$40
Yavapai Co., AZ

LOCATION: N.W. New Mexico into Arizona. **DESCRIPTION:** A medium size, broad, triangular point with a short, contracting, rounded stem. Shoulders are prominent and slightly barbed. Opposite edges are beveled. Related to the *Gypsum Cave* type. **I.D. KEY:** Blade beveling, short stem.

MARSHALL - Mid-Archaic to Woodland, 6000 - 2000 B. P.

(Also see Cienega, Elko Corner Notched, Figueroa, Mount Albion)

LOCATION: Western New Mexixo into Texas. **DESCRIPTION:** A medium to large size, broad, high quality, corner to basal notched point with long barbs that turn inward towards the base. Notching is less angled than in *Marcos*. Bases are straight to concave to bifurcated. **I.D. KEY:** Drooping tangs.

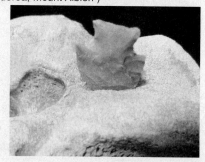

G7, $30-$50
Lea Co. NM.
Showing a Marshall point embedded in an animal bone

MARTIS- Late Archaic, 3000 - 1500 B. P.

(Also see Northern, San Rafael, Ventana Side Notched)

Red jasper

G6, $20-$35
NW Chihuahua, Mex, thick

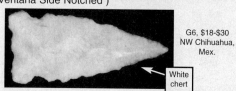

G6, $18-$30
NW Chihuahua, Mex.

White chert

MARTIS (continued)

G6, $15-$25
NW Chihuahua, Mex.

Clear obsidian

G6, $18-$30
NW Chihuahua, Mex.

Gray chert

G8, $30-$50
S. W. TX

LOCATION: W. Arizona into the Great Basin. **DESCRIPTION:** A small to medium size side notched point with a straight to concave base. Shoulders are tapered to horizontal.

MATAMOROS - Late Archaic to Classic Phase, 3000 - 400 B. P.

(Also see Abasolo, Catan, Early Triangular, Mescal Knife and Triangular Knife)

LOCATION: Western Texas into Arizona. **DESCRIPTION:** A small to medium size, broad, triangular point with concave, straight, or convex base. On some examples, beveling occurs on one side of each face as in *Tortugas* points. **I.D. KEY:** Triangular form.

G8, $25-$40
Mohave Co., AZ

G7, $12-$25
W. TX

Brown petrified Palmwood

Black chert

Banded red jasper

G5, $18-$30
Otero Co., NM

G8, $18-$30
Otero Co., NM

G8, $15-$30
Cochise Co., AZ

G10, $35-$60
N.W. Chihuahua, Mex.

MESCAL KNIFE - Desert Traditions- Classic and Historic Phases, 700 B. P. to historic times

(Also see Matamoros, Kinney and Triangular Knife)

LOCATION: Southwestern states. **DESCRIPTION:** A well made triangular blade which was hafted horizontally along one edge.

G9, $120-$200
Yavapai Co., AZ

SW

MESERVE - Early Archaic, 9500 - 8500 B.P.

(Also see Allen, Angostura, Midland and San Jose)

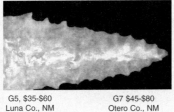

G5, $35-$60
Luna Co., NM

G7 $45-$80
Otero Co., NM

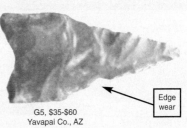

Edge wear

G5, $35-$60
Yavapai Co., AZ

MESERVE (continued)

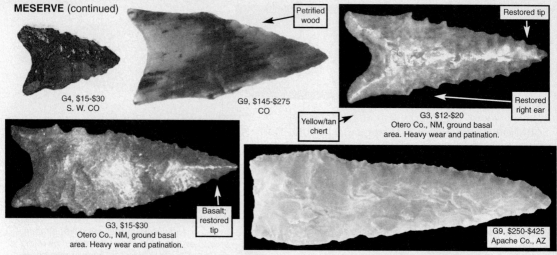

G4, $15-$30
S. W. CO

Petrified wood

G9, $145-$275
CO

Restored tip

G3, $12-$20
Otero Co., NM, ground basal
area. Heavy wear and patination.

Restored right ear

Yellow/tan chert

G3, $15-$30
Otero Co., NM, ground basal
area. Heavy wear and patination.

Basalt; restored tip

G9, $250-$425
Apache Co., AZ

LOCATION: Throughout the U.S. from the Rocky Mountains to the Mississippi River. **DESCRIPTION:** A member of the *Dalton* Family. Blade edges are straight to slightly concave with a straight to very slightly concave sided stem. They are basally thinned and most examples are beveled and have light serrations on the blade edges. The basal edge is concave. **I.D. KEY:** Squared, concave base.

MIDLAND - Paleo, 10,700 - 10,400 B. P.

(Also see Belen, Folsom, Goshen, Mescal Knife and Milnesand)

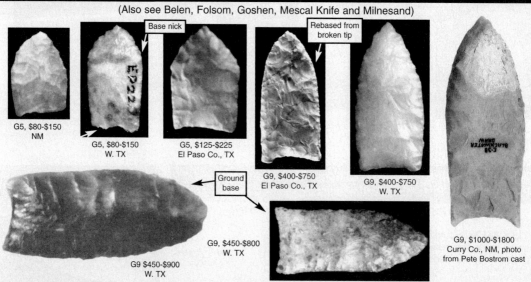

G5, $80-$150
NM

Base nick

G5, $80-$150
W. TX

G5, $125-$225
El Paso Co., TX

Rebased from broken tip

G9, $400-$750
El Paso Co., TX

G9, $400-$750
W. TX

Ground base

G9 $450-$900
W. TX

G9, $450-$800
W. TX

G9, $1000-$1800
Curry Co., NM, photo
from Pete Bostrom cast

LOCATION: New Mexico northward to Montana, the Dakotas and Minnesota. **DESCRIPTION:** An unfluted *Folsom*. A small to medium size, thin, unfluted lanceolate point with a straight to concave base. Basal thinning is weak and the blades exhibit fine, micro edgework. Bases are ground.

MILNESAND - Transitional Paleo, 11,000 - 8000 B. P.

(Also see Folsom, Goshen and Midland)

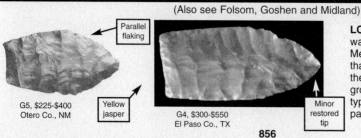

Parallel flaking

G5, $225-$400
Otero Co., NM

Yellow jasper

G4, $300-$550
El Paso Co., TX

Minor restored tip

LOCATION: Texas, New Mexico northward to Canada. **DESCRIPTION:** Medium size unfluted lanceolate point that becomes thicker and wider towards the tip. The base is basically square and ground. Thicker than *Midland*. A scarce type. **I.D. KEY:** Square base and Paleo parallel flaking.

MILNESAND
(continued)

Ground basal area

Banded pink chert

Ground stem sides & base

Yellow jasper

Yellow jasper

G6, $350-600
Tucumcari, NM

G9, $650-$1200
Otero Co., NM

G9, $800-$1500
El Paso Co., TX

G8, $700-$1200
Chihuahua, MX

MIMBRE - Developmental Phase, 800 B. P.

(Also see Del Carmen, Desert, Dry Prong, Nawthis and Sacaton)

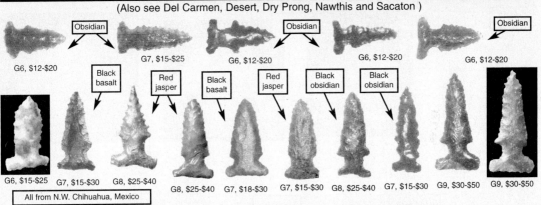

Obsidian

Obsidian

Obsidian

G6, $12-$20

G7, $15-$25

G6, $12-$20

G6, $12-$20

G6, $12-$20

Black basalt

Red jasper

Black basalt

Red jasper

Black obsidian

Black obsidian

G6, $15-$25   G7, $15-$30   G8, $25-$40   G8, $25-$40   G7, $18-$30   G7, $15-$30   G8, $25-$40   G7, $15-$30   G9, $30-$50   G9, $30-$50

All from N.W. Chihuahua, Mexico

LOCATION: N.W. Chihuahua, Mexico into Sou. New Mexico and far west Texas. **DESCRIPTION:** A small size, narrow, side notched arrow point with a base that flares out wider than the blade. The base is straight to slightly incurvate to excurvate. Blade edges are serrated. **I.D. KEY:** Broad base, wide notches.

MOUNT ALBION - Early to Middle Archaic, 5800 - 5350 B. P.

(Also see Cienega, Elko Corner Notched, Figueroa, Martis and San Pedro)

Tip wear

SW

G5, $8-$15
Hidalgo Co., NM

G8, $15-$25
N. AZ

G8, $20-$35
Hidalgo Co., NM

G7, $12-$20
Santa Fe Co., NM

G7, $25-$45
S. W. CO

G5, $8-$15
Cochise Co., AZ

G7, $25-$45
AZ

G8, $30-$55
NM

G7, $25-$45
S. W. CO

G6, $20-$35
Luna Co., NM

857

MOUNT ALBION (continued)

G7, $25-$45, NM

G7, $15-$30
Cochise Co., AZ

G8, $25-$45
Cochise Co., AZ

LOCATION: Northeastern Arizona, southeastern Utah, northern New Mexico and southern Colorado. **DESCRIPTION:** A medium sized dart/knife with small side to corner notches, an expanded stem and convex blade edges. The basal edge is convex. **I.D. KEY:** Large expanded, convex base

MOYOTE - Early to Mid-Archaic, 7000 - 4500 B. P.

(Also see Bell, Cienega, Elko Corner Notched, Figueroa, Marshall, Shumla)

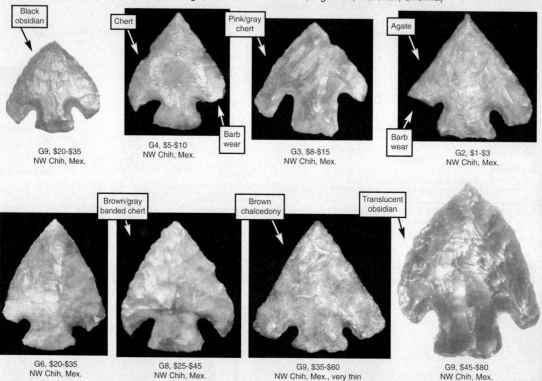

Black obsidian

G9, $20-$35
NW Chih, Mex.

Chert

Barb wear

G4, $5-$10
NW Chih, Mex.

Pink/gray chert

G3, $8-$15
NW Chih, Mex.

Agate

Barb wear

G2, $1-$3
NW Chih, Mex.

Brown/gray banded chert

G6, $20-$35
NW Chih, Mex.

G8, $25-$45
NW Chih, Mex.

Brown chalcedony

G9, $35-$60
NW Chih, Mex., very thin

Translucent obsidian

G9, $45-$80
NW Chih, Mex.

LOCATION: N.W. Chihuahua, Mex. **DESCRIPTION:** A medium size, thin, broad, corner notched point with an expanding stem. Blade edges can be straight to convex. Base is mostly convex but can be straight. Barbs are broad and squarrish and some examples show a clipped wing on at least one barb. **I.D. KEY:** Broadness and angle of notching.

NAWTHIS- Developmental Phase, 1100 - 700 B.P.

(Also see Buck Taylor Side Notched, Desert, Mimbre and Sacaton)

G8, $15-$30
NM

LOCATION: Northern New Mexico into Colorado. **DESCRIPTION:** A well made, side notched arrow point. It is triangular in shape with deep, narrow notches placed low on the blade. **I.D. KEY:** Low, deep and narrow side notches.

NEFF - Late Archaic, 3500 - 2300 B. P.

(Also see Ahumada, Duran, Escobas, Maljamar and San Jose)

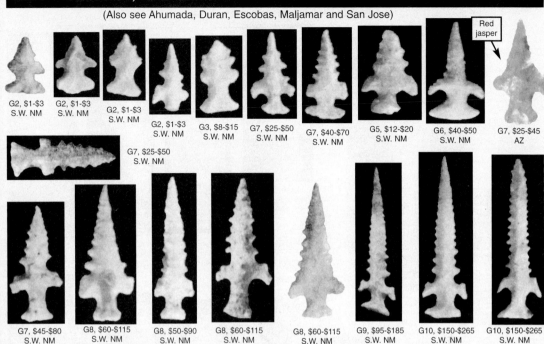

G2, $1-$3
S.W. NM

G2, $1-$3
S.W. NM

G2, $1-$3
S.W. NM

G2, $1-$3
S.W. NM

G3, $8-$15
S.W. NM

G7, $25-$50
S.W. NM

G7, $40-$70
S.W. NM

G5, $12-$20
S.W. NM

G6, $40-$50
S.W. NM

Red jasper

G7, $25-$45
AZ

G7, $25-$50
S.W. NM

G7, $45-$80
S.W. NM

G8, $60-$115
S.W. NM

G8, $50-$90
S.W. NM

G8, $60-$115
S.W. NM

G8, $60-$115
S.W. NM

G9, $95-$185
S.W. NM

G10, $150-$265
S.W. NM

G10, $150-$265
S.W. NM

LOCATION: Eastern New Mexico and western Texas. **DESCRIPTION:** A small to medium sized dart/knife with an expanded stem, drooping shoulders and multiple notches between the shoulders and tip. Another variation similar to *Duran, Sinner* and *Livermore* found in Texas. **I.D. KEY:** Large expanded, convex base.

NORTHERN SIDE NOTCHED - Paleo to LateArchaic, 9000 - 3000 B. P.

(Also see San Pedro, San Rafael, Sudden, Ventana Side Notched,)

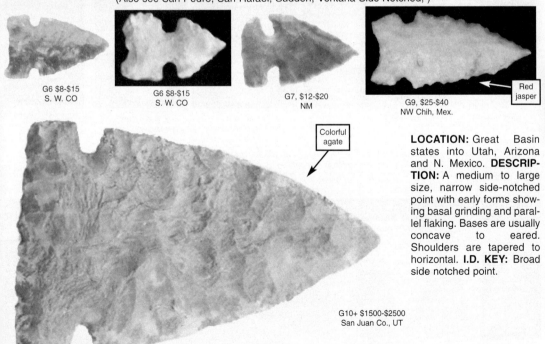

G6 $8-$15
S. W. CO

G6 $8-$15
S. W. CO

G7, $12-$20
NM

G9, $25-$40
NW Chih, Mex.

Red jasper

Colorful agate

LOCATION: Great Basin states into Utah, Arizona and N. Mexico. **DESCRIPTION:** A medium to large size, narrow side-notched point with early forms showing basal grinding and parallel flaking. Bases are usually concave to eared. Shoulders are tapered to horizontal. **I.D. KEY:** Broad side notched point.

G10+ $1500-$2500
San Juan Co., UT

SW

PALMILLAS - Middle to Late Archaic, 6000 - 3000 B. P.

(Also see Axtel, Godley, Williams, Yavapai)

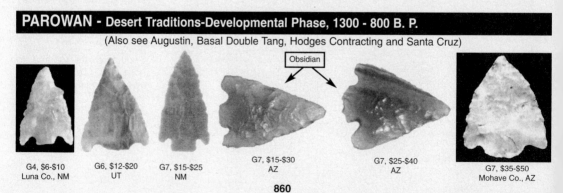

Red jasper

Perforator

Red base, clear chalcedony

Pink jasper

Banded chert

Milky chalcedony

G6, $5-$10
S. W. CO

G4, $8-$15
NW Chihuahua, Mex.

G6, $5-$10
S. W. CO

G7, $15-$25
NW Chihuahua, Mex.

White chalcedony

G8, $25-$45
El Paso Co., TX, serrated.

G10, $35-$60
Otero Co., NM, thin & perfect, serrated

G8, $30-$50
Otero Co., NM

G5, $8-$15
NW Chihuahua, Mex., serrated.

G10, $40-$75
S. W. CO

Serrated edge

White chert

Banded chert

Gray chert

Beige chert

G6, $25-$40
S. W. CO

G7, $30-$55
S. W. CO

G8, $30-$55
NW Chihuahua, Mex., thin.

G9, $60-$115
Otero Co., NM, ground base.

G9, $70-$135
NW Cihuahua, Mex.

G10, $150-$275
Otero Co., NM, thin and excellent.

LOCATION: Texas to Oklahoma. **DESCRIPTION:** A small to medium size triangular point with a bulbous stem. Shoulders are prominent and can be horizontal to barbed or weak and tapered. Stems expand and are rounded. **I.D. KEY:** Bulbous stem.

PAROWAN - Desert Traditions-Developmental Phase, 1300 - 800 B. P.

(Also see Augustin, Basal Double Tang, Hodges Contracting and Santa Cruz)

Obsidian

G4, $6-$10
Luna Co., NM

G6, $12-$20
UT

G7, $15-$25
NM

G7, $15-$30
AZ

G7, $25-$40
AZ

G7, $35-$50
Mohave Co., AZ

PAROWAN (continued)

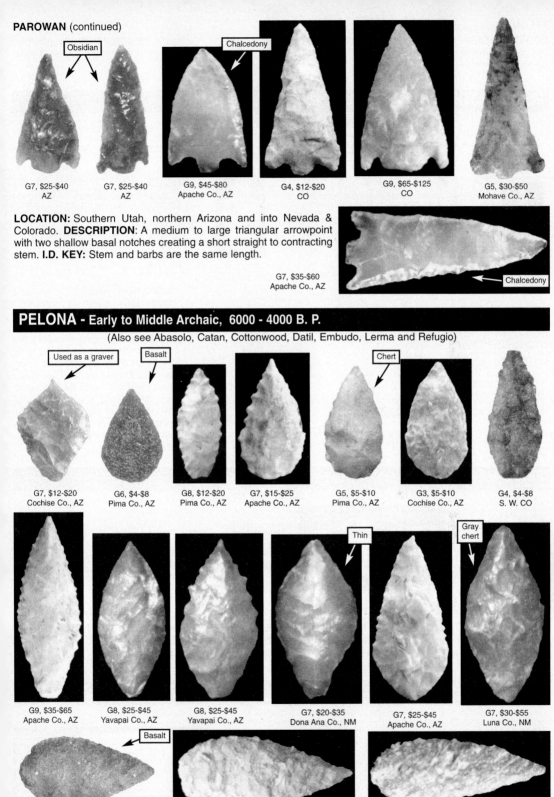

Obsidian

G7, $25-$40
AZ

G7, $25-$40
AZ

Chalcedony

G9, $45-$80
Apache Co., AZ

G4, $12-$20
CO

G9, $65-$125
CO

G5, $30-$50
Mohave Co., AZ

LOCATION: Southern Utah, northern Arizona and into Nevada & Colorado. **DESCRIPTION:** A medium to large triangular arrowpoint with two shallow basal notches creating a short straight to contracting stem. **I.D. KEY:** Stem and barbs are the same length.

G7, $35-$60
Apache Co., AZ

Chalcedony

PELONA - Early to Middle Archaic, 6000 - 4000 B. P.

(Also see Abasolo, Catan, Cottonwood, Datil, Embudo, Lerma and Refugio)

Used as a graver

Basalt

Chert

G7, $12-$20
Cochise Co., AZ

G6, $4-$8
Pima Co., AZ

G8, $12-$20
Pima Co., AZ

G7, $15-$25
Apache Co., AZ

G5, $5-$10
Pima Co., AZ

G3, $5-$10
Cochise Co., AZ

G4, $4-$8
S. W. CO

Thin

Gray
chert

SW

G9, $35-$65
Apache Co., AZ

G8, $25-$45
Yavapai Co., AZ

G8, $25-$45
Yavapai Co., AZ

G7, $20-$35
Dona Ana Co., NM

G7, $25-$45
Apache Co., AZ

G7, $30-$55
Luna Co., NM

Basalt

G7, $15-$25
Pima Co., AZ

G6, $25-$40
Cochise Co., AZ

G5, $20-$35
Cochise Co., AZ

PELONA (continued)

LOCATION: Southern Arizona, southwestern New Mexico and southeastern California. **DESCRIPTION:** Ranges from lozenge to ovoid in shape. It may have serrations on the blade, or, less frequently, on the hafting area, or, in most cases, not serrated.

PERFORATOR - Archaic to Historic, 9000 - 400 B. P.

(Also see Drill, Graver and Scraper)

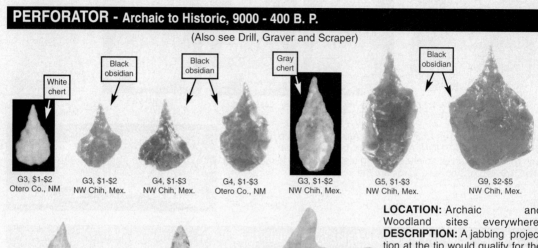

White chert

Black obsidian

Black obsidian

Gray chert

Black obsidian

G3, $1-$2
Otero Co., NM

G3, $1-$2
NW Chih, Mex.

G4, $1-$3
NW Chih, Mex.

G4, $1-$3
Otero Co., NM

G3, $1-$2
NW Chih, Mex.

G5, $1-$3
NW Chih, Mex.

G9, $2-$5
NW Chih, Mex.

G9, $2-$5
AZ

G6, $2-$4
S.W. CO

G4, $1-$3
AZ

LOCATION: Archaic and Woodland sites everywhere. **DESCRIPTION:** A jabbing projection at the tip would qualify for the type. It is believed that *perforators* were used for tattooing, incising or to punch holes in leather or other materials or objects. Paleo peoples used *Gravers* for the same purpose. All Archaic and Woodland cultures converted their points into this type. Therefore, most point types could occur in this form.

PINTO BASIN - Early to Late Archaic, 8000 - 3000 B. P.

(Also see Duncan and Hanna)

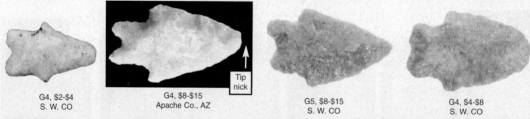

G4, $2-$4
S. W. CO

G4, $8-$15
Apache Co., AZ

Tip nick

G5, $8-$15
S. W. CO

G4, $4-$8
S. W. CO

LOCATION: Arizona, New Mexico into E. California, Utah, Nevada, Idaho and Oregon. **DESCRIPTION:** A medium size auriculate point. Shoulders can be tapered, horizontal or barbed. Bases are either deeply bifurcated with parallel to expanding ears or tapered with a concave basal edge. **I.D. KEY:** Bifurcated base.

PLAINVIEW - Late Paleo, 10,000 - 7000 B. P.

(Also see Allen, Angostura, Clovis, Golondrina, Goshen)

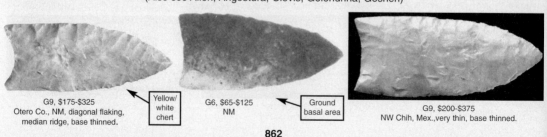

G9, $175-$325
Otero Co., NM, diagonal flaking, median ridge, base thinned.

Yellow/ white chert

G6, $65-$125
NM

Ground basal area

G9, $200-$375
NW Chih, Mex.,very thin, base thinned.

PLAINVIEW (continued)

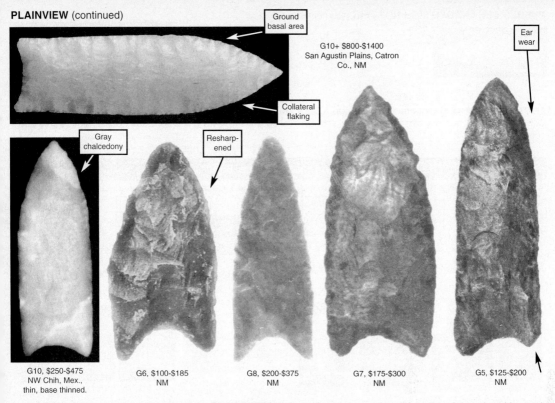

Ground basal area

G10+ $800-$1400
San Agustin Plains, Catron Co., NM

Ear wear

Collateral flaking

Gray chalcedony

Resharpened

G10, $250-$475
NW Chih, Mex.,
thin, base thinned.

G6, $100-$185
NM

G8, $200-$375
NM

G7, $175-$300
NM

G5, $125-$200
NM

LOCATION: Mexico northward to Canada. **DESCRIPTION:** A medium to large size, thin, lanceolate point with usually parallel sides and a concave base that is ground. Some examples are thinned or fluted and is believed to be related to the earlier *Clovis* and contemporary *Dalton* type. Flaking is of high quality and can be collateral to oblique transverse. **I.D. KEY:** Base form, thinness.

POINT OF PINES SIDE NOTCHED - Dev. Phase, 850 - 700 B. P.

(Also see Kin Kletso, Pueblo Side notched, Salado, Snaketown Triangular & Walnut Canyon)

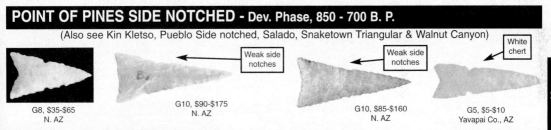

Weak side notches

Weak side notches

White chert

G8, $35-$65
N. AZ

G10, $90-$175
N. AZ

G10, $85-$160
N. AZ

G5, $5-$10
Yavapai Co., AZ

SW

LOCATION: Arizona. **DESCRIPTION:** A small size, thin, triangular, arrow point with a concave base, needle tip and weak side notches. Notches occur about half way up from the base. Basal corners are sharp. **I.D. KEY:** Triangular form with weak side notches.

PUEBLO ALTO SIDE NOTCHED - Developmental Phase, 1000 - 800 B. P.

(Also see Awatovi Side Notched, Bonito, Desert, Pueblo Arroyo, Temporal)

LOCATION: S.W. colorado into Utah, Arizona & New Mexico. **DESCRIPTION:** A small, thin, triangular arrow point with side notches. Bases are mostly convex, rarely straight with rounded corners

G9, $15-$30
Apache Co., AZ

Shoulder wear

G6, $5-$10
Apache Co., AZ

PUEBLO DEL ARROYO SIDE NOTCHED - Developmental Phase, 1000 - 800 B. P.

(Also see Bonito, Desert, Pueblo Alto, Pueblo Side Notched)

PUEBLO DEL ARROYO SIDE NOTCHED (continued)

Chalc.

G8, $25-$40
S.W. CO

G10, $40-$75
Montez. Co., CO

G9, $35-$60
Montez. Co., CO

LOCATION: S.W. colorado into Utah, Arizona & New Mexico. **DESCRIPTION:** A small, thin, triangular arrow point with side notches that are close to the base and are angled upward toward the tip. Bases are straight with square corners.

PUEBLO SIDE NOTCHED - Dev. to Classic Phase, 850 - 500 B. P.

(Also see Awatovi Side Notched, Buck Taylor Notched, Desert, Salado, Walnut Canyon)

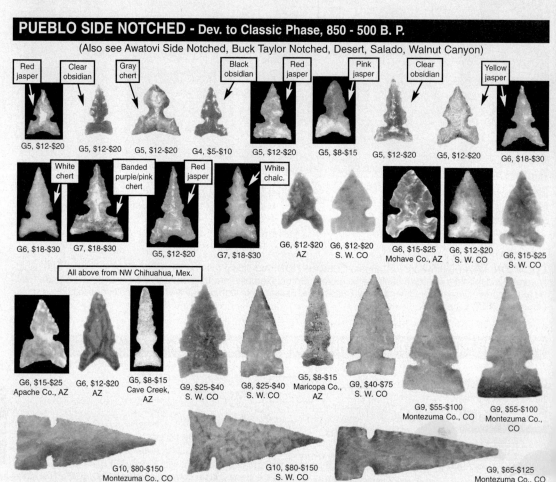

Red jasper — G5, $12-$20

Clear obsidian — G5, $12-$20

Gray chert — G5, $12-$20

G4, $5-$10

Black obsidian — G5, $12-$20

Red jasper — G5, $8-$15

Pink jasper — G5, $12-$20

Clear obsidian — G5, $12-$20

Yellow jasper — G6, $18-$30

White chert — G6, $18-$30

G7, $18-$30

Banded purple/pink chert — G5, $12-$20

Red jasper — G7, $18-$30

White chalc. — G6, $12-$20 AZ

G6, $12-$20 S. W. CO

G6, $15-$25 Mohave Co., AZ

G6, $12-$20 S. W. CO

G6, $15-$25 S. W. CO

All above from NW Chihuahua, Mex.

G6, $15-$25 Apache Co., AZ

G6, $12-$20 AZ

G5, $8-$15 Cave Creek, AZ

G9, $25-$40 S. W. CO

G8, $25-$40 S. W. CO

G5, $8-$15 Maricopa Co., AZ

G9, $40-$75 S. W. CO

G9, $55-$100 Montezuma Co., CO

G9, $55-$100 Montezuma Co., CO

G10, $80-$150 Montezuma Co., CO

G10, $80-$150 S. W. CO

G9, $65-$125 Montezuma Co., CO

LOCATION: Sou. California into Arizona, New Mexico and N. Mex. **DESCRIPTION**: A small size, thin, triangular, side notched arrow point with a straight to concave base. Notches can occur one fourth to half way up from the base. Basal corners can be squared to eared. **I.D. KEY:** Triangular form with side notches.

RED HORN (see Buck Taylor Notched and White Mountain Side Notched)

REFUGIO - Middle Archaic, 5000 - 2000 B. P.

(Also see Abasolo, Lerma, Pelona)

LOCATION: New Mexico into Texas. **DESCRIPTION:** A medium to large size, narrow, lanceolate blade with a rounded base.

G7, $20-$35
Otero Co., NM

RIO GRANDE - Early Archaic, 7500 - 6000 B. P.

(Also see Agate Basin, Angostura, Bajada, Escobas, Hell Gap, Jay, Lake Mohave, Madden Lake)

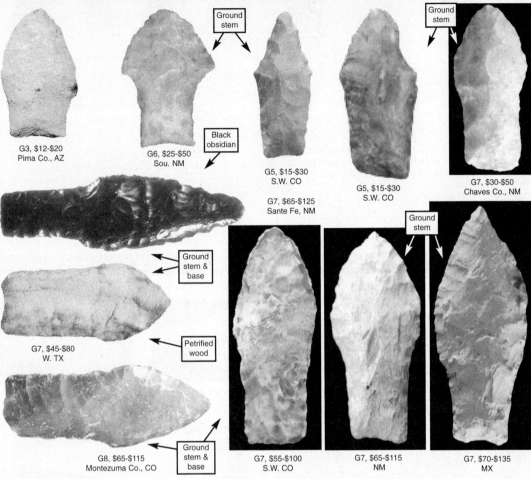

G3, $12-$20
Pima Co., AZ

Ground stem

G6, $25-$50
Sou. NM

Black obsidian

G5, $15-$30
S.W. CO

G7, $65-$125
Sante Fe, NM

G5, $15-$30
S.W. CO

Ground stem

G7, $30-$50
Chaves Co., NM

Ground stem & base

G7, $45-$80
W. TX

Petrified wood

Ground stem & base

G8, $65-$115
Montezuma Co., CO

Ground stem

G7, $55-$100
S.W. CO

G7, $65-$115
NM

G7, $70-$135
MX

LOCATION: Southern Colorado, New Mexico and western Texas. **DESCRIPTION:** A lanceolate point with a relatively long stem formed by obtuse shoulders. The stem contracts slightly and stem edges are ground. Developed from the earlier *Jay* point and related to the later *Escobas* point. **I.D. KEY:** The shoulders are more pronounced then on *Hell Gap* points.

SW

ROSE SPRINGS CORNER NOTCHED - Developmental Phase, 1600 - 700 B. P.

(Also see Chaco Corner Notched, Convento, Bonito and Desert)

G4, $4-$8
Otero Co., NM

Clear obsidian

G8, $12-$20
UT

G7, $15-$25
NM

G7, $12-$20
AZ

G7, $15-$25
NM

Black obsidian

G7, $12-$20
UT

G9, $30-$50
Grand Co., UT

G8, $20-$35
S.W. CO

Black obsidian

G8, $25-$40
S.W. CO

Black obsidian

G9, $25-$40
N.W. AZ, Virgin Riv.

G9, $25-$40
N.W. AZ, Virgin Riv.

865

ROSE SPRINGS CORNER NOTCHED (continued)

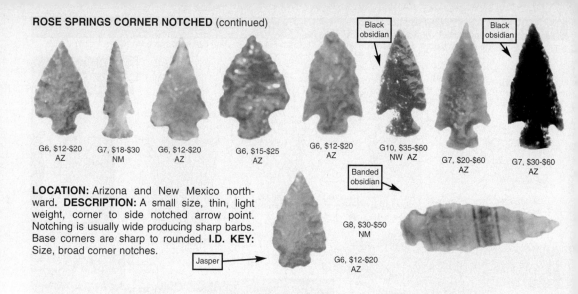

G6, $12-$20
AZ

G7, $18-$30
NM

G6, $12-$20
AZ

G6, $15-$25
AZ

G6, $12-$20
AZ

Black obsidian

G10, $35-$60
NW AZ

G7, $20-$60
AZ

Black obsidian

G7, $30-$60
AZ

Banded obsidian

G8, $30-$50
NM

LOCATION: Arizona and New Mexico northward. **DESCRIPTION:** A small size, thin, light weight, corner to side notched arrow point. Notching is usually wide producing sharp barbs. Base corners are sharp to rounded. **I.D. KEY:** Size, broad corner notches.

Jasper

G6, $12-$20
AZ

ROSE SPRINGS STEMMED - Developmental Phase, 1600 - 700 B. P.

(Also see Cohonina Stemmed & Snaketown)

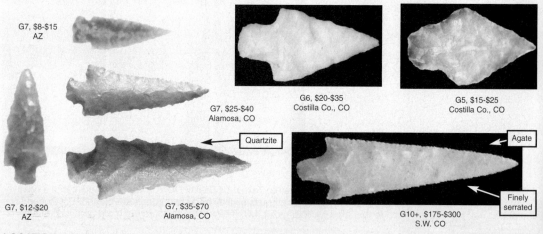

G7, $8-$15
AZ

G7, $25-$40
Alamosa, CO

G6, $20-$35
Costilla Co., CO

G5, $15-$25
Costilla Co., CO

Quartzite

Agate

Finely serrated

G7, $12-$20
AZ

G7, $35-$70
Alamosa, CO

G10+, $175-$300
S.W. CO

LOCATION: Arizona and New Mexico northward. **DESCRIPTION:** A small to medium size, thin, narrow, light weight, stemmed arrow point. Stems are parallel sided to tapered to expanding. Bases are incurvate to rounded. Larger examples are dart/knives. **I.D. KEY:** Thinness and narrowness.

ROUND-BACK KNIFE - Arachaic, 8000 - 2300 B. P.

(Also see Agate Basin, Early Leaf, Lerma, Refugio)

G8, $40-$75
NW Chihuahua, Mex.,

866

G8, $35-$65
S.W. CO

Brown jasper

G8, $40-$75
NW Chihuahua, Mex.,
very thin, ground edge from use. Soto
site.

Thin

Pink jasper

G8, $85-$160
NW Chihuahua, Mex.,

LOCATION: Arizona into N.W. Chihuahua, Mexico. **DESCRIPTION:** A large size lanceolate blade with a convex base. Some examples are very thin and well made. **I.D. KEY:** Convex base.

Agate jasper

G10, $70-$135
NW Chihuahua, Mex.,
thin, Soto site.

SW

Rootbeer colored flint

G10, $100-$185
NW Chihuahua,
Mex.

ROUND-BACK KNIFE (continued)

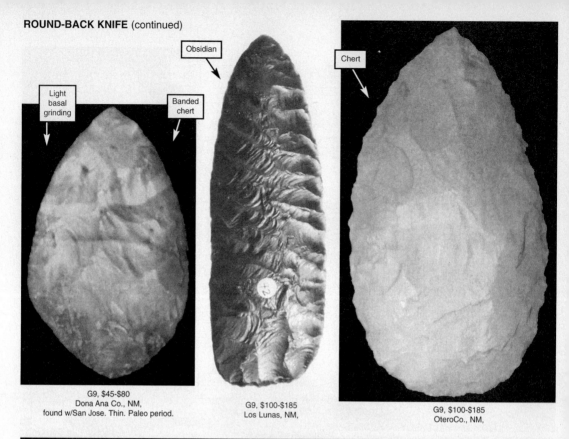

Light basal grinding

Obsidian

Banded chert

Chert

G9, $45-$80
Dona Ana Co., NM,
found w/San Jose. Thin. Paleo period.

G9, $100-$185
Los Lunas, NM,

G9, $100-$185
OteroCo., NM,

SACATON - Desert Traditions-Developmental Phase, 1100 - 900 B. P.

(Also see Desert, Dry Prong, Mimbre and Temporal)

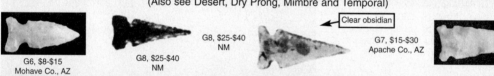

Clear obsidian

G6, $8-$15
Mohave Co., AZ

G8, $25-$40
NM

G8, $25-$40
NM

G7, $15-$30
Apache Co., AZ

LOCATION: Arizona and central and southwestern New Mexico. **DESCRIPTION:** A small, triangular arrow point with relatively large side notches placed close to the basal edge. The base is the widest part of the point and is slightly concave. **I.D. KEY:** Wide base.

SALADO - Developmental-Classic Phase, 850 - 500 B.P.

(Also see Desert, Pueblo Side Notched and Walnut Canyon Side Notched)

G6, $15-$25
Cedar Ridge, AZ

G5, $15-$25
AZ

G8, $25-$45
AZ

G8, $25-$45
AZ

G8, $25-$45
Cedar Ridge, AZ

G8, $25-$45
Cedar Ridge, AZ

G8, $25-$45
Cedar Ridge, AZ

G7, $25-$45
AZ

G8, $40-$70
AZ

G9, $35-$65
Cedar Ridge, AZ

G7, $15-$30
Cedar Ridge, AZ

G8, $25-$45
Gila River, AZ.

G6, $20-$35
AZ

LOCATION: Arizona to California. **DESCRIPTION:** A small, thin, arrow point with a straight to concave base and tiny side notches set well up from the base. Related to *Hohokam*. Given this name in Perino #3. Also known as *Pueblo Side Notched*; see Justice, 2002. **I.D. KEY:** Large basal area.

SALADO (continued)

G9, $80-$150
AZ

G7, $35-$65
AZ

G10, $80-$150
AZ

G10, $125-$200
AZ

G10, $80-$150
AZ

G9, $65-$125
AZ

G10, $90-$180
AZ

G10, $90-$180
AZ

G10, $90-$180
AZ

SALT RIVER INDENTED BASE - Developmental, 1150 - 1000 B. P.

(Also see Gila River Corner Notched, Snaketown Side Notched)

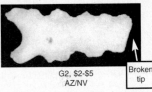

G8, $20-$35
Pima Co., AZ

Red basalt

G2, $1-$3
AZ/NV

Broken tip

G3, $2-$5
Yavapai Co., AZ

Broken tip

G2, $2-$5
AZ/NV

Broken tip

LOCATION: Arizona and New Mexico. **DESCRIPTION:** A medium size, narrow, spike, auriculate Hohokam arrow point with multiple barbs that are larger close to the base. The base is eared and deeply concave. **I.D. KEY:** Exaggerated barbs and auriculate base.

SAN BRUNO- Classic to Historic Phase, 600 - 200 B. P.

(Also see Desert, Gatlin, Gila River, Pueblo Side Notched & Rose Springs, Snaketown)

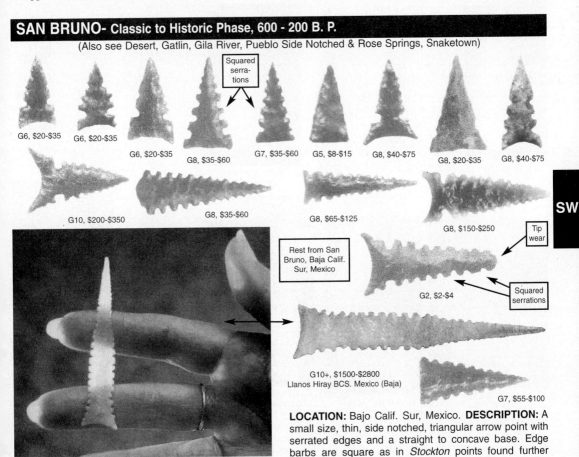

Squared serra-tions

G6, $20-$35

G6, $20-$35

G6, $20-$35

G8, $35-$60

G7, $35-$60

G5, $8-$15

G8, $40-$75

G8, $20-$35

G8, $40-$75

G10, $200-$350

G8, $35-$60

G8, $65-$125

G8, $150-$250

Tip wear

SW

Rest from San Bruno, Baja Calif. Sur, Mexico

G2, $2-$4

Squared serrations

G10+, $1500-$2800
Llanos Hiray BCS. Mexico (Baja)

G7, $55-$100

Hand held to show size and transparency

LOCATION: Bajo Calif. Sur, Mexico. **DESCRIPTION:** A small size, thin, side notched, triangular arrow point with serrated edges and a straight to concave base. Edge barbs are square as in *Stockton* points found further north. **I.D. KEY:** Square serrations.

869

SAN JOSE - Early Archaic, 9000 - 6000 B. P.

(Also see Armijo, Bajada, Baker, Barreal, Chiricahua, Duncan, Escobas, Hanna, Maljamar, Meserve, Neff, Snaketown, Soto and Uvalde)

G3, $5-$10
Yavapai Co., AZ

G3, $5-$10
NM

G5, $5-$10
Yavapai Co., AZ

Serrated edge

G6, $15-$30
Apache Co., AZ

G6, $8-$15
S. W. CO

G5, $18-$30
Otero Co., NM

Serrated edge

G9, $35-$60
Yavapai Co., AZ

Red jasper

Serrated edge

Restored tip

G7, $35-$60
Santa Fe Co., NM

G6, $15-$30
S.W. CO

G9, $30-$50
Montezuma Co., CO

G6, $35-$60
S.W. CO

G3, $12-$20
Otero Co., NM

G6, $30-$50
S.W. CO

Ground stem

Ground stem & base

Obsidian

Jasper

Serrated edge

G7, $40-$75
Otero Co., NM

G9, $125-$225
Otero Co., NM

G7, $40-$70
Luna Co., NM

G7, $40-$70
NW Chih, Mex.

G7, $35-$60
S.W. CO

G6, $30-$50
S.W. CO

Thinned base

Serrated edge

Pink jasper

Thinned base

Restored tip

Serrated edge

G10, $125-$225
Otero Co., NM

Ground stem

G10, $125-$225
Otero Co., NM

G3, $8-$15
Otero Co., NM,
ground basal area.

Ground stem

G3, $12-$20
Otero Co., NM

G10, $90-$165
S.W. CO

LOCATION: Arizona, New Mexico, sou. Utah, Nevada and Colorado. **DESCRIPTION:** A small to medium size dart/knife with wide, shallow side notches creating an auriculate base. The shoulders are obtuse and the blade edges always have relatively large serrations. Stem and base edges are usually ground. Similar to the *Barreal* point of the same age. **I.D. KEY:** Auriculate base.

SAN JOSE (continued)

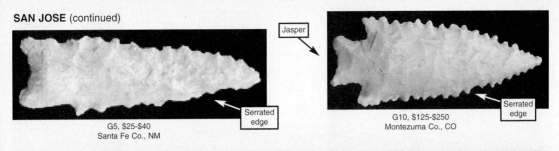

Jasper

Serrated edge

G5, $25-$40
Santa Fe Co., NM

G10, $125-$250
Montezuma Co., CO

Serrated edge

SAN PEDRO - Late Archaic, 2500 - 1800 B. P.

(Also see Black Mesa Narrow Neck, Carlsbad, Cienega, Mount Albion and Yavapai Stemmed)

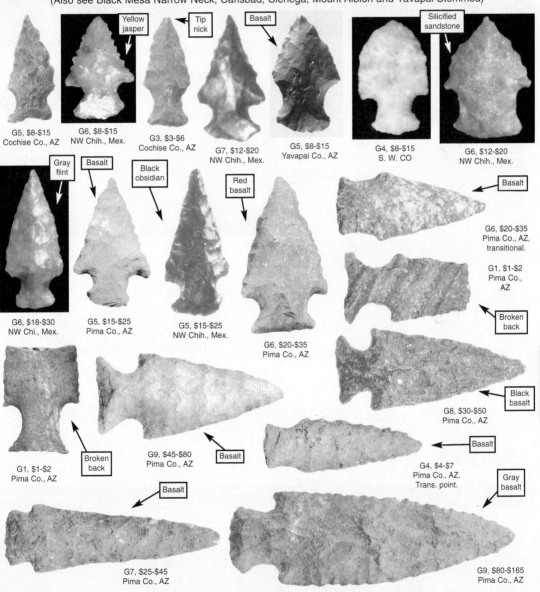

Yellow jasper

Tip nick

Basalt

Silicified sandstone

G5, $8-$15
Cochise Co., AZ

G6, $8-$15
NW Chih., Mex.

G3, $3-$6
Cochise Co., AZ

G7, $12-$20
NW Chih., Mex.

G5, $8-$15
Yavapai Co., AZ

G4, $8-$15
S. W. CO

G6, $12-$20
NW Chih., Mex.

Gray flint

Basalt

Black obsidian

Red basalt

Basalt

G6, $20-$35
Pima Co., AZ,
transitional.

G1, $1-$2
Pima Co.,
AZ

Broken back

G6, $18-$30
NW Chi., Mex.

G5, $15-$25
Pima Co., AZ

G5, $15-$25
NW Chih., Mex.

G6, $20-$35
Pima Co., AZ

Black basalt

G8, $30-$50
Pima Co., AZ

Broken back

G9, $45-$80
Pima Co., AZ

Basalt

Basalt

G1, $1-$2
Pima Co., AZ

G4, $4-$7
Pima Co., AZ.
Trans. point.

Gray basalt

Basalt

G7, $25-$45
Pima Co., AZ

G9, $80-$165
Pima Co., AZ

SW

LOCATION: New Mexico, Arizona and northern Mexico. **DESCRIPTION:** A small to medium sized dart/knife made on a triangular preform and having side notches which begin at the basal corners and range from shallow to as deep as wide. Blade edges may be lightly serrated and the basal edge is straight to slightly convex. This type has been found hafted to foreshafts with sinew and pitch in Utah and New Mexico.

SAN PEDRO (continued)

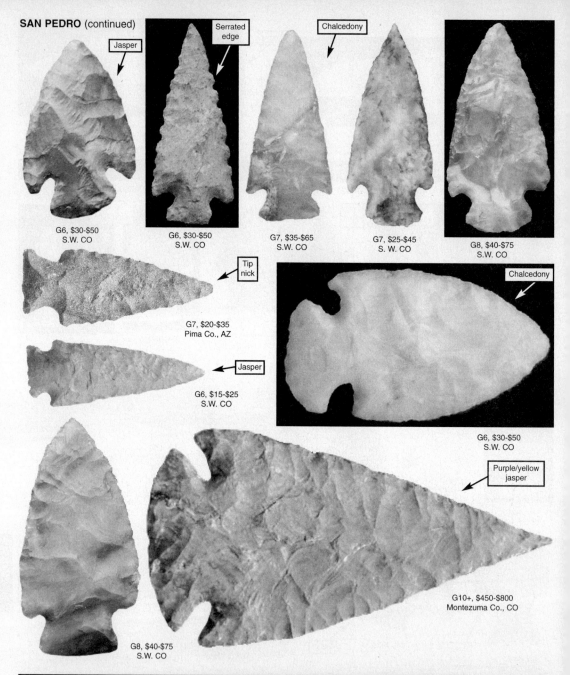

Jasper

Serrated edge

Chalcedony

G6, $30-$50
S.W. CO

G6, $30-$50
S.W. CO

G7, $35-$65
S.W. CO

G7, $25-$45
S. W. CO

G8, $40-$75
S.W. CO

Tip nick

G7, $20-$35
Pima Co., AZ

Chalcedony

Jasper

G6, $15-$25
S.W. CO

G6, $30-$50
S.W. CO

Purple/yellow jasper

G8, $40-$75
S.W. CO

G10+, $450-$800
Montezuma Co., CO

SAN RAFAEL - Middle Archaic, 4,400 - 3500 B. P.

(Also see Frio, Martis, Northern Side Notched and Ventana Side Notched)

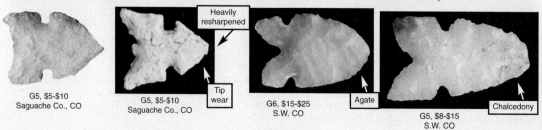

G5, $5-$10
Saguache Co., CO

Heavily resharpened

Tip wear

G5, $5-$10
Saguache Co., CO

G6, $15-$25
S.W. CO

Agate

Chalcedony

G5, $8-$15
S.W. CO

SAN RAFAEL (continued)

LOCATION: Utah, Colorado into Arizona. **DESCRIPTION:** A medium size, broad, side-notched point with usually a deeply concave to eared base. Some examples include a small notch at the center of the basal concavity. Side Notches occur high up from the base and the cross section is very thin. **I.D. KEY:** High-up side notches, eared base, thinness.

G10, $175-$300
S.W. CO

SANDIA I-III - Paleo, 11,500? - 10,000 B. P.

(Also see Clovis, Folsom and Madden Lake)

Fluted with single shoulder

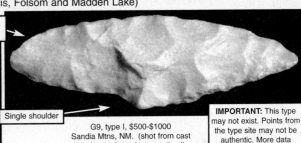

Convex base

Single shoulder

G9, type III, $750-$1500
Sandia Mtns, NM. (shot from cast of real point from the type site)

G9, type I, $500-$1000
Sandia Mtns, NM. (shot from cast of real point from the type site discovered between 1936 and 1940)

IMPORTANT: This type may not exist. Points from the type site may not be authentic. More data needed.

Base nick

G6, type II, $350-$700
Sandia Mtns, NM.
(shot from cast of real point from the type site)

LOCATION: Type site is Sandia Mtns., New Mexico, south of Albuquerque. **DESCRIPTION:** This point occurs in three forms: The first form is a narrow, elliptical shape with only one shoulder and a rounded base. The second form has a slightly concave base, otherwise it is the same as the first form. The third form has a deeply concave base with drooping auricles. This, as well as the second form, have been found fluted on one or both faces. This type is extremely rare everywhere and may be later than *Clovis*. Another site with datable contex has not yet been found. Originally (questionably?) carbon dated to 20,000 B.P. **I.D. KEY:** Single shoulder.

SANDIA IV - Paleo, 11,500? - 10,000 B. P.

(Also see Clovis and Folsom)

Fluting channel

Ground basal area

G9, $700-$1300
Colfax Co., NM.

LOCATION: Type site is Sandia Mtns., New Mexico, south of Albuquerque. **DESCRIPTION:** This authenticated point is very thin, single shouldered and fluted on both sides. Percussion flaked with fine pressure flaking. Basal area is ground. The classic *Sandia* form, but is thinner and better made than Sandia I points which lack the fine pressure flaking. **I.D. KEY:** Single shoulder, fine retouch.

SANTA CRUZ -Desert Traditions-Developmental Phase, 1400-600 B. P.

(Also see Augustin, Gypsum Cave, Hodges Contr. Stem, Manzano and Truxton)

White chert

G7, $25-$40
Apache Co., AZ

G5 $8-$15
Cochise Co., AZ

G5, $12-$20
Coconino Co., AZ

G3, $2-$5
Cochise Co., AZ

G3, $2-$5
Apache Co., AZ

G5, $12-$20
Tucson, AZ

G3, $2-$5
Mohave Co., AZ

G5, $8-$15
Apache Co., AZ

LOCATION: Arizona and contiguous parts of adjoining states. **DESCRIPTION:** A small, triangular arrow point with straight to obtuse shoulders and a short, tapering stem. These may prove to be small *Hodges Contracting Stem* points. **I.D. KEY:** Tiny, triangular stem.

(Also see Drill, Perforator, Scraper)

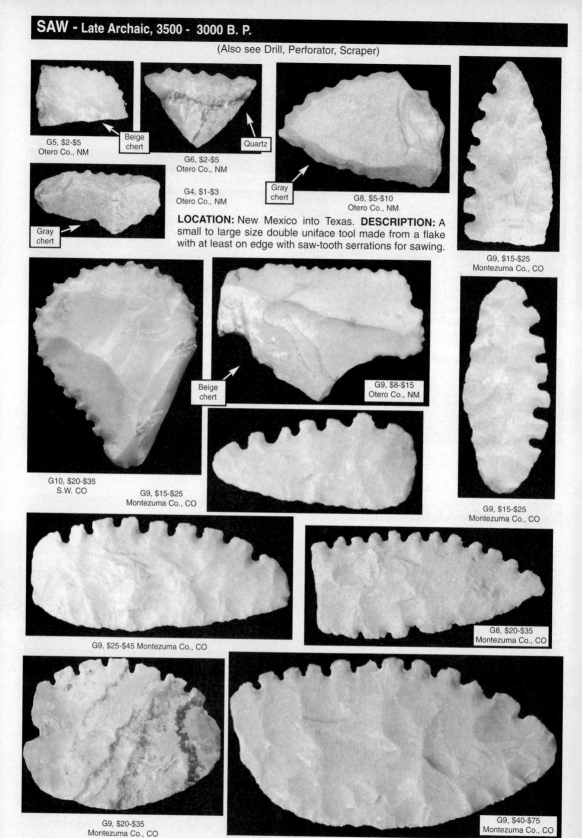

G5, $2-$5
Otero Co., NM

Beige chert

Quartz

G6, $2-$5
Otero Co., NM

G4, $1-$3
Otero Co., NM

Gray chert

G8, $5-$10
Otero Co., NM

Gray chert

LOCATION: New Mexico into Texas. **DESCRIPTION:** A small to large size double uniface tool made from a flake with at least on edge with saw-tooth serrations for sawing.

G9, $15-$25
Montezuma Co., CO

Beige chert

G9, $8-$15
Otero Co., NM

G10, $20-$35
S.W. CO

G9, $15-$25
Montezuma Co., CO

G9, $15-$25
Montezuma Co., CO

G9, $25-$45 Montezuma Co., CO

G8, $20-$35
Montezuma Co., CO

G9, $20-$35
Montezuma Co., CO

G9, $40-$75
Montezuma Co., CO

SCOTTSBLUFF II - Early Archaic, 9500 - 8500 B. P.

(Also see Bajada, Eden and Firstview)

LOCATION: Midwestern states. **DESCRIPTION:** A medium to large size triangular point with shoulders a little stronger than on Type I and a broad parallel sided/expanding stem.

G5, $175-$300
Montezuma co., CO

Red jasper

Note parallel flaking

G8, $900-$1600, Taos, NM

SCRAPER- Archaic, 8000 - 2300 B. P.

(Also see Drill, Lancet and Saw)

All NM & TX Thumb scrapers found on a Folsom site

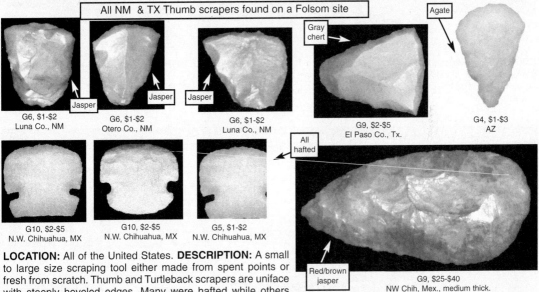

Agate

Gray chert

Jasper

Jasper

Jasper

G6, $1-$2
Luna Co., NM

G6, $1-$2
Otero Co., NM

G6, $1-$2
Luna Co., NM

G9, $2-$5
El Paso Co., Tx.

G4, $1-$3
AZ

All hafted

G10, $2-$5
N.W. Chihuahua, MX

G10, $2-$5
N.W. Chihuahua, MX

G5, $1-$2
N.W. Chihuahua, MX

Red/brown jasper

G9, $25-$40
NW Chih, Mex., medium thick.

SW

LOCATION: All of the United States. **DESCRIPTION:** A small to large size scraping tool either made from spent points or fresh from scratch. Thumb and Turtleback scrapers are uniface with steeply beveled edges. Many were hafted while others were hand-held in use.

SHUMLA - Woodland, 3000 - 1000 B. P.

(Also see Acatita, Marshall, Parowan)

G6, $15-$25
San Luis Potosi, MX

LOCATION: Northern Mexico to Oklahoma. **DESCRIPTION:** A small size, basal notched point with convex, straight or recurved sides. Basal corners can be rounded to sharp. Bases are straight to slightly convex. Barbs turn in towards and usually extend to the base. Related to *Acatita* in Mexico?

SILVER LAKE- Early Archaic, 11,000 - 7000 B. P.

(Also see Early Stemmed, Firstview, Lake Mohave and Yavapai)

G9, $85-$150
Yavapai Co., AZ

G6, $30-$50
NV

LOCATION: Arizona, Nevada to California. **DESCRIPTION:** A medium to large size, stemmed point with weak, tapered shoulders and usually a serrated edge. The stem can be up to half its length. The base is usually rounded and ground. **I.D. KEY:** Long stem, weak shoulders.

SNAKETOWN-Desert Traditions-Developmental Phase, 1200-1050 B. P.

(Also see Gila River, Hodges Contracting Stem and Salt River Indented Base)

G10, $125-$225
Kearny, AZ

Serrated edge

LOCATION: Arizona. **DESCRIPTION:** A very rare, form of *Hohokam* arrow point. The stem is straight to expanded and sometimes concave to bifurcated and has large serrations on both sides of the blade. Some examples are serrated on the lower half of the point. **I.D. KEY:** Narrowness, length, broad serrations.

SNAKETOWN SIDE NOTCHED - Dev.-Classic Phase, 800-600 B. P.

(Also see Bonito Notched, Gatlin, Gila River, Pueblo Side Notched)

G6, $5-$10
Yavapai Co., AZ

G5, $12-$20
Apache Co., AZ

G9, $25-$45
Pima Co., AZ

G6, $15-$30
Apache Co., AZ

G9, $35-$50
Yavapai Co., AZ

LOCATION: Southern California into Arizona and New Mexico. **DESCRIPTION:** A small, serrated, side notched, *Hohokam* triangular arrow point with a concave to straight base. Basal corners are wide and rounded. Notches are broad. **I.D. KEY:** Broad notches.

G6 $15-$30
S. W. CO

SNAKETOWN TRIANGULAR - Developmental Phase, 1050-850 B. P.

(Also see Bull Creek, Salt River Indented Base, Sobaipuri, Soto)

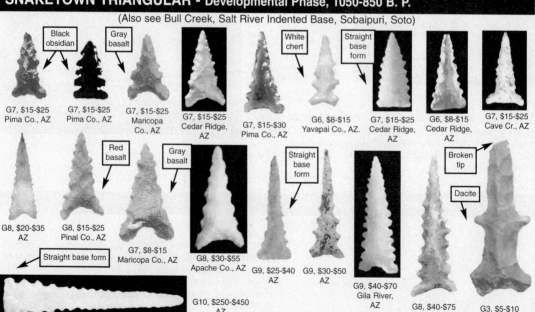

Black obsidian

Gray basalt

White chert

Straight base form

G7, $15-$25
Pima Co., AZ

G7, $15-$25
Pima Co., AZ

G7, $15-$25
Maricopa Co., AZ

G7, $15-$25
Cedar Ridge, AZ

G7, $15-$30
Pima Co., AZ

G6, $8-$15
Yavapai Co., AZ.

G7, $15-$25
Cedar Ridge, AZ

G6, $8-$15
Cedar Ridge, AZ

G7, $15-$25
Cave Cr., AZ

Red basalt

Gray basalt

Straight base form

Broken tip

Dacite

G8, $20-$35
AZ

G8, $15-$25
Pinal Co., AZ

G7, $8-$15
Maricopa Co., AZ

G8, $30-$55
Apache Co., AZ

G9, $25-$40
AZ

G9, $30-$50
AZ

G9, $40-$70
Gila River, AZ

G8, $40-$75
Pima Co., AZ

G3, $5-$10
AZ

Straight base form

G10, $250-$450
AZ

SNAKETOWN TRIANGULAR (continued)

G7, $15-$30
Cedar Ridge, AZ

G10, $25-$40, Pinal Co., AZ

White chert

LOCATION: Southern California into Arizona and New Mexico. **DESCRIPTION:** A small, serrated, triangular *Hohokam* arrow point with a concave to straight base. Made by the Hohokam people. **I.D. KEY:** Wild barbs.

SOBAIPURI - Classic to Historic Phase, 500 - 200 B. P.

(Also see Aguaje, Bull Creek, Cottonwood, Salt River Indented Base and Snaketown)

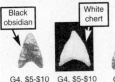

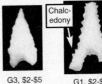

Black obsidian

White chert

Chalcedony

Gray basalt

White chert

G4, $5-$10
Maricopa Co., AZ

G4, $5-$10
Maricopa Co., AZ

G3, $2-$5
Maricopa Co., AZ

G3, $2-$5
Maricopa Co., AZ

G6, $5-$10
Maricopa Co., AZ

G3, $2-$5
Pima Co., AZ

G1, $2-$4
Maricopa Co., AZ

G7, $12-$20
Pima Co., AZ

G6, $8-$15
Pinal Co., AZ

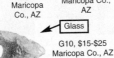

White chert

G6, $12-$20
Maricopa Co., AZ

Glass

G10, $15-$25
Maricopa Co., AZ

G10, $8-$15
Maricopa Co., AZ

G10, $8-$15
Maricopa Co., AZ

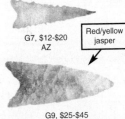

Green glass

Chalcedony

White chert

Red/yellow jasper

G7, $12-$20
AZ

G5, $2-$5
Maricopa Co., AZ

G1, $12-$20
Pinal Co., AZ

G7, $15-$35
Maricopa Co., AZ

G10, $15-$25
Maricopa Co., AZ

G6, $5-$10
Maricopa Co., AZ

G8, $20-$35
Maricopa Co., AZ

G8, $15-$25
AZ

G9, $25-$45
Pima Co., AZ, diagonal flaking.

LOCATION: Southern Arizona, New Mexico and northern Mexico. **DESCRIPTION:** A small triangular, finely serrated, arrow point with convex sides and a deep, concave basal notch. **I.D. KEY:** Small triangular point with serrations.

SOCORRO - Late Archaic, 3000 B. P.

(Also see Acatita, Cienega and Gobernadora, Yavapai)

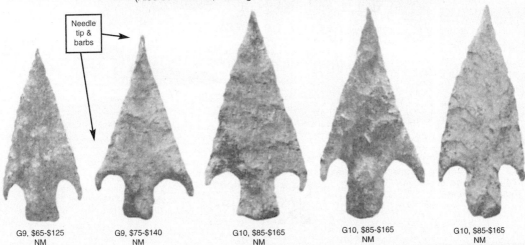

Needle tip & barbs

G9, $65-$125
NM

G9, $75-$140
NM

G10, $85-$165
NM

G10, $85-$165
NM

G10, $85-$165
NM

LOCATION: Northern Mexico into New Mexico. **DESCRIPTION:** A medium size dart/knife point with a long needle tip and sharp, drooping barbs that can turn inward. Stems are generally long and expanding to slightly contracting with a straight to bulbous base.

SW

SOTO- Classic Phase to Early Historic, 1000-700 B. P.

(Also see Awatovi, Del Carmen, Garza, Pueblo Side Notched, San Jose and Toyah)

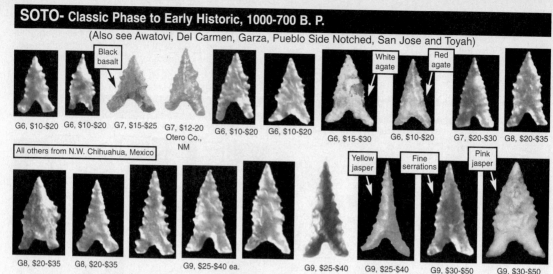

Black basalt

White agate

Red agate

G6, $10-$20   G6, $10-$20   G7, $15-$25   G7, $12-20 Otero Co., NM   G6, $10-$20   G6, $10-$20   G6, $15-$30   G6, $10-$20   G7, $20-$30   G8, $20-$35

All others from N.W. Chihuahua, Mexico

Yellow jasper   Fine serrations   Pink jasper

G8, $20-$35   G8, $20-$35   G9, $25-$40 ea.   G9, $25-$40   G9, $25-$40   G9, $30-$50   G9, $30-$50

LOCATION: NW Chihuahua Mexico. **DESCRIPTION:** A small, serrated arrow point with expanding ears, weak shoulders and a concave base. Most are made of agate and jasper. Similar to Garza & Toyah. Named by Alan Phelps. **I.D. KEY:** Thinness, drooping ears.

SQUAW MOUNTAIN - Middle Archaic, 5000 - 3000 B. P.

(Also see Barreal, Chiricahua, Hanna, San Jose & Ventana Side Notched)

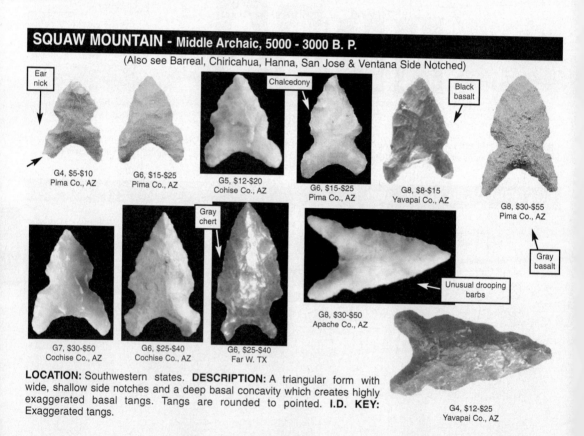

Ear nick

Chalcedony

Black basalt

G4, $5-$10 Pima Co., AZ   G6, $15-$25 Pima Co., AZ   G5, $12-$20 Cohise Co., AZ   G6, $15-$25 Pima Co., AZ   G8, $8-$15 Yavapai Co., AZ

G8, $30-$55 Pima Co., AZ

Gray chert

Gray basalt

Unusual drooping barbs

G8, $30-$50 Apache Co., AZ

G7, $30-$50 Cochise Co., AZ   G6, $25-$40 Cochise Co., AZ   G6, $25-$40 Far W. TX

G4, $12-$25 Yavapai Co., AZ

LOCATION: Southwestern states. **DESCRIPTION:** A triangular form with wide, shallow side notches and a deep basal concavity which creates highly exaggerated basal tangs. Tangs are rounded to pointed. **I.D. KEY:** Exaggerated tangs.

SUDDEN SERIES - Early to Mid Archaic, 6300 - 4180 B. P.

(Also see Northern Side Notch, San Rafael & Ventana Side Notched)

SUDDEN SERIES (continued)

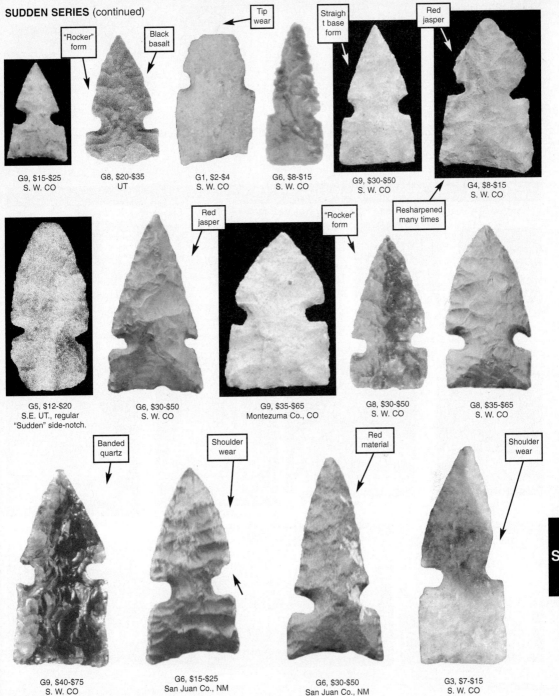

"Rocker" form

Black basalt

Tip wear

Straight base form

Red jasper

G9, $15-$25
S. W. CO

G8, $20-$35
UT

G1, $2-$4
S. W. CO

G6, $8-$15
S. W. CO

G9, $30-$50
S. W. CO

G4, $8-$15
S. W. CO

Resharpened many times

Red jasper

"Rocker" form

G5, $12-$20
S.E. UT., regular
"Sudden" side-notch.

G6, $30-$50
S. W. CO

G9, $35-$65
Montezuma Co., CO

G8, $30-$50
S. W. CO

G8, $35-$65
S. W. CO

Banded quartz

Shoulder wear

Red material

Shoulder wear

SW

G9, $40-$75
S. W. CO

G6, $15-$25
San Juan Co., NM

G6, $30-$50
San Juan Co., NM

G3, $7-$15
S. W. CO

LOCATION: SE Utah, SW colorado into Arizona. **DESCRIPTION:** A medium size side notched dart/knife point that comes in two forms. Side notches are high up from the base. The regular form has a large basal area and a straight to concave base. The "Rocker" form has a convex base.

TEMPORAL - Desert Traditions-Developmental Phase, 1000 - 800 B. P.

(Also see Bonito Notched, Desert, Dry Prong and Sacaton)

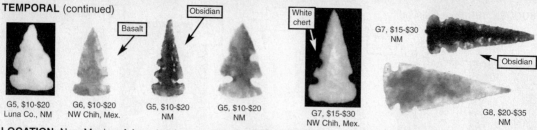

TEMPORAL (continued)

Basalt

Obsidian

White chert

G7, $15-$30
NM

Obsidian

G5, $10-$20
Luna Co., NM

G6, $10-$20
NW Chih, Mex.

G5, $10-$20
NM

G5, $10-$20
NM

G7, $15-$30
NW Chih, Mex.

G8, $20-$35
NM

LOCATION: New Mexico, Arizona and western Texas. **DESCRIPTION:** A small side notched arrow point with one or two extra notches on one side. It is triangular with straight sides and a convex basal edge. Notches are narrow and deeper than they are wide. **I.D. KEY:** Rounded or rocker like basal edge.

TEXCOCO - Late Archaic, 6000 - 5000 B.P.

(Also see Elko Corner Notched, Mount Albion and San Pedro)

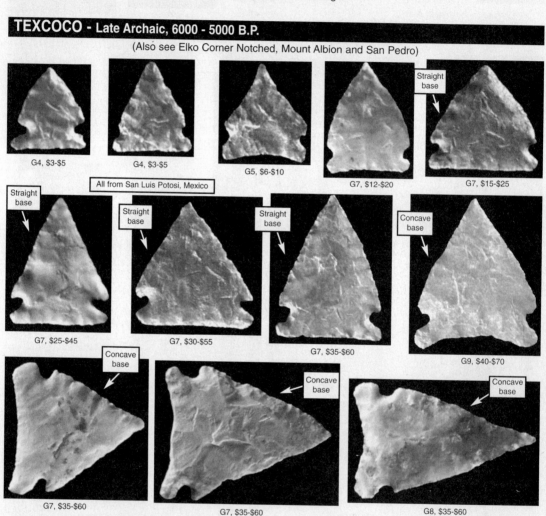

G4, $3-$5

G4, $3-$5

G5, $6-$10

All from San Luis Potosi, Mexico

Straight base

G7, $12-$20

G7, $15-$25

Straight base

G7, $25-$45

Straight base

G7, $30-$55

Straight base

G7, $35-$60

Concave base

G9, $40-$70

Concave base

G7, $35-$60

Concave base

G7, $35-$60

Concave base

G8, $35-$60

LOCATION: Central Mexico. **DESCRIPTION:** A triangular, wide based, thin, flat, corner to side notched point. The base is straight to concave. **I.D. KEY:** Width and thinness.

TORTUGAS - Middle Archaic to Woodland, 6000 - 1000 B. P.

(Also see Kinney, Early Triangular, Matamoros, Mescal & Trangular Knife)

LOCATION: New Mexico, Northern Mexico, Oklahoma to Tennessee. **DESCRIPTION:** A medium size, fairly thick, triangular point with straight to convex sides and base. Some examples are beveled on one side of each face. Bases are usually thinned. Smaller examples would fall in the *Matamoros* type.

TORTUGAS (continued)

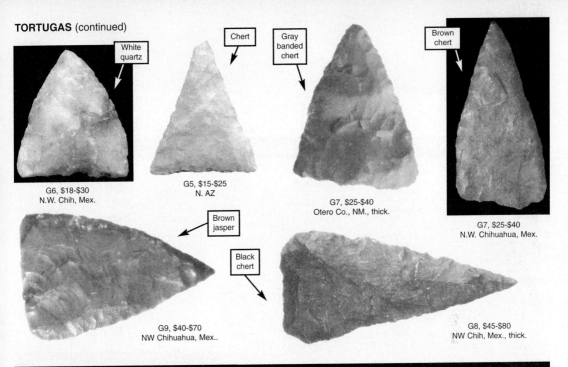

White quartz

G6, $18-$30
N.W. Chih, Mex.

Chert

G5, $15-$25
N. AZ

Gray banded chert

G7, $25-$40
Otero Co., NM., thick.

Brown chert

G7, $25-$40
N.W. Chihuahua, Mex.

Brown jasper

Black chert

G9, $40-$70
NW Chihuahua, Mex..

G8, $45-$80
NW Chih, Mex., thick.

TOYAH- Desert Traditions-Late Classic Phase, 600 - 400 B. P.

(Also see Awatovi Side Notched, Del Carmen, Desert , Pueblo Side notched and Soto)

G5, $5-$10
S.W. CO

G9, $25-$45
W. TX

LOCATION: Western Texas. **DESCRIPTION:** A small triangular arrow point with straight blade edges, side notches, and a concave base which often has a further central notch. Variations of this point may have multiple sets of side notches.

TRADE - Historic, 400 - 170 B. P.

(Also see Glass)

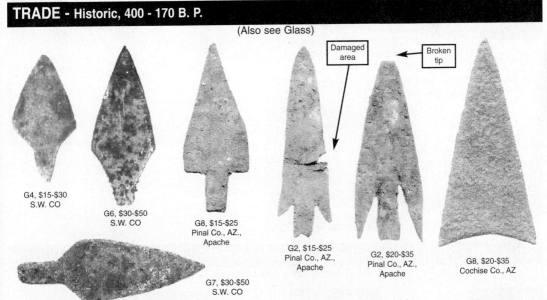

G4, $15-$30
S.W. CO

G6, $30-$50
S.W. CO

G8, $15-$25
Pinal Co., AZ.,
Apache

Damaged area

Broken tip

G7, $30-$50
S.W. CO

G2, $15-$25
Pinal Co., AZ.,
Apache

G2, $20-$35
Pinal Co., AZ.,
Apache

G8, $20-$35
Cochise Co., AZ

LOCATION: All over North America. **DESCRIPTION:** These points were made of copper, iron, and steel and were traded to the Indians by the French, British and others from the 1600s to the 1800s. Examples have been found all over the United States.

SW

G8, $40-$70
S.W. CO

G8, $80-$150
S.W. CO

TRIANGULAR KNIFE - Late Archaic, 3500 - 2300 B. P.

(Also see Early Triangular, Matamoros and Mescal Knife)

Gray chert

Brown chert

Beveled all four edges

Yellow jasper

G7, $10-$20
Otero Co., NM, thin.

G7, $15-$25
N. AZ

G8, $25-$40
Otero Co., NM, thin.

G9, $40-$70
NW Chih., Mex.

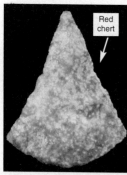

Red chert

G7, $25-$40
N.W. Chih., Mex.

G8, $35-$60
Otero Co., NM

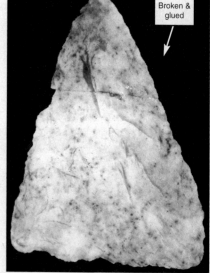

Broken & glued

LOCATION: Northwestern Arizona and, possibly, into adjacent areas of contiguous states. **DESCRIPTION:** A large, asymmetrical to triangular knife form which may have been hafted horizontally. The blade is very thin and flat for its size.

G6, $25-$40
Mohave Co., AZ

G2, $2-$5
Mohave Co., AZ

TRUXTON - Desert Traditions-Developmental Phase, 1500 - 1000 B. P.

(Also see Duran, Hodges, Maljamar and Santa Cruz)

G4, $6-$12
Mohave Co., AZ

G4, $8-$15
Mohave Co., AZ

G6, $25-$40
Mohave Co., AZ

TRUXTON (continued)

G5, $12-$25
Mohave Co., AZ

G4, $8-$15
Mohave Co., AZ

G4, $5-$10
Navajo Co., AZ

LOCATION: Northern Arizona and possibly into adjacent states. **DESCRIPTION:** A small arrow point with a short stem, most often with a convex basal edge. The central portion of the blade has multiple notches and the tip of the blade is straight-sided converging to a sharply pointed tip.

TULAROSA CORNER NATCHED (see Cienega)

UVALDE - Middle Archaic to Woodland, 6000 - 1500 B. P.

(Also see Frio, Hanna, San Jose and Zephyr)

G10 $275-$500
Otero Co., NM

LOCATION: Texas to Oklahoma and New Mexico. **DESCRIPTION:** A medium size, bifurcated stemmed point with barbed to tapered shoulders. Some examples are serrated. The *Frio* point is similar but is usually broader and the ears flare outward more than this type. **I.D. KEY:** Narrow bifurcated stem.

VENTANA-AMARGOSA - Early Archaic, 7000 - 5000 B. P.

(Also see Yavapai Stemmed)

Obsidian

Rhyolite

G3, $3-$6
Cochise Co., AZ

G6, $12-$20
NW Chihuahua, Mex.

G5, $8-$15
Yavapai Co., AZ

G6, $20-$35
Pima Co., AZ

G6, $20-$35
Pima Co., AZ

G5, $10-$20
Coconino Co., AZ

SW

G4, $5-$10
Yavapai Co., AZ

LOCATION: Arizona and contiguous parts of adjacent states. **DESCRIPTION:** A small to medium sized dart/knife with a triangular blade with straight to slightly convex edges and straight to angular shoulders. The stem is parallel sided and rectangular to square. The basal edge is straight to rounded. **I.D. KEY:** A very square appearing stem.

VENTANA SIDE NOTCHED - Mid-Archaic, 5500 - 4800 B. P.

(Also see Basketmaker, Northern Side Notched, San Rafael, Sudden)

Yellow jasper

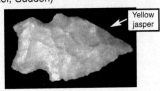

Black obsidian

G4, $3-$6
Sou. NM

G6, $5-$10
S. W. CO

G6, $5-$10
S. W. CO

G6, $8-$15
NW Chuahua, Mex.,
not ground

883

VENTANA SIDE NOTCHED (continued)

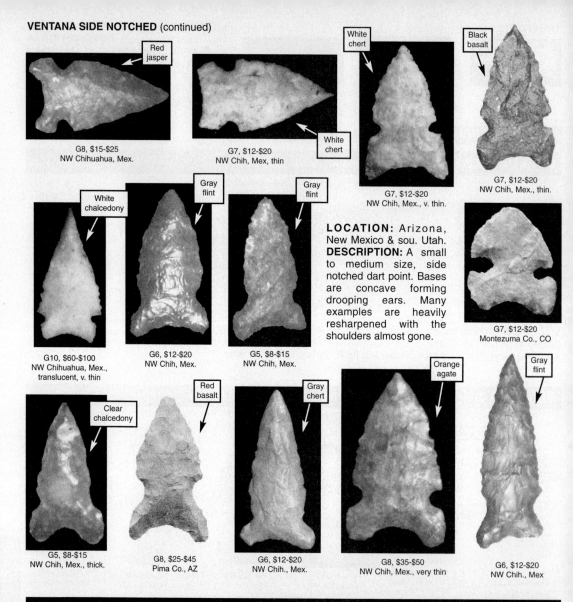

Red jasper

G8, $15-$25
NW Chihuahua, Mex.

White chert

G7, $12-$20
NW Chih, Mex, thin

White chert

G7, $12-$20
NW Chih, Mex., v. thin.

Black basalt

G7, $12-$20
NW Chih, Mex., thin.

White chalcedony

Gray flint

Gray flint

G10, $60-$100
NW Chihuahua, Mex.,
translucent, v. thin

G6, $12-$20
NW Chih, Mex.

G5, $8-$15
NW Chih, Mex.

LOCATION: Arizona, New Mexico & sou. Utah. **DESCRIPTION:** A small to medium size, side notched dart point. Bases are concave forming drooping ears. Many examples are heavily resharpened with the shoulders almost gone.

G7, $12-$20
Montezuma Co., CO

Clear chalcedony

Red basalt

Gray chert

Orange agate

Gray flint

G5, $8-$15
NW Chih, Mex., thick.

G8, $25-$45
Pima Co., AZ

G6, $12-$20
NW Chih., Mex.

G8, $35-$50
NW Chih, Mex., very thin

G6, $12-$20
NW Chih., Mex

WALNUT CANYON SIDE NOTCHED - Dev. to Classic Phase 850 - 700 B. P.

(Also see Awatovi Side Notched, Desert, Gatlin Side Notched, Point Of Pines, Pueblo Side Notched & Salado)

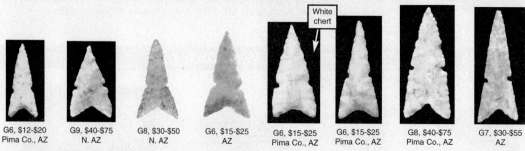

White chert

G6, $12-$20
Pima Co., AZ

G9, $40-$75
N. AZ

G8, $30-$50
N. AZ

G6, $15-$25
AZ

G6, $15-$25
Pima Co., AZ

G6, $15-$25
Pima Co., AZ

G8, $40-$75
Pima Co., AZ

G7, $30-$55
AZ

LOCATION: Arizona into New Mexico. **DESCRIPTION:** A small, narrow, side notched, triangular *Hohokam* arrow point with a deeply concave base. Notches occur high up from the base below mid-section. Basal corners are rounded to sharp. **I.D. KEY:** Narrowness and large basal area.

WALNUT CANYON SIDE NOTCHED (continued)

Agate

G9, $65-$125
AZ

G10, $100-$195
AZ

G10, $125-$225
AZ

G10, $125-$200
AZ

G10, $125-$200
AZ

G10, $125-$200
AZ

G10, $125-$200
Cedar Ridge, AZ

WHITE MOUNTAIN SIDE NOTCHED - Classic-Historic, 600 - 200 B. P.

(Also see Del Carmen, Desert and Rose Springs Side Notched)

LOCATION: Most of Arizona, southern New Mexico, S.W. Texas and northern Mexico. **DESCRIPTION:** A small, triangular arrow point with a deep basal notch and multiple side notches, most often with two pairs of side notches but examples with three pairs are not uncommon. Blade edges are generally straight. **I.D. KEY:** Multiple side notches.

G6, $12-$25
Navajo Co., AZ

G8, $25-$50
Navajo Co., AZ

YAVAPAI - Late Archaic to Transitional, 3300 - 1000 B. P.

(Also see Darl, Ventana-Amargosa)

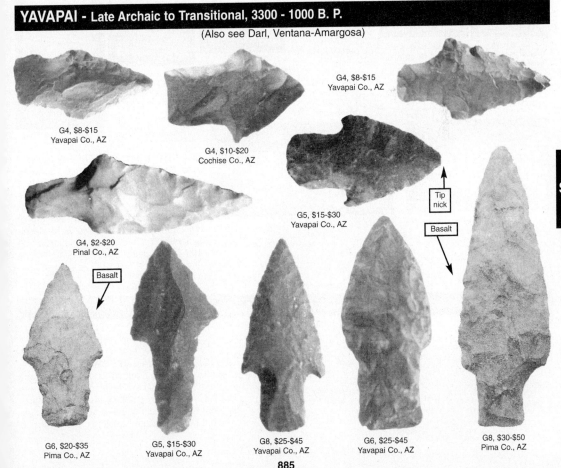

G4, $8-$15
Yavapai Co., AZ

G4, $10-$20
Cochise Co., AZ

G4, $8-$15
Yavapai Co., AZ

G4, $2-$20
Pinal Co., AZ

G5, $15-$30
Yavapai Co., AZ

Tip nick

Basalt

Basalt

G6, $20-$35
Pima Co., AZ

G5, $15-$30
Yavapai Co., AZ

G8, $25-$45
Yavapai Co., AZ

G6, $25-$45
Yavapai Co., AZ

G8, $30-$50
Pima Co., AZ

SW

885

YAVAPAI (continued)

Basalt

G7, $45-$85
Pima Co., AZ, torque blade.

LOCATION: Arizona and contiguous areas of adjacent states. **DESCRIPTION:** A medium sized dart point with a triangular blade and obtuse to lightly barbed shoulders. The stem is rectangular to slightly tapering or slightly expanding and longer than wide. The basal edge is straight to slightly concave or convex. **I.D. KEY:** Stem longer than wide.

ZEPHYR - Early Archaic, 9000 - 6000 B. P.

(Formerly Lampasos; also see San Jose and Uvalde)

White chert

Restored tip

Brown jasper

Jasper

Brown jasper

Restored tip

Red jasper

G2, $8-$15
Otero Co., NM,
ground basal area,
serrated.

G3, $12-$20
Otero Co., NM,
ground basal area, serrated.

G9, $60-$115
S.W. CO

G8, $60-$115
Otero Co., NM,
ground basal area

G3, $15-$30
NW Chih, Mex.
red jasper. ground basal
area, serrated.

Serrated edge

Jasper

White chert

Chalcedony

G10, $200-$350
S.W. CO

G7, $40-$75
Otero Co., NM,
ground basal area, serrated.

G9, $85-$165
Otero Co., NM,
ground basal area, serrated.

LOCATION: Texas. **DESCRIPTION:** A medium to large size, narrow, serrated point with square to tapered, barbed shoulders and an eared base. Blade edges are beveled on one side of each face on resharpened forms. Flaking is of high quality. These points were classified with *Darl* in the past. Also known as *Mahomet* locally. **I.D. KEY:** Fishtail base and serrations.

ZORRA - Middle Archaic, 6000 - 4000 B. P.

(See Augustin, Gypsum Cave, Yavapai)

Basalt

G8, $25-$40
W. TX

LOCATION: Texas. **DESCRIPTION:** A medium to large size point with tapered shoulders and stem that is usually flat on one face and beveled on both sides ot the opposite face. Most have needle tips and good quality flaking. **I.D. KEY:** Base beveling.

NORTHERN HIGH PLAINS SECTION:

This section includes point types from the following states:
Colorado, Idaho, Kansas, Montana, Nebraska, North Dakota,
South Dakota, Utah and Wyoming

The points in this section are arranged in alphabetical order and are shown **actual size**. All types are listed that were available for photographing. Any missing types will be added to future editions as photographs become available. We are always interested in receiving sharp, black and white or color glossy photos, color slides or high resolution (300 pixels/inch) digital pictures of your collection. Be sure to include a ruler in the photograph so that proper scale can be determined.

Lithics: Materials employed in the manufacture of projectile points from this region are: agate, basalt, chert, Dendritic chert, Flat Top chert, Flint, Knife River flint, obsidian, petrified wood, porcelanite, siltstone, Swan River chert and quartzite.

Regional Consultant:
John Byrd

Special Advisors:
Jerry Cubbuck, Jeb Taylor, Greg Truesdell

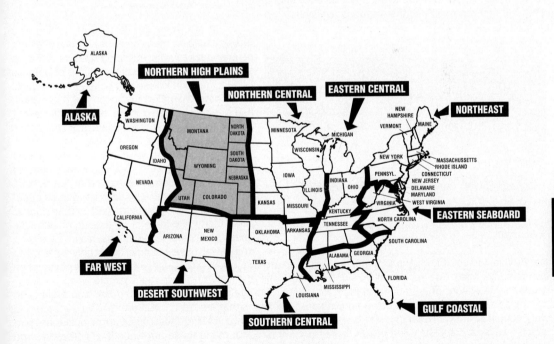

NP

887

HUNTING THE BUFFALO JUMPS
By John Byrd

Throughout all of the 14,000 plus years that prehistoric peoples lived in the geographical area now known as Montana, hunting has been the primary subsistence base. The open prairie grass lands and abundant water found in the eastern three quarters of this region provided an ideal habitat for all manner of grazing herd animals. Chief among these were the bison and later the buffalo, both of which were favorite prey for these early hunters.

To a limited degree, mass kills of these herds by coordinated communal hunting techniques were employed from the earliest of times. However, the sheer number of these kill sites dramatically increased around 1,200 to 1,300 years ago. Interestingly enough, this fits the time period when the bow and arrow technology was replacing the atlatl and a number of these kill sites will show evidence of use with both weapon types. The systematic use of this hunting method continued up until the 1600s when horses finally became readily available to the Indian population.

The technique employed was usually very similar from one location to another. Small groups of between 10 and 100 animals were gathered from their grazing areas or intercepted going to or from water. They were then driven or stampeded to the site chosen as the kill area (no small task given the nature of these animals). This actual kill would either be a low cliff 10 to 50 feet high or more frequently a steep bank or low lying depression. In the later cases, a stout corral was built to contain the herd long enough to complete the slaughter. The intent was not necessarily to kill the animals from the drop over a cliff or down a bank, but rather to injure them severely enough that they were easier to kill with the weapons available.

Digging in the bone beds of this Montana Buffalo Jump has yielded many fine projectile points.

In efficiency, this method of hunting was unsurpassed for many centuries. These sites are usually packed with multiple layers of bone as silent testimony to the sheer volume of animals killed. One such kill site had bone forty feet thick, and it was estimated that over 400,000 buffalo had been slaughtered there. Some of the especially strategic sites were used over thousands of years.

Of course, to kill these creatures a vast number of projectiles were used and many of these were either lost, damaged or left behind. Since the 1930s these kill sites have been popular locations for collectors and archaeologists alike. Many hundreds of thousands of projectile points have been found and placed in collections from what have become commonly referred to

Example of Buffalo Jump located in Montana. Animals were driven over this cliff for slaughter.

as "Buffalo Jumps". The highest percentage of these are true arrow points rather than the dart points used by the earlier atlatl. The very small size of these "arrowheads" is surprising to many people when considering the large stature of the animal being hunted. The average length will be between 3/4" and 1 1/4" with examples as small as 1/4" not being uncommon. Specimens that are over 1 1/2" are relatively scarce and very sought after. Many people who do not know the difference refer to these small arrow points as "bird points" which is completely erroneous. It was not the size that made these arrowheads effective on large animals but rather their ability to penetrate into the vital organs.

NORTHERN HIGH PLAINS POINT TYPES
(Archaeological Periods)(Carbon dates shown)

PLAINS PALEO (11,500 B. P. - 7,500 B. P.)

Agate Basin	Eden	Lancet	Scottsbluff I & II
Alberta	Firstview	Meserve	Scraper
AndersonBrowns Valley	Folsom	Midland	
Clovis	Frederick	Milnesand	
Clovis-Colby	Goshen	Plainview	
Cody Knife	Graver	Red River Knife	
Drill	Hell Gap	San Jose	

TRANSITIONAL PALEO (9,000 B. P. - 7,200 B. P.)

Allen	Angostura	Bajada	Lusk

MOUNTAIN PALEO (9,400 B. P. - 6,000 B. P.)

Alder Complex	Frederick	Lovell	Pryor Stemmed

EARLY ARCHAIC (8,000 B. P. - 5,000 B. P.)

Archaic Knife	Logan Creek	Plains Knife
Archaic Triangle	Lookingbill	Rio Grande
Hawken	Mount Albion	Simonsen

MIDDLE ARCHAIC (5,100 B. P. - 3,300 B. P.)

Buffalo Gap	Green River	Mallory	Wray
Duncan	Hanna	McKean	Yonkee
	Hanna-Northern	Oxbow	

LATE ARCHAIC (3,400 B. P. - 1,000 B. P.)

Base Tang Knife	Corner Tang Knife	Mid-Back Tang
Besant	Exotic Forms	Pelican Lake
Besant Knife	Hafted Knife	Plains Side Notched

LATE PREHISTORIC (1,900 B. P. - 150 B. P.)

Avonlea-Carmichael	Glendo Dart	Paskapoo	Swift Current
Avonlea-Classic	Harahey	Pekisko	Tompkins
Avonlea-Gull Lake	Harrell	Pipe Creek	Toyah
Avonlea-Timber Ridge	High River	Plains Side Notched	Washita
Billings	Hog Back	Prairie Side Notched	Washita Northern
Camel Back	Horse Fly	Samantha-Arrow	
Cottonwood Leaf	Huffaker	Samantha Dart	
Cottonwood Triangle	Irvine	Sattler	
Emigrant	Lewis	Side Knife	
Galt	Mummy Cave	Sonota	
Glendo Arrow	Nanton	Stott	

NP

PROTOHISTORIC (300 B. P. - 100 B.P.)

Bone Point	Cut Bank Jaw Notched	Plains Triangular	Trade Points

NORTHERN HIGH PLAINS
THUMBNAIL GUIDE SECTION

The following references are provided to aid the collector in easier and quicker identification of point types. All photos are exactly 30% of actual size and are proportional to each other. Each point pictured in this section represents a classic form for the type. When a match is found, go to the alphabetical location of that type for more examples in actual size.

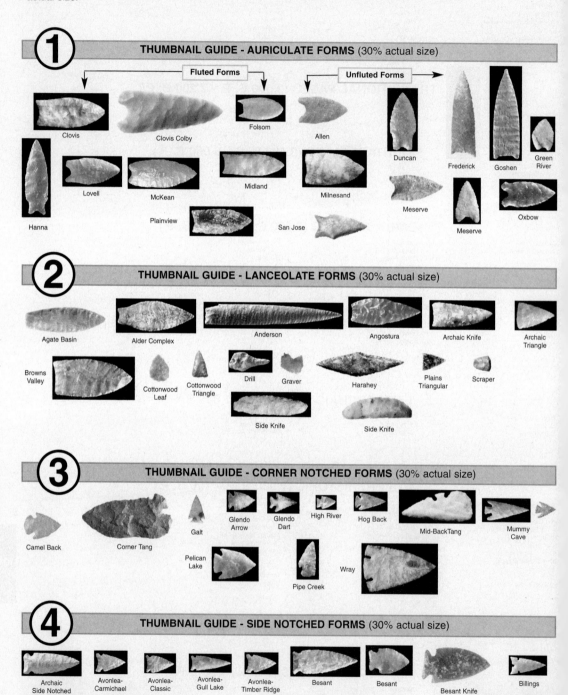

① THUMBNAIL GUIDE - AURICULATE FORMS (30% actual size)

Fluted Forms — Unfluted Forms

Clovis | Clovis Colby | Folsom | Allen | Duncan | Frederick | Goshen | Green River
Hanna | Lovell | McKean | Midland | Milnesand | Meserve | Meserve | Oxbow
Plainview | San Jose

② THUMBNAIL GUIDE - LANCEOLATE FORMS (30% actual size)

Agate Basin | Alder Complex | Anderson | Angostura | Archaic Knife | Archaic Triangle
Browns Valley | Cottonwood Leaf | Cottonwood Triangle | Drill | Graver | Harahey | Plains Triangular | Scraper
Side Knife | Side Knife

③ THUMBNAIL GUIDE - CORNER NOTCHED FORMS (30% actual size)

Camel Back | Corner Tang | Galt | Glendo Arrow | Glendo Dart | High River | Hog Back | Mid-BackTang | Mummy Cave
Pelican Lake | Pipe Creek | Wray

④ THUMBNAIL GUIDE - SIDE NOTCHED FORMS (30% actual size)

Archaic Side Notched | Avonlea-Carmichael | Avonlea-Classic | Avonlea-Gull Lake | Avonlea-Timber Ridge | Besant | Besant | Besant Knife | Billings
Bitterroot | Buffalo Gap | Cut Bank Jaw Notched | Desert-General | Desert-Sierra | Emigrant | Harrell | Huffaker | Hawkens

THUMBNAIL GUIDE - SIDE NOTCHED FORMS (continued)

Irvine   Lancet   Lewis   Logan Creek   Looking Bill   Mallory   Mount Albion   Nanton   Paskapoo   Pekisko

Plains Side Notched

Plains Knife

Yonkee

Prairie Side Notched

Samantha Arrow

Samantha Dart   Simonsen   Sonota   Stott   Swift Current   Toyah   Washita   Washita-Northern

⑤ THUMBNAIL GUIDE - STEMMED FORMS (30% of actual size)

Alberta   Bajada   Base Tang Knife   Besant   Cody Knife   Duncan   Eden   Firstview   Hanna   Hanna-Northern   Hell Gap   Horse Fly

Pryor Stemmed   Red River Knife   Rio Grande   Sattler   Scottsbluff I   Scottsbluff II   Trade

AGATE BASIN - Plains Paleo, 10,200 - 8500 B. P.

(Also see Alder Complex, Angostura, Browns Valley & Eden)

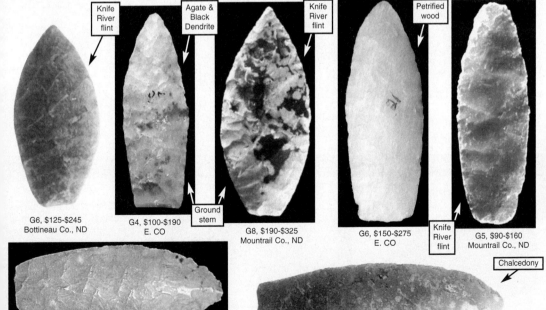

Knife River flint

G6, $125-$245
Bottineau Co., ND

Agate & Black Dendrite

Ground stem

G4, $100-$190
E. CO

Knife River flint

G8, $190-$325
Mountrail Co., ND

Petrified wood

G6, $150-$275
E. CO

Knife River flint

G5, $90-$160
Mountrail Co., ND

Ground stem

Edwards Plateau flint

G5, $150-$275
Pueblo Co., CO

Chalcedony

G5, $150-$275
S. E. ID

NP

AGATE BASIN (continued)

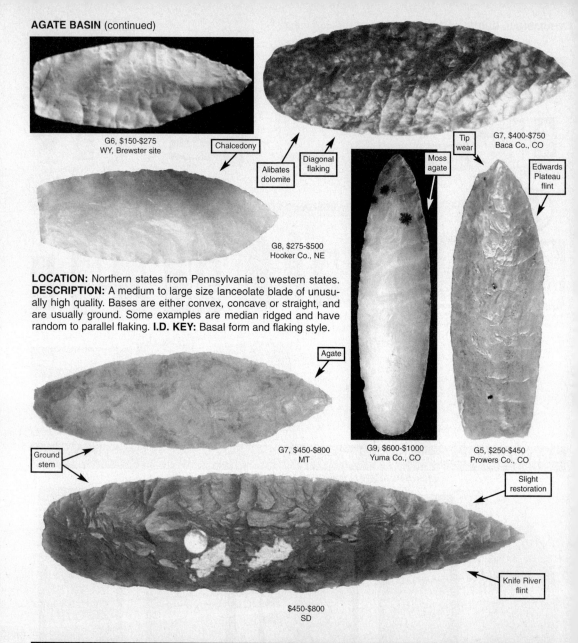

G6, $150-$275
WY, Brewster site

Chalcedony

Alibates dolomite

Diagonal flaking

Moss agate

Tip wear

G7, $400-$750
Baca Co., CO

Edwards Plateau flint

G8, $275-$500
Hooker Co., NE

LOCATION: Northern states from Pennsylvania to western states. **DESCRIPTION:** A medium to large size lanceolate blade of unusually high quality. Bases are either convex, concave or straight, and are usually ground. Some examples are median ridged and have random to parallel flaking. **I.D. KEY:** Basal form and flaking style.

Agate

G7, $450-$800
MT

G9, $600-$1000
Yuma Co., CO

G5, $250-$450
Prowers Co., CO

Ground stem

Slight restoration

Knife River flint

$450-$800
SD

ALBERTA - Plains Paleo, 10,000 - 8500 B. P.

(Also see Cody Knife, Eden, Rio Grande and Scottsbluff)

Basalt

G5, $125-$225
WY

G3, $90-$160
Lewis & Clark Co., MT

LOCATION: Northern states from Michigan to Montana and Nevada. **DESCRIPTION:** A medium to large size point with a broad, long parallel stem and weak shoulders. Believed to belong to the Cody Complex and is related to the *Eden* and *Scottsbluff* type. Stems are ground. **I.D. KEY:** Long stem, weak shoulders.

ALBERTA (continued)

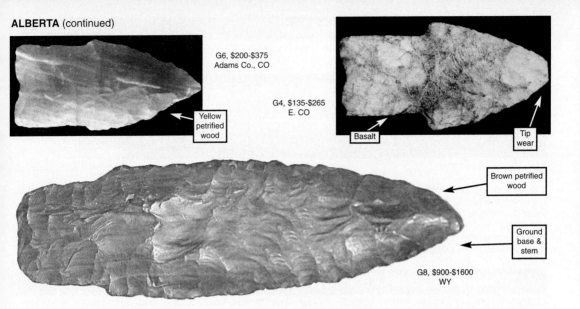

G6, $200-$375
Adams Co., CO

Yellow petrified wood

G4, $135-$265
E. CO

Basalt

Tip wear

Brown petrified wood

Ground base & stem

G8, $900-$1600
WY

ALDER COMPLEX - Mountain Paleo, 9400 B. P.

(Also see Agate Basin, Browns Valley, Clovis, Green River, Lovell and Meserve)

Oblique flaking

G8, $400-$650
Park Co., MT

G3, $60-$110
Lewis & Clark Co., MT

LOCATION: Plains states. **DESCRIPTION:** A medium to large size unfluted lanceolate point of high quality with convex sides and a straight to concave base. Flaking is usually the parallel oblique type. Basal areas are ground. **I.D. KEY:** Basal form and flaking style.

ALLEN - Transitional Paleo, 8500 - 7500 B. P.

(Also see Alder Complex, Browns Valley, Clovis, Frederick, Goshen, Green River, Lovell & Meserve)

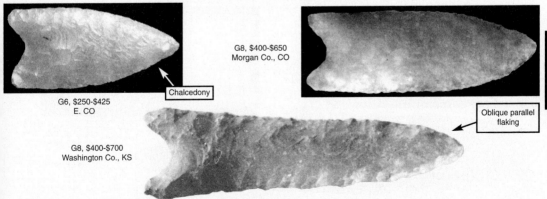

G8, $400-$650
Morgan Co., CO

Chalcedony

G6, $250-$425
E. CO

NP

Oblique parallel flaking

G8, $400-$700
Washington Co., KS

LOCATION: Plains states. Named after Jimmy Allen of Wyoming. **DESCRIPTION:** A medium to large size lanceolate point that has oblique tranverse flaking and a concave base with usually rounded ears. Basal area is ground. **I.D. KEY:** Basal form and flaking style.

ANDERSON - Plains Paleo, 9000 - 8000 B. P.

(Also see Allen, Angostura, Plainview)

Intentional buri-nated base

Oblique flaking

Famous point found by Perry Anderson published as 1st Yuma point; later named Allen or Angostura and recently named Anderson after its finder.

G10, $5,000-$10,000+
Yuma Co., CO

LOCATION: Colorado, Wyoming & South Dakota. **DESCRIPTION:** Very rare. A long slender lanceolate form exhibiting a uniform profile that is very thin with straight edges; stem edge grinding is short (similar to Cody Complex) and basal grinding is present; pressure flaking is superb and serial, parallel oblique. **Note:** This type was first identified years ago as *Yuma* and later changed to *Allen, Angostura* and other types. Recently it has been determined that this type is unique and different enough to have its own distinct name which has been proposed by Jeb Taylor. Named for Perry Anderson who found the first well known example.

ANGOSTURA - Transitional Paleo, 8800 - 7500 B. P.

(Also see Alder Complex, Allen, Anderson, Archaic Knife, Browns Valley, Clovis, Frederick, Goshen and Lusk)

Diagonal flaking

Petrified wood

Petrified wood

Diagonal flaking

Edge nick

Knife Riv. flint, ground stem

Diagonal flaking

Broken pieces of Angostura points from Wyoming. $10 ea.

G9, $200-$375
Mountrail Co., ND

G8, $165-$300
E. CO

G7, $175-$315
E. CO

G6, $250-$475
Dunn Co., ND

Diagonal flaking

G1, $40-$75
E. CO. Chert. Broken.

Base corner nick

G1, $40-$75
E. CO. Chert. Broken.

Knife River flint

Diagonal flaking

G6, $350-$650
Dunn Co., ND

LOCATION: Plains states. **DESCRIPTION:** A medium to large size lanceolate blade of unusually high quality. Bases are either convex, concave or straight and are usually ground. Most examples have oblique transverse flaking. **I.D. KEY:** Basal form and flaking style.

894

ARCHAIC KNIFE - Early Archaic, 8000 - 5000 B. P.

(Also see Angostura, Harahey, Plains Knife and Plains Triangular)

G3, $2-$4
Morton Co., ND

G5, $12-$20
E. CO

Agate

G10, $175-$325
Costilla Co., CO

LOCATION: Plains states. **DESCRIPTION:** A medium to large triangular blade with a concave to straight base. **I.D. KEY:** Large triangle with early flaking.

ARCHAIC TRIANGLE - Early to Middle Archaic, 6000 - 4000 B. P.

(Also see Cottonwood and Plains Triangular)

Chalcedony

G7, $18-$30
E. CO

G6, $8-$15
Custer Co., NE

G6, $12-$20
Lewis & Clark Co., MT

LOCATION: Plains states. **DESCRIPTION:** A small size triangular point that shows early flaking. **I.D. KEY:** Triangle with early flaking.

AVONLEA-CARMICHAEL - Late Prehistoric, 1800 - 1300 B. P.

(Also see Galt, High River, Irvine, Lewis, Nanton, Pekisko, Swift Current and Tompkins)

NP

G5, $20-$35
Meagher
Co., MT

G5, $20-$35
Cascade
Co., MT

G5, $30-$50
Cascade Co.,
MT

G6, $35-$60
Choteau, MT

G6, $40-$75
Choteau, MT

G8, $45-$85
Meagher Co., MT

G7, $40-$75
Cascade Co., MT

G7, $40-$75
Cascade Co., MT

LOCATION: Plains states. **DESCRIPTION:** A small size, very thin, high quality arrow point with shallow side notches close to the base which is concave. The blade is constructed with broad, parallel flakes that extend to the center. Quality is slightly lower than the other forms of this type. Frequently found on Bison kill sites. **I.D. KEY:** Low side notches, very thin.

AVONLEA-CARMICHAEL (continued)

G8, $45-$80
Meagher Co., MT

G8, $50-$90
Meagher Co., MT

G8, $50-$90
MT

G8, $50-$90
Teton Co., MT

AVONLEA-CLASSIC - Late Prehistoric, 1800 - 1230 B. P.

(Also see Galt, High River, Irvine, Lewis, Nanton, Pekisko, Swift Current and Tompkins)

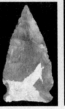

G6, $20-$35
Meagher Co., MT

G6, $20-$35
Custer Co., NE

G6, $30-$55
Meagher Co., MT

G8, $35-$60
Cascade Co., MT

G8, $40-$55
Meagher Co., MT

G6, $30-$55
Custer Co., NE

G6, $20-$35
Meagher Co., MT

G5, $15-$25
Custer Co., NE

G8, $40-$75
Meagher Co., MT

G8, $40-$75
Meagher Co., MT

G7, $35-$60
Saco, MT, Milk Rv.

G8, $50-$90
Teton Co., MT

LOCATION: Plains states. **DESCRIPTION:** A small size, very thin, high quality arrow point with shallow side notches close to the base which is concave. High quality parallel flaking is evident on the blade. Found at Bison kill sites. The first true Arrowpoint of the high plains along with Galt. **I.D. KEY:** Low side notches, very thin.

AVONLEA-GULL LAKE - Late Prehistoric, 1800 - 1230 B. P.

(Also see Besant, Galt, High River, Irvine, Lewis, Nanton, Pekisko, Swift Current & Tompkins)

G5, $20-$35
Meagher Co.,
MT.

G5, $20-$35
Cascade Co.,
MT.

G5, $35-$60
Meagher Co.,
MT.

G5, $40-$75
Meagher Co.,
MT.

G7, $45-$85
Meagher Co.,
MT.

G8, $55-$100
Phillips Co.,
MT.

G8, $60-$115
Cascade Co., MT.

G8, $60-$115
Meagher Co., MT

Obsidian

Parallel flaking

Parallel flaking

G9, $75-$140
Meagher Co.,
MT

G7, $65-$125
Meagher Co.,
MT

G9, $80-$155
Meagher Co., MT

G7, $50-$90
Choteau Co., MT.

G9, $125-$215
Cascade Co., MT.

G10, $115-$225
Cascade Co., MT.

G10, $150-$250
Meagher Co.,
MT

G10, $250-$425
Meagher Co., MT
Best known
example.

BESANT (continued)

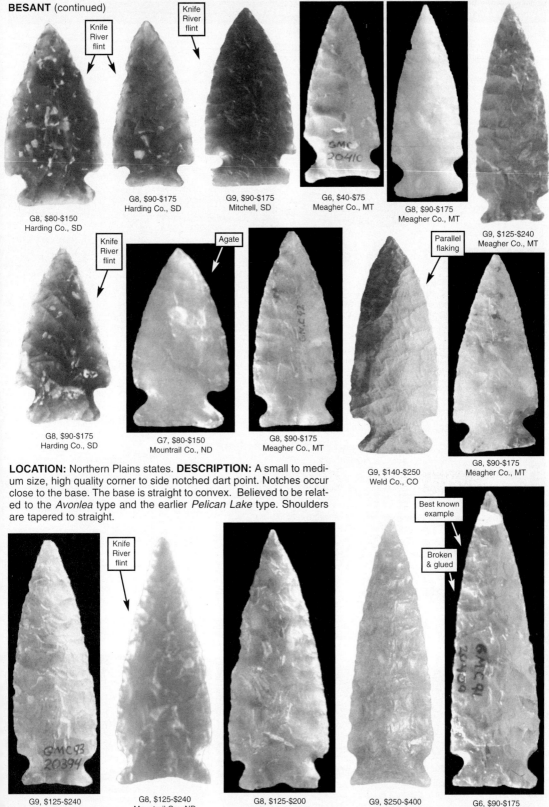

Knife River flint

Knife River flint

G8, $80-$150
Harding Co., SD

G8, $90-$175
Harding Co., SD

G9, $90-$175
Mitchell, SD

G6, $40-$75
Meagher Co., MT

G8, $90-$175
Meagher Co., MT

G9, $125-$240
Meagher Co., MT

Knife River flint

Agate

Parallel flaking

G8, $90-$175
Harding Co., SD

G7, $80-$150
Mountrail Co., ND

G8, $90-$175
Meagher Co., MT

G9, $140-$250
Weld Co., CO

G8, $90-$175
Meagher Co., MT

LOCATION: Northern Plains states. **DESCRIPTION:** A small to medium size, high quality corner to side notched dart point. Notches occur close to the base. The base is straight to convex. Believed to be related to the *Avonlea* type and the earlier *Pelican Lake* type. Shoulders are tapered to straight.

Knife River flint

Best known example

Broken & glued

G9, $125-$240
Meagher Co., MT

G8, $125-$240
Mountrail Co., ND

G8, $125-$200
Cascade Co., MT

G9, $250-$400
NE

G6, $90-$175
Meagher Co., MT

NP

899

BESANT KNIFE - Late Archaic, 1900 - 1500 B. P.

(Also see Plains Knife)

Petrified wood

Agate

G7, $150-$290
Bent Co., CO

G8, $200-$350
ND

LOCATION: Northern Plains states. **DESCRIPTION:** A medium to large size asymmetrical knife with wide corner to side notches. On some examples the blade leans heavily to one side. **I.D.KEY:** Symmetry of blade and notches.

G7, $175-$300
SD

Transparent Knife River flint

G9, $400-$700
Douglas Co., ND

G6, $150-$275
Grand Co., CO

G9, $400-$750
WY

Patinated Knife River flint

BILLINGS - Late Prehistoric, 300 - 150 B. P.

(Also see Emigrant, Harrell and Mallory)

| G6, $20-$35 Lewis & Clark Co., MT | G6, $25-$40 Lewis & Clark Co., MT | G6, $30-$45 Lewis & Clark Co., MT | G6, $30-$45 Lewis & Clark Co., MT | G6, $30-$55 Lewis & Clark Co., MT | G7, $35-$60 Lewis & Clark Co., MT | G8, $40-$75 Lewis & Clark Co., MT | G10, $45-$85 Lewis & Clark Co., MT |

BILLINGS (continued)

LOCATION: Northern Plains states. **DESCRIPTION:** A small, thin, tri-notched point with a straight to convex base. Blade edges can be serrated. Basal corners are sharp to pointed. Widest at the base, this point has excellent flaking, usually of the oblique transverse variety. If basal corners are rounded the type would be *Emigrant*.

G8, $40-$70
Lewis & Clark Co., MT

Knife River
flint

G10, $80-$150
Lewis & Clark Co., MT

BITTERROOT   (see Lookingbill for points found east of the Great Basin area)

BONE POINT - Proto Historic, 300 - 150 B. P.

(Also see Hafted Knife and Side Knife)

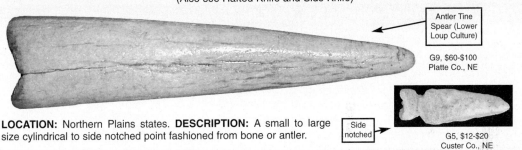

Antler Tine
Spear (Lower
Loup Culture)

G9, $60-$100
Platte Co., NE

LOCATION: Northern Plains states. **DESCRIPTION:** A small to large size cylindrical to side notched point fashioned from bone or antler.

Side
notched

G5, $12-$20
Custer Co., NE

BROWNS VALLEY - Plains Paleo, 10,000 - 8000 B. P.

(Also see Agate Basin, Alder Complex, Allen, Angostura, Goshen and Lovell)

Diagonal
flaking

Diagonal
flaking

Petrified
wood

Knife River
flint

G8, $165-$300
Mountrail Co., ND

Diagonal
flaking

G8, $400-$700
Cascade Co., MT

G8, $250-$475
E. CO

Jasper

LOCATION: Midwest to Northern Plains states. **DESCRIPTION:** A medium to large, thin, lanceolate blade with usually oblique to horizontal transverse flaking and a concave to straight base which can be ground. **I.D. KEY:** Paleo transverse flaking.

G9, $400-$700
Lewis & Clark Co., MT

NP

BUFFALO GAP - Middle Archaic, 5500 - 3500 B. P.

(Also see Lookingbill & Washita)

Knife River flint

Asymmetrical base

Asymmetrical base

Asymmetrical base

G3, $12-$20
Teton Co., MT

G6, $25-$40
Mountrail Co., ND

LOCATION: Northern Plains states. **DESCRIPTION:** A medium size, thin, side notched triangular point with a concave base. Basal corners are asymmetrical with one higher than the other, called a "single spur" base. **I.D. KEY:** Asymmetrical basal corners.

CAMEL BACK - Late Prehistoric, 700 - 500 B. P.

(Also see Hog Back and Pelican Lake)

LOCATION: Colorado. **DESCRIPTION:** A small corner notched point with a broad, bulbous base. Larger than *Hog Back*. **I.D. KEY:** Bulbous base.

Basalt

G8, $20-$35
Costilla Co., CO

CLOVIS - Plains Paleo, 11,500 - 10,600 B. P.

(Also see Alder Complex, Allen, Angostura, Folsom, Goshen and Plainview)

Broken tip

Flute channel

Jasper

G1, $30-$50
CO

G5, $175-$315
E. CO

G5, $175-$325
Pine Ridge, SD,
Bison kill site.

G6, $200-$375
E. CO

G6, $200-$375
Weld Co., CO

G6, $200-$375
E. CO

Flute channel

Petrified wood

Base wear

G5, $275-$500
Lyon Co., KS

G7, $450-$800
E. CO

LOCATION: All of North America. **DESCRIPTION:** A medium to large size, auriculate, fluted, lanceolate point with convex sides and a concave base that is ground. Most examples are fluted on both sides about 1/3 the way up from the base. The flaking can be random to parallel. Clovis is the earliest point type in the hemisphere. The origin of Clovis is unknown. It may have developed from earlier forms brought here from the Old World. The first Clovis find associated with Mastodon was in 1979 at Mastodon State Park, Jefferson Co., MO. in the Kimmswick bone bed carbon dated to 11,500 B.P. or approx. 14,000 actual years. **I.D. KEY:** Paleo flaking, shoulders, baton or billet fluting instead of indirect style.

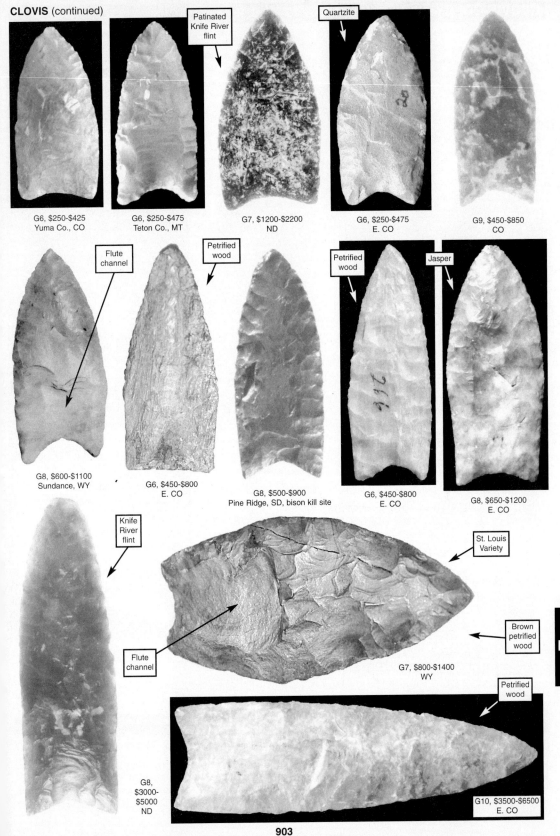

CLOVIS (continued)

Patinated Knife River flint

Quartzite

G6, $250-$425
Yuma Co., CO

G6, $250-$475
Teton Co., MT

G7, $1200-$2200
ND

G6, $250-$475
E. CO

G9, $450-$850
CO

Flute channel

Petrified wood

Petrified wood

Jasper

G8, $600-$1100
Sundance, WY

G6, $450-$800
E. CO

G8, $500-$900
Pine Ridge, SD, bison kill site

G6, $450-$800
E. CO

G8, $650-$1200
E. CO

Knife River flint

St. Louis Variety

Brown petrified wood

NP

Flute channel

G7, $800-$1400
WY

Petrified wood

G8,
$3000-
$5000
ND

G10, $3500-$6500
E. CO

903

CLOVIS-COLBY - Plains Paleo, 11,500 - 10,600 B. P.

(Also see Alder Complex, Allen, Angostura, Folsom, Goshen, Midland and Plainview)

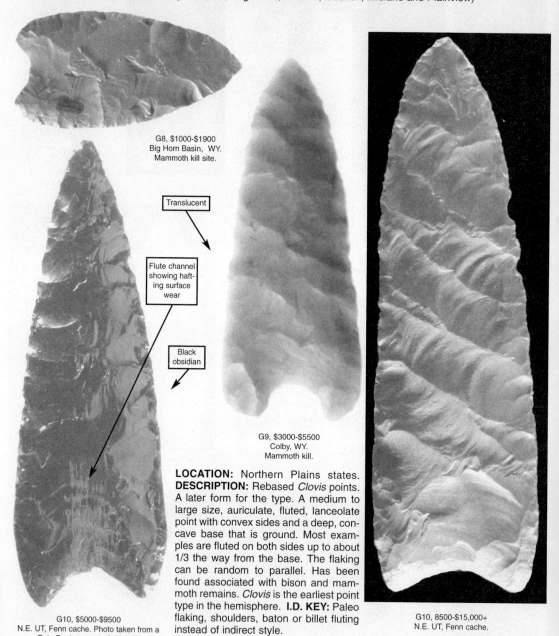

G8, $1000-$1900
Big Horn Basin, WY.
Mammoth kill site.

Translucent

Flute channel showing hafting surface wear

Black obsidian

G9, $3000-$5500
Colby, WY.
Mammoth kill.

G10, $5000-$9500
N.E. UT, Fenn cache. Photo taken from a
Pete Bostrom cast of original.

G10, 8500-$15,000+
N.E. UT, Fenn cache.

LOCATION: Northern Plains states. **DESCRIPTION:** Rebased *Clovis* points. A later form for the type. A medium to large size, auriculate, fluted, lanceolate point with convex sides and a deep, concave base that is ground. Most examples are fluted on both sides up to about 1/3 the way from the base. The flaking can be random to parallel. Has been found associated with bison and mammoth remains. *Clovis* is the earliest point type in the hemisphere. **I.D. KEY:** Paleo flaking, shoulders, baton or billet fluting instead of indirect style.

CODY KNIFE - Plains Paleo, 10,000 - 8000 B. P.

(Also see Base-Tang Knife, Corner Tang, Eden, Mid-Back Tang, Red River Knife and Scottsbluff)

LOCATION: Northern Plains states. **DESCRIPTION:** A medium to large size asymmetrical blade with one or two shoulders and a medium to short stem. Stem edges are ground on early examples. Made by the Cody complex people who made *Scottsbluff* points. Flaking is similar to the *Scottsbluff* type and some examples were made from *Scottsbluff* points. **I.D. KEY:** Paleo flaking, asymmetrical form.

CODY KNIFE (continued)

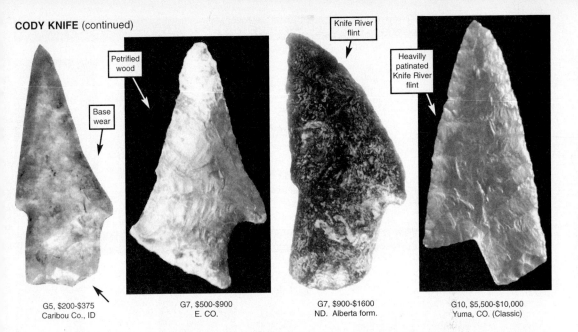

Base wear

Petrified wood

Knife River flint

Heavilly patinated Knife River flint

G5, $200-$375
Caribou Co., ID

G7, $500-$900
E. CO.

G7, $900-$1600
ND. Alberta form.

G10, $5,500-$10,000
Yuma, CO. (Classic)

CORNER TANG KNIFE - Late Archaic, 3400 - 1000 B. P.

(Also see Base-Tang Knife, Cody & Mid-Back Tang)

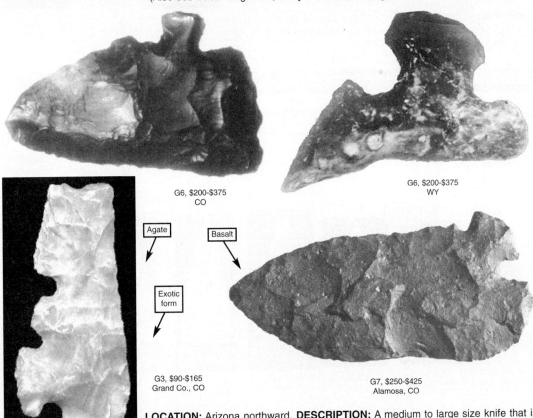

G6, $200-$375
CO

G6, $200-$375
WY

Agate

Basalt

Exotic form

G3, $90-$165
Grand Co., CO

G7, $250-$425
Alamosa, CO

NP

LOCATION: Arizona northward. **DESCRIPTION:** A medium to large size knife that is notched at one corner producing a tang for hafting to a handle. Tang knives are rare and have been reproduced in recent years. **I.D. KEY:** Angle of hafting.

COTTONWOOD LEAF - Late Prehistoric, 700 - 150 B. P.

(Also see Archaic Triangle and Plains Triangular)

    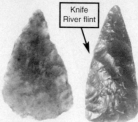  

Knife River flint

G5, $4-$6, CO

G4, $4-$6, CO

G3, $4-$6, CO

G6, $4-$6
Alamosa CO

G4, $4-$8
CO

G6, $6-$12,
Morton Co., ND

G6, $6-$12
Lewis & Clark Co.,
MT

LOCATION: Arizona northward. **DESCRIPTION:** A small to medium size triangular arrow point with a rounded base.

COTTONWOOD TRIANGLE - Late Prehistoric, 700 - 150 B. P.

(Also see Archaic Triangle and Plains Triangular)

G2, $2-$4, CO

G2, $4-$6, CO

G4, $5-$9, CO

G3, $6-$10, CO

G2, $4-$6
Weld Co., CO

G4, $4-$6, CO

G4, $4-$6
Lander, WY

LOCATION: Arizona northward. **DESCRIPTION:** A small to medium size triangular arrow point with a straight, slightly convex or concave base. Basal corners tend to be sharp.

CUT BANK JAW-NOTCHED - Proto Historic, 300 - 150 B. P.

(Also see Buffalo Gap, Emigrant, Paskapoo, Pekisko, Plains Side Notched & Washita)

G4, $8-$15
Custer Co., NE

G5, $12-$20 (Classic)
Cascade Co., MT

G4, $12-$20
Great Falls, MT

G6, $20-$35
S.E. CO

Chalc.

G8, $55-$100
Lewis & Clark Co., MT

Black obsidian

Parallel flaking

Classic

     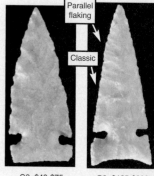 

G9, $80-$150
Weld Co., CO

G8, $30-$55
Lewis & Clark
Co., MT

G9, $55-$100
Teton Co., MT

G8, $35-$65
MT

G9, $90-$175
Teton Co., MT

G8, $40-$75
Teton Co., MT

G9, $125-$200
Teton Co., MT

LOCATION: Northern Plains states. **DESCRIPTION:** A small size, thin, triangular arrow point with deep, narrow side notches that expand towards the center of the blade. Base can be straight to concave. Flaking is of high quality, usually oblique parallel struck from the edge to the center of the blade.

DALTON   (see Meserve)

DESERT-GENERAL   (see Washita for the correct type in the Northern Plains)

DESERT-SIERRA   (see Harrell for the correct type in the Northern Plains)

DRILL - Plains Paleo to Historic Phase, 11,500 - 15 0 B. P.

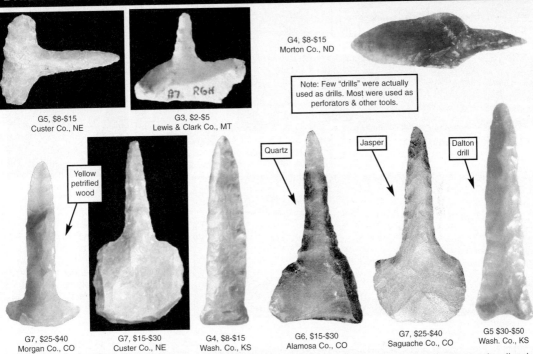

G5, $8-$15
Custer Co., NE

G3, $2-$5
Lewis & Clark Co., MT

G4, $8-$15
Morton Co., ND

Note: Few "drills" were actually used as drills. Most were used as perforators & other tools.

Yellow petrified wood

Quartz

Jasper

Dalton drill

G7, $25-$40
Morgan Co., CO

G7, $15-$30
Custer Co., NE

G4, $8-$15
Wash. Co., KS

G6, $15-$30
Alamosa Co., CO

G7, $25-$40
Saguache Co., CO

G5 $30-$50
Wash. Co., KS

LOCATION: Throughout North America. **DESCRIPTION:** Although many drills were made from scratch, all point types were made into the drill form. Usually, heavily resharpened and broken points were salvaged and rechipped into drills. **I.D. KEY:** Narrow blade form.

DUNCAN - Middle to Late Archaic, 4600 - 3500 B. P.

(Also see Hanna, Meserve and San Jose)

Restored ear

Quartzite

Clear chalc.

G8, $45-$85
Montrail Co., ND

Knife River flint

G8, $45-$85
Morgan Co., CO

G4, $8-$15
Sundance, WY

G4, $12-$20
Crowley Co., CO

G9, $55-$100
Otero Co., CO

G5, $15-$25
Dillon, MT

G5, $30-$55
Morgan Co., CO

G6, $25-$45
Moorcroft, WY

G5, $15-$25
Lewis & Clark Co., MT

NP

DUNCAN (continued)

G8, $65-$125
Lewis & Clark Co., MT

Knife River flint

G8, $60-$110
Mountrail Co., ND

Knife River flint

Very thin

G9, $65-$125
Casper, WY

Knife River flint

G8, $45-$85
Lewis & Clark Co., MT

Knife River flint

G9, $200-$375
Jamestown, ND

LOCATION: Northern Arizona to Canada and to eastern Oklahoma. **DESCRIPTION:** A small to medium size dart/knife point with a triangular blade and angular shoulders. The stem is straight with a V-shaped notch in the basal edge. Stem edges are usually ground. **I.D. KEY:** Straight stem edges.

G9, $250-$475
S. E. CO

EDEN - Plains Paleo, 10,000 - 8000 B. P.

(Also see Agate Basin, Alberta, Alder Complex, Angostura, Browns Valley and Scottsbluff)

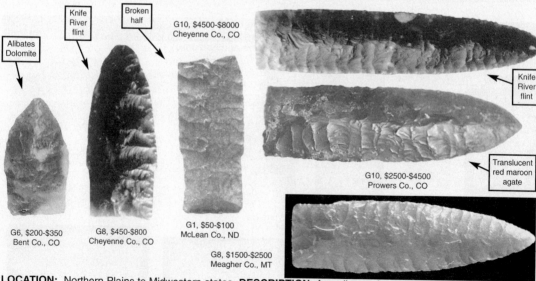

Alibates Dolomite

Knife River flint

Broken half

G10, $4500-$8000
Cheyenne Co., CO

Knife River flint

G10, $2500-$4500
Prowers Co., CO

Translucent red maroon agate

G6, $200-$350
Bent Co., CO

G8, $450-$800
Cheyenne Co., CO

G1, $50-$100
McLean Co., ND

G8, $1500-$2500
Meagher Co., MT

LOCATION: Northern Plains to Midwestern states. **DESCRIPTION:** A medium to large size, narrow, stemmed point with very weak shoulders and a straight to convex base. Basal sides are parallel to slightly expanding. Many examples have a median ridge and collateral to oblique parallel flaking. Bases are usually ground. A Cody Complex point. **I.D. KEY:** Paleo flaking, narrowness.

EDEN (continued)

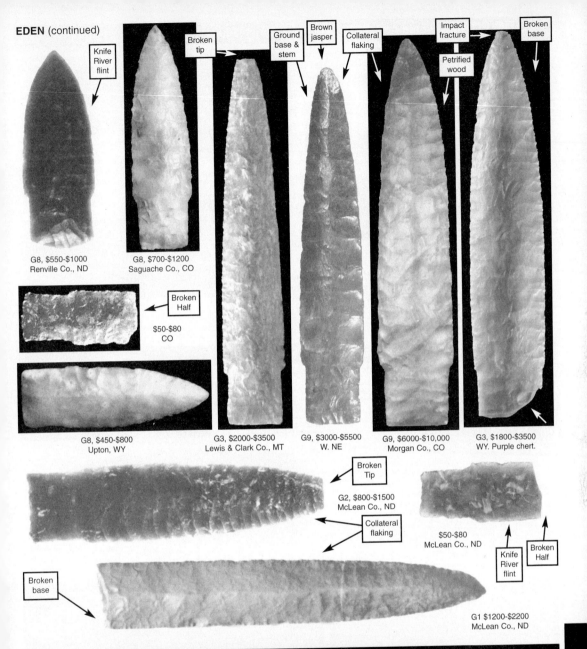

Knife River flint

Broken tip

Ground base & stem

Brown jasper

Collateral flaking

Impact fracture

Petrified wood

Broken base

G8, $550-$1000
Renville Co., ND

G8, $700-$1200
Saguache Co., CO

Broken Half

$50-$80
CO

G8, $450-$800
Upton, WY

G3, $2000-$3500
Lewis & Clark Co., MT

G9, $3000-$5500
W. NE

G9, $6000-$10,000
Morgan Co., CO

G3, $1800-$3500
WY. Purple chert.

Broken Tip

G2, $800-$1500
McLean Co., ND

Collateral flaking

$50-$80
McLean Co., ND

Knife River flint

Broken Half

Broken base

G1 $1200-$2200
McLean Co., ND

NP

EMIGRANT - Late Prehistoric, 900 - 400 B. P.

(Also see Billings, Buffalo Gap, Cut Bank, Plains Side Notched, Swift Current & Washita)

Classic form

Obsidian

G7, $25-$45
MT

G8, $30-$55
CO

G8, $40-$75
Meagher Co., MT

G9, $40-$75
Meagher Co., MT

G9, $50-$90
Teton Co., MT

G9, $40-$75
Teton Co., MT

LOCATION: Northern Plains states. **DES - CRIPTION:** A small size, thin, tri-notched point with rounded basal corners. If basal corners are pointed the type would be Billings. **I.D. KEY:** Rounded basal corners.

EXOTIC FORMS - Late Archaic to Late Prehistoric, 3000 - 1000 B. P.

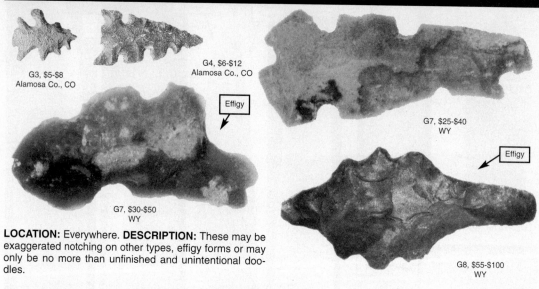

G3, $5-$8
Alamosa Co., CO

G4, $6-$12
Alamosa Co., CO

Effigy

G7, $25-$40
WY

Effigy

G7, $30-$50
WY

G8, $55-$100
WY

LOCATION: Everywhere. **DESCRIPTION:** These may be exaggerated notching on other types, effigy forms or may only be no more than unfinished and unintentional doodles.

FIRSTVIEW - Plains Paleo, 10,00 - 8000 B. P.

(Also see Alberta, Alder Complex, Cody Knife, Eden and Scottsbluff)

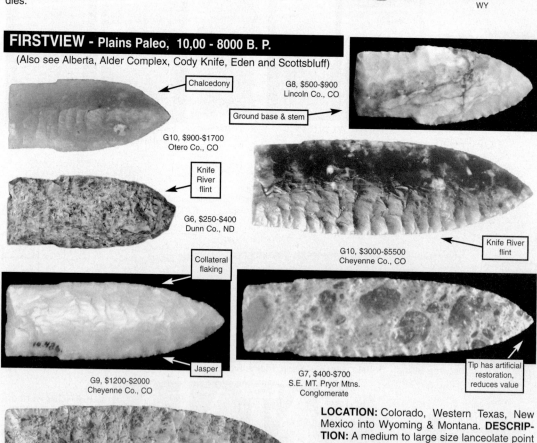

Chalcedony

G8, $500-$900
Lincoln Co., CO

Ground base & stem

G10, $900-$1700
Otero Co., CO

Knife River flint

G6, $250-$400
Dunn Co., ND

Knife River flint

G10, $3000-$5500
Cheyenne Co., CO

Collateral flaking

Jasper

G9, $1200-$2000
Cheyenne Co., CO

G7, $400-$700
S.E. MT. Pryor Mtns.
Conglomerate

Tip has artificial restoration, reduces value

G10, $2000-$3700
Rawlins, WY

Ground base & stem

LOCATION: Colorado, Western Texas, New Mexico into Wyoming & Montana. **DESCRIPTION:** A medium to large size lanceolate point with slightly convex blade edges, slight shoulders and a rectangular stem. Shoulders are sometimes absent from resharpening. It generally exhibits parallel-transverse flaking. A variant form of the *Scottsbluff* type made by Cody Complex people. **I.D. KEY:** Weak shoulders, diamond shaped cross-section.

G5, $400-$750
Cheyenne Co., CO

Base ding

Quartzite

FOLSOM - Plains Paleo, 11,000 - 10,000 B. P.

(Also see Alder Complex, Clovis, Goshen, Green River, Midland and Milnesand)

Petrified wood

G1, $600-$1000
CO

Broken tips, bases

G5, $500-$900
Saguache Co., CO

G2, $300-$500
San Luis Valley, CO

G1, $55-$100
CO

Preform, fluted one side

Edwards Plateau flint

G1, $55-$100
Logan Co., CO

G9, $3500-$6000
CO

G7, $3000-$5000
Hooker Co., NE

G7, $700-$1200
E. CO

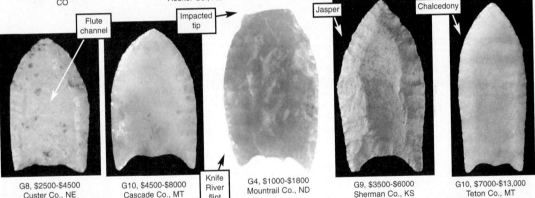

Flute channel

Impacted tip

Jasper

Chalcedony

G8, $2500-$4500
Custer Co., NE

G10, $4500-$8000
Cascade Co., MT

Knife River flint

G4, $1000-$1800
Mountrail Co., ND

G9, $3500-$6000
Sherman Co., KS

G10, $7000-$13,000
Teton Co., MT

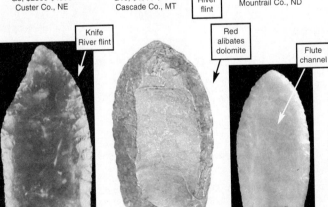

Knife River flint

Red alibates dolomite

Flute channel

Jasper

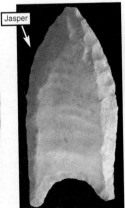

NP

G7, $2000-$3500
Mountrail Co., ND

G10, $8000-$15,000
E. CO

G10, $7000-$13,000
Jefferson Co., MT

G9, $8000-$15,000
CO

G8, $4000-$7500
Adams Co., CO

FOLSOM (continued)

Knife River flint

Broken tip & ear

G3, $400-$700
Mountrail Co., ND

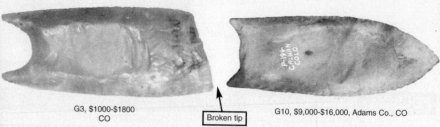

G3, $1000-$1800
CO

Broken tip

G10, $9,000-$16,000, Adams Co., CO

LOCATION: Canada to the Southwestern states and to N. Indiana. **DESCRIPTION:** A very thin, small to medium sized lanceolate point with convex edges and a concave basal edge creating sharp ears or basal corners. Most examples are fluted from the basal edge to nearly the tip of the point. Blade flaking is extremely fine. The hafting area is ground. A very rare type. Modern reproductions have been made and extreme caution should be exercised in acquiring an original specimen. Usually found in association with extinct bison fossil remains. **I.D. KEY:** Flaking style (Excessive secondary flaking).

FREDERICK - Plains Paleo, 9000 - 8000 B. P.

(Also see Allen, Anderson, Angostura, Goshen, Lovell, Lusk)

LOCATION: Colorado, Montana, North & South Dakota, Wyoming, Kansas & Nebraska. **DESCRIPTION:** A medium to large size lanceolate point with a concave base. Flaking is random to oblique transverse. Bases are thinned and are usually the widest part of the point. **I.D. KEY:** Triangular form, flaking style.

Oblique parallel flaking

G9, $400-$650
CO

GALT - Late Prehistoric, 1500 - 900 B. P.

(Also see Besant, Avonlea, Glendo)

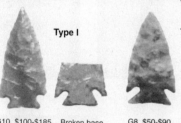

Type I

G10, $100-$185
White Sulfer
Springs, MT

Broken base
White Sulfer
Springs, MT

Type II

G8, $50-$90
White Sulfer
Springs, MT

Broken base
White Sulfer
Springs, MT

Type III

G8, $90-$175
White Sulfer
Springs, MT

Broken base
White Sulfer
Springs, MT

G7, $35-$65
White Sulfer
Springs, MT

G6, $35-$40
Meagher Co.,
MT

Type I

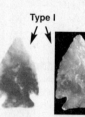

G7, $40-$70
White Sulfer
Springs, MT

Type I

G8, $65-$125
Meagher Co., MT

Type II

G10, $125-$200
White Sulfer
Springs, MT

Type II

G6, $25-$40
White Sulfer
Springs, MT

Type I

Type II

G9, $80-$150
Meagher Co.,
MT

LOCATION: North central Montana to northern half of Wyoming. **DESCRIPTION:** A small to medium size, thin, extremely well made, delicate arrow point. Flaking is random. Delicate "U" shaped angled notches that are deeper than those found on *Avonlea* points. Bases are straight to slightly concave. The high plains first true "arrow point" along with *Avonlea*. **Galt Type I** are corner notched removing equal portions of the basal and lateral blade edges. **Galt Type II** points start at the basal corner and remove the notch on the lateral edge. **Galt Type III** points are basal notched with the notch starting at the basal corner.

GALT (continued)

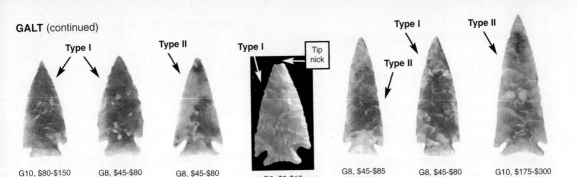

Type I   Type II   Type I   Tip nick   Type I   Type II   Type II

G10, $80-$150
White Sulfer
Springs, MT

G8, $45-$80
White Sulfer
Springs, MT

G8, $45-$80
White Sulfer
Springs, MT

G3, $5-$10
Meagher Co., MT

G8, $45-$85
White Sulfer
Springs, MT

G8, $45-$80
White Sulfer
Springs, MT

G10, $175-$300
White Sulfer
Springs, MT

GALT (Hastings Var.) - Late Prehistoric, 1500 - 900 B. P.

(Also see Avonlea, Besant, Glendo)

LOCATION: North central Montana to northern half of Wyoming. **DESCRIPTION:** Similar to the regular *Galt* point but with a decidedly convex base, type I corner notches, and are slightly thicker than the classic type.

G7, $35-$60
Ulm, MT

G8, $50-$90
Ulm, MT

GLENDO ARROW - Late Prehistoric, 1500 - 800 B. P.

(Also see Pelican Lake)

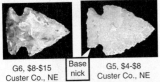

G8, $25-$40
Bent/Crowler
Co., CO

LOCATION: New Mexico into Colorado, Wyoming, southern Idaho and Montana. **DESCRIPTION:** A small size, broad, corner to side notched arrow point with a straight to convex base.

G6, $8-$15
Custer Co., NE

Base nick

G5, $4-$8
Custer Co., NE

GLENDO DART - Late Prehistoric, 1700 - 1200 B. P.

(Also see Pelican Lake and Besant)

G5, $5-$10
Custer Co., NE

G6, $20-$35
Bent Co., CO

G6, $25-$40
El Paso Co., CO

G7, $30-$55
Teller Co., CO

LOCATION: New Mexico into Colorado, Wyoming, southern Idaho and Montana. **DESCRIPTION:** A medium to large size, broad, corner to side notched dart point with a straight to convex base. Some examples have a concave base producing ears. Believed to be related to the *Besant* point.

G6, $15-$25
Custer Co., NE

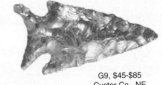

G9, $45-$85
Custer Co., NE

NP

GOSHEN - Plains Paleo, 11,250 - 9500 B. P.

(Also see Alder Complex, Clovis, Folsom, Green River, Midland and Milnesand)

LOCATION: Northern Plains states. **DESCRIPTION:** A small to medium size, very thin, auriculate dart point with a concave base. Basal corners are rounded to sharp. Basal area is ground. Flaking is oblique to horizontal transverse or random. Same as *Plainview* found in Texas. **I.D. KEY:** Thinness, auricles.

Alibates
dolomite

G10, $450-$850
Prowers Co., CO

GOSHEN (continued)

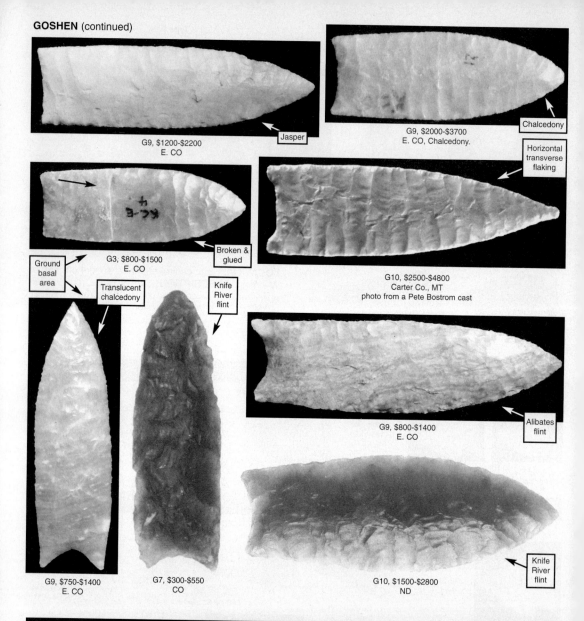

G9, $1200-$2200
E. CO

Jasper

G9, $2000-$3700
E. CO, Chalcedony.

Chalcedony

Horizontal transverse flaking

G3, $800-$1500
E. CO

Broken & glued

Ground basal area

Translucent chalcedony

Knife River flint

G10, $2500-$4800
Carter Co., MT
photo from a Pete Bostrom cast

G9, $800-$1400
E. CO

Alibates flint

G9, $750-$1400
E. CO

G7, $300-$550
CO

G10, $1500-$2800
ND

Knife River flint

GRAVER - Plains Paleo to Archaic, 11,500 - 4000 B. P.

(Also see Scraper)

Graver points

G6, $5-$10 ea.
Alamosa, CO, Folsom site.

LOCATION: Early man sites everywhere. **DESCRIPTION:** An irregular shaped uniface tool with sharp, pointed projections used for puncturing, incising, tattooing, etc.

GREEN RIVER - Mid-Archaic, 4500 - 4200 B.P.

(Also see Alder Complex, Clovis, Folsom, Green River, Midland and Milnesand)

LOCATION: Mont., WY, CO, NE, NM & AZ. **DESCRIPTION:** A small, very thin, auriculate point with contracting, almost pointed auricles and a small, deep basal concavity. **I.D. KEY:** Thinness, auricles.

GREEN RIVER (continued)

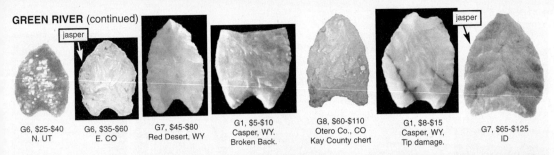

jasper

jasper

G6, $25-$40
N. UT

G6, $35-$60
E. CO

G7, $45-$80
Red Desert, WY

G1, $5-$10
Casper, WY.
Broken Back.

G8, $60-$110
Otero Co., CO
Kay County chert

G1, $8-$15
Casper, WY,
Tip damage.

G7, $65-$125
ID

HAFTED KNIFE - Late Archaic to Late Prehistoric - 2300 - 400 B.P.

(Also see Side Knife)

G8, $450-$800
Custer Co., NE

LOCATION: Northern Plains states. **DESCRIPTION:** A medium to large size blade hafted into a wooden, antler or bone handle. Usually asphaltum and fiber were used in the hafting process.

IMPORTANT: Hafted Knife shown half size

HANNA - Middle to Late Archaic, 4600 - 3500 B. P.

(Also see Duncan & San Jose)

Banded obsidian

Porcellanite

G6, $15-$30
CO

G6, $12-$20
CO

G5, $8-$15
Weld Co., CO

G4, $6-$10
CO

G6, $15-$30
WY

G5, $15-$25
Sweetgrass Hills, MT

G5, $20-$35
Weld Co., CO

G7, $30-$50
Lewis & Clark Co., MT

G5, $12-$20
Sou. Alberta, CAN

Basalt

G10, $65-$125
Natrona Co., WY

G7, $25-$40
Lewis & Clark Co., MT

G7, $25-$40
Lewis & Clark Co., MT

Beautiful chalcedony

G8, $45-$75
E. CO

G8, $40-$75
E. CO

G8, $90-$165
Bottineau Co., ND

G8, $90-$165
Mountrail Co., ND

Knife River Flint

Knife River Flint

NP

LOCATION: Nebraska to Canada and as far south as the Southwestern states. **DESCRIPTION:** A small to medium size, narrow, bifurcated stemmed dart/knife point with tapered to horizontal shoulders and an expanding stem which is notched to produce diagonally projecting rounded "ears". **I.D. KEY:** Expanding stem.

915

HANNA (continued)

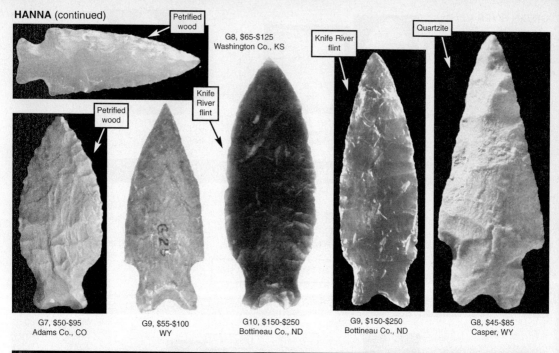

Petrified wood

G8, $65-$125
Washington Co., KS

Knife River flint

Quartzite

Petrified wood

Knife River flint

Knife River flint

G7, $50-$95
Adams Co., CO

G9, $55-$100
WY

G10, $150-$250
Bottineau Co., ND

G9, $150-$250
Bottineau Co., ND

G8, $45-$85
Casper, WY

HANNA NORTHERN - Middle to Late Archaic , 4600 - 3500 B. P.

(Also see Duncan)

Basalt

G4, $5-$10
Bent Co., CO

G5, $12-$20
Bent Co., CO

G6, $30-$55
Alberta, Canada

LOCATION: Northern Plains states to Canada. **DESCRIPTION:** A small to medium size, narrow, long stemmed point with tapered to horizontal shoulders. Stem can be bifurcated.

HARAHEY - Late Prehistoric, 700 - 300 B. P.

(Also see Archaic Knife and Neosho)

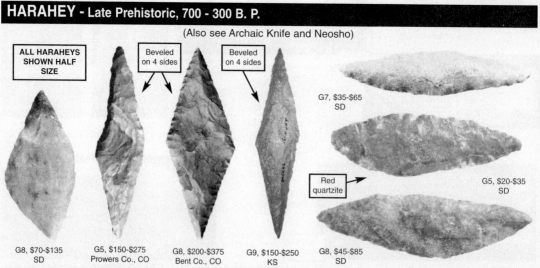

ALL HARAHEYS SHOWN HALF SIZE

Beveled on 4 sides

Beveled on 4 sides

G7, $35-$65
SD

G5, $20-$35
SD

Red quartzite

G8, $70-$135
SD

G5, $150-$275
Prowers Co., CO

G8, $200-$375
Bent Co., CO

G9, $150-$250
KS

G8, $45-$85
SD

LOCATION: Northern Plains states to Texas to Illinois to Canada. **DESCRIPTION:** A large size, double pointed buffalo knife that is beveled on all four edges. The cross section is rhomboid. See *Neosho* for the two beveled form. **I.D. KEY:** Rhomboid cross section.

916

HARAHEY (continued)

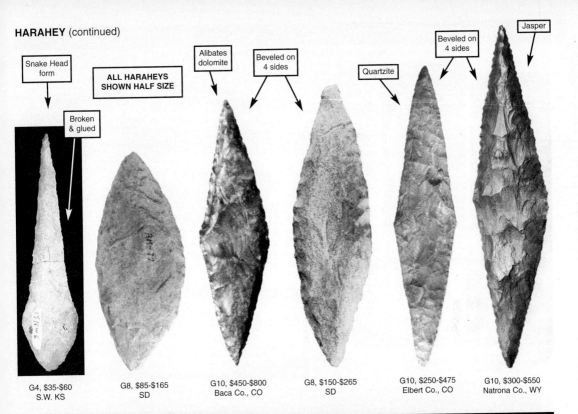

Snake Head form

ALL HARAHEYS SHOWN HALF SIZE

Broken & glued

Alibates dolomite

Beveled on 4 sides

Quartzite

Beveled on 4 sides

Jasper

G4, $35-$60
S.W. KS

G8, $85-$165
SD

G10, $450-$800
Baca Co., CO

G8, $150-$265
SD

G10, $250-$475
Elbert Co., CO

G10, $300-$550
Natrona Co., WY

HARRELL- Late Prehistoric, 900 - 500 B. P.

(Also see Billings and Washita)

G9, $15-$30
Sherman Co., NE

G6, $12-$20
Bismark, ND

G9, $30-$50
Sherman Co., NE

G9, $30-$50
Buffalo Co., NE

G9, $40-$70
Custer Co., NE

LOCATION: Eastern Colorado, Arkansas, Oklahoma, Kansas, Nebraska and Missouri. **DESCRIPTION:** A small size, thin, triangular arrow point with side notches and a basal notch. Bases are slightly concave to straight.

HAWKEN - Early to Middle Archaic, 6500 - 6200 B. P.

(Also see Besant, Logan Creek and Lookingbill)

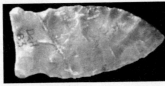

NP

G5, $60-$100, Custer Co., NE

G7, $120-$225
Teton Co., MT

G7, $150-$265
Meagher Co., MT

G8, $300-$550
Meagher Co., MT

Tip nick

LOCATION: Northern Plains state. Type site is in Wyoming. **DESCRIPTION:** A small to medium size, narrow point with broad, shallow side notches and an expanding stem. Blade flaking is of high quality and is usually the oblique to horizontal parallel type. Along with *Logan Creek* and *Lookingbill* this is one of the earliest side-notched points of the Plains states. **I.D. KEY:** Broad side notches, expanding base.

917

HELL GAP - Plains Paleo, 10,300 - 9500 B. P.

(Also see Agate Basin, Angostura, Bajada, Browns Valley, Pryor Stemmed and Rio Grande)

G9, $700-$1300
McPherson Co., NE

Brown agate

G5, $100-$180
Washington Co., CO

G5, $100-$180
Weld Co., CO

G4, $80-$150
MT

G7, $250-$400
MT

G7, $200-$350
E. CO

Alibates dolomite

Jasper

G9, $400-$750
Prowers Co., CO

Burlington chert

G7, $175-$300
WY

G9, $500-$900
Custer Co., NE

LOCATION: Northern Plains states to Canada. **DESCRIPTION:** A medium to large size, narrow, long stemmed point with weak, tapered shoulders. Base can be concave, convex or straight. The basal area is usually ground. **I.D. KEY:** Early flaking and base form. Can be easily confused with *Rio Grande* Points found in southern Colorado southward through New Mexico.

HIGH RIVER - Late Prehistoric, 1300 - 800 B. P.

(Also see Avonlea, Hog Back, Pelican Lake and Samantha)

G4, $4-$7
Chouteau Co., MT

G4, $6-$10
Meagher Co., MT

G4, $4-$7
Ft. Peck Res., MT

G7, $8-$15
Meagher Co., MT

G7, $8-$15
Lewis & Clark Co., MT

G8, $15-$20
Meagher Co., MT

LOCATION: Northern Plains states to Canada. **DESCRIPTION:** A small, thin, corner notched triangular arrow point with a straight to convex base. Basal grinding is evident on some specimens. **I.D. KEY:** Small corner notched point.

HOG BACK - Late Prehistoric, 1000 - 600 B. P.

(Also see Camel Back, High River, Mummy Cave, Pelican Lake & Samantha)

LOCATION: Northern Plains states to Canada. **DESCRIPTION:** A small, thin, corner notched triangular arrow point with barbed shoulders and a convex base. The preform is ovoid and blade edges can be serrated. **I.D. KEY:** Small corner notched point, barbs.

918

HOG BACK (continued)

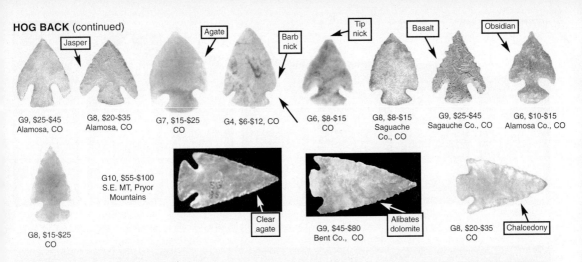

Jasper

G9, $25-$45
Alamosa, CO

G8, $20-$35
Alamosa, CO

Agate

G7, $15-$25
CO

G4, $6-$12, CO

Barb nick

G6, $8-$15
CO

Tip nick

G8, $8-$15
Saguache
Co., CO

Basalt

G9, $25-$45
Sagauche Co., CO

Obsidian

G6, $10-$15
Alamosa Co., CO

G10, $55-$100
S.E. MT, Pryor
Mountains

G8, $15-$25
CO

Clear agate

G9, $45-$80
Bent Co., CO

Alibates dolomite

G8, $20-$35
CO

Chalcedony

HORSE FLY - Late Prehistoric, 1500 - 1000 B. P.

(Also see High River and Lewis)

G7, $18-$30
E. CO. Petrified wood.

Quartzite

G8, $30-$50
Prowers Co., CO

Edwards Plateau flint

G7, $25-$40
Crowley Co., CO

LOCATION: Colorado. **DESCRIPTION:** A medium to large size, narrow, stemmed point with a short, expanding stem and a straight to slightly convex base. Shoulders are horizontal to slightly barbed. **I.D. KEY:** Short, expanding stem.

HUFFAKER - Late Prehistoric, 1000 - 500 B. P.

(Also see Washita)

LOCATION: Midwest to Northern Plains states. **DESCRIPTION:** A small size, thin, arrowpoint with a straight to concave base and double side notches. Bases can have a single notch. **I.D. KEY:** Double side notches.

Note double notches on each side

G6, $15-$25
Bismark, ND

IRVINE - Late Prehistoric, 1400 - 800 B. P.

(Also see Avonlea, Emigrant, Lookingbill, Plains Side Notched, Samantha & Washita)

Petrified wood

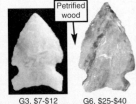     

G3, $7-$12
Meagher Co., MT

G6, $25-$40
Phillips Co., MT

G5, $15-$25
Cascade Co., MT

G6, $20-$35
Cascade Co., MT

G8, $30-$50
Phillips Co., MT

G6, $25-$45
Cascade Co., MT

G6, $25-$45
Saco, MT,
Milk Riv., kill
site

G5, $25-$45
Cascade Co.,
MT

Parallel flaking

G7, $30-$55
Cascade Co., MT.

LOCATION: Northern Plains states. **DESCRIPTION:** A small size, thin, side notched arrow point with a concave base. The notching is distinct forming squarish basal ears. **I.D. KEY:** Square basal ears.

NP

919

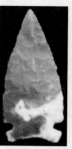

Parallel flaking

Obliquel flaking

G8, $35-$60
Meagher Co., MT

G9, $50-$90
MT

G9, $50-$90
Saco, MT, Milk Riv

G9, $50-$90
Cascade Co., MT

G10, $50-$95
Meagher Co., MT

G10, $60-$110
Meagher Co., MT

G10, $65-$125
Meagher Co., MT

LANCET - Plains Paleo to Historic Phase, 11,500 - 200 B. P.

(Also see Drill and Scraper)

G7, $8-$12 ea. (All hafted)
Lewis & Clark Co., MT

LOCATION: Everywhere. **DESCRIPTION:** Also known as a lammeler flake blade, it was produced by striking a flake or spall off a parent stone and was used as a knife for cutting. Some examples are notched for hafting. Recent experiments proved that these knives were sharper than a surgeon's scalpel. Similar to *burins* which are fractured at one end to produce a sharp point.

LEWIS - Late Prehistoric, 1400 - 400 B. P.

(Also see Avonlea, High River, Irvine, Nanton, Paskapoo, Swift Current and Tompkins)

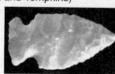

Petrified wood

G6, $12-$20
Phillips Co., MT

G5, $5-$10
Lewis & Clark Co., MT

G6, $12-$20
Phillips Co., MT

G6, $6-$12
Phillips Co., MT

LOCATION: Midwestern to Northern Plains states. **DESCRIPTION:** A small to medium size, thin, side notched point with a convex to concave base. The width of the base is less than the shoulders and the basal corners are rounded. Some specimens have basal grinding.

LOGAN CREEK - Early Archaic, 7000 - 5000 B. P.

(Also see Hawken, Lookingbill, Mallory, Plains Side Notched and Simonsen)

G6, $20-$35
Washington Co., KS

G6, $25-$40
Washington Co., KS

G8, $35-$65
Jefferson Co., NE

LOGAN CREEK (continued)

G6, $30-$50
Washington Co., KS

Drill form

G7, $40-$75
Jefferson Co., KS

G4, $12-$20
Washington Co., KS

G6, $25-$40
Washington Co., KS

Oblique flaking

Knife River flint

G7, $35-$65
Washington Co., KS

G7, $35-$65
Washington Co., KS

G7, $35-$65
Washington Co., KS

G8, $45-$85
Jefferson Co., KS

G7, $40-$75
Washington Co., KS

G8, $90-$175
Douglas Co., ND

G7, $45-$85
Washington Co., KS

Tip wear

G5, $10-$15
Pryor Mtns, MT

Tip nick

G6, $35-$65
Washington Co., KS

G7, $35-$65
Washington Co., KS

G9, $150-$265
S.D

G9, $125-$200
N. OK

G7, $150-$250
Washington Co., KS

NP

LOCATION: NE, IA, WY, MT, SD, KS. **DESCRIPTION:** A medium to large size, broad side-notched point with a straight, concave or convex base. Along with *Hawken* and *Lookingbill* , this is one of the earliest side-notched points of the Plains states. Oblique to horizontal blade flaking is evident on some examples. **I.D. KEY:** Broad side-notches close to the base, early flaking.

(Also see Archaic Side Notched, Hawken, Logan Creek & Simonsen)

G7, $20-$35
Tongue Riv., WY

G8, $55-$100
Mountrail Co., ND

G8, $65-$125
Jamestown, ND

Patinated
Knife River
flint

Knife
River flint

G6, $45-$80
Mountrail Co., ND

Knife
River
flint

G7, $80-$150
Sweetwater Co., WY

G7, $150-$250
WY

Knife River flint

G8, $150-$250
Mountrail Co., ND

Knife River
flint

G7, $125-$200
Mountrail Co., ND

G9, $175-$300
Mountrail Co., ND

Knife
River flint

Patinated Knife
River flint

G10, $250-$400
Nashua, MT,
Tongue River.

G9, $150-$250
Bottineau Co., ND

Knife
River
flint

LOCATION: Midwestern to Northern Plains states. **DESCRIP-TION:** A medium to large size, broad side-notched point with a straight to concave base. Along with *Hawkens* and *Logan Creek* this is one of the earliest side-notched points of the Plains states. **I.D.KEY:** Broad side notches close to the base, parallel flaking.

Knife
River
flint

Knife
River
flint

Moss
agate

G9, $125-$200
Pryor Mtns., S.E. MT

G7, $80-$150
Lewis & Clark Co., MT

G8, $150-$250
Mountrail Co., ND

G10, $250-$450
Bottineau Co., ND

G6, $175-$300
Mountrail Co., ND

LOVELL - Mountain Paleo, 8400 - 7800 B. P.

(Also see Agate Basin, Alder Complex, Clovis, Folsom, Goshen and Green River)

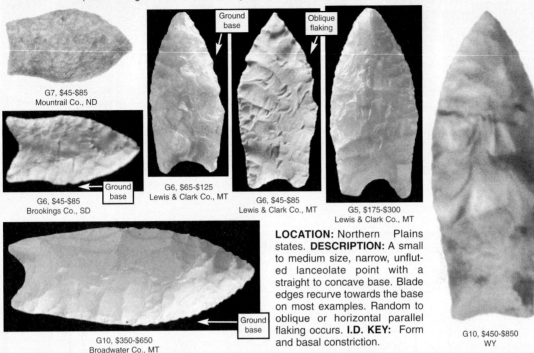

G7, $45-$85
Mountrail Co., ND

G6, $45-$85
Brookings Co., SD

Ground base

G6, $65-$125
Lewis & Clark Co., MT

Ground base

Oblique flaking

G6, $45-$85
Lewis & Clark Co., MT

G5, $175-$300
Lewis & Clark Co., MT

Ground base

G10, $350-$650
Broadwater Co., MT

G10, $450-$850
WY

LOCATION: Northern Plains states. **DESCRIPTION:** A small to medium size, narrow, unfluted lanceolate point with a straight to concave base. Blade edges recurve towards the base on most examples. Random to oblique or horizontal parallel flaking occurs. **I.D. KEY:** Form and basal constriction.

LUSK - Transitional Paleo, 8500 - 7400 B. P.

(Also see Angostura)

G8, $175-$300
Mountrail Co., ND

G8, $275-$350
Washington Co., CO

LOCATION: ND, SD, CO, NE, KS, WY. **DESCRIPTION:** A medium to large size, point with a contracting stem. Bases are usually concave and thinned. Related to *Angostura* points. **I.D.KEY:** Lanceolate point with contracting stem.

MALLORY - Middle Archaic, 4600 - 3500 B. P.

(Also see Billings, Emigrant, Logan Creek and Lookingbill)

NP

Alibates dolomite

Edwards Plateau

Alibates

Chalc.

G8, $65-$125
E. CO

G9, $150-$250
E. CO

G10, $80-$150
E. CO

G10, $350-$600
E. CO

LOCATION: Northern Plains states. **DESCRIPTION:** A small to medium size, broad, tri-notched to side notched point with a concave base and sharp basal corners. Side notches occur high up from the base. **I.D. KEY:** Size and tri-notching.

MALLORY (continued)

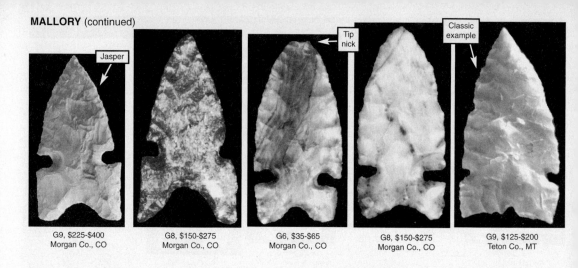

G9, $225-$400
Morgan Co., CO

G8, $150-$275
Morgan Co., CO

Tip nick

G6, $35-$65
Morgan Co., CO

G8, $150-$275
Morgan Co., CO

Classic example

G9, $125-$200
Teton Co., MT

Jasper

MCKEAN - Middle Archaic, 4600 - 3500 B. P.

(Also see Folsom, Goshen, Green River and Lovell)

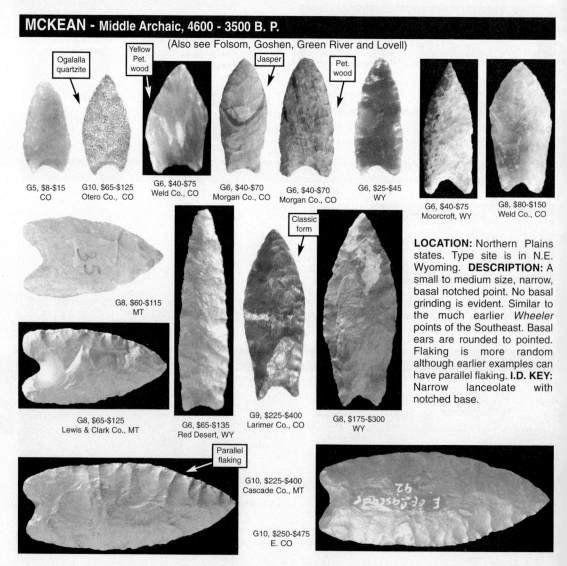

Ogalalla quartzite

Yellow Pet. wood

Jasper

Pet. wood

G5, $8-$15
CO

G10, $65-$125
Otero Co., CO

G6, $40-$75
Weld Co., CO

G6, $40-$70
Morgan Co., CO

G6, $40-$70
Morgan Co., CO

G6, $25-$45
WY

G6, $40-$75
Moorcroft, WY

G8, $80-$150
Weld Co., CO

G8, $60-$115
MT

Classic form

G8, $65-$125
Lewis & Clark Co., MT

G6, $65-$135
Red Desert, WY

G9, $225-$400
Larimer Co., CO

G8, $175-$300
WY

LOCATION: Northern Plains states. Type site is in N.E. Wyoming. **DESCRIPTION:** A small to medium size, narrow, basal notched point. No basal grinding is evident. Similar to the much earlier *Wheeler* points of the Southeast. Basal ears are rounded to pointed. Flaking is more random although earlier examples can have parallel flaking. **I.D. KEY:** Narrow lanceolate with notched base.

Parallel flaking

G10, $225-$400
Cascade Co., MT

G10, $250-$475
E. CO

(Also see Clovis, Folsom, Goshen, Lovell and San Jose)

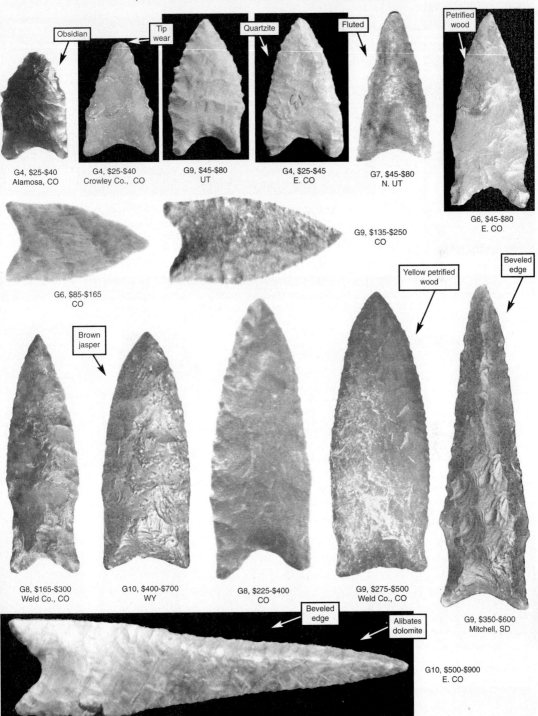

Obsidian

Tip wear

Quartzite

Fluted

Petrified wood

G4, $25-$40
Alamosa, CO

G4, $25-$40
Crowley Co., CO

G9, $45-$80
UT

G4, $25-$45
E. CO

G7, $45-$80
N. UT

G6, $45-$80
E. CO

G9, $135-$250
CO

G6, $85-$165
CO

Brown jasper

Yellow petrified wood

Beveled edge

G8, $165-$300
Weld Co., CO

G10, $400-$700
WY

G8, $225-$400
CO

G9, $275-$500
Weld Co., CO

G9, $350-$600
Mitchell, SD

Beveled edge

Alibates dolomite

G10, $500-$900
E. CO

NP

LOCATION: Co, SD, ND, MT, WY. **DESCRIPTION:** The Plains extension of the *Dalton* family. Blade edges are straight to slightly concave with a straight to very slightly concave sided stem. They are basally thinned and most examples are beveled and have light serrations on the blade edges. Beveling extends to the basal area on some examples. **I.D. KEY:** Concave base with pointed to rounded ears.

MID-BACK TANG - Late Archaic, 3400 - 1000 B. P.

(Also see Base Tang Knife, Cody Knife and Corner Tang)

Quartzite

G7, $250-$450
E. CO

Agate

G10, $1700-$3200
WY

LOCATION: Midwestern states and Canada. **DESCRIPTION:** A variation fo the corner tang knife with the hafting area occurring near the center of one side of the blade. **I.D. KEY:** Tang in center of blade.

MIDLAND - Plains Paleo, 10,900 - 10,200 B. P.

(Also see Alder Complex, Clovis, Folsom, Goshen and Milnesand)

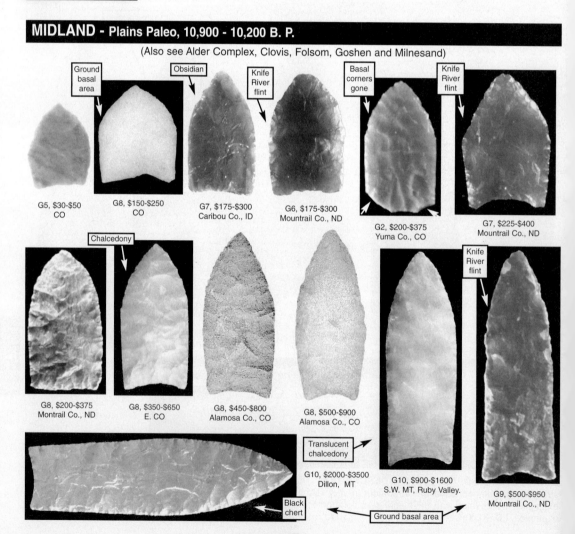

Ground basal area

G5, $30-$50
CO

Obsidian

G8, $150-$250
CO

Knife River flint

G7, $175-$300
Caribou Co., ID

G6, $175-$300
Mountrail Co., ND

Basal corners gone

G2, $200-$375
Yuma Co., CO

Knife River flint

G7, $225-$400
Mountrail Co., ND

Chalcedony

G8, $200-$375
Montrail Co., ND

G8, $350-$650
E. CO

G8, $450-$800
Alamosa Co., CO

G8, $500-$900
Alamosa Co., CO

Knife River flint

Translucent chalcedony

G10, $2000-$3500
Dillon, MT

G10, $900-$1600
S.W. MT, Ruby Valley.

G9, $500-$950
Mountrail Co., ND

Black chert

Ground basal area

926

MIDLAND (continued)

LOCATION: Texas to the Northern Plains states. **DESCRIPTION:** A small to medium size, very thin, unfluted lanceolate point with the widest part near the tip. Believed to be unfluted *Folsoms.* Bases have a shallow concavity. Basal thinning is weak and the blades exhibit fine micro-edgework. **I.D. KEY:** Form and thinness.

MILNESAND - Plains Paleo, 11,000 - 9500 B. P.

(Also see Alder Complex and Midland)

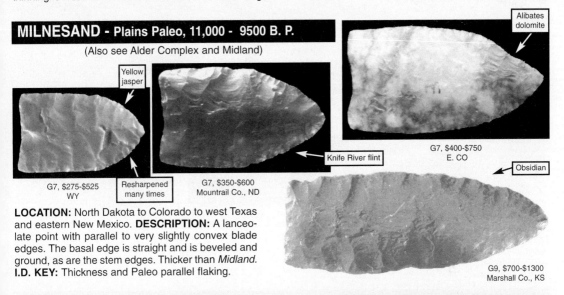

Yellow jasper

Alibates dolomite

Knife River flint

Obsidian

G7, $275-$525
WY

Resharpened many times

G7, $350-$600
Mountrail Co., ND

G7, $400-$750
E. CO

G9, $700-$1300
Marshall Co., KS

LOCATION: North Dakota to Colorado to west Texas and eastern New Mexico. **DESCRIPTION:** A lanceolate point with parallel to very slightly convex blade edges. The basal edge is straight and is beveled and ground, as are the stem edges. Thicker than *Midland.* **I.D. KEY:** Thickness and Paleo parallel flaking.

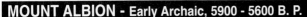

MOUNT ALBION - Early Archaic, 5900 - 5600 B. P.

(Also see Besant & Samantha)

G4, $2-$5
CO

G3, $1-$3
CO

G3, $4-$8
Weld Co., CO

G3, $3-$6
Weld Co., CO

G3, $4-$8
Weld Co., CO

G6, $6-$12
Weld Co., CO

G5, $6-$12
Weld Co., CO

G6, $6-$12
E. CO, Alibates.

Alibates dolomite

G7, $12-$20
E. CO

G9, $45-$80
E. CO

LOCATION: Southwestern states to Colorado. **DESCRIPTION:** A small to medium size, narrow, broad side notched point with a convex base. Shoulders are tapered. Basal corners are rounded.

NP

MUMMY CAVE - Late Prehistoric, 1400 - 1200 B. P.

(Also see Hog Back and Pelican Lake)

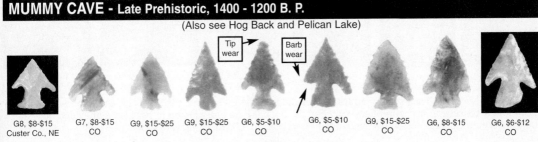

Tip wear

Barb wear

G8, $8-$15
Custer Co., NE

G7, $8-$15
CO

G9, $15-$25
CO

G9, $15-$25
CO

G6, $5-$10
CO

G6, $5-$10
CO

G9, $15-$25
CO

G6, $8-$15
CO

G6, $6-$12
CO

MUMMY CAVE (continued)

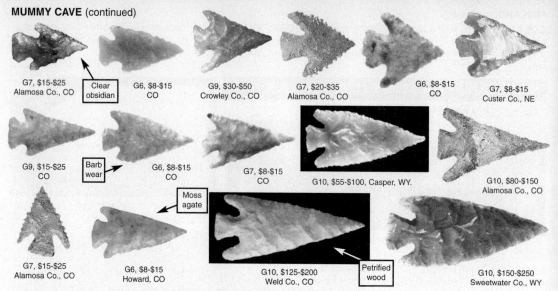

G7, $15-$25
Alamosa Co., CO

Clear obsidian

G6, $8-$15
CO

G9, $30-$50
Crowley Co., CO

G7, $20-$35
Alamosa Co., CO

G6, $8-$15
CO

G7, $8-$15
Custer Co., NE

G9, $15-$25
CO

Barb wear

G6, $8-$15
CO

G7, $8-$15
CO

G10, $55-$100, Casper, WY.

G10, $80-$150
Alamosa Co., CO

Moss agate

G7, $15-$25
Alamosa Co., CO

G6, $8-$15
Howard, CO

G10, $125-$200
Weld Co., CO

Petrified wood

G10, $150-$250
Sweetwater Co., WY

LOCATION: Northern Plains states. **DESCRIPTION:** A small size, thin, corner notched dart point with sharp, pointed tangs and an expanding base. Blade edges can be serrated. Similar to *Rose Springs* found in the Great Basin. **I.D. KEY:** Thinness, sharp tangs, early flaking.

NANTON - Late Prehistoric, 1400 - 300 B. P.

(Also see Avonlea, Cut Bank, Pekisko, Irvine and Swift Current)

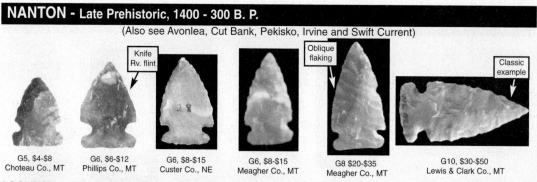

Knife Rv. flint

G5, $4-$8
Choteau Co., MT

G6, $6-$12
Phillips Co., MT

G6, $8-$15
Custer Co., NE

G6, $8-$15
Meagher Co., MT

Oblique flaking

G8 $20-$35
Meagher Co., MT

Classic example

G10, $30-$50
Lewis & Clark Co., MT

LOCATION: Northern Plains states. **DESCRIPTION:** A small to medium size, thin, narrow, side-notched point with rounded basal ears. Basal grinding occurs on some examples.

OXBOW - Middle Archaic, 5200 - 5100 B. P.

(Also see Meserve, San Jose, McKean)

G7, $20-$35
Weld Co., CO

Chalcedony

Knife River flint

G7, $15-$25
MT

G7, $15-$25
Cascade, WY

G7, $20-$35
Lewis & Clark Co., MT

G7, $35-$65
E. CO

G7, $50-$95
Jamestown, ND

G7, $40-$75
Divide Co., ND

LOCATION: Northern Plains states and Canada. **DESCRIPTION:** A small to medium size, side notched, auriculate point with a concave to bifurcated base that may be ground. Ears are squared to rounded and extend outward or downward from the base. Flaking is random to parallel oblique. **I.D. KEY:** Basal form.

OXBOW (continued)

Yellow petrified wood

G10, $90-$175
Mountrail Co., ND

G8, $90-$175
Divide Co., ND

Knife River flint

G8, $55-$100
Lewis & Clark Co., MT

Knife River flint

G7, $55-$100
Mountrail Co., ND

Knife River flint

G7, $35-$60
Mountrail Co., ND

Agate

G10, $90-$175
Mountrail Co., ND

Knife River flint

Classic form

G10, $250-$400
Meagher Co., MT

Knife River flint

G9, $150-$250
Mountrail Co., ND

Knife River flint

G9, $175-$300
ND

G8, $150-$250
Mountrail Co., ND

Knife River flint

G10, $175-$325
Bottineau Co., ND

Colorful chert

G8, $150-$250
Broadus, MT

G10, $200-$350
Bottineau Co., ND

Knife River flint

G10, $175-$300
Pollack, SD

G5, $30-$50
N. UT

Patinated Knife River flint

G10, $300-$550
Bottineau Co., ND

NP

PASKAPOO - Late Prehistoric, 1000 - 400 B. P.

(Also see Cut Bank, Irvine, Nanton, Pekisko and Plains Side Notched)

G8, $12-$20
Lewis & Clark Co., MT

G6, $10-$18
Choteau, MT

Tip nick

G3, $2-$5
Custer Co., NE

PASKAPOO (continued)

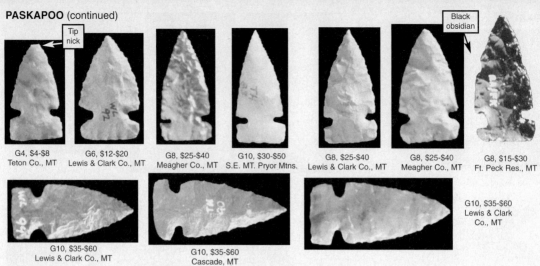

G4, $4-$8
Teton Co., MT

G6, $12-$20
Lewis & Clark Co., MT

G8, $25-$40
Meagher Co., MT

G10, $30-$50
S.E. MT. Pryor Mtns.

G8, $25-$40
Lewis & Clark Co., MT

G8, $25-$40
Meagher Co., MT

G8, $15-$30
Ft. Peck Res., MT

Black obsidian

Tip nick

G10, $35-$60
Lewis & Clark Co., MT

G10, $35-$60
Cascade, MT

G10, $35-$60
Lewis & Clark
Co., MT

LOCATION: Northern Plains states. **DESCRIPTION:** A small to medium size, thin arrow point with side-notches that occur higher up from the base than other Plains forms. The base is straight with rounded corners and are usually ground.

PEKISKO - Late Prehistoric, 800 - 400 B. P.

(Also see Buffalo Gap, Cut Bank, Nanton, Paskapoo & Washita)

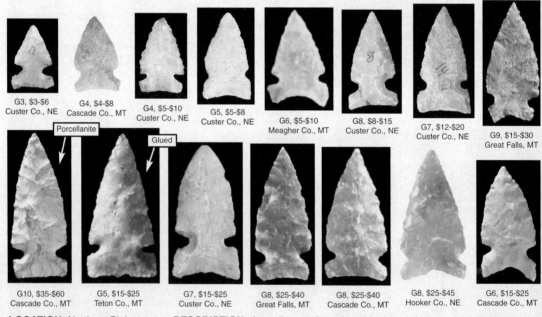

G3, $3-$6
Custer Co., NE

G4, $4-$8
Cascade Co., MT

G4, $5-$10
Custer Co., NE

G5, $5-$8
Custer Co., NE

G6, $5-$10
Meagher Co., MT

G8, $8-$15
Custer Co., NE

G7, $12-$20
Custer Co., NE

G9, $15-$30
Great Falls, MT

Porcellanite

Glued

G10, $35-$60
Cascade Co., MT

G5, $15-$25
Teton Co., MT

G7, $15-$25
Custer Co., NE

G8, $25-$40
Great Falls, MT

G8, $25-$40
Cascade Co., MT

G8, $25-$45
Hooker Co., NE

G6, $15-$25
Cascade Co., MT

LOCATION: Northern Plains states. **DESCRIPTION:** A small to medium size, thin, triangular arrow point with v-notches on both sides above the base. Bases are concave to straight and are as wide as the shoulders. **I.D.KEY:** V-notches.

PELICAN LAKE - Late Archaic, 2600 - 2300 B. P.

(Also see Camel Back, Elko, Glendo Arrow, Hog Back, Samantha & Washita)

LOCATION: Northern Plains states to Canada. **DESCRIPTION:** A small to medium size, thin, corner notched dart point with a straight to convex, expanding base. Barbs are usually pointed. Grinding may occur in notches and around base. Believed to have evolved into the *Samantha Dart* point. **I.D. KEY:** Sharp barbs.

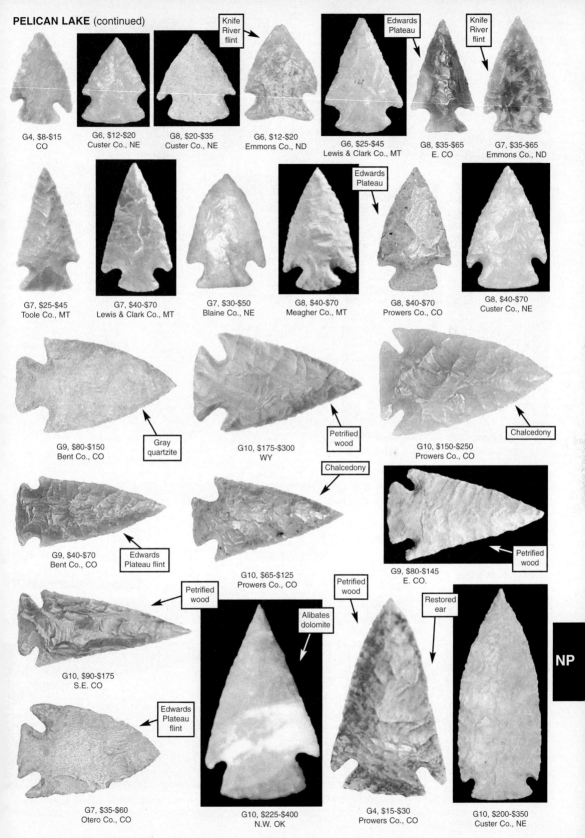

PELICAN LAKE (continued)

Knife River flint

Edwards Plateau

Knife River flint

G4, $8-$15
CO

G6, $12-$20
Custer Co., NE

G8, $20-$35
Custer Co., NE

G6, $12-$20
Emmons Co., ND

G6, $25-$45
Lewis & Clark Co., MT

G8, $35-$65
E. CO

G7, $35-$65
Emmons Co., ND

Edwards Plateau

G7, $25-$45
Toole Co., MT

G7, $40-$70
Lewis & Clark Co., MT

G7, $30-$50
Blaine Co., NE

G8, $40-$70
Meagher Co., MT

G8, $40-$70
Prowers Co., CO

G8, $40-$70
Custer Co., NE

Gray quartzite

Petrified wood

Chalcedony

G9, $80-$150
Bent Co., CO

G10, $175-$300
WY

G10, $150-$250
Prowers Co., CO

Chalcedony

Edwards Plateau flint

Petrified wood

G9, $40-$70
Bent Co., CO

G10, $65-$125
Prowers Co., CO

G9, $80-$145
E. CO.

Petrified wood

Petrified wood

Restored ear

Alibates dolomite

G10, $90-$175
S.E. CO

Edwards Plateau flint

G7, $35-$60
Otero Co., CO

G10, $225-$400
N.W. OK

G4, $15-$30
Prowers Co., CO

G10, $200-$350
Custer Co., NE

NP

PELICAN LAKE (continued)

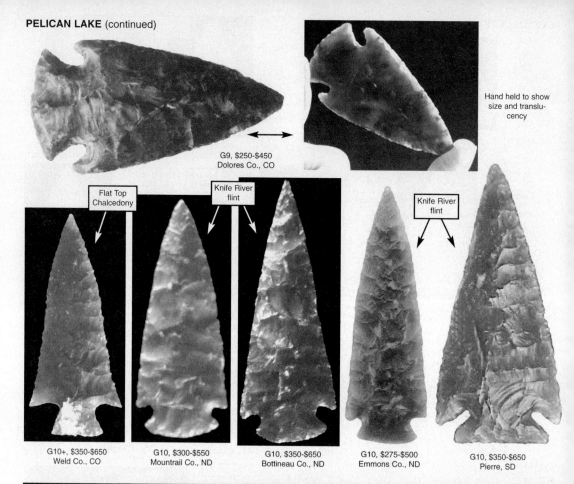

G9, $250-$450
Dolores Co., CO

Hand held to show size and translucency

Flat Top Chalcedony

Knife River flint

Knife River flint

G10+, $350-$650
Weld Co., CO

G10, $300-$550
Mountrail Co., ND

G10, $350-$650
Bottineau Co., ND

G10, $275-$500
Emmons Co., ND

G10, $350-$650
Pierre, SD

PIPE CREEK - Late Prehistoric, 1200 - 1000 B. P.

(Also see Corner Tang Knife)

LOCATION: Colorado into Texas and Tennessee. **DESCRIPTION:** A medium size knife with a notch in one basal corner. Bases can be straight to sloping. **I.D. KEY:** Single corner notch.

G5, $5-$10
Custer Co., NB

G6, $12-$20
Weld Co., CO

PLAINS KNIFE - Early to Middle Archaic, 6000 - 4000 B. P.

(Also see Archaic Knife, Archaic Side, Logan Creek, Lookingbill and Mallory)

Black obsidian

G8, $70-$135
Lewis & Clark Co., MT

G9, $150-$275
Lewis & Clark Co., MT

LOCATION: Northern Plains states. **DESCRIPTION:** A medium to large size, triangular, side-notched point with a straight to concave base. Flaking is horizontal transverse. The widest part of the point is at the basal corners. Bases are ground. **I.D. KEY:** Size, wide base.

(Also see Bitterroot, Buffalo Gap, Cut Bank, Desert, Nanton, Paskapoo, Pekisko & Washita)

G5, $5-$10
Bismark, ND

G5, $5-$10
Choteau Co., MT

G7, $12-$20
Sherman Co., NE

G7, $12-$20
Bismark, ND

G5, $8-$15
Choteau Co., MT

G7, $8-$15
Mobridge, SD

Knife River flint

G7, $12-$20
Morton Co., ND

Basalt

G8, $12-$20
Prowers Co., CO

Knife River flint

Edwards Plateau

G8, $15-$25
Bismark, ND

G7, $15-$25
Bismark, ND

G8, $12-$20
Otero Co., CO

Clear chalcedony

G8, $20-$35
Bent Co., CO

Knife River flint

G7, $15-$30
Morton Co., ND

Siltstone

G7, $15-$30
Morton Co., ND

Quartzite

G8, $20-$35
Prowers Co., CO

G8, $20-$35
Weld Co., CO

Siltstone

G7, $15-$30
Cascade Co., MT

G8, $20-$35
Morton Co., ND

G8, $20-$35
Weld Co., CO

G8, $20-$35
Sherman Co., NE

Agate

Edwards Plateau

G10, $35-$60
Otero Co. ,CO

Quartzite

G8, $20-$35
Pueblo Co., CO

Basalt

G10, $20-$35
Otero Co., CO

G9, $25-$45
Bent Co., CO

G10 $90-$175
Teton Co., MT

Black obsidian

G9, $55-$100
Meagher Co., MT

G8, $45-$85
Teton Co., MT

Black obsidian

G8, $40-$70
MT

G8, $40-$70
Teton Co., MT

G8, $40-$70
Teton Co., MT

G8, $40-$70
Teton Co., MT

Repaired tip

Chalc.

G5, $15-$30
E. CO

Ogalalla quartzite

G9, $55-$100
E. CO

G10, $80-$150
Bent Co., CO

Dark chalc.

G9, $55-$100
Teton Co., MT

G9, $80-$150
Teton Co., MT

One notch higher

G10, $80-$150
Teton Co., MT

One notch higher

G10, $125-$200
MT

G10, $125-$200
Teton Co., MT

NP

PLAINS SIDE NOTCHED (continued)

LOCATION: Northern Plains states. **DESCRIPTION:** A small to medium size, thin, triangular, side-notched arrow point with a concave base. Notches are narrow and occur high up from the base. Basal corners are usually sharp and blade edges are not serrated. Many have been dug in buffalo kill sites. **I.D. KEY:** Notches.

PLAINS TRIANGULAR - Proto Historic, 200 - 150 B. P.

(Also see Archaic Triangle, Cottonwood)

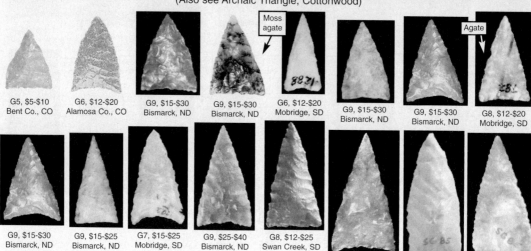

G5, $5-$10
Bent Co., CO

G6, $12-$20
Alamosa Co., CO

G9, $15-$30
Bismarck, ND

Moss agate

G9, $15-$30
Bismarck, ND

G6, $12-$20
Mobridge, SD

G9, $15-$30
Bismarck, ND

G9, $15-$30
Bismarck, ND

Agate

G8, $12-$20
Mobridge, SD

G9, $15-$30
Bismarck, ND

G9, $15-$25
Bismarck, ND

G7, $15-$25
Mobridge, SD

G9, $25-$40
Bismarck, ND

G8, $12-$25
Swan Creek, SD

G9, $30-$50
Bismarck, ND

G8, $20-$35 ea.
S.E. MT, Pryor Mtns.

LOCATION: Northern Plains states. **DESCRIPTION:** A small size, thin, triangular arrow point with a straight to concave base and sharp basal ears. **I.D. KEY:** Small triangle

PLAINVIEW - Plains Paleo, 11,250 - 9500 B. P.

(Also see Clovis, Folsom, Goshen, Lovell, Midland, Milnesand)

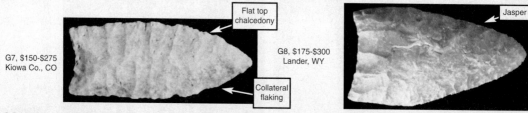

Flat top chalcedony

G7, $150-$275
Kiowa Co., CO

G8, $175-$300
Lander, WY

Collateral flaking

Jasper

LOCATION: Colorado into Texas. **DESCRIPTION:** A medium to large size, thin, lanceolate point with usually parallel sides and a concave base that is ground. Some examples are thinned or fluted and are believed to be related to the earlier *Clovis* and contemporary *Dalton/Merserve* types. Examples found further north are called *Goshen* which is the same type. Flaking is of high quality and can be collateral to oblique transverse. A cross type between *Clovis* and *Dalton*. **I.D. KEY:** Basal form and parallel flaking.

PRAIRIE SIDE NOTCHED - Late Prehistoric, 1300 - 620 B. P.

(Also see Irvine, Nanton, Paskapoo, Pekisko, Plains Side Notched & Washita)

Knife River flint

Knife River flint

Knife River flint

Knife River flint

G5, $6-$10
Mitchell, SD

G5, $7-$12
Mitchell, SD

G5, $12-$20
Phillips Co., MT

G6, $12-$20
Mitchell, SD

G6, $15-$25
Mitchell, SD

G5, $12-$20
Phillips Co., MT

G6, $15-$25
Mitchell, SD

G6, $15-$25
Great Falls, MT

PRAIRIE SIDE NOTCHED (continued)

G6, $12-$20	G5, $12-$20	G7, $20-$35	G7, $15-$25	G6, $12-$20
Lewis & Clark Co., MT	Phillips Co., MT	Lewis & Clark Co., MT	Lewis & Clark Co., MT	Lewis & Clark Co., MT

LOCATION: Northern Plains states. **DESCRIPTION:** A medium size triangular arrow point with broad side notches. Bases are straight to slightly concave.

PRYOR STEMMED - Mountain Paleo, 8500 - 7500 B. P.

(Also see Eden eared and Hell Gap)

Oblique transverse flaking

G7, $50-$90
WY

Quartz

G7, $90-$175
CO/NE border

LOCATION: Northern Plains states into W. Oregon. **DESCRIPTION:** A medium size, short stemmed point with slight, tapered shoulders, a concave base and rounded basal corners. Flaking is usually oblique transverse. Stems are ground.

RED RIVER KNIFE - Plains Paleo, 10,000 - 8000 B. P.

(Also see Alberta, Cody Knife, Eden, Firstview and Scottsbluff)

LOCATION: Texas to Colorado. **DESCRIPTION:** A medium size, asymmetrical blade with weak shoulders and a short, expanding stem. Bases are straight to slightly convex. It has been reported that these knives were made by the Cody Complex people from *Scottsbluff* points. Look for early parallel flaking and stem grinding.

Spanish Diggins quartzite

G9, $250-$400
Bent Co., CO

RIO GRANDE - Early Archaic, 7500 - 6000 B. P.

(Also see Bajada & Hell Gap)

Basalt

G5, $60-$100
Alamosa CO., CO

Yellow agatized Texas palmwood

G10, $500-$900
Otero CO., CO

NP

LOCATION: Southern Colorado into western Texas. **DESCRIPTION:** A lanceolate point with a relatively long stem formed by tapered shoulders. The stem contracts slightly and edges are ground. **I.D. KEY:** Shoulders more pronounced than on *Hell Gap* points but can easily be confused with *Hell Gap*. Both types cross over in Colorado. Some *Hell Gaps* have prominent shoulders similar to this type.

RIO GRANDE (continued)

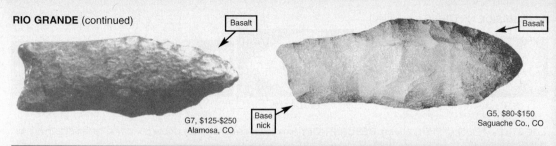

Basalt

Basalt

G7, $125-$250
Alamosa, CO

Base nick

G5, $80-$150
Saguache Co., CO

SAMANTHA-ARROW - Late Prehistoric, 1500 - 1200 B. P.

(Also see Avonlea, High River, Lewis and Tompkins)

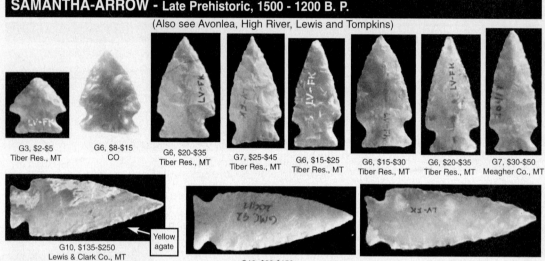

G3, $2-$5
Tiber Res., MT

G6, $8-$15
CO

G6, $20-$35
Tiber Res., MT

G7, $25-$45
Tiber Res., MT

G6, $15-$25
Tiber Res., MT

G6, $15-$30
Tiber Res., MT

G6, $20-$35
Tiber Res., MT

G7, $30-$50
Meagher Co., MT

G10, $135-$250
Lewis & Clark Co., MT

Yellow agate

G10, $80-$150
Meagher Co., MT

G10, $80-$150
Tiber Res., MT

G9, $55-$100
Tiber Res., MT

LOCATION: Canada to the Northern Plains states. **DESCRIPTION:** A small to medium size, narrow, thin, corner to side-notched arrow point. Flaking is random to oblique transverse. Related and developed from the earlier *Samantha Dart* point. Shoulders are tapered and the stem expands to a straight to slightly concave base.

SAMANTHA-DART - Late Prehistoric, 2200 - 1500 B. P.

(Also see Besant, Mount Albion and Pelican Lake)

Gem

G5, $12-$20
CO

G7, $12-$20
CO

G8, $20-$35
CO

G5, $12-$20
Sundance, WY

G5, $12-$20
Lewis & Clark Co., MT

G5, $12-$20
Lewis & Clark Co., MT

G5, $12-$20
Lewis & Clark Co., N

Georgetown Flint

G6, $20-$35
Bent Co., CO

G6, $15-$25
Lewis & Clark Co., MT

G7, $15-$25
Lewis & Clark Co., MT

G6, $20-$35
CO

G6, $15-$25
UT

Knife River Flint

G7, $20-$35
ND

SAMANTHA DART (continued)

Chalcedony

G10, $80-$150
Prowers Co., CO

Rare double tip

G6, $15-$30
Hooker Co., NE

G7, $30-$50
Teton Co., MT

G8, $20-$35
CO

G8, $30-$50
Meagher Co., MT

G7 $55-$100
Jamestown, ND

G6, $25-$45
Teton Co., MT

Edge wear

G7, $40-$70
Phillips Co., MT

Knife River Flint

Knife River flint

Petrified wood

G8, $65-$125
Renville Co., ND

G7, $40-$75
Lewis & Clark Co., MT

G9, $125-$200
Bottineau Co., ND

G10, $250-$425
Adams Co., CO

G10, $250-$425
SD

LOCATION: Canada to the Northern Plains states. **DESCRIPTION:** A medium to large size, corner to side-notched dart point with with horizontal, tapered or slightly barbed shoulders. Believed to have evolved from the *Pelican Lake* type changing into the *Besant* type at a later time.

SAN JOSE - Plains Paleo - Transitional Paleo, 9000 - 6000 B. P.

(Also see Bajada, Clovis, Folsom, Goshen, Hanna, Lovell and Meserve)

Basalt

G10, $15-$30
Conejos Co., CO

G6, $25-$45
Seguache Co., CO

Tip wear

G8, $50-$90
Crowley Co., CO

G7, $40-$75
Weld Co., CO

LOCATION: Arizona, Colorado, Nevada, New Mexico, Sou. Utah. **DESCRIPTION:** A small to medium size dart/knife point with wide, shallow side notches creating an auriculate base. The shoulders are obtuse and the blade edges always have serrations. Stem and base edges are usually ground. **I.D. KEY:** Auriculate base.

SATTLER - Late Prehistoric, 1400 - 400 B. P.

(Also see Hog Back)

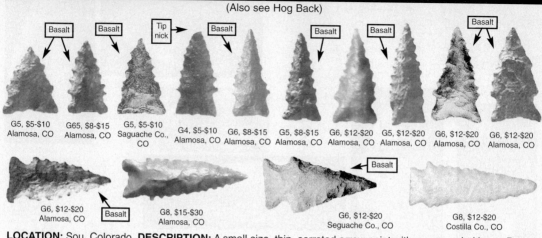

G5, $5-$10
Alamosa, CO

G65, $8-$15
Alamosa, CO

G5, $5-$10
Saguache Co.,
CO

G4, $5-$10
Alamosa, CO

G6, $8-$15
Alamosa, CO

G5, $8-$15
Alamosa, CO

G6, $12-$20
Alamosa, CO

G5, $12-$20
Alamosa, CO

G6, $12-$20
Alamosa, CO

G6, $12-$20
Alamosa, CO

G6, $12-$20
Alamosa, CO

G8, $15-$30
Alamosa, CO

G6, $12-$20
Seguache Co., CO

G8, $12-$20
Costilla Co., CO

LOCATION: Sou. Colorado. **DESCRIPTION:** A small size, thin, serrated arrow point with an expanded base. Base is straight to concave. Tips are sharp.

SCOTTSBLUFF I - Plains Paleo, 10,000 - 8000 B. P.

(Also see Alberta, Bajada, Cody Knife, Eden, Firstview, Hell Gap & Red River Knife)

G6, $150-$250
E. CO

G7, $150-$250
E. CO

G7, $150-$275
Broadwater Co., MT

G5, $90-$175
El Paso Co., CO

G5, $90-$175
ND

G8, $250-$400
E. CO

G8 $200-$350
Upton, WY

G7, $350-$600
Broadwater Co., MT

G7, $350-$600
Broadwater Co., MT

G7, $350-$600
S. E. OK

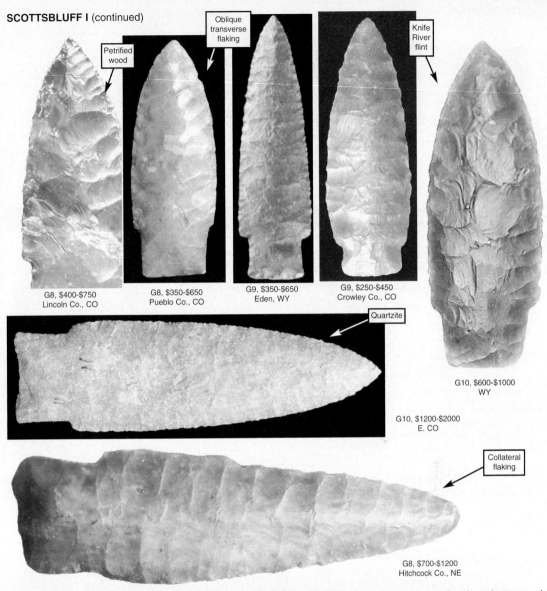

Petrified wood

Oblique transverse flaking

Knife River flint

G8, $400-$750
Lincoln Co., CO

G8, $350-$650
Pueblo Co., CO

G9, $350-$650
Eden, WY

G9, $250-$450
Crowley Co., CO

G10, $600-$1000
WY

Quartzite

G10, $1200-$2000
E. CO

Collateral flaking

G8, $700-$1200
Hitchcock Co., NE

LOCATION: Midwestern states to Texas and Colorado. **DESCRIPTION:** A medium to large size, broad, stemmed point with parallel to convex sides and weak shoulders. The stem is parallel sided or expands slightly. The base is straight to concave. Made by the Cody complex people. Flaking is of the high quality parallel horizontal to oblique transverse type. Bases are ground. **I.D. KEY:** Broad stem, weak shoulders.

SCOTTSBLUFF II - Plains Paleo, 10,000 - 8000 B. P.

(Also see Alberta, Bajada, Cody Knife, Eden, Hell Gap & Red River Knife)

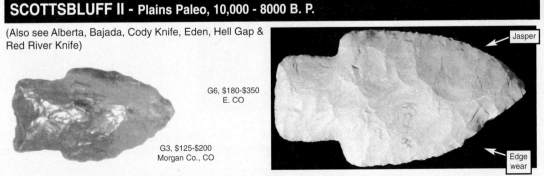

Jasper

G6, $180-$350
E. CO

G3, $125-$200
Morgan Co., CO

Edge wear

NP

SCOTTSBLUFF II (continued)

Photo from a Pete Bostrom cast of original

Collateral flaking

G10+, $7,000-$12,000+
Beaverhead Co., MT

LOCATION: Midwestern states to Texas and Colorado. **DESCRIPTION:** A medium to large size triangular point with shoulders a little stronger than on Type I and a broad parallel sided/expanding stem that is ground. **I.D. KEY:** Broad stem, stronger shoulders.

SCRAPER - Plains Paleo to Middle Archaic, 11,500 - 5000 B. P.

(Also see Drill, Hafted Knife, Paleo Knife and Side knife)

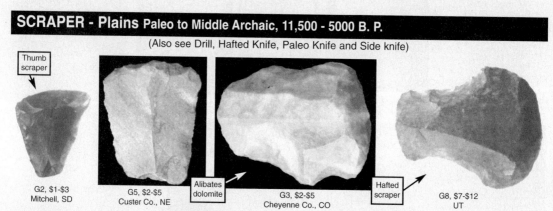

Thumb scraper

G2, $1-$3
Mitchell, SD

G5, $2-$5
Custer Co., NE

Alibates dolomite

G3, $2-$5
Cheyenne Co., CO

Hafted scraper

G8, $7-$12
UT

LOCATION: All early-man sites. **DESCRIPTION:** Thumb, duckbill and turtleback forms are small to medium size, thick, ovoid shaped, uniface, scraping tools that are steeply beveled, especially at the broadest end. Side scrapers are long hand-held uniface flakes with beveling on all blade edges of one face. Scraping was done primarily from the sides of these blades. Many of these tools were hafted.

SIDE KNIFE - Late Prehistoric, 500 - 300 B. P.

(Also see Crescent, Hafted Knife & Scraper)

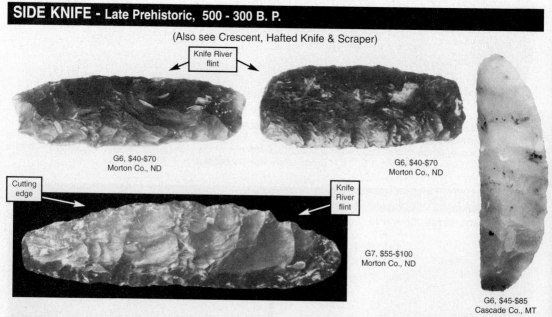

Knife River flint

G6, $40-$70
Morton Co., ND

G6, $40-$70
Morton Co., ND

Cutting edge

Knife River flint

G7, $55-$100
Morton Co., ND

G6, $45-$85
Cascade Co., MT

LOCATION: Northern Plains states. **DESCRIPTION:** Side Knives were generally hafted into bison rib-bone handles as illustrated below. Gut and plant fibers were also used when needed to bind the hafting. Also known as *Round-End Knife.*

SIDE KNIFE (continued)

G10, $550-$1000
ND. 500-800 years old.

G10, $800-$1500
E. CO. Bone handle, stone blade.

Siltstone

G7, $50-$90
Cascade Co., MT

Quartzite

Very rare examples of hafted knives, both in a bone handle and found perfectly preserved. Asphaltum or pitch was used as an adhesive to glue the stone tool in the handle.

G6, $35-$65
Morton Co., ND

SIDE NOTCH (See Archaic Side Notch)

SIMONSEN - Early Archaic, 6800 - 6400 B. P.

(Also see Besant and Bitterroot)

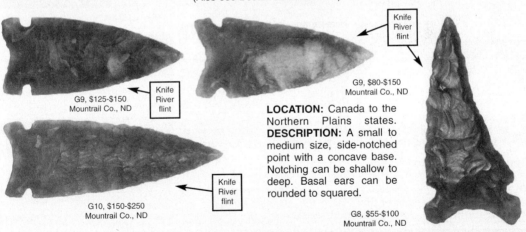

G9, $125-$150
Mountrail Co., ND

Knife River flint

Knife River flint

G9, $80-$150
Mountrail Co., ND

G10, $150-$250
Mountrail Co., ND

Knife River flint

LOCATION: Canada to the Northern Plains states. **DESCRIPTION:** A small to medium size, side-notched point with a concave base. Notching can be shallow to deep. Basal ears can be rounded to squared.

G8, $55-$100
Mountrail Co., ND

NP

SONOTA - Late Prehistoric, 1000 - 400 B. P.

(Also see Besant and Bitterroot)

Clasic example

Very thin

G8, $40-$75
Mountrail Co., ND

LOCATION: Canada to the Northern Plains states. **DESCRIPTION:** Most examples are small, thin, side to corner notched points with a straight to slightly concave base. Basal corners can form ears on some examples and notching is usually close to the base. Base usually is not as wide as the shoulders.

SONOTA (continued)

Knife River flint

G6, $55-$65
Mountrail Co., ND

G8, $65-$125
Mountrail Co., ND

G8, $150-$275
Lewis & Clark Co., MT

Knife River flint

G9, $250-$400
McKenzie Co., ND

G9, $250-$400
McClean Co., ND

STOTT - Late Prehistoric, 1300 - 600 B. P.

(Also see Besant, Bitterroot, Nanton, Paskapoo, Pekisko and Tompkins)

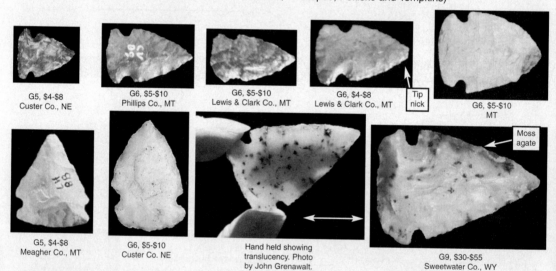

G5, $4-$8
Custer Co., NE

G6, $5-$10
Phillips Co., MT

G6, $5-$10
Lewis & Clark Co., MT

G6, $4-$8
Lewis & Clark Co., MT

Tip nick

G6, $5-$10
MT

G5, $4-$8
Meagher Co., MT

G6, $5-$10
Custer Co. NE

Hand held showing translucency. Photo by John Grenawalt.

Moss agate

G9, $30-$55
Sweetwater Co., WY

LOCATION: Canada to the Northern Plains states. **DESCRIPTION:** A small size, v-notched point with a convex base. Size of base is large in proportion to the blade size. **I.D. KEY:** V-notches, large base.

SWIFT CURRENT - Late Prehistoric, 1300 - 800 B. P.

(Also see Avonlea, Cut Bank, Irvine and Pekisko)

G6, $12-$20
Phillips Co., MT

Petrified wood

G6, $15-$25
Phillips Co., MT

G6, $15-$30
Lewis & Clark Co., MT

G6, $15-$30
Saco, MT, Milk Rv.

G6, $12-$20
Lewis & Clark Co., MT

SWIFT CURRENT (continued)

From a Buffalo jump kill site

G6, $20-$35
Nelson Res., MT

G7, $20-$35
Lewis & Clark Co., MT

G6, $15-$30
Saco, MT

G7, $20-$35
Cascade Co., MT

G7, $20-$35
Saco, MT, Milk Rv.

G8, $25-$45
Lewis & Clark Co., MT

G7, $30-$55
Lewis & Clark Co., MT

Classic form

Variant base form

G7, $20-$35
Great Falls, MT

G7, $30-$55
Lewis & Clark Co., MT

G9, $30-$55
Phillips Co., MT

G8, $35-$65
Lewis & Clark Co., MT

G9, $25-$45
Fort Peck Res., MT

G8, $35-$65
Meagher Co., MT

G8, $30-$55
Lewis & Clark Co., MT

LOCATION: Northern Plains states. **DESCRIPTION:** A small size, thin, side notched arrow point with a concave base. Blade edges can be serrated. Ancient buffalo jump kill sites have been discovered in the Plains states where this type is found. Early man drove the buffalo over cliffs and into corrals for easy killing. **I.D. KEY:** Drooping ears.

TOMPKINS - Late Prehistoric, 1200 - 800 B. P.

(Also see Cut Bank, High River, Irvine, Nanton, Pekisko, Paskapoo, Prairie Side Notched and Swift Current)

G6, $4-$8
Choteau Co., MT

G6, $4-$8
Phillips Co., MT

G6, $5-$10
Phillips Co., MT.

Knif. Riv. flint

LOCATION: Northern Plains states. **DESCRIPTION:** A small size, thin, serrated, side to corner notched arrow point with a concave base. On some examples, one notch is from the corner and the other definitely from the side. Some have basal grinding. Found on ancient Buffalo jump kill sites.

TOYAH - Late Prehistoric, 600 - 400 B. P.

(Also see Harrell and Washita)

Chalcedony

G6, $5-$10
Conejos Co., CO

LOCATION: Northern Mexico to Texas and Colorado. **DESCRIPTION:** A small size, thin, triangular point with expanded barbs and one or more notches on each side and a basal notch. **I.D. KEY:** Has drooping, pointed barbs.

NP

TRADE POINTS - Proto Historic, 300 - 100 B. P.

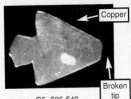

Copper

Broken tip

G5, $25-$40
Mountrail Co., ND

G5, $25-$40
Custer Co., NE

G5, $25-$40
Custer Co., NE

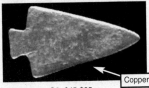

Copper

G9, $45-$85
Mountrail Co., ND

All above points were probably made by the indians.

Lettering adds value

"Little Big Horn" form

Broken base

G6, $45-$80
Custer Co., NE

*G7, $60-$110
Custer Co., NE

*G7, $95-$185
Custer Co., NE

*G8, $85-$165
Custer Co., NE

These points were made of copper, iron, and steel and were traded to the Indians by the French, British and others from the 1600s to the 1800s. Examples have been found all over the United States. **NOTE:** All points with * were probably blacksmith made trade points.

*G9, $90-$165
Custer Co., NE

*G9, $125-$200
Meagher Co., MT

*G3, $12-$20
Costilla Co., CO

G6, $25-$40
Lewis & Clark Co., MT

Note: All points with * were probably blacksmith made trade points.

Base wear

Tip wear

"Little Big Horn" form

"Little Big Horn" form

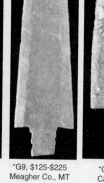

*G6, $35-$65
Custer Co., NE

*G6, $35-$50
Custer Co., NE

*G4, $40-$70
Custer Co., NE

*G9, $125-$225
Meagher Co., MT

*G10, $175-$300
Cascade Co., MT

*G10, $200-$325
Cheyenne, MT. Little Big
Horn site. ca. 1850/Iron.

WASHITA - Late Prehistoric, 800 - 400 B. P.

(Also see Harrell and Toyah)

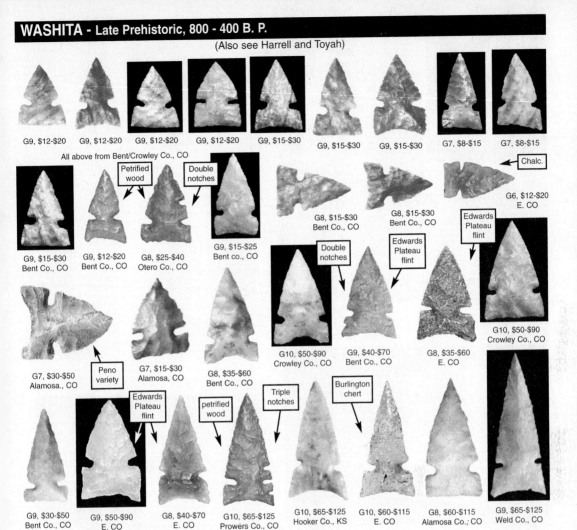

G9, $12-$20   G9, $12-$20   G9, $12-$20   G9, $12-$20   G9, $15-$30   G9, $15-$30   G9, $15-$30   G7, $8-$15   G7, $8-$15

All above from Bent/Crowley Co., CO

Petrified wood

Double notches

Chalc.

G6, $12-$20
E. CO

G9, $15-$30
Bent Co., CO

G9, $12-$20
Bent Co., CO

G8, $25-$40
Otero Co., CO

G9, $15-$25
Bent co., CO

G8, $15-$30
Bent Co., CO

G8, $15-$30
Bent Co., CO

Edwards Plateau flint

Double notches

Edwards Plateau flint

G10, $50-$90
Crowley Co., CO

G7, $30-$50
Alamosa., CO

Peno variety

G7, $15-$30
Alamosa, CO

G8, $35-$60
Bent Co., CO

G10, $50-$90
Crowley Co., CO

G9, $40-$70
Bent Co., CO

G8, $35-$60
E. CO

Edwards Plateau flint

petrified wood

Triple notches

Burlington chert

G9, $30-$50
Bent Co., CO

G9, $50-$90
E. CO

G8, $40-$70
E. CO

G10, $65-$125
Prowers Co., CO

G10, $65-$125
Hooker Co., KS

G10, $60-$115
E. CO

G8, $60-$115
Alamosa Co.; CO

G9, $65-$125
Weld Co., CO

LOCATION: Kansas, E. Colorado northward into the Dakotas. **DESCRIPTION:** A small size, thin, side notched arrow point with a concave base and sharp basal corners. Notches usually occur far up from the base. Can be confused with the Desert series.

WASHITA-NORTHERN - Late Prehistoric, 800 - 400 B. P.

(Also see Harrell & Toyah)

G6, $25-$45
Cascade Co., MT

G7, $15-$25
ND

Knife River flint

G6, $30-$50
Bismark, ND

G6, $35-$60
Lewis & Clark Co., MT

G6, $35-$60
Cascade Co., MT

Classic form

LOCATION: Northern Plains states. **DESCRIPTION:** A small size, thin, triangular side notched arrow point with a concave base. Basal area is usually large in proportion to the blade size. Basal corners are sharp. Notches are narrow.

WRAY - Mid-Archaic, 5000 - 3500 B. P.

(Also see Base Tang Knife, Mount Albion, Pelican Lake and Samantha Dart)

LOCATION: Northern Plains states to Canada. **DESCRIPTION:** A broad, medium size basal notched point with a convex base. Shoulders are sharp to squared and the base that is usually ground is convex.

WRAY (continued)

G9, $70-$135
Sweetwater Co., WY

Hand held to show
translucency

G9, $80-$150
Goshen Co., WY

Banded agate

Flat Top Chalcedony

Alibates dolomite

Very thin

Jasper

G7, $35-$60
Crowley Co., CO

G8, $150-$275
Bent Co., CO

G7, $80-$140
Alamosa, CO

G10, $150-$275
N. OK

G10, $300-$550
Boar's Tusk, WY

Petrified wood

G10, $250-$400
Mountrail Co., ND

Porcellanite

YONKEE - Late Archaic, 3200 - 2500 B. P.

(Also see Besant and Bitterroot)

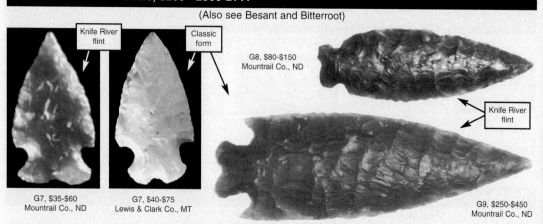

Knife River flint

Classic form

G8, $80-$150
Mountrail Co., ND

Knife River flint

G7, $35-$60
Mountrail Co., ND

G7, $40-$75
Lewis & Clark Co., MT

G9, $250-$450
Mountrail Co., ND

LOCATION: Northern Plains states. **DESCRIPTION:** A medium size, narrow point that is corner or side-notched. The stem expands and the base is convex and bifurcated forming ears. Shoulders are barbed to horizontal. Related to *Samantha* points. **I.D. KEY:** Lobed ears.

946

FAR WEST SECTION:

This section includes point types from the following states:
Great Basin, California, W. Idaho, W. Utah, Nevada, Oregon, Washington, and British Columbia, Canada

The points in this section are arranged in alphabetical order and are shown **actual size**. All types are listed that were available for photographing. Any missing types will be added to future editions as photographs become available. We are always interested in receiving sharp, black and white, color glossy photos or high resolution (300 pixels/inch) digital images of your collection. Be sure and include a ruler in the photograph so that proper scale can be determined.

Lithics: Materials employed in the manufacture of projectile points from this region are: obsidian, basalt, dacite and ignimbrite with lesser amounts of agate, jasper, chert, chalcedony, nephrite, opal, petrified wood.

Important sites: Clovis: Borax Lake, N. California, Wenatchee Clovis cache, WA.

Regional Consultants:
John Byrd, Jim Hogue

Special Advisors:
Mark Berreth, Tony Hardie, Bill & Donna Jackson,
Randy McNeice, Rodney Michel, Ben Stermer, Jeb Taylor
Gregory J. Truesdell

FW

FAR WEST POINT TYPES
(Archaeological Periods)

PALEO (13,200 B. P. - 8,000 B. P.)

Agate Basin	Crescent	Haskett	Lind Coulee	Plainview	Windust
Alder Complex	Drill	Hell Gap	Midland	Scraper	Windust-Alberta
Black Rock Concave	Fells Cave (N.W.)	Intermontane	Milnesand	Silver Lake	Windust Contracting
Bone Pin	Folsom	Stemmed	Owl Cave	Spedis I	Stem
Chopper	Goshen	Kennewick	Paleo Knife	Spedis II	Windust-Hatwai
Clovis	Graver	Lake Mohave	Pay Paso (N.W.)	Spedis Fishtail	
Cougar Mountain	Hand Axe	Lancet	Pieces Esquillees	Tulare Lake	

EARLY ARCHAIC (10,500 B. P. - 5,500 B. P.)

Alberta	Cody Complex Knife	Jalama Side Notched	Pluvial Lakes Side	Tulare Lake Bi-Point
Albion-Head Side Notched	Cordilleran	Kelsey Creek Barbed	Notched	Wendover
Atlatl Valley Triangular	Early Eared	Mahkin Shouldered Lance.	Pryor Stemmed	Wildcat Canyon
Base Tang Knife	Early Leaf	Nightfire	Rose Valley	Youngs River Stemmed
Bitterroot	Eden	Northern Side Notched	Rough Stemmed Knife II	
Borax Lake	Firstview	Okanogan Knife	Salmon River	
Cascade	Hawken	Parman	Scottsbluff I	
Cascade Knife	Humboldt Basal Notched	Perforator	Scottsbluff II	
Cascade Shouldered	Humboldt Constricted	Pinto Basin	Scottsbluff Knife	
Chilcotin Plateau	Base	Pinto Basin Sloping	Sierra Contracting	
Chumash Tools	Humboldt Triangular	Shoulder	Stemmed	

MIDDLE ARCHAIC (5,500 B. P. - 3,300 B. P.)

Big Valley Stemmed	Gatecliff	Notched	Steamboat Lanceolate	Willits Side Notched
Bullhead	Gatecliff Split-Stem	McGillivray Expanding	Triple "T"	
Cold Springs	Gold Hill	Stem	Tucannon Corner Notched	
Coquille Broadneck	Gypsum Cave	McKee Uniface	Tucannon Side Notched	
Coquille Knife	High Desert Knife	Mendocino Concave	Tucannon Stemmed	
Coquille Side Notched	Houx Contracting Stem	Base	Vandenberg Contracting	
Fish Gutter	Mayacmas Corner	Rossi Square-Stemmed	Stem	

LATE ARCHAIC (3,500 B. P. - 2,300 B. P.)

Ahsahka	Elko Split-Stem	Hendricks	Need Stemmed	Rough Stemmed	Tuolumne Notched
Año Nuevo	Elko Wide-Notch	Lady Island Pent.	Lanceolate	Knife I	Wooden Dart/Arrow
Buchanan Eared	Excelsior	Martis	Ochoco Stemmed	Shaniko Stemmed	
Contra Costa	Exotic Forms	Merrybell, Var. I	Point Sal Barbed	Spedis III	
Elko Cor. Notched	Fountain Bar	Merrybell, Var. II	Priest Rapids	Square-End Knife	
Elko Eared	Harpoon	Merrybell, Var. III	Quilomene Bar	Triangular Knife	

DESERT TRADITIONS:

TRANSITIONAL PHASE (2,300 B. P. - 1,600 B. P.)

Coquille Narrowneck	Sauvie's Island Basal	Notched	Strong Barbed	Vendetta
Hafted Knife	Notched	Sizer	Auriculate	
Rabbit Island Dart	Sauvie's Island Shoulder	Snake River Dart	Three-Piece Fish Spear	

DEVELOPMENTAL PHASE (1,600 B. P. - 700 B. P.)

Alkali	Dagger	Notched	Rose Springs Corner	Stockton
Bear River	Eastgate	Hell's Canyon Corner	Notched	Trojan
Bliss	Eastgate Split-Stem	Notched	Rose Springs Side	Uinta
Bone Arrow	Emigrant Springs	Kamloops Side Notched	Notched	Wahmuza
Calapooya	Freemont Triangular	Malaga Cove Leaf	Rose Springs Sloping	Wallula Gap Rect. Stem
Calapooya Knife	Gunther Barbed	Malaga Cover Stemmed	Shoulder	Wealth Blade
Cottonwood Leaf	Gunther Triangular	One-Que	Rose Springs Stemmed	Wintu
Cottonwood Triangle	Hell's Canyon Basal	Parowan	Side Knife	Yana

CLASSIC PHASE (700 B. P. - 400 B. P.)

Canalino Triangular	Deschutes Knife	Desert Sierra	NW Four-Way Knife	Snake River Arrow
Columbia Mule Ear	Desert Delta	Lake Rivier Side Notched	Piquinin	
Columbia Plateau	Desert General	Lewis River Short Stem	Plateau Pentagonal	
Columbia Riv. Pin Stem	Desert Redding	Miniature Blade	Rabit Island Arrow	

HISTORIC (400 B. P. - Present)

Diamond Back	Ishi	Nottoway	Trade Points
Ground Stone	Klickitat	Panoche	Ulu

FAR WEST
THUMBNAIL GUIDE SECTION

The following references are provided to aid the collector in easier and quicker identification of point types. All photos are exactly 30% of actual size and are proportional to each other. Each point pictured in this section represents a classic form for the type. When a match is found, go to the alphabetical location of that type for more examples in true actual size.

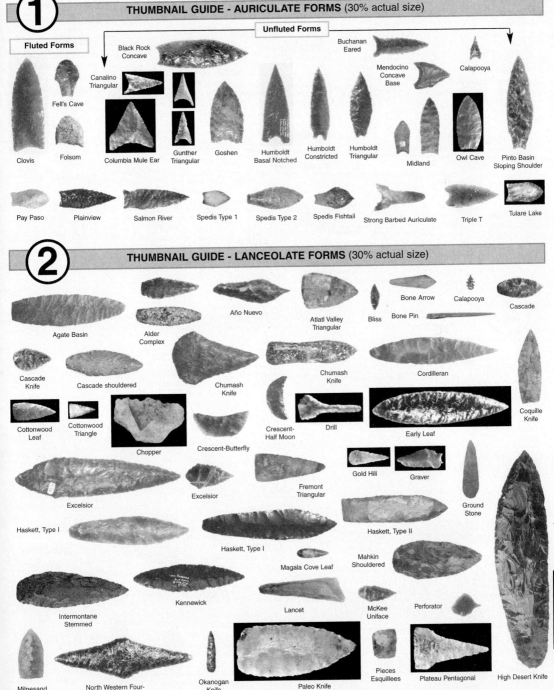

① THUMBNAIL GUIDE - AURICULATE FORMS (30% actual size)

Unfluted Forms

Fluted Forms

Black Rock Concave · Canalino Triangular · Buchanan Eared · Mendocino Concave Base · Calapooya · Fell's Cave · Clovis · Folsom · Columbia Mule Ear · Gunther Triangular · Goshen · Humboldt Basal Notched · Humboldt Constricted · Humboldt Triangular · Midland · Owl Cave · Pinto Basin Sloping Shoulder

Pay Paso · Plainview · Salmon River · Spedis Type 1 · Spedis Type 2 · Spedis Fishtail · Strong Barbed Auriculate · Triple T · Tulare Lake

② THUMBNAIL GUIDE - LANCEOLATE FORMS (30% actual size)

Agate Basin · Alder Complex · Año Nuevo · Atlatl Valley Triangular · Bliss · Bone Arrow · Bone Pin · Calapooya · Cascade · Cascade Knife · Cascade shouldered · Chumash Knife · Chumash Knife · Cordilleran · Coquille Knife · Cottonwood Leaf · Cottonwood Triangle · Chopper · Crescent-Butterfly · Crescent-Half Moon · Drill · Early Leaf · Excelsior · Excelsior · Fremont Triangular · Gold Hill · Graver · Ground Stone · Haskett, Type I · Haskett, Type I · Haskett, Type II · Magala Cove Leaf · Mahkin Shouldered · Intermontane Stemmed · Kennewick · Lancet · McKee Uniface · Perforator · Milnesand · North Western Four-Way Knife · Okanogan Knife · Paleo Knife · Pieces Esquillees · Plateau Pentagonal · High Desert Knife

FW

949

LANCEOLATE FORMS (continued)

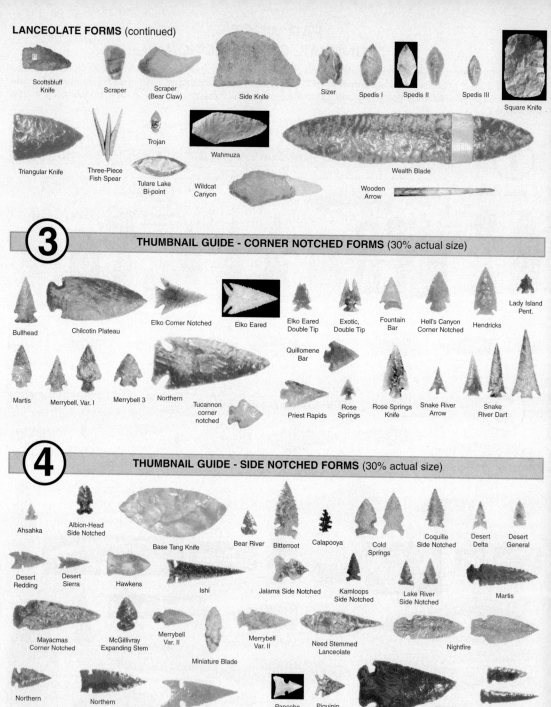

Scottsbluff Knife

Scraper

Scraper (Bear Claw)

Side Knife

Sizer

Spedis I

Spedis II

Spedis III

Square Knife

Triangular Knife

Three-Piece Fish Spear

Trojan

Tulare Lake Bi-point

Wahmuza

Wildcat Canyon

Wealth Blade

Wooden Arrow

③ THUMBNAIL GUIDE - CORNER NOTCHED FORMS (30% actual size)

Bullhead

Chilcotin Plateau

Elko Corner Notched

Elko Eared

Elko Eared Double Tip

Exotic, Double Tip

Fountain Bar

Hell's Canyon Corner Notched

Hendricks

Lady Island Pent.

Martis

Merrybell, Var. I

Merrybell 3

Northern

Tucannon corner notched

Quillomene Bar

Priest Rapids

Rose Springs

Rose Springs Knife

Snake River Arrow

Snake River Dart

④ THUMBNAIL GUIDE - SIDE NOTCHED FORMS (30% actual size)

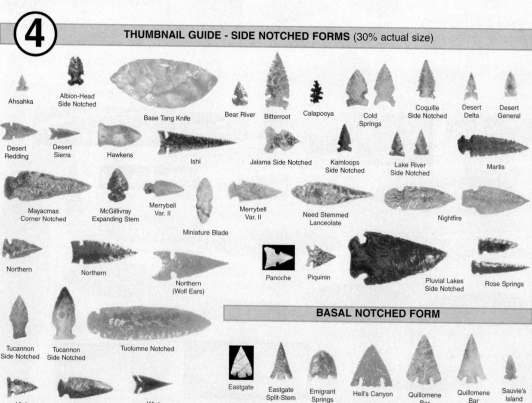

Ahsahka

Albion-Head Side Notched

Base Tang Knife

Bear River

Bitterroot

Calapooya

Cold Springs

Coquille Side Notched

Desert Delta

Desert General

Desert Redding

Desert Sierra

Hawkens

Ishi

Jalama Side Notched

Kamloops Side Notched

Lake River Side Notched

Martis

Mayacmas Corner Notched

McGillivray Expanding Stem

Merrybell Var. II

Miniature Blade

Merrybell Var. II

Need Stemmed Lanceolate

Nightfire

Northern

Northern

Northern (Wolf Ears)

Panoche

Piquinin

Pluvial Lakes Side Notched

Rose Springs

Tucannon Side Notched

Tucannon Side Notched

Tuolumne Notched

Uinta

Wendover

Wintu

BASAL NOTCHED FORM

Eastgate

Eastgate Split-Stem

Emigrant Springs

Hell's Canyon

Quillomene Bar

Quillomene Bar

Sauvie's Island Basal Notched

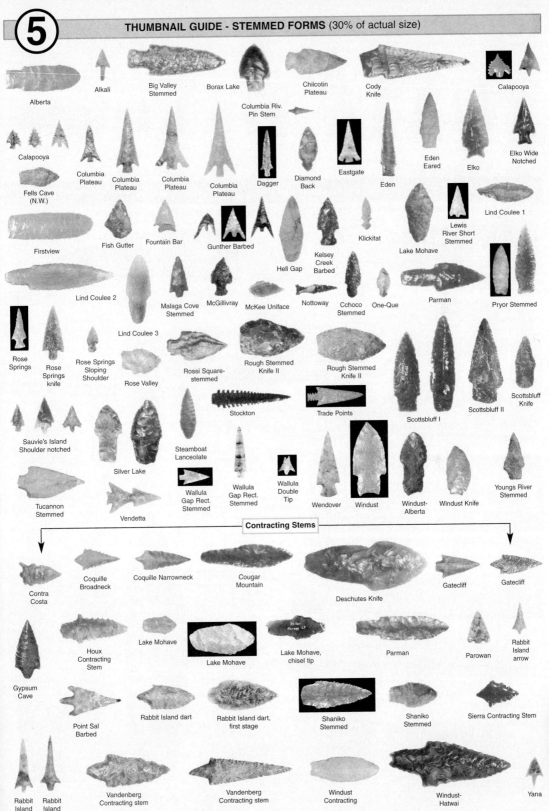

Alberta

Alkali

Big Valley Stemmed

Borax Lake

Chilcotin Plateau

Cody Knife

Calapooya

Calapooya

Columbia Riv. Pin Stem

Columbia Plateau

Columbia Plateau

Columbia Plateau

Columbia Plateau

Dagger

Diamond Back

Eastgate

Eden

Eden Eared

Elko

Elko Wide Notched

Fells Cave (N.W.)

Fish Gutter

Fountain Bar

Gunther Barbed

Klickitat

Lake Mohave

Lewis River Short Stemmed

Lind Coulee 1

Firstview

Lind Coulee 2

Hell Gap

Kelsey Creek Barbed

Lind Coulee 3

Malaga Cove Stemmed

McGillivray

McKee Uniface

Nottoway

Cchoco Stemmed

One-Que

Parman

Pryor Stemmed

Rose Springs

Rose Springs knife

Rose Springs Sloping Shoulder

Rose Valley

Rossi Square-stemmed

Rough Stemmed Knife II

Rough Stemmed Knife II

Scottsbluff Knife

Scottsbluff II

Sauvie's Island Shoulder notched

Silver Lake

Steamboat Lanceolate

Stockton

Trade Points

Scottsbluff I

Wendover

Windust

Windust-Alberta

Windust Knife

Youngs River Stemmed

Tucannon Stemmed

Vendetta

Wallula Gap Rect. Stemmed

Wallula Gap Rect. Stemmed

Wallula Double Tip

Contracting Stems

Contra Costa

Coquille Broadneck

Coquille Narrowneck

Cougar Mountain

Deschutes Knife

Gatecliff

Gatecliff

Gypsum Cave

Houx Contracting Stem

Lake Mohave

Lake Mohave

Lake Mohave, chisel tip

Parman

Parowan

Rabbit Island arrow

Point Sal Barbed

Rabbit Island dart

Rabbit Island dart, first stage

Shaniko Stemmed

Shaniko Stemmed

Sierra Contracting Stem

Rabbit Island arrow

Rabbit Island dart

Vandenberg Contracting stem

Vandenberg Contracting stem

Windust Contracting

Windust-Hatwai

Yana

FW

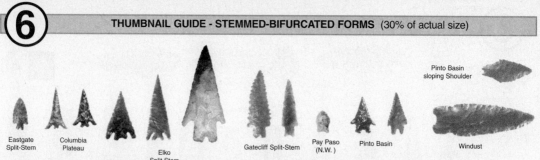

Eastgate Split-Stem

Columbia Plateau

Elko Split Stem

Gatecliff Split-Stem

Pay Paso (N.W.)

Pinto Basin

Pinto Basin sloping Shoulder

Windust

AGATE BASIN - Transitional Paleo-Early Archaic, 10,200 - 8500 B. P.

(Also see Cordilleran, Haskett, Intermontane Stemmed, Owl Cave, Scottsbluff)

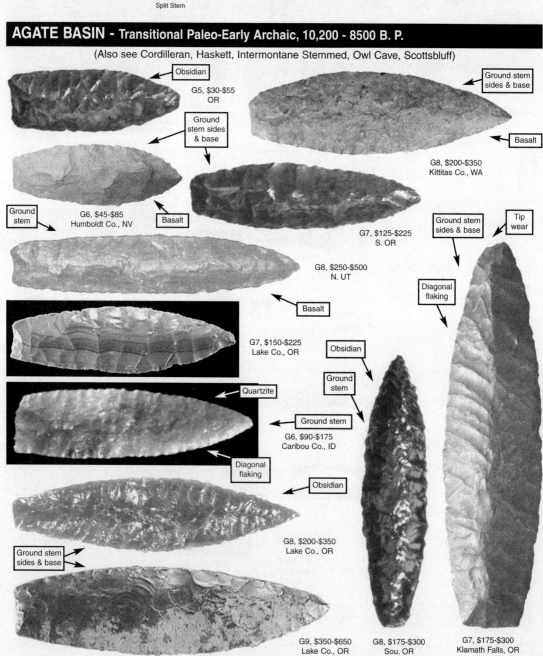

Obsidian

G5, $30-$55
OR

Ground stem sides & base

Ground stem sides & base

Basalt

G8, $200-$350
Kittitas Co., WA

Ground stem

G6, $45-$85
Humboldt Co., NV

Basalt

G7, $125-$225
S. OR

Ground stem sides & base

Tip wear

Diagonal flaking

G8, $250-$500
N. UT

Basalt

G7, $150-$225
Lake Co., OR

Quartzite

Obsidian

Ground stem

Ground stem

G6, $90-$175
Caribou Co., ID

Diagonal flaking

Obsidian

G8, $200-$350
Lake Co., OR

Ground stem sides & base

G9, $350-$650
Lake Co., OR

G8, $175-$300
Sou. OR

G7, $175-$300
Klamath Falls, OR

AGATE BASIN (continued)

LOCATION: From Pennsylvania westward into Idaho, Nevada, Oregon to Canada. **DESCRIPTION:** A medium to large size lanceolate blade of high quality. Bases are either convex, concave or straight, are often beveled, and stems are usually ground. Some examples are median ridged and have random to parallel flaking. Believed to have evolved from the earlier *Haskett/Lind Coulee types*. **I.D. KEY:** Basal form and flaking style. **NOTE:** The Alaska *Mesa* point is a similar form and has been reportedly dated to 13,700 years B.P., but more data is needed to verify this extreme age.

AHSAHKA - Late Archaic-Classic Phase, 3,000 - 500 B. P.

(Also see Cold Springs, Desert, Lake River Side, Northern Side, Piqunin & Sauvie's Island)

G5, $2-$5
Spokane, WA

G5, $2-$5
Spokane, WA

G4, $2-$5
Spokane, WA

G4, $2-$5
Spokane, WA

G6, $3-$6
Snake River, ID

G6, $4-$8
Snake River, ID

LOCATION: Northern Idaho & Washington. **DESCRIPTION:** A medium size dart point with shallow side notches and a straight to convex base. A descendent of *Hatwai* which is a descendent of *Cold Springs*. **I.D. KEY:** Shallow side notches.

ALBERTA - Early Archaic, 10,000 - 8500 B. P.

(Also see Big Valley, Cody Complex Knife, Eden, Firstview, Lind Coulee, Parman, Scottsbluff & Windust)

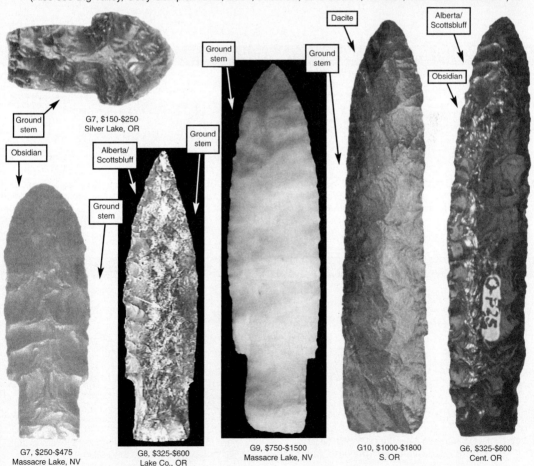

G7, $150-$250
Silver Lake, OR

G7, $250-$475
Massacre Lake, NV

G8, $325-$600
Lake Co., OR

G9, $750-$1500
Massacre Lake, NV

G10, $1000-$1800
S. OR

G6, $325-$600
Cent. OR

FW

Burinated tip

Ground stem

G6, $165-$275
Warner Valley, OR

G2, $40-$75
S. OR

LOCATION: Northern States from Michigan to Montana to Nevada and Oregon. **DESCRIPTION:** A medium to large size point with a broad, long parallel stem that is ground and weak shoulders. Developed from the *Haskett, Lind Coulee* in the Great Basin and later changed into the Cody Complex and is related to the *Eden* and *Scottsbluff* types. **I.D. KEY:** Long, broad rectangular stem, weak shoulders, serial flaking.

ALBION-HEAD SIDE NOTCHED - Early Archaic to Transitional, 6500 - 2000 B. P.

(Also see Cold Springs, Northern and Rose Springs)

Rare double tip

G7, $8-$15
Bethel Isle, CA

LOCATION: N. California. **DESCRIPTION:** A medium size dart point with side notches and a concave base with rounded ears.

ALDER COMPLEX - Late Paleo, 9,500 - 8000 B. P.

(Also see Agate Basin, Cascade, Haskett, Owl Cave and Pryor Stemmed)

Collateral flaking

Diagonal flaking

Tip wear

G7, $35-$50
S. E. OR

G5, $20-$35
S. E. OR

LOCATION: S. E. Oregon into Idaho, utah, Wyoming and Montana. **DESCRIPTION:** A medium to large size unfluted lanceolate point of high quality with convex sides and a straight to concave base. Flaking is usually the parallel oblique type. Basal areas are ground. **I.D. KEY:** Basal form and flaking style.

ALKALI - Developmental to Classic Phase, 1500 - 500 B. P.

(Also see Eastgate, Elko and Rose Springs)

Yellow agate

Serrated edge

Serrated edge

G7, $5-$10
Col. Riv. OR

G8, $8-$15
S. E. OR

G8, $8-$15
Lake Co., OR

G8, $8-$15
Lake Co., OR

G8, $12-$20
Lake Co., OR

G8, $15-$25
Columbia Riv., OR

G6, $15-$25
Butte Falls, OR

G10, $30-$50
Columbia Riv., OR

G10, $25-$45
Lake Co., OR

LOCATION: California to Canada. **DESCRIPTION:** A small size, barbed arrow point with a long parallel sided stem. This type was included with *Rose Springs* in early reports. **I.D. KEY:** Flaking style and long stem.

AÑo NUEVO - Late Archaic, 2950 - 2500 B. P.

(Also see Cougar Mountain, Deschutes Knife, Lind Coulee, Parman and Wildcat Canyon)

Apiculate tip

Monterey chert

G8, $25-$45
Coastal CA

Light rootbeer colored Monterey chert

Basalt

G8, $60-$100
Mendocino Co., CA

G6, $15-$25
San Mateo Co., CA

Apiculate tip

Dark rootbeer colored Monterey chert

G6, $65-$125
S. Coast, CA

G9, $65-$125
San Mateo Co., CA

G6, $15-$30
Pismo Beach, CA

G10, $125-$225
San Mateo Co., CA

LOCATION: Type site is in San Mateo Co., CA. **DESCRIPTION:** A medium to large size point with a long, tapered stem and weak tapered shoulders. The base is convex and stem sides are not ground. The distal end can be apiculate and flaking is random. Thicker than *Cougar Mountain* points. Made almost exclusively of Monterey Chert which is rootbeer colored, similar to Knife River flint from the Dakotas. **I.D. KEY:** Tip style and long stem.

ATLATL VALLEY TRIANGULAR - Early to late Archaic, 7000 - 3500 B. P.

(Also see Coquille Knife, Cottonwood, Fremont Triangular, Plateau Pentagonal, Triangular Knife)

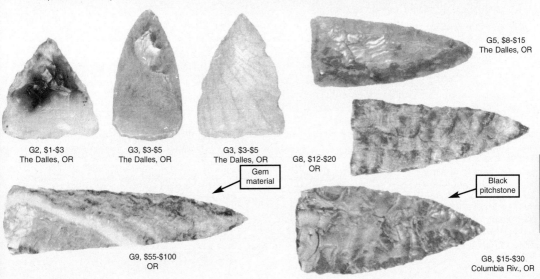

G5, $8-$15
The Dalles, OR

G2, $1-$3
The Dalles, OR

G3, $3-$5
The Dalles, OR

G3, $3-$5
The Dalles, OR

G8, $12-$20
OR

Gem material

Black pitchstone

G9, $55-$100
OR

G8, $15-$30
Columbia Riv., OR

FW

ATLATL VALLEY TRIANGULAR (continued)

Tip wear

Beveled edge

Dark brown/red jasper with inclusions

Beveled base

Opposing bevels

G8, $20-$35
The Dalles, OR

G8, $45-$80
OR

G10, $175-$300
Jefferson Co., ID

Beveled base

G9, $80-$150
OR

LOCATION: Snake River in the East to the Cowlitz River in W. Oregon. **DESCRIPTION:** A small to medium size triangular knife with an occasional bevel on one side of each face. Some are uniface. Bases are straight to convex and are well thinned to beveled. Some bases are beveled half way across, then change at the midway point to an opposing bevel.These are never hafted & are resharpened all the way to the basal corners. Smaller examples have been found with *Rabbit Island* points. **I.D. KEY:** Beveling and blade form.

BASE TANG KNIFE - Early Archaic to Transitional Phase, 10,000 - 2000 B. P.

(Also see Paleo Knife)

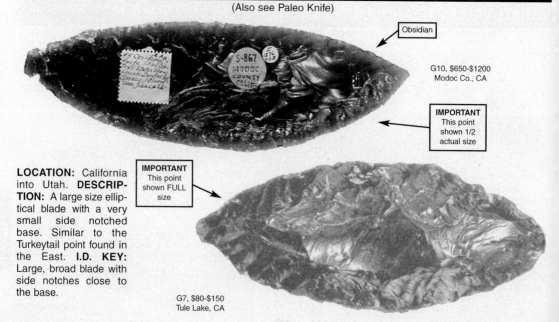

Obsidian

G10, $650-$1200
Modoc Co., CA

IMPORTANT
This point shown 1/2 actual size

LOCATION: California into Utah. **DESCRIPTION:** A large size elliptical blade with a very small side notched base. Similar to the Turkeytail point found in the East. **I.D. KEY:** Large, broad blade with side notches close to the base.

IMPORTANT
This point shown FULL size

G7, $80-$150
Tule Lake, CA

956

BASE TANG KNIFE (continued)

IMPORTANT
This point shown FULL size

Moss agate

Blunt tip

G8, $150-$250
Iron Co., UT

BEAR RIVER - Developmental to Classic Phase, 1300 - 400 B. P.

(Also see Desert, Emigrant, Lake River, Rose Spring, Sauvie's Island Side)

| G6, $5-$10 Gooding Co., ID | G7, $5-$10 OR | G9, $15-$30 ID | G9, $15-$25 Gooding Co., ID | G9, $15-$30 Gooding Co., ID | G6, $12-$20 N. UT, Bear Riv. | G10, $30-$50 OR | G8, $15-$25 N. UT, Bear Riv. |

LOCATION: Found in the Fremont area of Utah (Bear River) into SW Idaho. **DESCRIPTION:** A small size, thin, side-notched arrow point with deep notches. The base is large in relation to its overall size. Basal corners are rounded. **I.D. KEY:** Large base, small overall size.

BIG VALLEY STEMMED - Middle Archaic, 4000 - 3500 B. P.

(Also see Alberta, Cody Complex, Lind Coulee, Mayacmas Corner, Parman and Silver Lake)

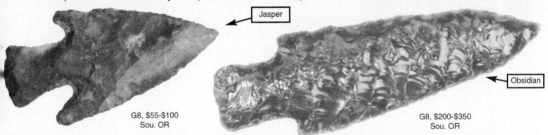

Jasper

Obsidian

G8, $55-$100
Sou. OR

G8, $200-$350
Sou. OR

LOCATION: Northern California into southern Cascades, Oregon. **DESCRIPTION:** A medium to large size, long stemmed point with rounded basal corners. Shoulders are horizontal and bases are straight. **I.D. KEY:** Large stem.

BITTERROOT - Early to middle Archaic, 7500 - 5000 B. P.

(See Ahsahka, Desert, Emigrant, Nightfire, Northern Side Notched & Salmon River)

LOCATION: Northwestern states. **DESCRIPTION:** A variant of the *Northern Side Notched.* A medium size side-notched point with a straight, concave or convex base. Notches are placed at an angle into each side of the blade. Early Archaic flaking is evident on many examples.

Banded obsidian

G10, $600-$1000
Warner Valley, OR

FW

BITTERROOT (continued)

Obsidian

Basalt

G8, $60-$115
S.E. OR

Obsidian

Basalt

G7, $35-$60
Lake Co., OR

G9, $80-$150
Lake Co., OR

G7, $25-$45
S.E. OR, Thorn Lake

G8, $80-$150
Lake Co., OR

BLACK ROCK CONCAVE - Paleo, 11,000 - 10,500 B. P.

(Also see Cascade, Clovis, Folsom, Humboldt, Midland, OwL Cave, Plainview, Triple T, Tulare Lake)

Jasper

Many resharpen-ings

Resharpened

Red Basalt

G8, $800-$1500
S. E. OR

Ground basal sides

Obsidian

G5, $200-$350
Elmer, WA

Altered by a later culture

Ground basal sides

G3, $65-$125
Columbia Plateau, OR

Black & mahogany obsidian

G7, $350-$600
Silver Lake, OR

Jasper

Tan & orange varigated agate

Cut for water hydration age test

Ground basal sides

G9, $700-$1200
Elmer, WA

G9, $1400-$2500
Black Rock Desert, NV

Ground

G9, $1500-$2500
N.W. NV, ground basal sides

Ground

G9, $1600-$3000
Lake Co., OR, Alkali Lake

Translucent orange tinged mahogany obsidian

G8, $1600-$3000
Black Rock Desert, NV

G9, $2500-$4000
Klamath Co., OR. Hydration test dated to 10,100 B.P.

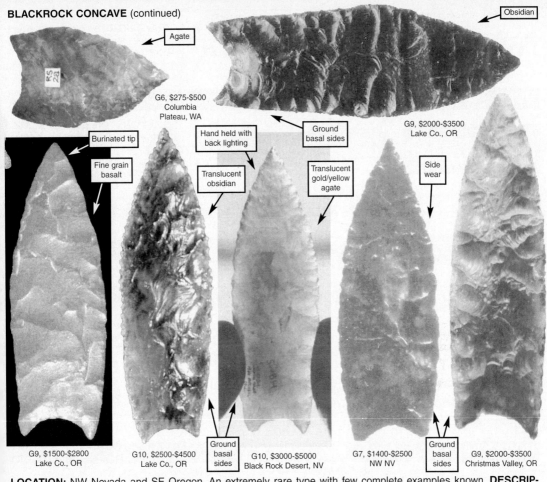

Agate

Obsidian

G6, $275-$500
Columbia
Plateau, WA

Ground
basal sides

G9, $2000-$3500
Lake Co., OR

Burinated tip

Fine grain
basalt

Hand held with
back lighting

Translucent
obsidian

Translucent
gold/yellow
agate

Side
wear

G9, $1500-$2800
Lake Co., OR

G10, $2500-$4500
Lake Co., OR

Ground
basal
sides

G10, $3000-$5000
Black Rock Desert, NV

G7, $1400-$2500
NW NV

Ground
basal
sides

G9, $2000-$3500
Christmas Valley, OR

LOCATION: NW Nevada and SE Oregon. An extremely rare type with few complete examples known. **DESCRIPTION:** A medium size, thin, lanceolate point with a concave base. Basal edges are usually ground. Blade flaking is horizontal transverse. Similar in flaking style and form to *Midland* and *Goshen* points and is considered to be the unfluted *Folsom* of the Great Basin. **I.D. KEY:** Micro secondary flaking, ground basal sides, thinness.

BLISS - Developmental to Historic Phase, 900 - 350 B. P.

(Also see Spedis III)

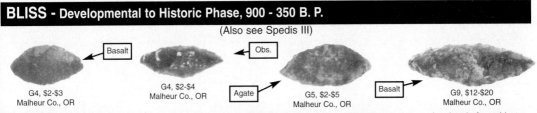

Basalt

Obs.

G4, $2-$3
Malheur Co., OR

G4, $2-$4
Malheur Co., OR

Agate

G5, $2-$5
Malheur Co., OR

Basalt

G9, $12-$20
Malheur Co., OR

LOCATION: SW Idaho into SE Oregon border area. **DESCRIPTION:** A small size lanceolate point that is found in two forms: Bipointed, widest near the center, and with a rounded to straight base, widest near the tip. Blade edges are convex. Thicker than *Spedis*, has been found hafted to a wooden foreshaft of an arrow.

BONE ARROW - Developmental to Historic Phase, 1500 - 200 B. P.

(Also see Bone Pin, Three-Piece Fish Spear and Wooden Arrow)

FW

G8, $25-$40
Astoria, OR

G6, $15-$30, OR

G6, $12-$20
Chehalis, WA, Historic.

G7, $15-$30
OR

G10, $40-$70
OR

BONE ARROW (continued)

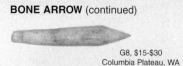

G8, $15-$30
Columbia Plateau, WA

G9, $35-$60
OR

LOCATION: Oregon into Alaska.
DESCRIPTION: A long narrow foreshaft and point crafted from bone or ivory.

BONE PIN - Paleo, 11,500- 10,000 B. P.

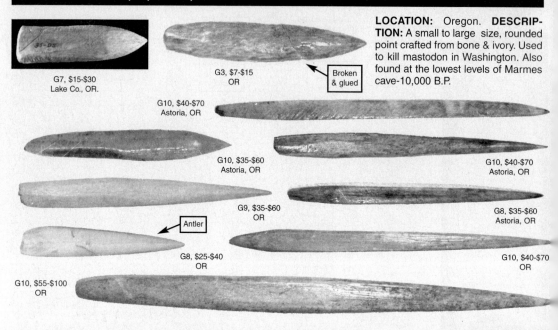

G7, $15-$30
Lake Co., OR.

G3, $7-$15
OR

Broken & glued

LOCATION: Oregon. **DESCRIPTION:** A small to large size, rounded point crafted from bone & ivory. Used to kill mastodon in Washington. Also found at the lowest levels of Marmes cave-10,000 B.P.

G10, $40-$70
Astoria, OR

G10, $35-$60
Astoria, OR

G10, $40-$70
Astoria, OR

G9, $35-$60
OR

G8, $35-$60
Astoria, OR

Antler

G8, $25-$40
OR

G10, $40-$70
OR

G10, $55-$100
OR

BORAX LAKE - Early Archaic, 8000 - 5000 B. P.

(Also see Houx Contracting Stem, Scottsbluff)

Translucent obsidian

Brown chert

Chert

G8, $100-$180
OR

G7, $25-$40
W. NV

G7, $25-$45
W. NV

Chert

G6, $15-$25
W. NV

LOCATION: N. California into S. Oregon. **DESCRIPTION:** This type has an elongated, triangular blade when pristine with a wide, approximately square stem. Stem sides are often ground. Bases are straight to slightly convex. A very similar point with a concave base is called the *Stanislaus Broad Stem*. There are narrower versions of both types and they range from the central valley of California to the Pacific Ocean, north into southern Oregon, and sporadically into W. Nevada. Have been found with Crescents. **I.D. KEY:** Strong Hertzican core scars in notches, wide, thin primary flake removal on pristine specimens, and chevron pattern resharpening on worn-out pieces.

(Also see Black Rock Concave, Early Eared, Humboldt and Strong)

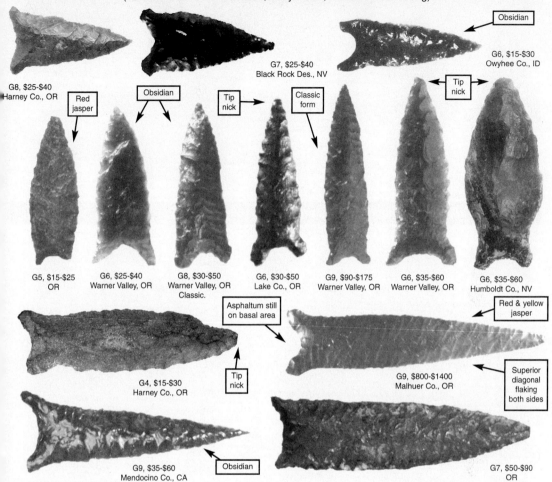

Obsidian

G6, $15-$30
Owyhee Co., ID

G7, $25-$40
Black Rock Des., NV

Tip nick

G8, $25-$40
Harney Co., OR

Red jasper

Obsidian

Tip nick

Classic form

Tip nick

G5, $15-$25
OR

G6, $25-$40
Warner Valley, OR

G8, $30-$50
Warner Valley, OR
Classic.

G6, $30-$50
Lake Co., OR

G9, $90-$175
Warner Valley, OR

G6, $35-$60
Warner Valley, OR

G6, $35-$60
Humboldt Co., NV

Asphaltum still on basal area

Red & yellow jasper

Tip nick

G4, $15-$30
Harney Co., OR

G9, $800-$1400
Malhuer Co., OR

Superior diagonal flaking both sides

Obsidian

G9, $35-$60
Mendocino Co., CA

G7, $50-$90
OR

LOCATION: Great Basin states, esp. N.W. Nevada. **DESCRIPTION:** A small to medium size, narrow, lanceolate point with an expanded, eared, concave base. Some examples show excellent parallel flaking. A later form of *Humboldt*.

(Also see Chilcotin Plateau, Elko Corner, Hell's Canyon, Hendricks, Merrybell)

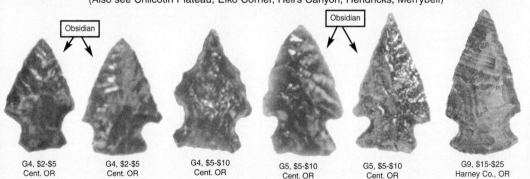

Obsidian

Obsidian

G4, $2-$5
Cent. OR

G4, $2-$5
Cent. OR

G4, $5-$10
Cent. OR

G5, $5-$10
Cent. OR

G5, $5-$10
Cent. OR

G9, $15-$25
Harney Co., OR

FW

LOCATION: Central to southern Oregon. **DESCRIPTION:** A medium size, thick, heavy duty corner notched dart/knife. Shoulders are tapered to horizontal. Stems expand and bases are convex to slightly concave. Very heavily ground stems and base. **I.D. KEY:** Heavily ground stem and base.

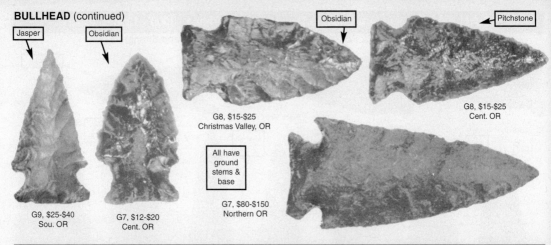

BULLHEAD (continued)

Jasper

Obsidian

Obsidian

Pitchstone

G8, $15-$25
Christmas Valley, OR

G8, $15-$25
Cent. OR

All have
ground
stems &
base

G9, $25-$40
Sou. OR

G7, $12-$20
Cent. OR

G7, $80-$150
Northern OR

CALAPOOYA - Developmental to Historic Phase, 1000 - 200 B. P.

(Also see Columbia Plateau, Gunther, Wallula and Wintu)

G6, $2-$5   G6, $5-$10   G6, $2-$5   G6, $6-$20   G6, $6-$12   G6, $6-$12   G6, $6-$12   G6, $6-$12   G6, $6-$12   G6, $8-$15

G6, $8-$15   G6, $8-$15   G8, $12-$20   G8, $12-$20   G8, $12-$20   G6, $8-$15   G8, $12-$20   G8, $12-$20   G6, $5-$10

G6, $15-$25   G6, $15-$25   G6, $15-$30   G6, $20-$35   G6, $20-$35   G6, $15-$25   G6, $20-$35   G6, $15-$25   G7, $12-$20

Brown
jasper

G6, $15-$25

G9, $18-$35   G8, $15-$30   G6, $8-$15   G6, $15-$25
Sauvie's Isle, OR   G6, $20-$35
Sauvie's Isle, OR

Orange
chalc.

Knife
form

Dacite

Knife
form

All others made from obsidian
and from Fern Ridge, OR

G8, $30-$50
Fern Ridge, OR   G8, $40-$70
Fern Ridge, OR   G9, $45-$85
OR   G9, $80-$150
OR   G10, $135-$250
Fern Ridge, OR   G9, $80-$150
Willamette Valley, OR

LOCATION: Willamette Valley, Oregon between the Columbia and Rogue rivers. **DESCRIPTION:** A small size, thin, arrow point that occurs either as stemmed, side notched, triangular and ovate. Most examples are heavily serrated and imitate local styles such as *Gunther, Desert, Columbia Plateau, Wallula* and other types. The barbed edge, short stemmed variant is locally called a *Fern Leaf* point. This type has three spellings: Calapooya, Calapooia & Kalapooya. **I.D. KEY:** Wild serrations.

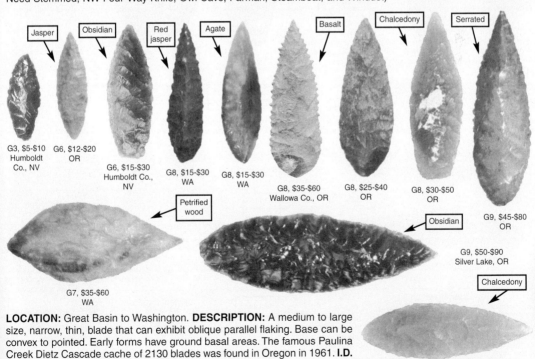

CANALINO TRIANGULAR - Classic to Historic Phase, 700 - 200 B. P.

(Also see Bull Creek, Cottonwood, Gold Hill, Gunther Triangular)

Jasper agate

G8, $15-$30
Ventura Co.,
CA

Agate

G9, $25-$40
Ventura Co.,
CA

Quartz

G6, $12-$20
Santa Barbara
Co., CA.

Fused shale

G9, $15-$30
Ventura Co., CA
Green Chalc.

Moss agate

G6, $8-$15
Santa Barbara
Co., CA.

G10, $25-$40
Ventura Co., CA

Fused shale

G7, $15-$25
Santa Barbara
Co., CA.

Monterey chert

G7, $20-$35
Los Angeles
Co., CA.

G7, $20-$35
Santa Barbara Co., CA.

Fused shale

G9, $15-$30
Ventura Co., CA.

G9, $30-$50
Mendocino Co., CA

Monterey chert

G9, $35-$60
Los Angeles Co., CA.

Fused shale

G10, $35-$60
Ventura Co., CA.

G10, $40-$75
Ventura Co., CA.

Agate

G10, $40-$75
Santa Barbara Co., CA.

LOCATION: California. **DESCRIPTION:** A small size, thin, triangular arrow point with a shallow to deep concave base. Some are serrated. Also known as *Coastal Cottonwood.*

CASCADE - Early Archaic, 8000 - 4000 B. P.

(Also see Agate Basin, Cordilleran, Early Leaf, Excelsior, Haskett, Intermontane, Kennewick, Mankin Shouldered, Need Stemmed, NW Four-Way Knife, Owl Cave, Parman, Steamboat, and Windust)

Jasper

Obsidian

Red jasper

Agate

Basalt

Chalcedony

Serrated

G3, $5-$10
Humboldt
Co., NV

G6, $12-$20
OR

G6, $15-$30
Humboldt Co.,
NV

G8, $15-$30
WA

G8, $15-$30
WA

G8, $35-$60
Wallowa Co., OR

G8, $25-$40
OR

G8, $30-$50
OR

G9, $45-$80
OR

Petrified wood

Obsidian

G9, $50-$90
Silver Lake, OR

G7, $35-$60
WA

Chalcedony

FW

G8, $45-$80
WA

LOCATION: Great Basin to Washington. **DESCRIPTION:** A medium to large size, narrow, thin, blade that can exhibit oblique parallel flaking. Base can be convex to pointed. Early forms have ground basal areas. The famous Paulina Creek Dietz Cascade cache of 2130 blades was found in Oregon in 1961. **I.D. KEY**: Narrow, lanceolate form.

CASCADE (continued)

Opalized agate

Obsidian

Basalt

Agate

Obsidian

G9, $65-$110
OR

G6, $20-$35
N. CA

G7, $20-$35
WA

G6, $15-$25
Harney Co., OR

G8, $65-$115
OR

G7, $35-$60
Harney Co., OR

G8, $45-$80
Silver Lake, OR

Basalt

Chert

Chalcedony

Obsidian

Notched base

G7, $55-$100
WA

G8, 55-$100
Columbia Riv., OR

G8, $65-$115
WA

G9, $125-$200
OR

G7, $30-$50
OR

G7, $30-$50
Christmas Valley, OR

Agate

Yellow jasper

Obsidian

G7, $50-$90
OR

Serrated edge

G10, $150-$250
Klamath Falls, OR

Notched base form

G8, $65-$125
Tule Lake, CA

G9, $125-$225
OR

G7, $50-$90
OR

CASCADE (continued)

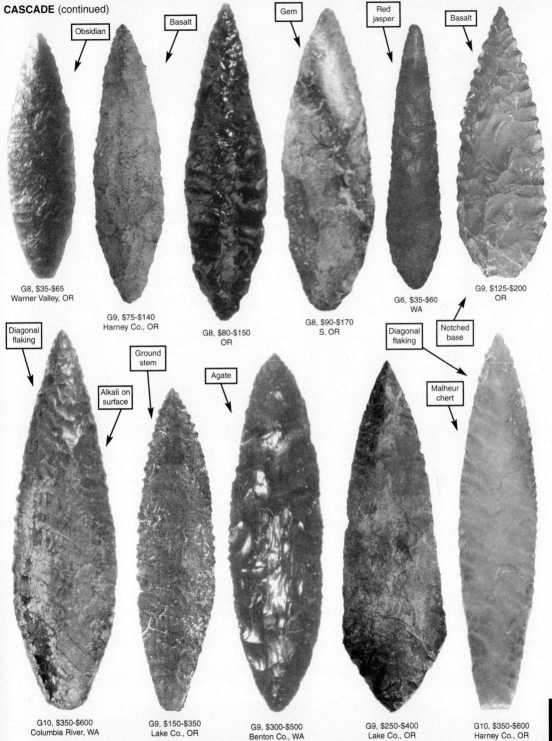

Obsidian

Basalt

Gem

Red jasper

Basalt

G8, $35-$65
Warner Valley, OR

G9, $75-$140
Harney Co., OR

G8, $80-$150
OR

G8, $90-$170
S. OR

G6, $35-$60
WA

G9, $125-$200
OR

Diagonal flaking

Ground stem

Agate

Diagonal flaking

Notched base

Alkali on surface

Malheur chert

G10, $350-$600
Columbia River, WA

G9, $150-$350
Lake Co., OR

G9, $300-$500
Benton Co., WA

G9, $250-$400
Lake Co., OR

G10, $350-$600
Harney Co., OR

NOTE: There is a difference between the *Cascade base-notched* and the *Humboldt* points. The *Humboldt* point usually has a straight more visible hafting area than the *Cascade*. The *Cascade* hafting area tapers to the base, while the *Humboldt* usually expands slightly near the base. Most *Humboldts* have wider base notches than the *Cascades*. The *Cascade* base-notch appears to be a field improvisation while the *Humboldt* notch is preplanned and usually has multiple strokes. While approximately 90% of *Humboldt* stems are ground, less than 10% of the Cascades have ground stems. Completely worn out or damaged specimens could be mistaken for one another.

Obsidian

G9, $200-$350
Lake Co., OR

Basalt

Gray sucrosic
obsidian

Diagonal
flaking

G8, $175-$300
OR

G7 $90-$175
Lake Co., OR

G7, $80-$150
OR

G10, $400-$700
Oregon desert.

Obsidian

G8, $300-$550
Lake Co., OR

CASCADE KNIFE - Early Archaic, 8000 - 4000 B. P.

(Also see Cascade Knife, Cascade Shouldered, Early Leaf, Excelsior, Haskett, High Desert Knife, Kennewick, and NW Four-Way Knife)

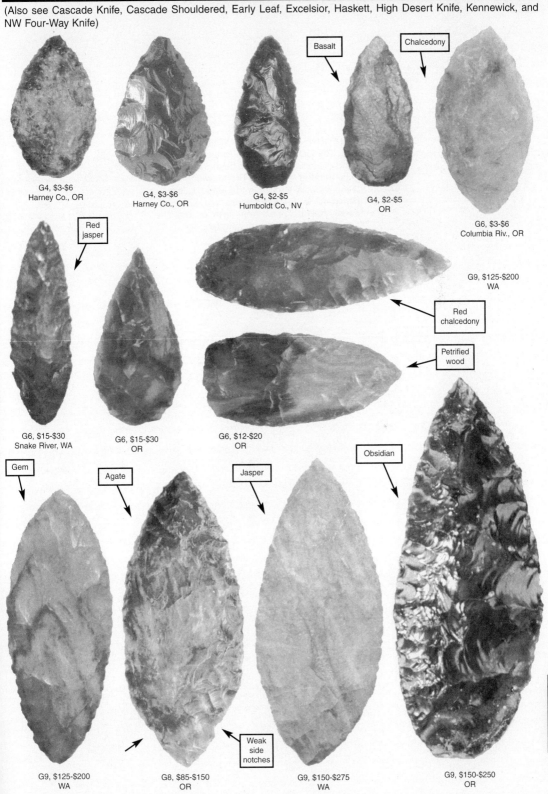

G4, $3-$6
Harney Co., OR

G4, $3-$6
Harney Co., OR

G4, $2-$5
Humboldt Co., NV

Basalt

Chalcedony

G4, $2-$5
OR

G6, $3-$6
Columbia Riv., OR

Red jasper

G9, $125-$200
WA

Red chalcedony

Petrified wood

G6, $15-$30
Snake River, WA

G6, $15-$30
OR

G6, $12-$20
OR

Gem

Agate

Jasper

Obsidian

Weak side notches

G9, $125-$200
WA

G8, $85-$150
OR

G9, $150-$275
WA

G9, $150-$250
OR

FW

967

CASCADE KNIFE (continued)

Agate

G9, $150-$250
Harney Co., OR

Chalcedony

LOCATION: Great Basin to Washington.
DESCRIPTION: A medium to large size, broad blade with a rounded base. The distal is rounded to pointed. Broad, wide, flat flakes were taken to thin the blade. Edge alignment and resharpening are short, steeply taken flakes from one or both faces. **I.D. KEY**: Resharpening technique.

Basalt

G10, $300-$500
OR

Basalt

First stage

Obsidian

First stage

G5, $55-$100
WA

G9, $200-$350
OR

G9, $400-$700
S. OR

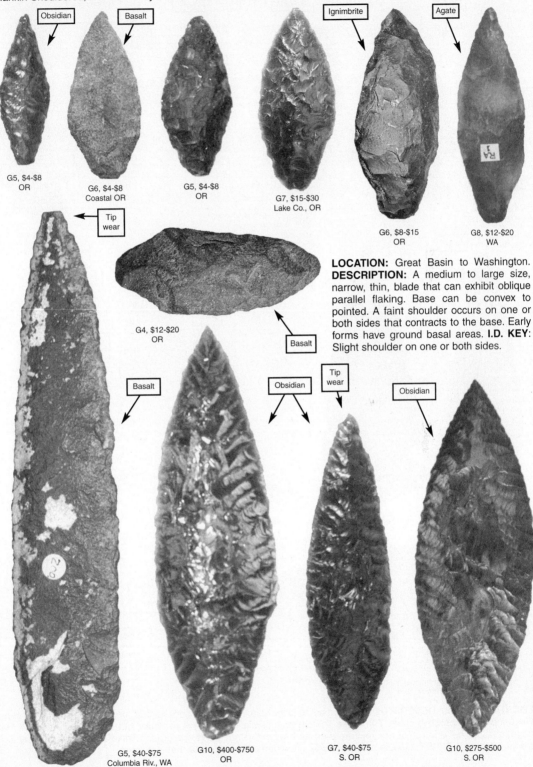

CASCADE SHOULDERED - Early Archaic, 8000 - 4000 B. P.

(Also see Cascade, Cascade Knife, Early Leaf, Excelsior, Harahey, Haskett, Intermontane Stemmed, Kennewick, Mahkin Shouldered, NW Four-Way Knife, Parman, Shaniko Stemmed and Windust)

Obsidian

Basalt

Ignimbrite

Agate

G5, $4-$8
OR

G6, $4-$8
Coastal OR

G5, $4-$8
OR

G7, $15-$30
Lake Co., OR

G6, $8-$15
OR

G8, $12-$20
WA

Tip wear

G4, $12-$20
OR

Basalt

LOCATION: Great Basin to Washington.
DESCRIPTION: A medium to large size, narrow, thin, blade that can exhibit oblique parallel flaking. Base can be convex to pointed. A faint shoulder occurs on one or both sides that contracts to the base. Early forms have ground basal areas. **I.D. KEY:** Slight shoulder on one or both sides.

Basalt

Obsidian

Tip wear

Obsidian

G5, $40-$75
Columbia Riv., WA

G10, $400-$750
OR

G7, $40-$75
S. OR

G10, $275-$500
S. OR

FW

(See Bullhead, Elko Corner, Hell's Canyon, Hendricks, Northern Side Notched, Snake River & Wendover)

Agate

Basalt

Agate

Basalt

Asymmetrical base

Basalt

Ground base

Red jasper

Diagonal flaking

Yellow jasper

Perfect base example, round & beveled

Brown petrified wood

G7, $12-$20
British Colum., CA

G7, $15-$30
Sou. OR

G7, $15-$25
Harney Co., OR

G10, $175-$300
WA

G6, $15-$30
Sou. OR

G6, $15-$30
Sou. OR

G6, $15-$25
Harney Co., OR

G6, $25-$45
OR

G8, $65-$115
OR

G6, $20-$35
Hood Riv., OR

G10+, $550-$1000
Lake Co., OR

G10, $275-$525
The Dalles, OR

LOCATION: Oregon. **DESCRIPTION:** A medium to large size, corner notched, barbed point with a straight to convex base and expanding stem. The cross section is lenticular (fairly thick at times, but occasionally flat). Blade edges are convex and rarely are resharpened by beveling. Stem sides are ground while bases are only occassionally ground. **I.D. KEY:** Grinding on stem sides, rounded or convex base that is beveled.

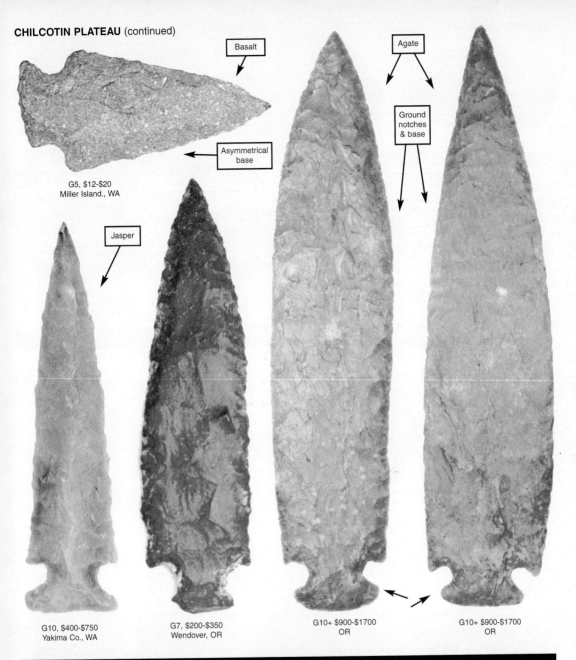

Basalt

Asymmetrical base

G5, $12-$20
Miller Island., WA

Jasper

Agate

Ground notches & base

G10, $400-$750
Yakima Co., WA

G7, $200-$350
Wendover, OR

G10+ $900-$1700
OR

G10+ $900-$1700
OR

CHOPPER - Paleo, 11,500 - 10,000 B. P.

(Also see Hand Axe and Scraper)

LOCATION: California. **DESCRIPTION:** A medium to large size, thick, early chopping and pounding tool. Most are irregular shaped to oval to circular.

G6, $2-$5 ea.
San Bernadino, CA

Famed Calico site choppers dated to 50,000 B.P. by L.S.B. Leakey, San Bernadino Co., CA.

IMPORTANT: Shown 40% actual size

FW

CHOPPER (continued)

Basalt

Chert

IMPORTANT: Shown 30% actual size

G6, $2-$5
San Bernadino Co., Ca,
Calico Mountain site

G8, $5-$10
San Bernadino Co., Ca,
Calico Mountain site

G5, $2-$5
Kern Co., CA,
Mojave Desert

Jasper/agate

Agate

Chert

Chert

G8, $2-$5
Kern Co., CA, Mojave
Desert

G8, $5-$10
San Bernadino Co., Ca,
Calico Mountain site

G8, $5-$10
San Bernadino Co., Ca,
Calico Mountain site

G4, $2-$5
San Bernadino Co., Ca,
Calico Mountain site

CHUMASH TOOLS - Early to middle Archaic, 9000 - 5000 B. P.

(See Columbia Mule Ear, High Desert Knifes and Plateau Pentagonal)

Knife

Black agate

Brown jasper

Knife

Black agate

G5, $2-$3
Ventura Co., CA

G5, $2-$5
Ventura Co., CA

Knife

G5, $5-$10
Ventura Co., CA

Knife/drill

Agate

Knife

Dark green agatized chert

Drill

Drill

G6, $1-$2
Ventura Co., CA

G5, $8-$15
Ventura Co., CA

G6, $1-$3
Ventura Co., CA

G8, $50-$90 (Rare)
Santa Barbara Co., CA

G6, $1-$3
Ventura Co., CA

CHUMASH (continued)

Knife

Black
fused
shale

G8, $100-$180
Santa Barbara Co., CA

LOCATION: Southern California. **DESCRIPTION:** The knives are medium to large size lanceolate to pentagonal shaped forms with straight to rounded bases. Scrapers are large ovoid shaped forms with cutting/scraping edges.

Scraper

G7, $25-$40
Ventura Co., CA

CLOVIS - Paleo, 11,500 - 10,600 B. P.

(Also see Black Rock Concave, Cascade, Folsom, Humboldt, Midland, Plainview, Tulare Lake & Windust)

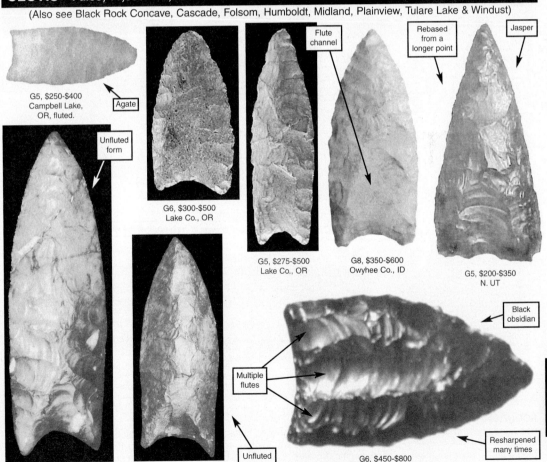

G5, $250-$400
Campbell Lake,
OR, fluted.

Agate

Unfluted
form

G6, $300-$500
Lake Co., OR

Flute
channel

G5, $275-$500
Lake Co., OR

G8, $350-$600
Owyhee Co., ID

Rebased
from a
longer point

Jasper

G5, $200-$350
N. UT

Black
obsidian

Multiple
flutes

Resharpened
many times

G9, $2000-$3500
Tulare Lake, CA

G8, $350-$600
Tulare Lake, CA

Unfluted
form

G6, $450-$800
OR, Rebased from a longer point

FW

CLOVIS (continued)

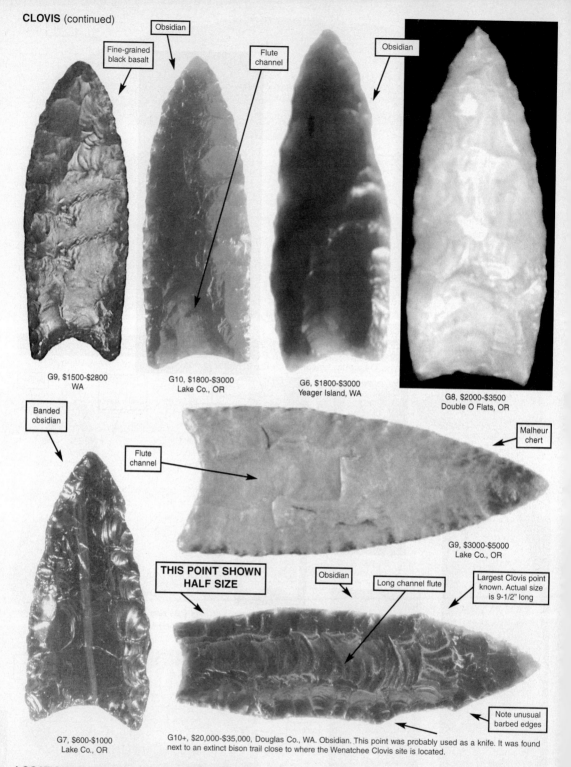

Fine-grained black basalt

Obsidian

Flute channel

Obsidian

G9, $1500-$2800
WA

G10, $1800-$3000
Lake Co., OR

G6, $1800-$3000
Yeager Island, WA

G8, $2000-$3500
Double O Flats, OR

Banded obsidian

Flute channel

Malheur chert

G9, $3000-$5000
Lake Co., OR

THIS POINT SHOWN HALF SIZE

Obsidian

Long channel flute

Largest Clovis point known. Actual size is 9-1/2" long

Note unusual barbed edges

G7, $600-$1000
Lake Co., OR

G10+, $20,000-$35,000, Douglas Co., WA. Obsidian. This point was probably used as a knife. It was found next to an extinct bison trail close to where the Wenatchee Clovis site is located.

LOCATION: All of North America. **DESCRIPTION:** A small to large size, auriculate, fluted, lanceolate point with convex sides and a concave base that is ground. Most examples have multiple flutes, usually on both sides. The basal concavity varies from shallow to deep. The oldest known point in North America. This point has been found associated with extinct mammoth & bison remains in several western states. **I.D. KEY:** Lanceolate form, baton fluting instead of indirect style.

974

CODY COMPLEX KNIFE - Early Archaic, 10,000 - 8000 B. P.

(Also see Eden, Firstview, Scottsbluff and Scottsbluff Knife)

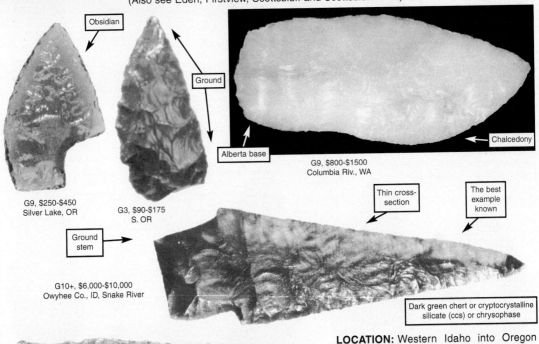

Obsidian

Ground

Alberta base

Chalcedony

G9, $800-$1500
Columbia Riv., WA

G9, $250-$450
Silver Lake, OR

G3, $90-$175
S. OR

Thin cross-section

The best example known

Ground stem

G10+, $6,000-$10,000
Owyhee Co., ID, Snake River

Dark green chert or cryptocrystalline silicate (ccs) or chrysophase

G7, $425-$800
Lake Co., OR

LOCATION: Western Idaho into Oregon and Washington. **DESCRIPTION:** A medium to large size, well made, triangular knife with a broad base. Resharpened examples have prominent shoulders forming a pentagonal form. The classic blade form has a diagonal slant. **I.D. KEY:** Early flaking, diagonal slant.

COLD SPRINGS - Middle Archaic, 5000 - 4000 B. P.

(Also see Ahsahka, Bear River, Bitterroot, Jalama Side Notched, Nightfire and Northern Side Notched)

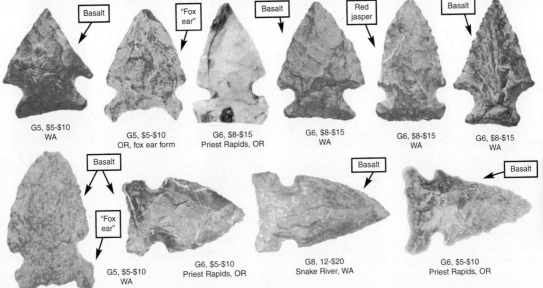

Basalt

"Fox ear"

Basalt

Red jasper

Basalt

G5, $5-$10
WA

G5, $5-$10
OR, fox ear form

G6, $8-$15
Priest Rapids, OR

G6, $8-$15
WA

G6, $8-$15
WA

G6, $8-$15
WA

Basalt

"Fox ear"

Basalt

Basalt

G5, $5-$10
WA

G6, $5-$10
Priest Rapids, OR

G8, 12-$20
Snake River, WA

G6, $5-$10
Priest Rapids, OR

FW

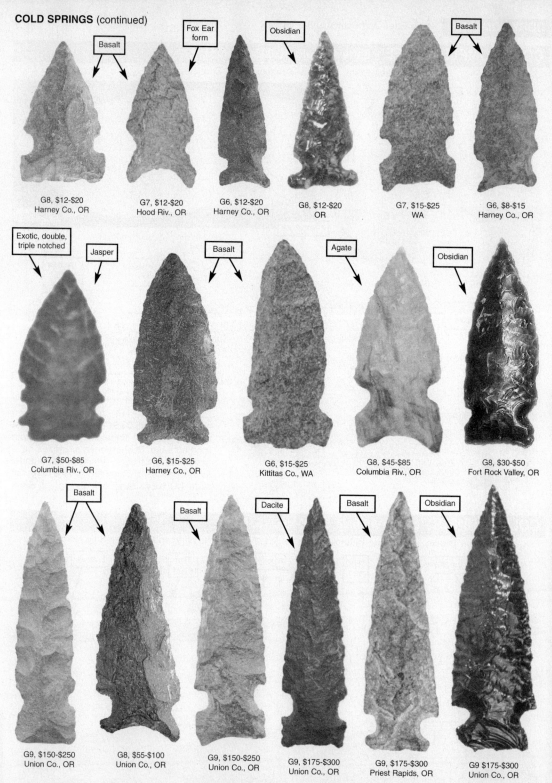

Basalt

Fox Ear form

Obsidian

Basalt

G8, $12-$20
Harney Co., OR

G7, $12-$20
Hood Riv., OR

G6, $12-$20
Harney Co., OR

G8, $12-$20
OR

G7, $15-$25
WA

G6, $8-$15
Harney Co., OR

Exotic, double, triple notched

Jasper

Basalt

Agate

Obsidian

G7, $50-$85
Columbia Riv., OR

G6, $15-$25
Harney Co., OR

G6, $15-$25
Kittitas Co., WA

G8, $45-$85
Columbia Riv., OR

G8, $30-$50
Fort Rock Valley, OR

Basalt

Basalt

Dacite

Basalt

Obsidian

G9, $150-$250
Union Co., OR

G8, $55-$100
Union Co., OR

G9, $150-$250
Union Co., OR

G9, $175-$300
Union Co., OR

G9, $175-$300
Priest Rapids, OR

G9 $175-$300
Union Co., OR

LOCATION: Idaho, Oregon & Washington. **DESCRIPTION:** A small to medium size broadly side to corner notched point with a straight to concave base. Hafting areas can vary considerably from "Fox Ear" forms to auriculate bases. Most are made from Basalt. **I. D. KEY:** Point of origin.

COLUMBIA MULE EAR - Classic Phase, 700 - 400 B. P.

(Also see Chumash knife, Plateau Pentagonal and Strong)

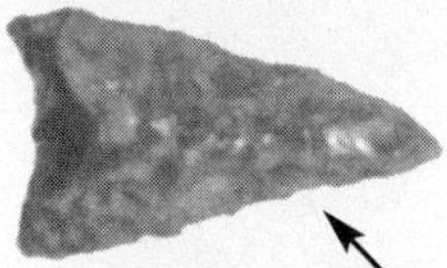

G3, $8-$15
OR

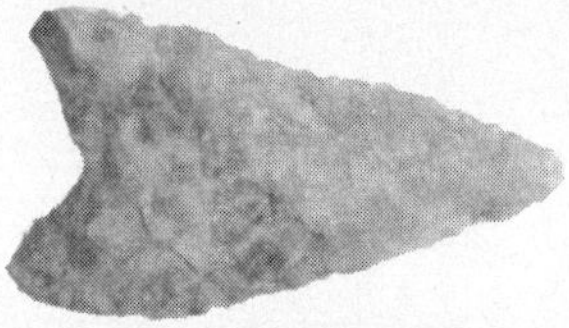

Red jasper

G5, $12-$20
Columbia Riv., OR

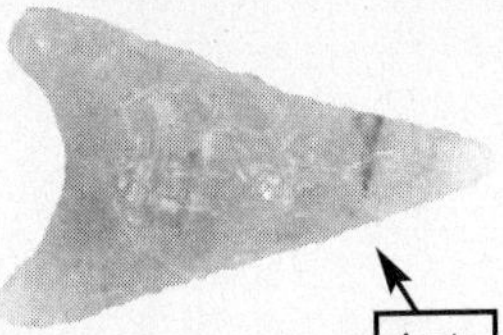

G6, $25-$40
N. OR

Agate

G6, $12-$20
Columbia Riv., OR

Agate

G5, $25-$40
Columbia Riv. Basin, OR

G6, $25-$40
Columbia Riv., OR

Jasper

G5, $15-$25
Columbia Riv., OR

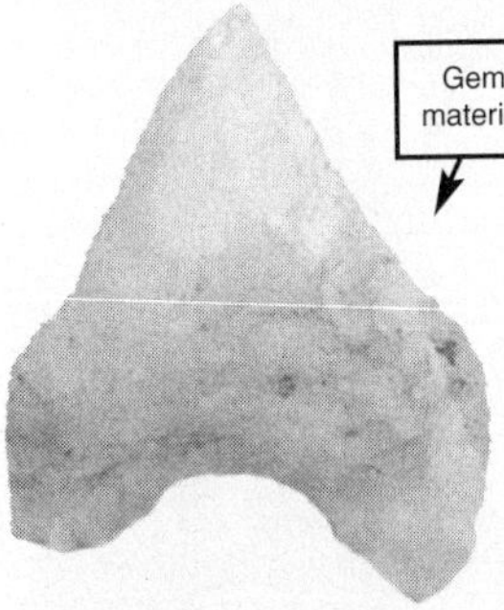

Gem material

G5, $18-$35
Columbia River Basin, OR

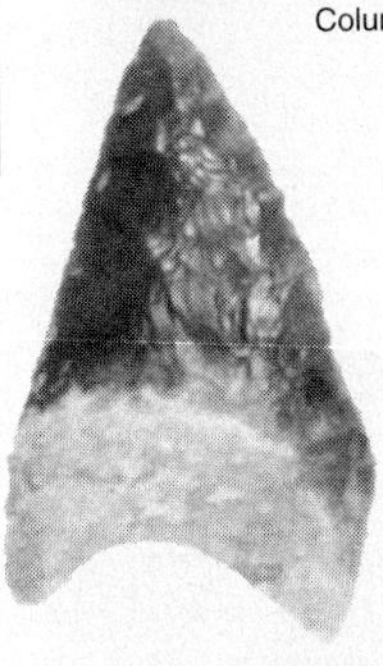

G6, $18-$35
OR

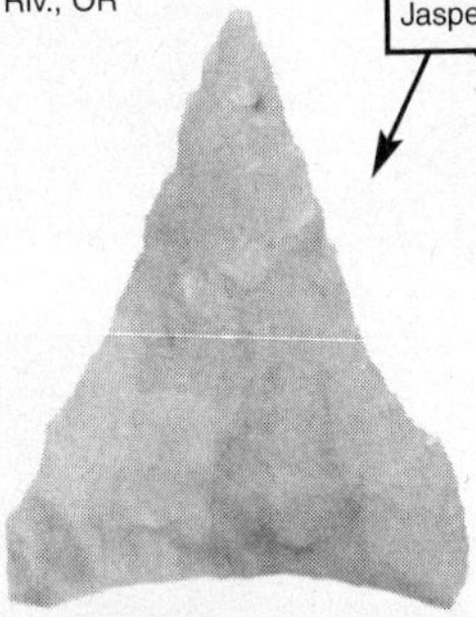

Jasper

G8, $35-$65
OR

G7, $30-$50
Bonneville Dam, OR

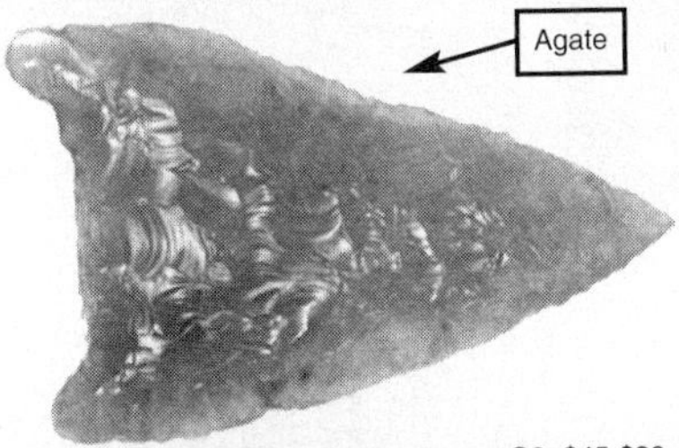

Agate

G5, $35-$65
Columbia River, OR

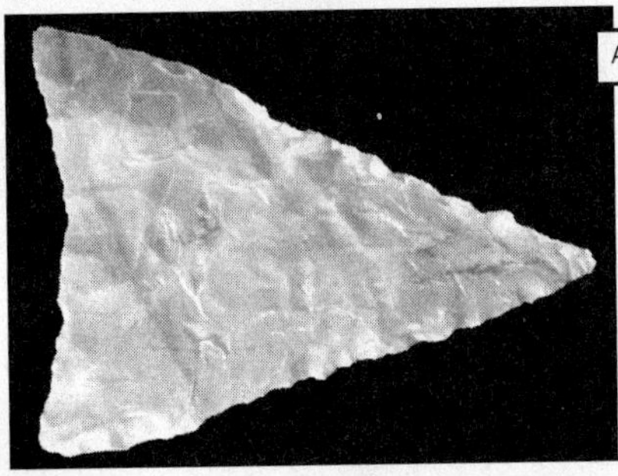

G8, $45-$80
Biggs Junction, OR

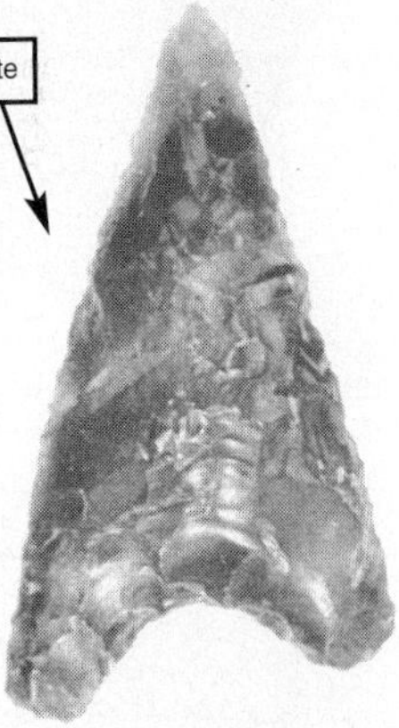

Agate

G8, $40-$70
Columbia River, OR

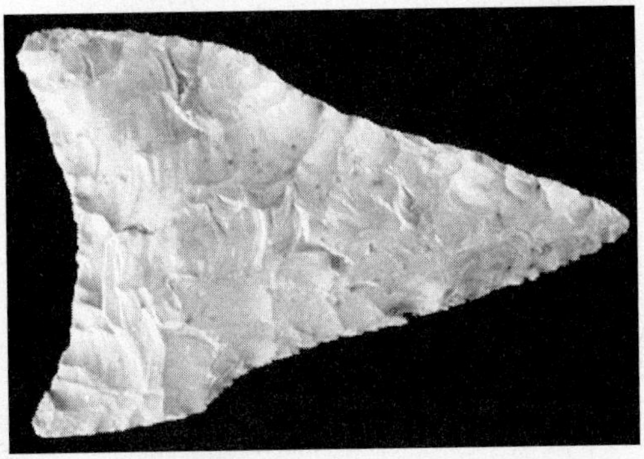

G9, $175-$300
Wasco Co., OR

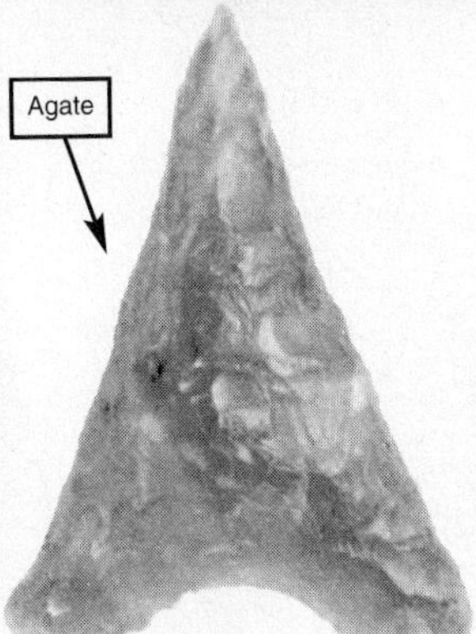

Agate

G8, $35-$65
Bonneville Dam, OR

LOCATION: Oregon and Washington. **DESCRIPTION:** A small to medium size, well made, triangular knife with a broad base. Resharpened examples have prominent shoulders forming a pentagonal form. Found only along the Columbia River in Washington & Oregon. **I.D. KEY:** Pentagonal form and prominent auricles.

FW

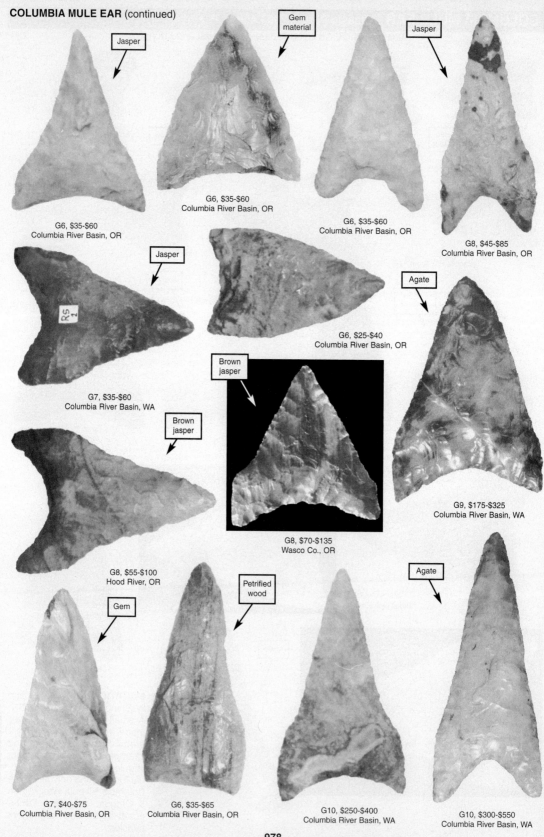

Jasper

Gem material

Jasper

G6, $35-$60
Columbia River Basin, OR

G6, $35-$60
Columbia River Basin, OR

G6, $35-$60
Columbia River Basin, OR

G8, $45-$85
Columbia River Basin, OR

Jasper

Agate

G6, $25-$40
Columbia River Basin, OR

G7, $35-$60
Columbia River Basin, WA

Brown jasper

Brown jasper

G8, $70-$135
Wasco Co., OR

G9, $175-$325
Columbia River Basin, WA

G8, $55-$100
Hood River, OR

Gem

Petrified wood

Agate

G7, $40-$75
Columbia River Basin, OR

G6, $35-$65
Columbia River Basin, OR

G10, $250-$400
Columbia River Basin, WA

G10, $300-$550
Columbia River Basin, WA

(Also see Eastgate, Gatecliff, Gunther, Rose Springs, Sauvies Island, Snake River Arrow and Wallula)

Chalc.

Chalc.

Chalc.

Obsidian

Chalc.

G6, $15-$30
OR

G6, $15-$30
Columb. Riv.,
OR

G6, $25-$45
OR

G5, $20-$35
Columb. Riv., OR

G6, $20-$35
OR

G5, $15-$25
OR

G8, $35-$65
OR

G7, $65-$120
WA

Jasper

Split
stem

Jasper

Jasper

Split
stem

G7, $35-$65
WA

G8, $80-$150
WA

G9, $125-$200
WA

G8, $35-$65
OR

G8 $35-$65
OR

G7, $55-$100
OR

G9, $120-$225
WA

Restored

Split
stem

Agate

Dacite

Tip
nick

Split
stem

Split
stem

Split
stem

G9, $125-$200
OR

G3, $25-$40
Hood Riv., OR

G9, $70-$130
John Day Riv., OR

G9, $95-$175
OR

G7, $20-$35
OR

G8, $80-$150
N. OR

Jasper

Split
stem

Agate

G9, $30-$50
Columb. Riv., WA

G8, $35-$60
OR

G8, $55-$100
Columb. Riv., WA

G8, $55-$100
Hood Riv., OR

G8, $55-$100
OR

Split
stem

Agate

Chalcedony

Agate

G10, $175-$300
Columb. Riv., WA

G8, $50-$95
Colum. Riv., WA

G8, $45-$80
WA

G8, $80-$150
Klamath Lake, OR

G7, $55-$100
N. OR

G9, $125-$225
Columb. Riv., WA

G8, $55-$100
Hood Riv., OR

Chalcedony

Gem

Obsidian

G9, $65-$125
Columb. Riv., WA

G10, $150-$250
Columb. Riv., WA

G9, $125-$200
OR

G10, $250-$400
Hood Riv., OR

FW

LOCATION: Columbia River in Oregon and Washington. **DESCRIPTION:** A small size, thin, triangular corner notched arrow point with strong barbs and a short, expanding to parallel sided stem. Shoulder barbs are usually pointed and can extend to the base. Blade edges can be serrated and the base can be bifurcated. Broader tangs than Wallula. Related to the earlier *Snake River* dart points.

COLUMBIA PLATEAU (continued)

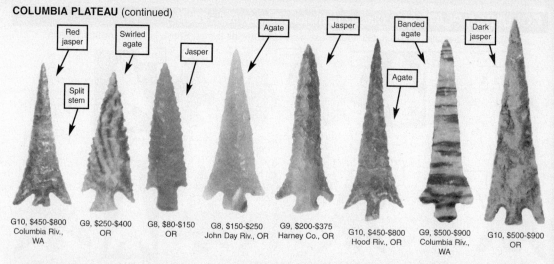

Red jasper

Split stem

G10, $450-$800
Columbia Riv.,
WA

Swirled agate

G9, $250-$400
OR

Jasper

G8, $80-$150
OR

Agate

G8, $150-$250
John Day Riv., OR

Jasper

G9, $200-$375
Harney Co., OR

Banded agate

Agate

G10, $450-$800
Hood Riv., OR

G9, $500-$900
Columbia Riv.,
WA

Dark jasper

G10, $500-$900
OR

COLUMBIA RIVER PIN STEM - Classic to Historic Phase, 500 - 200 B. P.

(Also see Alkali, Dagger, Lewis River Short Stemmed, Rabbit Island, Wallula, Yana)

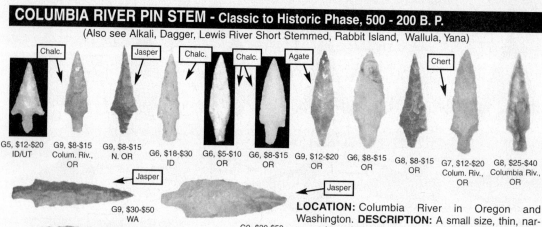

Chalc.

G5, $12-$20
ID/UT

G9, $8-$15
Colum. Riv.,
OR

Jasper

G9, $8-$15
N. OR

G6, $18-$30
ID

Chalc.

Chalc.

G6, $5-$10
OR

G6, $8-$15
OR

Agate

G9, $12-$20
OR

G6, $8-$15
OR

G8, $8-$15
OR

Chert

G7, $12-$20
Colum. Riv.,
OR

G8, $25-$40
Columbia Riv.,
OR

Jasper

G9, $30-$50
WA

G7, $45-$85
OR

G9, $30-$50
WA

Jasper

Red agate

LOCATION: Columbia River in Oregon and Washington. **DESCRIPTION:** A small size, thin, narrow triangular arrow point with rounded shoulders and a rounded stem.

CONTRA COSTA - Late Archaic to Developmental Phase, 2500 - 1500 B. P.

(Also see Coquille, Gypsum Cave, Point Sal Barbed, Vandenberg Contracting Stem)

Made into a drill

G3, $2-$5
CA coast

G8, $30-$50
Warner Valley, OR

G8, $40-$75
Modoc Co., CA

G3, $10-$20
CA coast

Restored tip

LOCATION: Central California Coastal area. **DESCRIPTION:** A medium size, dart/knife with a contracting stem and double side notches. Shoulders droop towards base.

COQUILLE BROADNECK - Mid-Archaic to Transitional Phase, 4500 - 2200 B. P.

(Also see Contra Costa, Gatecliff, Gypsum Cave, Rabbit Island, Sierra Contracting, Vandenberg Contracting)

COQUILLE BROADNECK (continued)

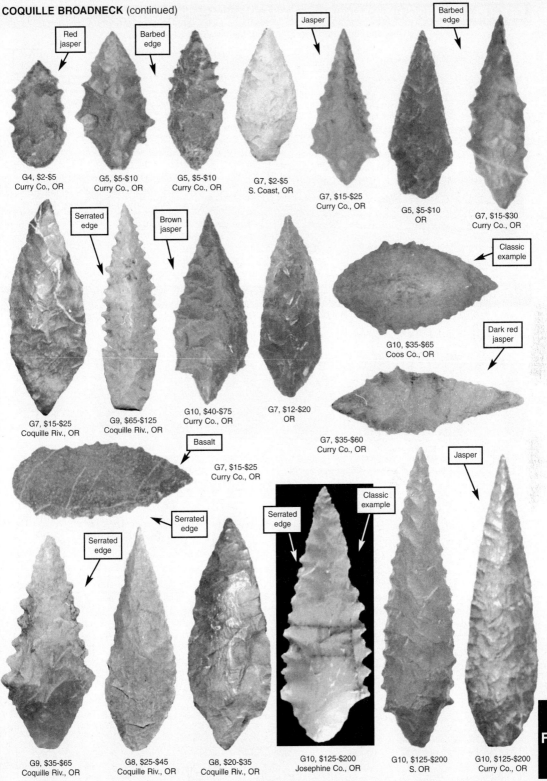

Red jasper

Barbed edge

Jasper

Barbed edge

G4, $2-$5
Curry Co., OR

G5, $5-$10
Curry Co., OR

G5, $5-$10
Curry Co., OR

G7, $2-$5
S. Coast, OR

G7, $15-$25
Curry Co., OR

G5, $5-$10
OR

G7, $15-$30
Curry Co., OR

Serrated edge

Brown jasper

Classic example

Dark red jasper

G7, $15-$25
Coquille Riv., OR

G9, $65-$125
Coquille Riv., OR

G10, $40-$75
Curry Co., OR

G7, $12-$20
OR

G10, $35-$65
Coos Co., OR

G7, $35-$60
Curry Co., OR

Basalt

G7, $15-$25
Curry Co., OR

Jasper

Serrated edge

Serrated edge

Serrated edge

Classic example

G9, $35-$65
Coquille Riv., OR

G8, $25-$45
Coquille Riv., OR

G8, $20-$35
Coquille Riv., OR

G10, $125-$200
Josephine Co., OR

G10, $125-$200
S. OR

G10, $125-$200
Curry Co., OR

FW

LOCATION: Coos & Curry Co. OR & N.W. California. **DESCRIPTION:** A medium size, triangular dart/knife with a convex to straight blade edge. The stem is broad and triangular to tapering and rounded. Shoulders are barbed to horizontal. Many are serrated. **I.D. KEY:** Broad, tapering to rounded stem.

COQUILLE KNIFE - Mid-Archaic to Transitional Phase, 4500 - 400 B. P.

(Also see Cascade, Intermontane Stemmed, Mahkin Shouldered, Triangular Knife)

Red jasper

Red jasper

G7, $3-$7
Rogue Riv., OR

G8, $15-$25
Curry Co., OR

Red Franciscan chert

LOCATION: Coos & Curry Co. OR. **DESCRIPTION:** A medium sized lanceolate knife with a straight base. **I.D. KEY:** Medium lanceolate form.

G3, $1-$2
OR

G6, $1-$2
Rogue Riv., OR

COQUILLE NARROWNECK - Transition Phase, 2200 - 400 B. P.

(Also see Gatecliff, Gold Hill, Rabbit Island, Rose Springs Sloping Shoulder, Sierra Contracting)

Jasper

Red jasper

G3, $1-$2
Rogue Riv., OR

G5, $2-$5
OR

G6, $2-$5
Rogue Riv., OR

G4, $2-$5
Rogue Riv., OR

G6, $5-$10
OR

G7, $3-$6
Rogue Riv., OR

G7, $5-10
OR

G7, $3-$6
Rogue Riv., OR

Serrated edge

Jasper

Chalc.

G7, $2-$5
Rogue Riv., OR

G6, $2-$5
S. Coast, OR

G5, $1-$2
OR

G7, $12-$20
OR

G6, $2-$5
Rogue Riv., OR

G6, $5-$10
S.W. OR

G5, $1-$2
Rogue Riv., OR

G6, $5-$10
OR

Serrated edge

Red agate

Gem

Jasper

G9, $20-$35
OR

G9, $20-$35
Camas Valley, OR

G9, $15-$30
OR

G9, $20-$35
OR

G9, $20-$35
OR

G8, $20-$35
OR

G8, $15-$30
Camas Valley, OR

COQUILLE NARROWNECK (continued)

Serrated edge

G7, $30-$50
OR

G6, $5-$10
OR

G7, $25-$40
OR

G6, $10-$20
OR
Rogue Riv., OR

G7, $30-$50
OR

G7, $10-$20
OR

G7, $15-$30
OR

Red jasper

Brown jasper

G7, $15-$25
OR

G7, $15-$25
OR

G7, $25-$45
OR

G7, $15-$25
OR

G9, $20-$35
Curry Co., OR

G7, $15-$25
Coquille Riv., OR

G9, $25-$40
Coquille Riv., OR

LOCATION: Coos Co. & Curry Co. OR. & N.W. California. **DESCRIPTION:** A medium size, triangular dart/knife with a convex to straight blade edge. The stem is narrow and triangular to tapering and rounded. Shoulders are barbed to horizontal. Many are serrated. **I.D. KEY:** Narrow, tapering to rounded stem.

COQUILLE SIDE NOTCHED - Mid-Archaic to Transition Phase, 4500 - 2200 B. P.

(Also see Cold Springs, Merrybell, Rose Springs Side Notched & Tucannon Side)

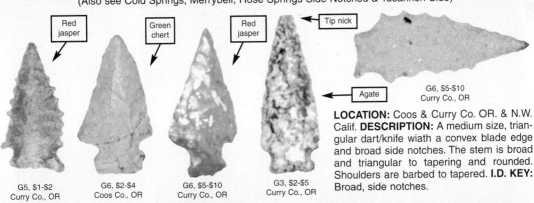

Red jasper

Green chert

Red jasper

Tip nick

Agate

G6, $5-$10
Curry Co., OR

G5, $1-$2
Curry Co., OR

G6, $2-$4
Coos Co., OR

G6, $5-$10
Curry Co., OR

G3, $2-$5
Curry Co., OR

LOCATION: Coos & Curry Co. OR. & N.W. Calif. **DESCRIPTION:** A medium size, triangular dart/knife wiath a convex blade edge and broad side notches. The stem is broad and triangular to tapering and rounded. Shoulders are barbed to tapered. **I.D. KEY:** Broad, side notches.

CORDILLERAN - Early Archaic, 9,500 - 7,500 B. P.

FW

(Also see Agate Basin, Cascade, Early Leaf, Excelsior, Haskett, Intermontane, Kennewick)

LOCATION: Great Basin states northward. **DESCRIPTION:** A usually large, mostly bi-pointed lanceolate spear or dart/knife with parallel and occasionally oblique flaking. Basal configuration is always contracting and can be dully pointed, rounded or straight with rounded corners. Stem sides are usually ground and blade cross-sections are lenticular and are not as thin as *Kennewick*. Possible descendant of *Haskett* points and later evolving into *Cascade* points. This point is transitional overlapping the late *Hasketts* with the early *Cascades*. **I.D.KEY:** Hafting area is shorter than *Haskett* but longer than *Cascade*.

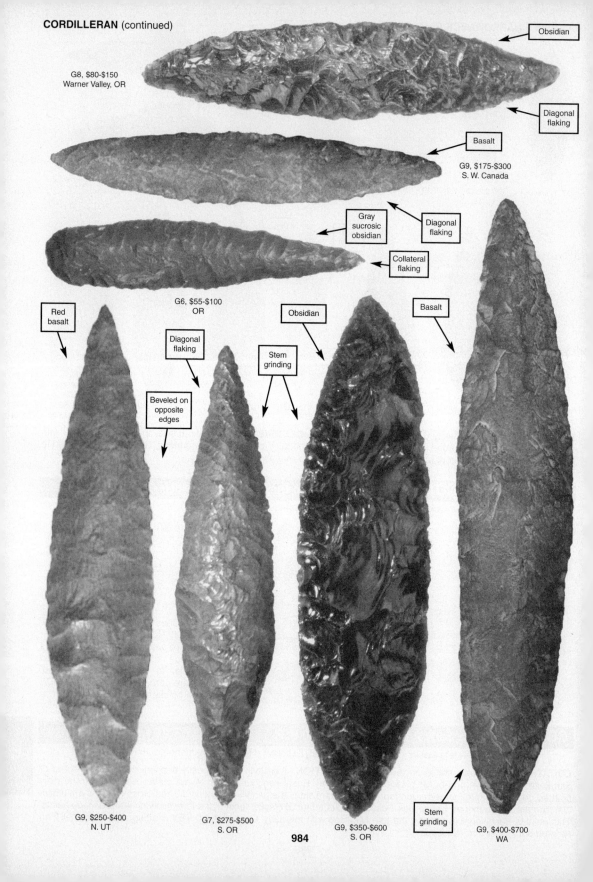

Obsidian

G8, $80-$150
Warner Valley, OR

Diagonal
flaking

Basalt

G9, $175-$300
S. W. Canada

Gray
sucrosic
obsidian

Diagonal
flaking

Collateral
flaking

G6, $55-$100
OR

Red
basalt

Diagonal
flaking

Stem
grinding

Obsidian

Basalt

Beveled on
opposite
edges

G9, $250-$400
N. UT

G7, $275-$500
S. OR

984

Stem
grinding

G9, $350-$600
S. OR

G9, $400-$700
WA

CORDILLERAN (continued)

Dacite →

G9, $250-$400
OR

Ground stem →

Chalcedony

G10, $275-$500
Hood Riv., WA

Cordilleran/Haskett cross type

COTTONWOOD LEAF - Developmental to Historic Phase, 1100 - 200 B. P.

(Also see Canalino, Cascade, Cottonwood Triangle, Gold Hill, Magala Cove Leaf and Trojan)

Basalt — Obsidian — Jasper — Agate

G5, $2-$4
NV

G6, $3-$6
OR

G6, $3-$6
Humboldt Co., NV

G6, $3-$6
Lake Co., OR

G5, $4-$8
NV

G6, $4-$8
NV

G6, $8-$15
Humboldt Co., NV

G8, $12-$20
S. OR

G8, $20-$35
CA

Obsidian

Obsidian

Petrified wood

G5, $6-$12
S. W. OR

G6, $5-$15
Colum. Riv., OR.

G7, $20-$30
S. W. OR

G6, $50-$90
OR

LOCATION: Great Basin states northward. **DESCRIPTION:** A small size, thin, ovoid point with a convex base. Similar to the *Nodena* type from Arkansas. **I.D. KEY:** Small ovoid form.

COTTONWOOD TRIANGLE - Developmental to Historic Phase, 1100 - 200 B. P.

(Also see Bull Creek, Canalino Triangular, Cottonwood Leaf, Desert & Gunther Triangular)

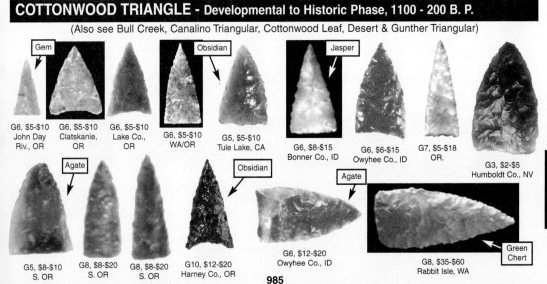

Gem

Obsidian

Jasper

G6, $5-$10
John Day Riv., OR

G6, $5-$10
Clatskanie, OR

G6, $5-$10
Lake Co., OR

G6, $5-$10
WA/OR

G5, $5-$10
Tule Lake, CA

G6, $8-$15
Bonner Co., ID

G6, $6-$15
Owyhee Co., ID

G7, $5-$18
OR.

G3, $2-$5
Humboldt Co., NV

Agate

Obsidian

Agate

G5, $8-$10
S. OR

G8, $8-$20
S. OR

G8, $8-$20
S. OR

G10, $12-$20
Harney Co., OR

G6, $12-$20
Owyhee Co., ID

G8, $35-$60
Rabbit Isle, WA

Green Chert

FW

985

COTTONWOOD TRIANGLE (continued)

G6, $8-$15
Napa Valley, CA

G8, $12-$20
OR
Chalc.

G8, $12-$20
OR

G7, $12-$20
CA

Edge
wear

Banded
obsidian

Obsidian

Jasper

Banded
obsidian

G7, $12-$20
S. OR

G7, $12-$20
S. OR

G5, $12-$20
CA

G8, $15-$25
Owyhee Co., ID

G7, $12-$20
CA

G7, $12-$20
Harney Co., OR

LOCATION: Great Basin states northward. **DESCRIPTION:** A small to medium size, thin, triangular point with a straight to concave base. Basal corners are sharp to rounded. The preform for the *Desert* series. **I.D. KEY:** Small triangle form.

COUGAR MOUNTAIN - Paleo, 11,000 - 9000 B. P.

(Also see Agate Basin, Año Nuevo, Cody Complex, Deschutes Knife, Haskett, Lake Mohave, Lind Coulee and Parman, Shaniko Stemmed and Wildcat Canyon)

Ignimbrite

Miniature
form

Yellow
agate

Red
jasper

Red and
blue on one
side, green
on the other

White
banded
agate

G5, $200-$350
S. OR

Ground
stem

G7, $300-$550
S. Cent. OR

G7, $250-$550
S. OR

Ground
stem

G7, $300-$550
S. Cent. OR

Ground
stem

Ground
stem

G8, $450-$800
CA/OR state line

Ground
stem

Obsidian

G7, $600-$1000
Lake Co., OR

Ground
stem

G9, $2500-$4500
Harney Co., OR

LOCATION: Southern Oregon, N.W. Nevada. **DESCRIPTION:** A large size, long stemmed form with weak tapered shoulders and a convex base. Basal area is ground. Associated with *Haskett* points found on the same sites. Among the earliest points found at Cougar Mountain Cave in Southern Oregon. Very rare. **I.D. KEY:** Long tapered stem & obtuse shoulders.

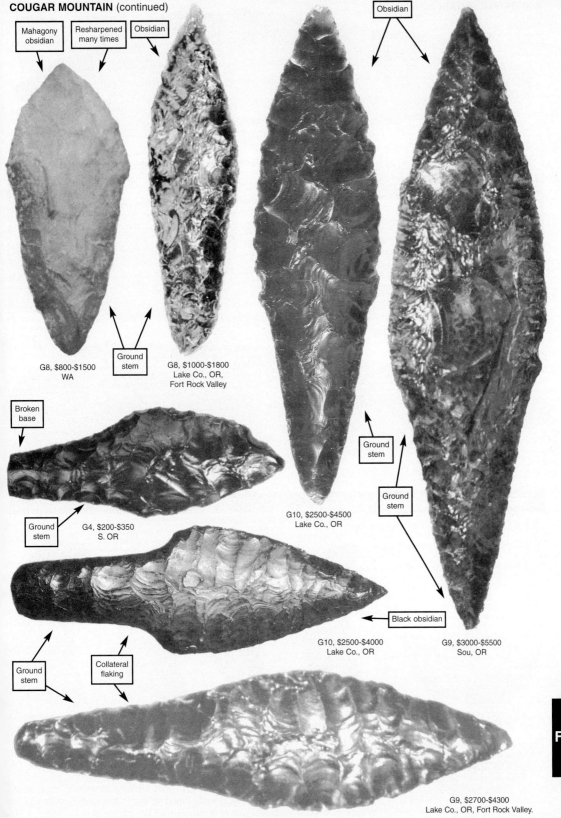

Mahagony obsidian

Resharpened many times

Obsidian

Obsidian

Ground stem

G8, $800-$1500
WA

G8, $1000-$1800
Lake Co., OR,
Fort Rock Valley

Ground stem

Broken base

Ground stem

G4, $200-$350
S. OR

G10, $2500-$4500
Lake Co., OR

Ground stem

Ground stem

Black obsidian

G10, $2500-$4000
Lake Co., OR

G9, $3000-$5500
Sou, OR

Ground stem

Collateral flaking

G9, $2700-$4300
Lake Co., OR, Fort Rock Valley.

FW

987

COUGAR MOUNTAIN (continued)

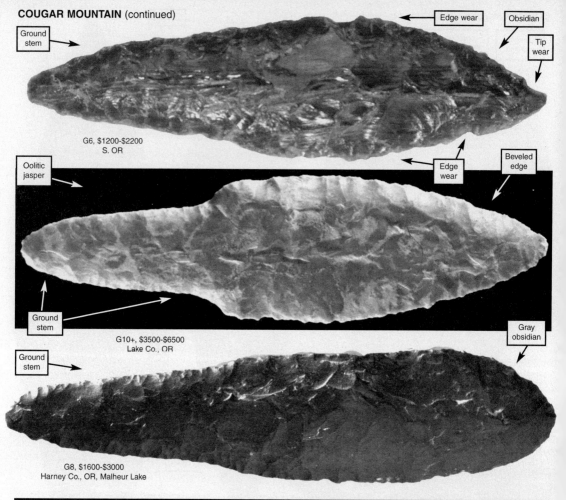

Ground stem

Edge wear

Obsidian

Tip wear

G6, $1200-$2200
S. OR

Oolitic jasper

Edge wear

Beveled edge

Ground stem

Gray obsidian

G10+, $3500-$6500
Lake Co., OR

Ground stem

G8, $1600-$3000
Harney Co., OR, Malheur Lake

CRESCENT - Paleo, 11,000 - 10,500 B. P.

(Also see Black Rock Concave)

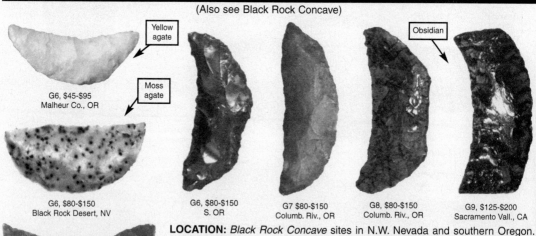

Yellow agate

Moss agate

Obsidian

G6, $45-$95
Malheur Co., OR

G6, $80-$150
Black Rock Desert, NV

G6, $80-$150
S. OR

G7 $80-$150
Columb. Riv., OR

G8, $80-$150
Columb. Riv., OR

G9, $125-$200
Sacramento Vall., CA

G9, $80-$150
S. OR

LOCATION: *Black Rock Concave* sites in N.W. Nevada and southern Oregon.
DESCRIPTION: Crescent moon to butterfly shaped, *Crescents* are controversial with different theories as to their use. The earlier forms show grinding on the edge only at the center of both sides as well as one or more burinated tips. Possible use could be as knives (thatch (tule) cutters), scrapers, transverse points or gravers. Crescent forms were found at the Paleo *Lind Coulee* site in Washington state. and with *Clovis* points in the Fenn cache of N.E. Utah.

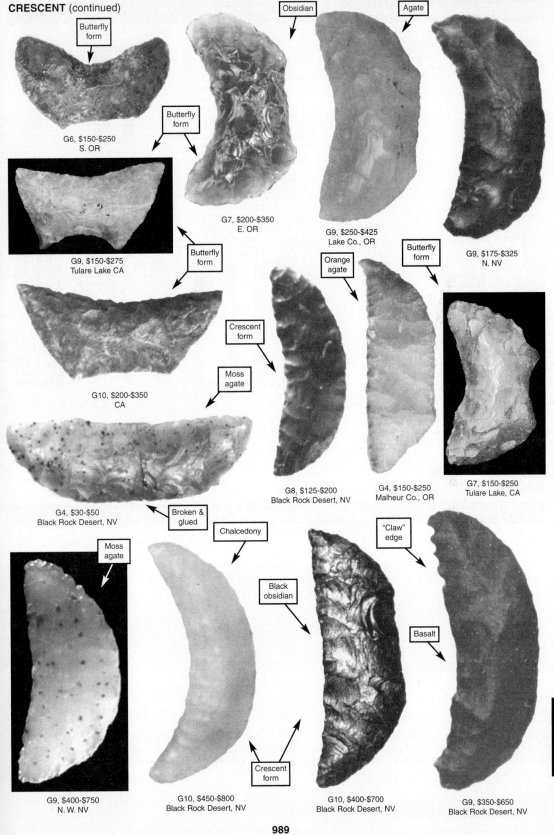

CRESCENT (continued)

Butterfly form

G6, $150-$250
S. OR

Obsidian

Agate

Butterfly form

G7, $200-$350
E. OR

G9, $250-$425
Lake Co., OR

G9, $175-$325
N. NV

G9, $150-$275
Tulare Lake CA

Butterfly form

Orange agate

Butterfly form

Crescent form

Moss agate

G10, $200-$350
CA

G4, $30-$50
Black Rock Desert, NV

Broken & glued

G8, $125-$200
Black Rock Desert, NV

G4, $150-$250
Malheur Co., OR

G7, $150-$250
Tulare Lake, CA

Chalcedony

"Claw" edge

Black obsidian

Basalt

Moss agate

G9, $400-$750
N. W. NV

Crescent form

G10, $450-$800
Black Rock Desert, NV

G10, $400-$700
Black Rock Desert, NV

G9, $350-$650
Black Rock Desert, NV

FW

989

DAGGER - Developmental to Classic Phase, 1200 - 400 B. P.

(Also see Columbia River Pin Stem, Diamond Back, Klickitat and Nottoway)

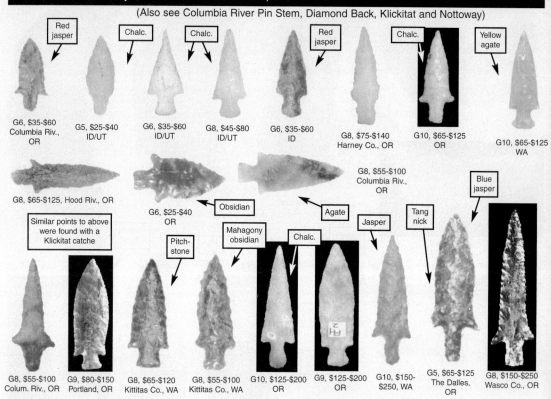

Red jasper

G6, $35-$60
Columbia Riv.,
OR

Chalc.

G5, $25-$40
ID/UT

Chalc.

G6, $35-$60
ID/UT

G8, $45-$80
ID/UT

Red jasper

G6, $35-$60
ID

G8, $75-$140
Harney Co., OR

Chalc.

G10, $65-$125
OR

Yellow agate

G10, $65-$125
WA

G8, $65-$125, Hood Riv., OR

G6, $25-$40
OR

G8, $55-$100
Columbia Riv.,
OR

Blue jasper

Similar points to above were found with a Klickitat catche

Obsidian

Pitch-stone

Mahagony obsidian

Chalc.

Agate

Jasper

Tang nick

G8, $55-$100
Colum. Riv., OR

G9, $80-$150
Portland, OR

G8, $65-$120
Kittitas Co., WA

G8, $55-$100
Kittitas Co., WA

G10, $125-$200
OR

G9, $125-$200
OR

G10, $150-$250, WA

G5, $65-$125
The Dalles,
OR

G8, $150-$250
Wasco Co., OR

LOCATION: Columbia River basin along the Columbia River. **DESCRIPTION:** A small size, narrow, thin, barbed point or knife. Bases vary from expanded to contracted. Diamond shaped bases would place point in *Klickitat* type. **I.D. KEY:** Blade form.

DAGGER   (see Klickitat)

DESCHUTES KNIFE - Classic to Historic Phase, 500 - 250 B. P.

(Also see Ano Nuevo & Cougar Mountain)

Rootbeer colored flint

G8, $250-$400
Lake Co., OR

Must have notch in base

LOCATION: Mid-Columbia River basin in Oregon. **DESCRIPTION:** Very rare. A large size, long stemmed to lanceolate knife with slight to tapered shoulders and a concave base. Length can be 4 to 9". There is edge grinding on the stem. This blade had a wrapped handle and was held as a knife. **I.D. KEY:** Size, basal notch & blade form.

DESERT CORNER NOTCHED   (see Elko Corner Notched)

DESERT DELTA - Classic to Historic Phase, 700 - 200 B. P.

(Also see Bitterroot, Cold Spring, Panoche, Piquinin, Uinta)

Pink jasper

Agate

Calcedony

G7, $15-$25
Columbia
Riv., OR

G7, $15-$25
OR

G7, $15-$25
OR

G7, $15-$25
N. OR

G7, $15-$25
Twin Falls Co., ID

G7, $15-$25
N. OR

G8, $25-$45
Harney Co., OR

G8, $25-$45
Modoc Co., CA

Red
agate

Base
nick

Agate

G7, $18-$30
OR

G7, $18-$30
OR

G7, $15-$25
Lake Co., OR.

G6, $25-$45
Sou. OR

G10, $90-$175
Columbia Riv., OR

G10, $40-$70
OR

G9, $20-$45
OR

G8, $20-$45
WA

Red
jasper

Jasper

Chert

Serrated
edge

ca. 1850-1890

Minor
shoulder
nicks

Historic,
glass

G7, $25-$45
OR

G8, $35-$60
OR

G9, $50-$90
OR

G10, $90-$175
OR

G10, $50-$165
OR

G9, $55-$110
CA

G9, $55-$110
OR

G9, $60-$110
Portland, OR

LOCATION: Great Basin westward. **DESCRIPTION:** A small, thin, triangular, side notched arrow point with a deeply concave base, straight blade edges and expanded, pointed ears making the base the widest part of the point. Blade edges can be serrated. **I.D. KEY:** Small triangle, side notched form.

DESERT GENERAL - Classic to Historic Phase, 700 - 200 B. P.

(Also see Ahsahka, Bear River, Bitterroot, Cold Spring, Kamloops, Panoche, Piquinin, Rose, Uinta & Wintu)

Basalt

Red
jasper

Gem

G4, $2-$4
Gooding Co.,
ID

G4, $2-$5
Owyhee Co.,
ID

G7, $15-$25
OR

G7, $8-$15
OR

G7, $10-$15
OR

G5, $6-$12
Lake Co., OR

G8, $15-$25
Humboldt Co., NV

G5, $6-$12
N. OR

G5, $6-$12
OR

Banded
obsidian

Double
notched

Serrated

Chalc.

Double
notched

Agate

G7, $15-$25
Owyhee Co.,
ID

G9, $20-$35
OR

G8, $45-$85
WA

G8, $15-$30
N. OR

G7, $15-$30
Humboldt Co.,
NV

G8, $20-$35
Columbia
Riv., WA

G9, $25-$45
OR

G9, $60-$110
WA

G8, $15-$30
Gooding Co., ID

FW

DESERT GENERAL (continued)

Obsidian
G6, $12-$20
Gooding Co., ID

Clear
G8 $30-$50
Columbia Riv., WA

G10, $35-$60
OR

Banded obsidian
G7, $20-$35
Sou. Cent. OR

Rare snowflake obsidian
G9, $40-$75
OR

Clear agate
G10, $55 $110
OR

G8, $15-$25
OR

G8, $15-$30
Columbia Riv., WA

G10, $50-$90
OR

G10, $50-$90
OR

Basalt
G8, $35-$60
Gooding Co., ID

Obsidian
G8, $25-$40
OR

Double notched
G10, $90-$175
WA

G10, $50-$95
OR

Still hafted to arrow shaft with asphaltum
G10, $150-$275
N. UT, Hogup cave, 30" long & complete w/agate point

G6, $25-$40
OR

G10, $150-$275
N. UT, Hogup cave, 30" long & complete w/agate point

LOCATION: Great Basin westward. **DESCRIPTION:** A small, thin, side notched arrow point with a straight to slightly concave base. Blade edges can be serrated. Similar to the *Reed* point found in Oklahoma. Reported to have been used by the Shoshoni Indians of the Historic period.

DESERT REDDING - Classic to Historic Phase, 700 - 200 B. P.

(Also see Bear River, Bitterroot, Cold Spring, Panoche, Piquinin)

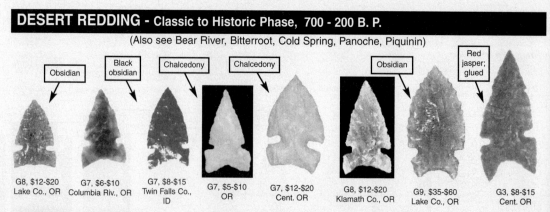

Obsidian
G8, $12-$20
Lake Co., OR

Black obsidian
G7, $6-$10
Columbia Riv., OR

Chalcedony
G7, $8-$15
Twin Falls Co., ID

Chalcedony
G7, $5-$10
OR

G7, $12-$20
Cent. OR

Obsidian
G8, $12-$20
Klamath Co., OR

G9, $35-$60
Lake Co., OR

Red jasper; glued
G3, $8-$15
Cent. OR

LOCATION: Great Basin westward. **DESCRIPTION:** A small, thin, side notched arrow point with a concave base. Blade edges curve into the base and can be serrated. Reported to have been used by the Shoshoni Indians of the Historic period.

(Also see Bitterroot, Cold Spring and Panoche)

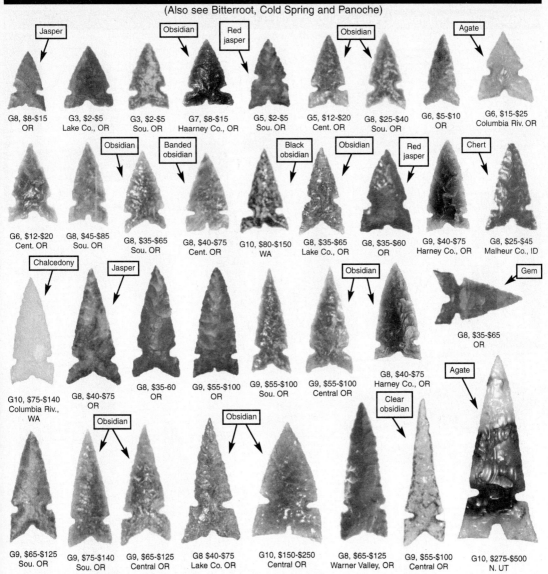

Jasper

G8, $8-$15
OR

G3, $2-$5
Lake Co., OR

G3, $2-$5
Sou. OR

Obsidian **Red jasper**

G7, $8-$15
Haarney Co., OR

G5, $2-$5
Sou. OR

Obsidian

G5, $12-$20
Cent. OR

G8, $25-$40
Sou. OR

G6, $5-$10
OR

Agate

G6, $15-$25
Columbia Riv. OR

G6, $12-$20
Cent. OR

G8, $45-$85
Sou. OR

Obsidian

G8, $35-$65
Sou. OR

Banded obsidian

G8, $40-$75
Cent. OR

Black obsidian

G10, $80-$150
WA

Obsidian

G8, $35-$65
Lake Co., OR

G8, $35-$60
OR

Red jasper

G9, $40-$75
Harney Co., OR

Chert

G8, $25-$45
Malheur Co., ID

Chalcedony

G10, $75-$140
Columbia Riv.,
WA

Jasper

G8, $40-$75
OR

G8, $35-60
OR

G9, $55-$100
OR

G9, $55-$100
Sou. OR

G9, $55-$100
Central OR

Obsidian

G8, $40-$75
Harney Co., OR

Gem

G8, $35-$65
OR

Agate

Obsidian

G9, $65-$125
Sou. OR

G9, $75-$140
Sou. OR

G9, $65-$125
Central OR

Obsidian

G8 $40-$75
Lake Co. OR

G10, $150-$250
Central OR

G8, $65-$125
Warner Valley, OR

Clear obsidian

G9, $55-$100
Central OR

G10, $275-$500
N. UT

LOCATION: Great Basin westward. **DESCRIPTION:** A small size, thin, triangular side and basal notched arrow point with distinctive basal pointed barbs and a basal notch. **I.D. KEY:** Triple notches, pointed basal corners.

(Also see Klickitat, One-Que)

Red jasper

G6, $15-$25
Sauvie's Island, OR

Agate

G8, $35-$65
Hood River, OR

FW

LOCATION: Columbia River basin. **DESCRIPTION:** A small, thin, arrow point with a diamond shaped stem. Shoulders are horizontal to tapered. Bases are pointed to rounded. The knife form of *Klickitat Daggers*. More utilitarian, lacking the refinements of true daggers.

DRILL - Paleo to Historic Phase, 11,500 - 200 B. P.

(Also see Chopper, Graver, Hand Axe, Lancet, Perforator and Scraper)

Agate

Northern Side Notched

Chalc.

G6, $8-$15
OR

G4, $8-$15
Malheur Co., OR

G3, $5-$10
OR

G3, $2-$5
Hood Riv., OR

G6, $12-$20
Death Valley, NV

G6, $15-$30
OR

G7, $15-$30
Colum. Riv.,
OR

Columbia Mule Ear type

Jasper

Chalc.

G9, $25-$40
Curry Co.,OR

G6, $15-$25
OR

G6, $20-$35
WA

G6, $20-$35
Harney Co., OR

G6, $25-$50
Columbia Riv., OR

Cascade

Bog agate

Cascade

Jasper

G9, $60-$110
WA

Jasper

Orange agate

Haskett drill

G9, $50-$90
Colum. Riv., OR

Red chalc.

Cascade

G10, $120-$225
WA

G10, $120-$225
Harney Co., OR

G8, $30-$50
OR

G9, $40-$70
Hood Riv., OR

G9, $80-$150
Lake Co., OR

G10, $150-$275
WA

G10, $150-$275
Celilo Falls, OR

LOCATION: Everywhere. **DESCRIPTION:** Although many drills were made from scratch, all point types were made into the drill form. Usually, heavily resharpened and broken points were salvaged and rechipped into drills. These objects were certainly used as drills (evidence of extreme edge wear), but there is speculation that some of these forms may have been used as pins for clothing, ornaments, ear plugs and other uses.

(Also see Goshen, Hawken, Humboldt Expanded Base, Midland, Pryor Stemmed and Shaniko Stemmed)

Tip nick

Franciscan chert

Tip nick

G5, $15-$25
OR

G9, $75-$140
Nixon, NV

LOCATION: Great Basin westward. **DESCRIPTION:** A medium size, thin, lanceolate point with broad, shallow side notches expanding into rounded ears that may be ground. The base is concave. These haven't been officially named yet.

EARLY LEAF - Early to middle Archaic, 8000 - 5000 B. P.

(Also see Agate Basin, Cascade, Cordilleran, Excelsior, High Desert Knife, Intermontane Stemmed, Kennewick, Shaniko Stemmed and Wildcat Canyon)

Diagonal flaking

G8, $65-$125
S.E. OR

Basalt

Diagonal flaking

Basalt

Basalt

Side nicks

G6, $30-$50
S. OR

G6, $25-$45
S.E. OR

G9, $85-$165
British Colum.,
Canada

G6, $40-$75
N. NV

Dacite

G6, $55-$100
S. OR

FW

EARLY LEAF
(continued)

G8, $200-$350
Harney Co., OR

Probably Clovis or Windust knife

Found with Windust points

Basalt

NOTE: Early Leaf points are currently being re-classified. The points shown on this page will in the future fall under various types such as *Cascade, Clovis Knife, Cordilleran, High Desert Knife, Windust Knife* and other types.

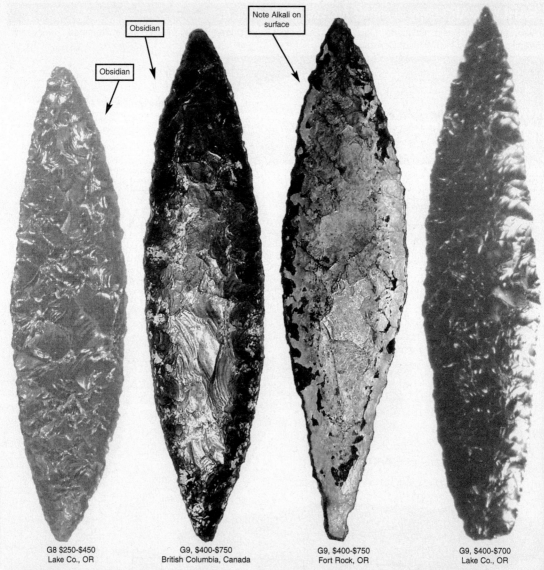

Obsidian

Obsidian

Note Alkali on surface

G8 $250-$450
Lake Co., OR

G9, $400-$750
British Columbia, Canada

G9, $400-$750
Fort Rock, OR

G9, $400-$700
Lake Co., OR

LOCATION: Great Basin to Washington. **DESCRIPTION:** A medium to large size lanceolate point or blade with a convex, pointed or straight base. Early parallel flaking is evident on many examples. These haven't been officially named yet and could be early *Cascade* forms.

EASTGATE - Developmental to Classic Phase, 1500 - 400 B. P.

(Also see Columbia Plateau, Eastgate, Elko, Emigrant Springs, Gunther, Rose Springs, Wallula)

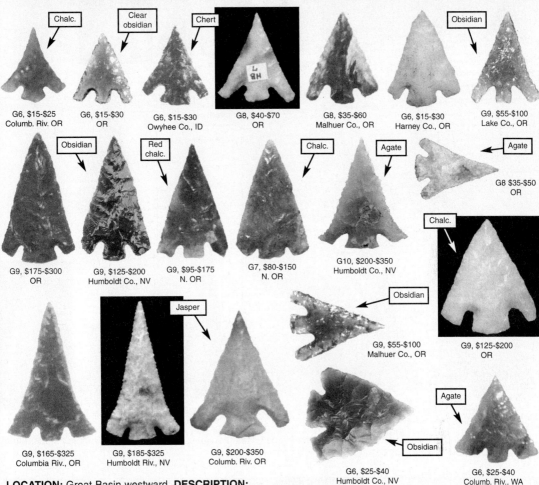

Chalc.
G6, $15-$25
Columb. Riv. OR

Clear obsidian
G6, $15-$30
OR

Chert
G6, $15-$30
Owyhee Co., ID

G8, $40-$70
OR

G8, $35-$60
Malhuer Co., OR

G6, $15-$30
Harney Co., OR

Obsidian
G9, $55-$100
Lake Co., OR

Obsidian
G9, $175-$300
OR

G9, $125-$200
Humboldt Co., NV

Red chalc.
G9, $95-$175
N. OR

G7, $80-$150
N. OR

Chalc.
Agate
G10, $200-$350
Humboldt Co., NV

Agate
G8 $35-$50
OR

Chalc.
G9, $125-$200
OR

Jasper
G9, $165-$325
Columbia Riv., OR

G9, $185-$325
Humboldt Riv., NV

G9, $200-$350
Columb. Riv. OR

Obsidian
G9, $55-$100
Malhuer Co., OR

Agate
Obsidian
G6, $25-$40
Humboldt Co., NV

G6, $25-$40
Columb. Riv., WA

LOCATION: Great Basin westward. **DESCRIPTION:**
A small, thin, triangular corner-notched arrow point
with a short parallel sided to expanded stem. Barbs
can be pointed or squared and usually extend to
base.

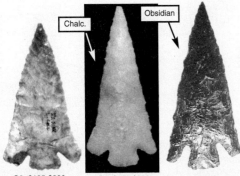

Chalc.
Obsidian
G9, $125-$200
Humboldt Sink, NV

G9, $175-$300
Columb. Riv., OR

G9, $175-$300
N. UT

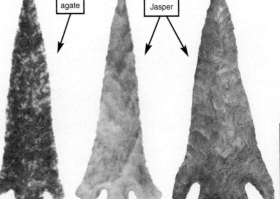

Moss agate
Jasper
G10, $400-$700
Klamath Co., OR

G10+, $800-$1500+
Owyhee Riv., OR

G8, $175-$300
Snake Riv., OR

FW

EASTGATE SPLIT STEM - Developmental to Classic Phase, 1500 - 400 B. P.

(Also see Columbia Plateau, Gunther, Wallula)

G8, $15-$30
Rabbit Isle, OR

G9, $20-$35
Lake Co., OR

G6, $15-$30
British Columbia,
Canada

G9, $30-$50
Lake Co., OR

G9, $45-$80
Lake Co., OR

G9, $30-$55
Harney Co., OR

G8, $40-$75
Columbia Riv., WA

G6, $35-$60
OR

G10, $90-$175
Lake Co., OR

G5, $30-$50
Columb. Riv., WA

G7, $45-$80
OR

G8, $65-$125
Sou. OR

G8, $45-$80
Sou. OR

G9, $55-$100
Humboldt Co., NV

G9, $65-$125
Lake Co., OR

G7, $90-$175
Owens Valley, CA

G10, $250-$475
Warner Valley, OR

G9, $250-$400
WA

G8, $55-$100
OR

G9, $150-$250
Central OR

G8, $90-$175
Sherman Co., OR

LOCATION: Great Basin westward. **DESCRIPTION:** A small, thin, triangular arrow point with expanding barbs and a small bifurcated base. Blade edges are usually finely serrated.

EDEN - Early Archaic, 10,000 - 8000 B. P.

(Also see Alberta, Cody Knife, Firstview, Shaniko Stemmed, Scottsbluff & Windust)

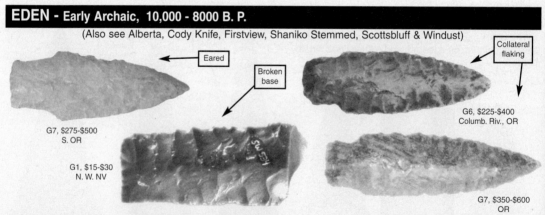

G7, $275-$500
S. OR

G1, $15-$30
N. W. NV

G6, $225-$400
Columb. Riv., OR

G7, $350-$600
OR

LOCATION: Midwest into the Plains states and the Great Basin to Oregon and Washington. **DESCRIPTION:** A medium to large size, narrow, short-stemmed point with a straight to concave base. Many examples have a median ridge and collateral to oblique parallel flaking. Shoulders are very weak and are not as prominent as in the *Scottsbluff* type. Bases can be eared and are usually ground. Stems are parallel sided. **I. D. KEY:** Weak shoulders, and have 3-4 layers of serial flaking.

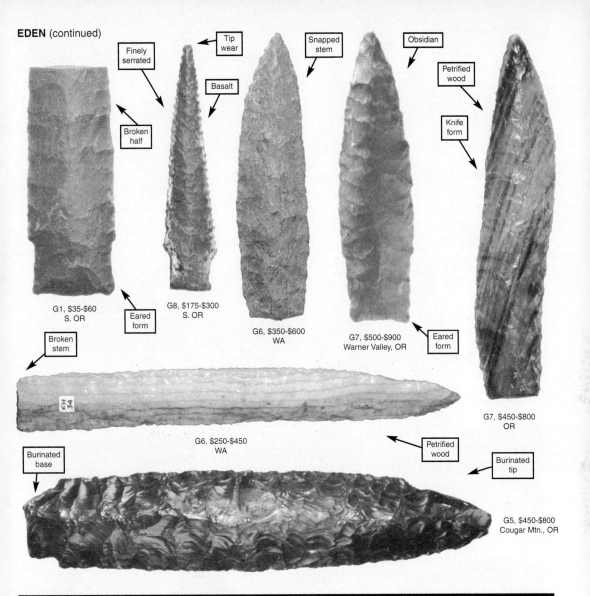

Finely serrated

Tip wear

Basalt

Snapped stem

Obsidian

Petrified wood

Knife form

Broken half

Eared form

G1, $35-$60
S. OR

G8, $175-$300
S. OR

G6, $350-$600
WA

G7, $500-$900
Warner Valley, OR

Eared form

G7, $450-$800
OR

Broken stem

G6, $250-$450
WA

Petrified wood

Burinated base

Burinated tip

G5, $450-$800
Cougar Mtn., OR

ELKO CORNER NOTCHED - Late Archaic to Developmental Phase, 3500 - 1200 B. P.

(Also see Chilcotin Plateau, Columbia Plateau, Eastgate, Hell's Canyon, Hendricks, Merrybell, and Snake River)

Obsidian

Obsidian

Obsidian

G5, $8-$15
Harney Co., OR

G5, $8-$15
Colum. Riv., OR

G6, $12-$20
Owyhee Co., ID

G6, $12-$20
Lake Co., OR

G8, $20-$35
Harney Co., OR

G7, $15-$25
Humboldt Co., NV

FW

LOCATION: Great Basin westward. **DESCRIPTION:** A small to large size, thin, corner notched dart point with shoulder tangs and a convex, concave or auriculate base. Shoulders and tips are sharp. Some examples exhibit excellent parallel flaking on blade edges.

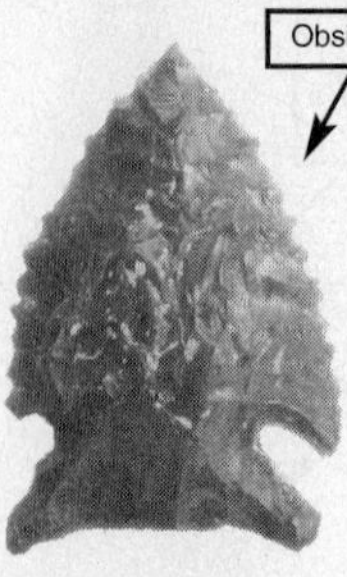

Obsidian

Obsidian

Obsidian

Obsidian

G7, $35-$40
Lake Co., OR

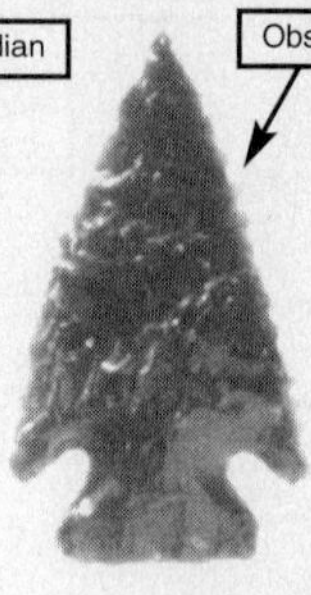

G9, $60-$110
Warner Val., OR

G9, $80-$150
Warner Valley, OR

G8, $40-$75
Harney Co., OR

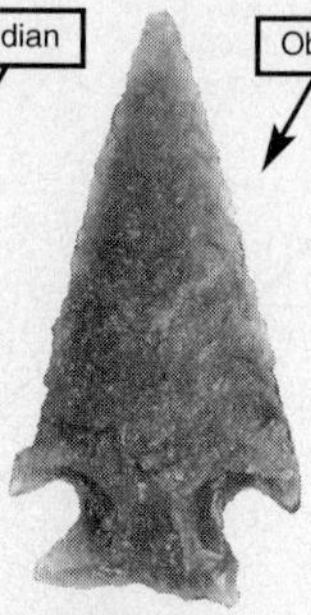

G8, $35-$60
Harney Co., OR

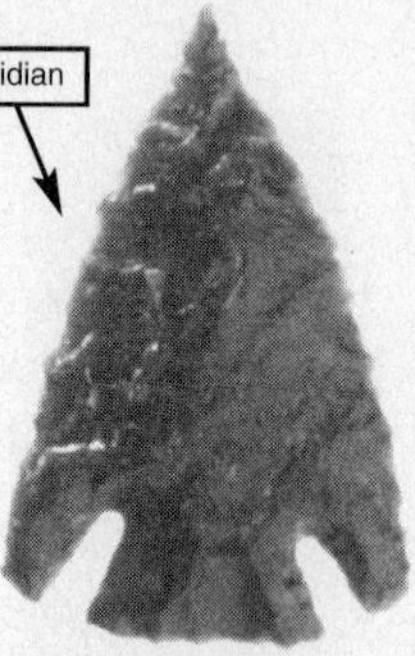

G9, $125-$200
Warner Valley, OR

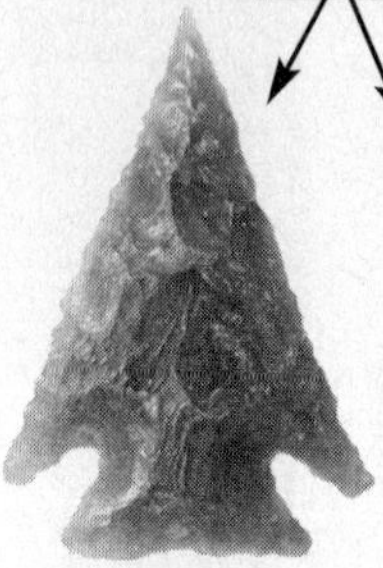

Obsidian

Obsidian

Obsidian

Barb nick

Clear banded obsidian

Serrated edge

G9, $50-$90
Harney Co., OR

G8, $35-$60
Humboldt Co., NV

G8, $40-$75
Harney Co., OR

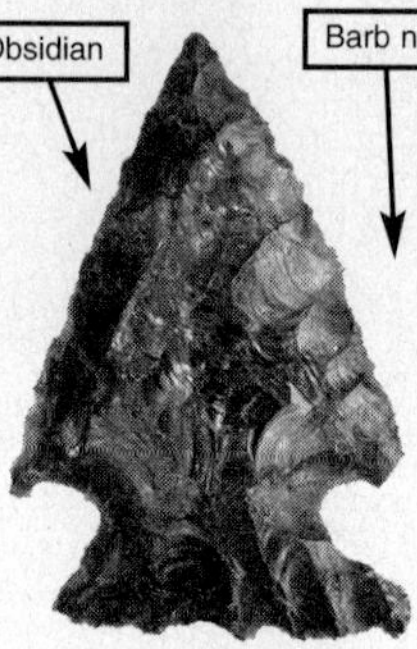

G6, $35-$60
Harney Co., OR

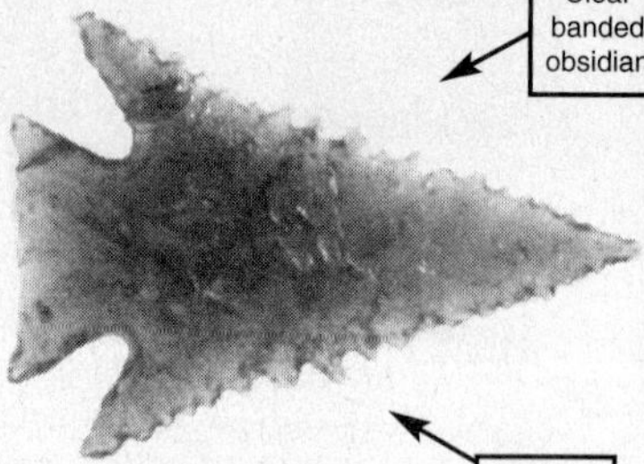

G10, $275-$500
Warner Valley, OR

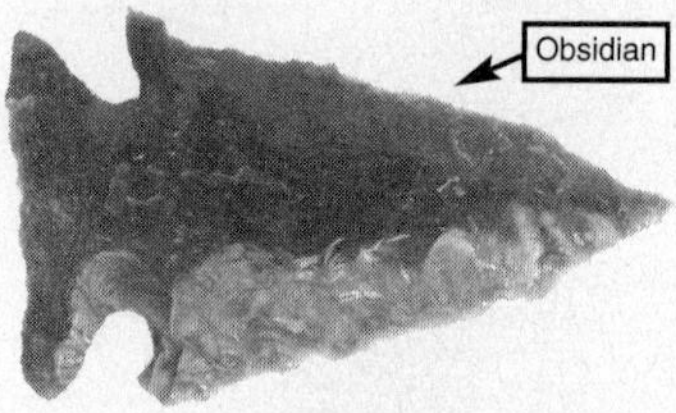

Obsidian

Obsidian

Obsidian

G7, $40-$75
LakeCo., OR

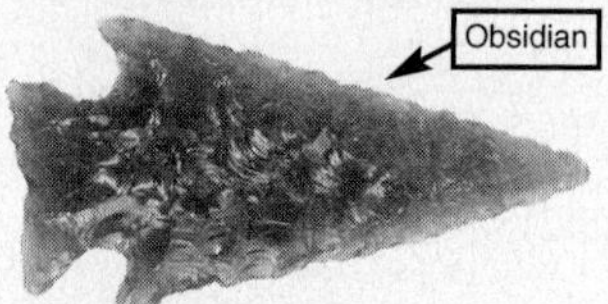

G7, $25-$40
Harney Co., OR

G8, $35-$65
Silver Lake, OR

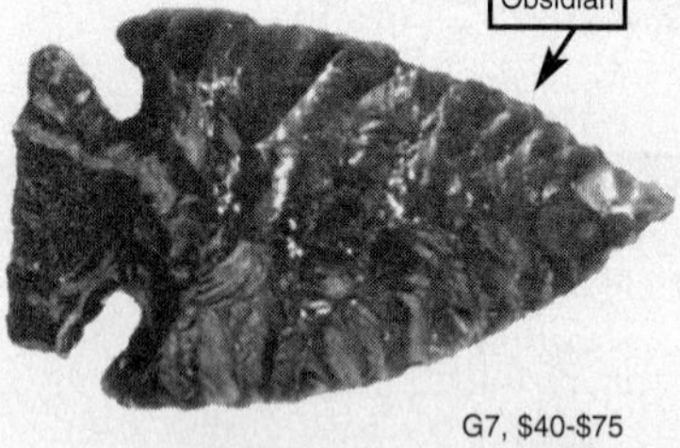

Obsidian

Quartz crystal

Obsidian

Pink chert

G7, $40-$75
Sou. OR

G6, $80-$150
LakeCo., OR

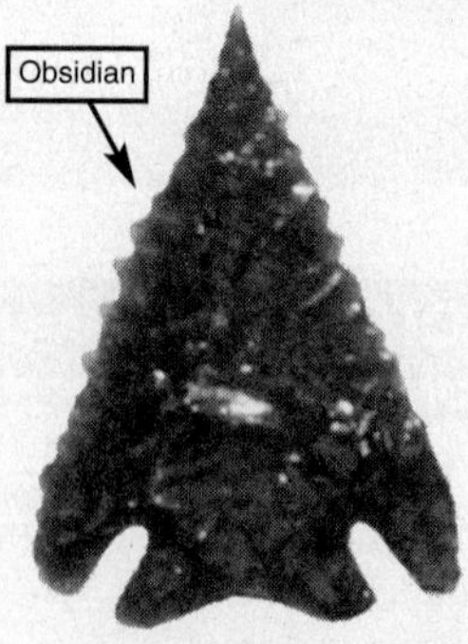

G9, $200-$375
Sou. OR

Dark brown chert

G8, $60-$110
Sou. UT

G10, $400-$700
N. W. UT

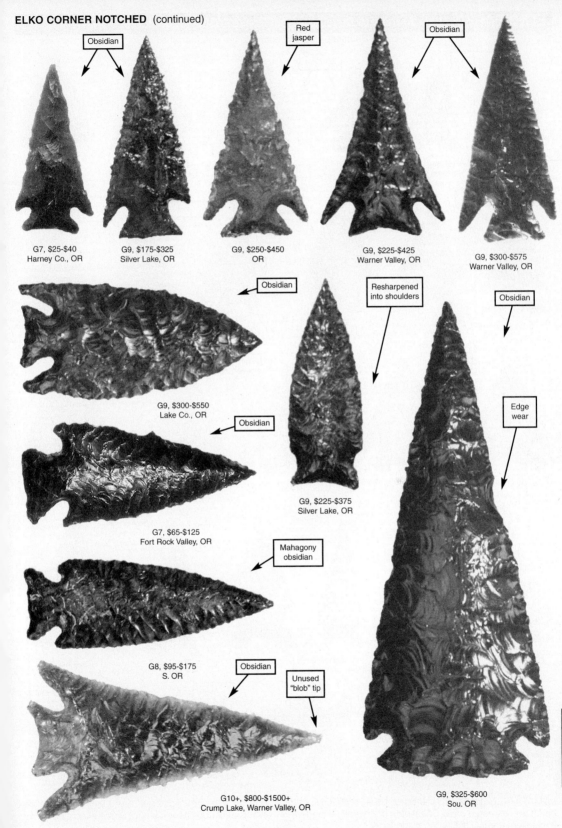

ELKO CORNER NOTCHED (continued)

Obsidian

Red jasper

Obsidian

G7, $25-$40
Harney Co., OR

G9, $175-$325
Silver Lake, OR

G9, $250-$450
OR

G9, $225-$425
Warner Valley, OR

G9, $300-$575
Warner Valley, OR

Obsidian

Resharpened into shoulders

Obsidian

G9, $300-$550
Lake Co., OR

Obsidian

G9, $225-$375
Silver Lake, OR

Edge wear

G7, $65-$125
Fort Rock Valley, OR

Mahagony obsidian

G8, $95-$175
S. OR

Obsidian

Unused "blob" tip

G10+, $800-$1500+
Crump Lake, Warner Valley, OR

G9, $325-$600
Sou. OR

FW

1001

Obsidian

G6, $5-$10
S. OR

G6, $5-$10
Harney Co., OR

Obsidian

G6, $5-$10
OR

G6, $12-$20
OR

G6, $12-$20
Harney Co., OR

G6, $12-$20
Humboldt Co., NV

Obsidian

G6, $15-$30
Harney Co., OR

G5, $8-$15
Harney Co., OR

G6, $12-$20
Humboldt Co., NV

Banded obsidian

G7, $35-$60
Warner Valley, OR

Obsidian

G6, $12-$20
Harney Co., OR

Double tip

G8, $40-$75
Lake Co., OR

Obsidian

G7, $15-$25
Harney Co., OR

G7, $15-$25
Harney Co., OR

Obsidian

G7, $15-$25
Harney Co., OR

Obsidian

G10, $90-$175
Lake Co., OR

G6, $12-$20
Harney Co., OR

Obsidian

G9, $60-$110
Lake Co., OR

G9, $60-$110
Humboldt Co., NV

Obsidian

G7 $15-$25
Harney Co., OR

G8, $30-$50
OR

Obsidian

G8, $15-$25
Harney Co., OR

G8, $30-$50
Warner Valley, OR

Obsidian

G8, $35-$60
Warner Valley, OR

Obsidian

G8, $15-$30
Humboldt Co., NV

Obsidian

G4, $12-$20
S. OR

LOCATION: Great Basin westward. **DESCRIPTION:** A small to large size corner notched dart point with shoulder barbs and an eared base. Basal ears are usually exaggerated, and corners and tips are sharp. Some examples exhibit excellent parallel flaking on blade faces.

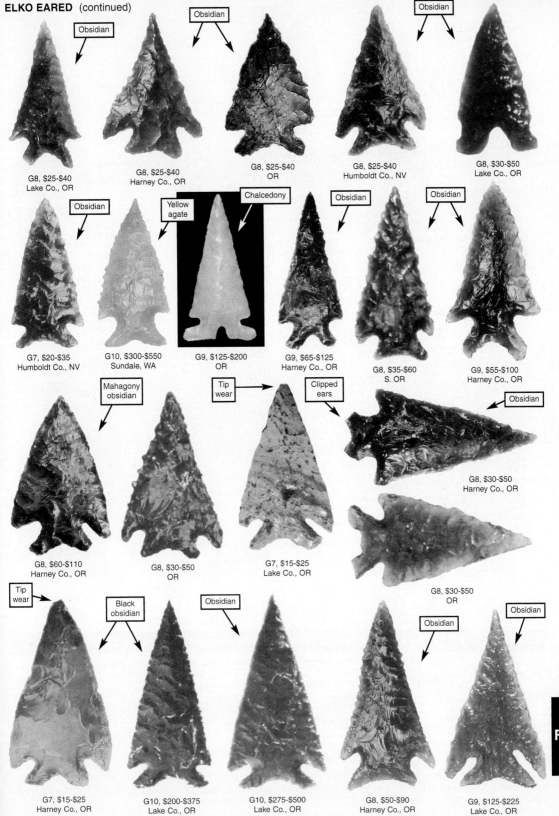

ELKO EARED (continued)

Obsidian

G8, $25-$40
Lake Co., OR

Obsidian

G8, $25-$40
Harney Co., OR

Obsidian

G8, $25-$40
OR

Obsidian

G8, $25-$40
Humboldt Co., NV

Obsidian

G8, $30-$50
Lake Co., OR

Obsidian

G7, $20-$35
Humboldt Co., NV

Yellow agate

G10, $300-$550
Sundale, WA

Chalcedony

G9, $125-$200
OR

Obsidian

G9, $65-$125
Harney Co., OR

Obsidian

G8, $35-$60
S. OR

Obsidian

G9, $55-$100
Harney Co., OR

Mahagony obsidian

G8, $60-$110
Harney Co., OR

G8, $30-$50
OR

Tip wear

Clipped ears

G7, $15-$25
Lake Co., OR

Obsidian

G8, $30-$50
Harney Co., OR

G8, $30-$50
OR

Tip wear

G7, $15-$25
Harney Co., OR

Black obsidian

G10, $200-$375
Lake Co., OR

Obsidian

G10, $275-$500
Lake Co., OR

Obsidian

G8, $50-$90
Harney Co., OR

Obsidian

G9, $125-$225
Lake Co., OR

FW

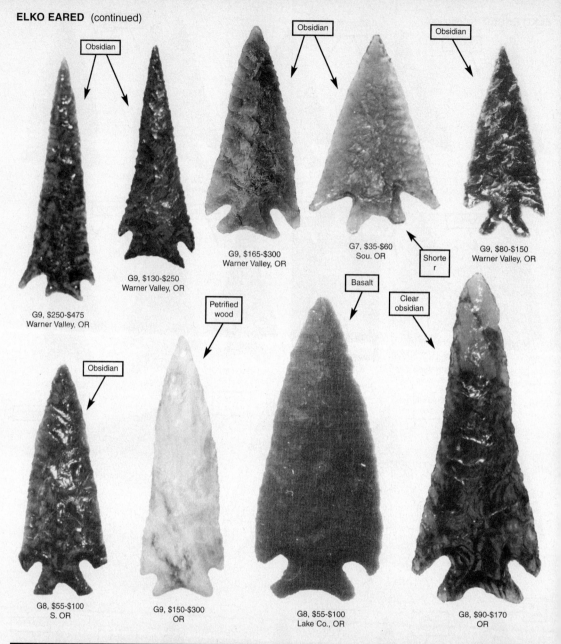

Obsidian

Obsidian

Obsidian

G9, $165-$300
Warner Valley, OR

G7, $35-$60
Sou. OR

Shorter

G9, $80-$150
Warner Valley, OR

G9, $130-$250
Warner Valley, OR

Basalt

Clear obsidian

G9, $250-$475
Warner Valley, OR

Petrified wood

Obsidian

G8, $55-$100
S. OR

G9, $150-$300
OR

G8, $55-$100
Lake Co., OR

G8, $90-$170
OR

ELKO SPLIT-STEM - Late Archaic to Developmental Phase, 3500 - 1200 B. P.

(Also see Eastgate, Elko Corner Notched, Elko Eared, Gatecliff Split-Stem)

Obsidian

Obsidian

Obsidian

G6, $8-$10
Harney Co., OR

G6, $8-$10
Harney Co., OR

G5, $8-$15
Warner Valley, OR

G6, $8-$15
Lake Co., OR

LOCATION: Great Basin westward. **DESCRIPTION:** A small to large size corner notched dart point with shoulder tangs and a short base that is bifurcated. Shoulders are rounded to sharp. Some examples exhibit excellent parallel flaking on blade edges. Believed to have evolved from the earlier *Gatecliff* point.

ELKO SPLIT STEM (continued)

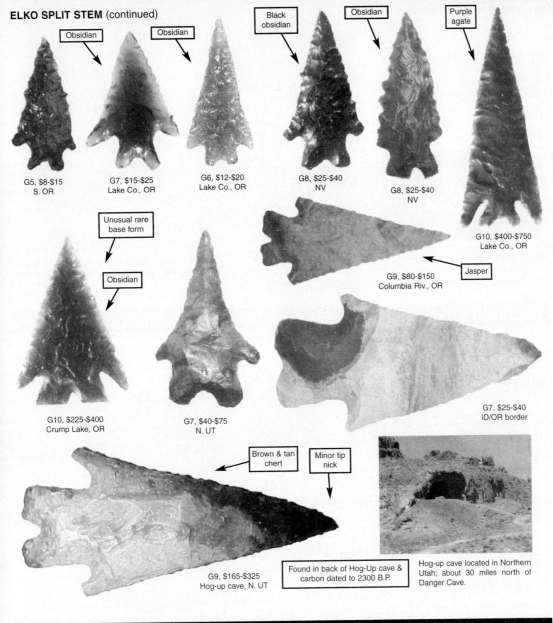

Obsidian

Obsidian

Black obsidian

Obsidian

Purple agate

G5, $8-$15
S. OR

G7, $15-$25
Lake Co., OR

G6, $12-$20
Lake Co., OR

G8, $25-$40
NV

G8, $25-$40
NV

G10, $400-$750
Lake Co., OR

Unusual rare base form

Obsidian

G9, $80-$150
Columbia Riv., OR

Jasper

G10, $225-$400
Crump Lake, OR

G7, $40-$75
N. UT

G7, $25-$40
ID/OR border

Brown & tan chert

Minor tip nick

G9, $165-$325
Hog-up cave, N. UT

Found in back of Hog-Up cave & carbon dated to 2300 B.P.

Hog-up cave located in Northern Utah; about 30 miles north of Danger Cave.

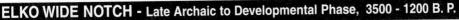

ELKO WIDE NOTCH - Late Archaic to Developmental Phase, 3500 - 1200 B. P.

(Also see Eastgate, Elko, Elko Corner Notched and Elko Eared)

G7, $12-$20
Lake Co., OR

Obsidian

G6, $8-$15
Lake Co., OR

Obsidian

G7, $12-$20
S. OR

Basalt

G7, $15-$25
Lake Co., OR

Black obsidian

G9, $55-$100
E. OR

FW

ELKO WIDE NOTCH (continued)

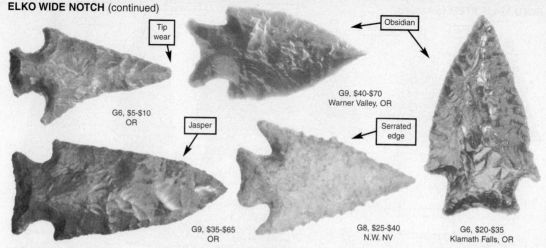

Tip wear

G6, $5-$10
OR

Jasper

Obsidian

G9, $40-$70
Warner Valley, OR

Serrated edge

G9, $35-$65
OR

G8, $25-$40
N.W. NV

G6, $20-$35
Klamath Falls, OR

LOCATION: Great Basin westward. **DESCRIPTION:** A medium size knife with broad corner to side notches and a concave base. Shoulders are usually barbed and bases are eared. It appears to be a knife-only variant and is made from existing Elko types. All have been resharpened several times.

EMIGRANT SPRINGS - Developmental Phase, 1200 - 1000 B. P.

(Also see Hells Canyon Basal and Eastgate)

Obsidian

Obsidian

G7, $15-$30
N. UT

G7, $12-$20
N. NV

G7, $12-$20
N. NV

G7, $12-$20
N. UT

LOCATION: Utah and surrounding area. **DESCRIPTION:** A broad, short basal notched point. Tangs can extend beyond the base. The base is straight to rounded. Shoulders are rounded.

EXCELSIOR - Late Archaic to Transitional Phase, 3000 - 1700 B. P.

(Also see Agate Basin, Cascade, Cordilleran, Early Leaf, Intermontane Stemmed, Kennewick)

G5, $5-$10
OR

G6, $12-$25
CA

Obsidian

G4, $8-$15
Susanville, CA

Serrated edge

Basalt

G6, $12-$25
Mendocino Co., CA

G5, $12-$20
Mendocino Co., CA

Serrated edge

G5, $8-$15
OR

Red jasper

Serrated edge

G8, $35-$60
CA

G9, $55-$100
CA

Yellow jasper

EXCELSIOR (continued)

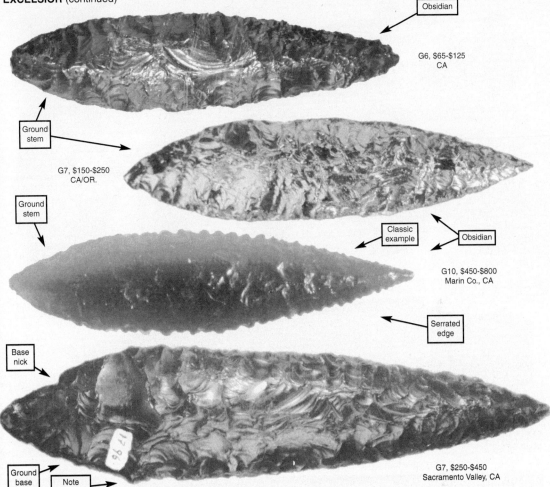

Obsidian

G6, $65-$125
CA

Ground stem

G7, $150-$250
CA/OR.

Ground stem

Classic example

Obsidian

G10, $450-$800
Marin Co., CA

Serrated edge

Base nick

Ground base

Note shoulders

G7, $250-$450
Sacramento Valley, CA

LOCATION: Northern California and Sou. Oregon. **DESCRIPTION:** A medium to large size, narrow, lanceolate, double pointed blade. Some examples are serrated. Basal areas are usually ground.

EXOTIC FORMS - Late Archaic to Developmental Phase, 3000 - 1000 B. P.

(Also see Stockton and Vendetta)

Chalc.   Eastgate

G8, $8-$15
OR

G8, $8-$15
Humboldt Co., NV

Petrified wood   Eastgate

G8, $20-$35
Humboldt Co., NV

G8, $8-$15
OR

Elko double tip

Elko Eared double notch

G6, $25-$40
OR

G6, $8-$15
OR

G8, $25-$40
Lake Co., OR

Double notch

G9, $70-$125
Sou. OR

Base & side notches

G7, $40-$70
Lower Columbia Riv, OR

Base & side notches

G9, $70-$135
Lower Columbia Riv, OR

FW

EXOTIC FORMS (continued)

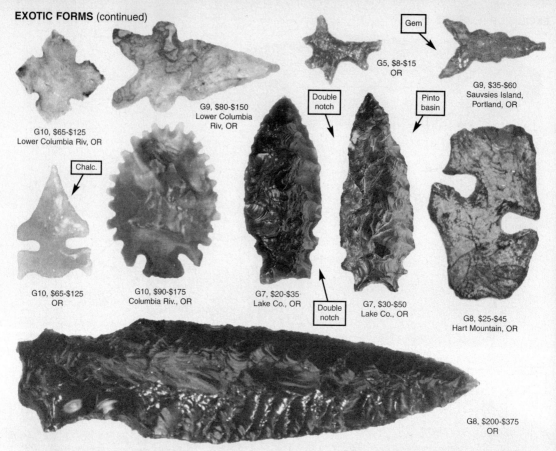

G10, $65-$125
Lower Columbia Riv, OR

G9, $80-$150
Lower Columbia
Riv, OR

G5, $8-$15
OR

Gem

G9, $35-$60
Sauvsies Island,
Portland, OR

Double notch

Pinto basin

Chalc.

G10, $65-$125
OR

G10, $90-$175
Columbia Riv., OR

G7, $20-$35
Lake Co., OR

Double notch

G7, $30-$50
Lake Co., OR

G8, $25-$45
Hart Mountain, OR

G8, $200-$375
OR

LOCATION: Everywhere. **DESCRIPTION:** The forms illustrated are rare. Some are definitely effigy forms or exotic point designs while others may be no more than unfinished and unintentional doodles.

FELL'S CAVE (N.W.) - Paleo, 10,800 - 10,100 B. P.

(Also see Midland, Milnesand, Pay Paso (N.W.), Spedis)

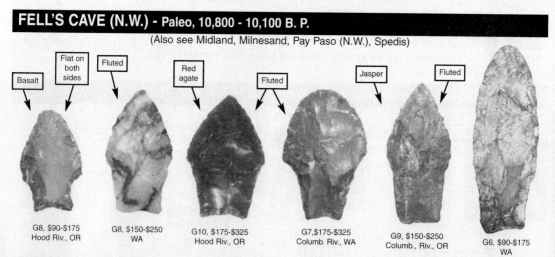

Basalt

Flat on both sides

Fluted

Red agate

Fluted

Jasper

Fluted

G8, $90-$175
Hood Riv., OR

G8, $150-$250
WA

G10, $175-$325
Hood Riv., OR

G7,$175-$325
Columb. Riv., WA

G9, $150-$250
Columb., Riv., OR

G6, $90-$175
WA

LOCATION: Great Basin westward. **DESCRIPTION:** This point is the Paleo point of South America. Early knives are strongly shouldered and have one, two or no flutes. Flutes vary in length, but usually pass the shoulders into the blade. Stems are ground or smoothed into the shoulders and stem sides are incurvate to straight, rarely contracting. Most, but not all, bases have delicate auricles, giving these points the nickname "fishtail." There is a small or unfluted, basally thinned variety made on spalled flakes, that can be flat on one or both sides, with minimal edge retouch edge alignment. **I.D. KEY:** Auriculate stem, strong shoulders.

FIRSTVIEW - Early Archaic, 10,000 - 8000 B. P.

(Also see Alberta, Cody Complex , Eden and Scottsbluff)

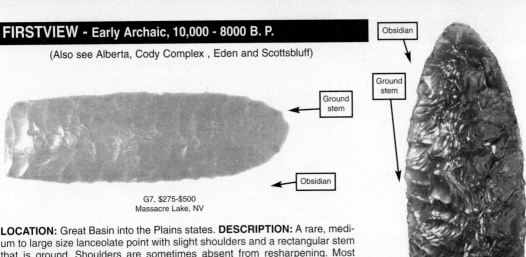

Obsidian

Ground stem

Ground stem

Ground stem

Obsidian

G7, $275-$500
Massacre Lake, NV

G7, $350-$600
OR

LOCATION: Great Basin into the Plains states. **DESCRIPTION:** A rare, medium to large size lanceolate point with slight shoulders and a rectangular stem that is ground. Shoulders are sometimes absent from resharpening. Most examples exhibit excellent parallel transverse flaking. A variant form of the *Scottsbluff* type made by the Cody Complex people. **I.D. KEY:** Weak shoulders, diamond shaped cross-section.

FISH GUTTER - Mid to Late Archaic, 4000 - 3000 B. P.

(Also see Cascade Shouldered & Mahkin Shouldered)

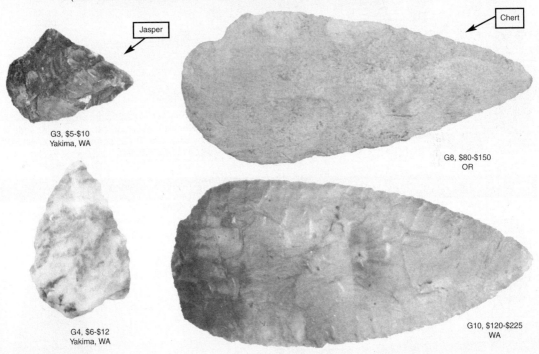

Jasper

Chert

G3, $5-$10
Yakima, WA

G8, $80-$150
OR

G4, $6-$12
Yakima, WA

G10, $120-$225
WA

LOCATION: Columbia River watershed. **DESCRIPTION:** Medium to large size knives with scraper bases. The scraper bases are round to pointed with all of the variations between the two extremes. All of the bases have one sharp shoulder to facilitate opening the abdominal cavity of Salmon. The "rounded portion" of the base was used to scrape the oily, dark blood vein from the Salmon's abdomen. If the dark vein was left in place, it would spoil the fish. The blood was saved and used as a highly nutritious food supplement and dipping sauce. These points range in quality from very well-made to rough. initial blade thinning is random baton percussion, with edge retouch and resharpening by pressure flaking. This is a hand-held knife and hand-holds are sometimes ground. Cross sections are plano-convex to lenticular and blade edges are convex.

FW

FOLSOM - Paleo, 11.000 - 10,000 B. P.

(Also see Black Rock Concave, Clovis, Humboldt and Midland)

Broken base

G1, $15-$30
Blue Creek, UT

Resharpened many times

G4, $350-$600
NV

Fully fluted

G6, $600-$1000
Stinking Pig Site, WA

LOCATION: Canada into Southwestern states and eastward to N. Indiana. **DESCRIPTION:** A very thin, small to medium sized lanceolate point with convex to straight sides and a convex basal edge creating sharp ears or basal corners. Most examples are fluted from the basal edge to nearly the tip of the point. Blade flaking is extremely fine and the hafting area is ground. Very Rare for the area. **I.D. KEY:** Thinness and form.

FOUNTAIN BAR - Late Archaic, 3000 B. P.

Red jasper

Basalt

Agate

G4, $5-$10
The Dalles, OR

G3, $2-$5
Columbia Riv., OR

G6, $8-$15
NV

G4, $8-$15
N. OR

G7, $30-$50
OR

G6, $12-$20
OR

G8, $35-$65
Hood River, OR

LOCATION: Oregon and Washington. **DESCRIPTION:** A small to medium size assymetrical knife point that is notched only on one side. These points are manufactured as single side or corner notched.

FREMONT TRIANGULAR - Developmental Phase, 1600 - 800 B. P.

(Also see Plateau Pentagonal & Triangular Knife)

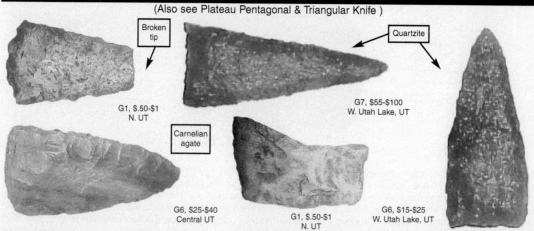

Broken tip

Quartzite

G1, $.50-$1
N. UT

G7, $55-$100
W. Utah Lake, UT

Carnelian agate

G6, $25-$40
Central UT

G1, $.50-$1
N. UT

G6, $15-$25
W. Utah Lake, UT

LOCATION: Southern to Northern Utah into Nevada where the Fremont culture lived. **DESCRIPTION:** A large, thin, narrow, triangular knife with a straight to convex base. There are three variants: Square base, rounded base and unfinished base. Some examples were notched to facilitate hafting.

FREMONT TRIANGULAR (continued)

Broken base

G1, $.30-$1
N. UT

Edge wear

Purple & white agate

Yellow jasper

Edge wear

IMPORTANT:
This point is shown half size

Very thin

"Loring's sword"

Hand held to show size and quality

G5, $25-$45
S. UT

G8, $150-$250
N. UT

G3, $15-$30
N. UT

G10+, $7000-$12,000
N. UT, 9-1/8" long

GATECLIFF - Middle to Late Archaic, 5000 - 3000 B. P.

(Also see Coquille, Eastgate, Elko Split-Stem, Gypsum Cave, Houx Contaracting Stem, Pismo, Rabbit Isle,Tucannon Stemmed, Vandenberg Contracting Stem)

Chalc.

Red jasper

G6, $5-$10
Harney Co., OR

G9, $20-$35
Colum. Riv., OR

G6, $8-$15
Lake Co., OR

G5, $8-$15
Harney Co., OR

G5, $12-$20
Harney Co., OR

G6, $12-$20
Harney Co., OR

G6, $12-$20
Humbolt Co., NV

FW

LOCATION: Great Basin westward. **DESCRIPTION:** A medium to large size dart point with horizontal to barbed shoulders and a contracted stem. Bases are straight, rounded or pointed. Blade edges are convex to recurved. Most of the contracting stem points are known as *Gypsum Cave* further south. Parallel, oblique flaking does occur on this type. **I.D. KEY:** Tapered stem.

GATECLIFF (continued)

Tip wear

Agate

Red jasper

Straight base

Red jasper

Straight base

G8, $25-$40
OR

G7, $20-$35
Harney Co., OR

G5, $2-$5
Christmas Valley, OR

G9, $30-$55
Harney Co., OR

G8, $35-$60
Lake Co., OR

G8, $30-$50
Hood Riv., OR

Obsidian

Agate

Obsidian

Diagonal flaking

G6, $35-$60
Black Rock Desert, NV

G6, $15-$30
OR

G7, $30-$50
OR

G7, $30-$55
Lake Co., OR

G6, $15-$30
Harney Co., OR

G9, $35-$60
Bend, OR

Petrified wood

Straight base

Straight base

Obsidian

G8, $30-$50
Lake Co., OR

G7, $20-$35
Lake Co., OR

G6, $15-$30
Lake Co., OR

G6, $15-$25
Lake Co., OR

G8, $35-$60
OR

Obsidian

Agate

Obsidian

Obsidian

G8, $35-$65
Lake Co., OR

G9, $75-$140
Klamath Lake, OR

G9, $175-$300
OR

G8, $65-$125
Harney Co., OR

G8, $40-$75
OR

G10, $150-$250
Silver Lake, OR

(Also see Coquille, Eastgate, Elko Split-Stem, Pinto Basin, Rabbit Island & Vandenberg Contracting Stem)

Obsidian
G8, $25-$40
Sou. OR.

Obsidian
G6, $15-$30
Cent. NV

Obsidian
G8, $30-$50
Harney Co., OR

Basalt

Serrated edge

Obsidian
G7, $30-$50
Warner Valley, OR

Obsidian

Obsidian

G4, $15-$25
Sou. OR.

Serrated edge

Oblique flaking

Obsidian

G9, $55-$100
Sou. OR

G9, $65-$125
Bend, OR

G8, $65-$120
Warner Valley, OR

G9, $150-$250
N.W. NV

G8, $125-$200
Tule Lake, CA

G9, $200-$375
Warner Valley, OR

LOCATION: Great Basin westward. **DESCRIPTION:** A medium to large size stemmed, bifurcated dart point that is usually serrated with horizontal to barbed shoulders. Believed to have evolved into *Elko* points. The *Gatcliff* usually has a longer stem and a shallowerer base notch than *Pinto Basin* of which it was a part. Parallel, oblique blade flaking does occur. Slightly contracting or expanding is acceptible. **I.D. KEY:** Shallow bifurcated stem.

GOLD HILL - Middle Archaic, 4,500 - 2200 B. P.

(Also see Coquille, Cottonwood Leaf, Malaga Cove Leaf and Trojan)

Jasper

G2, $2-$4
Rogue Riv., OR

G3, $3-$5
Rogue Riv., OR

G6, $4-$8
Rogue Riv., OR

G5, $4-$8
Rogue Riv., OR

G5, $4-$8
Rogue Riv., OR

Jasper

Jasper

Red jasper

Red jasper

Tip wear

Agate

G7, $8-$15
Rogue Riv., OR

G7, $8-$15
OR

G7, $8-$15
Rogue Riv., OR

G7, $15-$20
Rogue Riv., OR

G7, $8-$15
Rogue Riv., OR

G6, $5-$10
Rogue Riv., OR

G7, $8-$15
Rogue Riv., OR

G7, $8-$15
OR

FW

Red jasper

Jasper

Chalc.

G7, $15-$20
Rogue Riv., OR

G7, $15-$25
Rogue Riv., OR

G7, $15-$30
Rogue Riv., OR

G7, $25-$40
OR

G7, $25-$40
OR

G7, $15-$30
OR

G7, $15-$30
OR

G7, $15-$30
Rogue Riv., OR

Jasper

G7, $15-$20
OR

Serrated edge

Jasper

G7, $15-$20
Rogue Riv., OR

Knife form

Petrified wood

Knife form

G7, $25-$40
OR

G7, $25-$40
OR

G7, $25-$40
OR

G7, $30-$50
Rogue Riv., OR

G7, $35-$60
OR

G7, $35-$60
OR

G7, $45-$80
Coquille Riv., OR

LOCATION: S.W. Oregon and N.W. Calif. **DESCRIPTION:** A descendant of the *Cascade* type. A small to medium size lanceolate dart point with a rounded base. Similar in form to *Malaga Cove Leaf* found in southern California.

GOSHEN - Paleo, 11,250 - 9,500

(Also see Alder Complex, Folsom, Midland, Milnesand, Plainview & Spedis)

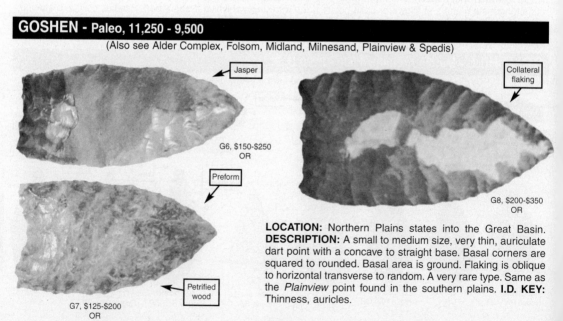

Jasper

Collateral flaking

G6, $150-$250
OR

Preform

G8, $200-$350
OR

Petrified wood

G7, $125-$200
OR

LOCATION: Northern Plains states into the Great Basin. **DESCRIPTION:** A small to medium size, very thin, auriculate dart point with a concave to straight base. Basal corners are squared to rounded. Basal area is ground. Flaking is oblique to horizontal transverse to random. A very rare type. Same as the *Plainview* point found in the southern plains. **I.D. KEY:** Thinness, auricles.

G9, $400-$700
Columbia Riv., WA

Agate

GRAVER - Paleo to Archaic, 11,500 - Historic

(Also see Drill, Lancet, Perforator, Scraper & Sizer)

Graver tip

Graver tip

Graver tip

G6, $8-$15
Lake Co., OR

Graver tips

G6, $12-$20
N.W. NV

G6, $8-$15
Lake Co., OR

G6, $8-$15
OR

Graver tip

Agate

Graver tip

Red agate

G6, $8-$15
Lady Island, WA

Graver tips

Paleo

G6, $12-$20
OR

Graver tip

Graver tips

G6, $8-$15
Sou. OR

G7, $15-$25
WA

Graver tip

G10, $25-$40
Columbia River, OR

LOCATION: Paleo and Archaic sites everywhere. **DESCRIPTION:** An irregular shaped uniface tool with sharp, pointed projections used for puncturing, incising, tattooing, etc. Some examples served a dual purpose for scraping as well. Gravers have been found on *Black Rock Concave* sites in the Great Basin.

GROUND STONE - Historic Phase, 300 - 100 B. P.

(Also see Cascade & Side Knife)

Ground slate

G6, $15-$25
Puget Sound, WA

LOCATION: Washington state. **DESCRIPTION:** A medium to large size, stemmed point made from stone. Some examples have a median ridge running along the center of the blade. These points were probably used as knives and harpoons by the Eskimos and others along the coastal waters.

FW

GUNTHER BARBED - Developmental to Historic Phase, 1000 - 200 B. P.

(Also see Calapooya, Columbia Plateau, Point Sal Barbed, Rabbit Island and Wallula)

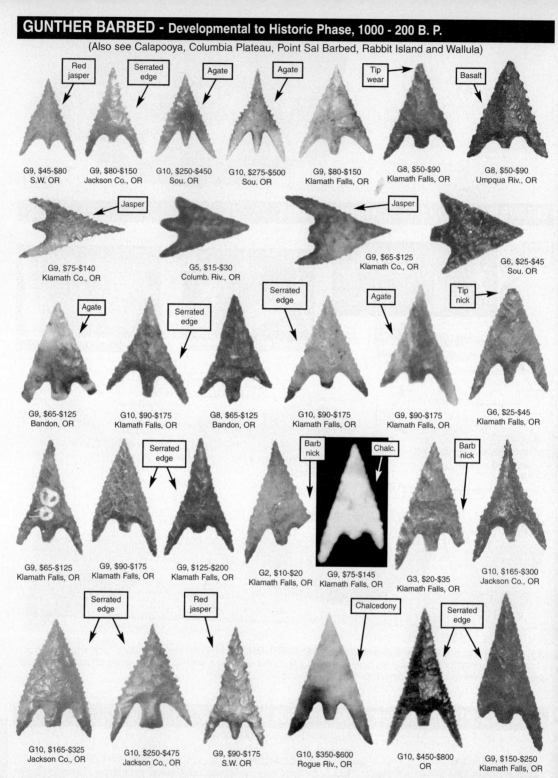

Red jasper

Serrated edge

Agate

Agate

Tip wear

Basalt

G9, $45-$80
S.W. OR

G9, $80-$150
Jackson Co., OR

G10, $250-$450
Sou. OR

G10, $275-$500
Sou. OR

G9, $80-$150
Klamath Falls, OR

G8, $50-$90
Klamath Falls, OR

G8, $50-$90
Umpqua Riv., OR

Jasper

Jasper

G9, $75-$140
Klamath Co., OR

G5, $15-$30
Columb. Riv., OR

G9, $65-$125
Klamath Co., OR

G6, $25-$45
Sou. OR

Agate

Serrated edge

Serrated edge

Agate

Tip nick

G9, $65-$125
Bandon, OR

G10, $90-$175
Klamath Falls, OR

G8, $65-$125
Bandon, OR

G10, $90-$175
Klamath Falls, OR

G9, $90-$175
Klamath Falls, OR

G6, $25-$45
Klamath Falls, OR

Serrated edge

Barb nick

Chalc.

Barb nick

G9, $65-$125
Klamath Falls, OR

G9, $90-$175
Klamath Falls, OR

G9, $125-$200
Klamath Falls, OR

G2, $10-$20
Klamath Falls, OR

G9, $75-$145
Klamath Falls, OR

G3, $20-$35
Klamath Falls, OR

G10, $165-$300
Jackson Co., OR

Serrated edge

Red jasper

Chalcedony

Serrated edge

G10, $165-$325
Jackson Co., OR

G10, $250-$475
Jackson Co., OR

G9, $90-$175
S.W. OR

G10, $350-$600
Rogue Riv., OR

G10, $450-$800
OR

G9, $150-$250
Klamath Falls, OR

LOCATION: Great Basin westward. **DESCRIPTION:** A small to medium size, thin, broad, triangular arrow point with long barbs that extend to and beyond the base. The blade sides are straight to concave and the stem is parallel sided to slightly contracting or expanding. These points exhibit high quality flaking. Other local names used for this type are "Camas Valley," "Mad River," "Molalla," "Rogue River," and "Shasta."

GUNTHER TRIANGULAR - Developmental to Historic Phase, 1000 - 200 B. P.

(Also see Canalino Triangular and Cottonwood)

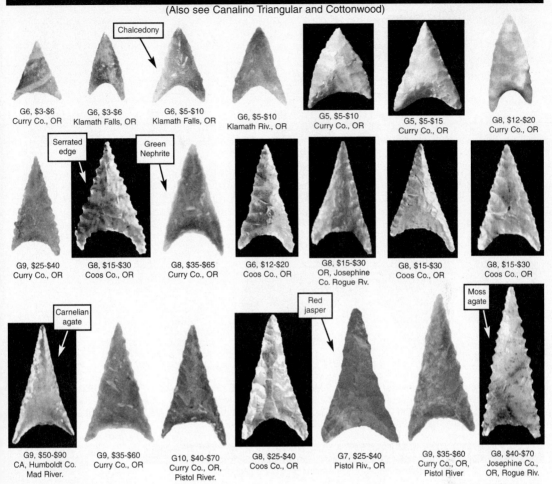

G6, $3-$6
Curry Co., OR

G6, $3-$6
Klamath Falls, OR

Chalcedony

G6, $5-$10
Klamath Falls, OR

G6, $5-$10
Klamath Riv., OR

G5, $5-$10
Curry Co., OR

G5, $5-$15
Curry Co., OR

G8, $12-$20
Curry Co., OR

G9, $25-$40
Curry Co., OR

Serrated edge

Green Nephrite

G8, $15-$30
Coos Co., OR

G8, $35-$65
Curry Co., OR

G6, $12-$20
Coos Co., OR

G8, $15-$30
OR, Josephine
Co. Rogue Rv.

G8, $15-$30
Coos Co., OR

G8, $15-$30
Coos Co., OR

Carnelian agate

G9, $50-$90
CA, Humboldt Co.
Mad River.

G9, $35-$60
Curry Co., OR

G10, $40-$70
Curry Co., OR,
Pistol River.

Red jasper

G8, $25-$40
Coos Co., OR

G7, $25-$40
Pistol Riv., OR

G9, $35-$60
Curry Co., OR,
Pistol River

Moss agate

G8, $40-$70
Josephine Co.,
OR, Rogue Riv.

LOCATION: Great Basin westward. **DESCRIPTION:** A small to medium size, thin, triangular point with basal barbs that can be asymmetrical with one longer than the other. The basal ears have a tendency to turn in towards the base which is concave. Early forms are called U-Back locally. Usually made from jasper, agate, green chert, rarely from obsidian.

GYPSUM CAVE - Middle Archaic, 5000 - 3300 B. P.

(Also see Coquille, Gatecliff, Parowan, Rabbit Island, Sierra Contracting, Tucannon, Vandenberg)

G3, $5-$10
NV

Beatty chert

G5, $8-$15
NV

Obsidian

Obsidian

G6, $12-$20
OR

G7, $15-$30
S. OR

Obsidian

G8, $25-$40
Silver Lake, OR

G9, $45-$80
Silver Lake, OR

FW

Obsidian

G6, $12-$20
N. UT

Blue chert

Tip wear

Sugar quartz

Obsidian

Chalcedony

Obsidian

Obsidian

G9, $65-$125
NV

G8, $80-$150
Klamath Co., OR

G10, $250-$475
S. OR

G6, $15-$25
N. UT

G7, $20-$35
W. Cent. UT

LOCATION: Type site is Gypsum Cave, Nev. Found in ID, E. CA, E. OR, N. AZ, W. UT **DESCRIPTION:** A medium sized dart/knife with straight blade edges and a short stem which contracts to a rounded base. The shoulders are obtuse. this point may be related to the *Augustin* point found further south and the Gatecliff point from Oregon, though, in general, it seems to have better workmaship. **I.D. KEY:** Stubby stem.

HAFTED KNIFE - Transitional-Historic Phase, 2300 - 500 B. P.

(Also see Hafted Knife in Northern High Plains section)

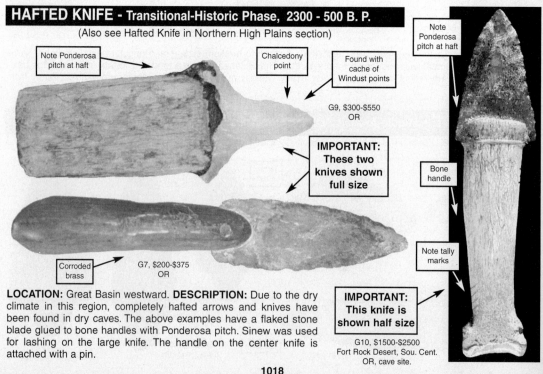

Note Ponderosa
pitch at haft

Note Ponderosa
pitch at haft

Chalcedony
point

Found with
cache of
Windust points

G9, $300-$550
OR

**IMPORTANT:
These two
knives shown
full size**

Corroded
brass

G7, $200-$375
OR

Bone
handle

Note tally
marks

**IMPORTANT:
This knife is
shown half size**

G10, $1500-$2500
Fort Rock Desert, Sou. Cent.
OR, cave site.

LOCATION: Great Basin westward. **DESCRIPTION:** Due to the dry climate in this region, completely hafted arrows and knives have been found in dry caves. The above examples have a flaked stone blade glued to bone handles with Ponderosa pitch. Sinew was used for lashing on the large knife. The handle on the center knife is attached with a pin.

HAND AXE - PALEO, 11,000 - 20,000+ ? B. P.

(Also see Chopper and Scraper)

Paleo flaking

Chert

Jasper

G6, $2-$5
San Bernadino Co., CA,
Calico Mountains,

G9, $5-$10
San Bernadino Co., CA
Calico Mountains

IMPORTANT:
All hand axes
are shown half
size

G4, $2-$5
Calico Mountains
CA

G4, $2-$5
Calico Mountains
CA

G8, $5-$10
San Bernadino
Co., CA, Calico
Mountains

G9, $5-$10
San Bernadino
Co., CA, Calico
Mountains

LOCATION: Calico Mountain area of California in San Bernadino Co. **DESCRIPTION:** Irregular percussion shaped axes used for cutting and chopping. This site is famed for producing very early man-made objects that were dated by L. S. B. Leakey to 50,000 years ago. This age remains controversial waiting a corroborative date from another site which has yet to be found.

HARAHEY (see Northwestern 4-Way Knife)

HARPOON - Late Archaic to Historic Phase, 3000 - 200 B. P.

(Also see Harpoons in Alaska Section)

FW

LOCATION: Coastal areas and around large lakes and rivers. **DESCRIPTION:** Harpoon points were carved from bone, antler or fashioned from metal. They were used in fishing. Some have stone tips and were hafted either directly to the shaft or inserted as a foreshaft.

HARPOON (continued)

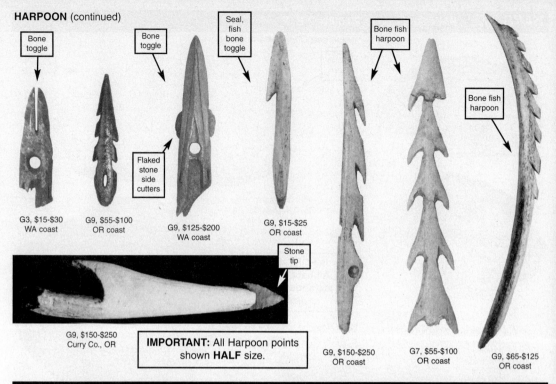

Bone toggle
Bone toggle
Seal, fish bone toggle
Bone fish harpoon
Bone fish harpoon

G3, $15-$30
WA coast

G9, $55-$100
OR coast

Flaked stone side cutters

G9, $125-$200
WA coast

G9, $15-$25
OR coast

Stone tip

G9, $150-$250
Curry Co., OR

IMPORTANT: All Harpoon points shown **HALF** size.

G9, $150-$250
OR coast

G7, $55-$100
OR coast

G9, $65-$125
OR coast

HASKETT - Late Paleo, 12,000 - 8000 B. P.

(Also see Agate Basin, Año Nuevo, Cordilleran, Cougar Mountain, Cascade, Excelsior, Humboldt, Intermontane, Kennewick, Lake Mojave, Lind Coulee, Owl Cave and Wildcat Canyon)

Type II Hasket
Black obsidian
Type I
Type I
Basalt
Dacite

G6, $175-$300
S. OR

G6, $200-$350
Burns, OR

G7, $250-$400
Christmas Valley, OR

G7, $250-$400
S. OR

Ground stem

G9, $250-$500
S. OR

Type I

G7, $250-$500
Christmas Valley, OR

LOCATION: Idaho, N.W. Nevada and Southern Oregon. **DESCRIPTION:** A medium to large size, narrow, thick, lance-olate point with parallel flaking and a ground, convex to straight base. It comes in two types: **Type I** expands towards the tip (Could be resharpened **type IIs**). **Type II** is basically parallel sided to excurvate. Consistantly dated older than *Clovis* from hydration dates obtained from controlled conditions. One such test dated *Haskett* to 12,100 years old. The *Haskett* point is related to *Cougar Mountain* points found on the same sites. *Haskett /Lind Coulee* points later evolved into *Alberta* & *Agate Basins*. An extremely rare type with only a few dozen complete examples known. **I.D. KEY:** Early parallel flaking and base form.

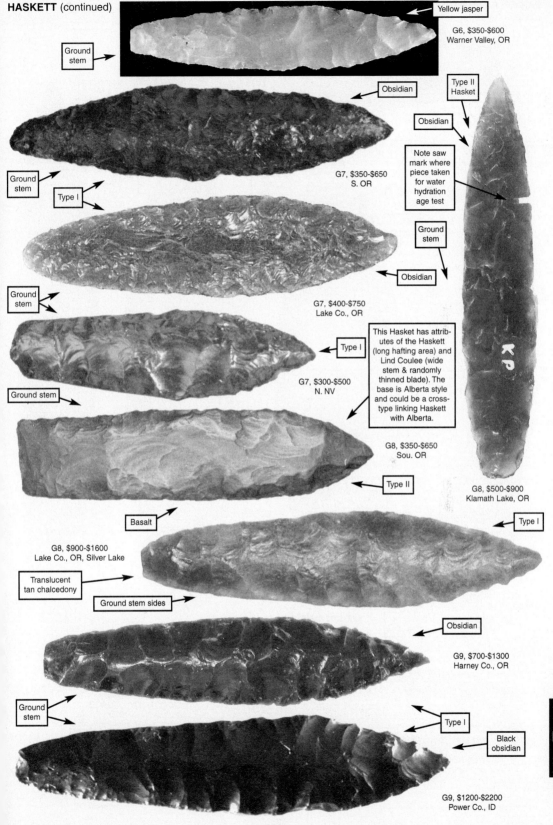

HASKETT (continued)

Yellow jasper

Ground stem

G6, $350-$600
Warner Valley, OR

Obsidian

Type II Hasket

Obsidian

Note saw mark where piece taken for water hydration age test

Ground stem

G7, $350-$650
S. OR

Ground stem

Type I

Obsidian

Ground stem

G7, $400-$750
Lake Co., OR

Type I

This Hasket has attributes of the Haskett (long hafting area) and Lind Coulee (wide stem & randomly thinned blade). The base is Alberta style and could be a cross-type linking Haskett with Alberta.

G7, $300-$500
N. NV

Ground stem

G8, $350-$650
Sou. OR

Type II

G8, $500-$900
Klamath Lake, OR

Basalt

Type I

G8, $900-$1600
Lake Co., OR, Silver Lake

Translucent tan chalcedony

Ground stem sides

Obsidian

G9, $700-$1300
Harney Co., OR

Ground stem

Type I

Black obsidian

G9, $1200-$2200
Power Co., ID

Type I

Ignimbrite

G7, $400-$700
Twin Falls Co., ID

Ground
basal area

Gray
obsidian

Type I

Basalt

Type I

Blue &
tan
jasper

Type II
Hasket

Collateral
flaking

Side
wear

G8, $900-$1600
Lake Co., OR

Ground
basal area

G8, $900-$1600
Sou. OR

G8, $1000-$1800
Owyhee Riv., OR

Ground
basal area

G9, $1500-$2800
Sou. OR

Obsidian

Ground
basal area

Type I

G9, $1500-$2500
Harney Co., OR

HASKETT (continued)

Basalt

Type II

Type II

Diamond cross section

Collateral flaking

Type II

Basalt

Collateral flaking

Ground basal area

Ground basal area

G6, $175-$300
S. OR

G9, $1300-$2500
Sou. OR

G8, $1600-$3000
Sou. OR

G10+, $5000-$8000+
Harney Co., OR

G10+, $4000-$7000+
Lake Co., OR

FW

HATWAI (see Windust-Hatwai)

HAWKEN - Early to mid-Archaic, 7000 - 5000 B. P.

(Also see Chilcotin Plateau, Early Eared, Kelsey Creek Barbed, Wendover)

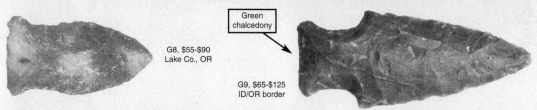

G8, $55-$90
Lake Co., OR

Green
chalcedony

G9, $65-$125
ID/OR border

LOCATION: Wyoming westward into eastern Oregon. **DESCRIPTION:** A small to medium size, narrow point with broad, shallow side notches and an expanding stem. Blade flaking is of high quality and can be the oblique to horizontal parallel style. One of the earliest side notched points of the plains states. **I.D. KEY:** Broad side notches, expanding base.

HELL GAP - Late Paleo, 10,300 - 9500 B. P.

(Also see Agate Basin, Cascade Shouldered, Intermontane, Lake Mohave, Mahkin Shouldered, Silver Lake, Windust)

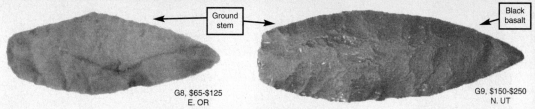

Ground
stem

Black
basalt

G8, $65-$125
E. OR

G9, $150-$250
N. UT

LOCATION: Northwest eastward into the Plains states. **DESCRIPTION:** A medium size lanceolate dart point with a long, contacting basal stem and a short, triangular blade. Bases are generally straight and are ground. High quality flaking. **I. D. KEY:** Long stem.

HELL'S CANYON BASAL NOTCHED - Developmental to Historic Phase, 1200 - 200 B. P.

(Also see Eastgate, Elko Corner Notched, Emigrant Springs, Fountain Bar and Quillomene Bar)

LOCATION: Great Basin westward. **DESCRIPTION:** A medium to large size, broad, basal notched point with tangs usually dropping to the base line. Stems are parallel sided to expanding.

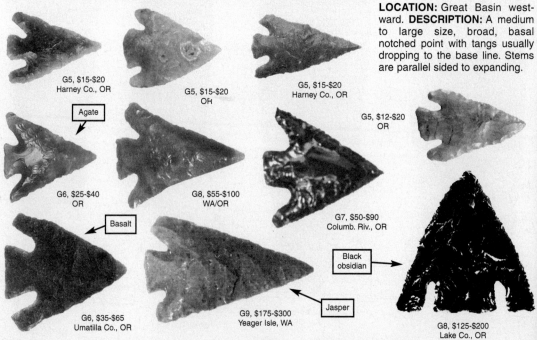

G5, $15-$20
Harney Co., OR

G5, $15-$20
OR

G5, $15-$20
Harney Co., OR

G5, $12-$20
OR

Agate

G6, $25-$40
OR

G8, $55-$100
WA/OR

G7, $50-$90
Columb. Riv., OR

Basalt

Black
obsidian

G6, $35-$65
Umatilla Co., OR

G9, $175-$300
Yeager Isle, WA

Jasper

G8, $125-$200
Lake Co., OR

HELL'S CANYON BASAL NOTCHED (continued)

Petrified wood

Chalcedony

G5, $20-$35
N. UT

G9, $150-$275
Priest Rapids, WA

G9, $150-$275
WA/OR

G9, $250-$400
The Dalles, OR

G8, $90-$175
Lake Co., OR

Note unusual barb notches

G10, $450-$850
Klameth Co., OR

Agate

Classic form

G10, $600-$1000
Franklin Co., WA

HELL'S CANYON CORNER NOTCHED - Develop. to Historic, Phase, 1200 - 200 B. P.

(Also see Bullhead, Elko Corner Notched & Quillomene Bar, Wendover)

G9, $20-$35
OR

G6, $12-$20
Gooding Co., ID

G7, $12-$20
OR

G6, $10-$20
OR

G6, $10-$20
Humboldt Co., NV

G7, $15-$25
OR

G8, $20-$35
Columb. Riv., OR

LOCATION: Great Basin westward. **DESCRIPTION:** A medium to large size, broad, corner notched point with barbed shoulders and an expanding stem. Shoulder barbs are rounded. First recognized and found on Hell's Canyon Reservoir in Idaho.

G7, $15-$30
Silver Lake, OR

G8, $15-$25
OR

G8, $20-$35
OR

Chalcedony

G8, $20-$35
OR

G6, $15-$25
OR. Gem.

G7, $20-$35
WA

G6, $20-$35
WA

G5, $20-$35
Gooding Co., ID

G6, $15-$35
McNary Dam, OR

FW

Basalt

G10, $125-$200
WA

Agate

G8, $30-$60
WA

HENDRICKS - Late Archaic to Woodland, 3500 - 1500 B. P.

(Also see Elko Corner Notched, Merrybell and Snake River)

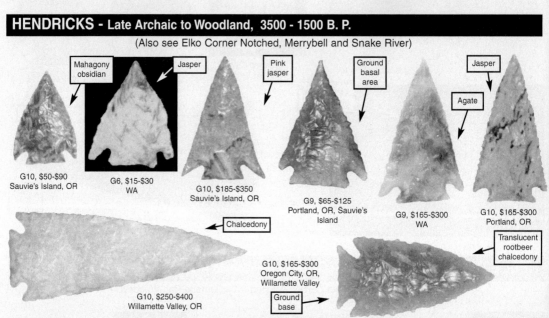

Mahagony obsidian

Jasper

Pink jasper

Ground basal area

Jasper

Agate

G10, $50-$90
Sauvie's Island, OR

G6, $15-$30
WA

G10, $185-$350
Sauvie's Island, OR

G9, $65-$125
Portland, OR, Sauvie's Island

G9, $165-$300
WA

G10, $165-$300
Portland, OR

Chalcedony

Translucent rootbeer chalcedony

G10, $250-$400
Willamette Valley, OR

G10, $165-$300
Oregon City, OR, Willamette Valley

Ground base

LOCATION: Northern Willamette Valley in Oregon. **DESCRIPTION:** A medium sized corner notched point with fine blade serrations. Basal corners and barbs are sharp. Bases are straight and are usually ground. Similar to the *Snake River* point which mostly have concave bases. **I.D. KEY:** Location and straight bases and quality.

HIGH DESERT KNIFE - Mid-Archaic to Classic Phase, 5500 - 500 B. P.

(Also see Cascade and Northwestern Four-Way Knife)

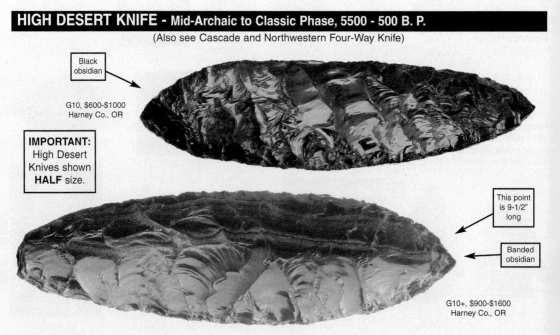

Black obsidian

G10, $600-$1000
Harney Co., OR

IMPORTANT:
High Desert Knives shown **HALF** size.

This point is 9-1/2" long

Banded obsidian

G10+, $900-$1600
Harney Co., OR

HIGH DESERT KNIFE (continued)

Dacite

Basalt

IMPORTANT: High Desert Knives shown **HALF** size.

Rug-hook scraper

Obsidian

G8, $55-$100
OR

G6, $45-$80
S. OR

G8, $150-$250
S. OR

LOCATION: Columbia River in Washington, E. Calif. and all of Nevada. **DESCRIPTION:** A very large biface knife blade with excurvate sides and a rounded to pointed base. Flaking quality is usually very high. This knife was made by several pre-historic groups in the Great Basin, Columbia Plateau and adjoining territory. Formational flaking, pressure flaking, blade edge alignment and silhouette profiles are a close approximation of each other. Until there is a manufacturing formulation, these blades cannot be assigned to any one culture or group unless found in situ.

G7, $250-$400
OR

G8, $350-$600
NV

G9, $400-$750
Harney Co., OR

HOUX CONTRACTING STEM - Mid-Archaic to Developmental, 4500 - 1500 B. P.

(Also see Coquille, Gatecliff, Gypsum Cave & Sierra Contracting Stem)

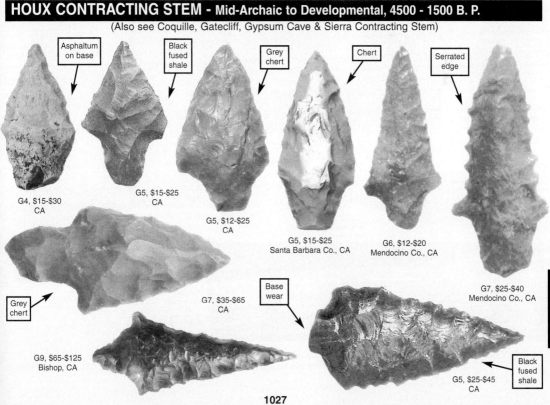

Asphaltum on base

Black fused shale

Grey chert

Chert

Serrated edge

G4, $15-$30
CA

G5, $15-$25
CA

G5, $12-$25
CA

G5, $15-$25
Santa Barbara Co., CA

G6, $12-$20
Mendocino Co., CA

Grey chert

G7, $35-$65
CA

Base wear

G7, $25-$40
Mendocino Co., CA

G9, $65-$125
Bishop, CA

Black fused shale

G5, $25-$45
CA

FW

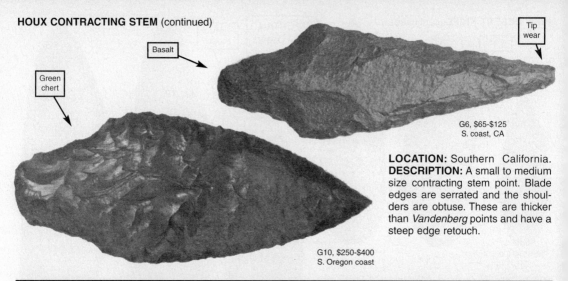

Basalt

Tip wear

Green chert

G6, $65-$125
S. coast, CA

LOCATION: Southern California.
DESCRIPTION: A small to medium size contracting stem point. Blade edges are serrated and the shoulders are obtuse. These are thicker than *Vandenberg* points and have a steep edge retouch.

G10, $250-$400
S. Oregon coast

HUMBOLDT-BASAL NOTCHED - Early to mid-Archaic, 8000 - 5000 B. P.

(Also see Black Rock Concave, Buchanan Eared, Clovis, Pinto Basin)

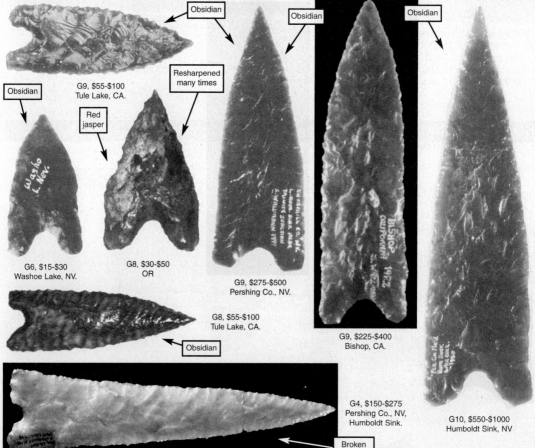

Obsidian

Obsidian

Obsidian

Obsidian

Obsidian

G9, $55-$100
Tule Lake, CA.

Red jasper

Resharpened many times

G6, $15-$30
Washoe Lake, NV.

G8, $30-$50
OR

G9, $275-$500
Pershing Co., NV.

G8, $55-$100
Tule Lake, CA.

G9, $225-$400
Bishop, CA.

Obsidian

G4, $150-$275
Pershing Co., NV,
Humboldt Sink.

G10, $550-$1000
Humboldt Sink, NV

Broken and glued

LOCATION: Great Basin states, esp. Nevada. **DESCRIPTION:** A medium to large size, narrow, lanceolate point with a concave base and rounded basal tangs. Widest at the base, this form is scarce in the type area. **I.D. KEY:** Rounded basal ears.

HUMBOLDT-CONSTRICTED BASE - Early to mid-Archaic, 7000 - 5000 B. P.

(Also see Buchannan Eared, Early Leaf, Pinto Basin and Pryor Stemmed)

Orange chert

Basalt

Obsidian

G5, $8-$15
Union Co., OR

G6, $15-$25
CA

G6, $15-$30
Humboldt Co., NV

G6, $15-$30
Warner Vall., OR

G6, $15-$25
Humboldt Co., NV

G5, $12-$20
Lake Co., OR

G6, $15-$30
S. W. NV

G7, $15-$30
OR

Ground stem

G6, $20-$35
Sou. OR

Obsidian

Obsidian w/alkali

G6, $25-$45
Owyhee Co., ID

G6, $25-$45
Humboldt Co., NV

G6, $20-$35
Harney Co., OR

G8, $50-$90
Warner Vall., OR

G9, $50-$90
Humboldt Co., NV

G8, $55-$100
Warner Valley, OR.

G9, $55-$100
Warner Vall., OR

G9, $125-$245
Klamath Co., OR

Excellent oblique flaking & clear with black bands

Obsidian

Obsidian

Obsidian

Obsidian

G8, $90-$175
S. OR

G8, $80-$150
Warner Vall., OR

G9 $50-$90
Tule Lake, CA

G8, $90-$175
Warner Vall., OR

G10, $600-$1000
Modoc Co., CA

G9, $185-$350
S. OR

FW

LOCATION: Great Basin states, esp. Nevada. **DESCRIPTION:** A small to medium size, narrow, lanceolate point with a constricted, concave, eared base. Some examples have faint shoulders. Parallel, oblique flaking occurs on many examples.

HUMBOLDT-TRIANGULAR - Mid to late Archaic, 7000 - 5000 B. P.

(Also see Black Rock Concave, Cascade, Clovis, Early Leaf and Owl Cave)

Obsidian

Chert

Chert

G6, $15-$25
Harney Co., OR.

G6, $12-$20
OR

G8, $15-$25
OR

G6, $15-$30
Lake Co., OR

G8, $15-$30
Owyhee Co., ID

G6, $15-$30
Warner Val., OR.

G8, $25-$45
Humboldt Co., NV

G8, $15-$30
Klamath Lake, OR

Obsidian

Tip nick

Obsidian

Obsidian

G6, $25-$40
Harney Co., OR

G6, $25-$40
OR

G8, $50-$90
Crump Lake, OR

G7, $35-$60
OR

G7, $35-$60
S. OR

G8, $50-$90
Owyhee Co., ID

G5, $20-$35
Fort Rock, OR

G6, $35-$60
Humboldt Co., NV

Tip nick

Obsidian

Obsidian

Obsidian

Obsidian

Agate

G8, $55-$100
Humboldt Co., NV

G6, $35-$60
S. OR

G8, $45-$85
Crump Lake, OR

G8, $45-$85
S. OR

G9, $80-$150
S. OR

G9, $80-$150
S. OR

G10, $600-$1100
Lake Co., OR

LOCATION: Great Basin states, esp. Nevada. **DESCRIPTION:** A small to medium size, narrow, lanceolate point with a tapered, concave base. Basal concavity can be slight to extreme. Many examples have high quality oblique parallel flaking.

HUMBOLDT-TRIANGULAR (continued)

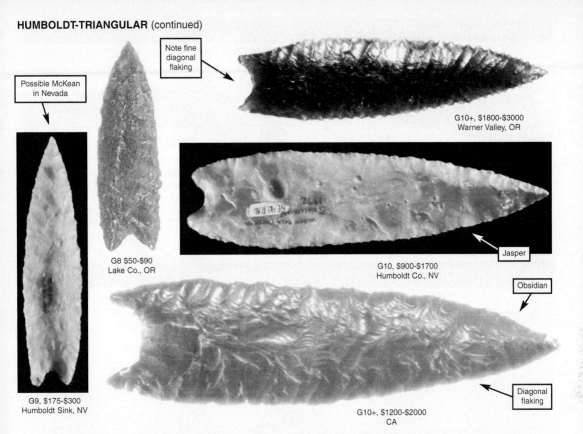

Possible McKean in Nevada

Note fine diagonal flaking

G10+, $1800-$3000
Warner Valley, OR

G8 $50-$90
Lake Co., OR

Jasper

G10, $900-$1700
Humboldt Co., NV

Obsidian

Diagonal flaking

G9, $175-$300
Humboldt Sink, NV

G10+, $1200-$2000
CA

INTERMONTANE STEMMED - Paleo, 10,500 - 10,000 B.P.

(Also see Agate Basin, Cascade, Hell Gap, Lake Mohave, Mahkin Shouldered and Shaniko)

Basalt

G8, $125-$200
S. E. OR

Basalt

G7, $55-$100
British Columbia, Canada

G8, $150-$250
British Columbia, Canada

FW

LOCATION: British columbia, Canada. **DESCRIPTION:** A medium to large size lanceolate point with a tapering stem. Bases are rounded to pointed. Shoulders are non-existant to obtuse. Basal areas are ground.

ISHI - Historic Phase, 100 - 80 B.P.

(Also see Glass)

Very rare. Real examples would need excellent provenance

G10, $800-$1500
CA. 1911
Applies to points only made by Ishi

G10, $1200-$2000
CA. 1911
Applies to points only made by Ishi

LOCATION: Northern California. **DESCRIPTION:** A medium size, thin, corner to side notched point with deep notches set close to the base. Bases vary from concave to convex. Ishi, known as the last wild Indian in North America and the last survivor of his tribe, in fear for his life, turned himself in to the local authorities in Oroville, California. The year was 1911. The University of California museum offered him sanctuary for the rest of his life. While there, he knapped arrowpoints which were given to friends and acquaintances he met at the museum. For more information, read "Ishi in Two Worlds", 1963, University of Calif. Press at Berkeley.

JALAMA SIDE NOTCHED - Early to mid-Archaic, 6000 - 4500 B. P.

(Also see Bitterroot, Cold Springs, Northern Side Notched, Pluvial Lakes Side, Tucannon Side)

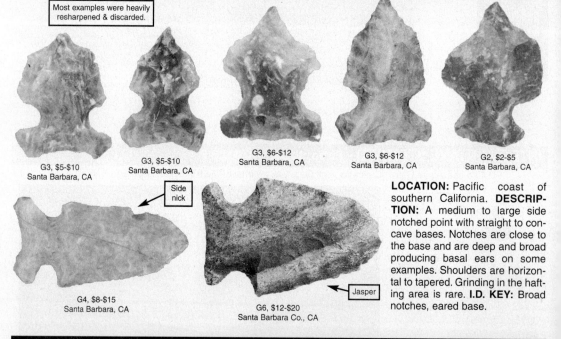

Most examples were heavily resharpened & discarded.

G3, $5-$10
Santa Barbara, CA

G3, $5-$10
Santa Barbara, CA

G3, $6-$12
Santa Barbara, CA

G3, $6-$12
Santa Barbara, CA

G2, $2-$5
Santa Barbara, CA

Side nick

G4, $8-$15
Santa Barbara, CA

Jasper

G6, $12-$20
Santa Barbara Co., CA

LOCATION: Pacific coast of southern California. **DESCRIPTION:** A medium to large side notched point with straight to concave bases. Notches are close to the base and are deep and broad producing basal ears on some examples. Shoulders are horizontal to tapered. Grinding in the hafting area is rare. **I.D. KEY:** Broad notches, eared base.

KAMLOOPS SIDE NOTCHED - Developmental to Historic Phase, 1000 - 200 B. P.

(Also see Ahsahka, Bear River, Desert & Rose Springs)

Basalt

G6, $4-$7
British Colum., CAN

Basalt

G6, $5-$10
British Colum., CAN

Basalt

G6, $5-$10
British Colum., CAN

Basalt

G6, $5-$10
British Colum., CAN

G7, $12-$20
British Colum., CAN

LOCATION: British Columbia in the high desert areas of Fraser River canyon & Thompson River drainage. **DESCRIPTION:** A small to medium size, thin, triangular side notched arrowpoint with a straight to concave base. 90% are made from native black basalt with a few made of agate and jasper. Some may be serrated. A decendent of the *Prairie Side Notch* or *Desert Side Notch* from the south.

KAMLOOPS SIDE NOTCHED (continued)

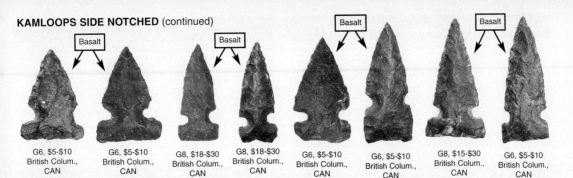

Basalt

Basalt

Basalt

Basalt

G6, $5-$10
British Colum.,
CAN

G6, $5-$10
British Colum.,
CAN

G8, $18-$30
British Colum.,
CAN

G8, $18-$30
British Colum.,
CAN

G6, $5-$10
British Colum.,
CAN

G6, $5-$10
British Colum.,
CAN

G8, $15-$30
British Colum.,
CAN

G6, $5-$10
British Colum.,
CAN

KELSEY CREEK BARBED - Early to mid-Archaic, 6000 - 4500 B. P.

(Also see Big Valley Stemmed and Mayacmas Corner Notched, McGillivray)

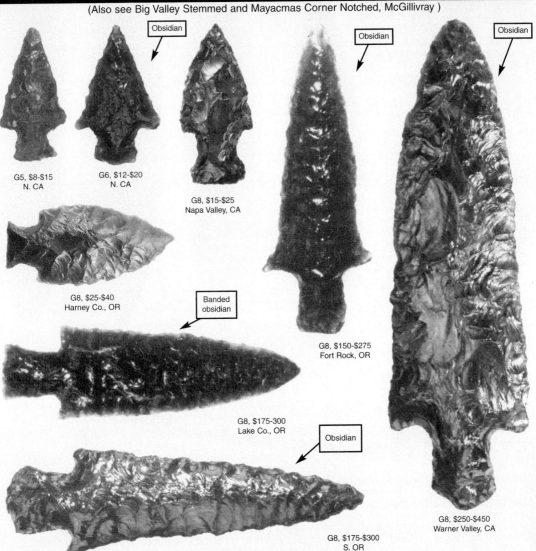

Obsidian

Obsidian

Obsidian

G5, $8-$15
N. CA

G6, $12-$20
N. CA

G8, $15-$25
Napa Valley, CA

G8, $25-$40
Harney Co., OR

Banded
obsidian

G8, $150-$275
Fort Rock, OR

G8, $175-300
Lake Co., OR

Obsidian

G8, $175-$300
S. OR

G8, $250-$450
Warner Valley, CA

FW

LOCATION: Northern California into southern Oregon. **DESCRIPTION:** A medium to large size broadly corner notched point. Stems expand and bases are straight to convex. Basal corners are sharp to rounded. Shoulders are horizontal to strongly barbed. Stems can be fairly long on some examples.

Orange jasper

Heavy edge grinding all the way to the tip

G5, $55-$100
S. OR

Basal area is ground

Black obsidian

Black obsidian

Black obsidian

Edge wear

Black obsidian

Ground stem

G7, $125-$225
Lake Co., OR,
Fort Rock

G7, $150-$275
Lake Co., OR,
Fort Rock

Ground stem

G8, $200-$325
Lake Co., OR, Fort
Rock

G6, $125-$200
S.W. OR

Ground stem

G9, $250-$400
Lake Co., OR, Fort Rock

Basal fluting

G9, $350-$600
Warner Valley, OR

G10, $375-$700
Lake Co., OR

Ground stem

LOCATION: Columbia Plateau in Washington, south into Oregon, Nevada and Utah. **DESCRIPTION:** The lanceolate form of *Windust* or *Lind Coulee*. A medium to large size, thin, double pointed lanceolate blade with convex sides. The basal end is usually a little more rounded than the tip. Flaking is to a median ridge with a very thin to medium thin cross-section. Stem sides are heavily ground for hafting. Previously known as *Cascade* bi-point. **I.D. KEY:** Basal grinding and double pointed form. A similar point was found in the hip of "Kennewick Man," a 9300 year old Caucasoid. Named by Jim Hogue and John Cockrell. Similar points were found at the lowest levels in Cougar Mtn. Cave.

KLICKITAT (continued)

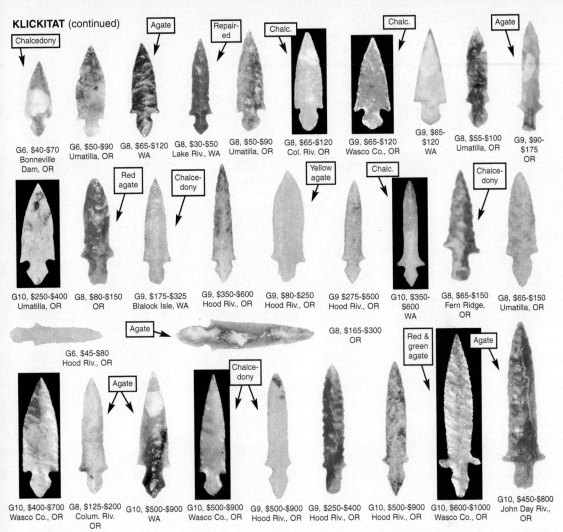

Chalcedony

G6, $40-$70
Bonneville
Dam, OR

G6, $50-$90
Umatilla, OR

Agate

G8, $65-$120
WA

Repaired

G8, $30-$50
Lake Riv., WA

G8, $50-$90
Umatilla, OR

Chalc.

G8, $65-$120
Col. Riv. OR

Chalc.

G9, $65-$120
Wasco Co., OR

G9, $65-$120
WA

Agate

G8, $55-$100
Umatilla, OR

G9, $90-$175
OR

Red agate

G10, $250-$400
Umatilla, OR

G8, $80-$150
OR

Chalcedony

G9, $175-$325
Blalock Isle, WA

G9, $350-$600
Hood Riv., OR

Yellow agate

G9, $80-$250
Hood Riv., OR

G9 $275-$500
Hood Riv., OR

Chalc.

G10, $350-$600
WA

Chalcedony

G8, $65-$150
Fern Ridge, OR

G8, $65-$150
Umatilla, OR

G6, $45-$80
Hood Riv., OR

Agate

G8, $165-$300
OR

Red & green agate

Agate

Agate

Chalcedony

G10, $400-$700
Wasco Co., OR

G8, $125-$200
Colum. Riv. OR

G10, $500-$900
WA

G10, $500-$900
Wasco Co., OR

G9, $500-$900
Hood Riv., OR

G9, $250-$400
Hood Riv., OR

G10, $500-$900
Hood Riv., OR

G10, $600-$1000
Wasco Co., OR

G10, $450-$800
John Day Riv., OR

LOCATION: The Columbia River in Oregon and Washington. **DESCRIPTION:** A small size, narrow, thin, lanceolate, barbed arrow point with a usually diamond shaped base. Bases can also be rectangular with horizontal barbs. Some examples have excellent oblique, parallel flaking. Other base forms would fall under the Dagger type.

LADY ISLAND PENTAGONAL - Late Archaic to Classic Phase, 2500 - 400 B. P.

(Also see Merrybell)

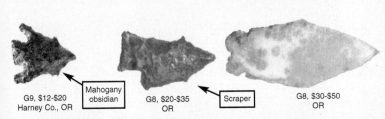

Mahogany obsidian

G9, $12-$20
Harney Co., OR

G8, $20-$35
OR

Scraper

G8, $30-$50
OR

LOCATION: Type site is Lady Island, Columbia River. Oregon and Washington. **DESCRIPTION:** All points are undercut at the shoulder to form a single serration cutter. A "shoulder" is formed in the blade by resharpening. This modification can be found on dart and arrow points in the lower Columbia and other parts of the northwest.

FW

LAKE MOHAVE - Paleo to Early Archaic, 13,200 - 7000 B. P.

(Also see Haskett, Hell Gap, Intermontane, Lind Coulee, Parman, Silver Lake and Windust)

LAKE MOHAVE (continued)

Ground stem

Ground stem

Chisel tip

Agate

G5, $35-$60
Lake Co., OR

G6, $45-$75
Owens Valley, CA

G6, $40-$75
S. OR

G4, $40-$70
Lake Co., OR

G6, $45-$80
Lake Co., OR

G5, $45-$80
San Bernadino Co., CA

Classic example

Obsidian

Chert

Chalcedony

G6, $50-$90
Lake Co., OR

G7, $75-$140
Lake Co., OR

G6, $65-$120
Lake Co., OR

G6, $90-$175
San Bernadino Co., CA

G8, $175-$300
San Bernadino Co., CA

G7, $90-$175
Lake Co., OR.

Obsidian

G6, $175-$300
Maybee Site, OR

G6, $65-$120
Black Rock
Desert, NV

Obsidian

Edge wear

Chalcedony

Stem is ground half way up

Ground stem

G6, $125-$225
N. CA.

Ground stem

G6, $90-$175
San Bernadino Co., CA

G8, $175-$300
Carson Sink, NV

G9, $175-$300
Cougar Mtn., OR

G10, $250-$525
Steens Mountain, OR

1036

LAKE MOHAVE (continued)

LOCATION: S.E. Calif. to Sou. Oregon. Type site: S.E. California. **DESCRIPTION:** A medium size, narrow to broad, parallel to contracting stemmed point. Shoulders are weak to none. Stem is much longer than the blade. Basal sides are ground. Most examples are worn-out, resharpened points. Found with *Butterfly Crescents*. Associated with Bison hunting. One of the oldest dated projectile point types in the Great Basin. Carbon dated to 13,200 B.P. Variants exist where a burin was removed from opposite sides of the tip, called chisel tips. This type may prove to be worn-out *Parmans*.

LAKE RIVER SIDE NOTCHED - Classic to Historic Phase, 700 - 200 B. P.

(Also see Ahsahka, Bear River, Desert, Panoche, Rose Springs)

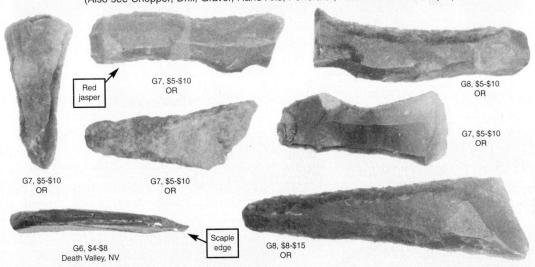

Chalc.	Chalc.	Jasper					Chalc.	Chalc.

G4, $2-$4
Lewis Riv., WA

G4, $2-$4
Lewis Riv., WA

G6, $3-$5
Col. Riv., OR

G5, $3-$5
Col. Riv., OR

G7, $2-$5
Lake Riv., WA

G6, $2-$5
Lake Riv., WA

G8, $2-$5
Lake Riv., WA

G8, $5-$10
Lewis Riv., WA

G8, $5-$10
Lewis Riv., WA

G6, $2-$5
Lewis Riv., WA

G7, $4-$8
Lake Riv., WA

G5, $2-$5
Lake Riv., WA

G8, $4-$8
Lake Riv., WA

G6, $8-$15
Scappoose, OR

G6, $8-$15
Sauvies Isle, OR

G8, $5-$10
Clatskanie, OR

G9, $15-$30
Lake Riv., WA

G7, $12-$20
Lake Riv., WA

LOCATION: Lower Columbia River and some tributaries near the name site, Lake River near Vancouver, Wash. **DESCRIPTION:** A small triangular arrow point that has low placed side notches that vary in depth and width. The bases are convex to concave with straight being dominant. These points are made on narrow to widely triangular pre-forms and flakes. This type is smaller, on average, than the Desert Side Notched series. Despite the great deal of variation in the silhouette of these points, they were found together in caches. This point was found in situ with late era trade beads. Defined and named in 2001 by A. Erickson, J.L. Hogue and R. Snyder.

LANCET - Paleo to Archaic, 11,500 - 5000 B. P.

(Also see Chopper, Drill, Graver, Hand Axe, Perforator, Paleo Knife and Scraper)

Red jasper

G7, $5-$10
OR

G8, $5-$10
OR

G7, $5-$10
OR

G7, $5-$10
OR

G7, $5-$10
OR

G6, $4-$8
Death Valley, NV

Scaple edge

G8, $8-$15
OR

LOCATION: Great Basin westward. **DESCRIPTION:** A medium to large size sliver used as a knife for cutting. Recent experiments proved that these knives were sharper than a surgeon's scalpel. Similar to *Burins* which are fractured at one end to produce a sharp point.

FW

LEWIS RIVER SHORT STEMMED - Classic to Historic Phase, 700 - 200 B. P.

(Also see Columbia River Pin Stem, Gunther, Rabbit Island, Rose Springs Stemmed)

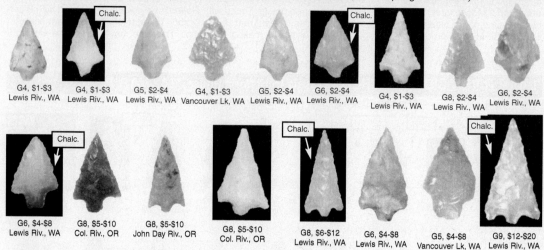

G4, $1-$3
Lewis Riv., WA

Chalc.
G4, $1-$3
Lewis Riv., WA

G5, $2-$4
Lewis Riv., WA

G4, $1-$3
Vancouver Lk, WA

G5, $2-$4
Lewis Riv., WA

Chalc.
G6, $2-$4
Lewis Riv., WA

G4, $1-$3
Lewis Riv., WA

G8, $2-$4
Lewis Riv., WA

G6, $2-$4
Lewis Riv., WA

Chalc.
G6, $4-$8
Lewis Riv., WA

G8, $5-$10
Col. Riv., OR

G8, $5-$10
John Day Riv., OR

G8, $5-$10
Col. Riv., OR

Chalc.
G8, $6-$12
Lewis Riv., WA

G6, $4-$8
Lewis Riv., WA

G5, $4-$8
Vancouver Lk, WA

Chalc.
G9, $12-$20
Lewis Riv., WA

LOCATION: Lower Columbia River and tributaries in Oregon and Washington. **DESCRIPTION:** This point is a small triangular arrow point with straight to slightly convex blade edges. The shoulders are straight to slightly barbed. The stems are short, square or occasionally contracting to a rounded base. Many bases are truncated and finished with short steep strokes. Found in situ with late era trade beads. Defined and named by Jim Hogue in 2000.

LIND COULEE - Late Paleo, 11,000 - 10,500 B.P.

(Also see Año Nuevo, Cougar Mountain, Early Stemmed, Haskett, Hell Gap, Intermontane, Kennewick, Lake Mohave, Parman, Silver Lake and Windust)

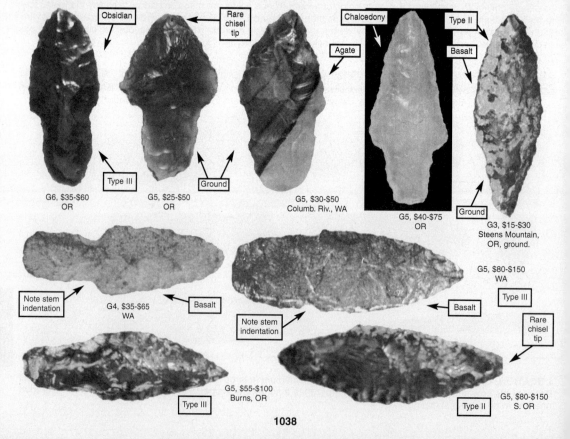

G6, $35-$60
OR

G5, $25-$50
OR

G5, $30-$50
Columb. Riv., WA

G5, $40-$75
OR

G3, $15-$30
Steens Mountain,
OR, ground.

G5, $80-$150
WA

G4, $35-$65
WA

G5, $55-$100
Burns, OR

G5, $80-$150
S. OR

LIND COULEE (continued)

Type III — G8, $125-$200
Steens Mountain, OR

Ground

Type II — G5, $65-$125
Steens Mountain, OR

Obsidian / **Ground** — G5, $35-$60
S. OR

Jasper — G9, $250-$450
Cowlitz Co., Wa

Obsidian / **Type II** — G8, $175-$250
N. OR

Chalcedony — G6, $175-$250
OR

G6, $175-$200
OR

Ground — G6, $150-$250
OR

Obsidian — G7, $150-$250
OR

Type I / **Ground** — G9, $300-$550
WA

Obsidian — G8, $175-$300
Lake Co., OR

Type II — G4, $25-$40
OR

LOCATION: The Columbia Plateau in Oregon and Washington. **DESCRIPTION:** A medium to large size stemmed point with weak horizontal to sloping to very weak shoulders and a contracting to bulbous base. Stem sides are ground. The base is rounded. This point has been confused with the *Parman* point found in the Great Basin of Nev., N. California and S.E. Oregon. Both types have stem grinding, but the *Lind Coulee* is believed to be earlier. *Crescents* were found on the type site in Washington associated with this type. This type develops into *Alberta* and *Parman* and coexisted with *Clovis* in the Great Basin. **Note:** Hasketts and Lind Coulees were found together at Cooper's Ferry, Idaho and dated at 11,500 B.P., 1,000 years before Parman. **I.D. KEY:** Long stem that is ground.

FW

Tip & edge wear

Obsidian

Yellow agate

Type II

Rare chisel tip

Lind Coulee going into Alberta

G9, $450-$800
Lake Co., OR

Type I

Type III

Obsidian

Ground stem

Ground stem

G8, $250-$400
Warner Valley, OR

Type II

G8, $200-$350
OR

G8, $200-$350
S. OR

G6, $200-$350
Malheur Co., OR

MAHKIN SHOULDERED LANCEOLATE - Early Archaic, 6500 - 5000 B. P.

(Also see Cascade Shouldered, Fish Gutter, Hell Gap, Plateau Pentagonal & Wahmuza)

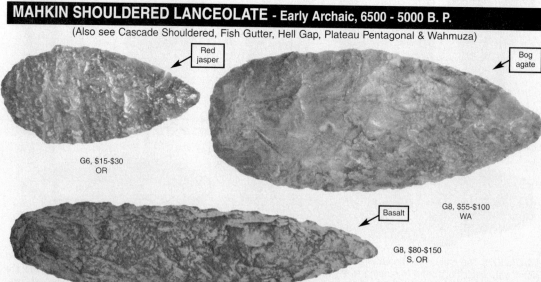

Red jasper

Bog agate

G6, $15-$30
OR

Basalt

G8, $55-$100
WA

G8, $80-$150
S. OR

LOCATION: Oregon & Washington. **DESCRIPTION:** A medium to large size lanceolate point with a rounded base and very weak, but definite shoulders. Stems are usually ground. A very rare type as part of the *Humboldt* series.

MAHKIN SHOULDERED LANCEOLATE (continued)

Obsidian

G6, $25-$40
S. OR

G8, $35-$65
N. OR

MALAGA COVE LEAF - Developmental Phase, 1500 - 700 B. P.

(Also see Cascade, Cottonwood, Gold Hill, and Trojan)

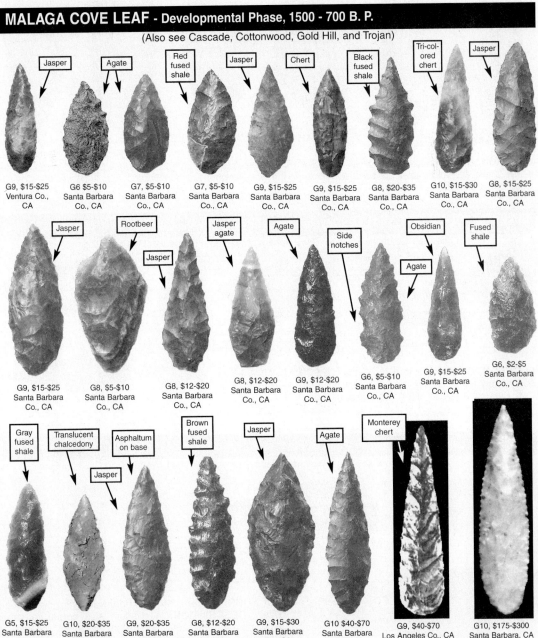

Jasper

Agate

Red fused shale

Jasper

Chert

Black fused shale

Tri-colored chert

Jasper

G9, $15-$25
Ventura Co.,
CA

G6 $5-$10
Santa Barbara
Co., CA

G7, $5-$10
Santa Barbara
Co., CA

G7, $5-$10
Santa Barbara
Co., CA

G9, $15-$25
Santa Barbara
Co., CA

G9, $15-$25
Santa Barbara
Co., CA

G8, $20-$35
Santa Barbara
Co., CA

G10, $15-$30
Santa Barbara
Co., CA

G8, $15-$25
Santa Barbara
Co., CA

Jasper

Rootbeer

Jasper

Jasper agate

Agate

Side notches

Obsidian

Agate

Fused shale

G9, $15-$25
Santa Barbara
Co., CA

G8, $5-$10
Santa Barbara
Co., CA

G8, $12-$20
Santa Barbara
Co., CA

G8, $12-$20
Santa Barbara
Co., CA

G9, $12-$20
Santa Barbara
Co., CA

G6, $5-$10
Santa Barbara
Co., CA

G9, $15-$25
Santa Barbara
Co., CA

G6, $2-$5
Santa Barbara
Co., CA

Gray fused shale

Translucent chalcedony

Asphaltum on base

Jasper

Brown fused shale

Jasper

Agate

Monterey chert

G5, $15-$25
Santa Barbara
Co., CA

G10, $20-$35
Santa Barbara
Co., CA

G9, $20-$35
Santa Barbara
Co., CA

G8, $12-$20
Santa Barbara
Co., CA

G9, $15-$30
Santa Barbara
Co., CA

G10 $40-$70
Santa Barbara
Co., CA

G9, $40-$70
Los Angeles Co., CA

G10, $175-$300
Santa Barbara, CA

FW

1041

MALAGA COVE LEAF (continued)

Monterey chert

Chert

Chert

Rootbeer chert

Agate

Jasper

Jasper

Black fused shale

G7, $12-$20
Ventura Co., CA

G9, $40-$70
Santa Barbara, CA

G9, $25-$45
Santa Barbara Co., CA

G7, $15-$25
Santa Barbara Co., CA

G7, $15-$25
Ventura Co., CA

G6, $20-$35
Ventura Co., CA

G10, $175-$325
Santa Barbara Co., CA

G10, $200-$350
Ventura Co., CA

LOCATION: Coastal southern California. **DESCRIPTION:** A small to medium size lanceolate point with a rounded to pointed base. Some examples are serrated. Similar to the *Gold Hill* point found in Oregon. Also known as the *Coastal Cottonwood* point.

MALAGA COVE STEMMED - Developmental Phase, 1500 - 700 B. P.

(Also see Columbia Plateau, Rose Springs, Steamboat Lanceolate, Wallula Gap)

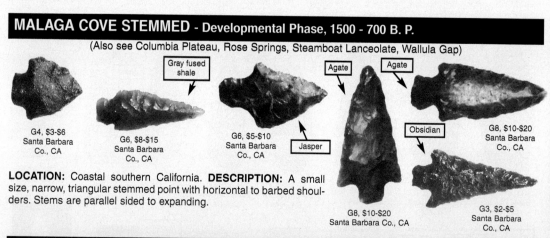

Gray fused shale

Agate

Agate

Obsidian

Jasper

G4, $3-$6
Santa Barbara
Co., CA

G6, $8-$15
Santa Barbara
Co., CA

G6, $5-$10
Santa Barbara
Co., CA

G8, $10-$20
Santa Barbara
Co., CA

G8, $10-$20
Santa Barbara Co., CA

G3, $2-$5
Santa Barbara
Co., CA

LOCATION: Coastal southern California. **DESCRIPTION:** A small size, narrow, triangular stemmed point with horizontal to barbed shoulders. Stems are parallel sided to expanding.

MARTIS - Late Archaic, 3000 - 1500 B. P.

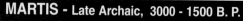

(Also see Elko Corner Notched, Hell's Canyon, Merrybell, Wendover)

G6, $5-$10
OR

G6, $5-$10
Harney Co., OR

Red jasper

G6, $5-$10
Susanville, CA

G9, $20-$35
S. OR

LOCATION: Western Arizona northward into the Great Basin. **DESCRIPTION:** A medium size corner to side notched point with small tapered to horizontal shoulders. Bases are often asymmetrical.

(Also see Big Valley and Kelsey Creek barbed & McGillivray)

Obsidian

LOCATION: Northern California into southern Oregon. **DESCRIPTION:** A medium size, narrow, corner notched dart/knife point with rounded basal corners. Stems are short with notching from the basal corners. Shoulders are usually horizontal and barbed but can be rounded. Edges can be serrated. Related to the *Big Valley* point.

G8, $55-$100
OR

(Also see Base Tang, Kelsey Creek, Mayacmas, Need Stemmed, Nightfire, Tuolumne, Wendover, Willits Side)

Obsidian

Obsidian

Red jasper

Obsidian

Tan chert

G4, $1-$2
N. CA

G5, $1-$2
Humboldt Co., NV

G5, $1-$2
N. CA

G5, $2-$5
N. CA

G7, $5-$10
Harney Co., OR

G6, $7-$15
N. CA

G9, $125-$225
Harney Co., OR

G8, $150-$250
Lake Co., OR

G7, $80-$150
S. OR

G4, $20-$35
S. OR

FW

LOCATION: Central to Northern California. **DESCRIPTION:** A medium to large size, side notched point with an expanding stem that is straight to rounded to pointed. Stem sides usually expand moderately. **I.D. KEY:** Bulbous to "turkey tail" stem.

MCKEE UNIFACE - Middle Archaic, 5000 - 4000 B. P.

(Also see Cascade, Excelsior and Marybelle)

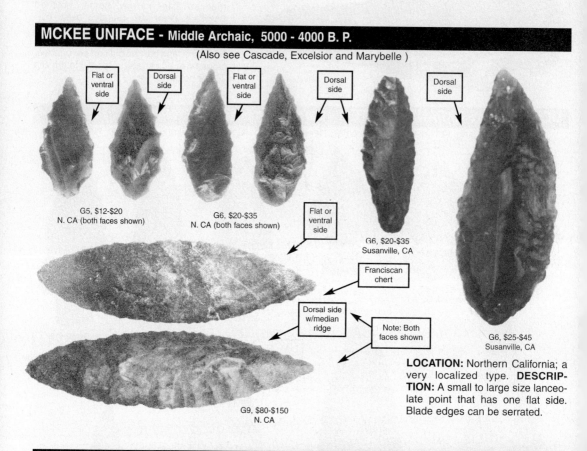

Flat or ventral side

Dorsal side

Flat or ventral side

Dorsal side

Dorsal side

G5, $12-$20
N. CA (both faces shown)

G6, $20-$35
N. CA (both faces shown)

Flat or ventral side

G6, $20-$35
Susanville, CA

Franciscan chert

Dorsal side w/median ridge

Note: Both faces shown

G6, $25-$45
Susanville, CA

G9, $80-$150
N. CA

LOCATION: Northern California; a very localized type. **DESCRIPTION:** A small to large size lanceolate point that has one flat side. Blade edges can be serrated.

MENDOCINO CONCAVE BASE - Late Archaic, 5000 - 2500 B. P.

(Also see Humboldt & Triple T)

LOCATION: Southern to northern California. **DESCRIPTION:** A medium size, eared lanceolate dart point with a concave base. A California variant of the *Humboldt* point.

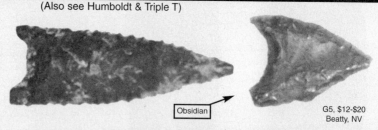

G9, $40-$75
OR

Obsidian

G5, $12-$20
Beatty, NV

MERRYBELL, VAR. I - Late Archaic to Transitional Phase, 2500 - 1750 B.P.

(Also see Elko Corner Notched, Martis and Snake River)

Made into a perforator

G6, $5-$10
Columbia Riv., OR

Yellow agate

G4, $3-$5
OR

G6, $7-$15
Vancouver, WA

G2, $.50-$1
OR

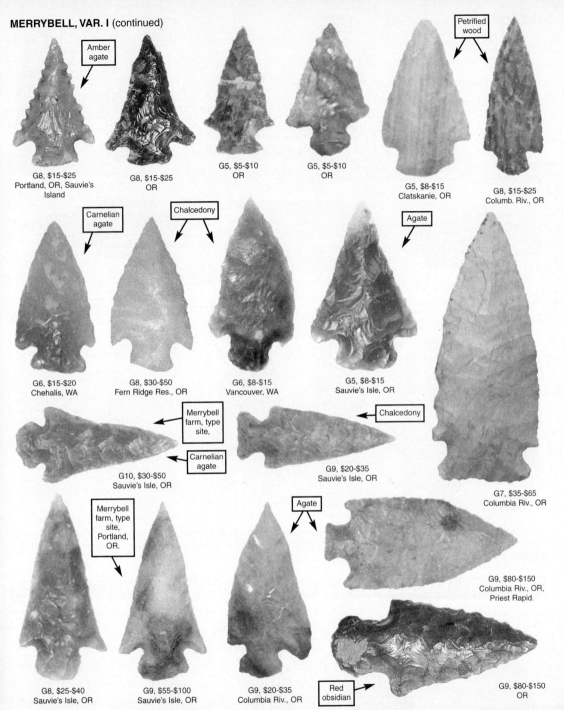

Amber agate

G8, $15-$25
Portland, OR, Sauvie's
Island

G8, $15-$25
OR

G5, $5-$10
OR

G5, $5-$10
OR

Petrified wood

G5, $8-$15
Clatskanie, OR

G8, $15-$25
Columb. Riv., OR

Carnelian agate

Chalcedony

Agate

G6, $15-$20
Chehalis, WA

G8, $30-$50
Fern Ridge Res., OR

G6, $8-$15
Vancouver, WA

G5, $8-$15
Sauvie's Isle, OR

Merrybell farm, type site,

Chalcedony

Carnelian agate

G10, $30-$50
Sauvie's Isle, OR

G9, $20-$35
Sauvie's Isle, OR

G7, $35-$65
Columbia Riv., OR

Merrybell farm, type site, Portland, OR.

Agate

G9, $80-$150
Columbia Riv., OR,
Priest Rapid.

Red obsidian

G8, $25-$40
Sauvie's Isle, OR

G9, $55-$100
Sauvie's Isle, OR

G9, $20-$35
Columbia Riv., OR

G9, $80-$150
OR

LOCATION: The Columbia River in Oregon and Washington. Type site is the Merrybell farm on Sauvie's Island near Portland, Oregon. **DESCRIPTION:** A small to medium sized corner notched point with a straight to convex edge. Shoulders become modified with resharpenings. Bases are straight to convex and can be ground. Cross sections are lenticular. Blade edges are sometimes serrated. First published by Ken Matsen in 1968 in the Oregon Archaeological Society's "Screenings," Vol., 17 #7.

FW

MERRYBELL, VAR. II - Late Archaic to Transitional Phase, 2500 - 1750 B.P.

(Also see Cold Springs, Uinta and Wendover)

MERRYBELL, VAR. II (continued)

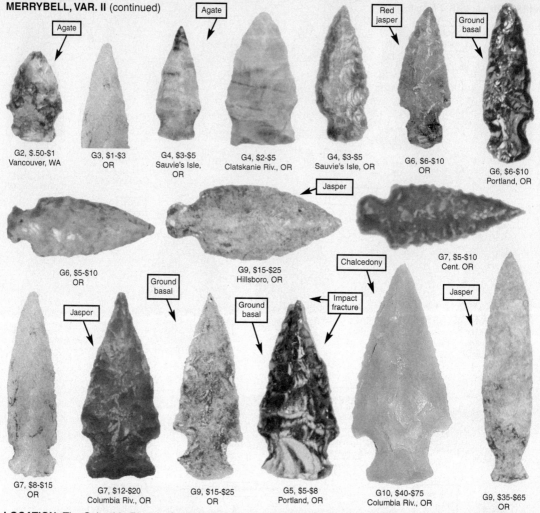

Agate

G2, $.50-$1
Vancouver, WA

G3, $1-$3
OR

Agate

G4, $3-$5
Sauvie's Isle,
OR

G4, $2-$5
Clatskanie Riv., OR

G4, $3-$5
Sauvie's Isle, OR

Red
jasper

G6, $6-$10
OR

Ground
basal

G6, $6-$10
Portland, OR

Jasper

G6, $5-$10
OR

G9, $15-$25
Hillsboro, OR

G7, $5-$10
Cent. OR

Jasper

Ground
basal

Chalcedony

Impact
fracture

Ground
basal

Jasper

G7, $8-$15
OR

G7, $12-$20
Columbia Riv., OR

G9, $15-$25
OR

G5, $5-$8
Portland, OR

G10, $40-$75
Columbia Riv., OR

G9, $35-$65
OR

LOCATION: The Columbia River in Oregon and Washington. **DESCRIPTION:** A small to medium sized widely side-notched point with a convex base. Stem sides and base can be ground. Blade edges are convex to incurvate and can be serrated.

MERRYBELL, VAR. III - Late Archaic to Transitional Phase, 2500 - 1750 B.P.

(Also see Elko Corner Notched, Elko Eared)

Jasper

Agate

Red
jasper

G4, $2-$5
Sauvie's Isle, OR

G8, $8-$15
Sauvie's Isle, OR

G8, $8-$15
Sauvie's Isle, OR

G7, $8-$15
OR

G9, $12-$20
Sauvie's Isle, OR

LOCATION: The Columbia River in Oregon and Washington. **DESCRIPTION:** A small to medium sized corner notched point with a convex to concave edge. Corner notches are usually wide and start at or slightly above the corner. Bases are concave to notched and almost always smoothed. Cross sections are lenticular. Blade edges are sometimes serrated. **I.D. KEY:** Basal treatment is only significant difference from the type I

MERRYBELL, VAR. III (continued)

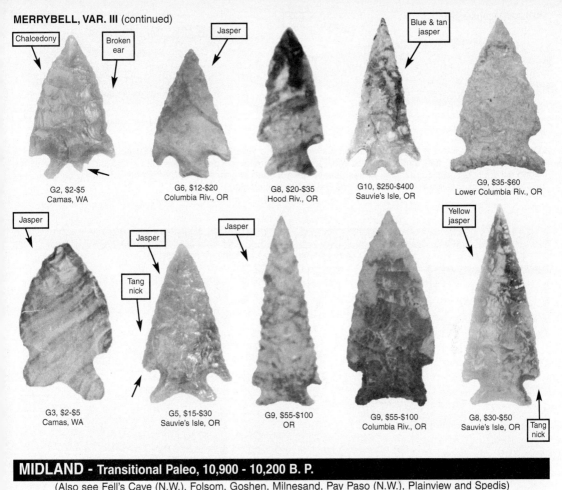

Chalcedony

Broken ear

G2, $2-$5
Camas, WA

Jasper

G6, $12-$20
Columbia Riv., OR

G8, $20-$35
Hood Riv., OR

Blue & tan jasper

G10, $250-$400
Sauvie's Isle, OR

G9, $35-$60
Lower Columbia Riv., OR

Jasper

G3, $2-$5
Camas, WA

Jasper

Tang nick

G5, $15-$30
Sauvie's Isle, OR

Jasper

G9, $55-$100
OR

G9, $55-$100
Columbia Riv., OR

Yellow jasper

G8, $30-$50
Sauvie's Isle, OR

Tang nick

MIDLAND - Transitional Paleo, 10,900 - 10,200 B. P.

(Also see Fell's Cave (N.W.), Folsom, Goshen, Milnesand, Pay Paso (N.W.), Plainview and Spedis)

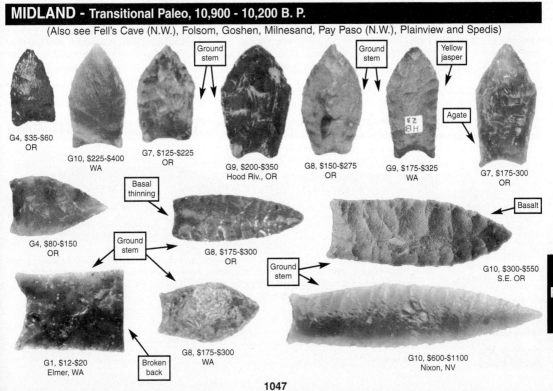

G4, $35-$60
OR

G10, $225-$400
WA

Ground stem

G7, $125-$225
OR

G9, $200-$350
Hood Riv., OR

Ground stem

G8, $150-$275
OR

Yellow jasper

G9, $175-$325
WA

Agate

G7, $175-300
OR

G4, $80-$150
OR

Basal thinning

Ground stem

G8, $175-$300
OR

Ground stem

Basalt

G10, $300-$550
S.E. OR

Ground stem

G1, $12-$20
Elmer, WA

Broken back

G8, $175-$300
WA

G10, $600-$1100
Nixon, NV

FW

MIDLAND (continued)

Obsidian

Obsidian

Ground stem

G10, $550-$1000
OR

Ground stem

G10, $800-$1500
OR

First stage form

LOCATION: Texas into the plains states and Nevada into the Great Basin. **DESCRIPTION:** An unfluted *Folsom*. A small to medium size, thin, unfluted lanceolate point with parallel to convex sides. Basal thinning is weak and the blades exhibit fine micro edgewqork. Bases usually have a shallow concavity, can be eared, and are ground most of the way to the tip. **I.D. KEY:** Square base and Paleo horizontal flaking.

MILNESAND - Transitional Paleo, 11,000 - 9,500 B. P.

(Also see Folsom, Goshen, Midland, Plainview and Spedis)

Agate

G6, $90-$175
Humboldt Co., NV

Agate

Ground stem

Amber agate

Petrified wood

G9, $175-$300
Klickitat Co., WA

Jasper

G9, $175-$325
Columb. Riv., WA

G9, $175-$325
OR

G10, $225-$400
WA

G10, $275-$500
WA

LOCATION: Texas into the plains states and Nevada into the Great Basin. **DESCRIPTION:** A medium size unfluted lanceolate dart point that becomes thicker and wider towards the tip. The base is basically square and ground. Thicker than Midland. **I.D. KEY:** Square base and Paleo horizontal flaking.

MINIATURE BLADE - Classic to Historic Phase, 500 - 100 B. P.

(Also see Cascade)

G9, $30-$50
Coastal OR

G9, $55-$100
Lake Co., OR

G9, $15-$25 ea.
Coastal WA

LOCATION: Northern California into Oregon and Washington. **DESCRIPTION:** A small size, double pointed lanceolate blade made in miniature to possibly symbolize the larger dance or Wealth blades. These objects could also have been used as buttons to fasten garmets or nose ornaments.

MOLALLA (See Gunther)

MULE EAR (See Columbia Mule Ear)

NEED STEMMED LANCEOLATE - Late Archaic to Developmental , 2500 - 1500 B. P.

(Also see Cascade, McGillivray, Nightfire, Tuolumne Notched & Willits Side Notched)

Side notches

G8, $15-$30
Humboldt Co., NV

Side notches

G7, $25-$40
N. CA

Jasper

LOCATION: Northern California into Sou. Oregon. **DESCRIPTION:** A medium to large size, narrow leaf shaped point with shallow side notches, and random flaking, that is occasionally oblique. Cross sections are varied, flattened to oval to plano-convex. Bases are tapered to round or straight and somewhat bulbous **I.D. KEY:** Weak side notches and round bulbous base.

G8, $250-$450
OR

NEWBERRY   (See Rabbit Island)

NIGHTFIRE - Early to mid-Archaic, 7000 - 4000 B. P.

(Also see Bitterroot, Cold Springs, Need Stemmed Lanceolate, McGillvray, Northern Side Notched, Tuolumne Notched and Willits Side Notched)

Obsidian

Basalt

Obsidian

Obsidian

Straight base form

Side wear

Obsidian

G6, $25-$40
Klamath Co., OR

G7, $30-$50
Sou. OR

G6, $35-$60
Sou. OR

G6, $55-$100
N. CA

G8, $90-$175
OR

Ignimbrite

Obsidian

G8, $125-$200
Lake Co., OR

G7, $150-$250
OR

Round base form

G10, $450-$850
Lake Co., OR

FW

NIGHTFIRE (continued)

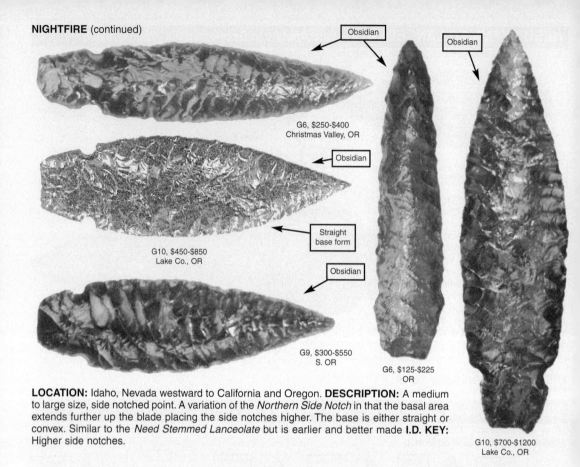

Obsidian

G6, $250-$400
Christmas Valley, OR

Obsidian

Obsidian

Straight base form

G10, $450-$850
Lake Co., OR

Obsidian

G9, $300-$550
S. OR

Obsidian

Obsidian

G6, $125-$225
OR

G10, $700-$1200
Lake Co., OR

LOCATION: Idaho, Nevada westward to California and Oregon. **DESCRIPTION:** A medium to large size, side notched point. A variation of the *Northern Side Notch* in that the basal area extends further up the blade placing the side notches higher. The base is either straight or convex. Similar to the *Need Stemmed Lanceolate* but is earlier and better made **I.D. KEY:** Higher side notches.

NORTHWESTERN FOUR-WAY KNIFE - Classic Phase, 700 - 400 B. P.

(Also see Cascade, Cordilleran, Early Leaf, Excelsior, High Desert Knife, Mahkin Shouldered, Wahmuza)

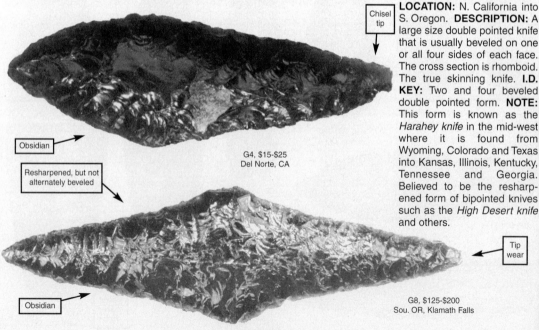

Chisel tip

Obsidian

Resharpened, but not alternately beveled

G4, $15-$25
Del Norte, CA

Obsidian

Tip wear

Obsidian

G8, $125-$200
Sou. OR, Klamath Falls

LOCATION: N. California into S. Oregon. **DESCRIPTION:** A large size double pointed knife that is usually beveled on one or all four sides of each face. The cross section is rhomboid. The true skinning knife. **I.D. KEY:** Two and four beveled double pointed form. **NOTE:** This form is known as the *Harahey knife* in the mid-west where it is found from Wyoming, Colorado and Texas into Kansas, Illinois, Kentucky, Tennessee and Georgia. Believed to be the resharpened form of bipointed knives such as the *High Desert knife* and others.

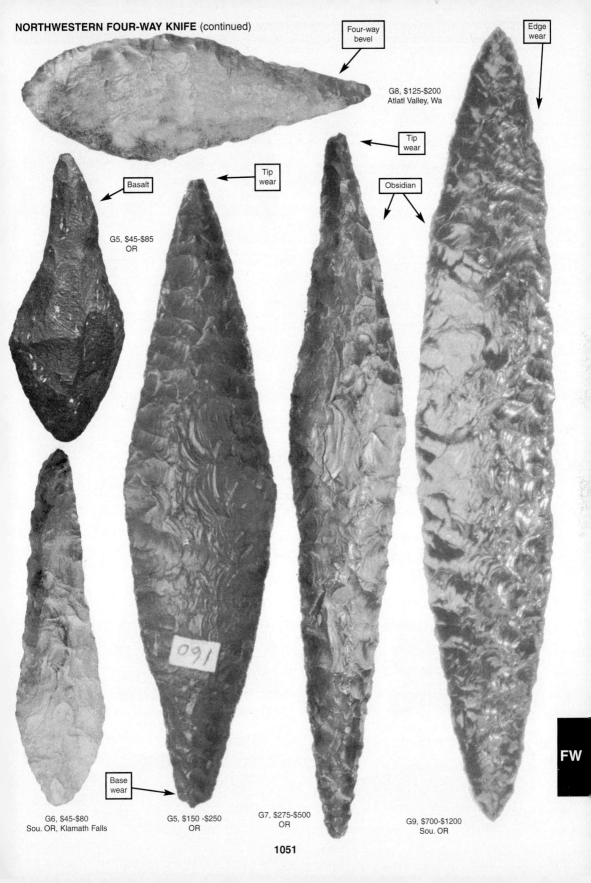

NORTHWESTERN FOUR-WAY KNIFE (continued)

Four-way bevel

G8, $125-$200
Atlatl Valley, Wa

Edge wear

Tip wear

Tip wear

Obsidian

Basalt

G5, $45-$85
OR

091

Base wear

G6, $45-$80
Sou. OR, Klamath Falls

G5, $150 -$250
OR

G7, $275-$500
OR

G9, $700-$1200
Sou. OR

FW

(Also see Ahsahka, Bitterroot, Chilcotin Plateau, Cold Springs, Jalama Side Notched, Nightfire & Willits Side Notched)

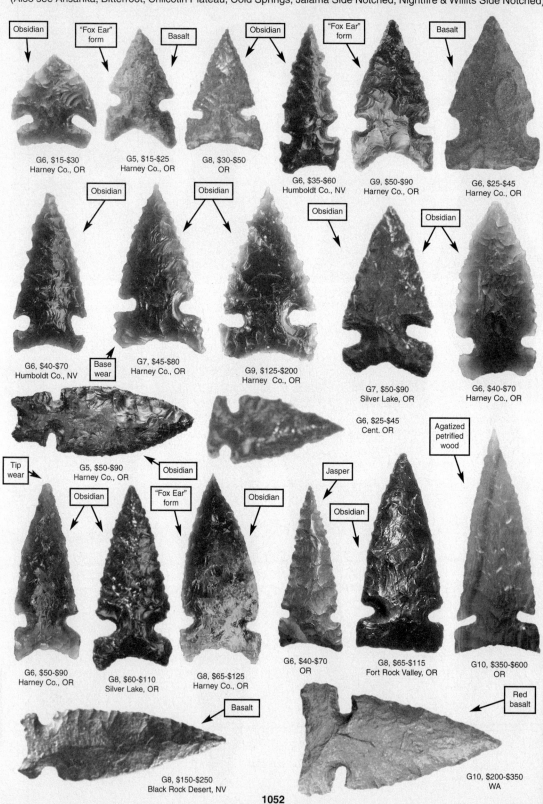

Obsidian
G6, $15-$30
Harney Co., OR

"Fox Ear" form
G5, $15-$25
Harney Co., OR

Basalt
G8, $30-$50
OR

Obsidian

"Fox Ear" form
G6, $35-$60
Humboldt Co., NV

G9, $50-$90
Harney Co., OR

Basalt
G6, $25-$45
Harney Co., OR

Obsidian
G6, $40-$70
Humboldt Co., NV

Base wear

Obsidian
G7, $45-$80
Harney Co., OR

Obsidian
G9, $125-$200
Harney Co., OR

Obsidian
G7, $50-$90
Silver Lake, OR

Obsidian
G6, $40-$70
Harney Co., OR

G5, $50-$90
Harney Co., OR

G6, $25-$45
Cent. OR

Agatized petrified wood

Tip wear

Obsidian

"Fox Ear" form

Obsidian

Jasper

Obsidian

G6, $50-$90
Harney Co., OR

G8, $60-$110
Silver Lake, OR

G8, $65-$125
Harney Co., OR

G6, $40-$70
OR

G8, $65-$115
Fort Rock Valley, OR

G10, $350-$600
OR

Basalt
G8, $150-$250
Black Rock Desert, NV

Red basalt
G10, $200-$350
WA

Obsidian

Obsidian

Gray obsidian

Obsidian

Basalt

Drill form

G8, $80-$150
Harney Co., OR

G8, $60-$115
Harney Co., OR

G8, $50-$90
Lake Co., OR

G7, $50-$90
Tule Lake, CA

G6, $40-$70
Harney Co., OR

G6, $30-$50
Columbia Riv., OR

Obsidian

"Fox Ear" form

Obsidian

G7, $125-$200
Harney Co., OR

G8, $125-$200
OR

G9, $300-$550
Crump Lake, Warner Valley, OR

G8, $90-$175
Harney Co., OR

G6, $65-$125
Harney Co., OR

Basalt

"Fox Ear" form

Obsidian

Obsidian

G9, $250-$400
Harney Co., OR

G8, $250-$450
Warner Valley, OR

G9, $275-$500
Lakeview, OR

G9, $250-$400
Silver Lake, OR

G10, $350-$600
Sou. OR

FW

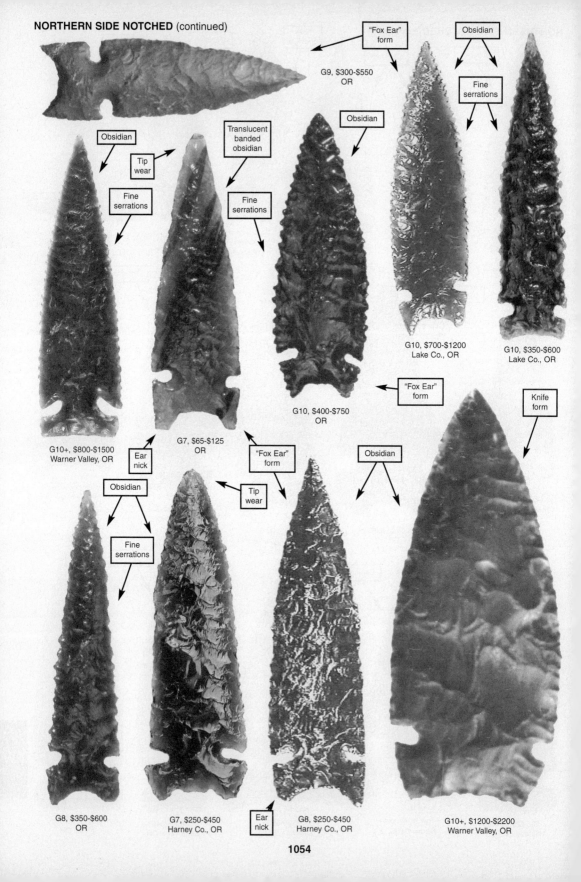

NORTHERN SIDE NOTCHED (continued)

"Fox Ear" form

G9, $300-$550
OR

Obsidian

Fine serrations

Obsidian

Tip wear

Obsidian

Translucent banded obsidian

Fine serrations

Fine serrations

Obsidian

G10, $700-$1200
Lake Co., OR

G10, $350-$600
Lake Co., OR

G10+, $800-$1500
Warner Valley, OR

G7, $65-$125
OR

Ear nick

G10, $400-$750
OR

"Fox Ear" form

Knife form

Obsidian

Fine serrations

"Fox Ear" form

Tip wear

Obsidian

G8, $350-$600
OR

G7, $250-$450
Harney Co., OR

Ear nick

G8, $250-$450
Harney Co., OR

G10+, $1200-$2200
Warner Valley, OR

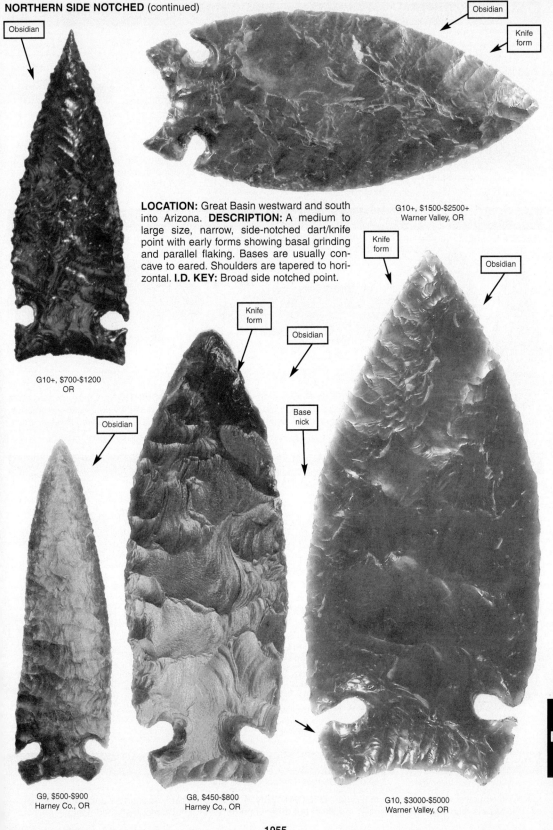

Obsidian

Obsidian

Knife form

LOCATION: Great Basin westward and south into Arizona. **DESCRIPTION:** A medium to large size, narrow, side-notched dart/knife point with early forms showing basal grinding and parallel flaking. Bases are usually concave to eared. Shoulders are tapered to horizontal. **I.D. KEY:** Broad side notched point.

G10+, $1500-$2500+
Warner Valley, OR

Knife form

Obsidian

G10+, $700-$1200
OR

Knife form

Obsidian

Base nick

Obsidian

G9, $500-$900
Harney Co., OR

G8, $450-$800
Harney Co., OR

G10, $3000-$5000
Warner Valley, OR

FW

NOTTOWAY - Historic Phase, 300 - 160 B. P.

(Also see Merrybell, Rose Springs & Tucannon)

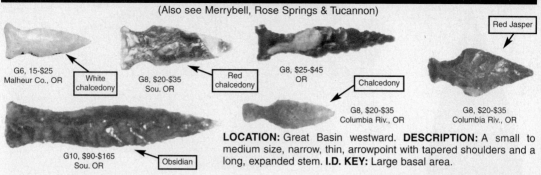

Red Jasper

G6, 15-$25
Malheur Co., OR

White chalcedony

G8, $20-$35
Sou. OR

Red chalcedony

G8, $25-$45
OR

Chalcedony

G8, $20-$35
Columbia Riv., OR

G8, $20-$35
Columbia Riv., OR

G10, $90-$165
Sou. OR

Obsidian

LOCATION: Great Basin westward. **DESCRIPTION:** A small to medium size, narrow, thin, arrowpoint with tapered shoulders and a long, expanded stem. **I.D. KEY:** Large basal area.

OCHOCO STEMMED - Late Archaic to Developmental Phase, 2500 - 1500 B.P.

(Also see Parman and Rabbit Island)

Obsidian

G8, $25-$40
Sou. OR

G6, $15-$25
Cent. OR

G6, $12-$20
Sou. OR

G8, $15-$30
Lake Co., OR

LOCATION: John Day River watershed in Oregon. **DESCRIPTION:** A medium size point with an elongated, triangular blade. Stem is straight sided to slightly contracting to bulbous. Looks like late *Parmans*, but slightly later in age. Possibly related to the *Rabbit Island* point.

OKANOGAN KNIFE - Early to mid-Archaic, 8000 - 4000 B. P.

(Also see Coquille Knife & Paleo Knife)

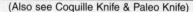

Petrified wood

G5, $8-$15
Columb. Riv., OR

G7, $70-$100
Columbia Riv., WA

LOCATION: Great Basin westward. **DESCRIPTION:** A small to large size, narrow, lanceolate knife with a convex base. Stems are unusuably long and heavily ground. **I.D. KEY:** The slight single shoulder on pristine specimens. Resharpened shoulderless points can be identified by the length of the ground stem.

Broken & glued

Petrified wood

G2, $50-$90
Columbia Riv., WA

ONE-QUE - Developmental to Historic Phase, 1320 - 1000 B. P.

(Also see Dagger, Diamond Back and Klickitat)

LOCATION: Lower Columbia River in Oregon. **DESCRIPTION:** A small to medium size, arrow point with side notches. The base is diamond shaped, similar to Klikitat but rougher made. **I.D. KEY:** Diamond shaped base.

ONE QUE (continued)

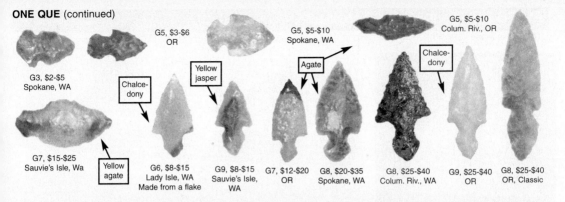

G3, $2-$5
Spokane, WA

G5, $3-$6
OR

G5, $5-$10
Spokane, WA

G5, $5-$10
Colum. Riv., OR

Yellow jasper

Agate

Chalce-dony

G7, $15-$25
Sauvie's Isle, Wa

Yellow agate

Chalce-dony

G6, $8-$15
Lady Isle, WA
Made from a flake

G9, $8-$15
Sauvie's Isle,
WA

G7, $12-$20
OR

G8, $20-$35
Spokane, WA

G8, $25-$40
Colum. Riv., WA

G9, $25-$40
OR

G8, $25-$40
OR, Classic

OWL CAVE - Late Paleo, 9500 - 8000 B. P.

(Also see Alder Complex, Cody Complex, Haskett, Humboldt Triangular, Pryor Stemmed)

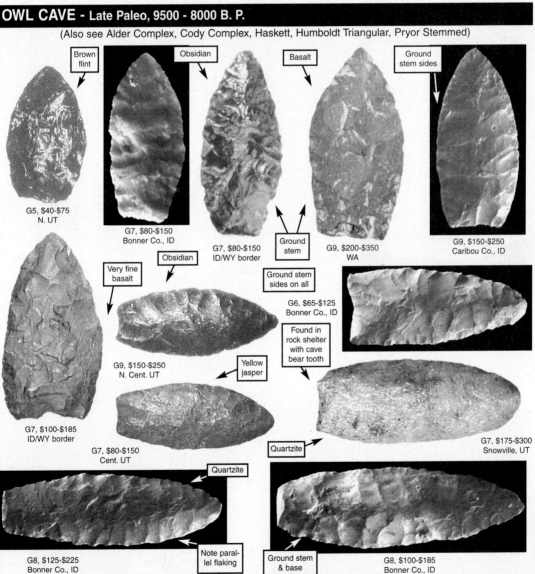

Brown flint

Obsidian

Basalt

Ground stem sides

G5, $40-$75
N. UT

G7, $80-$150
Bonner Co., ID

Ground stem

G7, $80-$150
ID/WY border

G9, $200-$350
WA

G9, $150-$250
Caribou Co., ID

Very fine basalt

Obsidian

Ground stem sides on all

G6, $65-$125
Bonner Co., ID

G9, $150-$250
N. Cent. UT

Yellow jasper

Found in rock shelter with cave bear tooth

G7, $100-$185
ID/WY border

G7, $80-$150
Cent. UT

Quartzite

G7, $175-$300
Snowville, UT

Quartzite

G8, $125-$225
Bonner Co., ID

Note paral-lel flaking

Ground stem & base

G8, $100-$185
Bonner Co., ID

FW

LOCATION: Oregon, Nevada, Idaho, Wyoming. The Wasden Site in southern Idaho is the type area. **DESCRIPTION:** A medium size, narrow, lanceolate point with a straight to concave base. Blade edges are convex. Basal sides are ground. Very similar to and can be confused with small *Agate Basin* points. **I.D. KEY:** Basal form and flaking style.

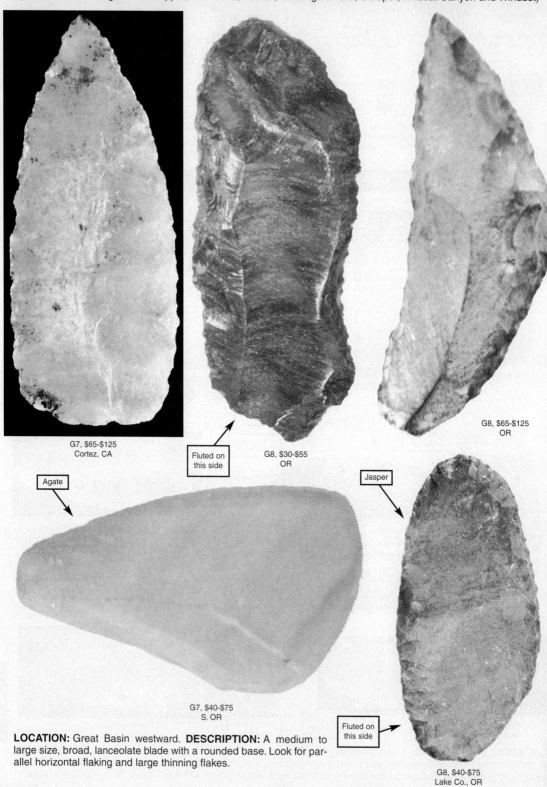

PALEO KNIFE - Paleo, 10,000 - 8000 B. P.

(Also see Base Tang Knife, Chopper, Hand Axe, Lancet, Okanogan Knife, Scraper, Wildcat Canyon and Windust)

G7, $65-$125
Cortez, CA

Fluted on
this side

G8, $30-$55
OR

G8, $65-$125
OR

Agate

Jasper

G7, $40-$75
S. OR

Fluted on
this side

G8, $40-$75
Lake Co., OR

LOCATION: Great Basin westward. **DESCRIPTION:** A medium to large size, broad, lanceolate blade with a rounded base. Look for parallel horizontal flaking and large thinning flakes.

PANOCHE - Historic, 300 - 200 B. P.

(Also see Bear River, Cold Springs, Desert, Lake River, Sauvie's Island, Uinta)

G5, $2-$5

G5, $5-$10

All Monterey Co., CA

G6, $8-$15

G6, $12-$20

LOCATION: Panoche Reservoir in Fresno Co., California. **DESCRIPTION:** A small size, thin side notched arrow point with a straight to concave base. Notches are larger than other *Desert Side Notched* forms that they are related. Similar to *Salado* found further East.

PARMAN - Early Archaic, 10,500 - 9000 B. P.

(Also see Cougar Mountain, Early Stemmed, Lake Mohave, Lind Coulee & Silver Lake)

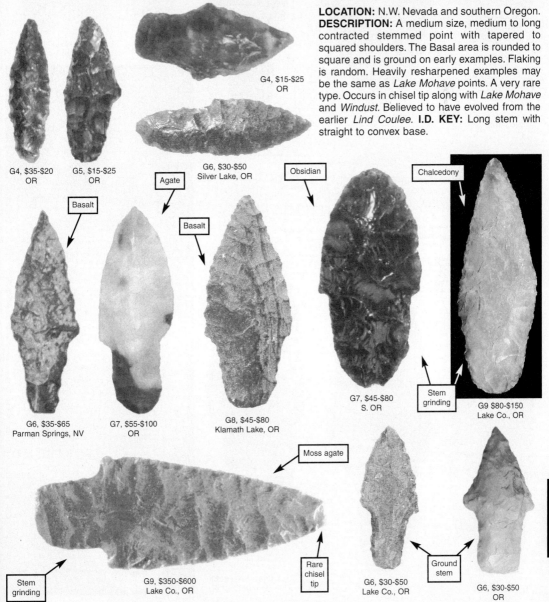

LOCATION: N.W. Nevada and southern Oregon. **DESCRIPTION:** A medium size, medium to long contracted stemmed point with tapered to squared shoulders. The Basal area is rounded to square and is ground on early examples. Flaking is random. Heavily resharpened examples may be the same as *Lake Mohave* points. A very rare type. Occurs in chisel tip along with *Lake Mohave* and *Windust*. Believed to have evolved from the earlier *Lind Coulee*. **I.D. KEY:** Long stem with straight to convex base.

G4, $15-$25
OR

G4, $35-$20
OR

G5, $15-$25
OR

Agate

G6, $30-$50
Silver Lake, OR

Obsidian

Chalcedony

Basalt

Basalt

G6, $35-$65
Parman Springs, NV

G7, $55-$100
OR

G8, $45-$80
Klamath Lake, OR

G7, $45-$80
S. OR

Stem grinding

G9 $80-$150
Lake Co., OR

Moss agate

Stem grinding

G9, $350-$600
Lake Co., OR

Rare chisel tip

Ground stem

G6, $30-$50
Lake Co., OR

G6, $30-$50
OR

FW

1059

PARMAN (continued)

Rare chisel tip

Obsidian

Basalt

Obsidian

Rare chisel tip

Ground stem

Ground stem

G6, $55-$100
Lake Co., OR

G9, $150-$275
Lake Co., OR

G9, $200-$350
Cougar Mtn., OR

G9, $200-$350
Lake Co., OR

G9, $300-$550
Lake Co., OR

Obsidian

Knife form

G8, $125-$200
Lake Co., OR

Late in the series

Basalt

Broken & glued

Obsidian

G6, $80-$150
S. OR

G4, $80-$150
OR

G6, $125-$200
S. OR

G10+, $700-$1200
Harney Co., OR

1060

PARMAN (continued)

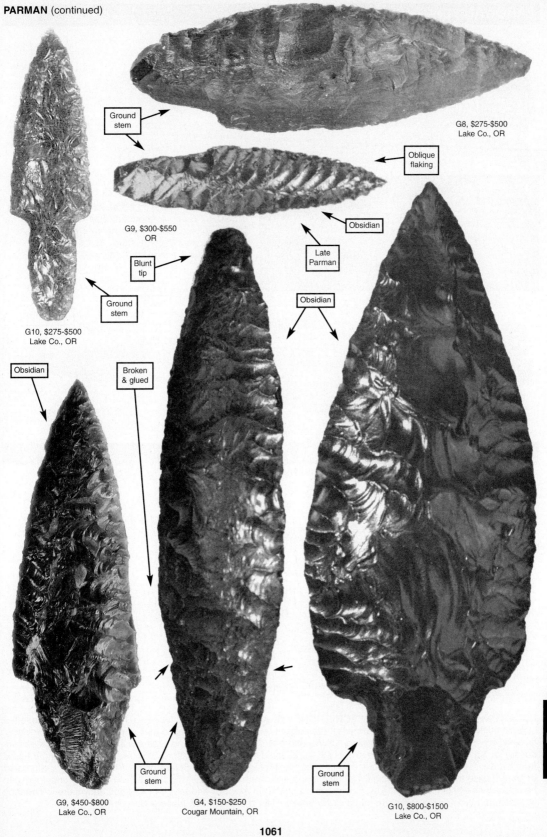

Ground stem

G8, $275-$500
Lake Co., OR

Oblique flaking

Obsidian

G9, $300-$550
OR

Late Parman

Blunt tip

Obsidian

Ground stem

G10, $275-$500
Lake Co., OR

Obsidian

Broken & glued

Ground stem

G9, $450-$800
Lake Co., OR

Ground stem

G4, $150-$250
Cougar Mountain, OR

Ground stem

G10, $800-$1500
Lake Co., OR

FW

PAROWAN - Developmental Phase, 1300 - 800 B. P.

(Also see Gatecliff, Gypsum Cave, Rabbit Island)

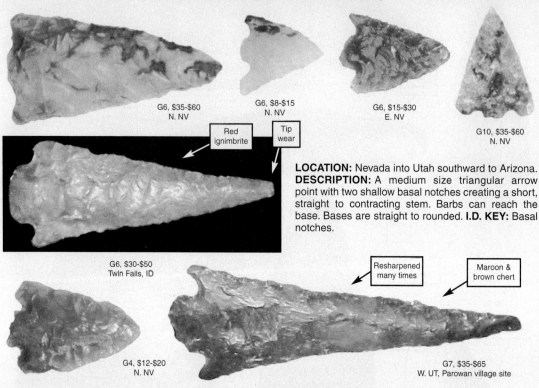

G6, $35-$60
N. NV

G6, $8-$15
N. NV

G6, $15-$30
E. NV

G10, $35-$60
N. NV

Red ignimbrite

Tip wear

LOCATION: Nevada into Utah southward to Arizona. **DESCRIPTION:** A medium size triangular arrow point with two shallow basal notches creating a short, straight to contracting stem. Barbs can reach the base. Bases are straight to rounded. **I.D. KEY:** Basal notches.

G6, $30-$50
Twln Falls, ID

Resharpened many times

Maroon & brown chert

G4, $12-$20
N. NV

G7, $35-$65
W. UT, Parowan village site

PAY PASO (N.W.) - Paleo, 9500 - 8600 B. P.

(Also see Fell's Cave (N.W.), Midland, Milnesand, Pryor Stemmed & Spedis)

Ground stem

Burinated tip

Ground stem

Chalc.

Agate

Ground stem

Ground stem

Ground stem

G6, $15-$25
Sauvie's Isle, OR

G6, $25-$40
Chehalis, WA

G1, $8-$15
The Dalles, OR
Broken

G9, $80-$150
WA

G10, $150-$250
OR

G6, $125-$200
The Dalles, OR

LOCATION: Oregon & Washington. **DESCRIPTION:** This is a South American type found with all diagonistics in the Columbia River Valley and the Chehalis River drainage. It is a well flaked, small to medium sized dart knife previously identified as *Pryor* or *Pryor*-like. Location (N.W.) and basal thinning technique separate the two types. This point is basally thinned by steeply flaking one side of the basal and then using that platform to drive one or more longer flakes from the opposing side. This technique occurs on some *Midland* and some *Spedis* points. This type has a bifurcated or "eared" base and stem that is usually incurvate and well ground. Cross sections are lenticular. Blade shoulders can be obtuse to barbed. These points are not well-known in North America and may be re-named after more information is gathered. *Pryor* or Pryor-like are found in the Snake River drainage in W. Idaho & S.E. Oregon.

PERFORATOR - Archaic to Historic, 9000 - 400 B. P.

(Also see Drill, Graver and Scraper)

Obsidian

Agate

Obsidian

G5, $1-$3
OR

G5, $1-$2
OR

G5, $1-$2
WA

G5, $1-$2
OR

G5, $1-$2
OR

Red
jasper

Hells
Canyon
Corner
notched

Jasper

G10, $20-$35
OR

G5, $1-$2
OR

G5, $1-$2
OR

G5, $1-$3
OR

G5, $1-$3
OR

G7, $3-$6
Columbia Riv., WA

LOCATION: Archaic and Woodland sites everywhere. **DESCRIPTION:** A jabbing projection at the tip would qualify for the type. It is believed that *perforators* were used for tattooing, incising or to punch holes in leather or other materials or objects. Paleo peoples used Gravers for the same purpose. All Archaic and Woodland cultures converted their points into this type. Therefore, most point types could occur in this form, although many examples were made from scratch. **I.D. KEY:** Long , slender tip.

PIECES ESQUILLEES - Paleo to Historic, 10,000 - 400 B. P.

(Also see Drill, Graver and Scraper)

LOCATION: Oregon & Washington **DESCRIPTION:** A splitting wedge. Some in the old world may be 30,000 years old. The bottom cutting edge should be beveled or V shaped. The opposing edge or hammering surface should be flattened or knobbed enough to receive a hammer blow. The larger pieces could be used to split house timbers or planks, or perhaps spear shafts and foreshafts. The smaller pieces could be used to split bone for needles and arrow or small dart points. Look for hammer scars on the edge opposing the "V" or beveled edge. **I.D. KEY:** Wedge form.

G5, $1-$3
WA

Red/brown
jasper

Basalt

Blade
edge

G6, $2-$5
Vancouver, WA

Hammer
strokes

G6, $5-$10
Columbia Riv., OR

PINTO BASIN - Early to late Archaic, 8000 - 2650 B. P.

(Also see Eastgate Bifurcated, Elko, Gatecliff, Humboldt and Rose Valley)

PINTO BASIN (continued)

Obsidian

G3, $1-3
Harney Co., OR

G8, $12-$20
Lake Co., OR

G5, $2-$5
Humboldt Co., NV

G6, $2-$5
Santa Barbara Co., CA

G5, $2-$5
Harney Co., OR

Jasper

G6, $5-$10
OR

Obsidian

G7, $12-$20
Harney Co., OR

Obsidian

G8, $25-$40
Warner Valley, OR

G8, $25-$45
Warner Valley, OR

G7, $12-$20
OR

Obsidian

G7, $12-$20
Harney Co., OR

Obsidian

G9, $25-$40
Harney Co., OR

G7, $12-$20
Cent. OR

Obsidian

Obsidian

Obsidian

Obsidian

G7, $25-$40
S. OR

G7, $15-$30
Warner Valley, OR

G8, $25-$30
Cent. OR

G10, $80-$150
Warner Valley, OR

G9, $30-$50
Harney Co., OR

G8, $25-$40
Warner Valley, OR

Obsidian

Obsidian

Obsidian

G8, $30-$55
Warner Valley, OR

G9, $35-$65
Warner Valley, OR

G8, $25-$45
OR

G8, $25-$45
OR

G9, $45-$80
Warner Valley, OR

LOCATION: Great Basin states. **DESCRIPTION:** A medium to large sized, narrow, auriculate point. Shoulders can be tapered, horizontal or barbed. Bases are either deeply bifurcated with parallel to expanding ears or tapered with a concave basal edge. The bifurcated form may prove to be *Gatecliff* forms. Most examples show excellent flaking. **I.D. KEY:** Long pointed ears; tapered base.

1064

PINTO BASIN (continued)

Obsidian

G7, $25-$45
Christmas Vall., OR

Obsidian

G7, $25-$45
S. OR

Obsidian

G8, $40-$75
Lake Co., OR

Obsidian

G8, $35-$65
Harney Co., OR

G9, $65-$125
OR

Obsidian

G9, $175-$300
Warner Valley, OR

G8, $55-$100
OR

Basalt

G7, $25-$45
Sou. CA

Obsidian

G8, $65-$115
S. OR

Obsidian

G9, $65-$125
S. OR

Obsidian

Ground
stem

G9, $125-$200
OR

Obsidian

G8, $65-$125
Lake Co., OR

Ground
stem

G10, $250-$400
OR

Ground
stem

G10, $175-$300
Snake Riv., OR

Obsidian

G8, $125-$200
Lake Co., OR

1065

FW

PINTO BASIN SLOPING SHOULDER - Early to late Archaic 8000 - 3000 B. P.

(Also see Eastgate Bifurcated, Elko, Gatecliff, Humboldt and Windust)

Obsidian

G7, $25-$45
Humboldt Co., NV

Obsidian

Basalt

G6, $20-$35
Duck Flat, OR

Obsidian

G7, $30-$50
Lake Co., OR

G9, $65-$125
Warner Valley, OR

Obsidian

G5, $12-$20
S. OR

Obsidian

G8, $45-$80
S. OR

Obsidian

G8, $55-$100
Warner Valley, OR

Obsidian

Black
obsidian

LOCATION: Great Basin states. **DESCRIPTION:** The typical *Pinto Basin* point, but with a distinctive single shoulder on one side and a convex blade edge on the opposite side. **Note:** This may later prove to be a late *Windust* cross-type.

G7, $40-$70
Warner Valley, OR

G9, $250-$400
Cent. OR

G10, $275-$500
Lake Co., OR

Agate

Obsidian

G9, $175-$300
Lake Co., OR

Obsidian

G7, $45-$85
Lake Co., OR

Shoulder
nick

G9, $80-$150
Lake Co., OR

G9, $200-$350
Lake Co., OR

PIQUNIN - Classic to Historic Phase, 700 - 150 B. P.

(Also see Cold Springs, Elko Eared, Merrybell, Panoche and Sauvie's Island)

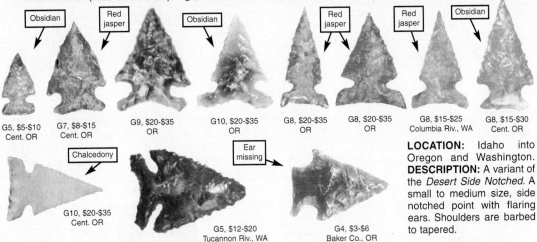

Obsidian

Red jasper

Obsidian

Red jasper

Red jasper

Obsidian

G5, $5-$10
Cent. OR

G7, $8-$15
Cent. OR

G9, $20-$35
OR

G10, $20-$35
OR

G8, $20-$35
OR

G8, $20-$35
OR

G8, $15-$25
Columbia Riv., WA

G8, $15-$30
Cent. OR

Chalcedony

G10, $20-$35
Cent. OR

Ear missing

G5, $12-$20
Tucannon Riv., WA

G4, $3-$6
Baker Co., OR

LOCATION: Idaho into Oregon and Washington. **DESCRIPTION:** A variant of the *Desert Side Notched*. A small to medium size, side notched point with flaring ears. Shoulders are barbed to tapered.

PISMO (see Rabbit Island)

PLAINVIEW - Late Paleo, 10,000 - 7000 B. P.

(Also see Alder Complex, Black Rock Concave, Clovis, Goshen, Midland, Milnesand, Spedis)

Basalt

Obsidian

Petrified wood

Restored base

Agate

Obsidian

G6, $55-$100
Columbia Riv., OR

G8, $55-$100
Columbia Riv., WA

G9, $125-$200
S. OR

G7, $80-$150
Columbia Riv., WA

G3, $55-$100
S. OR

G7, $250-$400
Columbia Riv., WA

Petrified wood

Ground

Obsidian

Very thin

G10, $275-$500
WA

G8, $200-$350
Columbia Riv., OR

Jasper

Tip wear

G8, $250-$450
OR

LOCATION: Mexico northward through the plains states into the Great Basin. **DESCRIPTION:** A medium size, thin, lanceolate point with usually parallel sides and a concave base that is ground. Some examples are thinned or fluted and is believed to be related to the earlier *Clovis* type. Flaking is of high quality and can be collateral to oblique transverse.

FW

PLATEAU PENTAGONAL - Classic Phase, 600 - 400 B. P.

(Related to Columbia Mule Ear; see Chumash Tools, Fremont Triangular, Wahmuza and Wildcat Canyon)

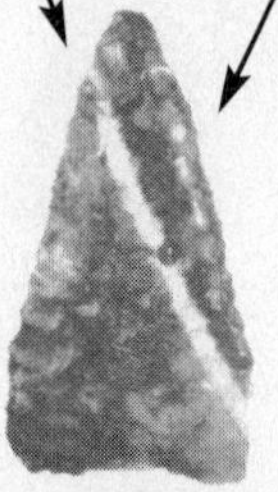
Agate
Beveled
G5, $8-$15
Owyhee Co., ID

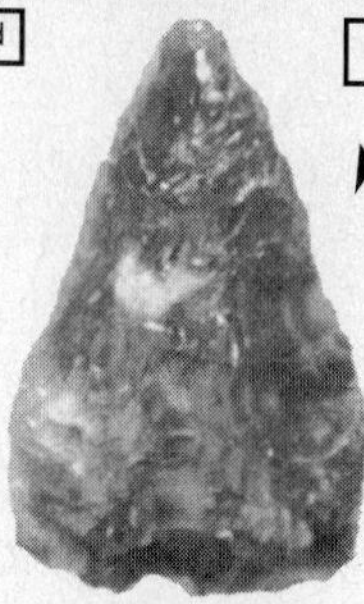
Gem
G5, $12-$20
WA

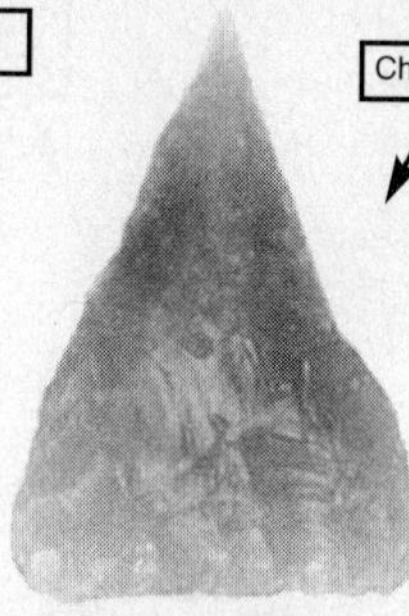
Chalcedony
G6, $15-$25
Umatilla, OR

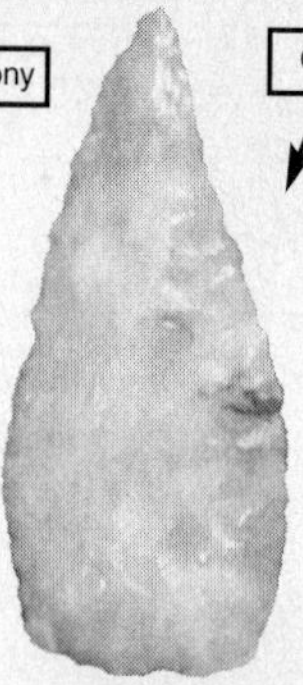
Gem
G7, $15-$25
N. OR

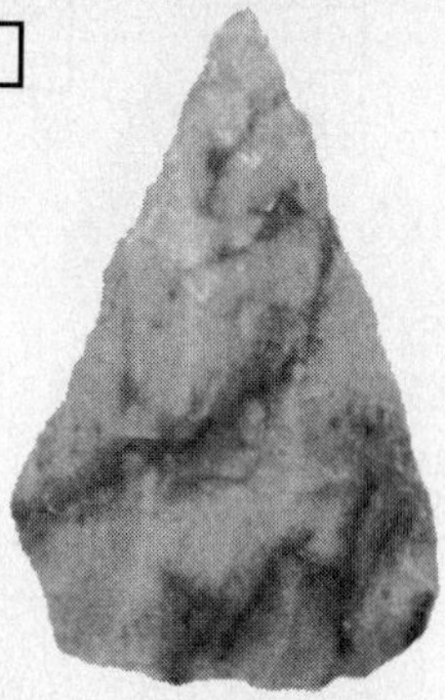
G7, $15-$30
OR

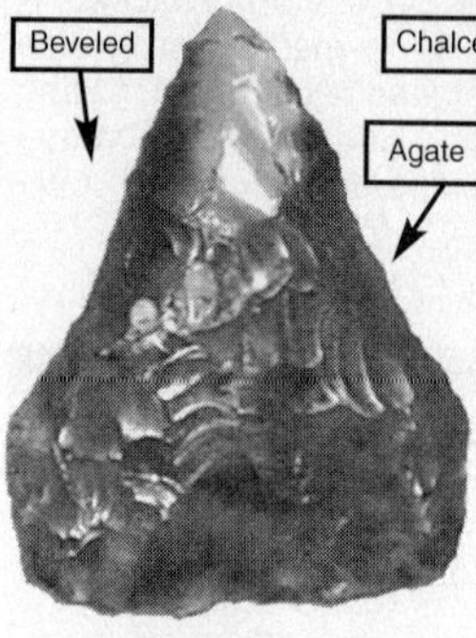
Beveled
Agate
G7, $55-$100
E. Columbia Riv., OR

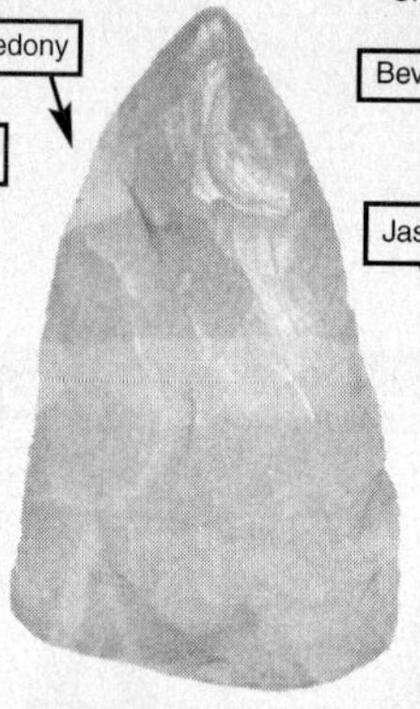
Chalcedony
G7, $30-$50
WA

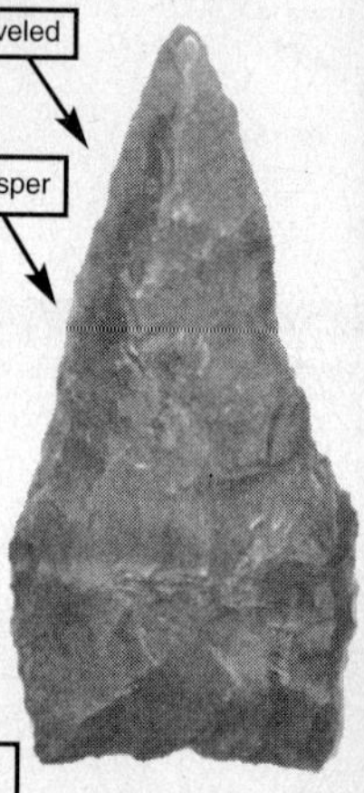
Beveled
Jasper
G7, $35-$60
OR

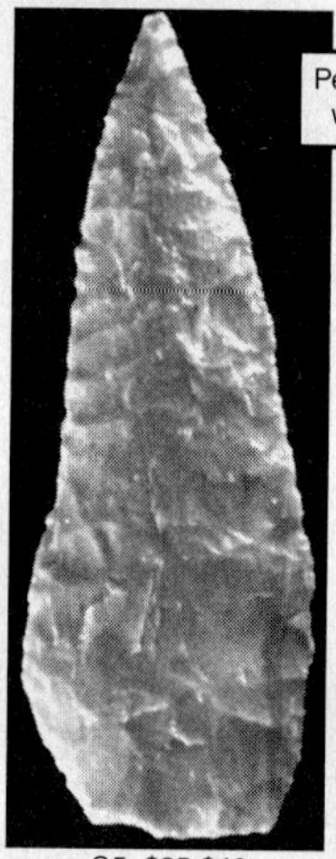
G5, $25-$40
Wasco Co., OR

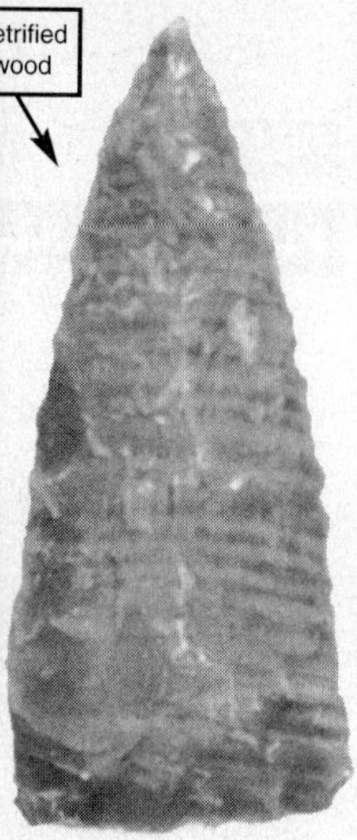
Petrified wood
G7, $40-$70
5 Mile Locks,
OR

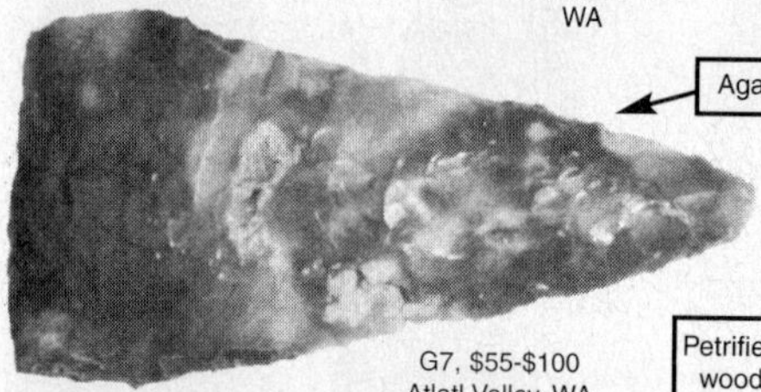
Agate
G7, $55-$100
Atlatl Valley, WA

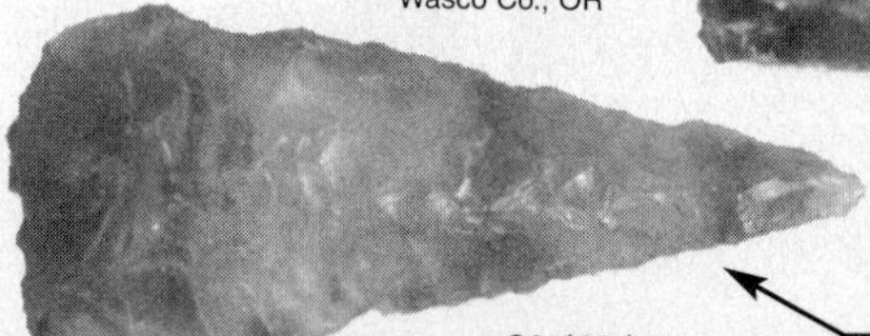
Agate
G6, $25-$40
OR

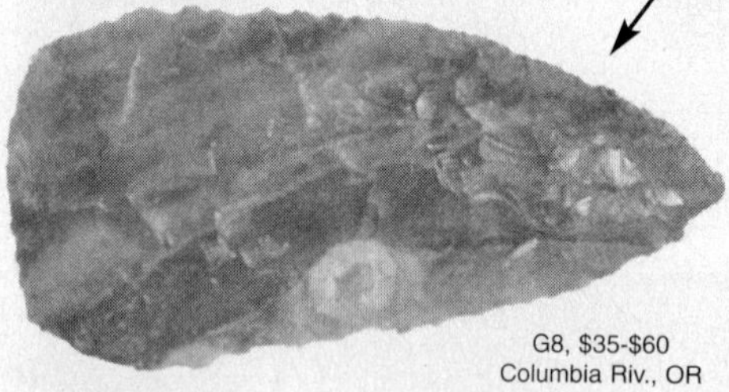
Petrified wood
G8, $35-$60
Columbia Riv., OR

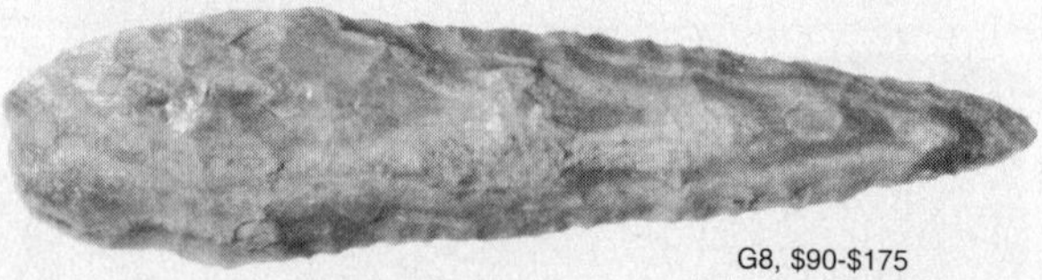
G8, $90-$175
Lake Pend Oreill, ID

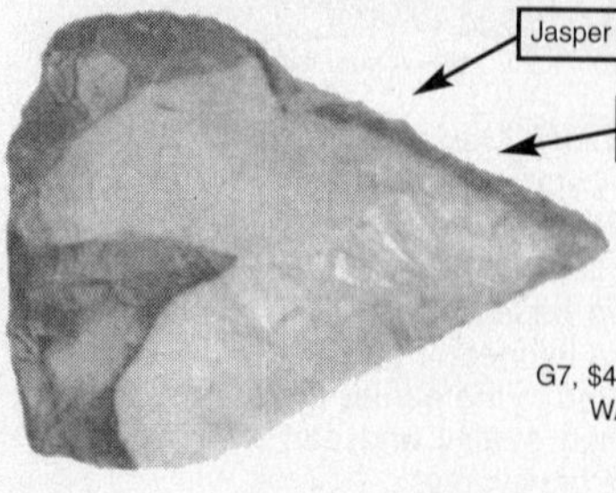
Jasper
Beveled
G7, $40-$75
WA

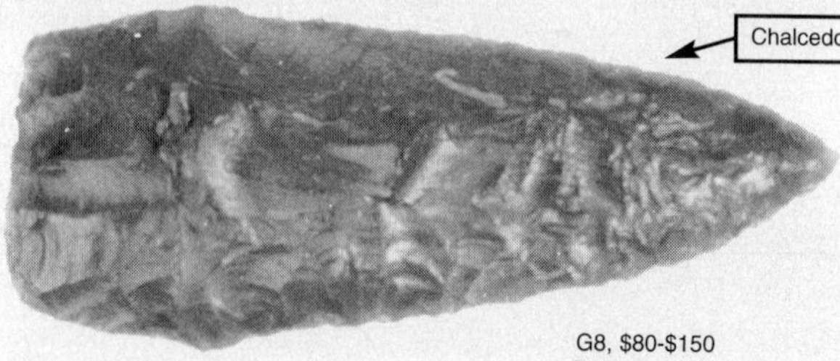
Chalcedony
G8, $80-$150
Patterson, WA

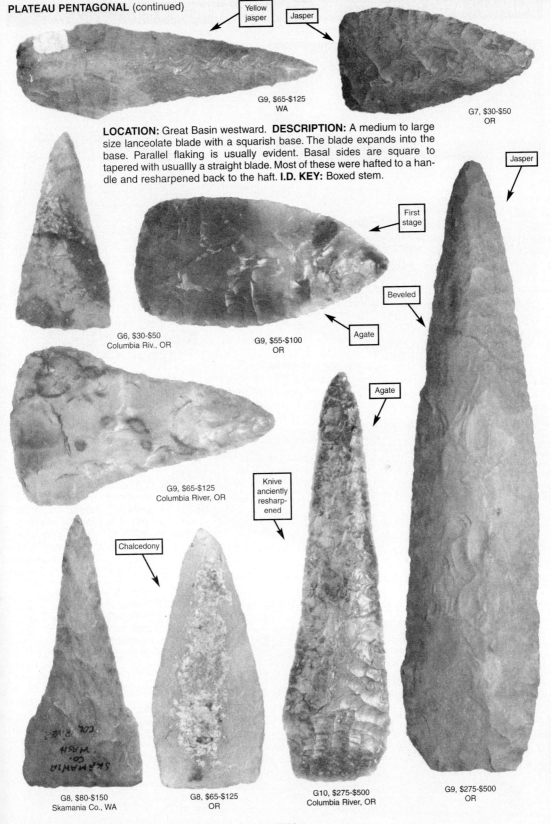

PLATEAU PENTAGONAL (continued)

Yellow jasper

Jasper

G9, $65-$125
WA

G7, $30-$50
OR

LOCATION: Great Basin westward. **DESCRIPTION:** A medium to large size lanceolate blade with a squarish base. The blade expands into the base. Parallel flaking is usually evident. Basal sides are square to tapered with usuallly a straight blade. Most of these were hafted to a handle and resharpened back to the haft. **I.D. KEY:** Boxed stem.

Jasper

First stage

Beveled

G6, $30-$50
Columbia Riv., OR

Agate

G9, $55-$100
OR

Agate

G9, $65-$125
Columbia River, OR

Knive anciently resharpened

Chalcedony

G8, $80-$150
Skamania Co., WA

G8, $65-$125
OR

G10, $275-$500
Columbia River, OR

G9, $275-$500
OR

FW

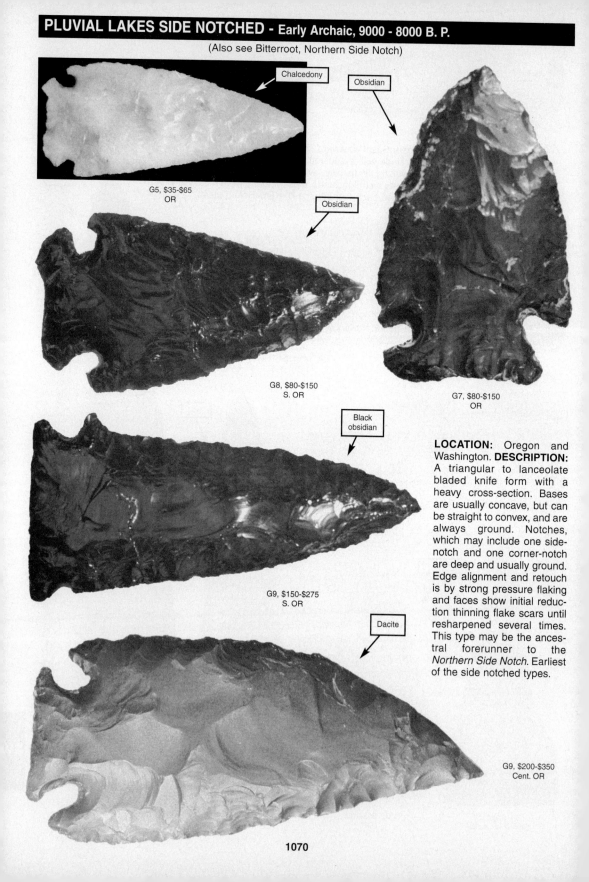

PLUVIAL LAKES SIDE NOTCHED - Early Archaic, 9000 - 8000 B. P.

(Also see Bitterroot, Northern Side Notch)

Chalcedony

Obsidian

G5, $35-$65
OR

Obsidian

G8, $80-$150
S. OR

G7, $80-$150
OR

Black
obsidian

G9, $150-$275
S. OR

Dacite

G9, $200-$350
Cent. OR

LOCATION: Oregon and Washington. **DESCRIPTION:** A triangular to lanceolate bladed knife form with a heavy cross-section. Bases are usually concave, but can be straight to convex, and are always ground. Notches, which may include one side-notch and one corner-notch are deep and usually ground. Edge alignment and retouch is by strong pressure flaking and faces show initial reduction thinning flake scars until resharpened several times. This type may be the ancestral forerunner to the *Northern Side Notch*. Earliest of the side notched types.

POINT SAL BARBED - Late Archaic to Developmental Phase, 3500 - 1500 B. P.

(Also see Columbia Plateau, Contra Costa, Coquille, Gunther, Rabbit Island, Sierra Contracting Stem & Yana)

LOCATION: California coast. **DESCRIPTION:** A medium to large size, triangular point with drooping barbs and a narrow, contracting stem that is rounded to pointed. Blade edges are recurved. The distal end is acuminate.

G9, $80-$150
Santa Barbara Co., CA

PRIEST RAPIDS - Late Archaic to Trans. Phase, 3000 - 1750 B.P.

(Also see Hells Canyon, Merrybell, Quilomene Bar)

Jasper

Gem

Red jasper

Classic example

Thinned heavily in center

G8, $35-$60
Columbia Riv., OR

G7, $30-$50
WA

G9, $55-$100
OR

G8, $35-$75
Priest Rapids, WA

G10, $150-$275
Celilo Falls, OR

LOCATION: Columbia River basin, Oregon & Priest Rapids, WA. **DESCRIPTION:** A medium size, short stemmed to basal notched point with drooping shoulders that turn inward and a rounded stem that is notched or well-thinned. A very rare type with only a few examples known.

PRYOR STEMMED - Early Archaic, 8000 - 7000 B. P.

(Also see Alder Complex, Eden, Humboldt Constricted, Owl Cave, Parman, Pay Paso N.W., Shaniko Stemmed)

Gem

G8, $60-$110
OR

G9, $75-$145
Lake Pend Oreill, ID

G7, $60-$110
Caribou Co., ID

Tip nick

Ground stem

These two may prove to be Lovel points

G6, $35-$60
Hogup Cave, N.W. UT, dated to 9755 B.P.

Tip wear

Very thin w/ground stem

G7, $35-$65
Lake Co., OR

G7, $30-$50
OR

G7, $175-$300
Hogup Cave, N.W. UT, dated to 9755 yrs. old

G6, $30-$50
Lake Co., OR

Broken & glued ear

FW

PRYOR STEMMED (continued)

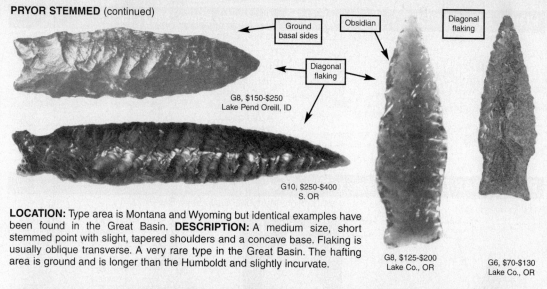

Ground basal sides

Obsidian

Diagonal flaking

Diagonal flaking

G8, $150-$250
Lake Pend Oreill, ID

G10, $250-$400
S. OR

LOCATION: Type area is Montana and Wyoming but identical examples have been found in the Great Basin. **DESCRIPTION:** A medium size, short stemmed point with slight, tapered shoulders and a concave base. Flaking is usually oblique transverse. A very rare type in the Great Basin. The hafting area is ground and is longer than the Humboldt and slightly incurvate.

G8, $125-$200
Lake Co., OR

G6, $70-$130
Lake Co., OR

QUILOMENE BAR - Late Archaic to Transitional Phase, 3000 - 2000 B. P.

(Also see Elko Corner Notched & Hell's Canyon)

Chalcedony

Agate

Petrified wood

G4, $5-$15
OR

G5, $15-$30
OR

G5, $15-$30
Columbia Riv., OR

G9, $55-$100
Columbia Riv., OR

G10, $45-$85
Priest Rapids, WA

Chalcedony

Agate

Gem wastcoite

Obsidian

Jasper

G6, $35-$60
Columbia Riv., OR

G7, $45-$85
OR

Resharpened several times

G9, 200-$375
Columbia Riv., OR

G10, $175-$325
OR

G9, $150-$250
Columbia Riv., OR

G10, $250-$425
Priest Rapids, Wa

Agate

Jasper

G10, $200-$375
Walla Walla, WA

LOCATION: Columbia River in Oregon and Washington. **DESCRIPTION:** A medium size base to corner notched point. The classic form has a convex base but can be straight to slightly concave. The stem is straight to expanded & the shoulders are squared

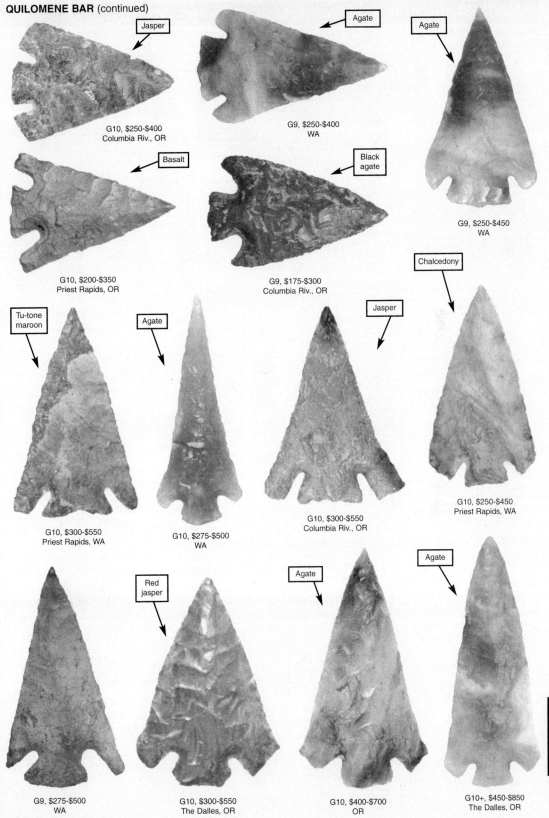

Jasper

G10, $250-$400
Columbia Riv., OR

Agate

G9, $250-$400
WA

Agate

G9, $250-$450
WA

Basalt

G10, $200-$350
Priest Rapids, OR

Black agate

G9, $175-$300
Columbia Riv., OR

Tu-tone maroon

G10, $300-$550
Priest Rapids, WA

Agate

G10, $275-$500
WA

Jasper

G10, $300-$550
Columbia Riv., OR

Chalcedony

G10, $250-$450
Priest Rapids, WA

G9, $275-$500
WA

Red jasper

G10, $300-$550
The Dalles, OR

Agate

G10, $400-$700
OR

Agate

G10+, $450-$850
The Dalles, OR

FW

RABBIT ISLAND ARROW - Classic to Historic Phase, 700 - 150 B. P.

(Also see Columbia Riv. PinStem, Coquille, Gatecliff, Gypsum Cave, Sauvie's Island Shoulder Notched, Rose Springs & Yana)

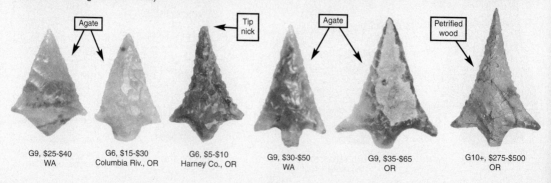

Chalc.

G5, $5-$10
OR

G5, $5-$10
Columbia
Riv., OR

Agate

G5, $5-$10
Columbia
Riv., OR

G8, $35-$65
Columbia
Riv., OR

Agate

G9, $55-$100
WA

Chalc.   Serrated edge

G9, $55-$100
OR

Agate

G8, $35-$65
Colum. Riv., OR

G8, $30-$50
Columbia
Riv., OR

Agate

G9, $55-$100
OR

Red agate

G5, $12-$20
Columbia Riv.,
OR

Red jasper

G9, $55-$100
Columbia
Riv., OR

Agate

G9, $55-$100
Columbia
Riv., OR

G5, $30-$50
Sauvie's Isle,
OR

G8, $25-$40
Columbia
Riv., OR

Chalce-dony

G8, 35-$55
Colum. Riv., OR

Obsidian

G9, $30-$55
Columbia
Riv., OR

G5, $25-$40
Sauvie's Isle,
OR

Red jasper

G8, $35-$60
Columbia Riv.,
OR

G8, $30-$55
OR

G8, $35-$60
OR

Obsidian

Red agate

G9, $80-$150
OR

Red agate

G9, $55-$100
OR

G9, $35-$60
OR

Yellow agate

G10, $200-$350
OR

G10, $175-$300
WA

Serrated edge

Agate

G10+, $250-$475
Rabbit Island, OR

Red agate

Gem

G9, $35-$60
Columb. Riv., OR

G10+, $250-$475
OR

LOCATION: Columbia River of Oregon and Washington. **DESCRIPTION: Dart:** A small to medium size, thin barbed point with a short, tapered base that can be pointed, to rounded. **Note:** This type is similar to the *Wallula* point which has a square stem; this type has a tapered stem. Evolved from the earlier dart point and was used to historic times.

RABBIT ISLAND DART - Transitional to Classic Phase, 2000 - 700 B. P.

(Also see Coquille, Gatecliff, Gypsum Cave, Point Sal Barbed, Rose Springs, Sauvie's Island Shoulder Notched, Sierra Contracting Stem & Yana)

Agate

G9, $25-$40
WA

G6, $15-$30
Columbia Riv., OR

Tip nick

G6, $5-$10
Harney Co., OR

Agate

G9, $30-$50
WA

G9, $35-$65
OR

Petrified wood

G10+, $275-$500
OR

RABBIT ISLAND DART (continued)

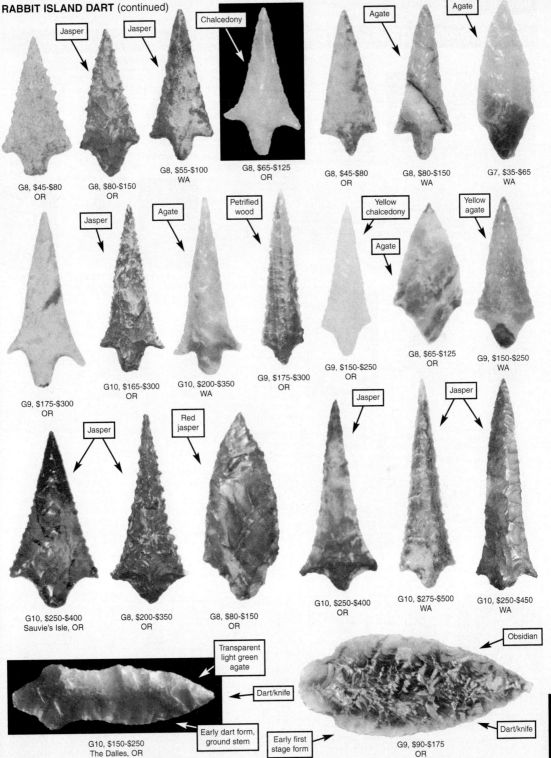

Jasper

G8, $45-$80
OR

Jasper

G8, $80-$150
OR

Jasper

G8, $55-$100
WA

Chalcedony

G8, $65-$125
OR

Agate

G8, $45-$80
OR

Agate

G8, $80-$150
WA

Agate

G7, $35-$65
WA

Jasper

G9, $175-$300
OR

Jasper

G10, $165-$300
OR

Agate

G10, $200-$350
WA

Petrified
wood

G9, $175-$300
OR

Yellow
chalcedony

Agate

G9, $150-$250
OR

G8, $65-$125
OR

Yellow
agate

G9, $150-$250
WA

Jasper

G10, $250-$400
Sauvie's Isle, OR

Jasper

Red
jasper

G8, $200-$350
OR

G8, $80-$150
OR

Jasper

G10, $250-$400
OR

Jasper

G10, $275-$500
WA

Jasper

G10, $250-$450
WA

Transparent
light green
agate

Dart/knife

G10, $150-$250
The Dalles, OR

Early dart form,
ground stem

Early first
stage form

Obsidian

Dart/knife

G9, $90-$175
OR

FW

LOCATION: Columbia River of Oregon and Washington. **DESCRIPTION:** A medium size, contracted stemmed point with tapered to horizontal, pointed shoulders and a short base that can be pointed or rounded. Early forms have a tapered stem with a straight base. Blade edges can be serrated. Also known as *Pismo.* **Note:** This type evolves into an arrow point in later times and lasted to the historic period.

1075

ROSE SPRINGS CORNER NOTCHED - Develop. to Classic Phase, 1600 - 600 B. P.

(Also see Columbia Plateau, Eastgate, Elko, Snake River & Wendover)

G5, $5-$10
OR

G7, $12-$20
OR

G8, $15-$30
OR

G8, $15-$25
Harney Co., OR

G8, $15-$25
Harney Co., OR

G8, $18-$30
OR

G9, $40-$70
Clearwater Co., ID

Opalite

G5, $18-$30
Owyhee Co., ID

Banded obsidian

G8, $20-$35
Owyhee Co., ID

G8, $20-$35
Lake Co., OR

G9, $25-$40
OR

G9, $30-$55
OR

G9, $30-$55
OR

Obsidian

G8, $30-$55
Sou. OR

G10, $30-$55
Grand Co., UT

G9, $30-$55
Harney Co., OR

G8, $25-$40
Lake Co., OR

Agate

G8, $25-$40
UT

G8, $30-$55
Central OR

Chalcedony

G9, $40-$75
OR

G9, $40-$75
OR

G8, $30-$55
Humboldt Co., NV

G9, $40-$75
OR

G9, $40-$75
Klamath Lake, OR

Obsidian

Obsidian

Knife

Red jasper

Obsidian

G9, $50-$90
Malheur Co., OR

G9, $50-$90
Sou. OR

G8, $55-$100
OR

G6, $15-$30
Humboldt Co., NV

G9, $80-$150
Lake Co., OR

G10, $150-$250
Oregon desert.

G10, $175-$300
Lake Co., OR

G9, $65-$125
Lake Co., OR

Chalcedony

Knife

Obsidian

Knife

Arrow

Red Obsidain

Arrow

Banded obsidian

Red jasper

G8, $50-$90
OR

G7, $25-$45
OR

G10, $80-$150
Oregon Desert.

G10, $80-$150
OR

LOCATION: S. OR into NV. **DESCRIPTION:** A small to medium size, thin, corner notched arrow point. Larger examples are knives/dart points. Shoulder tangs can be sharp to rounded. Same as *Columbia Plateau* points except where found.

G9, $80-$150
Sou. OR

G9, $80-$150
Lake Co., OR

G8, $50-$95
Sou. OR

G8, $50-$95
Sou. OR

ROSE SPRINGS CORNER NOTCHED (continued)

Jasper

G7, $30-$55
Harney Co., OR

G7, $40-$70
Columbia Riv., OR

Knife

G8, $45-$80
Harney Co., OR

Knife

G7, $35-$65
Humboldt Co., NV

Obsidian

G9, $55-$100
Humboldt Co., NV

Dart/knife

G8 $45-$80
Sou. OR

Dart

Arrow

G9, $100-$180
OR

Mottled obsidian

G9, $150-$250
S. OR

Lacks symmetry

Knife

Knife

Obsidian

Lacks symmetry

Dart

Red obsidian

Dart

Obsidian

Knife

Obsidian

Dart

No damage

G8, $50-$95
OR

G8, $90-$175
Lake Co., OR

G7 $30-$55
OR

G9, $150-$275
Lake Co., OR

G9, $200-$375
Lake Co., OR

G7, $40-$70
S. OR

ROSE SPRINGS SIDE NOTCHED - Developmental to Classic Phase, 1600 - 600 B. P.

(Also see Albion-Head, Coquille, Eastgate, Elko, Nottoway, Piqunin, & Wendover)

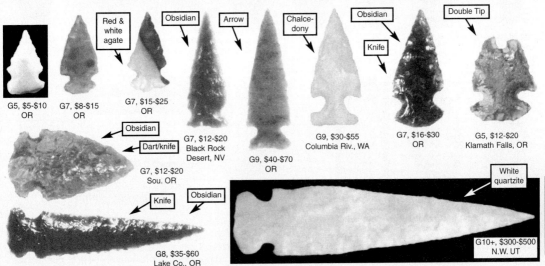

G5, $5-$10
OR

G7, $8-$15
OR

Red & white agate

G7, $15-$25
OR

Obsidian

Arrow

G7, $12-$20
Black Rock Desert, NV

G9, $40-$70
OR

Chalce-dony

G9, $30-$55
Columbia Riv., WA

Obsidian

Knife

G7, $16-$30
OR

Double Tip

G5, $12-$20
Klamath Falls, OR

Obsidian

Dart/knife

G7, $12-$20
Sou. OR

Knife

Obsidian

G8, $35-$60
Lake Co., OR

White quartzite

G10+, $300-$500
N.W. UT

FW

LOCATION: Great Basin westward. **DESCRIPTION:** A small to medium size, narrow, side notched arrow point. Larger examples are dart/knives. Notches are very distinctive in that they are very close to the base.

ROSE SPRINGS SIDE NOTCHED (continued)

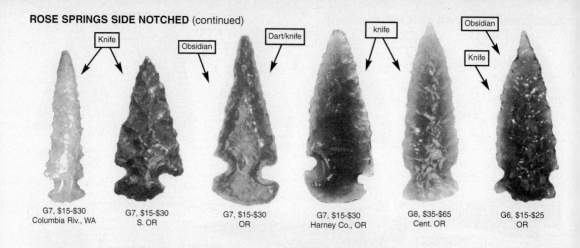

Knife

Obsidian

Dart/knife

knife

Obsidian

Knife

G7, $15-$30
Columbia Riv., WA

G7, $15-$30
S. OR

G7, $15-$30
OR

G7, $15-$30
Harney Co., OR

G8, $35-$65
Cent. OR

G6, $15-$25
OR

ROSE SPRINGS SLOPING SHOULDER - Develop. to Classic Phase, 1600 - 600 B. P.

(Also see Eastgate, Elko, Wallula & Wendover)

G8, $5-$10
S. E. OR

G7, $5-$10
Humboldt Co.,
NV

G5, $4-$8
Humboldt Co.,
NV

G8, $5-$10
S. E. OR

G8, $8-$15
Lake Co., OR

G7, $5-$10
Lake Co., OR

G5, $4-$8
Harney
Co., OR

G8, $6-$12
S. E. OR

G6, $5-$10
Harney
Co., OR

G6, $5-$10
Lake Co., OR

Obsidian

Obsidian

Obsidian

G6, $6-$12
Lake Co., OR

G5, $5-$10
Humboldt Co.,
NV

G8, $8-$15
S. E. OR

G8, $8-$15
S. E. OR

G6, $6-$12
S. E. OR

G7, $6-$12
S. E. OR

G8, $12-$20
Harney Co., OR

G6, $8-$15
Susanville, CA

Obsidian

Chalcedony

Chalcedony

Obsidian

Obsidian

G5, $5-$10
S. E. OR

Obsidian

G8, $12-$20
S. E. OR

G8, $12-$20
Harney Co., OR

G5, $8-$15
Lake Co., OR

G7, $8-$15
S. E. OR

G9, $12-$20
S. E. OR

G10, $25-$40
Lake Co., OR

LOCATION: Northern Great Basin. **DESCRIPTION:** This arrow sized point has a barbless triangular blade. The blade transitions smoothly into a straight, slightly expanding (seldom contracting) stem. Approximately 90% of points examined had well ground stems. This type is usually well made. The point has a lenticular cross section. The age of the point is the same as other Rose Springs or Rosegate material.

(Also see Calapooya Knife, Eastgate, Elko, Malaga Cove, Nottoway, Wendover)

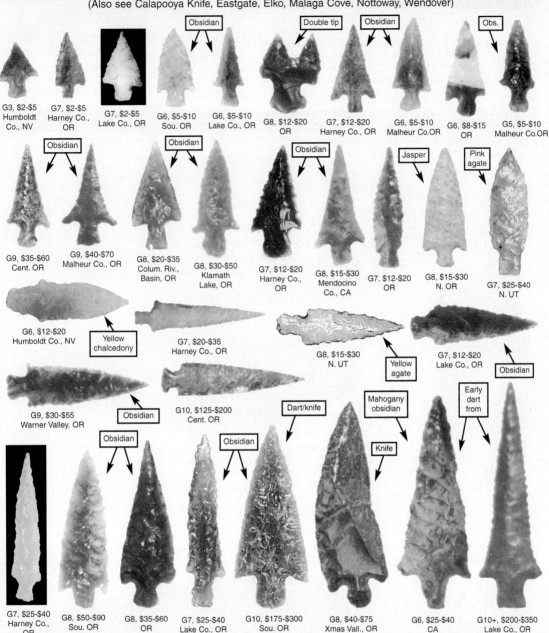

G3, $2-$5 Humboldt Co., NV

G7, $2-$5 Harney Co., OR

G7, $2-$5 Lake Co., OR

Obsidian

G6, $5-$10 Sou. OR

G6, $5-$10 Lake Co., OR

Double tip

G8, $12-$20 OR

G7, $12-$20 Harney Co., OR

Obsidian

G6, $5-$10 Malheur Co.OR

G6, $8-$15 OR

Obs.

G5, $5-$10 Malheur Co.OR

Obsidian

G9, $35-$60 Cent. OR

G9, $40-$70 Malheur Co., OR

Obsidian

G8, $20-$35 Colum. Riv., Basin, OR

G8, $30-$50 Klamath Lake, OR

Obsidian

G7, $12-$20 Harney Co., OR

G8, $15-$30 Mendocino Co., CA

G7, $12-$20 OR

Jasper

G8, $15-$30 N. OR

Pink agate

G7, $25-$40 N. UT

G6, $12-$20 Humboldt Co., NV

Yellow chalcedony

G7, $20-$35 Harney Co., OR

G8, $15-$30 N. UT

Yellow agate

G7, $12-$20 Lake Co., OR

Obsidian

G9, $30-$55 Warner Valley, OR

Obsidian

G10, $125-$200 Cent. OR

Dart/knife

Mahogany obsidian

Knife

Early dart from

Obsidian

Obsidian

G7, $25-$40 Harney Co., OR

G8, $50-$90 Sou. OR

G8, $35-$60 OR

G7, $25-$40 Lake Co., OR

G10, $175-$300 Sou. OR

G8, $40-$75 Xmas Vall., OR

G6, $25-$40 CA

G10+, $200-$350 Lake Co., OR

LOCATION: Great Basin westward. **DESCRIPTION:** A small to medium size, narrow, expanded to contracted stemmed arrow point. Larger examples are dart/knives. The base can be incurvate to rounded.

ROSE VALLEY - Early Archaic, 7000 - 5000 B. P.

(Also see Pinto Basin and Silver Lake)

LOCATION: Southern California. **DESCRIPTION:** A small to medium size, stubby point with a short stem that contracts, expands or is parallel sided. Bases are straight to incurvate and can form small ears on some examples. Believed to be the link between *Silver Lake* and *Pinto Basin* points.

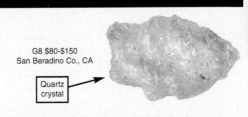

G8 $80-$150 San Beradino Co., CA

Quartz crystal

FW

ROSSI SQUARE-STEMMED - Mid-Archaic-Transitional Phase, 4000 - 2000 B. P.

(Also see Shaniko Stemmed)

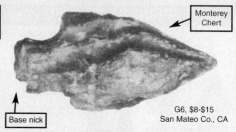

Monterey Chert

LOCATION: San Mateo Co., California and surrounding area into central and sou. coastal California. Usually made of Monterey Chert. **DESCRIPTION:** A medium size, square stemmed dart/knife point with horizontal shoulders.

Base nick

G6, $8-$15
San Mateo Co., CA

ROUGH STEMMED KNIFE I - Late Archaic to Classic Phase, 3000 - 400 B. P.

(Also see Cascade, Cordilleran, Early Leaf, Excelsior, Intermontane, Mahkin Shouldered)

G7, $45-$80
S. OR

G7, $35-$65
S. OR

G8, $55-$100
S. OR

LOCATION: Great Basin westward. **DESCRIPTION:** This knife is a leaf shaped cache or trade blade. The blades are made by one individual and then roughly hafted by a second individual. The blades are medium to large with wide, thin baton reduction flakes. Edge alignment and resharpening is bi-facial pressure flaking. The hafting areas are contracting to a rounded or a rounded pointed base and will show a distinct change in flaking patterns. Cross sections are flattened or lenticular and are heavily made without being "thick."

ROUGH STEMMED KNIFE II - Early Archaic to Classic Phase, 9,500 - 500 B. P.

G4, $1-$3
Columbia Riv., OR

G8, $40-$70
S. OR

LOCATION: Great Basin westward and probalby all over the World. **DESCRIPTION:** This type has no stem and is a recycled blade used by prehistoric opportunists. it consists of various types of broken blades with inappropriate or no stems. Some hafting areas are hammered with percussion strokes that do not match the original manufacturing strokes. Shoulders are flaked into original edgework. These modified points occur from Paleo to Historic and many times cannot be classified as to original type.

ROUGH STEMMED KNIFE II (continued)

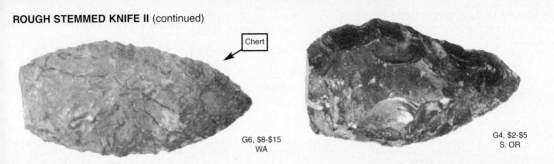

Chert

G6, $8-$15
WA

G4, $2-$5
S. OR

SALMON RIVER - Early Archaic, 8000 - 5800 B. P.

(Also see Bitterroot, Shaniko Stemmed & Wendover)

G6, $15-$20
Humboldt Co., NV

G8, $20-$35
S.E. OR

Basalt

Basalt

G6, $15-$25
WA

Basalt

Basalt

G6, $15-$25
WA

G9, $125-$225
Black Rock Desert,
NV

Basalt

Worn
tip

G5, $15-$25
Union Co., OR

LOCATION: Oregon and Washington state. **DESCRIPTION:** A *Bitterroot* variant. A medium size, narrow, dart point with weak, tapered shoulders, an expanding stem and a straight base. Basal corners are sharp to rounded. Stems can be short to long.

SAUVIE'S ISLAND BASAL NOTCHED - Trans. to Classic Phase, 1950 - 500 B. P.

(Also see Parowan)

G6, $12-$20
S.E. OR

G8, $20-$35
S.E. OR

LOCATION: Oregon and Washington state. **DESCRIPTION:** A thin, small size, basal and side notched arrow point. Stems are very short and side edges are convex.

SAUVIE'S ISLAND SHOULDER NOTCHED - Trans. to Classic Phase., 1750 - 400 B. P.

(Also see Columbia Plateau, Rabbit Island and Wallula)

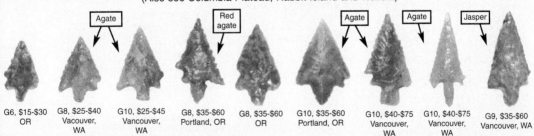

Agate

Red
agate

Agate

Agate

Jasper

G6, $15-$30
OR

G8, $25-$40
Vacouver,
WA

G10, $25-$45
Vancouver,
WA

G8, $35-$60
Portland, OR

G8, $35-$60
OR

G10, $35-$60
Portland, OR

G10, $40-$75
Vancouver,
WA

G10, $40-$75
Vancouver,
WA

G9, $35-$60
Vancouver, WA

FW

LOCATION: Oregon and Washington state. **DESCRIPTION:** A thin, small size, stemmed arrow point with one or both shoulders that contain a notch. These are consistently *Rabbits* & *Wallula Gaps* with shoulder notches. Shoulders can be tapered to barbed. Bases are straight to convex. Stems are short and are either squared or tapered. Named by Jim Hogue.

SAUVIE'S ISLAND SHOULDER NOTCHED(continued)

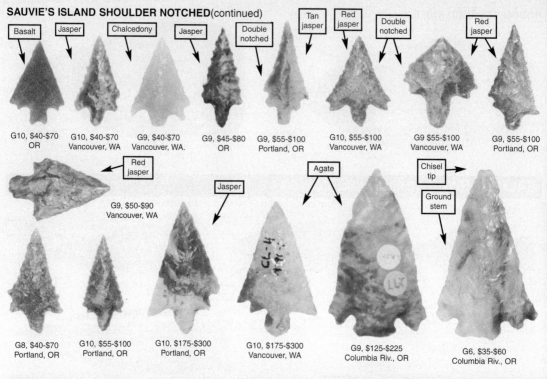

Basalt

Jasper

Chalcedony

Jasper

Double notched

Tan jasper

Red jasper

Double notched

Red jasper

G10, $40-$70
OR

G10, $40-$70
Vancouver, WA

G9, $40-$70
Vancouver, WA.

G9, $45-$80
OR

G9, $55-$100
Portland, OR

G10, $55-$100
Vancouver, WA

G9 55-$100
Vancouver, WA

G9, $55-$100
Portland, OR

Red jasper

G9, $50-$90
Vancouver, WA

Jasper

Agate

Chisel tip

Ground stem

G8, $40-$70
Portland, OR

G10, $55-$100
Portland, OR

G10, $175-$300
Portland, OR

G10, $175-$300
Vancouver, WA

G9, $125-$225
Columbia Riv., OR

G6, $35-$60
Columbia Riv., OR

SCOTTSBLUFF I - Early Archaic, 10,000 - 8000 B. P.

(Also see Alberta, Cody Knife, Eden, Firstview, Lind Coulee, Parman, Shaniko Stemmed & Windust)

Opalized wood

G3, $30-$50
S. OR

G4, $35-$60
Warner Valley, OR

G3, $25-$40
Humboldt Co., NV

G6, $45-$80
Columbia Riv., WA

G6, $65-$125
WA

G7, $125-$200
Lake Co., OR

yellow agate

yellow jasper

G5, $125-$200
OR

Obsidian

G6, $80-$150
Lake Co., OR

G8, $150-$250
WA

G6, $125-$200
OR

G10, $275-$500
Lake Co., OR

SCOTTSBLUFF I (continued)

Petrified palmwood

G10, $275-$500
WA

Agate

G5, $150-$250
Klickitat Co., WA

Red jasper

G8, $200-$350
Klickitat Co., WA

Obsidian

G7, $175-$300
N. OR

Rebased

Obsidian

G6, $125-$200
S. OR

Red agate

G8, $250-$400
WA

Basalt

G6, $150-$250
Kittitas Co., WA

Brown jasper

Basalt

Ground stem

G6, $150-$250
N. OR

Ground stem

G8, $250-$400
Sou. OR

G9, $275-$500
Lake Co., OR

Basalt

Ground stem

G5, $200-$350
Lake Co., OR

Obsidian

G8, $250-$400
Malheur Co., OR

Obsidian

"Anderson" style "Yuma" point

Obsidian

Burinated & ground w/stem

G9, $250-$400
Warner Valley, OR

FW

LOCATION: Western Washington & Oregon into Idaho, Nevada, Utah, Montana & Wyoming. **DESCRIPTION:** A medium to large size, broad, stemmed point with weak shoulders and a broad parallel sided to expanding stem that is ground. Developed from earlier *Alberta* points. *Cody* points in this area have shorter and more variable stems (including miniatures) than anywhere else in the country. Flaking is usually the horizontal to oblique style. Chisel tips are known. **I.D. KEY:** Early flaking, square stem that is ground.

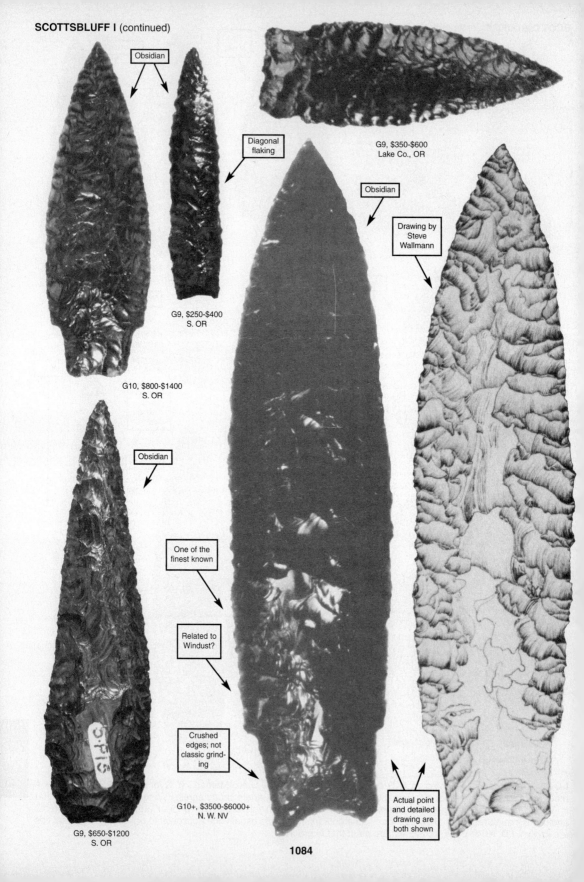

Obsidian

Diagonal flaking

G9, $350-$600
Lake Co., OR

Obsidian

Drawing by Steve Wallmann

G9, $250-$400
S. OR

G10, $800-$1400
S. OR

Obsidian

One of the finest known

Related to Windust?

Crushed edges; not classic grinding

Actual point and detailed drawing are both shown

G10+, $3500-$6000+
N. W. NV

G9, $650-$1200
S. OR

1084

SCOTTSBLUFF I I - Early Archaic, 10,000 - 8000 B. P.

(Also see Alberta, Cody Knife, Eden, Firstview, Lind Coulee, Parman, Shaniko Stemmed & Windust)

Chalcedony

Ground basal sides

G7, $35-$60
WA. Larson cache style
(barbs)

Obsidian

G6, $80-$150
Lake Co., OR

Obsidian

G6, $120-$200
Klickitat Co., WA

Obsidian

Ground stem

G4, $150-$250
Henrys Lake, ID

Basalt

Minor nicks

G6, $125-$200
Columbia Riv., OR

Black obsidian

Ground stem

G8, $350-$650
Lake Co., OR

Obsidian

G6, $250-$450
Lake Co., OR

G4, $175-$300
Klickitat Co., WA

Black obsidian

Ground stem

G7, $275-$500
Warner Valley, OR,
Flagstaff Lake

Ground stem

G9, $400-$700
Lake Co., OR

Obsidian

G8, $400-$700
Harney Co., OR

Red jasper

G6, $250-$400
Harney Co., OR

Black obsidian

G7, $250-$400
Lake Co., OR

FW

1085

SCOTTSBLUFF II (continued)

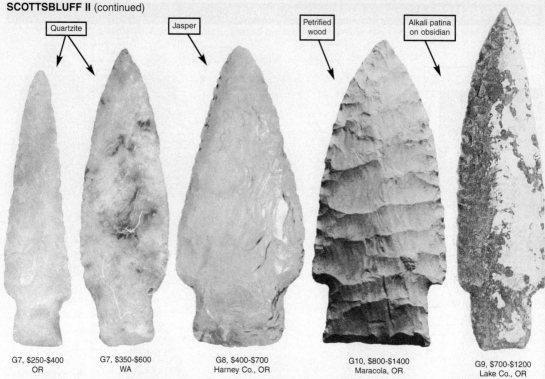

Quartzite

Jasper

Petrified wood

Alkali patina on obsidian

G7, $250-$400
OR

G7, $350-$600
WA

G8, $400-$700
Harney Co., OR

G10, $800-$1400
Maracola, OR

G9, $700-$1200
Lake Co., OR

LOCATION: Western Oregon into Idaho, Nevada and Montana. **DESCRIPTION:** A medium to large size, broad, stemmed point with stronger shoulders and a broad parallel sided to expanding stem that is ground. Developed from earlier *Alberta* points. *Cody* points in this area have shorter and longer stems than anywhere else in the country. Flaking is usually the horizontal to oblique style. Chisel tips are known. **I.D. KEY:** Early flaking, square stem that is ground.

SCOTTSBLUFF KNIFE - Early Archaic, 10,000 - 8000 B. P.

(Also see Cody Knife)

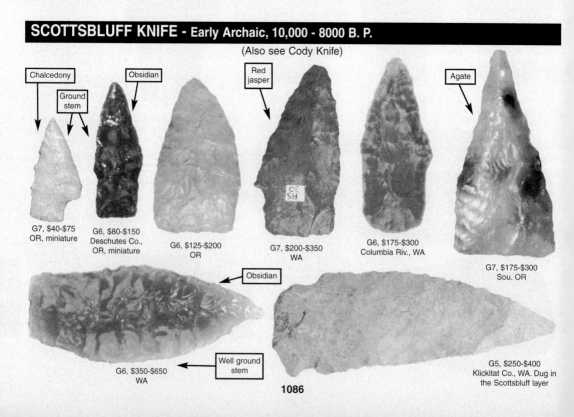

Chalcedony

Ground stem

Obsidian

Red jasper

Agate

G7, $40-$75
OR, miniature

G6, $80-$150
Deschutes Co.,
OR, miniature

G6, $125-$200
OR

G7, $200-$350
WA

G6, $175-$300
Columbia Riv., WA

G7, $175-$300
Sou. OR

Obsidian

Well ground stem

G6, $350-$650
WA

G5, $250-$400
Klickitat Co., WA. Dug in
the Scottsbluff layer

SCOTTSBLUFF KNIFE (continued)

LOCATION: Western Oregon into Idaho, Nevada and Montana. **DESCRIPTION:** These are reworked Scottsbluff points where the blade was resharpened at an angle. unlike the traditional Cody Complex knife that was designed and made from scratch.

SCRAPER - Paleo to Developmental Phase, 11,500 - 1000 B. P.

(Also see Chopper, Drill, Graver, Hand Axe, Lancet, Paleo Knife, Perforator and Sizer)

Thumb scraper

Scraping edge

G6, $1-$2
WA

G6, $4-$8
OR

G6, $2-$5
OR

G6, $2-$5
Coos Co., OR

G8, $5-$10
Harney Co., OR

G6, $1-$3
Humboltd Co., NV

Cascade scraper

Scraping edge

Hafted scraper

G8, $5-$10
OR

G8, $4-$8
Christmas Valley, OR

Cascade scraper

G8, $4-$8
Christmas Valley, OR

G6, $5-$10
Harney Co., OR

G8, $2-$5
The Dalles, OR

G6, $1-$2
Santa Barbara Co., CA

Scraping edge

G6, $5-$10
OR

Corner Notched

Chalcedony

G6, $2-$5
The Dalles, OR

G6, $4-$8
OR

G6, $4-$8
Atlatl Valley, OR

G8, $5-$10
OR

FW

LOCATION: All early-man sites. **DESCRIPTION:** Thumb, duckbill, claw and turtleback forms are small to medium size, thick, ovoid shaped, uniface, scraping tools that are steeply beveled, especially at the broadest end. Side scrapers are long to oval hand-held uniface flakes with beveling on the edges intended for use. Scraping was done primarily from the sides of these blades. Some of these tools were hafted.

SCRAPER (continued)

Agate

G10, $20-$30
Christmas Valley, OR

G8, $8-$15
San Bernadino Co., CA

G8, $12-$20
San Bernadino Co., CA

SHANIKO STEMMED - Late Archaic to Woodland, 3500 - 2300 B. P.

(Also see Cascade, Eden, Lake Mohave, Lind Coulee, Owl Cave, Parman, Pryor Stemmed, Rossi Square-Stemmed, Scottsbluff, Sierra Contracting Stem, Silver Lake and Windust)

Chalcedony

Yellow jasper

Ground stem

Dark yellow/red agate

G7, $30-$50
WA

G7, $30-$50
OR

G9, $60-$110
Lake Co., OR

G8, $40-$70
OR

G8, $55-$100
Columbia Riv., WA

Ground stem

G9, $65-$125
WA

Petrified wood

G5, $40-$70
N. OR

G6, $55-$100
OR

Basalt

Chalcedony

G8, $30-$50
Plymouth, OR

G5, $25-$40
Columbia Riv., WA

1088

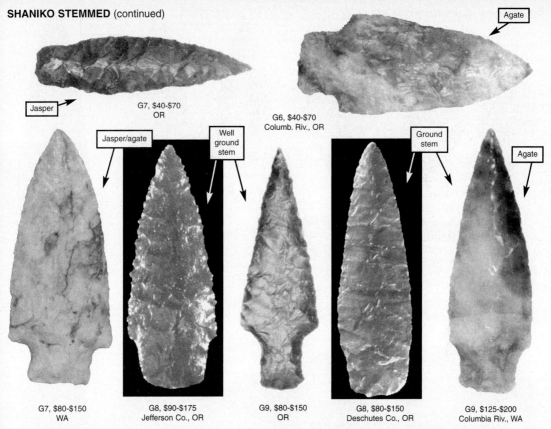

Agate

Jasper

G7, $40-$70
OR

G6, $40-$70
Columb. Riv., OR

Jasper/agate

Well ground stem

Ground stem

Agate

G7, $80-$150
WA

G8, $90-$175
Jefferson Co., OR

G9, $80-$150
OR

G8, $80-$150
Deschutes Co., OR

G9, $125-$200
Columbia Riv., WA

LOCATION: Mid-Columbia River area in Oregon. **DESCRIPTION:** A medium size point with sloping to slightly barbed shoulders. Stems are straight to contracting to a straight to convex base. Stem sides are sometimes ground and bases can be thinned. Flaking is random and the cross section is flat. Named by A.R. Snyder and J.L. Hogue in April, 2000. Formerly called *Early Stemmed*. **I.D. KEY:** Base form and size.

SIDE KNIFE - Devlopmental to Historic Phase, 1000 - 300 B. P.

(Also Scraper, Square-End Knife)

Chalcedony

LOCATION: Great Basin westward. **DESCRIPTION:** A large size blade made for hafting along one side. Gut and plant fibers were used when needed to bind the hafting. Pitch or asphaltum were used as an adhesive to glue the stone tool in the handle.

G7, $20-$35
Hood Riv., OR

FW

SIERRA CONTRACTING STEM - Early to Late Archaic, 6000 - 3000 B. P.

(Also see Coquille, Houx Contracting Stem, Rabbit Island, Shaniko, Silver Lake, Tucannon)

SIERRA CONTRACTING STEM (continued)

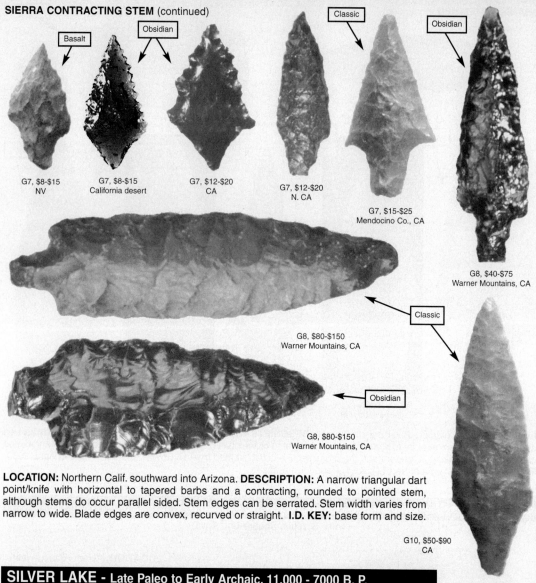

Basalt

Obsidian

Classic

Obsidian

G7, $8-$15
NV

G7, $8-$15
California desert

G7, $12-$20
CA

G7, $12-$20
N. CA

G7, $15-$25
Mendocino Co., CA

G8, $40-$75
Warner Mountains, CA

G8, $80-$150
Warner Mountains, CA

Classic

Obsidian

G8, $80-$150
Warner Mountains, CA

LOCATION: Northern Calif. southward into Arizona. **DESCRIPTION:** A narrow triangular dart point/knife with horizontal to tapered barbs and a contracting, rounded to pointed stem, although stems do occur parallel sided. Stem edges can be serrated. Stem width varies from narrow to wide. Blade edges are convex, recurved or straight. **I.D. KEY:** base form and size.

G10, $50-$90
CA

SILVER LAKE - Late Paleo to Early Archaic, 11,000 - 7000 B. P.

(Also see Borax Lake, Eden, Hell Gap, Lake Mohave, Lind Coulee, Parman, Rose Valley, Scottsbluff, Shaniko, Sierra Stemmed)

Ground stem

Obsidian

Obsidian

Scraper

Perforator

G6, $45-$80
Harneye Co., OR

G6, $65-$125
Harney Co., OR

G6, $125-$200
S. OR

G5, $125-$200
OR

Ground stem

G6, $80-$150
Beatty, NV

G6, $80-$150
Harney Co., OR

SILVER LAKE (continued)

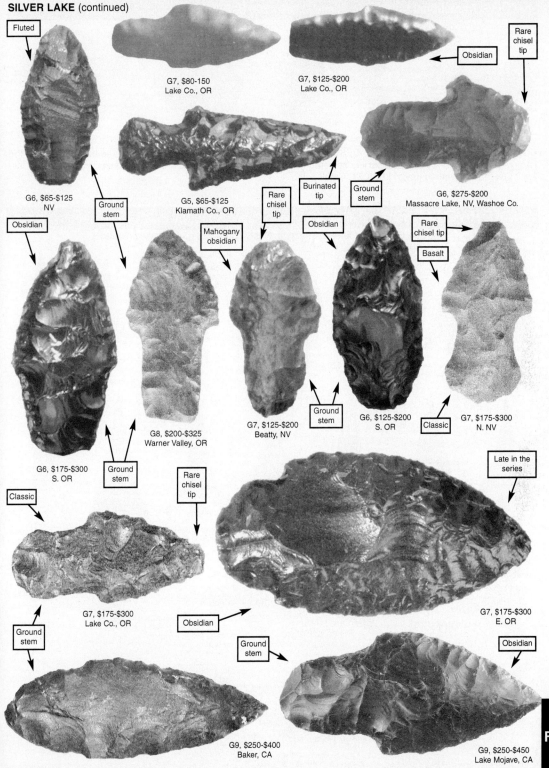

Fluted

G6, $65-$125
NV

Ground stem

G7, $80-150
Lake Co., OR

G7, $125-$200
Lake Co., OR

Obsidian

Rare chisel tip

G5, $65-$125
Klamath Co., OR

Rare chisel tip

Burinated tip

Ground stem

Ground stem

G6, $275-$200
Massacre Lake, NV, Washoe Co.

Obsidian

Mahogany obsidian

Obsidian

Rare chisel tip

Basalt

G7, $125-$200
Beatty, NV

Ground stem

G6, $125-$200
S. OR

Classic

G7, $175-$300
N. NV

G8, $200-$325
Warner Valley, OR

G6, $175-$300
S. OR

Ground stem

Classic

Rare chisel tip

Late in the series

Ground stem

G7, $175-$300
Lake Co., OR

Obsidian

G7, $175-$300
E. OR

Ground stem

Obsidian

G9, $250-$400
Baker, CA

G9, $250-$450
Lake Mojave, CA

FW

LOCATION: Sou. California into sou. Oregon. **DESCRIPTION:** A small to medium size, narrow point with slight to moderate tapered or square shoulders and a long, contracting to expanding bulbous stem that is ground. Later examples have shorted stems.. **I.D. KEY:** Long stem, weak shoulders.

1091

SIZER - Transitional to Historic Phase, 2,300 - 200 B. P.

(Also see Drill, Graver and Scraper)

G6, $1-$2
OR

G5, $1-$2
OR

G10, $2-$5
OR, fully flaked

G4, $1-$2
OR

G4, $1-$2
OR

G5, $1-$3
OR

LOCATION: North to central Oregon. **DESCRIPTION:** A small, notched scraper used to make basket material the same size. Spruce or cedar roots vary considerably. A uniform diameter would produce a tighter, higher quality basket. Look for use wear in notch. **I.D. KEY:** Small notch.

SNAKE RIVER ARROW - Classic to Historic Phase, 700 - 150 B. P.

(Also see Columbia Plateau, Eastgate, Rose Springs, Sauvie's Island, Wallula)

Agate

Agate

Chalcedony

Red
Chalcedony

Jasper

G9, $40-$70
WA

G9, $55-$100
John Day Riv., OR

G10, $150-$250
WA

G10, $200-$350
WA

G10, $250-$400
John Day Riv., OR

G10, $110-$200
WA

G7, $90-$175
Columb. Riv., WA

G10, $175-$300
Columb. Riv., WA

Agate

Agate

Bifurcated
base

Agate

G9, $110-$200
WA

G9, $275-$500
WA

G10, $200-$350
Columb. Riv., WA

G8, $110-$200
Columb. Riv.,OR

G10, $200-$350
Columb. Riv.,OR

G10, $350-$600
Columb. Riv., WA

G10, $350-$600
John Day Riv., OR

Bifurcated
base

Red
agate

Agate

Bifurcated
base

Chalc.

Jasper

G10, $400-$700
WA

G8, $125-$200
John Day Riv., OR

G10, $500-$900
WA

G10, $275-$500
WA

Nick

Yellow
agate

Obsidian

Agate

Agate

G10, $400-$750
WA

G8, $80-$150
WA

G8, $40-$75
Harney Co., OR

G8, $150-$250
Sauvie's Island, OR

LOCATION: Great Basin westward. **DESCRIPTION:** A small to medium size barbed, corner notched arrow point. Blade edges are convex or recurved and can be serrated. **Stems are straight to contracting.** Bases are convex, straight, concave or are bifurcated. Evolved from the earlier dart point. *Columbia Plateau* points are similar but have expanding bases. These have parallel sides to contracting bases. Otherwise the points are identical.

SNAKE RIVER ARROW (continued)

Chalc.

G10, $275-$500
OR

Agate

G9, $125-$200
Hood Riv., OR

Red agate

G9, $350-$650
WA

SNAKE RIVER DART - Transitional to Classic Phase, 2000 - 700 B. P.

(Also see Columbia Plateau, Eastgate, Elko, Hendricks, Rose Springs, Sauvie's Island, Wallula)

Serrated edge

Agate

Chalcedony

Agate

G6, $20-$35
Columbia Riv.,
OR

G9, $65-$125
Columbia Riv., OR

G9, $125-$200
Columbia Riv., OR

G10, $165-$300
Columbia Riv., OR

G8, $35-$65
Columbia Riv., OR

G8, $35-$65
WA

Serrated edge

Agate

Serrated edge

Red jasper

Agate

G7, $20-$35
OR

G6, $30-$50
Columbia Riv., OR

G6, $30-$50
OR

G6, $30-$50
Columbia Riv., OR

G8, $35-$65
WA

G9, $150-$250
Columbia Riv., OR

G8, $65-$125
Columb. Riv., WA

Obsidian

G10, $200-$350
Columbia Riv., OR

Gem

Yellow agate

Tip wear

Agate

Chalcedony

G10, $200-$350
Columbia Riv., OR

G9, $125-$200
Priest Rapids, WA

G10, $175-$300
Columbia Riv., OR

G8, $80-$150
WA

G7, $65-$125
WA

FW

LOCATION: Great Basin westward. **DESCRIPTION:** A small to medium size barbed, corner notched dart point. Blade edges can be serrated. Bases are usually straight to concave to auriculate. Evolves into the arrow point at a later time and also believed to have evolved into *Columbia Plateau* arrow points.

SNAKE RIVER DART (continued)

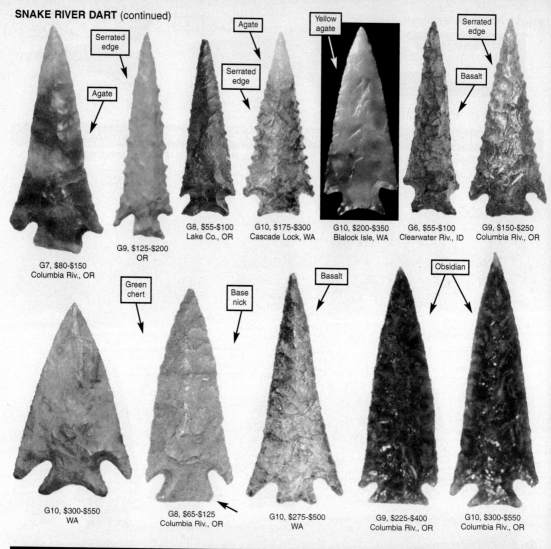

G7, $80-$150
Columbia Riv., OR

Serrated edge

Agate

G9, $125-$200
OR

Agate

Serrated edge

G8, $55-$100
Lake Co., OR

G10, $175-$300
Cascade Lock, WA

Yellow agate

G10, $200-$350
Blalock Isle, WA

Serrated edge

Basalt

G6, $55-$100
Clearwater Riv., ID

Serrated edge

Basalt

G9, $150-$250
Columbia Riv., OR

Green chert

G10, $300-$550
WA

Base nick

G8, $65-$125
Columbia Riv., OR

Basalt

G10, $275-$500
WA

Obsidian

G9, $225-$400
Columbia Riv., OR

G10, $300-$550
Columbia Riv., OR

SPEDIS I - Paleo, 10,000 - 8000 B. P.

(Also see Cascade, Fells Cave (N.W.), Gypsum Cave, Haskett, Midland, Milnesand, Pay Paso & Rabbit Island)

G4, $12-$20
WA

Ground stem

G8, $25-$40
Umatilla, OR

Jasper

G8, $30-$50
Columb. Riv., OR

G9, $30-$50
Hood Riv., OR

Basalt

G7, $30-$50
OR

G9, $35-$60
OR

Jasper

G7, $30-$50
WA

LOCATION: Oregon and Washington, Columbia River basin. **DESCRIPTION:** A small to medium size, thin, narrow, lanceolate dart/knife point with a distinctive "pumpkin seed" shape. The stems are contracting and have straight to slightly concave sides and are ground. The bases are straight, truncated, diagonally biased or notched and are usually smoothed. Single shoulder examples occur. Usually exotic materials were employed. They are thinned by a combination of percussion and pressure. The cross sections are flattened to lenticular. **I.D. KEY:** "Pumpkin seed" blade-form. Usually thinner than Spedis II.

1094

(See Cascade, Fells Cave (N.W.), Gypsum Cave, Haskett, Midland, Milnesand, Pay Paso (N.W.), Rabbit Island)

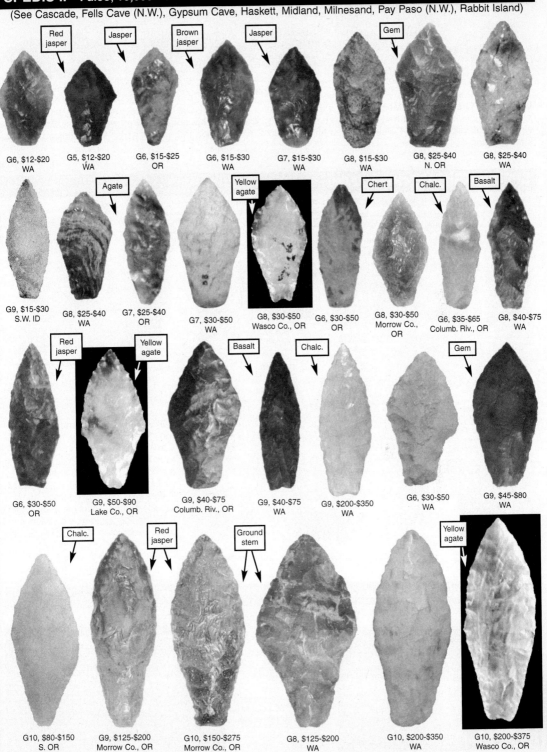

Red jasper

Jasper

Brown jasper

Jasper

Gem

G6, $12-$20 WA

G5, $12-$20 WA

G6, $15-$25 OR

G6, $15-$30 WA

G7, $15-$30 WA

G8, $15-$30 WA

G8, $25-$40 N. OR

G8, $25-$40 WA

Agate

Yellow agate

Chert

Chalc.

Basalt

G9, $15-$30 S.W. ID

G8, $25-$40 WA

G7, $25-$40 OR

G7, $30-$50 WA

G8, $30-$50 Wasco Co., OR

G6, $30-$50 OR

G8, $30-$50 Morrow Co., OR

G6, $35-$65 Columb. Riv., OR

G8, $40-$75 WA

Red jasper

Yellow agate

Basalt

Chalc.

Gem

G6, $30-$50 OR

G9, $50-$90 Lake Co., OR

G9, $40-$75 Columb. Riv., OR

G9, $40-$75 WA

G9, $200-$350 WA

G6, $30-$50 WA

G9, $45-$80 WA

Chalc.

Red jasper

Ground stem

Yellow agate

G10, $80-$150 S. OR

G9, $125-$200 Morrow Co., OR

G10, $150-$275 Morrow Co., OR

G8, $125-$200 WA

G10, $200-$350 WA

G10, $200-$375 Wasco Co., OR

FW

LOCATION: Oregon and Washington, Columbia River basin. **DESCRIPTION:** Has the same "pumpkin seed" shaped blade, but the stems are slightly longer and narrower. The stem sides contract to a straight base with rounded corners. Both stem sides and base are usually ground. **I.D. KEY:** "Pumpkin seed" form with longer stem.

SPEDIS III - Late Archaic to Transitional Phase, 3000 - 2000 B. P.

(Also see Bliss, Cascade, Gold Hill and Trojan)

G4, $2-$5
Sauvie's Isle, OR

G6, $12-$20
Sauvie's Isle, OR

G6, $4-$8
Sauvie's Isle, OR

G4, $3-$6
Sauvie's Isle, OR

Tip wear

G9, $15-$25
Sauvie's Isle, OR

Red jasper

LOCATION: Oregon and Washington, Columbia River basin. **DESCRIPTION:** This type commonly called "Spedis" is a small Woodland point that only has the "pumpkin seed" silhouette. This point is not as well made as the first two types and qualifies as lower Columbia types #5 and/or #6. Stems are not ground. **I.D. KEY:** "Pumpkin seed" form, no stem grinding.

SPEDIS FISHTAIL - Paleo, 10,000 - 8000 B. P.

(Also see Fells Cave (N.W.), Goshen, Midland, Milnesand, Pay Paso (N.W.), and Spedis)

Agate

Yellow agate

Red jasper

G7, $40-$75
OR

G9, $125-$200
WA

G7, $40-$75
WA

G8, $30-$50
Hood Riv., OR

G9, $125-$200
OR

G8, $40-$75
Columb. Riv., OR

G9, $80-$150
WA

Rootbeer agate

G8, $65-$125
WA

G9, $150-$250
OR

G10, $175-$300
WA

G9, $125-$200
OR

LOCATION: Oregon and Washington, Columbia River basin. **DESCRIPTION:** A small to medium size, thin, lanceolate dart/knife point with most having expanded auricles and a recurved blade producing a waist. Bases are generally concave and are usually ground. This type is separated from the *Pay Paso* type by basal thinning technique. **I.D. KEY:** Eared base.

SQUARE-END KNIFE - Late Archaic to Historic, 3500 - 400 B. P.

(Also see Drill, Hand Axe, Scraper, Paleo Knife & Side Knife)

G6, $12-$20
Lake Co., OR

G6, $10-$20
Lake Co., OR,
Christmas Lake.

White chert

SQUARE-END KNIFE (continued)

LOCATION: Great Basin westward.
DESCRIPTION: A medium to large size squared blade that is beveled on all four sides for cutting. **I.D. KEY:** Squared form.

Basalt

G8, $30-$50
Lake Co., OR

STEAMBOAT LANCEOLATE - Mid to late Archaic, 5000 - 2500 B. P.

(Also see Cascade, Cordilleran, intermontane Stemmed, Malaga Cove Leaf, Sierra Contracting Stem)

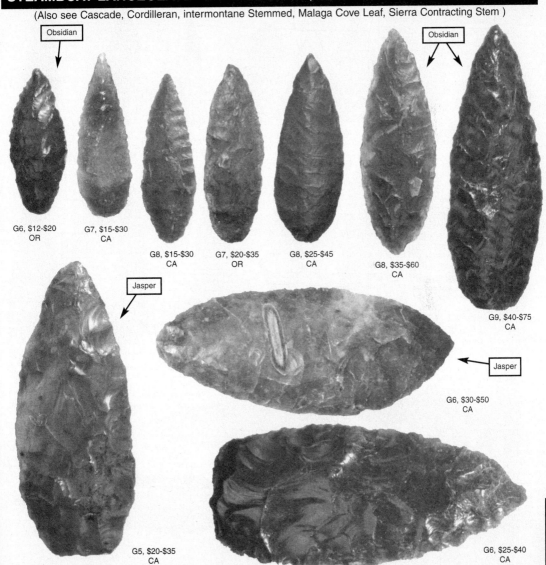

Obsidian

Obsidian

G6, $12-$20
OR

G7, $15-$30
CA

G8, $15-$30
CA

G7, $20-$35
OR

G8, $25-$45
CA

G8, $35-$60
CA

G9, $40-$75
CA

Jasper

Jasper

G6, $30-$50
CA

G5, $20-$35
CA

G6, $25-$40
CA

FW

LOCATION: Northern California, Western Nevada into southern Oregon. **DESCRIPTION:** A medium to large size, narrow to broad, lanceolate dart/knife point with a rounded, pointed or straight base. Some examples show stem grinding.

G9, $200-$375
CA

STOCKTON - Developmental to Historic Phase, 1200 - 200 B. P.

(Also see Exotic and Vendetta)

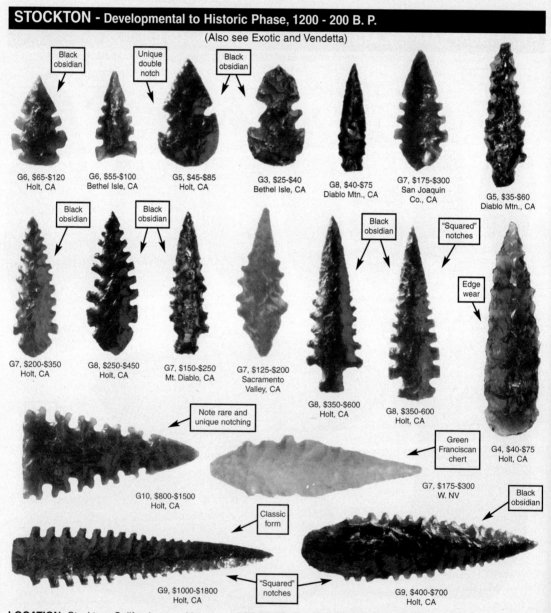

Black
obsidian

Unique
double
notch

Black
obsidian

G6, $65-$120
Holt, CA

G6, $55-$100
Bethel Isle, CA

G5, $45-$85
Holt, CA

G3, $25-$40
Bethel Isle, CA

G8, $40-$75
Diablo Mtn., CA

G7, $175-$300
San Joaquin
Co., CA

G5, $35-$60
Diablo Mtn., CA

Black
obsidian

Black
obsidian

Black
obsidian

"Squared"
notches

Edge
wear

G7, $200-$350
Holt, CA

G8, $250-$450
Holt, CA

G7, $150-$250
Mt. Diablo, CA

G7, $125-$200
Sacramento
Valley, CA

G8, $350-$600
Holt, CA

G8, $350-600
Holt, CA

Note rare and
unique notching

Green
Franciscan
chert

G4, $40-$75
Holt, CA

G10, $800-$1500
Holt, CA

Classic
form

G7, $175-$300
W. NV

Black
obsidian

G9, $1000-$1800
Holt, CA

"Squared"
notches

G9, $400-$700
Holt, CA

LOCATION: Stockton, California area. Very rare. **DESCRIPTION:** A small to large size, thin, narrow, point that has exaggerated, squared barbs along the blade edges. Believed to have been used for sawing as well as an arrow point. Forms vary from stemmed to auriculate to corner notched. **I.D. KEY:** Deep square barbs. **Warning:** Reproductions exist in the market today. Credible provenience is recommended before acquiring a specimen.

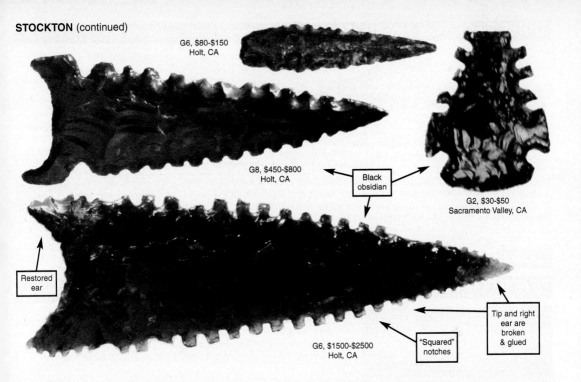

G6, $80-$150
Holt, CA

G8, $450-$800
Holt, CA

Black
obsidian

G2, $30-$50
Sacramento Valley, CA

Restored
ear

Tip and right
ear are
broken
& glued

G6, $1500-$2500
Holt, CA

"Squared"
notches

STRONG BARBED AURICULATE - Transitional to Classic Phase, 1750 - 700 B. P.

(Also see Columbia Mule Ear, Humboldt and Triple T)

Note: Absolute authentication of this rare type is necessary as modern reproductions may exist.

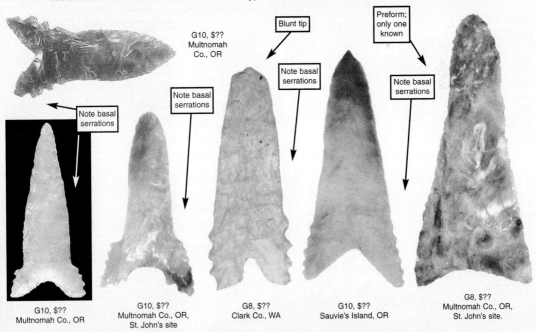

G10, $??
Multnomah
Co., OR

Blunt tip

Preform;
only one
known

Note basal
serrations

Note basal
serrations

Note basal
serrations

Note basal
serrations

Note basal
serrations

G10, $??
Multnomah Co., OR

G10, $??
Multnomah Co., OR,
St. John's site

G8, $??
Clark Co., WA

G10, $??
Sauvie's Island, OR

G8, $??
Multnomah Co., OR,
St. John's site.

FW

LOCATION: Sauvie's Island, Oregon and adjacent areas. **DESCRIPTION:** A very rare type with only 11 examples known. A medium size auriculate point with a concave, notched to v-shaped base and an obtuse to apiculate tip. The basal ears are serrated. **I.D. KEY**: Basal ears serrated. **Note:** Unique; none have been sold and value will be determined when sales data becomes available.

THREE-PIECE FISH SPEAR - Transitional to Historic Phase, 2300 - 200 B.P.

(Also see Harpoon)

Center pieces
G5-8, $2-$8 ea.
All from Astoria, OR

G9, $175-$300 Complete
Camas, WA

G10, $250-$400 Complete
Curry Co., OR

IMPORTANT:
These two pieces shown half size

LOCATION: East & west coast into Canada. **DESCRIPTION:** A small size bone point consisting of two flanges and a short center shaft. The flanges comprise the barbs and a portion of the point. The flanges are grooved at one end to fit over the center shaft. They were tied together to form the point. This point was then hafted over a spear shaft. Rarely found complete. **I.D. KEY**: Widely extended barbs.

TOGGLE (See Harpoon)

TRADE POINTS - Classic to Historic Phase, 400 - 170 B.P.

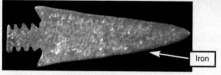

Iron

G8, $50-$90
Bonner Co., ID

LOCATION: These points were made of copper, iron, and steel and were traded to the Indians by the French, British and others from the 1600s to the 1800s. Examples have been found all over the United States. Forms vary from triangular to conical to stemmed.

TRIANGULAR KNIFE - Late Archaic, 3500 B.P.

(Also see Atlatl Valley Triangular, Cascade Knife, Chumash Tools, Square Knife)

Chalcedony

Agate

G8, $25-$45
Harney Co., OR

LOCATION: Southern Oregon southward to Mexico. **DESCRIPTION:** A large size triangular knife with a straight base. Beveling occurs on some resharpened examples.

Obsidian

Beveled edge

G6, $20-$35
N.W. NV

G10, $125-$225
Lake Co., OR

G6, $45-$80
UT

Base nick

TRIANGULAR KNIVE (continued)

Obsidian

Agate

G8, $80-$150
Silver Lake, OR

G9, $125-$200
OR

G8, $80-$150
OR

TRIPLE "T" - Middle Archaic, 5500 - 5000 B. P.

(Also see Black Rock Concave, Cascade, Humboldt, Mendocino Concave Base and Strong)

Obsidian

Banded obsidian

Heavy resharpening

G9, $90-$175
Warner Valley, OR

G9, $125-$200
N.W. NV

Obsidian

Obsidian

G8, $65-$125
CA

G8, $35-$65
Lake Co., OR

G9, $150-$250
Tule Lake, CA

LOCATION: Great Basin westward. **DESCRIPTION:** A medium size, lanceolate point with rounded basal corners and a concave base. Blade edges curve from point to base. Another variation of the *Humboldt* series.

TROJAN - Developmental to Classic Phase, 1320 - 300 B. P.

(Also see Cottonwood, Gold Hill, Magala Cove Leaf)

$1-$3ea.
Trojan Point,
OR, Type site.

FW

LOCATION: Lower Columbia River from Portland to Astoria. **DESCRIPTION:** A small, thin, triangular to ovate arrow point. Many are made from flakes with unfinished bases and minimal retouch. Over 2200 were found at the Trojan site. Possible use as tips in bone harpoons for hunting seal and fish.

TROJAN (continued)

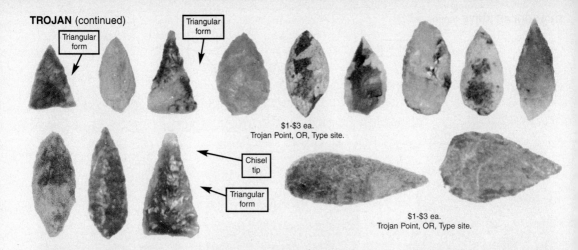

Triangular form

Triangular form

Chisel tip

Triangular form

$1-$3 ea.
Trojan Point, OR, Type site.

$1-$3 ea.
Trojan Point, OR, Type site.

TUCANNON CORNER NOTCHED - Mid to Late Archaic, 5000 - 200 B.P.

(Also see Martis, Merrybell)

G3, $1-$2
WA

G3, $1-$2
WA

LOCATION: Oregon and Washington. **DESCRIPTION:** A small tariangular point with wide corner notches and in some points, "ears" are left on the stem bases. Bases are usually straight but can be slightly concave or convex. Cross sections are usually flat and edge retouch is from both faces.

TUCANNON SIDE NOTCHED - Mid to Late Archaic, 5000 - 2500 B.P.

(Also see Bitterroot, Cold Springs, Maratix and Nottoway)

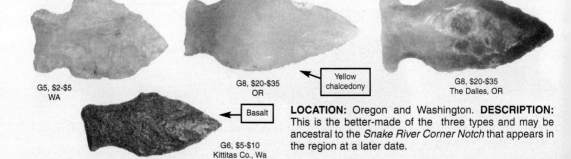

G5, $2-$5
WA

G8, $20-$35
OR

Yellow chalcedony

G8, $20-$35
The Dalles, OR

Basalt

G6, $5-$10
Kittitas Co., Wa

LOCATION: Oregon and Washington. **DESCRIPTION:** This is the better-made of the three types and may be ancestral to the *Snake River Corner Notch* that appears in the region at a later date.

TUCANNON STEMMED - Mid to Late Archaic, 5000 - 2500 B.P.

(Also see Gatecliff, Gypsum Cave, Rabbit Island & Sierra Contracting Stem)

Gem

G6, $5-$10
Columb. Riv., OR

G5, $5-$10
Columb. Riv., OR

G6, $8-$15
Columb. Riv., OR

G6, $8-$15
OR

TUCANNON STEMMED (continued)

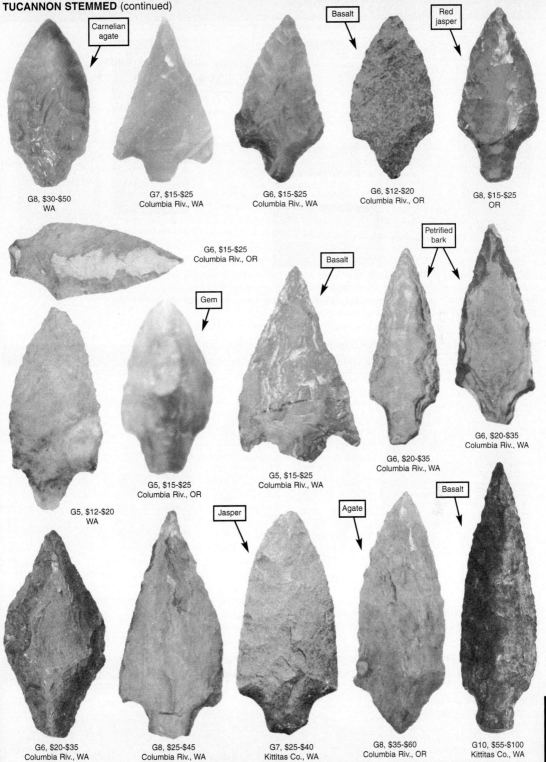

Carnelian agate

G8, $30-$50
WA

G7, $15-$25
Columbia Riv., WA

Basalt

G6, $15-$25
Columbia Riv., WA

G6, $12-$20
Columbia Riv., OR

Red jasper

G8, $15-$25
OR

G6, $15-$25
Columbia Riv., OR

Gem

Basalt

Petrified bark

G5, $12-$20
WA

G5, $15-$25
Columbia Riv., OR

G5, $15-$25
Columbia Riv., WA

G6, $20-$35
Columbia Riv., WA

G6, $20-$35
Columbia Riv., WA

Jasper

Agate

Basalt

G6, $20-$35
Columbia Riv., WA

G8, $25-$45
Columbia Riv., WA

G7, $25-$40
Kittitas Co., WA

G8, $35-$60
Columbia Riv., OR

G10, $55-$100
Kittitas Co., WA

FW

LOCATION: Oregon and Washington. **DESCRIPTION:** A small to medium size stemmed dart/knife point with a wide triangular blade and a contracting stem. The stem base can be concave, convex or left untouched. Shoulders vary from slightly barbed to horizontal. Cross sections are usually flat and edge retouch is from both faces. Believed to be ancestral to the *Rabbit Island* dart/knife. The type site is Tucannon River in Washington.

TULARE LAKE - Paleo, 11,200 - 10,000 B. P.

(Also see Black Rock Concave, Clovis, Humboldt and Mendocino Concave Base)

G6, $175-$300
Tulare Lake, CA

G6, $175-$300
Tulare Lake, CA

G6, $175-$300
Tulare Lake, CA

G5, $125-$200
Tulare Lake, CA

G5, $250-$450
Tulare Lake, CA

G6, $150-$250
Tulare Lake, CA

G10, $350-$650
Kern Co., CA

LOCATION: Central California. **DESCRIPTION:** A late *Clovis* variant. A small to medium size unfluted, auriculate point with a concave base. Basal area is ground. Some bases are thinned. Basal area is usually over half the length of the point. Has been found with *Crescents* and unfluted *Clovis* points at the Witt site.

TULARE LAKE BI-POINT - Early Archaic, 8,000 - 6,000 B. P.

(Also see Cascade, Cordilleran, Early Leaf, Excelsior, Kennewick, Wildcat Canyon)

G2, $1-$3
Tulare Lake, CA

G4, $8-$15
Tulare Lake, CA

G6, $12-$20
Tulare Lake, CA

G6, $15-$30
Tulare Lake, CA

G6, $25-$40
Tulare Lake, CA

G8, $35-$60
Tulare Lake, CA

LOCATION: Central California. **DESCRIPTION:** A medium to large size double pointed lanceolate blade found on the Clovis Witt site in California.

TUOLUMNE NOTCHED - Late Archaic, 3100 - 2500 B. P.

(Also see McGillivray, Need Stemmed Lanceolate, Nightfire & Willits Side Notched)

LOCATION: Central Northern California. **DESCRIPTION:** A large corner to side notched point with a convex, bulbous base. Some examples have excellent oblique, parallel flaking on the blade faces. Similar to but later than the Nightfire point found further North. **I.D. KEY:** Bulbous base.

G8, $125-$200
Fort Rock Valley, OR

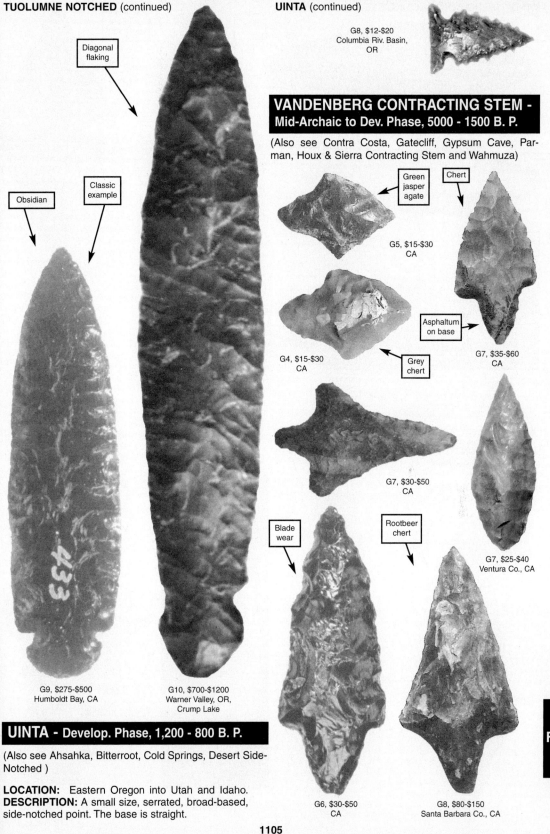

TUOLUMNE NOTCHED (continued)

Diagonal flaking

UINTA (continued)

G8, $12-$20
Columbia Riv. Basin, OR

Obsidian

Classic example

VANDENBERG CONTRACTING STEM -
Mid-Archaic to Dev. Phase, 5000 - 1500 B. P.

(Also see Contra Costa, Gatecliff, Gypsum Cave, Parman, Houx & Sierra Contracting Stem and Wahmuza)

Green jasper agate

Chert

G5, $15-$30
CA

Asphaltum on base

G4, $15-$30
CA

Grey chert

G7, $35-$60
CA

G7, $30-$50
CA

Blade wear

Rootbeer chert

G7, $25-$40
Ventura Co., CA

G9, $275-$500
Humboldt Bay, CA

G10, $700-$1200
Warner Valley, OR,
Crump Lake

UINTA - Develop. Phase, 1,200 - 800 B. P.

(Also see Ahsahka, Bitterroot, Cold Springs, Desert Side-Notched)

LOCATION: Eastern Oregon into Utah and Idaho.
DESCRIPTION: A small size, serrated, broad-based, side-notched point. The base is straight.

G6, $30-$50
CA

G8, $80-$150
Santa Barbara Co., CA

FW

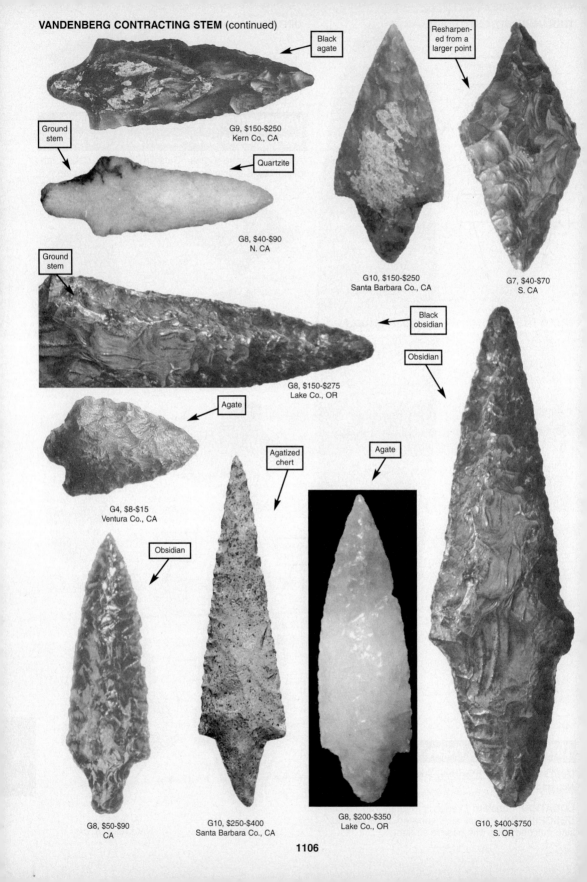

VANDENBERG CONTRACTING STEM (continued)

Black agate

G9, $150-$250
Kern Co., CA

Ground stem

Quartzite

G8, $40-$90
N. CA

Ground stem

Resharpened from a larger point

G10, $150-$250
Santa Barbara Co., CA

G7, $40-$70
S. CA

Black obsidian

Obsidian

G8, $150-$275
Lake Co., OR

Agate

G4, $8-$15
Ventura Co., CA

Agatized chert

Agate

Obsidian

G8, $50-$90
CA

G10, $250-$400
Santa Barbara Co., CA

G8, $200-$350
Lake Co., OR

G10, $400-$750
S. OR

VANDENBERG CONTRACTING STEM (continued)

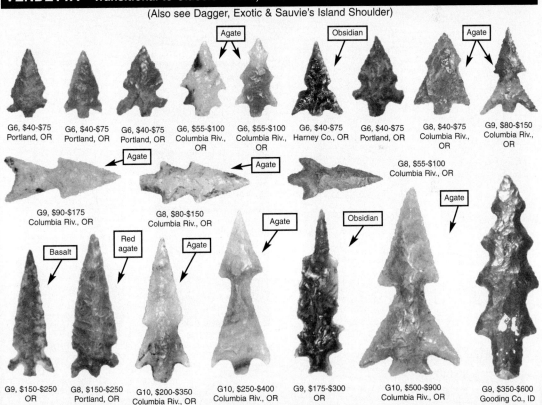

Rootbeer chert

Obsidian

G9, $175-$300
Ventura Co., CA

G10, $400-$700
Lake Co., OR

LOCATION: California, Nevada, Oregon. Named after Vandenberg Air Force base where the type site is located. **DESCRIPTION:** A medium to large size, contracting stemmed point. Shoulders are barbed to contracting. Bases are convex and stems are usually ground. Similar to the *Gypsum Cave* point but much larger and earlier in age. Usually finer made than the *Houx* point.

VENDETTA - Transitional to Classic Phase, 1750 - 200 B. P.

(Also see Dagger, Exotic & Sauvie's Island Shoulder)

Agate

Obsidian

Agate

G6, $40-$75
Portland, OR

G6, $40-$75
Portland, OR

G6, $40-$75
Portland, OR

G6, $55-$100
Columbia Riv., OR

G6, $55-$100
Columbia Riv., OR

G6, $40-$75
Harney Co., OR

G6, $40-$75
Portland, OR

G8, $40-$75
Columbia Riv., OR

G9, $80-$150
Columbia Riv., OR

Agate

Agate

G8, $55-$100
Columbia Riv., OR

G9, $90-$175
Columbia Riv., OR

G8, $80-$150
Columbia Riv., OR

Agate

Basalt

Red agate

Agate

Agate

Obsidian

Agate

G9, $150-$250
OR

G8, $150-$250
Portland, OR

G10, $200-$350
Columbia Riv., OR

G10, $250-$400
Columbia Riv., OR

G9, $175-$300
OR

G10, $500-$900
Columbia Riv., OR

G9, $350-$600
Gooding Co., ID

LOCATION: Columbia River Basin, Oregon. Researched and described by Jim Hogue and Del Greer in 1998. **DESCRIPTION:** A small to medium size barbed-notched triangular blade that has had a second set of notches flaked into the blade halfway between the shoulders and the tip. This style is usually made on larger sized *Wallula Gap* and/or *Rabbit Islands*, although other types are sometimes used. The cross section is flattened lenticular. The depth of the second set of barbs varies, and triple notches do occur. These points are well made and usually of gem material, and were locally called *"Vendetta"* points as they were designed to snap at the weakened halfway point, on contact with bone, cartilage or heavy muscle. **I.D. KEY:** Double shoulders.

FW

(Also see Cascade, Gypsum Cave, Owl Cave, Plateau Pent., Vandenberg Contracting Stem & Wildcat Canyon)

Chalcedony

Agate

Ground basal sides

G3, $8-$15
WA

G8, $40-$75
OR

G7, $35-$60
Columbia River Valley, OR

Tip wear

G7, $25-$45
Lake Co., OR

Jasper

G6, $30-$55
Sou. OR

G4, $12-$20
OR

G8, $50-$90
Five Mile Locks, OR

Agate

Ground stem

Ground basal sides

G8, $55-$100
OR

G8, $80-$150
WA

G8, $65-$125
Caribou Co., ID

Petrified wood

G8, $110-$200
OR

G9, $200-$350
WA

LOCATION: Great Basin area. **DESCRIPTION:** A medium size lanceolate point with a recurved edge and a long, straight-sided, tapered base that is ground. The basal edge is short and straight to rounded. **I.D. KEY:** Pronounced contracting base.

1108

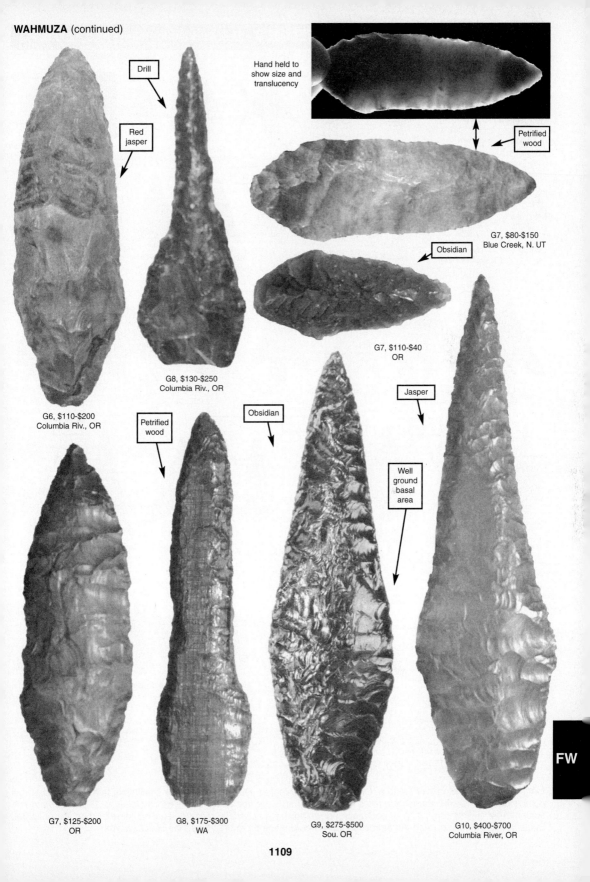

Drill

Red
jasper

Hand held to
show size and
translucency

Petrified
wood

G7, $80-$150
Blue Creek, N. UT

Obsidian

G8, $130-$250
Columbia Riv., OR

G7, $110-$40
OR

G6, $110-$200
Columbia Riv., OR

Petrified
wood

Obsidian

Jasper

Well
ground
basal
area

G7, $125-$200
OR

G8, $175-$300
WA

G9, $275-$500
Sou. OR

G10, $400-$700
Columbia River, OR

FW

WALLULA GAP RECTANGULAR STEMMED - Dev. to Historic Phase, 1000 - 200 B. P.

(Also see Columbia Plateau, Eastgate, Rabbit Island, Rose Spring & Sauvie's Island)

Red agate — G9, $30-$50 Portland, OR

Agate — G9, $45-$80 WA

G6, $12-$20 OR

Obsidian — G9, $25-$45 Colum. Riv., OR

Agate — G9, $25-$45 Hood Riv., OR

G8, $15-$30 Colum. Riv., OR

G6, $15-$30 Lake Co., OR

G9, $30-$55 Colum. Riv., OR

G9, $25-$40 Colum. Rv., OR

Agate — G3, $5-$10 OR

G5, $8-$15 Hood Rv., OR

G9, $50-$90 OR

Black jasper — G8, $8-$15 Peterson, WA

Chalc. — G6, $15-$30 WA

Agate — G9, $35-$65 John Day Rv., OR

G9, $35-$65 John Day Rv., OR

G9, $50-$90 WA

Agate — G8, $30-$50 Hood Rv., OR

Jasper — G8, $30-$50 OR

G9, $85-$165 John Day Riv., OR

G9, $45-$80 Hood Riv., OR

Red jasper — G8, 45-$80 Hood Riv., OR

G6, $15-$30 N. OR

Jasper — G7, $25-$40 Hood Riv., OR

Serrated edge — G5, $15-$30 Columb. Riv., OR

G7, $35-$65 John Day, Riv., OR

Chalc. — G8, $45-$80 WA

G6, $15-$30 Columb. Riv., OR

G9, $75-$140 OR

Agate — G9, $65-$115 Colum. Rv., OR

Banded agate — G7, $40-$75 OR

Jasper — G8, $65-$115 OR

Chalc. — G10, $125-$200 WA

G6, $45-$80 OR

G10, $250-$450 John Day Riv., OR

Agate — G8, $75-$140 OR

G8, $50-$90 Cent. WA

Chalc. — G9, $45-$80 OR

Serrated edge — G9, $125-$200 Hood Riv., OR

Jasper — G9, $125-$200 OR

G9, $75-$140 John Day Riv., OR — Agate

G10, $275-$500 Colum. Rv., OR

Agate — G9, $55-$100 Colum. Rv., OR

G9, $200-$350 WA

LOCATION: Columbia River basin of Oregon and Washington. **DESCRIPTION:** A small size, thin, stemmed, arrow point usually with barbs. Blades are more narrow and barbs are not as prominent as on *Columbia Plateau* points. The stem can be slightly expanding or contracting or bulbous but is usually rectangular. Shoulders barbed to horizontal. Blade edges can be serrated. A contracting stem would place the point in the *Rabbit Island* type.

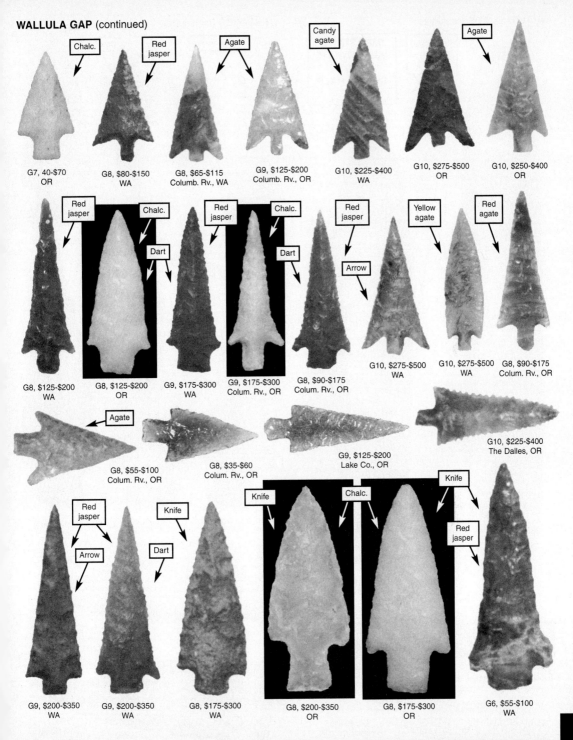

Chalc.

Red jasper

Agate

Candy agate

Agate

G7, 40-$70
OR

G8, $80-$150
WA

G8, $65-$115
Columb. Rv., WA

G9, $125-$200
Columb. Rv., OR

G10, $225-$400
WA

G10, $275-$500
OR

G10, $250-$400
OR

Red jasper

Chalc.

Dart

Red jasper

Chalc.

Dart

Red jasper

Arrow

Yellow agate

Red agate

G8, $125-$200
WA

G8, $125-$200
OR

G9, $175-$300
WA

G9, $175-$300
Colum. Rv., OR

G8, $90-$175
Colum. Rv., OR

G10, $275-$500
WA

G10, $275-$500
WA

G8, $90-$175
Colum. Rv., OR

Agate

G8, $55-$100
Colum. Rv., OR

G8, $35-$60
Colum. Rv., OR

G9, $125-$200
Lake Co., OR

G10, $225-$400
The Dalles, OR

Red jasper

Arrow

Knife

Dart

Knife

Chalc.

Knife

Red jasper

G9, $200-$350
WA

G9, $200-$350
WA

G8, $175-$300
WA

G8, $200-$350
OR

G8, $175-$300
OR

G6, $55-$100
WA

FW

WEALTH BLADE - Developmental to Present, 1200 B.P. - Present

(Also see Cascade, Early Leaf)

LOCATION: Southern Oregon. **DESCRIPTION:** A large to very large size lanceolate, double pointed blade. Some examples have a waist in the center of the blade to facilitate holding. Recent examples have been used in dance ceremonies. The classic examples are 11"–16" long, well made, generally always waisted. **I.D. KEY:** Extreme size.

WEALTH BLADE (continued)

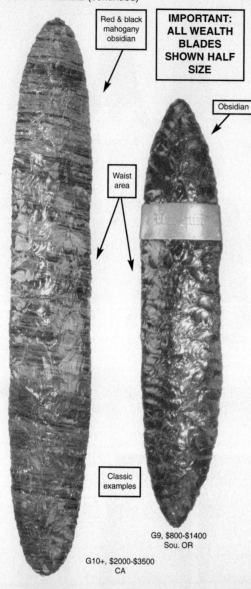

Red & black mahogany obsidian

IMPORTANT: ALL WEALTH BLADES SHOWN HALF SIZE

Obsidian

Waist area

Classic examples

G9, $800-$1400
Sou. OR

G10+, $2000-$3500
CA

WENDOVER (continued)

Chalcedony

Obsidian

G7, $15-$25
OR

G6, $15-$25
Sou. OR

G7, $15-$30
OR

Red agate

Obsidian

Basalt

G10, $125-$200
Umatilla Co., OR

G8, $25-$40
Sou. OR

G9, $40-$75
Harney Co., OR

Obsidian

G9, $55-$100
Cent. OR

Obsidian

G10, $80-$150
Lake Co., OR

WENDOVER - Early to middle Archaic, 7000 - 5000 B. P.

(Also see Bitterroot, Bullhead, Chilcotin Plateau, Eastgate, Merrybell and Rose Springs)

Basalt

G6, $8-$15
Wallowa Co., OR

G5, $10-$20
Pyramid Lake, NV

LOCATION: Great Basin westward. **DESCRIPTION:** A medium size, narrow, expanded stem to side notched dart point with a convex base. Shoulders can be slightly tapered to barbed. Base corners are sharp to rounded. Found on buffalo jump sites in Owyhee Co., ID.

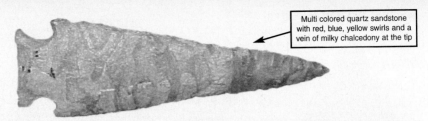

Multi colored quartz sandstone with red, blue, yellow swirls and a vein of milky chalcedony at the tip

G9, $175-$300
N.W. UT, Hogup Mountains,

WILDCAT CANYON - Early Archaic, 9000 - 7500 B. P.

(Also see Cascade, Early Leaf, Paleo Knife, Plateau Pentagonal & Wahmuza)

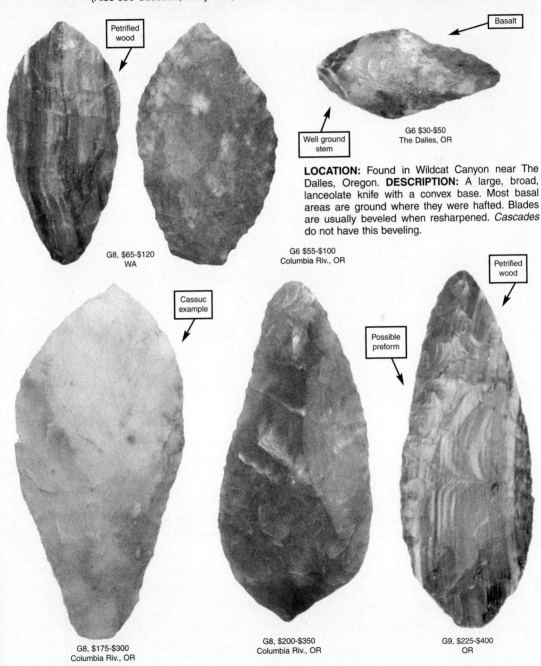

Petrified wood

Basalt

Well ground stem

G6 $30-$50
The Dalles, OR

G8, $65-$120
WA

LOCATION: Found in Wildcat Canyon near The Dalles, Oregon. **DESCRIPTION:** A large, broad, lanceolate knife with a convex base. Most basal areas are ground where they were hafted. Blades are usually beveled when resharpened. *Cascades* do not have this beveling.

G6 $55-$100
Columbia Riv., OR

Cassuc example

Possible preform

Petrified wood

G8, $175-$300
Columbia Riv., OR

G8, $200-$350
Columbia Riv., OR

G9, $225-$400
OR

FW

1113

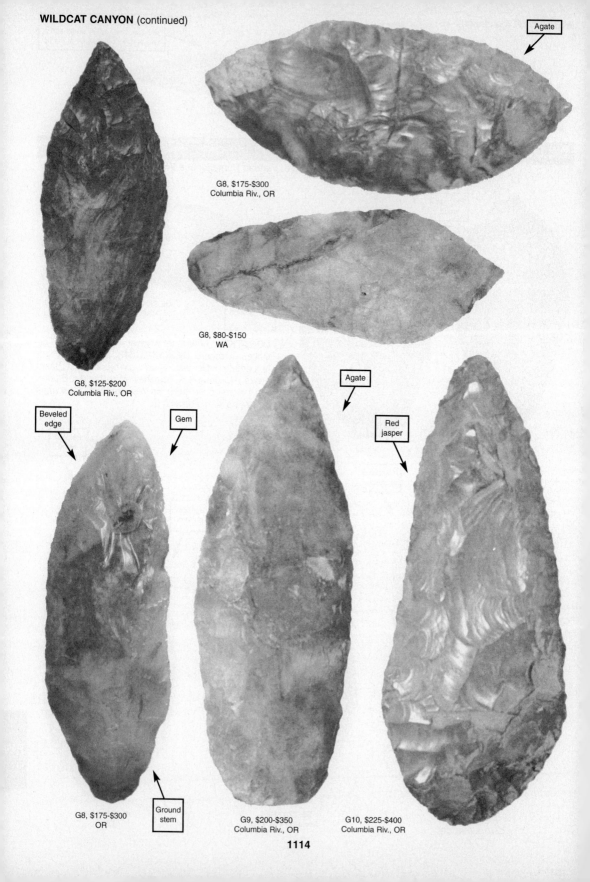

Agate

G8, $175-$300
Columbia Riv., OR

G8, $80-$150
WA

G8, $125-$200
Columbia Riv., OR

Beveled
edge

Gem

Agate

Red
jasper

G8, $175-$300
OR

Ground
stem

G9, $200-$350
Columbia Riv., OR

G10, $225-$400
Columbia Riv., OR

WILLITS SIDE NOTCHED - Mid-Archaic, 4000 - 1500 B. P.

(See Kelsey Creek, Mayacmas, McGillivray, Need Stemmed Lanceolate, Nightfire & Tuolumne Notched)

Basalt

Obsidian

Heavily resharpened

Obsidian

G5, $12-$20
Humboldt Co., NV

G6, $20-$35
Sou. CA coast

G7, $30-$50
CA

G7, $35-$60
Silver Lake, OR

G7, $35-$75
Lake Co., OR

Agate

G9, $125-$200
Washoe Lake, N. NV

Basalt

Broken tip

G1, $2-$5
OR

G9, $175-$300
Columbia Riv., OR

Thin

G10, $350-$650
CA

G8, $250-$450
N. CA

FW

LOCATION: Northern California into southern Oregon. **DESCRIPTION:** A medium to large size, narrow, weakly side-notched point with a convex base. Notches usually appear high up from the base creating a large, bulbous stem. Some examples are lightly serrated. **I.D. KEY:** Bulbous stem.

(See Eden, Hell Gap, Lake Mohave, Lind Coulee, Owl Cave, Parman, Scottsbluff, Shaniko Stemmed, Silver Lake & Youngs River)

Bifurcated stem

Broken ear

Jasper

Obsidian

G4, $25-$40
Sou. OR

Ground stem

G6, $55-$100
Lake Co., OR

Windust/ Cody

G5, $35-$60
Humboldt Co., NV

G4, $35-$60
WA

G6, $40-$75
Sou. OR

G5, $30-$50
Sou. OR

Basal grinding

Obsidian

Basalt

Obsidian

G8 $80-$150
Sou. OR

G8, $125-$200
S. OR

Base wear

G5, $40-$75
E. OR

Ground stem

G8, $150-$250
E. OR

G8, $125-$200
Lake Co., OR

Beveled edge

Ground stem

Tip nick

Yellow jasper

Obsidian

G9, $175-$300
Humboldt Co., NV

Red & black banded obsidian

G5, $80-$150
Fort Rock Valley, OR

G5, $55-$100
Sou. OR

Ground stem

G9, $175-$300
WA

G4, $125-$200
Sou. OR

LOCATION: Oregon and Washington. **DESCRIPTION:** A medium size, broad point that has weak shoulders and a stemmed, concave basal area. Basal concavity can be shallow to deep and rarely can be fluted. Some examples are non-stemmed with a concave base. Basal area can be ground. Chisel tips occur along with *Lake Mojave* and *Parman* points. This point co-existed with *Clovis*.

WINDUST (continued)

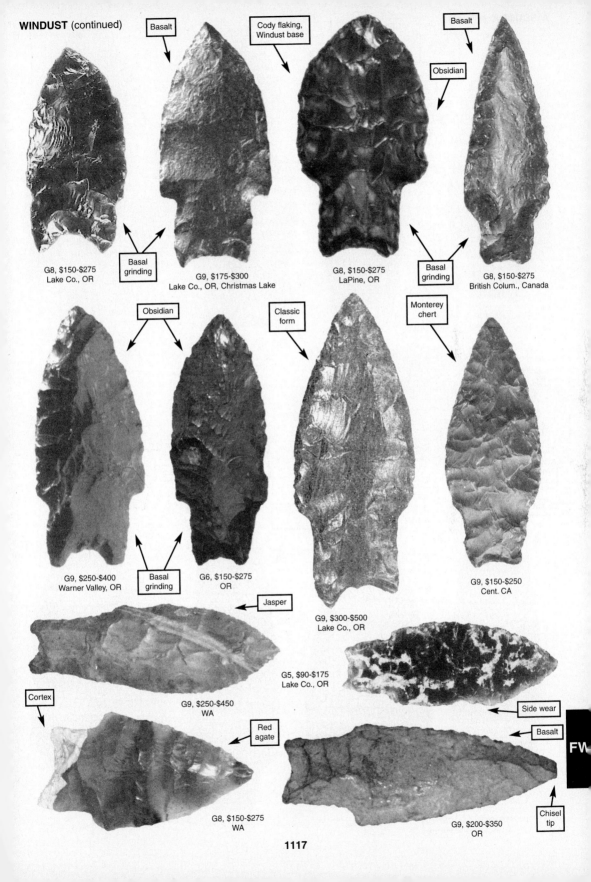

Basalt

Cody flaking,
Windust base

Basalt

Obsidian

Basal
grinding

G8, $150-$275
Lake Co., OR

G9, $175-$300
Lake Co., OR, Christmas Lake

Basal
grinding

G8, $150-$275
LaPine, OR

Basal
grinding

G8, $150-$275
British Colum., Canada

Obsidian

Classic
form

Monterey
chert

Basal
grinding

G9, $250-$400
Warner Valley, OR

G6, $150-$275
OR

G9, $150-$250
Cent. CA

G9, $300-$500
Lake Co., OR

Jasper

G5, $90-$175
Lake Co., OR

G9, $250-$450
WA

Cortex

Red
agate

Side wear

Basalt

G8, $150-$275
WA

Chisel
tip

G9, $200-$350
OR

FW

1117

Black obsidian

Very thin

Obsidian

G10, $275-$500
N. UT, Danger cave

Basal grinding

G5, $150-$375
S. OR

G8, $275-$500
Lake Co., OR

G8, $275-$500
Sou. OR

Classic form

G10, $450-$800
Lake Co., OR

Alkali on surface

Ground stem

Hart Mountain jasper

Obsidian

Obsidian

Basalt

Windust/ Cody

G6, $250-$450
S. OR

Basal grinding

G9, $350-$650
S. OR

G10, $350-$600
S. OR

G8, $250-$450
S. OR

WINDUST (continued)

Obsidian

Chisel tip

G9, $325-$450
Lake Co., OR

Obsidian

Ground stem

Thinning strikes at base

G9, $400-$700
S.E. OR. Classic form.

G8, $325-$500
Lake Co., OR

Ground stem

G9, $550-$1000
Lake Co., OR

G7, $400-$750
Millers Island, WA

WINDUST-ALBERTA - Paleo to Early Archaic, 10,500 - 9000 B. P.

(See Alberta, Lake Mohave, Lind Coulee, Owl Cave, Parman, Scottsbluff, Shaniko Stemmed and Silver Lake)

Obsidian

Ground stem

G6, $150-$250
S. OR

Ground stem

G4, $40-$75
OR

FW

LOCATION: Great Basin into Oregon & Washington. **DESCRIPTION:** A lanceolate point with long, straight contracting stems. The blades are formed by random percussion and the edges are aligned by non-serial pressure flaking. Shoulders are formed by strong pressure flaking. The residual Hertzian core scars are usually eliminated by finer finish flaking. Stem sides are ground and basal corners are usually rounded. Some points have basal thinning that leaves a slight "lobed" appearance. Cross sections are lenticular and heavy without being "thick."

WINDUST -ALBERTA (continued)

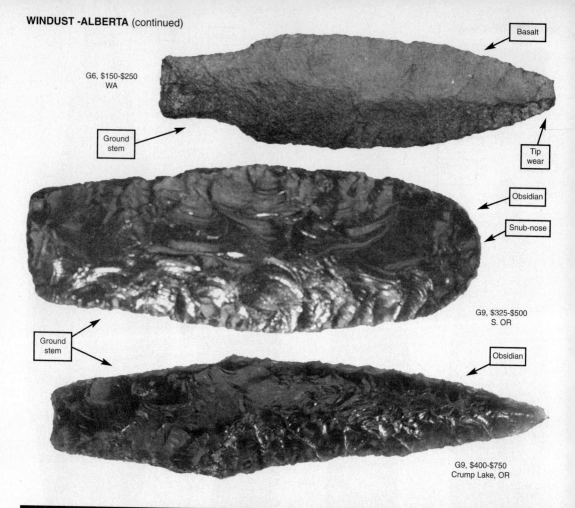

Basalt

G6, $150-$250
WA

Ground stem

Tip wear

Obsidian

Snub-nose

G9, $325-$500
S. OR

Ground stem

Obsidian

G9, $400-$750
Crump Lake, OR

WINDUST CONTRACTING STEM - Paleo to Early Archaic, 10,500 - 8000 B. P.

(See Lake Mohave, Intermontane, Lind Coulee, Owl Cave, Parman, Shaniko Stemmed and Silver Lake)

Tan chert

G6, $30-$50
Xmas Vall., OR

G5, $25-$40
OR

G5, $25-$40
Columbia Riv., OR

G6, $30-$50
OR

G6, $15-$25
OR

G5, $25-$40
OR

G7 $80-$150
OR

LOCATION: Great Basin into Oregon & Washington.
DESCRIPTION: A medium size, broad point that has weak shoulders and a contracting stem. This style of *Windust* has many characteristics common to the Cody Complex.

WINDUST CONTRACTING STEM (continued)

Ground stem

Obsidian

G5, $30-$50
OR

G6, $35-$65
Humboldt Co., NV

G8, $80-$150
OR

G7, $55-$100
Snake River, ID

Basalt

Windust/Cody

Basalt

G6, $125-$200
Lake Co., OR

G6, $125-$200
Snake River, WA

Obsidian

Gem

First stage

Obsidian

G8, $80-$150
Lake Co., OR

G6, $80-$150
OR

Ground stem

G8, $150-$250
OR

G8 225-$400
Lake Co., OR

Ground stem

G10, $350-$600
WA

G9, $275-$500
Klickitat Co., WA

Ground stem

Ground stem

Obsidian

G8, $200-$375
OR

Ground stem

G9, $250-$400
OR

FW

1121

WINDUST-HATWAI - Paleo to Early Archaic, 10,500 - 8000 B. P.

(See Lake Mohave, Lind Coulee, Owl Cave, Parman, Shaniko Stemmed and Silver Lake)

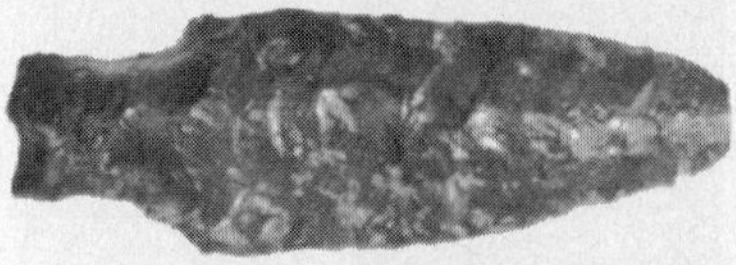

Tip wear

G5, $25-$40
OR

Jasper

G8, $65-$125
OR

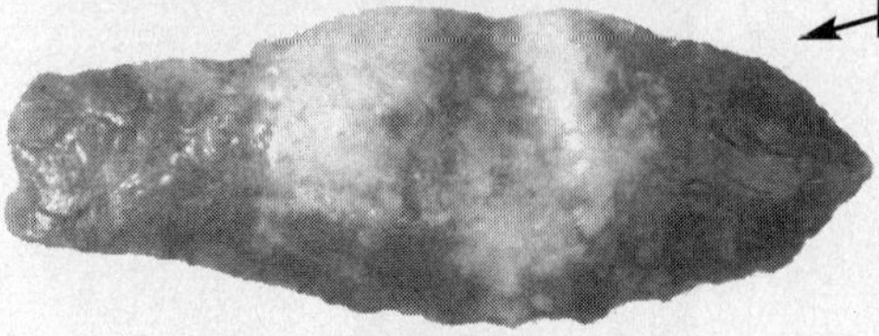

Agate

Obsidian

G6, $65-$125
WA

G8, $125-$200
Steens Mtn., OR

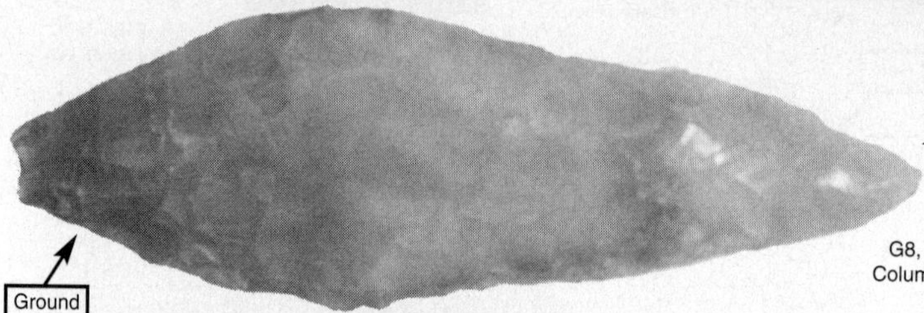

Chalcedony

G8, $250-$450
Columbia Riv., WA

Obsidian

Ground stem

Obsidian

G8, $200-$350
Crump Lake, OR

Ground stem

Obsidian

G9, $275-$500
Lake Co., OR

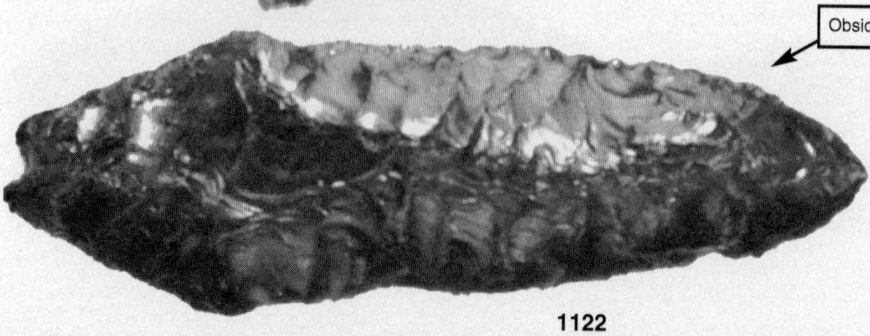

Obsidian

G8, $350-$600
Crump Lake, OR

Obsidian

G8, $250-$450
OR

WINDUST-HATWAI (continued)

Agate

Obsidian

Ground stem

G9, $275-$500
Crump Lake, OR

LOCATION: Great Basin into Oregon & Washington. **DESCRIPTION:** A medium to large size dart/knife that has a long, contracting, bifurcated stem. Shoulders are obtuse to horizontal to barbed. Stem edges are ground. Basal concavity usually shows a strong hertzian cone of percussion that is often off-center.

Ground stem

G8, $125-$200
OR

Resharpened many times

Obsidian

Obsidian

Base wear

G6, $200-$375
Crump Lake, OR

Ground stem

G8, $400-$700
Crump Lake, OR

Ground stem

G9, $550-$1000
Crump Lake, OR

FW

WINTU - Developmental to Historic Phase, 1000 - 200 B. P.

(Also see Desert Side Notched and Piquinin

Obsidian

Serrated edge

G10+, $275-$500
Redding, CA, from a Pete Bostrom cast

G10, $250-$400
Warner Valley, OR

G10++, $700-$1200
Modoc Co., CA

LOCATION: Central California to sou. Oregon. **DESCRIPTION:** A rare, thin, needle tipped point with unique upward sloping, narrow side notches and a concave base. Usually made of jasper and obsidian.

WOODEN DART/ARROW - Late Archaic to Transitional Phase, 3500 - 2000 B. P.

(Also see Bone Arrow, Bone Pin)

G9, $15-$25
N. UT, Hogup Cave
6" long, dated to 2200 B.P.
made of willow wood

G9, $15-$25, N. UT, Hogup
Cave, 6" long, dated to 2200 B.P.

G8, $15-$25
N. UT, Hogup Cave
Atlatl tip made of grease
wood. Dated to 3500 B.P.

LOCATION: Utah. **DESCRIPTION:** Fashioned from sand bar willow wood and grease wood, these dart/arrows were carved and polished to sharp tips. Stone tips were not utilized. These were carbon dated to 3,500 & 2,200 years old.

YANA - Developmental to Historic Phase, 1500 - 400 B. P.

(Also see Coquille, Gatecliff, Gunther, Gypsum Cave, Point Sal Barbed, Rabbit Island and Wallula)

G9, $15-$25
Shasta Co., CA,
Redding, CA

G8, $35-$50
Mendocino Co., CA

LOCATION: Northern California **DESCRIPTION:** A rare, thin, small to medium size, barbed point with a short to long, narrow, tapered stem. A rare type. Part of the *Gunther* cluster. **I.D. KEY:** Stem form.

YOUNGS RIVER STEMMED - Early Archaic, 8000 - 6000 B. P.

(Also see Windust)

Basalt

G3, $8-$15
OR coast

G4, $12-$20
OR coast

resilicified
sandstone

G5, $12-$20
Columbia Riv. Basin, OR, near type site.

G4, $12-$20
Lake Co., OR

G5, $15-$25
Wahkiakum Co. WA

LOCATION: Great Basin westward. **DESCRIPTION:** A medium size, broad stemmed point with tapered shoulders. A *varitey* of *Windust*.

ALASKA THE FAR NORTH SECTION:

This section includes artifact types from the following regions:
St. Lawrence Island, Bering Sea - southward into the Aleutian Islands, Northern Slope and eastward.

With a few exceptions, archaeological sites in the Northern Reaches are either sparse or involve shallow multiple occupations, often over large areas, that are disturbed and mixed through frost action. Organic materials are seldom preserved except in late sites.

Lithics: Material employed in the manufacture of projectile points and related artifacts from these regions are: Basalt, chalcedony, chert, Jadeite, jasper, nephrite, obsidian, slate.

Important sites: Anangula, Broken Mammoth, Gerstle River Quarry, Healy Lake, Lime Hills, Mesa, Onion Portage.

Regional Consultant:
Joel Castanza

Special Advisor:
Ben Stermer

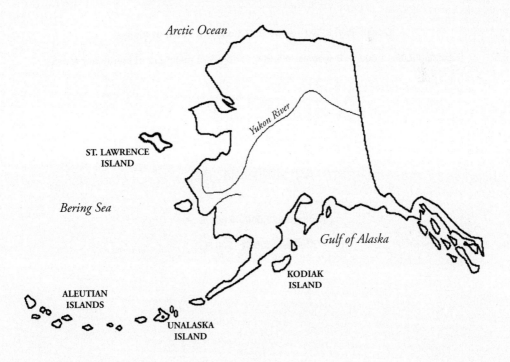

AK

ALASKAN CULTURAL PERIODS

Including: Aleutian Islands, Kodiak Region, Bering Sea Region, Siberia, Northern Alaska, Canada

Bering Sea Region, Siberia, Northern Alaska, Canada

Paleo-Arctic – 10,000 - 7,000 years B. P.

Northern Archaic: 6,500 - 4,000 B. P.

Arctic Small Tool: 6,000 - 4,200 B. P.

Norton Tradition: 3,000 - 1,200 B. P.

Dorset Tradition: 3,000 - 1000 B. P.

Thule Tradition: 2,500 - 1000 B. P. Includes the Old Bering Sea, Okvik, Punuk, Birnirk

Inuit/Eskimo: 2,800 B.P. - Historic

Athapaskan: 2,000 B.P. - Historic

Kodiak Region

Ocean Bay: 6,000 - 3,000 B. P. Southern coast of Alaska

Kodiak: 6,000 - 1,000 B. P. Kodiak Island and adjacent mainland of southeast Alaska

Aleutian Islands

Anangula: 9,000 - 5,000 B .P.

Aleutian: 5,000 - 200 B.P.

ALEUTIAN REGION

The artifacts from Chignik are all site points.

CHIGNIK DART - Aleutian Tradition, 5000 - 200 B. P.

(Also see Dutch Harbor Stemmed, Kotzebue Dart and Whale)

Basalt

LOCATION: Lower Alaskan peninsula. **DESCRIPTION:** A medium size, broad point with rounded, tapered shoulders and a rounded stem.

G9, $200-$300
Chignik Lake Outlet, Aleutian Peninsula.
Very rare

CHIGNIK LANCEOLATE - Aleutian Tradition, 5000 - 200 B. P.

(Also see Dutch Harbor Lanceolate and Independence)

LOCATION: Lower Alaskan peninsula. **DESCRIPTION:** A medium size, lanceolate projectile with a tapering hafting area and a straight to convex base.

G7, $20-$35
Aleutian Peninsula

G10, $150-$300
Aleutian Peninsula

Basalt

CHIGNIK LEAF - Aleutian Tradition, 5000 - 200 B. P.

(Also see Dutch Harbor Lanceolate, Naknek & St. Michael Leaf)

G10, $40-$75
Aleutian Peninsula

Basalt

LOCATION: Lower Alaskan peninsula. **DESCRIPTION:** A medium size, narrow, lanceolate point with a convex base.

G9, $55-$100
Aleutian Peninsula

CHIGNIK STEMMED - Aleutian Tradition, 5000 - 200 B. P.

(Also see Kayuk, Kotzebue Bay, Portage, Ugashik & Unalaska)

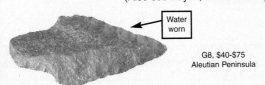

Water worn

G8, $40-$75
Aleutian Peninsula

LOCATION: Lower Alaskan peninsula. **DESCRIPTION:** A medium size, stemmed point with medium, tapered shoulders. The stem tapers into a rounded base.

DUTCH HARBOR BI-POINT - Aleutian Tradition, 5000 - 200 B. P.

(Also see Chignik Lanceolate, Chignik Leaf, Mesa & Portage & Cascade in Far West Section)

LOCATION: Lower Alaskan peninsula islands. **DESCRIPTION:** A medium to large size, bipointed blade with excurvate edges.

AK

DUTCH HARBOR BI-POINT(continued)

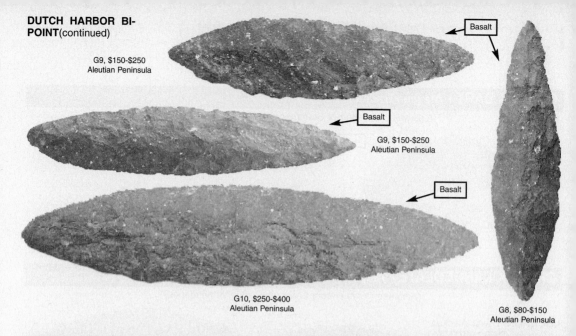

G9, $150-$250
Aleutian Peninsula

Basalt

Basalt

G9, $150-$250
Aleutian Peninsula

Basalt

G10, $250-$400
Aleutian Peninsula

G8, $80-$150
Aleutian Peninsula

DUTCH HARBOR LARGE STEMMED - Aleutian Tradition, 5000 - 200 B. P.

(Also see Dutch Harbor Stemmed)

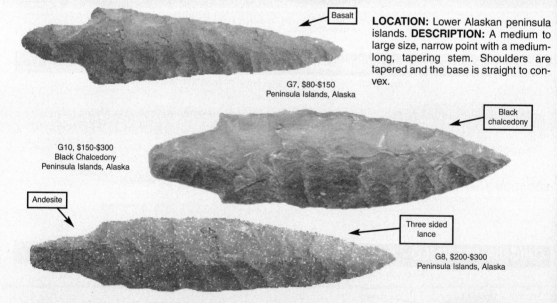

Basalt

G7, $80-$150
Peninsula Islands, Alaska

LOCATION: Lower Alaskan peninsula islands. **DESCRIPTION:** A medium to large size, narrow point with a medium-long, tapering stem. Shoulders are tapered and the base is straight to convex.

G10, $150-$300
Black Chalcedony
Peninsula Islands, Alaska

Black chalcedony

Andesite

Three sided lance

G8, $200-$300
Peninsula Islands, Alaska

DUTCH HARBOR SIDE NOTCHED - Aleutian Tradition, 5000 - 200 B. P.

(Also see Kotzebue Bay)

Chert

LOCATION: Lower Alaskan peninsula islands. **DESCRIPTION:** A medium size point with shallow side notches. Base can be convex to concave.

G9, $70-$120
Peninsula Islands, Alaska

Glassy basalt

G9, $150-$250
Peninsula Islands, Alaska

1128

DUTCH HARBOR STEMMED - Aleutian Tradition, 5000 - 200 B. P.

(Also see Chignik Dart and Point Hope)

Basalt

G6, $35-$65
Peninsula Islands, Alaska

Basalt

Basalt

G10, $175-$300
Unalaska Captain's Cove, Alaska
Lower Alaskan Peninsula Islands

G8, $150-$250
Peninsula Islands, Alaska

G8, $150-$250
Unalaska Island, AK

G10, $125-$200
Peninsula Islands, Alaska

LOCATION: Lower Alaskan peninsula islands. **DESCRIPTION:** A medium size, broad point with a short to median, tapering stem. Shoulders are tapered and the base is straight to convex.

UNALASKA (Dutch Harbor) - Aleutian Tradition, 5000 - 200 B. P.

(Also see Chignik Stemmed)

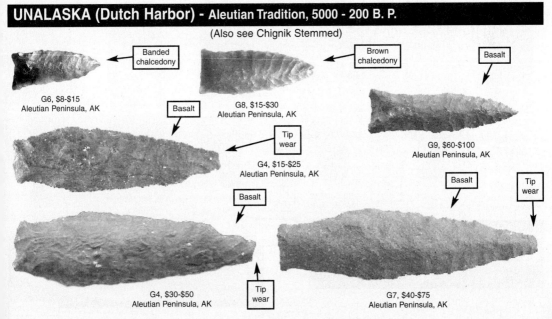

Banded chalcedony

G6, $8-$15
Aleutian Peninsula, AK

Brown chalcedony

Basalt

G8, $15-$30
Aleutian Peninsula, AK

Basalt

Tip wear

G4, $15-$25
Aleutian Peninsula, AK

G9, $60-$100
Aleutian Peninsula, AK

Basalt

Basalt

Tip wear

Tip wear

G4, $30-$50
Aleutian Peninsula, AK

G7, $40-$75
Aleutian Peninsula, AK

LOCATION: Lower Alaskan peninsula islands. **DESCRIPTION:** A medium to large size, narrow, auriculate, stemmed point with broad side notches to an expanding stem. Bases are straight to concave.

AK

ARCTIC ESKIMO REGION

BEAR-TYPE 1 (Under 2") - Norton Tradition, 3000 B.P. - Inuit/Eskimo - Historic

(Also see Kavik, Kayuk, Point Hope & Unalakleet)

Tip nick

Gray chert

Gray/ brown flint

Chert

Shovel- nose tip

G4, $30-$50
Alaska

Chert

Gray chert

G4, $5-$10
High Arctic, Alaska

G4, $5-$10
Point Hope, Alaska

G6, $12-$20
Alaska

G5, $12-$20
Alaska

G5, $5-$10
Utkiavwin,AK

G6, $20-$35
High Arctic, Alaska

G5, $15-$30
Point Hope, Alaska

Tip wear

LOCATION: Bear points are found mostly along the North Alaskan coast and St. Lawrence and Punuk Island. **DESCRIPTION:** A small size, narrow point with weak, tapered shoulders and a short parallel stem. Flaking is collateral on the better-made specimens. Bear points were inserted into a bone, antler or ivory shaft and were used in hunting walrus, seals, caribou & other large animals and in war. **Note:** Dating has been difficult. The Yupuk of the St. Lawrence Island have been digging archaeological sites for at least 300 years due to demand for fossil ivory which has destroyed the archaeological record on most sites. This type may date to 5,000-6,000 B.P.

BEAR-TYPE 2 (2"-3") - Norton Tradition, 3000 B.P. - Inuit/Eskimo - Historic

(Also see Kavik, Kayuk, Point Hope & Unalakleet)

Tip wear

Collateral flaking to a median ridge

Gray chert

Dark chalc.

Gray chert

G4, $8-$15
St. Lawrence, Island, Alaska

G6, $25-$40
Alaska

black chert

G8, $40-$75
Nuwuk, Alaska

Black chalc.

G6, $30-$50
Alaska

G6, $35-$65
Alaska

G7, $65-$125
Alaska

G5, $25-$45
Alaska

Bifurcated base

G8, $65-$125
Alaska

Chalcedony

LOCATION: Same as type 1. **DESCRIPTION:** A medium size (2"-3"), narrow point with horizontal shoulders and a medium-length, parallel stem. Base is straight to slightly convex. Blade edges can be serrated. Cross section forms a median ridge with usually collateral flaking. **I.D. KEY:** Long, narrow stemmed point.

Green chert
w/red streak

G8, $75-$140
Alaska

G6, $80-$150
Alaska

Collateral flaking to
a median ridge

BEAR-TYPE 3 (Over 3") - Norton Tradition, 3000 B. P. - Inuit/Eskimo - Historic

(Also see Kavik, Kayuk, Point Hope & Unalakleet)

Black
chert

Translucent
chalcedony

Green/gray
chert

Collateral
flaking to a
median
ridge

Black
chert

Gray
chert

Base
fracture

Material
flaw

G9, $125-$200
Alaska

G5, $150-$250
Alaska

G9, $200-$350
Alaska

G10, $175-$300
Alaska

G10+, $250-$400
Alaska

LOCATION: See type 1. **DESCRIPTION:** A large size, narrow point with horizontal shoulders and a medium-length, parallel stem. Base is straight to slightly convex. Blade edges can be serrated. Cross section forms a median ridge. **I.D. KEY:** Long, narrow stemmed point.

BEAR-TYPE 4 - Norton Tradition, 3000 B. P. - Inuit/Eskimo - Historic

(Also see Kayuk, Point Hope, Unalaklett)

Gray
chert

Fired
chert

G4, $20-$35
Alaska

G7, $65-$125
Alaska

Green/gray
chert

Gray
chert

G8, $35-$65
Alaska

G6, $60-$110
Alaska

BEAR-TYPE 4 (continued)

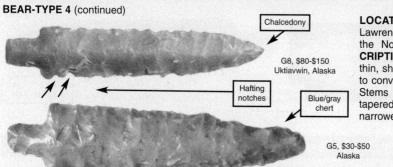

Chalcedony

G8, $80-$150
Uktiavwin, Alaska

Hafting notches

Blue/gray chert

G5, $30-$50
Alaska

LOCATION: Northern Alaska (St. Lawrence Island), North Slope, and the Northern Yukon Territory. **DESCRIPTION:** A medium to large zie, thin, short stemmed point with parallel to convex sides and strong shoulders. Stems are parallel sided to slightly tapered. This variation is longer and narrower than the standard *Bear* point.

BIRD ARROW-BLUNT - Inuit/Eskimo, 2800 B. P. - Historic

(Also see Bone Arrow and Harpoon)

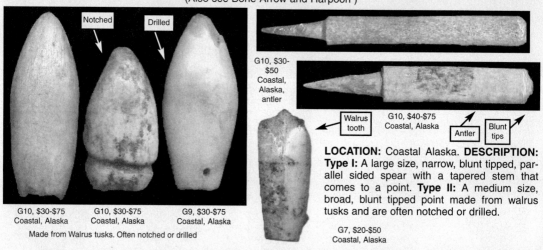

Notched

Drilled

G10, $30-$75
Coastal, Alaska

G10, $30-$75
Coastal, Alaska

G9, $30-$75
Coastal, Alaska

Made from Walrus tusks. Often notched or drilled

G10, $30-$50
Coastal, Alaska, antler

Walrus tooth

G10, $40-$75
Coastal, Alaska

Antler

Blunt tips

G7, $20-$50
Coastal, Alaska

LOCATION: Coastal Alaska. **DESCRIPTION:** **Type I:** A large size, narrow, blunt tipped, parallel sided spear with a tapered stem that comes to a point. **Type II:** A medium size, broad, blunt tipped point made from walrus tusks and are often notched or drilled.

BIRD SPEAR - Inuit/Eskimo, 2800 B. P. - Historic

(Also see Bone Arrow and Harpoon)

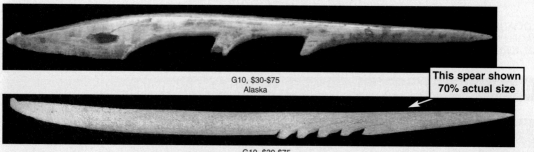

G10, $30-$75
Alaska

This spear shown 70% actual size

G10, $30-$75
Alaska

LOCATION: Coastal Alaska. **DESCRIPTION:** A large size, narrow spear with barbs. Made from bone or antler.

BONE ARROW - Inuit/Eskimo, 2800 B. P. - Historic

(Also see Harpoon)

LOCATION: Bering Sea Region. **DESCRIPTION:** A long, narrow foreshaft and point crafted from fossilized ivory, tusk and antler.

BONE ARROW (continued)

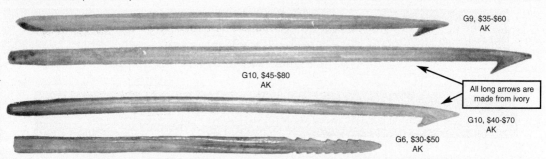

G9, $35-$60
AK

G10, $45-$80
AK

All long arrows are
made from ivory

G10, $40-$70
AK

G6, $30-$50
AK

Deer arrow. Deer arrows have a long trihedral pile of antler from 4-8" long, with a sharp thin-edged point slightly concaved on the faces like the point of a bayonet. Two of the edges are rounded, but the third is sharp and cut into one or more simple barbs. Behind the barb the pile takes the form of a rounded shank, ending in a shoulder and a sharp rounded tang a little enlarged above the point. Ref: 9th Annual Report, 1887-88 Bureau of Etnology.

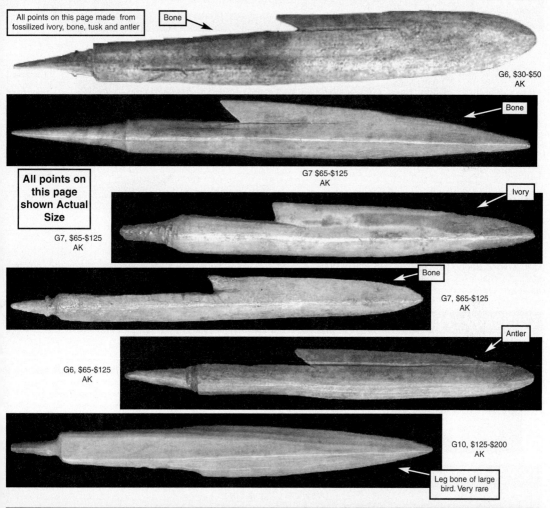

All points on this page made from
fossilized ivory, bone, tusk and antler

Bone

G6, $30-$50
AK

Bone

**All points on
this page
shown Actual
Size**

G7 $65-$125
AK

Ivory

G7, $65-$125
AK

Bone

G7, $65-$125
AK

Antler

G6, $65-$125
AK

G10, $125-$200
AK

Leg bone of large
bird. Very rare

BONE ARROW w/Metal or Stone points - Inuit/Eskimo, 2800 B. P. - Historic

(Also see Hafted Knife, Harpoon, Unalakleet)

Unalakleet
point tip

G10, $300-$500 (complete)
AK

(see Unalakleet page for price
of point only

AK

BONE ARROW with metal or stone points (continued)

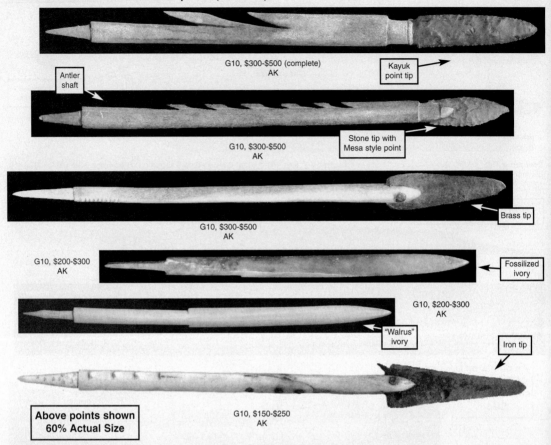

G10, $300-$500 (complete)
AK

Antler shaft

Kayuk point tip

G10, $300-$500
AK

Stone tip with Mesa style point

Brass tip

G10, $300-$500
AK

G10, $200-$300
AK

Fossilized ivory

G10, $200-$300
AK

"Walrus" ivory

Iron tip

Above points shown 60% Actual Size

G10, $150-$250
AK

LOCATION: Bering Sea Region. **DESCRIPTION:** A large size, narrow, parallel sided spear with a tapered, pointed stem that that inserts into the main shaft. Made from fossilized ivory, tusk and antler. Metal or stone points were used as tips.

CHINDADN - Paleo-Arctic Tradition, 11,300 - 11,000 B. P.

(Also see Mesa and Sub-Triangular)

G8, $25-$50
Nenana Valley, AK

Picture from a cast made by Pete Bostrom

LOCATION: Alaska. **DESCRIPTION:** A small size, broad, thin, ovate point made from a flake that has a convex base. Made during the Nenana occupation. **I.D. KEY:** Broad, ovate form.

DORSET TRIANGULAR - The Dorset Tradition, 2500 - 1000 B. P.

(Also see Chignik Leaf)

Dark chalcedony

LOCATION: Bering Sea Region, Canadian Arctic. **DESCRIPTION:** A medium sized, thin, triangular point with a concave base.

G9, $25-$50
Yupuk-Eskimo, AK
Bering Sea Region, Canadian Arctic

G7, $25-$50
Kotzebue Bay, AK,
toggle point

Black chert

1134

DRILL - Paleo-Arctic Tradition - Historic, 10,000 - 200 B. P.

(Also see Hafted Knife, Scraper)

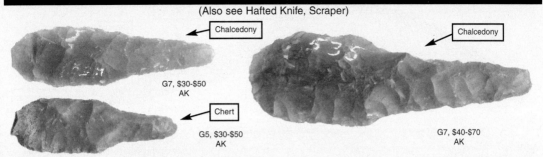

Chalcedony

Chalcedony

G7, $30-$50
AK

Chert

G5, $30-$50
AK

G7, $40-$70
AK

LOCATION: Everywhere. **DESCRIPTION:** Although many drills were made from scratch, all point types were made into the drill form. Usually, heavily resharpened and broken points were salvaged and rechipped into drills. These objects were certainly used as drills (evidence of extreme edge wear), but there is speculation that some of these forms may have been used as pins for clothing, ornaments, ear plugs and other uses.

FIRSTVIEW - Paleo-Arctic to Northern Archaic Tradition, 10,000 - 8000 B. P.

(Also see Mesa and Eden, Firstview & Scottsbluff In Northern Plains Section)

Gray chert

Ground stem

G9, $300-$500
Alaska

LOCATION: Alaska. **DESCRIPTION:** A small to medium sized stemmed projectile with weak shoulders and a straight to convex base. Basal sides are parallel, median ridged and collateral to oblique parallel flaking. stem is often ground. Made by the Cody Complex people.

FLAKING TOOL - INUIT/ESKIMO, 2800 B. P. - Historic

(Also see Drill, Hafted Knife, Scraper)

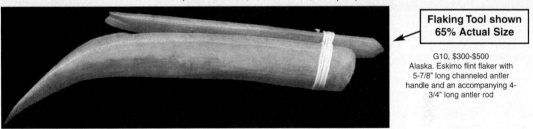

Flaking Tool shown 65% Actual Size

G10, $300-$500
Alaska. Eskimo flint flaker with 5-7/8" long channeled antler handle and an accompanying 4-3/4" long antler rod

LOCATION: Alaska. **DESCRIPTION:** A large hand tool for knapping stone into projectiles and other tools.

HAFTED KNIFE - INUIT/ESKIMO, 2800 B.P. - Historic

(Also see Arrow, Bone Arrow, Drill, Scraper)

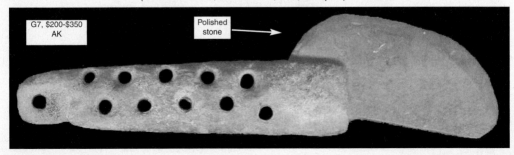

G7, $200-$350
AK

Polished stone

LOCATION: Alaska. **DESCRIPTION:** Hafting handles were crafted from wood, fossilized ivory, tusk or bone and were afixed to the blade with pitch or other adhesive. Flaked and polished stone were used as cutting blades.

HAFTED KNIFE (continued)

Reamer

Chert tip

G6, $150-$250
AK

Unalakleet knife

G9, $250-$400
AK

Unalakleet point type

G9, $250-$400
AK

Slate tip

HARPOON - Inuit/Eskimo - Historic, 3000 - 200 B. P.

(Also see Bird Spear, Hafted Knife)

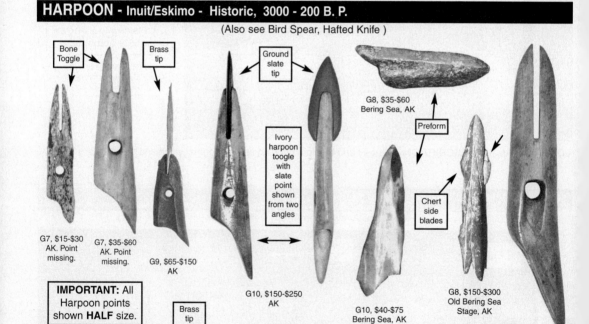

Bone Toggle

Brass tip

Ground slate tip

G8, $35-$60
Bering Sea, AK

Preform

Ivory harpoon toggle with slate point shown from two angles

Chert side blades

G7, $15-$30
AK. Point missing.

G7, $35-$60
AK. Point missing.

G9, $65-$150
AK

IMPORTANT: All Harpoon points shown **HALF** size.

Brass tip

G10, $150-$250
AK

G10, $40-$75
Bering Sea, AK

G8, $150-$300
Old Bering Sea Stage, AK

G10, $55-$100
AK. Point missing.

G9, $150-$250
AK

Broken base

Seal, fish bone Toggle

G4, $15-$25
AK

Walrus size ivory harpoon toggle

1136

HARPOON (continued)

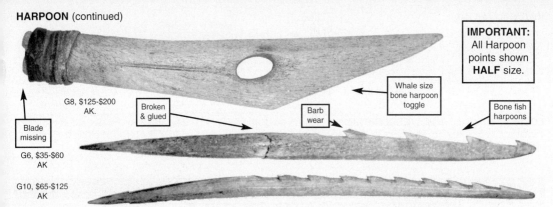

IMPORTANT: All Harpoon points shown **HALF** size.

G8, $125-$200 AK.

Broken & glued

Barb wear

Whale size bone harpoon toggle

Bone fish harpoons

Blade missing

G6, $35-$60 AK

G10, $65-$125 AK

LOCATION: Coastal areas and around large lakes and rivers, Bering Sea Region. **DESCRIPTION:** Harpoon points were carved from bone, antler or fashioned from metal. They were used in fishing. Some have stone tips and were hafted either directly to the shaft or inserted as a foreshaft.

INDEPENDENCE - Arctic Small Tool Tradition, 6000 - 4200 B. P.

(Also see Chignik Lanceolate)

Petrified wood

G10, $250-$400 AK

LOCATION: Alaska. **DESCRIPTION:** A medium size lanceolate to pentagonal point with a tapered stem and a straight base.

KAVIK - Historic Phase, 300 - 200 B.P.

(Also see Bear and Unalakleet)

chert

chertt

G5, $5-$10 Klo-kut, AK

G5, $10-$20 High Arctic, Alaska

G6, $12-$20 High Arctic, Alaska

LOCATION: Alaska. **DESCRIPTION:** A medium size stemmed point with the blade expanding towards the base. Shoulders are horizontal and the stem is narrow and parallel sided. Base is straight to convex. **I.D. KEY:** Base and shoulder form.

KAYUK - Northern Archaic Tradition, 6500 - 4000 B. P.

(Also see Bear, Chignik Stemmed)

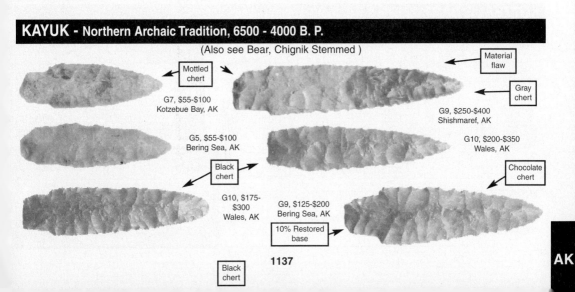

Mottled chert

Material flaw

Gray chert

G7, $55-$100 Kotzebue Bay, AK

G9, $250-$400 Shishmaref, AK

G5, $55-$100 Bering Sea, AK

G10, $200-$350 Wales, AK

Black chert

Chocolate chert

G10, $175-$300 Wales, AK

G9, $125-$200 Bering Sea, AK

10% Restored base

Black chert

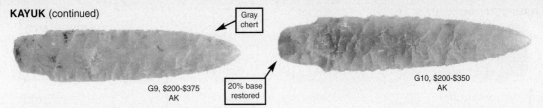

KAYUK (continued)

Gray chert

20% base restored

G9, $200-$375
AK

G10, $200-$350
AK

LOCATION: Coastal Alaska. **DESCRIPTION:** A small to medium size (2"+) lanceolate point. Parallel sided with horizontal transverse flaking. The stem is short to moderate, parallel sided and narrow. The base is straight. Similar to *Alberta, Eden, First View* and *Scottsbluff* types.

KOTZEBUE BAY - Arctic Small Tool Tradition, 6000 - 4200 B. P.

(Also see Chignik Stemmed, Dutch Harbor Side Notched, Palisades & Ugashik)

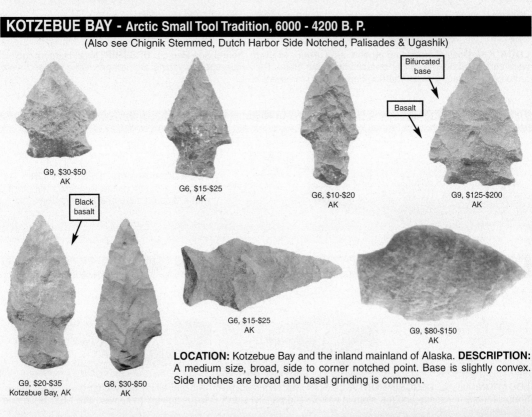

Bifurcated base

Basalt

G9, $30-$50
AK

G6, $15-$25
AK

G6, $10-$20
AK

G9, $125-$200
AK

Black basalt

G6, $15-$25
AK

G9, $80-$150
AK

G9, $20-$35
Kotzebue Bay, AK

G8, $30-$50
AK

LOCATION: Kotzebue Bay and the inland mainland of Alaska. **DESCRIPTION:** A medium size, broad, side to corner notched point. Base is slightly convex. Side notches are broad and basal grinding is common.

KOTZEBUE DART - Arctic Small Tool Tradition, 6000 - 4200 B. P.

(Also see Chignik Dart and Whale)

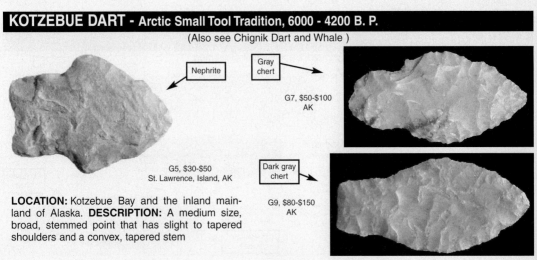

Nephrite

Gray chert

G7, $50-$100
AK

G5, $30-$50
St. Lawrence, Island, AK

Dark gray chert

G9, $80-$150
AK

LOCATION: Kotzebue Bay and the inland mainland of Alaska. **DESCRIPTION:** A medium size, broad, stemmed point that has slight to tapered shoulders and a convex, tapered stem

KOTZEBUE DART (continued)

Olive
chert

G7, $65-$125
Aleutian Peninsula, AK

MESA - Paleo-Arctic Tradition, 10,000 - 7000 B. P.

(Also see Chindadn, Firstview, Sub-Triangular and Agate Basin, Scottsbluff in Great Basin section)

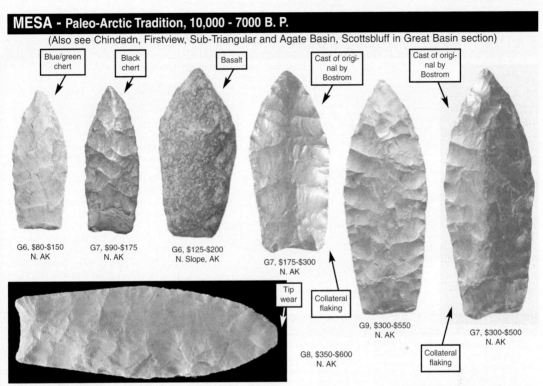

Blue/green
chert

Black
chert

Basalt

Cast of original
by Bostrom

Cast of original
by Bostrom

G6, $80-$150
N. AK

G7, $90-$175
N. AK

G6, $125-$200
N. Slope, AK

G7, $175-$300
N. AK

Tip
wear

Collateral
flaking

G9, $300-$550
N. AK

G7, $300-$500
N. AK

G8, $350-$600
N. AK

Collateral
flaking

LOCATION: Alaska. **DESCRIPTION:** A medium to large size lanceolate blade of high quality. Bases are either convex, concave or straight, and stems are usually ground. Some examples are median ridged and have random to parallel flaking. **I.D. KEY:** Basal form and flaking style. **Note:** The *Agate Basin* point, found in southern Canada into the western United States, is similar in form but not as old. The *Mesa* point has been reportedly dated to 13,700 years B.P., but more data is needed to verify this extreme age.

NAKNEK - Arctic Small Tool Tradition, 6000 - 4200 B. P.

(Also see Chignik Leaf, Dutch Harbor Lanceolate and Portage)

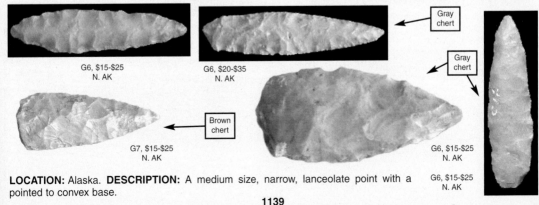

Gray
chert

Gray
chert

G6, $15-$25
N. AK

G6, $20-$35
N. AK

Brown
chert

G7, $15-$25
N. AK

G6, $15-$25
N. AK

G6, $15-$25
N. AK

LOCATION: Alaska. **DESCRIPTION:** A medium size, narrow, lanceolate point with a pointed to convex base.

1139

AK

PALISADES - Late Northern Archaic Tradition, 7000 - 4000 B. P.

(Also see Kotzebue Bay)

G7, $12-$20
AK

LOCATION: Alaska. **DESCRIPTION:** Northern extension of the *Snake River* type. A small to medium size dart point with an expanding stem that is concave. Shoulders are horizontal to slightly barbed. Blade edges are convex. Basal corners are pointed to rounded. Notches and stem edges are ground.

POINT HOPE - Bear (type 5) - Norton Tradition, 3000 - Inuit/Eskimo - Historic

(Also see Bear, Dutch Harbor Stemmed and Unalakleet)

Basalt

G10, $150-$250
AK

Green chert

Black chert

G10, $175-$300
AK

Siberian point not typed

G10, $250-$400
Point Hope, AK

LOCATION: NorthernAlaska. **DESCRIPTION:** A medium to large size, broad, dart/knife stemmed point that is parallel sided and median ridged. Shoulders are rounded. Stem is parallel sided with a convex base. This point is broader than the other *Bear* forms.

POLISHED STONE - The Thule Tradition, 2000 - 400 B. P.

(Also see Snow Knife & Ulu)

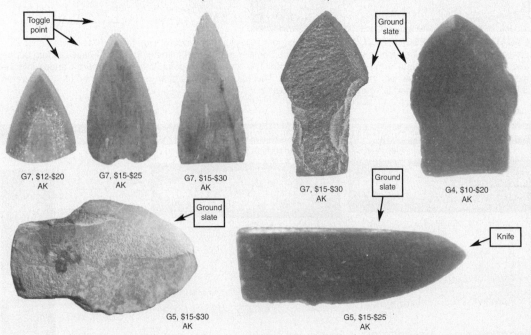

Toggle point

G7, $12-$20
AK

G7, $15-$25
AK

G7, $15-$30
AK

Ground slate

G7, $15-$30
AK

Ground slate

G4, $10-$20
AK

Ground slate

Ground slate

Knife

G5, $15-$30
AK

G5, $15-$25
AK

POLISHED STONE (continued)

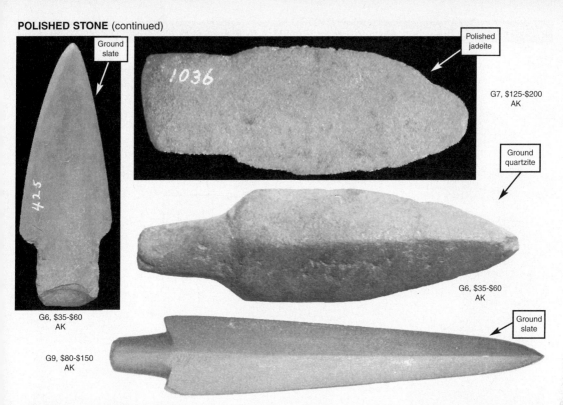

Ground slate

Polished jadeite

G7, $125-$200
AK

Ground quartzite

Ground slate

G6, $35-$60
AK

G6, $35-$60
AK

G9, $80-$150
AK

LOCATION: Alaska. **DESCRIPTION:** A medium to large size, stemmed to triangular point usually made from slate, although other lithics may be used, but are uncommon. Some examples have a median ridge running along the center of the blade. These points were probably used as knives and harpoons by the Eskimos along the coastal waters.

PORTAGE - Late Northern Archaic Tradition, 6000 - 4000 B. P.

(Also see Chignik Stemmed, Kayuk and Naknek)

LOCATION: Alaska. **DESCRIPTION:** A medium size lanceolate point with a tapered stem and a straight to slightly rounded base. Similar to *Spedis* found further south.

Gray chert

G9, $20-$35
Alaska

ST. MICHAEL LEAF - The Thule Tradition, 2000 - 400 B. P.

(Also see Chignik Leaf, Dutch Harbor Lanceolate and Naknek)

*Note: Black chert is scarce in the area

G9, *$80-$150
Alaska

Black chert

G9, $20-$35
Alaska

G9, $20-$35
Alaska

LOCATION: Alaska. **DESCRIPTION:** A medium size, broad, lanceolate point with a convex base. Blade edges are convex.

SCRAPER - Inuit/Eskimo - Historic, 2800 - 200 B.P.

(Also see Drill and Hafted Knife)

Hafted scraper with stone tip

Hafted scraper with stone tip

Hafted scraper with stone tip

All shown actual size

Baleen (whalebone)

G10, $250-$400
AK

G10, $250-$400
AK

G10, $250-$450
AK

LOCATION: Bering Sea Region, Alaska. **DESCRIPTION:** Thumb, duckbill, claw and turtleback forms are small to medium size, thick, ovoid shaped, uniface, scraping tools that are steeply beveled, especially at the the broadest end. Side scrapers are long to oval hand-held uniface flakes with beveling on the edges intended for use. Scraping was done primarily from the sides of these blades. Some of these tools were hafted.

SNOW KNIFE - Historic, 400 - 200 B. P.

(Also see Ground Stone and Ulu)

Ivory

G10, $80-$150
AK

LOCATION: Alaska. **DESCRIPTION:** A medium size knife made of ivory or bone for hafting.

SUB-TRIANGULAR - Paleo-Arctic Tradition, 11,300 - 11,000 B. P.

(Also see Chindadn and Mesa)

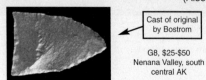

Cast of original by Bostrom

G8, $25-$50
Nenana Valley, south central AK

LOCATION: Alaska. **DESCRIPTION:** A small size, broad, thin, triangular point made from a flake that has a straight to slightly concave base. Made during the Nenana occupation. **I.D. KEY:** Broad triangle.

UGASHIK - Northern Archaic Tradition, 6000 - 4500 B. P.

(Also see Chignik Stemmed, Kotzebue Bay and Naknek)

G6, $5-$15
AK

Black chalc.

G6, $5-$15
AK

Black chalc.

G7, $12-$20
AK

LOCATION: Alaska. **DESCRIPTION:** A small to medium size point with tapered shoulders that are rounded and a broad stem with a convex base. The stem is paralled sided to slightly expanding and is usually ground.

ULU - Kodiak Tradition, 6000 - 1000 B. P.

(Also see Ground Stone, Side Knife and Snow Knife)

G5, $35-$65
AK

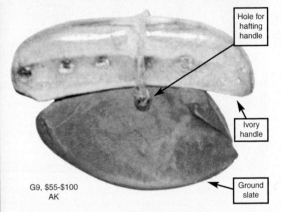

Hole for hafting handle

Ivory handle

Ground slate

G9, $55-$100
AK

LOCATION: Alaska. **DESCRIPTION:** Made from flat, thin, rocks, slate, or even jade. Handles were fashioned out of wood, ivory, or bone and often decorated with distinctive markings of the craftsmen.

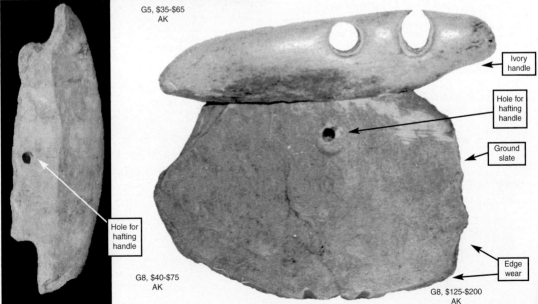

Hole for hafting handle

G8, $40-$75
AK

Ivory handle

Hole for hafting handle

Ground slate

Edge wear

G8, $125-$200
AK

AK

(Also see Bear, Chignik Stemmed, Dutch Harbor Large Stemmed, Hafted, Kavik)

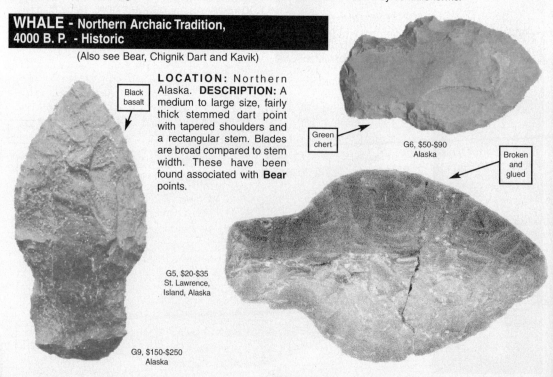

Blue/green chert

Chalcedony

Brown chert

Petrified wood

Collateral flaking to a median ridge

G10, $125-$200
N. Alaska

G5, $30-$50
N. Alaska

G5, $30-$50
N. Alaska

G9, $250-$400
N. Alaska

G9, $65-$125
N. Alaska

G10, $225-$400
N. Alaska

Collateral flaking to a median ridge

G9, $125-$200
St. Lawrence Island, Alaska

LOCATION: Northern Alaska (St. Lawrence Island), North Slope, and the Northern Yukon Territory. **DESCRIPTION:** A small to medium size (2"+) lenticular point. Parallel sided horizontal transverse flaking. The stem is short to moderate and narrow. Blade edges are serrated and recurvate near the base. These may be knife forms.

WHALE - Northern Archaic Tradition, 4000 B. P. - Historic

(Also see Bear, Chignik Dart and Kavik)

LOCATION: Northern Alaska. **DESCRIPTION:** A medium to large size, fairly thick stemmed dart point with tapered shoulders and a rectangular stem. Blades are broad compared to stem width. These have been found associated with **Bear** points.

Black basalt

Green chert

G6, $50-$90
Alaska

Broken and glued

G5, $20-$35
St. Lawrence, Island, Alaska

G9, $150-$250
Alaska

COLLECTING
OLD WORLD
PREHISTORIC ARTIFACTS

by Duncan Caldwell

This section gives an overview of artifact types from Western Europe, the Sahara & the Sahel from 2.6 million to 3,000 years ago. A few tools from elsewhere appear for comparison.

This chapter includes photographic sections illustrating:
- how radically patina can differ from one face of an artifact to the other (& often should),
- various hand-ax grips, showing how a few types were held,
- evidence for Neanderthal hafting of blades into compound tools,
- & proof of how large Neolithic prestige axes were hafted – in the middle, not at the end.

As in the previous edition, artifacts are presented in chronological, rather than alphabetical order, to give the reader an idea of their evolution. Furthermore, many of the artifacts are again larger than this book, so they can not be presented actual size. Instead, dimensions are given. Also, only superior specimens have been chosen in most cases, because there is not enough space to show the quality range for each type. In addition to sculptural hand-axes – which are the oldest evidence for the birth of aesthetics – there are several works of figurative & abstract prehistoric art to emphasize the expansion of assemblages with the addition of such artifacts starting roughly 45,000 years ago. Lastly, the multitude of preserved types that arose over a prehistoric period that spanned 2.6 million years as opposed to the Americas' 13,000 to 18,000 is correspondingly bigger, so this section, as opposed to the North American ones, is an overview containing gaps. All the same, by compiling this chapter with its predecessors in the 6th, 7th & 8th editions of this guide, enthusiasts may start to get a clear idea of the artifacts in the 3 regions.

RULES OF THUMB:
1)   Patinas Usually Differ from One Side to the Other:
The European and African artifacts that follow all have some kind of patina, usually a pronounced one that is different from one face to the other. This is because most prehistoric tools have just 2 main faces & tend to lie on the surface with one side exposed & the other buried both before burial and again before discovery. The part exposed to the air would be slowly adulterated by gamma radiation, lichens and wind weathering, for example, while the face lying against soil might experience silica loss and the intrusion of lime salts. An artifact's buried face could also acquire a crusty ring of minerals leached out of the surrounding soil that adhered to the artifact by tensile force and longer humidity in its shade. At the very least a stone tool would acquire soil sheen and in cold regions manganese or iron oxide concretions might "grow" from cleavage lines in frost pits. In most cases, each face would undergo several of these changes as its position shifted over hundreds of millenia.
But don't be fooled by almost unpatinated resharpening into thinking that such chipping is inevitably modern or even from a much later date than the rest of the knapping. Long experience in the field has shown that certain flake scars that are as old or nearly as old as the rest may hardly patinate. There could be several overlapping reasons for their relative failure to change

color: these facets might exhibit different geometry vis-à-vis the crystalline structure of the material – reducing porosity in their zone: even short exposure to solar radiation, gastric or other body acids, heat from fires, etc. during the tool's use may have predisposed older chipping to patination once the tool was abandoned and buried, but the surface of the latest resharpening might not have been stressed enough before burial to patinate as easily. Finally, it is true that a few tools found in highly preservative stable clay or cave deposits show only soil sheen and fine hydration mists. These account for such a negligible proportion that most collectors should simply avoid collecting Lower & Middle Paleolithic artifacts unless they exhibit intense patination, and, for surface finds, a different one on each side. There are enough fine patinated specimens that you should never have to worry about whether your pieces are authentic.

A) Dark face of an Acheulean cleaver vs. lighter face of same cleaver. Differential patination – the patina on one face is quite different from that on the other. Gravel pit find.

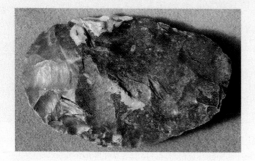

B) Browner side of a Mousterian Triangular biface vs. its creamier side.

C) More colorful side of a Malian Neolithic flared celt vs. its milky side.

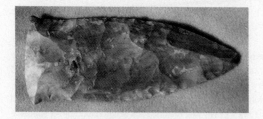

2) Only suckers look for "perfection":

Don't expect artifacts that are often 100 times older than the oldest American ones to be unchipped. After all, many have undergone glacial periods, surviving long weathering by frost & high winds on plateaus or rolling in tumultuous thawing rivers before being deposited in gravel-beds. In fact, a collector should be comforted by a little breakage, because depending on whether the posterior chips are ancient or modern, they will show a surprising depth & variety of patinas, often on the same piece.

3) Be circumspect about famous origins:

Another point to remember is that a famous origin may increase the value of an artifact, but buyers should be circumspect. For example, in my early days, I purchased hand-axes in an auction held by France's most famous "expert" that he described as having come from the type sites of La Micoque & St. Acheul & as having been in the collection of one the greatest 19th prehistorians, de Mortillet. Later I was invited to examine large collections from those sites that had remained intact since the original excavations. The pieces I had were almost dead ringers for certain specimens from the 2 sites – but not quite. Although they had been chosen shrewdly to fool most prehistorians, the palette of patinas was slightly off, indicating subtly different lithics & geological processes. But I had no proof. Then I got a call. It was the finder of the hand-axes who had sold them directly to the "expert" with full provenance. When he had seen them being sold to me under false pretenses during the "expert's" next auction, the collector had fumed & obtained my name. The field collector pointed out tiny innocuous initials that he had put on the bifaces & provided the key for deciphering them. They were the abbreviations of his sites in the Nievre region, far from the type-sites. I was able to confirm this by checking the rest of the man's collection & even finding identical tools at the true sites. Talk about a silver lining.

But I'd learned my lesson. Even if you have just spent $50,000,000 out of an $80 million dollar budget, as one European collector is said to have done recently, read up, familiarize yourself with well provenanced collections & take claims from merchants who may be more interested in lucre than prehistory with salt. It is absolutely essential that the seller be honorable and provide a *lifetime* guarantee of authenticity.

Finally, collecting artifacts from a time span over 140 times longer than all of American prehistory combined will begin to reveal the vast iceberg of humanity's past, of which American prehistory is just the peak of the tip. As the collector of Paleolithic artifacts explores that vast new domain, he will discover unending nuances and whole zones of mystery, while developing increasing respect for the prowess of ancestors we can all truly share. To aide new-comers to this passionate field of study, I recommend not only the Handbook of Paleolithic Typology by Debénath and Dibble and Tools of the Old and New Stone Age by Bordaz, but broader books by Susan Allport, The Primal Feast, Juan Luis Arsuaga, The Neanderthal's Necklace, & Jared Diamond, Guns, Germs & Steel.

Lithics: Some of the materials from the 2 continents that this chapter concentrates on are: **For Europe:** Grand Pressigny flint - Indre et Loire & Vienne regions of France; Jablines flint - Seine et Marne; Thanatian flint - Oise & Somme valleys; jadeite, metahornblendite & dolerite - Brittany; Font-Maure jasper, France; Pelite-quartz - W. Alps; Obsidian - Italy, S. France, Greece; Green slate - W. Russia, Baltic states; etc. **For North Africa:** quartzite, flint, siltstone, jasper, etc. **Important sites:** Because the region and time frame are so vast, only a few almost random sites are listed. However, an effort has been made to choose fully provenanced tools from famous sites, which are referred to in the captions. "T.S." after a site indicates that it is a cultural type-site, although it should be kept in mind that other locations are often type-sites for particular traits and tools.

Prices: Price ranges have been extrapolated from the results of auctions and consultations with dealers from around the world - but with less focus on US sales than in previous editions as the dollar has plummeted, ensuring that the highest prices for the best pieces are now usually paid in Europe.

The 8th Edition described how the massive importation of Saharan artifacts from Morocco south & eastwards to Niger had driven down their prices, but the situation has again changed. American, Mauritanian and French customs recently publicized large seizures of prehistoric artifacts, many of which had apparently come from Mali and Niger. However, the reality behind the news is ironic. For example, in 2004 a Malian merchant coming from Niger had his prehistoric merchandise confiscated in Paris as he was on his way to the US. French customs invited the press to see the contraband and then asked the Niger embassy to press charges against the suspect. Caught in the limelight of the media blitz, the diplomats apparently felt obliged to comply. The French then handed the artifacts to the embassy for repatriation. Not surprisingly, the merchant hastened to the embassy to see if he could get them back. The same diplomats who had just pressed charges apologized to him and said they would have gladly returned the artifacts if not for the media attention. As it was, they told the dealer that they'd give it all back to him in Niger. Two thirds of the goods apparently evaporated at that point, while the rest were indeed returned to him. The merchant then took his returned merchandise to the States any way, but by a different route.

The story's morale is apparently a simple tale of Western political correctness vs. African corruption. But it actually highlights how many representatives of under-developed countries will pay lip-service to western attitudes while casting a blind eye on peasants, nomads and small merchants who scavenge for artifacts - since the alternative for their compatriots can be starvation. Global warming due to emissions from the sanctimonious West that imposes its archeological morals on undeveloped countries is increasing desertification, killing crops and flocks… and people. So many Africans see artifacts that are exposed by the same desertification as a thin silver lining – manna in the midst of a foreign-induced catastrophe. When the deputy director of one of France's top institutions for the study of prehistory (she could just as easily have been from any other western country, including America) was asked pointblank recently if stopping surface collecting by desperately poor Africans was worth the death of some of their children, she replied, "Absolutely, whatever it takes: they must be taught." It should be noted that she is a warm and highly reflective person – making her answer that much more telltale. Science and humanism have been aspects of the same trend since the Renaissance: when did they drift apart in terms of archeology? The last edition suggested that "it would have been better for the vestiges to be studied & *then exported with proper provenance"* rather than being wantonly swept from the desert. I still believe that. But that also means that researchers must wake up to the benefits of working with surface collectors and of making sure there is something in it for everyone. The cruelty of ideological rigidity and the contradictions of hypocrisy must give way to a new legal framework focused on incentives, not sanctions, and results. Give people a reason to cooperate and the underground market will shrivel, creating more transparency and the collection of more information. But once again such pragmatism is certainly neither politically correct nor commercially expedient.

So back to reality: the seizures will probably reduce African imports – worsening conditions for the starving while making Saharan antiquities already in the West more valuable. The rarest forms of Tenerian arrowheads in rock crystal or with multiple tiers have already tripled in value – from $25 a few years ago to at least $75 and sometimes up to $250 a piece. The most grotesque irony is that the French seizures have also forced the same northern European merchants whose goods were confiscated to turn to a new source. With newly opened borders and a common currency in Europe what better source could there be than the country nextdoor with the type sites themselves: France itself! Dutch, Belgian and German dealers who used to stock up in the Sahara now flock to Normandy to buy artifacts which they can drive home the same day and then export internationally without hindrance, since their countries can't be bothered with policing the export of artifacts sold at government licensed auctions in France. So the seizures of Saharan artifacts that brought such glory to French customs (before the objects were discreetly returned) have led to the unbridled export of French artifacts themselves.

As a result of this and other trends, including the fact that the most decorative pieces have now been recognized by art connisseurs as unbelievably cheap at $10,000-30,000 compared to other types of art like paintings, the cream of European artifacts have gone through the roof. The price range for fine *French* triangular handaxes at a provincial auction in 2004 was $11,000 to $17,028. Five years ago, the same pieces would have cost $1,100 to $2,800 at the grassroots level and double to triple that in galleries. Now, it's anyone's guess as to what sophisticated galleries could charge, although very few have enough familiarity with the field to ride or even be aware of the wave. On a side note, a French museum also pre-empted a newly reported paleolithic "venus" after setting the price themselves at roughly $624,000.

Way down at the other end of the spectrum, there's the internet – that world of usually low end and hopelessly misdescribed artifacts – often at extremely affordable prices – which are mainly used as crumbs to lure clients into more lucrative hidden transactions for objects of supposedly greater interest. You may be able to land some bargains, but buyers beware! The result is great confusion among newer collectors as to values and what is even genuine. I can only hope that these pages make things clearer.

Hand-ax & Mousterian Scraper Grips:

Hand-axes & other Paleolithic bifaces, which superficially resemble hand-axes but may have been hafted, are traditionally grouped by the geometry of their faces. But classifying a tool only on this basis can be misleading because its silhouette may change as the tool is worn, resharpened and used up. Hand-axes that are apparently quite different may just illustrate stages in the reduction sequence of a single true type. It is important to identify those types from their first stage, to determine if methods of reducing tools were also culturally specific, & to emphasize that some types are indeed particular to regions, periods & traditions. The hand-axes & bifaces below are classified not only by their silhouettes, but more importantly by:
- **their contours when seen edge-on.** Such examination reveals that certain hand-held bifaces (hand-axes) have bases that are tipped up relative to the cutting plane. This creates a protective pocket for the user's fingers above the material being cut & is just as intentional a design element as the contours of an artifact's face. So a protective pocket must be considered in classification. Another trait best seen from this perspective is inverse beveling due to the sharpening of one edge of a hand-ax, then flipping the hand-ax on its axis to sharpen the other edge. This results in opposite edges being flaked along opposite faces. Many typologists group such skewed hand-axes in a type, but inversely beveled hand-axes probably just represent advanced stages in reduction sequences.
- **the position of their grips.** True hand-axes have some sort of direct grip – whether it is an ergonomic patch of rough, rounded cortex left along a base or edge or else a *"mi-plat"* – a flat section along the rim that is perpendicular to the tool's plane. Beginners often dismiss the grip's departure from expected symmetry as breakage or an un-finished section. Instead grips testify to the care taken by the earliest toolmakers to achieve comfortable & effective designs. Since a grip's position also remains stable during reduction sequences, it is even more useful for classifying hand-axes than their changing contours.
- **an edge-on analysis of peripheral flaking, retouch, crushing, etc.** If one edge has been straightened with secondary

soft-hammer retouch for cutting, whereas the opposite one has only been roughed out with hard hammer flaking or seems to have been *thinned* as opposed to sharpened, the rougher edge may have been prepared for insertion in a slotted grip that rotted away. If there is no direct grip at all – just all-around sharpness that bites into your palm when you press on one edge to cut with another - then a hafting scenario becomes almost inescapable. The use of such rim analysis led to distinctions between triangular bifaces in the 8th edition. Other tools which could be differentiated based on the distribution of straightened, thinned, crushed, resharpened, & ground edges have probably been lumped together too because their faces looked so similar that typologists thought the artifacts were the same kind. As a result, the inventiveness & cultural variety of Neanderthals probably continues to be under-estimated even by their champions.

1) Dagger grip hand-axes. These have a long "handle" composed of two facing oblique planes. Thrusting & slashing cuts. Very rare.

2) Oblique cortical grip on a concave crescent hand-ax. The grip is common, the concavity not so. A lateral cut.

3) Side grip. A rocking or sawing cut.

4) Basal pocket grip. The base twists about 30 degrees away from the cutting plane, allowing fingers to be tucked into a safe pocket away from the meat or hide being prepared. Inwards lateral cuts. Aisne.

5) Crescent side-scraper grip. Such a Neanderthal tool may also have been inserted in a slotted handle like an ulu.

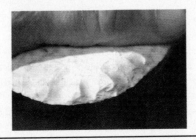 

6) Inverse beveling seen from tip.
The result of resharpening.

Proof of Hafting:

Neanderthal compound tools: The 2 photos show a much reduced Mousterian convergent side-scraper. Its most interesting feature is the thinning of the flat side of the base. This must have been done to turn the base into a peg that could be inserted and glued (with reduced birch sap or rabbit glue for example) into a handle as was the case with the 400,000 + BP flint at Schöningen. The recognition of an artifact's most telling but elusive features is one of an enthusiast's greatest pleasures, but students of prehistory should look forward to contesting their theories.

Neolithic polished axes:

1) The detail of a giant celt from Calvados shows grooves where lashing gradually ground into the ax's edge on either side of a lighter zone where the wooden handle surrounded the blade.

2) A belt of lighter patination around the middle of this ax found in a peat bog shows where the wooden handle survived long enough to impede patination until it had disintegrated.

AFRICAN, ASIAN & EUROPEAN POINT AND TOOL TYPES:

Grouping artifacts into Technological Modes:
Stone Age artifacts are currently grouped as follows:

MODE I: Oldowan. Unifacial or bifacial flaking along a cobble to make a cutting edge or remove flakes for use

MODE II: Acheulean. The first tools of a pre-determined shape not suggested by the block of stone. Working towards a mental template, the maker had to carry out dozens of gestures to achieve his goal, just like an origami master turning a sheet of paper into a swan. A sense of correctness was born – in other words, aesthetics.

MODE III: Levallois/ Mousterian/ Kombewa. The first tools of a standardized & repeated shape struck in succession from a pre-adapted core. The maker had to envision 2 successive phases at once: the core to be shaped & the products to be struck from it once the core was made. This involved planning & first occurred when modern human & Neanderthal ancestors independently reached cranial capacities of about 1,400 cc.

MODE IV: Upper Paleolithic. Blade, antler & bone tools of enormous diversity.

Archeological Periods:

The entire Stone Age fits fairly neatly into the geological **Quaternary Period**, which is currently defined as having begun 2.5 million years ago at the boundary of the Gauss/Matuyama paleomagnetic epochs. The Quaternary consists of 2 epochs: the **PLEISTOCENE** from 2.5 million until 10,000 years ago with its succession of Ice Ages, & the **HOLOCENE** from 10,000 BP till now.

Unlike in the Americas, where "Paleolithic" refers to the period from 18,000 to 8,000 B.P., in the Old World it is split into three sub-sections, each of which is linked to one or more technological Modes. The dates are approximate & shift from region to region since the modes appeared in them at different times:

1) the **Lower Paleolithic** linked to Mode I & Mode II technologies from 2.6 million to roughly 250,000 B.P.,

2) the **Middle Paleolithic** linked to Mode II & Mode III technologies from 250,000 to approximately 45,000 B.P., and

3) the **Upper Paleolithic** linked to Mode IV technologies from 45,000 B.P. to 12,000 B.P.

LOWER PALEOLITHIC (ca. 2,600,000 B.P. - 250,000 B.P.)

CHOPPER AND FLAKE TRADITION (a Mode I technology): At first *Homo habilis &/or Homo rudolfensis*, then *Homo ergaster* in Africa & its basic equivalent, *Homo erectus*, in Eurasia - 2.6 - 1.4 million B.P. in Africa, 1.8 million+ BP – 780,000 BP in S. Europe, with much later vestiges in Hungary, E. Asia, etc.

Oldowan I and II industries - Pebble choppers, Bifacial chopping-tools, Inverse choppers; **Clactonian flake tools:** notches, denticulates, becs. **Important sites:** Olduvai Gorge, Tanzania T.S.); Damanisi, Georgia; Longgupo, China (1.8 million); Sangiran, Indonesia; Gran Dolina, Sierra de Atapuerca, Spain (800,000 BP); Tatoui, Romania; Orce, Greece; Clacton-on-Sea, U.K. (T.S.); Vértesszöllös, Hungary; Wimereux, France; etc.

ASIAN CHOPPER/CHOPPING TOOL TRADITION:

Important sites: Choukoutien, Patjitan, etc.

ABBEVILLEAN (Also known as the EARLY ACHEULEAN – the period of the first MODE II Technology. Mode II is defined by tapered bifaces (LCTs), which are commonly called hand-axes. Abbevillean ones were made only with direct hard hammer flaking.):

Homo ergaster & Homo erectus - 1,600,000 - 780,000 B.P. in Africa/ later in Eurasia)

Abbevillean hand-axes (Africa & Europe) - **Trihedral picks** (Africa) - **Amygdaloid hand-axes, Ficrons. Important sites:** Ubeidiya, Israel; Bose Basin, S. China (app. 803,000 BP), Pingliang, China; Abbeville, France (T.S.); Konso, Ethiopia; Beni Ihklef, Algeria; etc.

MID TO LATE ACHEULEAN: *Homo erectus* to archaic *Homo sapiens* in Africa & *Homo antecessor* to *Homo heidelbergensis* in Eurasia, etc. - 780,000 - 250,000 B.P.:

NOTES: 1) The MODE II hand-axes of the later Acheulean often show *both* direct hard hammer & secondary soft hammer flaking.

2) The first MODE III technologies such as Levallois & Kombewa flake tools appeared earlier - at around 300,000 BP - in both Africa & Europe than the conventional date for the start of the Middle Paleolithic at 250,000 BP, suggesting that the Middle Paleolithic should be extended backwards.

HAND-AX TYPES: Tihodaine type cleavers (Africa), Tabel Balalt type cleaver (Africa), Kombewa flake cleavers (Africa), Chalossian pic, Lanceolate, Backed bifaces, Cordiform hand-axes, Limandes, Ovates, Discoids, Triangular (late transitional form), Elongated triangular, Fusiform hand-axes, Naviforms, Shark's tooth hand-axes, Pélécyformes, Ogivo-triangulaire, Lagéniformes, Micoquekeile, etc.

ASSOCIATED TOOLS: Kombewa flakes (Africa), Centripetal Levallois flakes, Levallois point, Levallois blades, Side-scrapers, Wooden spears (Schöningen, Germany - ca. 400,000 B.P.), Hafted knives (Schöningen).

IMPORTANT SITES (Mid-Acheulean - 780,000 - 500,000 B.P.): St. Acheul (T.S.), Soleihac & Artenac France; Petrolona, Greece; Boxgrove, U.K.; Sima de los Huesos, Burgos, Spain; Latamne, Syria; Kudaro, Georgia; Beni Ikhlef, Algeria; etc.

IMPORTANT SITES (Late Acheulean - 500,000 - 250,000 B.P.): Terra Amata & Tautavel, France; Gesher Benot Ya'aqov, Israel (tranchet cleavers); Torralba, Spain; Fontana Ranuccio, Italy; Swanscombe, U.K.; Schöningen & Karlich-Seeufer, Germany; El Ma el Abiod, Algeria; etc.

MIDDLE PALEOLITHIC (ca. 250,000 B.P. - 45,000 B.P.) – Mode III Technologies: Late *Homo heidelbergensis* to Classic *Homo neanderthalensis* (after 130,000 BP) in Eurasia, Archaic to Modern *Homo sapiens* in Africa & Middle East

TRUE MOUSTERIAN INDUSTRIES (EUROPE) First signs at **250,000 BP.** Full flower 170,000 - 45,000 B.P.: **1)** Mousterian in the Acheulean Tradition, **2)** Denticulate Tool Tradition, **3)** Quina Tool Tradition **4)** Ferrassie Mousterian - **"MOUSTEROID" FLAKE TOOL INDUSTRY** (North Africa, Middle East) - **SANGOAN INDUSTRY** (Central Africa) - **ATERIAN INDUSTRY** (N. Africa), etc.

Elongated Mousterian points, Levallois points, Mousterian points (wholly retouched), Soyons points, Tayac points, Emireh points, Bifacial leaf-points - Blattspitzen (Eastern Europe), Aterian points, Raclette side-scrapers (21 types), Limaces, Burins, Cleaver hand-axes, Continuation of Micoquian hand-axes, Small to medium cordiform hand-axes (with direct soft-hammer retouching), Mousterian discs, Convex scrapers, Concave scrapers, Backed knives, First "retouchoirs" for pressure flaking, Levallois blade tools, Wooden spears (Lehringen), Borers, Non-Levallois truncated backed blades, etc.

Important sites: Le Moustier (T.S.), Fontéchevade, La Quina, Combe-Grenal, Laussel, Pech-de-l'Azé, La Chapelle-aux-Saints, Arcy-sur-Cure (France); Spy (Belgium); Monte Circeo (Italy); Neandertal (Germany); Tata, Molodova (Ukraine); High Lodge, Saccopastore, Krapina (Croatia); Mt. Carmel (Israel); Solo (Indonesia); Ain Meterchem, Kalambo Falls (Sangoan) & Charaman (T.S. Zambia), Lupemba (T.S. Congo), Pietersburg (T.S.), Howieson's Port (T.S.) & Klasies River Mouth (S. Africa); etc. **NOTE:** *According to traditional dating, based on European sites, the last 4 references are Mid Paleolithic, but typologically they anticipate the Upper Paleolithic.*

UPPER PALEOLITHIC: Mode IV Technologies (45,000 B.P. - 12,000 B.P.)

ULUZZIAN (late Neanderthals - ITALY - Circa 45,000 - 35,000 B.P.)
Crescents, Backed pionts, Burins, End-scrapers, Flake tools; Bone tools: awls, Conical points, biconical points, Etc. **Important site:** Grotta del Cavallo.

CHATELPERRONIAN (late Neanderthals - France - ca. 45,000 - 35,000 B.P.)
Châtelperronian knives, Châtelperronian points, End-scrapers, Truncated pieces, Burins, Incised tooth ornaments, Ivory pendants; Bone tools: awls, ivory pins, digging sticks, tubes, lozenge-shaped points, etc. **Important sites:** Châtelperron (T.S.), Grotte du Renne, St.-Césaire, Isturitz, Gargas, Caminade Est, Belvis, Quinçay, etc.

OTHER TRANSITIONAL MID-TO-UPPER PALEOLITHIC CULTURES: SZELETIAN (C. & E. Europe)/ LUPEMBIAN (Africa)

AURIGNACIAN (first European *Homo Sapiens sapiens*, also known as Cro-Magnons - ca. 40,000 - 28,000 B.P.)
Dufour bladelets, Retouched blades, Strangulated blades, Caminade scraper, Carinated (keeled) scraper, Nosed scraper, Plane, Dihedral burins; Bone tools: Split based atlatl points, etc. **Important sites:** Chauvet, Arcy-sur-Cure, La Ferrassie, Caminade Ouest, Dufour, Baden-Württemberg, Geissenklösterle, Vogelherd, etc.

GRAVETTIAN & PERIGORDIAN (W. Europe), PAVLOVIAN (C. Europe), KOSTIENKI (Ukraine & Russia), ETC. - *Homo sapiens* 28,000 - 23,000 B.P. - *Despite different names, the cultures of this period shared many features from the Pyrenees to Siberia, with Venus figurines made at Brassempouy in S. France sharing many stylistic aspects with those found at Kostienki, for example, although Kostienki craftsmen had a better understanding of how to align their sculptures with the grain of tusks for durability.*
Noaille gravers, Kostienki shouldered points, Font Robert points, Gravette points, Micro-Gravette points, Pointed median groove bone points, Obliquely truncated blades, Scrapers on large thin flakes, "Batons de Commandment" (wrenches), Dihedral burins, etc.
Important sites: La Gravette (T.S.), Chateau de Corbiac, Cougnac, Peche Merle, La Font-Robert, La Ferrassie, Laugerie Haute, Tursac, Predmosti, Dolni Vestonice, Avdievo, Kostienki, etc.

SOLUTREAN (France & Spain) & EPI-GRAVETTIAN (Italy, Central & E. Europe): 23,000 - 17,000 B.P.
Early Solutrean unifacial points, Mid-Sol. bifacial laurel leaf points (13 types), late Sol. shouldered points (4 types), Bifacial willow leaf points, Tanged bifacial points (Spain), Bevel based bone points, Backed bladelets, Borers, Bifacial knives, End-scrapers, Various dihedral burins, Laugerie Haute micro-scraper, Carinated scraper, Raclettes, Becs, Eyed needles, etc. **Important sites:** La Solutré (T.S.), Volgu, Lascaux, etc.

MAGDALENIAN (W. Europe), EPI-GRAVETTIAN (Italy, C. & E. Europe), KEBARIAN (Levant), IBEROMAURSIAN (N. Africa), etc. 17,000 - 12,000 B.P.
Teyjat points, dihedral burins, Magdalenian shouldered points, Many new microliths, Backed bladelets, Saw-toothed backed bladelets, End-scrapers, Dual burin-scraper tools, Parrot-beaked burin, Lacan burin, Carinated scraper, Thumb-nail scrapers; Bone & antler tools: Atl-atls, Harpoons (many types), Polished awls, Polished bone chisels, "lissoirs" & spatulas, Pincer tipped "navette" double ended blade grips, Engraved split bone rods, Eyed needles, wrenches, etc. **Important sites:** Gönnersdorf, Altamira, La Madeleine, Marsoulas, Pincevent, Isturitz, Niaux, Castillo, La Vache, Le Portel, Kesslerloch, etc.

MESOLITHIC: MANY DISTINCT CULTURES (end of glacial period - W. Europe: ca. 12,000 - 8,000 B.P. , Middle East: ca. 13,000 - 10,000 B.P.)
Microliths: small blade fragments retouched into geometric shapes (100s of types): Azilian points, Chaville points, Sauveterre points, Tardenois points, Capsian arrowheads, Trapezes (over 13 types), Rouffignac backed knives, Lunates, Triangles (over 11 types), Microburins, Tranchet chisels, Thumb-nail & other scrapers, Azilian Harpoons, Bone fish hooks, bone & antler mattocks, hafted adzes, etc. **Important sites:** Mas d'Azil (T.S. - Early Meso.), Milheeze (Federmesser), Ahrensbourg (T.S. - early mid-Meso.), Remouchamps, Sonchamp (T.S.), Sauveterre-la-Lémance (T.S. - late mid-Meso.), Fère-en-Tardenois (T.S. - late Meso.), Shoukba & Jericho (Natufian), Gough's Cave (Creswellian), Horsham, Shippea Hill, Star Carr (Maglemosian); Otwock (Poland - Swiderian); Relilai, El Oued, Medjez (N. Africa); Mureybet (Mesopotamia: Meso. to Neo.)

NEOLITHIC: MANY CULTURES (Europe: ca. 8,000 - 5,000 B.P., Middle East: ca. 11,000 - 6,000 B.P.)
Amouq points (I & II), Byblos points, Temassinine points, Labied points, Bifacial leaf points, Tell Mureybet points; Saharan points (at least 9 families consisting of 103 groups, encompassing many more types), Chisel-ended arrowheads, French flint daggers, Sickle blades, Gouges, Chisels, Antler sleeve shock absorbers for celts, First polished celts, Antler harpoons, Eyed needles, First ceramic pottery outside Jomon (Mesolithic) Japan **Important sites:** *Europe* —> Stonehenge, Skara Brae (U.K.); Newgrange (Ireland); Barnenez, Carnac, Fort-Harrouard, Gavrinis, Filatosa (France); Michelsberg (T.S.) Belgium, Sittard (Holland); Starcevo, Sesklo, Vinca (T.S.), Butmir (T.S.), Cucuteni (T.S.), Cernavoda (Balkans); Nea Nikomedeia (Greece); *W. Asia* —> Catal Huyuk (T.S.), Hacilar, Mersin (Turkey), Jericho (West Bank), Jarmo, Hassuna, Halaf (T.S.), Jemdet Nasr (Mesopototamia), Khirokitia (Cyprus); Ali Kosh, Tépé Hissar (Iran); Dzejtun, Kelteminar; *N. Africa* —> Merimde, Badari, Fayoum (Egypt); Jaatcha, Tazina, Djerat, Redeyef, Adrar Bous III, etc. **China** —> Yangshao (T.S.)

CHALCOLITHIC & BRONZE AGE (E. Europe & Anatolia 7,500 - 3,000 B.P. / W. Europe: 5,000 - 2,800 B.P.)
NOTE: All but the most prestigious tools (& even some of those) during these periods still tended to be made of stone.
Egyptian fishtail flint knives, Gerzean flint knives, Armorican flint arrowheads, Scandanavian flint daggers based on copper & bronze models, Hardstone shaft-hole battleaxes, First Copper, then Bronze tools: Axes, Adzes, Chisels, Razors, Bronze arrowheads, Etc. **Important sites:** Cambous & Mont Bego (France); Nagada (Egypt); Hagar Qim & Mnajdra (Malta), Su Nuraxi, Sardinia; etc.

Putting The Artifacts Into Perspective
The artifacts shown below were made by a succession of human species with ever-bigger brains, who also had to adapt, in the case of the Neanderthals, to several Ice Ages. The following figures are helpful for situating each artifact in these progressions. **Brian Sizes of Hominids Who Made Stone Tools:** Cranial capacity progressed from roughly **500 cc** at the beginning of the Stone Age, 2.6 million years ago, to approximately **1,400 cc** about 150,000 years ago. But it is also important to remember that a species did not necessarily go extinct as soon as a new species had evolved from it, so directly related species overlapped & probably made different types of tools simultaneously. Finally, brains did not expand much until more than 2.5 million years after hominids had become bipedal over 5 million years ago, so the Australopithecines & their descendant, *Homo habilis*, had brains only marginally bigger than a **gorilla's 500 cc** or a **chimp's 410 cc**.

Homo habilis (Africa)	2.3 - 1.5 million BP	**510 cc to 674 cc**.
Homo rudolfensis (Africa)	ca. 2 million BP	**752 cc** (skull KNM-ER 1470).
Homo ergaster (Africa)	1.9 million - 800,000 BP	**804 cc to 900 cc**.
Homo erectus (Eurasia)	1.9 million - to 54,000? BP	**813 cc to 1,225 cc** at start
		1,013 cc to 1,251 cc later on

Javan specimens of *erectus* have more robust crania than African *ergaster* but are otherwise basically the same. The name *ergaster* may be folded back into the older term *erectus*.

Homo antecessor (Europe)   ca. 800,000 BP   **App. 1,000+ cc.**

Possibly the last common ancestor of Neanderthals & our lineage, Homo sapiens

Archaic Homo sapiens (Africa) 400,000 - 250,000 BP   **1,285 cc** (Broken Hill) to **1,400 cc** (Lake Turkana).

Pre-modern Homo sapiens (Africa) 250,000 - 100,000 BP   **1,300 cc** to **1,430 cc.**

Homo heidelbergensis (Europe) 700,000 - 200,000 BP.   App. **1,000** (Steinheim) to **1,390 cc** (Sima de los Huesos).

Proto-Homo neanderthalensis (Europe) 250,000 (Ehringsdorf) & 200,000 (Biache-St.-Vaast)

Classic Neanderthals   ca. 130,000 – 30,000 BP.   Av. **1,450 cc.** Max. **1,750 cc** (Amud, Israel).

Modern Homo sapiens   120,000+ - Present   Average **1,350 cc.**

The conventional average cranial capacity of modern humans is 100 cc less than the Nean derthal average. But the average Neanderthal weighed over 168 lb. – more than the average for modern humans from any continent. So in relation to their body weight, Neanderthal brains were slightly smaller than ours. It must also be emphasized that cranial capacity by itself is NOT indicative of intelligence. Einstein's brain was twice the size of that of the great 19th century French writer, Anatole France. Because of sexual dimorphism, men have brains about 100 cc larger than a woman's of equal body weight – the same relative difference as in macaque monkeys. This difference is unconnected to cognitive functions. But it may be related to natural selection of males with better spatial orientation. Such males would have been able to mentally map landscapes & rotate images. Mental rotation may have been useful in producing the first tapered bifaces (also known as **LCTs** – large cutting tools – which are the defining trait of Mode II technology).

GLACIAL PERIODS & INTER-GLACIALS OF THE PLEISTOCENE:

Glacial periods were first defined both by moraines they left in the Alps & in outwash sediment deposited around the N. Sea. So each period has both an Alpine & Lowland name. The Alpine name appears in ***BOLD ITALICIZED CAPITALS*** & is the most common one for Old World usage. The Lowland name appears next in SIMPLE CAPITALS & the equivalent American name third. Warm to temperate inter-glacial periods, like the one we are in now, were first defined from the lowland deposits & appear between the Glacial Periods. Dates are based on oxygen isotope levels recorded from core samples extracted from ocean floors.

0 – 18,000 BP:	Inter-glacial (Although glaciers generally did not grow after 18,000 BP, fluctuating cold conditions continued until 10,000 BP when tundra animals disappeared from western Europe);		
18,000 – 67,000 BP:	***WÜRM***	= WEICHSEL	= Wisconsin
67,000 – 128,000 BP:	Inter-glacial ***UZNACH***	= EEM	= Sangamon;
128,000 – 180,000 BP:	***RISS***	= SAALE	= Illinoian;
180,000 – 230,000 BP:	Inter-glacial ***HOETTING***	= HOLSTEIN	= Yarmouth;
230,000 – 300,000 BP:	***MINDEL***	= ELSTER	= Kansan;
300,000 – 330,000 BP:	Inter-glacial ***G-M***	= CROMER	= Aftonian;
330,000 – 470,000 BP:	***GUNZ***	= MENAP	= Nebraskan;
470,000 – 540,000 BP:	Inter-glacial ***D-G***	= WAALIAN;	
540,000 – 550,000 BP:	***DONAU II***	= WEYBOURNE;	
550,000 – 585,000 BP:	Inter-glacial	= TIGLIAN;	
585,000 – 600,000 BP:	***DONAU I (DANUBE)***;		

600,000 to 2 million BP: Roughly 20 more glacial advances

OLD WORLD TYPOLOGY
& PRICE GUIDE

CHOPPERS - Chopper & Flake Tradition:
ca. 2,600,000 to 1,400,000 / 100,000 B.P. (depending on region): *Essentially Homo habilis or Homo ergaster through Homo erectus*

1) 4 1/2" *Oldowan* **chopper**. Foum-al-Hassan, Morocco. 1.4 to 2.2 million BP. Major wind gloss on quartzite. The flake scars aren't as clear as on the following specimen. $650 - $800 If crude or small, from $75.

2) 4" *Oldowan* **chopper**. Basalt with heavy wind stippling. Taouz, Morocco. 1.4 to 2.2 million BP. A well made and dramatic specimen. $1,300 - $1,800. Lesser examples from $150.

3) 3 1/2" **chopper**. Arranches, Portugal. Europe's oldest tool type – perhaps contemporaneous with Dmanisi, Georgia fossils. This one apparently closer to mid Paleolithic. Monochromatic patinated quartzite. $290 - $450. Poor specimens from $35.

LOCATION: Africa and Europe as far north as Hungary.
DESCRIPTION: A cobble with 2 or more flakes struck from one side. Although choppers & chopping tools (see below) are found throughout the Stone Age, those from early sites are especially sought after as the oldest surviving vestiges of hominid tool-use:
I.D. KEY: Lower & Middle Paleolithic specimens always patinated.

CHOPPING TOOLS - Chopper & Flake Tradition:
ca. 2,600,000 to 1,400,000 / 100,000 B.P. (depending on region): *Essentially Homo habilis or Homo ergaster through Homo erectus*

4) 6" x 5 1/2" **pre-Acheulean chopper**. Pointes aux Oies, France. Beneath the waves of the English Channel, the tools are in situ in peat underlying a bluff. Over 750,000 BP. Black flint turned calico in flaked area by peat acids. Massive, colorful. Unique site now covered by Nazi surf defenses & bunkers fallen from the eroded bluff & sand diverted to prevent silting of port. $850 - $1,300. Small or crude from $150.

5) 6" **pre-Acheulean chopper**. Pointes aux Oies, France. Over 750,000 BP. Black flint turned calico. Massive, sculptural. $750 - $1,100.

LOCATION: Africa, Europe as far north as Hungary. **DESCRIPTION:** A cobble with flakes struck bifacially from both sides of at least one edge, usually by alternate flaking forming a sinuous cutting edge. **I.D. KEY:** Lower & Middle Paleolithic specimens always patinated

CLACTONIAN TOOLS - European Chopper & Flake Tradition, depending on region:
1,700,000 to 500,000 B.P.: *Homo ergaster to Homo erectus to Homo antecessor*

6) 7" **Clactonian denticulated knife**. Sainte Adresse, France. Over 500,000 BP. Soil sheen & hydration fogging. Found 200 meters off-shore at low tide in a unique site. Cortical side grip & retouched cutting edge. $600 - $1,000. Small/crude from $50. **I.D. KEY:** Thick flakes with percussion bulb & ripples obtained by striking a nodule against a stone anvil. Coarsely retouched with heavy hammer stone.

LOCATION: An industry without bifaces, whose official southwestern limit is Clacton-on-Sea, England. It survived in the middle latitudes of Europe as Acheulean hand-axes spread into S. Europe & east into India &, exceptionally, China. **NOTES:** The Clactonian tool set consists of choppers, chopping tools, becs (borers), dendiculates, side-scrapers & notches. Fire was known by the tradition's end. At least 3 handaxes, one clearly Micoquian, were also found in the sea at Ste. Adresse.

PRIMITIVE "ABBEVILLEAN" HAND-AXES - Early Acheulean, 1.4 million + B.P. - 780,000 B.P./Later outside Africa: *Homo ergaster to Homo erectus to Homo antecessor*

The oldest tapered idealized artifacts known are large bifaces & trihedral picks that herald the start of Mode II technology. The term LCT (Large Cutting Tool) may be applied to either of them. Both types of hand-axes were made by direct hard-stone percussion & were found with a 1.4 million year old Homo ergaster mandible in Konso, Ethiopia. The oldest datable African specimens were found in the same complex of sites below a level of volcanic tuff dated at 1.6 million BP. The oldest European specimens are more conservatively dated at roughly 650,000 BP.

AFRICAN TYPE:

7) 11" *trihedral pick* **hand-ax**. Quartzite. Beni Ikhlef, Algeria. Dated by comparison with dated series at KGA 10 in Konso, Ethiopia: at least 1.4 million years old. On the unshown ridge side, there is wind luster & desert varnish caused by Metallogenium & Pedomicrobium bacteria absorbing manganese, iron & clay particles as a sun-shield. Leaching crust. The only one this big ever seen with decorative burgundy and beige coloring. $7,500 - $9,000 **NOTES:** If crude, from $50. If plain, from $300.

8) 11 1/4" *Early Acheulian Lanceolate* **handax**. Bifacial as opposed to trihedral form. Western Sahara. Banded quartzite. Such huge bifaces are one of the two earliest tool types in the Konso area of Ethiopia, where they have been dated to over 1.4 million BP! $5,900 - $7,000. Small monochromatic Saharan handaxes from $140.

AFRICAN MID TO LATE ACHEULEAN HAND-AXES - Lower Paleolithic, ca. 750,000 - 250,000 B.P.: *late Homo erectus*

The discovery that a biface's edges could be straightened by retouching them with a soft hammer made of antler, bone or wood revolutionized bifaces around 750,000 years ago. Not only were the new hand-axes more efficient knives, but their makers could now adapt their silhouettes for specific tasks and, perhaps more importantly, as an expression of their group's particular technological culture. The oldest artifact to have been found expressly deposited with the dead is a hand-ax dropped on top of bodies that had been dragged deep into a Spanish cave before the invention of lamps & pitched into shafts. Such hand-axes must have been charged with symbolism & represent another step in the evolution of the mind.

9) Giant lanceolate handax. Quartzite with micro-exfoliation. One of biggest ever seen at 12". Northern Tchigheti, Mauritania. Colonial collection. Dramatic & no longer exported. $6,900 - $8,400. Only 2 seen on market in 3 years. Common dark & smaller handaxes from further north start at $120.

10) *Giant spatulate* **handax**. Quartzite with micro-exfoliation. One of biggest ever seen at 12". Northern Tchigheti, Mauritania. Colonial collection. Dramatic & no longer exported. $6,900 - $8,400. None seen surpassed this in size over the past several years. Smaller but fine specimens from $900.

11) 9" *Bifacial lagéniforme (tongue-shaped)* **handax**. Late Acheulian. Mylonite. Iringa Highlands, Tanzania. A spectacular specimen from a rare source. $1,800 - $2,900.

12) 10" *Giant cleaver* **handax**. Mid-to-late Acheulian. Quartzite with micro-exfoliation. Northern Tchigheti, Mauritania. Colonial collection. Dramatic & no longer exported. $3,900 - 5,000. Small Moroccan cleavers from $110.

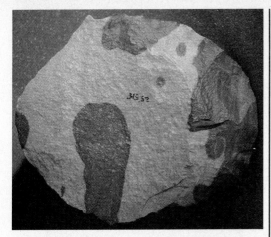

13) 8 3/4" *Flake-based* **cleaver** with bifacially thinned base. Late Acheulian. Tabelbalalt area Algeria based on appearance. Red & tan quartzite. This side wind stippled, other side darkened. Colorful. $1,800 - $2,300. Dull brown specimens from $100.

14) 6 1/4" *Cordiform* **handax**. Banded jasper and quartzite with high wind polish. Marked Mali, but probably extremely south of former Spanish Sahara. Among the prettiest materials. $1,800 - $2,700.

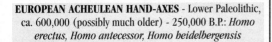

EUROPEAN ACHEULEAN HAND-AXES - Lower Paleolithic, ca. 600,000 (possibly much older) - 250,000 B.P.: *Homo erectus, Homo antecessor, Homo heidelbergensis*

15) *Lanceolate* **handax with** *inverse double oblique grips*. Remarkable ergonomy. Chert. Among the biggest European bifaces at 9 3/4". 1920s field find in now urbanized zone; Le Tillay, Seine-et-Marne, France. Bifaces from this famous site are illustrated in Fr. Bordes' typology guides. $7,000-$9,000. Poor specimens from $350.

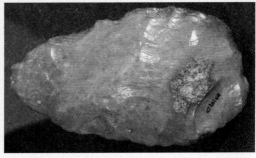

16) 6" *Lanceolate* **handax**. Pressignien flint tumbled in alluvia. Claise, Indre-et-Loire, France. An excellent example & transparent orange. $3,000 - $4,800. Smaller specimens fall rapidly in price to around $500.

17) *Lanceolate* **handax**. Flint. 7 1/4". Orange patina over originally mat black Thanatian flint is typical of the brick clay of the Somme region. From the type site of the longest period in human development, St. Acheul, plus one of the finest from anywhere. $14,000 - $18,000.

18) *Elongated ovate* **handax**. Gray Thanatian flint patinated by watertable. 7 1/4". One of the biggest & best proportioned from the type site of St. Acheul. $15,000 - $20,000. Poor quality Acheulian handaxes start at $150.

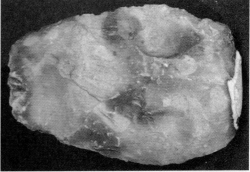

19) *Bifacial Cleaver* **handax**. If the angles to straight bit were not so abrupt it would be a classic *Limande*. Flint with typical orange brick clay patina of type site. 6 1/4". Cleavers are rarities in Europe as opposed to Africa and this is the best ever seen from the type site of St. Acheul itself. $13,000 - $15,000. Lesser specimens from $100 for the Sahara.

20) 6 1/4" *crescent* hand-ax. Boves next door to Amiens & St. Acheul. Dark gray flint turned white by lime salt substitution for leached-out silica. Found 1883. **ID:** A concave cutting edge opposite a convex edge with an oblique grip. It is difficult to explain such hand-axes as being a step in a reduction sequence since they seem to be specific to certain sites and are exceedingly rare in those assemblages. $2,000 - $2,900. Small cordiforms down to $30 if frost damaged or ugly material, especially in mat brown, NW African quartzite.

21) 10" *arch-backed naviform* hand-ax. Vailly-sur-Aisne, France. Sparkling quartzite with patina & crusts. The American prehistorian and frequent companion of Abbé Breuil, Harper Kelley, reported on similar giant hand-axes from the Aisne in1963. **ID:** Arch-backed hand-axes with an oblique grip on a convex edge opposite a much straighter cutting edge that runs from the tip to the base, have been reported from the Seine northwards through the Aisne, the English Wolvercote assemblage and into central Europe. $3,600 - $4,500. Small & crude bifaces from same valley from $250.

22) 8" *arched-edge naviform* hand-ax. Montieres, France. Dark gray flint patinated white by silica loss and lime salt intrusion. For other hand-axes from the same site see François Bordes. **ID:** Whereas the *arch-backed* naviform has an oblique basal grip along the arched edge, the *arched-edge* naviform has the grip along the straighter one. On this specimen, the long bulging edge across from the grip works best with a rocking saw motion. True naviforms are double bitted & usually have a lateral grip. $3,900 - $4,900.

23) *Naviform* handax. Quartzite. 6 3/4". Port d'Envaux. A large example of one of the rarest Acheulian types. Best seen in 3 years. $5,000 - $8,000. Lesser naviforms from $1,300.

24) 5" *shark's tooth lanceolate ficron* hand-ax. **ID:** Edges not as well made as on a typical lanceolate or Micoquian. Lanceolate ficrons have slightly covex edges, Micoquian ficrons, slightly concave ones. Basal grip. Boves, next door to St. Acheul from1883 excavation. Tri-color peat patina with fossilized worm burrow in flint. Original label, painterly colors, bold example of rare form. $5,800 - $7,000.

25) *"Bishop's Mitre" sub-cordiform* handax, to quote the 1917 inscription on the base. Flint patinated to several colors. 4". France. Decorative & historically interesting. $2,900 - $3,900.

26) 6" *Cordiform* handax. Acheulian. Flint. Sanvic, Seine-Maritime. Found around 1900 in a sand-pit. A large perfectly proportioned example. $7,000 - $9,000 in France. Run-of-the-mill Mousterian cordiforms which are not illustrated start at $500.

27) 6 1/2" *amygdaloid* hand-ax. St. Même la Carrière, Charente. Mid-Acheulean. Extremely varied patinas from many processes. The 6 major collections in the area are black holes, sucking local artifacts in & never parting with anything. $3,800 - $5,000.

28) 7" extremely *elongated cordiform* biface with hole through it & *tip gloss*. Bon Secour, Dreux, France. Found 1885. Dark, mat gray flint turned snowy white. All around cutting edge. The blade is so thin, it foreshadows Central European mid to upper paleo leaf points & knives. Late Acheulean to Mid Paleolithic. **HYPOTHESIS:** Although gloss on hand-axes & similar but possibly hafted bifaces may derive from soil mechanics or even the silica particles in corn roots, the author has noticed that gloss usually appears around tips, rather than elsewhere. It is hard to explain a predilection of roots for tips, so cases of tip gloss may be due to their use for digging among the silica in soil - probably for root storage organs & post pits. Hole, artisanal perfection, thinness, & 2 intriguing features. $5,500 - $7,500.

29) *Limande* handax. Gray flint patinated orange by watertable. 4 1/2". Bon Secour, Vernouillet, Eure-et-Loir. An especially colorful example of more typical Acheulian handaxes. $1,900 - $3,400.

30) 9 1/4" *"Micoquian" finger-pocket hand-ax* with concave edges & lens cross-section. Heavily patinated black flint. Pommiers, Aisne. Tip thin for 2/5ths of tool's length. Seen from the side, the handle goes up at a 35 degree angle from the plane of the cutting edges – creating a sheltered space for the fingers when the knife is used for cutting flesh sideways off hide. See the Grip Demo section for a side view of a similar hand-ax. One of the biggest specimens of a type seen (rarely) from the Seine into central Europe. $7,500 - $9,500.

31) 7 1/4" *bi-pointed, side-grip limande hand-ax*. Chevrière, Oise. Faces patinated differently: the one with cortex black, the other olive. The edge with the most cortex is actually the main cutting side. The only blunt ergonomic surface that could serve as a grip is a small patch of cortex along the opposite edge. Side-grip limande & naviform hand-axes work best with a downwards rocking & sawing motion. Rare sub-type, large size. $2,400 - $2,800.

32) *Cordiform* handax. Late Acheulian or Mousterian. Mat black flint with some peat patina & much soil sheen. 5 1/4". An example of an only slightly patinated specimen which was probably protected where it was left by percipitated clay. The finest seen for this form for the region. Vailly-sur-Aisne, France. $9,000 – $14,000.

33) *Miniature biconcave pebble* handax. Acheulian. Only 3". Swanscombe, Kent, UK. A rare English form due to the use of small cobbles there. This specimen belonged to Martin A.C. Hinton, the main suspect in the Piltdown Man Hoax! $6,500 - $8,500. Common small handaxes start at $450.

OTHER EUROPEAN ACHEULEAN TOOLS - Lower Paleolithic, ca. 650,000 (possibly older) - 250,000 B.P.: *Homo erectus, Homo antecessor, Homo heidelbergensis*

34) *Limace* Monoface with deeply invasive knapping to the base. Acheulian. Flint patinated by watertable. 4 3/4". St. Même-les-Carrières, Charente. Limace-like monofaces are far rarer than handaxes in the Acheulian tool kit. $2,600 - $3,600. Simple Acheulian flake tools start at $30.

35) 5" *Bifacial crescent* knife. Flint. St. Même-les-Carrières, Charente. The grip is around the knob in the middle of the edge opposite the ulu-like knife. An extremely rare Acheulian tool type. $3,900 - $4,900.

THE MIDDLE PALEOLITHIC - ca. 250,000 - 45,000 B.P.: *Neanderthals & Archaic Homo sapiens*

AFRICAN MID-PALEOLITHIC TOOLS - ca. 250,000 - 45,000 B.P.: *Advanced Homo erectus variants (Broken Hill Man, Saldana Man) & "Gracile" Neanderthals (in N. Africa) to Archaic Homo sapiens*

36) A: 2" **Aterian stemmed scraper**. Petrified wood. Wind gloss. S. Algeria. **ID:** A Levallois flake which has been given a stem. One of the first indisputably hafted tools.

B: 2" **Aterian stemmed point**. Petrified wood. Wind gloss. S. Algeria. **ID:** A Levallois point that has been given a stem. The oldest stemmed point type seen. Late Middle Stone Age into Upper Paleolithic. Particularly fine specimens $150 - $250. But mostly broken & crude Aterian points & scrapers were sold a few years ago by Africans for just $3 a piece in lots of 1,000 - a mind-boggling bargain. Even at $250, the cheapest Paleolithic points available.

37) A 3" & a 3 3/4" **T-shaped tool**. W. Sahara. Tabular flint with 3 concave "spoke-shave" concavities. Wind gloss & color alteration. Some early prehistorians speculated that the longest spoke represented a bird goddess's beak while the other spokes represented her brows. Still speculating, they could be a culturally specific whittling tool or parts of a thrown snare, similar in conception to bolas. Middle Stone Age. Rare. $350 - $500.

38) 3 1/4" T-shaped tool (or symbol). An extremely unusual specimen for 2 reasons: There are 2 concavities, not 3, & the convex section, although worked, bears significantly darker & older patina. If the narrow spoke had been a stem for hafting, one would expect the convex edge to show preparation for use as a chisel or scraper. Neither is the case. Could it be a zoomorphic or anthropomorphic representation after all? For years, the only one seen on the market. Now there are more: $450 - $600.

39) 3 1/2" mid-Paleolithic drill made of Libyan Glass, an impactite from a meteorite explosion that vitrified dunes 29 million years ago. Earliest glass tools are from late Acheulean. W. Egypt. Transparent. Extreme wind smoothing & stippling. $1,300 - $1,900. If debitage from $150.

40) 7" ovate biface. Wind patinated quartzite. Erg Titersine, Libya. Middle Stone Age ovates seem to be typical of the Libyan & Egyptian Sahara rather than the Western Sahara. Could they be a guide-artifact to a specific culture? The most colorful and perfect have a shield-like boldness. Travelers have sold some fine specimens for as low as $130! More traditional & reliable markets such as galleries sell from $1,450 to $1,900.

41) 6 1/2" ovate biface. Libyan Desert in Egypt. Quartzite. Intense differential weathering of rock on photoed side. Other side unweathered! This piece lay like a turtle hunkered in the wind for tens of thousands of years. $1,450 - $1,900.

42) 8 1/4" "Micoquian" lanceolate hand-ax. Libya. Beige & red quartzite. Leaching crust & aeolized on domed face. Tip unbroken, colorful, & rare type. One of 2 seen in 5 years. **NOTE:** Unlike true Micoquian hand-axes, from SW Europe which are localized late Acheulean to Mousterian transitional artifacts, bifaces with concave edges appeared earlier in Africa. $3,200 - $4,900.

43) 8 1/2" fishtail cleaver hand-ax. One of two reported. Akin to both Tabelbala-Tachenghit (type 4) & tihodaine (type 5) cleavers which are common. Quartzite with micro-exfoliation & patina. Late Acheulean to early Middle Stone Age. Mauritania. **ID:** Like Saharan cleavers illustrated in Overstreet editions 6 & 7, made from a huge flake with bifacial thinning along both edges. But the thinning is a

tour-de-force to create a flared bit. Elegance & only 2 reported. $5,800 - $7,000. *Most* Saharan cleavers from $30 to $800. **NOTE:** Type 4 has an asymmetrically tilted bit, one convex & one concave edge, an oblique base & thinning around the sides & base of the flat bottom. Type 5 has a straight bit, parallel sides, a semi-circular base & is bifacial except at the bit. Acheulean cleavers are also found in Spain, Sicily & the Middle East.

EUROPEAN MOUSTERIAN HAND-AXES, OTHER TOOLS & CORES - Middle Paleolithic, ca. 250,000 - 45,000 B.P.: *Neanderthals*

Only one of the several Mousterian cultures continued to make "hand-axes" with any regularity, the Mousterian in the Acheulean Tradition, as opposed to the Quina tradition, the Denticulate tradition, and others.

44) 6 1/2" diameter Levallois flake-tool core. From a unique site 500 meters offshore at Ault, Somme. Barnacles on back & peaty patina. This site provided so many flint nodules from a chalk cliff that have now eroded back half a kilometer that pre-Neanderthals often used cores to remove just one tool – instead of dozens as elsewhere. So the cores are among the biggest known. The workmanship is also superb. $2,300 - $2,900 for finest. Small ones from elsewhere from $10.

45) 3 1/2" Quina side-scraper. One of the biggest from the type-site of this Mousterian culture: La Quina, Les Gardes, Charente. Most are half size. Found 1912. Gray chert patinated white. $1,750 - $2,100. If small from $300. If from elsewhere, from $75.

46) 5" Levallois flake convergent side-scraper/crescent knife. Vailly-sur-Aisne. Black flint with soil sheen & water-table patina. Incredible preservation due to the Neanderthals' camp being covered by still waters & precipitating clay. Never tumbled or chipped. Both edges show fine scaling from the base to the tip. Rarer than most hand-ax types. $1,600 - $2,300.

47) 4 1/2" Mousterian convergent side-scraper/leaf-blade knife. Thanatian flint typical of Picardy & the Somme. Calcite caliche on unphotoed side. Bifacial basal thinning – probably for hafting! Soissons, Aisne. Such an elegant tool bears so little resemblance to typical side-scrapers, that it seems reasonable to see it more as a finely contoured, leaf-blade knife. Dibble is correct about the reduction sequence of convergent side-scrapers to Mousterian points in some – but far from all – cases. One would expect to find the reduction sequence in all sites with double-edged side-scrapers. That is NOT the case. One would also expect many more points since they would be end products, jettisoned like cigarette butts. That is not the case either. Highly symmetrical leaf blade & crescent knives are regularly found at a few Middle Paleolithic sites, but unheard of in most others with double side-scrapers. The dismissive reduction sequence theory looks better in a drawing than in the field. Incredibly rare. $1,900 - $2,400.

48) 4 1/2" **Mousterian monoface**. Boulogne-la-Grasse, Oise. Water table patina. A cultural indicator for an un-named aspect of the Mousterian – I'd dub it the Oise Mousterian - since it comes from an assemblage with many fine monofaces & few bifaces. Unlike on a convergent side-scraper, the flaking is invasive and not simply scaled around edges. Cortical concavity near base. $2,400 - $3,000. Poor specimens from $70.

49) *Cordiform* **handax**. Mousterian. Gray flint turned white. 5 1/4". Villiers-Louis, Yonne. Thin cross-scetion & retouch around the edges worthy of a Gerzean knife. As fine as they get. $7,000 - $11,000. Smaller Mousterian cordiforms start around $500.

50) *Micoquian* **handax**. Cap de la Heve, Le Havre, France. True Micoquian handaxes have concave edges and are typically small. Note the barnacles on this remarkable specimen found in the English Channel. It is the best of 3 found many decades ago at a submerged site within a kilometer of the published Clactonian site off Ste. Adresse. One of the most highly sought-after forms. $8,000 - $12,000.

51) 5" *Triangular* **handax**. Pressignian flint patinated with lime & hydration webbing mainly on one side. Chaumussay, Indre-et-Loire, France. François Bordes wrote that the triangular handaxes reached their zenith of perfection at Chaumussay. This quality $9,000 - $11,000 at grassroots French provincial auctions during 2004. Poor specimens from $1,500.
DESCRIPTION: Straight or slightly convex sides, fairly straight base, often sharp, with suggestion of thinning for hafting. After the discovery of a hafted Acheulean flint in a coalmine in Schöningen, Germany, the creation of such complex tools by even the earliest Neanderthals is incontestable. Complete triangular bifaces/hand-axes are especially rare because - **(1)** of their thinness & consequent delicacy, **(2)** they were produced during the transition from the Acheulean to Mousterian, and **(3)** they are the first hand-axes to consistently show tip fractures suggesting impact damage (thus hafting).

52) 6" *Triangular* **handax**. Transitional Acheulian to Mousterian form. Flint. One side with tan patina, other creamy with concretions. Lanneray, Eure-et-Loir. All around cutting edge & geometric perfection. Even with a few chips at least $11,000 at the provincial French level. Possibly $15,000 - $18,000 in galleries.

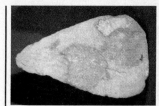

53) *Giant triangular* **handax**. Quartzite with mineral deposits. Huge at 7 3/4". Vailly-sur-Aisne. $7,000 - $10,000. at the French provincial level. Higher by the time such a tool gets elsewhere.

54) 2 3/4" **Mousterian in the Acheulean Tradition (MAT) cordiform biface**. Senonais. Max. thickness half inch. Basal thinning for probable hafting. Too small & thin to be a "handax". Narrow examples may even be projectile points related to late Neanderthals' leaf points in central Europe. Colorful $850 - $1,300. If crude & monochrome from $200.

55) 2" **MAT biface**. Quartz (rare material). Manzac-sur-Vern. $700 - $1,200.

56) 5" **ovate biface**. Gray flint turned yellow. Hydration webbing. Upper terrace of Loire, Nievre. The find of a decade of intensive searching. Perfect geometry. $1,900 - $3,000.

57) 4 3/4" **ovate biface**. Bu, Eure et Loir. Completely de-silicified in spots. A geometrical gem. $1,600 - $1,900.

58) 7 1/2" **bifacial naviform leaf-blade**. 3 color quartzite – milky, tan & dark gray. Water-table patinas. Aisne, France. So thin & finely knapped, it resembles a gigantic Solutrean laurel leaf knife. Possibly a precursor to SZELETIAN leaf points. This is the finest & most colorful specimen seen for such a late mid-Paleolithic biface. $9,000 - $12,000

59) Bifacial Mousterian knife/side-scraper. Dark gray flint patinated by lime salts. 4 3/4". Malay-le-Petit, Yonne. A rare nearly rectangular biface with one sharpened long edge opposite another with crushing or other evidence of preparation for hafting. 6 are now known from a 10 kilometer square, suggesting a local variant. $2,900 – $3,800 but none on the market. Simple Mousterian side-scrapers from $75.

60) A: Mousterian point. Creamy patination over dark gray flint. Retouched to base on one edge & halfway on other. 4". Maillot, Yonne. A splendid example. $1,900 – 2,900 **B: Mousterian blade**, heralding the first Upper Paleolithic blade-based industries. Patinated orange in boggy depression. 3 3/4". Malay-le-Petit, Yonne. $350 - $490. Tumbled specimens without proper provence start at $40.

61) Mousterian point. All edges are retouched, plus basal thinning for probable hafting! Gray flint with soil sheen & creamy patination. Grignieuzeville, France. Superb specimen. $1,900 - $2,900. Such points with breakage & other defects start at $190.

62) 2" Levallois point. Mousterian. Flint patinated orange in a peaty depression. Both edges are retouched to the base! Malay-le-Petit, Yonne, France. $1,600 - $2,400. Simple largely untouched & monochromatic Levallois points start at $140.

63) Levallois point core. Villevallier, Yonne. 4 1/3". The ability to extract multiple points from such cores represented one of humanity's great technical innovations. $290 - $450.

64) Levallois outre-passé flake tool. Gray flint patinated white by silica leaching & lime salt substitution. At 6 7/8", the biggest ever seen from its region. Mesnil-St.-Loup, Aube, France. Levallois flake tools, Levallois blades and Levallois points were the mainstays and basic building blocks of the Mousterian-in-the-Acheulian-Tradition tool kit. Highly decorative centripedal flake scars. $2,600 - $3,700. Small Levallois flakes start at $25.

65) Mousterian "Bola". Quartzite. 3 1/2" in diameter. Malay-le-Grand, Yonne. Extremely rare to non-existant in most Mousterian sites. Often confused with concussed Neolithic hammers which are usually made of flint, whereas Mousterian "bolas" are usually quartzite. $1,900 - $2,900. Neolithic hammerstones from $60.

THE UPPER PALEOLITHIC
(Sub-periods: Châtelperronian [*last Neanderthals*], Aurignacian, Gravettian, Solutrean, Magdalenian) ca. 45,000 - 12,000 B.P.: *Mainly Cro-Magnons, the name for European Upper Paleolithic modern humans were as much Homo sapiens as we are.*

SOME INVENTIONS: MEASURING SYSTEMS, ATL-ATL POINTS, NEEDLES, HARPOONS, BASKETRY & OTHER "WEAVING" TECHNOLOGIES, JEWELRY & ART:
NOTE: *Despite the fact that Upper Paleolithic tools are often much smaller than the preceding ones, they are also much rarer than most of them because:*
• *populations were extremely sparse due to often extreme glacial conditions*
• *the periods were much shorter and*
• *most sites have been off-limits to collectors for 60 or more years.*

AURIGNACIAN - ca. 40,000 (N. Europe) / 43,000 (SW Europe) - 28,000 B.P. Hitherto associated exclusively with our species, Homo sapiens sapiens, & dated from 34,000 BP in SW Europe, but the deepest proto-Aurignacian strata in the El Castillo Cave in Spain have now been dated to 43,000 BP – about 8,000 years before firm evidence of sapiens sapiens in western Europe. Could the proto-Aurignacian have been another Neanderthal invention like the Chatelperronian? Our species may have copied Neanderthal technology as much as the other way around."

66) 5 1/2" **Aurignacian calibrated antler tine**. Blanchard rock shelter, Dordogne. One of the oldest examples of non-functional (in the traditional sense) notation, counting or measurement. Mathematical, musical and linguistic literacy eventually took off from the breakthrough represented by this specimen. Ca. 32,000 BP. Only one this old seen in private hands. Inestimable.

CHATELPERRONIAN - ca. 40,000 - 30,000 B.P.
Neanderthals

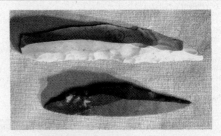

67) A: 4" **Châtelperronian point**. Palis, Aube – not far from Châtelperronian site at Arcy-sur-Cure. Knapping of back usually from one face. The steeply retouched back on Gravettes is usually from *both* faces. Perhaps the biggest specimen of the rarest point. $18,000 up
NOTE: The Châtelperronian is one of several Neanderthal cultures that represent a final flourish before they went extinct (except for a few genetic markers they seem to have left in people of European descent). Most prehistorians have a tendency to dismiss the final Neanderthal cultures as desperate attempts to cope with intruding members of our species, Homo sapiens sapiens. There has been much speculation of a deficiency of Neanderthal language, despite their well-developed hyoid bone used to anchor vocal muscles and brains that were larger than ours on average. Supposedly, our species was also far more efficient because of its ability to manipulate symbols and a newly invented blade technology that lent itself to the manu-

facture of complex compound tools with insertable standardized parts. The problem is that almost all Châtelperronian layers seem to pre-date the Aurignacian ones associated with modern humans.

So the theory *may* be flawed. In fact, Neanderthals may have made jewelry and invented a blade technology *before* our lineage arrived. They may have been just as capable of invention, yet simply had less virulent microbes. Whereas our lineage had recently come out of the tropics' incredible microbial diversity - which the migrants carried within themselves (along with immunities acquired over millenia of epidemics), Neanderthals had developed in cold regions with much lower exposure to microbes. So our ancestors were walking biological bombs infecting Neanderthals directly & indirectly. Neanderthal bands would have become too small to compete in favorable areas. Mortality would have exceeded the birth rate and they would have gone extinct like the Taino before the onslaught of the Conquistadors. In the mean time, our lineage may actually have acquired some behaviors from Neanderthals – as well as vice versa. At the very least, the final Neanderthal flourishes – either independently, or in the face of disease and advancing intruders - proved Neanderthal adaptability once and for all.

B: 3 1/4" Gravette point. From the type-site: La Gravette, Bayac, Dordogne. Steep retouch along one edge creating a back for insertion & gluing in a slotted shaft. A true projectile point. Ca. 25,000 BP. One of the rarest Paleolithic point types. $4,900 - $6,000

68) A: Blade end-scraper. Upper Solutrean. East section of Laugerie Haute, Les Eyzies, Dordogne. 4 1/8". $2,900 - $3,900.

B: Fully Retouched Aurignacian Blade. Castelmerle, Sergeac, Dordogne. Found 1902. Still has original label. 4". Perfection & one of the rarest tools from one of the most important sites. $3,900 - $6,700.

69) A: Double burin & parallel side-scraper all in one tool. Early Aurignacian. Lartet Rock Shelter, Les Eyzies, Dordogne. Dark gray flint patinated creams & whites. 19th C find. 5 1/4". Finest ever seen in private hands. $5,900 - $7,800. Little single upper Paleo burins start at $80.
B: Blade end-scraper with lateral retouch to base on both sides. Upper Solutrean. Laugerie Basse, Dordogne. Flint with soil sheen & mineral patina. 6". Longest seen. $5,900 - $7,900. Small end-scrapers start at $45. **NOTE:** It should be noted that any collecting around the Dordogne's famous sites today is not only strictly forbidden but heavily policed! All the illustrated pieces come from such 19th C collections as Christy & Lartet's and often have the original labels.

70) 4 7/8" Aurignacian to Gravettian retouched blade. Retouch around all edges. Black flint turned white. Abri Labattut, Sergeac, Dordogne, 1912. Now a museum site. $2,900 - $3,800

71) 4 3/4" Gravettian convergent side-scraper / "point". Bergerac flint with rich patina. Reglued. From the well documented site under the lawn of the Chateau de Corbiac, Ponponne, Dordogne. Both specimens are fully retouched down to their tiny punctiform striking platforms. $2,300 - $3,300.

72) Two Font Robert points. Both from the type site of Font Robert in the Correze. The first stemmed European point type. Gravettian. Flint with soil sheen & microscopic mineralization. Tan one 2 3/4". Black 2 7/8". Fewer than 10 seen on the market in 15 years. $13,000 - $16,000. Neolithic stemmed arrowheads from 6,000 BP, as opposed to 25,000 BP, start at $50.

73) A: Font Robert Point. From Font Robert type site in Correze. Gravettian. Flint. 2 7/8". Far rarer than contemporaneous Gravette Points or later Solutrean Laurel Leaf Points. Under ten seen in 15 years. $13,000 - $16,000.
B: Solutrean Laurel Leaf Projectile Point. Flint with rich but not masking patinas. 2 3/8". Carsac, Dordogne. A beautiful example of the point type which may have presaged Clovis. Prices all over the map: $4,000 - $11,000, partly because of increasingly accomplished fakes. Two which were sold for around $20,000 recently were almost certainly forgeries. Soil sheen is not enough – go for patina, integrity and provenance.
C: An atypical Solutrean Shouldered Point. Dordogne with cave deposits still adhering to point. 3". Slightly cruder shoulderd points continued into the Magdalenian. This is far from the best, but the best are almost all represented by fragments. $4,900 - $5,900. The best over $25,000.

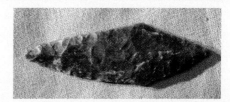

74) 2 1/2" Solutrean bifacial lozenge point. Only projectile of this sort seen in private hands. See Philip Smith's Le Solutréen en France for similar specimens. Laugerie Haute shelter, Dordogne. Don't confuse with almost equally rare but thicker lozenge points from Copper Age dolmens. $7,000 - $9,000.

A MISSING LINK BETWEEN EUROPE & THE AMERICAS?
75) 3 1/4" Solutrean laurel leaf point with *basal grinding* like on American Paleo points. This feature has never been reported before on laurel leaves – even in Smith's encyclopedic Le Solutréen en France. Basal grinding was invented independently in several places in the world, but has never been found with so many traits shared with the earliest undisputed American tool kits. Many prehistorians suspect that a small Solutrean band may have succeeded in crossing a continuous land & ice bridge from the Pyrenees area because only American Clovis and SW European Laurel Leaf points share outre-passé flaking & lens-shaped cross sections at about the same time. Except for a single fluted point, which may represent

later flux *out* of America, these features are missing at the Asian end of Berengia, where points typically have diamond-shaped cross-sections. Now that Clovis points share *3 features* with European Laurel Leaves, the case for a Solutrean migration is even harder to dismiss. The Paleolithic population of Europe would have been demographically squeezed by advancing ice towards the peninsular dead-end of SW Europe & out onto its vast exposed continental shelves. But for a short period during the coldest phase of the last Ice Age – which occurred during the Solutrean – those shelves merged with continuous floes, ice-locked islands and other shelves rich in auks, belugas, cod and seals to make a dry passage to the Americas. Such a bridge could only have been negotiated after the invention of weather-tight clothing made possible by the eyed needle: a Solutrean invention. Similarities between the Solutrean tool set and the pre-Clovis assemblage found at Cactus Hill, Dinwiddie County, Virginia lend support to the hypothesis. A genetic marker only reported among American Indians & Basques of the Pyrenees lends further support. Although a Solutrean band may have been the first to arrive, a 9,000 year old Brazilian skeleton with features reminiscent of Micronesians suggests a possible sea voyage around the Pacific rim. NE Asian populations living in 300 mile wide Berengia obviously got through too when the Yukon Corridor opened between the Alaskan and Canadian Ice Shields after the Solutrean. Then around 4,500 BP proto-Eskimos developed technologies to begin their remarkable expansion around the Arctic. Flint patinated with lime salt intrusion & hydration. Carsac, Dordogne. A missing link & reference specimen: Over $20,000. True Solutrean laurel leaves are scarce as hen's teeth in private collections, but poor specimens are seen from $1,000. Beware of later Clovis preforms & Saharan & Afghani Neolithic leaf points in different flints & patinas masquerading as infinitely rarer Solutrean laurel leaves!

76) 1 1/2" Crystal Solutrean laurel leaf point. Laugerie Haute, Dordogne. Utterly transparent. Much resharpened prehistorically but only crystal one seen outside a dozen in museums. $5,500 - $7,500. Fakes could become a problem.

77) Magdalenian Harpoon. Antler. 7" of the overall 7 3/4" are original including the barbs, with only 3/4" at the tip being restored. The shaft is also broken & glued near the base and is bent by long burial. Laugerie Haute, les Eyzies. This is nearly twice as long as the only other nearly complete harpoon that came to the market (to my knowledge) over the past 5 years. It is also the only one with clear provenance. Inestimable, but at least $25,000.

78) 2 1/2" Azilian Harpoon. Transitional Upper Paleolithic to Mesolithic. Bone. La Tourasse rock shelter, Haute Garonne. The Azilian was almost named the Tourassian, since Tourasse was the first site to be described, but turned out to be both less rich than the Mas d'Azil and misdescribed, since the first excavators seem to have mixed Azilian and slightly earlier Magdalenian artifacts. $16,000 - $21,000. Old Inuit bone harpoons start at $250.

79) A broken **"Shaft Straightener" or "Wrench"** according to some, although I prefer the French **"Baton de Commandment"** – suggesting a scepter. Magdalenian. Antler. 5". Laugerie Basse, les Eyzies. A North American specimen exists from the Richey Clovis cache. All 3 that have come to the market in the last decade were broken, this one was the only one with partial drilling from both sides to make a second new hole! $14,500 - $19,000. Higher if decorated. If decorated figuratively, off the charts, even if broken. Beware of fakes!

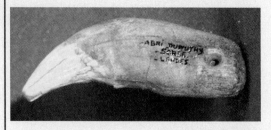

80) Cave bear fang pendant. Magdalenian. 4 1/2". From the highly documented Duruthy Rock Shelter, Sord, Landes, France (see Piette collection). Remarkable both as one of the rare examples of the earliest jewelry and as amazing evidence of the role cave bears played in Paleolithic culture. The invention of jewelry implies a new sense of self and otherness and a desire to change ones image. It also allowed individuals to differentiate themselves symbolically from each other, leading to different social roles. The reprecussions of such an artifact for humans are unfathomable. After being allowed to see hundreds of collections, the author is only aware of 3 authentic cave bear fang pendants outside museums. Estimated at $45,000 - $65,000. Small fox teeth pendants start at $500, but are rarely seen.

81) Two Cave Bear phalange whistles. Among the oldest known musical instruments. The smaller, 1 2/3". specimen still has its original 1863 Christy-Lartet label marked "le Moustier, Dordogne" – the first excavation at le Moustier in the first year of prehistoric studies in the Dordogne. The 2nd specimen is from the Tarté rock shelter, Haute Garonne. 2". Both pieces are heavily incised. Probably fewer than 20 authentic examples in private hands. $14,000 - $19,000 but a Stradivarius may be easier to find.

UPPER PALEOLITHIC ART - ca. 34,000 - 12,000 B.P.

82) A delicate engraving of a **chamois on bone in its cave breccia**. Published upon discovery in main French Prehistory journal. Magdalenian. The depiction of beings & drafting of symbols may have occurred in a scattered & tentative way before the upper Paleolithic but only took hold and became essential behaviors at the dawn of the new era. The oldest evidence for such behaviors comes from S. Africa and consists of geometrical incisions comparable to the calibrated Aurignacian antler tine shown above. No undisputed pieces of Upper Paleolithic art have appeared at auction in over 50 years. Inestimable.

83) Two reindeer meet as a harpoon head approaches from bottom left. Placard rock shelter, France. One of the most remarkable pieces of prehistoric art seen in private hands for 3 reasons: it appears to be a narrative – something rare in the period's art. Two, the meeting deer resemble a famous polychrome scene in the Font-de-Gaume cave. And, three, it supports the hypothesis that the first "harpoons" were used on big game. This theory is based on the concentration of harpoons at sites in dry interiors as opposed to along water. Inestimable.

84) *Paleolithic* Aboriginal **flake tool**. Basalt with red patination in flake scar on hidden base. Australia. Circa 15,000 BP. 3 3/4". $850 - $1,000.

85) Post-Contact bifacial disc scraper/knife & arrowhead. Bottle glass with concretions. Rottnest Island, Australia. Only 100 years old, based on known Aboriginal activity & a dateable manufacturer's mark on the other side of the disc. As remarkable as Ishi's points in their testimony to the quick adaptation of Stone Age craftsmen to modern materials. $750 - $900 each.

THE MESOLITHIC, ca. 14,000 – 11,000 B.P. Middle East / 12,000 - 8,000 B.P. (W. Europe) - *Homo sapiens*

SOME INVENTIONS: EARLIEST POTTERY VESSELS (JOMON, JAPAN - 12,000 B.P.); RESOURCE EFFICIENT MICROLITHIC TECHNOLOGIES; ARCHERY; SPREAD OF NARRATIVE ROCK-ART

86) Two conical Mesolithic bladelet cores. Flint. 1" & 1 1/4". From a site now flooded by a dam in Iran. Gem-stone facetting represents one of the peaks of prehistoric knapping. $450-$600. Common blade cores from $25.

NEOLITHIC - ca. 11,000 - 6,000 B.P. (Middle East) / 8,000 - 5,000 B.P. (W. Europe): *Homo sapiens*

SOME INVENTIONS: AGRICULTURE, CERAMIC VESSELS, URBANIZATION

SAHARAN POINTS, AXES & OTHER TOOLS:

87) A: Double-edged denticulate. Mauritania. Mesolithic to Neolithic. Although arrowheads from Niger to Mauritania have swamped the market in the last 6 years, few other tools have appeared – although they can be more interesting conceptually than another pointed arrowhead. Narrower serrated bladelets are also known from the European Magdalenian. Only one seen. $490 - $650.
B: A **strangled blade**. Mauritania. Strangled blades are also one of the key artifacts of the European Aurignacian. $480 - $600.

88) Six **lunates with steeply retouched crescent backs**. Made from blade segments. W. African Mesolithic to Neolithic. The same form occurs in the European Mesolithic – suggesting a link. Mauritanian lunates are extreme varieties of the Transverse razor arrowhead. Arrows have survived in the Sahara's aridity with lunate razors still in position. So, despite preconceptions, NOT all arrowheads are pointed! Ethnographic clues suggest that these were dipped in toxins and used to sever vessels of animals as large as giraffes. The prey would succumb over 2 or 3 days to bleeding & poisoning. Lunates could also be slotted along shafts or curved sickles to create segmented (& easily replaceable) cutting edges. The original, adaptable & light spare part. Usually unseen in collections. $230 - $450. If European & fine, double to triple.

89) 7 *average* N. African Capsian Mesolithic to Neolithic arrowheads PLUS a **serrated point from India** for comparison. The *Transverse razor point* is similar to S. European ones & is terribly rare in NW Africa. The *barbed & stemmed point* is also found on both sides of the Mediterranean. But the notched base *Eiffel Tower points* & long tanged points are typical of NW Africa. Eiffel Tower points are never as deeply notched as *Fayoum points* (see Overstreet 6th Ed P 38 ph 97) from Egypt. The point in the center is one of the world's more unusual types – an *Escutcheon Point* described from Bir es-Sof. A bladelet has been steeply retouched to create both stem & tip. These 7 points are probably NOT contemporaries but their distribution may never be studied due to their rapid disappearance from the desert, inaccessibility to westerners and lack of funds. **NOTE:** Capsian (but not transverse) points have flooded the market, with Africans selling them in lots of 3,000 for $2 an arrowhead, many of which are broken. A famous Californian web site advertises average specimens for $175 - $250. Such prices will still give you the pick of the litter from other dealers. Beware of dealers reselling these genuine & wonderful artifacts as Texas bird points and Columbia River gem points. For comparison: 1 1/16" *Spiked Xmas tree point* from India. Super rare. $500 - $700.

90) *Fine* **green jasper points from the "Sudanese" Neolithic Tradition** of the S. Sahara & Sahel. Longest is 2 1/16". Light green point is from Niger. All others from Kiffa region, Mauritania. Amazing micro-denticulation on needle point. The workmanship of the S. Sahara, especially in the Teneré Desert, is often more impressive than that of the Capsian Tradition of the NW Sahara. But because of the poverty of the countries in question, the prices at the grassroots was lower – until recently! Suddenly the best points have jumped from $4 to $150 in the desert itself! Only gem-quality will tend to appreciate – despite the amazingly high premium paid by top collectors until just recently.

91) 2 1/2" **serrated V-stemmed point**. Niger. Only one of its type in huge collection. $85 - $150.

92) 1 1/2" *side-toothed point* **with a long bulbous stem**. Best seen intact.
B) 2" white **double side-toothed point with in-curving ears**. One of the 3 master-pieces from a large collection. $85 - $150 & climbing. C) 1 1/4" **double side-toothed quartz point**. Rarity. First described by H.J. Hugot (who found 5) in Libyca. $45 - $85. All Mali & Niger.

93) A) 1 7/8" **Fan-eared point**. One of the few with intact barbs. $75 - $100
B) 1 7/8" **Fan-eared point**. One barb broken, but best overall shape & color. $80 - $100. Probably rare as Calf Creeks. The best 2 of a huge collection. **ID:** Long wire-thin ears, often accompanied by bulbous blade. Mali & Niger.

94) 2" **double-tiered, serrated, Xmas tree point**. Best of only 2 seen from 1,000s of points. The ultimate point from the Sahel. $250-500 & climbing fast.

95) 7 3/4" **flared celt**. Mali. Rainbow flint. Paler patina on unphotoed side. Flared celts are rare suggesting a ceremonial use. Colorful common celts have flooded the market. A couple of Africans sell lots of 1,000 for as low as 75 cents a celt. But local prices range much higher. Exceptional pieces are culled out locally & sold in the hundreds to thousands of dollars. In the USA, common celts have been selling for as low as $15 wholesale to $250 retail. Exceptional ones like this $1,900 - $3,400.

96) 8 7/8" *Polished & pecked* **ax**. Hard dark green stone with leaching crust. Saharan axes are often pecked into shape & polished only at the bit. One of the finest seen in recent years from the W. Sahara. $1,300 - $2,300. Shorter more rudimentary celts from the same area appear from $210.

97) 5" **omphalos ax or adze**. Heavy crusting & wind erosion. S. Algeria. The central hole is too small for a strong shaft. Could this have been a totemic ax head or an elaborate pectoral ax? Although the celt form is so utilitarian that it occurs around the world, there are fabulous local variants on the polished ax. UNIQUE. $8,900 - $13,000.

98) 7 1/8" **Early** *Gerzean Pre-Dynastic Egyptian Proto-Ripple-Flake* **Knife**. Patinated flint. Gerzean knives represent one of the highpoints of prehistoric knapping. Rarely seen on the market. $13,000 - $18,000.

99) 8 1/4" *Tbinnite shouldered* **knife** from the proto-historic phase before the first Egyptian dynasty. Patinated flint. Rarely seen. $12,000 - $17,000.

100) 5 1/4" **grinding basin with an abstract design pecked into its domed back**. The zigzag may be a snake circling a solar egg, based on more figurative examples. The Saharan Neolithic convention for the sun was a circle or oval amid concentric pecked zones that replicate solar halos caused by suspended dust. 2 hand-held grinding basins bearing this specific design are known. Fewer than 300 portable art objects are known for the culture. $16,000 or more.

WARNING: NON-portable rock art is being extracted from cliffs in the NW Sahara with diamond saws. Poverty, lack of local appreciation, Islamic traditions against figurative art & unscrupulous dealers have abetted pillaging of immobile petroglyphs which I hope no western dealer or collector would tolerate from his own country. There is no reason to hypocritically encourage the destruction of rock art from elsewhere, regardless of mitigating circumstances. Draw the line & stop the traffic.

EUROPEAN POINTS, AXES & OTHER TOOLS:

101) 2 **French Neolithic arrowheads: A:** 1 1/2" *transverse razor arrowhead*. Even rarer than Saharan equivalents. Only one seen with steep inverse beveling along sides. Yvelines, France. The razor arrowhead is so unusual on a world scale that its existence on both sides of the Mediterranean attests to cultural flows during the Mesolithic & Neolithic between N. Africa & Europe. Iberian & Saharan rock art from the period is also similar. $350 - $650. If crude from $20.
B: 2" *long-stemmed & barbed point*. Grand Pressigny, Indre et Loire. The find of a couple of lifetimes in terms of French arrowheads. $1,400 - $2,500. Lesser ones from $80.

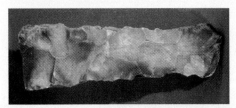

102) **First Stage Ax Preform**. Flint with different patination each side. Big at 10 3/4". Denmark. Rarely left at this stage with only heavy hammer knapping which makes this both a spectacularly decorative & pedagogical piece. $3,700 - $4,900. Small monochrome Danish celts start at $450.

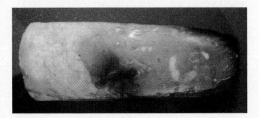

103) **Polished ax**. Denmark. Flint colorfully patinated by peat. 8 7/8". $3,800 - $5,500. Spectacular 25 to 40 cm. polished Scandanavian celts fetch $6,000 to $15,000.

104) **Polished gouge**. Banded flint. 5 1/2". Egtved, Jutland, Denmark. Finest seen. $3,800 - $5,000. Less decorative specimens from $550.

105) **Giant preform for a polished ax**. Tabular flint. Each side has its own patina; other side is darker. At 15 1/2", one of the biggest recorded. Jablines, Seine-et-Marne. Found beside a Neolithic flint mine in the 1930s. Interestingly, no polished axes are found at the site. $17,000 - $21,000. Small ax preforms start at $110.

106) 8 1/4" **Un-polished ax**. Flint with different patina on each side. Nottonville, Eure-et-Loir, France. Certain axes are so well knapped that they certainly were not preforms, representing instead fully finished prestige or currency axes. With the weak dollar $6,500 - $9,000. Even many fully polished but smaller, duller and chipped specimens are just $400 to $800.

107) **Prestige ax**. Banded gray flint transformed by a rich watertable patina. 7 1/8". 19th C find in Eure-et-Loir. $4,800 - $8,000.

108) **Polished ax**. Gray flint patinated by bog. Orange one side, light yellow on other. Restored chip at bit. 7 1/4". Gaudonville, Loir-et-Cher. $4,500 - $7,200.

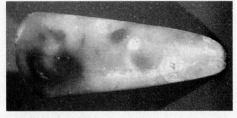

109) 7" **Polished ax**. Gray flint patinated orange by 5 millenia on the bottom of the Seine. Dredged from Seine at Bercy in Paris during 1890s. Where the Finance Minister's office cantilevers over the river today. Est. $9,000 - $14,000 to Parisian collectors.

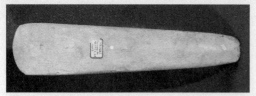

110) Polished prestige ax. Flint with creamy patination. At 11", it is too long and thin to have been for wood working. Maule, Yvelines, France. One of the finest French specimens. $12,000 - $16,000. The author does not know of a single field find of this size anywhere in the country in 20 years.

111) 5 3/8" Prestige ax. Jadeite. Dolmen at Teillay, Ille-et-Vilaine, France. Red ochre patina on one side. As finely made as they come. This quality not seen in 7 years. Among other defects, fakes still tend to be more rectangular rather than lense-like in cross section. Beware of any deal that seems too good to be true. I'm not aware of current benchmarks for the finest authentic dolmenic axes, so guesstimated at $9,000 - $11,000.

112) Side-view of a 10" polished **prestige ax showing differences in color where the ax was hafted** & "rope burns" where cordage bit into the stone on either side of the ax handle! Courson, Calvados. Although a few axes have been found in their handles in peat bogs & lake sites, the author does not know of another LARGE ax blade with direct evidence not only of where the handle was placed (not at the poll, but near the middle) but also of how it was lashed. $10,000 - $13,000.

113) 9" polished **prestige ax with a band of lighter patina around the middle of the ax where the handle survived** in peat long enough to show where it had been. Pithiviers, Loiret. Large, perfect, beautiful colors & probably unique. $13,000 - $15,000. Polished axes start from $200.

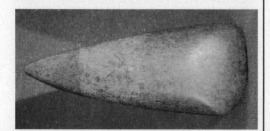

114) Polished prestige ax. Jadeite. 6 1/8". Lighter patination around the middle provides rare evidence of how the ax was hafted! Rousset, St. Martin-de-Coux, Charente Inferieur, France. $7,000 - $10,000. Flint field grade celt from $300.

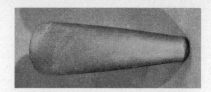

115) 6 1/2" Polished Button Ax. Jadeite. Vienne-en-Val, Loiret, France. One of the rarest forms of polished Neolithic axes. Only 3 seen on the market in a decade. Est. value $9,000 - $14,000.

116) 6 1/2" Prestige ax. Light green jadeite patinated black on one side. 19th C find at Auneau, Eure-et-Loir with original label. $6,300 - $8,000. Small jade axes, under 8 cm. start at $1,200.

117) 10 1/2" Ceremonial flint double pick with bi-conical pecked shaft hole. Heavily patinated. Late Neolithic. Maintenon, Eure et Loir. The only other one known to the author is in the Chartres museum. These two totemic instruments appear to have been modeled on the first copper implements imported from Eastern Europe via the Danube corridor. One of 3 imported copper ax/adzes found in France was discovered in the same area during the 19th century. Over $17,000.

118) 6" Polished chisel. Flint. Dredged from Seine at Villeneuve-St.-Georges. French Neolithic chisels must have been rare variants on prestige axes, rather than a common woodworking tool, since one will find hundreds of common celts before finding an intact "chisel". $3,900 - $6,000.

119) Green ax in antler sleeve. Late Neolithic form. Found during the late 19th C in a submerged site in Chalain Lake, Jura, France. 4 3/8". Perishable material plus the finest seen in several years. $7,900 - $9,700. Cracked sleeves from $450.

120) 4 7/8" French engraved shaft-hole battle-ax. Eure-et-Loir with original 19th C. label. While battle-axes are common gravegoods in northern European single male Neolithic graves, they are the find of a life-time (or more) in southern Europe. This 19th C find is even engraved. $7,900 - $9,000. Ukrainian specimens, some very nice, from $450.

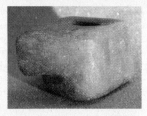

121) 4" Mace-head battle-ax with a rare separated bit. Ukraine. Hardly ever seen. $3,900 - $4,800. Simple wedge shaft-hole axes from $450.

122) Macehead. Light green jadeite. 7". Dolmen in the Eure-et-Loir. Almost certainly not utilitarian, since the ends are round and highly polished. A unique piece. Est. $7,500 - $9,000.

123) A: 1 5/8" **Neolithic pendant** broken at the hole, but with a prehistorically engraved ax. Found in a dolmen, Eure-et-Loir.
B: 1 3/4" **Ax-amulet pendant.** Jadeite. From a tumulus in Brittany. Formerly in the Nicaise collection described in the Lord McAlpine collection catalog. French Neolithic pendants of any kind are basically only found in funerary contexts, not fields. Pendants refering to the ax-cult are rarer still. $4,800 - $6,900. Miniature ax pendants in other rock types are quite common in Mali & Niger, starting at just $350!

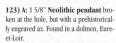

124) 2 3/4" **Double "drill"** – in fact, probably a **pottery decorating tool.** Foissy-sur-Vanne, Yonne. Flint. Great finesse & apparently unique. $1,900 - $2,300. Simple drills start at $70.

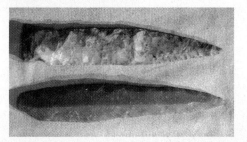

125) EUROPEAN DAGGERS: A: 6 1/2" **Scandinavian *semi-fishtail dagger*.** Natural concavity in handle. Peat patina. Many thousands are known. $3,700 - $4,800 Best specimens over $10,000. Danish fakers place forgeries in tide pools to acquire soil sheen. Beginners should go for peat patina.
B: 7" *Grand Pressigny dagger.* One of about 300. Pithiviers, Loiret. **ID:** Made from Neo-Levallois cores called Livres de Beurres (Pounds of Butter), which are almost unique to the Grand Pressigny region. A few similar cores have been found around Bergerac, Dordogne & Spiennes, Belgium. They were used to produce the longest & straightest blades known. The blades were delicately retouched & exported as far as Holland & the Alps for 500 years at the end of the Neolithic. Several were found at the Charavines lake site with wicker & wood handles. Micro-tracelogy shows they were used for harvesting, but most daggers in private collections – including this perfect specimen – were found before WW II in megalithic graves – underlining their ceremonial importance. $6,500 - $8,500

126) 6 1/2" **Danish dagger.** Gray flint patinated by peat bog. Egtved, Denmark. An above average specimen despite ding at tip. The finest examples have "stitching" up the middle of the handles. Scandanavian daggers are far more common than Southern European forms because they were regularly placed in individual male graves. This specimen $3,900 - $4,800. Finest for up to $25,000.

127) 7 5/8" **Grand Pressigny dagger.** Grand Pressigny, Indre-et-Loire flint patinated white on top side which is also fully polished, except for a bifacial retouch around all edges. The finest French dagger I've ever seen. Est. $18,000 - $21,000. Unpolished French daggers start at $2,500. An increasingly faked artifact. Reliance on provenance, previous publication & microscopic examination eliminates problems.

128) 5 3/4" **Neolithic "venus" pendant.** Silicified limestone with bituminous deposits. Northern Fertile Crescent. The shoulder holes may double as a second set of "eyes," linking it to "eye idols." Head glued back. Est. $40,000 - $60,000.

129) 10 1/2" **Stemmed hoe.** Basalt patinated light green & encrusted with mineral deposits. New Caledonia. An extremely ancient pre-contact artifact, plus the best & biggest seen. $4,800 - $6,700. Small recent specimens from $300.

PARADOXES OF DISCOVERY & THE LAW:

A disproportionate number of the western European artifacts above are 19th century finds because prehistoric vestiges were more easily found before quarrying was highly mechanized and gravel was conveyed blindly to crushers. A century ago, gravel pits were locally owned & their owners gave their neighbors & other collectors access. Unfortunately, European sandpits have been consolidated under huge companies including the world's largest construction materials group. These multi-nationals forbid access to non-institutional collectors – supposedly for reasons of liability and equipment theft, but also (according to their foremen) to obstruct the discovery of vestiges which might lead to calls for preservation. The institutional researchers that the monopolies must allow in (occasionally) by law are so few, have such tiny travel budgets and are so constrained by industrial lobbies that the chief archeologist of a region north of Paris told the author he rubber-stamped a huge construction project between 3 megalithic graves because he was too afraid for his job even to look. He lost his office anyway.

So it is hardly surprising that institutional researchers, who have seen their efforts attacked (even from within their governments) & salvage budgets cut, seem to have accepted a devil's bargain with quarriers: in return for the right to check top soil that doesn't interest the companies, archeologists usually don't check lower, commercially exploitable strata before a pit is opened. Such archeologists dismiss all the artifacts in lower "alluvial" strata as being displaced by currents and therefore, somehow, of no scientific interest. By this thinking, St. Acheul itself would have been a waste of time to excavate. The absurdity of such thinking is demonstrated first by such in situ Acheulean sites as ones exceptionally excavated in gravel pits at Soucy. And, secondly, by what trespassing amateurs could tell the "institutionals" they missed in some places by keeping their eyes closed. After periods of quarrying through truly tumbled alluvia, the quarrying equipment will inevitably scoop up dozens of un-eroded tools mixed with mammoth and rhino bones in clay. A true concentration that has never been tumbled, and it happens again & again. But what nobody sees, nobody has to bother with. Too bad. When artifacts are found in such clay, which typically precipitated from becalmed backwaters on flood plains, the objects have often lain where they were put by ancient hands. Even gestures can sometimes be reconstructed. If only amateurs were working respectfully with everyone & spending their own time & gas money to watch for changes at quarries, the handful of institutional archeologists in the region, who simply can't be everywhere, would have a chance to speedily salvage some of that information with the help of volunteers – especially if the workers were motivated by finding things they could keep after proper central recording. Instead, of gaining more knowledge & saving some of what is being annihilated, everything goes to the crusher. But at least institutionals haven't compromised themselves by feeding the market or working beside enthusiasts with suspect motives. As one prehistorian explained to the author, the discipline has also become such a question of statistics, that researchers have lost touch with pieces – and their potential aesthetics or poetry as relics of ancient human endeavor. Some institutionals make the mistake of actually disdaining finer pieces because they believe *justifiably* that too much emphasis on fine artifacts skews our perception of a site's full tool assemblage and its culture. It is true that beginning and investment-driven collecting can be uninformed & that beginners tend to be overly attracted to "prettiness." But the resulting contempt for the artifacts themselves which is a by-product of prevailing views in museums is scandalous: the author himself has found labeled bifaces in national museum dumpsters (which as a result were moved behind high spiked fences) & one of the most exalted museums is reported by some professional archeologists to have bought a crusher to destroy its "excess" hand-axes. According to them, the museum's excuse is that those artifacts lack provenance and hence any "scientific" interest. To begin with, what hubris it is for today's scientists to imagine that such pieces will never be of scientific interest!

Another excuse is said to be that the museum does not want to feed anything into the crass market where such artifacts could encourage collectors even though that market will not go away. How twisted! If the museum really wanted to subvert the market (instead of wallowing in ideological purity) it could do nothing more destructive than *dump* the museum's "useless" surpluses on collectors & make prices collapse. Such de-acquisitions would even provide such shrewd museums - which are constantly begging - with extra income while sparing the taxpayer.

But the real motive for institutional destruction of artifacts – beyond over-familiarity with them, is the doctrinaire contempt that has been growing for the group from which many great prehistorians issued and whose generosity has given birth to so many museum collections: collectors. Not surprisingly, the European laws invoked against them often date to the Fascistic period (France 1941, Italy 1939) – but are somehow perceived as "progressive". These draconian laws are easy for politicians of all stripes to continue supporting since they categorically "protect" things which are generally seen by the non-collecting public as being so rare that they should only be kept in museums.

But go figure: How can states afford to look for or curate the millions of artifacts created by humans over hundreds of thousands of years which risk destruction every year? The fact is they can't afford to and don't. The public has been kept in the dark. But is the abundance of many artifacts any reason for a museum to toss them in a crusher? I think the public would still be aghast at the destruction of such wondrously resistant reminders of our deep past and would insist on the distribution of surpluses to school collections or even to citizens who could appreciate artifacts for their tie to antiquity or sculptural beauty.

Instead, the destruction goes on – in museums & outside. At a time when agricultural, mining and construction equipment is more ubiquitous and powerful – turning over more sediment than ever before, much less is being discovered with each year. Why? Given that so many more artifacts were found in the old days when far less earth was turned over – but turned over by hand - it's obvious that industrial nations are undergoing the archeological

equivalent of genocide! Why is it happening? After all, our dutiful politicians and zealous institutionals have passed those blanket restrictions protecting vestiges. The reason is the laws themselves.

By being so categorical, sweet-sounding legislation absolves us all from having to check for perverse side effects or actual consequences. Their framers can feel honorable & move on to the next order of business. And it is undeniable that draconian laws should apply to some kinds of sites – for example, in situ deposits in caves. But when a vast pool of enthusiasts with their private funds for traveling to fields and exposures, their extra eyes and their endless legwork, are threatened and treated with contempt, then government researchers who frame the laws for politicians may have the pleasure of being purists, but deny themselves & humanity a resource that could extend researchers' range enormously. When collectors also hide their objects for fear of dispossession, rather than be encouraged by a legal system of transparency to have their pieces studied, then most potential discoveries will go unreported and unrecognized. Finally, if a market is not allowed to operate to provide pieces with values that everyone can understand, much will even be thrown away by institutions & collectors' heirs alike – witness collections lost near Sens, Gisors & from municipal museums at Blois & the Cote d'Or.

Yet the press, which relies on museum sources for stories, seems to be unaware that there is any problem – except with collectors. In some places today any farmer with a disk-tiller or quarrier has a license to kill vestiges, but that same person is forbidden to salvage & keep a single artifact on the surface during the window between plowing and harrowing. Up in their cabs, today's workers are no longer even in touch with the soil they ravish. Embittered museum workers have even shown the author a letter from their country's Ministry of Industry to their own branch of government telling the (lesser) ministry to stop intervening to save one tiny site in a gravel pit because it was a nuisance for a multi-national. Needless-to-say, the effort was abandoned & the site destroyed. But according to government archeologists & the tame press, collectors are the enemy. Talk about scapegoats.

Luckily, such laws give themselves the lie: most published sites are found during a few publicly funded construction projects for which a salvage budget is set aside out of the same good intentions that led to backfiring draconian measures. You might ask yourself: why is it that almost all prehistoric beings in European countries from dinosaurs to Neanderthals seem to have lived only on land that would end up in such projects – in other words, in the public domain? Were all those beings proto-socialists who died on land they knew would someday become public? The answer is that we are only seeing discoveries from public land because vestiges in private projects are being systematically destroyed due to the same draconian laws that mandate a salvage budget along the routes of future railroads & highways. On private construction sites, foreman after foreman has told the author that he had unwritten orders from management to obliterate anything that might ruin his schedule & even to prevent any evidence from getting out. With invasive laws, the alternative could be an imposed closure for months or even forever. Worse yet, the regulations often make the owner pay for the privilege! Whether you're in France or America, it's the same old story: apparently roughly 70 mammoths have turned up during construction just in Stark County, Ohio, but only one has been reported or saved because researchers didn't know how to get in & out in 48 hours & stick only to the patch where the first find was reported. So they weren't told of later findings. After all, what is in it for builders or any citizen under the present laws? Will their schedules be respected? Can they keep or sell vestiges? Even when they report things & their project is not postponed & their land is not requisitioned, they are often treated as culpable instead of being celebrated. So the Fascistic laws, which have been similarly framed by purists on both sides of the Atlantic, go on shooting themselves, science & the public in the foot – massively contributing to the very destruction they are (supposedly) against.

Is there an answer? Should we hire enough institutional salvage archeologists to check every public *& private* construction site? What about all the artifacts that would turn up if people looked as closely as they did in the 1880s? The museums are already so over-burdened by their reserves that they're destroying them. Does anyone really think taxpayers want to pay for still more archeologists & storage?

If only we could start over & search for synergies that would respect industry's schedules, encourage much more salvaging even if it is sometimes done speedily & by channeled amateurs who could keep their finds (& store them at their own expense) & end the atmosphere of contempt & secrecy. I bet discoveries would increase ten to a hundred-fold.

MCKEAN
4,600 B.P.,
CO,
quartzite

MALLORY
4,600 B.P., CO, Chalcedony

HANNA
4,600 B.P., KS

MALLORY
4,600 B.P., CO,
Edwards Plateau

COQUILLE NAR-ROWNECK
4,500 B.P., OR,
brown jasper

COQUILLE BROADNECK
4,500 B.P., OR,
jasper

COQUILLE NAR-ROWNECK
4,500 B.P., OR,
jasper

BASCOM
4,500 B.P., SC

COQUILLE NAR-ROWNECK
4,500 B.P., OR, jasper

COQUILLE BROADNECK
4,500 B.P., OR,
jasper

GODAR
4,500 B.P., IL

GOLD HILL
4,500 B.P., OR

GREEN RIVER
4,500 B.P., CO,
Kay County chert

GYPSUM CAVE
4,500 B.P., AZ, basalt

LITTLE RIVER
4,500 B.P., AR, novaculite

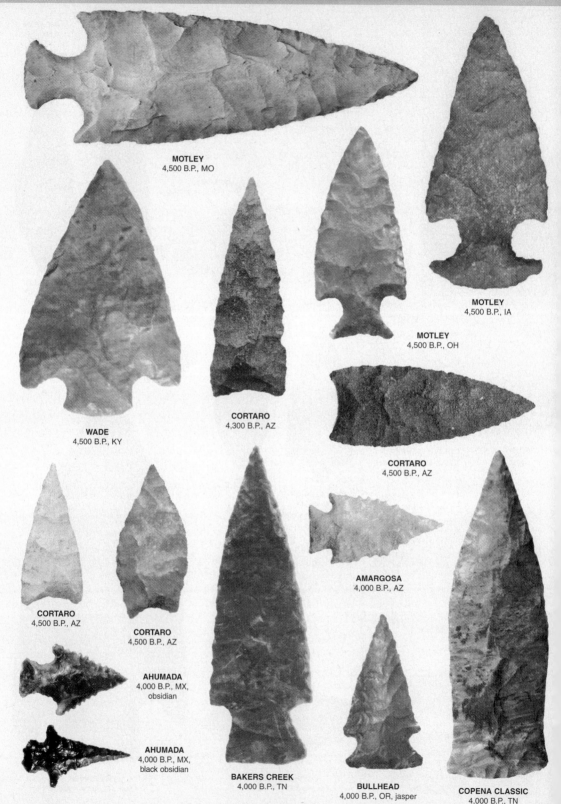

MOTLEY
4,500 B.P., MO

MOTLEY
4,500 B.P., IA

MOTLEY
4,500 B.P., OH

WADE
4,500 B.P., KY

CORTARO
4,300 B.P., AZ

CORTARO
4,500 B.P., AZ

CORTARO
4,500 B.P., AZ

CORTARO
4,500 B.P., AZ

AMARGOSA
4,000 B.P., AZ

AHUMADA
4,000 B.P., MX,
obsidian

AHUMADA
4,000 B.P., MX,
black obsidian

BAKERS CREEK
4,000 B.P., TN

BULLHEAD
4,000 B.P., OR, jasper

COPENA CLASSIC
4,000 B.P., TN

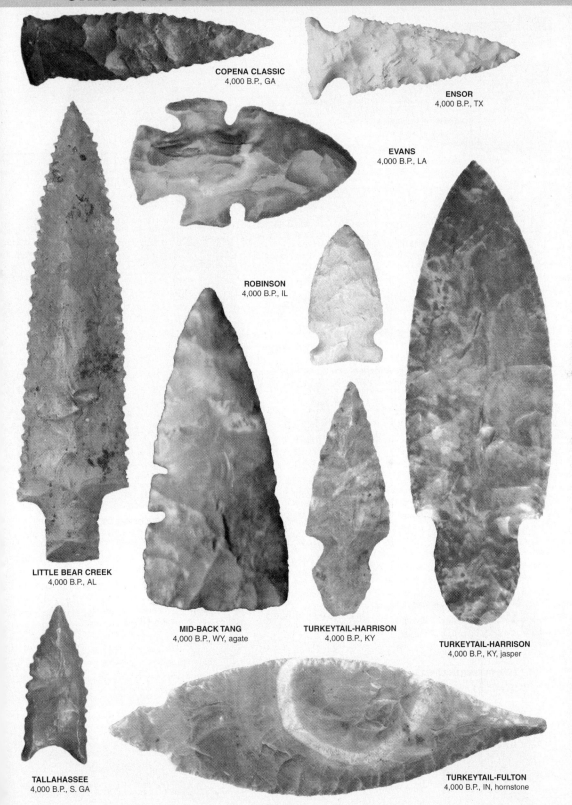

COPENA CLASSIC
4,000 B.P., GA

ENSOR
4,000 B.P., TX

EVANS
4,000 B.P., LA

ROBINSON
4,000 B.P., IL

LITTLE BEAR CREEK
4,000 B.P., AL

MID-BACK TANG
4,000 B.P., WY, agate

TURKEYTAIL-HARRISON
4,000 B.P., KY

TURKEYTAIL-HARRISON
4,000 B.P., KY, jasper

TALLAHASSEE
4,000 B.P., S. GA

TURKEYTAIL-FULTON
4,000 B.P., IN, hornstone

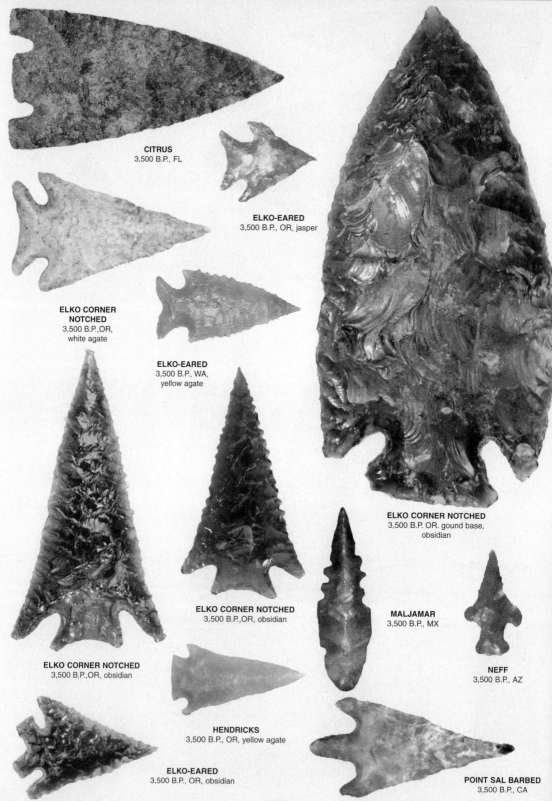

CITRUS
3,500 B.P., FL

ELKO-EARED
3,500 B.P., OR, jasper

ELKO CORNER
NOTCHED
3,500 B.P.,OR,
white agate

ELKO-EARED
3,500 B.P., WA,
yellow agate

ELKO CORNER NOTCHED
3,500 B.P. OR. gound base,
obsidian

ELKO CORNER NOTCHED
3,500 B.P.,OR, obsidian

MALJAMAR
3,500 B.P., MX

NEFF
3,500 B.P., AZ

ELKO CORNER NOTCHED
3,500 B.P.,OR, obsidian

HENDRICKS
3,500 B.P., OR, yellow agate

ELKO-EARED
3,500 B.P., OR, obsidian

POINT SAL BARBED
3,500 B.P., CA

TRIANGULAR KNIFE
3,500 B.P., MX

SHANIKO STEMMED
3,500 B.P., WA, gem

FROST ISLAND
3,200 B.P., PA,
black chert

YAVAPAI
3,300 B.P., AZ

SQUARE-END KNIFE
3,500 B.P., OK

GARY
3,200 B.P., TX

GARY
3,200 B.P., TX

ADENA
3,000 B.P.,TN

ADENA
3,000 B.P., MO

ADENA BLADE
3,000 B.P., OH, Flintridge flint

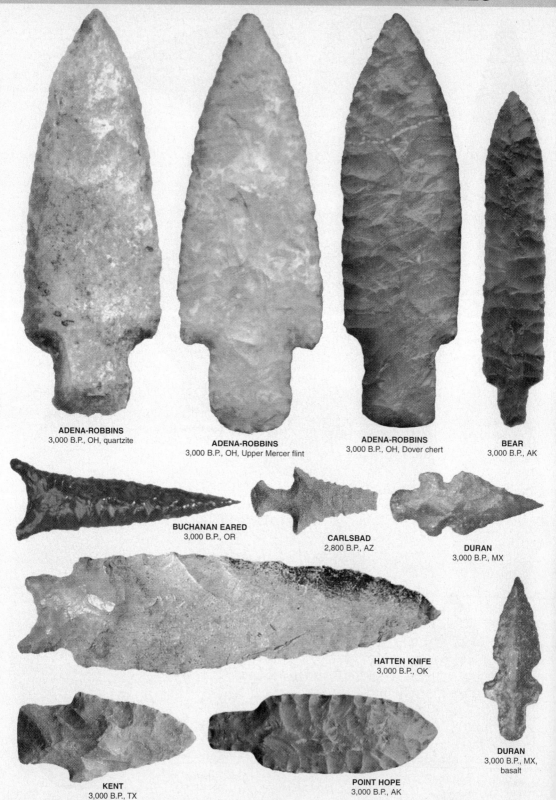

ADENA-ROBBINS
3,000 B.P., OH, quartzite

ADENA-ROBBINS
3,000 B.P., OH, Upper Mercer flint

ADENA-ROBBINS
3,000 B.P., OH, Dover chert

BEAR
3,000 B.P., AK

BUCHANAN EARED
3,000 B.P., OR

CARLSBAD
2,800 B.P., AZ

DURAN
3,000 B.P., MX

HATTEN KNIFE
3,000 B.P., OK

DURAN
3,000 B.P., MX, basalt

KENT
3,000 B.P., TX

POINT HOPE
3,000 B.P., AK

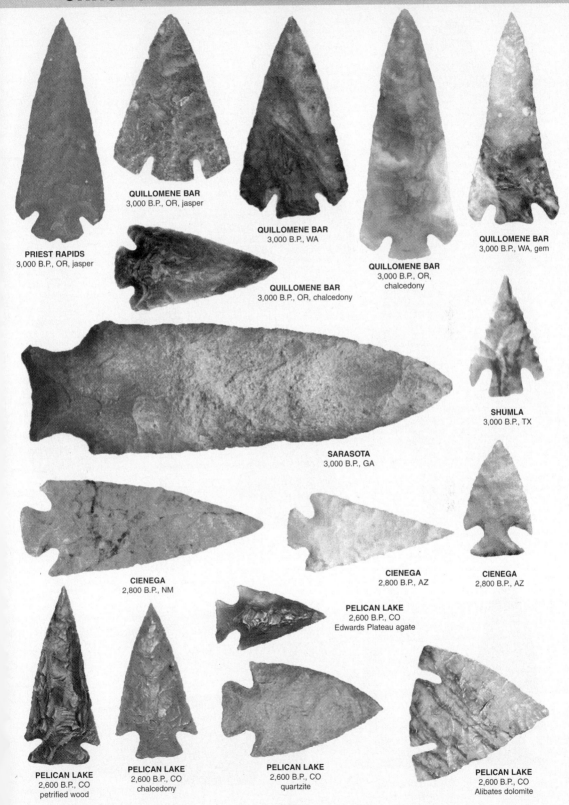

PRIEST RAPIDS
3,000 B.P., OR, jasper

QUILLOMENE BAR
3,000 B.P., OR, jasper

QUILLOMENE BAR
3,000 B.P., WA

QUILLOMENE BAR
3,000 B.P., OR,
chalcedony

QUILLOMENE BAR
3,000 B.P., WA, gem

QUILLOMENE BAR
3,000 B.P., OR, chalcedony

SHUMLA
3,000 B.P., TX

SARASOTA
3,000 B.P., GA

CIENEGA
2,800 B.P., NM

CIENEGA
2,800 B.P., AZ

CIENEGA
2,800 B.P., AZ

PELICAN LAKE
2,600 B.P., CO
Edwards Plateau agate

PELICAN LAKE
2,600 B.P., CO
petrified wood

PELICAN LAKE
2,600 B.P., CO
chalcedony

PELICAN LAKE
2,600 B.P., CO
quartzite

PELICAN LAKE
2,600 B.P., CO
Alibates dolomite

MERRYBELL I
2,500 B.P., OR, red agate

MERRYBELL I
2,500 B.P., WA,
carnelian agate

HOPEWELL
2,500 B.P., IL

MERRYBELL I
2,500 B.P., OR, chalcedony

MERRYBELL I
2,500 B.P., OR

NEED STEMMED
LANCEOLATE
2,500 B.P., CA

DICKSON
2,500 B.P., MO,
beveled edge

SAN PEDRO
2,500 B.P., AZ

SAN PEDRO
2,500 B.P., AZ, basalt

SAN PEDRO
2,500 B.P., AZ, basalt

SAN PEDRO
2,500 B.P., AZ, basalt

SAN PEDRO
2,500 B.P., AZ, basalt

CHRONOLOGICAL GALLERY OF POINT TYPES

SNYDERS
2,500 B.P., IL

SNYDERS
2,500 B.P., IL

WAUBESA
2,500 B.P., TN

YADKIN EARED
2,500 B.P., SC

WAUBESA
2,500 B.P., TN

DICKSON
2,500 B.P., TN

BRADFORD
2,000 B.P., FL

SAMANTHA DART
2,200 B.P., ND, Knife
River flint

BLACK MESA
NARROW NECK
2,000 B.P., CA

COLUMBIA
2,000 B.P., GA

1179

CHRONOLOGICAL GALLERY OF POINT TYPES

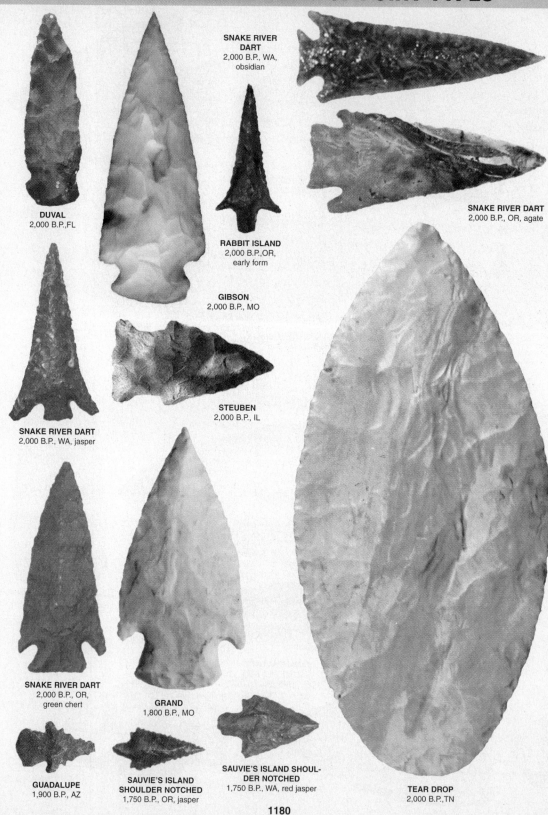

DUVAL
2,000 B.P.,FL

SNAKE RIVER DART
2,000 B.P., WA,
obsidian

RABBIT ISLAND
2,000 B.P.,OR,
early form

SNAKE RIVER DART
2,000 B.P., OR, agate

GIBSON
2,000 B.P., MO

STEUBEN
2,000 B.P., IL

SNAKE RIVER DART
2,000 B.P., WA, jasper

SNAKE RIVER DART
2,000 B.P., OR,
green chert

GRAND
1,800 B.P., MO

GUADALUPE
1,900 B.P., AZ

**SAUVIE'S ISLAND
SHOULDER NOTCHED**
1,750 B.P., OR, jasper

**SAUVIE'S ISLAND SHOUL-
DER NOTCHED**
1,750 B.P., WA, red jasper

TEAR DROP
2,000 B.P.,TN

1180

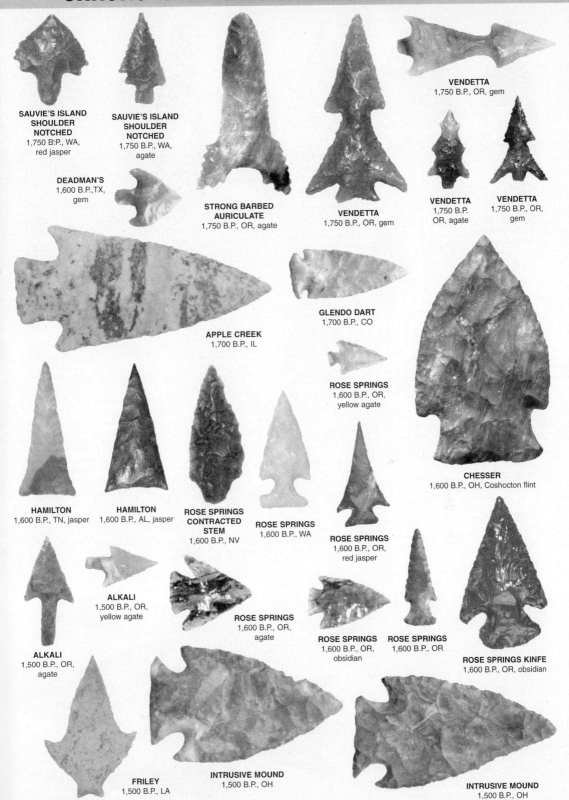

SAUVIE'S ISLAND SHOULDER NOTCHED
1,750 B.P., WA, red jasper

SAUVIE'S ISLAND SHOULDER NOTCHED
1,750 B.P., WA, agate

DEADMAN'S
1,600 B.P.,TX, gem

STRONG BARBED AURICULATE
1,750 B.P., OR, agate

VENDETTA
1,750 B.P., OR, gem

VENDETTA
1,750 B.P., OR, gem

VENDETTA
1,750 B.P. OR, agate

VENDETTA
1,750 B.P., OR, gem

APPLE CREEK
1,700 B.P., IL

GLENDO DART
1,700 B.P., CO

ROSE SPRINGS
1,600 B.P., OR, yellow agate

CHESSER
1,600 B.P., OH, Coshocton flint

HAMILTON
1,600 B.P., TN, jasper

HAMILTON
1,600 B.P., AL, jasper

ROSE SPRINGS CONTRACTED STEM
1,600 B.P., NV

ROSE SPRINGS
1,600 B.P., WA

ROSE SPRINGS
1,600 B.P., OR, red jasper

ALKALI
1,500 B.P., OR, yellow agate

ALKALI
1,500 B.P., OR, agate

ROSE SPRINGS
1,600 B.P., OR, agate

ROSE SPRINGS
1,600 B.P., OR, obsidian

ROSE SPRINGS
1,600 B.P., OR

ROSE SPRINGS KINFE
1,600 B.P., OR, obsidian

FRILEY
1,500 B.P., LA

INTRUSIVE MOUND
1,500 B.P., OH

INTRUSIVE MOUND
1,500 B.P., OH

JACK'S REEF COR. NOTCHED
1,500 B.P., OH, Flint Ridge flint

**JACK'S REEF COR-
NER NOTCHED**
1,500 B.P., IL

**JACK'S REEF
PENTAGONAL**
1,500 B.P., TN,
jasper

KNIGHT ISLAND
1,500 B.P., TN,
jasper

**MALAGA COVE
LEAF**
1,500 B.P., CA

**MALAGA COVE
LEAF**
1,500 B.P., CA

SALADO
1,500 B.P., AZ

SALADO
1,500 B.P., AZ

YANA
1,500 B.P., CA

SALADO
1,500 B.P., AZ

EASTGATE
1,400 B.P., ID

DOLORES
1,400 B.P. CO,
agate

DOLORES
1,400 B.P., CO

DOLORES
1,400 B.P., AZ

**EASTGATE
SPLIT STEM**
1,400 B.P., OR,
obsidian

EASTGATE
1,400 B.P., OR,
jasper

**EASTGATE
SPLIT STEM**
1,400 B.P., OR,
jasper

ONE-QUE
1,320 B.P.,
OR, agate

ONE-QUE
1,320 B.P.,
WA, agate

**CHACO CORNER
NOTCHED**
1,250 B.P., CO, jasper

**CHACO COR-
NER NOTCHED**
1,250 B.P., CO,
agate

DAGGER
1,200 B.P., WA,
pitchstone

**CHACO COR-
NER NOTCHED**
1,250 B.P., CO,
agate

**CHACO COR-
NER NOTCHED**
1,250 B.P., CO

AGEE
1,200 B.P., AR,
novaculite

**HODGES CONTRACTING
STEM**
1,300 B.P., AZ

**HELL'S CANYON
BASAL NOTCHED**
1,200 B.P., WA, agate

HAYES
1,200 B.P., TX,
jasper

**HELLS CANYON
BASAL NOTCHED**
1,200 B.P., WA,
petrified wood

STOCKTON
1,200 B.P., CA,
obsidian

CHRONOLOGICAL GALLERY OF POINT TYPES

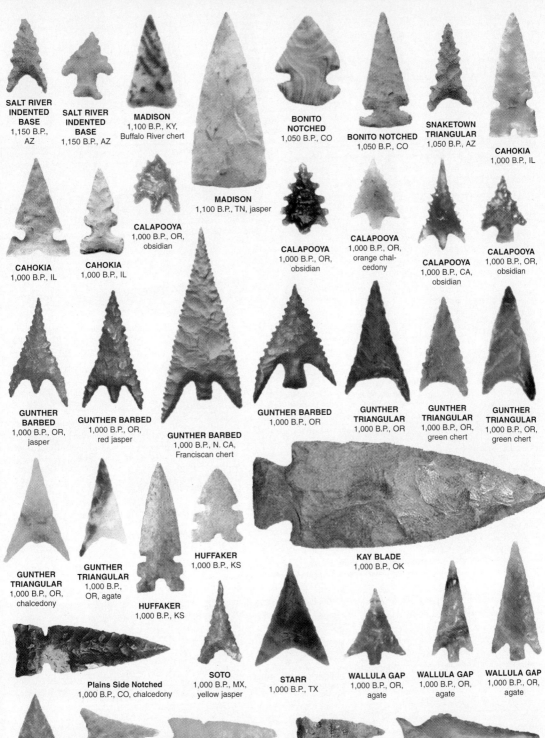

SALT RIVER INDENTED BASE
1,150 B.P., AZ

SALT RIVER INDENTED BASE
1,150 B.P., AZ

MADISON
1,100 B.P., KY, Buffalo River chert

BONITO NOTCHED
1,050 B.P., CO

BONITO NOTCHED
1,050 B.P., CO

SNAKETOWN TRIANGULAR
1,050 B.P., AZ

CAHOKIA
1,000 B.P., IL

CAHOKIA
1,000 B.P., IL

CAHOKIA
1,000 B.P., IL

CALAPOOYA
1,000 B.P., OR, obsidian

MADISON
1,100 B.P., TN, jasper

CALAPOOYA
1,000 B.P., OR, obsidian

CALAPOOYA
1,000 B.P., OR, orange chalcedony

CALAPOOYA
1,000 B.P., CA, obsidian

CALAPOOYA
1,000 B.P., OR, obsidian

GUNTHER BARBED
1,000 B.P., OR, jasper

GUNTHER BARBED
1,000 B.P., OR, red jasper

GUNTHER BARBED
1,000 B.P., N. CA, Franciscan chert

GUNTHER BARBED
1,000 B.P., OR

GUNTHER TRIANGULAR
1,000 B.P., OR

GUNTHER TRIANGULAR
1,000 B.P., OR, green chert

GUNTHER TRIANGULAR
1,000 B.P., OR, green chert

GUNTHER TRIANGULAR
1,000 B.P., OR, chalcedony

GUNTHER TRIANGULAR
1,000 B.P., OR, agate

HUFFAKER
1,000 B.P., KS

KAY BLADE
1,000 B.P., OK

HUFFAKER
1,000 B.P., KS

Plains Side Notched
1,000 B.P., CO, chalcedony

SOTO
1,000 B.P., MX, yellow jasper

STARR
1,000 B.P., TX

WALLULA GAP
1,000 B.P., OR, agate

WALLULA GAP
1,000 B.P., OR, agate

WALLULA GAP
1,000 B.P., OR, agate

WALLULA GAP
1,000 B.P., OR, jasper

BULL CREEK
950 B.P., AZ

POINT OF PINES SIDE NOTCHED
850 B.P., AZ

PUEBLO SIDE NOTCHED
850 B.P., AZ

BAYOGOULA
800 B.P., LA

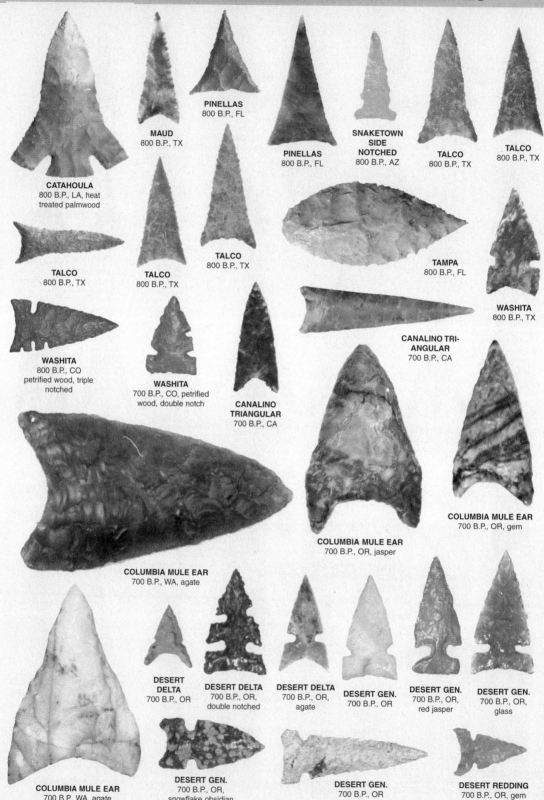

PINELLAS
800 B.P., FL

MAUD
800 B.P., TX

PINELLAS
800 B.P., FL

SNAKETOWN SIDE NOTCHED
800 B.P., AZ

TALCO
800 B.P., TX

TALCO
800 B.P., TX

CATAHOULA
800 B.P., LA, heat treated palmwood

TALCO
800 B.P., TX

TAMPA
800 B.P., FL

TALCO
800 B.P., TX

TALCO
800 B.P., TX

WASHITA
800 B.P., TX

WASHITA
800 B.P., CO petrified wood, triple notched

WASHITA
700 B.P., CO, petrified wood, double notch

CANALINO TRIANGULAR
700 B.P., CA

CANALINO TRI-ANGULAR
700 B.P., CA

COLUMBIA MULE EAR
700 B.P., OR, gem

COLUMBIA MULE EAR
700 B.P., OR, jasper

COLUMBIA MULE EAR
700 B.P., WA, agate

DESERT DELTA
700 B.P., OR

DESERT DELTA
700 B.P., OR, double notched

DESERT DELTA
700 B.P., OR, agate

DESERT GEN.
700 B.P., OR

DESERT GEN.
700 B.P., OR, red jasper

DESERT GEN.
700 B.P., OR, glass

COLUMBIA MULE EAR
700 B.P., WA, agate

DESERT GEN.
700 B.P., OR, snowflake obsidian

DESERT GEN.
700 B.P., OR

DESERT REDDING
700 B.P., OR, gem

CHRONOLOGICAL GALLERY OF POINT TYPES

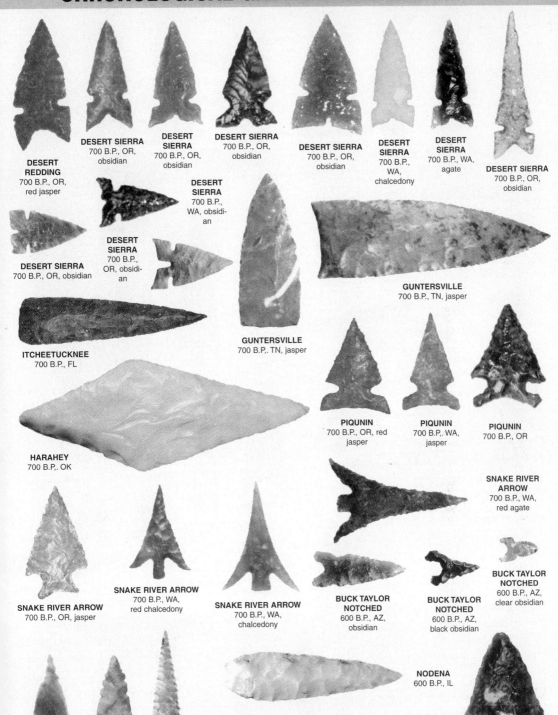

DESERT REDDING
700 B.P., OR, red jasper

DESERT SIERRA
700 B.P., OR, obsidian

DESERT SIERRA
700 B.P., OR, obsidian

DESERT SIERRA
700 B.P., OR, obsidian

DESERT SIERRA
700 B.P., OR, obsidian

DESERT SIERRA
700 B.P., WA, chalcedony

DESERT SIERRA
700 B.P., WA, agate

DESERT SIERRA
700 B.P., OR, obsidian

DESERT SIERRA
700 B.P., WA, obsidian

DESERT SIERRA
700 B.P., OR, obsidian

DESERT SIERRA
700 B.P., OR, obsidian

GUNTERSVILLE
700 B.P., TN, jasper

ITCHEETUCKNEE
700 B.P., FL

GUNTERSVILLE
700 B.P., TN, jasper

HARAHEY
700 B.P., OK

PIQUNIN
700 B.P., OR, red jasper

PIQUNIN
700 B.P., WA, jasper

PIQUNIN
700 B.P., OR

SNAKE RIVER ARROW
700 B.P., WA, red agate

SNAKE RIVER ARROW
700 B.P., OR, jasper

SNAKE RIVER ARROW
700 B.P., WA, red chalcedony

SNAKE RIVER ARROW
700 B.P., WA, chalcedony

BUCK TAYLOR NOTCHED
600 B.P., AZ, obsidian

BUCK TAYLOR NOTCHED
600 B.P., AZ, black obsidian

BUCK TAYLOR NOTCHED
600 B.P., AZ, clear obsidian

NODENA
600 B.P., IL

CARACARA
600 B.P., TX

CARACARA
600 B.P., TX

DARDANELLE
600 B.P., OK

NODENA
600 B.P., TN

PLATEAU PENTAGONAL
600 B.P. OR, agate

CHRONOLOGICAL GALLERY OF POINT TYPES

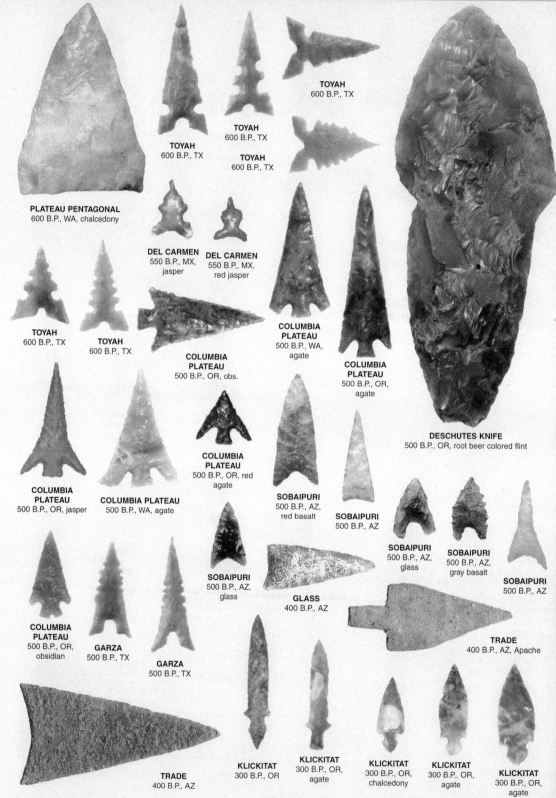

TOYAH
600 B.P., TX

TOYAH
600 B.P., TX

TOYAH
600 B.P., TX

TOYAH
600 B.P., TX

TOYAH
600 B.P., TX

PLATEAU PENTAGONAL
600 B.P., WA, chalcedony

DEL CARMEN
550 B.P., MX, jasper

DEL CARMEN
550 B.P., MX, red jasper

COLUMBIA PLATEAU
500 B.P., WA, agate

DESCHUTES KNIFE
500 B.P., OR, root beer colored flint

TOYAH
600 B.P., TX

TOYAH
600 B.P., TX

COLUMBIA PLATEAU
500 B.P., OR, obs.

COLUMBIA PLATEAU
500 B.P., OR, agate

COLUMBIA PLATEAU
500 B.P., OR, red agate

COLUMBIA PLATEAU
500 B.P., OR, jasper

COLUMBIA PLATEAU
500 B.P., WA, agate

SOBAIPURI
500 B.P., AZ, red basalt

SOBAIPURI
500 B.P., AZ

SOBAIPURI
500 B.P., AZ, glass

SOBAIPURI
500 B.P., AZ, gray basalt

SOBAIPURI
500 B.P., AZ

COLUMBIA PLATEAU
500 B.P., OR, obsidian

GARZA
500 B.P., TX

GARZA
500 B.P., TX

SOBAIPURI
500 B.P., AZ, glass

GLASS
400 B.P., AZ

TRADE
400 B.P., AZ, Apache

TRADE
400 B.P., AZ

KLICKITAT
300 B.P., OR

KLICKITAT
300 B.P., OR, agate

KLICKITAT
300 B.P., OR, chalcedony

KLICKITAT
300 B.P., OR, agate

KLICKITAT
300 B.P., OR, agate

1186

Index of Point Types

Regional Codes

Alaska - AK
Desert Southwest - SW
Eastern Central - EC

Eastern Seaboard - ES
Far West - FW

Gulf Coastal - GC
Northeastern - NE
Northern Central - NC

Northern High Plains - NP
Southern Central - SC

Abasolo (7,000) SC, SW
Abbey (6,000) GC
Acatita (3,000) SW
Addison Micro-Drill (2,000) EC
Adena (3,000) EC, ES, GC, NC, NE
Adena Blade (3,000) EC, NC, NE, SC
Adena-Mason Var. (3,000) EC
Adena-Narrow Stem (3,000) EC, NC
Adena-Notched Base (3,000) EC, NC
Adena-Robbins (3,000) EC, ES, NE, SC
Adena-Vanishing Stem (3,000) EC
Afton (5,000) NC
Agate Basin (10,200) EC, FW, NC, NE,
    NP, SC, SW
Agee (1,200) NC, SC
Aguaje (600) SW
Ahsahka (3,000) FW
Ahumada (4,000) SW
Alachua (5,500) GC
Alamance (10,000) EC, ES
Alba (See Hughes)
Alba (1,100) NC, SC
Albany Knife (10,000) SC
Alberta (10,000) EC, FW, NP, SC
Albion-Head Side Notched (6,500) FW
Alder Complex (9,500) FW, NP
Alkali (1,500) FW
Allen (8,500) NC, NP, SC, SW
Almagre (6,000) SC
Amargosa (4,000) FW, SW
Amos (10,000) NE
Anderson (9,000) NP
Andice (8,000) SC
Angostura (8,800) EC, NC, NE, NP,
    SC, SW
Año Nuevo (2950) FW
Antler (1,400) SC
Appalachian (6,000) EC, ES
Apple Creek (1,700) SC
Archaic Knife (8,000) NP
Archaic Knife (10,000) SC
Archaic Side Notched (6,000) NP
Archaic Triangle (6,000) NP
Arden (9,000) NE
Arenosa (see Langtry-...)
Arkabutla (10,500) SC
Armijo (3,800) SW
Armstrong (2450) ES
Arredondo (6,000) GC
Ashtabula (4,000) EC, NE
Atlantic Phase Blade (4,300) NE
Atlatl Valley Triangular (7,000) FW
Augustin (7,000) SW
Autauga (9,000) EC
Avonlea-Carmichael (1,800) NP
Avonlea Classic (1,800) NP
Avonlea-Gull Lake (1,800) NP
Avonlea-Timber Ridge (1,800) NP
Axtel (7,000) SC
Badin (1,000) ES
Bajada (6,000) SW
Baker (7,500) SC, SW
Bakers Creek (4,000) EC
Bandy (7,500) SC
Barber (10,000) SC
Bare Island (4,500) NE
Barnes Cumberland (see Cumberland)
Barreal (9,000) SW
Basal Double Tang (3,500) SW
Bascom (4,500) GC
Base Tang Knife (4,000) NP, SC
Base Tang Knife (10,000) FW

Basketmaker (1,500) SW
Bassett (800) SC
Bat Cave (9,000) SW
Bayogoula (800) NC, SC
Beacon Island (4,000) EC
Bear Type 1 (3000) AK
Bear Type 2 (3000) AK
Bear Type 3 (3000) AK
Bear Type 4 (3000) AK
Bear River (1,300) FW
Beaver Lake (11,500) EC, GC, NC, NE
Beekman Triangular (4,800) NE
Belen (10,500) SW
Bell (7,000) SC
Benjamin (3,000) EC
Benton (6,000) EC
Benton Blade (6,000) EC
Benton Bottle Neck (6,000) EC
Benton Double Notch (6,000) EC
Benton Narrow Blade (6,000) EC
Benton Side Notched (6,000) EC, ES
Besant (1,900) NP
Besant Knife (1,900) NP
Big Creek (3,500) SC
Big Sandy (10,000) EC, ES, SC
Big Sandy Broad Base (10,000) EC
Big Sandy Contracted Base
    (10,000) EC
Big Sandy E-Notched (10,000) EC
Big Sandy Leighton (10,000) EC
Big Slough (7,000) EC
Big Valley Stemmed (4,000) FW
Billings (300) NP
Bird Arrow-Blunt (2,800) AK
Bird Spear (2,800) AK
Bitterroot (7,500) FW, NP
Black Mesa Narrow Neck (2,000) SW
Black Rock Concave (11,000) FW
Blevins (1,200) SC
Bliss (950) FW
Blunt (11,500) EC
Boats Blade (4,300) NE
Boggy Branch Type I (9,000) GC
Boggy Branch Type II (9,000) GC
Bolen Beveled (10,500) ES, GC
Bolen Plain (9,000) ES, GC
Bone/Antler (4,500) NE
Bone Arrow (1,500) FW
Bone Arrow (2,800) AK
Bone Arrow w/Metal or Stone points
    (2,800) AK
Bone Pin (11,500) FW, GC
Bonham (1,200) SC
Bonito Notched (1,050) SW
Borax Lake (8,000) FW
Bradford (2,000) GC
Bradley Spike (4,000) EC
Brazos (see Darl Stemmed)
Brewerton Corner Notched (6,000) EC,
    NE
Brewerton Eared Triangular (6,000)
    EC, ES, NE, SC
Brewerton Side Notched (6,000) EC,
    ES, NE, SC
Broad River (3,000) GC
Brodhead Side Notched (9,000) NE
Broward (2,000) GC
Browns Valley (10,000) EC, NC, NP, SC
Brunswick (5,000) EC
Buchanan Eared (3,000) FW
Buck Creek (6,000) EC
Buck Gulley (1,500) FW
Buck Taylor Notched (600) SW

Buffalo Gap (5,500) NP
Buffalo Stemmed (6,000) ES
Buggs Island (5,500) EC
Bull Creek (950) FW, SW
Bullhead (4,000) FW
Bulverde (5,000) SC
Burin (2,500, Merrybell Phase) FW
Burkett (2,300) SC
Burroughs (8,000) NC
Burwell (5,000) NE
Buzzard Roost Creek (6,000) EC
Cache River (10,000) EC, NC, SC
Caddoan Blade (800) SC
Cahokia (1,000) NC
Calapooya (1,000) FW
Calcasieu (5500) SC
Calf Creek (8,000) NC, SC
Camel Back (700) NP
Camp Creek (3,000) EC
Canalino Triangular (700) FW
Candy Creek (3,000) EC
Caracara (600) SC
Caraway (1,000) ES
Carlsbad (3,000) SW
Carrizo (7,000) SC
Carrolton (5,000) SC
Carter (2,500) NC
Cascade (8,000) FW
Cascade Knife (8,000) FW
Cascade-Shouldered (8,000) FW
Castroville (4,000) SC
Catahoula (800) SC
Catan (4,000) SC, SW
Cave Spring (9,000) EC
Cedral (see Acatita)
Chaco Corner Notched (1,250) SW
Charcos (3,000) SC, SW
Charleston Pine Tree (10,000) NE
Chesser (1,600) EC
Chignik Dart (5,000) AK
Chignik Lanceloate (5,000) AK
Chignik Leaf (5,000) AK
Chignik Stemmed (5,000) AK
Chilcotin Plateau (8,000) FW
Chillesquaque (6,000) NE
Chindadn (11,300) AK
Chipola (10,000) GC
Chiricahua (4,800) SW
Chopper (14,000) FW, SC
Chumash Tools (9,000) FW
Cienega (2,800) SW
Circular Uniface Knife (6,000) FW
Citrus (3,500) GC
Citrus Side Notched (800) SW
Clarksville (1,000) ES
Clay (5,000) GC
Cliffton (1,200) SC
Clovis (11,500) EC, ES, FW, GC, NC,
    NE, NP, SC, SW
Clovis-Colby (11,500) NP
Clovis-Hazel (11,500) EC
Clovis-St. Louis (11,500)NC
Clovis Unfluted (11,500)
    EC, ES
Coahuila (4,000) SC
Cobbs Triangular (9,000) EC, NC
Cody Knife (10,000) FW, NP
Cohonina Stemmed (1,300) SW
Colbert (1,000) SC
Cold Springs (5,000) FW
Coldwater (10,000) EC, SC
Collins (1,500) NC
Columbia (2,000) GC

Columbia Mule Ear (700) FW
Columbia Plateau (500) FW
Columbia River Pin Stem (500) FW
Conejo (4,000) SC, SW
Conerly (7,500) EC, GC
Conodoquinet/Canfield (4,000) NE
Contra Costa (2,500) FW
Convento (950) SW
Coosa (2,000) EC
Copena Auriculate (5,000) EC
Copena Classic (4,000) EC
Copena Round Base (4,000) EC
Copena Triangular (4,000) EC
Coquille Knife (4,500) GB
Coquille Broadneck (4,500) FW
Coquille Narrowneck (4,500) FW
Coquille Side-Notched (4,500) FW
Cordilleran (9,500) FW
Corner Tang Knife (3,400) EC, NP, SC
Cortaro (4,300) SW
Coryell (7,000) SC
Cossatot River (9,500) NC
Cotaco Creek (2,500) EC
Cotaco Blade (2,500) EC
Cotaco Preform (2,500) EC
Cotaco-Wright (2,500) EC
Cottonbridge (6,000) GC
Cottonwood Leaf (1,100) FW, NP, SW
Cottonwood Triangle (1.100) FW, NP,
    SW
Cougar Mountain (11,000) FW
Covington (4,000) SC
Cowhouse Slough (10,000) GC
Cow's Skull (600) SW
Crawford Creek (8,000) EC
Cresap (3,000) EC
Crescent (11,000) FW, NP
Crescent (5,000) SW
Crescent Knife (10,200) SC
Crooked Creek (9,000) NE
Crowfield (11,000) NE
Cruciform I (6,000) SW
Cruciform II (3,000) SW
Culbreath (5,000) GC
Cumberland (11,250) EC, NC
Cumberland Barnes (11,250) NE
Cumberland Unfluted (11,250) NC
Cuney (400) SC
Cupp (1,500) EC, NC, SC
Cut Bank Jaw Notched (300) NP
Cypress Creek (5,000) EC
Cypress Creek (5,500) GC
Dagger (arrow) (1,200) FW
Dagger (large) (4,000) SC
Dallas (4,000) SC
Dalton-Breckenridge (10,000) NC, SC
Dalton Classic (10,000) EC, NC, NE,
    NP, SC
Dalton-Colbert (10,000) EC, SC
Dalton-Greenbrier (10,000) EC, SC
Dalton-Hemphill (10,000) EC, NC, SC
Dalton-Hempstead (10,000) SC
Dalton-Kisatchie (10,000) SC
Dalton-Nansemond (10,000) ES
Dalton-Nuckolls (10,000) EC, NC, NE
Dalton-Sloan (10,000) NC
Damron (8,000) EC
Dardanelle (600) SC
Darl (2,500) SC
Darl Blade (2,500) SC
Darl Fractured Base (2,500) SC
Darl Stemmed (8,000) SC
Datil (7,000) SW

1187

Dawson (7,000) SC
Deadman's (1,600) SC, SW
Dear Arrow (see Bone Arrow)
Debert (11,000) EC, NE
Decatur (9,000) EC, ES, NC, NE
Decatur Blade (9,000) EC
Del Carmen (550) SW
Delhi (3,500) SC
Deschutes Knife (500) FW
Desert-Delta (700) FW, SW
Desert-General (700) FW, NP, SW
Desert-Redding (700) FW, SW
Desert-Sierra (700) FW, NP, SW
Desert-Stemmed (see Rose Springs)
Desmuke (4,000) SC
Dewart Stemmed (5,000) NE
Diamond-Back (300) FW
Dickson (2,500) EC, ES, NC, SC
Disc (5,000) SW
Dismal Swamp (3,500) ES
Dolores (1,400) SW
Dorset Triangular (2,500) AK
Double Tip (see Elko, Pedernales, Samantha)
Dovetail (see St. Charles)
Drill (11,500) AK, EC, ES, FW, GC, NC NE, NP, SC, SW
Dry Prong (1,000) SW
Drybrook Fishtail (3,500) NE
Duck River Sword (1,100) EC
Duncan (4,600) NP, SW
Duncan's Island (6,000) NE
Duran (3,000) SC, SW
Durango (4,500) SW
Durant's Bend (1,600) EC, GC
Durst (3,000) EC
Dutch Harbor Bi-Point (5,000) AK
Dutch Harbor Large Stemmed (5,000) AK
Dutch Harbor Side Notched (5,000) AK
Dutch Harbor Stemmed (5,000) AK
Duval (2,000) EC, GC
Early Eared (8,000) FW
Early Leaf (8,000) FW
Early Ovoid Knife (11,000) EC
Early Side Notched (see Archaic --)
Early Stemmed (9,000) SC
Early Stemmed (see Shaniko Stemmed)
Early Stemmed Lanceolate (9,000) FW, SC
Early Triangular (9,000) SC
Eastern Stemmed Lanceolate (9,500) EC
Eastgate (1,400) FW, NP
Eastgate Split Stem (1,400) FW, SW
Ebenezer (2,000) EC
Eccentric (see Exotic)
Ecusta (8,000) EC, ES
Eden (10,000) NC, NP, SW
Edgefield Scraper (10,500) ES, GC
Edgewood (3,000) SC
Edwards (2,000) SC
Elam (4,000) SC
Elk River (8,000) EC
Elko (3,500) FW, NP
Elko Corner Notched (3,500) FW, SW
Elko Eared (3,500) FW, SW
Elko Split Stem (3,500) FW
Elko Wide Notched (3,500) FW
Ellis (4,000) SC
Elora (6,000) EC, GC
Embudo (7,000) SW
Emigrant (900) NP
Emigrant Springs (1,200) FW
Ensor (4,000) SC
Ensor Split Base (4,000) SC
Epps (3,500) NC, SC
Erb Basal Notched (2,000) NE
Erie Triangle (1,500) NE
Escobas (6,500) SW
Eshback (5,500) NE
Etley (4,000) EC, NC
Eva (8,000) EC
Evans (4,000) EC, NC, SC
Excelsior (3,000) FW

Exotic (5,000) EC, ES, FW, NC, SC
Fairland (3,000) EC, SC
Fell's Cave (10,800) FW
Ferry (5,500) NC
Figueroa (3,000) SC, SW
Firstview (10,000) AK, FW, NP, SC, SW
Fish Gutter (4,000) FW
Fishspear (9,000) EC, ES
Flaking Tool (2,800) AK
Flint Creek (3,500) EC
Flint River (4,000) SC
Flint River Spike (see McWhinney)
Folsom (10,800) EC, FW, NC, NP, SC, SW
Forest Notched (3,000) NE
Fort Ancient (800) EC
Fort Ancient Blade (800) EC
Fountain Bar ((3,000) FW
Fountain Creek (9,000) EC, ES
Fox Creek (2,500) ES, NE
Fox Valley (9,000) NC
Frazier (7,000) EC
Frederick (9,000) EC
Frederick (9,000) NP, SC
Fremont Triangular (1,100) FW
Fresno (1,200) SC
Friday (4,000) SC
Friley (1,500) SC
Frio (5,000) SC, SW
Frio Transitional (3,000) SW
Frost Island (3,200) NE
Gahagan (4,000) SC
Galt (1,500) NP
Galt (Hastings) (1,500) NP
Gar Scale (1,800) SC
Garth Slough (9,000) EC, ES
Garver's Ferry (1,800) NE
Gary (3,200) NC, SC
Garza (500) SC, SW
Gatecliff (5,000) FW
Gatlin Side Notched (800) SW
Genesee (5,000) NE
Gibson (2,000) EC, NC, SC
Gila Butte (see Hodges Contr. Stem)
Gila River Corner Notched (1,350) SW
Gilchrist (10,000) GC
Glass (400) FW
Glendo Arrow (1,500) NP
Glendo Dart (1,700) NP
Gobernadora (3,000) SW
Godar (4,500) NC, SC
Goddard (1,000) NE
Godley (2,500) SC
Gold Hill (4,500) FW
Golondrina (9,000) EC, SC
Goshen (11,250) FW, NP, SC, SW
Gower (8,000) SC
Graham Cave (9,000) EC, NC, SC
Grand (1,800) NC, SC
Graver (11,500) EC, GB, NE, NP, SC, SW
Green River (4,500) NP, SW
Greenbrier (9,500) EC, NC
Greene (1,700) NE
Greeneville (3,000) EC, ES
Ground Slate (6,000) NE
Ground Stone (300) FW
Guadalupe (1,900) SW
Guerrero (300) SC
Guilford Round Base (6,500) ES, NE
Guilford Stemmed (6,500) ES
Guilford Straight Base (6,500) ES
Guilford Yuma (7,500) ES, NE
Guntersville (700) EC
Gunther Barbed (1,000) FW
Gunther Triangular (1,000) FW
Gypsum Cave (4,500) SW
Gypsy (2,500) ES
Hafted Knife (2,800) AK
Hafted Knife (2,300) FW
Hale (Bascom) (4,000) SC
Halifax (6,000) EC, ES
Hamilton (1,600) EC
Hamilton (8,000) GC
Hamilton Stemmed (3,000) EC
Hand Axe (12,000+) FW

Hanna (4,600) NP, SW
Hanna Northern (4,600) NP
Harahey (700) EC, GC, NC, NP, SC
Harahey (see Northwestern Four-Way Knife)
Hardaway (9,500) EC, ES, GC, NE
Hardaway Blade (9,500) ES
Hardway Dalton (9,500) EC, ES
Hardaway Palmer (9,500) ES
Hardee Beveled (5,500) GC
Hardin (9,000) EC, ES, GC, NC, SC
Hare Bi-Face (3,000) SC
Harpeth River (9,000) EC
Harpoon (3,000) AK, FW
Harrell (900) NC, SC
Haskell (800) NC, SC
Haskett (12,000) FW
Hatten Knife (3,000) NC
Hatwai (see Windust--) FW
Haw River (11,000) EC, NE
Hawken (6,500) FW, NP
Hayes (see Turner)
Hayes (1,200) NC, SC
Heavy Duty (7,000) EC, ES, NC
Hell Gap (10,300) FW, NC, NP, SC, SW
Hellgramite (3,000) NE
Hell's Canyon Basal Notched (1,200) FW
Hell's Canyon Corner Notched (1,200) FW
Helton (4,000) NC
Hemphill (7,000) NC, SC
Hendricks (3,500) FW
Hernando (4,000) GC
Hi-Lo (10,000) EC, NC
Hickory Ridge (7,000) NC, SC
Hidden Valley (8,000) NC, SC
High Desert Knife (5,500) FW
High River (1,300) NP
Hillsboro (300) ES
Hillsborough (5,500) GC
Hinds (10,000) EC
Hodges Contracting Stem (1,300) SW
Hog Back (1,000) NP
Hohokam (1,200) SW
Hohokam Knife (1,200) SW
Holcomb (11,000) NE
Holland (10,000) EC, NC, NP, SC
Hollenberg Stemmed (9,500) NP
Holmes (4,000) ES
Homan (1,000) NC, SC
Hoover's Island (6,000)NE
Hopewell (2,500) EC, NC
Hopewell Blade (2,500) NE
Horse Fly (1,500) NP
Houx Contracting Stem (4,500) FW
Howard (700) SC
Howard County (7,500) NC
Hoxie (8,000) SC
Huffaker (1,000) NC, NP, SC
Hughes (1,100) SC
Humboldt (7,000) FW, SW
Humboldt Basal Notched (8,000) FW
Humboldt Constricted Base (7,000) FW, SW
Humboldt Expanded Base (see Buchanan Eared)
Humboldt Triangular (7,000) FW
Independence (6,000) AK
Intermontane Stemmed (10,500) FW
Intrusive Mound (1,500) EC
Irvine (1,400) NP
Ishi (100) FW
Itcheetucknee (700) GC
Jacks Reef Corner Notched (1,500) EC, ES, NC, NE
Jacks Reef Pentagonal (1,500) EC, NE
Jackson (2,000) GC
Jakie Stemmed (8,000) SC
Jalama (6,000) FW
Jay (8,000) SW
Jeff (10,000) EC
Jetta (8,000) SC
Jim Thorpe (6,000) NE

Johnson (9,000) EC, SC
Jude (9,000) EC, ES
Kamloops Side Notched (1,000) FW
Kampsville (3,000) NC
Kanawha Stemmed (8,200) EC, ES, NE
Kaskaskia (see Trade Points)
Kavik (300) AK
Kay Blade (1,000) NC, SC
Kays (5,000) EC
Kayuk (6,500) AK
Keithville (see San Patrice)
Kelsey Creek Barbed (4,500) FW
Kennewick (11,000) FW
Kent (3,000) SC
Keota (800) EC, SC
Kerrville Knife (5,000) SC
Kessel (10,000) NE
Kin Kletso Side Notched (900) SW
Kings (4,500) NC, SC
Kinney (5,000) SC
Kirk Corner Notched (9,000) EC, ES, GC, NC, NE
Kirk Snapped Base (9,000) EC
Kirk Stemmed (9,000) EC, ES, GC, NE
Kirk Stemmed-Bifurcated (9,000) EC, ES
Kiski Notched (2,000) NE
Kittatiny (6,000) NE
Klickitat (300) FW
Kline (9,000) NE
Knight Island (1,500) EC, SC
Koens Crispin (4,000) NE
Kotzebue Bay (6,000) AK
Kotzebue Dart (6,000) AK
Kramer (3,000) NC
La Jita (7,000) SC
Lackawaxen (6,000) NE
Lady Island Pentagonal (2,500) FW
Lafayette (4,000) SC
Lake Erie (9,000) EC, NC, NE
Lake Mohave (13,200) FW, SW
Lake River Side Notched (700) FW
Lamine Knife (8,000) SC
Lamoka (5,500) NE
Lancet (11,500) EC, NP, SW
Lange (6,000) SC
Langtry (5,000) SC
Langtry-Arenosa (5,000) SC
Lecroy (9,000) EC, ES, NE
Ledbetter (6,000) EC
LeFlore Blade (500) SC
Lehigh (2,500) NC
Lehigh (4,000) NE
Leighton (8,000) EC
Leon (1,500) GC
Lerma (4,000) SW
Lerma Pointed (9,000) SC
Lerma Rounded (9,000) EC, NC, NP, SC, SW
Levanna (1,300) EC, NE
Levy (5,000) SC
Lewis (1,400) NP
Lewis River Short Stemmed (700) FW
Limestone (5,000) EC
Limeton Bifurcate (9,000) EC
Lind Coullee (11,000) FW
Little Bear Creek (4,000) EC
Little River (4,500) SC
Livermore (1,200) SC
Logan Creek (7,000) NP
Lookingbill (7,200) NP, SW
Lost Lake (9,000) EC, ES, NC, NE
Lott (500) SC
Lovell (8,400) NP
Lowe (1,650) EC
Lozenge (1,000) FW
Lundy (800) NC
Lusk (8,500) NP
Lycoming Co. (6,000) NE
MacCorkle (8,000) EC, NE
Mace (1,100) EC
Madden Lake (10,700) SW
Madison (1,100) EC, ES, NC, NE
Mahaffey (10,500) NP, SC
Mahkin Shouldered Lanceolate (6,500) FW

Malaga Cove Leaf (1,500) FW
Malaga Cove Stemmed (1,500) FW
Maljamar (3,500) SW
Mallory (4,600) NP
Manasota (3,000) GC
Manker (2,500) NC
Mansion Inn Blade (3,700) NE
Manzano (5,000) SW
Maples (4,500) EC
Marcos (3,500) SC
Marianna (10,000) EC, GC
Marion (7,000) SC
Marshall (6,000) SC, SW
Martindale (8,000) SC
Martis (3,000) FW
Massard (900) SC
Matamoros (3,000) SC,SW
Matanzas (4,500) EC, NC, SC
Maud (800) SC
Mayacmas Corner Notched (4,500) FW
McGillivray Expand Stem (4,500) FW
McIntire (6,000) EC
McKean (4,600) NP, SC
McKee Uniface (5,000) FW
McWhinney Heavy Stemmed
   (5,000) EC
Meadowood (4,000) EC, NE
Mehlville (4,000) NC
Mendocino Concave Base (5,000) FW
Merkle (4,000) EC, SC, NC
Merom (4,000) EC
Merrimack Stemmed (6,000) NE
Merrybelle, Type I (2,500) FW
Merrybelle, Type II (2,500) FW
Merrybelle, Type III (2,500) FW
Mesa (10,000) AK
Mescal Knife (700) SW
Meserve (9,500) EC, NC, NP, SC, SW
Mid-Back Tang (4,000) NP, SC
Midland (10,700) FW, NP, SC, SW
Milnesand (11,000) FW, NP, SC, SW
Mimbre (800) SW
Mineral Springs (1,300) SC
Miniature Blade (300) FW
Molalla (see Gunther)
Montell (5,000) SC
Montgomery (2,500) EC
Moran (1,200) SC
Morhiss (4,000) SC
Morrill (3,000) SC
Morris (1,200) SC
Morrow Mountain (7,000) EC, ES, GC,
   NE
Morrow Mountain Round (7,000) EC
Morrow Mountain Straight (7,000) EC,
   ES
Morse Knife (3,000) EC, NC
Motley (4,500) EC, NC, SC
Mount Albion (5,900) NP, SW
Mount Floyd (see Cohonina Stemmed)
Mountain Fork (6,000) EC
Mouse Creek (1,500) EC
Moyote (7,000) SW
Mud Creek (4,000) EC
Mulberry Creek (5,000) EC
Mule Ear (see Columbia Mule Ear)
Mummy Cave (1,400) NP
Muncy Bifurcate (8,500) NE
Munker's Creek (5,400) NC
Naknek (6,000) AK
Nanton (1,400) NP
Nawthis (1,100) SW
Nebo Hill (7,500) NC
Need Stemmed Lanceolate (2,500) FW
Neff (3,500) SW
Neosho (400) SC
Neuberger (9,000) EC, NC
Neville (7,000) NE
New Market (3,000) EC
Newmanstown (7,000) NE
Newnan (7,000) GC
Newton Falls (7,000), EC
Nightfire (7,000) FW
Nodena (600) EC, NC, SC
Nolan (6,000) SC
Nolichucky (3,000) EC

Normanskill (4,000) NE
North (2,200) EC, NC
Northern Side Notched (7,000) FW
Northumberland Fluted Knife
   (11,250) NE
Northwestern Four-Way Knife (700)
   FW
Notchaway (5,000) GC
Nottoway (300) FW
Nova (1,600) EC
Ocala (2,500) GC
Occaneechee Large Triangle (600) ES
Ochoco Stemmed (2,500) FW
Ohio Double Notched (3,000) EC
Ohio Lanceolate (10,500) EC, NE
Okanogan Knife (4,000) FW
O'leno (2,000) GC
Oley (2,200) NE
One-Que (1,320) FW
Orient (4,000) EC, NE
Osceola (7,000) NC
Osceola Greenbrier I (9,500) GC
Osceola Greenbrier II (9,500) GC
Otter Creek (5,000) ES, NE
Ouachita (3,000) SC
Ovates (3,000) NE
Owl Cave (9,500) FW
Oxbow (5,200) NP
Paint Rock Valley (10,000) EC
Paisano (6,000) SC
Paleo Knife (10,000) FW, NC, SC
Palisades (7,000) AK
Palmer (9,000) EC, ES, NE
Palmillas (6,000) SC, SW
Pandale (6,000) SC
Pandora (4,000) SC
Panoche (300) FW
Papago (see Sobaipuri)
Parman (10,500) FW
Parowan (1,300) FW, SW
Parallel Lanceolate (9,500) NE
Paskapoo (1,000) NP
Patrick (5,000) EC
Patrick Henry (9,500) ES
Patuxent (4,000) NE
Pay Paso (9,500) FW
Pedernales (6,000) SC
Pee Dee (1,500) ES
Peisker Diamond (2,500) NC, SC
Pekisko (800) NP
Pelican (10,000) NC, SC
Pelican Lake (2,600) NP
Pelican Lake "Keaster" Variety (see
   Samantha)
Pelona (6,000) SW
Penn's Creek (9,000) NE
Penn's Creek Bifurcate (9,000) NE
Pentagonal knife (6,500) EC, NE
Perdiz (1,000) SC
Perforator (9,000) EC, FW, SC, SW
Perkiomen (4,000) NE
Pickwick (6,000) EC, ES GC
Pièces Esquillées (10,000) FW
Piedmont Northern Variety (6,000) NE
Piedmont Southern Variety
   (see Hoover's Island) NE
Pigeon Creek (2,000) SC
Pike County (10,000) NC, SC
Pine Tree (8,000) EC
Pine Tree Charleston Variety
   (8,000) NE
Pine Tree Corner-Notched (8,000) EC,
   NC
Pinellas (800) GC
Piney Island (6,000) NE
Pinto Basin (8,000) FW, NP, SW
Pinto Basin Sloping Shoulder
   (8,000) FW
Pipe Creek (1,200) EC, NP
Piqunin (700) FW
Piscataway (2,500) NE
Pismo (see Rabbit Island)
Plains Knife (6,000) NP
Plains Side Notched (1,000) NP
Plains Triangular (200) NP
Plainview (10,000) EC, FW, NC, NP,

SC, SW
Plateau Pentagonal (6,000) FW
Pluvial Lakes Side Notched (9,000)
   FW
Pogo (2,000) SC
Point Hope (3,000) AK
Point Of Pines Side Notched (850) SW
Point Sal Barbed (4,500) FW
Polished Stone (2,000) AK
Pontchartrain Type I (3,400) EC, SC
Pontchartrain Type II (3,400) EC
Poplar Island (6,000) NE
Port Maitland (2,500) NE
Portage (6,000) FW
Potts (3,000) ES
Prairie Side Notched (1,300) NP
Priest Rapids (3,000) FW
Pryor Stemmed (8,500) FW
Pueblo Alto Side Notched (1,000) SW
Pueblo Del Arroyo Side Notched
   (1,000) SW
Pueblo Side Notched (850) SW
Putnam (5,000) GC
Quad (10,000) EC, ES, NC
Quillomene Bar (3,000) FW
Rabbit Island Arrow (1,200) FW
Rabbit Island Dart (4,000) FW
Raccoon Notched (1,500) NE
Raddatz (5,000) NC, SC
Ramey Knife (5,000) EC, NC
Randolph (2,000) ES, NE
Rankin (4,000) EC
Red Horn (see Buck Taylor)
Red Ochre (3,000) EC, NC
Red River Knife (9,500) SC
Redstone (11,500) EC, ES, GC, NC, NE
Reed (1,500) SC
Refugio (4,000) SC
Rheems Creek (4,000) EC
Rice Contracted Stem
   (see Hidden Valley) NC
Rice Lobbed (9,000) EC, NC, SC
Rice Shallow Side-Notched
   (1,600) NC
Rio Grande (7,500) SC, SW
Robinson (4,000) NC
Rochester (8,000) NC
Rocker (see Sudden)
Rockwall (1,400) SC
Rodgers Side Hollowed (10,000) SC
Rogue River (see Gunther)
Rose Springs (1,600) FW, SW
Rose Springs Contracted Stem
   (1,600) SW
Rose Springs Corner Notched
   (1,600) FW, NP, SW
Rose Springs Knife (1,600) FW
Rose Springs Side Notched
   (1,600) FW, SW
Rose Springs Sloping Shoulder
   (1,600) FW
Rose Springs Stemmed (1,600) FW
Rose Valley (7,000) FW
Ross (2,500) SC, NC
Ross County (see Clovis)
Rossi Expanding Stem (4,000) FW
Rossi Square-Stemmed (4,000) FW
Rossville (1,500) NE
Rough Stemmed Knife (700) FW
Round-Back Knife (8,000) SW
Round-End Knife (see Side Knife)
Rowan (3,000) ES
Russell Cave (9,000) EC
St. Albans (8,900) EC, ES, NE
St. Anne (1,400) NE
St. Charles (9,500) EC, NC, NE, SC
St. Helena (8,000) EC
St. Michael Leaf (2,000) AK
St. Tammany (8,000) EC
Sabinal (1,000) SW
Sabine (4,000) SC
Sacaton (1,100) SW
Safety Harbor (800) GC
Salado (1,500) SW (also see
   Pueblo Side Notched)
Sallisaw (800) SC

Salmon River (8,000) FW
Salt River Indented Base (1,150) SW
Samantha Arrow (1,500) NP
Samantha Dart (2,200) NP
San Bruno (600) FW
San Gabriel (2,000) SC
San Jacinto (3,000) SW
San Jose (9,000) SW
San Patrice-Geneill Var. (10,000) SC
San Patrice-Hope Var. (10,000) SC
San Patrice-Keithville Var. (10,000)
   SC
San Patrice-St. Johns Var. (10,000)
   SC
San Pedro (2,500) SW
San Rafael (4,400) SW
San Saba (3,000) SC
Sand Mountain (1,500) EC
Sandhill Stemmed (2,200) NE
Sandia (11,500) SW
Santa Cruz (1,400) SW
Santa Fe (4,000) GC
Sarasota (3,000) GC
Sattler (1,400) NP
Sauvie's island Basal Notched
   (1,750) FW
Sauvie's Island Shoulder Notched
   (1,750) FW
Savage Cave (7,000) EC, SC
Savannah River (5,000) EC, ES, GC,
   NE, SC
Saw (3,500) SW
Scallorn (1,300) NC, SC
Schustorm (1,200) SW
Schuykill (4,000) NE
Scottsbluff I (10,000) FW, NC, NE, NP,
   SC, SW
Scottsbluff II (10,000) FW, NC, NE, NP,
   SC, SW
Scottsbluff Knife (10,000) FW
Scraper (11,500) AK, EC, FW, NE, NP,
   SC, SW
Scraper-Turtleback (10,000) SW
Searcy (7,000) EC, SC
Sedalia (5,000) EC, NC
Seminole (5,000) GC
Sequoyah (1,000) NC, SC
Shaniko Stemmed (3,500) FW
Shark's Tooth (2,000) NE
Shoals Creek (4,000) EC
Shumla (3,000) SW
Side Knife (500) FW, NP
Sierra Contracting Stem (6,000) FW
Silver Lake (11,000) FW SW
Simonsen (6,800) NP
Simpson (10,000) ES, GC
Simpson-Mustache (10,000) GC
Sinner (3,000) SC
Six Mile Creek (7,500) GC
Sizer (2,300) FW
Smith (4,000) EC, NC
Smithsonia (4,000) EC
Snake Creek (4,000) EC
Snake River Arrow (700) FW
Snake River Dart (2,000) FW
Snaketown (1,200) SW
Snaketown Side Notched (800) SW
Snaketown Triangular (1,050) SW
Snook Kill (4,000) NE
Snow Knife (400) AK
Snyders (2,500) EC, NC
Snyders (Mackinaw Var.) (2,500) EC,
   NC
Sobaipuri (500) SW
Socorro (3,000) SW
Sonota (1,000) NP
Soto (1,000) SW
South Prong Creek (5,000) GC
Southhampton (8,000) ES
Spedis I, II (10,000) FW
Spedis III (3,000) FW
Spedis Fishtail (10,000) FW
Spokeshave (4,000) EC, SC
Square-end Knife (3,500) EC, FW, NC,
   NP, SC
Squaw Mountain (5,000) SW

Squibnocket Stemmed (4,200) NE
Squibnocket Triangle (4,200) NE
Stanfield (10,000) EC, GC
Stanly (8,000) EC, ES, NE
Stanly Narrow Stem (8,000) ES
Stark (7,000) NE
Starr (1,000) SC
Steamboat Lanceolate (5,000) FW
Steiner (1,000) SC
Steuben (2,000) NC, SC
Steubenville (9,000) EC
Stilwell (9,000) EC, NC
Sting Ray Barb (2,500) GC
Stockton (1,200) FW
Stone Square Stem (6,000) NC
Stott (1,300) NP
Strike-a-Lite Type I (9,000) NE
Strike-a-Lite Type II (3,000) NE
Stringtown (9,500) EC, NE
Strong Barbed Auriculate (1,750) FW
Sublet Ferry (4,000) EC
Sub-Triangular (11,300) AK
Sudden Series (6,300) SW
Sumter (7,000) EC
Sun Disc (1,100) EC
Susquehanna Bifurcated (9,000) NE
Susquehanna Broad (3,700) NE
Susquehannock Triangle (1,500) NE
Suwannee (10,000) GC
Swan Lake (3,500) EC
Swatara-Long (5,000) NE
Swift Current (1,300) NP
Sykes (6,000) EC
Table Rock (4,000) EC, NC, SC
Taconic Stemmed (5,000) NE
Talahassee (4,000) GC
Talco (800) SC
Tampa (800) GC
Taunton River Bifurcate (9,000) NE
Taylor (9,000) ES
Taylor Side Notched (9,000) GC
Taylor Stemmed (2,500) GC

Tear Drop (2,000) EC
Temporal (1,000) SW
Tennessee River (9,000) EC, NC
Tennessee Saw (8,000) EC
Tennessee Sword, (see Duck River Sword)
Texcoco (6,000) SW
Thebes (10,000) EC, ES, NC, NE
Thonotosassa (8,000) GC
Three-Piece Fish Spear (2,300) FW
Timponogus Blade (800) FW
Tock's Island (1,700) NE
Tompkins (1,200) NP
Tortugas (6,000) EC, SC
Toyah (600) SC, SW
Trade Points (400) EC, ES, FW, NE, NP, SC, SW
Travis (5,500) SC
Triangular Knife (3,500) FW, SW
Trinity (4,000) SC
Triple T (5,500) FW, SW
Trojan (1,320) FW
Truxton (1,500) SW
Tucannon Corner Notched (5,000) FW
Tucannon Side Notched (5,000) FW
Tucannon Stemmed (5,000) FW
Tulare Lake (11,200) FW
Tulare Lake Bi-point (8,000) FW
Tuolumne Notched (3,100) FW
Turin (8,500) NC
Turkeytail-Fulton (4,000) EC, NC
Turkeytail-Harrison (4,000) EC, NC
Turkeytail-Hebron (3,500) EC, NC
Turkeytail-Tupelo (4,750) EC
Turner (900) SC
Ugashik (6,000) AK
Uinta (1,200) FW
Ulu (6,000) AK
Unalakleet (3,000) AK
Unalaska (4,000) AK
Union Side Notched (10,000) GC
Uvalde (6,000) SC

Uwharrie (1,600) ES
Val Verde (5,000) SC, SW
Valina (2,500) EC
Van Lott (9,000) ES
Vandenberg Contracting Stem (5,000) NW
Vendetta (1,750) FW
Ventana-Amorgosa (7,000) SW
Ventana Side Notched (5,500) SW
Vernon (2,800) NE
Vestal Notched (4,500) NE
Victoria (10,000) SC
Virginsville (5,000) NE
Vosburg (5,000) NE
Wacissa (9,000) GC
Wade (4,500) EC
Wading River (4,200) NE
Wadlow (4,000) NC
Wahmuza (9,000) FW
Waller Knife (9,000) ES, GC
Wallula Gap Rectangular Stemmed (1,000) FW
Wallula Gap Rectangular Stemmed Knife (1,000) FW
Walnut Canyon Side Notched (850) SW
Wapanucket (6,000) NE
Waratan (3,000) ES, NE
Warito (5,500) EC
Warrick (9,000) EC, NC
Wasco Knife (see Plateau Pentagonal)
Washington (3,000) EC
Washita (800) NC, NP, SC
Washita Northern (800) NP
Washita (Peno) (800)SC
Wateree (3,000) ES
Watts Cave (10,000) EC
Waubesa (2,500) EC, NC
Wayland Notched (3,700) NE
Wealth Blade (1,200) FW
Web Blade (1,500) NE
Weeden Island (2,500) GC

Wells (8,000) SC
Wendover (7,000) FW
Westo (5,000) GC
Whale (4,000) AK
Wheeler Excurvate (10,000) EC, GC, NC
Wheeler Expanded Base (10,000) EC, GC
Wheeler Recurvate (10,000) EC
Wheeler Triangular (10,000) EC
White Mountain Side Notched (600) SW
White River (6,000) SC
White Springs (8,000) EC
Wildcat Canyon (9,000) FW
Will's Cove (3,000) ES
Williams (6,000) SC
Willits Side Notched (4,000) FW
Windust (10,500) FW
Windust-Alberta (10,500) FW
Windust Contracting Stem (10,500) FW
Windust-Hatwai (10,500) FW
Windust Knife (10,500) FW
Wintu (1,000) FW
Withlacoochie (10,500) GC
Wooden Dart/Arrow (3,500) FW
Wray (5,000) NP
Yadkin (2,500) EC, ES
Yadkin Eared (2,500) ES
Yana (1,500) FW
Yarbrough (2,500) SC
Yavapai (3,300) SW
Yonkee (3,200) NP
Young (1,000) SC
Youngs River Stemmed (8,000) FW
Zella (4,000) SC
Zephyr (9,000) SC, SW
Zorra (6,000) SC

Bibliography

Alabama Projectile Point Types, by A. B. Hooper, III. Albertville, AL, 1964.

Album of Prehistoric Man, by Tom McGowen, illustrated by Rod Ruth, Rand McNally and Co., Chicago-New York-San Francisco, 1975.

American Indian Almanac, by John Upton Terrell, Thomas Y. Crowell Co., New York, N.Y., 1974.

American Indian Point Types of North Florida, South Alabama and South Georgia, by Son Anderson, 1987.

American Indian Ways of Life, by Thorne Deuel, Illinois State Museum, Springfield, IL, 1968.

Americans Before Columbus, by Elizabeth Chesley Baity. The Viking Press, New York, N.Y., 1951.

America's Beginnings-the Wild Shores, by Loften Snell, National Geographic Society, Washington, D.C., 1974.

America's Fascinating Indian Heritage, The Readers Digest Association, Inc., Pleasantville, N.Y., 1978.

Americans in Search of their Prehistoric Past, by Stuart Struever and Felicia Antonelli, Holter Anchor Press, Doubleday, New York, 1979.

The Anthropology of Florida Points and Blades, by Lloyd E. Schroder, American Systems of the Southeast, Inc. West Columbia, SC 29169

The Arkansas Archeologist, Bulletin, Vol. 19, Univ. of Arkansas, Fayetteville, AR., 1978.

The Ancient Civilizations of Peru, by J. Alden Mason, Penguin Books, Ltd., Middlesex, England, 1968.

The Ancient Kingdoms of the Nile, by Walter A. Fairservis, Jr., N.A.L. Mentor Books, The North American Library, Thomas Y. Crowell Co., New York, N.Y., 1962.

Ancient Native Americans, by Jesse D. Jennings, editor, W.H. Freeman & Co., San Francisco, CA, 1978.

Antiquities of Tennessee, by Gates P. Thurston, The Robert Clarke Co., Cincinnati, OH, 1964.

An Archaeological Survey and Documentary History of the Shattuck Farm, Andover, Mass., (Catherine G. Shattuck Memorial Trust), Mass. Historical Commission, March, 1981.

Archaeology, by Dr. Francis Celoria, Bantam Books, New York, N.Y., 1974.

Archaeology-Middle America (A science program) - U.S.A., Nelson Doubleday, Inc., 1971.

The Archaeology of Essex County, by Gwenn Wells, Essex Life, summer, 1983.

Arrowheads and Projectile Points, by Lar Hothem, Collector Books, Paducah, KY, 1983.

Arrowhead Collectors Handbook, produced by John L. Sydman, Charles Dodds (author), Danville, Iowa, 1963.

Artifacts of North America (Indian and Eskimo), by Charles Miles, Bonanza Books, Crown Publ., Inc., New York, N.Y., 1968.

Beginners Guide to Archaeology, by Louis A. Brennan, Dell Publishing Co., Inc., New York, N.Y., 1973.

The Bog People (Iron-Age Man Preserved), by P.V. Glob, Faber and Faber, London, 1965.

The Book of Indians, by Holling C. Holling, Platt and Munk Co., Inc., New York, N.Y., 1935.

The Chattanooga News-Free Press, Thursday, Nov. 14, 1989, page B5, U.P.I. dateline, Los Angeles, CA article by James Ryan.

Cherokee Indian Removal from the Lower Hiwassee Valley, by Robert C. White, A Resource Intern Report, 1973.

The Cherokees, Past, and Present, by J. Ed Sharpe, Cherokee Publications, Cherokee, NC., 1970.

The Columbia Encyclopedia Edition, Clarke F. Ansley, Columbia University Press, New York, N.Y., 1938.

The Corner-Tang Flint Artifacts of Texas, University of Texas, Bulletin No. 3618, Anthropological Papers, Vol.1., No. 3618, 1936.

Cro-Magnon Man, Emergence of Man Series, by Tom Prideaux, Time-Life Books, New York, N.Y., 1973.

The Crystal Skull, by Richard Garvin, Pocket Books-Simon & Schuster, Inc., New York, N.Y. 1974.

Cypress Creek Villages, by William S. Webb and G. Haag, University of Kentucky, Lexington, KY., 1940.

Death on the Prairie, by Paul I. Wellman, Pyramid Books, Pyramid Publications, Doubleday and Co., Inc. New York, 1947.

Digging into History, by Paul S. Martin, Chicago National History Museum, Chicago, IL., 1963.

Duck River Cache, by Charles K. Peacock, published by T. B. Graham, Chattanooga, TN., 1954.

Early Man, by F. Clark Howell, Time-Life Books, New York, N.Y., 1965.

Early Man East of the Mississippi, by Olaf H. Prufer, Cleveland Museum of Natural History, Cleveland, Ohio, 1960.

Etowah Papers, by Warren K. Moorehead, Phillips Academy, Yale University Press, New Haven, CT. 1932.

Eva-An Archaic Site, by T.M.N. Lewis and Madelin Kneberg Lewis, University of Tennessee Press, Knoxville, TN., 1961.

Field Guide to Point Types of the State of Florida, by Son Anderson and Doug Puckett, 1984.

Field Guide to Point Types (The Tennessee River Basin), by Doug Puckett, Custom Productions (printer), Savannah, TN.,1987.

A Field Guide to Southeastern Point Types, by James W. Cambron, Decatur, AL.

A Field Guide to Stone Artifacts of Texas Indians, by Sue Turner and Thomas R. Hester, 1985, Texas Monthly Press.

Field Identification of Stone Artifacts of the Carolinas, by Russell Peithman and Otto Haas, The Identifacs Co., 1978.

The First American (Emergence of Man), by Robert Claiborne, Time-Life Books, New York, N.Y., 1973.

Flint Blades and Projectile Points of the North American Indian, by Lawrence N. Tully, Collector Books, Paducah, KY, 1986.

Flint Type Bulletin, by Lynn Mungen, curator, Potawatomi Museum, Angola, IN., 1958.

Flint Types of the Continental United States, by D.C. Waldorf and Valerie Waldorf, 1976.

Fluted Points in Lycoming County, Penn., by Gary L. Fogelman and Richard P. Johnston, Fogelman Publ. Co., Turbotville, Pennsylvania.

The Formative Cultures of the Carolina Piedmont, by Joffre Lanning Coe, New Series-Vol. 54, part 5, The American Philosophical Society, 1964.

Fossil Man, by Michael H. Day, Bantam Books, Grosset & Dunlap, Inc., New York, N.Y, 1971.

Frontiers in the Soil, (Archaeology of Georgia), by Roy S. Dickens and James L. McKinley, Frontiers Publ. Co., Atlanta, GA, 1979.

Geological Survey of Alabama, Walter B. Jones, Geologist, University of Alabama, 1948.

The Great Histories-The Conquest of Mexico, The Conquest of Peru, Prescott, edited by Roger Howell, Washington Square Press, Inc., New York, N.Y., 1966.

Guide to the Identification of Certain American Indian Projectile Points, by Robert E. Bell, Oklahoma AnthropologicalSociety, Norman, OK., 1958, 1960, and 1968.

A Guide to the Identification of Florida Projectile Points, by Ripley P. Bullen, Kendall Books, 1975.

A Guide to the Identification of Virginia Projectile Points, by Wm. Jack Hranicky and Floyd Painter, Special Publ. No. 17, Archaeological Society of Virginia, 1989.

Handbook of Alabama Archaeology, by Cambron and Hulse, edited by David L. DeJarnette, Universtiy of Alabama, 1986.

A Handbook of Indian Artifacts from Southern New England, drawings by William S. Fowler, Mass. Archaeological Society.

A History of American Archaeology, by Gorgen R. Willey and J.A. Sabloff, Thomas and Hudson, Great Britain, 1974.

Hiwassee Island, by T.M.N. Lewis and Madeline Kneberg, University of Tenn. Press, Knoxville, TN. 1946.

How to Find and Identify Arrowheads and Other Indian Artifacts (Southeastern United States), by Frank Kenan Barnard, 1983.

A Hypothetical Classification of some of The Flaked Stone Projectiles, Tools and Ceremonials From the Southeastern United States, by Winston H. Baker, Williams Printing Inc., 1225 Furnace Brook Parkway, Quincy, MA, 1995.

In Search of the Maya, by Robert L. Brunhouse, Ballentine Books-Random House, Inc., New York, N.Y., 1974.

The Incredible Incas, by Loren McIntyre, National Geographic Society, Washington, D.C., 1980.

Indian Artifacts, by Virgil U. Russell & Mrs. Russell, Johnson Publ. Co., Boulder, CO., 1962.

Indian Relics and Their Story, by Hugh C. Rogers, Yoes Printing and Lithographing Co., Fort Smith, AR., 1966.

Indian Relics and Their Values, by Allen Brown, Lightner Publishing Co., Chicago, IL., 1942.

Indian Relics Price Guide, by Lynn Munger, published by Potawatomi Museum, Angola, IN., 1961.

Indiana Archaeological Society Yearbook, The Indiana Archaeological Society, 1975-1986.

Indianology, by John Baldwin, Messenger Printing Co., St. Louis, MO. 1974.

Indians and Artists In the Southeast, by Bert W. Bierer, published by the author, State Printing Co., Columbia, SC, 1979.

Indians of the Plains, by Harry L. Shapiro, McGraw-Hill Book Co., Inc., New York, NY, 1963.

An Introduction to American Archaeology (Middle & North America), by Gordon R. Willey, Prentice-Hall, Inc. Englewood Cliffs, NJ, 1966.

Ishl-In Two Worlds (The Last Wild Indian in North America), by Theodora Kroeber, Univ. of Calif. Press, Berkeley & Los Angeles 1965.

Journal of Alabama Archaeology, David L. DeJarnette, editor, University of Alabama, 1967.

Man's Rise to Civilization, by Peter Faro, Avon Books, The Hearst Corp., New York, N.Y., 1966.

Massachusetts Archaeological Society, Bulletin of the, by William S. Fowler, Vol. 25, No. 1, Bronson Museum, Attleboro, Mass, Oct., 1963.

The Mighty Aztecs, by Gene S. Stuart, National Geographic Society, Washington, D.C., 1981.

The Mississippian Culture, by Robert Overstreet & Ross Bentley, Preston Printinq, Cleveland, TN, 1967.

The Missouri Archaeologist (The First Ten Years, 1935-1944), The Missouri Archaeological Society, Inc., Columbia, MO, 1975.

The Missouri Archaeologist Edition, Carl H. Chapman, University of Missouri, Columbia MO.

The Mound Builders, by Henry Clyde Shetrone, D. Appleton-Century Co., New York, N.Y., 1941.

Mysteries of the Past, by Lionel Casson, Robert Claiborne, Brian Fagan and Walter Karp, American Heritage Publ., Co., Inc., New York, N.Y., 1977.

The Mysterious Maya, by George E. and Gene S. Stuart, National Geographic Society, Washington, D.C., 1983.

The Mystery of Sandia Cave, by Douglas Preston, The New Yorker, June 12, 1995.

National Geographic, National Geographic Society, Numerous issues, Washington, D.C.

The Neanderthals, The Emergence of Man Series, by George Constable, Time-Life Books, New York, N.Y., 1973.

New World Beginnings (Indian Cultures in the Americas), by Olivia Viahos, Fawcett Publ., Inc., Greenwich, CT, 1970.

North American Indian Artifacts, by Lar Hothem, Books Americana, Florence, AL, 1980.

North American Indian Arts, by Andrew Hunter Whiteford, Golden Press-Western Publ. Co. Inc., New York, N.Y., 1970.

North American Indians-Before the Coming of the Europeans, by Phillip Kopper (The Smithsonian Book), Smithsonian Books, Washington, D.C.

Notes In Anthropology, by David L. Dejarnette & Asael T. Hansen, The Florida State University, Tallahassee, FL, 1960.

Paleo Points, Illustrated Chronology of Projectile Points, by G. Bradford, published by the author, Ontario Canada,1975.

The Papago Indians of Arizona, by Ruth Underhill, Ph. D., U.S. Dept. of the Interior, Bureau of Indian Affairs, Washington, D.C.

The Plants, (Life Nature Library), by Frits W. Went, Time-Life Books, New York, N.Y, 1971.

Pocket Guide to Indian Points, Books Americana, Inc., Florence AL, 1978.

Points and Blades of the Coastal Plain, by John Powell, American Systems of the Carolinas, Inc., 1990.

Prehistoric Art, R.E. Grimm, editor, Greater St. Louis Archaeological Society, Wellington Print., St. Louis, MO, 1953.

Prehistoric Artifacts of North America, John F. Berner, editor, The Genuine Indian Relic Society, Inc., Rochester, IN, 1964.

Prehistoric Implements, by Warren K. Moorehead, Publisher, Charley G. Drake, Union City GA, 1968.

Prehistoric Implements, by Warren K. Moorehead, Publisher, Charley G. Drake, American Indian Books, Union City, GA, Amo Press, Inc., New York, NY, 1978.

Projectile Point Types In Virginia and Neighboring Areas, by Wm. Jack Hranicky and Floyd Painter, Special Publ. No. 16, Archaeological Society of Virginia, 1988.

Projectile Point Types of the American Indian, by Robert K. Moore published by Robert K. Moore, Athens AL.

A Projectile Point Typology for Pennsylvania and the Northeast, by Gary L. Fogelman, Fogelman Publ., Co., Turbotville, Pennsylvania, 1988.

Projectile Points of the Tri-Rivers Basin, (Apolachicola, Flint and Chattahoochee), by John D. Sowell & Udo Volker Nowak, Generic Press, Dothan, Alabama, 1990.

The Redskin, Genuine Indian Relic Society, Inc., published by the Society, East St. Louis, IL, 1964.

Relics of Early Man Price Guide, by Philip D. Brewer, Athens, AL, 1988.

Secrist's Simpilfied Identification Guide (Stone Relics of the American Indian), by Clarence W. Secrist, published by the author, Muscatine, Iowa.

Second Preliminary Report: The St. Albans Site, Kanawha County, West Virginia by Bettye J. Broyles. Number 3, West Virginia Geological and Economic Survey, 1971.

Selected Preforms, Points and Knives of the North American Indian, by Gregory Perino, Vol. No. 1, Idabel, OK, 1985.

Selected Preforms, Points and Knives of the North American Indian, by Gregory Perino, Vol. No. 2, Idabel, OK, 1991.

Selected Preforms, Points and Knives of the North American Indian, by Gregory Perino, Vol. No. 3, Idabel, OK, 2002.

Shoop Pennsylvania's Famous Paleo Site, Fogelman Publ., Co., Turbotville, Pennsylvania.

Solving The Riddles of Wetherill Mesa, by Douglas Osborne, Ph. D., National Geographic, Feb. 1964, Washington, D.C.

Southern Indian Studies, by The Archaelogoical Society of N.C., University of North Carolina, Chapel Hill, NC, 1949.

Stone Age Spear and Arrow Points of California and the Great Basin, by Noel D. Justice, Indiana University Press, 2002.

Stone Age Spear and Arrow Points of the Southwestern United States by Noel D. Justice, Indiana University Press, 2002.

Stone Artifacts of the Northwestern Plains, by Louis C. Steege, Northwestern Plains Publ., Co., Colorado Springs, CO.

Stone Implements of the Potomac Chesapeake Province, by J.W. Powell, 15th Annual Report, Bureau of Ethnology, Washington, DC, 1893-1894.

Story In Stone (Flint Types of Central & Southern U.S.), by Valene and D.C. Waldorf, Mound Builder Books, Branson, MO, 1987.

Sun Circles and Human Hands, Emma Lila Fundaburk & Mary Douglas Foreman, editors. Published by the editors, Paragon Press, Montgomery, AL, 1957.

Ten Years of the Tennessee Archaeologist, Selected Subjects, J.B. Graham, Publisher, Chattanooga, TN.

Tennessee Anthropologist, Vol. XIV, No. 2, Fall, 1989, U.T., Knoxville, 1989.

Tennessee Archaeologist, T. M.N. Lewis and Madeline Kneburg, University of Tennessee, Knoxville, TN.

Tennessee Anthropologist, Vol. 14, No. 2, 1989, The Quad Site Revisted, by Charles Faulkner

A Topology and Nomenclature of New York Projectile Points, by William A. Ritchie, Bulletin No. 384, New York State Museum, NY, 1971.

U.S. News and World Report (Weekly News Magazine) article by William F. Amman and Joannie M. Schrof-"Last Empires of the Americas," April 2, 1990 issue, Washington, DC.

The Vail Site (A Paleo Indian Encampment in Maine), by Dr. Richard Michael Gramly, Bulletin of the Buffalo Society of Natural Science, Vol. No. 30, Buffalo, NY, 1982.

Walk with History, Joan L. Franks, editor, Chattanooga Area Historical Assn., Chattanooga, TN, 1976.

Who's Who In Indian Relics, by H.C. Wachtel, publisher, Charley G. Drake, American Indian Books, Union City, GA, 1980.

The World Atlas of Archaeology (The English Edition of "Le Grand Atlas de Parcheologie"), executive editor- James Hughes, U.S. & Canada, G.K. Hall & Co., Boston, Mass, 1985.

World Book Encyclopedia, Field Enterprises, Inc., W.F. Quarrie and Company, Chicago, Ill.,1953.

The World of the American Indian (A volume in the Story of Man Library), National Geographic Society, Jules B. Billard-Editor, Washington, DC, 1989.

DREAMSPEARS

PRESENTS
AN ART ARTIFACT

Texas
Amateur
Archeological
Association

DIG TEXAS!

HOT!

Plan your next dig with the TAAA!
Check out the photos on the web at
www.texasaaa.com

TAAA was founded in 1994. This is our 11ᵗʰ year!
Dig with the professionals - dig with the TAAA!
We specialize in backhoe screen digs!
YOU KEEP WHAT YOU FIND!

Membership in the TAAA and daily dig fee required.

Contact: *Bob McWilliams* at texasaaa@aol.com
or call 210-275-5657 for current dig info.

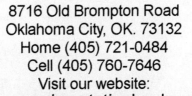

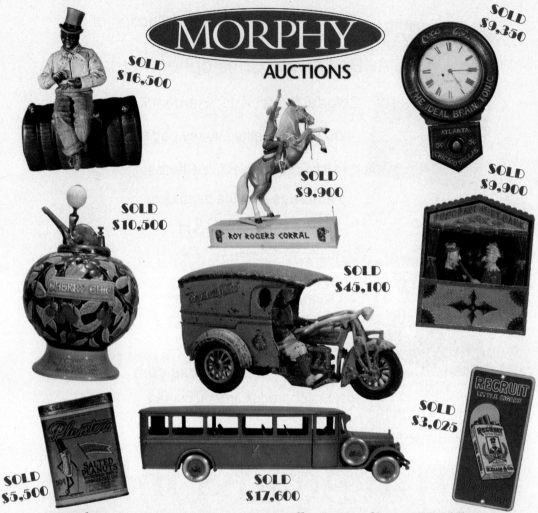

MORPHY
AUCTIONS

SOLD $16,500

SOLD $9,350

SOLD $9,900

SOLD $9,900

SOLD $10,500

ROY ROGERS CORRAL

SOLD $45,100

SOLD $3,025

SOLD $5,500

SOLD $17,600

Seeking auction consignments - No collection too big or too small.

Consider Morphy Auctions for the sale of your collection. We take the utmost care in handling your items, giving you the personalized attention you deserve and publicizing our sales world-wide. From the prime auction location to the compelling advertising campaign, you are sure to be proud of your collection's presentation, and pleased with the outcome of the sale.

THE PREVIEW: Consignments are on display at the Adamstown Antique Gallery months prior to the auction, as well as online at www.morphyauctions.com. In addition, we print many thousands of full-color auction catalogs and fliers before the sale.

THE BIDDING: Bids accepted internationally via mail, phone, fax or live on the Internet.

THE SALE: We sell your items on the auction floor at the Adamstown Antique Gallery located on the Adamstown antique strip in Denver, Pa., "Antiques Capital of America."

MORPHY AUCTIONS

2000 N. Reading Road ◆ Denver, PA 17517   Tel: (717) 335-3435 ◆ Fax: (717) 336-7115
www.morphyauctions.com   E-mail: morphy@morphyauctions.com
Catalog: $35.00 + $5.00 shipping and handling.

MORPHY AUCTIONS is a division of DIAMOND INTERNATIONAL GALLERIES

FIRST MESA

1996 LIST #1
$10.00

INC.

· AMERICAN INDIAN ART ·
· PREHISTORIC ARTIFACTS · BOOKS ·

Specializing
in:

Pottery · Basketry

Weavings · Flint · Stone Tools

Fetishes Ornamentals · Masks

Ceremonials · Pipes · Beadwork

Geological Specimens · Fossils · Horns

Skulls · Bones · Mounts · Antiquities

Sculptures · Jewelry · Paintings

Americana · Pre-Columbian Art

Tribal Art · Folk Art · Kachinas

Weaponry · Primitives

P.O. Box 1256
South Bend, IN 46624

LARRY A. LANTZ
(574) 243-2296

First Mesa Inc. offers two catalogs. The first is an extensive Photo
Illustrated In-Stock Sales Catalog of American Indian Art, Prehistoric
Artifacts, Pre-Columbian Art, Tribal Art, etc. The second is our Web Site
Printout of 400-500 Photo Illustrated In-Stock Points/Knives/Blades.
All have Authentication Papers, most by Greg Perino.
Each Catalog is $6.00 post paid. Both for $10.00.

www.firstmesa.com